PROFESSIONAL
MICROSOFT® SQL SERVER® 2012
ANALYSIS SERVICES WITH MDX AND DAX

► **PART V**   **ADVANCED TOPICS WITH TABULAR BISM AND INTEGRATION WITH POWER VIEW**

PROFESSIONAL

Microsoft® SQL Server® 2012 Analysis Services with MDX and DAX

PROFESSIONAL

Microsoft® SQL Server® 2012 Analysis Services with MDX and DAX

Sivakumar Harinath
Ronald Pihlgren
Denny Guang-Yeu Lee
John Sirmon
Robert M. Bruckner

WILEY

John Wiley & Sons, Inc.

Professional Microsoft® SQL Server® 2012 Analysis Services with MDX and DAX

Published by
John Wiley & Sons, Inc.
10475 Crosspoint Boulevard
Indianapolis, IN 46256
www.wiley.com

Copyright © 2012 by Sivakumar Harinath, Ronald Pihlgren, Denny Guang-Yeu Lee, John Sirmon, and Robert M. Bruckner

Published by John Wiley & Sons, Inc., Indianapolis, Indiana

Published simultaneously in Canada

ISBN: 978-1-118-10110-0
ISBN: 978-1-118-22343-7 (ebk)
ISBN: 978-1-118-23708-3 (ebk)
ISBN: 978-1-118-26209-2 (ebk)

Manufactured in the United States of America

10 9 8 7 6 5 4 3 2

For general information on our other products and services please contact our Customer Care Department within the United States at (877) 762-2974, outside the United States at (317) 572-3993 or fax (317) 572-4002.

Wiley publishes in a variety of print and electronic formats and by print-on-demand. Some material included with standard print versions of this book may not be included in e-books or in print-on-demand. If this book refers to media such as a CD or DVD that is not included in the version you purchased, you may download this material at http://booksupport.wiley.com. For more information about Wiley products, visit www.wiley.com.

Library of Congress Control Number: 2012933620

ABOUT THE AUTHORS

SIVAKUMAR HARINATH was born in Chennai, India. He has a Ph.D. in Computer Science from the University of Illinois at Chicago. His thesis title was "Data Management Support for Distributed Data Mining of Large Datasets over High Speed Wide Area Networks." He has worked for Newgen Software Technologies (P) Ltd; IBM Toronto Labs, Canada; National Center for Data Mining, University of Illinois at Chicago; and has been at Microsoft since February of 2002. Siva started as a Software Design Engineer in Test (SDET) in the Analysis Services Performance team, and currently is a Senior Program Manager in the Analysis Services team. His other interests include high-performance computing, distributed systems, and high-speed networking.

Siva is married to Shreepriya and has twins, Praveen and Divya. His personal interests include travel, games, and sports (in particular carrom, chess, racquet ball, and board games). Siva has co-authored books *Professional Microsoft SQL Server Analysis Services 2005 with MDX* (Wrox, 2006), *MDX Solutions 2nd edition* (Wiley, 2006), *Professional Microsoft SQL Server Analysis Services 2008 with MDX* (Wrox, 2009), and *Professional Microsoft PowerPivot for Excel and SharePoint* (Wrox, 2010). You can reach Siva at sivakumar.harinath@microsoft.com.

RONALD PIHLGREN is a native of Chicago, Illinois. He has a Bachelor of Science degree in Computer Science from DePaul University. A 17-year veteran at Microsoft, he is currently a Senior Software Development Engineer in Test on the SQL Server Analysis Services team. He was one of the principal tech reviewers for the book *Professional Microsoft SQL Server Analysis Services 2008 with MDX* (Wrox, 2009) and was one of the co-authors of the book *Professional Microsoft PowerPivot for Excel and SharePoint* (Wrox, 2010). He has a blog at http://ronaldpihlgren.wordpress.com.

DENNY GUANG-YEU LEE is a Technical Principal Program Manager within Microsoft based out of Redmond, WA. He is one of the original core members of Microsoft Hadoop on Windows and Azure and had helped bring Hadoop into Microsoft. In addition to Big Data, he was the Data Warehousing and BI Group Lead for the SQL Customer Advisory team and co-creator of the SSAS Maestros course.

As consulting architect enjoying working on complex technical problems, Lee has also become a SME in web analytics and healthcare. He is avid in social media (@dennylee) and continuously uses the forum to share deep technical learning. Examples of his work can be found in books ranging from Analysis Services to Healthcare Informatics (http://dennyglee.com/books-2/), comprehensive technical guides including Analysis Services Performance and Operations Guides (http://dennyglee.com/articles/), and in his blogs at both sqlcat.com and dennyglee.com.

JOHN SIRMON is a Senior Program Manager with the SQL Server Customer Advisory team at Microsoft. He has worked for Microsoft since March 2001 and began working with Microsoft SQL Server over 10 years ago when he began his professional career as a consultant at PricewaterhouseCoopers. He has extensive development experience with Microsoft Visual Studio and all the components of the Microsoft BI Stack. His specialties include Analysis Services performance tuning, Reporting Services, SharePoint integration, troubleshooting Kerberos Authentication, and PowerPivot for SharePoint. John has presented topics ranging from Reporting Services SharePoint integration to Analysis Services at SQL Server PASS Summits and Microsoft TechReady conferences. John holds a BS degree in Business Administration with a minor in MIS from the Citadel, the Military College of South Carolina. In his spare time he is the lead singer/guitarist of a local rock band in Charlotte, NC. John lives in Lake Wylie, SC, with his wife, two sons, and their two bloodhounds.

ROBERT M. BRUCKNER is a Principal Software Architect and developer with the Microsoft SQL Server division. Robert is responsible for the technical architecture of SQL Server Reporting Services including Power View. One of Robert's core areas has been the design and development of the scalable report processing engine utilized by Reporting Services and Power View. Power View is an enhancement of Reporting Services 2012, enabling end users to easily and interactively visualize data, quickly gain analytical insights, and simply have fun exploring data!

Prior to joining Microsoft in 2003, Robert researched, designed, and implemented database and business intelligence systems as a system architect at T-Mobile Austria, and as a researcher at Vienna University of Technology, Austria. Robert holds Masters and PhD degrees with highest distinctions in Computer Science from Vienna University of Technology, and holds several patents.

Anyone good with a search engine can find thousands of Robert's past postings on public newsgroups and MSDN forums sharing his insights, tips, tricks, and expert advice related to Reporting Services and other SQL Server technologies. Robert has co-authored books on SQL Server Reporting Services as well as Analysis Services. Robert regularly presents at industry conferences and also maintains a popular blog at `http://blogs.msdn.com/robertbruckner`. In his spare time, Robert enjoys mountain biking, skiing, and reading.

ABOUT THE CONTRIBUTORS

ADAM JORGENSEN is a SQL Server MVP and President of Pragmatic Works Consulting. He also serves as a Director for the Professional Association of SQL Server (PASS). His focus is on using his over 12 years of experience to mentor executives and teams to maximize their insight and execution based on improved analytics and data performance. He lives in Jacksonville, FL and is a regular speaker at SQL Saturdays, SQL Rally, and PASS Summit events. You can catch up with Adam at AdamJorgensen.com or @AJBigData.

DUSTIN RYAN is Senior Business Intelligence Consultant with Pragmatic Works. He began working with Pragmatic Works as a Junior Business Intelligence Consultant in 2008. Dustin's specialties include Reporting Services, Integration Services, and Analysis Services. Dustin has worked as a technical editor for the book *Knight's 24-Hour Trainer: Microsoft SQL Server 2008 Integration Services* (Wiley, 2009). You can find Dustin speaking at community events such as SQL Saturdays, Code Camps, and various PASS events. Dustin blogs regularly at http://sqldusty.wordpress .com and http://www.bidn.com.

Dustin is a native of Jacksonville, Florida and is married to his beautiful wife, Angela, and is the father of their two amazing children, Dallas and Bradley. In his spare time, Dustin enjoys spending time with his family and serving at his church.

CHRIS PRICE is a Senior Business Intelligence Consultant with Pragmatic Works based out of Lakeland, Florida. He has a BS degree in Management Information Systems and a Masters of Business Administration, both from the University of South Florida. He began his career 12 years ago as a developer and has extensive experience across a wide range of Microsoft technologies. His current interests include ETL, Data Integration, Analysis Services, SharePoint and Big Data. Chris regularly presents at SQL Saturdays, Code Camps, and other community events such as 24 Hours of PASS. You can follow Chris on his blog at http://bidn.com/blogs/cprice1979/ or on Twitter at @BluewaterSQL.

CREDITS

EXECUTIVE EDITOR
Robert Elliott

PROJECT EDITOR
Tom Dinse

TECHNICAL EDITORS
Leon Cyril
Wayne Robertson
Sergey Volegov

PRODUCTION EDITOR
Daniel Scribner

COPY EDITOR
San Dee Phillips

EDITORIAL MANAGER
Mary Beth Wakefield

FREELANCER EDITORIAL MANAGER
Rosemarie Graham

ASSOCIATE DIRECTOR OF MARKETING
David Mayhew

MARKETING MANAGER
Ashley Zurcher

BUSINESS MANAGER
Amy Knies

PRODUCTION MANAGER
Tim Tate

**VICE PRESIDENT AND EXECUTIVE GROUP
PUBLISHER**
Richard Swadley

VICE PRESIDENT AND EXECUTIVE PUBLISHER
Neil Edde

ASSOCIATE PUBLISHER
Jim Minatel

PROJECT COORDINATOR, COVER
Katie Crocker

PROOFREADERS
Scott Klemp, Word One
Paul Sagan, Word One
Louise Watson, Word One

INDEXER
Robert Swanson

COVER DESIGNER
Ryan Sneed

COVER IMAGE
© braverabbit / iStockPhoto

ACKNOWLEDGMENTS

WOW!!! IT HAS BEEN AN AMAZING 10 MONTHS from when we started writing this book. The first edition of this book started when Siva jokingly mentioned to his wife the idea of writing a book on SQL Server Analysis Services 2005. She took it seriously and motivated him to start working on the idea in October 2003. Because the first two editions were well received, we identified co-authors for the new edition. All the co-authors of this book are part of the Microsoft SQL Server team.

As always, there are so many people who deserve mentioning that we are afraid we will miss someone. If you are among those missed, please accept our humblest apologies. We first need to thank the managers of each co-author for their support. Next we thank our colleagues on the Analysis Services and Reporting Services team for their help and support with improving the content of the book, drawing on their expertise from proven best practices from large-scale customer deployments of Analysis Services and Reporting Services. We thank our editors, Bob Elliott and Tom Dinse, who supported us right from the beginning, and also prodded us along, which was necessary to make sure the book published on time. We thank Kay Unkroth, Wei Zou, Wee Hyong Tok, Karen Aleksanyan from SQL Server team for their contributions for Chapters 3, 12, 13, 18, and 19. In addition, the authors thank Adam Jorgensen, Dustin Ryan, and Chris Price from Pragmatic Works for their contributions to Chapters 8, 9, 10, 11, 17, 20, and 21. We would like to thank our technical reviewers Leon Cyril, Sergey Volegov, and Wayne Robertson who graciously offered us their assistance and significantly helped in improving the content and samples in the book.

Most importantly, we owe our deepest thanks to our wonderful families. Without their support and sacrifice, this book would have become one of those many projects that begins and never finishes. Our families truly took the brunt of it and sacrificed shared leisure time, all in support of our literary pursuit. We especially want to thank them for their patience with us, and the grace it took to not kill us during some of the longer work binges.

CONTENTS

INTRODUCTION

ANALYSIS SERVICES 2005 WAS A SIGNIFICANT LEAP from Analysis Services 2000, from the concept of building your cubes in Business Intelligence Development Studio (BIDS) to the concept of the Unified Dimensional Model (UDM) with attribute and user hierarchies. The first edition of this book, *Professional SQL Server Analysis Services 2005 with MDX*, was aimed at novice to advanced users and was very well received by its readers. Analysis Services 2005 was a large and complex product that needed a lot of fine-tuning to get the best performance.

Analysis Services 2008 added enhancements to the developer toolset and the server itself that made it easier to build your databases right with efficient performance. The second edition of this book was written to provide insight into those enhancements and to help you understand how to utilize them effectively for your business needs. Because Analysis Services 2008 was an incremental release, the second edition of the book had a similar structure to the first, but enhancements were made to each chapter of the book. The second edition was still targeted at novice to advanced users.

Between Analysis Services 2008 and the current major version, Analysis Services 2012, Microsoft released SQL Server 2008 R2, which introduced PowerPivot, Microsoft's entry into the self-service business intelligence arena. PowerPivot's goal was to bring the benefits of business intelligence (BI) to a larger audience with a simpler, easier to understand data model, the DAX expression language (designed to be familiar to users of Excel expressions) and the VertiPaq engine (which featured the speed of an in-memory, column-oriented database engine and state-of-the-art compression capabilities to allow larger databases to be memory-resident).

Now, we have Analysis Services 2012, which introduces Microsoft's new, overarching business intelligence semantic model (BISM). BISM subsumes the venerable Unified Dimensional Model and brings the tabular mode — introduced with PowerPivot in SQL Server 2008 R2 — to the professional BI developer outside the context of Excel and SharePoint. This release brings with it many questions about Microsoft's direction in the BI space, and about how to use Analysis Services 2012 to implement your BI solutions using SQL Server Data Tools (formerly called BIDS). This book answers those questions and gives you hands-on experience with both sides of the business intelligence semantic model — multidimensional and tabular. We also follow the tradition of previous versions of the book in aiming to provide value to both the novice and the advanced user.

WHO THIS BOOK IS FOR

This book targets the same audience as previous versions of the book: those who want to understand and master data warehousing and BI using Microsoft's tools. You may be passionate about becoming a BI professional and want to understand the full depth and breadth of Microsoft's approach to BI. You may be someone who is already working in a BI environment and you want help solving challenges in your job right now. Or you may be someone who has worked in BI before, using tools from other companies or previous versions of Microsoft's BI technology, and want to learn what Analysis Services 2012 and related products bring to the table. We think all of these audiences will find value in this book.

What are the prerequisites for reading and understanding this book? If you have no prior experience or exposure to the concepts of relational databases, you will likely be challenged by this book and you may want to start with a more basic book on that topic before you dive into this book. On the other hand, we don't expect you to have detailed knowledge of data warehousing, BI, or application development. If you want to learn about those topics and how Microsoft's products and technologies work together to enable you to develop BI solutions, this book is definitely for you!

WHAT THIS BOOK COVERS

Analysis Services 2012 is the premier analytical database product from Microsoft. Analysis Services 2012 builds on previous Analysis Services releases, providing powerful tools to design, build, test, and deploy your multidimensional and tabular mode databases. By using the tools integrated into Visual Studio, you get a true developer experience when you build BI projects.

This book walks you through the entire product and its important features with the help of step-by-step instructions. Along the way, you not only learn how to use the features, but you also learn more about the features at a user level and what happens behind the scenes to make things work. We believe this provides extra insight into how features really work and hence provides insight into how they are best used. It will also enhance your ability to debug problems that you might not have been able to otherwise.

MDX and DAX are the languages used for data retrieval from Analysis Services. In this book, you get an introduction to the basic concepts and various functions of these languages. By learning the expressions and functions sent to the server for the various operations, you will begin to understand the intricacies of these languages and improve your own coding skills by extension. Finally, you will learn to optimize your queries to get the best performance from your Analysis Services.

One of the key value-adds of this book, which we think is worth the price of admission by itself, is that you will begin to understand what design trade-offs are involved in BI application development. Further, the many scenarios in this book will help you to do better BI design for your company in the face of those trade-off decisions. The scenarios are geared toward some of the common business problems that are currently faced by existing Analysis Services customers. Although there is no claim that this book will teach you business per se, it is a book on BI and we explain certain business concepts that you are sure to run into eventually. For example, the often misunderstood concept of *depreciation* is explained in some detail. Again, this aspect of the book is shallow, but we hope what pure business concepts are covered will provide you with a more informed basis from which to work.

Finally, this book covers integration of Analysis Services with other SQL Server 2012 components: Data Mining, Integrations Services and Reporting Services (including Power View, the interactive reporting tool new in SQL Server 2012), as well as Microsoft Office products. These chapters will help you go beyond just a passing level of understanding of Analysis Services 2012; it is really integration of these disparate components that allows you to build start-to-finish BI solutions that are scalable, maintainable, have good performance characteristics, and highlight the right information. Do not skip the chapters that do not at first seem crucial to understanding Analysis Services 2012 itself; it is the whole picture that brings the real value. Get that whole picture for stellar success and return on your investment of time and energy.

HOW THIS BOOK IS STRUCTURED

The authors of books in the Wrox Professional series attempt to make each chapter as standalone as possible. This book is no exception. However, the sophistication of the subject matter and the manner in which certain concepts are necessarily tied to others has somewhat undermined this most noble intention. In fact, unless you are a seasoned data warehousing professional, or otherwise have experience with earlier versions of Analysis Services, we advise you to take a serial approach to reading chapters. Work through the first seven chapters and chapters 15, 16, 17, and 18 in order because they will collectively provide you with some architectural context, a good first look at creating multidimensional and tabular databases, as well as an introduction to MDX and DAX. Just to remind you, in the simplest terms, MDX and DAX are to Analysis Services what SQL is to SQL Server. OK, that was just too simple an analogy, but let's not get ahead of ourselves! As for the actual layout of the book, we have divided the book into roughly four major sections.

We begin with a chapter that introduces the basic concepts and provides an overview of the product.

Part I gets you kick-started using Analysis Services with most of the common operations that you need to design your multidimensional databases. You will become familiar with the product if you aren't already, and we hope it will provide you some sense of achievement, which will certainly help motivate you to go beyond the simple stuff and move to the advanced.

Part II contains chapters that prepare you for the more advanced topics about creating multidimensional databases, such as multiple measure groups, Business Intelligence wizards, Key Performance Indicators, and Actions. You will learn about the calculation model in Analysis Services 2012 and enhance your dimensions and cube designs using SQL Server Data Tools. Finally, you will learn how SQL Server Integration Services, SQL Server Reporting Services, and Data Mining provide integration with your multidimensional models.

In **Part III,** we provide an introduction to self-service business intelligence and PowerPivot that was released with SQL Server 2008 R2. Then, we immediately dive into creating and managing tabular databases, followed by querying data via DAX and some common business solutions that can be achieved using DAX in tabular databases. Finally, we cover how to analyze your multidimensional or tabular databases using Microsoft Office products.

Finally, in **Part IV**, we provide an introduction to Power View, a browser-based Silverlight application for ad-hoc reporting for business users such as data analysts, business decision makers, and information workers. Power View helps you to visualize and analyze data in your SQL Server Analysis Services tabular databases.

Together with the introductory chapter, the four sections that make up this book provide you with a full-blown BI learning experience so you can create, deploy, and manage your multidimensional and tabular databases. Because BI and BI applications constitute such an incredibly complex and massive field of endeavor, no one book can possibly cover it all. In terms of BI through the eyes of SQL Server Analysis Services 2012, we hope this book has got it covered!

WHAT YOU NEED TO USE THIS BOOK

You need a computer running some version of the Windows operating system, like Windows 7 Professional, for example, and a copy of SQL Server 2012 installed on that system. In addition, you also need the SQL Server 2012 Business Intelligence samples, which are available from this book's web page at www.wrox.com.

CONVENTIONS

To help you get the most from the text and keep track of what's happening, we've used a number of conventions throughout the book.

> *Warnings hold important, not-to-be-forgotten information that is directly relevant to the surrounding text.*

> *Notes indicates notes, tips, hints, tricks, and asides to the current discussion.*

As for styles in the text:

> ➤ We *italicize* new terms and important words when we introduce them.

> ➤ We show keyboard strokes like this: Ctrl+A.

> ➤ We show file path names, URLs, and code within the text like so: `persistence.properties`.

> ➤ We present code in snippets a special monofont style:

```
We use a monofont type for code examples.
```

SOURCE CODE

As you work through the examples in this book, you may choose either to type in all the code manually, or to use the source code files that accompany the book. All the source code used in this book is available for download at www.wrox.com.

You can search for the book at www.wrox.com by ISBN (the ISBN for this book is 978-1-118-10110-0) to find the code. And a complete list of code downloads for all current Wrox books is available at www.wrox.com/dynamic/books/download.aspx.

Throughout each chapter, you'll find references to the names of code files as needed in the text.

Most of the code on www.wrox.com is compressed in a .ZIP, .RAR, or similar archive format appropriate to the platform. Once you download the code, just decompress it with an appropriate compression tool.

 Because many books have similar titles, you may find it easiest to search by ISBN; this book's ISBN is 978-1-118-10110-0.

ERRATA

We make every effort to ensure that there are no errors in the text or in the code. However, no one is perfect, and mistakes do occur. If you find an error in one of our books, like a spelling mistake or faulty piece of code, we would be very grateful for your feedback. By sending in errata, you may save another reader hours of frustration, and at the same time, you will be helping us provide even higher quality information.

To find the errata page for this book, go to www.wrox.com and locate the title using the Search box or one of the title lists. Then, on the book details page, click the Book Errata link. On this page, you can view all errata that has been submitted for this book and posted by Wrox editors.

If you don't spot "your" error on the Book Errata page, go to www.wrox.com/contact/techsupport.shtml and complete the form there to send us the error you have found. We'll check the information and, if appropriate, post a message to the book's errata page and fix the problem in subsequent editions of the book.

P2P.WROX.COM

For author and peer discussion, join the P2P forums at http://p2p.wrox.com. The forums are a web-based system for you to post messages relating to Wrox books and related technologies and interact with other readers and technology users. The forums offer a subscription feature to e-mail you topics of interest of your choosing when new posts are made to the forums. Wrox authors, editors, other industry experts, and your fellow readers are present on these forums.

At http://p2p.wrox.com, you will find a number of different forums that will help you, not only as you read this book, but also as you develop your own applications. To join the forums, just follow these steps:

1. Go to http://p2p.wrox.com and click the Register link.

2. Read the terms of use and click Agree.

3. Complete the required information to join, as well as any optional information you wish to provide, and click Submit.

4. You will receive an e-mail with information describing how to verify your account and complete the joining process.

 You can read messages in the forums without joining P2P, but in order to post your own messages, you must join.

Once you join, you can post new messages and respond to messages other users post. You can read messages at any time on the Web. If you would like to have new messages from a particular forum e-mailed to you, click the Subscribe to this Forum icon by the forum name in the forum listing.

For more information about how to use the Wrox P2P, be sure to read the P2P FAQs for answers to questions about how the forum software works, as well as many common questions specific to P2P and Wrox books. To read the FAQs, click the FAQ link on any P2P page.

PART I
Introduction

1

Introduction

WHAT'S IN THIS CHAPTER?

- ➤ Introducing business intelligence and Analysis Services 2012
- ➤ Learning about the BISM multidimensional mode
- ➤ Understanding data warehousing and OLAP
- ➤ Learning about the BISM tabular mode
- ➤ Understanding self-service BI and the evolution of tabular mode
- ➤ Understanding the Microsoft Business Intelligence Semantic Model

Business intelligence (BI) refers to systems and technologies used to gain insights from data. Those systems and technologies have traditionally been built around the concept of taking operational data, typically stored in relational databases, and using it to build a data warehouse. The data in a data warehouse is usually the result of the transformation of the operational data into a form optimized for reporting and analysis, the main business activities on the data in a BI system. Key aspects of BI systems are performance and scalability. The approach to organizing data in BI systems is referred to as Online Analytical Processing, or OLAP. The OLAP approach was created to meet the needs of BI — making sense of a large amount of existing data. This is different than the approach taken by relational databases, referred to as Online Transaction Processing (OLTP), which is optimized for efficient creating and updating of individual transactions.

Microsoft SQL Server Analysis Services has grown to be the industry-leading OLAP server based on its capabilities in helping implement the requirements of traditional BI systems. In addition to the server features and support for the performance and scalability needed by BI systems, Analysis Services provides a platform and ecosystem that supports integration with applications and tools from Microsoft and other third-party companies and independent software vendors (ISVs).

Since the previous edition of this book, the BI world has changed. The push now is to expand the scope of BI to an even wider audience. In the Microsoft BI world, this started with PowerPivot, which first shipped with SQL Server 2008 R2. PowerPivot changed the way BI was done. It consisted of a client piece in the form of a free, downloadable add-in to Microsoft Excel, and a mid-tier and server piece, which shipped in the SQL Server box and was built on top of Microsoft Office SharePoint. Aside from building a product that was dependent on Microsoft Office, other new features included with PowerPivot were the VertiPaq engine, a column-oriented in-memory database technology, DAX (a new expression language that was designed to be close to Excel's expression syntax but with added functionality focused on analytics), and a new data model. This new data model differed from the UDM model in previous Microsoft BI offerings because it dealt with tables and relationships rather than dimensions, facts, and cubes. The new model was designed to be simpler and to make the benefits of BI available to a larger audience.

PowerPivot and the Managed Self-Service BI message were successful, and the Analysis Services team began work on the next version of the product. Their goal was to evolve the new tabular model beyond just PowerPivot and make its benefits available to professional BI developers. The next step in this evolution is the tabular mode of the Business Intelligence Semantic Model (BISM). BISM is the term for the new over-arching Microsoft BI model. Analysis Services 2012 is a step in the direction of where Microsoft is going with BISM. Microsoft's goal is to provide a common model for all end-user experiences using Microsoft BI technologies. Under the hood, this model consists of three layers (data access, business logic, and data model) with two different implementations of each layer corresponding to the two different modes of BISM. This evolution will take longer than a single product cycle. The Analysis Services team has laid out its roadmap for BISM at `http://bit.ly/ktIzTG`.

This book covers the multidimensional and tabular modes of the BI Semantic Model. The multidimensional mode is the continuing evolution of the former UDM model of Analysis Services, which was the subject of the previous two versions of this book. Parts I and II of the book cover multidimensional mode in detail. The tabular mode is the evolution of the model introduced in PowerPivot. This book covers the changes to the tabular model as implemented for BI developers in Analysis Services 2012, although PowerPivot is also covered. The tabular mode is the topic of part III of the book. The remainder of this chapter gives a conceptual overview of these two modes of the BI Semantic Model.

BISM MULTIDIMENSIONAL MODE

If you are familiar with previous versions of Analysis Services, you are familiar with the multidimensional mode of BISM. This approach to multidimensional BI revolves around an entity known as a *data warehouse.*

A data warehouse is a system of records (a BI gathering system) that takes data from a company's operational databases and other data sources and transforms it into a structure conducive to business analysis. Business calculations are often performed on the organized data to further its usefulness for making business decisions. Finally, the data is made available to the end user for querying, reporting, and analysis. A data warehouse system that is cleansed and organized has optimized storage of historical records that gives the organization an intelligence gathering system to understand the dynamics of the business. *Business Analytics* is a function in which information workers, business analysts, and other business users investigate business data to identify patterns and trends, and make business decisions to improve their business processes. *Predictive Analytics* (also known as data mining) is done using mathematical models to predict future trends based on existing business data. The general approach to storing business data in a dimensional model and providing quick answers by slicing and dicing the business data is known as Online Analytical Processing (OLAP). OLAP systems are architected in different ways. The most common types are Multidimensional

OLAP (MOLAP), Relational OLAP (ROLAP), and Hybrid OLAP (HOLAP). SQL Server 2012 multidimensional mode is a business intelligence platform that provides a scalable infrastructure with servers (Analysis Services and Reporting Services) and tools (Data Quality Services, Integration Services, Master Data Services, and Reporting Services) to extract, transform, cleanse, load, build, audit, query, and report on the data in your data warehouse.

In this section you learn what data warehousing is and how it relates to multidimensional business intelligence. You also look at the best approaches to warehousing with the introduction of those concepts. Data warehousing is explained in several different ways. You see how SQL Server 2012 Analysis Services puts it all together in terms of architecture — at both client and server levels.

A Closer Look at Data Warehousing

Data warehousing has existed since the early days of computers and information systems. Initially, concepts of data warehousing were referred to as Decision Support Systems (DSS). In the book *Building the Data Warehouse*, Bill Inmon described the data warehouse as "a *subject oriented*, *integrated*, *non-volatile*, and *time variant* collection of data in support of management's decisions." According to Inmon, the subject orientation of a data warehouse differs from the operational orientation in OLTP systems; so a subject in a data warehouse might relate to customers, whereas an operation in an OLTP system might relate to a specific application such as sales processing and all that goes with it.

The word *integrated* means that throughout the enterprise, data points should be defined consistently or there should be some integration methodology to force consistency at the data warehouse level. One example would be how to represent the entity Microsoft. If Microsoft were represented in different databases as MSFT, MS, Microsoft, and MSoft, it would be difficult to meaningfully merge these in a data warehouse. The best-case solution is to have all databases in the enterprise refer to Microsoft as, say, MSFT, thereby making the merger of this data seamless. A less desirable, but equally workable, solution is to force all the variants into one during the process of moving data from the operational system to the data warehouse.

A data warehouse is referred to as nonvolatile because it differs from operational systems, which are often transactional in nature and updated regularly. The data warehouse is generally loaded at some preset interval, which may be measured in weeks or even months. This is not to say it is never measured in days; but even if updates do occur daily, that is still a sparse schedule compared to the constant changes made to transactional systems.

The final element in this definition is time variance, which is a sophisticated way to say how far back the stored data in the system reaches. For operational systems, the time period is quite short, perhaps days, weeks, or months. For the warehouse, it is quite long — typically on the order of years. This last item might strike you as self-evident because you would have a hard time analyzing business trends if your data didn't date back further than 2 months.

OLAP systems are architected in different ways depending on how the data warehouse is built. A classic OLAP system's data warehouse is built using a multidimensional store that is optimized for performance and uses dimensional models. Alternatively, the data warehouse is built using the Relational Tables in the operational databases using a specialized schema design that is optimized for storage. Hybrid OLAP is an architecture that provides performance and optimized storage. There is more to come in this chapter on the differences between relational and multidimensional databases.

Data warehousing is the process by which data created in an operational database is transformed and stored and provides a context to facilitate the extraction of business-relevant information from the source data. An operational or transactional database, such as a point-of-sale (POS) database, is transaction-based and typically normalized to reduce the amount of redundant data storage generated. The result makes for fast updates, but this speed of update capability is offset by a reduction in speed of information retrieval at query time. For speed of information retrieval, especially for the purpose of business analytics, a multidimensional database is called for. A multidimensional database is highly denormalized and therefore has rows of data that may be redundant. This makes for fast query responses because relatively few joins are involved. And fast responses are what you want while doing BI work.

Figure 1-1 shows information extracted from transactional databases and consolidated into multidimensional databases, which is then stored in data marts or data warehouses. Data marts can be thought of as mini-data warehouses and quite often act as part of a larger warehouse. Data marts are subject-oriented data stores for well-manicured (cleaned) data. Examples include a sales data mart, an inventory data mart, or basically any subject rooted at the departmental level. A data warehouse, on the other hand, functions at the enterprise level and typically handles data across the entire organization.

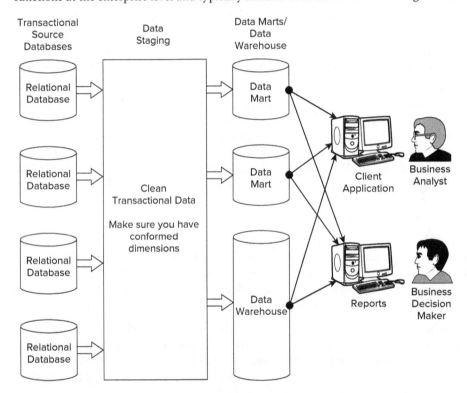

FIGURE 1-1

The data warehouse designer can see a consolidated view of all the objects in a data warehouse in the form of an entity relationship diagram, as shown in Figure 1-2. The appropriate level of access might be provided to the end users based on the levels of access they can see and query from the data warehouse. Even though your data warehouse might contain information about all the departments in your organization, the finance department might see only the objects relevant to finance and any other related objects for which it has access.

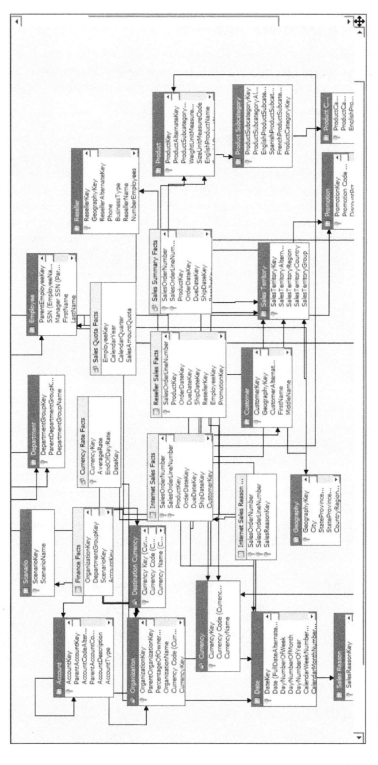

FIGURE 1-2

Key Elements of a Data Warehouse

Learning the elements of a data warehouse or data mart is, in part, about building a new vocabulary; the vocabulary associated with data warehousing can be less than intuitive, but when you get it, it all makes sense. Two kinds of tables form a data warehouse: fact tables and dimension tables.

Figure 1-3 shows a fact and a dimension table and the relationship between them. A fact table typically contains the business fact data such as sales amount, sales quantity, the number of customers, and the foreign keys to dimension tables. A *foreign key* is a field in a relational table that matches the primary key column of another table. Foreign keys provide a level of indirection between tables that enable you to cross-reference them. One important use of foreign keys is to maintain referential integrity (data integrity) within your database. Dimension tables contain detailed information relevant to specific attributes of the fact data, such as details of the product, customer attributes, store information, and so on. In Figure 1-3, the Product dimension table contains the Product SKU and Product Name attributes. The following sections go into more detail about fact and dimension tables.

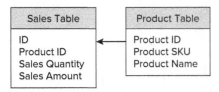

FIGURE 1-3

Fact Tables

With the end goal of extracting crucial business insights from your data, you need to structure your data initially in such a way as to facilitate later numeric manipulation. Leaving the data embedded in some normalized database will never do! Your business data, often called detail data or fact data, goes in a de-normalized table called the fact table. Don't let the term "facts" throw you; it literally refers to the facts. In business, the facts are things such as number of products sold and amount received for products sold. Yet another way to describe this type of data is to call them *measures*. Calling the data measures versus detail data is not an important point. What is important is that this type of data is often numeric (though it could be of type string) and the values are quite often subject to aggregation (precalculated rollups of data over hierarchies, which subsequently yield improved query performance). A fact table often contains columns like the ones shown in the following table:

PRODUCT ID	DATE ID	STATE ID	NUMBER OF CASES	SALES AMOUNT
1	07/01/2011	6	3,244	$90,842
1	07/01/2011	33	6,439	$184,000
1	07/01/2011	42	4,784	$98,399
1	08/01/2011	31	6,784	$176,384
1	08/01/2011	6	2,097	$59,136
1	08/01/2011	33	7,326	$8,635

PRODUCT ID	DATE ID	STATE ID	NUMBER OF CASES	SALES AMOUNT
1	08/01/2011	42	4,925	$100,962
1	09/01/2011	31	8,548	$176,384
1	09/01/2011	6	945	$26,649
1	09/01/2011	33	8,635	$246,961
1	09/01/2011	42	4,935	$101,165
1	10/01/2011	31	9,284	$257,631
1	10/01/2011	33	9,754	$278,965
1	10/01/2011	42	4,987	$102,733
...	...	...	...	...

This table shows the sales of different varieties of beer between the months of July and October 2011 in four different states. The product ID, date ID, and state IDs together form the primary key of the fact table. The number of cases of beer sold and the sales amount are facts. The product ID, date ID, and state ID are foreign keys that join to the products, date, and state tables. In this table the state IDs 6, 31, 33, and 42 refer to the states MA, CA, OR, and WA, respectively, and represent the order in which these states joined the United States. Building the fact table is an important step toward building your data warehouse.

Dimension Tables

The fact table typically holds quantitative data; for example, transaction data that shows the number of units sold per sale and amount charged to the customer for the unit sold. To provide reference to higher-level rollups based on things like time, a complementary table can be added that provides linkage to those higher levels through the magic of the join (how you link one table to another). In the case of time, the fact table might show only the date on which some number of cases of beer was sold; to do business analysis at the monthly, quarterly, or yearly level, a time dimension is required. The following table shows what a beer products dimension table would minimally contain. The product ID is the primary key in this table. The product ID of the fact table shown previously is a foreign key that joins to the product ID in the following table:

PRODUCT ID	PRODUCT SKU	PRODUCT NAME
1	SBF767	SuperMicro Ale
2	SBH543	SuperMicro Lager
3	SBZ136	SuperMicro Pilsner
4	SBK345	SuperMicro Hefeweizen
...	...	...

For illustrative purposes, assume that you have a dimension table for time that contains monthly, quarterly, and yearly values. There must be a unique key for each value; these unique key values are called primary keys. Meanwhile, back in the fact table you have a column of keys with values mapping to the primary keys in the dimension table. These keys in the fact table are called foreign keys. For now it is enough if you get the idea that dimension tables connect to fact tables, and this connectivity provides you with the ability to extend the usefulness of your low-level facts resident in the fact table.

A multidimensional database is created from fact and dimension tables to form objects called dimensions and cubes. Dimensions are objects that are created mostly from dimension tables. Some examples of dimensions are time, geography, and employee, which would typically contain additional information about those objects by which users can analyze the fact data. The cube is an object that contains fact data as well as dimensions so that data analysis can be performed by slicing or dicing fact data by dimensions. For example, you could view the sales information for the year 2011 in the state of Washington. Each of those slices of information is a dimension.

Dimensions

To make sense of a cube, which is at the heart of business analysis and discussed in the next section, you must first understand the nature of dimensions. We say that OLAP is based on multidimensional databases because it quite literally is. You do business analysis by observing the relationships between dimensions like Time, Sales, Products, Customers, Employees, Geography, and Accounts. Dimensions are most often made up of several hierarchies. Hierarchies are logical entities by which a business user might want to analyze fact data. Each hierarchy can have one or more levels. A hierarchy in the geography dimension, for example, might have the following levels: Country, State, County, and City.

A hierarchy like the one in the geography dimension would provide a completely balanced hierarchy for the United States. Completely balanced hierarchy means that all leaf (end) nodes for cities would be an equal distance from the top level.

Some hierarchies in dimensions can have an unbalanced distribution of leaf nodes relative to the top level. Such hierarchies are called *unbalanced hierarchies*. An organization chart is an obvious example of an unbalanced hierarchy. There are different depths to the chain of supervisor to employee; that is, the leaf nodes are different distances from the top-level node. For example, a general manager might have unit managers and an administrative assistant. A unit manager might have additional direct reports such as a development and a test manager, whereas the administrative assistant would not have any direct reports.

Some hierarchies are typically balanced but are missing a unique characteristic of some members in a level. Such hierarchies are called ragged hierarchies. An example of a ragged hierarchy is a geography hierarchy that contains the levels Country, State, and City. Within the Country USA you have State Washington and City Seattle. If you were to add the Country Greece and City Athens to this hierarchy, you would add them to the Country and City levels. However, there are no states in the Country Greece, and hence, member Athens is directly related to the Country Greece. A hierarchy in which the members descend to members in the lowest level with different paths is referred to as a ragged hierarchy.

Figure 1-4 shows an example of a Time dimension with the hierarchy Time. In this example, Year, Quarter, Month, and Date are the levels of the hierarchy. The values 2010 and 2011 are members of the Year level. When a particular level is expanded (indicated by a minus sign in the figure) you can see the members of the next level in the hierarchy chain.

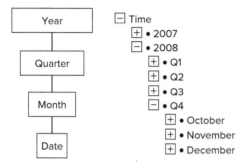

FIGURE 1-4

To sum up, a dimension is a hierarchical structure that has levels that may or may not be balanced. It has a subject matter of interest and is used as the basis for detailed business analysis.

Cubes

A cube is a multidimensional data structure which you can query for business information. You build cubes out of your fact data and dimensions. A cube can contain fact data from one or more fact tables and often contains a few dimensions. Any given cube usually has a dominant subject under analysis associated with it. For example, you might build a Sales cube with which you analyze sales by region, or a Call Processing cube with which you analyze length of call by problem category reported. These cubes are what you make available to your users for analysis.

Figure 1-5 shows a Beer Sales cube that was created from the fact table data shown previously. Consider the front face of the cube that shows numbers. This cube has three dimensions: Time, Product Line, and State where the product was sold. Each block of the cube is called a *cell* and is uniquely identified by a member in each dimension. For example, analyze the bottom-left corner cell that has the values 4,784 and $98,399. The values indicate the number of sales and the sales amount. This cell refers to the sales of Beer type Ale in the state of Washington (WA) for July 2011. This is represented as [WA, Ale, Jul '11]. Notice that some cells do not have any value; this is because no facts are available for those cells in the fact table.

The whole point of making these cubes involves reducing the query response time for the information worker to extract knowledge from the data. To make that happen, cubes typically contain precalculated summary data called aggregations. Querying existing aggregated data is close to instantaneous compared to doing cold (no cache) queries with no precalculated summaries in place. This is actually the heart of BI, the ability to query data with possibly gigabytes or terabytes of presummarized data behind it and yet get an instant response from the server. It is quite the thrill when you realize you have accomplished this feat!

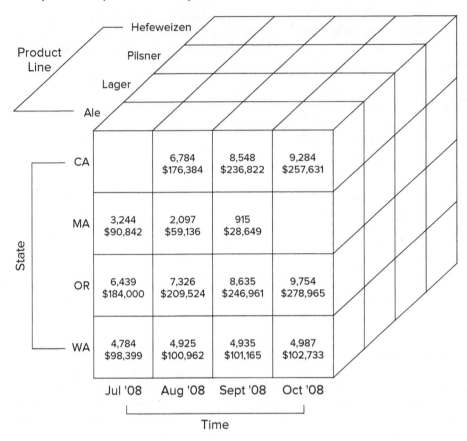

FIGURE 1-5

You learned about how cubes provide the infrastructure for storing multidimensional data. Well, it doesn't just store multidimensional data from fact tables; it also stores something called aggregations of that data. A typical aggregation would be the summing of values up a hierarchy of a dimension. An example would be summing of sales figures up from stores level, to district level, to regional level; when querying for those numbers, you would get an instant response because the calculations would have already been done when the aggregations were formed. The fact data does not necessarily need to be aggregated as the sum of the specific fact data. You can have other ways of aggregating the data such as counting the number of products sold. Again, this count would typically roll up through the hierarchies of a dimension.

The Star Schema

The entity relationship diagram representation of a relational database shows you a different animal altogether as compared to the OLAP (multidimensional) database. It is so different that there is a name for the types of schemas used to build OLAP databases: the star schema and the snowflake schema. The latter is largely a variation on the first. The main point of difference is the complexity of the schema; the OLTP schema tends to be dramatically more complex than the OLAP schema. Now that you know the infrastructure that goes into forming fact tables, dimension tables, and cubes, the concept of a star schema should offer little resistance. That is because when you configure a fact table with foreign key relationships to one or more of a dimension table's primary keys, as shown in Figure 1-6, you have a star schema. This type of schema is called a "star schema" since you see a number of dimension tables (like the points of a star) joined to one central fact table (the star's body).

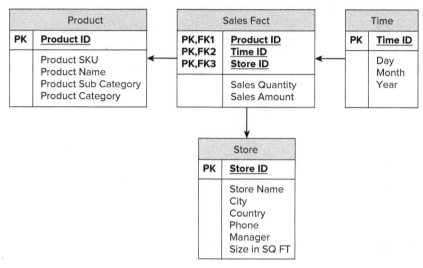

FIGURE 1-6

The star schema provides you with an illustration of the relationships between business entities in a clear and easy-to-understand fashion. Further, it enables number crunching of the measures in the fact table to progress at amazing speeds.

The Snowflake Schema

If you think the star schema is nifty, and it is, there is an extension of the concept called the snowflake schema. The snowflake schema is useful when one of your dimension tables starts looking as detailed as the fact table it is connected to. With the snowflake, one or more levels are forked off from one of the dimension tables, so they are separated by one or more tables from the fact table. In Figure 1-7 the Product dimension is joined to a Product Sub Category level. The Product Sub Category level is hence one table removed from the Sales Fact table. In turn, the Product Sub Category level is joined to a final level called the Product Category — which has two tables of separation between it and the Sales Fact table. These levels, which can be used to form a hierarchy in the dimension, do not make for faster processing or query response times, but they can keep a complex schema sensible.

You have so far learned the fundamental elements of a data warehouse. The biggest challenge is to understand these well, and design and implement your data warehouse to cater to your end users. There are two main design techniques for implementing data warehouses: the Inmon approach and the Kimball approach.

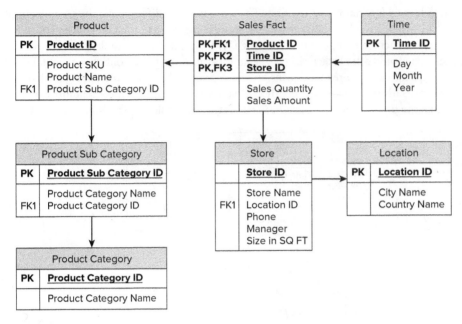

FIGURE 1-7

Inmon Versus Kimball — Different Approaches

In data warehousing there are two commonly acknowledged approaches to building a decision support infrastructure, and you can implement both using the tools available in SQL Server Analysis Services 2012 multidimensional. It is worth understanding these two approaches and the often-cited difference of views that result. These views are expressed most overtly in two seminal works: *The Data Warehouse Lifecycle Toolkit* by Ralph Kimball, Laura Reeves, Margy Ross, and Warren Thornthwaite, and *Corporate Information Factory* by Bill Inmon, Claudia Imhoff, and Ryan Sousa.

Kimball identified early on the problem of the stovepipe. A stovepipe is what you get when several independent systems in the enterprise go about identifying and storing data in different ways. Trying to connect these systems or use their data in a warehouse results in something resembling a Rube-Goldberg device. To address this problem, Kimball advocates the use of conformed dimensions. *Conformed* refers to the idea that dimensions of interest — sales, for example — should have the same attributes and rollups (covered in the "Cubes" section earlier in this chapter) in one data mart as another. Or at least one should be a subset of the other. In this way, a warehouse can be formed from data marts. The real gist of Kimball's approach is that the data warehouse contains dimensional databases for ease of analysis and that the user queries the warehouse directly.

The Inmon approach has the warehouse laid out in third normal form (not dimensional) and the users query data marts, not the warehouse. In this approach the data marts are dimensional in nature. However, they may or may not have conformed dimensions in the sense Kimball talks about.

Happily, it is not necessary to become a card-carrying member of either school of thought to do work in this field — this book is not strictly aligned to either approach. What you can find as you work through this book is that by using the product in the ways in which it was meant to be used and are shown here, certain best practices and effective methodologies can naturally emerge.

Business Intelligence Is Data Analysis

Having designed a data warehouse, the next step is to understand and make business decisions from your data warehouse. Business intelligence is nothing more than analyzing your data and making actionable decisions. An example of business analytics is shown through the analysis of results from a product placed on sale at a discounted price, as commonly seen in any retail store. If a product is put on sale for a special discounted price, there is an expected outcome: increased sales volume. This is often the case, but whether it worked in the company's favor isn't obvious. That is where business analytics come into play. You can use SSAS 2012 to find out if the net effect of the special sale was to sell more product units. Suppose you sell organic honey from genetically unaltered bees; you put the 8-ounce jars on special — two for one — and leave the 10- and 12-ounce jars at regular price. At the end of the special, you can calculate the *lift* provided by the special sale — the difference in total sales between a week of sales with no special versus a week of sales with the special. How is it you could sell more 8-ounce jars on special that week, yet realize no lift? It's simple — the customers stopped buying your 10- and 12-ounce jars in favor of the two-for-one deal; and you didn't attract enough new business to cover the difference for a net increase in sales.

You can surface that information using SSAS 2012 by creating a Sales cube that has three dimensions: Product, Promotion, and Time. For the sake of simplicity, assume you have only three product sizes for the organic honey (8-ounce, 10-ounce, and 12-ounce) and two promotion states ("no promotion" and a "two-for-one promotion for the 8-ounce jars"). Further, assume the Time dimension contains different levels for Year, Month, Week, and Day. The cube itself contains two measures, "count of products sold" and the "sales amount." By analyzing the sales results each week across the three product sizes, you could easily find out that there was an increase in the count of 8-ounce jars of honey sold, but perhaps the total sales across all sizes did not increase due to the promotion. By slicing on the Promotion dimension, you could confirm that there was a promotion during the week that caused an increase in the number of 8-ounce jars sold. When looking at the comparison of total sales for that week (promotion week) to the earlier (nonpromotion) weeks, lift or lack of lift is seen quite clearly. Business analytics are often easier described than implemented, however.

BISM TABULAR MODE

The Analysis Services BISM multidimensional mode is a great BI platform and has been for five releases of SQL Server. However, there may be some BI development situations that are not the best match for the full power and corresponding overhead of the multidimensional model. You may want to do BI work in a more exploratory rather than in a highly planned way. You may have an application that may benefit from BI but you don't have the time, budget, or expertise to build a solution with the Analysis Services multidimensional tools and platform. You may want to start small and scale your app as it proves to be more useful for a larger audience. For these types of situations, Analysis Services tabular mode might be a better fit.

The first appearance of the BISM tabular mode was in PowerPivot for Microsoft Office 2010 along with SQL Server 2008 R2. That release marked the introduction by Microsoft of Managed Self-Service approach to Business Intelligence. PowerPivot provided the ability to information workers to create their own analytical models using Microsoft Office Excel and sharing their models for collaboration using Microsoft Office SharePoint. The PowerPivot data model was designed to be simpler and easier to understand by users familiar with Excel and the relational data model.

PowerPivot enabled building models using data from many different data sources than just relational databases such as data feeds, text files, and tables in Excel. The corresponding models were composed of tables and relationships and those relationships could be between tables from different types of data sources. PowerPivot models could also contain calculations written in the DAX (Data Analysis eXpressions), which was designed to match the simpler tabular data model and be similar and familiar to Excel expressions. Data in PowerPivot models was embedded in the Excel workbooks that contained the model.

PowerPivot models, in the form of Excel workbooks, created with Excel and the PowerPivot add-in could be uploaded to PowerPivot for SharePoint. This allowed the PowerPivot model to be shared using the collaboration features of SharePoint. Data could be automatically refreshed from the source data on a regular schedule determined by the workbook owner. Models could be browsed in the PowerPivot gallery using different visualizations than just a standard SharePoint list. Information on usage of workbooks could be viewed using the PowerPivot management dashboard.

> *For more information on PowerPivot, see the book* Professional Microsoft PowerPivot for Excel and SharePoint *by Sivakumar Harinath, Ronald Pihlgren, and Denny Lee.*

In Analysis Services 2012, the tabular model introduced in PowerPivot is being enhanced and made available to the professional BI developer audience. You can now create tabular models using SQL Server Data Tools (SSDT) just as you can multidimensional and data mining models. Those models can be deployed to a standalone Analysis Services tabular mode instance, not just as part of an Excel workbook. Tabular mode models can be imported from PowerPivot workbooks using SSDT or restored from a PowerPivot workbook using SQL Server Management Studio (SSMS). BISM tabular mode in Analysis Services 2012 has added features that professional BI developers and users expect such as KPIs, Hierarchies, and Row-Level Security.

Tabular mode applications have a lower barrier to entry than multidimensional applications. You can start with just Excel and the PowerPivot for Excel add-in. You can build a model in a highly interactive way using data from disparate data sources including data pasted from other documents or applications, external OData feeds, or data from Excel tables in the same workbook. You can modify the data using Excel-like DAX calculations. And your model and all the data are contained within the Excel workbook. Working with tabular mode using PowerPivot for Excel can be thought of as *Personal BI*.

If you build a PowerPivot model that becomes useful to a larger audience, you can take your workbook to the next level, *Team BI*, and upload it to a PowerPivot for SharePoint-enabled SharePoint farm. Now you can take advantage of the collaborative features of SharePoint and PowerPivot features such as scheduled data refresh. With SQL Server 2012 you can also work with the model in your workbook using the new interactive reporting tool Power View.

If you need to scale your tabular model beyond what is possible using PowerPivot, you can import the model in your PowerPivot workbook into an Analysis Services 2012 instance running in VertiPaq mode and work with it using the SQL Server Data Tools (SSDT) development environment. Analysis Services tabular mode provides a powerful set of tools and capabilities that can handle the evolution of your business intelligence application from a simple model in an Excel workbook to a large application that can work with gigabytes of data. This use of tabular mode is referred to as *Organizational BI*. You will learn a lot more about tabular mode BISM in Part IV of this book, starting with Chapter 15.

SQL SERVER ANALYSIS SERVICES 2012

SQL Server 2012 is the heart of the Microsoft BI platform. Analysis Services 2012 is the BI database engine that can operate in traditional MOLAP mode or the new VertiPaq mode. In addition to Analysis Services, SQL Server 2012 contains other services such as Data Quality Services (tools to enable the integrity and quality of data sources), Integration Services (tools and an engine to Extract, Transform, and Load), Master Data Services (tools to implement master data management) and Reporting Services (traditional reporting platform and now, Power View), among other things. These services and tools form the core of the BI platform with SQL Server as the relational backend.

SQL Server Analysis Services (SSAS) 2012 multidimensional mode is a scalable, reliable, and secure enterprise-class multidimensional database server. The architecture of Analysis Services allows it to provide scalability in terms of scale-out and scale-up features and in terms of large database capabilities. Several instances of Analysis Services can be integrated together to provide an efficient scale-out solution. Similarly, Analysis Services is also 64-bit enabled and scales up on a large-scale system. On the other hand, the service has been architected with efficient algorithms to handle large dimensions and cubes on a single instance. Analysis Services provides a rich set of tools for creating multidimensional databases, efficient and easy manageability, as well as profiling capabilities.

SSAS 2012 tabular mode is a high-performance in-memory database server utilizing state-of-the-art, column-oriented storage technology and patented compression technology that makes it easy to build and administer scalable BI solutions with a relational data model that brings BI capabilities to more people. Tabular mode servers can be installed and configured to be a part of a SharePoint farm or as standalone servers.

The SQL Server Data Tools (SSDT) integrated within Visual Studio 2010 is the professional BI development tool for both modes of Analysis Services 2012. SQL Server Management Studio (SSMS) provides an integrated environment for managing SQL Server, Analysis Services, Integration Services, and Reporting Services. SQL Server Profiler in the SQL Server 2012 release supports profiling SSAS 2012, which helps in analyzing the types of commands and queries sent from different users or clients to SSAS 2012. You learn more about using SSDT and SSMS to develop and administer SSAS 2012 multidimensional databases in Chapter 2 . Chapter 16 is the corresponding chapter for SSAS 2012 tabular databases. You learn about profiling an instance of SSAS 2012 using SQL Server Profiler in Chapter 11. In addition to the previously mentioned tools, SSAS 2012 provides the Deployment Wizard, which helps to deploy the database files created using SSDT to your production Analysis Services 2012 instances.

SSMS provides efficient, enterprise-class manageability features for Analysis Services. Key aspects of an enterprise-class service are availability and reliability. SSAS 2012 supports fail-over clustering on Windows clusters through an easy setup scheme, and fail-over clustering certainly helps provide high availability. In addition, SSAS 2012 has the capability of efficiently recovering from failures. You can set up fine-grain security so that you can provide administrative access to an entire service or administrative access to specific databases, process permissions to specific databases, and read-only access to metadata and data. In addition to this, certain features are turned off by default so that the service is protected from hacker attacks.

Analysis Services multidimensional natively supports the XML for Analysis (XMLA) specification defined by the XMLA Advisory Council. What this means is that the communication interface to Analysis Services from a client is XML. This facilitates ease of interoperability between different clients and Analysis Services. The architecture of Analysis Services includes various modes of communication to the service, as shown in Figure 1-8. Analysis Services 2012 provides three main client connectivity components to communicate to the server. Analysis Management Objects (AMO) is an object model that helps you manage Analysis Services and the databases resident on it. OLE DB for OLAP 11.0 is the client connectivity component used to interact with Analysis Services instances for queries that conform to the OLE DB standard. ADOMD.NET is .NET object model support for querying data from Analysis Services. The data pump is a component that is set up with *Internet Information System (IIS)* to provide connection to Analysis Services multidimensional instances over *Hypertext Transfer Protocol (HTTP)*.

Although the Analysis Services tabular mode has a different data model, it still communicates to clients using the same XMLA protocol as multidimensional mode. This enables a key aspect of the BI Semantic Model: a common view and interface for client applications to both modes of the model.

The Business Intelligence Semantic Model

Analysis Services 2012 introduces the Business Intelligence Semantic Model (BISM). This model joins the proven platform of the multidimensional model and a new relational data model with the aim of expanding BI to a much broader community of BI practitioners.

Figure 1-9, courtesy of the Analysis Services product team, illustrates the high-level architecture of Microsoft's BI Semantic Model. You can see that both multidimensional and tabular modes fit into the overall BI framework, where Analysis Services is the central hub connecting to multiple sources of input data and multiple clients that consume the model. For each mode, there is a data model, a query language, and a data access technology tailored for that mode's intended use.

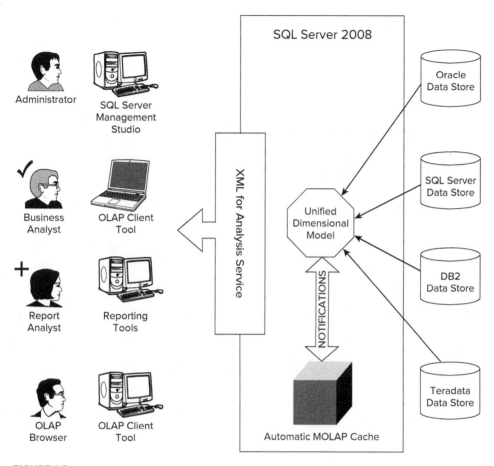

FIGURE 1-8

Data Model

The multidimensional mode's data model involves dimensions and facts which make up a cube. Multidimensional data models are built using SQL Server Data Tools using various wizards and designers. Multidimensional data models have powerful capabilities for building advanced BI applications and can support data volumes into the terabyte range.

Tabular mode data models are relational rather than multidimensional and can be created using PowerPivot for Excel or SQL Server Data Tools. Some features such as row-level security and partition definition needed by advanced tabular models can only be defined when building your model using SSDT. The tabular data model is simpler to understand and quicker to build than the multidimensional data model. Tabular mode cannot support the massive data volumes that multidimensional models can in Analysis Services 2012.

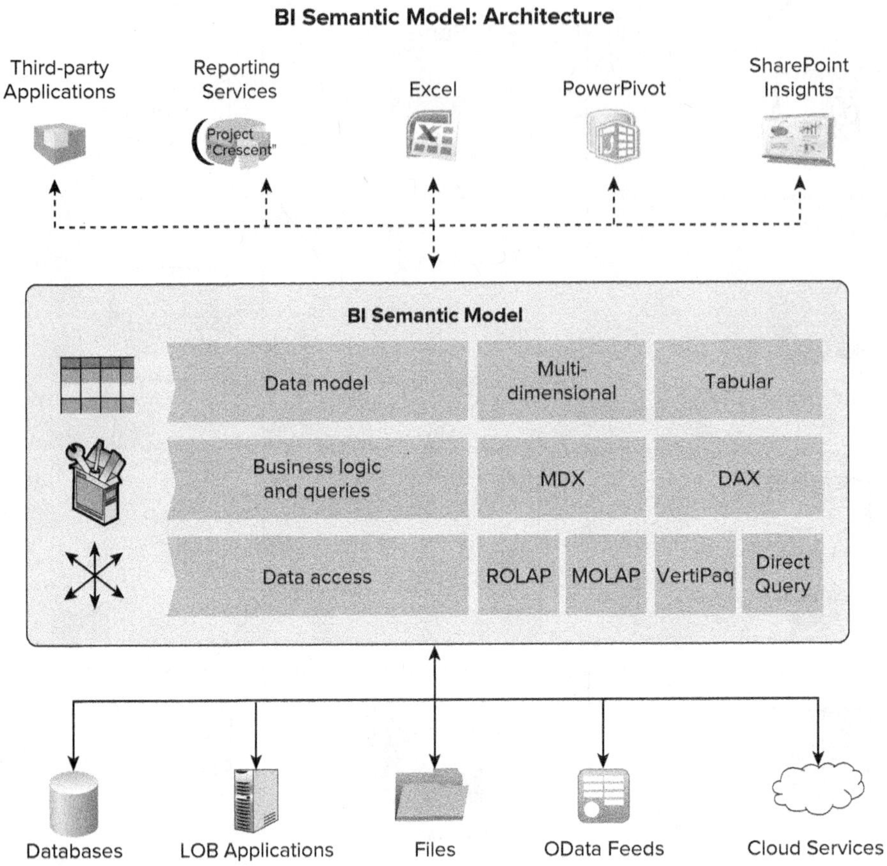

BI Semantic Model: Architecture

FIGURE 1-9

Query Language

MDX is the language of multidimensional mode. It is a well-established standard for specifying multidimensional calculations and can be used to create sophisticated analytical calculations.

DAX, the language of tabular mode, was based on Excel's formula language and designed to be easy to use by those familiar with Excel. Although the DAX language has added new functionality in Analysis Services 2012, it is not as capable as MDX for advanced analytical calculations.

Data Access Technology

Multidimensional BISM allows data access from data cached in Analysis Services (MOLAP mode), from queries directly to the backend relational data (ROLAP mode), or from the backend for non-aggregated data and from Analysis Services for aggregated data (HOLAP mode). Analysis Services multidimensional data can be pre-aggregated and is stored on disk.

Tabular BISM uses the VertiPaq engine to access data. It is not pre-aggregated but since data is stored in memory rather than disk, queries are fast. Tabular BISM also offers a pass-through mode that retrieves source data directly from relational data sources similar to ROLAP mode. This mode of data access is called DirectQuery. In SQL Server 2012, DirectQuery mode is limited to SQL Server relational data sources.

The multidimensional model currently has the most capability as you might expect from a mature technology that has been developed over many product releases. It is capable of handling the most demanding application needs with its complex metadata model, highly capable query language, MDX. It also has capabilities such as translations and actions that allow you to build highly complex world-ready applications.

The tabular model is evolving rapidly. It has a simpler data model and query language that is more appropriate for people without a lot of knowledge and training in multidimensional concepts. If the needs of your application don't require the power of multidimensional Analysis Services, you can get results faster using the tabular model. It is also not as far down its development life cycle as the multidimensional model. You can see that Analysis Services 2012 adds a lot of new features over what was delivered in PowerPivot for the 2008 R2 release. That will continue in subsequent releases.

The BI Semantic Model is designed to provide client applications with a common way to talk to both multidimensional and tabular modes. In SQL Server 2012, that capability is not complete. For example, you cannot yet talk to multidimensional models using the DAX language. The Analysis Services team has committed to provide that functionality in subsequent releases of the product.

SUMMARY

Reading this chapter may have felt like the linguistic equivalent of drinking from a fire hose; it is good you hung in there because now you have a foundation from which to build as you work through the rest of the book. Now you know about Microsoft's Business Intelligence Semantic Model and its two modes: multidimensional and tabular.

The multidimensional mode allows a traditional BI model of development. Data warehousing is all about structuring data for decision support. The data is consumed by the business analyst and business decision-maker and can be analyzed through OLAP and Data Mining techniques.

OLAP is a multidimensional database format that is a world apart in form and function when compared to an OLTP relational database system. You saw how OLAP uses a structure called a cube, which in turn relies on fact tables (which are populated with data called facts) and dimension tables. These dimension tables can be configured around one or more fact tables to create a star schema. If a dimension table is deconstructed to point to a chain of subdimension tables, the schema is called a snowflake schema.

The tabular mode provides a simpler relational model made up of tables and relationships that for many are more intuitive to work with. In the end, though, both models are designed to support BI work and having a hybrid model such as BISM allows more flexibility and tailoring of an approach to business needs.

By choosing SQL Server 2012, you have chosen a business intelligence platform with great features as well as reliability, availability, and scalability. The SQL Server business intelligence platform is the fastest growing (with the highest market share) OLAP server in the market. The rest of this book illustrates the power of SQL Server Analysis Services 2012, which is the core part of the BI platform from Microsoft.

Chapter 2 begins the journey into the multidimensional mode of the BI Semantic Model starting with an overview of multidimensional mode features.

PART II
Designing Multidimensional BISM

2
A First Look at Multidimensional BISM

WHAT'S IN THIS CHAPTER?

➤ Upgrading to SQL Server 2012 from previous versions

➤ Introduction to SQL Server Data Tools (SSDT)

➤ Creating an Analysis Services multidimensional project

➤ Creating data sources, Data Source Views, and cubes in a multidimensional project

➤ Deploying and browsing cubes

➤ Managing Analysis Services with SSMS

➤ Querying a cube using MDX

In Chapter 1 you learned general data warehousing concepts, including some key elements that go into successful data warehouse projects, the different approaches taken to build data warehouses, and how the data warehouses are subsequently mined for information. You also learned about the Microsoft Business Intelligence Semantic Model (BISM) and the two components that make up the model: tabular and multidimensional. This chapter introduces you to the multidimensional side of SQL Server Analysis Services 2012 and related tools. These are the tools, resident in two different environments, which you need to develop and manage Analysis Services multidimensional databases.

In this chapter you become familiar with the Analysis Services multidimensional development environment by working through a tutorial based on a sample relational database for SQL Server Analysis Services called AdventureWorksDW, which you can download from this book's page on Wrox.com. This tutorial covers many basic Analysis Services concepts by taking you through the process of building and browsing a cube. The tutorial shows you how to use the tools and also provides you with insight into what the product does behind the scenes.

In the management environment, you learn the basic operations associated with managing Analysis Services multidimensional applications. Further, you learn about the objects that make up an Analysis Services database and what management actions can be taken against them. Finally, you are introduced to the MDX query editor that you can use to query cube data.

 MultiDimensional eXpressions (MDX) is the query language used to retrieve data from multidimensional databases.

By the end of this chapter, you will be familiar with the key components that constitute the Analysis Services tools, the process of building Analysis Services multidimensional databases, and how to use MDX to retrieve data. So, buckle your seatbelt and let's start!

Analysis Services 2012 is a powerful, enterprise-class business intelligence (BI) product that you can use to build large-scale online OLAP and tabular databases to implement strategic business analysis applications against those databases. You learn about the multidimensional side of the Analysis Services BISM in this and subsequent chapters. Later, in Part III of this book, you learn about the tabular side of the BISM. This chapter gives you hands-on experience with the multidimensional development and management environments.

DEVELOPMENT, ADMINISTRATIVE, AND CLIENT TOOLS

Analysis Services has separate environments for development and management. The development environment is called *SQL Server Data Tools* (SSDT) and is integrated with Microsoft Visual Studio. Similar to building a Visual Basic or C++ project, you can build a BI project. The management environment is called *SQL Server Management Studio* (SSMS), which is a complete, integrated management environment for several services (including SQL Server Analysis Services, Reporting Services, and Integration Services). SSMS was built to provide ease of use and manageability for database administrators in one environment. The capability of analyzing and retrieving data from Analysis Services is integrated into both SSDT and SSMS. You can also browse source data from both of these environments. In SSMS you are provided with a query builder for writing queries to retrieve data from Analysis Services. The query builder provides IntelliSense support for the MDX language including auto completion and syntax coloring.

Another useful Analysis Services tool is the SQL Server Profiler. You can use Analysis Services Profile information captured by the profiler to analyze and improve performance. You learn more about the SQL Server Profiler in Chapter 11.

UPGRADING TO ANALYSIS SERVICES 2012

You can upgrade to Analysis Services 2012 from Analysis Services 2005, Analysis Services 2008, or Analysis Services 2008 R2. If you currently do not have a requirement to upgrade your previous

Analysis Services instances to Analysis Services 2012 or if you are a first-time user of Analysis Services, you can jump to the next section.

> *The Migration Wizard, which enabled upgrading from Analysis Services 2000, has been removed from the product for the 2012 release.*

The Analysis Services upgrade process in general is not always a seamless process and not without its share of gotchas. Fortunately, Analysis Services 2012 provides a tool called Upgrade Advisor to prepare you to upgrade databases from Analysis Services 2005 and later to Analysis Services 2012. Upgrade Advisor is available in the <processor architecture>\redist\Upgrade Advisor folder on the SQL Server installation media or as a downloadable component of the SQL Server 2012 feature pack www.microsoft.com/download/en/details.aspx?id=29065.

> *The SQL Server 2012 Upgrade Advisor requires that the Transact SQL Script DOM (SQLDOM.msi) is installed in order for its setup program to work. This component is also a part of the SQL Server 2012 Feature Pack. Note also that the Transact SQL Script DOM setup program requires .NET 4.0 to be installed.*

Install the Upgrade Advisor on your machine. When you run Upgrade Advisor on your existing Analysis Services 2005, 2008, or 2008 R2 instance, it informs you whether your databases will upgrade successfully without any known issues. Upgrade Advisor provides errors and warnings in cases where an upgrade of some of the objects or definitions is not feasible or when potential changes exist in the names of dimensions or cubes during the upgrade process due to the Analysis Services 2012 architecture. After you review all the information from Upgrade Advisor, you are ready to start the upgrade. Follow these steps to use Upgrade Advisor for analyzing the effects of upgrading your existing Analysis Services 2005 or later instance to Analysis Services 2012:

1. On your machine, choose Start ➪ All Programs ➪ Microsoft SQL Server 2012 ➪ SQL Server 2012 Upgrade Advisor. The welcome screen appears, as shown in Figure 2-1. At the bottom of the page, click the Launch Upgrade Advisor Analysis Wizard link.

2. You now see the Welcome to Upgrade Advisor for Microsoft SQL Server 2012 page. Click the Next button.

3. In the SQL Server Components selection page, as shown in Figure 2-2, enter the name of a machine that contains the Analysis Services 2005, 2008, or 2008 R2 instance you want to upgrade. In this illustration, an Analysis Services 2008 R2 server name is specified. If you click the Detect button, Upgrade Advisor populates the SQL Server Components page with the services running on the server whose name you provided. You can also manually select which services you want the Upgrade Wizard to analyze. Select the Analysis Services component, as shown in Figure 2-2, and click Next.

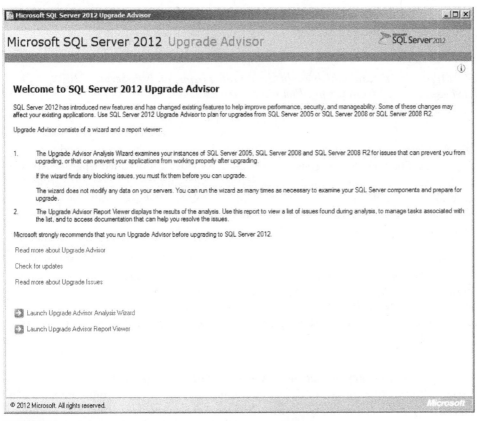

FIGURE 2-1

FIGURE 2-2

4.   On the Analysis Services Parameters page, as shown in Figure 2-3, you can select the Analysis Services instance name. (Analysis Services supports only Windows Authentication.) Click Next.

FIGURE 2-3

5.   On the Confirm Upgrade Advisor Settings page, as shown in Figure 2-4, you can review your selections. If your selections are not correct, go back to the previous page to make the appropriate changes. Click the Run button for an upgrade analysis.

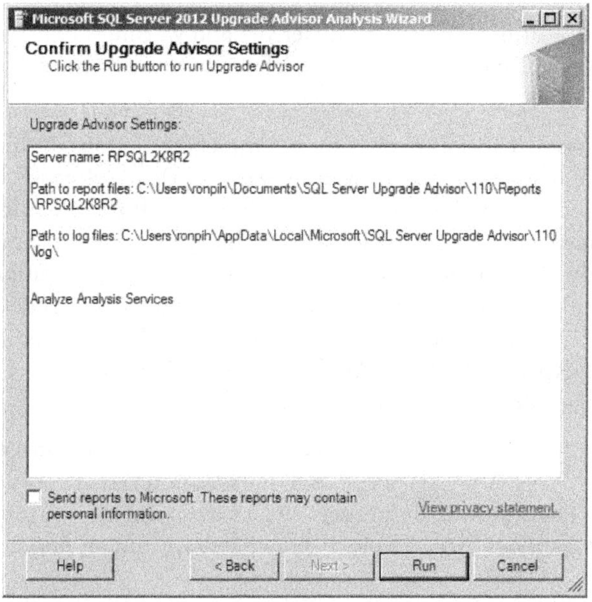

FIGURE 2-4

In the next screen you see the Upgrade Advisor analyzing the databases on your Analysis Services instance. At the end of the analysis, you see the results, as shown in Figure 2-5. Any errors or warnings appear on this page.

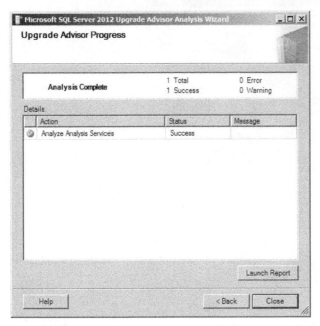

FIGURE 2-5

6. Click the Launch Report button to see the detailed report of the analysis and the actions you need to take for a smooth migration of your databases, as shown in Figure 2-6.

You need to run the Upgrade Advisor utility, analyze all the errors and warnings reported, and take the appropriate actions. In certain cases, you might need to perform some operations on your existing Analysis Services database.

After you analyze the Upgrade Advisor report and take any recommended actions on your existing Analysis Services databases you are ready to upgrade. Install the product and select the Upgrade from SQL Server 2005, SQL Server 2008, or SQL Server 2008 R2 option. If warnings in Upgrade Advisor indicate that names of dimensions or hierarchies will be changed, your applications might also need to be updated accordingly. Plan to spend time to verify that all your applications work for your customers after the upgrade process. An additional experience-based recommendation from the authors is to perform the entire upgrade process on a test machine. In this way, you can verify if your existing applications work as expected using the Analysis Services 2012 instance. Finally, with confidence, you can perform the upgrade on your production machine.

To test the upgrade process you must install Analysis Services 2012 as a named instance. You then need to back up your existing Analysis Services databases and restore them on your Analysis Services 2012 instance. Then test the databases. After you confirm that your applications work against your Analysis Services 2012 instance as expected, you can upgrade your existing Analysis Services instance to Analysis Services 2012 using the SQL Server 2012 setup upgrade path.

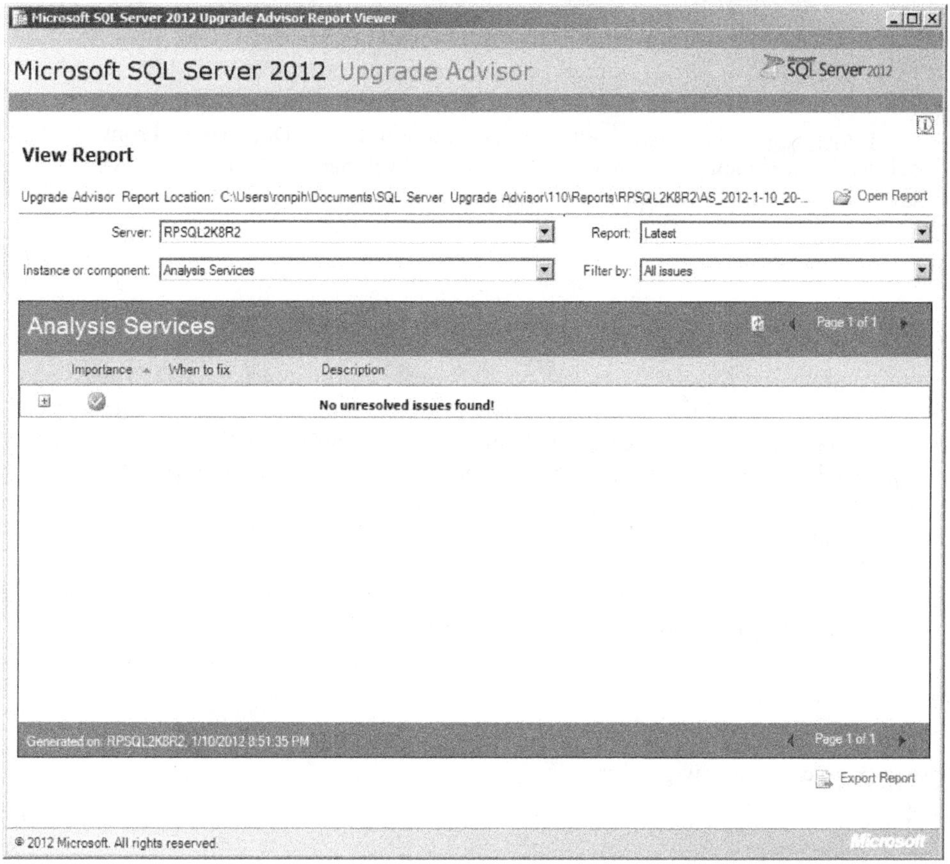

FIGURE 2-6

USING SQL SERVER DATA TOOLS TO BUILD ANALYSIS SERVICES MULTIDIMENSIONAL APPLICATIONS

SQL Server Data Tools (SSDT) is the development environment for designing your Analysis Services databases. To start SSDT, click the Windows Start button and go to All Programs ➪ Microsoft SQL Server 2012 ➪ SQL Server Data Tools. If you're familiar with Visual Studio, you might think that SSDT looks a lot like the Visual Studio environment. You're right: In Analysis Services 2012, you create Analysis Services projects in an environment that is Visual Studio. Working in Visual Studio offers many benefits, such as easy access to source control and support for multiple projects within the same Visual Studio solution. (A Visual Studio solution is a collection of projects such as an Analysis Services project, a C# project, an Integration Services project, or a Reporting Services project.)

WHAT HAPPENED TO BUSINESS INTELLIGENCE DEVELOPMENT STUDIO (BIDS)?

The Analysis Services extensions to Visual Studio for BI application development were formerly known as Business Intelligence Development Studio (BIDS). In SQL Server 2012, those features are combined with new tools for creating SQL Server database projects, and that single tool is now called SQL Server Data Tools. From an Analysis Services viewpoint, this is just a rename. SQL Server Data Tools looks familiar to users of BIDS from previous versions of SQL Server.

Creating a Project Using SQL Server Data Tools

To design your Analysis Services database, you need to create a project using SSDT. Typically, you design your database within SSDT, make appropriate changes, and finally send the database definition to your Analysis Services instance. Each Analysis Services project within SSDT becomes a database on the Analysis Services instance when the definition (metadata) of all the objects within the project is sent to the server. You can also use SSDT to directly connect to an existing Analysis Services database and make changes.

 If you use SSDT in this way, the changes you make are to a live Analysis Services database. Proceed with caution!

Follow these steps to create a new project:

1. From the main menu in SSDT, select File ⇨ New ⇨ Project. You see the Business Intelligence projects templates, as shown in Figure 2-7.

2. Select the Analysis Services Multidimensional and Data Mining Project template.

3. Type **AnalysisServicesMultidimensionalTutorial** as the project name, and select the directory in which you want to create this project.

4. Click OK to create the project.

You are now in an Analysis Services project, as shown in Figure 2-8. When you create a Business Intelligence project, it is created inside a solution with the same name. (A Visual Studio solution is a container for one or more projects.) When you create a new project with a solution open in Visual Studio, you have the option to add the project to the existing solution or create a new one. The SSDT environment contains several tool windows; of most concern here are the Solution Explorer, the Properties window, and the Output window.

FIGURE 2-7

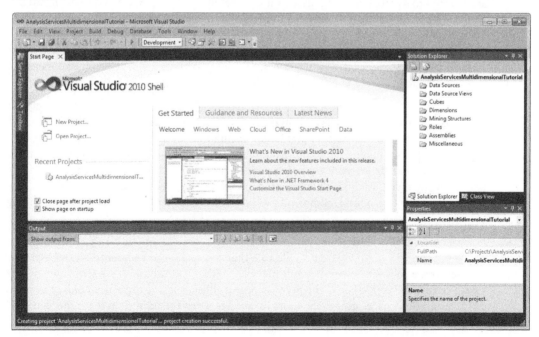

FIGURE 2-8

The Solution Explorer

The Solution Explorer shows eight folders (refer to Figure 2-8):

➤ **Data Sources:** Your data warehouse is likely made up of disparate data sources such as Microsoft SQL Server, Oracle, DB2, Teradata, and so forth. Analysis Services can easily deal with retrieving relational data from various relational databases. Data source objects contain information needed to connect to a data source such as server name, catalog or database name, and login credentials. You establish connections to relational servers by creating a data source for each one.

➤ **Data Source Views:** When working with a large operational data store, you don't always want to use all the tables in the database. With Data Source Views (DSVs), you can limit the number of visible tables by including only the tables that are relevant to your analysis. DSVs enable you to create a logical data model upon which you build your multidimensional database. A DSV can contain tables from one or more data sources. Data sources and DSVs are discussed in Chapter 4.

➤ **Cubes:** Cubes are the foundation for analysis. A collection of *measure groups* (discussed later in this chapter) and a collection of dimensions form a cube. Each measure group is composed of a set of *measures*. Cubes can have more than three dimensions; they are mathematical constructs and not necessarily the three-dimensional objects their name suggests. You learn more about cubes later in this chapter and throughout the book.

➤ **Dimensions:** Dimensions are the categories by which you slice your data to view specific quantities of interest. Each dimension contains one or more *hierarchies*. Two types of hierarchies exist: attribute hierarchies and user hierarchies. In this book, attribute hierarchies are referred to as attributes, and user or multilevel hierarchies are referred to as hierarchies. Attributes correspond to columns in a dimension table, and hierarchies are formed by grouping several related attributes. For example, most cubes have a Time dimension. A Time dimension typically contains the attributes Year, Month, Date, and Day and a hierarchy for Year-Month-Date. Sales cubes often contain Geography dimensions, Customer dimensions, and Product dimensions. You learn about dimensions in Chapter 5.

➤ **Mining Structures:** Data mining (covered in Chapter 12) is the process of analyzing raw data using algorithms that help discover interesting patterns not typically found by ad-hoc analysis. Mining Structures are objects that hold information about a data set. A collection of mining models forms a mining structure. Each mining model is built using a specific data mining algorithm and can be used for analyzing patterns in existing data or predicting new data values. Knowing these patterns can help companies make their business processes more powerful. For example, the book recommendation feature on Amazon.com relies on data mining.

➤ **Roles:** Roles are objects in a database that control access permissions to the database objects (read, write, read/write, and process). If you want to provide only read access to a set of users, you could create a single role that has read access and add all the users in that set to the role. There can be multiple roles within a database. If a user is a member of several roles, the user inherits the permissions of those roles. If there is a conflict in permissions, Analysis Services grants the most liberal access to the user. You learn more about roles in Chapters 7 and 14.

➤ **Assemblies:** Assemblies are user-defined functions that can be created using a .NET language such as Visual Basic .NET, Visual C# .NET, or through languages such as Microsoft C++ that can produce Component Object Model (COM) binaries. These are typically used for custom operations needed for specific business logic and are executed on the server for efficiency and performance. Assemblies can be added at the server instance level or within a specific database. The scope of an assembly is limited to the object to which the assembly has been added. For example, if an assembly is added to the server, that assembly can be accessed within every database on the server. On the other hand, if an assembly has been added within a specific database, it can be accessed only within the context of that database. In SSDT you can add only .NET assembly references. You learn more about assemblies in Chapter 7.

➤ **Miscellaneous:** This folder is used for adding any miscellaneous objects (design or meeting notes, queries, temporary deleted objects, and so on) relevant to the database project. These objects are stored in the project and are not sent to the Analysis Services instance.

The Properties Window

If you click an object in the Solution Explorer, the properties for that object appear in the Properties window. Items that cannot be edited are grayed out. If you select a particular property, the description of that property appears in the Description pane at the bottom of the Properties window.

The Output Window

The Output window reports warnings and errors during builds. When a project is deployed to the server, progress reporting and error messages display in this window.

Creating an Analysis Services Database Using SQL Server Data Tools

You are now ready to create a cube. The cube you create in this chapter is based on the relational AdventureWorksDW database available from this book's page on www.wrox.com.

> *Many versions of AdventureWorks are available on CodePlex, but you should download and install the AdventureWorksDW sample database from this book's page on* www.wrox.com.

AdventureWorksDW contains the sales information of a fictional bicycle company, AdventureWorks Cycles. Figure 2-9 shows the structure of the data warehouse you build in this chapter, which consists of two fact tables and eight dimension tables. FactInternetSales and FactResellerSales are fact tables. They each contain several measures and foreign keys that relate them to their dimension tables. Both fact tables contain three dimension keys — ShipDateKey, OrderDateKey, and DueDateKey — which are joined to the DimDate dimension table. The FactInternetSales and the FactResellerSales fact tables join to the other appropriate dimension tables by a single key, as shown in Figure 2-9. The ParentEmployeeKey in the Employee table is joined with EmployeeKey in the same table, which is modeled as a parent-child hierarchy. You learn about parent-child hierarchies in Chapter 5.

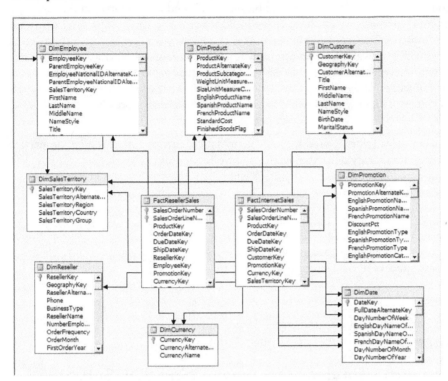

FIGURE 2-9

Creating a Data Source

Cubes and dimensions of an Analysis Services database must retrieve their data from tables in a relational data store. This data store, typically part of a data warehouse, must be defined as a data source. An OLE DB or .NET data provider is used to retrieve data from a data source. OLE DB and .NET data providers are industry-standard technologies for retrieving data from relational databases. If your relational database provider does not provide a specific OLE DB data provider or a .NET data provider, you can use the generic Microsoft OLE DB provider to retrieve data. In this chapter you use a SQL Server database, and therefore you can use the Native OLE DB provider for SQL Server, also known as the SQL Server Native Client. If you need to use the .NET data provider, select SqlClient Data Provider.

To create a data source, follow these steps:

1. In the Solution Explorer, select the Data Sources folder.

2. Right-click the Data Sources folder, and click New Data Source, as shown in Figure 2-10.

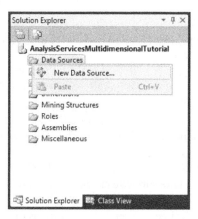

FIGURE 2-10

This launches the Data Source Wizard. This wizard is self-explanatory, and you can easily create a data source by making the appropriate selection on each page of the wizard. The first page of the wizard is the welcome page that provides additional information about data sources in general. Click Next to continue.

3. You're now on the connection definition page of the Data Source Wizard, as shown in Figure 2-11. On this page, you provide the connection information about the relational data source that contains the AdventureWorksDW database. Under Data connection properties click the New button to specify the connection details. The Connection Manager dialog box launches.

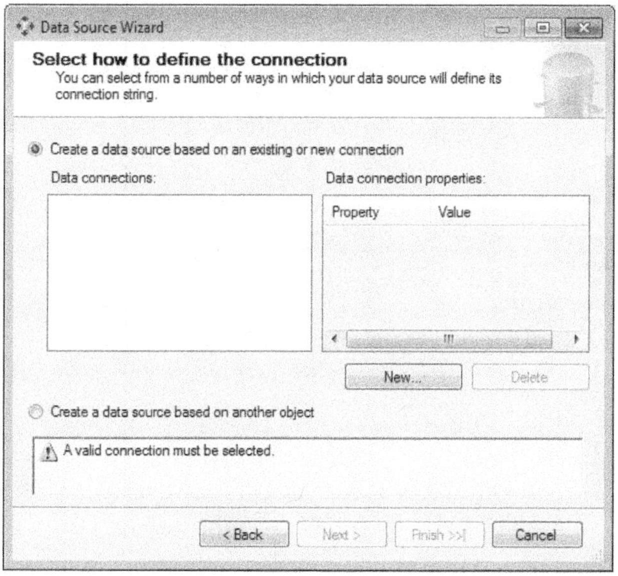

FIGURE 2-11

4.   On the page shown in Figure 2-12, specify the connection properties of the SQL Server containing the AdventureWorksDW database. The provider used to connect to any relational database by default is the Native OLE DB\SQL Native Client 11.0 provider. If that provider is not selected, click the Provider drop-down, and select SQL Server Native Client 11.0. If you have installed the SQL Server 2012 database engine and the AdventureWorksDW sample database on the same machine, type **localhost** or the machine name in the Server name field, as shown in Figure 2-12. If you have restored the sample AdventureWorksDW database on a different SQL Server machine, type that machine name instead. You can choose either Windows Authentication or SQL Server Authentication for connecting to the relational data source. Select Use Windows Authentication. If you choose Use SQL Server Authentication, you need to specify a SQL Server login name and password. Make sure you check the Save My Password option. Due to security restrictions in Analysis Services 2012, if you do not select this option, you will be prompted to key in the password each time you send the definitions of your database to the Analysis Services instance. Under Select or enter a database name, from the drop-down list box, select AdventureWorksDW. You have now provided all the details needed to establish a connection to the relational data in AdventureWorksDW. Click OK.

FIGURE 2-12

5.   The connection properties you provided in the connection dialog are now shown on the Select how to define the connection page of the Data Source Wizard, as shown in Figure 2-13. Click the Next button.

FIGURE 2-13

6. On the Impersonation Information page, you need to specify the impersonation details that Analysis Services will use to connect to the relational data source. There are four options, as shown in Figure 2-14. You can provide a domain username and password to impersonate or select the Analysis Service instance's service account for connection. The option Use the credentials of the current user is primarily used for data mining where you retrieve data from the relational server for prediction. If you use the Inherit option, Analysis Services uses the impersonation information specified for the database. Select the Use a specific Windows user name and password option, enter the credentials of an account that has permissions to access the AdventureWorksDW database, and click Next.

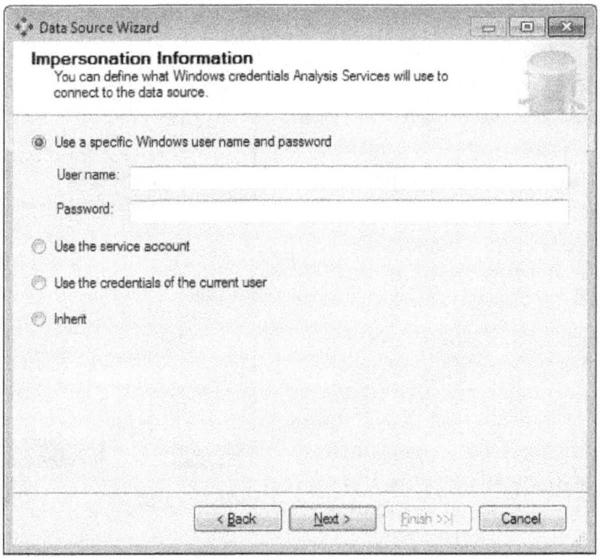

FIGURE 2-14

7. On the final page, the Data Source Wizard chooses the relational database name you have selected as the name for the data source object you are creating. You can accept the default name specified or provide a new name here. Enter the name **Adventure Works DW**, as shown in Figure 2-15. The connection string to be used for connecting to the relational data source is shown under Preview. Click Finish.

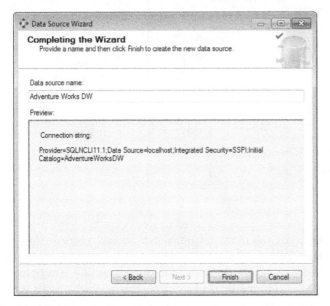

FIGURE 2-15

Super! You have successfully created a data source.

Creating a Data Source View (DSV)

Data Source Views (DSVs) give you a logical view of the tables used within your OLAP database. A DSV can contain tables and views from one or more data sources. Although you could accomplish the same functionality by creating views in the relational database, DSVs provide additional functionality, flexibility, and manageability, especially when you do not have privileges to create views on the relational backend.

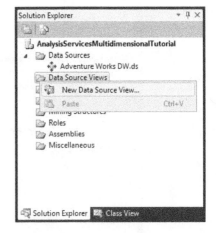

FIGURE 2-16

To create a DSV, follow these steps:

1. In the Solution Explorer, select the Data Source Views folder.

2. Right-click Data Source Views, and select New Data Source View, as shown in Figure 2-16. This launches the Data Source View Wizard. Similar to the Data Source Wizard, this wizard enables you to create a DSV by choosing an appropriate selection on each page of the wizard. Click the Next button to go to the next page of the wizard.

3. The second page of the DSV Wizard (see Figure 2-17) shows the list of data source objects from which you might want to create a view. The New Data Source button enables you to launch the Data Source Wizard so that you can create new data source objects from the wizard. You have already created a data source for the AdventureWorksDW database that you use for this example. Select this data source and click Next.

FIGURE 2-17

4. When you click the Next button, the DSV Wizard connects to the AdventureWorksDW relational database using the connection string contained in the data source object. The wizard then retrieves all the tables, views, and relationships from the relational database and shows them on the third page. You can now select the tables and views needed for the Analysis Services database you are creating. For this tutorial, navigate through the Available objects list and select the FactInternetSales and FactResellerSales tables. Click the > button to move the selected tables to the Included objects list. Select the two tables in the Included objects list. Notice that the Add Related Tables button is enabled. This button enables you to add all the tables and views that have relationships with the selected tables to the Included objects list. Click the Add Related Tables button. All the related dimension tables mentioned earlier as well as the FactInternetSalesReason table are added to the Included objects list. In this tutorial you do not use the FactInternetSalesReason table, so you should remove this table. Select the FactInternetSalesReason table in the Included objects list, and click the < button to remove it from the Included Objects. You have now selected all the tables needed to build the cube in this tutorial. Your Included objects list of tables should match what's shown in Figure 2-18.

5. Click the Next button, and you are at the final page of the DSV Wizard. Similar to the final page of the Data Source Wizard, you can specify your own name for the DSV object or use the default name. Enter **Adventure Works DW** for the DSV Name in the wizard, and click Finish.

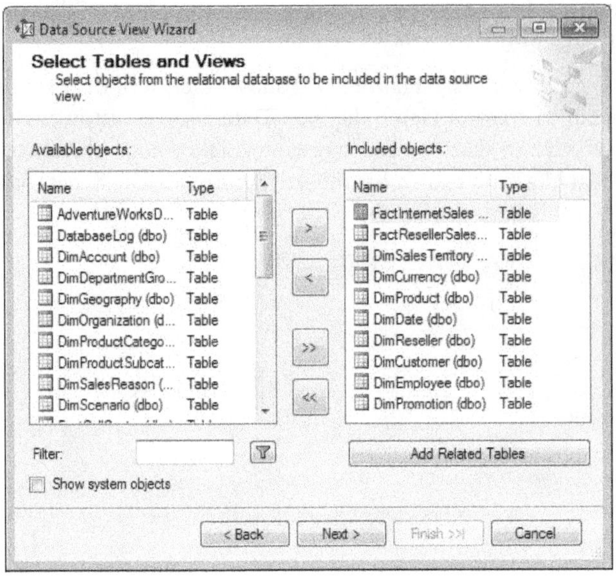

FIGURE 2-18

You have now successfully created the DSV that will be used in this chapter. The DSV object is shown in the Solution Explorer, and the newly created DSV is opened in the DSV Designer, as shown in Figure 2-19. The DSV Designer contains three panes: the Diagram Organizer, the Tables pane, and the Diagram view. The Diagram view shows a graphical representation of the tables and their relationships. Each table is shown with its columns and an indication of the key attribute. The connecting lines show the relationships between tables. If you double-click a connecting line, you can find the columns of each table used to form the join that defines the relationship. You can make changes to the DSV by adding, deleting, or modifying tables and views in the DSV Designer. In addition, you can establish new relationships between tables. You learn more about the DSV Designer in Chapter 4.

The number of tables you can see in the Diagram view depends on the resolution of your machine. In this view, you can zoom in to see a specific table enlarged or zoom out to see all the tables within the Diagram view. To use the zoom feature, you can right-click anywhere within the Diagram view, select Zoom, and set the zoom percentage you want. Alternatively, on the main menu you can select View ⇨ Zoom and then select the zoom percentage. Select a zoom percentage of 150%. Figure 2-20 shows a zoomed-in Diagram view so that you can see clearly the FactResellerSales table.

The Diagram view in the DSV arranges the tables to best fit within the view. Sometimes the number of tables in the DSV can be quite large. In such circumstances, navigating to the tables in the Diagram view can be difficult. For easier navigation you can use the Locator window (see Figure 2-20). The Locator window shows the full DSV diagram as a thumbnail. You can open it by performing a left mouse-click on the four-headed arrow in the lower-right corner of the diagram, as highlighted in Figure 2-19. The Locator window remains open while the mouse button is held down. This enables you to navigate through the visible area in the Diagram view by moving the mouse.

You have now learned the basic operations used within a DSV. Next, you move on to creating a cube using the Cube Wizard.

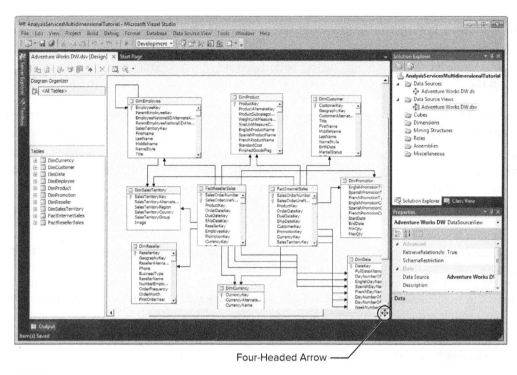

Four-Headed Arrow ———

FIGURE 2-19

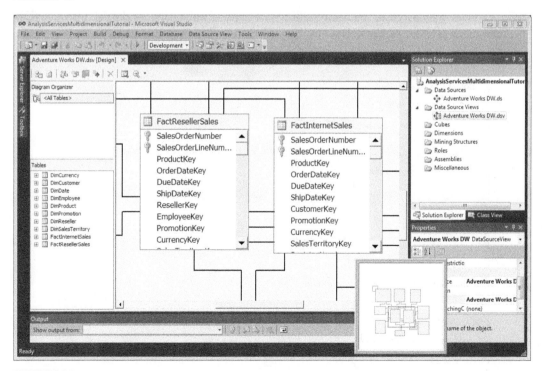

FIGURE 2-20

Creating a Cube Using the Cube Wizard

In Analysis Services you can build cubes via three approaches: top-down, bottom-up, or starting from an empty cube. The traditional way to build cubes is bottom-up from existing relational databases. In the bottom-up approach, you need a DSV from which a cube can be built. Cubes within a project can be built from a single DSV or from multiple DSVs. In the top-down approach, you create the cube and then generate the relational schema based on the cube design. In Analysis Services you also have the option to first create an empty cube and then add objects to it.

A cube in Analysis Services consists of one or more measure groups whose data is sourced from one or more fact tables in the relational data source (typically you will have one measure group per fact table) and one or more dimensions (such as Product and Time) sourced from relational dimension tables. Measure groups consist of one or more measures (for example, sales, cost, count of objects sold). When you build a cube, you specify the fact and dimension tables you want to use. Each cube must contain at least one fact table, which determines the contents of the cube. The facts stored in the fact table are mapped as measures in the cube. Typically, measures from the same fact table are grouped together to form an object called a measure group. If a cube is built from multiple fact tables, the cube contains multiple measure groups. Before building the cube, the dimensions must be created from the dimension tables. The Cube Wizard packages all the steps involved in creating a cube into a simple sequential process:

1. Launch the Cube Wizard by right-clicking the Cube folder in the Solution Explorer and selecting New Cube.

2. Click the Next button in the welcome page.

3. You are now asked to select the method to create the cube. Choose the default value (Use existing tables) and click Next (see Figure 2-21).

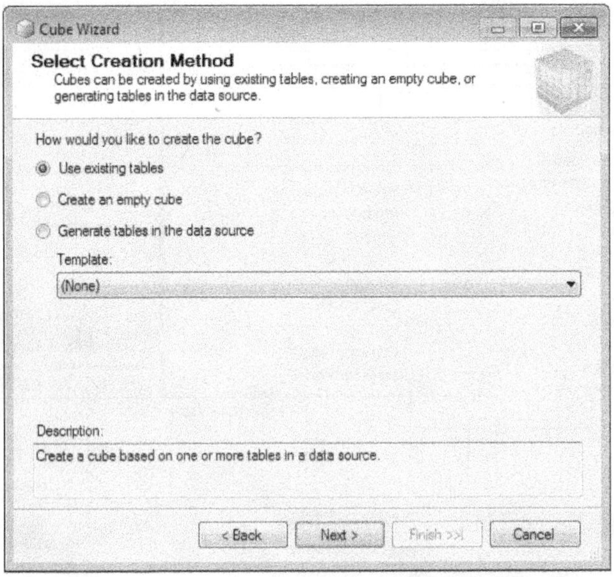

FIGURE 2-21

4. On the Select Measure Group Tables page, select the Adventure Works DW DSV, as shown in Figure 2-22.

FIGURE 2-22

5. The Suggest button helps you identify the measure group tables. If you click the Suggest button, the Cube Wizard analyzes the relationships between the tables in the DSV and selects the potential measure group tables. For this example, select Fact Internet Sales and Fact Reseller Sales as measure group tables, and click Next.

6. The Select Measures page enables you to select specific columns from the measure group tables as measures, as shown in Figure 2-23. By default, all the columns in the selected measure group tables except the key column are shown as measures and selected. Accept the default selection shown by the wizard, and click Next.

7. In the Select New Dimensions page, the Cube Wizard shows the potential dimensions along with their attributes. The Cube Wizard, by default, includes the key attribute in each dimension, which is highlighted on this page, as shown in Figure 2-24. Deselect the Fact Internet Sales and Fact Reseller Sales dimensions, as shown in Figure 2-24, and click Next.

8. In the Final page of the Cube Wizard, provide the cube name Adventure Works DW, as shown in Figure 2-25, and click Finish.

9. After the wizard completes the Adventure Works DW cube, the Dim Date, Dim Currency, Dim Customer, Dim Sales Territory, Dim Product, Dim Promotion, Dim Employee, and Dim Reseller dimensions are created and appear in the Solution Explorer, as shown in Figure 2-26.

FIGURE 2-23

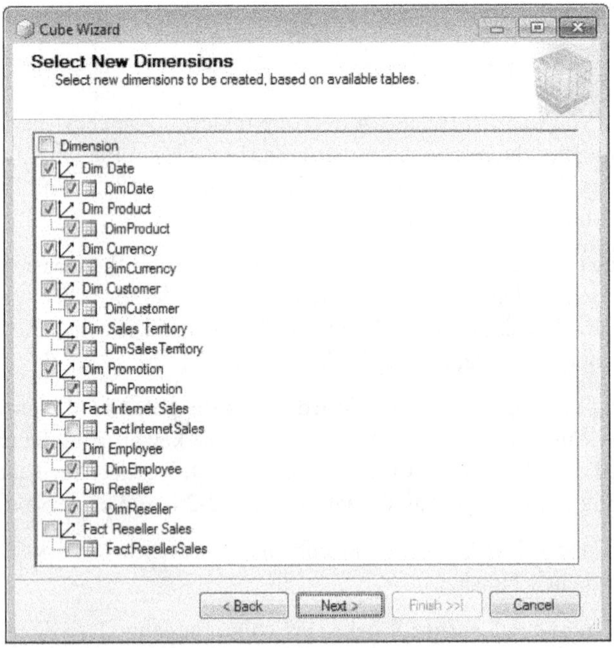

FIGURE 2-24

FIGURE 2-25

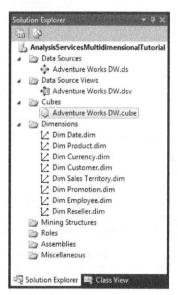

FIGURE 2-26

The Adventure Works DW cube opens in the Cube Designer, as shown in Figure 2-27.

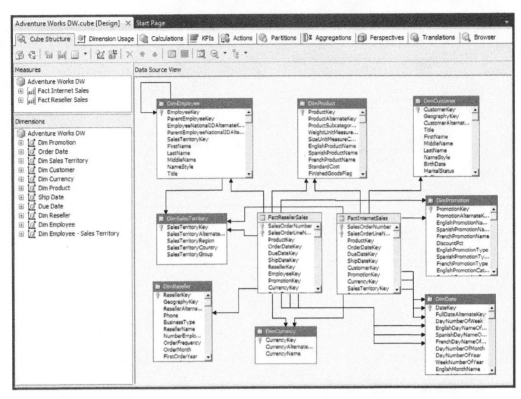

FIGURE 2-27

The Cube Designer has several pages that enable you to perform various operations on a cube. The default page that opens upon completion of the Cube Wizard is the Cube Structure page. Other pages in the Cube Designer are Dimension Usage, Calculation, KPIs, Actions, Partitions, Aggregations, Perspectives, Translations, and Browser. In this chapter you become familiar with basic operations in the Cube Structure and the Browser pages. You learn more about the Cube Designer in Chapters 6 and 9.

The Cube Structure page contains three panes: Measures, Dimensions, and Data Source View. You add or modify measure groups or measures in the Measures pane. Use the Dimensions pane to add or modify the cube's dimensions. The Data Source View pane shows the fact and dimension tables used in the cube, color-coded (yellow for fact tables and blue for dimension tables). Actions such as zoom in, zoom out, navigation, finding tables, and different diagram layouts of the tables are available in the DSV pane of the Cube Designer.

If you right-click within the Measures, Dimensions, or Data Source View panes, you can see the various actions that can be accomplished within each pane. The actions within the Measures, Dimensions, or DSV panes of the Cube Designer can also be accomplished using the corresponding buttons in the Cube Designer's toolbar.

You have now successfully created a cube using SSDT. The Cube Wizard has added only the most essential attributes to the dimensions it created. These dimensions need to be refined further to analyze the data in the cube. Because this is the first cube you create and you want simple instructions, the following steps include most of the attributes from the dimensions. When you create a production cube, include only those dimension attributes required for your application. Continue with the following steps to refine the dimensions created by the Cube Wizard so that you can perform a simple analysis.

10. In the Solution Explorer, double-click the Dim Date.dim dimension.

11. The Dim Date dimension opens in the Dimension Designer with the default page, the Dimension Structure page, selected. The Dimension Structure page contains three panes: Attributes, Hierarchies, and Data Source View, as shown in Figure 2-28. In the Data Source View pane, select all the columns in the DimDate table except the DateKey column.

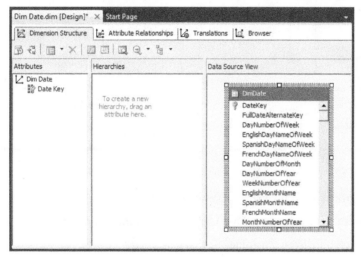

FIGURE 2-28

12. Drag and drop the selected columns to the Attributes pane. This action creates an attribute for each of the columns in the DimDate table.

13. Rename the key attribute from Date Key to **Date**.

14. Drag and drop the Fiscal Quarter attribute from the Attributes pane to the Hierarchies pane. This creates a new hierarchy called Hierarchy.

15. Drag and drop the Month Number of Year attribute onto the Hierarchies pane below Fiscal Quarter. This creates a second level in the hierarchy.

16. Drag and drop the Date attribute onto the Hierarchies pane below Month Number of Year.

17. Right-click the hierarchy and select Rename. Rename the hierarchy to **Fiscal Quarter – Month Number of Year**. The Dimension Designer with the Dim Date dimension should appear, as shown in Figure 2-29.

18. In the Solution Explorer, double-click the Dim Currency.dim dimension to open it in the Dimension Designer.

19. Drag and drop the Currency Alternate Key column from the Data Source View pane to the Attributes pane.

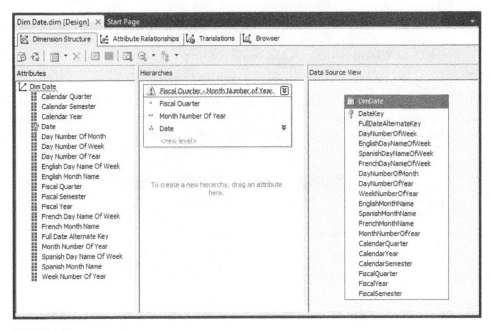

FIGURE 2-29

20. Rename the key attribute from Currency Key to **Currency**.

21. In the Dimension Designer, open the Dim Customer.dim dimension.

22. Rename the key attribute from Customer Key to **Customer**.

23. Drag and drop all the columns except Customer Key from the DimCustomer table in the Data Source View pane to the Attributes pane.

24. In the Dimension Designer, open the DimSalesTerritory.dim dimension.

25. Drag and drop all the columns from the DimSalesTerritory table except SalesTerritoryKey and Image from the Data Source View pane to the Attributes pane.

26. Rename the Sales Territory Key attribute to **Sales Territory**.

27. In the Dimension Designer, open the Dim Product.dim dimension.

28. Rename the key attribute from Product Key to **Product**.

29. Drag and drop all the columns of the DimProduct table except ProductKey, ProductImage, and LargePhoto from the Data Source View pane to the Attributes pane.

30. In the Dimension Designer, open the Dim Promotion.dim dimension.

31. Rename the key attribute from Promotion Key to **Promotion**.

32. Drag and drop all the columns of the DimPromotion table except PromotionKey from the Data Source View pane to the Attributes pane.

33. Drag and drop the English Promotion Category attribute from the Attributes pane to the Hierarchies pane. This creates a new Hierarchy.

34. Drag and drop the Discount Pct attribute from the Attributes pane to the Hierarchies pane below English Promotion Category. This creates a new level in the hierarchy.

35. Drag and drop the Promotion attribute from the Attributes pane to the Hierarchies pane below the Discount Pct level.

36. Rename the hierarchy to **English Promotion Category – Discount Pct.** The Dimension Designer with the Dim Promotion dimension should look like Figure 2-30.

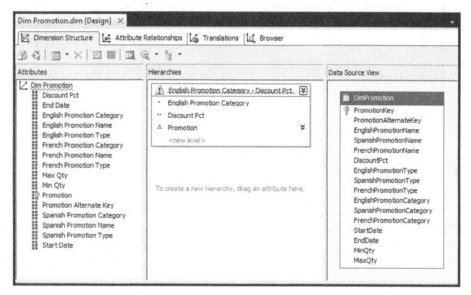

FIGURE 2-30

37. Open the Dim Reseller.dim dimension in the Dimension Designer.

38. Rename the key attribute from Reseller Key to **Reseller.**

39. Drag and drop all the columns of the DimReseller table except ResellerKey from the Data Source View pane to the Attributes pane.

40. Drag and drop the Annual Revenue attribute from the Attributes pane to the Hierarchies pane. A new hierarchy is created.

41. Drag and drop the Number Employees attribute from the Attributes pane to the Hierarchies pane under Annual Revenue. This creates a new level called Number Employees.

42. Drag and drop the Reseller attribute from the Attributes pane to the Hierarchies pane under Number Employees.

43. Rename the hierarchy to **Annual Revenue – Number of Employees.** Your Dim Reseller dimension should look like Figure 2-31.

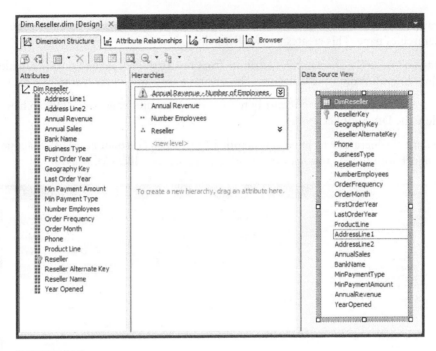

FIGURE 2-31

44. In the Dimension Designer, open the Dim Employee.dim dimension.

45. This dimension has three key attributes created by the Cube Wizard compared to the single key attribute created for all the other dimensions you opened. This is because the Cube Wizard detected a parent-child relationship within the Dim Employee dimension. You learn more about parent-child dimensions in Chapter 5.

46. Drag and drop all the columns in the DimEmployee table except EmployeeKey, ParentEmployeeKey, Sales TerritoryKey, and Photo from the Data Source View pane to the Attributes pane.

47. Rename the Employee Key attribute to **Employee**.

48. Drag and drop the Department Name attribute from the Attribute pane to the Hierarchies pane. This creates a new hierarchy.

49. Drag and drop the Title attribute from the Attributes pane to the Hierarchies pane below Department Name.

50. Drag and drop the Employee attribute from the Attributes pane to the Hierarchies pane below Title.

51. Rename the hierarchy to **Department Name – Title**.

You have successfully created a cube using SSDT and refined the dimensions to do simple analysis. You might have noticed warning symbols in the Dimension editor for the dimensions where you created hierarchies. You learn more about these warnings and the creation of dimensions, attributes, hierarchies, and attribute relationships in Chapters 5 and 9. All you have done, though, is create the structure of the cube. There has not been any interaction with the Analysis Services instance at this point. This method to create the cube structure without any interaction with the Analysis Services instance is referred to as project mode. Using SSDT you can also create these objects directly on the Analysis Services instance. That method of interacting with the Server is called online mode, which is discussed in Chapter 7. Now you need to send the schema definitions of the newly created cube to the Analysis Services instance. This process is called *deployment*.

Deploying and Browsing a Cube

To deploy the database to the Analysis Server, in the Solution Explorer, right-click the project name and select Deploy, as shown in Figure 2-32. You can also deploy the project to the server from the main menu in SSDT by selecting Debug ⇨ Start or by pressing the F5 function key on your keyboard.

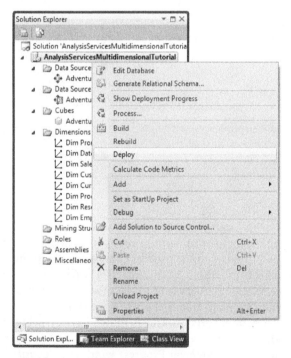

FIGURE 2-32

When you deploy an Analysis Service project, SSDT first builds the project you have created and checks for preliminary warnings and errors such as invalid definitions. If no errors exist for project definitions, SSDT packages all the objects and definitions you created in the project and sends them to the Analysis Services instance. By default, these definitions are sent to the Analysis Services instance on the same machine (localhost). A database with the name of the project is created, and all the objects defined in the project are created within this database. When deploying, SSDT not only sends all the schema definitions of the objects you created, but also sends a command to process the database.

If you want to deploy your project to a different machine that runs Analysis Services 2012, right-click the project and select Properties. This brings up the Property Pages dialog in which you can specify the Analysis Services instance to deploy the project to, as shown in Figure 2-33. Change the Server property to the appropriate machine, and follow the steps to deploy the project.

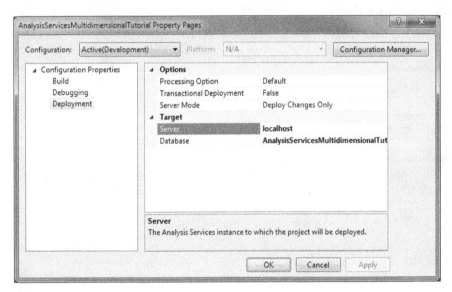

FIGURE 2-33

After you deploy the project, you see a Deployment Progress window at the location of the Properties window. The Output window in SSDT shows the operations that occur after selecting Deploy — building the project, deploying the definitions and the process command sent to the server. SSDT retrieves information about the objects processed by the Analysis Services instance and shows the details (the object processed; the relational query sent to the relational database to process that object including the start and end time; and errors, if any) in the Deployment Progress window. When the deployment completes, appropriate status is shown in the Deployment Progress window as well as in the Output window. If there were errors reported from the server, you see these in the Output window. You can use the Deployment Progress window to identify which object caused the error. SSDT waits for results from the server. If the deployment succeeded (successful deployment of schema and processing of all the objects), that information is shown as Deploy: 1 succeeded, 0 failed, 0 skipped. The message Deployment Completed Successfully displays in the Deployment Progress window. If there are any errors reported from Analysis Services, deployment fails and you are prompted with a dialog box. The errors returned from the service display in the Output window. In your current project, deployment succeeds, as shown in Figure 2-34, and you can browse the cube.

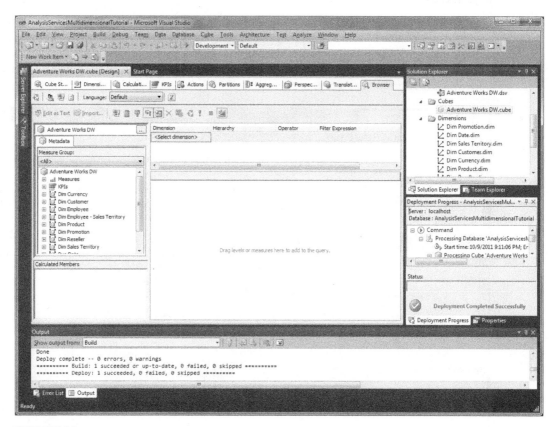

FIGURE 2-34

To browse your successfully deployed cube, use the following steps:

1. In the Cube Designer, open the Adventure Works DW cube.

2. Switch to the Browser page, as shown in Figure 2-35. The left side of the Browser page enables you to select which perspective to work with (you learn about perspectives in Chapter 6) and shows the available measures and dimensions in the Metadata pane. You can expand the tree nodes to see the measure groups, measures, dimensions, and hierarchies. On the right side, you have two panes split horizontally. The top pane is the Filter window where you can specify filter conditions to use while browsing the cube. The Report pane, at the bottom right of the browser page, is used for analyzing results. You can drag and drop measures and dimensions from the Metadata pane to the Report pane to analyze data.

Drag and drop the English Promotion Category attribute of the Dim Promotion dimension and the Sales Territory Group attribute of the Dim Sales Territory dimension to the Report pane of the Cube Browser (refer to Figure 2-35).

3. Drag and drop the Sales Amount measure from the Fact Internet Sales measure group to the Report pane. You now see the measure values that correspond to the intersection of the different values of the English Promotion Category and Sales Territory Group attributes (refer to Figure 2-35). Each measure value corresponding to the intersection of the dimension attribute values is referred to as a cell.

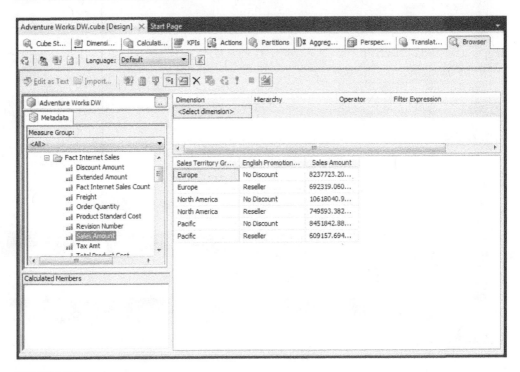

FIGURE 2-35

If you are familiar with the Cube Browser in previous versions of the product you will notice that the Cube Browser has changed in Analysis Services 2012. Chapter 6 has more details on this change.

USING SQL SERVER MANAGEMENT STUDIO

SQL Server Management Studio (SSMS) is ground zero for administering the Analysis Services servers resident on your network. You can also administer instances of SQL Server, Reporting Services, and Integration Services from within SSMS. In this book you learn how to administer and manage Analysis Services instances. This chapter specifically discusses the Analysis Services objects shown in the SSMS user interface. Administering Analysis Services is discussed in more detail in Chapter 7.

The first step in the process to work with objects in SSMS is to connect to the servers you want to manage. When you start SQL Server Management Studio, a dialog prompts you to connect to one of the server types, as shown in Figure 2-36. Create a connection to the Analysis Services through your login.

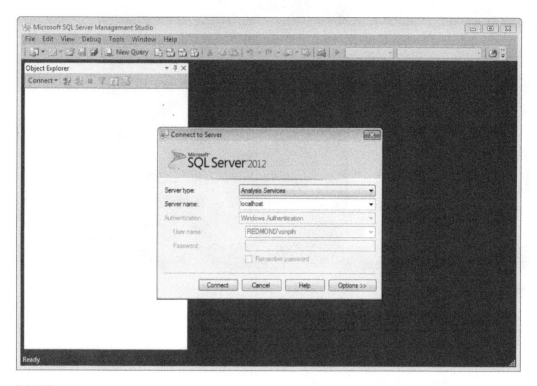

FIGURE 2-36

SSMS provides you with a way to register your servers so that you do not have to specify the login credentials each time you need to connect. Click the View menu, and select Registered Servers. The Registered Servers pane appears above the Object Explorer, as shown in Figure 2-37. In the Registered Servers pane, click the Toolbar icon second from left; this enables you to register an Analysis Services instance. Now, expand the Analysis Services node, right-click the Local Server Groups folder, and select New Server Registration. In the resulting New Server Registration dialog (see Figure 2-38) specify the name of the Analysis Services instance you want to connect to, and optionally specify connection parameters such as Connection time-out and enabling encryption. If the server instance you want to connect to is a named instance, enter its name in the Server name field; otherwise, type in **localhost**, which means you want to register the default instance of Analysis Services on your machine. After you have filled in the Server name field, you can test the connection by clicking the Test button at the bottom of the dialog. If the connection does not succeed, you need to make sure Analysis Services is running and that your authentication scheme is correct. When the connection is working, click Save.

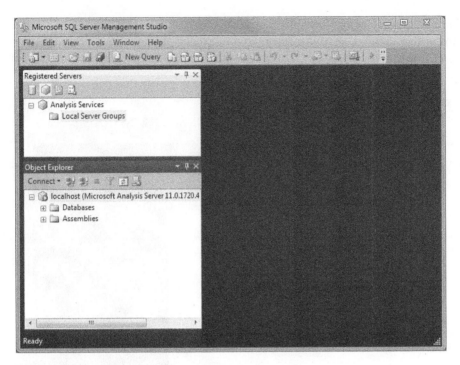

FIGURE 2-37

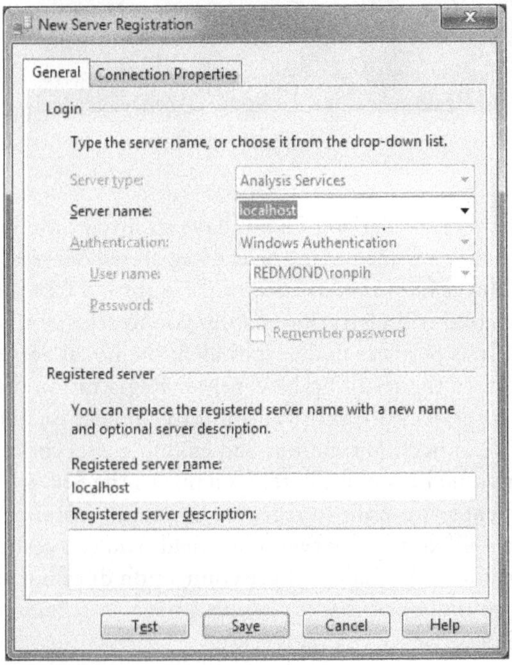

FIGURE 2-38

The Object Explorer Pane

When you connect to an Analysis Services instance, you see it in the Object Explorer pane (see Figure 2-39). This section reviews the various Analysis Services objects shown in the Object Explorer. Open the Databases folder to see the AnalysisServicesMultidimensionalTutorial database, and expand each object type's folder. You should see a list of the seven major object types (Data Sources, Data Source Views, Cubes, Dimensions, Mining Structures, Roles, and Assemblies), as shown in Figure 2-39.

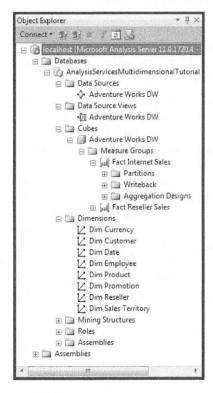

FIGURE 2-39

The following list describes each of the objects:

➤ **Databases:** Database objects are where your deployed Analysis Services projects are listed; these objects could have been created in On-line mode or Project mode.

➤ **Data Sources:** The Data Sources folder, at minimum, contains a single object pointing to a data source such as SQL Server 2012 if you have cubes or dimensions or mining models. Behind the scenes, these objects store connection information to a relational data source, which can apply to a .NET provider or an OLE DB provider. In Analysis Services you can use either technology to establish a connection to a data source. In Figure 2-39, you can see the data source called Adventure Works DW. Many databases have multiple data sources.

➤ **Data Source Views:** A Data Source View object refers to a subset of the data identified by its parent data source object. This object type exists because, in the enterprise environment, a data source might contain thousands of tables, though you're interested in working with only a small subset of those tables. Using a DSV object, you can restrict the number of tables shown in a given view. This makes working on even the largest source databases a manageable task. On the other hand, you might want to create a DSV that contains not only all tables in a single database, but also tables from other databases.

➤ **Cubes:** You have already looked at the details of cubes in SSDT; they are the lingua franca of business intelligence. You can also view cubes in the Object Explorer pane. Further, four subfolders under the Cubes object provide information about how the cube is physically stored and whether writing data back to the cube is allowed:

➤ **Measure Groups:** Measure groups are composed of one or more columns of a fact table that, in turn, are composed of the data to be aggregated and analyzed. Measure groups combine multiple measures under a single entity.

➤ **Partitions:** Partitioning is a way to distribute data to achieve efficient management as well as improved query performance. You typically partition fact data if you have a large fact table. In this way you can make the queries run faster. This works because scanning partitions in parallel is faster than scanning serially. There is a maintenance benefit as well; when you do incremental updates (process only data changed since the last update) it is more efficient for the system to update only those partitions that have changed. A typical partitioning strategy adopted is partitioning the data based on a time dimension. A variation of the partitioning strategy is to also have different storage modes for some partitions. In this way, a single fact table might have only up to 5 years of the most recent data in a few MOLAP partitions and is therefore subject to queries, whereas the older, less often accessed data can lie fallow in a ROLAP partition. If you right-click the Partitions folder in the FactInternetSales measure group, you can see a number of administrative tasks associated with partitions that can be dealt with directly in SSMS.

➤ **Writeback:** Writeback provides the flexibility to perform a what-if analysis of data or to perform a specific update to a measure such as budget when your budget for next year changes. The Writeback folder is empty in AnalysisServicesMultidimensionalTutorial because it has not been enabled. By default, writeback is not turned on. To see what options are available, right-click the Writeback object.

➤ **Aggregation Designs:** Aggregation designs help in pre-aggregating fact data based on various dimension members and storing them on disk. Aggregation designs are created using the Aggregation Designer or Usage-Based Optimization Wizard. You learn about the benefits of aggregations and how to design them in Chapter 9, Chapter 10, and Chapter 11.

After aggregations are designed for a cube, you can see the aggregation designs of a partition in this folder. You can assign aggregation designs to a partition or edit existing aggregation designs using SSMS. Right-click the Aggregation Designs folder or specific aggregation designs to see the various options.

➤ **Dimensions:** Dimensions are what cubes are made of, and you can see what dimensions are available for use in a given project by looking at the contents of this folder. You can browse, process, and delete dimensions from here with a right-click of the mouse.

➤ **Mining Structures:** Data mining requires a certain amount of infrastructure to make the algorithms work. Mining structures are objects that contain one or more mining models. The mining models contain properties such as column content type, your data mining algorithm of choice, and predictable columns. You create mining models based on a mining structure. You learn about data mining in Chapter 12.

➤ **Roles:** Roles are objects that define a database-specific set of permissions. These objects can be for individual users or groups of users. Three types of permissions can be set for a role: Administrator level or Full control, Process Database level, and Read Database Metadata level. Roles are discussed with the help of a scenario in Chapter 14.

➤ **Database Assemblies:** You learned earlier in this chapter that assemblies are actually stored procedures (created with .NET or COM-based programming languages) used on the server side for custom operations. The scope of these assemblies is database-specific; that is, an assembly can operate only on the Analysis Services database for which it is run.

➤ **Server Assemblies:** If you want to operate on multiple databases in Analysis Services, you must create a server assembly. Server assemblies are virtually the same as assemblies, except their scope is increased; they work across databases in Analysis Services.

QUERYING USING THE MDX QUERY EDITOR

Just to recap, MDX is a language that enables you to query multidimensional databases similar to the way SQL is used to query relational databases. MDX extracts information from Analysis Services cubes or dimensions. Whereas SQL returns results along two axes — rows and columns — MDX returns data along multiple axes. You learn about MDX in depth in Chapter 3. For now, look at a simple MDX query to learn how to execute it and view its results.

Following is the syntax of a typical MDX query:

```
SELECT [<axis_specification>
    [, <axis_specification>...]]
FROM [<cube_specification>]
[WHERE [<slicer_specification>]]
```

The MDX SELECT clause is where you specify the data you need to retrieve across each axis. The FROM clause specifies the cube from which you retrieve the data. The optional WHERE clause slices a small section of data from which you need results.

Query editors are integrated into SSMS for sending queries to SQL Server and Analysis Services instances. These query editors have IntelliSense (dynamic function name completion) capabilities built in. When MDX queries are saved from SSMS, they are saved with the extension .mdx. You can open the MDX query editor in SSMS by selecting File ➪ New ➪ Analysis Services MDX Query, as shown in Figure 2-40, or by clicking the MDX query button, as shown in Figure 2-41.

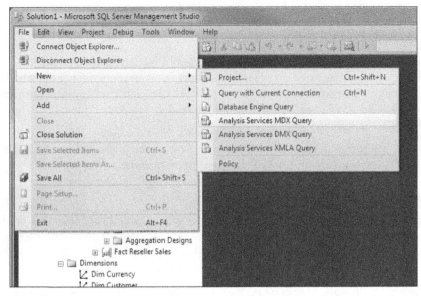

FIGURE 2-40

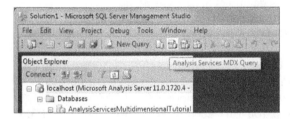

FIGURE 2-41

You will be prompted to connect to your Analysis Services instance. After you establish a connection, you can select the name of the database you want to use from the Available Databases drop-down on the toolbar, as shown in Figure 2-42. Select the AnalysisServicesMultidimensionalTutorial database that you created in this chapter. In this database you created a single cube called Adventure Works DW, which is shown in the Cube drop-down box. The query editor is composed of two window panes: the Metadata pane on the left and the Query pane on the right. In the Query pane, you can make use of the IntelliSense feature by pressing Ctrl+Spacebar after typing in a few characters of an MDX keyword.

Now you can type the following query in the Query pane:

```
SELECT [Measures].members on COLUMNS
FROM [Adventure Works DW]
```

You can now execute the query by pressing the Ctrl+E key combination or clicking the Execute button. On execution, the query pane splits in two, and the results from the server display in the bottom half. You can execute all MDX queries cited in this book using this method. Congratulations;

you just ran your first MDX query! You can see the results of the MDX query in the Results pane where you can see the members on axes and the corresponding cell values, as shown in Figure 2-42.

FIGURE 2-42

SUMMARY

In this chapter you were introduced to Analysis Services 2012. Analysis Services 2012 provides a rich suite of tools for development and management of Analysis Services databases.

You were also introduced to SQL Server Data Tools, which is the core tool for designing Analysis Services cubes and dimensions. You successfully created a cube using the Cube Wizard. While building that cube, you learned about data sources, Data Source Views, dimensions, and the wizards used to create these objects. You successfully deployed the cube to Analysis Services and then browsed it within SSDT.

In the second part of this chapter, you learned about the integrated management environment of SQL Server 2012, SQL Server Management Studio, which manages SQL Server and Analysis Services. You were familiarized with the various objects within an Analysis Services database by browsing them in the Object Explorer.

Finally, you learned that MDX does not require a Ph.D. in nuclear physics to use. You can easily use the MDX query editor to execute an MDX query, in this case, against the cube you built. Finally, you viewed query results. In the next chapter you learn the basics of MDX, which form the foundation of your deeper understanding of the Analysis Services multidimensional model.

3

Understanding MDX

WHAT'S IN THIS CHAPTER?

- ➤ What is MDX?

- ➤ MDX concepts

- ➤ MDX queries

- ➤ MDX expressions

- ➤ MDX operators

- ➤ MDX functions

- ➤ MDX scripts

- ➤ Restricting cube space/slicing cube data

- ➤ Parameters and MDX queries

- ➤ MDX comments

In Chapter 2 you ran a simple MDX query to retrieve data from Analysis Services. Building on that, in this chapter you learn the fundamentals underlying the MDX language to manipulate and query Analysis Services objects. You also learn about some advanced concepts, such as MDX operators and functions. This forms the basis for many of the subsequent chapters in this book.

SQL Server 2012 provides a sample Analysis Services project that demonstrates the majority of the Analysis Services features available from www.wrox.com to learn MDX. In addition, this chapter along with Appendix A provides you with examples of MDX queries based on the sample Adventure Works DW Multidimensional project updated for Analysis Services 2012. Some of the MDX queries you need to write to solve business problems necessitate the use of cube space restriction, empty cell removal, and parameterized queries — all concepts covered in this chapter.

WHAT IS MDX?

Just as Structured Query Language (SQL) is a query language used to retrieve data from relational databases, Multi-Dimensional eXpressions (MDX) is a query language used to retrieve data from Analysis Services databases. MDX supports two distinct modes:

➤ **Expressions language:** Define and manipulate Analysis Services objects and data to calculate values.

➤ **Query language:** Retrieve data from Analysis Services.

MDX was originally designed by Microsoft and introduced in 1998 with SQL Server Analysis Services 7.0, but it is nevertheless a general, standards-based query language to retrieve data from OLAP databases. Many other OLAP providers support MDX, including Microstrategy's Intelligence Server, Hyperion's Essbase Server, and SAS's Enterprise BI Server. There are those who want to extend the standard for additional functionality, and MDX extensions have indeed been developed by individual vendors, but the constituent parts of any extension are expected to be consistent with the MDX standard. Analysis Services provides several extensions to the MDX standard defined by the OLE DB for OLAP specification. In this book you learn about the form of MDX supported by SQL Server Analysis Services 2012.

MDX CONCEPTS

A multidimensional database in SQL Server Analysis Services contains one or more cubes. A *cube* is the object that is designed and used by the users for data analysis. Each cube must contain at least two dimensions (one of which is a special dimension called Measures), but typically will contain more than two dimensions. For example, the callouts in Figure 3-1 show the dimensions that are part of the Adventure Works cube.

You can download and install the AdventureWorksDW relational database and the SSAS Multi-dimensional model Projects of SQL Server 2012 from this book's page on www.wrox.com. Open the Adventure Works DW Multidimensional project in SQL Server Data Tools (SSDT) to see the measures and dimensions that make up the cube on the Cube Structure tab.

Measures and Measure Groups

The *Measures* object within a cube is a special cube dimension representing a collection of measures. Measures are quantitative entities that are used for analysis. You can see some measures in the sample project in Figure 3-1.

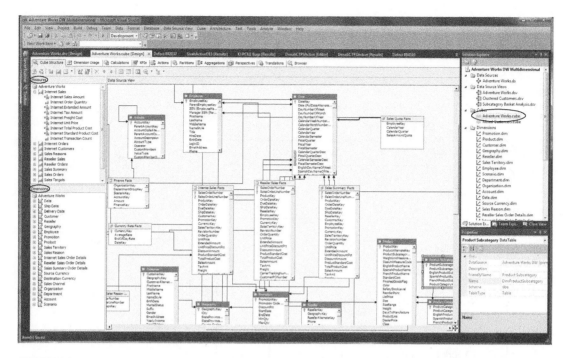

FIGURE 3-1

Each measure is part of an entity called a measure group. *Measure groups* are collections of related measures, and each measure can only be part of a single measure group. Measure groups are primarily used for navigational purposes for better readability or ease of use in client tools. Measure groups are never used in MDX queries when querying measures. However, they can be used in certain MDX functions discussed later in this chapter.

Hierarchies and Hierarchy Levels

You can see that the dimensions in the Adventure Works cube have one or more hierarchies, and each hierarchy contains one or more levels. Figure 3-2 shows a simplified cube with three hierarchies — Calendar, Product Line, and Country — analyzing the data for illustration in this chapter. In the Adventure Works DW sample, the Calendar hierarchy of the Date dimension contains five levels: Calendar Year, Calendar Semester, Calendar Quarter, Month, and Date, whereas the Product Line and Country hierarchies are attribute hierarchies with only two levels: the All level and the Product Line or Country level, respectively. You learn more about dimensions, hierarchies, and levels in Chapters 5 and 8.

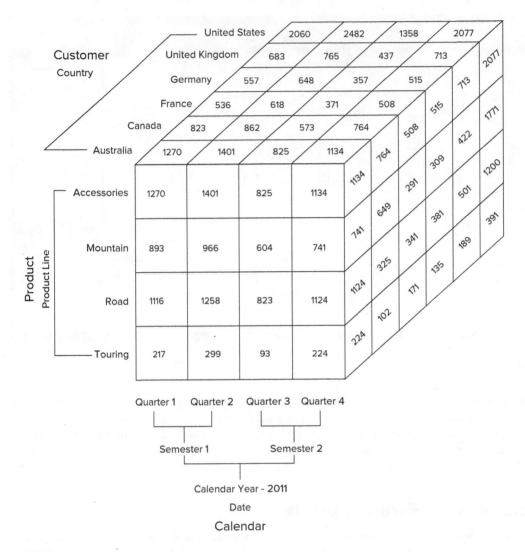

FIGURE 3-2

 Figure 3-2 does not reflect the actual data in the sample cube. For illustration purposes, some members from the hierarchies are removed.

Members

Each hierarchy contains one or more items that are referred to as *members*, and each member corresponds to one or more occurrences of the referenced value in the underlying dimension table.

Figure 3-3 shows the members of the Calendar hierarchy in the Date dimension. In the Calendar hierarchy, the items CY 2005, H1 CY 2005, H2 CY 2005, Q1 CY 2005, Q2 CY 2005 Q3 CY 2005, and Q4 CY 2005 are the members. You can see that the items at each level together form the collection of the members of the hierarchy. You can also query the members of a specific level. For example, Q1 CY 2005, Q2 CY 2005, Q3 CY 2005, and Q3 CY 2005 are members of the Calendar Quarter level for the calendar year CY 2005.

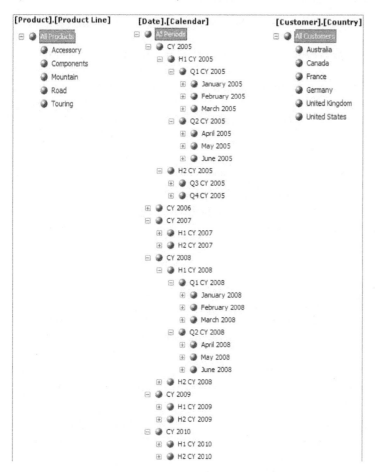

FIGURE 3-3

In MDX, each specific member of a hierarchy is identified by a unique name. You can access a member in a dimension with its dimension name, hierarchy name, and level name using the name path (using the name of the member) or the key path (using the key of the member). For example, member Q1 CY 2006 in the Calendar hierarchy is represented as:

```
[Date].[Calendar].[Calendar Quarter].[Q1 CY 2006]
```

Use the square brackets to enclose the names whenever you have a name that contains a space, has a number in it, or is an MDX keyword. Otherwise, you can omit the square brackets. In the preceding expression the dimension name Date is an MDX keyword and hence must be enclosed within brackets. (Although the brackets are optional, it's good practice to use them.)

The following three representations are also valid for the member Q1 CY 2006:

```
[Date].[Calendar].[Q1 CY 2006]                          (1)
[Date].[Calendar].[CY 2006].[H1 CY 2006].[Q1 CY 2006]   (2)
[Date].[Calendar].[Calendar Quarter].&[2006]&[1]        (3)
```

In the first, the member is represented in the format *[DimensionName].[HierarchyName].[MemberName]*. You can use this format as long as there are no two members with the same name. For example, if quarter 1 in each year is called Q1, you cannot use this format; you would need to qualify using the level name in the MDX expression. If you do use the preceding format, it always retrieves Q1 for the first year in the hierarchy. In the second format, you can see the navigational path for the member clearly because you see all the members in the path. The final format uses the key path where the keys of the members in a path are represented as *&[MemberName]*. When you use the key path, the members are always preceded with the ampersand (&) symbol. In general, you can use the following format for accessing a member:

```
[DimensionName].[HierarchyName].[LevelName].[MemberName]
```

This format is predominantly used in this chapter as well as the rest of the book. The formats described in this section are called as *Uniquename* of a specific dimension member and are included as examples only. We recommend that you retrieve and use the *Uniquename* the server generates when you are querying a specific member.

Cells

Figure 3-2 shows three faces of a cube. The front face is divided into 16 squares, and each square holds a number. Assume the number within each square is the measure [Internet Sales Amount]. If you view the remaining visible faces of the cube, you can see that each square you analyzed in the front face of the cube is actually a small cube. The top-right-corner square of the front face contains the value 1134; the same number is represented on the other sides as well. This smaller cube is referred to as a *cell*. Cells hold the data values of all measures in the cube. If the data value for a measure within a cell is not available, the corresponding measure value is Null.

The number of cells within a cube depends on the number of hierarchies within each dimension and the number of members in each hierarchy. Similar to a three-dimensional coordinate space, where each point is represented by an X, Y, and Z coordinate value, each cell within a cube is represented by dimension members. In the illustration shown in Figure 3-4, you can see three dimensions: Product, Customer, and Date. Assume that each of these dimensions has exactly one hierarchy; then you can see that Product Line has four members, Calendar has four members (considering only quarters), and Country has six members. Therefore, the number of cells is equal to 4 * 4 * 6 = 96 cells.

Assume you want to retrieve the data shown by the shaded area in the cube. The Sales amount value in this cell is 966. This cell is located at the intersection of Product=Mountain, Date=Quarter2, and Customer=Australia. To get this data, your MDX query needs to uniquely identify the cell that contains the value 966. That MDX query is:

```
SELECT Measures.[Internet Sales Amount] ON COLUMNS
FROM [Adventure Works]
WHERE ( [Date].[Calendar].[Calendar Quarter].&[2011]&[2],
    [Product].[Product Line].[Mountain],
    [Customer].[Country].[Australia] )
```

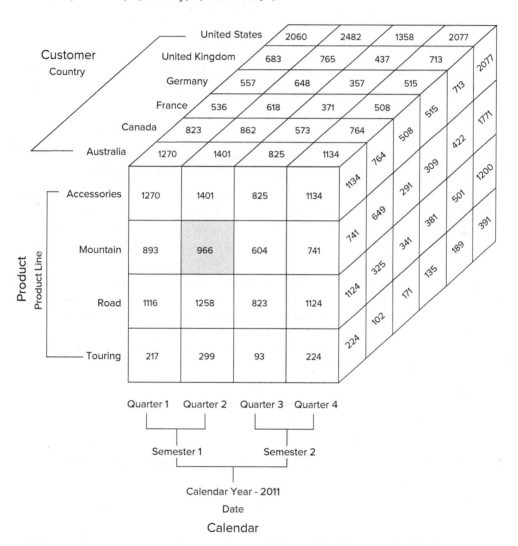

FIGURE 3-4

You can see from this query that you are selecting the Measures.[Internet Sales Amount] value from the Adventure Works cube based on a specific condition mentioned in the query's WHERE clause, which uniquely identifies the cell.

Tuples

An MDX expression that uniquely identifies a cell or a section of a cube is called a *tuple*. A tuple is represented by one member from each dimension, separated by a comma, and enclosed within parentheses. A tuple does not necessarily need to explicitly contain members from all the dimensions. Following are some examples of tuples based on the Adventure Works:

➤ `([Customer].[Country].[Australia])`

➤ `([Date].[Calendar].[2011].[H1 CY 2011].[Q1 CY 2011], [Customer].[Country]`
`.[Australia])`

➤ `([Date].[Calendar].[2011].[H1 CY 2011].[Q1 CY 2011], [Product]`
`.[ProductLine].[Mountain], [Customer].[Country].[Australia])`

Tuples 1 and 2 do not contain members from all the dimensions in the cube. Therefore, they represent sections of the cube. A cube section represented by a tuple is called a *slice*.

A tuple represented by a single member is called a *simple tuple* and does not need to be enclosed within parentheses. For example, `([Customer].[Country].[Australia])` is a simple tuple and can be referred to as `[Customer].[Country].[Australia]` or simply `Customer.Country` `.Australia`. When there is more than one dimension in a tuple, it needs to be enclosed in parentheses however.

When you refer to the tuple `([Customer].[Country].[Australia])`, you actually refer to the 16 cells that correspond to the country Australia in Figure 3-4. Therefore when you retrieve the data held by the cells pointed to by this tuple, you are retrieving the Internet Sales Amount of all the customers in Australia. The Internet Sales Amount value for the tuple `[Customer].[Country]` `.[Australia]` is an aggregate of the cells encompassed in the front face of the cube. The MDX query to retrieve data represented by this tuple is

```
SELECT Measures.[Internet Sales Amount] ON COLUMNS
FROM [Adventure Works]
WHERE ([Customer].[Country].[Australia])
```

The result of this query is $9,061,000.58.

The order of the members used to represent a tuple does not matter, and because a tuple uniquely identifies a cell, it cannot contain more than one member from each dimension.

Sets

A collection of tuples forms a new object called a *set*. This collection of tuples is defined using the exact same set of dimensions, both in type and number. Sets are frequently used in MDX queries and expressions.

A set is specified within curly brace characters ({ and }). Set members are separated by commas. The following examples illustrate sets:

➤ **Example 1:** The tuples `(Customer.Country.Australia)` and `(Customer.Country` `.Canada)` are resolved to the exact same hierarchy `Customer.Country`. A collection of these two tuples is a valid set and is specified as:

```
{(Customer.Country.Australia), (Customer.Country.Canada)}
```

➤ **Example 2:** Each of the following tuples has the three dimensions: Date, Product, and Customer:

1. `([Date].[Calendar].[2008].[H1 CY 2008].[Q1 CY 2008], [Product]`
   `.[Product Line].[Mountain], [Customer].[Country].[Australia]),`
2. `([Product].[Product Line].[Mountain], [Customer].[Country].[Australia],`
   `([Date].[Calendar].[2006].[H1 CY 2006].[Q1 CY 2006])`
3. `([Customer].[Country].[Australia], [Date].[Calendar].[2007]`
   `.[H1 CY 2007].[Q1 CY 2007], [Product].[Product Line].[Mountain] )`

The members in the `[Date].[Calendar]` hierarchy of the three preceding tuples are different; therefore, these tuples refer to different cells. As per the definition of a set, a collection of these tuples is a valid set and is shown here:

```
{ ([Date].[Calendar].[2008].[H1 CY 2008].[Q1 CY 2008], [Product].[Product
Line].[Mountain], [Customer].[Country].[Australia]), ([Product].[Product
Line].[Mountain], [Customer].[Country].[Australia],
([Date].[Calendar].[2006].[H1 CY 2006].[Q1 CY
2006]),([Customer].[Country].[Australia], [Date].[Calendar].[2007].[H1 CY
2007].[Q1 CY 2007], [Product].[Product Line].[Mountain] )}
```

A set can contain zero, one, or more tuples. A set with zero tuples is referred to as an empty set. An empty set is represented as:

```
{   }
```

A set can contain duplicate tuples. An example of such a set is:

```
{Customer.Country.Australia, Customer.Country.Canada,
        Customer.Country.Australia}
```

This set contains two instances of the tuple `Customer.Country.Australia`. A few important points to understand about tuples and sets are:

➤ A member of a dimension (Example: `([Date].[Calendar].[2008].[H1 CY 2008].[Q1 CY 2008]`) by itself forms a tuple and a set. Hence, it can be used as such in MDX queries.

➤ If there is a tuple that is specified by only one hierarchy, you do not need the parentheses to specify it as a set. This tuple can be directly used in MDX queries.

➤ When there is a single tuple specified in a query, you do not need curly braces to indicate it should be treated as a set. When the query is executed, the tuple is implicitly converted to a set.

In general it is a good practice to use the parenthesis and curly braces while you write MDX queries to ensure the tuples or set specified in your MDX queries are accurate.

MDX QUERIES

. Chapter 2 introduced you to the MDX SELECT statement with its syntax:

```
[WITH <formula_expression> [, <formula_expression> ...]]
SELECT [<axis_expression>, [<axis_expression>...]]
FROM [<cube_expression>]
[WHERE [slicer_expression]]
```

You might be wondering whether the SELECT, FROM, and WHERE clauses are the same as those in Structured Query Language (SQL). Even though they look identical, the MDX language is different and supports more complex operations. The keywords WITH, SELECT, FROM, and WHERE along with the expressions following them are referred to as *clauses*. In the preceding MDX query template, anything specified within square brackets means it is optional.

Considering that the WITH and WHERE clauses are optional, the simplest possible MDX query should be the following:

```
SELECT
FROM [Adventure Works]
```

This MDX query returns a single value. Which value, you might ask? Recall that fact data is stored in a special dimension called Measures. When you send this query to Analysis Services, you get the value of the default member from the Measures dimension which, for the Adventure Works cube, is Reseller Sales Amount from the Reseller Sales measure group. The result of this query is the aggregated value of all the cells in the cube for this measure for the default values of each cube dimension.

SELECT Statement and Axis Specification

The MDX SELECT statement allows retrieving data with more than just two dimensions. Indeed, MDX provides you with the capability of retrieving data on one, two, or many axes. When referring to an axis dimension, this actually corresponds to a hierarchy for Analysis Services because you include hierarchies in the MDX statement.

The syntax for axis specification in a SELECT statement is:

```
SELECT [<axis_expression>, [<axis_expression>...]]
```

The axis_expressions refer to the dimension data you want to retrieve. The data from these dimensions are projected onto the corresponding axes. The syntax for an axis_expression is:

```
<axis_expression> := <set> ON (axis | AXIS(axis number) | axis number)
```

Axis dimensions are used to retrieve result sets. The set, a collection of tuples, is defined to form an axis dimension. MDX provides you with the ability to specify up to 128 axes in a SELECT statement. The first five axes have aliases: COLUMNS, ROWS, PAGES, SECTIONS, and CHAPTERS. Axes can also be specified as a number, which allows you to specify more than five dimensions in your SELECT statement. Take the following example:

```
SELECT   Measures.[Internet Sales Amount] ON COLUMNS,
         [Customer].[Country].MEMBERS ON ROWS,
         [Product].[Product Line].MEMBERS ON PAGES
FROM [Adventure Works]
```

Three axes are specified in the SELECT statement. Data from dimensions Measures, Customers, and Product are mapped on to the three axes to form the axis dimensions. This statement could equivalently be written as shown below. Please do note that most of the client tools including SQL Server Management Studio (SSMS) may not be able to retrieve data from this query since it contains three axes.

```
SELECT   Measures.[Internet Sales Amount] ON 0,
         [Customer].[Country].MEMBERS ON 1,
```

```
        [Product].[Product Line].MEMBERS ON 2
FROM [Adventure Works]
```

 No Shortcuts! In MDX you cannot create a workable query that omits lower axes. If you want to specify a PAGES axis, you must also specify COLUMNS and ROWS.

FROM Clause and Cube Specification

The FROM clause determines the cube from which you retrieve and analyze data. It's a necessity for any MDX query. The syntax of the FROM clause is

```
FROM <cube_expression>
```

The *cube_expression* denotes the name of a cube from which you want to retrieve data. You can define just one cube name, which is called the *cube context,* and the query is executed within this cube context. That is, every part of *axis_expressions* are retrieved from the cube context specified in the FROM clause:

```
SELECT [Measures].[Internet Sales Amount] ON COLUMNS
FROM [Adventure Works]
```

This is a valid MDX query that retrieves data from the [Internet Sales Amount] measure on the X-axis. The measure data is retrieved from the cube context [Adventure Works].

Subselect Clauses

MDX queries can also contain a FROM clause called *subselect,* which allows you to restrict your query to a subcube instead of the entire cube. The syntax of the subselect clause is:

```
[WITH <formula_expression> [, <formula_expression> ...]]
SELECT [<axis_expression>, <axis_expression>...]]

FROM [<cube_expression> | (<sub_select_statement>)]
[WHERE <expression>]
[[CELL] PROPERTIES <cellprop> [, <cellprop> ...]]

<sub_select_statement> =
SELECT [<axis_expression> [, <axis_expression> ...]]
FROM [<cube_expression> | (< sub_select_statement >)]
[WHERE <expression>]
```

The *cube_expression* in the SELECT statement can now be replaced by another SELECT statement called the *sub_select_statement.* You can have nested subselect statements up to any level. The subselect clause restricts the cube space to the subselect's specified dimension members. Outer queries can therefore see only the dimension members that are specified in the inner subselect clauses, as illustrated in the following MDX query that uses subselect syntax:

```
SELECT NON EMPTY { [Measures].[Internet Sales Amount] } ON COLUMNS,
NON EMPTY { ([Customer].[Customer Geography].[Country].ALLMEMBERS ) }
```

```
DIMENSION PROPERTIES MEMBER_CAPTION, MEMBER_UNIQUE_NAME ON ROWS
FROM (
    SELECT ( { [Date].[Fiscal].[Fiscal Year].&[2008],
              [Date].[Fiscal].[Fiscal Year].&[2009]
            }
          )
    ON COLUMNS
    FROM (
          SELECT ( { [Product].[Product Categories].[Subcategory].&[26],
                    [Product].[Product Categories].[Subcategory].&[27] } )
          ON COLUMNS
          FROM [Adventure Works]
          )
      )
WHERE ( [Product].[Product Categories].CurrentMember,
        [Date].[Fiscal].CurrentMember
      )
CELL PROPERTIES VALUE, BACK_COLOR, FORE_COLOR, FORMATTED_VALUE
```

WHERE Clause and Slicer Specification

The WHERE clause adds a whole new level of power to restricting queries to return only wanted data. Although the MDX SELECT statement identifies the dimensions and members a query returns, the WHERE statement limits the result set by some criteria. The concept is the same in SQL, but keep in mind that, in MDX, members are elements that make up a dimension's hierarchy.

A Product table, when modeled as a cube, might contain two measures, Sales and Weight, and a Product dimension with the hierarchies ProductID, ProductLine, and Color. In this example the Product table is used as a fact as well as a dimension table. The following MDX query restricts the results only to those products with a silver color:

```
SELECT Measures.[Sales] ON COLUMNS,
[Product].[Product Line].MEMBERS on ROWS
FROM   [ProductsCube]
WHERE ([Product].[Color].[Silver])
```

The axes COLUMNS and ROWS refer to the Sales amount per Product Line, and the MDX WHERE clause refers to a slice on the cube that contains those products that have silver color. As you can see, even though the SQL and MDX queries look similar, their semantics are quite different.

Slicer Dimension

The *slicer dimension* is what you build when you define the WHERE statement. It is a filter that removes unwanted members in a dimension. In Analysis Services, the dimensions are actually hierarchies. What makes things interesting is that the slicer dimension includes any axis in the cube including those that are not explicitly included in any of the queried axes. Each hierarchy in a dimension always has a default member. (You learn about default members in Chapters 8). The default members of hierarchies not included in the query axes are used in the slicer axis. Regardless of how it gets its data, the slicer dimension accepts only MDX expressions that evaluate to a single set. When there are tuples specified for the slicer axis, MDX evaluates those tuples as a set, and the results of the tuples are aggregated based on the measures included in the query and the aggregation function of that specific measure.

WITH Clause, Named Sets, and Calculated Members

The MDX WITH clause provides you with the ability to create calculations that must be formulated within the scope of a specific query. In addition, you can retrieve data from outside the context of the current cube by using the LookupCube MDX function.

Typical calculations that are created using the WITH clause are named sets and calculated members. In addition to these, the WITH clause enables you to define cell calculations, load a cube into an Analysis Services cache for improving query performance, alter the contents of cells by calling functions in external libraries, and additional advanced capabilities such as solve order and pass order.

The syntax of the WITH clause is:

```
[WITH <formula_expression> [, <formula_expression> ...]]
```

You can specify several calculations in one WITH clause. The formula_expression can vary depending on the type of calculation. Calculations are separated by commas.

Named Sets

A set expression, even though simple, can often be quite lengthy and might increase query complexity, but you can mitigate this issue by defining sets dynamically and assigning a name that is then used within the query. Think of it as an alias for the collection of tuples in the set that can be used anywhere within the query as an alternative to specifying the actual set expression. This is called a *named set*.

Suppose you want to retrieve the Sales information for selected customers in Europe. Your MDX query could look like this:

```
SELECT Measures.[Internet Sales Amount] ON COLUMNS,
{[Customer].[Country].[Country].&[France],
[Customer].[Country].[Country].&[Germany],
[Customer].[Country].[Country].&[United Kingdom]} ON ROWS
FROM [Adventure Works]
```

This query is not too lengthy, but you can imagine a query that would contain a lot of members and functions being applied to this specific set several times within the query. Instead of specifying the complete set every time, you can create a named set and then use it in the query as follows:

```
WITH SET [EUROPE] AS '{[Customer].[Country].[Country].&[France],
[Customer].[Country].[Country].&[Germany],[Customer].[Country].[Country].
    &[United Kingdom]}'

SELECT Measures.[Internet Sales Amount] ON COLUMNS,
[EUROPE] ON ROWS
FROM [Adventure Works]
```

The formula_expression for the WITH clause with a named set is:

```
formula_expression := [DYNAMIC] SET <set_alias_name> AS [']<set>[']
```

The set_alias_name can be any alias name and is typically enclosed within square brackets. The keywords SET and AS are used in this expression to specify a named set. The keyword DYNAMIC (explained later in this chapter) is optional. The actual set of tuples does not need to be enclosed within single quotes. The single quotes in the MDX query are optional.

Global Named Sets

Named sets created within an MDX query can be accessed only within the scope of the query. Other queries within the same session or other users in different sessions cannot access these named sets in their queries. However, some of the named sets might be useful for others users.

Analysis Services provides ways to define named sets within a specific session where you can send multiple queries, or in a cube's MDX script where they can be accessed by multiple users. This is done using the CREATE statement, as shown here:

```
CREATE SET [Adventure Works].[Europe]
AS { [Customer].[Country].[Country].&[France],
    [Customer].[Country].[Country].&[Germany],
    [Customer].[Country].[Country].&[United Kingdom] };
```

Instead of the WITH clause that you used in the MDX query for set creation, the CREATE statement allows you to create a set within the scope of a session or the entire cube. You need to specify the cube name as a prefix, but you do not specify the name of a dimension because the created set is not considered to be part of any single dimension.

After the set has been created, it can be accessed in any query. If it were created within a session, it would be valid only within that specific session and could not be used by users in other sessions. If named sets are to be used by several users, you should create them in the cube scope by defining them in an MDX script. Named sets can be in one of three scopes when an MDX query is being executed:

➤ They can be within the query scope where they are defined with the WITH clause in MDX.

➤ They can be within the session scope where they can be created within a specific session using the CREATE SET statement you just learned.

➤ They can be scoped as global and defined within an MDX script using the CREATE SET statement.

Static and Dynamic Named Sets

Analysis Services supports the useful ability to define dynamically evaluated sets, yet before speaking further about dynamic sets, it makes sense to discuss static sets briefly. Use the following CREATE SET statement to illustrate the point, which creates a named set of a global scope (in the MDX script of the cube):

```
CREATE SET CURRENTCUBE.[Static Top 10 Customers]
  AS TopCount
    (
      [Customer].[Customer].[Customer].MEMBERS,
      10,
      [Measures].[Internet Sales Amount]
    ) ;
```

Prior to Analysis Services 2008, a set would be evaluated once in the context it was created. Imagine this example defined in a query scope using WITH SET rather than CREATE SET. Evaluating the top ten customers once in the context of a query is just fine because the query sets the dimensional context and uses it once. Defining the set in the scope of a session or at the cube level (to be used across all future client sessions) is clearly problematic for this type of data-bound set. The set will be evaluated when the client connects or in the current session context so any subsequent filters (say by product or time period) will not result in the set membership being updated and will effectively return the wrong data.

Dynamic sets solve this issue. Hence, the keyword DYNAMIC, which is typically used within MDX scripts to evaluate the expression at query execution time. In practice, this means that the set will not be static and will be evaluated in the context of every query that directly or indirectly references them and with respect to the WHERE clause and subselects.

Here is the preceding set, defined as DYNAMIC:

```
CREATE DYNAMIC SET CURRENTCUBE.[ Dynamic Top 10 Customers]
  AS TopCount
     (
       [Customer].[Customer].[Customer].MEMBERS,
       10,
       [Measures].[Internet Sales Amount]
     ) ;
```

We recommend you create both sets to see the differences in the MDX query results. Using a DYNAMIC set can have a performance impact if the set is very large. Hence, you should evaluate whether you truly need the results to be evaluated dynamically at query time, and then create appropriate named sets for your business.

Caption and Display Folder for Named Sets

Named sets also support the following two properties:

➤ CAPTION: This property is primarily for scenarios involving session-scoped calculations where greater flexibility in naming (for example, when defining reports) may be wanted and as such is not exposed in the user interface.

➤ DISPLAY_FOLDER: This property allows for defining a customizable folder structure in which to display metadata. A hierarchical organization may be specified by separating display folders by backslashes (\).

Deleting Named Sets

Named sets are useful for querying because they are easy to read and allow multiple users to access them. However, be aware that there is a memory cost associated with holding them in Analysis Services. If you need to create a large number of named sets that are quite large in terms of number of tuples, exercise caution. Drop any named sets whenever they are not used. Just as there is a CREATE SET statement, there is a DROP SET statement to delete named sets as well. The syntax is simple:

```
DROP SET <setname>
```

Calculated Members

Calculated members are calculations specified by MDX expressions. They are resolved as a result of MDX expression evaluation rather than just by the retrieval of the original fact data. A typical example of a calculated member is the calculation of year-to-date sales of products. Say the fact data contains only sales information of products for each month and you need to calculate the year-to-date sales. You can do this with an MDX expression using the WITH clause.

The *formula_expression* of the WITH clause for calculated members is:

```
Formula_expression := MEMBER <MemberName> AS ['] <MDX_Expression> ['],
                [ , SOLVE_ORDER = <integer>]
                [ , <CellProperty> = <PropertyExpression>]
```

MDX uses the keywords MEMBER and AS in the WITH clause for creating calculated members. The *MemberName* should be a fully qualified name that includes the dimension, hierarchy, and level under which the specific calculated member needs to be created. The *MDX_Expression* should return a value that calculates the value of the member.

The SOLVE_ORDER, which is an optional parameter, should be a positive integer value if specified. It determines the order in which the members are evaluated when multiple calculated members are defined. The *CellProperty* is also optional and is used to specify cell properties for the calculated member such as the text formatting of the cell contents including the background color.

All the measures in a cube are stored in a special dimension called Measures. Calculated members can also be created on the measures dimension, in which case they are referred to as calculated measures. The following is an example of a calculated member statement:

```
WITH MEMBER MEASURES.[Profit] AS [Measures].[Internet Sales Amount]-
[Measures].[Internet Standard Product Cost]
SELECT measures.profit ON COLUMNS,
  [Customer].[Country].MEMBERS ON ROWS
FROM [Adventure Works]
```

In this example, a calculated member, Profit, has been defined as the difference of the measures [Internet Sales Amount] and [Internet Standard Product Cost]. When the query is executed, the Profit value will be calculated for every country based on the MDX expression.

Global Calculated Members

As with named sets, you can create calculated members using the CREATE statement followed by the keyword MEMBER and the member name, as follows:

```
CREATE MEMBER [Adventure Works].[Measures].[Profit] AS
  '([Measures].[Internet Sales Amount] - [Measures].[Total Product Cost])';
```

You are expected to specify the cube and dimension name for calculated members. In an MDX script, you can use the CURRENTCUBE keyword instead of the cube name as shown here:

```
CREATE MEMBER CURRENTCUBE.[Measures].[Profit] AS
  '([Measures].[Internet Sales Amount] - [Measures].[Total Product Cost])';
```

However, all measures within a cube are always within a special dimension called Measures. Hence, in the preceding CREATE statement, the cube name and the dimension Measures are specified. The calculated members that are most often created by users are calculated measures, that is, calculated members on the Measures dimension. For convenience, Analysis Services assumes that a calculated member will be in the Measures dimension if it is not explicitly prefixed with Measures. Hence, the following statement is valid syntax in your cube's MDX script:

```
CREATE MEMBER [Profit]
AS '( [Measures].[Internet Sales Amount] - [Measures].[Total Product Cost] )';
```

After the calculated members have been created, you can use them as shown in the following query. The query scope, session scope, and global scope seen for named sets also apply to calculated members.

```
SELECT [Measures].[Profit] ON COLUMNS,
       [Customer].[Country].MEMBERS ON ROWS
FROM [Adventure Works]
```

Analysis Services provides another way to define calculated members at the global scope (in an MDX script). This involves declaring a member first without any definition and later defining the expression, as the following MDX statements demonstrate. Using this technique is a matter of convenience if, say, you want to create a calculated measure and are not sure about the actual expression which later is specified in the MDX script. You can define the calculated member, use it in statements, and finally create the actual expression.

```
CREATE MEMBER [Profit] AS NULL;

[Measures].[Profit] = [Measures].[Sales Amount] - [Measures].
       [Total Product Cost];
```

Properties of Calculated Members

Analysis Services further extends the calculated member syntax by enabling the definition of three properties:

➤ CAPTION: Changing the caption is most useful for session-scoped calculations, and for this reason it's not exposed in the development tools.

➤ DISPLAY_FOLDER: Simply controls the name of the display folder, as you have likely guessed.

➤ ASSOCIATED_MEASURE_GROUP: A direct reference to an existing measure group that is used to visually group calculated measures with the appropriate physical measures. This property is an XML property, not in the MDX language.

Deleting Calculated Members

Similar to named sets, calculated members can also be dropped using the DROP MEMBER statement. The syntax for DROP MEMBER is:

```
DROP MEMBER <member name>
```

Ranking and Sorting

Ranking and Sorting are pretty common features in most business analyses, and MDX provides several functions for this purpose, such as TopCount, BottomCount, TopPercent, BottomPercent, and Rank. The following are basic examples for TopCount and BottomCount based on Adventure Works DW.

If you are looking for the top N product categories based on the sales in all countries, the following query can provide you with the answer.

```
SELECT [Measures].[Internet Sales Amount] ON COLUMNS,
TopCount( [Product].[Product Categories].[Category].MEMBERS, 3,
    [Measures].[Internet Sales Amount] ) ON ROWS
FROM [Adventure Works]
```

On the other hand, to maximize your business you might want to discontinue products that are not providing your best sales. Now see the bottom 10% in terms of Internet sales:

```
//Total number of products contributing towards internet sales - 159 products

SELECT { [Measures].[Internet Sales Amount] } ON COLUMNS,
NON EMPTY [Product].[Product Categories].[Product].MEMBERS ON ROWS
FROM [Adventure Works]

//Bottom 10% (Sales) of the products sold through the internet - 95 products
SELECT { [Measures].[Internet Sales Amount] } ON COLUMNS,
NON EMPTY BottomPercent(
    [Product].[Product Categories].[Product].MEMBERS, 10,
    [Measures].[Internet Sales Amount] ) ON ROWS
FROM [Adventure Works]
```

You can see that there are 159 products that contribute toward Internet sales, and out of these, 95 products contribute to the bottom 10% of the overall sales. Now you can further drill down at each product and identify the cost of selling them over the Internet to see if it makes sense to keep selling these products.

MDX EXPRESSIONS

MDX expressions are partial MDX statements that evaluate to a value. They are typically used in calculations or in defining values for objects such as default members and default measures, or for defining security expressions to allow or deny access. MDX expressions typically take a member, a tuple, or a set as a parameter and return a value. If the result of the MDX expression evaluation is no value, a Null value is returned. Following are some examples of MDX expressions:

➤ **Example 1:** This example returns the default member specified for the Customer Geography hierarchy of the Customer dimension.

```
Customer.[Customer Geography].DEFAULTMEMBER
```

➤ **Example 2:** This MDX expression compares the sales to customers of different countries with sales of customers in Australia.

```
(Customer.[Customer Geography].CURRENTMEMBER, Measures.[Sales Amount]) -
(Customer.[Customer Geography].Australia, Measures.[Sales Amount])
```

You typically use such an expression in a calculated measure. Complex MDX expressions can include various operators in the MDX language along with the combination of the functions available in MDX as follows.

➤ **Example 3:** This example is an MDX cell security expression that allows employees to see Sales information made by them or by the employees reporting to them and not other employees. This MDX expression uses several MDX functions. (You learn some of these in the next section.) You can see that this is not a simple MDX expression. The preceding MDX expression returns a value True or False based on the employee logged in. Analysis Services allows appropriate cells to be accessed by the employee based on the evaluation.

```
COUNT(INTERSECT( DESCENDANTS( IIF( HIERARCHIZE(EXISTS[Employee].
      [Employee].MEMBERS,
```

```
STRTOMEMBER("[Employee].[login].[login].&["+USERNAME+"]")),
        POST).ITEM(0).ITEM(0).PARENT.DATAMEMBER is
HIERARCHIZE(EXISTS([Employee].[Employee].MEMBERS,
        STRTOMEMBER("[Employee].[login].[login].&["+USERNAME+"]")),
        POST).ITEM(0).ITEM(0),
HIERARCHIZE(EXISTS([Employee].[Employee].MEMBERS,
        STRTOMEMBER("[Employee].[login].[login].&["+username+"]")),
        POST).ITEM(0).ITEM(0).PARENT,
HIERARCHIZE(EXISTS([Employee].[Employee].MEMBERS,
STRTOMEMBER("[Employee].[login].[login].&["+USERNAME+"]")),
        POST).ITEM(0).ITEM(0))
).ITEM(0) , Employee.Employee.CURRENTMEMBER))  > 0
```

MDX OPERATORS

The MDX language has several types of operators including arithmetic operators, logical operators, and special MDX operators. An operator is a function that performs a specific action, takes arguments, and returns a result.

Arithmetic Operators

Regular arithmetic operators such as +, –, *, and / are available in MDX. Just as with other programming languages, you can apply these operators on two numbers. You can also use the + and – operators as unary operators on numbers. Use unary operators, as the name indicates, with a single operand (single number) in MDX expressions such as + 100 or – 100.

Set Operators

The +, –, and * operators, in addition to being arithmetic operators, can also perform operations on the MDX sets. The + operator returns the union of two sets: The – operator returns the difference of two sets, and the * operator returns the cross product of two sets. The cross product of two sets results in all possible combinations of the tuples in each set and helps to retrieve data in a matrix format. For example, if you have two sets, {Male, Female} and {2007, 2008, 2009}, the cross product, represented as {Male, Female} * {2007, 2008, 2009}, is {(Male,2007), (Male,2008), (Male,2009),(Female,2007),(Female,2008),(Female,2009)}. The following examples show MDX expressions that use the set operators:

➤ **Example 1:** The result of the MDX expression:

{[Customer].[Country].[Australia]} + {[Customer].[Country].[Canada]}

is the union of the two sets as shown here:

{[Customer].[Country].[Australia], [Customer].[Country].[Canada]}

➤ **Example 2:** The result of the MDX expression:

{[Customer].[Country].[Australia],[Customer].[Country].[Canada]}*
{[Product].[Product Line].[Mountain],[Product].[Product Line].[Road]}

is the cross product of the sets as shown here:

{([Customer].[Country].[Australia],[Product].[Product Line].[Mountain])
([Customer].[Country].[Australia],[Product].[Product Line].[Road])

```
([Customer].[Country].[Canada],[Product].[Product Line].[Mountain])
([Customer].[Country].[Canada],[Product].[Product Line].[Road])}
```

Comparison Operators

MDX supports the comparison operators <, <=, >, >=, =, and <>. These operators take two MDX expressions as arguments and return TRUE or FALSE based on the result of comparing the values of each expression.

➤ **Example:** The following MDX expression uses the greater than comparison operator, >:

```
Count (Customer.[Country].members) > 3
```

In this example, Count is an MDX function that can count the number of members in the Country hierarchy of the Customer dimension. Because there are more than three members, the result of the MDX expression is TRUE.

Logical Operators

The logical operators that are part of MDX are AND, OR, XOR, NOT, and IS, which are used for logical conjunction, logical disjunction, logical exclusion, logical negation, and comparison, respectively. These operators take two MDX expressions as arguments and return TRUE or FALSE based on the logical operation. You typically use logical operators in MDX expressions for cell and dimension security, which you learn about in Chapter 14.

Special MDX Operators — Curly Braces, Commas, and Colons

You can use the curly braces, represented by the characters { and }, to enclose a tuple or a set of tuples to form an MDX set. Whenever you have a set with a single tuple, the curly brace is optional because Analysis Services implicitly converts a single tuple to a set when needed. When there is more than one tuple to be represented as a set or when there is an empty set, you need to use the curly braces.

You have already seen the comma character used in several earlier examples. The comma character can form a tuple that contains more than one member. By doing this you create a slice of data on the cube. In addition, the comma character can separate multiple tuples specified to define a set. In the set { (Male,2007), (Male,2008), (Male,2009),(Female,2007),(Female,2 008),(Female,2009)} the comma character is not only used to form tuples, but also to form the set of tuples.

The colon character defines a range of members within a set. Use it between two nonconsecutive members in a set to indicate inclusion of all the members between them, based on the set ordering (key-based or name-based). For example, if you have the following set:

```
{[Customer].[Country].[Australia], [Customer].[Country].[Canada],
[Customer].[Country].[France], [Customer].[Country].[Germany],
[Customer].[Country].[United Kingdom], [Customer].[Country].[United States]}
```

the following MDX expression:

```
{[Customer].[Country].[Canada] : [Customer].[Country].[United Kingdom]}
```

results in the following set:

```
{[Customer].[Country].[Canada], [Customer].[Country].[France],
[Customer].[Country].[Germany], [Customer].[Country].[United Kingdom]}
```

MDX FUNCTIONS

MDX functions help address some of the common operations needed in MDX expressions or queries including ordering tuples in a set, counting the number of members in a dimension, and string manipulation required to transform user input into corresponding MDX objects. Because MDX functions are so central to the successful use of Analysis Services, it is best if you jump in and learn some of them now.

MDX Function Categories

In this section, the MDX functions have been categorized in a specific way similar to the product documentations of MDX functions to help you understand them efficiently. You also see some details on select functions of interest, where interest level is defined by the probability you will use a given function in your future BI development work. You can see all the MDX functions in detail in Appendix A (available online at www.wrox.com).

MDX functions can be called in several ways:

➤ .Function (read *dot* function)

   Example: `Dimension.Name` returns the name of the object being referenced (could be a hierarchy or level/member expression). Perhaps this reminds you of the dot operator in VB.NET or C# programming — that's fine. It's roughly the same idea.

➤ Function

   Example: `Username` acquires the username of the logged-in user. It returns a string in the following format: *domain-name\user-name*. Most often you use this in dimension- or cell security-related MDX expressions.

➤ Function ( )

   Example: The function `CustomData ( )` requires parentheses, but takes no arguments. You can find more on `CustomData ( )` in Appendix A (available online at www.wrox.com).

➤ Function (arguments)

   Example: `.( [Level_Expression [ , Member_Expression] ] )` is an MDX function that takes an argument that can specify both the `level_expression` with the `member_expression` or just the `member_expression` itself, and returns the first member at the level of the `member_expression`. For example, `.(Day, [April])` returns the first member of the Day level of the April member of the default time dimension. (Note the opening period in this example function.)

Set Functions

Set functions, as the category name suggests, operate on sets. They take sets as arguments and often return a set. Some of the widely used set functions are `Crossjoin` and `Filter`.

Crossjoin

Crossjoin returns all possible combinations of sets as specified by the arguments to the Crossjoin function. If there are N sets specified in the Crossjoin function, this results in a combination of all the possible members within that set on a single axis. You see this in the following example:

```
Crossjoin ( Set_Expression [ ,Set_Expression ...] )

SELECT Measures.[Internet Sales Amount] ON COLUMNS,
CROSSJOIN( {Product.[Product Line].[Product Line].MEMBERS},
{[Customer].[Country].MEMBERS}) on ROWS
FROM [Adventure Works]
```

NONEMPTYCROSSJOIN and NONEMPTY

The previous Crossjoin example produces the cross product of each member in the Product dimension with each member of the Customer dimension along the sales amount measure. Sometimes such a cross join results in a large number of values being null, but instead of retrieving all the results and then checking for null values, you can restrict these on the server side and optimize the query so that only the appropriate result is retrieved and sent. To eliminate the null values, you can use the keyword NON EMPTY on the axis or the MDX functions NONEMPTYCROSSJOIN, NONEMPTY, and FILTER.

Use the NON EMPTY operator on an axis to remove the members that result in rows with empty (null) cell values. When you apply NON EMPTY, cells with null values are eliminated in the context of members on other axes. You can see this in the following query:

```
SELECT [Measures].[Internet Sales Amount] ON 0,
NON EMPTY [Customer].[Customer Geography].[Country].MEMBERS *
[Product].[Product Categories].MEMBERS ON 1
FROM [Adventure Works]
```

The NonEmptyCrossjoin and NonEmpty functions remove rows with empty cells in these query results. The syntax is:

```
NonEmpty(Set_Expression [ ,FilterSet_Expression])
NonEmptyCrossjoin(
        Set_Expression [ ,Set_Expression ...][ ,Crossjoin_Set_Count ] )
```

When using the NonEmptyCrossjoin function, it uses the default measure unless you specify the wanted measure directly, such as [Internet Sales Amount] in the following example. Most users and client tools use the NonEmptyCrossjoin function extensively. When using the NonEmpty function, you first do the Crossjoin and then filter out the tuples that have null values for the Internet Sales amount, as shown in the second query in the following code.

```
SELECT Measures.[Internet Sales Amount] ON COLUMNS,
NONEMPTYCROSSJOIN( {Product.[Product Line].[Product Line].MEMBERS},
{[Customer].[Country].MEMBERS},Measures.[Internet Sales Amount],2 )  ON ROWS
FROM [Adventure Works]

SELECT Measures.[Internet Sales Amount] ON COLUMNS,
NONEMPTY(CROSSJOIN ( {Product.[Product Line].[Product Line].MEMBERS},
{[Customer].[Country].MEMBERS}),Measures.[Internet Sales Amount]) ON ROWS
FROM [Adventure Works]
```

Filter and Having

The `Filter` function helps to restrict the query results based on one or more conditions. The `Filter` function takes two arguments: a set expression and a logical expression. The logical expression is applied on each item of the set and returns a set of items that satisfy the logical condition. The function arguments for the `Filter` function are:

```
Filter( Set_Expression , { Logical_Expression | [ CAPTION | KEY | NAME ]
        =String_Expression } )
```

If you are interested only in the products for which the sales amount is greater than a specific value and are still interested in finding out amounts by countries, you can use the `Filter` function as shown here:

```
SELECT Measures.[Internet Sales Amount] ON COLUMNS,
FILTER(CROSSJOIN( {Product.[Product Line].[Product Line].MEMBERS},
{[Customer].[Country].MEMBERS}),[Internet Sales Amount] >2000000) on ROWS
FROM [Adventure Works]
```

This query filters out all the products for which the sales amount is less than 2,000,000 and returns only the products that have the sales amount greater than 2,000,000.

Another option to eliminate cells that have null values and then apply the filter condition on the resulting set is to use the `HAVING` clause. The syntax for the `HAVING` clause is:

```
SELECT <axis_specification> ON 0,
NON EMPTY <axis_specification> HAVING <filter condition> ON 1
FROM <cube identifier>
```

The following MDX query uses the `HAVING` clause to analyze the gross profit of all the products that have sales amounts greater than $100,000 for a product in a given year:

```
SELECT { [Measures].[Gross Profit] } ON 0,
NON EMPTY [Product].[Product Categories].[Product] *[Date].[Calendar].[Calendar
Year]

    HAVING [Sales Amount] > 100000 ON 1
FROM [Adventure Works]
```

Member Functions

You can use member functions for operations on members such as retrieving the current member, ancestor, parent, children, sibling, next member, and so on. All the member functions return a member. One of the most widely used member functions is `ParallelPeriod`, which helps you to retrieve a member in the Time dimension based on a given member and certain conditions. The function definition for `ParallelPeriod` is:

```
ParallelPeriod( [ Level_Expression [ ,Numeric_Expression [ , Member_Expression ] ]
        ] )
```

Figure 3-5 shows an illustration of the `ParallelPeriod` function, which returns a member from a Time dimension relative to a given member for a specific time period. The *Numeric_Expression* is the number of time periods to move to. You learn more about time dimensions in Chapter 5.

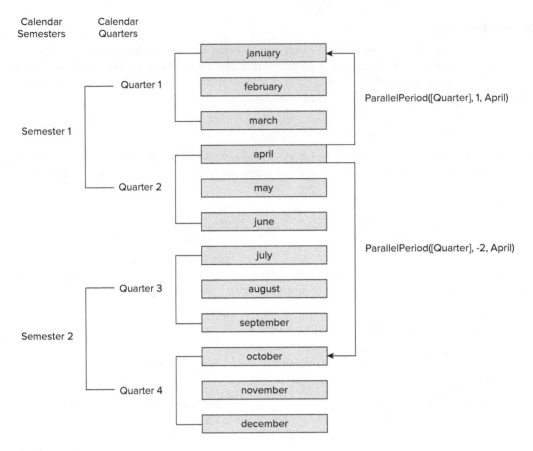

FIGURE 3-5

Numeric Functions

Numeric functions are handy when you define the parameters for an MDX query or create any calculated measure. Plenty of statistical functions are in this group, including standard deviation, sample variance, and correlation. The most common is a simple one, Count, along with its close cousin, DistinctCount. You can use the Count function to count the number of items in the collection of a specific object such as a dimension, a tuple, a set, or a level. The DistinctCount function, on the other hand, takes a *Set_Expression* as an argument and returns a number that indicates the number of distinct items in the *Set_Expression*, not the total count of all items. Following are the function definitions for each:

```
Count ( Dimension | Tuples | Set| Level)
DistinctCount ( Set_Expression )
```

Take a look at the following query:

```
WITH MEMBER Measures.CustomerCount AS DistinctCount(
Exists([Customer].[Customer].MEMBERS, [Product].[Product Line].Mountain,
```

```
"Internet Sales"))
SELECT Measures.CustomerCount ON COLUMNS
FROM [Adventure Works]
```

The `DistinctCount` function counts the number of distinct members in the Customer dimension who have purchased products in the Mountain product line. If a customer has purchased multiple products from the specified product line, the `DistinctCount` function counts the customer just once. The MDX function `Exists` filters customers who have purchased only product line Mountain through the Internet.

Dimension Functions, Level Functions, and Hierarchy Functions

Functions in these groups are typically used for navigation and manipulation. Following is an example of just such a function, the `Level` function from the Level group:

```
SELECT [Date].[Calendar].[Calendar Quarter].[Q1 CY 2008].LEVEL ON COLUMNS
FROM [Adventure Works]
```

This query results in a list of all the quarters displayed in the results. The reason is that `[Date]`.`[Calendar]`.`[Calendar Quarter]`.`[Q1 CY 2008]`.`LEVEL` evaluates to `[Date]`.`[Calendar Year]`.`[Calendar Semester]`.`[Calendar Quarter]`. When a level is specified in an MDX expression, it is implicitly converted to a set and hence all the members at that level are implied in MDX. Due to this, you get the list of all quarters for the specified calendar year and semester.

String Manipulation Functions

To extract the names of sets, tuples, and members in the form of a string, you can use functions such as `MemberToStr` (`<Member_Expression>`). To do the inverse — take a string and create a member expression — you can use `StrToMember` (`<String>`). String manipulation functions are useful when accepting parameters from users and transforming them to corresponding MDX objects. However, there is a significant performance cost. Hence, you use these functions only if necessary.

```
SELECT STRTOMEMBER ('[Customer].[Country].[Australia]' ) ON COLUMNS
FROM [Adventure Works]
```

Other Functions

Four other function categories exist: `Subcube` and `Array` both have one function each. The final two categories are logical functions, which allow you to do Boolean evaluations on MDX objects, and tuple functions, which you can use to access tuples from an MDX set or convert a string to a tuple. You have seen some of them in this chapter, such as `NonEmpty` and `Exists`. Detailed information about these functions is provided in Appendix A (available online at www.wrox.com).

MDX SCRIPTS

MDX scripts can contain complex calculations and consist of various types of MDX statements and commands, each separated by semicolons. CALCULATE, SCOPE, IF-THEN-ELSE, and CASE are just a few of the MDX statements that you can use within an MDX script. MDX scripts are meant to be structured in a way that the flow of the statements is simple and readable. The scripting language is based on a procedural programming model, and although it may sound complex, it is actually simpler to use than certain predecessor technologies.

When you create a cube using the Cube Wizard within the SSDT, a default MDX script is created for you. You can see the script definitions on the Calculations tabs of the Cube Designer, as shown in Chapters 6 and 9.

Analysis Services also includes tools to help you debug MDX scripts interactively, more like debugging a program, to identify any semantic errors in calculations defined in the script. Syntactic errors are automatically flagged when the cube is deployed to an Analysis Services instance. The real value of an MDX script is to define calculations that assign values to cells in the cube space based upon potentially complex business logic.

MDX Script Execution

MDX script typically contain the calculations that need to be applied to a cube including creation of calculated members, named sets, and calculations for the cells. However, users of the cube can have different security permissions defined for dimensions and cubes within a database. Therefore, when a user connects to a cube, Analysis Services evaluates the security permissions for the user and assigns the user a cube context. This ensures that the data populated within the cube for the user is based on the security permissions of that user. If a cube context with that specific set of permissions already exists, the user is automatically assigned to that cube context. You learn more about securing data in Chapters 9 and 14.

CALCULATE Statement

The CALCULATE statement is added to a cube's MDX script by the Cube Wizard to indicate that Analysis Services should aggregate the data from the lowest level of attributes and hierarchies to higher levels. Aggregation of data to various levels of a hierarchy is illustrated in Figures 3-6 through 3-8.

When a user accesses the cube, the fact data first loads into the cube (refer to Figure 3-6), which represents data for a specific year. This is referred to as PASS 0 within Analysis Services. After the fact data has been loaded into the cube, Analysis Services applies calculations for the cells based on an MDX script or dimension attributes. When the CALCULATE statement is encountered in the script, a new PASS, PASS 1, is created where the fact data, aggregated for appropriate levels of the dimension hierarchies, is accessible to end users. For hierarchies with only one level, there is no need to aggregate the data, but the Date hierarchy in Figure 3-7 and Figure 3-8 has the levels Semester and Year for which the data needs to be aggregated. Analysis Services aggregates the data for the Semester and Year levels as shown so that you can query the aggregated data.

If the CALCULATE statement is not specified in the MDX script, you cannot query the aggregated data for Semester and Year. If you attempt such a query you, get null values for those levels. If you are missing a CALCULATE statement in the MDX script, you can retrieve the fact data for aggregated levels only when you include all hierarchies of all dimensions in your query.

If a cube does not have an MDX script defined, Analysis Services uses a default MDX script with a CALCULATE statement. It is not expected that users have MDX scripts without the CALCULATE statement other than by mistake. If you do not have any calculations defined and your queries return null values for various hierarchies, you should check if the CALCULATE statement is included in the MDX script.

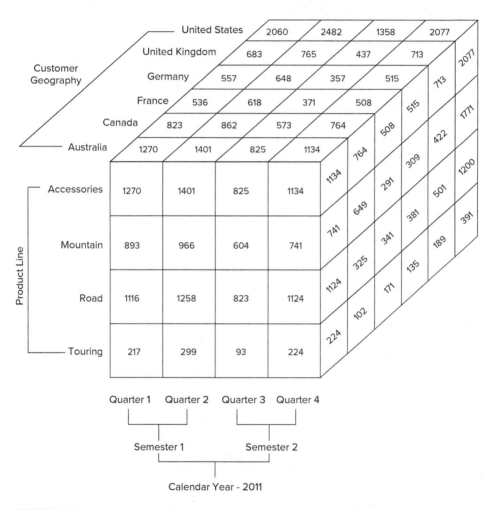

FIGURE 3-6

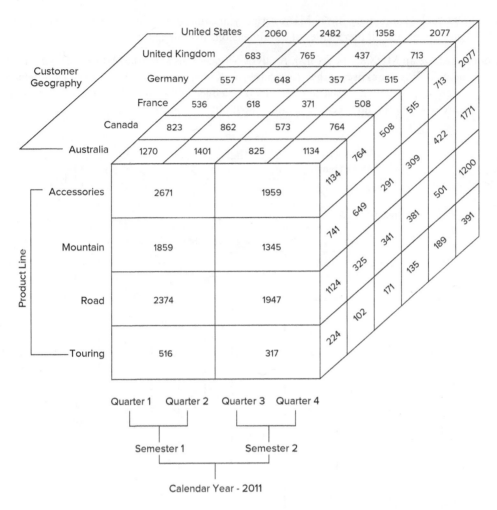

FIGURE 3-7

Cube Space

The cube space (cells) can be quite large, even for a small Analysis Services cube that contains less than ten dimensions, with each dimension containing approximately ten attributes. When referring to the data in the cube space, we do not just refer to the data in the fact table. Some cells in the cube space retrieve data through calculations of the data in the fact table or are aggregated up across dimensions due to the cube modeling scheme. Still, the cells that have data are quite sparse compared to the entire cube space.

Referring to the cube space accessible to the users and that can be manipulated through calculations as the real cube space, you can access certain cells in the cube space through MDX queries that are actually not part of the real cube space. For example, assume a Customer dimension that has attributes Name, Gender, and Marital Status. There is a customer named

Aaron Flores who is Male in the Adventure Works DW Multidimensional sample database, but the cell corresponding to Customer.Customer.[Aaron Flores] and Customer.Gender.Female does not exist in the cube space. If you request the cell corresponding to this coordinate, you get a null value.

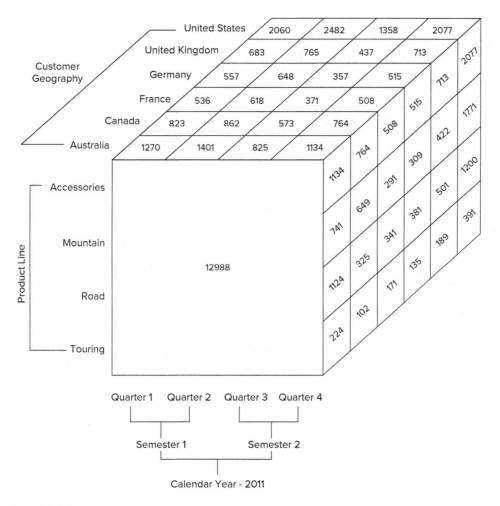

FIGURE 3-8

AUTO EXISTS

If you do a cross-join of multiple attributes, you get the entire cross product of all the members of the attributes involved in the cross-join. However, if you do a cross-join of the attributes within the same dimension, Analysis Services eliminates the cells corresponding to the attributes' members that do not exist with one another. This specific behavior is called AUTO EXISTS, which can be interpreted as an EXISTS MDX function automatically being applied to attributes within the same dimension. For example, if you query [Internet Sales Amount] along with customers across states and countries, your MDX query will be:

```
SELECT [Measures].[Internet Sales Amount] ON COLUMNS,
[Customer].[Country].[Country].MEMBERS *
[Customer].[State-Province].[State-Province].MEMBERS
ON ROWS
FROM [Adventure Works]
```

The results of this MDX query have only the states within a specific country instead of a regular cross-join of the members of both hierarchies. Alberta, which is a state in Canada, does not exist in Australia, and hence you do not have a tuple containing Australia and Alberta in your result.

Cell Calculations and Assignments

MDX provides several ways to specify calculations, such as calculated members, calculated measures, custom rollups (discussed in Chapter 8), and unary operators (also discussed in Chapter 8). Using these features to affect a group of cell values or even a single cell value is not easy.

Query, Session, and Cube Scope

The CREATE CELL CALCULATION statement, similar to calculated members and named sets, can be specified at a query, session, or cube scope. The syntax for the CREATE CELL CALCULATION statement is

```
CREATE CELL CALCULATION  <CubeName>.<formula name>
FOR <SetExpression> AS <MDX Expression>, <cell property list>
CONDITION = <Logical Expression>
```

In the preceding syntax, the <formula name> is an identifier for the cell calculation statement. The SetExpression resolves to a set of tuples for which the cell values will be changed. The cell property list is an optional set of properties for the cell such as DISABLED, DESCRIPTION, CALCULATION_PASS_NUMBER, and CALCULATION_PASS_DEPTH, which can be applied to the cells being evaluated separated by commas.

For global scope you need to define the cell calculation statements within MDX scripts. If you want to use this within the query scope, you need to use the CREATE CELL CALCULATION statement with the WITH clause, like this:

```
WITH CELL CALCULATION [SalesQuota2009]
FOR '( [Date].[Fiscal Year].&[2009],
     [Date].[Fiscal].[Month].MEMBERS,
      [Measures].[Sales Amount Quota] )'
AS '( ParallelPeriod( [Date].[Fiscal].[Fiscal Year], 1,
     [Date].[Fiscal].CurrentMember), [Measures].[Sales Amount] ) * 2'

SELECT { [Measures].[Sales Amount Quota],
     [Measures].[Sales Amount] } ON 0,
DESCENDANTS( { [Date].[Fiscal].[Fiscal Year].&[2008],
     [Date].[Fiscal].[Fiscal Year].&[2009] }, 3, SELF ) ON 1
FROM [Adventure Works]
```

Cell calculations not only help you evaluate specific cell values, but also avoid the addition of members in the cube space. The properties CALCULATION_PASS_NUMBER and CALCULATION_PASS_DEPTH provide the functionality to specify complex recursive calculations such as goal-seeking equations. The CALCULATION_PASS_NUMBER specifies the PASS number at which the calculation is to be performed. Cell calculation is provided here for overall MDX understanding. This is deprecated by the product in favor of the assignments which you will learn in the next section.

Simple Assignments

The cell calculation syntax also allows you to model complex business logic through the SCOPE statement, the CASE statement, and MDX functions such as Root and Leaves. You must be familiar with the SCOPE statement along with assignments using the THIS keyword. Each assignment statement in MDX scripts results in a new PASS value. The cell calculation example with SCOPE is as follows:

```
SCOPE([Date].[Fiscal Year].&[2009],
    [Date].[Fiscal].[Month].MEMBERS,
    [Measures].[Sales Amount Quota]);
THIS = (ParallelPeriod( [Date].[Fiscal].[Fiscal Year],
1,[Date].[Fiscal].CurrentMember),[Measures].[Sales Amount])*2;
END SCOPE;
```

The preceding cell calculation is simple in the sense that it does not require special conditions. It is referred to as a simple assignment because the cell value for the current coordinate indicated by THIS is assigned a value, which is evaluated from the MDX expression on the right side.

Complex Assignments with IF Statements

If you have a complex expression with several conditions to apply to the cell calculation, a simple assignment will not be sufficient. You can use the IF statement to check for conditions before applying the cell calculation. For example, if you want the Sales Amount Quota to be two times the previous year's Sales Amount just for the first quarter, your calculation using the IF statement is:

```
SCOPE( [Date].[Fiscal Year].&[2008],
    [Date].[Fiscal].[Month].MEMBERS,
    [Measures].[Sales Amount Quota] );

    THIS = ( ParallelPeriod( [Date].[Fiscal].[Fiscal Year], 1,
        [Date].[Fiscal].CurrentMember ),
        [Measures].[Sales Amount] ) * 1.3;
    IF ( [Date].[Fiscal].CurrentMember.Parent IS
        [Date].[Fiscal].[Fiscal Quarter].&[2008]&[1] )
    THEN THIS = ( ParallelPeriod( [Date].[Fiscal].[Fiscal Year], 1,
        [Date].[Fiscal].CurrentMember ),
        [Measures].[Sales Amount] ) * 2.0
    END IF;

END SCOPE;
```

In the preceding example, you first assign values to all the cells corresponding to the subcube to be 1.3 times the value of the Sales Amount in the previous year. Then you use the conditional IF statement to update the first quarter's cell values to be two times the Sales Amount. As you can see, the statement is straightforward. It is quite easy to debug statements in MDX scripts with the help of the MDX debugger within the Cube Designer. (You learn how to debug MDX scripts in Chapter 9.)

Complex Assignments with CASE Statements

You can get into more complex expressions that may require multiple IF statements, which can lead to updating cells multiple times. To support efficient assignments, Analysis Services provides the CASE statement. The syntax for the CASE statement is:

```
CASE <value_expression>
WHEN <value_expression> THEN <statement>
ELSE  <statement>
END;
```

Here an MDX statement is assigned one of the values specified by the CASE statement. You can specify the conditions easily, as in the following example:

```
SCOPE ( [Date].[Fiscal Year].&[2008],
    [Date].[Fiscal].[Month].MEMBERS,
    [Measures].[Sales Amount Quota] );

    THIS = CASE

    WHEN ( [Date].[Fiscal].CurrentMember.Parent IS
        [Date].[Fiscal].[Fiscal Quarter].&[2008]&[1] )
    THEN ( ParallelPeriod( [Date].[Fiscal].[Fiscal Year], 1,
        [Date].[Fiscal].CurrentMember ),
        [Measures].[Sales Amount] ) * 1.3

    WHEN ( [Date].[Fiscal].CurrentMember.Parent IS
        [Date].[Fiscal].[Fiscal Quarter].&[2008]&[2] )
    THEN ( ParallelPeriod( [Date].[Fiscal].[Fiscal Year], 1,
        [Date].[Fiscal].CurrentMember ),
        [Measures].[Sales Amount] ) * 2.0

    ELSE ( ParallelPeriod( [Date].[Fiscal].[Fiscal Year], 1,
        [Date].[Fiscal].CurrentMember ),
        [Measures].[Sales Amount] ) * 1.75

    END;

END SCOPE;
```

Direct Assignments to a Subcube

In all the previous examples, you have seen SCOPE – END SCOPE being used. Use SCOPE when you have multiple calculations that need to be applied within the SCOPE. However, if it is a single MDX expression, you can write the cell calculation by direct assignment to the subcube, as shown here:

```
( [Date].[Fiscal Year].&[2009],
    [Date].[Fiscal].[Month].MEMBERS,
    [Measures].[Sales Amount Quota] ) =
( ParallelPeriod( [Date].[Fiscal].[Fiscal Year], 1,
    [Date].[Fiscal].CurrentMember ),
    [Measures].[Sales Amount] ) * 2;
```

Root and Leaves Assignments

Two additional MDX functions can help you write cell calculations with ease. These functions are Root and Leaves, which are great if you want to apply cell calculation to the leaf-level members or the root of a hierarchy. These functions appropriately position a coordinate so that the cell calculations can be applied to that coordinate. The following example uses the Root and Leaves MDX functions:

```
CREATE MEMBER CURRENTCUBE.[Measures].[Ratio To All Products] AS
    [Measures].[Sales Amount] /
        ( Root( [Product] ), [Measures].[Sales Amount] ),
    FORMAT_STRING = "Percent",
    NON_EMPTY_BEHAVIOR = [Sales Amount];

SCOPE( Leaves( [Date] ), [Measures].[Sales Amount Quota] );
    THIS = THIS * 1.2;
END SCOPE;
```

In the first part of the example, you see a calculated measure that computes the contribution of Sales of a product as a portion of total product sales. This is accomplished through the use of Root(Product), which provides the sales information for all the products. Root(Product) is often used to calculate ratios of a measure for a single member against all the members in the dimension. In the second part of the example, the Sales Amount Quota is being applied to Leaf members of the Date dimension so that the Sales Amount Quota is increased by 20%. The Leaves MDX function would help in budgeting and financial calculations where you want the calculations applied only to the leaf-level members and then rolled up to the members at other levels. The Leaves MDX function (like the Root function) takes a dimension as its argument and returns the leaf-level members of the dimension that exist with the granularity attribute of the dimension. (You learn about the granularity attribute in Chapter 9.)

Recursion

Recursive calculations occur when a calculated member references itself for calculations. For example, if you want to calculate the cumulative sales over time, you can apply an MDX expression that calculates the sales of the current time member and the cumulative sales for the previous time member. This leads to recursion because the cumulative sales of the previous time member needs to be evaluated with the same MDX expression.

You can avoid infinite recursions by the use of a PASS value. Consider the following MDX statements in your MDX script:

```
SCOPE ([Date].[Fiscal Year].&[2004]);
    [Sales Amount Quota] = [Sales Amount Quota] * 1.2;
END SCOPE;
```

The evaluation of [Sales Amount Quota] would result in an infinite recursion, but Analysis Services can automatically handle these types of scenarios by virtue of internally assigning a value from the previous calculation pass.

Freeze Statement

Use the Freeze statement in circumstances in which you might want to change the cell value that was used in an MDX expression to determine results for another cell value without changing the cell value from an earlier calculation. This `Freeze` statement is used only within MDX scripts. The syntax is:

```
Freeze <subcube expression>
```

For more information on the `Freeze` statement including detailed examples and how to use it effectively, we recommend *MDX Solutions: With SQL Server Analysis Services 2005 and Hyperion Essbase, Second Edition*, by George Spofford et al. (Wiley Publishing, Inc., 2006).

RESTRICTING CUBE SPACE/SLICING CUBE DATA

Considering that a typical cube contains several dimensions with possibly hundreds or even thousands of members, you should want to restrict the cube space for your queries by slicing the data or drilling down into specific sections. You can do this in several ways using MDX, the choice of which would depend on the context of your problem and what you want to accomplish.

SCOPE Statement

The `SCOPE` statement is used within MDX scripts to restrict the cube space so that all MDX statements and expressions specified within the `SCOPE` statement are evaluated exactly once against the restricted cube space. The syntax of the `SCOPE` statement is:

```
SCOPE <SubCubeExpression>
 <MDX Statement>
 <MDX Statement> ...
END SCOPE
```

You can have one or more MDX statements within the `SCOPE` statement, and you can have nested `SCOPE` statements. Nested `SCOPE` statements can often be simplified as a single `SCOPE` statement as long as all the MDX statements are within the innermost `SCOPE` statement. MDX statements expressed within `SCOPE` statements are actually cell calculations, which you learned earlier in this chapter. Named sets in the MDX script are not affected by the `SCOPE` statement.

CREATE and DROP SUBCUBE

The `CREATE SUBCUBE` statement enables you to restrict the cube space for subsequent queries. This statement is typically used within the scope of a query session. The syntax of this statement is:

```
CREATE SUBCUBE <SubCubeName> AS <SELECT Statement>
```

where the `SELECT` statement is an MDX `SELECT` clause that returns the results for the restricted cube space based on specific criteria. The cube name specified in the `SELECT` statement should have the same *SubCubeName* specified in the `CREATE SUBCUBE` statement.

Assume you are analyzing Internet sales in the Adventure Works DW Multidimensional database for various quarters by using the following MDX query:

```
SELECT [Measures].[Internet Sales Amount] ON 0,
[Date].[Fiscal].[Fiscal Quarter].MEMBERS ON 1
FROM [Adventure Works]
```

If you want to restrict the cube space and analyze only the Internet sales data for the fiscal year 2008, you can use a CREATE SUBCUBE statement, as follows:

```
CREATE SUBCUBE [Adventure Works] AS
SELECT { [Date].[Fiscal].[Fiscal Year].&[2008] } ON 0
FROM [Adventure Works]

SELECT [Measures].[Internet Sales Amount] ON 0,
[Date].[Fiscal].[Fiscal Quarter].MEMBERS ON 1
FROM [Adventure Works]

DROP SUBCUBE [Adventure Works]
```

Notice the DROP SUBCUBE statement followed by the name of the subcube after the query to revert back to the original cube space.

Using EXISTS

As mentioned earlier, the cube space is typically quite large and sparse. Remember AUTO EXISTS? Well, EXISTS is a function that allows you to explicitly do the same operation of returning a set of members that exists with one or more tuples of one or more sets. The EXISTS function can take two or three arguments according to the following syntax:

```
EXISTS( Set, <FilterSet>, [MeasureGroupName])
```

The first two arguments are sets that get evaluated to identify the members that exist with each other. EXISTS identifies all the members in the first set that exist with the members in the *FilterSet* and returns those members as results. The third optional parameter is the Measure group name, so EXISTS can be applied across the measure group.

Using EXISTING

By now, you should be quite familiar with the WHERE clause in the MDX SELECT statement. The WHERE clause changes the default members of the dimensions for the current subcube but does not restrict the cube space. It does not change the default for the outer query and gets a lower precedence as compared to the calculations specified within the query scope.

To restrict the cube space so that calculations are performed within the scope of the conditions specified in the WHERE clause, you can use the keyword EXISTING, by which you force the calculations to be done on a subcube under consideration by the query rather than the entire cube. Following is an MDX query using EXISTING:

```
WITH MEMBER [Measures].[X] AS
COUNT ( EXISTING [Customer].[Customer Geography].[State-Province].MEMBERS)
SELECT [Measures].[X] ON 0
FROM [Adventure Works]
WHERE ( [Customer].[Customer Geography].[Country].&[United States] )
```

If you execute the above query against the sample Adventure Works DW Multidimensional database you will get a result of 36. If you remove EXISTING and execute the query you will get the result 71.

The first MDX query returns the states associated with the country United States and the later returns the total number states in the databases.

Using SUBSELECT

MDX queries can contain a clause called subselect, which allows you to restrict your query to a sub-cube instead of the entire cube. The syntax of the subselect clause along with SELECT is:

```
[WITH <formula_expression> [, <formula_expression> ...]]
SELECT [<axis_expression>, <axis_expression>...]]

FROM [<cube_expression> | (<sub_select_statement>)]
[WHERE <expression>]
[[CELL] PROPERTIES <cellprop> [, <cellprop> ...]]

<sub_select_statement> =
SELECT [<axis_expression> [, <axis_expression> ...]]
FROM [<cube_expression> | (< sub_select_statement >)]
[WHERE <expression>]
```

The *cube_expression* in the MDX SELECT statement can now be replaced by another SELECT statement called the sub_select_statement, which queries a part of the cube. You can have nested sub_select_statements up to any level. The subselect clause in the SELECT statement restricts the cube space to the specified dimension members in the subselect clause. Outer queries can therefore see only the dimension members specified in the inner subselect clauses. Look at the following MDX query that uses subselect syntax:

```
SELECT NON EMPTY { [Measures].[Internet Sales Amount] } ON COLUMNS,
NON EMPTY { ([Customer].[Customer Geography].[Country].ALLMEMBERS ) }
DIMENSION PROPERTIES MEMBER_CAPTION, MEMBER_UNIQUE_NAME ON ROWS
FROM (
    SELECT ( { [Date].[Fiscal].[Fiscal Year].&[2008],
              [Date].[Fiscal].[Fiscal Year].&[2009]
            }
          )
    ON COLUMNS
    FROM (
          SELECT ( { [Product].[Product Categories].[Subcategory].&[26],
                    [Product].[Product Categories].[Subcategory].&[27] } )
          ON COLUMNS
          FROM [Adventure Works]
          )
    )
WHERE ( [Product].[Product Categories].CurrentMember,
        [Date].[Fiscal].CurrentMember
      )
CELL PROPERTIES VALUE, BACK_COLOR, FORE_COLOR, FORMATTED_VALUE
```

The query contains two subselect clauses. The innermost clause returns a subcube that contains only Products whose SubCategory ids are 26 or 27. Assume that this subcube is named subcube A. The second subselect uses subcube A and returns another subcube with the restriction of Fiscal Years 2008 and 2009. Finally, the outermost SELECT statement retrieves the Internet Sales Amount for Customers in various countries. Here, subselect clauses restrict the cube space to certain members on Product and Date dimensions and thereby the outermost SELECT statement queries data from a subcube rather than the entire cube space. If you execute the preceding query in SSMS, you can see the results. You can rewrite most queries using subselect clauses with the WHERE clause in Analysis Services 2012, which accept sets as valid MDX expressions. There are instances in which subselects and WHERE clauses can return different results. More information is provided in the book *MDX Solutions: With SQL Server Analysis Services 2005 and Hyperion Essbase, Second Edition,* by George Spofford et al. (Wiley Publishing, Inc., 2006). Analysis Services 2012 supports calculated members within subselects.

PARAMETERIZED MDX QUERIES

Parameterized queries in MDX, as the name suggests, help in passing parameters to a query where the values for the parameters are substituted before query execution. Why are parameterized queries important? You might have heard about injection attacks on web sites in which an attacker hacks the sites by entering their own raw inputs that are executed along with the full query. One of the main reasons why such attacks are possible is because user input is not validated, but Analysis Services overcomes MDX injection threats by allowing parameters to be passed along with queries. Analysis Services validates these parameters, replaces the parameters in the query with the actual values, and then executes the query.

The parameters to a query are represented within the query prefixed with the @ symbol. The following is an example that uses a parameter for filtering the country.

```
select [Measures].members on 0,
       Filter(Customer.[Customer Geography].Country.members,
              Customer.[Customer Geography].CurrentMember.Name =
              @CountryName) on 1
from [Adventure Works]
```

Your client application would send the preceding query along with the list of parameters and values. The following XMLA script shows how this is sent to Analysis Services. You have a name and value pair specified for each parameter under the Parameters section of the XMLA script.

```
<Envelope xmlns="http://schemas.xmlsoap.org/soap/envelope/">
  <Body>
    <Execute xmlns="urn:schemas-microsoft-com:xml-analysis">
      <Command>
        <Statement>
select [Measures].members on 0,
       Filter(Customer.[Customer Geography].Country.members,
              Customer.[Customer Geography].CurrentMember.Name =
              @CountryName) on 1
from [Adventure Works]
</Statement>
      </Command>
      <Properties />
      <Parameters>
        <Parameter>
          <Name>CountryName</Name>
```

```
            <Value>'United Kingdom'</Value>
         </Parameter>
       </Parameters>
     </Execute>
   </Body>
 </Envelope>
```

MDX COMMENTS

MDX can quickly end up with a complex query or expression. Therefore, you should add comments to your MDX expressions and queries so that you can look back at a later point in time and interpret or understand what you were implementing with a specific MDX expression or query.

You can comment your MDX queries and expressions in three different ways:

```
// (two forward slashes) comment goes here
-- (two hyphens) comment goes here
/* comment goes here */ (slash-asterisk pairs)
```

SUMMARY

Congratulations, you have made it through the first three chapters! Ostensibly, you should now feel ready to take on the rest of the chapters in no particular order. But you got this far, so why not go immediately to Chapter 4 and jump right in? Now you know the fundamental elements of MDX: cells, members, tuples, and sets. Further, you learned that MDX has two forms: queries and expressions. You also learned about calculation fundamentals and the use of MDX scripts to apply global scope calculations.

You saw that MDX queries retrieve data from Analysis Services databases. MDX expressions, on the other hand, are simple yet powerful constructs that are partial statements; by themselves they do not return results like queries. The expressions are what enable you to define and manipulate multidimensional objects and data through calculations, like specifying a default member's contents, for example.

To solidify your understanding of MDX, you learned the common query statements WITH, SELECT, FROM, and WHERE, as well as the MDX operators such as addition, subtraction, multiplication, division, set and the logical operators AND and OR. These details are crucial for effective use of the language. You got a good look at the MDX function categories, saw the four forms MDX functions can take, and even saw detailed examples of some commonly used functions. All the MDX functions supported in Analysis Services are provided with examples in Appendix A, available online at www.wrox.com.

Don't think you are done learning about MDX with this chapter. You learn additional MDX in subsequent chapters through illustrations and examples wherever applicable. Your journey through the Analysis Services landscape will become even more interesting and exciting as you work your way through the book. Coming up in Chapter 4 are the details to create a data source and a Data Source View, and how to deal with multiple data source views in a single project.

Data Sources and Data Source Views

You have completed Chapter 2 of the book, where you worked hands on with SQL Server Analysis Services (SSAS) 2012 multidimensional tools, and Chapter 3, where you learned the basics of the MDX language and used it to retrieve data from Analysis Services. The next three chapters of the book guide you in the use of the product to design dimensions and cubes.

The traditional approach of dimension and cube design is based on an existing single-source data set. In the real world, you will likely work with multiple relational data sources when you develop business intelligence applications. In this chapter you learn what data sources are in the Analysis Services multidimensional world and how they feed into the creation of Data Source Views (DSVs). These DSVs provide you with a consolidated, single-source view on just the data of interest across one or more data sources you define. The data sources and DSVs form the foundation for subsequent construction of both dimensions and cubes. More than one data source per project is supported as are multiple DSVs. You learn how this infrastructure plays out in this chapter.

DATA SOURCES

For Analysis Services to retrieve data from a source, you need to provide it with information about that source such as its name, the method used to retrieve the data, security permissions needed to retrieve the data, and so on. In Analysis Services, all this information is encapsulated into an object called a *data source*. An Analysis Services database contains a collection of data sources, which holds all the data sources used to build the dimensions and cubes within that database. Analysis Services can retrieve source data from data sources via the native OLE DB provider interface or the .NET Managed Provider interface.

In the simplest case you can have one data source that contains one fact table with some number of dimensions linked to it by joins. That data source is populated by data from an OLTP database and is called an *Operational Data Store* (ODS). Figure 4-1 shows a graphical representation of this data source usage. The ODS is a single entity storing data from various sources so that it can serve as a single source of data for your data warehouse.

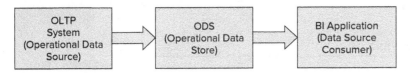

Data Source path commonly used prior to introduction of the multidimensional model; data is first transformed to a more usable format and stored in the OD.

FIGURE 4-1

A variant of data source usage, which is enabled by the Business Intelligence Semantic Model (BISM) multidimensional model, is the ability to take data directly from the OLTP system as input to a business intelligence (BI) application, which is shown in Figure 4-2.

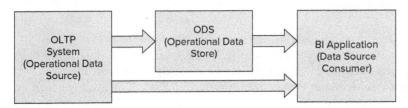

Data Sources enabled with BISM multidimensional; data is transformed to a more usable format and stored in the ODS and data can be easily obtained from different data sources without going through the ODS.

FIGURE 4-2

Analysis Services supports building cubes based on multiple fact tables which can come from different data sources. As shown in Figure 4-2, those data sources can come from the operational data store as well as from other places. You can also do things like re-use one cube's measure groups in a different cube. Such measure groups are called *shared objects* and are explained more in Chapter 9. As you can see, the BISM multidimensional model gives you a lot of flexibility when you design your application's data model. This flexibility can be a double-edged sword, however, and we recommend that you understand all the implications of the decision to build models with multiple data sources and very complex schemas. Those implications are discussed in Parts II and III of this book.

Data Sources Supported by Analysis Services

In general, Analysis Services 2012 supports all data sources that expose a connectivity interface through OLE DB or a .NET Managed Provider. This is because Analysis Services uses those interfaces to retrieve the schema information (tables, relationships, columns within tables, and data types) and data it needs to work with those data sources. If the data source is a relational database, then by default it uses standard SQL to query the database. Analysis Services uses a "cartridge" mechanism that enables it to translate its standard SQL language to the SQL dialects of different relational database systems. Cartridges are, in essence, XSLT transforms that are applied to the standard SQL stored internally to Analysis Services in an XML format.

Officially, Analysis Services 2012 supports specific relational data sources. The major relational data sources supported by Analysis Services include Microsoft SQL Server and Parallel Data Warehouse, IBM's DB2, Teradata, Oracle, Sybase, and Informix. Figure 4-3 shows various data sources supported by Analysis Services 2012 on a machine that has SQL Server 2012 installed. For a specific data source, you may need to install additional client components of the data provider so that the OLE DB provider and/or .NET provider for that specific data source is available on your machine. These client components should not only be available on the development machine where you use SQL Server Data Tools (SSDT) to design your database, but they also must be available on the server machine where the Analysis Services instance runs. For relational databases DB2 and Oracle, it is recommended you use Microsoft's OLE DB data provider for Oracle or DB2 (Microsoft's DB2 driver is available in the SQL Server Feature Pack) instead of the OLE DB providers provided with those databases. Install appropriate connectivity components from Oracle and IBM's DB2 on your machine in addition to the OLE DB providers from Microsoft.

FIGURE 4-3

In Chapter 2 you used the Data Source Wizard to create a data source that included impersonation information. You use that Analysis Services project created in Chapter 2 for the illustrations and examples in this chapter.

In addition to providing impersonation information, you can optionally specify additional connection properties; such as query time out for connection, isolation level, and maximum number of connections; in the Connection Manager dialog, as shown in Figure 4-4, at the time you create your data source. Alternatively, you can define additional connection properties after the data source has been created using the Data Source Designer dialog, as shown in Figure 4-5. The isolation-level property has two modes: Read Committed and Snapshot. By default, Read Committed is used for all the data sources. The Snapshot isolation mode, which is supported by SQL Server and Oracle relational data sources, ensures that the data read by Analysis Services is consistent across multiple queries sent over a single connection. This means that if the data in the relational data source changes while multiple queries are sent by Analysis Services to that relational data source, all the queries see the same data that was seen by the first query. Any changes to the data between the time the first query and Nth query were sent over the same connection are not included in the results of subsequent queries. The specified connection properties, including isolation level, are stored and applied whenever a connection is established to a specific data source.

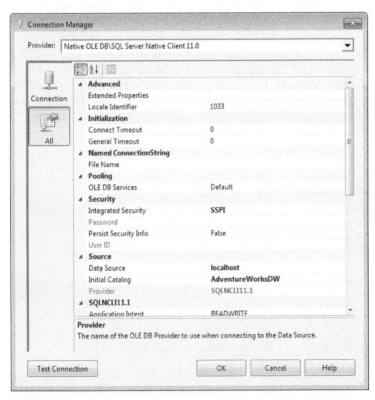

FIGURE 4-4

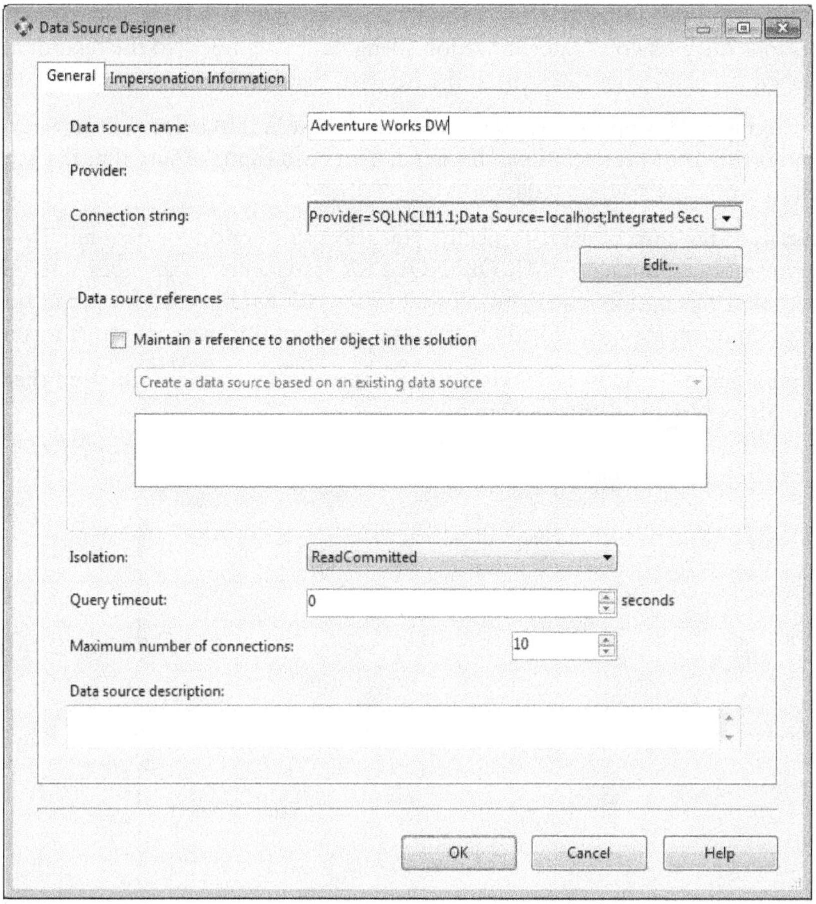

FIGURE 4-5

The Data Source Wizard enables you to create data sources based on an existing data source connection. This means that multiple Analysis Services databases can share a single data source connection. The wizard also enables you to establish connections to objects within the current Analysis Services project, such as establishing an OLE DB connection to a cube created in the project. Such a connection is typically useful when creating mining models (discussed in Chapter 12) from cubes.

The Impersonation Information tab in the Data Source Designer has four options, as shown in Figure 4-6. You briefly learned about these options in Chapter 2. At development time, SSDT uses the current user's credentials to connect to the relational data source and retrieve data. However, after the Analysis Services project deploys it needs credentials to connect to and retrieve data. Here you specify the impersonation information that Analysis Services uses to make that connection. The following list gives more details on the four options and when to use them:

➤ **Use a specific Windows username and password:** You typically would choose this option when the account used by the Analysis Services instance does not have permissions to access the relational backend. When you select this option, you need to specify a Windows username and password that Analysis Services can use to connect to the relational backend. For security reasons the password and connection string used to connect to the relational backend are encrypted before they are sent to the Analysis Services instance.

➤ **Use the service account:** This option uses the credentials of the Analysis Services service startup account to connect to the relational backend. You need to make sure that the account has permission to access the relational data source.

➤ **Use the credentials of the current user:** Typically, you select this option for data mining. Use this option for out-of-line bindings, DMX OPENQUERY statements, local cubes, and mining models. Do not select this option when you connect to a relational backend for processing, ROLAP queries, remote partitions, linked objects, and synchronization from target to source.

➤ **Inherit:** This option instructs Analysis Services to use the impersonation information specified in the parent Analysis Services database object.

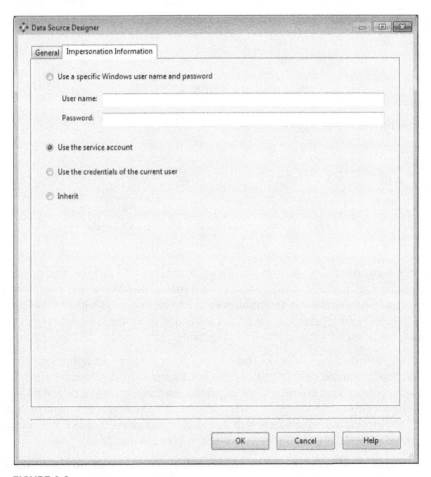

FIGURE 4-6

.NET Versus OLE DB Data Providers

Most data sources support one or both of the two types of data providers that Analysis Services can use to connect to external data: OLE DB providers or .NET Framework data providers. The OLE DB standard defines a set of COM interfaces for data access. The .NET Framework data provider interface is similar to OLE DB although providers using that interface are implemented in .NET managed code rather than native COM. Analysis Services has the capability to use OLE DB or .NET Framework data providers to access data sources ranging from flat files to large-scale databases such as SQL Server, Oracle, Teradata, DB2, Sybase, and Informix. Analysis Services retrieves data from the data sources using the chosen provider's interface (OLE DB or .NET) when processing Analysis Services objects. If any of the Analysis Services objects are defined as ROLAP, the provider is also used to retrieve data at query time. Analysis Services also provides the ability to update the data in a multidimensional model. This feature is called *writeback*. Analysis Services also uses the provider interfaces to update the source data during writeback. (You learn about writeback in Chapter 9.)

.NET Framework Data Providers

The Microsoft .NET Framework and programming languages that use the framework run in the Common Language Runtime (CLR) environment. The relationship between .NET languages and the CLR is analogous to that of the Java language and the Java Runtime (the JVM or Java Virtual Machine). The .NET Framework is a huge class library that provides support for almost every kind of functionality that most application programs need and does so in the context of managed code. The term *managed code* refers to the fact that memory is managed by the CLR and not the application program. You can write your own managed code provider for your data source, or you can leverage existing .NET Framework data providers. With the installation of SQL Server 2012, you have .NET providers that support Microsoft SQL Server and Oracle (refer to Figure 4-3). If you need to use a different relational data source and it has a .NET provider, you can install it and use that provider. In the Connection Manager page of the Data Source Wizard, you can choose from the installed .NET providers to connect to your data source.

OLE DB Data Providers

OLE DB is an industry-standard application programming interface that defines a set of Component Object Model (COM) interfaces for accessing data from various data sources. The OLE DB standard was created for client applications to have a uniform interface from which to access data. Such data can come from a wide variety of data sources such as Microsoft Access, Microsoft Project, and various database management systems.

Microsoft provides a set of OLE DB data providers to access data from several widely used data sources. This set of providers includes SQL Server OLE DB provider, Oracle OLE DB provider, and the OLE DB provider for ODBC. These OLE DB providers have been included in the operating system since Windows Server 2003 and Windows XP SP2 as a component known as Windows Data Access Components (WDAC). (This component was formerly known as Microsoft Data Access Components [MDAC] and was renamed with the release of Windows

Vista.) Even though the interfaces exposed by the providers are common, each provider is different in the sense they have specific optimizations relevant to the specific backend data source. OLE DB providers, being implementations of the OLE DB COM interfaces, are written in unmanaged code.

The Microsoft OLE DB provider for SQL Server included with WDAC provides basic connectivity to SQL Server for users of the Windows family of operating systems. You don't need SQL Server installed to use that provider. If you do install SQL Server, you have the option to install the SQL Server Native Client (SNAC), which is a single component containing enhanced versions of the SQL Server ODBC provider and the SQL Server OLE DB provider. The SQL Server Native client also provides the SQL Server team the ability to enhance the functionality of its native connectivity components on a different ship schedule than the providers that ship in the operating system as part of WDAC and are tied to OS releases. The SQL Server 2012 release provides version 11 of SQL Server Native Client and is used in the data source connection string (refer to Figure 4-5). Analysis Services provides the ability to connect to any data source that provides an OLE DB interface, including the Analysis Services OLE DB provider.

The Trade-Offs

Versions of Analysis Services prior to Analysis Services 2005 supported connecting to data sources through OLE DB providers only. Analysis Services 2005 and later have much tighter integration with the .NET Framework and support connections via both OLE DB and .NET data providers. If you deployed the .NET Framework across your entire organization, you should use the .NET providers to access data from relational data sources. You might encounter a small amount of performance degradation using the .NET provider; however, the uniformity, maintainability, inherent connection pooling capabilities, and security provided by .NET data providers are worth taking the small hit on performance. If you are concerned about the fastest possible performance, use OLE DB providers for your data access.

DATA SOURCE VIEWS

Data Source Views (DSVs) enable you to create a logical view of the tables and views from your data source. They are a powerful tool. You can, for example, filter out any tables not involved in your data warehouse design. In this way, you can exclude from the virtual workspace system tables and other tables not pertinent to your efforts. You can create DSVs that contain tables from multiple data sources, which you learn about later in this chapter in the "Multiple Data Sources Within a DSV" section.

You need to create DSVs in your Analysis Services databases because cubes and dimensions are created from a DSV rather than directly from data source objects. When you create a DSV, the DSV Wizard retrieves the schema information from the data source including relationships. This schema information is stored in the DSV and helps the Cube and Dimension Wizards identify fact and dimension tables as well as hierarchies. If the right relationships do not exist in the data source, you can create them within the DSV. Taking the time to create an effective DSV ultimately pays for itself in terms of speeding up the design of your data warehouse.

You use the DSV Wizard to create DSVs. After you create a DSV, you can perform operations on it, such as adding or removing tables, specifying virtual primary keys, and establishing relationships using the DSV Designer. You learn more about the DSV Wizard and the DSV Designer and how to work with them in the following sections.

DSV Wizard

In Chapter 2, you used the DSV Wizard to create a DSV based on the sales fact and related dimension tables in the Adventure Works DW relational database. You need a data source object to create a DSV. If you had not created a data source object in your database before running the DSV Wizard, you can do so from within the DSV Wizard's Select a Data Source page by clicking the New Data Source button. In addition, the DSV Wizard enables you to restrict your DSV to specific schemas as well as filter tables included in the DSV, which helps you to work more effectively using only the tables you need in your DSV.

DSV Designer

The DSV Designer contains three panes, as shown in Figure 4-7. The rightmost pane contains a graphical view of all the tables in the DSV. This pane is called the *diagram pane*. Relationships between tables are represented by lines connecting two tables with an arrow at the end. Primary key columns are indicated by a small key icon to the left of the column name.

The top-left pane is the *Diagram Organizer*, which is helpful in creating and saving concise views of subsets of the objects in your DSVs. This is especially helpful when DSVs contain many tables. When a DSV contains, for example, more than 20 tables it can be difficult to visualize the complete DSV in the diagram pane. When you have a large number of tables, you likely perform operations only on a subset of them at any given time. The Diagram Organizer is a handy way to create additional diagrams that include just such subsets of relevant tables. Operations done on tables within a diagram are reflected in real-time in the entire DSV. By default one diagram called All Tables contains all the objects in the DSV.

Figure 4-7 shows part of the default All Tables diagram that is created when you complete the DSV Wizard.

The lower-left pane of the DSV Designer is called the *Tables pane* and shows a tree view of all the tables in the DSV along with their relationships to other tables. Figure 4-8 shows the Tables pane with detailed information of the DimCurrency table. You can see the primary key of the DimCurrency table, CurrencyKey, which is distinguished by a key icon. In addition, there is a folder that contains the relationships between the DimCurrency table and other tables in the DSV. If you expand the Relationships folder (as shown in Figure 4-8) you can see that the DimCurrency table joins to the FactInternetSales and FactResellerSales tables through the CurrencyKey column (indicated in parentheses).

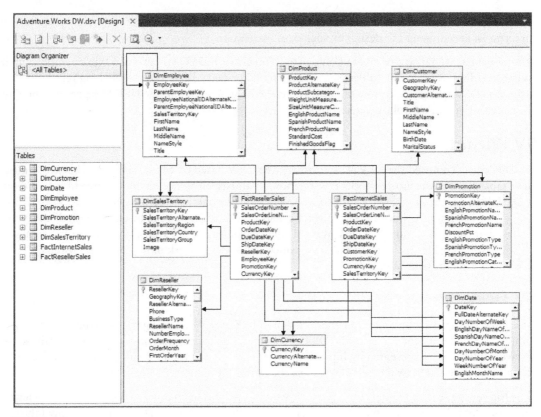

FIGURE 4-7

FIGURE 4-8

Adding/Removing Tables in a DSV

The DSV Wizard creates DSVs. It generates the initial DSV based on what it can discover from the schema of the source data. The real power of DSVs, though, comes from the ability to modify the initial DSV to align with the needs of the BI solution you build. You use the DSV Designer to tap into that power. To modify existing tables in the DSV, right-click the diagram pane, and select Add/Remove Tables, as shown in Figure 4-9.

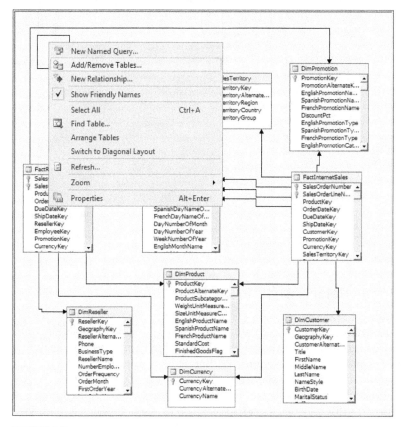

FIGURE 4-9

This invokes the Add/Remove Tables dialog shown in Figure 4-10. Using this dialog you can add additional tables to the DSV by moving tables from the Available objects list to the Included objects list or remove existing tables by moving them from the Included objects list to the Available objects list. You can also remove a table in the DSV Designer's diagram pane or Table pane using the following steps:

1. Select the table to be deleted.

2. Right-click the table, and on the context menu select Delete Table from DSV.

3. In the confirmation dialog that appears, click OK.

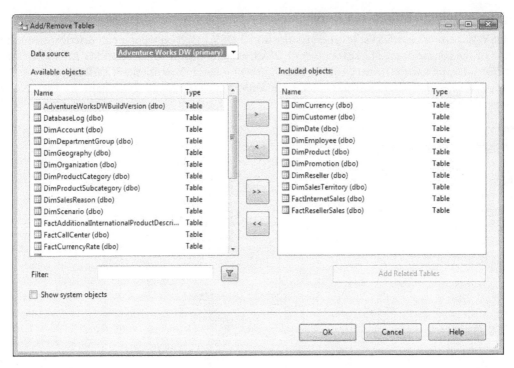

FIGURE 4-10

Specifying Primary Keys and Relationships in the DSV

It is likely that you will encounter underlying databases without the primary key to foreign key relationships that you need in place for preparation of data for analysis — that is, for building dimensions and cubes. The DSV Wizard can extract the primary keys and relationships specified in the underlying relational database and add them to your DSV. But perhaps some of the OLTP data you use does not have primary keys and relationships specified for the relevant tables. The DSV Designer provides you with the functionality to specify logical primary keys for the tables that do not have primary keys defined for them. In this way you can effectively modify or add new relationships between the tables in the DSV.

To specify a logical primary key for a table, do the following in the DSV Designer:

1.   Select the column(s) in the table that you want to specify as the logical primary key. If there is more than one column that forms the primary key, you can select multiple columns by holding down the Ctrl key while selecting.

2.   Right-click and select Set Logical Primary Key. When there is a relationship between two tables, Table1 and Table2, you typically have columns A in Table1 and B in Table2 involved in the join. If column B is the primary key in Table2, column A in Table1 is referred to as the foreign key. An example would be a Sales fact table that has a Product ID column that joins with the Product ID column in the Products dimension table. To specify relationships between the tables in this hypothetical example, you would use the following steps.

A. Select column A in Table1.

B. With column A selected, drag and drop it to column B in Table2. This forms a relation-ship between Table1 and Table2. A line will be created between these two tables with an arrow pointing toward Table2. If you double-click this line, you see the details of the relationship — the tables involved in the relationship and the columns used for the join. Figure 4-11 shows the relationship between the FactResellerSales and DimReseller tables. You can modify the relationship using this Edit Relationship dialog by either changing the columns involved in the join or by adding additional columns involved in the join.

You can also create a new relationship by right-clicking a table and selecting New Relationship. You will be asked to specify the source and destination columns that make up the relationship in the Create Relationship dialog, which is similar to the Edit Relationship dialog shown in Figure 4-11. You can also add a description for the relationship.

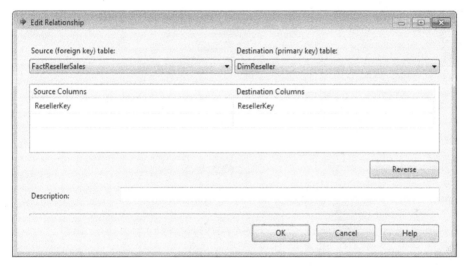

FIGURE 4-11

 All operations that you can accomplish in the diagram pane such as specifying primary keys or using drag and drop to create relationships you can also do using the Tables pane of the DSV Designer.

Customizing Your Tables in the DSV Designer

When building your data warehouse, you often want to select a subset of all the columns in a table or restrict the fact table rows based on some specific criteria. Or you might want to merge columns from several tables into a single table. You can do all these operations by creating views in the relational database. In some cases, doing these operations on the relational database side makes sense but in some cases you can't. For example, you may build your model from source data that you have only read-only access to. Or you may build your model using data from different sources. For these cases, Analysis Services provides the functionality to perform these operations within the DSV using a *Named Query*. You can invoke the Named Query editor by right-clicking a table in the diagram pane and selecting Replace Table ➪ With New Named Query, as shown in Figure 4-12. If you want to add a named query-based table without replacing an existing table in your DSV, right-click in the diagram pane of the DSV Designer but not on a table, and select New Named Query.

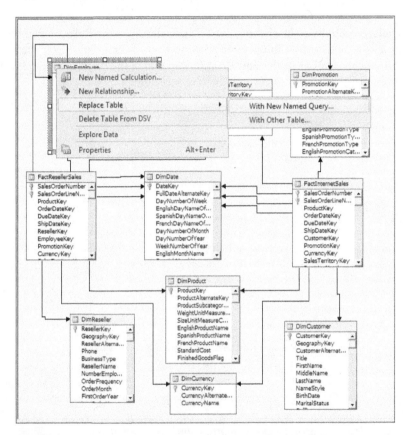

FIGURE 4-12

The Create Named Query dialog is shown in Figure 4-13. In this dialog you can add tables from the data source, select specific columns from a table, and apply restrictions or filters to the rows of a table. A SQL query is created based on your selections and displays in the SQL pane in the editor. If you're a SQL wizard, you can enter or paste a valid SQL query directly into the SQL pane. You can then execute the query to make sure the query is correct. The results from the underlying relational database are then visible in a new pane beneath the SQL pane. Click OK after you form and validate your query. The table is now replaced with results from the Named Query you have specified.

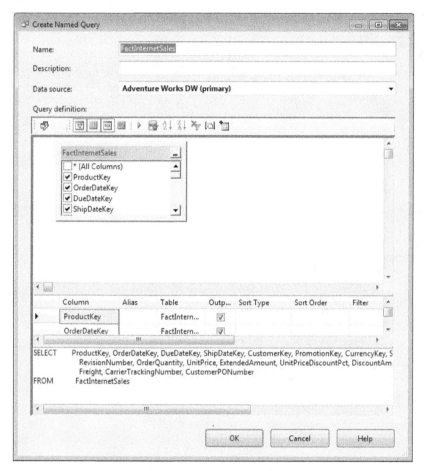

FIGURE 4-13

In certain instances you might want to create a new column in a table. For example, you may want to create a column that contains the full name of an employee based on the first name, middle name, and last name. One way to accomplish this task would be to replace the entire table with a named query and write the appropriate SQL to include this additional column. However, Analysis Services provides a simpler way to do the same operation. Right-click the Employee table, and select New Named Calculation, as shown in Figure 4-14. This action invokes the Create Named Calculation dialog, as shown in Figure 4-15. To add a column called FullName to the Employee table, you just need to combine the FirstName, MiddleName, and LastName columns. You can type the expression for this named calculation in the Expression pane, as shown in Figure 4-15, and then click the OK button.

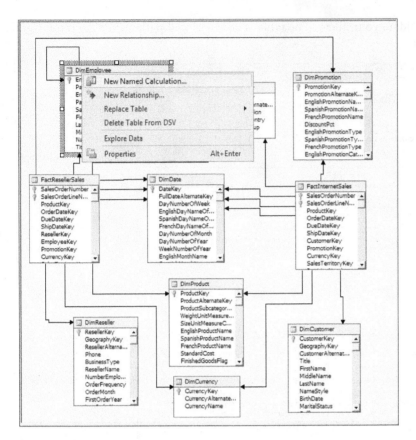

FIGURE 4-14

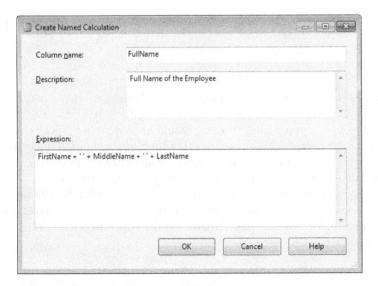

FIGURE 4-15

A new column is added to the Employee table, as shown in Figure 4-16. The data type of this calculated column will be determined based on the data types of the actual columns involved in the calculation or data used within the expression. If the expression results in a number, the data type for this column is an integer. In the preceding example the data type of this column is a string.

The DSV maintains the named calculation definition in the metadata of the Analysis Services database; it does not write it out to the underlying tables. When you want to view the data of this table (which you see later in this chapter), the expression is added to the SQL query that Analysis Services sends to the relational backend. You can see the data in the computed column in the results that are returned.

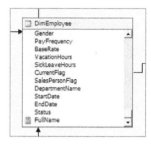

DATA SOURCE VIEWS IN DEPTH

FIGURE 4-16

Data warehouse designs consist of one or more fact tables and associated dimension tables. Small data warehouses are usually composed of 10 to 20 tables, whereas larger data warehouses can have more than a hundred tables. Even though you have a large number of tables in your data warehouse, you likely work with a small subset of those tables at a time; each of which has relationships to other tables in the group. For example, assume you have sales, inventory, and human resources (HR) data to analyze and the HR data is not strongly related to the sales and inventory data but there is a desired linkage. Further, there may be one group of your customers who want to see just the HR-related view of the data and another group that wants to focus on just the sales and inventory information. You may even have a business policy that restricts the details of the HR information to a subset of your customers. To conform to these requirements, you might create two cubes, one for sales and inventory information and another one for HR. It is quite possible you can store the Sales, Inventory, and HR information in a single data source — in the ODS or OLTP system.

Employee HR information could be related to the sales and inventory information within the company in so far as there is a link between a given sales event and the employee who made the sale. You might want to slice the sales data by a specific employee, but to do so you must access information that is a part of a separate table only accessible to the HR department (for security reasons). You can get around this problem by making a single DSV containing all the tables that store sales, inventory, and HR information of a company. From that DSV, you can formulate both cubes and set permissions such that only members of the HR group can drill down on personal employee data.

Diagrams

Having a lot of tables in the DSV definitely makes the navigation and usability a bit complex. When you work on HR data, you want to see only the tables related to this alone. For easy manageability you need customizable views within your DSV that show only certain tables. Analysis Services provides you with the ability to have several views within the DSV that each contains a subset of the DSV's tables. These views are called *diagrams*. By default, you get a diagram called <All Tables> when you complete the DSV Wizard that contains all the tables available in the DSV. You can create additional diagrams and choose the tables that you want to include within them. Next, you learn how to create a new diagram.

To create a new diagram, do the following:

1. Right-click the Diagram Organizer pane, and select New Diagram, as shown in Figure 4-17.

FIGURE 4-17

2. Name the new diagram **Internet Sales**.

3. You now have an empty diagram view. Right-click the Diagram pane and select Show Tables (see Figure 4-18). A dialog displays where you can choose the table(s) you want to include in this diagram.

FIGURE 4-18

4. Select the FactInternetSales table, and click OK.

5. Right-click the caption of the table you just added, and select Show Related Tables.

This gives you a diagram that contains the FactInternetSales fact table and the related dimension tables, as shown in Figure 4-19. The Internet Sales diagram you have created has seven of the ten tables in the DSV. This diagram allows you to work with only the tables that related to Internet sales.

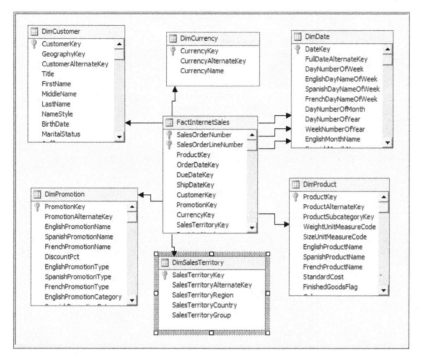

FIGURE 4-19

If you do not want a specific table in your diagram, you can right-click the table and select Hide. Instead of Steps 3 through 5 in the preceding list, you could have added tables to the diagram view by dragging and dropping them from the Table pane to the Diagram pane. Create another diagram called Reseller Sales and add the FactResellerSales table and related tables.

Data Source View Properties

Each object in your Analysis Services project has certain properties. Within the DSV Designer you can view the properties of the objects in the DSV such as tables, views, columns, and relationships. Properties of these objects are shown in the Properties window within SSDT, as shown in Figure 4-20.

Figure 4-20 shows the properties of various DSV objects: a column in a table, a named calculation, a table, and a relationship. For regular columns in a table, you have the properties AllowNull, DataType, DateTimeMode, Description, FriendlyName, Length, and Name. SSDT populates the properties of a column by retrieving the corresponding properties from the data source. Based on the properties defined in the data source, the properties AllowNull, DataType, Length, Name, and FriendlyName are populated. The Length property is applicable only for the string data type. For all other data types, the Length property has a value of –1. You cannot change certain properties of a column. They are not editable in the Properties window and are grayed out to indicate they are read-only.

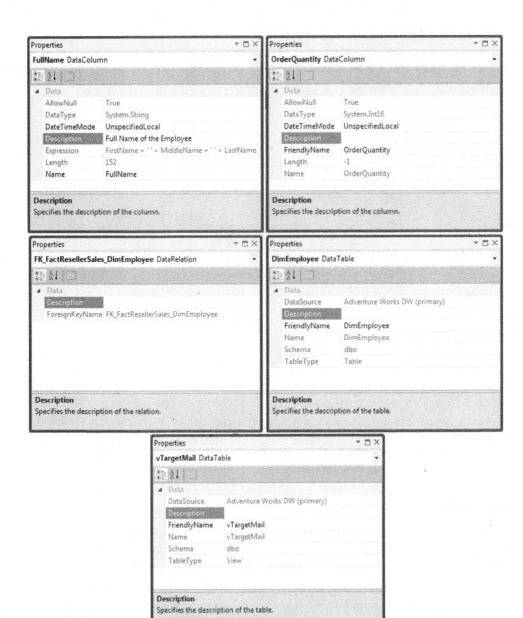

FIGURE 4-20

You can change the FriendlyName property and also provide a description for each column. Often, columns of a table in the relational database might not have user-friendly names. User-friendly means the name of the column should indicate clearly or intuitively the data stored in the column. The FriendlyName property is initially populated by the DSV Wizard with the name of the column in the data source. You can change this property to a name that is easier to understand and more indicative of the purpose of the data in the column. The DSV Designer provides you with the option of switching between the original column names and the friendly names. You can right-click in the DSV diagram view and toggle between the friendly name and the original column name by selecting the Show FriendlyName option.

Named calculation columns do not have a FriendlyName property because you define the name of this column and should provide an intuitive and understandable name. Instead, named calculation columns have the Expression property because each named column is created from a SQL expression. You can change this expression only in the Named Column dialog and not in the Properties window.

Tables have the properties DataSource, Description, FriendlyName, Name, Schema, and TableType. The DataSource property is the name of the data source of the table. The TableType property indicates whether the object in the underlying data source is a table or a view. Similar to the columns, tables also have the option to specify a friendly name.

Relationships between tables are given a name that includes the tables that participate in the relationship. This name is also listed as the ForeignKeyName property. They do not have a FriendlyName property but they do allow you to add a description that will be included in the metadata of the DSV.

Different Layouts in DSVs

The DSV Designer provides two different layout types: rectangular and diagonal. In rectangular layout, the lines representing the relationships between tables are composed of horizontal and vertical lines, and the lines emerge from any of the four sides of the table. The second layout type offered by the DSV Designer is diagonal layout. In diagonal layout, lines emerge from only the right or left sides of the table and the lines themselves are not restricted to be only horizontal and vertical lines; they can be diagonal. You can switch between rectangular layout and diagonal layout in the DSV by right-clicking in the DSV Designer and selecting the layout type of your choice. Figures 4-21 and 4-22 show rectangular and diagonal layouts, respectively, of the Internet Sales diagram.

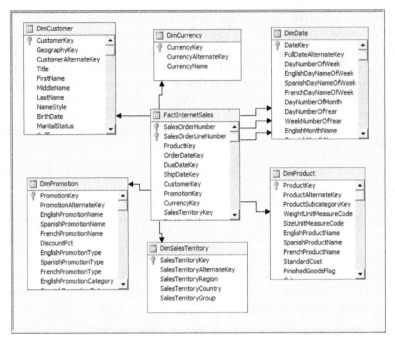

FIGURE 4-21

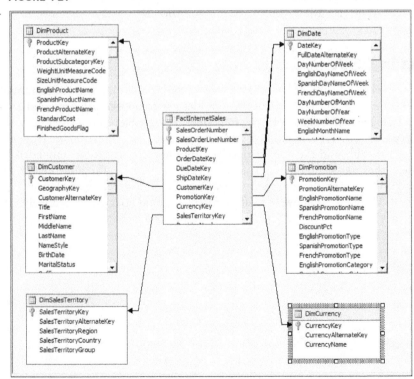

FIGURE 4-22

Diagonal layout works best for subset diagrams that contain a single fact table with its associated dimensions — a classic star or snowflake schema. For more complex diagrams, though, a proliferation of diagonal lines can make the diagram confusing. In that case, rectangular layout can be easier to view and understand. For this reason, the default layout type for the default diagram created by the DSV Wizard is rectangular.

Validating Your DSV and Initial Data Analysis

The relationships specified in the DSV are an important component of the structure of the dimensions and cubes in your multidimensional model. Therefore, validating your DSV is crucial to your data warehouse design. The DSV Designer provides a first level of validation when you specify relationships. If the data types of column(s) involved in the relationship do not match, the DSV will not allow you to establish the relationship. This forces you to make sure you appropriately cast the data types of the column(s) involved in the relationships. You might need another level of validation by looking at the data within each table. You can do this by issuing queries to the tables in the relational data source. The DSV provides a way to look at sample data for validation. A couple of validations you can do within the DSV by looking at sample data follow:

➤ Looking at the fact table data helps you make sure the table contains fact data, the primary key has been specified correctly, and appropriate relationships needed for dimensions are established.

➤ Analyzing a dimension table's sample data ensures that you have all the relationships established between the fact and dimension table and any relationships within each table are correctly established. For example, if you have an Employee table that contains an employee and his manager, you might want to establish a relationship so that your model can take advantage of this.

Looking at samples of data from the tables in the DSV helps you identify the measures of the cube as well as the hierarchies in each dimension. Analyzing sample data in the DSV also helps you identify dimensions that can be created from the fact table data. The analysis of sample data within the DSV is even more important when creating Data Mining models. You learn more about using Data Mining to analyze data in Chapter 12.

To see a sample of the data specified by your DSV, right-click a table in the DSV Designer, and select Explore Data. You can see rows from the underlying table presented within the Explore <tablename> Table window, as shown in Figure 4-23. The data presented is only a subset of the underlying table data. By default, the first 5,000 rows are retrieved and shown in this window. You can change the number of rows retrieved by clicking the Sampling Options button. Clicking the Sampling Options button launches the Data Exploration Options dialog where you can change the sampling method and the sample count. After you change the sample count value, you can click the Resample Data button to refresh the data based on the new settings. The Table tab shows the raw sampled data from the data source as rows and columns with column headings.

Resample Data

Sampling Options

Explore FactInternetSales Table ×	Adventure Works DW.dsv [Design]*							
Table								
ProductKey	OrderDateKey	DueDateKey	ShipDateKey	CustomerKey	PromotionKey	CurrencyKey	SalesTerritoryKey	
310	20050701	20050713	20050708	21768	1	19	6	
346	20050701	20050713	20050708	28389	1	39	7	
346	20050701	20050713	20050708	25863	1	100	1	
336	20050701	20050713	20050708	14501	1	100	4	
346	20050701	20050713	20050708	11003	1	6	9	
311	20050702	20050714	20050709	27645	1	100	4	
310	20050702	20050714	20050709	16624	1	6	9	
351	20050702	20050714	20050709	11005	1	6	9	
344	20050702	20050714	20050709	11011	1	6	9	
312	20050703	20050715	20050710	27621	1	100	4	
312	20050703	20050715	20050710	27616	1	100	4	
330	20050703	20050715	20050710	20042	1	98	10	
313	20050703	20050715	20050710	16351	1	6	9	
314	20050703	20050715	20050710	16517	1	6	9	
314	20050704	20050716	20050711	27606	1	100	1	
311	20050704	20050716	20050711	13513	1	29	8	
310	20050705	20050717	20050712	27601	1	100	4	
311	20050705	20050717	20050712	13591	1	98	10	
314	20050705	20050717	20050712	16483	1	6	9	
311	20050705	20050717	20050712	16529	1	6	9	
336	20050705	20050717	20050712	25249	1	6	9	
311	20050706	20050718	20050713	27668	1	100	1	
312	20050706	20050718	20050713	27612	1	100	4	
311	20050706	20050718	20050713	13264	1	29	8	

FIGURE 4-23

MULTIPLE DATA SOURCES WITHIN A DSV

Data warehouses can consist of data from several data sources. Some examples of data sources are SQL Server, Oracle, DB2, and Teradata. Traditionally, the OLTP data is transferred from the operational data store to the data warehouse — the staging area that combines data from disparate data sources. This is not only time-intensive in terms of design, maintainability, and storage but also in terms of other considerations such as replication of data and ensuring data is in sync with the source. Analysis Services helps you avoid this and gives you a better return on your investment.

The DSV Designer has the ability to include tables from multiple data sources in a single DSV, which you can then use to build your cubes and dimensions. You first need to define the data sources that include the tables that are part of your data warehouse design using the Data Source Wizard. When this has been accomplished, you create a DSV and include tables from one of the data sources. This first data source is called the primary data source and needs to be a SQL Server data source. You can then add tables and work with them in the DSV Designer as described earlier in this chapter. The Add/Remove Tables dialog allows you to choose a different data source, as shown in Figure 4-24 so that you can add its tables to the DSV. To illustrate the selection of tables from a second data source, as shown in Figure 4-24, a second data source in the AnalysisServicesMultidimensionalTutorial project was created from the SQL Server Master database. You should be aware that there might be performance implications when retrieving data from secondary data sources because all the queries are routed through the primary SQL Server data source.

After you add the tables from multiple data sources to your DSV, you can start creating your cubes and dimensions as if these came from a single data source. The limitation that the primary data source needs to be a SQL Server is due to the fact that Analysis Services instance uses a SQL Server-specific feature called OPENROWSET to retrieve data from other data sources.

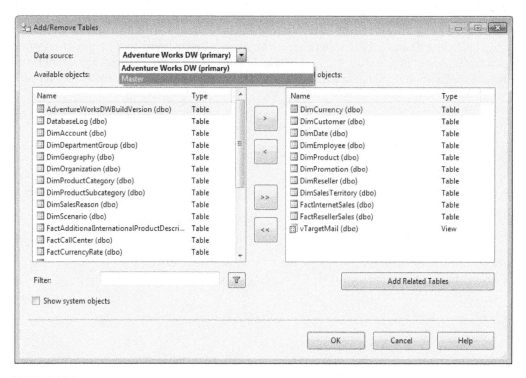

FIGURE 4-24

SUMMARY

You now have the skills to deal with the challenges real-world data warehouses can throw at you when using multiple data sources. You learned about OLE DB and managed data providers used by Analysis Services to retrieve data from data sources and the trade-offs of using one versus another. Indeed, you learned that you can tame the disparate data source beast by using multiple data sources. Then you learned to consolidate the tables and relationships of interest in Data Source Views (DSVs), and finally, to refine the tables and relationships in the DSVs so you have to deal with only what's relevant.

When you make changes in the DSV, that is where the changes stay — in the DSV. The changes are not written out to the underlying tables as you might expect. This is a good thing. To see why, take a look at the alternative to using the DSV capability. The alternative method is to create a view in SQL with real relationship transforms in the underlying tables. That's another viable approach, but if your data spans multiple databases, you may have to create linked servers and that can become time-consuming. Analysis Services provides an easy way to specify these cross-database relationships within a DSV without the overhead of having to use linked servers. However, when multiple data sources are included in a single DSV, the primary data source must support the ability to send queries and retrieve results from other servers. You can incur performance degradation due to this method; however, you do avoid the complexity of managing data on multiple servers to create your data warehouse.

You're doing great! You're now ready to tackle core business intelligence constructs such as dimension design (Chapter 5) and cube design (Chapter 6). If you already know these topics from working with earlier versions of SQL Server Analysis Services, work through the chapters anyway. There have been some important changes to the Cube and Dimension Wizards in Analysis Services 2012.

5

Dimension Design

Consider airline travel. Many people with different ultimate destinations embark on a journey together. They board a single airplane at a common location. The airline takes all of them to a common destination. (For the purposes of this metaphor, assume a nonstop flight.) After they arrive at that destination, they branch out to where their own business or personal agendas take them.

The data warehouse design process using Analysis Services multidimensional development tools is similar to that. The wizards that create each major object type take everyone to a common place. When you get there, you can use the corresponding designer to take your objects to their ultimate destination. You saw this approach in the previous chapter when you learned about creating data sources and Data Source Views. Likewise, in this chapter you learn how to create dimensions in a common way using the Dimension Wizard; then you use the Dimension Designer to take your dimensions to their final destination based on your business needs.

Cubes are made up of dimensions and measures, where the measure values are aggregated along each dimension. Without an understanding of dimensions and how measures are aggregated along them, you can't create and exploit the power of cubes, so jump right into learning about building and viewing dimensions. After you create dimensions, you add them to a cube and define the right relationship types between the fact data and dimensions. Analysis Services supports six relationship types: no relationship, regular, fact, referenced, many-to-many, and data mining. You learn about these relationship types in this chapter and in Chapters 8 and 12. In addition, you learn about the attributes and hierarchies that are an integral part of dimensions. You learn how to model Time dimensions and Parent-Child dimensions, which are different from regular dimensions and are important components of many data warehouses. Finally, you learn how to process and browse dimensions.

WORKING WITH THE DIMENSION WIZARD

Dimensions help you define the structure of your cube to facilitate effective data analysis. Specifically, dimensions provide you with the ability to slice a cube's data. You can build dimensions from one or more dimension tables. As you learned in Chapter 1, you can design your data warehouse using star or snowflake schemas. In a star schema, you create dimensions from single tables joined to a fact table. In a snowflake schema, you create dimensions from two or more joined dimension tables. When you build your cube using snowflake dimensions, one of the tables that make up the dimension joins to the fact table. You create both of these dimension types in this chapter.

You also learned in Chapters 2 and 3 that each dimension contains objects called *hierarchies*. In Analysis Services you have two types of hierarchies to contend with: attribute hierarchies, which correspond to a single column in a relational table, and multilevel or user hierarchies, which derive from two or more attribute hierarchies. Each level in the multilevel hierarchy is an attribute hierarchy. A typical example of an attribute hierarchy would be a ZIP code in a Geography dimension, and a typical example of a user hierarchy would be Country-State-City-ZIP code, also in a Geography dimension. In everyday discussions of user hierarchies, most people leave off the "user" and just call them "hierarchies."

For the exercises in this chapter, you start from the project you created in Chapter 2. If you don't have that project handy, you can download it from www.wrox.com. Regardless of whether you download it or use the project you built in Chapter 2, you need to add the Geography dimension (dbo.DimGeography) to the DSV. To add this dimension to your DSV, follow these steps:

FIGURE 5-1

1. In the Solution Explorer, double-click the Adventure Works DW.dsv DSV.

2. Click the Add/Remove Objects toolbar button (the top-left button in the DSV Designer toolbar) as shown in Figure 5-1.

3. In the Available objects list, select DimGeography, and click the > (right arrow) button, as shown in Figure 5-2. This moves the DimGeography dimension table into the Included objects list in the Add/Remove Tables dialog. Click OK to continue.

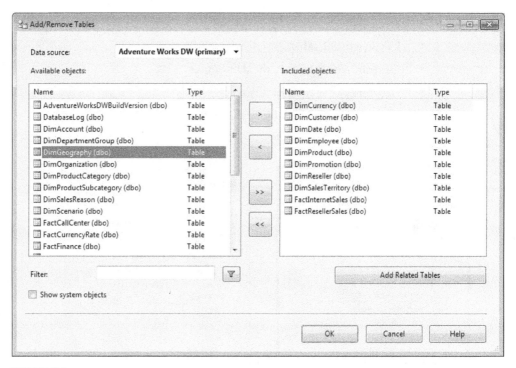

FIGURE 5-2

4. All dimension tables in a DSV should have a primary key set to allow Analysis Services to determine the key attribute column of the dimension, which will be joined to a foreign key column in the appropriate fact table(s). Review the DimGeography table in the DSV Designer to see that the DimGeography table's GeographyKey column has been set as the primary key, as shown in Figure 5-3.

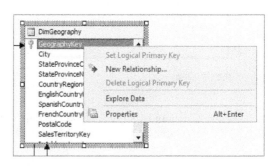

FIGURE 5-3

If a primary key is not defined in the source data table, you can right-click the desired key column(s) in that table and select Set Logical Primary Key (refer to Figure 5-3). This enables you to create the right primary key/foreign key relationships for tables in your data warehouse even if they are not defined in the source data. If the primary key for the table has been defined in the source data and recognized by the DSV Designer, the option to Set Logical Primary Key will be disabled.

Now you are ready to explore the use of the Dimension Wizard in SSDT. Continue to follow these steps to create the Geography dimension.

5. Launch the Dimension Wizard by right-clicking the Dimensions folder in the Solution Explorer and selecting New Dimension, as shown in Figure 5-4. If the welcome screen of the Dimension Wizard appears, click Next.

6. On the Select Creation Method page, as shown in Figure 5-5, you see four options:

> ➤ Use an existing table

> ➤ Generate a time table in the data source

> ➤ Generate a time table on the server

> ➤ Generate a non-time table in the data source

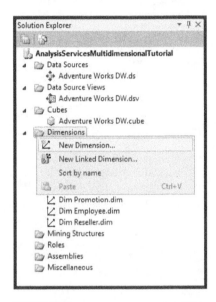

FIGURE 5-4

FIGURE 5-5

Using an existing table in the data source enables the creation of a standard dimension that can later be modified to become any sophisticated dimension type. This option is a great starting point for creating most dimensions.

A Time dimension, on the other hand, is a unique type of dimension typically created from a table that contains time information such as year, semester, quarter, month, week, and date. A Time dimension is unique because its members are fixed (for example, a year always has 12 months in it) and typical business analyses are performed over time. Due to the uniqueness of the Time dimensions and how they are used in business analysis, there are special MDX functions that can be used with them. Furthermore, aggregation of data on a Time dimension does not need to be a garden-variety additive aggregation like sum or count.

Most business decision makers want to analyze their data across a Time dimension to understand, for example, the month with maximum sales for a quarter or some other time period. Analysis Services provides you a distinct way to aggregate measure data across a Time dimension. This is done with semi-additive measures. You learn more about semi-additive measures in Chapters 6 and 9. In a Time dimension, some standard hierarchies are commonly used, such as fiscal year and calendar year, both of which can be built automatically. You can build the Time dimensions using either a table from the data source or without any associated tables in the data source. To create a table to serve as the source of your Time dimension, you choose the second option on the Select Creation Method page of the wizard. To create a server-based Time dimension, select the third option. You learn more about server-based Time dimensions in Chapter 8.

In addition to Time, Analysis Services is also aware of several other common dimension types used in business intelligence (BI) applications, such as Account, Customer, Employee, and Currency, and can create the necessary tables in the data source to support these dimension types. This chapter explores creating dimensions from existing tables in a data source.

In the Select Creation Method page, select Use an Existing Table, and click Next.

7. On the Specify Source Information page (shown in Figure 5-6), you need to select the DSV for creating the dimension, the main table from which the dimension is to be designed, the key columns for the dimension, and optionally a name column for the dimension key value. By default, the first DSV in your project is selected. Because the current project has only one DSV (the Adventure Works DW DSV), it is selected.

FIGURE 5-6

On the Main table drop-down on the page, you need to select the main table from which the dimension is to be designed. If a dimension is to be created from a star schema, the dimension is created from only one table. A dimension built using a snowflake schema contains several tables, one of which is the primary table of the dimension. This primary table is chosen as the main table in the Main table selection of the Dimension Wizard.

Select the DimGeography table from the Main table drop-down list, as shown in Figure 5-6.

After selecting the Main table for the dimension, the Key columns list and the Name column field are automatically set to the primary key of the selected table. If no primary key or logical primary key is set, you need to specify the key columns. If the primary key for the main dimension table is made up of multiple columns, you must select a single column in the Name column drop-down before proceeding. Because the DimGeography table has a primary key defined, the wizard used it to fill in the Key columns and Name column fields when you chose DimGeography as the Main table.

Click the Next button to proceed to the next step in the Dimension Wizard.

8.   The Dimension Wizard now analyzes the DSV to detect any outward-facing relationships from the DimGeography table. An outward-facing relationship is a relationship between the DimGeography table and another table, such that a column in the DimGeography table is a foreign key related to another table. The Select Related Tables page (see Figure 5-7) shows that the wizard detected an outward relationship between the DimGeography table and the DimSalesTerritory table. In this example you model the DimGeography table as a star schema table instead of a snowflake schema. Deselect the DimSalesTerritory table and click Next.

FIGURE 5-7

9.   The Select Dimension Attributes page of the Dimension Wizard (see Figure 5-8) displays the columns of the main table that have been selected for the dimension you're creating. The columns selected from the relational table are transformed by the dimension wizard into the attributes of the dimension that can then be used when querying the cube. You can control which of the attributes are available for browsing and querying by checking or unchecking the Enable Browsing option for each attribute. In addition, you can set the Attribute Type property to allow Analysis Services to provide special functionality based on the attribute's type. By default the wizard creates attribute names based on column names. You can change the attribute name for each selected attribute on this page.

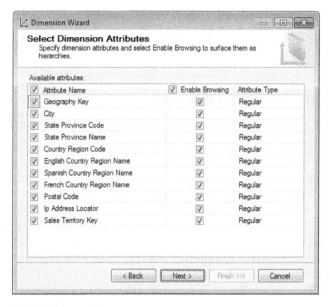

FIGURE 5-8

On the Select Dimension Attributes page, select all the columns of the DimGeography table. Leave their Attribute Type as Regular and allow them to be browsed, as shown in Figure 5-8. Click Next.

10. The final screen of the Dimension Wizard shows the attributes that will be created for the dimension based on your choices (see Figure 5-9). Click the Finish button.

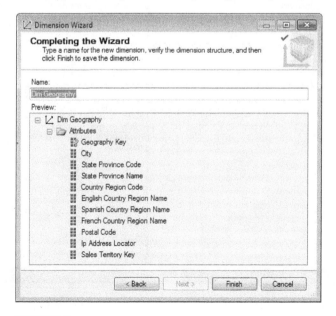

FIGURE 5-9

The wizard has created the Dim Geography dimension and opened it up in the Dimension Designer. Congratulations! You have successfully created your first dimension using the Dimension Wizard. Next, you learn how to use the Dimension Designer to enhance the dimension to fit your business needs.

WORKING WITH THE DIMENSION DESIGNER

The Dimension Designer, shown in Figure 5-10, is an important tool that helps you refine dimensions created by the Dimension Wizard. You can set properties such as unary operators, custom roll-ups, and so forth that help you define how data should be aggregated for cells referred to by members of hierarchies in the dimension. The Dimension Designer is composed of four pages, which you can access from the tabs at the top of the designer: Dimension Structure, Attribute Relationships, Translations, and Browser. The first of these pages, Dimension Structure, contains three panes: Attributes, Hierarchies, and Data Source View. The Attributes pane shows the dimension's attributes; the Hierarchies pane shows its hierarchies along with their levels; and the Data Source View pane shows the tables used in the dimension. In addition, you have a toolbar that contains buttons that help you enhance the dimension. If you hover over each toolbar button you can see a tooltip that describes the functionality of that button. Some of the buttons are the same as the ones you saw in the DSV Designer and are used for operations within the Dimension Designer's Data Source View pane. The functionality of the other buttons is discussed later in this chapter and in Chapter 8.

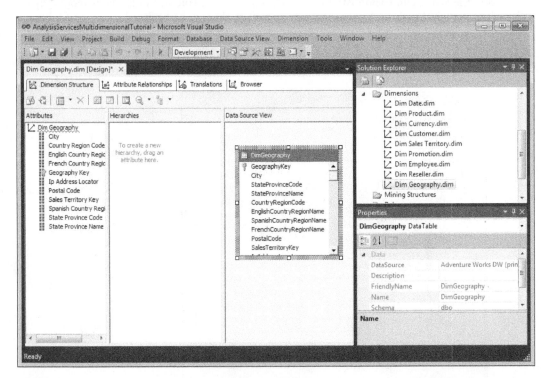

FIGURE 5-10

Attributes

Attribute hierarchies (or attributes, for short) are hierarchies that have only two levels: the leaf level, which contains one member for each distinct attribute value, and the All level, which contains the aggregated value of all the leaf level's members. The All level is optional. Each attribute directly corresponds to a table's column in the DSV. The Attributes pane in the Dimension Designer shows all the attribute hierarchies of the dimension. The default view in the Attributes pane is a Tree view, as shown in Figure 5-11. Two additional views are available: List view and Grid view. These views show the attributes and associated properties in different ways.

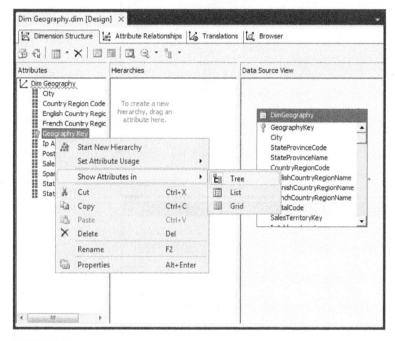

FIGURE 5-11

The List view repositions the Attributes pane below the Hierarchies pane and shows only the attributes of the dimension in a flat list. (It doesn't show the dimension name as a parent node.) This view is useful when your dimension has a lot of user hierarchies. Because you get a wider area for the Hierarchies pane, more hierarchies are visible without scrolling.

The Grid view is laid out similarly to the List view but includes additional columns that allow you to easily edit some of the important attribute properties right in the Attributes pane. When you work with more than one attribute, editing these properties in the Attributes pane is less cumbersome than having to select each attribute and then switching over to the Properties window to change the attribute's value. (All the properties shown in the Grid view are also present in the Properties window.)

You can toggle between the different views by right-clicking in the Attributes pane and selecting the view type you want, as shown in Figure 5-11. Choose the view that best helps you to visualize and design your dimension.

The List view and Grid view of the Dimension Designer are shown in Figure 5-12.

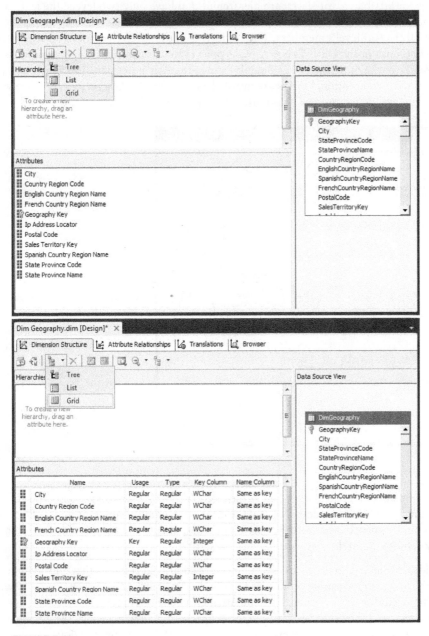

FIGURE 5-12

Attribute Relationships

Attribute relationships can be defined when attributes within the same dimension have a one-to-many relationship with each other. For example, if you have the attributes Country, State, and City, you have one-to-many relationships between Country and State, as well as between State and City. Each dimension must have at least one attribute defined as the key attribute. By definition, the key attribute is on the "many" side of a one-to-many relationship with every attribute in the dimension. The Dimension Wizard automatically establishes these relationships with all the attributes of the dimension.

If you are aware of one-to-many relationships between attributes, you should specify those relationships in the Dimension Designer. Specifying attribute relationships helps improve query performance as well as informing the aggregation design for user hierarchies. Because the Dim Geography dimension contains one-to-many relationships, you can specify attribute relationships to get improved query performance. You learn more about the benefits of attribute relationships in Chapter 10.

To view and edit a dimension's attribute relationships you use the Dimension Designer's Attribute Relationships page, as shown in Figure 5-13. The Attribute Relationships page contains three panes.

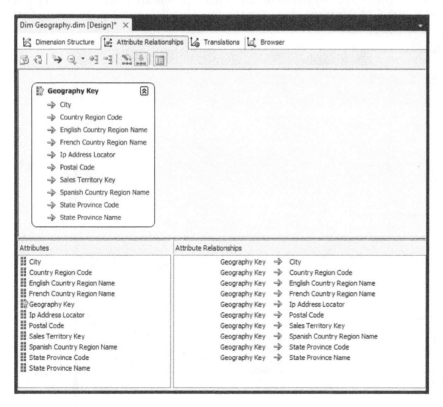

FIGURE 5-13

The top pane, called the Diagram pane, graphically shows the defined attribute relationships; the Attributes pane on the lower left shows the list of attributes in the dimension; and the Attribute Relationships pane in the lower right shows the list of defined relationships. The attributes shown in the Diagram pane when you open the designer are all the attributes of the dimension that have a one-to-many relationship with the key attribute (Geography Key). These attributes are also referred to as member property attributes or related attributes. Because an attribute relationship is defined between each member and the Geography Key attribute, you can retrieve the related attributes as properties using the member property MDX functions.

You can create new or modify existing attribute relationships using various methods within each of these panes. Follow these steps to update the Geography dimension's attribute relationships:

1. In the Diagram pane, you can modify attribute relationships by dragging and dropping attributes onto the attribute to which they are related.

   For example, State Province Name has a one-to-many relationship with City. Create the relationship as follows: In the Diagram pane, select the City attribute and drag and drop it onto the State Province Name attribute. This creates a new attribute relationship node, as shown in Figure 5-14. Note the change in the Attribute Relationships pane to reflect the

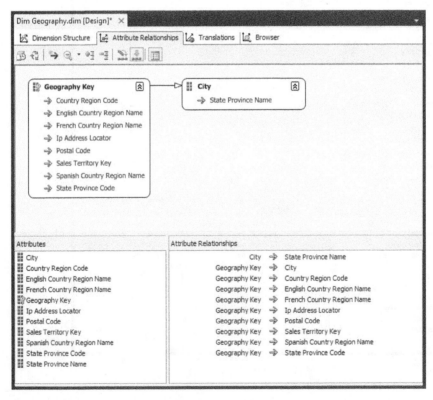

FIGURE 5-14

newly defined relationship. In the Diagram pane, you can edit and delete attribute relationships by right-clicking a relationship's line and selecting the wanted action from the
context menu.

2. To define a new relationship using the Attributes pane, right-click the attribute that makes
up the "many" side of the one-to-many relationship, and select New Attribute Relationship.
This launches the Create Attribute Relationship dialog. The Source Attribute corresponds to
the "many" side of the relationship, and the Related Attribute is the attribute corresponding
to the "one" side. You can also set the relationship type in this dialog to either Flexible or
Rigid. By default, Analysis Services tools define all relationships to be flexible. A relationship
is flexible if the value can change over time. A relationship is rigid if the relationship does not
change over time. For example, the birth date of a customer is fixed and hence the relationship between a customer's key/name and the birth date attribute would be defined as rigid.
However, the relationship between a customer and his city is flexible because the customer
can move from one city to another. In your dimension, there is a one-to-many relationship
between the English Country Region Name and State Province Name attributes. To specify
that relationship, perform the following steps.

3. In the Attributes pane, right-click the State Province Name attribute, and select New
Attribute Relationship from the context menu.

4. In the Create Attribute Relationship dialog, select English Country Region Name as the
Related Attribute (see Figure 5-15).

5. Click OK to create the relationship.

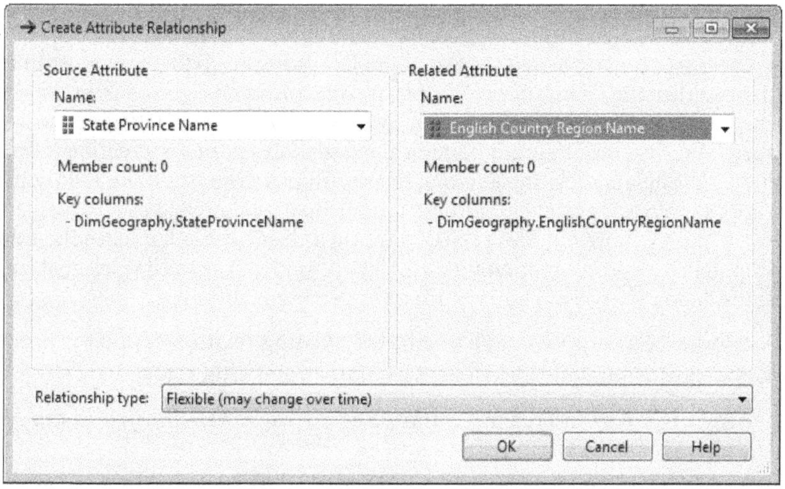

FIGURE 5-15

Your Attribute Relationships display should be similar to that shown in Figure 5-16.

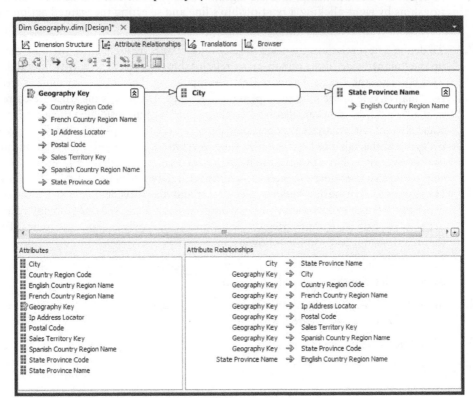

FIGURE 5-16

To define a new relationship using the Attribute Relationships pane, you must first select an attribute from either the Diagram or Attributes pane and then right-click in the Attribute Relationships pane in the area not occupied by existing attribute relationships. This can be a bit cumbersome. Use the Diagram pane or the Attributes pane for creating new attribute relationships. Editing and deleting existing relationships in the Attribute Relationships pane, however, is as simple as right-clicking the relationship and choosing the wanted action from the context menu, as shown in Figure 5-17. Editing a relationship launches the Edit Attribute Relationship dialog, whose functionality and layout is identical to the Create Attribute Relationships dialog shown in Figure 5-15; only the title is different.

Use the Attribute Relationships pane to edit the existing relationships for the French and Spanish Country Region Name attributes using the following steps:

6. Select the Geography Key to French Country Region Name relationship in the Attribute Relationships pane.

7. Right-click and select Edit Attribute Relationship.

8. In the Edit Attribute Relationship dialog, select the English Country Region Name as the Source Attribute (see Figure 5-18).

9. Click OK to save the change to the relationship.

10. In the Properties window, change the Cardinality property corresponding to the relationship between English Country Region Name and French Country Region Name from Many to One.

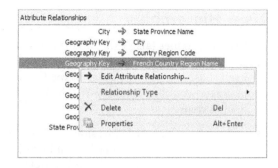

FIGURE 5-17

Repeat the previous five steps for the Spanish Country Region Name attribute relationship.

You have now used three different methods for working with attribute relationships. Often in business analysis when you analyze a specific member of a dimension, you need to see the properties of the dimension member to understand it better. In such circumstances, instead of traversing the complete hierarchy, you can retrieve the member by querying the member properties. This, once again, is a performance improvement from the end user's perspective. A wide variety of client tools support the ability to retrieve member properties of a specific member when needed by the data analyst. You can add additional attributes by dragging and dropping a column from the DSV to the Attributes pane or delete an existing attribute by right-clicking that attribute and selecting Delete.

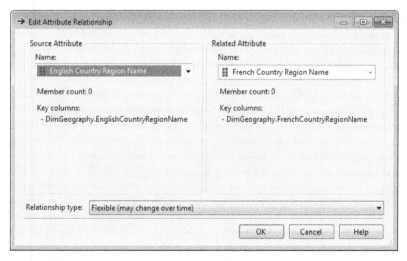

FIGURE 5-18

User Hierarchies

User hierarchies (also called multilevel hierarchies) are created from the attributes of a dimension. Each user hierarchy contains one or more levels, and each level is an attribute hierarchy itself. Based on the attributes of the Geography dimension you created, a logical user hierarchy to create would be Country-State-City-Postal Code. You can create this hierarchy using the following steps:

1. Switch to the Dimension Structure tab of the Dim Geography dimension, and drag and drop the English Country Region Name attribute from the Attributes pane to the Hierarchies pane. This creates a user hierarchy called Hierarchy with one level: English Country Region Name. This level corresponds to a country. To make this name more user-friendly, rename the English Country Region Name attribute to **Country** by right-clicking the attribute within the user hierarchy and selecting Rename.

2. Drag and drop State Province Name from the Attributes pane to the Hierarchies pane such that the State Province Name attribute is below Country in the user hierarchy. Rename State Province Name to **State Province** by right-clicking the attribute and selecting Rename.

3. Drag and drop City and Postal Code attributes to the user hierarchy in that order so that you now have a four-level hierarchy Country-State Province-City-Postal Code.

4. The default name of the hierarchy you have created is Hierarchy. Rename it to **Geography** by right-clicking its name and selecting Rename (see Figure 5-19). You can also rename hierarchy and level names in the Hierarchies pane by selecting the item and changing the value of its Name property in the Properties pane.

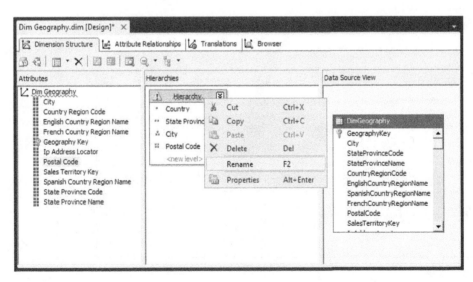

FIGURE 5-19

You have now created a user hierarchy called Geography that has four levels, as shown in Figure 5-20. You can click the arrows to expand the attribute in each level to see its related attributes.

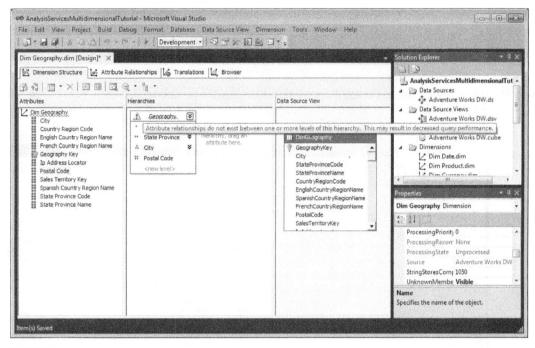

FIGURE 5-20

Notice the Warning icon next to the Geography hierarchy name and the squiggly line under the name of the hierarchy. If you place your mouse over this icon or the hierarchy name, you can see a tooltip message indicating that attribute relationships do not exist between one or more levels of the hierarchy and could result in decreased performance.

The current hierarchy design is called an unnatural hierarchy. An unnatural hierarchy exists when knowing the attribute value of one level of the hierarchy is not sufficient to know who its parent is in the next level up the hierarchy. Another example of an unnatural hierarchy would be a Customer Gender-Age hierarchy, where Gender is the top level of the dimension and Age is the second level. Knowing that a customer is 37 years old does not give any indication of gender.

Conversely, in a natural hierarchy, knowing the value of an attribute at one level clearly indicates who its parent is on the next level of the hierarchy. An example of a natural hierarchy would be a Product dimension hierarchy with Category, Sub-Category, and Product levels. By knowing that a product is in the Mountain Bike Sub-Category, you would know that it belongs to the Bike Category. This relationship between attribute values is defined through attribute relationships. For a hierarchy to be considered natural, attribute relationships must exist from the bottom level of the hierarchy all the way to the top. Analysis Services materializes only hierarchies considered natural. Use the following steps to refine the current Geography hierarchy so that it is natural:

1. Switch back to the Attribute Relationships page. The page should look similar to Figure 5-21.

2. There is no relationship between Postal Code and City. In the Diagram pane, drag and drop the Postal Code attribute to the City attribute.

   An attribute relationship between the Postal Code attribute and the City attribute is created, as shown in Figure 5-22.

   The visualization of the attribute relationships extends beyond the Diagram pane. (Depending on the resolution of your monitor, you might view all the attribute relationships.) You can zoom in or zoom out using the Zoom item in the context menu of the visualization pane

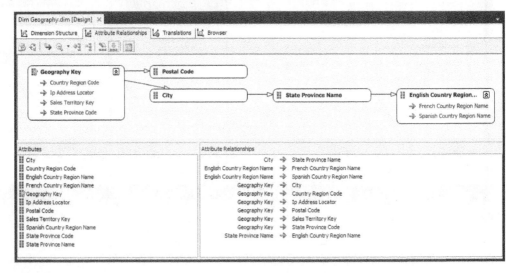

FIGURE 5-21

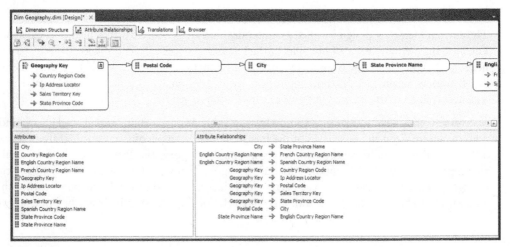

FIGURE 5-22

to adjust the size of the content of the Diagram pane to see all the attribute relationships. Sometimes the attribute relationships view can be quite large, depending on the number of attributes and the relationships you have established. You can easily navigate to the area of the visualization pane you're interested in by clicking the "+" symbol at the far right of the horizontal scrollbar and using the locator window (as shown in Figure 5-23).

3. Switch back to the Dimension Structure tab, verify the warning is gone, and save the dimension, as shown in Figure 5-24.

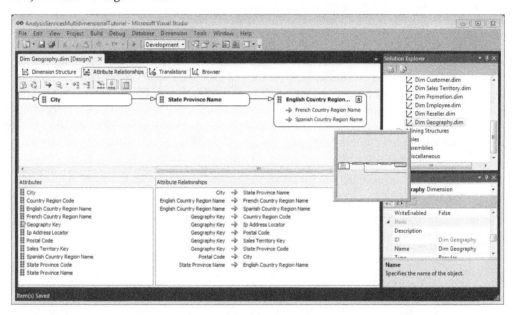

FIGURE 5-23

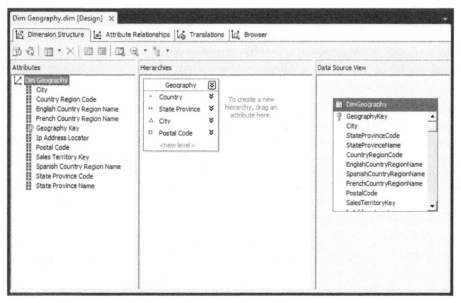

FIGURE 5-24

BROWSING THE DIMENSION

After successfully defining the Dim Geography dimension, you definitely would like to see the results of what you have created and find out how you can view the members of the dimension. At this point the dimension has been designed but not deployed to the server. Indeed, there has been no interaction with the instance of Analysis Services yet. To see the members of the dimension, Analysis Services needs to receive the details of the dimension (the attributes, member properties, and the multilevel hierarchies you have created).

The Analysis Services tools communicate to the instance of Analysis Services via XMLA (XML for Analysis). XMLA is an industry-standard, Simple Object Access Protocol (SOAP)–based XML Application Programming Interface (API) designed for OLAP and Data Mining. The XMLA specification defines two functions, Execute and Discover, which send actions to and retrieve data from the host instance. The Execute and Discover functions take several parameters that define the actions that the instance of Analysis Services can perform. One of the parameters of the Execute function is the command sent to an instance of Analysis Services. In addition to supporting the functionality defined in the XMLA specification, Analysis Services supports extensions to the standard. Following is a sample Execute request sent to an instance of Analysis Services using XMLA.

```
<Execute xmlns="urn:schemas-microsoft-com:xml-analysis">
  <Command>
    <Statement>
      SELECT Measures.MEMBERS ON COLUMNS FROM [Adventure Works DW]
    </Statement>
  </Command>
  <Properties>
    <PropertyList>
      <Catalog>AnalysisServicesMultidimensionalTutorial</Catalog>
      <Format>Multidimensional</Format>
      <AxisFormat>ClusterFormat</AxisFormat>
    </PropertyList>
  </Properties>
</Execute>
```

In the preceding XMLA, a request is sent to execute an MDX query specified within the Statement command on the AnalysisServicesMultidimensionalTutorial catalog. The request shown results in the query being executed on the server side and the results returned to the client via XMLA.

Several different commands communicate to the Analysis Services Server. Some of the common ones are Create, Alter, Process, and Statement. These commands change the structure of objects referenced in the command. Each Analysis Services object has a well-defined set of properties. The definition of the objects is accomplished by commands referred to as Data Definition Language (DDL) commands. Other commands work with data that has already been defined. Those commands are referred to as Data Manipulation Language (DML) commands. You learn some of the DML and DDL commands used in Analysis Services in various chapters of the book through examples. For an in-depth understanding of DML and DDL commands, see the Analysis Services documentation.

You might recall that you deployed the AnalysisServicesMultidimensionalTutorial project in Chapter 2. When you deploy a project, SSDT packages the design change information in the project into XMLA requests and sends them to the server. At this point, you might want to see the contents of the dimension you have created. To do this you need to deploy the project to an instance of Analysis Services. When you deploy the project to the Analysis Services server, several XMLA requests are sent:

1. Request a list of the databases from Analysis Services to determine if the database defined by the current project already exists on the instance. The project name you specified will be used as the database name. SSDT sends either a Create or Alter command for the database based on whether the database already exists on the server. Based on the deployment settings in your project, SSDT then sends either the entire definition of all the objects in your project or only the changes you have made since the last deploy. We have not included the contents of the Create/Alter XMLA request in the following code because it is quite large. You can use the SQL Server Profiler to view the XMLA requests sent by SSDT. (You learn to use SQL Server Profiler in Chapter 11.)

2. SSDT then sends an XMLA request to process the objects you have created and/or modified. Following is the request sent to the server to process the Dim Geography dimension:

```
<Batch xmlns="http://schemas.microsoft.com/analysisservices/2003/engine">
  <Process>
    <Type>ProcessDefault</Type>
    <Object>
      <DatabaseID>AnalysisServicesMultidimensionalTutorial</DatabaseID>
    </Object>
  </Process>
</Batch>
```

SSDT performs validations to make sure your dimension design is correct. If there are errors, SSDT shows those errors using red squiggly lines. You saw an example of this earlier in the chapter when you created a user hierarchy and hadn't yet defined attribute relationships between the hierarchy's levels. In addition to that, a set of error handling properties in the Analysis Services instance helps in validating your dimension design at deployment and processing time. SSDT sends the error handling property information to the Analysis Services instance to indicate how the server should respond to any referential integrity errors as part of the deployment process.

Deploy the AnalysisServicesMultidimensionalTutorial project to your Analysis Services instance by either pressing the F5 key or right-clicking the project in the Solution Explorer window and selecting Deploy. SSDT attempts to deploy the project to the Analysis Services instance. Deployment will fail, as you can see in the Deployment Progress window shown in Figure 5-25.

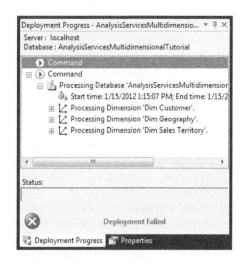

FIGURE 5-25

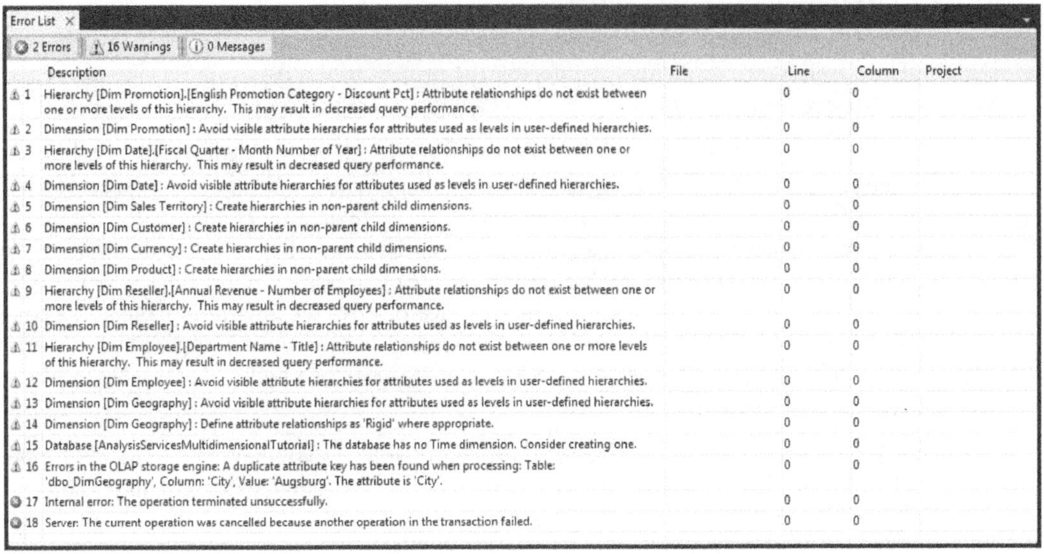

FIGURE 5-26

SSDT reports all the warnings and errors identified by SSDT from the Analysis Services instance using the Error List window, as shown in Figure 5-26.

The first 15 warnings shown in Figure 5-26 are an example of the Best Practices warnings feature mentioned earlier. This feature highlights common violations of best practices that the Analysis Services team has historically seen and are, by necessity, general. Some of these warnings shown by SSDT might be the result of valid design decisions you made for your particular Analysis Services database. Hence SSDT supports a warning infrastructure by which you can disable warnings for specific objects or even disable specific warnings from reappearing in future deployments. When you right-click one of the first 15 warnings, you can see an option to dismiss the warning. You cannot dismiss a warning reported by the Analysis Services instance (as opposed to SSDT) or any error. If you click the sixteenth warning, you can see that the warning cannot be dismissed. This is the first warning reported by the Analysis Services instance followed by the errors that fail the deployment of your AnalysisServicesMultidimensionalTutorial project. You learn more about the Best Practices warning feature in Chapter 9.

The Analysis Services instance warning (warning 16, shown in Figure 5-26) indicates that, while processing the City attribute, duplicate attribute key values were identified. This warning indicates that there are multiple cities with the same name. This error is raised because you have defined and guaranteed a one-to-many attribute relationship between the City attribute and the State Province Name attribute. The Analysis Services instance identifies that there are several different cities with the same name and cannot decide which State Province Name has the relationship to a specific city. If you query the City column in the DimGeography table, you can see that City names are not unique. For example, London, Paris, and Berlin all appear in excess of a dozen times in the DimGeography table of the AdventureWorksDW database. Hence the Analysis Services instance raises the error with the text "Errors in OLAP Storage Engine." Due to this error, the Analysis Services instance fails the processing of the City attribute, and subsequently the Dim Geography dimension, and the deployment fails.

To correct this issue, you need to make sure each city is unique. One way you can do this is by creating a surrogate key for the city that makes each city unique and use that key as the key column for the City attribute. Alternatively, you can use composite keys to uniquely identify a City attribute. In the following steps you use the second approach and build composite keys from multiple attributes that uniquely identify all members of those attributes that are not unique by themselves. To uniquely identify a city, you need to know the State Province Name to which it belongs. Therefore, the composite key for the City attribute should include the City and State Province Code. Follow these steps to make the City attribute have unique members:

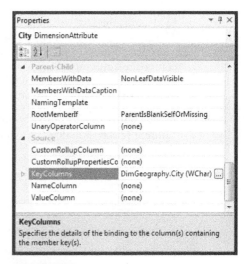

FIGURE 5-27

1. Open the Dim Geography dimension in the Dimension Designer, and select the City attribute in the Attributes pane.

2. In the Properties pane, locate the KeyColumns property, and click the ellipses (as shown in Figure 5-27) to open the Key Columns selection dialog.

3. In the Key Columns selection dialog, add the StateProvinceCode to the list of Key Columns, as shown in Figure 5-28. Click OK.

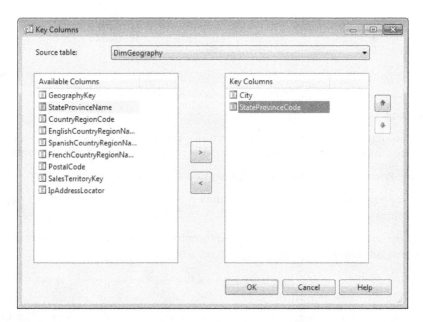

FIGURE 5-28

By default, the Dimension Wizard uses the column name as the key column for the attribute. The Analysis Services instance automatically infers the same column to be the name column (the column used to display the member names for the attribute). Whenever you define a composite key, you need to define a name column for the attribute because SSDT and the Analysis Services instance do not know which of the composite key columns should be used as the name column for the attribute.

4. In the NameColumn property for the City attribute, click the ellipses to open the Name Column selection dialog (shown in Figure 5-29) and select City as the source for the name of the City attribute. Click OK.

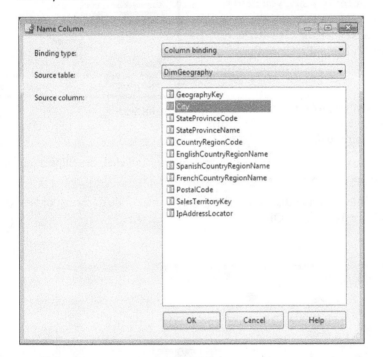

FIGURE 5-29

The DimGeography table in the data source also contains duplicate postal codes. As you just did for the City attribute, you need to make the Postal Code attribute members unique.

5. Select the Postal Code attribute in the Dimension Designer's Attributes pane.

6. In the Properties pane, locate the KeyColumns property, and click the ellipses to open the Key Columns selection dialog.

7. Change the key columns for the Postal Code attribute to include the StateProvinceCode, City, and PostalCode columns from the data source. Click OK.

8. Change the NameColumn property by clicking the ellipses next to the NameColumn property in the Properties window.

9. In the Name Column dialog, set the NameColumn property to PostalCode. Click OK.

10. Deploy the AnalysisServicesMultidimensionalTutorial database to the Analysis Services instance.

The AnalysisServicesMultidimensionalTutorial database now successfully deploys. Now that you have successfully deployed the database, you can browse the data for the Dim Geography dimension by switching to the Browser tab of the Dimension Designer, as shown in Figure 5-30. To display the data in the browser, SSDT sends several Discover requests to retrieve information, such as the hierarchies and levels available for the dimension. Finally, an MDX query is sent to the server by SSDT to retrieve dimension data. The MDX query follows:

```
Select Head( [Dim Geography].[Geography].Levels(0).Members, 1000 ) on 0
from [$Dim Geography]
```

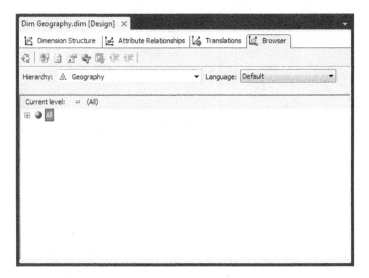

FIGURE 5-30

Because you have some familiarity with MDX, you might have deciphered most of the query. This query uses the HEAD function to request the first 1,000 members from Level 0 of the Geography hierarchy in the Dim Geography dimension. In the FROM clause you see [$Dim Geography]. In general, an MDX FROM clause should contain a cube name, but in this query the from clause specifies a dimension name, so how does this MDX query work? Here's how: When a dimension is created, the server internally stores the values of the dimension as a cube. This means that *every dimension is internally represented as a cube* with a single dimension that holds all the attribute values. The dimension you have created as part of the AnalysisServicesMultidimensionalTutorial database is called a database dimension. Because each database dimension is a one-dimensional cube, they can be queried with MDX using the special character $ before the dimension name. This is exactly what you see in the query: [$Dim Geography].

The hierarchy first shown in the dimension browser is the most recently created user hierarchy (in this case, Geography). You can choose to browse any of the user hierarchies or attribute hierarchies in a dimension by selecting them from the drop-down Hierarchy list. This list contains the dimension's user hierarchies followed by its attribute hierarchies. Each attribute hierarchy and user hierarchy within a dimension has a level called the All level. In Figure 5-30 you can see the All level for the Geography hierarchy. The All level is the topmost level of most hierarchies. (It can be removed in certain cases.) You can change the name of the All level by changing the AllMemberName property of the hierarchy. It makes sense to call the level "All" because it encompasses all the sublevels in the hierarchy. If a hierarchy does not contain the All level, the members of the topmost level display as the first level in the Dimension Designer's Browser page.

Assume you want to change the name of the All level of the Geography hierarchy to All Countries. The following steps show how to do this:

1. Go to the Dimension Structure page of the Dimension Designer.

2. Select the Geography hierarchy in the Hierarchies pane.

3. The Properties window now shows all the properties of this hierarchy. The first property is AllMemberName and it displays no value. Add a value by entering **All Countries** in the text box to the right of AllMemberName, as shown in Figure 5-31.

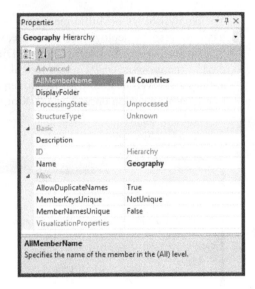

FIGURE 5-31

4. Deploy the project.

5. After successful deployment, switch from the Dimension Structure page to the Browser page. You see a message in the Dimension Browser to click Reconnect to see the latest changes. Click the Reconnect link.

You can now see that the All level of the Geography hierarchy has changed to All Countries, as shown in Figure 5-32. The figure also shows the All Countries level expanded to show the members in the next level.

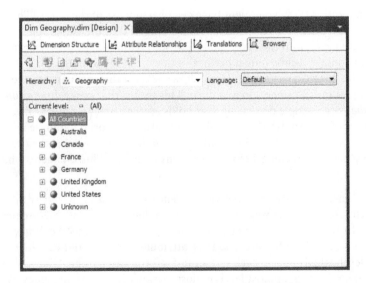

FIGURE 5-32

When you expand the All Countries level, the following MDX query is sent to the Analysis Services instance to retrieve the members in the next level:

```
WITH MEMBER [Measures].[-DimBrowseLevelKey 0-] AS
'[Dim Geography].[Geography].currentmember.properties("key0", TYPED)'

SELECT { [Measures].[-DimBrowseLevelKey 0-] } ON 0,
Head( [Dim Geography].[Geography].[All Countries].Children, 1000) ON 1
FROM [$Dim Geography]
CELL PROPERTIES VALUE
```

The goal of the MDX query is to retrieve all the members that are children of the All Countries level. Similar to the MDX query that was sent to retrieve members in level 0, this query uses the HEAD function to restrict the amount of returned results to a maximum of the first 1,000 children. This query includes a calculated measure called Measures.[-DimBrowseLevelKey 0-], which is selected in the MDX query. The calculated measure expression in this query retrieves the key of the current member by using the MDX Properties function. This function returns the value of the member property specified as the first argument to the expression. In this query the value requested is the key of the current member. The property requested is "key0" as opposed to "key." If the key of the member is a composite key, only the first column (column 0) of the composite key will be retrieved. If the query had specified "key" instead of "key0" and the key were a composite key, the value returned would be null.

Other parameters that can be passed to the Properties function are NAME, ID, and CAPTION, or the name of a member property or related attribute. The properties NAME, ID, KEY, and CAPTION are called *intrinsic member properties* because all attributes and hierarchies will have them. The second argument passed to the Properties function is optional, and the only value that can be passed is TYPED. If the Properties function is called without the second parameter, the function returns the string representation of the property. If the second argument, TYPED, is passed to the function, it returns the strongly typed value of the requested property (using the data type defined in the data source). For example, if the first argument is KEY and if the key of this attribute is of type integer, the Properties function returns the key as an integer value if you specify the TYPED parameter. Typically, specifying the second parameter is useful if you want to use the returned property value to filter the results based on a member property. For example, if the key of the Geography hierarchy is an integer and if you want to see only the children of member United States, you can use the Filter function along with the strongly typed calculated measure that has been created specifying the TYPED parameter.

The Dimension Browser sends the preceding MDX query to the Analysis Services server and uses the returned information to populate the second level of the hierarchy, as shown in Figure 5-32.

When you defined an attribute relationship between the State Province Name and City attributes earlier in the chapter, you implicitly set member properties for those attributes. You can see these member properties in the Dimension Designer's Browser page. To do that you can either click the Member Properties button in the Dimension Designer Browser toolbar (highlighted in Figure 5-33) or choose Member Properties from the Dimension menu. A dialog appears that has all the attributes of the dimension that participate in attribute relationships. Select the attributes English Country Region Name, State Province Name, and City. Click OK. The member properties you have selected are now shown in the Dimension Browser, as shown in Figure 5-33.

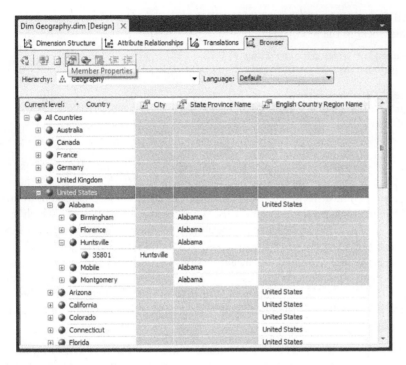

FIGURE 5-33

Expand the members of United States to see the member properties of the States and Cities under United States. The member properties of a member are also retrieved with the help of an MDX query. For example, when you want to see all the cities in Alabama, the following MDX query is sent to the server:

```
WITH MEMBER [Measures].[-DimBrowseLevelKey 0-] AS
 '[Dim Geography].[Geography].currentmember.properties("key0", TYPED)'
MEMBER [Measures].[-DimBrowseLevelKey 1-] AS
 '[Dim Geography].[Geography].currentmember.properties("key1", TYPED)'

SELECT { [Measures].[-DimBrowseLevelKey 0-],
 [Measures].[-DimBrowseLevelKey 1-] ON 0,
 Head( [Dim Geography].[Geography].[State Province].&[Alabama].Children,
 1000) ON 1
FROM [$Dim Geography]
CELL PROPERTIES VALUE
```

Similar to the MDX query you analyzed earlier to retrieve the members of the All level, this query retrieves all the Alabama City members. The City attribute's member property State Province Name is retrieved (along with the values that make up the City attribute's composite key: City, and State Province Code) with the same query as calculated members using the WITH MEMBER clause as seen in the preceding query.

SORTING MEMBERS OF A LEVEL

Members of a level are the members of the attribute that makes up that level. For example, the members of the level Country in the Geography hierarchy are actually the members of the attribute English Country Region Name. The member name that is shown in the Dimension Designer Browser is the text associated with the name of the country. It is not uncommon for dimension tables to have one column for the descriptive name and one column that is the key column of the table. You can use the descriptive name column to display the name of the attribute and the key column to sort the members of that attribute.

Each attribute in a dimension has the two properties: KeyColumns and NameColumn. The KeyColumns property is used to specify the columns that are used for sorting the members, and the NameColumn is used for the member's descriptive name. By default, the Dimension Wizard and the Dimension Designer set the KeyColumns property when an attribute is added to the dimension. They do not set the NameColumn property. If the NameColumn property is empty, Analysis Services returns the KeyColumns value for the member's descriptive name in response to client requests.

The KeyColumns property of the English Country Region Name attribute is set to be the column that the attribute itself is based on (EnglishCountryRegionName). Therefore, when you view the members in the Dimension Browser, they are sorted by the country names themselves. The Dim Geography dimension table also has the Country Region Code attribute. You can change the sort order of the countries to be based on the Country Region Code column instead of their names by changing the KeyColumns and NameColumn properties appropriately. The following exercise demonstrates how to do this.

1. In the Attributes pane, select English Country Region Name; then in the Properties pane, select the NameColumn property and click the Ellipsis button. This opens the Name Column dialog showing all the columns in the Dim Geography table. Select the EnglishCountryRegionName column, and click OK.

2. Select the KeyColumns property and click the Ellipsis button. This action launches the Key Columns dialog. Remove the EnglishCountryRegionName column from the collection. In the list of available columns, select CountryRegionCode and add it to the Key Columns list. The Key Columns selection dialog should look like Figure 5-34. Click the OK button.

3. In the Advanced section of the Properties window, make sure the value of the OrderBy property is Key, as shown in Figure 5-35. This instructs the server to order this attribute using the Key attribute (CountryRegionCode), which you specified in step 2.

4. Deploy the project to the Analysis Services instance.

Deploying the project to the Analysis Services instance sends the new changes defined in steps 1 through 3 to the server and then processes the dimension. Switch to the Browser page, and click the Reconnect option to update the dimension data. In the Dimension Browser select the Geography hierarchy. The order of the countries has now changed to be based on the order of Country Region Code (AU, CA, DE, FR, GB, and US followed by the Unknown members). The new order of countries is shown in Figure 5-36.

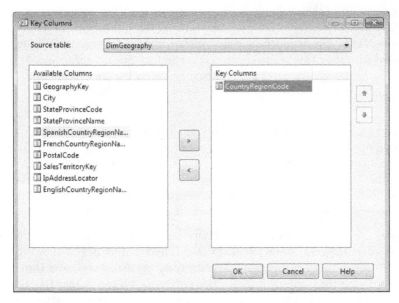

FIGURE 5-34

FIGURE 5-35

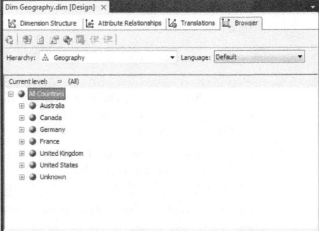

FIGURE 5-36

OPTIMIZING ATTRIBUTES

During the design of a dimension, you might want to include certain attributes but not have them available to end users for querying. Two attribute properties enable you to manipulate visibility of attributes to end users. One property, AttributeHierarchyEnabled, enables you to disable the attribute. By setting this property to False you can disable the attribute in the dimension; you cannot include this attribute in any level of a user hierarchy. This attribute can be defined only as a member property (related attribute) to another attribute. Members of this attribute cannot be retrieved by an MDX query, but you can retrieve the value as a member property of another attribute. If you disable an attribute you might see improvements in processing performance depending on the number of members in the attribute. You need to be sure that there will be no future need to slice and dice on this attribute.

FIGURE 5-37

Another property, AttributeHierarchyVisible, is useful for making an attribute hierarchy invisible for browsing. Even with this set, however, the attribute can be used as a level within a user hierarchy, and it can be used for querying. If you set this property to False, you will not see this attribute in the Dimension Browser. The properties AttributeHierarchyEnabled and AttributeHierarchyVisible are part of the Advanced group in the Properties window, as shown in Figure 5-37.

 If you want to create a dimension that contains only user hierarchies and no attribute hierarchies, you can set the AttributeHierarchyVisible property to False for all the attributes. When you go to the Dimension Browser you only see the multilevel hierarchies. Even though you have disabled the attributes for browsing, you can still query them using MDX.

DEFINING TRANSLATIONS IN DIMENSIONS

If your data warehouse is to be used globally, you may want to show the hierarchies, levels, and members in the languages that customers in those countries are familiar with. Analysis Services provides you with a feature called Translations that helps you create and view dimension members in multiple different languages. The benefit of this feature is that you do not have to build a new cube for every language you want to support if the only difference in functionality is the language of the data and metadata. For the translation feature to be used, you need only have columns in the relational data source that contain the translated member values for those attributes in the dimension whose values you would like to appear in the wanted languages.

For example, the Dim Geography table has two columns, Spanish Country Region Name and French Country Region Name, which contain the translated names of the countries that are members of the

English Country Region Name attribute. The following steps describe how to create new translations for those languages:

1. Switch to the Translations page in the Dimension Designer.

2. Click the New Translation toolbar button, as shown in Figure 5-38, or choose New Translation from the Dimension menu to create a new translation and choose a language. The Select Language dialog appears.

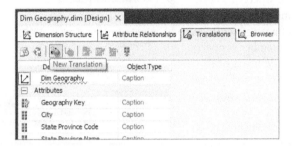

FIGURE 5-38

3. Select the language French (France) and click OK.

4. A new column with the title French (France) is added. Select the cell from the French (France) column in the English Country Region Name row. Then click the button that appears on the right side of the cell. You now see the Attribute Data Translation dialog.

5. Select the French Country Region Name column in the Translation Columns Tree view, as shown in Figure 5-39, and click OK.

6. Repeat steps 2 through 5 for the Spanish (Spain) translation.

You have now created translations for the French and Spanish languages. In addition to specifying the columns for member names, you can also change the metadata information of each level. For example, if you want to change the name of the Country level in the Geography hierarchy in the French and Spanish languages, you can enter the names in the row that shows the Country level. Type **Pays** and **Pais**, as shown in Figure 5-40, for French and Spanish translations, respectively.

You have now defined translations for the Country attribute in two languages, making use of the columns in the relational data source. To see how this metadata information is shown in the Dimension Browser, first deploy the project to your Analysis Services instance.

Next, to see the translations you have created, select French (France) from the Language dropdown in the Dimension Browser's toolbar, as shown in Figure 5-41. Select the Geography hierarchy, and expand the All level. Now you can see all the members in French. If you click any of the countries, the metadata shown for the level is Pays (French for country). There is a negligible amount of overhead associated with viewing dimension hierarchies, levels, and members in different languages.

FIGURE 5-39

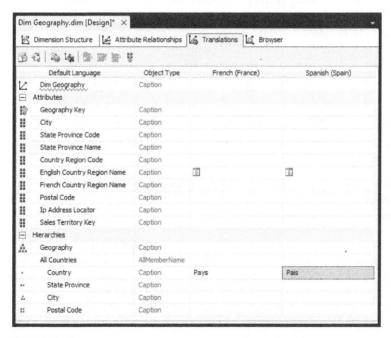

FIGURE 5-40

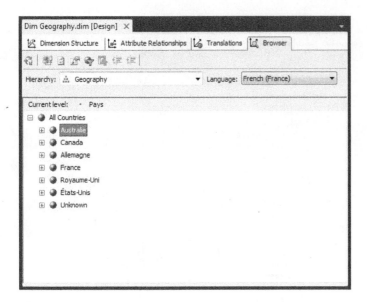

FIGURE 5-41

CREATING A SNOWFLAKE DIMENSION

A snowflake dimension is a dimension that is created using multiple dimension tables. A snowflake dimension normally suggests that the tables in the data source have been normalized. Normalization is the process by which tables of a relational database are designed to remove redundancy and are optimized for frequent updates. Most database design books, including *The Data Warehouse Toolkit (Second Edition)* by Ralph Kimball (Wiley, 2002) and *An Introduction to Database Systems* by C. J. Date (Addison Wesley, 2003), talk about the normalization process in detail.

The columns from different tables of a snowflake dimension often result in levels of a hierarchy in the dimension. The best way to understand a snowflake dimension is to create one yourself. To do this you need to add two additional tables to your DSV. Following is how to add the two tables:

1. Open the Adventure Works DW DSV, and click the Add/Remove Objects button (top-left button in the DSV Designer toolbar).

2. In the Available objects list of the Add/Remove Tables dialog, click DimProductCategory, Ctrl + Click DimProductSubcategory, and then the right arrow (>) button to move the two tables to the Included objects list. Click OK.

The DSV Designer identifies the relationships defined in the relational backend and shows the relationships between the DimProduct, DimProductSubcategory, and DimProductCategory tables within the DSV Designer's graphical design pane. Now that you have the necessary tables in the DSV with the relationships and primary keys defined, you can create a snowflake dimension using the DimProduct, DimProductCategory, and DimProductSubcategory tables. You can either delete the existing Product dimension in the AnalysisServicesMultidimensionalTutorial project and create a snowflake dimension using the Dimension Wizard, or refine the existing Product dimension to make it a snowflake dimension. In this example you use the latter approach. Follow these steps:

1. In the Solution Explorer, double-click the Dim Product dimension to open it in the Dimension Designer.

2. Within the Data Source View pane of the Dimension Designer, right-click and select Show Tables, as shown in Figure 5-42.

3. In the Show Tables dialog, select the DimProductCategory and DimProductSubcategory tables, as shown in Figure 5-43, and click OK.

   You now see the DimProductSubcategory and DimProductCategory tables added to the Data Source View pane of the Dimension Designer, as shown in Figure 5-44. The new tables added to the pane have a lighter colored caption bar. This indicates that none of the columns in the tables are included as attributes of the dimension.

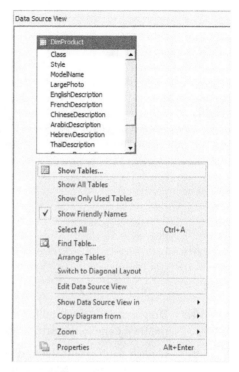

FIGURE 5-42

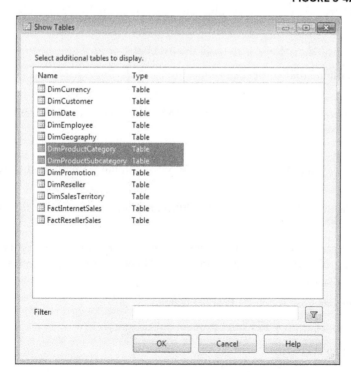

FIGURE 5-43

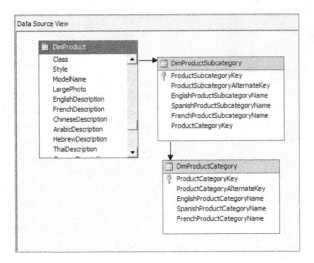

FIGURE 5-44

4. Drag and drop the ProductCategoryKey column from the DimProductSubcategory table in the DSV pane to the Attributes pane.

5. Launch the Name Column dialog for the Product Category Key attribute by clicking the ellipsis next to the NameColumn property in the Properties window.

6. Select DimProductCategory as the Source table, and then select EnglishProductCategoryName as the Source column. Click OK.

7. Select the Product Subcategory Key attribute in the Attributes pane.

8. Launch the Name Column dialog for the Product Subcategory Key attribute by clicking the ellipsis next to the NameColumn property in the Properties window.

9. Select DimProductSubcategory as the Source table, and then select EnglishProductSubcategory-Name as the Source column; then click OK.

10. Launch the Name Column dialog for Product (the key attribute) by selecting it in the Attributes pane and clicking the ellipsis next to the NameColumn property in the Properties window.

11. Select DimProduct as the Source table and EnglishProductName as the Source column and click OK.

12. Create a new user hierarchy with levels Product Category Key, Product Subcategory Key, and Product by dragging and dropping the attributes to the Hierarchies pane and renaming the hierarchy **Product Categories**.

13. Rename the Product Category Key level **Product Category**.

14. Rename the Product Subcategory Key level **Product Subcategory**.

15. Rename the Product level **Product Name**.

16. Figure 5-45 shows the Product dimension in the Dimension Designer after all the preceding changes.

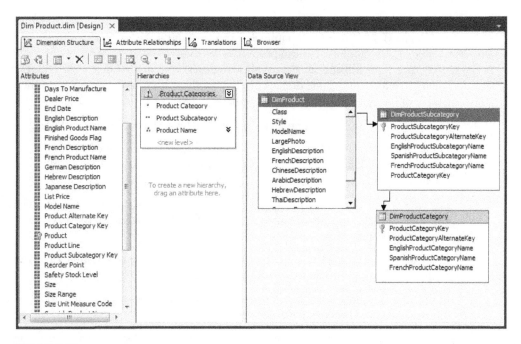

FIGURE 5-45

You have now successfully transformed the Dim Product dimension to use a snowflake schema. You can perform most of the same operations in a snowflake schema dimension as you can in a star schema dimension, including adding attributes, creating hierarchies, and defining member properties. We recommend you deploy the AnalysisServicesMultidimensionalTutorial project and browse the Dim Product snowflake dimension.

CREATING A TIME DIMENSION

Almost every data warehouse will have a Time dimension. The Time dimension can be composed of the levels Year, Semester, Quarter, Month, Week, Date, Hour, Minute, and Second. Most data warehouses contain the levels Year, Quarter, Month, and Date. The Time dimension allows analyzing business data across similar time periods — for example, determining how the current revenues or profit of a company compare to those of the previous year or previous quarter.

Even though it appears that the Time dimension has regular time periods, irregularities often exist. The number of days in a month varies, and the number of days in a year changes each leap year. In addition, a company can have its own fiscal year, which might not be identical to the calendar year. Even though there are minor differences in the levels, the Time dimension is often viewed as having regular time intervals. Several MDX functions help in solving typical problems related to analyzing data across time periods. ParallelPeriod is one such function, which you learned about in Chapter 3.

Time dimensions are treated specially by Analysis Services, and certain measures are aggregated across the Time dimension uniquely. Measures aggregated this way are called semi-additive measures. You learn more about semi-additive measures in Chapters 6 and 9.

The AnalysisServicesMultidimensionalTutorial project has a time dimension called Dim Date that was created by the Cube Wizard in Chapter 2. Even though the dimension has been created from the Dim Date table, it does not have certain properties set that would allow Analysis Services to see it as the source for a Time dimension. In the following exercise, you first delete the Dim Date dimension and then re-create it as a Time dimension. Follow these steps to create a Time dimension on the DimDate table of the AdventureWorksDW database:

1. In the Solution Explorer, right-click the Dim Date dimension, and select Delete.

2. In the Delete objects and files dialog, SSDT asks you to confirm the deletion of the corresponding Cube dimensions (you learn about Cube dimensions in Chapter 9). Select OK to delete the Dim Date dimension.

3. Launch the Dimension Wizard by right-clicking the Dimensions folder in the Solution Explorer and selecting New Dimension. When the Welcome screen of the Dimension Wizard opens, click Next.

4. In the Select Creation Method page of the wizard, select Use an Existing Table, and click Next.

5. In the Specify Source Information page, select DimDate as the main table from which the dimension is to be designed, and click Next.

6. In the Select Dimension Attributes page, in addition to the Date Key attribute, check the following attributes: Calendar Year, Calendar Semester, Calendar Quarter, English Month Name, and Day Number Of Month.

7. Set the Attribute Type for the Day Number of Month attribute to Date ⇨ Calendar ⇨ Day of Month, as shown in Figure 5-46.

8. Set the Attribute Type for the remaining enabled attributes so they match those shown in Figure 5-47, and click Next to continue.

9. Set the name of the dimension to Dim Date, and click Finish to close the Dimension Wizard. You have now successfully created a Time dimension using the Dimension Wizard.

10. Create a multilevel hierarchy Calendar Date with the levels Calendar Year, Calendar Semester, Calendar Quarter, Month (rename from English Month Name), and Day (rename from Day Number of Month).

11. Save the project and deploy it to the Analysis Services instance.

12. Switch to the Browser pane of the Dim Date dimension.

Figure 5-48 shows the Calendar Date hierarchy that you created. Notice that the order of months within a quarter is not the default calendar order. For example, the order of months of CY Q1 of year 2006 is February, January, and March. To change the order, change the KeyColumns, NameColumn, and OrderBy properties appropriately and redeploy the project. Define the necessary attribute relationships and attribute key values as defined by your business needs.

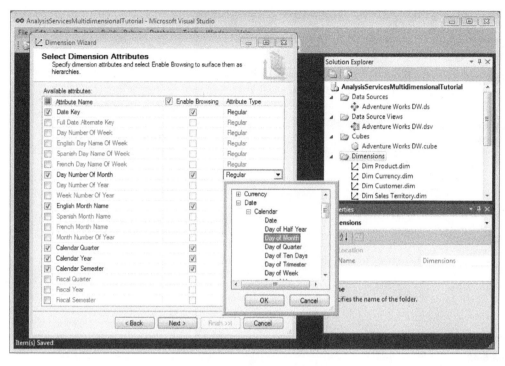

FIGURE 5-46

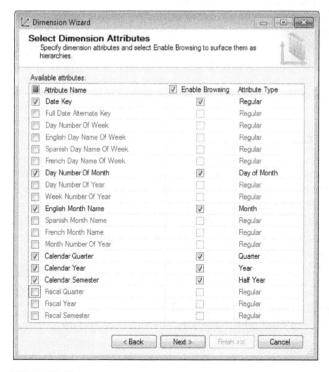

FIGURE 5-47

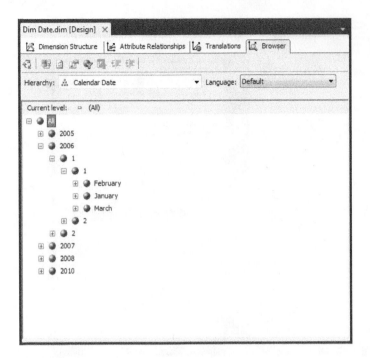

FIGURE 5-48

You have now successfully created a Time dimension. If you click the Dim Date dimension in the Attributes pane of the Dimension Structure page of the designer and review the properties of the Dim Date dimension, you see the Type property set to Time that indicates that the Dim Date dimension is a Time dimension. If you review the basic properties of each attribute in the Dim Date dimension, you notice that the Type property has values such as Quarter, Half Year, Year, Day Of Month, and Month. Setting the right Type property is important because client applications can use this property to apply the appropriate MDX functions for a Time dimension.

CREATING A PARENT-CHILD HIERARCHY

In the real world you come across relationships such as that between managers and their direct reports. This is similar to the relationship between a parent and child in that a parent can have several children, and a parent can also be a child because parents also have parents. In the data warehousing world, such relationships are modeled as Parent-Child dimensions, and in Analysis Services this type of relationship is modeled as a hierarchy called a Parent-Child hierarchy. The key difference between this relationship and any other multilevel hierarchy is how this relationship is represented in the data source. Well, that and certain other properties that are unique to the Parent-Child design. Both of these are discussed in this section.

When you created the Geography dimension, you might have noticed that there were separate columns for Country, State, and City in the relational table. Similarly, the manager and direct report can be modeled by two columns, ManagerName and EmployeeName, where the EmployeeName column is used for the direct report. If there were five direct reports for a manager, there would be five rows in the relational table. The interesting part of the Manager-DirectReport relationship is that the manager is also an employee and is a direct report to another manager. This is unlike the City, State, and Country columns in the Dim Geography table.

It is probably rare at your company, but employees can sometimes have new managers due to reorganizations. The fact that an employee's manager can change at any time is interesting when you want to look at facts such as sales generated under a specific manager, which is the sum of sales generated by the manager's direct reports. A dimension modeling such a behavior is called a *slowly changing dimension* because the manager of an employee changes over time. You can learn about slowly changing dimensions and different variations in detail in the book *The Microsoft Data Warehouse Toolkit: With SQL Server 2008 R2 and the Microsoft Business Intelligence Toolset* by Joy Mundy et al. (Wiley, 2011).

The DimEmployee table in the AdventureWorksDW relational database has a Parent-Child relationship because it has a join from the ParentEmployeeKey column to the EmployeeKey column. You have already created a DimEmployee dimension in the AnalysisServicesMultidimensionalTutorial project in Chapter 2 using the Cube Wizard. In the following exercise you refine the existing Dim Employee dimension and learn how to create a dimension with a Parent-Child hierarchy using the Dimension Wizard. You can actually refine, not create, the Dim Employee dimension in the illustration.

1. Launch the Dimension Wizard by right-clicking the Dimensions folder in the Solution Explorer and selecting New Dimension. If the Welcome screen of the Dimension Wizard opens up, click Next.

2. Make sure the Use an Existing Table option is selected, and click Next.

3. In the Specify Source Information page, select DimEmployee as the main table from which the dimension is to be designed, and click Next.

4. On the Select Related Tables screen, uncheck the DimSalesTerritory table, and click Next.

   In the Select Dimension Attributes dialog, the Dimension Wizard has detected three columns of the DimEmployee table to be included as attributes. The Dimension Wizard selects columns if they are either part of the primary key of the table or a foreign key related to the primary key in the table or a foreign key related to the primary key in another table in the DSV. Figure 5-49 shows two of the attributes selected by the Dimension Wizard from the DimEmployee table. The attributes suggested by the Dimension Wizard in this example are the key attribute Employee Key, the parent-child attribute Parent Employee Key, and the Sales Territory Key, which is a foreign key column to the DimSalesTerritory table.

5. Select all the columns of the DimEmployee table as attributes, and click Next.

6. In the preview pane of the Completing the Wizard dialog, the Parent Employee Key attribute has a unique icon (see Figure 5-50) indicating that Analysis Services detected a Parent-Child relationship in the DimEmployee table. The wizard identified the Parent-Child relationship due to the join within the same table in the DSV.

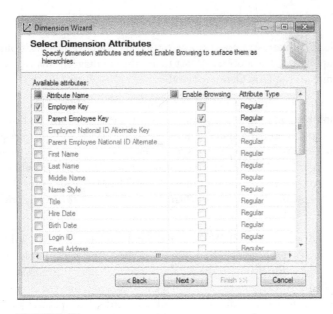

FIGURE 5-49

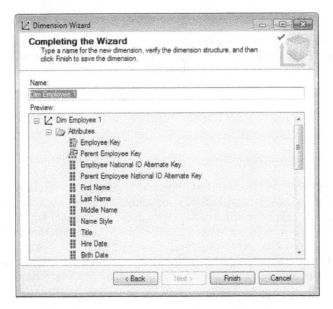

FIGURE 5-50

7. Click the Cancel button because you will not be creating another Dim Employee dimension.

   By default the Dimension Wizard defines the properties for the attribute modeling the Parent-Child hierarchy at the completion of the Dimension Wizard or the Cube Wizard.

8. Double-click the Dim Employee dimension in the Solution Explorer to open it in the Dimension Designer.

9. The properties of the Parent Employee Key attribute indicate that this attribute defines a Parent-Child hierarchy, as shown in Figure 5-51.

The hierarchy doesn't appear in the Hierarchies pane of the Dimension Designer. That's because the Parent-Child hierarchy is actually a special type of attribute hierarchy that can contain multiple levels, unlike the other attributes. The Parent-Child hierarchy that the wizard created is based on the attribute ParentEmployeeKey. The Usage property for this attribute is set to Parent, which indicates that this attribute is a Parent-Child hierarchy. If you browse the Parent-Child hierarchy of the DimEmployee dimension, you can see the IDs of the employees as a multilevel hierarchy, as shown in Figure 5-52.

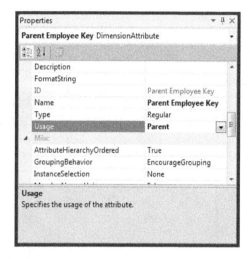

FIGURE 5-51

Typically, you would want to see the names of the employees rather than their IDs. You learned earlier that you can use the NameColumn property to specify the name that is shown in the browser and use the key column for ordering. Because the Parent-Child hierarchy retrieves all the information from the Key attribute, which is the Employee attribute in this example, you need to modify the NameColumn property of the Employee attribute rather than the NameColumn property of the Parent Employee Key attribute.

FIGURE 5-52

10. Change the NameColumn property of the Employee attribute to **LastName** and deploy the project to your Analysis Services instance.

When you browse the Parent-Child hierarchy, you see the members of the hierarchy showing the last names of the employees, as shown in Figure 5-53.

FIGURE 5-53

SUMMARY

Using the Dimension Wizard and other wizards in SSDT is only the starting point for designing objects in Analysis Services. For optimal results, you need to take your dimensions farther than the initial destination that the wizards take you to. To get to the ultimate destination of your dimension design, use the Dimension Designer you learned about in this chapter. A couple of examples of steps along this last leg of the journey are using the Properties window to assign descriptive names to an attribute whose name in the source database might be obscure to your end users and defining attribute relationships to optimize dimension performance. You can also use the Dimension Designer to create translations for the attributes and hierarchies of a dimension to enhance the user experience of your international customers.

In addition to learning about dimensions, you learned the necessity of deploying your dimension definition to the instance of Analysis Services where the dimension is processed by retrieving the data from the data source. Processing is essential to enable you to browse a dimension. The communication between SSDT and an instance of Analysis Services is accomplished through a SOAP-based XML API called XML for Analysis (XMLA), which is an industry standard. Even more interesting, dimensions stored in Analysis Services are represented internally as cubes — one-dimensional cubes; and, coincidentally, cubes are the topic of Chapter 6.

6

Cube Design

WHAT'S IN THIS CHAPTER?

➤ Understanding the BISM multidimensional mode

➤ Creating cubes with the Cube Wizard

➤ Browsing cubes with the Cube Browser and Excel

➤ Understanding cube dimensions and dimension relationships

➤ Learning measure and Measure Group properties

➤ Creating calculated members and measures

➤ Creating and browsing perspectives and translations

In Chapter 5 you learned to create dimensions using the Dimension Wizard and to refine and enhance dimensions using the Dimension Designer. Dimensions by themselves aren't that useful; you need to incorporate them into a cube to fulfill their purpose: enabling users to slice-and-dice data to gain insights. In this chapter you learn how to create cubes using the Cube Wizard and enhance your cubes using the Cube Designer. You learn to add calculations to your cube that facilitate effective data analyses followed by analyzing the cube data itself in the Cube Designer and Excel.

THE BISM MULTIDIMENSIONAL MODE

To generate profits for a business, you need to make key strategic decisions based on likely factors such as having the right business model, targeting the right consumer group, pricing the product correctly, and marketing through optimal channels. To make the right decisions and achieve targeted growth you need to analyze data. The data can be past sales, expected sales, or even information from competitors. The phrase "knowledge is power" is fitting here because in the world of business, analyzing and comparing, for example, current sales against the expected sales, helps executives make decisions directly aligned with the goals of the company. Such sales information is typically stored in a distributed fashion and must be collected from various sources. Executives making the business decisions typically do not have the ability to access the raw sales data spread across various locations and subsequently optimize it for their use. These decision-makers typically rely on the data that has already been aggregated into a form that is easy to understand and that facilitates the decision-making process. Presenting aggregated data to the decision-makers quickly is a key challenge for business intelligence providers. Analysis Services enables you to design a model that bridges the gap between the raw data and the information content that can be used for making business decisions. This model is called the Business Intelligence Semantic Model (BISM).

In this section you work with the multidimensional mode of the BISM. Later chapters deal with the other mode of the BISM: the tabular mode.

The BISM multidimensional mode enables you to bring data from multiple heterogeneous sources into a single model. Analysis Services buffers you from the difficulties of managing the integration of various data sources, so you can build your model easily. It provides you with the best of the OLAP and relational worlds, exposing rich data and metadata for exploration and analysis.

Figure 6-1 shows the architecture of the multidimensional model implemented in Analysis Services 2012. As shown in the figure, the multidimensional model helps you integrate data from various relational data sources — such as Oracle, SQL Server, DB2, and Teradata — as well as flat files into a single model that merges the underlying schemas into a single schema. The end users do not necessarily have to view the entire schema of the model. Instead, they can view the sections of it that are relevant to their needs through a feature provided by Analysis Services called perspectives.

In the OLAP world, data analyzed by end users is often historical data that might be a few days, months, or even years old. However, the responses to OLAP queries are typically returned within a few seconds. In the relational world the end users have instant access to the raw data, but the responses to queries can take much longer, on the order of minutes. As mentioned earlier, the multidimensional mode merges the best of both the OLAP and relational worlds and provides end users with real-time data with the query performance of the OLAP world. The multidimensional mode can provide that query performance with the help of a feature in Analysis Services that creates a cache of the relational data that also aggregates the data into an Analysis Services database. During the time the cache is being built, Analysis Services retrieves the data directly from the data sources. As soon as the cache is available, the results are retrieved from the cache in response to relevant queries. Whenever there is a change in the underlying data source, Analysis Services receives a notification and appropriate updates are made to the cache based on the settings defined for cache updates.

The multidimensional mode also provides rich, high-end analytic support through which complex business calculations can be exploited. Such complex calculations can be extremely difficult to formulate in the relational world at the data-source level. Even if such calculations are defined on the relational data source, responses from OLAP-style queries against the relational data source are typically slow compared to responses from Analysis Services.

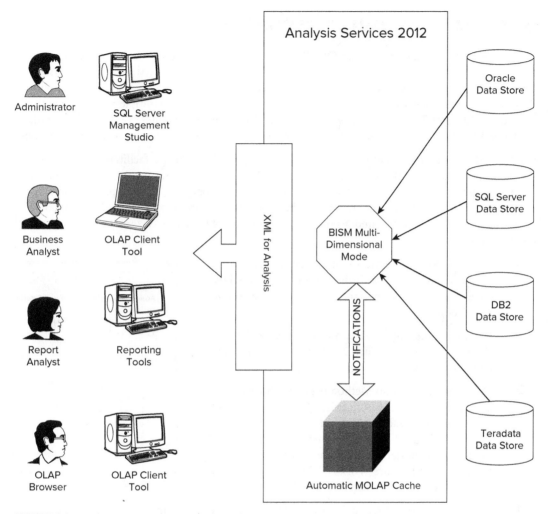

FIGURE 6-1

Analysis Services natively interfaces to end-user clients through the XML for Analysis (XMLA) standard, which allows client tools to retrieve data from Analysis Services. Client tools such as Excel allow end users to create ad-hoc queries for data analysis. In addition, the multidimensional mode supports rich analytic features such as Key Performance Indicators (KPIs), Actions, and Translations that help surface the status of your business data at any given time so that appropriate actions can be taken.

The multidimensional mode provides an efficient interface for detail-level reporting through dimension attributes that are common in the relational world. The ability to transform multidimensional results into views that are helpful to end users and the ability to perform ad-hoc queries on data from high-level aggregated data to detail-level items, make the multidimensional model a powerful construct indeed. The multidimensional mode also enables you to display the model's data and metadata in the end user's language, which is needed in a global market.

CREATING A CUBE USING THE CUBE WIZARD

Cubes are the principal objects of an OLAP database and are multidimensional structures primarily composed of dimensions and facts. *Measures* are the fact table data stored in a cube. *Measure Groups* are groups of measures typically sourced from the same fact table and associated with the same set of dimensions. In Analysis Services you can store data from multiple fact tables within the same cube. Chapter 2 introduced you to the Cube Wizard. In this chapter you see more details of the Cube Wizard and also learn how to make refinements to your cube using the Cube Designer.

Similar to the Dimension Wizard you used in Chapter 5, the Cube Wizard facilitates creation of cube objects from the DSV. For this exercise, you continue with the AnalysisServicesMultidimensionalTutorial project you updated in Chapter 5, which contained the Dim Geography, Dim Employee, and Dim Date dimensions. To start with a clean slate, delete the existing Adventure Works DW cube if it is still there from Chapter 2. To completely understand the functionality of the Cube Wizard, follow these steps to build a new cube from scratch:

1. Open the AnalysisServicesMultidimensionalTutorial project from Chapter 5. If the Adventure Works DW cube exists, delete it by right-clicking it in the Solution Explorer and selecting Delete.

2. Right-click the Cubes folder and select New Cube, as shown in Figure 6-2. Click Next on the introduction page to proceed.

3. On the Select Creation Method page, you have the option to build a cube from existing tables, create an empty cube, or build a cube from tables you generate in the data source (optionally based on an existing template. In this tutorial you build the cube from the existing tables in the Adventure Works DW data source). Click Next to proceed to the next step in the Cube Wizard.

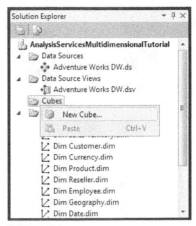

FIGURE 6-2

4. The next page of the Cube Wizard is the Select Measure Group Tables page. On this page, select the DSV the cube is based on and the tables in that DSV to serve as the fact tables for you measure group. Use the Suggest button on this page to have the Cube Wizard scan the DSV to detect the fact tables. Click the Suggest button to have the Cube Wizard automatically select potential Measure Group tables.

    The Cube Wizard scans the DSV to detect the fact tables and automatically selects the candidate tables in the Measure group tables list, as shown in Figure 6-3. Any table that has an outgoing relationship is identified as a candidate fact table.

5. You can check or uncheck a table to identify it as a measure group table. The wizard suggests that the FactInternetSales, FactResellerSales, and DimReseller tables are measure group tables. The DimReseller table was detected as a measure group table because there is an outgoing relationship from it. However, it is not used as a measure group table in this example. Uncheck the DimReseller table and click Next.

6. On the Select Measures page, the Cube Wizard shows all the columns from the fact tables that it detects as potential measures of the cube, as shown in Figure 6-4. The Cube Wizard

does not select the primary and foreign key columns in a table as potential measures. There is a one-to-one mapping between a column in the fact table and a measure in the cube. There is one measure group for each fact table included in the cube. In the DSV you use, two fact tables exist, and therefore two measure groups — Fact Internet Sales and Fact Reseller Sales — are created. You can select or deselect the measures you want to be part of the cube in this page. Use the default selection on this page, and click Next.

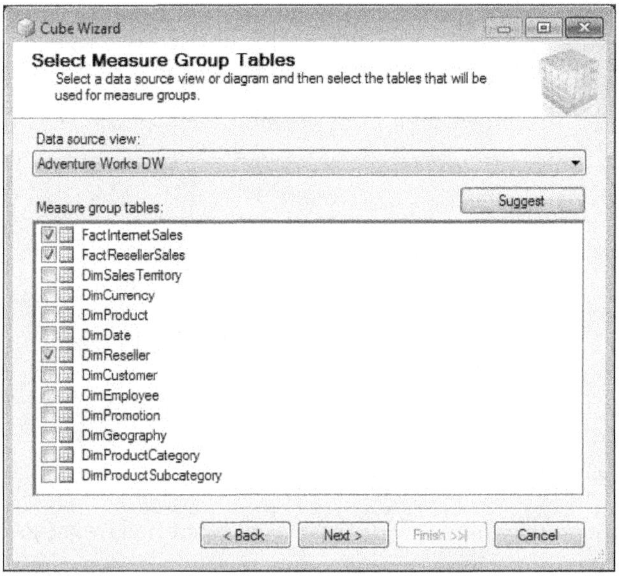

FIGURE 6-3

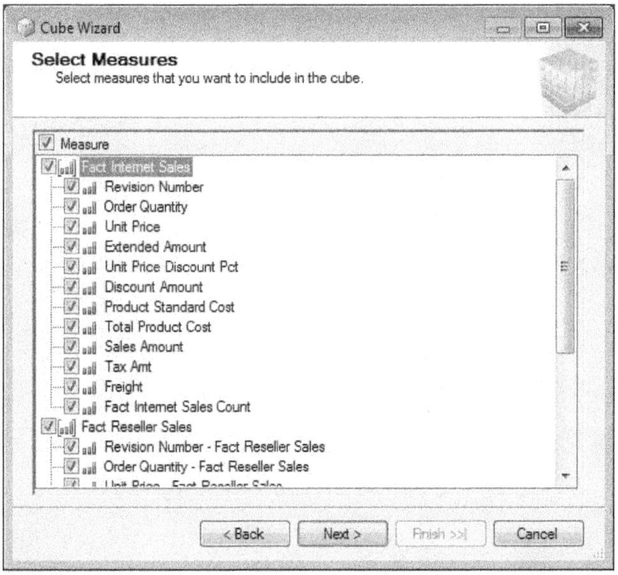

FIGURE 6-4

7. In the Select Existing Dimensions page (Figure 6-5), the Cube Wizard displays a list of all dimensions defined in the project. Accept the selection of all the dimensions, and click Next.

FIGURE 6-5

8. The Cube Wizard asks you to select any new dimensions to be created from existing tables in the data source that are not already used for dimensions, as shown in Figure 6-6. This illustration uses the fact tables only as measure groups and not for dimensions, so uncheck the Fact Reseller Sales and Fact Internet Sales dimensions on this page, and click Next.

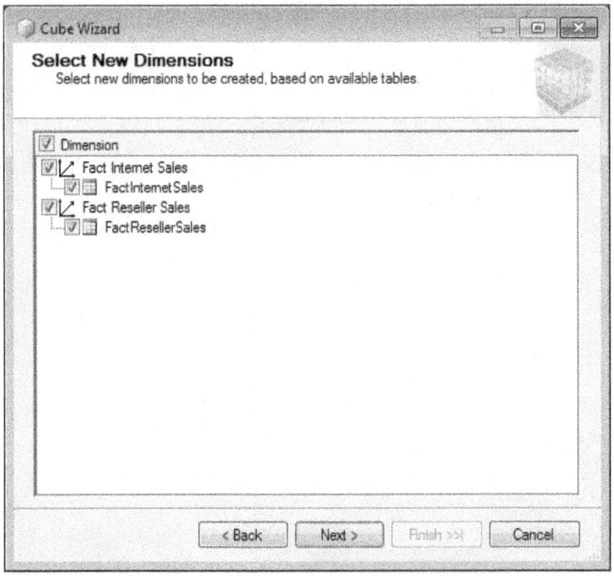

FIGURE 6-6

9. On the final page of the Cube Wizard (shown in Figure 6-7) you can specify the name of the cube to be created and review the measure groups, measures, dimensions, attributes, and hierarchies. Use the default name Adventure Works DW suggested by the Cube Wizard, and click Finish.

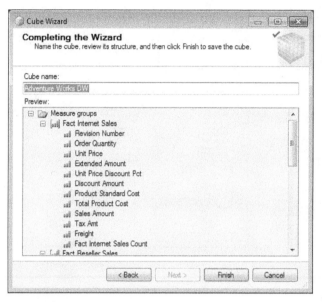

FIGURE 6-7

The Cube Wizard creates the cube when you click the Finish button. The created Adventure Works DW cube opens in the Cube Designer, as shown in Figure 6-8. The Cube Designer contains several pages that help perform specific operations that refine the initial cube created by the Cube Wizard. The default page is the Cube Structure page (refer to Figure 6-8). On the Cube Structure page, you can see three panes that show the Measures, Dimensions, and the Data Source View tables used in the cube. Operations such as adding or deleting tables in the DSV and zooming in or out with the DSV Designer are possible within the Cube Designer's Data Source View pane. The Dimensions pane shows the dimensions that are currently part of the cube, and the Measures pane shows the cube's measure groups and measures. You can add or delete measures and dimensions on the Cube Structure page. The dimensions in the cube are called cube dimensions. You can have multiple cube dimensions based on a single database dimension. For example, both the FactInternetSales and FactResellerSales fact tables have a relationship with the Dim Date dimension through their Order Date, Ship Date, and Due Date key fields. Hence you can see three cube dimensions: Ship Date, Due Date, and Order Date in the Dimensions pane, which refer to the Dim Date database dimension. A dimension such as Dim Date, which plays the role of multiple different cube dimensions, is called a role-playing dimension. You learn more about role-playing dimensions in Chapters 8 and 9. Within the Dimensions pane you can see the Hierarchies and Attributes of each dimension under separate folders when you expand each dimension.

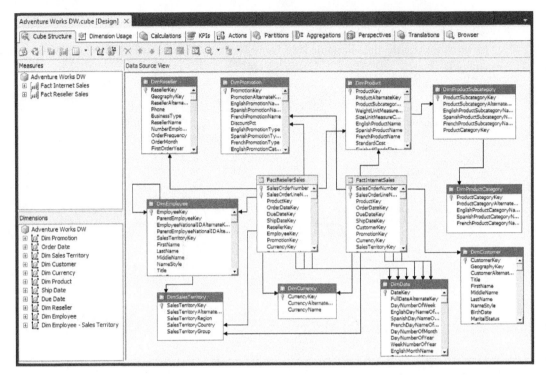

FIGURE 6-8

So far you have created an Analysis Services database containing the Adventure Works DW cube. You must deploy the project to the Analysis Services instance before you can analyze the data within the cube. You can deploy the project to the server in one of the following ways:

1. From the main menu, select Debug ⇨ Start Debugging.

2. In the Solution Explorer, right-click the AnalysisServicesMultidimensionalTutorial project node, and select Deploy.

3. Right-click the Adventure Works DW cube and choose Process — from which you will first be prompted to deploy the project, followed by the Process dialog to process the cube.

4. Use the shortcut key F5 to deploy and process.

When you deploy the project to the Analysis Services instance, SSDT sends an XMLA request containing object definitions to the Analysis Services server selected in the project. By default, the Analysis Services project deploys to the default instance of Analysis Services on your machine. The object definitions are of the cubes and dimensions you created. If you have installed Analysis Services as a named instance, you need to change the deployment server name. When the definitions of the objects in your project deploy to the server, SSDT sends another request to process the objects within the database.

Browsing Cubes

Now that you have deployed the cube to an Analysis Services instance, switch to the Cube Designer's Browser page. In the Browser page you can see panes on the left that enable you to select items for viewing and panes on the right that enable you to view and filter the results you chose on the left, as shown in Figure 6-9.

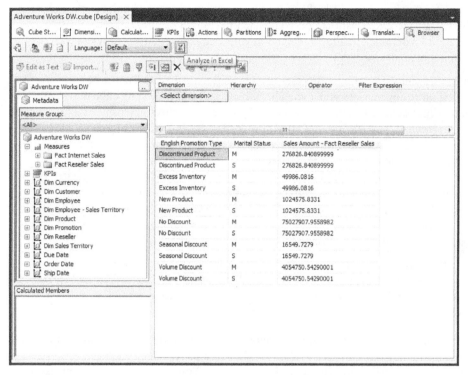

FIGURE 6-9

THE ANALYSIS SERVICES 2012 CUBE BROWSER

If you have used the cube browser in previous versions of Analysis Services, you will notice that the cube browser in Analysis Services 2012 is different than what you are used to seeing and working with. That is because a key component used in the implementation of previous versions of the cube browser, the Office Web Components, or OWC, is now discontinued and unsupported. It can no longer be shipped, either stand-alone or as a component of another product.

The Analysis Services team has, in place of the OWC, used the Analysis Services MDX query designer component (which is also used in Report Builder 3.0 and the PowerPivot Table Import Wizard) to implement cube browsing functionality in 2012 SSDT. Because the component was designed to be a query designer, it has some issues when used as a cube browser. For example, it enables you to create calculated members that aren't persisted after your browsing session is over. It also doesn't allow you to browse in the traditional row/column format of a PivotTable; you can only add columns to the tabular view.

continues

(continued)

The Analysis Services 2012 Cube Browser also includes a button, Analyze in Excel, which, if you have Excel installed on your machine, allows you to easily launch Excel with a PivotTable already connected to your deployed Analysis Services cube for testing and analysis.

When should you use the Cube Browser versus Analyze in Excel? The Cube Browser is more appropriate when you check certain features of your cube that are not easily shown in Excel. For example, if you want to check your cube's translations (which you learn about later in this chapter) in Excel you need to either be running on a localized version of the operating system that matches the translation you want to check or you need to manually modify the connection string Excel uses to talk to the Analysis Services server to include the appropriate `LocaleIdentifier` property and refresh the connection (for example, to show the French (France) translation you would modify the connection string to add `";LocaleIdentifier=1036"`). In the Cube Browser, it's simply a matter of selecting the wanted language in the Language drop-down on the toolbar.

On the other hand, Analyze in Excel is more appropriate when you want to test your cube using all the features of a powerful BI client such as Excel. Chances are that your end users will use Excel to work with your application when it is released.

On the upper left of the Cube Browser page, a control enables you to select the cube or perspective you want to browse. Below the cube selector is the Metadata pane, which enables you to select the measures, KPIs, and dimensions to browse in the Data pane. You can drag and drop measures and hierarchies from the Metadata pane onto the data area to analyze the data.

The right side of the Cube Browser is where you can view the data you want to analyze. There is also a Filter pane (above the data area) that you can use to filter the data being analyzed. The Filter pane enables you to use comparison operations such as equal, not equal, contains, in, not in, begins with, range operations, and any MDX expression to build a filter expression to help you analyze your multidimensional data.

In addition to the browsing functionality of the Cube Browser in SSDT, Analysis Services 2012 includes the capability of browsing the contents of your cube using Excel. You can accomplish this via the Analyze in Excel button on the Cube Browser's toolbar or the Analyze in Excel item in the Cube menu when you are in the Browser tab of the Cube Designer. For this feature to work correctly, you must have Excel installed on the machine you are running SSDT on. We recommend installing Excel to enable this very helpful feature.

Suppose you want to use the Analyze in Excel feature to analyze the Internet sales of products based on the promotions offered to customers and the marital status of those customers. First, you would click the Analyze in Excel toolbar button to bring up Excel with a PivotTable connected to your cube. Click Enable in the Security Notice dialog to enable data connections to the workbook. Excel opens with a blank PivotTable connected to your Analysis Services cube.

In the PivotTable Field List, expand the More fields folder under the Dim Promotion dimension, and drag and drop the English Promotion Type attribute to the Row Labels area in the PivotTable

Field List. You learn the MDX statements that are generated by Excel in this section. The SQL Server Profiler has the capability to trace the MDX statements sent to Analysis Services instances. For more information on how to obtain traces, refer to the section on using SQL Server Profiler in Chapter 15.

Dropping the English Promotion Type attribute into the Row Labels section of the PivotTable Field List causes Excel to send the following MDX query to the Analysis Services instance:

```
SELECT NON EMPTY Hierarchize(
   {DrilldownLevel(
   {[Dim Promotion].[English Promotion Type].[All]},,,INCLUDE_CALC_MEMBERS
   )}
   ) DIMENSION PROPERTIES PARENT_UNIQUE_NAME,HIERARCHY_UNIQUE_NAME ON COLUMNS
FROM [Adventure Works DW] CELL PROPERTIES VALUE
```

Here you can see that Excel asks for the child members of the English Promotion Type attribute (via the `DrilldownLevel()` MDX function). It displays the results of that query in the Row Labels column of the PivotTable. At this point you cannot see any measure values in the Excel PivotTable, but if you run the above query in SSMS, some measure values will be returned. Those values will be those of the default measure for the cube (which is Order Quantity) but Excel doesn't presume that's a measure you want to see unless you perform some action to indicate it explicitly. Note the ON COLUMNS clause in the query even though Excel displays the results in rows. This is because COLUMNS is just a synonym for "the first axis." (Excel could have also said ON 0.)

Next, drag and drop the Marital Status attribute from the Dim Customer folder in the PivotTable Field List to the Excel Column Labels area. Excel now sends an expanded MDX query that includes two axes clauses, one for Marital Status and one for English Promotion Type.

```
SELECT NON EMPTY Hierarchize(
   {DrilldownLevel(
   {[Dim Customer].[Marital Status].[All]},,,INCLUDE_CALC_MEMBERS
   )}
   ) DIMENSION PROPERTIES PARENT_UNIQUE_NAME,HIERARCHY_UNIQUE_NAME ON COLUMNS,
NON EMPTY Hierarchize(
   {DrilldownLevel(
   {[Dim Promotion].[English Promotion Type].[All]},,,INCLUDE_CALC_MEMBERS
   )}
   ) DIMENSION PROPERTIES PARENT_UNIQUE_NAME,HIERARCHY_UNIQUE_NAME ON ROWS
FROM [Adventure Works DW] CELL PROPERTIES VALUE
```

Excel now displays the members of both attributes in rows and columns.

Finally, drag and drop the Sales Amount measure from the Fact Internet Sales measure group to the Values area of the PivotTable Field List. Excel sends the following query to your Analysis Services instance:

```
SELECT NON EMPTY Hierarchize(
   {DrilldownLevel(
   {[Dim Customer].[Marital Status].[All]},,,INCLUDE_CALC_MEMBERS
   )}
   ) DIMENSION PROPERTIES PARENT_UNIQUE_NAME,HIERARCHY_UNIQUE_NAME ON COLUMNS,
NON EMPTY Hierarchize(
   {DrilldownLevel(
```

```
    {[Dim Promotion].[English Promotion Type].[All]},,,INCLUDE_CALC_MEMBERS
    )}
    ) DIMENSION PROPERTIES PARENT_UNIQUE_NAME,HIERARCHY_UNIQUE_NAME ON ROWS
FROM [Adventure Works DW]
WHERE ([Measures].[Sales Amount]) CELL PROPERTIES VALUE
```

Note the only difference between this query and the previous one is the addition of a WHERE clause specifying the measure you added to the Values field of the field list. Now Excel knows that you want a particular measure, so it asks for and displays it in the PivotTable.

If you hover over a particular cell in the PivotTable, you can see the cell values without formatting, along with the row and column member values that correspond to that cell, as shown in Figure 6-10.

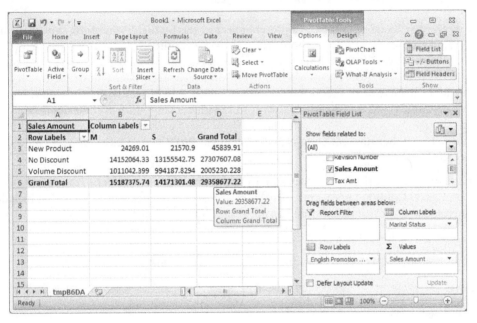

FIGURE 6-10

CUBE DIMENSIONS

The Cube Wizard helps you create your cube object from the DSV by creating appropriate dimension objects. The wizard detects the relationships between dimension tables and fact tables in the DSV, creates appropriate dimensions if needed, and establishes appropriate relationships between the dimensions and measure groups within the cube. The relationships between dimensions and measures groups define which dimensions in the cube can be used to slice and dice a measure group's data. As mentioned in the previous section, a cube contains instances of database dimensions referred to as cube dimensions. There can be multiple instances of a database dimension within a cube. There are relationships between a cube dimension and the measure groups within the cube. In this section you learn about various types of relationships between the cube dimensions and measure groups, as well as refine the Adventure Works DW cube created by the Cube Wizard by adding a new dimension.

The Cube Wizard establishes relationships between the measure groups and cube dimensions based on its analysis of relationships in the DSV. You might have to refine these relationships based on your business needs. You can change these relationships on the Dimension Usage tab of the cube editor. If you switch to the Dimension Usage tab, you see the Dimensions, Measure Groups of the cube, and the relationships between them, as shown in Figure 6-11.

The cube dimensions and measure groups are represented in a matrix format as rows and columns, respectively, where the relationship between them corresponds to the intersection cell. The intersection cell shows the dimension type along with the attribute used in the relationship to join.

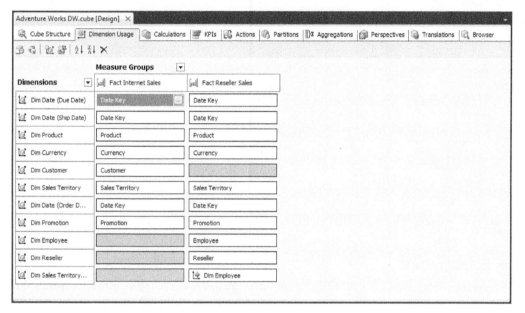

FIGURE 6-11

Relationship Types

Six different types of relationships can exist between a dimension and a measure group: No relationship, regular, fact, many-to-many, data mining, and referenced. In Figure 6-11 you see three of the six relationship types: No relationship (indicated by a gray box with no text), referenced (indicated by the glyph you see in the box at the intersection of the Fact Reseller Sales measure group and the Dim Sales Territory dimension), and regular (indicated by a white box with the name of the attribute used in the join that forms the relationship). The following sections describe each relationship type.

No Relationship

Cells shaded gray indicate no relationship exists between the dimension and measure group. Whenever no relationship exists between a dimension and measure group, the measure group property IgnoreUnrelatedDimension controls the results of queries involving any hierarchy of that dimension and any measure from the measure group. The measure values can either be null (IgnoreUnrelatedDimension=False) or the same value for each member of the dimension (IgnoreUnrelatedDimension=True). For example, no relationship exists between the Dim Employee dimension and the Fact Internet Sales measure group. If you browse the Gender hierarchy of Dim Employee and the Sales Amount measure, you see that the measure values for each member of Gender hierarchy are the same value as the Grand Total, as shown in Figure 6-12. This is because the `IgnoreUnrelatedDimension` property is set to `True` by the Cube Wizard as a default. You learn more about properties of measure groups and measures later in this chapter.

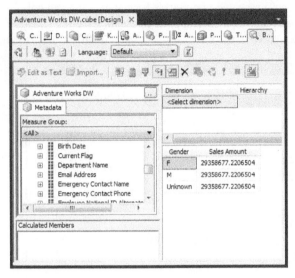

FIGURE 6-12

Regular Relationships

Cells corresponding to a specific dimension and measure group can have an attribute specified that indicates that the dimension type is Regular. Further, such attributes can be used in the join condition between the dimension and the measure group. Often this attribute is the key attribute of the dimension and is called the granularity attribute. The granularity attribute can be an attribute at a higher level of granularity than the key attribute of the dimension. When you browse a dimension along with measures of a measure group where the dimension and measure group have a regular relationship, Analysis Services aggregates the data appropriately. If you have your granularity attribute above the key attribute of your dimension, it is critical that you define appropriate attribute relationships in your dimension to make sure the data getting aggregated is accurate. The relationship between Dim Customer and Fact Internet Sales measure group is a regular relationship. The granularity attribute is shown in the cell intersecting the dimension and measure group, as shown in Figure 6-11.

Fact Relationships

When a table is used as both a fact and dimension table, a unique relationship exists between the dimension and measure group called a fact relationship. The relationship is similar to that of the regular dimension, but specifying it as a fact dimension helps improve query performance for a certain class of MDX queries. You learn more about fact dimensions in Chapter 9.

Many-to-Many Relationships

Typically, a one-to-many relationship exists between a dimension and a fact member for regular relationships. When you have a one-to-one relationship between a fact and a dimension member, you typically have a fact relationship. When a many-to-many relationship exists between a fact and a dimension member, the dimension member has a one-to-many relationship with various facts, and a single fact is associated with multiple dimension members. The definition for a many-to-many relationship can be understood via an example: Assume you have a fact table for sales of books that is related to a dimension table containing author information. Authors can have multiple books and books can have multiple authors. In order to model that many-to-many relationship you need to have both an intermediate fact table related to the book sales and authors and an intermediate dimension table related to both fact tables. You learn about how to work with many-to-many relationships in Chapter 9.

Data Mining Relationships

Data mining dimensions are another item type in the list of relationships; these are used to establish linkage between a cube and a dimension created from a data mining model. You learn more about this in Chapters 9 and 12.

Referenced Relationships

When a dimension is related to the fact data through another dimension, you define this indirect relationship between the measure group and the dimension as a referenced relationship. In Figure 6-11 the Dim Sales Territory dimension is related to the Fact Reseller Sales measure group through the Employee dimension. The icon at the intersection of the dimension and measure group indicates this referenced relationship. You might also recall that you added the Dim Geography dimension in the Select Existing Dimensions page of the Cube Wizard. However, the Cube Wizard was not smart enough to figure out there is a relationship between the fact tables and the Dim Geography dimension table through other dimension tables. Hence the Cube Wizard did not add the Dim Geography dimension as a cube dimension. Because the relationship between the Dim Geography dimension and the measure groups in the Adventure Works DW cube is through another dimension, you can say that there is an indirect relationship between the Dim Geography dimension and the measure groups.

Follow these steps to add the Dim Geography dimension to the cube and establish the referenced relationship:

1. To add the Dim Geography database dimension to the cube, right-click anywhere in the Dimension Usage page, and select Add Cube Dimension, as shown in Figure 6-13.

2. A dialog showing all the dimensions within the project launches, as shown in Figure 6-14. Select the Dim Geography dimension, and click OK.

   The Cube Designer cannot identify a relationship through an attribute between the existing measure groups and the Geography dimension and as a result leaves the relationship definition up to you. There exists an indirect relationship between the Dim Geography dimension and Fact Internet Sales measure group through the Dim Customer dimension. There is an indirect relationship between the Dim Geography dimension and the Fact Reseller measure group through the Dim Reseller dimension. You need to define these referenced relationships.

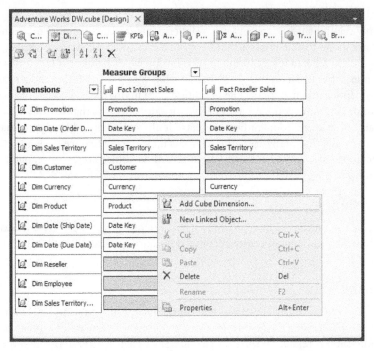

FIGURE 6-13

3. To define the relationship between the Dim Geography dimension and the Fact Internet Sales measure group, select the corresponding cell in the matrix, and you see a button with an ellipsis on the right side of that cell. Click the Ellipsis button (...).

4. This opens the Define Relationship dialog shown in Figure 6-15. On the Select relationship type drop-down, select Referenced. The Dim Geography dimension forms an indirect or referenced relationship with the Fact Internet Sales measure group through the Dim Customer dimension. You define the intermediate dimension through the Intermediate dimension field in the dialog. After you define

FIGURE 6-14

the intermediate dimension, you need to select the attributes involved in the join of the relationship. The Reference dimension attribute is the attribute in the reference dimension that is used in the join between the intermediate dimension (Dim Customer) and the reference dimension (Dim Geography). The Intermediate dimension attribute is the attribute of the intermediate dimension that is involved in the join between the reference dimension and the intermediate dimension. Select the Intermediate dimension as Dim Customer, the Reference dimension attribute as Geography Key, and the Intermediate dimension attribute as Geography Key as shown in Figure 6-15, and click OK. In Figure 6-15 you see a check box with the text Materialize. This check box is enabled by default in SQL Server Analysis Services. By enabling this check box, you ensure that Analysis Services builds appropriate indexes to get improved query performance when querying fact data along with reference dimension hierarchies.

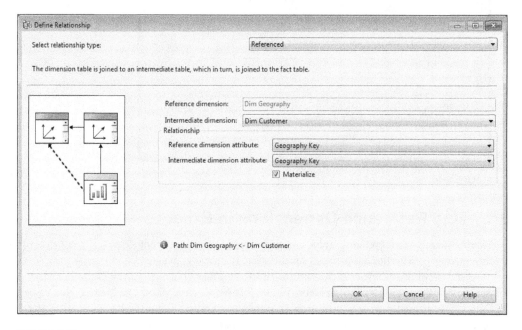

FIGURE 6-15

5. Similar to step 4, establish a referenced relationship between the Dim Geography dimension and the Fact Reseller Sales measure group through the Dim Reseller dimension. After you specify the relationship between Dim Geography and the two measure groups of the cube, your Dimension Usage tab should resemble Figure 6-16.

A referenced relationship between a dimension and a measure group is indicated by an arrow pointing to the intermediate dimension (refer to Figure 6-16). This graphical view of the reference relationship helps you identify the type of relationship between a dimension and measure group when you look at the Dimension Usage tab of the cube editor. Similar graphical representations are available for fact, many-to-many, and data mining dimensions, and you learn about these relationships in Chapters 9 and 12.

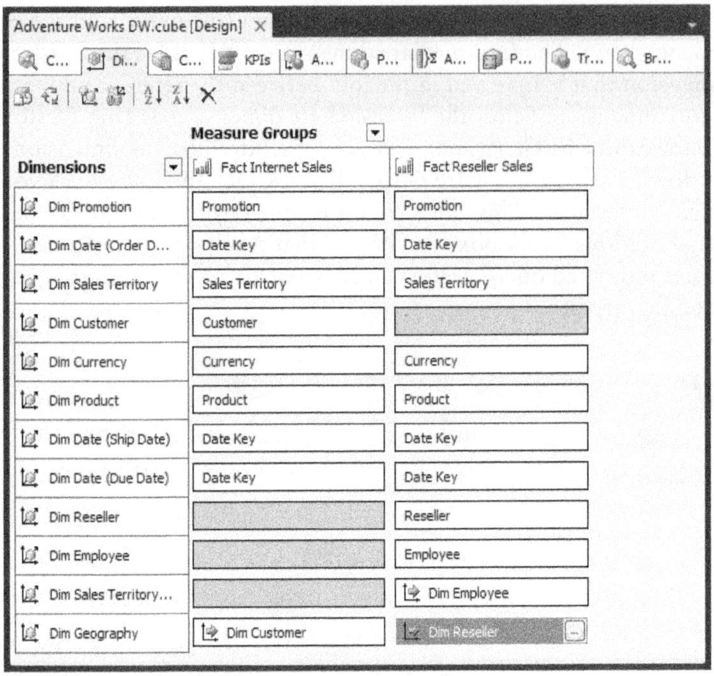

FIGURE 6-16

Browsing Reference Dimensions in Excel

Having added the Dim Geography dimension as a reference dimension to the cube, assume you want to analyze the Reseller Sales based on different business types in various countries. To do so you need to redeploy and process the cube with the changes. Then go to the Cube Browser, and click the Analyze in Excel button. In the Excel PivotTable field list, expand the More Fields folder under the Dim Geography dimension, and drag and drop the English Country Region Name attribute to the Row Labels area in the PivotTable Field List. Expand the More Fields folder under the Dim Reseller dimension, and drag and drop the Business Type attribute to the Column Labels area. Finally, drag and drop the Sales Amount – Fact Reseller Sales measure of the Fact Reseller Sales measure group to the Values area. You can now analyze the Sales data based on the business type in each country, as shown in Figure 6-17. Based on this sales knowledge — the costs associated with the products and your business goals — you can strategically promote the business type yielding the maximum profit for your company. Reference dimensions help you to analyze fact data even though they are not directly related to the facts.

Excel sends the following query to retrieve data for analyzing the reseller sales fact of various business types across various countries of the resellers.

```
SELECT
NON EMPTY Hierarchize(
  {DrilldownLevel({[Dim Reseller].[Business Type].[All]}
   ,,,INCLUDE_CALC_MEMBERS)})
    DIMENSION PROPERTIES PARENT_UNIQUE_NAME,HIERARCHY_UNIQUE_NAME ON COLUMNS ,
```

```
NON EMPTY Hierarchize(
  {DrilldownLevel({[Dim Geography].[English Country Region Name].[All]}
   ,,,INCLUDE_CALC_MEMBERS)})
    DIMENSION PROPERTIES PARENT_UNIQUE_NAME,HIERARCHY_UNIQUE_NAME,
  [Dim Geography].[English Country Region Name].
   [English Country Region Name].[French Country Region Name],
  [Dim Geography].[English Country Region Name].
   [English Country Region Name].[Spanish Country Region Name] ON ROWS
FROM [Adventure Works DW]
WHERE ([Measures].[Sales Amount - Fact Reseller Sales])
 CELL PROPERTIES VALUE, FORMAT_STRING, LANGUAGE, BACK_COLOR,
  FORE_COLOR, FONT_FLAGS
```

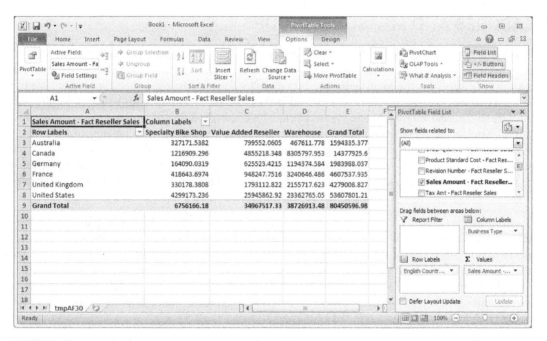

FIGURE 6-17

Because the query used by Excel retrieves data on three-dimensional axes, you cannot execute the same query in SQL Server Management Studio (SSMS) because SSMS can display only two-dimensional results. Therefore, if you need to see the same results in SSMS, you need to use an MDX query that can retrieve results in a two-dimensional format. You can rewrite the MDX query generated by Excel using the CrossJoin function or the cross join operator (*) so that the results can be retrieved on two axes. A simplified MDX query that returns the same results as the Excel query follows:

```
SELECT { [Measures].[Sales Amount - Fact Reseller Sales]} ON COLUMNS,
 NON EMPTY { [Dim Geography].[English Country Region Name].MEMBERS *
 [Dim Reseller].[Business Type].MEMBERS} ON ROWS
FROM [Adventure Works DW]
```

This simplified query asks for the members of the dimension attributes rather than drilling down to them from the All member as Excel's query does.

So far you have learned about cube dimensions, how to add them to a cube, how to define relationships between dimensions and measure groups, and then how to query data along with the dimensions. Cube dimensions and their attributes and hierarchies contain several properties. Some properties such as AttributeHierarchyEnabled, AttributeHierarchyVisible, and AttributeHierarchyOptimizedState reflect the default state of the cube dimension hierarchies or attributes. You can override these properties so that appropriate settings are applied for the dimensions within the cube. The AggregationUsage attribute property and AllMemberAggregationUsage dimension property control the behavior of aggregations designed on the cube. You learn more about these properties in Chapters 9 and 10.

MEASURES AND MEASURE GROUPS

You learned about editing cube dimensions and establishing the right relationships between dimensions and measure groups. Similarly, you can add or delete a cube's measures and measure groups. Measures are the focus point for data analysis and therefore they are the core objects of a cube. Measures are columns from the fact table that contain meaningful information for data analysis. Usually, measures are numeric types that can be aggregated or summarized along the attributes and hierarchies of a dimension. You can specify the type of aggregation to be applied for each measure. The most widely used aggregate functions are Sum, Count, and Distinct Count. A collection of measures forms an object called a measure group, and a collection of measure groups forms the dimension called *Measures* in the cube. Measures is a keyword in Analysis Services that refers to a special dimension that contains only the fact data.

If you click the Cube Structure tab in the cube editor, you can see the Measures pane on the top-left corner. Select the cube named Adventure Works DW in the Measures pane to see the cube's properties in the Properties window located on the bottom-right corner of SSDT. Figure 6-18 shows the Measures and Properties panes. The Measures pane shows the cube name and the measure groups within the cube. You can see the two measure groups, Fact Reseller Sales and Fact Internet Sales, which correspond to the two fact tables. There is typically a one-to-one relationship between a fact table and measure group in the cube.

In your source data, if you had partitioned your fact data into multiple fact tables across a specific dimension, it needs to be handled differently when designing the cube. For example, if you have Fact Internet Sales data stored in separate fact tables for each quarter (fact data has been partitioned into multiple fact tables across the Time dimension), then, with respect to the cube, all these tables can be considered a single fact table because they have the same schema. You typically partition your relational fact data into multiple fact tables due to design or scalability considerations, but when you want to analyze the data, you aggregate the data appropriately across various dimensions, especially the Time dimension. You can either merge the data from all the fact tables within the DSV with a named query, or you can utilize the partitioning feature in Analysis Services so that Analysis Services aggregates the data correctly during browsing. You learn more about partitions in Chapters 7 and 10.

You can see several properties of the cube in Figure 6-18. An important property is DefaultMeasure. The reason why the default measure is important is that whenever your MDX query does not explicitly contain a member from the measures dimension, the default measure is returned. In addition, the default measure is used whenever restrictions are applied in the query with the WHERE clause. Based on the setting of the default measure property your results can be different. If you select the DefaultMeasure property, you can see a drop-down list that shows all the measures of the cube. You can choose the measure you want to define as the default measure of the cube from this list. If the default measure is not specified, the first measure of the first measure group of the cube (as seen in the Measures pane) will be used as the default measure of the cube.

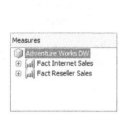

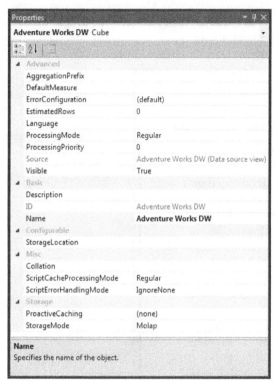

FIGURE 6-18

Another important property is the StorageMode property. This defines whether your fact data will be stored in Analysis Services, your relational data source, or both. The StorageMode property has three options: Multidimensional OLAP (MOLAP), Relational OLAP (ROLAP), and Hybrid OLAP (HOLAP). The default value is MOLAP, which means that when the cube is processed, Analysis Services reads the relational data and stores it in the Analysis Services database for fast retrieval. You learn more about the defining storage modes in Chapter 9. You have the option to instruct the Analysis Services instance to automatically update cube and dimension objects if there were a change in the relational data. The ProactiveCaching property lets you specify the frequency of the update of the cube data based on changes in the relational source data.

The ErrorConfiguration property helps in handling the various errors that can occur while processing the fact data and defining what actions should be taken under such error circumstances such as ignoring the error, converting to a specific value, or stopping processing when errors are encountered.

One of the main features of an OLAP database is the capability to create aggregations that facilitate fast query response times. You can use the AggregationPrefix property to prefix the name of the aggregations created for the cube.

The remaining properties are self-explanatory, and you can find detailed information for each property in Analysis Services 2012 product documentation.

If you select one of the measure groups in the Measures pane, you see the properties associated with that measure group in the Properties window. Most of the properties at the cube level are also applicable to the measure group level. If you specify a value for a common property at the measure group level that is different than the value for the same property at the cube level, the value specified at the measure group level will be applied to that measure group.

Expand the Fact Internet Sales measure group, and select the Sales Amount measure. The Properties window now shows the properties of the measure, as shown in Figure 6-19. Next, you learn the important properties of a measure in detail.

The AggregateFunction property defines how the measure value is to be aggregated from one level to another level of a hierarchy in a dimension. For example, assume a Product dimension contains a hierarchy called Products that contains two levels, Model Name and Product Name. Each model contains one or more products. If you want the sales amount of a specific product to be added to that of the parent model, you need to specify the Sum as the aggregate function. Whenever you browse the cube along the Products hierarchy, you can see that the sales of each product are added to the sales amount value of the corresponding model. However, sometimes you might not want

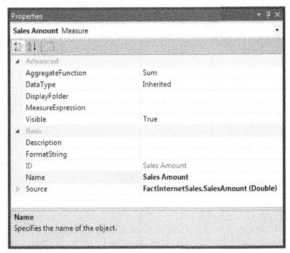

FIGURE 6-19

the measure value to be summed while browsing a hierarchy. Analysis Services supports several different aggregate functions. Aggregation functions supported in the measure properties can also be implemented in MDX scripts. (You learn about MDX scripts in Chapter 9.) However, you should use the built-in aggregation functions shown in the Properties window to get optimal performance from your Analysis Services instance.

Other than the Sum aggregate function, the most commonly used aggregate functions are Count and Distinct Count. Use the Count aggregate function, as the name indicates, whenever you want to count each occurrence of the measure value rather than add the measure values. For example, if you want to find the number of transactions in a day or number of customers in a day, you would use a Count aggregate function on a fact table column that indicates the customers who came to the store on a specific day. The Distinct Count aggregate function, on the other hand, identifies the unique number of occurrences of a specific measure value. For example, a customer can buy a specific product every month. If you want to find the number of customers who purchase a specific product, use the Distinct Count aggregate function. You see examples of Count and Distinct Count aggregate functions later in this section. The None aggregate function is used when you do not want to aggregate the values of a specific measure across a dimension. An example of where the None aggregate function would be used is for the price of a specific product or discount provided on a unit product.

When you build and browse a cube, you see all the measures occurring under the dimension called Measures in the Metadata pane of the Cube Browser. If you want to organize the related measures in a logical structure that is more meaningful for users, use the DisplayFolder property. You can specify a measure to be part of one or more display folders by editing its DisplayFolder property. If you enter a name in the DisplayFolder property, that specific measure becomes part of a display folder with that name. You can make a specific measure part of multiple display folders by specifying the display folders' names separated by semicolons. When display folders are specified, while browsing the cube you can see the display folders under the appropriate measure group name in the Metadata pane of the Browser. Therefore you cannot have measures from different measure groups in a single display folder.

In some business applications you may want to allow access to only the aggregated results of a measure. For such applications you need a way to aggregate the results of a measure but not show the base measure. You can aggregate the results of a measure by specifying a measure called a calculated measure (you learn more about calculations later in this chapter) and hide the base measure. The Visible measure property allows you to hide the base measure from viewing for such applications.

The FormatString property allows you to show the measure value in a format of your choice. If you select the FormatString property you can see the various format options available.

The MeasureExpression property specifies the expression that evaluates the value for the measure. For example, if you have Sales information you might want to ensure the Sales information is presented in the local currency based on the currency conversion rates. In such a case you can define an appropriate expression for the MeasureExpression property for the measure Sales. You learn more about the MeasureExpression property in Chapter 9.

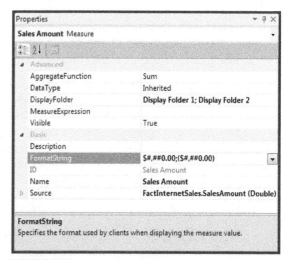

FIGURE 6-20

The easiest way to see the effect of the properties mentioned is to try them in your project. Specify two display folders named DisplayFolder 1 and DisplayFolder 2 for the Sales Amount measure in the Fact Internet Sales measure group. Because the Sales Amount measure is a currency data type, you can select the currency format. Select the $#,##0.00;($#,##0.00) format from the FormatString property drop-down. The Properties window for the Sales Amount measure should resemble Figure 6-20.

You learned examples of where the Count and Distinct Count aggregate functions can be useful. In your Adventure Works DW cube, if you want to count the number of customers and distinct customers who have bought specific products, you can use these aggregate functions. Customer Key identifies the customer who has bought a specific product in the fact table. Therefore, to see the customer counts mentioned, you need to create two new measures using the Customer Key fact table column. To create the two new measures follow these steps:

1. Right-click the Fact Internet Sales measure group, and select New Measure.

2. In the New Measure dialog, check the Show All Columns check box.

3. In the Source columns list, select Customer Key, and click OK. A new measure called Customer Key is created.

4. In the Measures pane, change the name for this measure from Customer Key to Distinct Customers by right-clicking the measure and selecting Rename.

5. Change the aggregate function for this measure to `Distinct Count`.

At this point you notice that a blue squiggly line shows up under the Distinct Customers measure. Analysis Services starting with the 2008 version has built-in checks for many of the best practices for dimension and cube design. These best practices are implemented as warnings in the Analysis Management Objects (AMO) API. SSDT surfaces these AMO warnings through warning icons and blue squiggly lines for objects that don't meet these design best practices. To discover the rules that generate these warnings, simply move the mouse over the blue squiggly line or warning icon to see a tooltip with the best practice design rule. In this case the rule suggests that distinct count measures should be broken out into separate measure groups (see Figure 6-21).

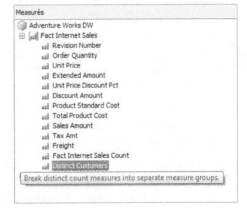

FIGURE 6-21

The reason for this warning is that distinct count measures are semi-additive and require storing records at a finer level of detail than measures using other aggregate functions. For a distinct count of customers to be accessible, the individual customer IDs must be available. Therefore, Analysis Services must use the Customer Key attribute for any and all aggregations. Consider the following example: If you are interested in the total Sales (sum) for a product in a given year, you do not need to retain the individual customer IDs that purchased the product within the chosen year. The Analysis Services engine can pre-aggregate data at the Product ID and Year attribute levels as part of the normal processing of the cube. However, if there is a requirement that you know the distinct number of customers who purchased the product within the year, you must retain the customer keys throughout any aggregated data.

If the product in question were purchased by 50,000 customers over the year, the aggregate goes from one row of data per product per year to 50,000 rows per product for the year. Separating `Distinct Count` measures into different measure groups allows maximum pre-aggregation of other additive measures with minimal storage and on-the-fly aggregation requirements.

For this illustration you can ignore this best practice warning and move on to the next steps.

1. Right-click the Fact Internet Sales measure group, and select New Measure.

2. In the New Measure dialog, select the Show All Columns check box.

3. Select the Customer Key column, and click OK. A new measure called Customer Key is now created.

4. In the Measures pane, change the name of this measure from Customer Key to Total Customers by right-clicking the measure and selecting Rename.

5. In the Properties window, change the AggregateFunction property for the Total Customers measure from Sum to Count.

6. The Unit Price of a product is the same value at every level of the hierarchy. Therefore, this value should not be aggregated. To implement this behavior set the Unit Price measure's aggregate function to FirstNonEmpty. Also change the property's FormatString property to Currency.

7. Create a new user hierarchy called Products in the Dim Product dimension with two levels, Model Name and English Product Name, where Model Name is the parent level of English Product Name. Rename the English Product Name level to Product Name.

8. Deploy the project to the Analysis Services instance.

9. When the deployment is complete, switch to the Cube Browser tab, and click the Analyze in Excel button on the toolbar. When you look at the Fact Internet Sales measure group in the PivotTable Field List, you see two folders called DisplayFolder 1 and DisplayFolder 2 that contain the Sales Amount measure, as shown in Figure 6-22.

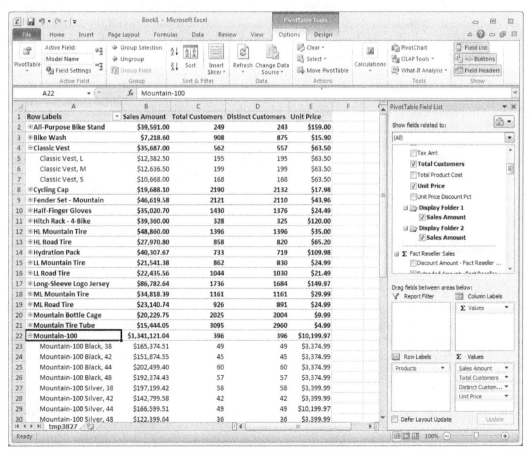

FIGURE 6-22

10. Drag and drop the Sales Amount, Total Customers, Distinct Customers, and Unit Price measures from the Fact Internet Sales measure group to the Values area of the PivotTable Field List.

11. Then drag and drop the Products hierarchy from the Dim Product dimension to the Row Labels area of the PivotTable Field List. Expand the Classic Vest member.

You can see that the values for the measures are aggregated for the two levels of the Products hierarchy, Model Name and Product Name, based on the aggregate function chosen. Choosing the aggregate functions Count and Distinct Count not only counts the values for the members of a hierarchy, but also aggregates the counts to the next level. Notice also that the values of Sales Amount and Unit Price are formatted based on the format strings you specified earlier. (Note that in order to see the formatting defined in the Analysis Services database you may have to click on the bottom of the Change Data Source button in the PivotTable Tools on the Options tab of the Excel ribbon, select Connection properties, and in the Connection Properties dialog, check the check boxes in the OLAP Server Formatting section of the dialog.) You can also see that the Unit Price measure is aggregated from the members in the Product Name level to Model Name level based on the FirstNonEmpty aggregate function. You see the value for the Unit Price measure for the Classic Vest model as $63.50, the same as the value of each of the specific products aggregated under it, as shown in Figure 6-22. On the other hand, if you expand the Mountain-100 model node, you see that the Products under it have different values. The Unit Price value shown for the Mountain-100 model is that of the Mountain-100 Silver 44 product, one of the members of the Mountain-100 model attribute. This is the value that was chosen by the FirstNonEmpty aggregate function.

You have now successfully enhanced your cube by adding cube dimensions and measures. In the process you have also learned about properties of cube dimensions, measures, and measure groups. Most often, businesses need complex logic to analyze their relational data. Analysis Services provides you with the ability to embed the complex calculations required for solving business problems in several ways. The most basic operation that every business needs is creating simple arithmetic calculations on base measures or dimension members. Objects created from such calculations are called calculated members.

CALCULATED MEMBERS

The term *calculated member* refers to the creation of any MDX object through a calculation. The calculated member can be part of the Measures dimension where a simple MDX expression such as addition or subtraction of two or more base measures results in a new measure. Such calculated members on the Measures dimension are referred to as *calculated measures*. You can also create calculated members on other dimensions by specifying an MDX expression. These members are simply referred to as calculated members. To create a calculated member, click the Calculations tab of the cube editor. This takes you to the Calculations page, as shown in Figure 6-23. The Calculations page contains three panes: Script Organizer, Calculation Tools, and Script Editor.

The Script Organizer pane shows the names of the calculation objects in the cube. Various types of calculations can be created in the Calculations view such as calculated members and calculated measures. You can also apply a name to a subset of dimension members, which is referred to as a named set. In addition to calculated members and named sets, you can define a script containing MDX expressions that perform complex business logic calculations. If you right-click in the Script Organizer pane, you can see menu items that allow you to create a calculated member, a named set, or a script command. These operations can also be performed using the corresponding toolbar buttons. In this chapter, you create calculated measures. The creation of script commands and named sets are detailed in Chapter 9.

FIGURE 6-23

The Calculation Tools pane contains three tabs: Metadata, Functions, and Templates. The Metadata tab shows the measures and dimensions of the current cube. The Functions tab shows all the MDX functions along with a template of the arguments needed for each function. In the Templates tab you can see templates for some common calculations used in certain applications such as budgeting and financial.

The Script Editor pane shows the actual calculation scripts. The default view of the Script window is called the Form View. It presents each calculated member in a form that makes it easy to enter the expression and set properties on the member. You can also switch the Script Editor pane to a different view called the Script View, which shows all the cube calculations in a single page showing the actual MDX for each calculation including the properties that could be specified via controls in form view. When Script View is in effect, the Script Organizer pane is hidden. You can toggle between the two views by clicking the Form View/Script View toolbar buttons or in the main menu using the Cube\Show Calculations command which contains options for Script or Form view.

All commands and selections available in Analysis Services are accessible via keyboard controls. You can switch between the three panes of the Calculations tab of the Cube Designer using the F6 function key or by making the appropriate selection via menu items.

Calculated Measures

Calculated measures are the most common type of calculated members in a cube. In your project you have the Sales Amount and Total Product Cost measures in the two measure groups, Fact Internet Sales and Fact Reseller Sales. An important question to ask about any business concerns profit, which is the difference between total sales and cost of goods sold. In the Adventure Works DW cube, you have Sales through the Internet as well as through resellers. Therefore, you need to add these two sales amounts to calculate the total sales of products. Similarly, you need to calculate the total product cost by adding the costs of products sold through the Internet and resellers. Two calculated measures must be formed to perform these operations. After you create these two calculations, you can calculate the profit. Follow these steps to create the calculated measure for profit:

1. Right-click in the Script Organizer pane, and select New Calculated Member, as shown in Figure 6-24. An object called [Calculated Member] is created. The Script window now shows a form with several controls for specifying the name of the calculated member, the MDX expression for the calculation, and other properties.

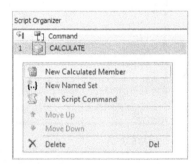

FIGURE 6-24

2. Specify the name of the calculated member as [Total Sales Amount] in the Name field of the Script Editor pane. In the Expression text box you need to enter the MDX expression that can calculate the Total Sales Amount. As mentioned earlier, the Total Sales Amount is the sum of sales amounts in the Fact Internet Sales and Fact Reseller Sales measure groups. Drag and drop these measures from the Metadata pane, and add the MDX operator "+" between them, as shown in Figure 6-25.

3. For cost of goods sold, create a new calculated member called [Total Product Costs] using a method similar to the one described in step 2 but with appropriate Product Cost measures from the two measure groups.

4. Create a calculated member called [Profit]. The MDX expression to evaluate Profit is the difference of the calculated measures you have created in steps 2 and 3. Enter the MDX expression [Total Sales Amount] - [Total Product Costs] in the Expression text box, as shown in Figure 6-26. Because Measures is a special dimension, you do not need to precede the measure name with [Measures].

5. You have the option to specify certain additional properties for calculated measures. By default, all the calculated measures created are visible. You can specify color, font, and

format strings for calculated measures based on certain conditions. For example, if you want to highlight the profit in red if the amount is less than one million dollars and in green if it is greater than or equal to one million, you can do so by specifying the appropriate background color for the calculated member.

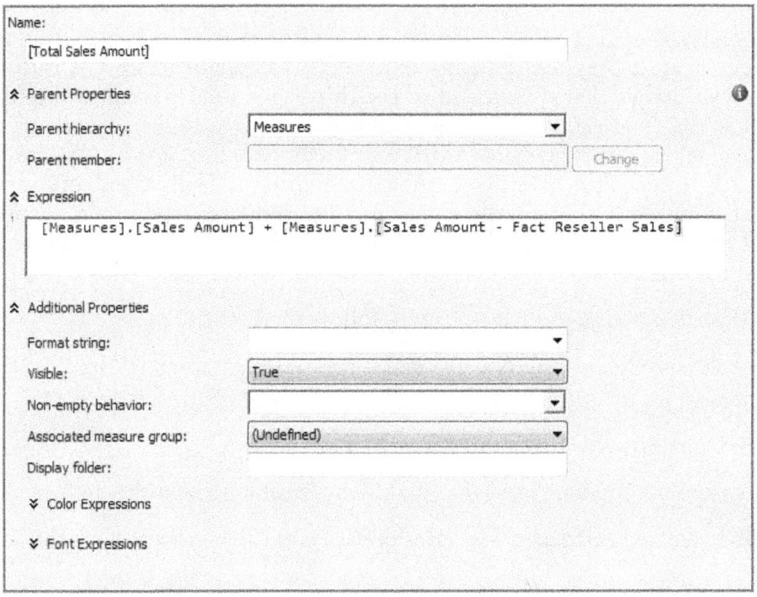

FIGURE 6-25

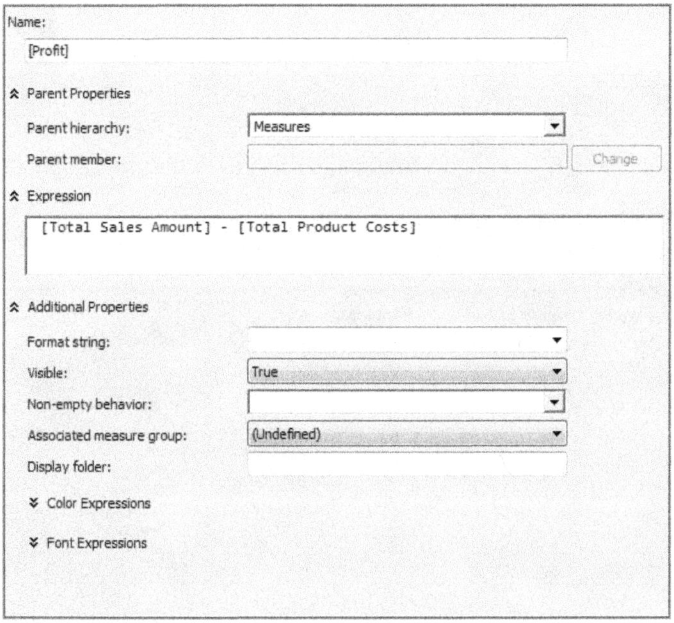

FIGURE 6-26

6. Enter the following MDX expression for the Color Expressions\Back color property in the Script Editor form:

```
iif ( [Measures].[Profit] < 1000000,    255 /*Red*/,
    65280 /*Green*/)
```

This MDX expression uses the IIF function. This function takes three arguments. The first argument is an expression that should evaluate to true or false. The return value of the IIF function is either the second or the third argument passed to the function. If the result of the expression is true, the IIF function returns the second argument; if the expression is false, it returns the third argument. The first argument passed to the IIF function is to see if the profit is less than one million. The second and third arguments passed to the function are the values for the colors red and green, respectively. You can also select the values for the color properties by clicking the color icon next to the background color text box.

To see the effect of the calculations you have created, follow these steps:

1. Deploy the AnalysisServicesMultidimensionalTutorial project to your Analysis Services instance.

2. To go to the Cube Browser page, and select the Browser tab.

3. When deployment is complete, click the Analyze in Excel button in the toolbar.

4. View the newly created calculated measures in the PivotTable Field List, as shown in Figure 6-27.

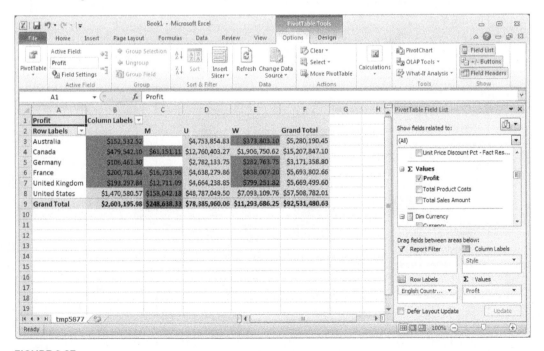

FIGURE 6-27

5. Drag and drop the Profit measure to the Values area, the English Country Region Name attribute of the Dim Geography dimension to the Row Labels area, and the Style attribute of the Dim Product dimension to the Column Labels area. (You must expand the More Fields folder to access the last two items.)

The results are shown in Figure 6-27. Although you can't see color in the figure, on the screen you will see that the background color for cells that contain values are either red or green based on the Profit value.

Querying Calculated Measures

You can query calculated measures similar to other measures in the cube by referencing them by name. For example, if you want to query the calculated member Profit based on Model Name, you execute the following query:

```
SELECT [Measures].[Profit] on COLUMNS,
[Dim Product].[Model Name].MEMBERS on ROWS
FROM [Adventure Works DW]
```

If you want to retrieve all the measures in the cube instead of specifying each measure, use [Measures].MEMBERS. However, calculated members are not returned in your query result when you specify [Measures].MEMBERS. You need to execute the following MDX query to retrieve the base measures along with the calculated members:

```
SELECT [Measures].ALLMEMBERS on COLUMNS,
[Dim Product].[Model Name].MEMBERS on ROWS
FROM [Adventure Works DW]
```

You have learned to enhance the Adventure Works DW cube by creating calculated measures and learned to set properties for the calculated measures via MDX expressions. The NonEmptyBehavior property for calculated measures is discussed in Chapter 11.

CREATING PERSPECTIVES

Analysis Services provides you with the option to create a cube that combines many fact tables. Each cube dimension can contain multiple attributes and hierarchies. Even though the cube might contain all the relevant data for business analysis combined into a single object, some users of the cube might be interested only in parts of it. For example, a cube might contain sales and budget information of a company. The Sales department is interested only in viewing sales-relevant data, whereas the users involved in budgeting or forecasting next year's revenue are interested only in budget-relevant sections of the cube. Typically, users do not like to see too much extra information. To accommodate this, Analysis Services allows you to create views of a cube that each contain a subset of all the cube's objects. These views are called *perspectives*.

In the Adventure Works DW cube, you have two fact tables, FactInternetSales and FactResellerSales. To understand the behavior of perspectives, create a perspective for Internet Sales and a perspective for Reseller Sales. The following steps show you how to do this:

1. Click the Perspectives tab in the Cube Designer. You see a column on the left showing the measures, dimensions, and calculated members in the cube, as shown in Figure 6-28.

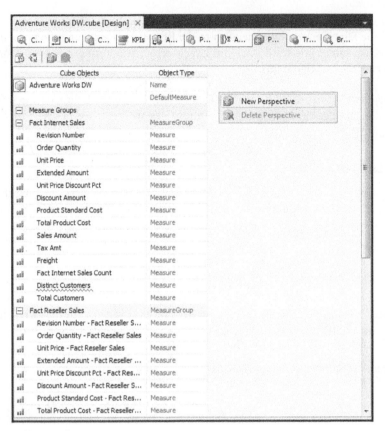

FIGURE 6-28

2. Right-click in the Perspectives page, and select New Perspective, as shown in Figure 6-28. You can also create a new perspective by clicking the New Perspective button in the toolbar. A new column with the name Perspective is created. A check box is in the Perspective column next to each object in the cube. Rename the new perspective to **Internet Sales**. Uncheck the Fact Reseller Sales measure group and the Dim Employee and Dim Reseller dimensions.

3. Create another perspective called Reseller Sales. Uncheck the Fact Internet Sales measure group and the Dim Customer dimension.

Your Perspective window should look similar to Figure 6-29. Now deploy the project. SSDT sends the definitions for the new perspectives to the server. Although perspectives are frequently shown as cubes in client applications such as the SSDT Cube Browser, they are not cubes but rather views of a subset of the objects in an existing cube.

In Chapter 5 you learned how to specify translations of attributes and metadata in a dimension. Similarly, you can create translations for metadata of a cube. You see the use of perspectives along with translations after learning how to create translations for a cube.

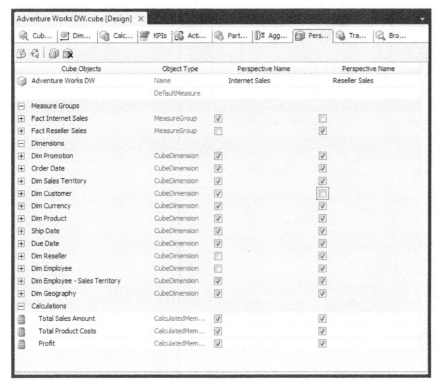

FIGURE 6-29

CREATING TRANSLATIONS

Translations facilitate the display of data and metadata in different languages. Unlike translations for dimensions, where you can specify translations for a dimension's data and metadata, cube translations are specified only for the cube's metadata.

To create a new translation for the Adventure Works DW cube, do the following:

1. Click the Translations tab in the Cube Designer. Similar to the Perspective view, the left column shows the names of all the metadata objects in the default language. There is another column that indicates the object type.

2. Right-click in the Translation page and select New Translation. You can also create a new translation using the New Translation button in the toolbar. In the Select Language dialog, select French (France) as the language, and click OK. You now have a new column where you can provide the translations of each object (measure, display folders, dimension name, attribute names). Specify the translations in French, as shown in Figure 6-30. (If you don't know French, you can enter the translations in a language of your choice.) You can define translations for each metadata object in the cube, such as measure names, measure group names, dimension names, perspective names, as well as calculated member names.

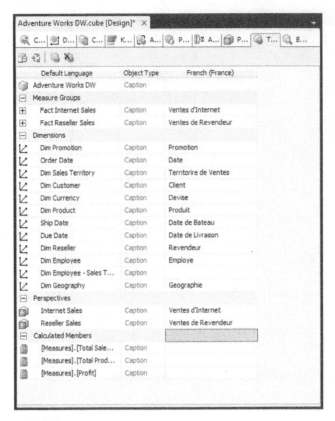

FIGURE 6-30

3. Deploy the project to your Analysis Services instance.

BROWSING PERSPECTIVES AND TRANSLATIONS

You have successfully created perspectives and translations for the Adventure Works DW cube. You can see these aspects of the cube in the Browser tab of the Cube Designer. In the Cube Browser, if you click the Cube Selection button above the Metadata pane on the left side of the Cube Browser page, you can bring up the Cube Selection dialog that allows you to choose from among three perspectives: Adventure Works DW (the default perspective that contains all cube objects), Internet Sales, and Reseller Sales. Select the Internet Sales perspective and click OK. If you expand the measures in the Measure Group window, all the measures relevant to the reseller are not visible. Drag and drop the Sales Amount, English Product Name attribute from the Dim Product dimension, and the English Education attribute of the Dim Customer dimension to the Report pane of the Cube Browser. You can see the sales amount data along with product names and education of customers, as shown in Figure 6-31.

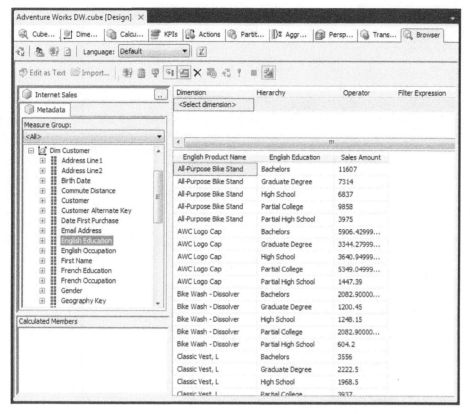

FIGURE 6-31

To see the translated names in French, select the French (France) language in the Language drop-down at the top of the Cube Browser. When you select the French (France) language, the metadata and data members for the hierarchies in the Cube Browser automatically change to values in French for those objects where translations have been defined, as shown in Figure 6-32. Thus, you have created translated values in French for a French client who wants to analyze the same values, but who can understand and interpret the results better in French than English. Each language has a corresponding ID called the locale ID. When you select a specific language in the Browser, SSDT connects to the server specifying the corresponding locale ID for the selected language. Analysis Services returns the metadata and data corresponding to the locale ID when queries are sent to the server on the same connection.

Instead of creating separate cubes for various users and clients understanding different languages or wanting to see subsets of the main cube you've built along with the overhead of maintaining those cubes for changes that need to be made, Analysis Services Translations and Perspectives features enable you to satisfy those types of customer needs with one cube.

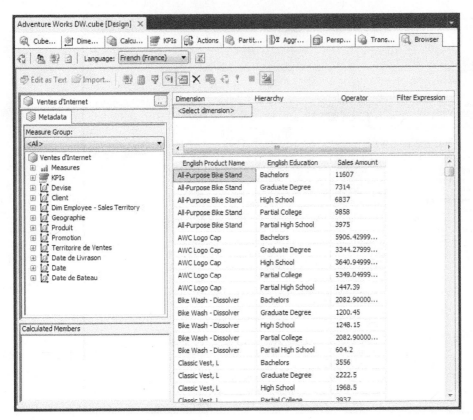

FIGURE 6-32

SUMMARY

You traversed the Cube Wizard for a second time in this book, but at a different level of granularity and hopefully with more understanding of what occurs. You learned how to create calculated members and set properties concerning the display of those members, for example, different color foregrounds and backgrounds. And finally, you learned how to create and browse perspectives and translations. In the real world of business, you have additional enhancement requirements to meet after running the Cube Wizard. These requirements may include creating calculated members on dimensions, creating cube scripts containing complex MDX expressions to meet your business needs, and adding Key Performance Indicators (KPIs), which can graphically represent the state of your business in real time. The Cube Designer contains additional tabs for KPIs and Actions. These features help enhance your cubes for business analyses. In addition, the Cube Designer helps in partitioning fact data and defining aggregations, which in turn help you achieve improved performance while querying your multidimensional model. These are covered in Chapter 9, with additional coverage in other chapters as well. In the next chapter you learn how to manage your Analysis Services databases using the SQL Server Management Studio.

Administration and Management

WHAT'S IN THIS CHAPTER?

➤ Administering Analysis Services with Management Studio

➤ Backing up your databases

➤ Basic Analysis Services database maintenance

➤ Monitoring Analysis Services databases

➤ Administering Analysis Services programmatically with AMO

Administration is an important task on any server product. As an administrator of SQL Server Analysis Services (SSAS) you need to make sure Analysis Services is secure and reliable, and provides efficient access to the end users. You can administer Analysis Services in two ways: through the SQL Server 2012 Tool set — SQL Server Management Studio (SSMS) and SQL Server Data Tools (SSDT) — or programmatically using an object model called Analysis Management Objects (AMO).

In Analysis Services 2012 you now have the option to run SSAS in tabular or multidimensional mode. Multidimensional mode is what was available in SSAS 2005/2008/2008r2. Sometimes you may hear this referred to as UDM, MOLAP, or legacy SSAS mode. Tabular mode uses the VertiPaq in-memory engine instead of the traditional SSAS engine; if you worked with PowerPivot for Excel/SharePoint, this is the same engine updated from personal and corporate BI applications to Enterprise applications. Now in SQL Server 2012 you have the ability to use the VertiPaq engine outside of Excel or SharePoint.

Management operations on multidimensional and tabular Analysis Services are different. If Analysis Services runs in tabular mode, you have the following options for managing your databases:

➤ SQL Server Management Studio (SSMS)

➤ Programmatically via Analysis Management Objects (AMO)

➤ PowerShell and AMO

➤ Deployment via SQL Server Data Tools (SSDT)

There is no option to connect and manage a tabular database in online mode with SSDT. To manage an existing tabular mode database with SSDT, you need to use Import from Analysis Services; this requires redeploying your database after any changes.

In either tabular or multidimensional mode, you can accomplish tasks such as processing objects, providing access to Analysis Services objects in databases, and synchronization of databases between Analysis Services instances using SSMS. You can use SSDT to connect to a multidimensional mode database to perform design changes and accomplish follow-on tasks such as processing and providing access to users. SSMS and SSDT both use AMO behind the scenes to accomplish all management tasks. The AMO object model itself is installed and registered into the Global Assembly Cache (GAC) when the product is installed. The AMO .NET assembly, by the way, is Microsoft.AnalysisSevices.dll. In this chapter you learn about key administrative tasks and how to accomplish those tasks using SSMS and SSDT. You also learn about administering SSAS programmatically using AMO.

ADMINISTRATION USING SQL SERVER 2012 TOOLS

In Chapter 2 you used SSMS to view the objects found in an Analysis Services 2012 database. You start here on a similar footing:

1. Launch SSMS from All Programs ➤ Microsoft SQL Server 2012 ➤ SQL Server Management Studio.

2. Using Object Explorer, connect to the Analysis Services instance.

3. Open the Databases folder.

In the Databases folder, you see a tree view of the databases you have saved on the server to date, as shown in Figure 7-1. One of those databases should be titled AnalysisServicesMultidimensionalTutorial—you should take a moment to review the tree nodes and what they contain because you will learn the administrative tasks associated with those objects.

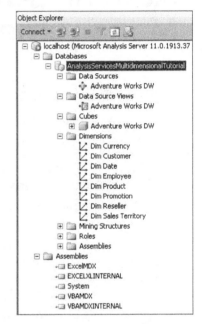

FIGURE 7-1

 You can launch Management Studio from a command prompt or the Start ➤ Run menu by typing **ssms**.

Figure 7-1 shows SSAS running in native SSAS mode. Figure 7-2 shows the difference between SSAS running in multidimensional versus tabular mode.

Managing Analysis Servers

SSMS, the integrated management environment for SQL Server 2012 products, provides you the flexibility to manage several Analysis Services instances. This chapter uses the word "server" to denote an instance of Analysis Services, and "servers" to denote one or more. If you have a set

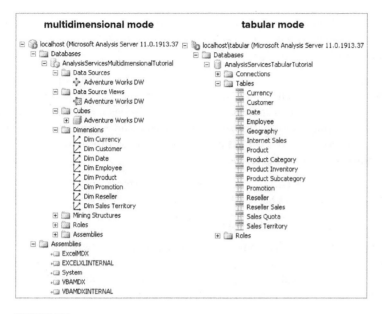

multidimensional mode / tabular mode

FIGURE 7-2

FIGURE 7-3

of production servers used by customers and a set of test servers used for development and testing purposes, you typically want to manage them differently. The most logical thing is to group these servers. Using the Registered Servers window of SQL Server Management Studio, you can group a set of Analysis Services servers to form a Server group, as shown in Figure 7-5. You can register Analysis Services servers and organize them into groups using the New Server Group and New Server Registration dialogs. Launch the new Server Registration window using the following steps:

1. In SSMS, open the Registered Servers window (Figure 7-3) by entering Ctrl+Alt+g or clicking View ≻ Registered Servers in the toolbar.

2. Right-click the Local Server Groups folder and select New Server Group as shown in Figure 7-4.

3. Enter "Test Server Group" as the Group Name and select OK (see Figure 7-5).

4. You can now move servers to this new server group or create new server registrations under this group.

Some of the common tasks of starting, stopping, restarting, and configuring Analysis Services servers can also be accomplished from the Registered Servers window. You can right-click the

FIGURE 7-4

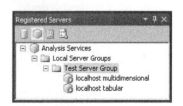

FIGURE 7-5

specific Analysis Services instance and choose the appropriate operation. In addition, you can switch to the Object Explorer window of the connected SSAS instance, or launch the MDX query editor or SQL Server Configuration Manager dialog from this window.

After you connect to an Analysis Services server in the Object Explorer window, you can accomplish various administrative tasks on that server, such as creating new databases, providing permissions, processing objects, and moving databases from test servers to production servers. First and foremost for the Analysis Server admin is providing access permissions to the users who will be administering the server. The following steps show how to add a user as an administrator of an Analysis Services server by making them part of the object called Server Role:

1. In the Object Explorer window, right-click the Analysis Services instance and select Properties. You see the Analysis Services Server Properties dialog.

2. Click Security in the left hand pane, as shown in Figure 7-6.

3. Click the Add button to add a user to the Analysis Services administrators group. You can add domain users, local machine users, or groups as part of the administrator group for Analysis Services. If your user is a local user you can specify *<machinename>\username* (or just the username) to add the user to this server administrator group, as shown in Figure 7-7.

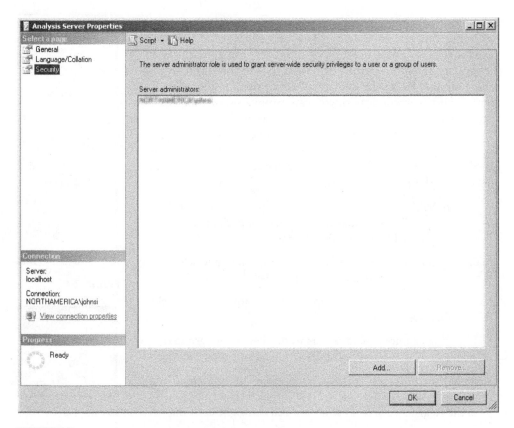

FIGURE 7-6

By default, if you try to add a group to the Analysis Services administrators group it will fail to resolve the group. To add a group, click the Object Types button in the Select Users or Groups dialog, then check Groups as seen in Figure 7-7.

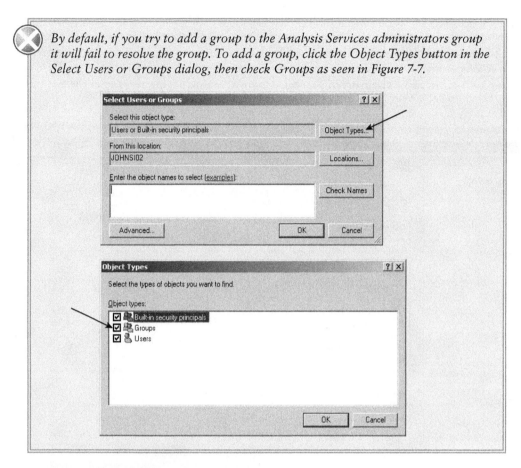

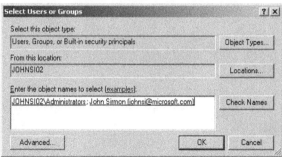

FIGURE 7-7

Another important management task is to set appropriate Analysis Server properties so that Analysis Services performs optimally. You can do this using the Analysis Server Properties dialog, as shown in Figure 7-8. Analysis Services needs to be restarted for certain properties to take effect. This is indicated by a "yes" in the Restart column for those properties in the Analysis Services Server Properties dialog. For more information on these properties and when you would want to consider changing them, see the Analysis Services Operations Guide at `http://msdn.microsoft. com/en-us/library/hh226085.aspx`. In addition, you can find all these properties and some additional properties in the msmdsrv.ini file. You can change the properties in either place. You learn some of these properties in this chapter and others in Chapter 10. The properties dialog has a check box that enables you to view and modify the advanced properties of the Analysis Services server. Adding users to the Server role or Database role and setting properties are considered part of securing your Analysis Services server. You learn more about managing security at the end of this chapter.

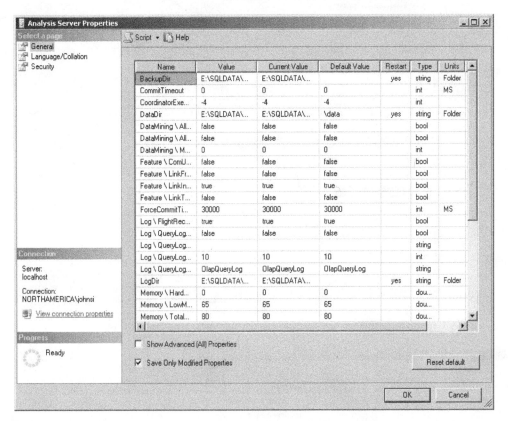

FIGURE 7-8

Managing Analysis Services Objects

Some of the most important tasks you can accomplish with SSMS are:

➤ Processing cubes and dimensions

➤ Setting permissions on various objects in a database

➤ Managing partitions of a cube based on usage

➤ Adding custom assemblies to your database

Even though the SQL Server Management Studio provides a great interface to manage Analysis Services 2012 and abstracts all the internal details, it is beneficial to understand the underlying operations that take place when you perform the management operations. Knowledge of these server internals gives you an edge in better understanding its operation and helps you more effectively manage the server when unforeseen problems occur.

All communications to Analysis Services is through XML for Analysis (XMLA). The management tasks executed through SSMS use the management object model AMO, which in turn sends XMLA Execute commands to the Analysis Services instance. You can see some of the commands sent to the Analysis Services server when performing management tasks in this chapter.

Database Creation

SQL Server Analysis Services 2012 enables a server administrator to create databases and assign database administrative permissions to a user. You can create a database only in SSMS for a multidimensional mode server. The following steps show how to create a database and assign permissions when SSAS runs in multidimensional mode.

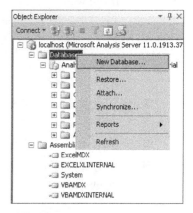

1. In the SSMS Object Explorer, right-click the Databases folder and select New Database, as shown in Figure 7-9.

2. Enter a new database name called DBATest, as shown in Figure 7-10, and click OK. SSMS sends an XMLA command to SSAS to create the new database called

FIGURE 7-9

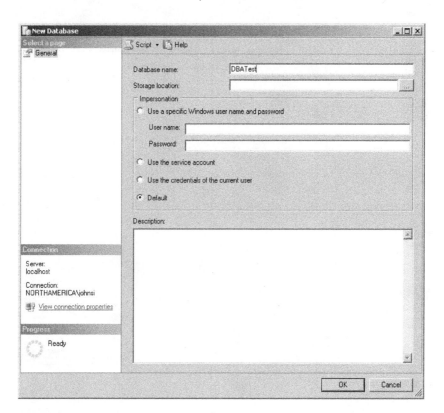

FIGURE 7-10

DBATest. SSMS then refreshes the Databases folder by retrieving the list of Databases from SSAS. You should see the DBATest database, as shown in Figure 7-11. If you are an administrator of SSAS, your account is a member of the Analysis Services server administrator role, as shown in Figure 7-6. If you want to provide a user with database administrator privileges and not Analysis Services server-wide privileges, you need to provide appropriate permissions at the database level. Continue following the next steps to provide database administrator permissions for a user.

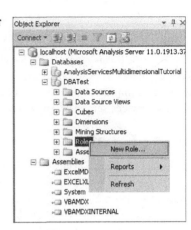

3. Expand the DBATest folder to see the various folders under DBATest.

FIGURE 7-11

4. Right-click the Roles folder, and select New Role.

5. In the Create Role dialog, check the Full control (Administrator) check box (shown in Figure 7-12) to provide full database administrator privileges.

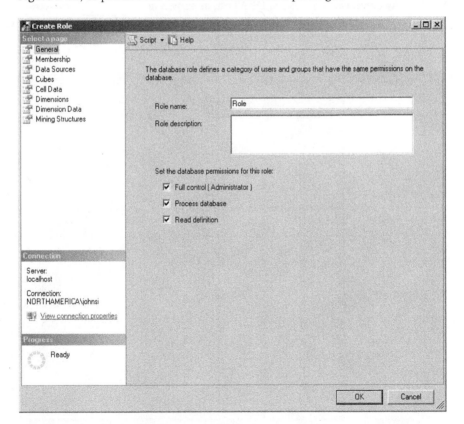

FIGURE 7-12

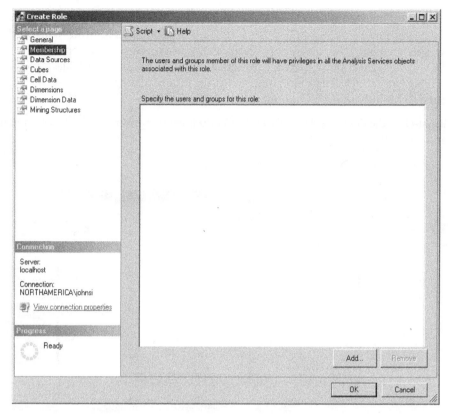

FIGURE 7-13

6. Select the Membership page in the dialog, as shown in Figure 7-13.

7. Click the Add button on the Membership page to bring up the Select Users or Groups dialog.

8. Enter the user or users for whom you want to provide database permissions, and click OK. You should now see the user you specified in the list of users who has database permissions listed in the Create Role dialog.

9. Click OK in the Create Role dialog.

You have successfully created a database called DBATest and provided full database permissions to a specific user. The user listed under the role Role will have full permissions to modify any of the objects that are part of the database DBATest including deleting the database. This user does not have permissions to perform any database operations outside of the DBATest database unless the same user is part of the Analysis Services Server administrator role.

Processing Analysis Services Database Objects

One of the important jobs of an Analysis Services Administrator is to process the objects (such as Cubes, Dimensions, and Mining Models) in an Analysis Services database. Analysis Services 2012 provides fine-grain control to the Analysis Services admin to process the objects within an

Analysis Services database using the Process dialog. You can launch the Process dialog by right-clicking the object folders such as Cubes, Dimensions, and Mining Structures — this works just as well on individual objects or groups of objects, too. Based on the location from which the Process dialog is launched, the options for processing the object or group of objects can vary. In addition to this you can select an object and launch the Process dialog. To process the database AnalysisServicesMultidimensionalTutorial, do the following:

1. Right-click the database AnalysisServicesMultidimensionalTutorial as shown in Figure 7-14, and select Process.

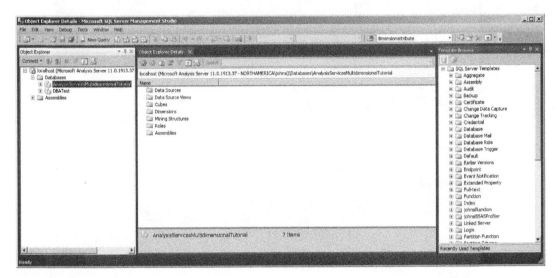

FIGURE 7-14

You see the Process dialog, as shown in Figure 7-15. This dialog shows the name of the object to be processed along with the type of object. Several processing options are available for each object. The default option for the database object is Process Full. As the name implies, the Process Full option enables you to process the selected object completely even if the object had been processed earlier. It can clear any data that was processed earlier.

2. When you click the OK button, the Process dialog sends an XMLA command to the Analysis Services instance to process the selected object. If you click the Script button and then select Script Action to New Query Window, you can see the Process XMLA command to be sent to the Analysis Services instance. You see the following script command:

```
<Batch xmlns="http://schemas.microsoft.com/analysisservices/2003/engine">
  <Parallel>
    <Process xmlns:xsd="http://www.w3.org/2001/XMLSchema"
    xmlns:xsi="http://www.w3.org/2001/XMLSchema-instance"
    xmlns:ddl2="http://schemas.microsoft.com/analysisservices/2003/engine/2"
```

```
    xmlns:ddl2_2="http://schemas.microsoft.com/analysisservices/2003/engine/2/2"
    xmlns:ddl100_100="http://schemas.microsoft.com/analysisservices/2008/
engine/100/100"
    xmlns:ddl200="http://schemas.microsoft.com/analysisservices/2010/engine/200"
    xmlns:ddl200_200="http://schemas.microsoft.com/analysisservices/2010/
engine/200/200"
    xmlns:ddl300="http://schemas.microsoft.com/analysisservices/2011/engine/300"
    xmlns:ddl300_300="http://schemas.microsoft.com/analysisservices/2011/
engine/300/300">
        <Object>
          <DatabaseID>AnalysisServicesMultidimensionalTutorial</DatabaseID>
        </Object>
        <Type>ProcessFull</Type>
        <WriteBackTableCreation>UseExisting</WriteBackTableCreation>
      </Process>
    </Parallel>
</Batch>
```

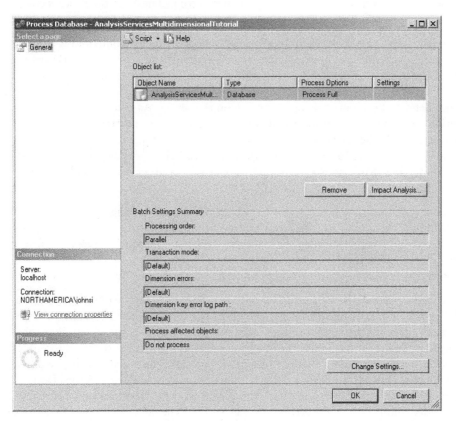

FIGURE 7-15

3. Click OK in this dialog to process the AnalysisServicesMultidimensionalTutorial database. When you click OK the Process dialog uses AMO to send the Process command to the Analysis Services instance.

The Process XMLA script contains several commands that are interpreted by Analysis Services. Because the medium of communication to Analysis Services is an XMLA request, the script is embedded within SOAP Envelope tags. This script can be executed from the XMLA editor within SQL Server Management Studio. SSMS adds the appropriate SOAP envelope tags to send the script to Analysis Services. The commands in the script are Batch, Parallel, and Process. The Process command is part of a set of commands that manipulates the data in Analysis Services. The Batch command enables multiple commands to be executed within a single statement. The Parallel command enables you to instruct the Analysis Services instance to execute all the commands within the command in parallel. The Process command is used to process an Analysis Services object and needs several properties such as DatabaseID, Process Type, and processing options (not shown in the previous XMLA script) such as parallelism for processing objects and actions to be taken during dimension key errors that can be changed using the Change Settings button in the Process dialog. You learn the processing options provided by the Process dialog in this chapter.

As mentioned earlier, when you click OK in the Process dialog, a Process command with appropriate options is sent to the Analysis Services instance. This command requests the server to process the database. When processing the objects within a database, the server needs to read data from the data source, which is done by issuing queries to it. You can now see the Process Progress dialog that shows details of each processing operation on the server. As you can see from Figure 7-16, the operations on each object within the database processed are reported along with the timing information and whether the operation succeeded or failed. You can also see the query sent to the relational data source to retrieve the data. The detailed information returned from Analysis Services is helpful if you need to investigate any issues in processing including the performance of processing an object.

When all the objects have been processed, you see the results of the processing command. If all the objects were successfully processed, you see Process succeeded in the status, as shown in Figure 7-16. If there were errors during processing, the status bar shows an appropriate message. The operations that resulted in an error are shown in red in the tree view of the Process Progress dialog. You can drill down into the details of the processing to understand the reasons for failure.

Several operations take place in the preceding processing command. All the objects within the database are processed in parallel based on the settings of the Analysis Services instance. If there are dependencies, the dependent objects are processed first. For example, the dimensions that are part of a cube need to be processed before the cube can be processed. Analysis Services processes all the objects of the database under a single transaction. What this means is that if one of the objects failed during processing, the remaining objects will not be processed and the effects of any previous operations will be rolled back. For example, if all the dimensions of a cube were successfully processed and if there were errors while processing the cube, the processing of the dimension objects will be rolled back. When all the objects have been successfully processed, the server commits the transaction, which means that the objects are marked as processed and are available for querying.

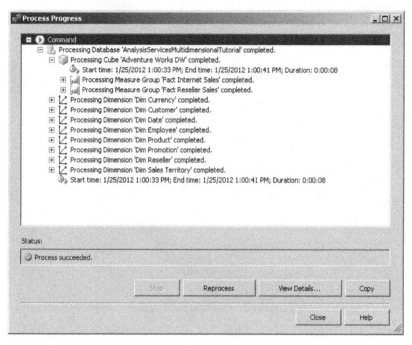

FIGURE 7-16

Assume an Analysis Services object has been processed and is queried by users. At the time users are querying the object, you can initiate processing on the same object. Because a version of the object is currently queried, Analysis Services stores the uncommitted processed object in a temporary file. At the time of commit, the server first ensures that the user is not using the objects, removes the previous version of the processed objects, and then marks the temporary files as primary. You see this in detail in the following section.

Processing a Cube

An Analysis Services database can contain several cubes and dimensions. You have the flexibility to control the processing of individual cubes and dimensions by launching the Process dialog from appropriate cube or dimension objects. There are several options for processing a cube, as shown in Figure 7-17. All the same processing options available for partitions and measure groups are available for the cube because a cube is a collection of measure groups, which in turn is a collection of partitions.

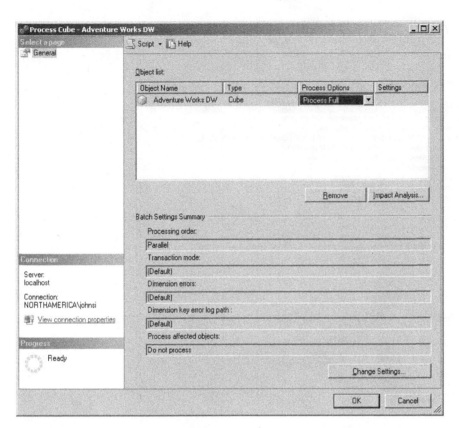

FIGURE 7-17

When a cube is created you typically do a full process (Process Full in the Process dialog) of it so that you can browse the cube. Usually, the cube structure does not change after the initial design completes. In this case, you process to get additional fact data that you would want to add to the cube. For example, you might have a Sales cube that you have created, and you might be getting sales fact data from each store every month. Processing the entire cube whenever new data comes in can take a considerable amount of time, causing end users to have to wait for a long period to see the most up-to-date data. Analysis Services 2012 provides you with an option to process only the new fact data instead of the entire cube. This is called incremental processing. To add new fact data to the cube, you can add a new partition to the cube and process that partition. Alternatively, you can use the Process Incremental option in the Process dialog and specify the query that provides the new fact data that needs to be processed. Process Incremental is a common management task for data warehouses. If you specify the Process Default option in the Process dialog, the server checks for all the objects that have not been processed and only processes those objects. If the cube data has been processed and if aggregations and indexes are not processed, then those are processed.

When you choose the Process Full option for processing a cube, the server performs three internal operations. If the storage mode for the cube is MOLAP, the server first reads the data from the relational data and stores it in a compact format. If there were aggregations defined for the cube, the server builds those aggregations during this processing. Finally, the server creates indexes for the data that helps speed access to data during querying. Even if there were no aggregations specified for the cube, the server still creates the indexes. The Process Data option actually is the first step of the Process Full option where the server reads data from relational data sources and stores it in proprietary format. The second and third steps of processing aggregations and indexes can be separately accomplished by the Process Index option. You might be wondering why you have the Process Data and Process Index options when the Process Full and Process Default options actually accomplish the same task. These options provide the administrator with a fine grain of control. These are especially important when you have limited time to access the relational data source and want to optimize the processing on your machine. Having multiple processing operations running in parallel can require more system resources. Specifically on a 32-bit (X86 machines) system, a large cube that fails on Process Full may be successfully processed by sending Process Data and Process Index commands one after another. In such instances, we recommend you first get the data from your relational backend into SSAS using the Process Data option. After you have all the data in the Analysis Services instance, you can then create your aggregations and indexes, which do not need access to the relational data source.

If you choose the Process Structure option, the server processes all the cube's dimensions and the cube definitions so that the cube's structure is processed without any processing of the data. The server will not process the partitions or measure groups of the cube; therefore, you cannot see any of the fact data. However, you can browse the cube because the cube definitions are processed. You can retrieve metadata information about the cube (measure names, measure groups, dimensions, KPIs, actions, and so on) after processing the cube's structure. However, you cannot query the cube data. For a cube that has been processed with Process Structure, you can see the cube in the SQL Server Management Studio MDX query editor when you select the drop-down list for the cube. If your cube contains linked measure groups and if they have been processed successfully, processing the cube with the Process Structure option enables you to query the measures in linked measure groups. Often when you design your UDM, you want to make sure your design is correct and your customers can see the right measures and dimensions. Process Structure is helpful in validating your design. As soon as the data for the cube is available, the cube can be processed with the Process Default option so that end users can query the data from the cube.

You can clear the data in the cube using the Unprocess option. The processing options provided in the Process dialog are different than the process types that are specified in the process command sent to Analysis Services. The following table shows how the various processing options map to the process types sent to Analysis Services:

PROCESS OPTIONS IN PROCESS DIALOG	PROCESS TYPE IN PROCESS COMMAND
Process Full	ProcessFull
Process Default	ProcessDefault
Process Data	ProcessData
Process Structure	ProcessStructure
Unprocess	ProcessClear
Process Index	ProcessIndexes
Process Incremental	ProcessAdd
Process Script Cache	ProcessScriptCache

The processed data of a cube are stored in a hierarchical directory structure equivalent to the structure you see in the Object Explorer. The metadata information about the cubes and dimensions are stored as XML files, and the data is stored in a proprietary format. Every time an object is processed, a new version number is appended to the object. The file `info.<versionnumber>` `.xml` stores the metadata information about the partition. Similar metadata files are stored within the directories of each object, cube, dimension, and measure group. You should browse through each object folder to see the metadata information. The fact data is stored in the file with extension `.data`. The key to an OLAP database is the fast access to data. You learned about a cell, which was represented by a tuple. A tuple is the intersection of various dimension members. For fast data access, Analysis Services builds indexes to access data across multiple dimensions. The index files in Analysis Services have the extension. `map`. The `.map` files that have the format `<version>` `.<Dimension>.<Hierarchy>.fact.map`. There is an associated header file for each map file. Analysis Services stores the data as blocks called segments for fast access. The associated header file contains offsets to the various segments for fast access during queries.

The processing dialog provides you the flexibility of processing objects in parallel or within the same transaction. If errors are encountered during processing, you can set options to handle these errors. You can configure the parallelism and error options by selecting the Change Settings button in the Process dialog. You see the Change Settings dialog, as shown in Figure 7-18, which enables you to configure certain processing options and error settings during processing. Setting the parallelism option is as simple as selecting the appropriate option in the Processing Order section of the dialog. By default, all the objects are processed in parallel and within the same transaction. If you do not want failure of one object to impact other objects, you should process the objects under different transactions by choosing the sequential option.

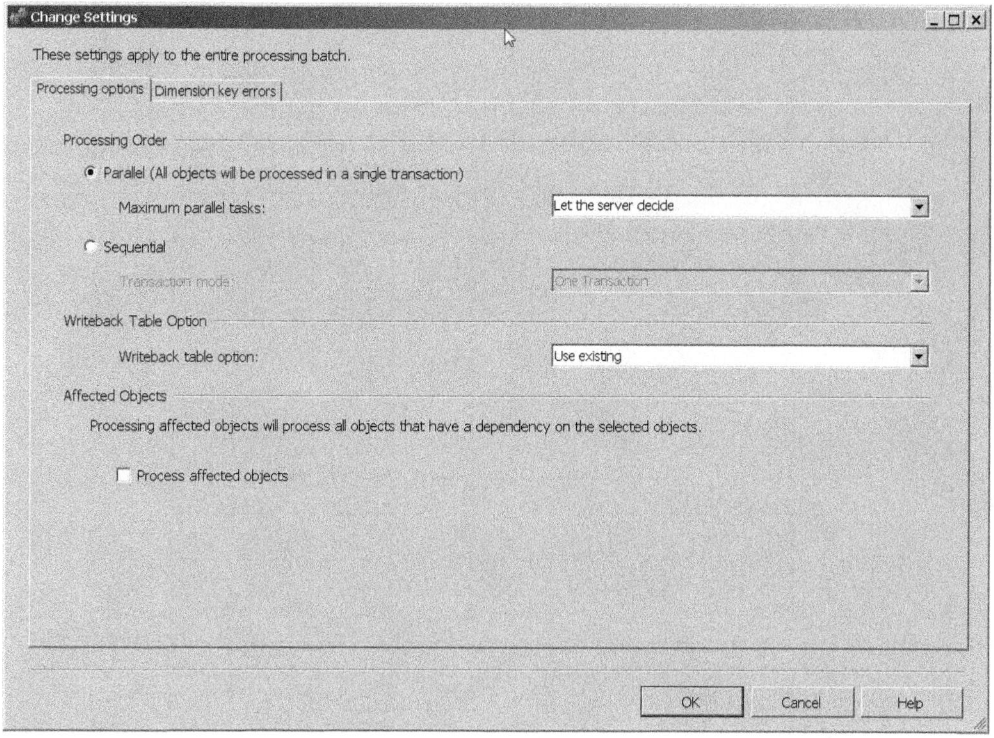

FIGURE 7-18

You might encounter errors while processing your Analysis Services objects due to incorrect design or referential integrity problems in the relational data source. For example, if you have a fact record that contains a dimension ID that is not available in the dimension table, you see a Key Not Found error while processing the cube. By default, when an error is encountered during processing, the processing operation fails. You can change the settings in the processing dialog to take appropriate action other than failing the processing operation. The Dimension key errors page of the Change Settings dialog, as shown in Figure 7-19, allows changing the error configuration settings for all the objects selected for processing. Whenever you encounter key errors, you can either convert the values to unknown or discard the erroneous records. You can run into key errors while processing facts or dimensions. If you encounter a key error while processing a cube, that means Analysis Services could not find a corresponding key in the dimension. You can assign the fact value to a member called the Unknown Member for that specific dimension. You can encounter key errors while processing a snowflake dimension when an attribute defined as a foreign key does not exist in the foreign table or when there are duplicate entries. The two most common types of key errors that you might encounter during dimension processing are Key not found and Duplicate key errors.

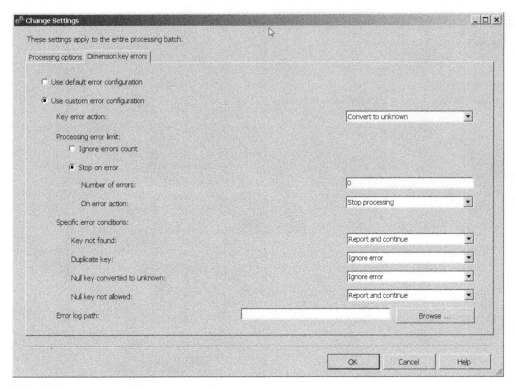

FIGURE 7-19

Processing a Dimension

You can process dimensions independent of the cubes they are a part of. After the initial processing of a dimension, you might process the dimensions on a periodic basis if additional records are added in the dimension table or there were changes to columns of an existing row. An example of additions to a dimension is new products being added to the products dimension. You would want this information to be reflected in the dimensions so that you can see the sales information for the new products. Another example of changes in dimension is when an employee moves from one city to another city; the attributes of the employee will need to change. Therefore, the Process Dimension dialog provides you with various options for processing the dimension, as shown in Figure 7-20.

While processing a dimension, Analysis Services reads data from the dimensions tables. When a dimension is processed, each attribute of the dimension is processed separately. Based on the parallelism specified on Analysis Services, these attributes can be processed in parallel. Each dimension contains an attribute called the All attribute. This is not exposed to the user but used internally by Analysis Services. You can see the files associated with this attribute as `<version>`. `(All)`.`<extension>`. When each attribute is processed, several files are created. Similar to fact data, dimension data is stored in a proprietary format. Each attribute of a dimension has a key column and a named column. These directly map into two different files with the extensions .kstore and .sstore,

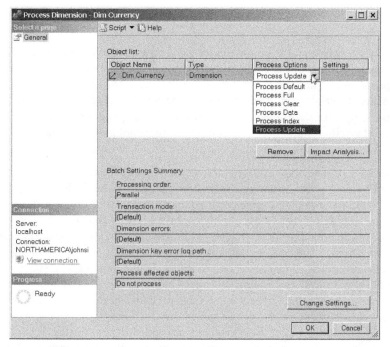

FIGURE 7-20

which refer to key store and string store, respectively. In addition, there are additional files that get created for each attribute of the dimension, which help in fast access to name, key, and levels of attributes and hierarchies. Files with the extension .map are created when indexes are processed for each attribute and help in fast retrieval of related attributes of the dimension for a dimension member.

The amount of time it takes to process a dimension depends on the number of attributes and hierarchies in the dimension as well as the number of members in each hierarchy. When a processing command is sent to the Analysis Services instance, the server reads the data from the relational data source and updates the dimension. When a dimension is processed, each attribute of the dimension is processed separately. Some attributes can be processed in parallel, whereas some cannot. The order of processing of various attributes is dependent on the relationships between the attributes in the dimensions and resources available on the machine. The relationships between attributes are defined at the dimension design time using the Attribute Relationships tab of the dimension designer, which you learned about in Chapter 5. For example, say you have a Customer dimension that contains the attributes Customer Name, SSN, City, State, and Country. Assume SSN is the Key attribute for this dimension and by default all attributes within the dimension are related to the key attribute. In addition, assume additional attribute relationships have been established. They are Country State, State City, City Customer Name, State Customer Name, and Country Customer Name. Based on the preceding relationships, the order of processing of the attributes in the Customer dimension is Country, State, City, Customer Name, and SSN. This is because Analysis Services needs to have information about Country to establish the member property relationship while processing the State, Customer Name, or SSN. The key attribute is always the last attribute processed within a dimension.

When the Process Default option is chosen for processing, the dimension's data or indexes are processed if they have not been processed or are out-of-date. If the Process Full option is chosen, the entire dimension is reprocessed. When the Process Full option is used, dimension data and indexes that have been processed initially will be dropped, and data is retrieved from the data source. The dimension processing time depends on the dimension size (number of dimension members as well as number of attributes and hierarchies in the dimension) and your machine resources.

Similar to incremental processing of the cubes, you can incrementally process dimensions using the Process Update option. The Process Update option in the Process dialog maps to the ProcessUpdate process type in the process command, which is applied only to dimensions. Some dimensions such as Employees or Customers or Products can potentially contain a large number of members. Additional members may have been added to these dimensions or some attributes of these dimension members might have changed. Often, a full processing of any dimension is not only unnecessary but cannot be afforded due to business needs. Under these circumstances, incremental processing of the dimension or an update of the attributes of the dimension should be sufficient. When you choose the Process Update option for the dimension, the server scans all the attributes in the dimension table. If there were changes to the dimension's properties, such as caption or description, they are updated. If new members are added to the dimension table, these members are added to the existing dimension using incremental processing. The attributes of each dimension member will also be updated. The key of each dimension member is assumed to be the same, but expect some attributes to be updated. The most important attribute that is updated is the member property for each member. When you have a parent-child hierarchy in a dimension and if the parent attribute has been changed, that information is updated during the Process Update processing option.

The Process Data option for dimensions queries the data source and updates the dimension with changes from the relational store. The indexes will not be processed when the Process Data option is used. The Process Index option creates indexes for attributes in the dimensions. If the ProcessMode dimension property is set to LazyAggregations, Analysis Services builds indexes for new attributes of the dimension as a lazy operation in the background thread. If you want to rebuild these indexes immediately you can do so by choosing the Process Index option. The Unprocess option is used to clear the data within the dimension.

Managing Partitions

Partitions enable you to distribute fact data within Analysis Services and aggregate data so that the resources on a machine can be efficiently utilized. When there are multiple partitions on the same server, you can reap the benefits of partitions because Analysis Services reads or writes data in parallel across multiple partitions. Fact data on the data source can be stored as several fact tables — Sales_Fact_2006, Sales_Fact_2007, and so on — or as a single, large fact table called Sales Fact. You can create multiple partitions within a measure group; one for each fact table in the data source or by splitting data from a single, large fact table through several queries. Partitions also enable you to split the data across two or more machines running Analysis Services, which are called Remote partitions.

As an administrator you might be thinking what the size of each partition should be to achieve the best results. In earlier versions of Analysis Services, Microsoft recommended each partition to be 3-5GB or 20 million records. More recent testing has shown that partition size does not have a substantial impact on query performance. Many Analysis Services administrators find it is much easier to maintain fewer large partitions as opposed to numerous smaller partitions. Your partition strategy should be based on the following:

➤ **Simplifying manageability of processing operations.** Try and keep the partition count small enough for efficient management. If you have 10,000 partitions that are 50MB each it becomes very tedious to manage.

➤ **Optimizing processing speed by maximizing parallelism within the boundaries of server's hardware.** If you have enough memory and CPU power to process four large partitions in parallel then go for it.

➤ **Improving query performance by partition elimination and support for different aggregation designs.** For more information on this see Partition elimination and Aggregation design under the Partitioning a Cube section in the Analysis Services Performance guide.

A sales cube's partitions, for example, often contain data spread across time. A new partition may be created for every month or a quarter as the data in the underlying data source is updated. As an administrator you would create a new partition from SQL Server Management Studio and process it so that it is available for users. To create a new partition, perform the following steps in SSDT:

1. Open the AnalysisServicesMultidimensionalTutorial project you have used in previous chapters.

2. Change the FactInternetSales table to a named query so that there is a where condition DueDateKey<20060101. In case you don't recall how this is done, here are the steps:

  a. Under the Data Source Views folder, Open Adventure Works DW.dsv.

  b. Right-click the FactInternetSales table in diagram view, and select the Replace Table with New Named Query menu item.

  c. In the Create Named Query dialog, in the DueDateKey Filter text entry box, enter <20060101. Your change automatically displays in the query window, as shown in Figure 7-21. Click OK to continue.

3. In the DSV, right-click in the diagram view, and select Add/Remove Tables from the context menu.

4. Add the FactInternetSales table to the Included objects: list, and click OK.

5. In the diagram view, replace the FactInternetSales table with a named query.

6. In the named query, set Filter to DueDateKey >=20060101.

7. Rename the named query as **FactInternetSalesNew**.

8. Deploy the AnalysisServices2012Tutorial project to your Analysis Services instance.

9. Connect to the AnalysisServices2012Tutorial database using SSMS.

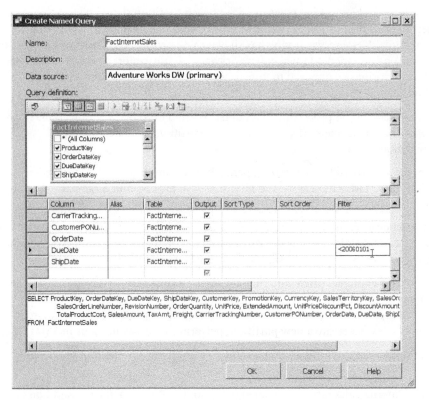

FIGURE 7-21

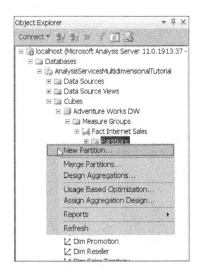

10. Navigate to the measure group FactInternetSales.

11. Right-click the Partitions folder, and select New Partition, as shown in Figure 7-22.

12. Click Next on the welcome screen of the Partition Wizard.

13. Choose the named query FactInternetSalesNew to create a new partition, as shown in Figure 7-23, and click Next. Select the check box Specify a query to restrict rows. As suggested by the warning in the Restrict Rows page (Figure 7-24) you may need to specify a restriction on the query to filter appropriate data for a partition. In this example, FactInternetSalesNew already has the appropriate query restriction.

14. Click the Next button.

FIGURE 7-22

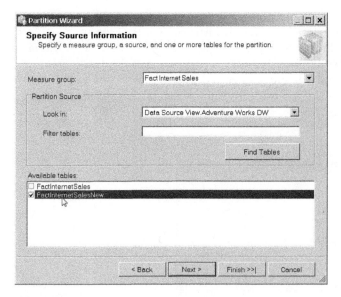

FIGURE 7-23

FIGURE 7-24

15. One way Analysis Services provides scalability is by use of remote partitions, where the partitions reside in two or more Analysis Services instances. On the Processing and Storage Locations page, as shown in Figure 7-25, you can specify where to store the partition. You can specify the remote Analysis Services instance on this page, but the data source to the remote Analysis Services instance should have been defined in this database. You can also change the storage location where you want the data for the partition to reside on any of the Analysis Services instances. Choose the default options, as shown in Figure 7-25, and click Next.

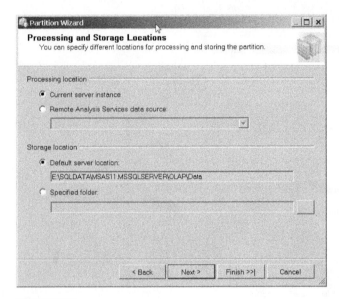

FIGURE 7-25

16. In the final page of the Partition Wizard, select Design aggregations later, Process Now, as shown in Figure 7-26, and click Finish.

17. In the Process Partition dialog, click OK to process the FactInternetSalesNew partition.

The partition processes, and you can browse the cube data. The number of partitions for a specific cube typically increases over time. Users might not browse historical data with the same granularity as that of the recent data. For example, you might be more interested in comparing Sales data for the current month to that of the previous month rather than data from 5 years ago. However, you might want to compare year-over-year data for several years. By merging the partition data, you can see some benefits during query performance. You learn about the considerations you should take into account to merge partitions in Chapter 10.

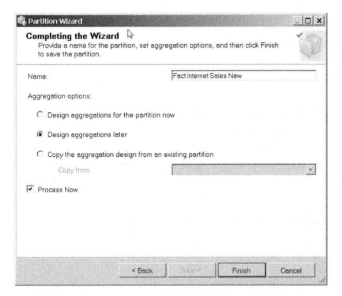

FIGURE 7-26

The two main requirements to merge partitions follow: The partitions should be of the same storage type, and they need to be on the same Analysis Services instance. Therefore, if you have remote partitions, they can be merged together only if they are on the same Analysis Services instance. To merge partitions, do the following:

1. Launch the Merge Partition dialog by right-clicking the Partitions folder under the Fact Internet Sales measure group.

2. In the Merge Partition dialog, as shown in Figure 7-27, select the Target partition that contains the merged data and the list of partitions to merge data, and click OK.

All the data from the source partitions merge into the target partition, and the source partitions are deleted due to this operation. SSMS sends the following command to Analysis Services to merge the partitions:

```
<MergePartitions xmlns="http://schemas.microsoft.com/analysisservices/2003/engine">
  <Sources>
    <Source>
      <DatabaseID>AnalysisServicesMultidimensionalTutorial</DatabaseID>
      <CubeID>Adventure Works DW</CubeID>
      <MeasureGroupID>Fact Internet Sales</MeasureGroupID>
      <PartitionID>Fact Internet Sales</PartitionID>
    </Source>
  </Sources>
  <Target>
```

```
        <DatabaseID>AnalysisServicesMultidimensionalTutorial</DatabaseID>
        <CubeID>Adventure Works DW</CubeID>
        <MeasureGroupID>Fact Internet Sales</MeasureGroupID>
        <PartitionID>Fact Internet Sales New</PartitionID>
      </Target>
    </MergePartitions>
```

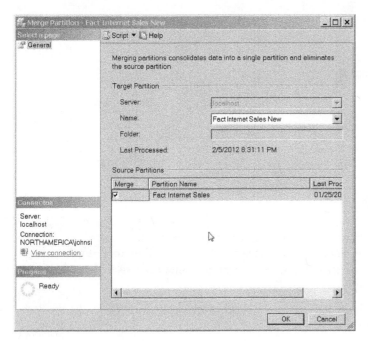

FIGURE 7-27

Managing Assemblies

Assemblies, also called stored procedures, help you to perform specific tasks on the Analysis Services database or across the server. For example, Analysis Services has four assemblies installed that provide you with the functionality of calling Excel or VBA functions within your MDX queries. The System Assembly is used for operations such as Backup or Restore in retrieving information such as folders containing Analysis Services backup files, as well as supporting data mining algorithm requests. Analysis Services 2012 supports two types of assemblies: COM user-defined functions (UDFs) and .NET assemblies. COM UDFs are primarily supported for backward compatibility with Analysis Services 2000. In this section you learn about managing assemblies on your Analysis Services instance.

Only Analysis Services administrators can add assemblies. You need to make sure your instance of Analysis Services is safe and secure irrespective of the operations done by the stored procedures. Security is always a concern, and you do not want any assemblies to bring down the server. The administrator needs to enable certain components and options to make assemblies available to users. By default, Analysis Services does not allow execution of stored procedures. The administrator first needs to enable the server property `Feature\ComUdfEnabled` to true. This can be accomplished by changing `Feature\ComUdfEnabled` from 0 to 1 in the `msmdsrv.ini` file or changing the `Feature\ComUdfEnabled` to true using the Analysis Services properties dialog.

The key to managing assemblies is to understand the nature of the assembly and setting appropriate properties while adding assemblies to your Analysis Services server. Figure 7-28 shows the dialog used to add assemblies to the server or to a specific database. You can launch this dialog by right-clicking the Assemblies folder under a specific database and choosing New Assembly.

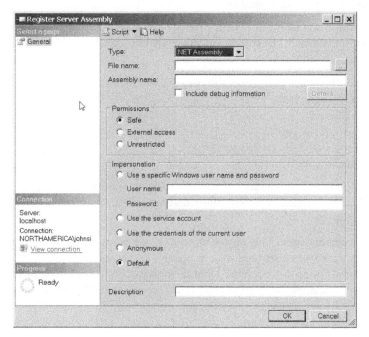

FIGURE 7-28

Analysis Services supports two types of assemblies: COM and .NET CLR assemblies. When you specify the type and name of the assemblies in the Register Assembly dialog, you need to specify the security information for these assemblies. Two parameters control the security of these stored procedures: Impersonation and Permissions. Permissions enable you to define the scope of access for the assembly, such as accessing the file system, accessing the network, and accessing unmanaged code. Following are three different values for permissions:

➤ **Safe:** The most secure of the three permissions. When the Safe permission set is specified for an assembly, it means that the assembly is intended only for computation and the assembly cannot access any protected resource. It guarantees protection against information leaks and elevation attacks by malicious code.

➤ **External access:** This permission value enables access to external resources by the assembly without compromising reliability but does not offer any specific security guarantees. You can use this if you as the DBA trust the programmer's ability to write good code and if there is a need to access external resources such as data from an external file.

➤ **Unrestricted:** This set value is primarily intended for people who have a good understanding of programming on servers and need access to all resources. This permission set does not guarantee any code security or reliability. Unrestricted access should be allowed only to assemblies that have been written by users who absolutely need access to external resources who have a good understanding of all security issues, such as denial-of-service attacks and information leakage and can handle all these within the stored procedures. Use this option only when it is absolutely essential and you have full confidence in the programming abilities of the developer who has developed the assembly.

All COM DLLs have the Permissions parameter set to Unrestricted. The Impersonation parameter allows you to specify the account under which the stored procedure will be executed. Following are five different values for Impersonation:

➤ **Default:** The Default value allows you to execute the stored procedure under a secure mode with the minimum privileges. If the assembly is of type COM, the default value is Use the Credentials of the Current User. For a .NET assembly, the default value depends on the permission set defined. If the permission set is Safe, the Impersonation mode is Impersonate Service Account, but if the permission set is External Access or Unrestricted, the Impersonation mode is Impersonate Current User.

➤ **Anonymous:** If you want the stored procedure to be executed as an anonymous user, you need to select Impersonate Anonymous. You have limited access when the stored procedure is executed under this setting.

➤ **Use the credentials of the current user:** This impersonation mode is typically used when you want the stored procedure to be executed with the user's credentials. This is a safe option to select. If the stored procedure accesses external resources and the current user executing the stored procedure does not have permissions, execution of the stored procedure does not cause any ill effects. A use of this impersonation mode is to define dynamic data security where the current user's credential is needed to access external resources.

➤ **Use the service account:** If you choose to use the service account, whenever the stored procedure executes, it executes under the credentials of service startup account for Analysis Services. An example of a stored procedure that would need this impersonation mode is an AMO stored procedure that does management operations on the server.

➤ **Use a specific Windows user name and password:** If your business needs a stored procedure to always be executed in the context of a specific user, you need to choose this option. You need to specify a Windows account name and password for this impersonation mode. A typical example in which you might use this option is when you access an external data source or web service to retrieve data with this account and use that value within the stored procedure for computation. If you choose this option, you need to make sure you update the password on the account when there is a password change.

COM assemblies should use the credentials of the current user impersonation, whereas for .NET CLR assemblies should use the appropriate impersonation mode based on your customer scenario. As an administrator of Analysis Services, you need to choose the impersonation and permission setting that suits your business needs and does not compromise the security of your Analysis Services instance.

When you register an assembly with a specific Analysis Services database or for the server using the Register Assembly dialog, AMO sets up the correct properties. This, in turn, sends a Create command to the Analysis Services instance as shown here:

```
<Create AllowOverwrite="true" xmlns="http://schemas.microsoft.com/analysisservices/
2003/engine">
    <ObjectDefinition>
        <Assembly xsi:type="ClrAssembly" xmlns:xsd="http://www.w3.org/2001/
XMLSchema" xmlns:xsi="http://www.w3.org/2001/XMLSchema-instance"
xmlns:ddl2="http://schemas.microsoft.com/analysisservices/2003/engine/2"
xmlns:ddl2_2="http://schemas.microsoft.com/analysisservices/2003/engine/2/2"
xmlns:ddl100_100="http://schemas.microsoft.com/analysisservices/2008/engine/100/100"
xmlns:ddl200="http://schemas.microsoft.com/analysisservices/2010/engine/200"
xmlns:ddl200_200="http://schemas.microsoft.com/analysisservices/2010/engine/200/200"
xmlns:ddl300="http://schemas.microsoft.com/analysisservices/2011/engine/300"
xmlns:ddl300_300="http://schemas.microsoft.com/analysisservices/2011/engine/300/300">
            <ID>AmoSproc</ID>
            <Name>AmoSproc</Name>
            <Description/>
            <ImpersonationInfo>
              <ImpersonationMode>Default</ImpersonationMode>
            </ImpersonationInfo>
            <Files>
              <File>
                <Name>AmoSproc.dll</Name>
                <Type>Main</Type>
                <Data>
    <Block>------------Content about the stored procedure------</Block>
    <Block>------------Content about the stored procedure------</Block>
     <Block>------------Content about the stored procedure------</Block>
     <Block>------------Content about the stored procedure------</Block>
                </Data>
              </File>
            </Files>
            <PermissionSet>Safe</PermissionSet>
        </Assembly>
    </ObjectDefinition>
</Create>
```

The information within the Block tag is a large amount of text content, which for illustration purposes has been restricted to a single line. This text within the Block tag is the assembly to be registered that will be stored within the Analysis Services instance. When queries use functions within the assembly, Analysis Services loads the assembly within the same process and executes the CLR assembly with the appropriate parameter passing. The results from the assembly are appropriately passed back to Analysis Services for further evaluation of a query.

Backup and Restore

Backup is an extremely critical operation for any data warehouse. There are several reasons why you should periodically back up your Analysis Services database. One reason is for disaster recovery; another is for auditing purposes. Irrespective of purpose, it is always a good idea to back up your database on a periodic basis. You can back up databases on your Analysis Services instance through SSMS. Follow these steps to back up the AnalysisServicesMultidimensionalTutorial database:

1. Using SSMS, connect to the Analysis Services instance.

2. In the Object Explorer window, navigate to the database AnalysisServicesMultidimensionalTutorial.

3. Right-click the database and select Back Up.

   You see the Backup Database dialog, as shown in Figure 7-29. By default, the dialog chooses the database name as the backup name. By default, the backup file is created in the Backup folder of your Analysis Services installation. If you want the backup to be stored in a location on a different drive or directory, you first need to change the Analysis Services server property AllowedBrowsingFolder by adding the appropriate directory. You can then choose the folder by clicking Browse in the Backup Database dialog.

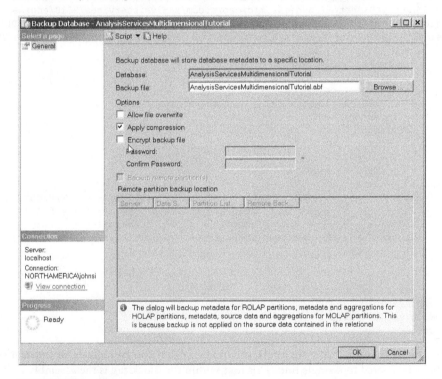

FIGURE 7-29

   You have the option to encrypt the database and specify a password. You need that password to restore the database. If you have remote partitions in the database, you have the option to specify the backup location for each remote partition. Backup of these partitions is done on respective Analysis Services instances on that machine.

4. Disable the option to encrypt the backup file.

5. Select the option Allow File Overwrite to overwrite any existing backup files with the same name.

6. Choose the default backup filename, and click OK.

SSMS sends the following command to the Analysis Services instance to back up the database AnalysisServices2012Tutorial:

```
<Backup xmlns="http://schemas.microsoft.com/analysisservices/2003/engine">
      <Object>
         <DatabaseID>AnalysisServicesMultidimensionalTutorial</DatabaseID>
      </Object>
      <File>AnalysisServicesMultidimensionalTutorial.abf</File>
   </Backup>
```

Analysis Services 2012 enables you to back up multiple databases at the same time. Through the SQL Server Management Studio, you can launch the backup command from multiple databases and run backups in parallel. Alternatively, you can create a DDL that executes backup of multiple databases within the same command.

Whenever you want to restore an Analysis Services database for which you have a backup, you can do so using the Restore Database dialog. Follow these steps to restore the AnalysisServicesMultidimensionalTutorial backup:

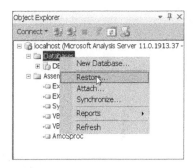

1. In SSMS Object Explorer, right-click the AnalysisServicesMultidimensionalTutorial, and select Delete.

2. In the Delete Objects dialog, click OK.

3. In the SSMS Object Explorer, right-click the Databases folder, as shown in Figure 7-30, and select Restore.

FIGURE 7-30

4. In the Restore Database dialog (see Figure 7-31) click the Browse button next to Backup file.

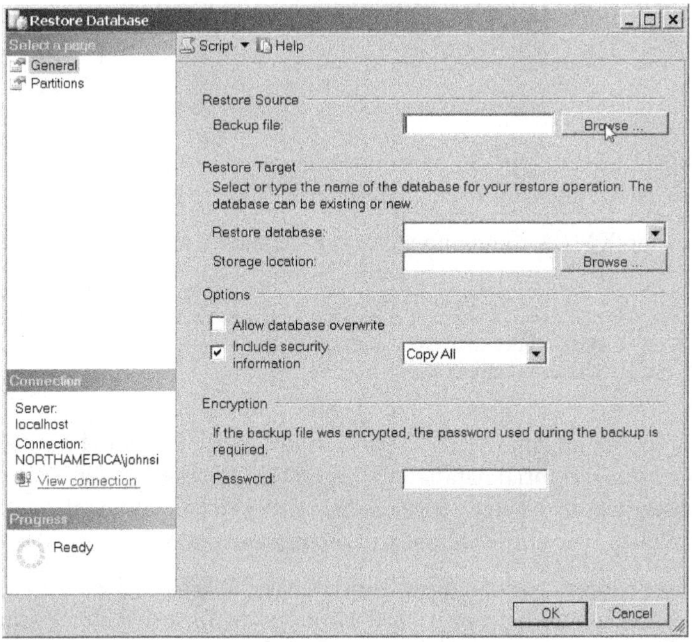

FIGURE 7-31

5. In the Locate Database Files dialog, navigate to the Backup folder, and select the AnalysisServicesMultidimensionalTutorial.abf file, as shown in Figure 7-32, and click OK.

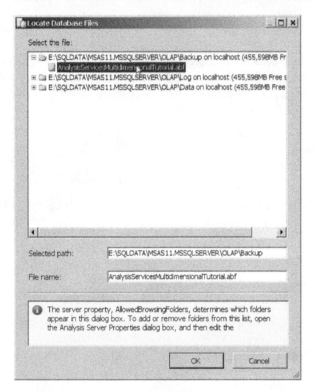

FIGURE 7-32

6. Click OK. You do not need to type the name in the combo box next to Restore Database unless you want to change the database name from the name that was restored.

SSMS now sends the following XMLA command to restore the database on your Analysis Services instance:

```
<Restore xmlns="http://schemas.microsoft.com/analysisservices/2003/engine">
<File>E:\SQLDATA\MSAS11.MSSQLSERVER\OLAP\Backup\
AnalysisServicesMultidimensionalTutorial.abf</File>
</Restore>
```

If you refresh the list of databases on your Analysis Services instance, you should now see the AnalysisServicesMultidimensionalTutorial database in the SSMS Object Explorer. If a database with the same name and ID exists on your Analysis Services instance, you can restore the newer database by clicking the Allow Database Overwrite check box in the Restore dialog.

After the database has been restored, you can query the database. You can take a backup of a database from your test servers and restore it on your production server. In such a circumstance you might choose to skip the security information if the security defined on production servers is different from those on your test servers. In such a circumstance you would need to ensure you secure the database by defining the right security on production servers. In a circumstance where the backup was taken on your production server and you are restoring the database on an upgraded production machine, expect that users must restore the database with the security information.

Detach and Attach

Analysis Services provides you the functionality to detach and attach a complete database from an Analysis Services instance. These detach and attach commands differ from backup and restore commands. The attach operation enables you to mark a specific database read-only, and the database's data files do not need to be stored in the default Data folder path of your Analysis Services instance. The read-only feature allows you to have a shared scalable architecture of Analysis Services for situations in which you have a need to scale out the server to multiple users who are querying a specific Analysis Services database.

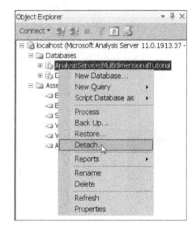

Follow these steps to detach the AnalysisServicesMultidimensionalTutorial database:

1. In SSMS, right-click the AnalysisServicesMultidimensionalTutorial database, and select Detach, as shown in Figure 7-33.

2. In the Detach Database dialog, as shown in Figure 7-34, click OK.

FIGURE 7-33

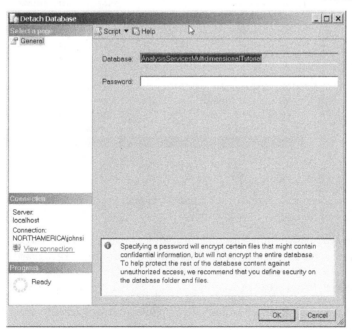

FIGURE 7-34

SSMS sends the following XMLA command to the Analysis Services instance:

```
<Detach xmlns="http://schemas.microsoft.com/analysisservices/2003/engine">
      <Object>
        <DatabaseID>AnalysisServicesMultidimensionalTutorial</DatabaseID>
      </Object>
    </Detach>
```

After receiving the detach command, Analysis Services first takes a write lock on the database to be detached. Taking a write lock means all existing DDL operations must complete before the detach command is started. The Analysis Services instance creates a detach log file that contains the version information, the key used for encrypting the database (if specified), and a few additional pieces of information about the database with the name AnalysisServicesMultidimensionalTutorial.detach_log. This log file is created within the database folder, as shown in Figure 7-35. Analysis Services then commits and deletes the database. The entire database folder is now independent and can be copied and attached to another Analysis Services instance.

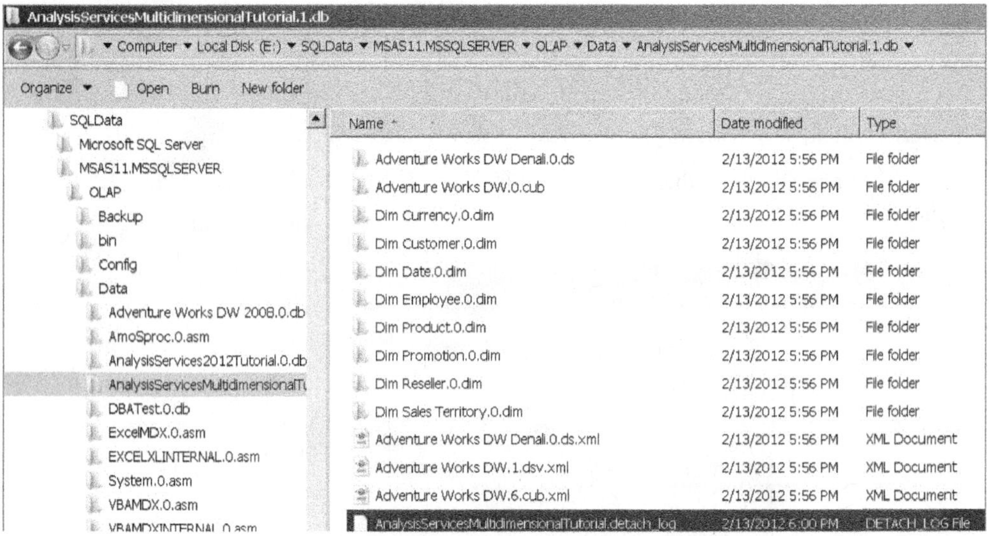

FIGURE 7-35

You can now attach the detached database to your Analysis Services instance. Follow these steps to attach the database in read-only mode:

1. Move the AnalysisServicesMultidimensionalTutorial database folder that was detached from its original location to a new location; for example, move from `%Program Files%\Microsoft SQL Server\MSAS11.SQLServer\OLAP\Data` to `%Program Files%\Microsoft SQL Server\MSAS11.SQLServer\OLAP`.

2. If prompted by the operating system to provide administrative privileges to move the folder, provide the permissions.

3. In the SSMS Object Explorer, right-click the Databases folder, and select Attach, as shown in Figure 7-36.

4. In the Attach Database dialog, specify the full path of the AnalysisServicesMultidimensionalTutorial database, as shown in Figure 7-37.

FIGURE 7-36

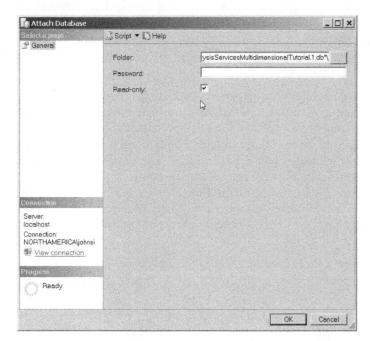

FIGURE 7-37

 When I have the database folder open in Windows Explorer, I like to Shift + right-click the name of the folder and select Copy as path and then paste in the folder location of the Attach Database dialog. You will need to remove the quotes but it still saves time.

5. Enable the check box next to Read-only, and click OK.

6. Refresh the Databases folder in the SSMS Object Explorer.

You can now see that the AnalysisServicesMultidimensionalTutorial database is read-only by right-clicking the database and selecting Properties and checking the Read-Write Mode property. You see the Read-Write Mode property set to ReadOnly. The read-only database feature in Analysis Services helps to have a shared scalable database architecture where you can have a single database folder on a Storage Area Network (SAN) attached to multiple Analysis Services instances. You learn how this is helpful in query performance in Chapter 11.

Synchronization

Synchronization sounds like a sophisticated, highly technical area of endeavor, but actually, it couldn't be simpler; consider synchronization as just replication for Analysis Services 2012 databases. The name actually is suitable because it allows you to "synchronize" the Analysis Services database resident on one Analysis Services instance to the same database on another Analysis Services instance. Typically, you can expect Analysis Services DBAs to test the designed Analysis Services database in a test environment before they move them to their production servers. The DBAs often need to back up their database on test servers and restore them on production servers. However, through the synchronization feature in Analysis Services 2012, you can move well-tested databases from test servers to production servers with ease.

If you have an Analysis Services instance actively supporting a population of users, you might want to update the database they're querying against without taking the system down to do so. Using the Synchronize Database Wizard, you can accomplish the database update seamlessly. The wizard can copy both data and metadata from your development and test machine (staging server) to the production server and automatically switch users to the newly copied data and metadata based on conditions defined on production server. To try this out, you need to have two instances of Analysis Services installed on another machine, or have a second instance of Analysis Services installed on your current machine. You should install another instance called SS2012 on the same machine. Follow these steps to synchronize a database from the default instance to the new named instance SS2012:

1. Launch SSMS and connect to your default instance (localhost) and named instance (localhost\ss2012) of Analysis Services, as shown in Figure 7-38.

2. Right-click the Databases folder of the named instance, and select Synchronize, as shown in Figure 7-38.

3. If you see the welcome screen, click Next.

4. On the Select Database to Synchronize page of the Synchronize Database Wizard, type the default instance **localhost** as the Source server, and select the Source database AnalysisServicesMultidimensionalTutorial, as shown in Figure 7-39, and click Next. On the Specify Locations for Local Partitions page, you can change locations of the partitions during synchronizations if the destination server allows it. In Figure 7-40 you can see that all the partitions of AnalysisServicesMultidimensionalTutorial are restored in the default location.

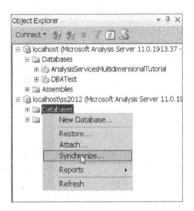

FIGURE 7-38

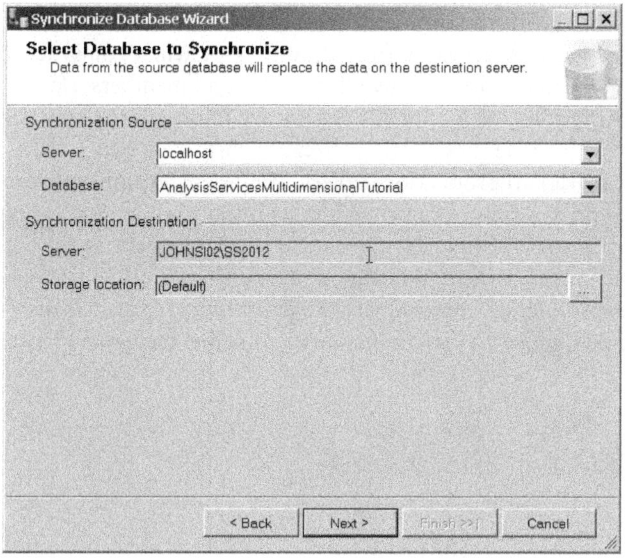

FIGURE 7-39

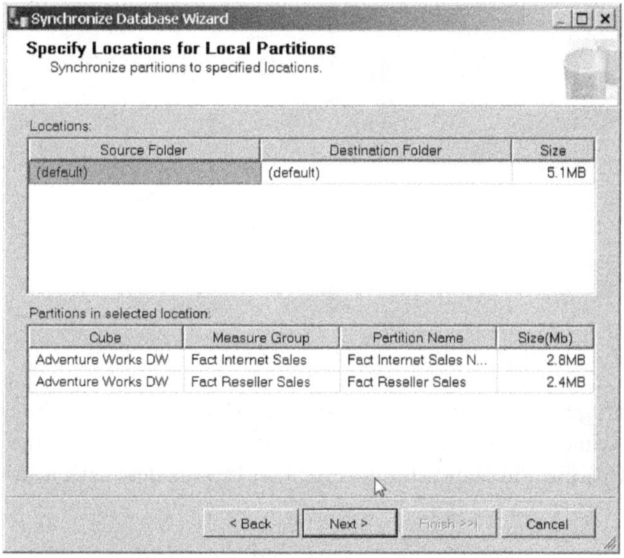

FIGURE 7-40

5. On the Specify Locations for Local Partitions page, click Next. On the Synchronization Options page, you can specify the level of security information to copy when you synchronize, as shown in Figure 7-41. You can choose to copy all the roles and members, skip the membership information for the roles, or ignore all the security information. Analysis Services 2012 has been designed to provide these options because customers might choose to synchronize databases from test servers to production servers. While synchronizing databases from test to production servers, you can choose to keep all roles if the security permissions in the test environment are identical to the ones in the production environment. If the security permissions have been defined in such a way that they can be utilized in the production environment but the users in the production environment are different, you can use the Ignore all option. If you choose the Ignore all option, you need to define membership after synchronization.

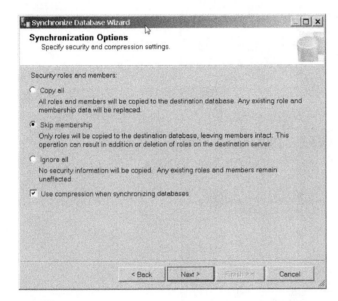

FIGURE 7-41

6. Select the Skip membership option, as shown in Figure 7-41, and click Next. On the Select Synchronization Method page, you can choose to start the synchronization process immediately or script the command to a file and later send the command to the destination server using SSMS or through other programs.

7. Select the Synchronize now method, as shown in Figure 7-42, and click Next.

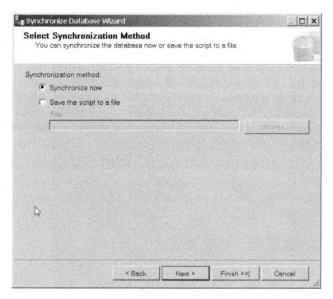

FIGURE 7-42

8. Review the synchronization options you have selected on the Completing the Wizard page, and click Finish.

SSMS sends the following XMLA command to the Analysis Services SS2012 instance to synchronize the AnalysisServices2012Tutorial database from the SQLServer2012 instance:

```
<Synchronize xmlns:xsi="http://www.w3.org/2001/XMLSchema-instance"
xmlns:xsd="http://www.w3.org/2001/XMLSchema" xmlns="http://schemas.microsoft.com/
analysisservices/2003/engine">
  <Source>
    <ConnectionString>Provider=MSOLAP.5;Data Source=localhost;
Integrated Security=SSPI;Initial Catalog=AnalysisServicesMultidimensionalTutorial
</ConnectionString>
    <Object>
      <DatabaseID>AnalysisServicesMultidimensionalTutorial</DatabaseID>
    </Object>
  </Source>
  <SynchronizeSecurity>SkipMembership</SynchronizeSecurity>
  <ApplyCompression>true</ApplyCompression>
</Synchronize>
```

You should be aware that the destination server contacts the source server for synchronization using the credentials of the service startup account and not the user who initiated the synchronize operation from SSMS.

You do need to make sure the service startup account of the destination server has credentials to access the databases on the source server. The source server creates a backup of the objects that have changed in the source server, compresses them, and then sends them to the destination server. On the destination server these objects are first restored under a temporary name. If there are active queries being executed against the database on the destination server, the server waits for those queries to complete and then updates the objects. On the source server, the objects are locked during synchronization. Until the time the objects are sent to the destination server, you cannot perform operations, such as processing, or other actions that modify the objects.

9. You see the progress of the synchronization operation in the Database Synchronization Progress dialog, shown in Figure 7-43. You can see the progress percentage of the synchronization shown on this page, which gets updated periodically. After the synchronization completes, you see the message in the page, as shown in Figure 7-43. Click Close.

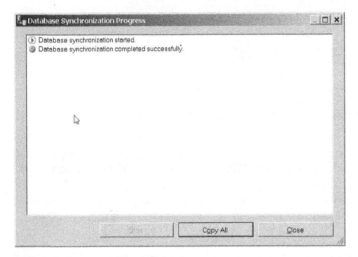

FIGURE 7-43

You can use the synchronization wizard periodically to synchronize the database from source server to destination server. You can typically expect the source server to be your test environment and the destination server to be the production environment. Synchronization is a pull model operation where the destination server pulls data from the source server. If a version of the database exists on the destination server, the source server sends only the data. Typically on the destination server, you might have established new membership or security permissions. If you choose appropriate options to skip membership or ignore roles during synchronization, security permissions on the destination servers will not be changed.

You must implement an important security requirement to complete a successful synchronization. The destination server's service startup account must have access to the databases on the source server that are expected to be synchronized. You may get an error such as "Either the user, NT SERVICE\MSOLAP$SS2012, does not have access to the AnalysisServicesMultidimensionalTutorial database, or the database does not exist."

Managing Security

As an administrator, managing security is the most critical operation for the Analysis Services database. The phrase "managing security" can mean several things: managing the roles of Analysis Services databases, using the Analysis Services security features dimension and cell security, enabling and disabling features in Analysis Services, and setting up Analysis Services with appropriate firewall protection. The latter ensures your Analysis Services instance can appropriately communicate via the Internet and intranet.

Server and Database Roles

Roles are of vital importance to securing databases on your Analysis Services instance. You deal with two kinds of roles when using the product: the server role and database roles. The server role is required for use by a login that performs administrative functions through the user interface (SSMS) or programmatically using AMO. The database roles are defined on an as-needed basis. You can provide read/write permissions to users for all objects in the database or as fine grain as certain cells in a cube. You learned about the server role and how to specify membership earlier in this chapter. In Chapters 9 and 14, you learn to define read/write access for dimensions and cubes in a database.

The Create Role dialog, accessed by right-clicking the Roles folder under a database node in Object Explorer, has the capability to provide full database access to a user, as shown earlier in this chapter. In addition, Roles objects in a database help the DBA define fine-grain access to various database objects. The pages in the Create Role dialog are identical to the Role designer, which you learn more about in Chapter 14. See Chapter 9 for more details on granting dimension and cube access to Analysis Services users. Chapter 14 provides extensive coverage of database role management through a scenario that shows how to restrict access to specific dimension members (dimension security) or cells in a cube (cell security).

To recap briefly, you as the database administrator can add roles to a specific database, add members to a role, and provide read, write, or read/write access to a role. In addition, you can specify the cell security and dimension security for this role using MDX expressions to limit access to specific cell data or dimension members. When a user is part of multiple roles, Analysis Services provides you access to data in a least restrictive manner. If a user has been restricted access to members of a dimension in one role and has been provided access to the same members in another role, the user can access the members.

Enabling or Disabling Features

Managing database roles is one aspect of securing data in Analysis Services. You can add users to the server role so that you can have several administrators for your Analysis Services instance. Administrators can define appropriate levels of access to databases and objects within a database. However, there is another level of protection that Analysis Services 2012 provides. You can disable features that are not used by your users. One of the most common ways to protect your server from security attacks is to reduce your attack surface by running your server or application with minimum functionality. For example, you can turn off unused services of an operating system that listen for requests from users by default. When features are needed, an administrator can enable them. Similarly, Analysis Services allows you to enable or disable certain features to prevent security attacks, thereby making your Analysis Services installation more secure. Following is the list of server properties that you can use to enable or disable certain features or services of your Analysis Services instance:

➤ `Feature\ManagedCodeEnabled`

➤ `Feature\LinkInsideInstanceEnabled`

➤ `Feature\LinkToOtherInstanceEnabled`

➤ `Feature\LinkFromOtherInstanceEnabled`

➤ `Feature\COMUDFEnabled`

➤ `Feature\ConnStringEncryptionEnabled`

➤ `Datamining\AllowAdhocOpenRowSetQueries`

➤ `Security\RequireClientAuthentication`

The properties LinkInsideInstanceEnabled, LinkToOtherInstanceEnabled, and LinkFromOtherInstanceEnabled enable or disable linked objects (measure groups and dimensions) within the same instance and between instances of Analysis Services. The properties ManagedCodeEnabled and COMUDFEnabled allow/disallow loading assemblies to Analysis Services. You can allow or deny ad-hoc open row set data mining queries using the property Datamining\AllowAdhocOpenRowSetQueries. The server property Security\RequireClientAuthentication allows or denies anonymous connections to Analysis Services. You can force clients to connect using encryption using the ConnStringEncryptionEnabled property. You can change these properties using the properties dialog for an Analysis Services instance.

ONLINE MODE

As an administrator, you need to ensure that databases and their objects are kept up to date. Otherwise, your end users will query out-of-date information. After creating an OLAP database in SSMS, you can use the Create Role dialog to create roles and provide permissions to specific users that allow them to be database administrators. To reduce confusion, deployed Analysis Services projects should be named the same as the database created by the server administrator. After the database is created, the server or the database administrator can perform administrative operations using SSMS such as adding new roles, adding assemblies, or processing objects periodically. There might be certain design changes that you must make to the database based on additional requirements from the end users. In such a circumstance you cannot make the changes in the original project and deploy that project to the Analysis Services instance because the new objects added to the database will likely be deleted. Analysis Services 2012 provides you two ways to make additional changes. You can connect to the Analysis Services database on the server directly through SSDT and then make the changes in a mode called online mode. The second option is to import the database into your Analysis Services instance using the Import Analysis Services 2012 Database project (one of the Business Intelligence Project templates that can be used from SSDT), make changes to the database in project mode, and then redeploy the project to the Analysis Services instance.

The former is recommended because you can not only make changes directly on the server, which updates the objects immediately, but you can also perform processing tasks on objects. Instead of designing your Analysis Services database in project mode and then deploying it to the Analysis Services instance, you can design the entire database by connecting to the database in online mode. Follow these steps to connect to an Analysis Services database in online mode using SSDT:

1. From All Programs ➤ Microsoft SQL Server 2012 ➤ SQL Server Data Tools, launch SSDT.

2. To open an Analysis Services database in online mode, select File ➤ Open ➤ Analysis Services Database, as shown in Figure 7-44. In the Connect to Database dialog, you have the choice of opening an existing database or creating a new database on the Analysis Services instance. You need to be a server administrator to create a database on the Analysis Services instance.

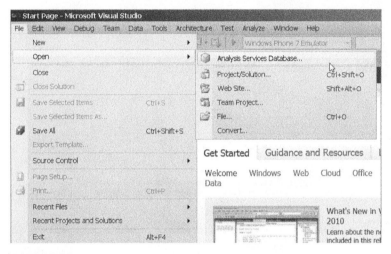

FIGURE 7-44

3. Type the Analysis Services instance name, and select a database to open in online mode, as shown in Figure 7-45, and click OK.

SSDT connects to the Analysis Services instance and retrieves all the database objects. You see all the objects of the database in the Solution Explorer similar to the project mode, as shown in Figure 7-46. With the database connected in online mode, the Analysis Services instance name is indicated next to the database name in the Solution Explorer. All the operations that you performed on the objects within a database in the project mode can be performed in the online mode. You do not have the deployment option for the database. Instead, you save all your changes directly to the server. You should explore making changes or adding new objects in the online mode and then saving the changes directly on the Analysis Services instance.

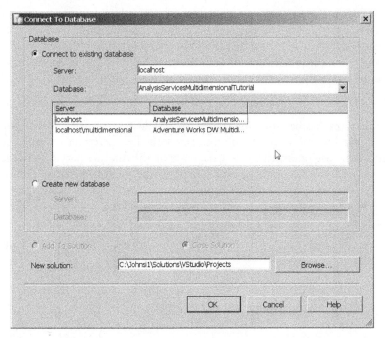

FIGURE 7-45

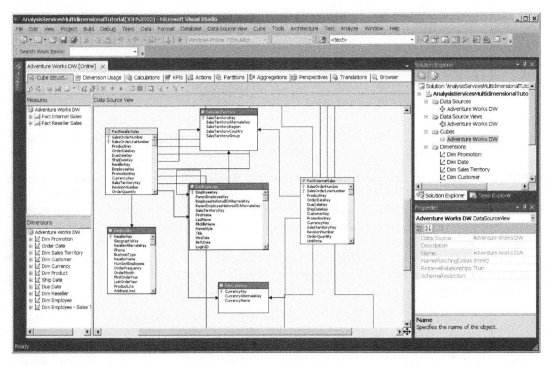

FIGURE 7-46

PROGRAMMATIC AND ADVANCED ADMINISTRATION

In Analysis Services 2005, 2008, and 2012 you have the option to automate administrative processes using XMLA commands or using AMO, which in turn communicates with the server using XMLA. AMO provides a well-defined, extremely helpful object model that extracts, executes, and discovers XMLA commands that need to be sent to the server. Almost all the user interfaces you saw in SQL Server Management Studio use the AMO object model while communicating to the server. In this chapter, you learn to manage Analysis Services using AMO. You learn about using XMLA commands and SQL Server Integration Services (SSIS) to automate some of the management tasks in Chapter 13. You don't need to type in the long code snippets that follow; they are available for download on the book's web site.

ANALYSIS MANAGEMENT OBJECTS (AMO)

As mentioned, AMO is an object model that can you can use for programmatic administration of an Analysis Services instance. AMO is the replacement for Decision Support Objects (DSO), which shipped in Analysis Services 2000. It is installed and registered into the Global Assembly Cache (GAC) when Analysis Services is installed. The GAC itself is part of the .NET infrastructure where all commonly used .NET assemblies are registered. The best way to actually learn AMO is to jump in and use it! In this section you learn a few sample AMO applications that can perform some of the administrative operations you learned to do using SSMS earlier in this chapter. With the help of AMO, you can automate almost all your administrative tasks.

Processing Analysis Services Databases

As you learned earlier in this chapter, processing is one of the most important operations for an administrator. Usually administrators want to automate this process using scripts or programs. In this section, you learn to build an AMO-based console application that takes four command-line parameters: server name, target type (cube or dimension), processing type (full, incremental, update, or unprocess), and finally, the object's name (to be processed). Before building this console app, read the following source code in advance, and don't worry if you don't get it right away; you will soon learn the purpose of all but the most self-explanatory lines of code. The following code is a sample to kick-start you into learning AMO with some of the processing options for processing dimension or cube objects within a database:

```
#region Using directives
using System;
using System.Collections.Generic;
using System.Text;
using AMO = Microsoft.AnalysisServices;
#endregion

namespace AnalysisServicesProcess
{
  public enum ASObjectType
  {
    Database,
```

```
    Cube,
    Dimension,
    MiningStructure
}

public class ProcessASObjects
{
    public static void Main(string[] args)
    {
        try
        {
            if (args.Length != 5)
            {
                throw new Exception(@"Usage: ProcessASObjects <serverName>
                    <ObjectType = 'Cube'|'Dimension'> <ProcessType =
                    'ProcessDefault'|'ProcessFull'|'ProcessAdd'|'ProcessUpdate'|
                    'ProcessClear'> <databaseName> <objectName>");
            }
            string serverName = args[0];
            ASObjectType objectType = (ASObjectType)Enum.Parse
                    (typeof(ASObjectType), args[1], true);
            AMO.ProcessType processType = (AMO.ProcessType)Enum.Parse
                    (typeof(AMO.ProcessType), args[2], true);
            string databaseName = args[3];
            string objectName = args[4];

            using (AMO.Server server = new AMO.Server())
            {
                server.Connect(serverName);
                AMO.Database database = server.Databases.GetByName( databaseName );
                AMO.IProcessable processableObject;
                switch (objectType)
                {
                    case ASObjectType.Database:
                        processableObject = database;   // objectName is not needed
                        break;
                    case ASObjectType.Cube:
                        processableObject = database.Cubes.GetByName(objectName);
                        break;
                    case ASObjectType.Dimension:
                        processableObject = database.Dimensions.GetByName(objectName);
                        break;
                    case ASObjectType.MiningStructure:
                        processableObject = database.MiningStructures.GetByName
                        (objectName);
                        break;
                    default:
                        throw new Exception("Unrecognized ASObjectType encountered: " +
                        objectType.ToString());
                }
                processableObject.Process(processType);
            }

            Console.WriteLine("Process completed.");
        }
```

```
      catch (Exception ex)
      {
        Console.WriteLine(ex.GetType().ToString());
        Console.WriteLine(ex.Message);
      }
    }
  }
}
```

To create an AMO-based console application for Analysis Server administration:

1. Open Visual Studio 2010 and under the File menu, select New Project.

2. In the New Project dialog, select Visual C# under installed templates and use the console application template.

3. Name your project AnalysisServicesProcess and ensure the Create Directory for Solution check box is checked, and click OK.

4. Next, add a reference to the AMO assembly to your project by right-clicking References in Solution Explorer and selecting Add Reference.

5. In the Add Reference dialog, click the .NET tab and find Analysis Management Objects (Microsoft.AnalysisServices.dll) and double-click it.

To accomplish the tasks required in this program, you need the following directives; add any you don't already have listed:

```
using System;
using System.Collections.Generic;
using System.Text;
using AMO = Microsoft.AnalysisServices;
```

Next, create a class called ProcessASObjects within the AnalysisServicesProcess namespace. For more information on namespaces or classes, see Microsoft's C# online documentation.

```
namespace AnalysisServicesProcess
{
  class ProcessASObjects
  {
    // the rest of the code in this application will go here...
  }
}
```

First, add an enum definition for the ASObjectType. This enum will be used to know what type of Analysis Services object is to be processed.

```
public enum ASObjectType
{
  Database,
  Cube,
  Dimension,
  MiningStructure
}
```

Then add the main method of the program. This static method is called by the CLR with the command-line parameters passed in using the args array. In this method you add basic exception handling that can report errors on the console. Use the try-catch syntax to do this, and then write the exception type followed by the error message to the console. Because AMO reports errors it encounters by throwing exceptions, this is a simple and easy way to manage errors for this small application.

```
public static void Main(string[] args)
{
  try
  {
    // code for processing will go here...
  }
  catch (Exception ex)
  {
    Console.WriteLine(ex.GetType().ToString());
    Console.WriteLine(ex.Message);
  }
}
```

Then add the code for processing the command-line parameters. First, check if the wrong number of parameters is used. If the number of command-line parameters does not equal 5, throw an exception with parameter usage information. The previously added exception handling code ensures this usage information is shown to the user on the command line. Next, convert the command-line arguments from the strings passed in to the program into forms you need. For serverName, databaseName, and objectName you just need these strings, so you can use them as-is. However, for objectType and processType, you need enumeration values. To get these, use the CLR's Enum.Parse method, which can convert the string to the appropriate enumeration value and throw an exception if no conversion can be made.

```
if (args.Length != 5)
  {
    throw new Exception("Usage: ProcessASObjects <serverName> <ObjectType =
               'Cube'|'Dimension'> <ProcessType = 'ProcessDefault'|
               'ProcessFull'|'ProcessAdd'|'ProcessUpdate'|'ProcessClear'>
               <databaseName> <objectName>");
  }
string serverName = args[0];
ASObjectType objectType = (ASObjectType)Enum.Parse(typeof(ASObjectType),
             args[1], true);
AMO.ProcessType processType = (AMO.ProcessType)Enum.Parse
                (typeof(AMO.ProcessType), args[2], true);
string databaseName = args[3];
string objectName = args[4];
```

Now that you have your input parameters cleaned up, it's time to actually process. The first thing you need to do here is to connect to the Analysis Services server. To do this you can simply create a new AMO.Server object and use the Connect method with the serverName passed in to you. When using connections, you must remember to close your connection to the server when you are done with it. You can do this by calling the Disconnect method on the server when you are done. However, if an exception occurs along the way, you still need to make sure your connection was closed. The easiest and safest way to do this is to put the server object in a C# using statement. This ensures that whatever happens, Dispose is called on the server object when execution leaves the using block. Dispose on the server object ensures that the connection is closed if it were opened. If there is any problem connecting or processing, AMO throws an exception; the using block ensures the connection is closed if necessary; and your try-catch reports the error nicely on the command line.

```
using (AMO.Server server = new AMO.Server())
{
  server.Connect(serverName);

  // processing code will go here...
}
```

You have a connection so now you need to get the appropriate Analysis Services object. To do this you must find the object using the name of the database that contains it and name and type of the object itself. First, you get the database by using AMO's GetByName method on the collection of databases on the server:

```
AMO.Database database = server.Databases.GetByName( databaseName );
```

GetByName looks for an object in a collection and throws a descriptive exception if the object is not found. You could also use FindByName, which returns null if the object is not found, but you want the exception to be thrown because you have code that handles that already. AMO objects can also be located in collections by using the indexer and passing in either the position or the ID of the object you are looking for. (IDs are similar to names in AMO, except they don't change when the object is renamed and are not displayed to end users.)

Now you can get the object to be processed by using a switch statement on the objectType and using FindByName in the appropriate collection. Then in the switch statement, you could call the Process method for each type of object this program can handle. AMO makes this easier by providing an IProcessable interface, which any object that can be processed can be cast to. This allows you to simply store a reference to the object as an instance of IProcessable and then you can use the same code to process all types of processable objects.

```
AMO.IProcessable processableObject;
switch (objectType)
{
  case ASObjectType.Database:
    processableObject = database;  // objectName is not needed
    break;
  case ASObjectType.Cube:
    processableObject = database.Cubes.GetByName(objectName);
    break;
  case ASObjectType.Dimension:
    processableObject = database.Dimensions.GetByName(objectName);
    break;
  case ASObjectType.MiningStructure:
    processableObject = database.MiningStructures.GetByName(objectName);
    break;
  default:
    throw new Exception("Unrecognized ASObjectType encountered: " +
            objectType.ToString());
}
processableObject.Process(processType);
```

To complete the program all you need to do now is report success when processing has completed:

```
Console.WriteLine("Process completed.");
```

After you have mastered the AMO and basic programming concepts shown in this section, you will find it easy to extend the code to take on other administrative tasks such as tracing server events, designing aggregations, and writing custom AMO programs for your management tasks.

Back Up and Restore

To convince you that it actually is not difficult to extend the concepts demonstrated in the preceding processing program and to complete other console apps for administrative purposes, please read through the following source code samples covering backup and restore capabilities.

Following is a simple program for backing up Analysis Services databases from the command line:

```
using System;
using System.Collections.Generic;
using System.Text;
using AMO = Microsoft.AnalysisServices;

namespace ASBackup
{
  class Program
  {
    static void Main(string[] args)
    {
      try
      {
        if (args.Length != 2)
        {
          Console.WriteLine("Usage: ASBackup <servername> <databasename>");
          return;
        }
        using (AMO.Server myServer = new AMO.Server())
        {
          myServer.Connect(args[0]);
          AMO.Database database = myServer.Databases.GetByName(args[1]);
          database.Backup(args[1] + ".abf", true); //Backup the database with
                                                    //the provided file name

        }
      }
      catch (Exception e)
      {
        Console.WriteLine("Exception occurred:" + e.Message);
      }

    } // end Main
  } // end class
} // end namespace
```

Following is a simple program for restoring Analysis Services database backups from the command line:

```
using System;
using System.Collections.Generic;
using System.Text;
using AMO = Microsoft.AnalysisServices;
```

```
namespace ASRestore
{
  class Program
  {
    static void Main(string[] args)
    {
      try
      {
        if (args.Length != 2)
        {
          Console.WriteLine("Usage: ASRestore <servername> <backupfilename>");
          return;
        }
        using (AMO.Server myServer = new AMO.Server())
        {
          myServer.Connect(args[0]);
          myServer.Restore(args[1]);
        }
      } //end try
      catch (Exception e)
      {
        Console.WriteLine("Exception occurred:" + e.Message);
      }
    } // end Main
  } // end class
} // end namespace
```

As you can see from the preceding code segments, it actually is quite simple — create an AMO
server object, and connect to the Analysis Services instance. Depending on the operation (backup
or restore) call the appropriate method to perform the operation using AMO. The more you experiment with AMO programming, the more interesting and useful solutions you can generate, so come
up with some solutions and code them up!

Adding Assemblies to Analysis Services

You can create your own application in AMO to register assemblies in an Analysis Services database. You just need to get the full path of the assembly, set the right permission and impersonation
mode, and then register the assembly. The following is sample code of a console application that reg-
isters the assembly to a specific database in an Analysis Services instance:

```
using System;
using System.IO;
using AMO = Microsoft.AnalysisServices;

namespace RegisterAssembly
{
  class RegisterAssembly
  {
    [STAThread]
    static void Main(string[] args)
    {
      try
```

```
    {
      if (args.Length != 5)
      {
        throw new Exception(@"Usage: RegisterAssembly <server>
            <assemblyPath>
            <database> <PermissionSet = 'Safe'|'ExternalAccess'|
            'Unrestricted'> <ImpersonationMode = 'Default'|
            'ImpersonateAccount'|'ImpersonateAnonymous'|
            'ImpersonateCurrentUser'|'ImpersonateServiceAccount'> ");
      }
      string serverName = args[0];
      string assemblyPath = args[1];
      string databaseName = args[2];
      AMO.PermissionSet permisionSet = (AMO.PermissionSet)Enum.Parse
            (typeof(AMO.PermissionSet), args[3], true);
      AMO.ImpersonationMode impersonationMode = (AMO.ImpersonationMode)
            Enum.Parse(typeof(AMO.ImpersonationMode), args[4], true);

      //Connect to the Analysis Services instance
      using (AMO.Server server = new AMO.Server())
      {
        server.Connect(serverName);

        //get the assembly name
        FileInfo fileInfo = new FileInfo(assemblyPath);
        string assemblyName = fileInfo.Name.Replace(fileInfo.Extension, "");
        assemblyName = assemblyName.Replace("AMO", "");
        AMO.ClrAssembly amoAssembly = new AMO.ClrAssembly(assemblyName,
            assemblyName);
        amoAssembly.LoadFiles(fileInfo.FullName, true);

        amoAssembly.ImpersonationInfo = new Microsoft.AnalysisServices
            .ImpersonationInfo(impersonationMode);
        amoAssembly.PermissionSet = permisionSet;

        //add assembly to database
        AMO.Database db = server.Databases.GetByName(databaseName);
        db.Assemblies.Add(amoAssembly);

        amoAssembly.Update(); //Sends the DDL to the Server
      }
      Console.WriteLine("Assembly registered.");
    }
    catch (Exception e)
    {
      Console.WriteLine(e.Message);
    }
  }
 }
}
```

In previous examples, the `Process` method, the `Backup` method, and the `Restore` method would cause AMO to send the appropriate XMLA commands to the server to perform these management operations. However, in this latest example, you actually modify the definition of an Analysis Services database. To tell AMO to send the change in the definition of the database to the server, you must use the `Update` method:

```
amoAssembly.Update(); //Sends the DDL to the Server
```

The `Update` method exists on AMO object types that Analysis Services considers important enough to allow updating on their own. These updatable objects are called major objects and derive from the `MajorObject` base class in AMO. Databases, Cubes, Dimensions, Mining Models, and in this case, Assemblies are a few examples of `MajorObjects`. For more details on how to use the `Update` method, see `MajorObject.Update` in SQL Server Books Online.

The AMO code samples provided in this section are primarily to help you start using AMO for the various management tasks. The samples provided in this chapter have been tested for appropriate operations. However, these are still code samples, and if you need to write your own AMO programs for management operations, you can write robust code for your production environment with appropriate error handling. AMO contains several classes that help you perform more than just management operations. You can design an entire database programmatically and deploy the entire database to an Analysis Services instance. `www.CodePlex.com` is a good resource to find more programming samples using AMO as well as other Microsoft technologies.

Synchronization is one of the administrative task operations to move databases from test environments to production environments. However, AMO does not have methods to perform the synchronize operation. AMO allows you to send XMLA scripts to the Analysis Services instances. You can take the script that can be generated from the Synchronization Wizard and send the script using AMO to perform management operations for synchronization. You can explore the AMO object model and write the code for synchronization.

PowerShell and Analysis Services

PowerShell is a powerful command-line shell and scripting language that is ideal for automating many administrative tasks. It is an extensible environment with built-in support for easily manipulating managed objects. If you've spent any significant amount of time working with batch files, PowerShell is worth looking into.

Analysis Services 2012 introduces an Analysis Services PowerShell provider and cmdlets that allow the use of PowerShell to administer and query Analysis Services. For more information and examples on using this new functionality see the SQL Server Books Online documentation at `http://msdn.microsoft.com/en-us/library/hh213141(SQL.110).aspx`.

RESOURCE AND ACTIVITY MONITORING

Analysis Services 2012 has added schema rowset support for Analysis Services running in tabular mode in addition to multidimensional mode. As with relational SQL Server, schema rowsets provide information about the contents and state of the server and its databases. These schema rowsets can show you the connections on a machine, the objects those connections use, the memory those objects consume, locks held by sessions, and other valuable information for understanding how your server performs and diagnoses issues.

In Analysis Services 2012, schema rowsets have been exposed as Dynamic Management Views (DMVs). DMVs allow you to write simple SQL statements to query schema rowsets. To try this, open SQL Server Management Studio and connect to an Analysis Services database. Then open a new MDX query window and try the following examples.

This query shows you all the tables in the current database including the schema rowsets:

```
SELECT * FROM $SYSTEM.DBSCHEMA_TABLES
```

As you can see, there's quite a list, and it includes tables representing actual objects in the database as well as schema rowsets. To just see the names of schema rowset tables, use the following query:

```
SELECT TABLE_NAME FROM $SYSTEM.DBSCHEMA_TABLES WHERE TABLE_TYPE = 'SCHEMA'
```

Now you can see there is a nice list of useful schema rowsets to choose from. To use any of these tables, just add the $SYSTEM schema prefix to the table name and query away. So to see the list of connections, try the following query:

```
SELECT * FROM $SYSTEM.DISCOVER_CONNECTIONS
```

If you want to learn more about the columns in a schema rowset, you can use the DBSCHEMA_COLUMNS rowset. This can be useful when there are many long column names or you want to know the data type of a column. To learn about the columns available in the DISCOVER_COMMANDS rowset, try the following query:

```
SELECT * FROM $SYSTEM.DBSCHEMA_COLUMNS WHERE TABLE_NAME = 'DISCOVER_COMMANDS'
```

Now you can build a more interesting query such as the following query that shows commands ordered by the amount of CPU time they've consumed:

```
SELECT * FROM $SYSTEM.DISCOVER_COMMANDS ORDER BY COMMAND_CPU_TIME_MS DESC
```

Another interesting query would be to look for commands that have taken longer than 1 second (1000 milliseconds) to be completed:

```
SELECT * FROM $SYSTEM.DISCOVER_COMMANDS WHERE COMMAND_ELAPSED_TIME_MS > 1000
```

If your server performs well and isn't handling any difficult commands, this query probably came back with no results. That's a good thing.

The SQL accepted for querying schema rowsets is fairly simple and does not include support for many SQL capabilities including joins. The lack of joins means that if you want to follow an investigation through several schema rowsets, you just need to write separate queries and use simple WHERE restrictions. For example, to see the commands belonging to a connection, first query connections, then query sessions restricting based on a connection ID, and then query commands restricting based on a session ID.

Some schema rowsets cannot be queried using SQL: DSCHEMA_ACTIONS and DISCOVER_XML_METADATA. These schema rowsets do not show up in the DBSCHEMA_TABLES and are not of much interest in the context of server monitoring and troubleshooting.

Though there are some limitations to the SQL syntax supported for schema rowset queries, these limitations are relatively minor, and the ability to use SQL to query information about the state of the server is extremely useful to managing Analysis Services 2012. If you face potential performance concerns or just want to better understand how your server operates, using SQL to query these rowsets is a valuable tool to have on your belt. I like to use the template browser to store the most common DMV queries I use when managing Analysis Services.

To open the Template Browser and add your DMV queries, perform the following steps:

1. Press CTRL+ALT+T to view the template browser.

2. Click the Analysis Services cube icon.

3. Right-click the Analysis Services Templates folder and select New Folder, and name it DMV Queries.

4. Right-click the newly created DMV Queries folder and select New DMX Template and name it SSAS Monitoring. Note that you can specify DMX or MDX and it will work; however, the DMVs use the Data Mining Parser to execute.

5. Next, right-click on the new template named SSAS Monitoring and select Edit.

6. Enter the following DMV queries and click Save.

```
//provide information about the currently opened connections
select * from $system.discover_connections;

//provide information about the currently executing or last executed commands in
the opened connections on the server
select * from $system.discover_commands;

//provide resource usage and information on the currently opened sessions on the
server
select * from $system.discover_sessions;

//provide information about the current standing locks on the server
select * from $system.discover_locks;

// order sessions by last command end time
select * from $system.discover_SESSIONS
order by SESSION_LAST_COMMAND_END_TIME DESC

// get schema rowsets available
select * from $system.Discover_schema_rowsets

// find all tables available for resource monitor
select * from $system.DBSCHEMA_TABLES where table_Schema ='$system'

// Top sessions that have consumed the most memory resource; this is an estimate as
it will not include any nested child objects of the session
select top 10 SESSION_SPID,
SESSION_CONNECTION_ID,
SESSION_USED_MEMORY,
SESSION_LAST_COMMAND_START_TIME,
SESSION_LAST_COMMAND_END_TIME,
SESSION_LAST_COMMAND_ELAPSED_TIME_MS,
SESSION_LAST_COMMAND
from $system.discover_sessions
order by Session_Used_Memory desc
```

```
// Top commands that have consumed the most CPU resource
select top 10 SESSION_SPID,
SESSION_CONNECTION_ID,
SESSION_LAST_COMMAND_CPU_TIME_MS,
SESSION_LAST_COMMAND_START_TIME,
SESSION_LAST_COMMAND_END_TIME,
SESSION_LAST_COMMAND_ELAPSED_TIME_MS,
SESSION_LAST_COMMAND
from $system.discover_sessions
order by SESSION_LAST_COMMAND_CPU_TIME_MS DESC
           // or
select top 10 SESSION_SPID,
COMMAND_CPU_TIME_MS,
COMMAND_START_TIME,
COMMAND_ELAPSED_TIME_MS
from $system.discover_commands
order by Command_CPU_TIME_MS desc

// Top running commands that have transferred the highest IO bytes
select TOP 10 SESSION_SPID, COMMAND_READ_KB + COMMAND_WRITE_KB AS [IO_Bytes]
from $system.discover_commands
order by COMMAND_READ_KB + COMMAND_WRITE_KB  desc

// Top running commands that have issued the highest IO operation calls
select TOP 10 SESSION_SPID, COMMAND_READS + COMMAND_WRITES AS [IO]
from $system.discover_commands
order by COMMAND_READS + COMMAND_WRITES  desc

// Top sessions that consumed the highest IO resource
SELECT Top 10 SESSION_ID,
SESSION_CONNECTION_ID,
SESSION_READS,
SESSION_WRITES,
SESSION_READ_KB,
SESSION_WRITE_KB
FROM $system.discover_sessions
```

HTTP CONNECTIVITY TO ANALYSIS SERVICES

You can enable HTTP access to Analysis Services by configuring the Data Pump (msmdpump.dll), an ISAPI extension that runs in a virtual directory within IIS. This allows web applications and other clients access to Analysis Services over Internet or extranet connections. The PUMP component needs to be loaded within Internet Information Server (IIS) as an ISAPI DLL. To provide web access to data from Analysis Services, you need to configure your IIS using the instructions provided in Books Online. You need to set up virtual directories, copy appropriate DLLs provided by Analysis Services, and set up appropriate permission on IIS so that users can access data from Analysis Services. The PUMP does not necessarily have to be set up on the same machine as Analysis Services. Using Analysis Services 2012 you can configure several data PUMPs to direct queries to various Analysis Services instances. Each PUMP has a configuration file where the server name and certain other properties are configured. To access Analysis Services data over the Web, a user would connect to IIS using HTTP. IIS in turn directs the request to the Analysis Services instance over TCP/IP with appropriate credentials set up on IIS.

You can configure security on IIS to use an anonymous connection to Analysis Services, perform username and password authentication on IIS, or perform Windows authentication.

ANALYSIS SERVICES AND FAILOVER CLUSTERING

As with Analysis Services 2005, 2008 and 2008r2, Analysis Services 2012 provides failover clustering out-of-the-box. SQL 2012 setup supports installing Analysis Services on a Windows clustered environment. You first need to have Microsoft Cluster Services (MSCS) set up to form a cluster of two or more nodes. Look at the Windows product documentation to set up and configure MSCS. You need to have a shared disk with sufficient disk space that can hold the Analysis Services data files. After setting up a cluster, you can then use Microsoft SQL Server setup to install Analysis Services with failover capability. In SQL Server 2012 setup, you need to install Analysis Services on each of the cluster nodes and then use the Cluster UI to create the failover virtual instance based on one of the standalone instances.

Users of Analysis Services will only be aware of the virtual server name. At a given time only one of the physical machines can service users' requests and have access to the shared disk containing Analysis Services data. When one of the nodes in the cluster fails due to network or power problems, MSCS makes the second node the primary and provides control to the shared disk. MSCS identifies failure in the primary node through the heart beat, which is typically a connection through a second network card between the machines involved in the cluster. The second node gains control of the Analysis Services data, and all future user requests are directed to the second node. Existing users originally connected to the first node would have to re-establish their connections. To make sure you are isolated from disk problems, it is recommended that the shared disk is a Redundant Array of Independent or Inexpensive Disks (RAID) to provide fault tolerance. Due to failover clustering support, you have higher availability of Analysis Services for your users whenever there are hardware problems.

SUMMARY

In this chapter you learned to administer SQL Server Analysis Services 2012 using SSMS and programmatically using AMO. You learned the various management operations that can be accomplished on the Analysis Services databases. You have seen that SSMS provides the ability to manage your Analysis Services instances effectively. In addition to learning the various management operations from SSMS, you also learned what XMLA commands are sent by SSMS to the Analysis Services instance, and you have a better understanding of the interactions between SSMS and an Analysis Services instance.

You learned that you can execute each administrative task through the user interface using SSMS or SSDT. You learned to perform Analysis Services management operations programmatically using the Analysis Services Management Object (AMO) model. You've seen how to use the Analysis Management Objects (AMO) object model to perform management tasks as well as to update the definition of Analysis Services databases. AMO provides you the power to program custom UIs and gain full access to the capabilities of the server. More important, AMO enables you to automate common tasks, such as processing, adding new users, or even the management of partitions. You've seen how .NET languages such as C# can be used to work with AMO, as well as how PowerShell can be used to work more interactively or to script AMO.

You learned how useful backup and restore can be for auditing purposes — specifically by providing snapshots in time of cubes to auditors and analysts. And you learned how security is configured for administrative versus user access to the server by using server and database roles, respectively.

You also learned how to perform some advanced administration tasks not available directly through the SQL Server Management Studio user interface. You learned to monitor the resources and activities of a server using schema rowsets. You saw how Analysis Services 2012 has extended the schema rowset support to provide much more transparency into the status of the server and how these rowsets can now be easily queried using SQL. You learned how Analysis Services can be configured to support connections over HTTP and also how a failover cluster can provide improved reliability without any visible difference to the end user.

In the next few chapters, you learn about enhancing your multidimensional models by enhancing your dimensions and cubes, and how to efficiently design your multidimensional models and fine tune your Analysis Services server to get maximum performance.

PART III
Advanced Topics in BISM

8

Advanced Dimension Design

WHAT'S IN THIS CHAPTER?

➤ Understanding custom hierarchy rollups

➤ Taking a look at enhancements to parent-child hierarchies

➤ Reviewing unary operators

➤ Customizing dimension through properties

➤ Using the Business Intelligence Wizards

➤ Taking a look at dimension writeback

In this chapter you learn to enhance dimensions to aggregate data up to the parent member through custom rollup (aggregate) operations, and to change dimension and hierarchy properties to customize dimensions for the needs of the end users. For example, you would normally expect data to be aggregated along a dimension from a child to its parent. If you have a hierarchy such as Time, then sales per month will typically be rolled up to calculate first the sales of a quarter, and sales of a quarter will be rolled up to calculate the sales of a year. Even though this is the most common way a user would expect the data to be aggregated, there are dimensions in which the data does not get rolled up by a simple sum. You also learn about the Business Intelligence Wizard, which helps you to enhance cubes and dimensions with logic and structure needed to solve common business problems. Finally, you are introduced to dimension writeback, which is a way to enable changes to the dimension structure.

Consider first the details you learned regarding dimension design in Chapter 5; you learned that dimensions are made up of hierarchies, which in turn consist of tiers called levels. The two types of hierarchies, attribute and multilevel, were described, as well as two specific types of dimension constructs: Time and Parent-Child dimensions. The material in this chapter builds on the initial baseline that has been established to this point. Consequently, this is a good time to refer to Chapter 5 if you're not completely comfortable with the material covered there.

If you don't get the in-depth details of this chapter just from reading the narrative descriptions, don't worry; the concepts are demonstrated through examples as well. This area is a classic example of "It seems profoundly difficult until you get it, but once you get it, it is so simple as to seem obvious." If you already know the aforementioned concepts or otherwise understand them after reading this paragraph, read the chapter anyway; it goes far beyond the basics.

Most of the examples in this chapter make use of the project created in Chapter 6, and a few of them use the download for this chapter, available at www.wrox.com. The project used will be explicitly mentioned preceding each example.

If you came to this chapter looking for information on calculated members or Data Mining dimensions (both being perfectly reasonable to expect here), they are not covered here. For information on calculated members, see Chapters 3 and 9, and for Data Mining dimensions, see Chapter 12.

CUSTOM ROLLUPS

The name *custom rollup* is self-describing. Custom refers to the user-defined nature of a rollup or aggregate formula, such that a measure value for a member is not a simple sum of values of its children as you move up a hierarchy. Rollup describes how those calculations typically start at the leaf or lower-level node and aggregate (roll) up toward the root. You can apply a custom rollup to a hierarchy in several ways: by using the attribute property CustomRollupColumn, using unary operators (used for parent-child hierarchies), and by using MDX scripts to specify custom rollup for members in a level.

A business scenario can help you better understand the need for and concept of the custom rollup. Perhaps you are familiar with *depreciation*. Technically, the definition of depreciation is "mapping an asset's expense over time to benefits gained through use of those assets." It simply means that the value of an asset decreases over time. You should be familiar with and understand two types of depreciation: straight-line and accelerated. Typically, businesses keep two (sometimes more) sets of accounting books, which, by the way, is completely legal. One set of books is for the IRS, and one set is for investors. The books for the IRS often use accelerated depreciation because this provides optimal tax benefits (less taxable income is initially reported), and the books for investors use straight-line depreciation because this yields higher net earnings per share for that quarter or year and a more favorable Return on Equity (ROE), which is the net income divided by the shareholder's equity.

Accelerated depreciation on a delivery van, as shown in Figure 8-1, is *front-loaded depreciation*; the percentages associated with each year indicate the percentage of total value depreciated or "written off" for that year. Because 40% is depreciated the first year and 10% the last year speaks to the notion that the depreciation is front-loaded. There is no cash involved in recognizing depreciation, yet there is a reduction in asset value and an expense is logged; therefore, it is called a noncash expense. The company can write off more of the van's value earlier on its taxes. That means less taxable income for the company in the earlier years and that is a good thing.

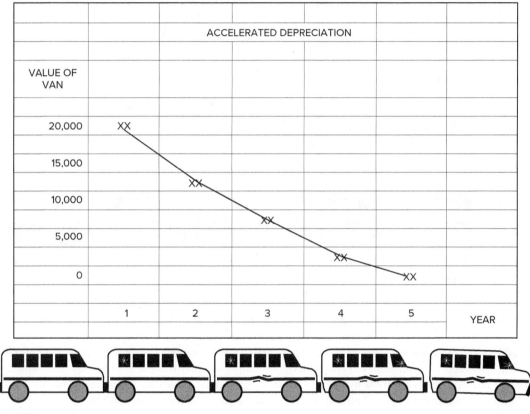

FIGURE 8-1

Straight-line depreciation on the same delivery van, as shown in Figure 8-2, again happens over time until the van is essentially worthless with no salvage value (in this case after 5 hard-driving years). The rate at which the van falls apart is the same, regardless of how depreciation is logged on the financial records. In this case, the noncash expense is logged in equal amounts over the life of the asset at 20% per year. The effect this method has is that an investor sees an asset retaining value for a longer period. That is a good thing because value ultimately relates to stock price.

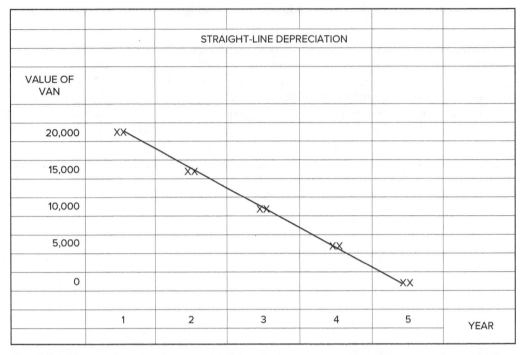

		STRAIGHT-LINE DEPRECIATION			

FIGURE 8-2

Having learned about depreciation you can understand the need for custom rollup of member values in a hierarchy to their parent — it all depends on the type of depreciation being logged and therefore will be custom, by definition. To calculate the net profit of your company, you would typically add up the sales revenue, any increase in asset values, and subtract the expenditures (Cost of Goods Sold) and depreciation values appropriately. You might wonder if these are just measure values, what is so complex about them? Why not just write an appropriate calculated measure? That would be a reasonable question to ask. And if it is just measures you deal with, you don't have a problem.

By definition, depreciation indicates that values change over time. So, your calculations that reflect the value of physical assets (such as delivery vans) should be adjusted for appropriate percentage changes based on the Time dimension you query. Similarly, there might be other dimensions or measure groups that calculations might depend on. For example, say you have a Budget measure group and a Sales measure group in your cube. To help better solve these types of problems, Analysis Services enables you to specify the calculations through MDX expressions as a property of the hierarchy.

Consider the following example: If there is an Account dimension that indicates the types of accounts of your company, such as asset, liability, income, and expenditure, and you have a measure called Amount, the rollup of the values to the parent member is not a simple sum. In such a case, you need to specify a custom rollup, typically per account type. If the hierarchy is a parent-child hierarchy, Analysis Services enable you to perform a custom rollup using a feature called unary operators. Unary operators enable specification of basic aggregate functions: add, subtract, multiply, multiply by a specified factor, divide, and a special case for a no-op for good measure. However, if the value of a member is not derived from its children or you have a user hierarchy where you need to rollup the values to the parent using a complex operation or custom formula, you would then likely specify the custom rollup using a property called CustomRollupColumn for an attribute hierarchy.

The CustomRollupColumn property of an attribute should be set to a column in the relational table that contains the custom rollup calculation — which is an MDX expression. For example, in the Account dimension in the Adventure Works DW Multidimensional sample project, the value for Account Average Unit is calculated from the Accounts Net Sales and Units, which are members in the Account dimension under different parents. To specify the custom formula for a member, the column in the relational table should contain an MDX expression that evaluates the value for the member. You need to specify an MDX expression for each member that a custom formula needs to be applied to. For the sake of clarity, it likely would have been better to name this property CustomFormula instead of CustomRollup. At any rate, follow these steps to understand the behavior of a custom rollup by using the sample Adventure Works DW relational database:

1. Open the AnalysisServicesMultidimensionalTutorial project you completed in Chapter 6. You can download this project from the book's accompanying web site in the Chapter 6 files.

2. Select the Adventure Works DW cube from the Solution Explorer, right-click, and select Delete.

3. Open the Adventure Works DW DSV. Right-click in the DSV Designer, and select Add/Remove Tables. Add all the dimension and fact tables in the Adventure Works DW data source except AdventureWorksBuildVersion, DatabaseLog, ProspectiveBuyer, SysDiagrams, and the views, as shown in Figure 8-3.

4. Create the dimensions Dim Account, Dim Department Group, Dim Organization, Dim Sales Reason, and Dim Scenario using the existing table path of the Dimension Wizard and selecting the tables Dim Account, Dim Department Group, Dim Organization, Dim Sales Reason, and Dim Scenario, respectively. While creating these dimensions, do not include any related tables detected by the Dimension Wizard, but instead select all the columns in the tables as attributes of the dimension and choose the default dimension names suggested by the Dimension Wizard.

5. After you have created all the dimensions, right-click the Dimensions folder in Solution Explorer, and select Sort by Name.

   You should end up with dimensions shown in Figure 8-4. In this example for illustration and quick understanding, you should select all the columns in the tables as attributes. When you design your dimensions, you should choose only the right set of columns as attributes, and only the ones that you want to use for slicing or dicing should be enabled for browsing. Choosing the right attributes for your dimension helps you to design your dimension from the start and thereby helps in optimal dimension and cube design. The Dimension Wizard can automatically detect parent-child relationships for dimensions DimAccount, DimDepartmentGroup, and DimOrganization and can create appropriate parent-child hierarchies.

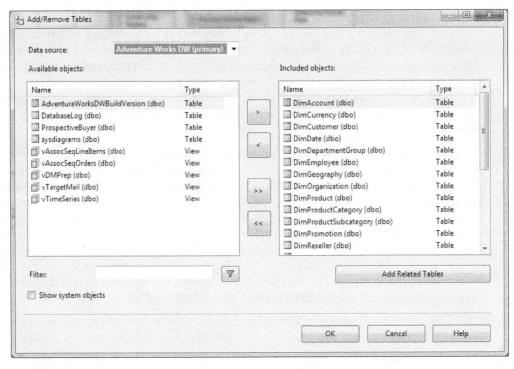

FIGURE 8-3

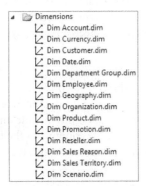

FIGURE 8-4

6. Create a new cube using the Cube Wizard and the Use existing tables wizard option. In the Select Measure Group Tables page, select the tables FactInternetSales, FactResellerSales, FactCurrencyRate, FactFinance, FactInternetSalesReason, and FactSalesQuota as measure group tables, as shown in Figure 8-5. Accept the defaults in the Select Measures and Select Existing Dimensions pages of the wizard. In the Select New Dimensions page, uncheck any potential dimension whose name starts with Fact. Click Next to advance the wizard and then Finish on the Completing the Wizard page.

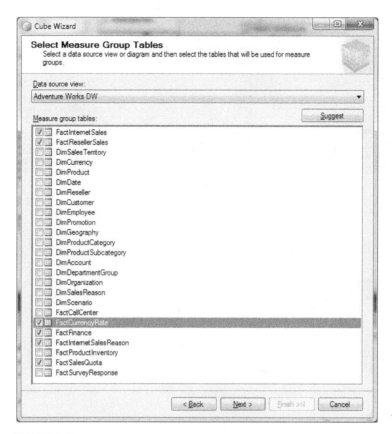

FIGURE 8-5

You now have the Adventure Works DW cube created. The Cube Wizard detects the relationship between the fact and dimension tables based on relationships in the DSV and creates appropriate dimension usage. If you do need to change the relationships, you can do so on the Dimension Usage tab within the cube editor. Now that the cube is created, deploy the project.

7. Double-click the Dim Account dimension in Solution Explorer. Notice the attribute hierarchies of the Dim Account dimension within the Dimension Designer. If you switch to the Dimension Browser and browse the parent-child hierarchy, you see the account numbers. To view the Account names while browsing the parent-child hierarchy, you need to specify the NameColumn property for the key attribute, which you learned about in Chapter 5. Select the key attribute Account Key and specify the relational column AccountDescription as the NameColumn property for the key attribute and then deploy the changes to the Analysis Services instance. If you go to the Dimension Browser you see the names of the accounts.

In the properties for an attribute you see a property called CustomRollupColumn, as shown in Figure 8-6. This property needs to be set to the relational column that has the MDX expression for the custom rollup formula. The MDX expression specified in this property is evaluated on the cells when the value's corresponding members of the hierarchy are retrieved in the query.

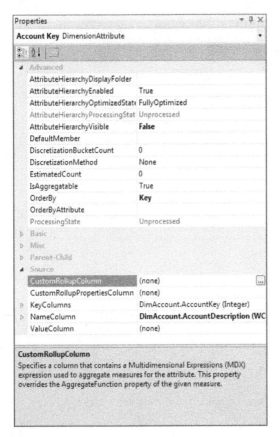

FIGURE 8-6

8. The sample Adventure Works DW relational database provides a column with custom rollups for the Account dimension. Right-click the DimAccount table in the DSV of the dimension DimAccount, and select Explore Data.

You see the data in the relational table, as shown in Figure 8-7. The relational column CustomMembers contains the MDX expression for custom rollup. In the Adventure Works DW database, there is an MDX expression defined for an Account, which has AccountKey = 98, as shown in Figure 8-7. There are no children for the Account with AccountKey = 98 (Account Name is Average Unit Price) and there are no corresponding fact rows in the fact table FactFinance. Therefore, if you browse the current Adventure Works DW cube in the Cube Browser, you see a null value for the Average Unit Price account. The MDX expression in the relational table for Average Unit Price account follows:

```
[Account].[Accounts].[Account Level 04].&[50]/[Account].[Accounts].
[Account Level 02].&[97]
```

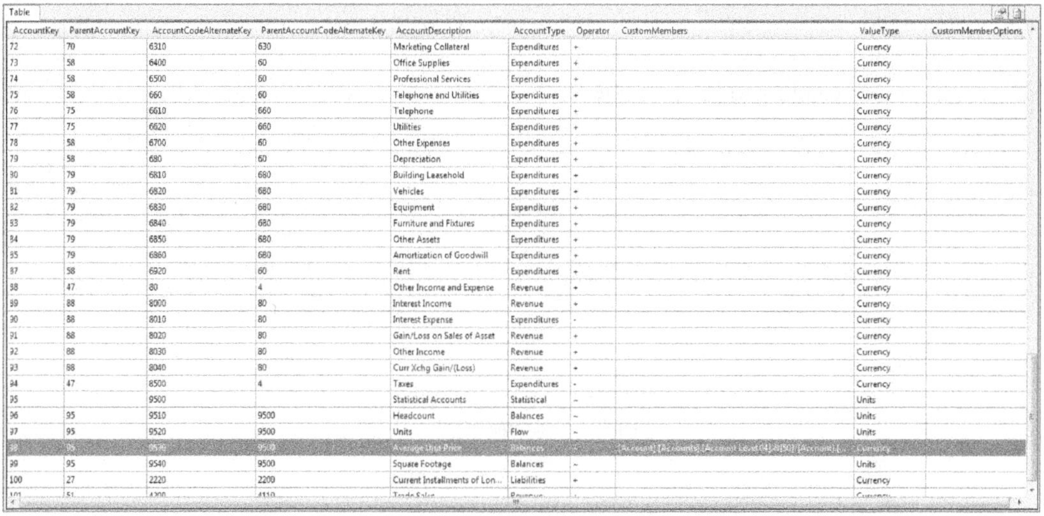

AccountKey	ParentAccountKey	AccountCodeAlternateKey	ParentAccountCodeAlternateKey	AccountDescription	AccountType	Operator	CustomMembers	ValueType	CustomMemberOptions
72	70	6310	630	Marketing Collateral	Expenditures	+		Currency	
73	58	6400	60	Office Supplies	Expenditures	+		Currency	
74	58	6500	60	Professional Services	Expenditures	+		Currency	
75	58	660	60	Telephone and Utilities	Expenditures	+		Currency	
76	75	6610	660	Telephone	Expenditures	+		Currency	
77	75	6620	660	Utilities	Expenditures	+		Currency	
78	58	6700	60	Other Expenses	Expenditures	+		Currency	
79	58	680	60	Depreciation	Expenditures	+		Currency	
80	79	6810	680	Building Leasehold	Expenditures	−		Currency	
81	79	6820	680	Vehicles	Expenditures	+		Currency	
82	79	6830	680	Equipment	Expenditures	+		Currency	
83	79	6840	680	Furniture and Fixtures	Expenditures	+		Currency	
84	79	6850	680	Other Assets	Expenditures	+		Currency	
85	79	6860	680	Amortization of Goodwill	Expenditures	+		Currency	
87	58	6920	60	Rent	Expenditures	+		Currency	
88	47	80	4	Other Income and Expense	Revenue	+		Currency	
89	88	8000	80	Interest Income	Revenue	+		Currency	
90	88	8010	80	Interest Expense	Expenditures	−		Currency	
91	88	8020	80	Gain/Loss on Sales of Asset	Revenue	+		Currency	
92	88	8030	80	Other Income	Revenue	+		Currency	
93	88	8040	80	Curr Xchg Gain/(Loss)	Revenue	+		Currency	
94	47	8500	4	Taxes	Expenditures	−		Currency	
95		9500		Statistical Accounts	Statistical			Units	
96	95	9510	9500	Headcount	Balances	~		Units	
97	95	9520	9500	Units	Flow	~		Units	
98	95	9530	9500	Average Unit Price	Balances	~	[Account].[Accounts].[Account Level 04].[9510],[Account].[...	Currency	
99	95	9540	9500	Square Footage	Balances	~		Units	
100	27	2220	2200	Current Installments of Lon...	Liabilities	+		Currency	
101	51	4200	4110	Trade Sales	Revenue			Currency	

FIGURE 8-7

When evaluated, this MDX expression provides the amount for Account Average Unit Price from Accounts Net Sales and Units. Accounts Net Sales and Units are not children of the Average Unit Price account; therefore, the custom formula mentioned earlier calculates the value for Average Unit Price Account. In the preceding expression you see that the dimension and hierarchy names specified are Account and Accounts, respectively. The members specified in the MDX expression for custom rollup include the level names Account Level 04 and Account Level 02. By default, the level names for parent-child hierarchies have the names Level xx. To make this work, you also need to make sure you specify the appropriate property to have the level names as shown in the MDX expression. Therefore, you will need to change the name of the dimension and the parent-child hierarchy in your database.

9. In the Solution Explorer, right-click the dimension name Dim Account.dim and click Rename. Enter the name **Account.dim**. When asked if the object name needs to be changed, click Yes. Open the Account dimension in the Dimension Designer. Right-click the parent-child hierarchy Parent Account Key and rename it **Accounts**. You now need to specify the level names for the parent-child hierarchy. Enter the value **Account Level *;** for the Accounts parent-child hierarchy property NamingTemplate and set the IsAggregatable property to False. You learn more about these properties later in this chapter. Don't think you have completed all the renaming yet. You have currently renamed the dimension and hierarchy. When an MDX expression within a cube is calculated, the dimension name addressed with the cube is the cube dimension and not the database dimension that you just renamed. You also need to rename the cube dimension name for dimension Account.

10. Open the Adventure Works DW cube. Click the Cube Structure tab; right-click the Dim Account dimension in the Dimensions pane, and select Rename. Enter the name **Account**. You have successfully made changes to your cube to define the custom rollup formula for the Accounts hierarchy.

11. Select the property CustomRollupColumn for the Accounts hierarchy in the Account dimension. Click the button at the right of the value column (with the "..." caption) in the Properties window to bring up the Custom Rollup Column dialog. In the Custom Rollup Column dialog select the CustomMembers column in the Dim Account table as the column for the CustomRollupColumn property, as shown in Figure 8-8, and click the OK button.

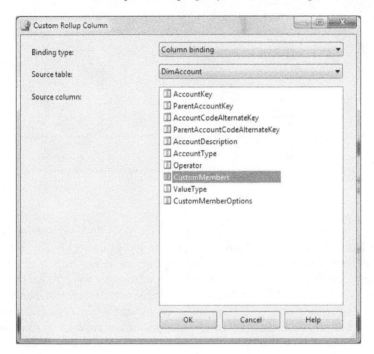

FIGURE 8-8

You have successfully specified a custom formula for members of the Accounts hierarchy. In addition to specifying a custom formula using CustomRollupColumn, you can also specify the CustomRollupPropertiesColumn property to apply custom properties on the cell value. The CustomRollupPropertiesColumn property also takes a column in the relational table as input and that column should contain an MDX expression specifying the cell properties such as background color and foreground color. The sample relational database does not contain values for CustomRollupPropertiesColumn so the exercise of exploring those properties is your choice.

12. Deploy the project to the Analysis Services instance. To make sure the CustomRollupColumn MDX expression is correctly evaluated for the Average Unit Price account attribute, go to the Cube Browser.

13. Click the Excel icon on the toolbar.

You now see Excel launched with a Pivot Table connected to the cube you have designed. The ability to connect to the cube designed using Excel is a new addition in SQL Server Analysis Services 2012 because certain limitations exist for browsing the cube in the Cube Browser. In this example, you cannot view the multiple levels of a parent-child hierarchy in the existing cube browser.

14. Drag and drop the Accounts hierarchy to Row Labels and Amount measure from the Fact Finance measure group, as shown in Figure 8-9. Right-click a row member, and select Expand/Collapse ➪ Expand to Account Level 04. You see the various levels of the Accounts dimension, as shown in Figure 8-9. Using a calculator you can easily verify that the value for Average Unit Price is equal to the value of Net Sales divided by the Units.

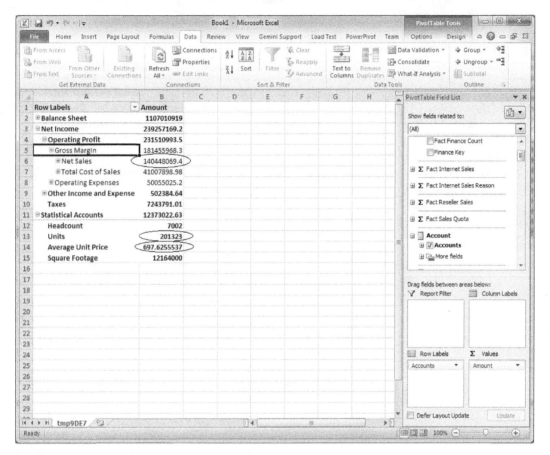

FIGURE 8-9

You have now successfully learned to apply a custom formula to members of a hierarchy. In this example, a parent-child hierarchy was used to help you understand the CustomRollupColumn property; however, the custom rollup is not limited to parent-child hierarchies and can be used on any hierarchy. As mentioned, Analysis Services provides a way to specify a custom formula for a level within a hierarchy. You can specify such a formula in your MDX script or specify the custom formula for the members in a relational column and use the CustomRollupColumn property for that hierarchy. If an attribute hierarchy is part of multiple user hierarchies and you need to apply different custom rollup behaviors based on the hierarchy, you need to apply these custom formulas in the MDX script. Analysis Services 2012 provides another way to aggregate data for members in parent-child hierarchies using a property called *UnaryOperatorColumn*. The next section provides further details.

ENHANCEMENTS TO PARENT-CHILD HIERARCHIES

The parent-child hierarchy structure is a particularly intuitive and quite common technique to model various business entities, and for this reason you need to master the modeling techniques related to it. In this section, the concepts discussed in the previous section are extended. Several important properties are supported by Analysis Services 2012 for parent-child hierarchies. One of those important properties is the UnaryOperatorColumn property.

Unary Operators

Unary operators are used for custom rollup of members to their parent where the rollup operation is a unary operation. A unary operator, as the name suggests, is an operator that takes a single argument — the member — and rolls up the value of the member to its parent. As with the custom rollup column, you need to have the unary operators specified as a column in the relational table, and this column must be set or mapped as a property for the parent-child hierarchy. Unary operators can be applied also to nonparent-child hierarchies, but this is not a common scenario, so it will not be covered here. The following table shows the various unary operators supported by Analysis Services and a description of their behaviors:

UNARY OPERATOR	DESCRIPTION
+	The value of the member is added to the aggregate value of the preceding sibling members. This is the default operator used if no unary operator column is specified.
−	The value of the member is subtracted from the aggregate value of the preceding sibling members.
*	The value of the member is multiplied by the aggregate value of the preceding sibling members.
/	The value of the member is divided by the aggregate value of the preceding sibling members.
~	The value of the member is ignored.
N	The value is multiplied by N and added to the aggregate values. N can be any numeric value (typically N is between 0 and 1).

A business scenario commonly used to demonstrate the usefulness of rollups using unary operators is the case in which Net Income equals Sales minus Cost of Goods Sold. In this example, Sales figures are added, hence the + operator is used, and for Cost of Goods Sold, which is subtracted, the − operator is used. Were depreciation included in the following example, given that it is a noncash expense, you might choose to ignore it in the hierarchy by using the tilde (~) unary operator. Follow these steps to set up unary operators for the parent-child hierarchies in the Account:

1. Open the Account dimension, and click the Accounts hierarchy. In the Properties window you see the properties associated with parent-child hierarchies under a section called

Parent-Child, as shown in Figure 8-10. First do a bit of housekeeping so that the dimension is a bit more user-friendly to browse. Locate the MembersWithData property, and set its value to NonLeafDataHidden.

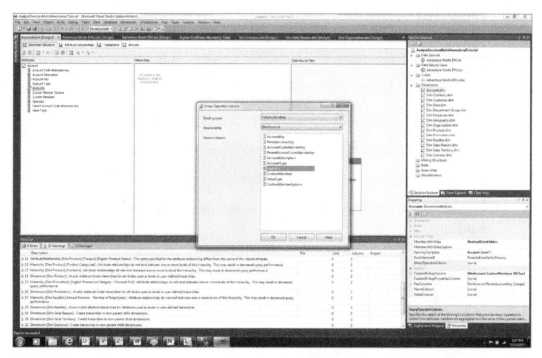

FIGURE 8-10

2. Select the Unary Operator Column property, and click the button at the right of the value column (with the "..." caption) in the Properties window to bring up the Unary Operator Column dialog box. In the Unary Operator Column dialog box, select Operator as the Source column, as shown in Figure 8-11. Click the OK button and deploy the changes to your Analysis Services instance.

If you explore the data for DimAccount table in the DSV Designer, you can see the unary operators associated for each account, as shown earlier in Figure 8-7. There are ~ operators indicating "ignore this," which is required for members that are calculations in and of themselves. Because the Operator column is an attribute hierarchy in the Account dimension, it becomes a member property of the key attribute. All member properties of the key attribute are automatically inherited by the parent attribute, the parent-child hierarchy. Therefore, you can view the unary operators associated with each account in the Dimension Browser while browsing the Accounts parent-child hierarchy by including the member property Unary Operator using the Member Property icon, as shown in Figure 8-12.

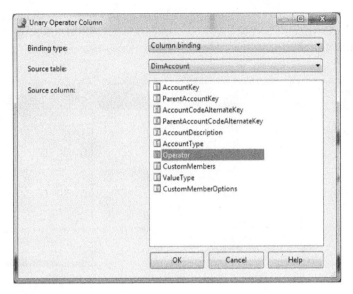

FIGURE 8-11

Member Property icon

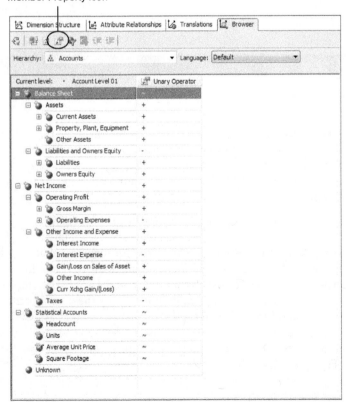

FIGURE 8-12

3. The next step is to ensure that you have set the unary operators correctly and the rollup to parent occurs as wanted. For verification, edit the Adventure Works DW cube, and click the Browser tab. Click the Excel icon to launch Excel and connect to the Adventure Works DW cube. Drag and drop the Amount measure and the parent-child hierarchy Accounts from the Measure Group pane to the Values and Row Labels area, respectively, and then expand the levels Net Income ⇨ Operating Profit ⇨ Gross Margin. Before specifying the unary operator, Analysis Services aggregates the values for Net Sales and Total Cost of Sales as a sum to calculate the value for Gross Margin. Because a unary operator has been specified, you should see the value for Gross Margin is the difference of Net Sales and Total Cost of Sales, as shown in Figure 8-13.

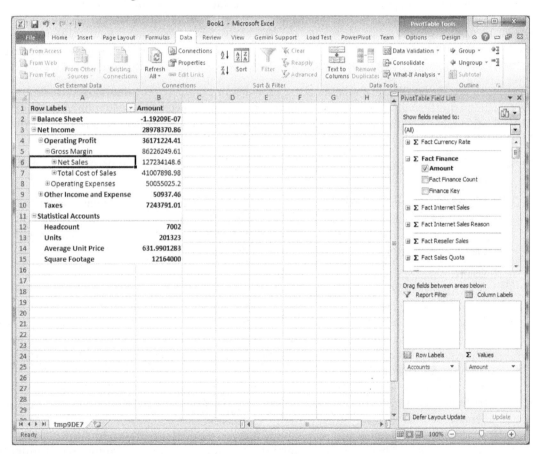

FIGURE 8-13

Understanding the Unary N Operator

Analysis Services has a unary operator referred to as N in the unary operator table. N is a numerical value used as a weighting factor so that the value of the member is multiplied by the value N and then aggregated to the parent. For example, a company might calculate overhead costs for utilities such as electricity at the level of an entire factory. Electricity consumption is not evenly distributed across the organizations within the factory, though; the manufacturing floor might be sucking up power at a rate completely disproportionate to the administrative section. This disparity is something that should be accounted for when doing internal costing analysis. One way managerial accountants address the problem is to calculate the overhead at the departmental level and at the factory level. The amount of electricity consumed can be weighted by some predetermined amount such that cost assignments are rolled up to the correct parents. For example, the manufacturing department could be assigned a ratio of 1 to 9 for factory-level overhead versus department-level overhead. That is, 10% of the electricity used by manufacturing facilities is assigned to factory overhead, and the other 90% is assigned as a department-specific cost.

In some organizations, even though a group is reporting to a parent (higher-level group), the measure value of the subgroup might be rolled up as a fraction of the total measure value to the parent. This is because parent groups only own a part of the organization. If you know the percentage of ownership for various organizations as a measure, you can specify CustomRollupColumn with an appropriate MDX expression. However, with the unary operator N, you can simply specify the rollup using numerical values.

The Adventure Works DW relational database provides an example of the unary operator N for the Organization dimension, where the percentage of ownership is specified in a column in the Dim Organization table. Follow these steps to enhance the Dim Organization dimension created by the Dimension Wizard so that the dimension is modeled to match the actual business results:

1. Open the Dim Organization dimension. Specify the NameColumn property for the key attribute as OrganizationName.

2. Rename the Parent Organization Key parent-child hierarchy to **Organizations**. Select the Unary Operator Column property, and click the button at the right of the value column (with the "..." caption) in the Properties window to bring up the Unary Operator Column dialog. In the Unary Operator Column dialog, select the PercentageOfOwnership column, and click OK.

   At this point, you have specified the weighted average for the Organization's parent-child hierarchy. You might immediately want to see the results by deploying the changes. However, if you do deploy as such, you might see odd results because of the way calculations are applied in the cube. This is because when Analysis Services retrieves data for measures across a specific hierarchy, it takes the default members of other hierarchies while doing this evaluation. For most hierarchies the All member is the default. In the Account dimension the IsAggregatable property is set to false because aggregating the data for the top-level members in the Account dimension does not make business sense. In such circumstances, Analysis Services uses the default member of the hierarchy. If a default member is not specified, Analysis Services retrieves the first member of the hierarchy. The first member of the Accounts hierarchy is Balance Sheet, and the unary operator for Balance Sheet, ~ (tilde) results in nonintuitive results. For you to see meaningful results, you need to make sure you choose the right default.

3. For the Accounts hierarchy in the Account dimension, click the DefaultMember property. In the Set Default Member dialog, select the Choose a Member to Be the Default option, select Net Income, and click the OK button. The Net Income member has a unary operator of +, which results in meaningful data being seen while browsing the Amount measure for other dimensions. Now, deploy the changes to the Analysis Services instance. This percentage of ownership will be applied for the measures being queried.

4. If you browse the Organization dimension along with the measure Amount, you can notice appropriate rollups based on the weighted unary operator. Figure 8-14 shows the amount for various organizations, and you can see that the amount from the French and German organizations is only partially aggregated to the European Operations organization.

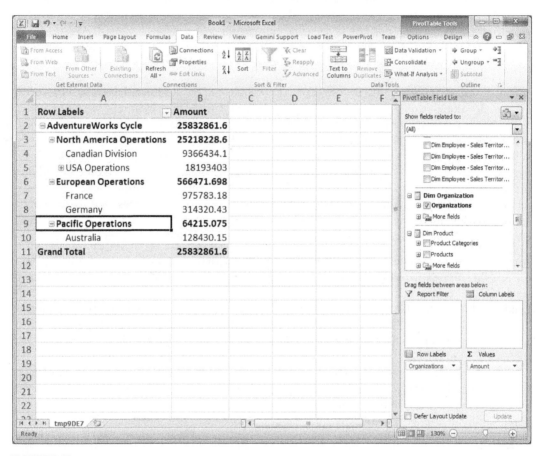

FIGURE 8-14

Calculation Precedence

When multiple calculations are specified for a cell, Analysis Services 2012 uses a specific order to evaluate calculations. Due to the order of calculations, cell values might not always be intuitive, and you can sometimes see unexpected results. You must know your cube design well, know Analysis Services' calculation precedence (order of calculations), and verify the results. Several calculations can be applied to a measure: semi-additive calculation, unary operator, and custom rollup. You learn more about semi-additive measures briefly in this chapter and in detail in Chapter 9. When Analysis Services is evaluating the measure value for a member, it initially calculates the regular aggregate of the measure value. This aggregate can be Sum, Count, or any of the built-in semi-additive functions (to be discussed later). If a unary operator is specified, the unary operator rollup is applied for the member across that specific dimension, and the value of the measure is overwritten. Finally, if a custom rollup is specified for the member, the value resulting from the custom rollup MDX expression is evaluated as the final result. The evaluation of a cell value is done across each dimension, and if dimensions have custom rollups and unary operators, then all the unary operators are applied, followed by custom rollups based on the order of the dimensions within the cube. As you might expect, you can modify the order of the dimensions by dragging and dropping dimensions to the wanted position in the cube editor's dimension list.

Specifying Names of Levels in a Parent-Child Hierarchy

When you create multilevel hierarchies, various attribute hierarchies form the levels of those hierarchies. For example, in a Geography hierarchy you may have Country, State, City, and ZIP Code as levels, and when you browse the dimension, you can see the names of the levels as the names of the attribute hierarchies. Parent-child hierarchies are different in this respect from user hierarchies. While creating regular hierarchies, you can see the various levels in the dimension editor, but for parent-child hierarchies you cannot visually see the number of levels unless you process and browse the hierarchy. The levels within a parent-child hierarchy are embedded within the self-referential relationships. However, Analysis Services allows you to define custom names for each level of the parent-child hierarchy. By default, Analysis Services 2012 provides basic names for the levels — Level 01, Level 02, and so on. Level N is based on the depth of the parent-child hierarchy.

If you want custom names to be specified for each level, Analysis Services provides a property for just that. For example, if you have an org-structure parent-child hierarchy, you can name the levels CEO, Presidents, Vice Presidents, General Managers, Product Unit Managers, Managers, Leads, and Individual Contributors. If you want to specify common prefix, use the parent-child property called NamingTemplate. If you click the selection for NamingTemplate, you launch the Level Naming Template dialog, as shown in Figure 8-15. In this dialog you can specify the name for each level in the parent-child hierarchy. If you want a constant prefix name followed by the level number, such as Employee Level 1, Employee Level 2, and so on, you just need to specify Employee Level * (refer to Figure 8-15) and Analysis Services automatically appends the level number at the end of each level. Follow these steps to create custom names for each level of a parent-child hierarchy:

1. Edit the Dim Employee dimension, select the Parent Employee Key hierarchy, and click the value for the NamingTemplate property.

2. In the Level Naming Template dialog, specify the level names as Employee Level * (refer to Figure 8-15).

3. Change the name of the parent-child hierarchy to Employees.

4. Add a new named calculation called Full Name in the DimEmployee table within the DSV, which is the concatenation of FirstName, a space, and LastName.

5. Make the Full Name relational column as the NameColumn for the key attribute of the Dim Employee dimension.

6. Deploy the changes to the Analysis Services instance.

When you browse the Employees hierarchy, you can see the new level names, as shown in Figure 8-16. When you click a member, you see the level name shown next to the Current Level.

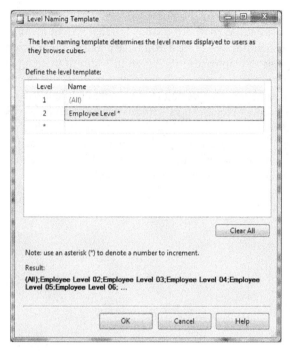

FIGURE 8-15

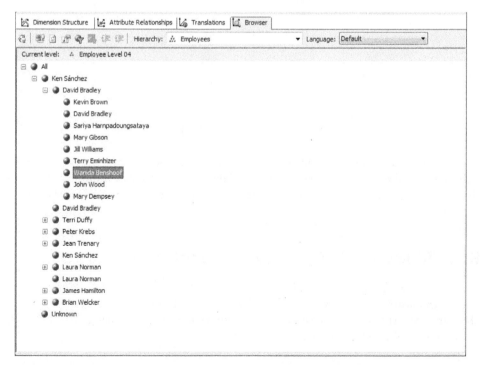

FIGURE 8-16

In Figure 8-16 you can see that the member David Bradley also reports to David Bradley. This is because each parent member is also included as its child, so that the value for that parent member is an aggregate of all its children and its own value. For example, if you have a Sales organization of employees and each manager manages a few sales employees in a region in addition to being in charge of certain sales, the total sales by the manager is a sum of all the direct reports plus the manager's own sales. That is why you sometimes see members reporting to themselves while browsing a parent-child hierarchy. If you know that the nonleaf members (as with managers in an employee organization) do not have fact data associated with them and are just an aggregate of the children, Analysis Services provides a property by which you can disable a member being a child of itself. This property is called MemberWithData and setting the value to NonLeafDataHidden, as shown in Figure 8-17, allows you to disable a member being shown as reporting to itself.

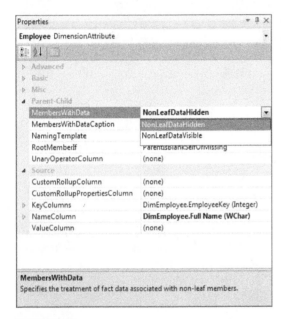

FIGURE 8-17

You have now learned several enhancements to parent-child hierarchies. The properties for parent-child hierarchies provided by Analysis Services help you model requirements for different business scenarios. In the next section you look at other properties of attributes and dimensions that help you enhance dimensions.

USING PROPERTIES TO CUSTOMIZE DIMENSIONS

Analysis Services provides several properties for use with hierarchies and dimensions. If every property were explained with illustrations and examples, this chapter would be quite large, so in this section you learn about the properties that are most important with respect to optimal design or more likely to be used in fulfillment of common business requirements.

Ordering Dimension Members

In Chapter 5 you learned to order dimension members of a hierarchy based on key or named columns specified for the attribute. Based on that, Analysis Services sorted the members in the hierarchy, and you could see the order while browsing the dimension. In certain business scenarios, you might have a need to sort the members based on a specific value or based on some other condition. Analysis Services provides properties to sort members of a hierarchy in a variety of ways other than by the attribute's key or name columns.

Specifically, you have the option to sort members of a given attribute based upon members of another, related attribute. The related bit is important here. For this technique to be used, you must define the ordering attribute as a related attribute (also known as member property) of the attribute to be ordered. For example, if you have an Employees parent-child hierarchy and if you have the age of the employees defined as an attribute, you can set the appropriate properties to the key attribute of the dimension to achieve a sorting of employees in the parent-child hierarchy based on age. You need to set the property OrderByAttribute to age and then set the property OrderBy to either AttributeKey or AttributeName depending on your requirements, and then deploy the changes to the Analysis Services instance. Figure 8-18 shows these properties. You can see the changes take effect by viewing the members in the Dimension Browser.

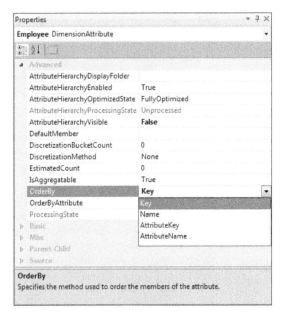

FIGURE 8-18

The All Member, Default Member, and Unknown Member

Each hierarchy within a dimension has a member that is called the *default member*. When a query is sent to Analysis Services, Analysis Services uses the default member for all the hierarchies that are not included in the query to evaluate the results for the query. If a default member is not specified, Analysis Services uses the first noncalculated member in the hierarchy based on the default ordering for the hierarchy. If the property IsAggregatable is set to True, that means that the values of members of the hierarchy can be aggregated to form a single member. This single member is, by default, called the All member and is most commonly the default member for the hierarchy. You can change the name of the All member for the attribute hierarchies within the dimension by changing the dimension property AttributeAllMemberName, as shown in Figure 8-19. To select the Properties window for the dimension, you can click the dimension name in the Attributes pane in the dimension editor or anywhere in the Hierarchies pane. If you deploy the project after changing the value for the AttributeAllMemberName property (refer to Figure 8-19), you can see that the All member for the Dim Employee dimension now shows up as All Employees in the Dimension Browser. For multilevel hierarchies the property to set the name of the (All) member is AllMemberName.

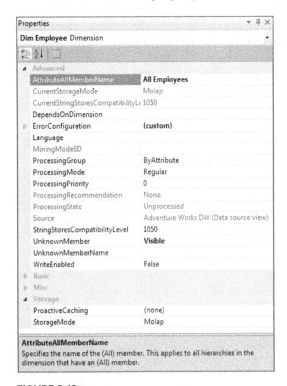

FIGURE 8-19

To change the default member for a hierarchy, you set the property DefaultMember to the correct member in the hierarchy. Click the ellipsis next to the DefaultMember property for the Employees hierarchy, and you see the Set Default Member dialog, as shown in Figure 8-20. You have three options for specifying the default member: using the system default member, selecting the member by browsing the hierarchy, or specifying an MDX expression to arrive at the default member. For the last option you can paste the MDX expression that evaluates the default member for the hierarchy or use the dialog to build the MDX expression that evaluates the default member. After the default member has been set for a specific hierarchy, Analysis Services uses that default member in query evaluation. You can send the following MDX query to ensure the default member you have set in the property is being used by Analysis Services:

```
SELECT [Dim Employee].[Employees].DefaultMember ON 0
FROM [Adventure Works DW]
```

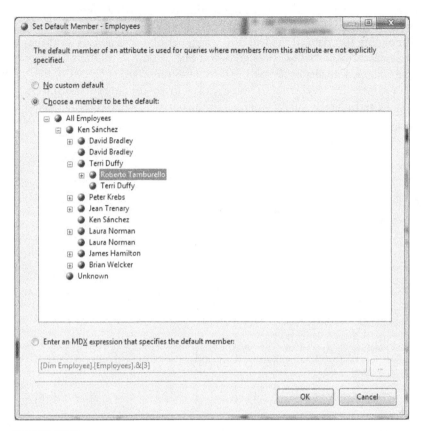

FIGURE 8-20

The UnknownMember is another property for each dimension in your database. If referential integrity issues are in your relational database, then during partition processing Analysis Services raises appropriate errors. If you have set specific processing options to ignore errors but include the fact data corresponding to errors in the cube, Analysis Services allocates the fact data to a member called the Unknown member in the dimensions for which it cannot find members due to referential integrity issues. You have the option to allow the Unknown member to be visible or hidden using the dimension property UnknownMember. When the UnknownMember is set to be visible, the member name is set to UnknownMember and is included in the results of the MDX queries that contain the hierarchy. Similar to the All member name, Analysis Services gives you the option to change the name of the Unknown member to a more meaningful name corresponding to that specific dimension. The name you choose is used across the entire dimension (that is, you cannot set per-attribute unknown member names), so make sure to pick a sufficiently general name.

Error Configurations for Processing

One of the challenges in designing a data warehouse is creating a perfect schema without any referential integrity issues. This is often not possible, and a significant amount of the time spent in designing a data warehouse is typically spent in data cleansing. Analysis Services, by default, stops processing dimensions whenever it encounters specific referential integrity issues. Some data warehouse designers might want to ignore the referential integrity issues by ignoring the records causing errors and include corresponding fact data to the Unknown member of dimensions so that they can see the results of their cube design. Analysis Services gives you fine-grain control for various referential integrity issues that can happen during processing. The dimension property ErrorConfiguration allows you that control for dimension processing. If you click the ErrorConfiguration property and select Custom, you see all the settings that allow you fine-grain control as well as the default values, as shown in Figure 8-21.

FIGURE 8-21

The possible errors Analysis Services can encounter while processing a dimension are related to key attributes of the dimension. Typically, you can encounter dimension key errors while processing, whenever Analysis Services cannot find corresponding keys in the dimension tables involved in the snowflake schema. The main errors that Analysis Services encounters are duplicate key errors (multiple occurrences of the key attribute in the dimension table), key not found error (unable to find a key in the dimension table in the schema), and null keys being encountered when you do not expect null keys to be present. You can set properties to stop processing after a specific number of errors have been reached, continue processing by reporting the errors, or ignore all errors. You can set various error configurations while building your data warehouses.

Storage Mode

Analysis Services supports two storage modes for dimensions. Your dimensions can be configured to be MOLAP or ROLAP dimensions. If a dimension is configured as MOLAP, Analysis Services reads all the dimension data from the relational data sources at the time of processing and stores the data in a compressed format. Due to the proprietary, patented format, Analysis Services can retrieve dimension data efficiently, resulting in fast query response times. When the storage mode is set to ROLAP, Analysis Services retrieves all data from the relational data source, in effect translating and redirecting at run time. Next, Analysis Services performs necessary calculations (aggregate computation, calculated members, and so on) prior to providing the results of the query to the client. Typically, ROLAP storage mode is chosen only when a large number of members exist in a dimension (with hundreds of millions of members). You need to evaluate the trade-off between query performance, which is significantly slower, versus storage or business requirement and set the correct storage mode for your dimensions. Disks have become quite cheap these days, and you can set the storage mode for dimensions to MOLAP. However, in certain business scenarios in which you have the dimension data constantly changing and you need real-time data, you might want to set the storage mode to ROLAP. Even in cases in which your customers need real-time data, you might set the property called Proactive Caching that helps to provide real-time data. Figure 8-22 shows the dimension property for storage mode. The InMemory StorageMode is only available for Tabular databases, which you learn in Chapter 17.

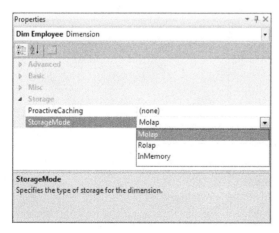

FIGURE 8-22

Grouping Members

Some of the hierarchies might have continuous data, and typically you might not be interested in viewing each member. An example of such a hierarchy is the salary of customers. Typically you would be interested in customers within a specific salary range rather than querying for customers with a specific salary. In such circumstances, Analysis Services allows you to model your hierarchy so that the members of the hierarchy are ranges rather than individual values. Analysis Services provides two properties to control this behavior so that you can group a set of members to a single group. These properties are DiscretizationBucketCount and DiscretizationMethod.

Follow these steps to understand the behavior:

1. In the Dimension Designer open the Dim Customer dimension.

2. The Yearly Income attribute hierarchy of the Dim Customer dimension has the annual income amount for each customer. To group these values into a few members, you need to set the properties DiscretizationBucketCount and DiscretizationMethod. Set the DiscretizationBucketCount to 10 and the DiscretizationMethod to Automatic, as shown in Figure 8-23. The DiscretizationBucketCount instructs Analysis Services to generate N members in the hierarchy. The DiscretizationMethod specifies the way in which you want the customer salaries to be grouped. The Automatic setting instructs Analysis Services to find the most efficient way to group the values after analyzing all the values. Deploy the changes to your Analysis Services instance.

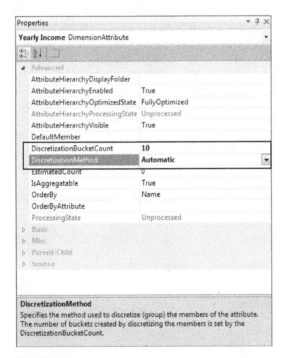

FIGURE 8-23

You can see the various buckets generated automatically by Analysis Services in the Dimension Browser, as shown in Figure 8-24.

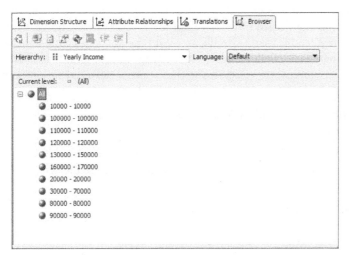

FIGURE 8-24

You have learned most of the commonly used properties that can help you to enhance your dimensions and hierarchies for your business. In the next section you add intelligence to your dimensions by means of the Business Intelligence Wizard. This wizard can help you model common business logic within your dimensions and cubes without writing any code.

DIMENSION INTELLIGENCE USING THE BUSINESS INTELLIGENCE WIZARD

The Business Intelligence Wizard contains multiple features, but you focus on three of the more commonly applicable ones in this chapter: Account Intelligence, Time Intelligence, and Dimension Intelligence. Analysis Services 2012 natively supports the Account dimension type in the engine. In this way, Analysis Services can aggregate data for members in Account dimensions based on account types. The Time Intelligence feature creates calculations for common business questions, such as year-over-year or quarter-over-quarter revenue. Analysis Services 2012 enables support for these calculations natively so that all client and custom tools can take advantage of these calculations. The Dimension Intelligence feature allows you to map your dimension to commonly used dimension types so that client tools can discover and present them to customers in a way that is easily interpreted.

Account Intelligence

In Chapter 6 you learned about measures and aggregation functions that are specified for measures such as Sum, Count, and Distinct Count. Analysis Services 2012 supports calculations specifically for the Account dimension type so that an appropriate aggregation function is applied based on account types. A special type of aggregation function is ByAccount. Based on the type of account, Analysis Services can apply the right aggregation function. The Account Intelligence Wizard allows you to qualify a dimension as an Account dimension and then map the dimension to well-known account types. Based on these mappings the wizard informs you of the type of aggregation function that is applied for the account. If your Account uses a specific account type and aggregation function, you can specify that at the database level. Follow these steps to map the Account dimension as a dimension of type Account and specify necessary attributes so that appropriate aggregation functions are applied:

1. In the AnalysisServicesMultidimensionalTutorial you have been working with, double-click the Account.dim dimension to open it in the Dimension Designer.

2. Launch the Dimension Intelligence Wizard from the menu item Dimension ➪ Add Business Intelligence or by clicking the first icon in the Dimension Designer. If you see the Welcome screen, click the Next button.

3. In the Choose Enhancement page, select Define Account Intelligence, as shown in Figure 8-25, and click Next.

FIGURE 8-25

4. In the Configure Dimension Attributes page, as shown in Figure 8-26, you need to define the mapping between the attributes in the current dimension named Account to the standard attributes of the Account dimension. Map the Chart of Accounts to the parent-child hierarchy Accounts; Account Name to the key attribute Account Key that contains the name of the Accounts; Account Number to the Account Code Alternate Key (Account Code Alternate Key uniquely identifies a member in the account); and the Account Type to the attribute Account Type, and click Next.

FIGURE 8-26

The Account Type identifies the type of an account member and is used by Analysis Services to use the appropriate aggregation function for measures that have the AggregationFunction property set to ByAccount.

5. In the Define Account Intelligence page (Figure 8-27), the account types from the source table are mapped to the built-in account types in Analysis Services. If the name of the account types in the source table do not directly map to the built-in account types, you would need to map them correctly in this page. Click Next.

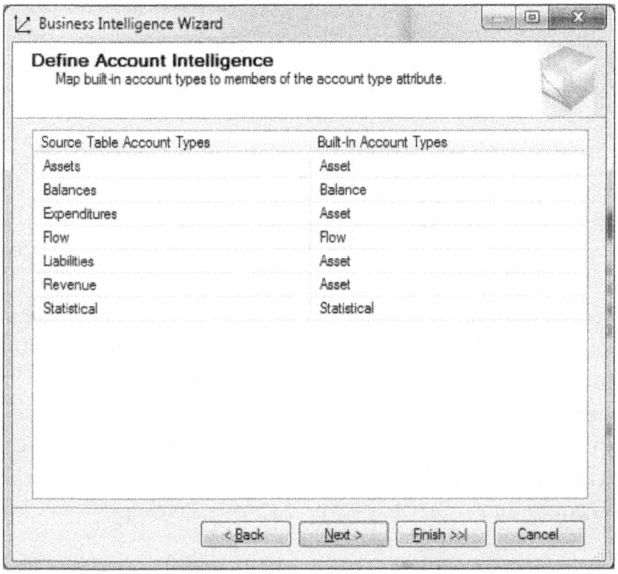

FIGURE 8-27

6. The final page of the Business Intelligence Wizard shows the various account types along with the aggregation functions associated with accounts (Figure 8-28). Please review the aggregation functions, and click Finish.

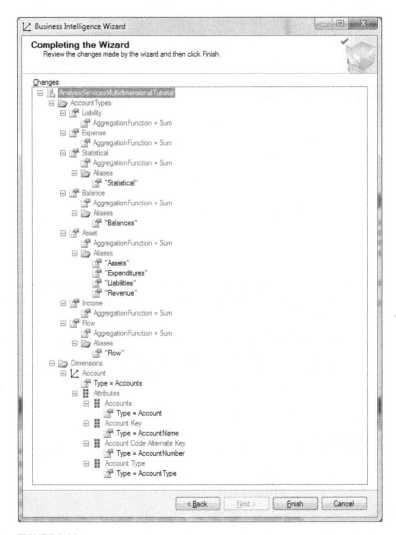

FIGURE 8-28

You have now successfully enhanced your Account dimension. If you look at the properties for the Account dimension you see that the Type property is set to Accounts. The aggregation functions for various account types are predefined in Analysis Services. However, Analysis Services allows you the flexibility to add additional account types as well as to make changes to the AggregationFunction for the account types to suit your business needs. To make modifications, right-click the project name AnalysisServicesMultidimensionalTutorial in the Solution Explorer, and select Edit Database. You now see a new designer where you could make changes at the database level, as shown in Figure 8-29.

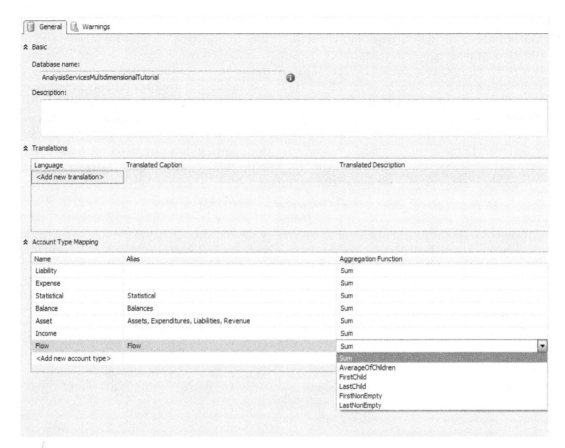

FIGURE 8-29

As mentioned earlier, the enhancement made to the Account dimension is applicable only for measures that have their aggregation function defined as ByAccount. Open the Adventure Works DW cube. In the Cube Structure pane, select the measure Amount in the Fact Finance measure group, and set the AggregateFunction, for this measure to ByAccount, as shown in Figure 8-30. Deploy your changes to the Analysis Services instance.

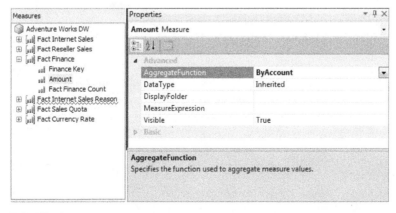

FIGURE 8-30

In the Cube Browser, launch Excel and browse the measure Amount along with the Account dimension members; the right aggregation functions are used to aggregate the measure values based on the account type. However, the member Statistical Accounts is not visible in the Pivot Table in Excel. This is because accounts of type Statistical should have the value rolled up based on the aggregation function Sum; however, all the children of member Statistical Accounts have a unary operator column set to ~, which means those values are not rolled up to the parent. To view the Statistical Accounts member and its children, you need to define a value for members. Switch to the Calculations tab in the Cube Designer. Right-click the Script Organizer pane and select New Script Command. In the script command window, enter the following statement to set the Amount for the Account member Statistical Account to be NA. Save the changes, switch to the Browser tab, and deploy the changes to your Analysis Services instance.

```
( [Account].[Accounts].&[95], [Measures].[Amount] ) = "NA"
```

You now refresh the Excel Pivot Table to the you see the Statistical Account member and its children, as shown in Figure 8-31. You can see the Amount for Statistical Accounts is set to NA even though the aggregation function is Sum. This is because Analysis Services applies Unary operator evaluation on a cell after the regular rollup across the dimension (in this specific case, ByAccount aggregation).

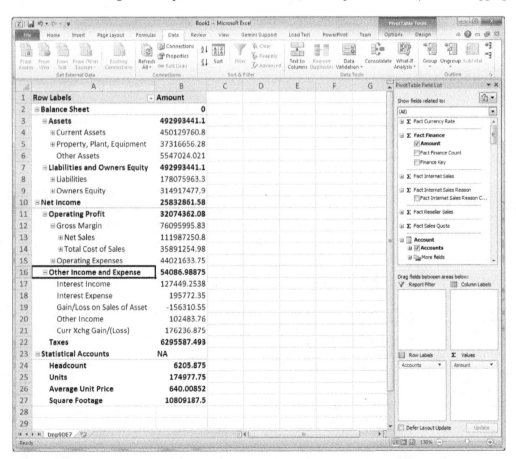

FIGURE 8-31

Because the aggregation functions specific to an Account Type are done natively with Analysis Services rather than in calculations in scripts, you should expect better query performance.

Time Intelligence

Certain calculations are frequently used in business such as calculating Year to Date and Year Over Year Growth for measures such as Sales. These calculations are related to Time dimensions and can be created within the scope of the query or session as necessary. Analysis Services 2012 provides a wizard to enhance your cube to add such calculations. The Time Intelligence enhancement is a cube enhancement because calculations such as Year to Date and Year Over Year Growth are all calculated in the context of measures. Because this enhancement adds appropriate calculations to the cube as well as attributes to the Time dimension, it is included this chapter. Follow these steps to define Time Intelligence enhancement:

1. Open the Adventure Works DW cube, and switch to the Cube Structure page.

2. Launch the Business Intelligence Wizard from the cube menu Add Business Intelligence or by clicking the Add Business Intelligence icon (first icon on the Cube Structure tab). If you see the Welcome screen, press Next.

3. On the Choose Enhancement page, select Define Time Intelligence, as shown in Figure 8-32, and click Next.

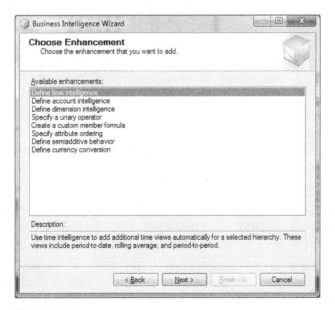

FIGURE 8-32

4. On the Choose Target Hierarchy and Calculations page, you need to select which time calculations to use as well as the hierarchy in the Time dimension that uses those calculations. In the drop-down list box for Use the Following Hierarchy to Analyze Time Calculations, you

can see the four Time dimensions: Dim Date, Order Date, Ship Date, and Due Date. All these cube dimensions are role-playing dimensions of the database dimension Dim Date. Select the multilevel hierarchy Calendar Date in the cube dimension Order Date, as shown in Figure 8-33. Select the calculations Year to Date, Year Over Year Growth, and Year Over Year Growth %, and click Next.

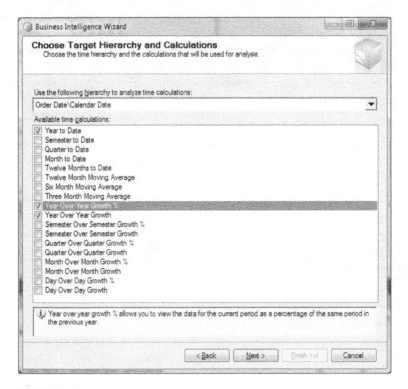

FIGURE 8-33

5. On the Define Scope of Calculations page, you need to select the measures for which you need the time calculations to be applied. Select the measure Sales Amount, as shown in Figure 8-34. Click Next.

6. The final page of the wizard shows the changes to the database Time dimension Dim Date as well as the calculations, as shown in Figure 8-35. You can see that the wizard adds a calculated column to the dbo_DimDate table in the DSV and adds that column as an attribute in the Dim Date dimension in addition to the calculations that will be added to the cube's script. Click the Finish button.

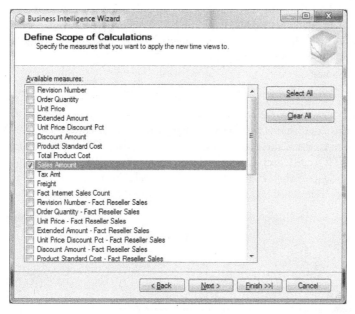

FIGURE 8-34

FIGURE 8-35

Switch to the Calculations tab of the cube, and explore the calculations created by the Business Intelligence Wizard. Also look at the Named Calculation added to the DimDate table in the DSV. These can help you to understand the calculations you need to create if you didn't have the Time Intelligence enhancement. The Business Intelligence Wizard makes it easy for data warehouse designers to add the enhancements related to Time dimensions without defining and verifying the calculations by hand, which can take a considerable amount of time.

You have successfully enhanced your cube and Time dimension to analyze growth of the Sales Amount measure. To use the calculations for analysis, deploy the enhancements to your Analysis Services instance, and switch to the Cube Browser. Launch Excel, drag and drop the measure [Sales Amount] to the Values area, [Order Date].[Calendar Date] hierarchy on Row Labels and [Order Date].[Calendar Date Order Date Calculations] on Column Labels. You can see the Year to Date, Year Over Year Growth, and Year Over Year Growth %, as shown in Figure 8-36.

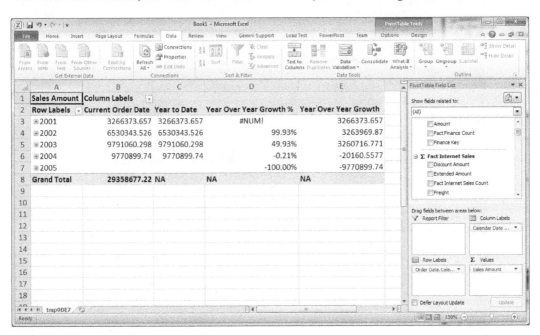

FIGURE 8-36

You see #NUM! and a value for Year Over Year Growth for the year 2001 (refer to Figure 8-36). The Time Intelligence Wizard defines calculations based on the assumption the hierarchy contains only years that have data. However in this example, the Calendar Year hierarchy has a year 2000 (you can verify this in the dimension browser) that does not have any Sales Amount value. Due to this inconsistency in the data, you get Year Over Year Growth and Year Over Year Growth % calculations incorrect. You would need to go into the Calculations tab and change the Calculation to set these values to Null. Enclosed here are the MDX script definitions you need to add to MDX script. Add these Script commands, deploy the project, and refresh that data in Excel to see the correct Null values for year 2001.

```
/*Year Over Year Growth % set to Null value for Year 2001 */
    (
        [Order Date].[Calendar Date Order Date Calculations].[Year Over Year Growth %],
```

```
    [Order Date].[Calendar Year].[Calendar Year].Members ( 1 ),
        [Order Date].[Date Key].Members
 ) = Null;


/*Year Over Year Growth set to Null value for Year 2001*/
(
    [Order Date].[Calendar Date Order Date Calculations].[Year Over Year Growth],
    [Order Date].[Calendar Year].[Calendar Year].Members ( 1 ),
        [Order Date].[Date Key].Members
 ) = Null;
```

Dimension Intelligence

Analysis Services provides you a way to map your dimensions to standard dimension types such as Customer, Organization, and Currency. These mappings can help client tools that might have customized views of presenting such dimension types to end users. To map your dimensions to standard dimension types, follow these steps:

1. Open the Dim Organization dimension in the Dimension Designer.

2. Launch the Business Intelligence Wizard by clicking the Add Business Intelligence icon or from the menu Dimension Add Business Intelligence. If you see the Welcome screen, click Next.

3. On the Choose Enhancement page, select Define Dimension Intelligence (as shown in Figure 8-37) and click Next.

FIGURE 8-37

4. On the Define Dimension Intelligence page, select the Dimension type as Organization, as shown in Figure 8-38, and enable the Attribute Types Company and Ownership Percentage and how they map to corresponding attributes in the Dim Organization dimension, and click Next.

FIGURE 8-38

5.   The final page of the wizard shows the definitions specified in the previous page. It shows that Dim Organization is of standard dimension type Organization. This dimension contains several companies, which are represented by the attribute Organizations, and the PercentOwnership is determined by the attribute Percentage of Ownership (see Figure 8-39). Click Finish.

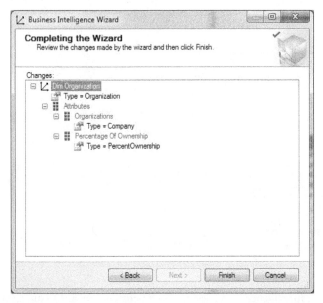

FIGURE 8-39

You have successfully defined dimension intelligence for the Dim Organization dimension. You can see that the property Type for the dimension and the attributes selected in the Dimension Intelligence enhancement have been set appropriately. You should apply the Dimension Intelligence enhancement to the remaining dimensions. You can view the effect of these only through client tools that utilize the dimension property Type.

SERVER TIME DIMENSION

In certain data warehouses you might not have a special table for Time. However, the fact table might contain Date as a column. Analysis Services 2012 provides you the functionality of creating a Time dimension with appropriate hierarchies based on a time range. For example, you can configure the range based on the beginning and end dates found in your fact tables. This range-based Time dimension is created in Analysis Services and is called a Server Time dimension. When a Server Time dimension is created, you can add it to the cube and specify appropriate granularity. Follow these steps to create a Server Time dimension:

1. In the Solution Explorer, right-click the Dimensions folder, and select New Dimension to launch the Dimension Wizard.

2. Select the option to Generate a Time Table on the Server, as shown in Figure 8-40, and click Next.

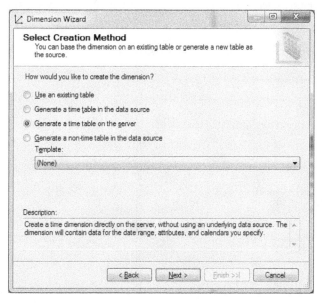

FIGURE 8-40

3. On the Define Time Periods page, select the date ranges, as shown in Figure 8-41, and the Time periods Year, Quarter, Month, Week, and Date, and click Next.

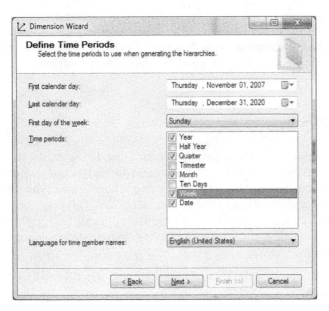

FIGURE 8-41

4. On the Select Calendars page, select Fiscal Calendar, as shown in Figure 8-42, and click Next.

FIGURE 8-42

5. On the final page of the wizard, enter the name of the dimension as **ServerTimeDimension**, as shown in Figure 8-43, and click Finish.

FIGURE 8-43

The ServerTimeDimension is now created, and you can see its hierarchies and attributes in the Dimension Designer, as shown in Figure 8-44. Because this dimension is created from Analysis Services instead of the DSV, you see a pane called Time Periods that lists all the periods available for selection. You can add additional Time Periods as attributes in the dimension. Date is the key attribute of this dimension and cannot be deleted. You likely need this attribute to define relationships to your fact tables.

Deploy the changes to the Analysis Services instance. You can now browse the hierarchies in ServerTimeDimension, as shown in Figure 8-45. The formats used for members of various levels cannot be changed, which is something to consider when opting to use this feature. You need to add this dimension to your cubes and then manually define the relationship between it and your measure groups. Server Time dimensions are especially useful when your data source does not already contain a Time dimension and you do not have write access to the underlying data source. If you do have write access and need to create a Time dimension, the Generate a Time Table in the Data Source option is more favorable because you can subsequently customize the dimension via named calculations.

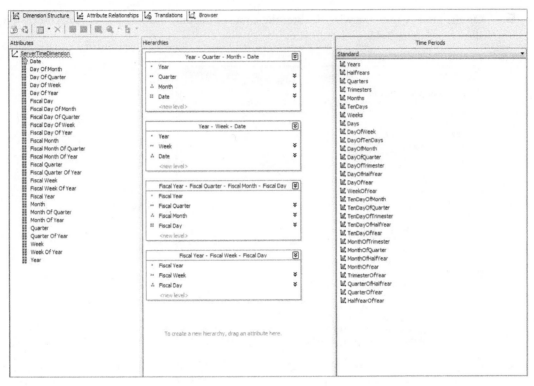

FIGURE 8-44

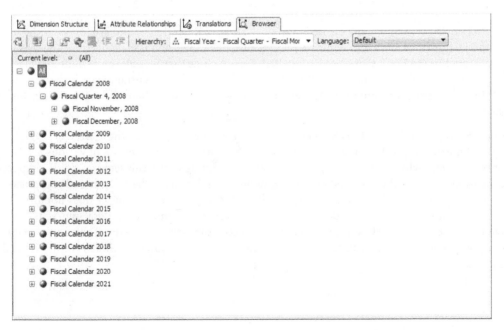

FIGURE 8-45

DIMENSION WRITEBACK

Dimension writeback is another enhancement to dimensions and is available through the Dimension Intelligence Wizard. This is an important though rarely used feature that allows you to create or modify members in your dimension without needing to go to your relational data source. After you enable your dimension for writeback, Analysis Services provides you the functionality to add or modify members through the Dimension Browser pane. Following are some business scenarios in which you can use dimension writeback:

➤ During budgeting or forecasting, to create or restructure accounts to model hypothetical business plans.

➤ When modeling a company reorganization or restructuring plan that involves moving employees for team to team or department to department.

➤ When you have an Account dimension and new types of accounts are introduced and you need to add members to the dimension.

When you write back data through the dimension, Analysis Services propagates the change in the data to the relational data source and does an incremental process of the dimension, such that affected members are processed. During this time, the dimension and cube are available for querying by other users. To understand dimension writeback you can use the official Adventure Works DW sample Analysis Services project. Because you make changes to the sample project, make a copy of the sample project files before you begin. The following steps show how to enable writeback on the Employee dimension and can also help you understand dimension writeback behavior by having you perform writeback operations on certain employees:

1. Open the Employee dimension of the Adventure Works sample Analysis Services project in the Dimension Designer, and look at the Properties pane.

2. Set the dimension property WriteEnabled to True, as shown in Figure 8-46.

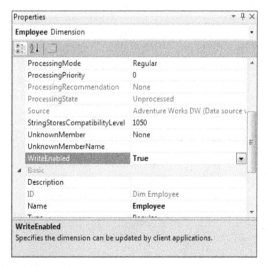

FIGURE 8-46

3. If you build your project, you see three errors in the Employee dimension that state the discretization method for the attributes Sick Leave Hours, Vacation Hours, and Base Rate needs to be set to None. Change the discretization method for the attributes Sick Leave Hours, Vacation Hours, and Base Rate to None.

> *Enabling dimension writeback has several restrictions. To make the Employee dimension fully write-enabled, you need to make a few additional changes.*

4. Change the property AttributeHierarchyEnabled to False for the attributes Start Date, End Date, Hire Date, Salaried Flag, Sales Person Flag, and Pay Frequency.

5. Change the NameColumn property of Gender from GenderDesc to the column Gender.

6. Save and deploy the changes to your Analysis Services instance.

7. After deployment succeeds, SSDT should automatically switch the view from the Dimension Structure pane to the Dimension Browser pane. If not, switch to the Dimension Browser pane. Click the Member Properties icon, and select the member properties Birth Date, Gender, Status, Phone, and Title, which are related to the Employees dimension.

8. Assume the employee John Wood got a new phone and you need to update his phone number. Navigate to the John Wood member (All Employees ⇨ Ken J. Sanchez ⇨ David M. Bradley). Click the Writeback toolbar button, or from the top menus select Dimension Writeback to enter writeback mode. Double-click the member property Phone for John Wood. The Phone for John is now editable, as shown in Figure 8-47.

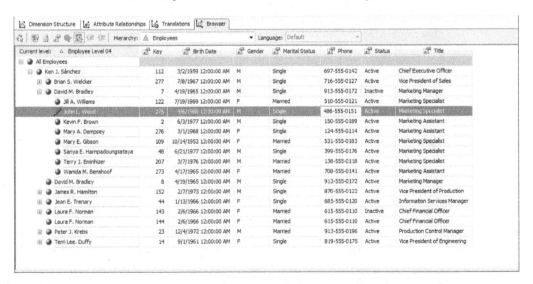

FIGURE 8-47

9.   Change the Phone value to 486-555-0151, and then move the cursor to a different row.

At this time SSDT sends the following dimension writeback request to the Analysis Services instance. If you run the SQL Profiler, you can see that an Update statement for the cube dimension $Employee is sent to the Analysis Services instance. The key attribute is critical for Analysis Server to make the appropriate update. If the operation was successful, you can make other operations. If there are errors, you should get feedback from the Analysis Services with the appropriate error messages. When a dimension member is updated via writeback, Analysis Services processes the dimension and related objects.

In the execute the following example in SQL Server Management Studio, you see an error that the writeback operation failed. If you analyze the operations on the Analysis Services instance using SQL Server Profiler (you learn about SQL Server Profiler and debugging operations on your Analysis Services in Chapter 11), you can see that the processing of the dimension Employee completes successfully, but while processing the related objects, you get a failure that causes the writeback to fail. This example is just to help you understand how to enable a dimension for writeback and use the Dimension Browser to perform dimension writeback.

```
<Update xsi:type="Update" xmlns:xsd="http://www.w3.org/2001/XMLSchema"
xmlns:xsi="http://www.w3.org/2001/XMLSchema-instance"
xmlns:ddl2="http://schemas.microsoft.com/analysisservices/2003/engine/2"
xmlns:ddl2_2="http://schemas.microsoft.com/analysisservices/2003/engine/2/2"
xmlns:ddl100_100="http://schemas.microsoft.com/analysisservices/2008/
engine/100/100"
xmlns="http://schemas.microsoft.com/analysisservices/2003/engine">
  <Object>
    <Database>Adventure Works DW</Database>
    <Cube>$Employee</Cube>
    <Dimension>Employee</Dimension>
  </Object>
  <Attributes>
    <Attribute>
      <AttributeName>Phone</AttributeName>
      <Keys>
        <Key xsi:type="xsd:string">486-555-0151</Key>
      </Keys>
    </Attribute>
  </Attributes>
  <Where>
    <Attribute>
      <AttributeName>Employee</AttributeName>
      <Keys>
        <Key xsi:type="xsd:int">275</Key>
      </Keys>
    </Attribute>
  </Where>
</Update>
```

You have successfully learned to enable a dimension for writeback in the Employee dimension. You can perform additional operations such as creating new members, moving a member along with descendants, and deleting members through dimension writeback. You can try these operations on a write-enabled dimension. You should be aware that you cannot change the values of the existing key attributes in the dimension because the key attribute is used by the Analysis Services instance to perform the writeback operation.

SUMMARY

You have experienced more chapter flashbacks than usual here, but that merely suggests certain loose ends are getting tied together and certain mental connections are being reinforced. In this chapter you learned about custom rollups using the common business concept of depreciation, which addresses the nature of value change over time. Any type of change over time is a recurrent theme in business intelligence, and this chapter discussed use of the Time Intelligence enhancement, which can be used on cubes with a Time dimension to provide views by time period. Similarly, the Account Intelligence enhancement was explored; it maps known business entities such as Income, Expense, Asset, and Liability to the dimensions in your cube so that appropriate rollup can be done for accounts natively in Analysis Services.

The Account Intelligence enhancement also allows you to add additional accounts and change aggregation functions for specific accounts based on your business requirements. You also learned how these calculations defined in MDX Script affect the results. The Server Time dimension helps you to define range-based Time dimensions quickly when there is no time table in your data source. The Dimension Wizard also provides you with the ability to create the standard dimension types such as Customers, Organizations, Time, Currency, and so on, along with appropriate attributes and hierarchies, and generates appropriate schemas in your data source, which is not discussed in this chapter. You would need to populate these tables with appropriate data before processing the dimensions. You can explore this option from the Dimension Wizard by selecting the option to Generate a Non-Time Table in the Data Source. Finally, dimension writeback was discussed, and you learned how data can be written back to the original relational table, and that an incremental process is kicked off so that related members in the dimension are processed along with the corresponding cube. Speaking of cubes, that is what the next chapter is about. Now that you have learned about dimension enhancement, it is time to move on to advanced cube design.

Advanced Cube Design

WHAT'S IN THIS CHAPTER?

➤ Working with measure groups and measures

➤ Understanding cube dimensions

➤ Exploring actions, Drillthrough, and Key Performance Indicators

➤ Extending cube intelligence

➤ Understanding cube storage and partitioning

➤ Building cube aggregations

➤ Exploring real-time cubes

You learned about creating and browsing a cube in Chapter 6, and in Chapters 5 and 8 you learned about dimensions and enhancing dimensions by using special dimension properties and by adding business intelligence. In addition you learned about MDX in Chapter 3. These topics form a solid foundation for this chapter, where you learn about enhancements to cube design that can help you become an expert in cube design. Review Chapters 3, 5, 6, and 8 if you are not confident that you understand them, because this chapter builds on what you learned there, focusing on enhancements to your cube in support of specific business requirements. The emphasis here is on working with measures in your cube by modifying properties to change how those measures appear in cubes and how values are aggregated. There is also a focus on using enhanced dimension relationships. In addition, you work with *actions* and *Key Performance Indicators* (KPIs), features that add functionality that help end users view and interpret data efficiently. To implement many of the techniques described in this chapter, you use advanced MDX. In some cases, you can use the Business Intelligence Wizard to simplify the addition of complex MDX. When you have the design techniques mastered, attention is turned to techniques for managing scalability through partitioning, assigning storage modes, and building aggregations.

If this book were the movie *The Matrix*, now is the time when Morpheus would hold out a red pill in one hand and a blue pill in the other, and say, "You put the book down and take the blue pill — the story ends, you wake up in your bed and believe whatever you want to believe. You take the red pill — and you see how to build powerful cubes." To be honest, this chapter might not be as dramatic as all that, but it brings together many of those gnarly concepts you have learned so that you can fine-tune the process to turn data into information (the essential theme of this book). At the risk of belaboring the point, this chapter actually is central, not just in the sense it is near the middle of the book, but in the sense it can help you understand some of the more important features in Analysis Services 2012. In this chapter, you use the AnalysisServicesMultidimensionalTutorial project you have been enhancing in previous chapters and the Adventure Works DW Multidimensional Analysis Services project available from this book's page on Wrox.com to understand how to apply advanced design techniques to cubes. So, gear up and get ready for a deep dive into the core of Analysis Services.

MEASURE GROUPS AND MEASURES

In Chapter 6, you learned about measure groups and measures within a cube. To recap, a cube can contain one or more measure groups, and each measure group can contain one or more measures. You also learned about the various aggregation functions for each measure and reviewed some MDX examples of how measure values are rolled up while browsing the cube. In this section, you learn how to use an MDX function to simplify querying measure groups and how to group measures within a measure group to help users navigate them more easily. You also learn how to use properties to control how measure values are aggregated when unrelated to dimensions in the same query or when performing currency conversions. Finally, you learn how to reuse measure groups in multiple cubes.

With Analysis Services 2012 it is quite possible to end up with a cube containing several measure groups. If you open the Adventure Works cube of the Adventure Works DW Multidimensional sample project, you have measures, as shown in Figure 9-1.

If you expand each measure group, you can see that most measure groups contain multiple measures. For example, the Internet Sales measure group has 9 measures, and the Reseller Sales measure group has 11. Often, business analysis questions are targeted at measures within a single measure group rather than all the measures within a cube. One way to write an MDX query targeting a specific measure group is to include each measure one by one. For instance, if you want all visible regular measures (that is, no calculated measures and no measures with the Visible property set to False) within the Internet Sales measure group, your MDX query could look like this:

```
SELECT
{[Measures].[Internet Sales Amount],
 [Measures].[Internet Order Quantity],
 [Measures].[Internet Extended Amount],
 [Measures].[Internet Tax Amount],
```

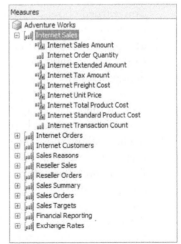

FIGURE 9-1

```
    [Measures].[Internet Freight Cost],
    [Measures].[Internet Total Product Cost],
    [Measures].[Internet Standard Product Cost]
} ON COLUMNS
FROM [Adventure Works]
```

It is time-consuming to form an MDX query that includes each measure of the measure group within the query because you need to drag and drop each measure individually or type the name of each measure into the query. Fortunately, an MDX function called `MeasureGroupMeasures` is provided to retrieve all the measures within a measure group. The following query shows how to use this function to return the same results as the preceding query:

```
SELECT MeasureGroupMeasures("Internet Sales") ON 0
FROM [Adventure Works]
```

Lots of measures in a single measure group can also be overwhelming for end users. Another feature can be used to create logical groupings of measures within each measure group, so users can locate measures more easily while browsing a cube. Simply assign the same value to the DisplayFolder property of each measure (in the same measure group) that you want to group together.

Not only do you need to consider measure groups and how measures appear in a cube, but also consider how they interact with dimensions. For example, when you have multiple measure groups within a single cube, certain dimensions do not have relationships with certain measure groups. Recall from Chapter 6 that relationships between dimensions and measure groups are defined on the Dimension Usage tab of the Cube Designer. If you look at Dimension Usage in the Adventure Works cube in the Adventure Works DW Multidimensional sample project, you see there is no relationship between the Internet Sales measure group and the Reseller dimension. A query that includes a measure from the Internet Sales measure group and members from the Reseller dimension, as shown in the following code, returns the same value for each Reseller member — the value for the All member:

```
SELECT {[Measures].[Internet Extended Amount]} ON 0,
[Reseller].[Reseller Type].MEMBERS ON 1
FROM [Adventure Works]
```

If users find this result confusing, you can override this default behavior by changing the value of the IgnoreUnrelatedDimensions property for the measure group, as shown in Figure 9-2.

If the IgnoreUnrelatedDimensions property is set to False, a query that includes a measure with a dimension having no relationship to it returns null values. If, for example, you change the IgnoreUnrelatedDimensions property of the Internet Sales measure group to False and then deploy the project, the preceding MDX query returns null cell values for each member of the Reseller dimension except the All Resellers member.

IgnoreUnrelatedDimensions is a property that modifies the functionality of the `ValidMeasure` MDX function. The `ValidMeasure` function returns a cell value corresponding to the All member for a dimension that does not have a relationship with the current measure. In other words, the dimension is not represented by a foreign key column in the fact table containing the current measure.

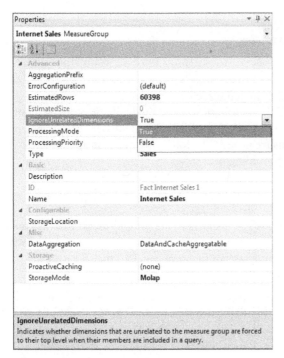

FIGURE 9-2

To continue the previous example, with the `IgnoreUnrelatedDimensions` property for the Internet Sales measure group set to False, you can execute the following MDX query to see that the cell values for all the members in the Reseller Type hierarchy have the same value for measure x, whereas the real measure Internet Extended Amount has null values:

```
WITH MEMBER measures.x AS ValidMeasure(([Measures].[Internet Extended Amount],
[Reseller].[Reseller Type]))
SELECT { measures.x,[Measures].[Internet Extended Amount]} ON 0,
[Reseller].[Reseller Type].MEMBERS ON 1
FROM [Adventure Works]
```

Another important measure property to know about is `MeasureExpression`. On the Cube Structure tab of the Cube Designer, click the Internet Sales Amount measure in the Internet Sales measure group to see its properties, as shown in Figure 9-3. A valid value for `MeasureExpression` is an MDX expression that typically includes the product (multiplication operator) or ratio (division operator) of two measures (or constant). This type of expression is used for currency conversions or when aggregating values with many-to-many dimensions, which are both discussed later in this chapter. When you specify a measure expression, Analysis Services 2012 evaluates the expression for each dimension member first and then aggregates the values across the dimension.

Measures used in the MDX expression can be from the same measure group or from different measure groups. The `MeasureExpression` divides Internet Sales Amount, from the Internet Sales measure group, by Average Rate, from the Exchange Rates measure group (refer to Figure 9-3). The Exchange Rates measure group contains the Average Rate and End of Day Rate to be used for currency conversions.

FIGURE 9-3

If you look at the Dimension Usage tab of the Cube Designer, you can see both measure groups, Internet Sales and Exchange Rates, have a direct relationship with the Date dimension. You can also see that dimension Destination Currency is directly related to the Exchange Rate measure group but has a many-to-many relationship with the Internet Sales measure group. These relationships are required when you store transaction data, such as sales amounts, in the fact table using the local currency, but need the ability to summarize that data in reports using a different currency. For instance, you have sales recorded in the fact table in Mexican pesos, but you need to report sales in Euros.

Because exchange rates vary over time, you might choose to average the exchange rate at the day or month level (depending on your business situation) to calculate the total sales in a specific currency. In the Adventure Works cube, the Average Rate measure is stored in the fact table at the day level. Because it's defined as a semiadditive measure, which you learn more about later in this chapter, its value is determined by calculating the average of the children of the current member of the Time dimension. That is, if the current member is a month member, the average rate is calculated by averaging the Average Rate measure for all days in that month.

You can best see the effect of Average Rate on Internet Sales Amount by browsing the cube in Excel. Place Destination Currency on rows, and add the measures Average Rate and Internet Sales Amount, as shown in Figure 9-4.

You can see the U.S. dollar is the base currency because it has an Average Rate of 1 (refer to Figure 9-4). The Internet Sales Amount for the other currencies is not derived from the division of Internet Sales Amount shown in U.S. dollars by the destination currency's Average Rate. The MeasureExpression defined for Internet Sales Amount causes Analysis Services to calculate a value for each individual transaction, dividing Internet Sales Amount in U.S. dollars by the Average Rate for that day, and then aggregating the calculated values to show the Internet Sales Amount in the wanted currency. (You learn later in this chapter how the individual transactions were converted to U.S. dollars before the MeasureExpression is applied.)

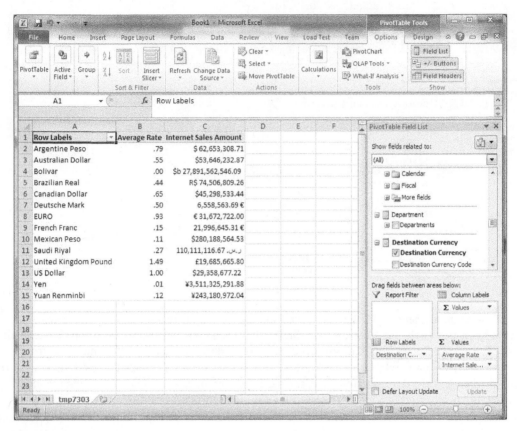

FIGURE 9-4

When you have a measure group and its measures designed just right, you can add that measure group into another cube. With Analysis Services 2012, you can use the Object Linked Wizard to add a measure group from another cube in the same database, a cube on the same server, or a cube in any other Analysis Services instance. You can launch the wizard from either the Cube Structure tab, as shown in Figure 9-5, or use the New Linked Object icon in the Cube Structure or Dimension Usage tabs of the cube editor.

Using the wizard, you can define a data source for the Analysis Services database containing the measure group you want to include in your current cube, and then select the wanted measure group from the list of available objects. The Linked Measure Group Wizard is self-explanatory, and you can add a linked measure group.

Take a look at the Mined Customers cube in the Adventure Works DW Multidimensional sample project

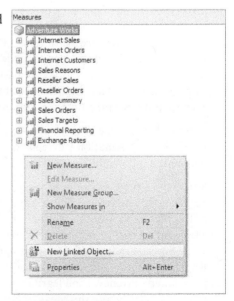

FIGURE 9-5

to see how all measure groups in a cube can be linked measure groups, as shown in Figure 9-6. Linked measure groups are identified by a linking chain icon.

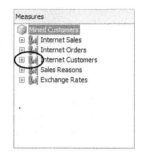

After adding a linked measure group, you still need to define the right relationships between the dimensions in the cube and the linked measure group. By using a linked measure group, you have access to data in the source cube without the maintenance overhead of multiple separate measure groups for the same data.

FIGURE 9-6

 You can have a cube where all the real measures are hidden. All the measures exposed to the end users are calculated measures. Some Analysis Services customers design their cubes this way to model specific business requirements.

ADDING AND ENHANCING DIMENSIONS

Dimensions are an integral part of a cube. In this section, you learn about specific properties that affect a dimension's behavior within a cube as well as special types of relationships that can be defined between a dimension and a measure group. These features enable you to address special business requirements and thereby enhance overall analytical capabilities.

When you create a dimension within an Analysis Services 2012 database, you are actually creating a *database dimension*, which can be shared across multiple cubes within the same database or used multiple times within a single cube. Each instance of a database dimension within a cube is called a *cube dimension*. Right-click within the Dimensions pane of the Cube Structure page, as shown in Figure 9-7, to add a new cube dimension.

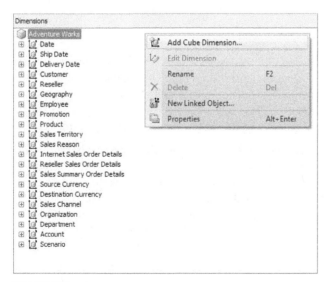

FIGURE 9-7

For each cube dimension, you can selectively exclude certain hierarchies or attributes by modifying properties. In the Dimensions pane on the Cube Structure tab, select the hierarchy or the attribute to be hidden and then change the applicable property in the Properties window to False. If you want to hide a hierarchy, use the Visible property. To hide an attribute, use the AttributeHierarchyVisible property.

Another important property of a cube dimension is AllMemberAggregationUsage. This property is associated with the cube dimension object. Changing the value of this property affects how Analysis Services builds aggregations to improve query performance. You learn more about cube dimension properties for hierarchies and attributes in Chapter 10.

Most changes to database dimensions, such as the addition or deletion of attributes or hierarchies as well as changes to most properties, are automatically reflected in the corresponding cube dimensions. However, certain changes, such as renaming a database dimension, do not result in a similar change to the cube dimension. In such circumstances you could either delete the existing cube dimension and then re-add the database dimension within the cube, or simply rename the cube dimension.

As soon as you add a cube dimension, Analysis Services attempts to detect relationships based on the DSV and to create appropriate relationships between the newly added dimension and the existing measure groups in the cube. You should switch to the Dimension Usage tab of the Cube Designer to verify that relationships between dimensions and measure groups were detected correctly.

The most common type of relationship between a dimension and a measure group is a regular relationship, but several other types could be defined: referenced, fact, many-to-many, data mining, and no relationship. You reviewed regular and referenced relationships in depth in Chapter 6. In this chapter, you learned how to use the IgnoreUnrelatedDimensions property to determine whether you see values or nulls when there is no relationship between a measure group and a dimension. The following sections discuss the remaining three relationship types.

Fact Dimensions

A fact relationship is a relationship that exists between a dimension and a measure group that are both based on the same relational table. In the Adventure Works DW Multidimensional sample project, the Internet Sales Order Details dimension and the Internet Sales measure group retrieve data from the FactInternetSales relational table. Fact dimensions are typically created to support detail-level reporting or scenarios in which the database does not have a well-structured star or snowflake schema but instead contains all information in a single table. Figure 9-8 shows the fact relationship defined between the measure group Internet Sales and the dimension Internet Sales Order Details.

To define a fact relationship, switch to the Dimension Usage tab, and click the cell that intersects the measure group and the dimension. When you select the Fact relationship type, the Define Relationship dialog automatically assigns the key attribute of the dimension as the granularity attribute. You can define a fact relationship only when the dimension and measure group are based on the same table; a validation in the Define Relationship dialog enforces this requirement. Otherwise, a fact relationship is similar to a regular relationship. For example, browsing the dimension with this measure group, whether in a Cube Browser or with your own custom MDX, looks similar to browsing data in a regular relationship. If that's the case why do you need a fact relationship type? Following are two reasons:

1. Specific optimizations are done by Analysis Services during Drillthrough (a command to get detailed data from your cube, which is discussed later in this chapter) when a fact relationship is defined between a measure group and a ROLAP dimension.

2. Certain client tools can present data from this relationship in a way that makes it easier for users to interpret the data during analysis.

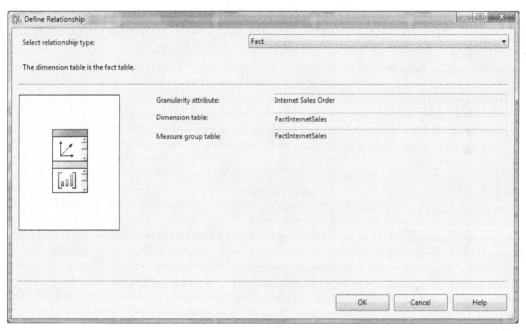

FIGURE 9-8

Many-to-Many Dimensions

Analysis Services 2012 includes support for a relationship type called many-to-many. You were introduced to many-to-many dimensions during the discussion of measure expressions. You can recognize a many-to-many relationship when a single fact row is associated with multiple members in the dimension table. Figure 9-9 shows an example of a many-to-many relationship that exists in the Adventure Works DW Multidimensional sample database.

As you learned in the previous section, the Internet Sales measure group is related to the Internet Sales Order Details dimension through a fact relationship. Figure 9-9 adds new relationships — the Sales Reasons measure group is related to the Sales Reason dimension through a regular relationship and to the Internet Sales Order Details dimension through a regular relationship. In other words, each line item in a sales order (in the Internet Sales measure group as a single fact row) can have one or more sales reasons (in the Sales Reason dimension). An *intermediate dimension*, Internet Sales Order Details, joins the two measure groups, one of which is an *intermediate fact table*. This intermediate fact table, Sales Reasons (the measure group) joins the intermediate dimension to the many-to-many dimension, Sales Reason (the dimension). When Analysis Services aggregates the values for each many-to-many dimension member, it aggregates the values in the measure group based on the set of distinct regular dimension members related to the current many-to-many dimension member. As a result, data is aggregated to each level exactly once. For example, consider a sales order that has two different sales reasons A and B. If you request Internet Sales measure values for that sales order by Sales Reason — specifically members A, B, and All — you can see that the measure values are aggregated to the "All" member exactly once because there is only one distinct sales order related to the All member. Similarly, there is only one distinct sales order related to A and to B, so all three members display the same values in this example.

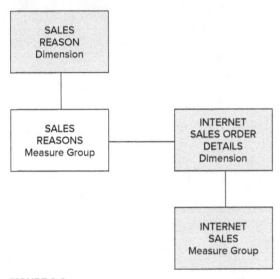

FIGURE 9-9

Many-to-many relationships are common in data warehouses, and now you have the ability to model and analyze the data from many-to-many dimensions. You can use a many-to-many relationship to perform currency conversion as you saw previously in this chapter when learning about measure expressions. Many-to-many relationships can be modeled for any schema that contains at least one common dimension between the regular measure group and the intermediate measure group. If there are multiple common dimensions between the measure groups, Analysis Services aggregates values for each distinct combination of members in those dimensions related to the current many-to-many dimension member.

On the Dimension Usage tab, click the cell that intersects the measure group and the dimension for which you want to define a many-to-many relationship. In the Adventure Works sample cube, take a look at the many-to-many relationship between the Sales Reason dimension and the Internet Sales measure group. You can see the relationship requires the intermediate measure group Sales Reasons, as shown in Figure 9-10.

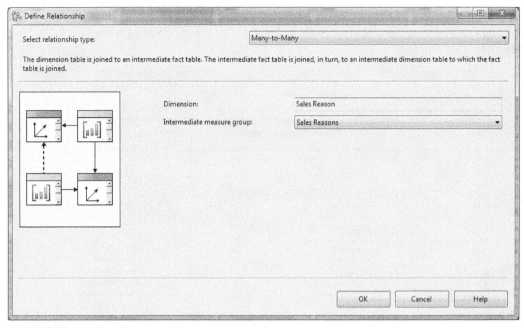

FIGURE 9-10

With this relationship defined, you can browse the many-to-many dimension Sales Reason along with the Internet Sales measure group in Excel, as shown in Figure 9-11.

The sum of the Internet Order Quantity values for the various sales reasons grouped with Sales Reason Type Other is 56,395, which is greater than the Total shown for Other, which is 51,314. Because a many-to-many relationship is defined between the Internet Sales measure group, which includes Internet Order Quantity, and the Sales Reason dimension, the aggregated measure values correctly use the distinct members to avoid double-counting.

Data Mining Dimensions

The technical definition of data mining is the process of automatic or semi-automatic discovery of hidden patterns in large data sets. Several data mining algorithms are available to discover different kinds of patterns. Some data mining algorithms predict future values based on the patterns detected in historical values. For example, you can first classify customers of a retail store as Platinum, Gold, Silver, and Bronze based on selected attributes, such as income, number of children, and so on. You can then use data mining to automatically classify new store customers based on the patterns discovered in existing customer data. In addition, a retail store could decide to boost sales by providing coupons to targeted customers based on the buying patterns of existing customers. Analysis Services 2012 supports several data mining algorithms, which you learn about in detail in Chapter 12.

In Analysis Services 2012, the multidimensional BISM (Business Intelligence Semantic Model) is tightly integrated with data mining features. You can, for example, create a data mining model not only from a relational data source, but also from an existing cube. When a data mining model is created from a cube, you can also create a data mining dimension from the mining model. You can then add this new dimension to the cube in order to perform analysis of cube data according to the data mining classification.

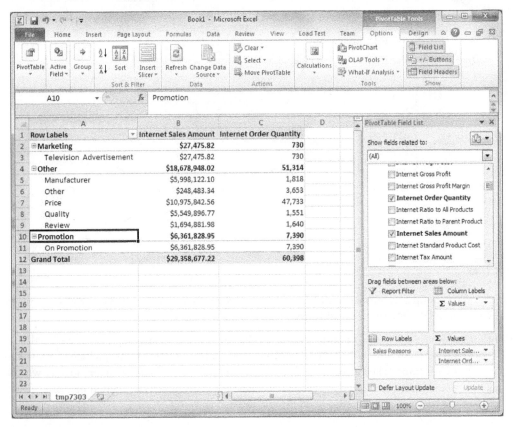

FIGURE 9-11

Figure 9-12 shows the relationship definition for a data mining relationship. The target dimension, Clustered Customers, is a dimension derived from a data mining model. The source dimension, Customers, is the dimension from which the data mining model was originally created.

If you open the Mined Customers cube in the Adventure Works DW Multidimensional sample project and switch to the Dimension Usage tab, you can see the data mining relationship defined between the Cluster Customers dimension and Internet Sales measure group. Open the Cube Browser to view the breakdown of Internet sales based on the Clustered Customers dimension, as shown in Figure 9-13. This dimension represents the data mining model's classification of all members in the Customers dimension into 10 different clusters. To see the characteristics of each cluster, you need to review the mining model. By combining data mining results with cube data, you can make specific business decisions. For example, using the sales information shown in Figure 9-13 in combination with the characteristics of clusters defined by the data mining model, you could decide to boost sales by developing promotions or other incentives for a specific set of customers.

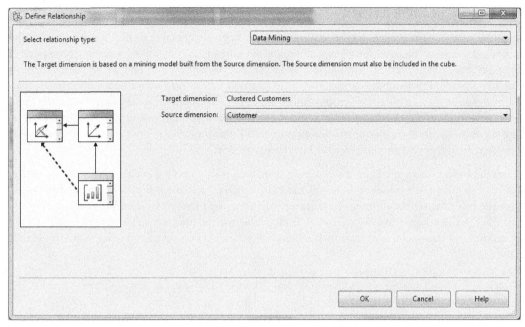

FIGURE 9-12

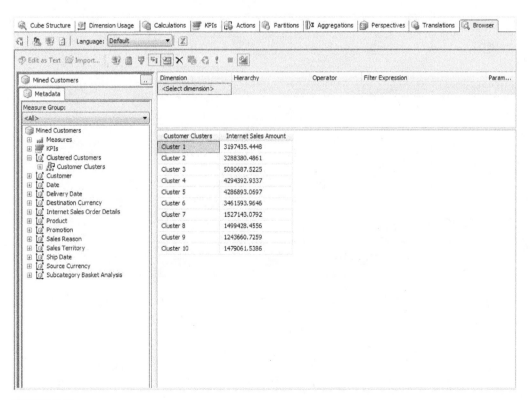

FIGURE 9-13

Role-Playing Dimensions

A role-playing dimension is a database dimension that acts as multiple dimensions within a cube. Instead of requiring the creation of two database dimensions that serve different purposes but depend on the same data source table, a single database dimension can be used to create separate cube dimensions. For example, if you have a geography dimension as a database dimension, you can add it to a cube as Customer Geography and Employee Geography cube dimensions. Similarly, you can have one Time dimension called Date, and then you can add Ship Date and Received Date as cube dimensions. In these examples, Geography and Date dimensions are role-playing dimensions because they can play different roles within the same cube.

Figure 9-14 shows how the Date dimension is used as a role-playing dimension in the Adventure Works cube of the Adventure Works DW Multidimensional sample project. The Date dimension plays the role of three date dimensions: Date, Ship Date, and Delivery Date. When a dimension plays multiple roles in a single measure group, the fact table for the measure group contains one foreign key column for each role, each of which must have a relationship to a single dimension table defined in the DSV.

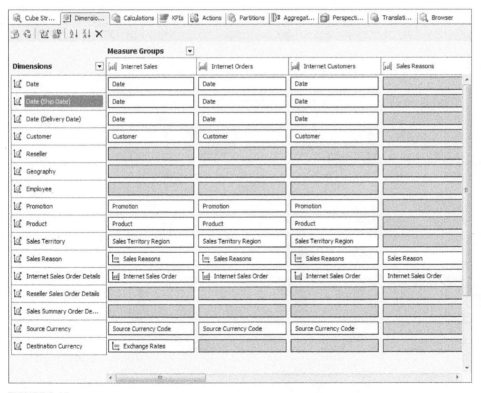

FIGURE 9-14

ADDING CALCULATIONS TO YOUR CUBE

In Chapter 3, you learned about the calculation model in Analysis Services 20122 and the concept of MDX scripts. In Chapter 6, you learned how to use the Calculations tab in the Cube Designer for creating calculated members and named sets. In this section, you learn how to review and test cell calculations.

You use the Calculations tab in the Cube Designer to define all calculations, which then become part of the MDX script of your cube. In this section, you continue using the Adventure Works DW Multidimensional sample project to explore the functionality available in the Calculations tab.

The following steps show how to review the definitions of some of the calculations defined in the Adventure Works sample cube and how to verify the results as the calculations are applied to the specific cells:

1. Open the Adventure Works DW Multidimensional sample project and, if you haven't done so already, deploy the project to the Analysis Services instance on your machine. If you have a default Analysis Services instance, you can deploy the project without changing the project properties. However, if you have installed named instances of Analysis Services and SQL Server, you must change the project's deployment properties to target the right instance of Analysis Services, and you must also change the relational data source in the project to point to your SQL Server instance.

2. Open the Adventure Works cube, and click the Calculations tab. You see all the calculated members, named sets, and calculations specified within the MDX script, as shown in Figure 9-15. The first command selected in the Script Organizer, which is also the first command in the MDX script, is the Calculate statement. The Calculate statement is automatically added to each cube created by the Cube Wizard. The Calculate statement can be anywhere within the MDX script, but it must be included, so be careful not to delete it. You can also add comments to the MDX script to make it easier to understand the purpose of the calculations by inserting your comments between the /* and */ characters, as shown in Figure 9-15. All comments within the MDX script are detected by the Cube Designer and converted to a green font color for easier reading.

3. The Calculations tab has two views: the Form View and the Script View. Figure 9-15 shows the Form View in which you can select a command listed in the Script Organizer pane to see its definition independently. Figure 9-16 shows the Script View, which displays when you click the Script View button in the Calculations toolbar. In Script View, you can see all the commands together in the script pane.

4. Click the Form View icon on the Calculations toolbar, scroll through the Script Organizer pane, and click the second Scope statement. As you can see in Figure 9-17, when you select an item in the Script Organizer, the corresponding script displays on the right side. This Scope statement restricts the cube space to Sales Amount Quota for Fiscal Quarters in Fiscal Year 2009.

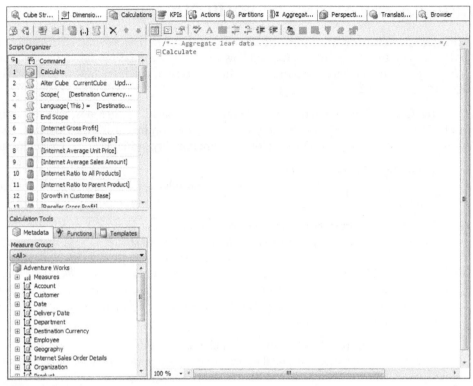

FIGURE 9-15

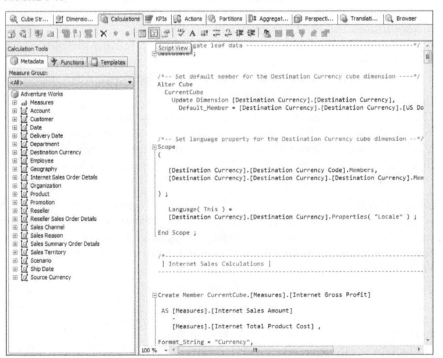

FIGURE 9-16

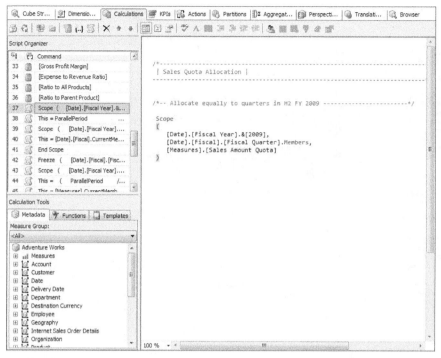

FIGURE 9-17

5. Click the statement that appears below the Scope statement in the Script Organizer to see the following assignment statement, which allocates the Sales Amount Quota for the Fiscal Year 2009 based on 135 percent of the Sales Amount Quota in the Fiscal Year 2008:

```
This = ParallelPeriod
        (
            [Date].[Fiscal].[Fiscal Year], 1,
            [Date].[Fiscal].CurrentMember
        ) * 1.35
```

6. As you add statements and commands to the MDX script, you should test the script to ensure the affected cells or members get the correct values. One way to test an MDX expression is to use it in a query and evaluate the results. This approach can become time-consuming, especially when you have complex expressions. A better alternative is to use the debugging capabilities of the Analysis Services Cube Designer, in which you can quickly validate results. Because a cube's MDX script is just a sequence of MDX statements, you can evaluate each statement separately by using the Cube Designer's debugging feature. Debugging your MDX script is similar to debugging application code. You can set breakpoints to evaluate a sequence of MDX statements that precede the statement specified as a breakpoint. To try the debugging capabilities, click the Script View icon in the Calculations toolbar, scroll through the list of MDX statements to locate the second Scope statement in the MDX script, and set a breakpoint, as shown in Figure 9-18. Set the breakpoint by clicking in the margin to the left of the Scope statement. The breakpoint appears as a solid red circle, as shown in Figure 9-18. After you have set the breakpoint, the statement is highlighted.

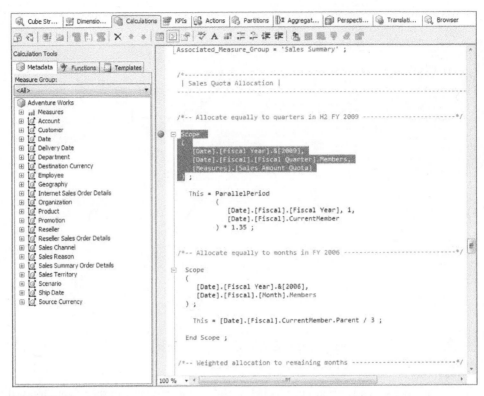

FIGURE 9-18

7. To start debugging mode, from the Calculations tab in the cube editor, press the F10 function key. After deploying the database, the Cube Designer switches to debugging mode, which divides the script pane into two sections, as shown in Figure 9-19. Standard Visual Studio environment debugging windows, such as Autos, Locals, and Breakpoints, among others, might also automatically open when debugging starts. Close these windows to allocate more screen space to the script pane. The top half of the script pane now contains the MDX script with the breakpoint statement highlighted in yellow. The bottom half now includes several subpanes labeled MDX1, MDX2, MDX3, and MDX4. The MDX panes 1 through 4 can be used to execute regular MDX queries during the debugging session. You also have the option to design the MDX using the DesignMDX icon.

8. The debugger stopped execution of the MDX script at the statement with the breakpoint. You can monitor the effect of the subsequent statements by entering the following MDX in MDX1 window and clicking the Execute button, as shown in Figure 9-20. The following MDX was formed by launching the MDX query window and dragging and dropping [Sales Amount Quota] measure and the hierarchies Date.[Fiscal Year] and Date.[Semester of Year] attribute hierarchies.

```
SELECT NON EMPTY
{ [Measures].[Sales Amount Quota] } ON COLUMNS,
NON EMPTY {
        ([Date].[Fiscal Year].[Fiscal Year].ALLMEMBERS
        * [Date].[Fiscal Semester of Year]
        .[Fiscal Semester of Year].ALLMEMBERS )
}
DIMENSION PROPERTIES MEMBER_CAPTION,
MEMBER_UNIQUE_NAME ON ROWS
FROM [Adventure Works] CELL PROPERTIES VALUE,
BACK_COLOR, FORE_COLOR, FORMATTED_VALUE,
FORMAT_STRING, FONT_NAME, FONT_SIZE, FONT_FLAGS
```

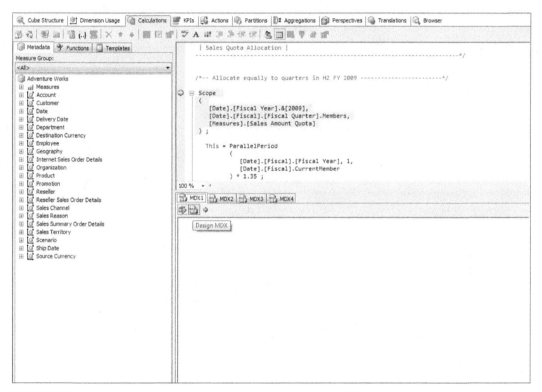

FIGURE 9-19

9.　The next statement, which is the assignment MDX expression to specify the Sales Amount Quota for the Fiscal Year 2009, is now ready for execution. Press F10 to step through the Scope statement. The assignment statement is now highlighted with a yellow background, as shown in Figure 9-21, but has not yet been executed.

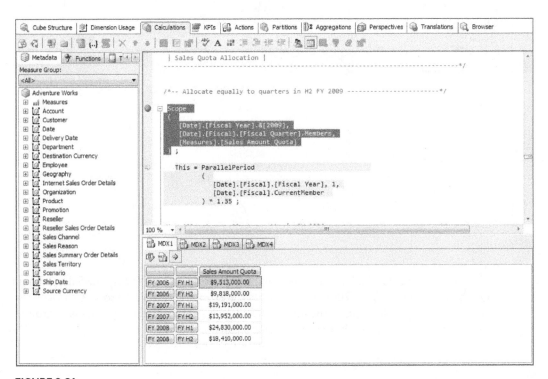

```
| Sales Quota Allocation |
-----------------------------------------------------------------------*/

/*-- Allocate equally to quarters in H2 FY 2009 ----------------------*/

Scope
(
    [Date].[Fiscal Year].&[2009],
    [Date].[Fiscal].[Fiscal Quarter].Members,
    [Measures].[Sales Amount Quota]
) ;

    This = ParallelPeriod
            (
                [Date].[Fiscal].[Fiscal Year], 1,
                [Date].[Fiscal].CurrentMember
            ) * 1.35 ;
```

FIGURE 9-20

```
| Sales Quota Allocation |
-----------------------------------------------------------------------*/

/*-- Allocate equally to quarters in H2 FY 2009 ----------------------*/

Scope
(
    [Date].[Fiscal Year].&[2009],
    [Date].[Fiscal].[Fiscal Quarter].Members,
    [Measures].[Sales Amount Quota]
) ;

    This = ParallelPeriod
            (
                [Date].[Fiscal].[Fiscal Year], 1,
                [Date].[Fiscal].CurrentMember
            ) * 1.35 ;
```

		Sales Amount Quota
FY 2006	FY H1	$9,513,000.00
FY 2006	FY H2	$9,818,000.00
FY 2007	FY H1	$19,191,000.00
FY 2007	FY H2	$13,952,000.00
FY 2008	FY H1	$24,830,000.00
FY 2008	FY H2	$18,410,000.00

FIGURE 9-21

10. Execute the assignment statement by pressing the F10 key, which executes one statement at a time. As soon as the assignment statement is executed, the Sales Amount Quota value for the two semesters of year 2009 have values as shown in Figure 9-22.

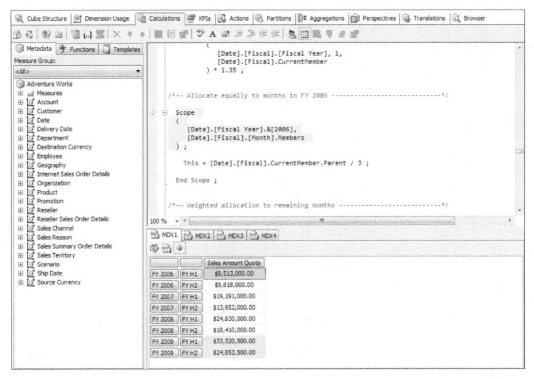

FIGURE 9-22

You have now successfully tested the MDX script calculations you learned about in Chapter 3. You can also use the MDX1 through MDX4 panes for additional debugging. You can make changes to the existing MDX query or have different MDX executed in other MDX windows. Figure 9-23 shows the following MDX query executed to show the Sales Amount Quota values for all the fiscal year 2009 and its children in the Date.Fiscal hierarchy.

```
SELECT NON EMPTY
{ [Measures].[Sales Amount Quota] } ON COLUMNS,
NON EMPTY { ([Date].[Fiscal].ALLMEMBERS ) }
DIMENSION PROPERTIES MEMBER_CAPTION,
MEMBER_UNIQUE_NAME ON ROWS
FROM [Adventure Works] CELL PROPERTIES VALUE,
BACK_COLOR, FORE_COLOR, FORMATTED_VALUE,
FORMAT_STRING, FONT_NAME, FONT_SIZE, FONT_FLAGS
```

The debugger also enables you to simulate a different user during execution. You can click the Change User icon (shown in Figure 9-24) to change to a different user or a role when you need to verify the results of an MDX script with appropriate security for your end users. Obviously, you don't want users to view data that they aren't supposed to see.

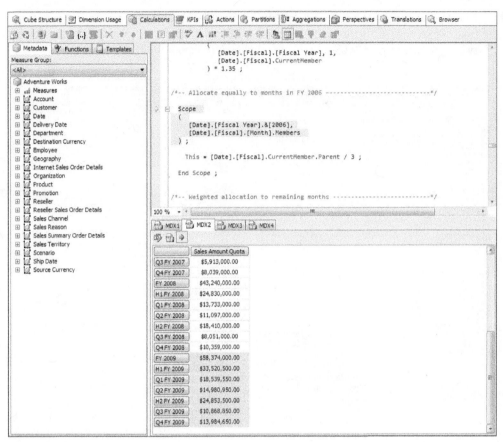

FIGURE 9-23

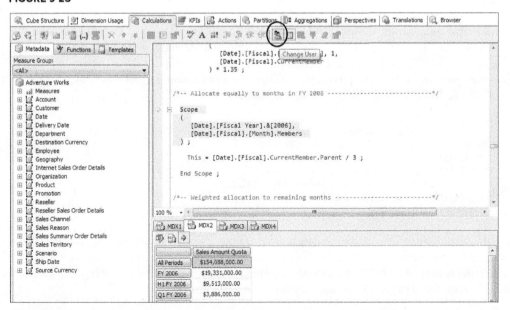

FIGURE 9-24

Now that you have learned how to use and debug calculations in Analysis Services, you're ready to learn about two other important types of cube enhancements, KPIs and actions.

KEY PERFORMANCE INDICATORS (KPIs)

Key Performance Indicators, most often called KPIs, may also be referred to as Key Success Indicators (KSIs). Regardless of what you call them, they can help your organization define and measure quantitative progress toward organizational goals. Business users often manage organizational performance using KPIs. Many business application vendors now provide performance management tools (namely dashboard applications) that collect KPI data from source systems and present KPI results graphically to end business users. Microsoft Office Excel 2010 and Microsoft Office PerformancePoint dashboard are examples of applications that can leverage the KPI capabilities of Analysis Services 2012.

Analysis Services provides a framework for categorizing the KPI MDX expressions for use with the business data stored in cubes. Each KPI uses a predefined set of data roles — actual, goal, trend, status, and weight — to which MDX expressions are assigned. Only the meta data for the KPIs is stored by an Analysis Services instance, whereas a set of MDX functions is available that allows applications to easily retrieve KPI values from cubes using this meta data.

The Cube Designer provided in SQL Server Data Tools (SSDT) also enables cube developers to easily create and test KPIs. You learn how to do this in the following section. Figure 9-25 shows the KPIs in the Adventure Works cube using the KPI browser in the Cube Designer. You can get to the KPI browser by clicking the KPI tab in the Cube Designer and then clicking the KPI browser icon (second button from the right in the toolbar in the KPI tab).

KPI Creation

Consider the following scenario: The Adventure Works sales management team wants to monitor the sales revenue for the fiscal year. Sales revenue for prior fiscal years is available in the Adventure Works cube. The management team has identified the goal of 15 percent growth for sales revenue year over year. If current sales revenue is more than 95 percent of the goal, sales revenue performance is satisfactory. If, however, the sales revenue is within 85 percent to 95 percent of the goal, management must be alerted. If the sales revenue drops under 85 percent of the goal, management must take immediate action to change the trend. These alerts and calls to action are commonly associated with the use of KPIs. The management team is interested in the trends associated with sales revenue; if the sales revenue is 20 percent higher than expected, the sales revenue status is great news and should be surfaced as well — it's not all doom and gloom.

Use the following steps to design the KPIs for the sales management team:

1. Open the Adventure Works DW Multidimensional Analysis Services sample project.

2. Double-click the Adventure Works cube in the Solution Explorer to open the Cube Designer.

3. Click the KPIs tab to open the KPI editor.

4. On the KPI toolbar click the New KPI button to open a template for a new KPI. As you can see in Figure 9-26, there are several properties to fill in.

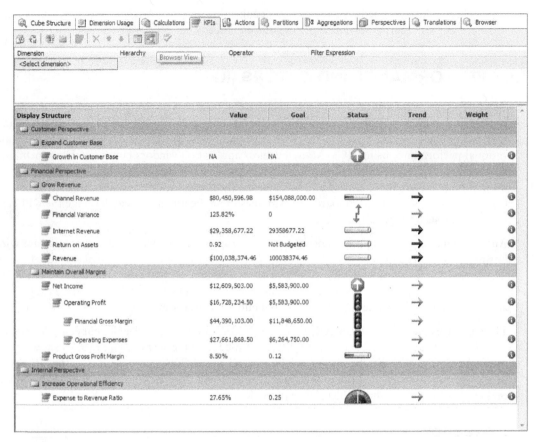

FIGURE 9-25

5. Type **Sales Revenue KPI** in the Name text box, and then choose Sales Summary in the drop-down box for Associated Measure Group. The revenue measure is Sales Amount, which is included in the Sales Summary measure group.

6. Type the following MDX expression in the Value Expression text box (refer to Figure 9-26):

```
[Measures].[Sales Amount]
```

When managers browse the KPI, the value of Sales Amount value will be retrieved from the cube.

7. Now you need to translate the sales revenue goal to increase 15 percent over last year's revenue into an MDX expression. Put another way, this year's sales revenue goal is 1.15 times last year's sales revenue. Use the ParallelPeriod function to get the previous year's time members for each current year time member. Type the MDX expression, shown here, in the Goal Expression text box (refer to Figure 9-26):

```
1.15 *
  (
    [Measures].[Sales Amount],
```

```
ParallelPeriod
(
    [Date].[Fiscal].[Fiscal Year],  1,
    [Date].[Fiscal].CurrentMember
)
)
```

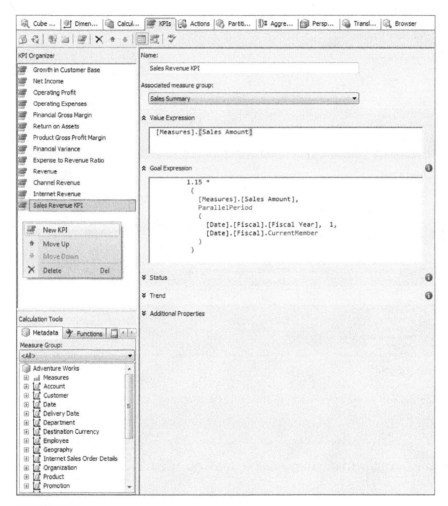

FIGURE 9-26

8. In the Status section of the KPI template, you can choose a graphical indicator for the status of the KPI to display in the KPI browser. You can see several of the available indicators in Figure 9-27. For your own KPI applications, you must programmatically associate the KPI status with your own graphical indicator. For now, select the Traffic Light indicator. The MDX expression that you define for status must return a value between –1 and 1. The KPI browser displays a red traffic light when the status is –1 and a green traffic light when the status is 1. When the status is 0, a yellow traffic light displays.

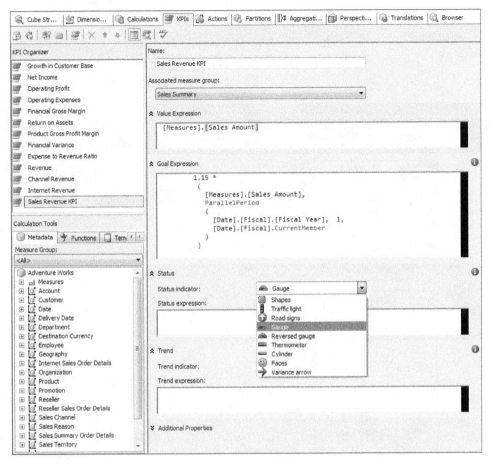

FIGURE 9-27

9. Type the following expression in the Status Expression text box:

```
CASE
  WHEN KpiValue("Sales Revenue KPI")/KpiGoal("Sales Revenue KPI")>=.95
    THEN 1
  WHEN KpiValue("Sales Revenue KPI")/KpiGoal("Sales Revenue KPI")<.95
    AND
      KpiValue("Sales Revenue KPI")/KpiGoal("Sales Revenue KPI")>=.85
    THEN 0
    ELSE -1
END
```

This expression uses the CASE MDX statement available for use with Analysis Services. In addition, you now have a set of MDX functions to use with KPI metric values. In the preceding MDX expression, the KpiValue function retrieves the value of Sales Revenue KPI, and the KpiGoal function retrieves the goal value of Sales Revenue KPI. More precisely, the KpiValue function is a member function that returns a calculated measure from the Measures dimension. By using these KPI functions, you can avoid a lot of typing if your value or goal expression is complex. This `Status` expression returns one of three discrete values: 1 if revenue exceeds 95 percent of goal; 0 if revenue is between 85 percent and 95 percent of goal; and –1 if revenue is below 85 percent of goal.

10. Choose the default indicator (Standard Arrow) for Trend indicator. Type the following MDX expression in the Trend Expression text box. This expression compares current KPI values with last year's values from the same time period to calculate the trend of the KPI:

```
CASE
    WHEN  (
            KpiValue ( "Sales Revenue KPI" ) -
            (
              KpiValue ( "Sales Revenue KPI" ),
              ParallelPeriod
              (
                [Date].[Fiscal].[Fiscal Year],
                1,
                [Date].[Fiscal].CurrentMember
              )
            )) /
            (
              KpiValue ( "Sales Revenue KPI" ),
              ParallelPeriod
              (
                [Date].[Fiscal].[Fiscal Year],
                1,
                [Date].[Fiscal].CurrentMember
              )
            )
          <=-.02
    THEN -1
    WHEN ( KpiValue ( "Sales Revenue KPI" ) -
            (
              KpiValue ( "Sales Revenue KPI" ),
              ParallelPeriod
              (
                [Date].[Fiscal].[Fiscal Year],
                1,
                [Date].[Fiscal].CurrentMember
              )
            )) /
            (
              KpiValue ( "Sales Revenue KPI" ),
              ParallelPeriod
              (
                [Date].[Fiscal].[Fiscal Year],
                1,
                [Date].[Fiscal].CurrentMember
              )
            )   >.02
    THEN 1
    ELSE 0
END
```

11. Expand the Additional Properties section at the bottom of the KPI template to type a name in the Display Folder combo box for a new folder, or to pick an existing display folder. The KPI browser shows all KPIs in a folder separate from other measures and dimensions, but you can further group related KPIs into folders and subfolders. A subfolder is created when the folder names are separated by a backslash, "\". In the Display Folder combo box, type **SampleKPI\RevenueFolder**, as shown in Figure 9-28.

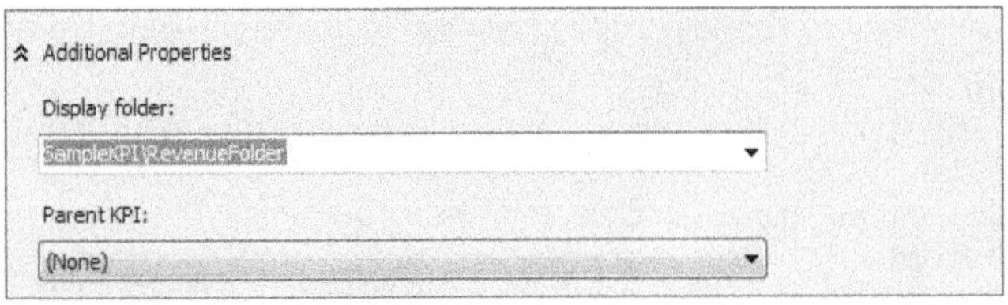

FIGURE 9-28

You can also choose to set Parent KPI so that the KPI browser displays KPIs hierarchically. Using the Parent KPI setting is for display purposes only and doesn't actually create a physical relationship between parent and child KPIs. You could, however, design a Parent KPI that uses values from child KPIs via KPI functions; there is even a Weight expression to adjust the value of a Parent KPI. The Display Folder setting is ignored if you select a Parent KPI because the KPI displays inside its parent's folder. To complete your KPI, leave the Parent KPI as (None).

Congratulations, you just created your first KPI! Deploy the project to an instance of Analysis Services so that you can view the KPI values. To deploy, select the Build menu item, and then select Deploy Adventure Works DW Multidimensional. Like MDX scripts, KPI definitions are only metadata, so changing and saving the KPI definitions updates only the meta data store. A cube reprocess is not required, allowing you to use a KPI right after deploying it to the Analysis Services instance.

To view the KPI, follow these steps:

1. In the Cube Designer, on the KPI toolbar, click the Browser View button, as shown in Figure 9-29.

FIGURE 9-29

Your new KPI is at the bottom of the view window and should look like Figure 9-30.

2. The KPI browser supports the standard slicer window at the top of the browser. You can select specific members to narrow down the analysis to areas of interest. For example, suppose you are interested in the sales revenue KPI for August 2007. In the slicer window, select the Date dimension, Fiscal hierarchy, and August 2007 (found in semester H1 FY 2008 and quarter Q1 FY 2008) as shown in Figure 9-31.

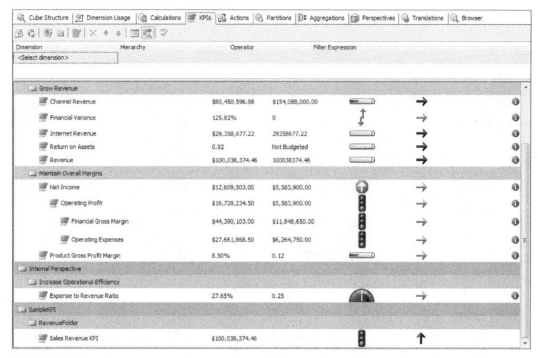

FIGURE 9-30

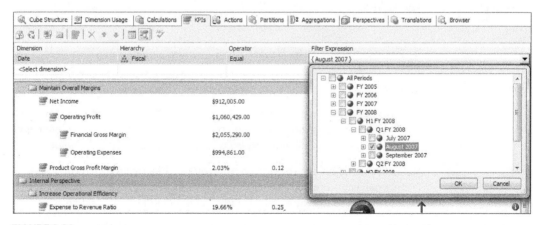

FIGURE 9-31

You notice the KPI values have changed, as shown in Figure 9-32, as have the Goals — August beats the goal!

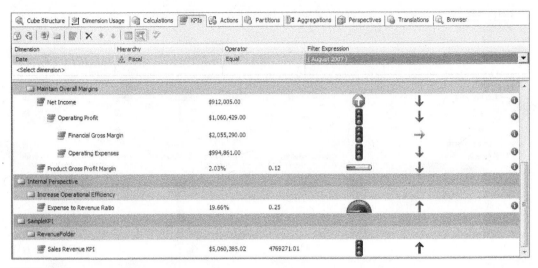

FIGURE 9-32

KPIs in Depth

Every Analysis Services cube can have an associated collection of KPIs, and each KPI has five properties as its set of meta data. These properties are MDX expressions that return numeric values from a cube, as described in the following table.

KPI-SPECIFIC PROPERTIES	DESCRIPTION
Value	An MDX expression that returns the actual value of the KPI. It is mandatory for a KPI.
Goal	An MDX expression that returns the goal of the KPI.
Status	An MDX expression that returns the status of the KPI. To best represent the value graphically, this expression should return a value between −1 and 1. Client applications use the status value to display a graphic indicator of the KPI value.
Trend	An MDX expression that returns the trend of the KPI over time. As with Status, the Trend expression should return a value between −1 and 1. Client applications use the trend value to display a graphic indicator of the KPI trend direction.
Weight	An MDX expression that returns the weight of the KPI. If a KPI has a parent KPI, you can define weights to control the contribution of this KPI to its parent.

Analysis Services creates hidden calculated members on the Measures dimension for each KPI metric (value, goal, status, trend, and weight). However, if a KPI expression directly references a measure, Analysis Services uses the measure directly instead of creating a new calculated measure. You can query the calculated measure used for KPIs in an MDX expression, even though it's hidden.

To see how this works, open SSMS and connect to Analysis Services. Click the Analysis Services MDX Query icon on the toolbar to open a new MDX query window. Make sure you connect to the Adventure Works DW Multidimensional database in the Available Databases list box; type the following query in the MDX query window, and click the Execute button:

```
SELECT  {Measures.[Sales Revenue KPI Goal] }  ON 0,
[Date].[Fiscal].[Fiscal Quarter].MEMBERS ON 1
FROM   [Adventure Works]
```

Figure 9-33 shows the results of executing the query.

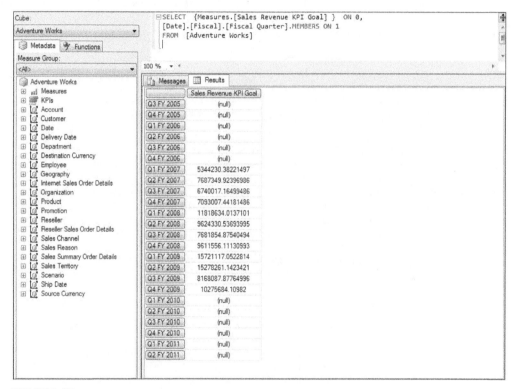

FIGURE 9-33

Using ADOMD.NET to Query KPIs

The Analysis Services instance hosting the database cubes also maintains the KPI definition metadata. As you learned in the previous section, you can access KPI values directly by using KPI functions. Client applications can also access this KPI meta data information and retrieve values program matically through an Analysis Services client-side component: ADOMD.NET.

ADOMD.NET provides support for KPIs. It includes a KPI class that contains a method called Kpi.Properties("KPI_XXX"), which is used to retrieve the properties of each KPI. This method returns a string of unique measures for the developer to use in the construction of MDX queries that retrieve the KPI values. The following code example demonstrates how to access a KPI using

ADOMD.NET and how to construct a parameterized MDX query. Because KPI metrics are just calculated measures, you execute a KPI query with ADOMD.NET the same way you execute regular MDX queries.

```csharp
using System;
using System.Collections.Generic;
using System.Text;
using Microsoft.AnalysisServices.AdomdClient;

namespace QueryKPIs
{
    class Program
    {
        static void Main(string[] args)
        {
            string connectionString =
                "Provider = MSOLAP;" +
                "Data Source=localhost;" +
                "Initial Catalog=Adventure Works DW Multidimensional";
            AdomdConnection acCon = new AdomdConnection(connectionString);
            try
            {
                acCon.Open();
                CubeDef cubeObject = acCon.Cubes["Adventure Works"];
                string commandText =
                    "SELECT { strtomember(@Value), strtomember(@Goal), " +
                    "strtomember(@Status), strtomember(@Trend) } " +
                    "ON COLUMNS FROM [" + cubeObject.Name + "]";
                AdomdCommand command = new AdomdCommand(commandText,
                    acCon);
                foreach (Microsoft.AnalysisServices.AdomdClient.Kpi kpi in
                    cubeObject.Kpis)
                {
                    command.Parameters.Clear();

                    command.Parameters.Add(new AdomdParameter("Value",
                        kpi.Properties["KPI_VALUE"].Value));
                    command.Parameters.Add(new AdomdParameter("Goal",
                        kpi.Properties["KPI_GOAL"].Value));
                    command.Parameters.Add(new AdomdParameter("Status",
                        kpi.Properties["KPI_STATUS"].Value));
                    command.Parameters.Add(new AdomdParameter("Trend",
                        kpi.Properties["KPI_TREND"].Value));
                    CellSet cellset = command.ExecuteCellSet();

                    Console.WriteLine("KPI Name:" + kpi.Name);
                    Console.WriteLine("Value:" +
                        cellset.Cells[0].FormattedValue);
                    Console.WriteLine("Goal:" +
                        cellset.Cells[1].FormattedValue);
                    Console.WriteLine("Status:" +
                        cellset.Cells[2].FormattedValue);
                    Console.WriteLine("Trend:" +
```

```
                            cellset.Cells[3].FormattedValue);
                    }


            }
            finally
            {
                acCon.Close();
            }
        }
    }
}
```

This example uses a parameterized MDX query and the StrToMember function to avoid MDX injection. The developer of a client-side application needs to be cautious with user input; a simple string concatenation would allow a malicious user to input and run harmful code. You can create a new C# program called QueryKPI, copy the preceding code, add the Microsoft.AnalysisServices. AdomdClient DLL as a reference, and run the program. Explore the .NET Adomd client object model by writing client programs that use it.

DRILLTHROUGH

Drill down is the process to navigate from a summary level to more detailed levels across a cube dimension. Drillthrough is a completely different animal. *Drillthrough* retrieves fact data corresponding to a cell or some specified range of cells. Often the lowest level of detail in a cube is still composed of aggregated values, but users occasionally have a need to see the associated row-level data from the fact table. In Analysis Services 2012, even if you use the MOLAP storage mode (discussed in the "Storage Modes and Storage Settings" section later in this chapter), you can still use Drillthrough. You can modify a server configuration advanced property, OLAP\Query\ DefaultDrillthroughMaxRows, to control the default size of the returned dataset.

By default, Drillthrough returns the granularity attribute of each dimension and all measures. And just how do you define Drillthrough? You could create an application that performs Drillthrough programmatically using the SQL query supported by Analysis Services 2012. Excel 2010 is an application that creates Drillthrough commands to Analysis Services when you double-click a cell in a pivot table. (You learn about analyzing a cube using Pivot Tables in Excel 2010 in Chapter 20.) Another option is to create a Drillthrough action. The following section describes the available action types, including how to create a Drillthrough action.

For some insight on how Drillthrough actually works in Analysis Services 2012, it is informative to contrast it to the implementation of Drillthrough in Analysis Services 2000. Analysis Services 2000 fetched all requested measures directly from the relational data source, which is potentially a slow process. Analysis Services 2005 and onward retrieve the requested measures from the MOLAP database directly and therefore runs much faster. Indeed, the system is self-contained and requires no connection to SQL Server. As mentioned, Drillthrough can be defined as an action (to be seen in the next section) and can drill through cells that have the Drillthrough action defined. You learn to define Drillthrough and understand its behavior in the next section.

ACTIONS

Actions are predefined meta data components stored on the server that send commands to client applications to perform certain operations based on a selection by the user in the Cube Browser. For example, the user could select dimension members, levels, a set, specific cube cells, and so on. An action command usually includes a command string, such as a URL, and the suggested command behavior, such as opening a web browser for the URL. MDX expressions are often built into commands to include the context of the user selection in the action. If a user initiates an action by selecting a product, for example, an MDX expression could be used to generate a URL for a catalog page describing the selected product.

Action Types

Analysis Services 2012 supports seven action types. These action types empower client applications with more analytical capabilities than traditional OLAP analysis drill up, drill down, and pivot activities. For example, if a sales manager is analyzing sales for cities in Washington State, the ability to click a city member to view an MSN city map would be helpful. Similarly, if your implementation includes Reporting Services, you could link a report that analyzes sales reasons by product category to the product category members by adding an action to the cube. When the sales manager clicks a product category, the action passes the selected product category as a parameter to the report, which then displays in a web browser. If a sales number for a specific region appears to be surprisingly high or low, the sales manager could use a Drillthrough action to retrieve all detailed transactions contributing to the value. The seven action types supported in Analysis Services are listed in the following table along with the information on what can be done by a client when such an action type is returned.

ACTION TYPE	DESCRIPTION
CommandLine	Returns a command that can be run under a command prompt.
HTML	Returns an HTML script that can be rendered using an HTML browser.
URL	Returns a URL that can be launched using a browser. Report Action (to be seen later) uses this action type.
Statement	Returns a statement that can be run as an OLE DB command.
Rowset	Returns a rowset to a client application.
Proprietary	Performs an operation by using an interface other than those listed in this table. The client application retrieving this action type should know how to use this proprietary action type.
Dataset	Returns a data set to a client application.

Action Target Types

Each action is tied to a target type. Target types refer to a specific object or objects inside the cube. If a user clicks an object that has been defined as a target for an action, the action will be enabled in the client application for that specific object. For example, if you define a URL action to be associated with attribute members of the geography.city attribute, that action will be available when the user selects any member of the city attribute. When you define an action, you must specify the type of objects that will be targets of the action. Analysis Services 2012 supports the following action target types:

TARGET TYPE	DESCRIPTION
Attribute Members	The only valid selection is a single attribute hierarchy. The target of the action will be all members of an attribute wherever they appear. (That is, it will apply to multilevel hierarchies as well.)
Cells	All cells is the only selection available. If you choose Cells as a target type, type an expression in Condition to restrict the cells with which the action is associated.
Cube	CURRENTCUBE is the only selection available. The action is associated with the current cube.
Dimension Members	You need to select a single dimension. The action will be associated with all members of the dimension.
Hierarchy	You need to select a single hierarchy. The action will be associated with the hierarchy object only. Attribute hierarchies appear in the list only if their AttributeHierarchyEnabled and AttributeHierarchyVisible properties are set to True.
Hierarchy Members	You need to select a single hierarchy. The action will be associated with all members of the selected hierarchy. Attribute hierarchies appear in the list only if their AttributeHierarchyEnabled and AttributeHierarchyVisible properties are set to True.
Level	You need to select a single level. The action will be associated with the level object only.
Level Members	You need to select a single level. The action will be associated with all members of the selected level.

URL Action

In these next sections you learn to create a few types of actions, starting with a URL action. The URL action is one of the most common actions you expect customers to use widely. Follow these steps to create a URL action:

1. Using SSDT, open the Adventure Works DW Multidimensional Analysis Services sample project, and double-click the Adventure Works cube in the Solution Explorer to open the Cube Designer. Click the Action tab to open the actions editor, as shown in Figure 9-34.

2. Click the New Action button in the Actions toolbar. Type a name for the new action: **My City Map**. Open the Target type list box (by clicking the down arrow) to see the available action target types, and then choose Attribute Members, as shown in Figure 9-35.

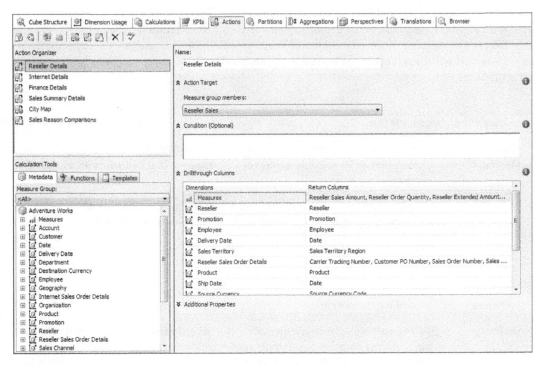

FIGURE 9-34

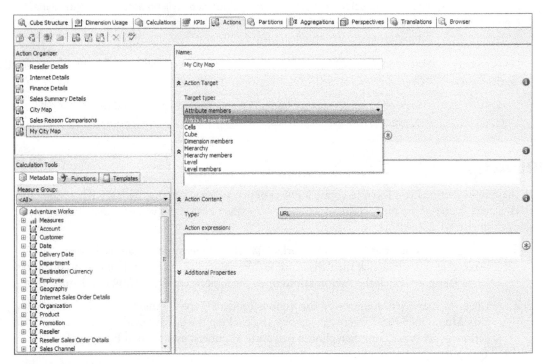

FIGURE 9-35

3. In the Target Object drill-down box, pick Geography.City as the attribute target (shown in Figure 9-36) and click the OK button.

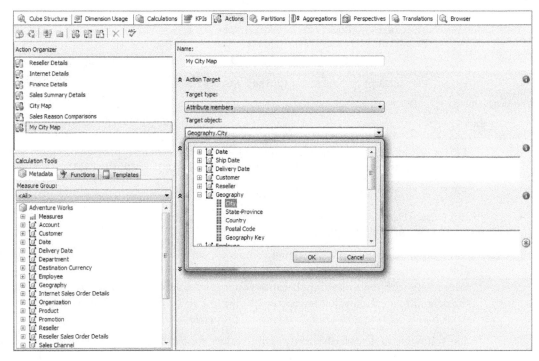

FIGURE 9-36

4. Leave the Action Condition text box blank. If you want to enable the action only under certain conditions, you can enter an MDX expression that returns a boolean value. Because you always want the My City Map action to be enabled, you don't need an Action Condition expression here.

5. In the Action Content section of the editor, keep the default action type, URL. In the Action Expression text box, type the following MDX expression:

```
// URL for linking to MSN Maps
"http://maps.msn.com/home.aspx?plce1=" +

// Retreive the name of the current city
[Geography].[City].CurrentMember.Name + "," +

// Append state-province name
[Geography].[State-Province].CurrentMember.Name + "," +

// Append country name
[Geography].[Country].CurrentMember.Name +

// Append region parameter
"&regn1=" +
```

```
// Determine correct region parameter value
Case
    When [Geography].[Country].CurrentMember Is
         [Geography].[Country].&[Australia]
    Then "3"
    When [Geography].[Country].CurrentMember Is
         [Geography].[Country].&[Canada]
         Or
         [Geography].[Country].CurrentMember Is
         [Geography].[Country].&[United States]
    Then "0"
    Else "1"
End
```

This MDX expression returns a string URL used by the client application to open MSN Map for the user-selected City. The user's selection is passed into the MDX expression as

`[Geography].[City].CurrentMember`

If the user selects a different city and launches the action, the MDX expression is re-evaluated and returns a different URL.

6. Scroll down to the section Additional Properties, and expand the section to review the available properties. There are three options for the property Invocation shown in the following table along with their meaning. Because you want the action to be triggered by the user, leave the default Invocation value Interactive. You can also leave the application and description fields blank because they are informational properties.

The following table describes the possible values for the Invocation property:

METHOD	DESCRIPTION
Interactive	The action is triggered by user interaction.
Batch	The action runs as a batch operation.
On Open	The action runs when a user opens the cube.

7. In the Caption text box, type the following MDX expression:

`[Geography].[City].CurrentMember.Member_Caption + " City Map ..."`

The specified caption is displayed to end users to indicate an action is available. The user clicks the caption to initiate the action. The `Caption Is` MDX property controls how the server evaluates the contents of the caption. If you leave this property value as `False`, the server treats the caption as a static string.

8. Change the `Caption Is` MDX value to `True`. The server evaluates the MDX expression in the Caption text box to construct the caption, which in this case results in different city names included in the caption as different cities are selected in the browser.

Now that you've created a My City Map action, deploy the project to save the action to the server. Just as with KPI definition, an action definition is meta data stored on the server with the cube.

Adding or changing the action won't impact the cube data and doesn't require a reprocess. When the project deploys, you can verify the newly created action right away.

Browse URL Action in the Cube Browser

Many standard OLAP client applications such as Excel support actions out-of-the-box. In this section, you learn to invoke the action My City Map from the Cube Browser.

1. In the Cube Designer, click the Browser tab to open the Cube Browser for the Adventure Works cube and launch Excel by clicking the Excel icon.

2. Drag and drop the Geography hierarchy to Rows and expand to the City level by right clicking one of the Countries and selecting Expand/Collapse ➤ Expand to "City," as shown in Figure 9-37.

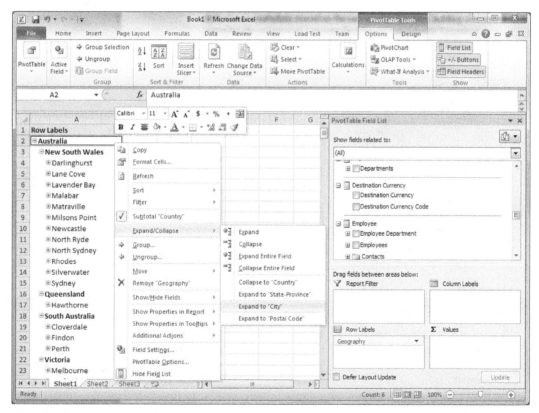

FIGURE 9-37

3. Right-click any City. Notice actions listed on the pop-up menu. The corresponding city map action captioned as *<CityName>* City Map is one of the actions listed. Figure 9-38 shows the action for the city Newcastle.

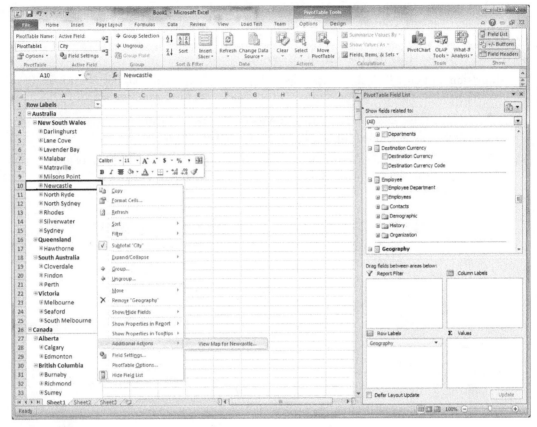

FIGURE 9-38

4. Click Newcastle City Map. Excel invokes a web browser and constructs a URL from the pre-defined MDX expression. Figure 9-39 shows the result of the action.

Report Actions

Report actions are similar to URL actions, except a Report action has additional properties to build the report server access to a URL for you. These properties are described in the following table:

PROPERTY	DESCRIPTION
ReportServer	The name of the Report Server
Path	The path exposed by the Report Server
ReportParameters	Extra parameters for the report
ReportFormatParameters	Extra parameters for the report format

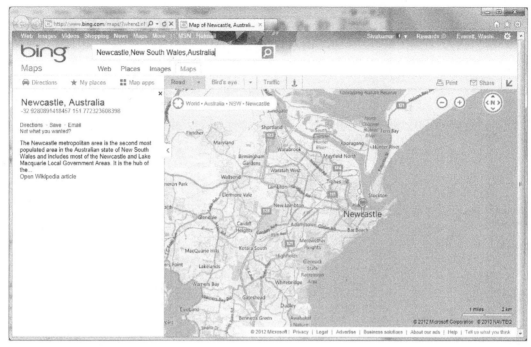

FIGURE 9-39

When a Report action is invoked, Analysis Services generates a URL string similar to the string here:

```
http://ReportServer/Path&ReportParameter1Name=ReportParameter1Value
&ReportParameter2Name=ReportParameter2Value.......&
ReportFormatParameter1Name=ReportFormatParameter1Value&
ReportFormatParameter2Name=ReportFormatParameter2Value ...
```

To review a Report action, follow these steps:

1. With the Adventure Works DW Multidimensional Analysis Services sample project still open in SSDT, click the Actions tab of the Cube Designer, and then click Sales Reason Comparisons Report in the Action Organizer. Now take a look at the properties of this Report action (see Figure 9-40). The optional parameter values are MDX expressions that provide the action with the context of the user selection.

2. As with a URL action, you can invoke a Report action from Excel connected to the Adventure Works cube. The Sales Reason Comparisons action's targets are members of the Product.Category hierarchy. Drag and drop the Product.[Product Categories] hierarchy to Rows in the Excel Pivot Table. Right-click the member Accessories to see the action's caption on the pop-up menu, as shown in Figure 9-41.

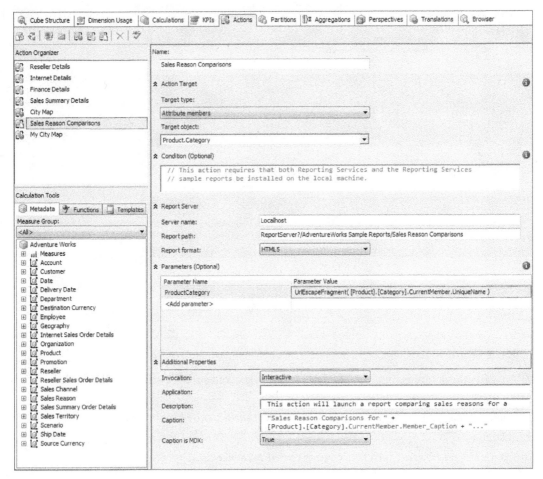

FIGURE 9-40

3. Click Sales Reason Comparisons for Accessories. A browser window opens. If Reporting Services is installed, you see a message: The Item "/AdventureWorks Sample Reports/Sales Reason Comparisons" Cannot Be Found; in other words, rsItemNotFound. This is because the report is fictitious. If this were a valid report, it would display the sales reasons for the Bike category.

Drillthrough Action

OLAP and multidimensional BISM are all about aggregating data and serving aggregated data to end users quickly. Users want to analyze data hierarchically by drilling up and drilling down, which may require aggregated data from millions of daily transaction rows. Sometimes it is useful for users to retrieve the transaction rows that have been aggregated into a particular cell. Access to such details often helps business users understand any abnormal business activities (such as extremely large or small numbers) and investigate root causes. Drillthrough provides this access to details by enabling users to fetch fact table rows that contribute to an aggregated value of a cube cell.

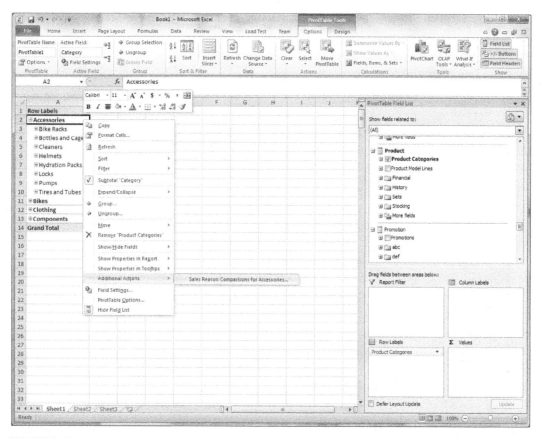

FIGURE 9-41

DRILLTHROUGH is an MDX command in Analysis Services 2012. However, Analysis Services 2012 also supports an action type called Drillthrough. A Drillthrough action's target is always one or more cube cells associated with a specific measure group. In other words, cells with measures in the target measure group display the available Drillthrough actions on the pop-up menu. Drillthrough actions return the related fact table rows in a tabular rowset. As the action developer, you specify which columns the action returns. The columns returned from a rowset Drillthrough action are not limited to the actual fact table columns. Any dimension attributes linked to the selected measure group target can be included. Many-to-many dimensions and referenced dimensions are also supported, so attributes from these special dimensions are available for Drillthrough return columns as well.

Cube designers in Analysis Services 2012 can allow or deny Drillthrough by defining a security role on each cube. Only an Analysis Services administrator can perform Drillthrough against any cube without explicit permissions. If a user does not have Drillthrough rights on a specific cube, the Drillthrough action does not execute and an error message displays.

Follow these steps to understand an existing Drillthrough action in the Adventure Works DW Multidimensional sample database, and enhance it:

1. With the AdventureWorks DW Multidimensional Analysis Services sample project still open in SSDT, click the Actions tab.

2. Click Finance Details in the Action Organizer, as shown in Figure 9-42.

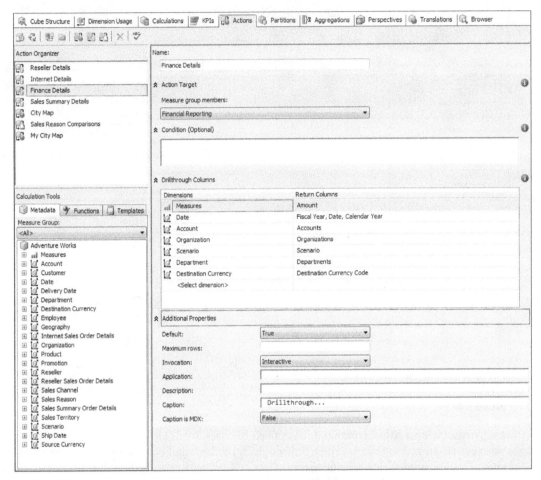

FIGURE 9-42

You can see the action target is the Financial Reporting measure group. The Drillthrough columns to be returned by the action are Amount, Fiscal Year, Date, and Calendar Year from the Date dimension, Accounts from the Account dimension, Organizations from the Organization dimension, Scenario from Scenario dimension, Departments from the Department dimension and Destination Currency Code from Destination Currency dimension.

3. Suppose the business user also wants Account Type and Account Number to be included as additional Drillthrough columns. Click the Accounts dimension attribute in the column labeled Return Columns to open the drop-down box. All available attributes for the Account dimension are listed here. Choose Account Type and Account Number, as shown in Figure 9-43. Click OK.

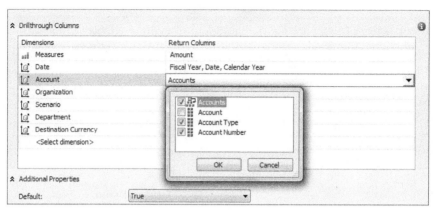

FIGURE 9-43

4. In the Additional Properties section, the Maximum Rows setting is useful for the designer to limit the maximum number of rows that can be returned for a Drillthrough action. This is important because a cell, especially a top-level cell, could be aggregated from millions of fact table rows. Setting the maximum rows value is always a good practice to protect your server from accidental or malicious operations, which can consume huge server resources. If the property is not set, the default max Drillthrough row count from server property Olap\ Query\DefaultDrillthroughMaxRows is used. The default value of the setting is 10000. In the Maximum Rows text box, type in **5000**, as shown in Figure 9-44. Deploy the project to save the action to the server.

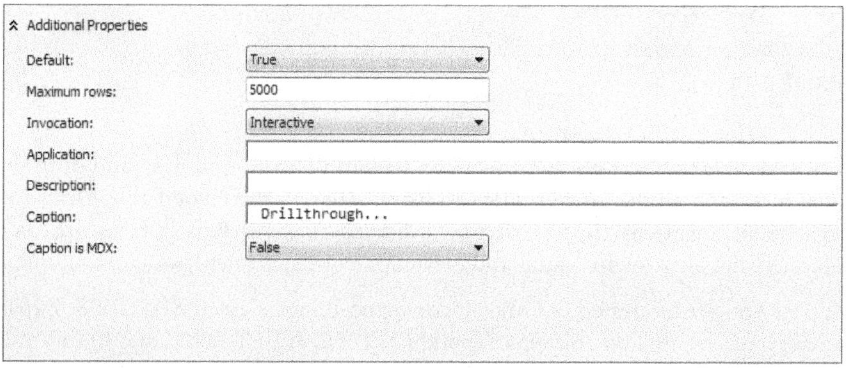

FIGURE 9-44

5. You can now view the Drillthrough results in the Cube Browser. Click the Browser tab to open the Cube Browser, and Launch Excel. Because the action for Finance details is on the measure group Financial Reporting, click the measure Measure.Amount in the Financial Reporting folder to add to the Values area of the Pivot Table. Right-click the cell, and you see Drillthrough as a menu item on the pop-up menu, as shown in Figure 9-45, indicating you can invoke the Drillthrough action for the cell. Before you actually invoke the action, you should limit your drillthrough to a much narrower data region to prevent the action from returning all fact table rows if no maximum row count limit is specified.

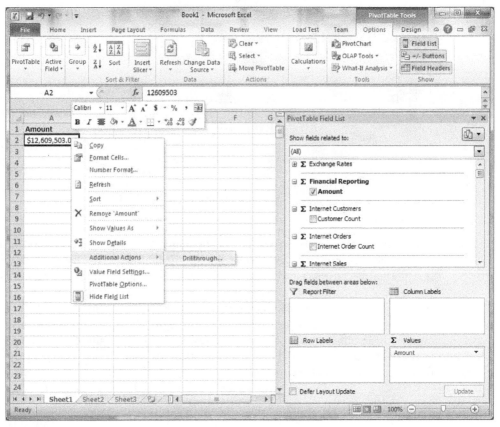

FIGURE 9-45

6. Drag and drop the Account dimension on Column Labels, and drag and drop the Date. Fiscal hierarchy (in the Fiscal folder) on Row Labels in the Pivot Table. Drag and drop Departments hierarchy from Department dimension to the Report Filter area in the Pivot Table. Set the filter for Research and Development department, as shown in Figure 9-46.

7. Suppose you are interested in Other Income and Expense from May 2008. Expand Net Income on rows, and on columns expand FY 2008, H2 FY 2008, and Q4 FY 2008. Right-click the cell intersection of May 2008 and Other Income and Expense, and then choose Drillthrough, as shown in Figure 9-46. A new Excel sheet is created that displays the fact table rows that aggregate to the cell value, as shown in Figure 9-47. The newly added account type and account number is returned.

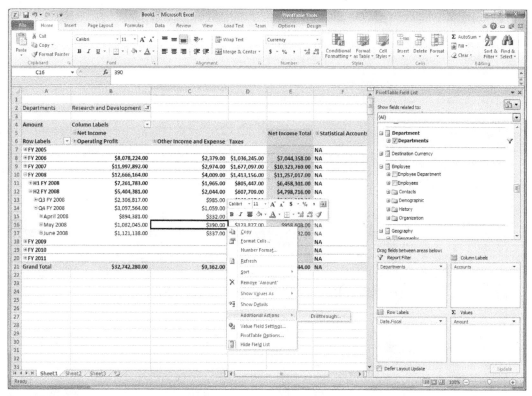

FIGURE 9-46

Under the hood, client applications, including the Cube Browser, use a schema rowset to get the proper drillthrough query for a specific action. Then the client application sends the drillthrough query to the server, which returns a rowset with the detailed fact table rows. Following is the query sent by the Cube Browser to get the previous drillthrough results. The Cube Browser sends the DRILLTHROUGH statement to retrieve the specified 5000 rows. The Cube Browser first sets a restriction to the cell coordinate corresponding to the value $390.00 and then issues the DRILLTHROUGH statement. The SELECT clause of the drillthrough query is therefore specific to the cell that was selected when activating drillthrough.

```
DRILLTHROUGH MAXROWS 5000
Select   ([Department].[Departments].&[6],
[Measures].[Amount],[Date].[Fiscal].[Month].&[2008]&[5],
[Account].[Accounts].&[88])  on 0
From [Adventure Works]
RETURN
```

```
[Financial Reporting].[Amount],[$Date].[Fiscal Year],
[$Date].[Date],[$Date].[Calendar Year],
[$Account].[Accounts],[$Account].[Account Type],
[$Account].[Account Number],[$Organization].[Organizations],
[$Scenario].[Scenario],
[$Department].[Departments],
[$Destination Currency].[Destination Currency Code]
```

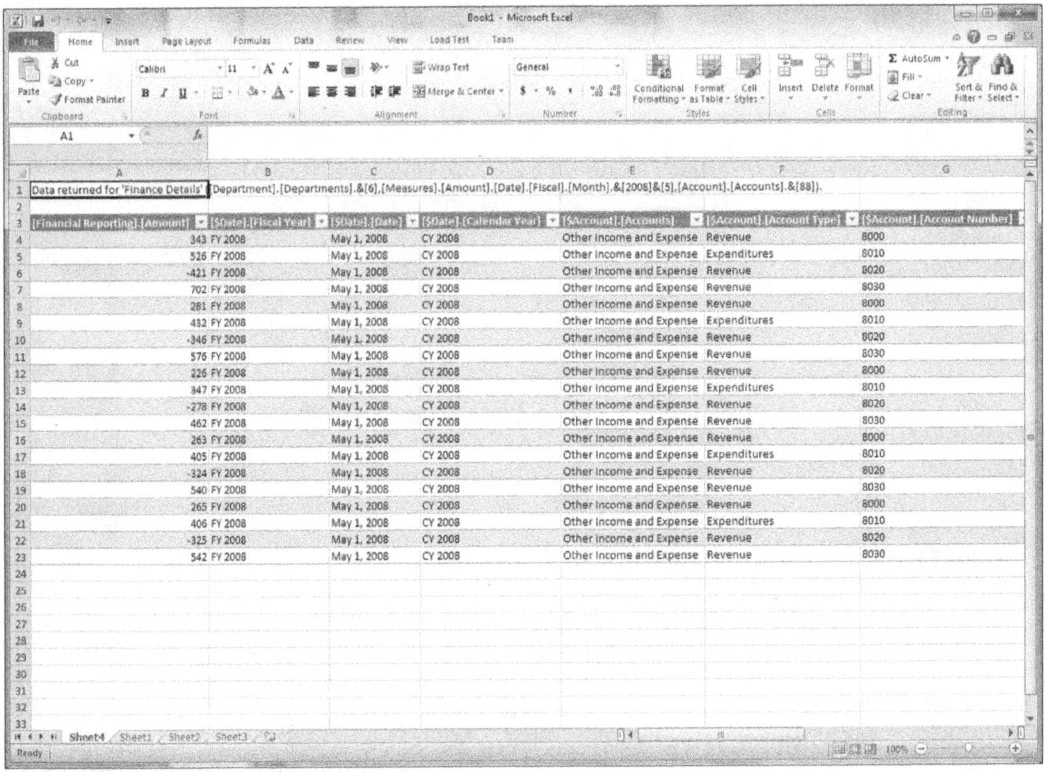

FIGURE 9-47

ADDING INTELLIGENCE TO THE CUBE

Similar to adding intelligence to dimensions (which you learned about in Chapter 8), you can add intelligence to the cube. Figure 9-48 shows the various enhancements that can be done to a cube using the Business Intelligence Wizard. You have learned most of these enhancements in earlier chapters. In this chapter you learn the enhancements used to define and understand semiadditive behavior as well as defining currency conversion whenever fact data needs to be converted to appropriate local currency.

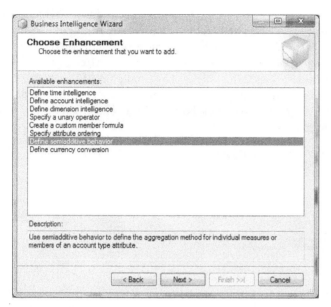

FIGURE 9-48

Semiadditive Measures

Semiadditive measures are measures whose data is not aggregated as a sum or a count over the various levels of a hierarchy. The semiadditive aggregate functions for measures are ByAccount, AverageOfChildren, FirstChild, LastChild, FirstNonEmpty, LastNonEmpty, and None. For example, assume you have a Time hierarchy and the measure Sales Value to be rolled up as an average of the sales of its children. Assume the levels in the Time hierarchy are Year, Half Year, Quarter, Month, and Date. If you have a member Quarter 1 of the year 2008 whose children are months July, August, and September, then the value for Quarter 1 will be the average of the sales values for the 3 months.

Using the Business Intelligence Wizard, you can change the behavior of the Aggregation Function of various measures in the cube. Launch the Business Intelligence Wizard, select Define Semiadditive Behavior on the Choose Enhancement page, and click Next. On the Define Semiadditive Behavior page (shown in Figure 9-49) you have three options. The default option is the detection of a dimension of type account, which contains semiadditive members. You learned in Chapter 8 to define semiadditive behavior for various Account types. If this selection is made, the Business Intelligence Wizard sets the aggregate function to ByAccount for all the measures of the measure group that have relationships defined with a dimension of type account. In the sample Adventure Works DW Multidimensional database, there is only one measure, Amount, that has the ByAccount aggregate function. The first option turns off all the semiadditive behavior for all the measures that have the Aggregate Function property set to a semiadditive behavior. When this option is selected, any measure that has a semiadditive aggregation function will be set to the Sum aggregate function. The last option, Define Semiadditive Behavior for Individual Measures, enables you to change the aggregation function for each measure. After you make the selection on the Define Semiadditive Behavior page, click Next. The final page of the Business Intelligence Wizard shows the new aggregate function for the measures that will be affected. Review the changes to be applied to the measures, and click Finish. SSDT then changes the Aggregate Function property for the measures.

FIGURE 9-49

You can verify the Aggregate Function property of the measures expected to be changed by the selections in the semiadditive behavior enhancement through the Business Intelligence Wizard. You learned the semiadditive behavior of the ByAccount aggregate function in Chapter 8. To see the results of LastNonEmpty and AverageOfChildren semiadditive aggregate functions, deploy the sample Adventure Works DW Multidimensional database, and browse the measures in the Exchange Rate in a Excel Pivot Table along with the Date.Fiscal hierarchy and DestinationCurrency.DestinationCurrency hierarchy, as shown in Figure 9-50. Select the members Australian Dollar and Euro in the Destination Currency hierarchy. You can see the value for the members in the Date.Fiscal hierarchy are calculated based on the aggregate functions LastNonEmpty (for End of Day Rate measure) and AverageOfChildren (for AverageRate measure) applied to their children.

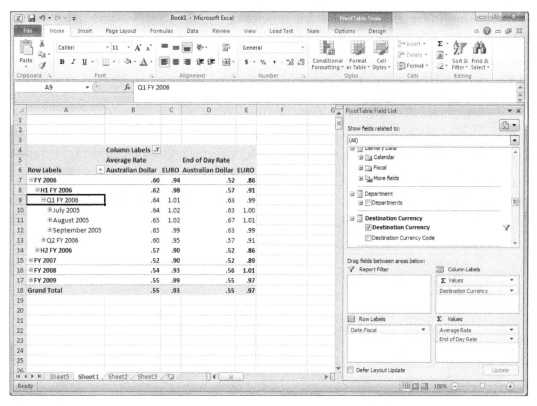

FIGURE 9-50

Currency Conversion

If your organization does business in more than one country, you might need to deal with converting currencies between countries. Analysts and managers may want to analyze transactions in the currency used for the transaction (also known as the local currency), whereas corporate management may want to convert all transactions to a single currency to get a complete view of all transactions globally. This scenario can be thought of as a many-to-one currency conversion. Or you might load data in the data warehouse in one currency but need to report financial results in different currencies. This scenario describes a one-to-many currency conversion. Yet another possibility is a combination of these two scenarios in which transaction data is in the local currency and needs to be reported in more than one different currency — a many-to-many currency conversion. Analysis Services 2012 provides a wizard to make it easy for you to add currency conversions to a cube for any of the three scenarios just described.

Before you can use the wizard, however, you need to build a currency dimension and an exchange rate measure group in your cube. These database objects are already in the Adventure Works cube that you've been using throughout this chapter, which gives you an opportunity to take a look at the proper structure before you build your own.

To review database objects used for currency conversion, follow these steps:

1. Using SSDT, open the Adventure Works cube in the Enterprise version of the Adventure Works DW Multidimensional sample project. Double-click the Adventure Works cube in the Solution Explorer to open the Cube Designer.

2. Click the Exchange Rates Measure Group in the Measures pane; then take a look at the Type property for the measure group, as shown in Figure 9-51. You must set the Type property value to ExchangeRate so that Analysis Services can correctly specify this measure group in the currency conversion calculations added to the MDX script when you use the wizard. The Exchange Rates measure group is based on a fact table that contains daily average and end-of-day exchange rates by day and by currency.

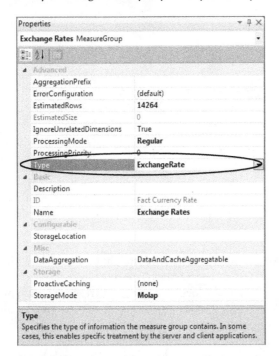

FIGURE 9-51

3. Open the Exchange Rates measure group; click the Average Rate measure and look at its AggregateFunction property. As you learned earlier in this chapter, Average Rate is a semi-additive measure that cannot be summed to get value for the month, quarter, or year level. Instead the aggregate function AverageOfChildren is used.

4. Now in the Solution Explorer, double-click the Source Currency dimension. In the Properties window, you can see the Type property for this dimension is set to Currency. Click the Source Currency attribute in the Attributes pane. You can see its Type property is CurrencySource. Lastly, click the Source Currency Code attribute, and verify its Type

property is CurrencyIsoCode. You can make sure you get the property settings right by selecting Currency as the Dimension Type when using the Dimension Wizard to create the dimension. The wizard prompts you for the column in your table containing the currency's ISO code and for the key attribute. Alternatively, you can change the properties after the dimension is created.

5. Now you're ready to start the Business Intelligence Wizard. The wizard creates a second currency dimension, one used for reporting the converted currencies, for you as well as updating the MDX script with calculations that ensure the currency conversion is correctly applied to affected measures. Right-click the Adventure Works cube in the Solution Explorer, click Add Business Intelligence, click Next, click Define Currency Conversion, and then click Next.

6. In the Set Currency Conversion Options page, the wizard looks for measure groups of type ExchangeRate and preselects that measure group. If such a measure group does not exist, it selects the first measure group. Click Exchange Rates in the "Select the Measure Group That Contains Exchange Rates" list. In the "Specify the Pivot Currency" list box, click USD, and then click OK. Now click the N USD Per 1 ARS radio button, as shown in Figure 9-52. The FactCurrencyRate table, on which the Exchange Rate measure group is based, has rates to convert one unit of local currency (such as one Australian dollar) into a standard currency (U.S. dollars in this case), which is called the pivot currency. If the table contained rates to convert 1 unit of the pivot currency into the local currency, you would select the N ARS Per 1 USD radio button. The drop-down list contains a predefined list of currencies to help you make the right selection. Click Next to continue.

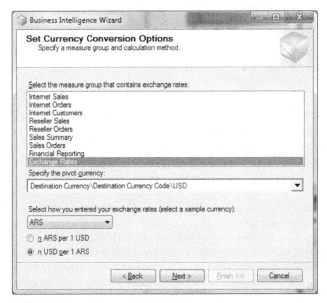

FIGURE 9-52

7. In the Select Members page (see Figure 9-53), select the check boxes next to Internet Sales Amount and Reseller Sales Amount. This page of the wizard identifies the members that will be converted. Another approach to currency conversion involves converting specific members in an attribute hierarchy of an Account dimension, such as certain expense accounts, or certain account types, such as all revenue accounts. You can select the measure from the measure group selected in the previous page of the dialog that is to be used for currency conversion. The Average Rate measure is selected by default. These options are useful when your cube is dedicated to financial data for balance sheets and profit and loss statements.

FIGURE 9-53

8. Click Next to view the next page of the wizard, as shown in Figure 9-54. Here you describe your conversion scenario for the wizard. Your selection here determines what information you must supply on subsequent pages of the wizard. The selections are self-explanatory. Choose the Many-to-Many selection, and click Next.

In the Define Local Currency Reference page (Figure 9-55), you define the location of the column that contains the currency key. After you specify whether it's in a fact table (which it is in the Adventure Works DW Multidimensional sample database) or in a dimension table, you select the attribute with which a currency is associated. If a currency attribute is in the fact table, it is likely to be a dimension key that is related to a dimension table. Otherwise, the attribute is a column in a dimension table that typically corresponds to geography, such as business divisions that are located in separate countries.

In this example, the Destination Currency is automatically selected because the currency conversion definition is already in the Adventure Works cube. If you were to start completely from scratch, you would choose the Source Currency dimension's key attribute on this page.

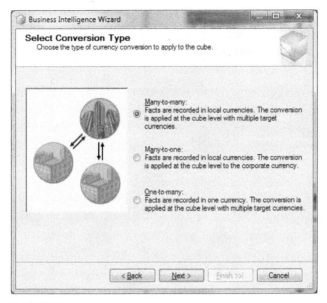

FIGURE 9-54

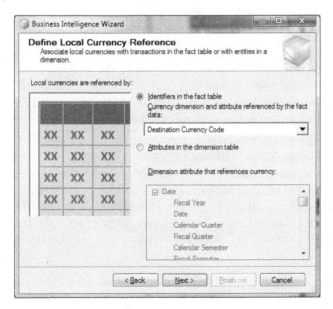

FIGURE 9-55

9. Click Next again, and then click the box to the left of Reporting Currencies to select all the available items, as shown in Figure 9-56. On this page, you identify the currencies to include in the reporting currency (called Destination Currency in the Adventure Works cube). The Business Intelligence Wizard builds a new dimension according to your selections here. If you forget to select a currency that exists in the exchange rate fact table, cube processing will fail — be careful!

FIGURE 9-56

10. Click Next, and then click Cancel on the final page of the wizard. Because the Destination Currency and currency conversion calculations are already in the cube, the wizard doesn't need to do anything. But if you add this capability to your own cube, there's still more to explore to better understand what the wizard would do if you start the process with only a Source Currency dimension and an Exchange Rates fact table.

11. Double-click the Adventure Works Data Source View in the Solution Explorer. In the Tables pane, right-click DestinationCurrency, and then click Edit Named Query. A query similar to the following query would be created by the Business Intelligence Wizard when creating a reporting currency. The WHERE clause of this query would detail currencies selected on the Specify Reporting Currencies page of the wizard (see Figure 9-56) if you picked some, but not all, available currencies. The main foundation for the named query is the DimCurrency table, which is also used for the Source Currency dimension in the Adventure Works DW Multidimensional database.

```
SELECT      CurrencyKey, CurrencyAlternateKey, CurrencyName,
            CASE WHEN CurrencyAlternateKey = 'ARS' THEN '11274' WHEN
                     CurrencyAlternateKey = 'AUD' THEN '3081' WHEN
                     CurrencyAlternateKey = 'DEM' THEN '1031' WHEN
                     CurrencyAlternateKey = 'GBP' THEN '2057' WHEN
                     CurrencyAlternateKey = 'MXN' THEN '2058' WHEN
                     CurrencyAlternateKey = 'CAD' THEN '4105' WHEN
                     CurrencyAlternateKey = 'SAR' THEN '1025' WHEN
                     CurrencyAlternateKey = 'EUR' THEN '2067' WHEN
```

```
                    CurrencyAlternateKey = 'FRF' THEN '1036' WHEN
                    CurrencyAlternateKey = 'BRL' THEN '1046' WHEN
                    CurrencyAlternateKey = 'JPY' THEN '1041' WHEN
                    CurrencyAlternateKey = 'CNY' THEN '2052' WHEN
                    CurrencyAlternateKey = 'VEB' THEN '16394' WHEN
                    CurrencyAlternateKey = 'USD' THEN '1033' END AS LCID
    FROM            dbo.DimCurrency
    WHERE           (CurrencyKey IN
                    (SELECT DISTINCT CurrencyKey
                        FROM   dbo.FactCurrencyRate))
```

12. Switch to the Cube Designer, click the Dimension Usage tab, and locate the relationships between the Exchange Rate measure group and other dimensions. Only the Date and Destination Currency dimensions have a regular relationship with Exchange Rate. Recall that you learned about many-to-many relationships earlier in this chapter. In the current example, Internet Sales has sales amounts in many local currencies, which need to be converted — by way of Exchange Rates — to multiple destination currencies. Accordingly, Internet Sales has a regular relationship with Source Currency (representing the local currency) and a many-to-many relationship with Destination Currency with Exchange Rate as the intermediate measure group.

WORKING WITH PARTITIONS

When building business intelligence solutions at the enterprise level, it is common to work with terabytes of source (also known as fact or detail) data. Even if you work with just a few hundred gigabytes, you can find the use of partitions to be critical to your success.

By adding partitions to your overall cube design strategy, you can manage how and where cube data is physically stored, how a cube is processed as well as the time required for processing, and how efficiently Analysis Services 2012 can retrieve data in response to user queries. One key benefit of partitioning is the distribution of data over and across one or more hard disk drives and the ability of Analysis Services to process or query the partitions in parallel using multiple processors or cores that help in processing and query performance. And in the case of remote partitions, the data can be spread over various machines. Partitions can even be processed in parallel on the remote machines. In this section, you first learn how to set up a local partition. Then, in the section that follows, you learn how to set up a remote partition configuration — which, by the way, is not the simplest procedure.

To work with partitions, you first need administrator privileges on both the local and remote instances of Analysis Services you intend to use. Administrator privileges are granted to member groups or users assigned to the Analysis Services server role. To join the Server role, first open SSMS under machine administrative privilege and connect to each Analysis Services instance you plan to use. For each instance, you need to perform the following steps:

1. Right-click the instance name and select Properties. In the Analysis Server Properties dialog, as shown in Figure 9-57, click the Security tab in the top-left pane. Then, click the Add button.

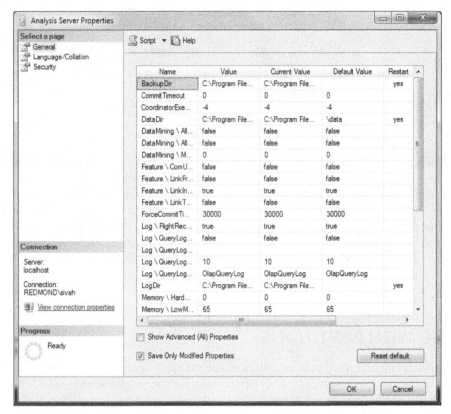

FIGURE 9-57

2. Next, you need to enter your fully articulated username in the "Enter the Object Names to Select" text box. In Figure 9-58, you can see how domain\username (enter a valid Windows account) was entered. To validate your entry, just click the Check Names button. Finally, click OK to close all dialogs. You now have serverwide administrator rights. Be sure to repeat these steps on the local and the remote servers.

FIGURE 9-58

Building a Local Partition

An important thing to know about partitions is that one partition per measure group in a cube is created behind the scenes to accommodate the storage of data and meta data of your cube — so without any action on your part, beyond the creation of the measure groups, you already have partitions on your computer. When you explicitly create a local partition, you add it to the group of existing partitions for a measure group. So, why should you take extra steps to add partitions? Well, by using partitions you can spread data across multiple hard disk drives on a single computer. Because large partitions slow down cube-related activities, dividing one large partition into multiple smaller partitions can improve processing and query times as well as simplify management and administration.

In the following exercise, your goal is to replace the single Internet Sales partition for 2008 into two partitions of equal size. This requires you to change the parameters on the existing partition to make room for the new partition; otherwise, Internet sales for 2008 would be double-counted because both partitions would contain the same data. Double-counting, by the way, is something you must be alert for because it results in incorrect results.

To create a local partition, follow these steps:

1. Using SSDT, open the Adventure Works DW Multidimensional sample database. Double-click the Adventure Works cube name in the Solution Explorer to open the Cube Designer.

2. Click the Partitions tab. Your screen should look similar to Figure 9-59.

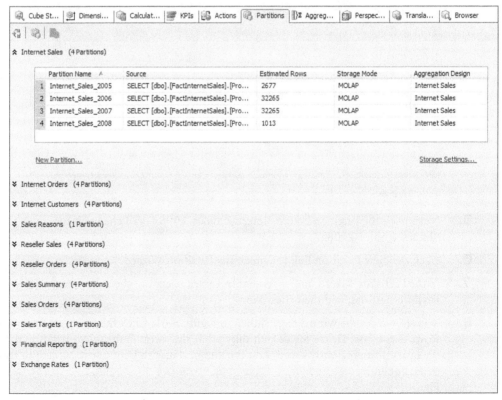

FIGURE 9-59

3. If necessary, expand the Internet Sales section by clicking the arrows to the left of Internet Sales. Click the Source box for Internet_Sales_2008, and then click the button with two dots appearing in the box to open the Partition Source dialog.

4. Because you need to use a similar filter query when you create the second Internet Sales 2008 partition, highlight the query, and copy it to the clipboard or Notepad. You can modify the query to change the partition such that it contains only data with OrderDateKeys between 20080101 and 20080531 (inclusive) as shown in Figure 9-60, and click OK.

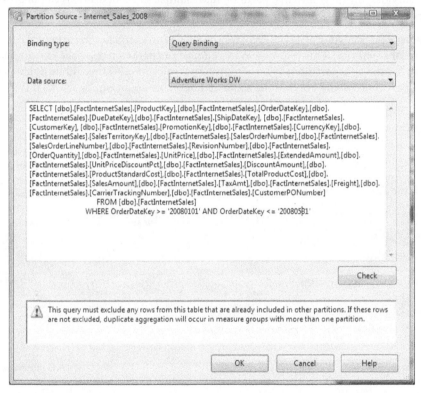

FIGURE 9-60

5. Next, click the Partition Name "Internet_Sales_2008," and change it to "Internet_Sales_2008a."

6. Click the New Partition link to launch the Partition Wizard.

7. In the Partition Wizard, under Available Tables select the check box next to FactInternetSales, and then click Next.

8. You should see the wizard page shown in Figure 9-61. Click the Specify a Query to Restrict Rows check box. Delete the default query that shows up in the query window, and paste in the query you previously saved. Edit the WHERE clause to limit partition data to rows with OrderDateKey >= '20080601' AND OrderDateKey <= '20081231', as shown in Figure 9-61.

FIGURE 9-61

9. Click Finish. (You're storing your partition to the default location.) In the Name box, type **Internet_Sales_2008b,** click the Design Aggregations Later radio button, and then click Finish.

Naturally, you want to design aggregations for your new partition, and deploy and process it. Designing aggregations for partitions is an important part of data warehouse design. You learn more about aggregation design later in the Building Aggregations section and in Chapter 10. In this case, you have learned how to use the Partition Wizard for creating a new partition without duplicating data in the process. Again, data duplication must be guarded against because it leads directly to wrong results. The next section takes on the formidable and useful remote partition.

Building a Remote Partition

The basic architecture of the remote partition keeps data definitions (meta data) in the cube on the master (or parent) machine and off-loads the measure or detail data to the remote partitions on subordinate machines. In terms of administration tasks related to remote partitions, the host machine containing the cube meta data acts as the point of control for all related remote partitions.

To implement a remote partition in the most meaningful way, you need two computers. Earlier in this chapter, you followed steps to make sure the permissions were set to work with the local and remote computers with appropriate credentials. In addition, you must have the firewall settings on the master computer (the host box) and subordinate box configured to accept outside connections for Analysis Services. The computer storing the remote partition on it is called the Subordinate (Target) computer. In the tutorial that follows, you use two instances on one machine (localhost and localhost\SSAS2012) to demonstrate remote partitions; in this case, firewall settings are not necessary. If you are going for a two machine configuration, of course, you need to set the firewalls appropriately. Before working with the subordinate computer, you set the stage for successful interserver interactions by starting your work on the Master computer.

1. In SSDT, open the Adventure Works DW Multidimensional Analysis Services sample project.

2. Right-click the project name, Adventure Works DW Multidimensional, in the Solution Explorer, and click Properties to access the Property Pages, as shown in Figure 9-62. Select the third item down below Configuration Properties in the pane on the left (Deployment). Make your settings consistent with those shown in the figure; be sure the correct name is listed for the Master Server which, if you're not using a named instance, should be localhost. Click OK.

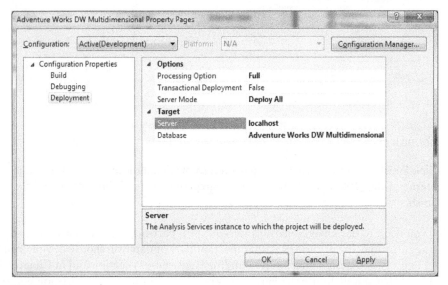

FIGURE 9-62

3. In the Solution Explorer, right-click the Adventure Works DW Multidimensional database icon, and select Deploy to deploy and process the project.

4. Now it's time to work on the target, or subordinate, machine (or instance). Open a new instance of SSDT, and then create a new Analysis Services Multidimensional and Data Mining project called Target.

5. Right-click the Data Sources folder in the Solution Explorer, and select New Data Source. In the Data Source Wizard dialog, click the New button to open the Connection Manager dialog.

6. Change the Provider to Native OLE DB\Microsoft OLE DB Provider for Analysis Services 11.0. In the Connection Manager dialog, there is a Server or File Name text box, into which you type the name of your master Analysis Services instance. If you use the default instance on the Master machine, type the machine name (or **localhost**). Set the authentication properties in Log on to the Server consistent with your own configuration. Then click the down

arrow for Initial Catalog, select Adventure Works DW Multidimensional (the dialog should look like Figure 9-63), and click OK.

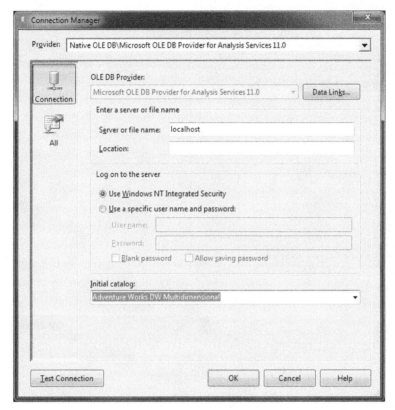

FIGURE 9-63

7. In the Data Source Wizard, click Next. Set the Impersonation Information at this time to verify correct security settings. Next.

8. You need to provide a new name on this page; such as ASDB_AdvWorksDW, and then click Finish.

9. Just to be clear, you're still on the subordinate machine or instance. Right-click the project name in the Solution Explorer, and choose Edit Database. Now in the Properties window change the MasterDataSourceID property from empty to **ASDB_AdvWorksDW**, as shown in Figure 9-64.

10. Right-click the database name in the Solution Explorer, and choose Properties. Click Configuration Properties, and then click Deployment. Click Server, and set the name to the subordinate instance of Analysis Services, as shown in Figure 9-65. Click OK to close the dialog.

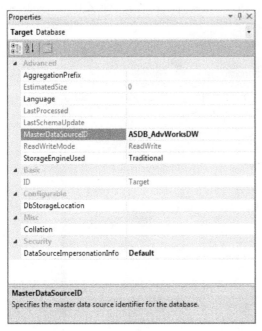

FIGURE 9-64

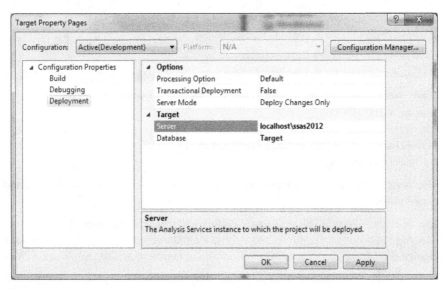

FIGURE 9-65

11. Deploy the project to move the meta data to the Analysis Services instance (localhost\
ssas2012).

12. For both localhost and localhost\ssas2012 do the following in SSMS:

a. Connect to the service.

b. Right-click the instance name and select Properties.

c. Change the Value (first column) of both Feature\LinkToOtherInstanceEnabled and Feature\LinkFromOtherInstanceEnabled to True.

d. Click OK to close the Analysis Server Properties dialog.

e. To make the server property changes take effect, you need to restart the instance of Analysis Services; just right-click the instance name in the SSMS Object Explorer and click Stop. When asked to run in administrator mode, click Continue. Click Yes when asked to verify you want to stop the service. Right-click the instances in the SSMS Object Explorer, and click Start to restart the instance.

13. In SSDT, create a second data source in the Adventure Works DW Multidimensional project to connect to the subordinate (target) instance of Analysis Services, and specifically at the target project (named Target here). Use the Native OLE DB\Microsoft OLE DB Provider for Analysis Services 11.0 (see Figure 9-66).

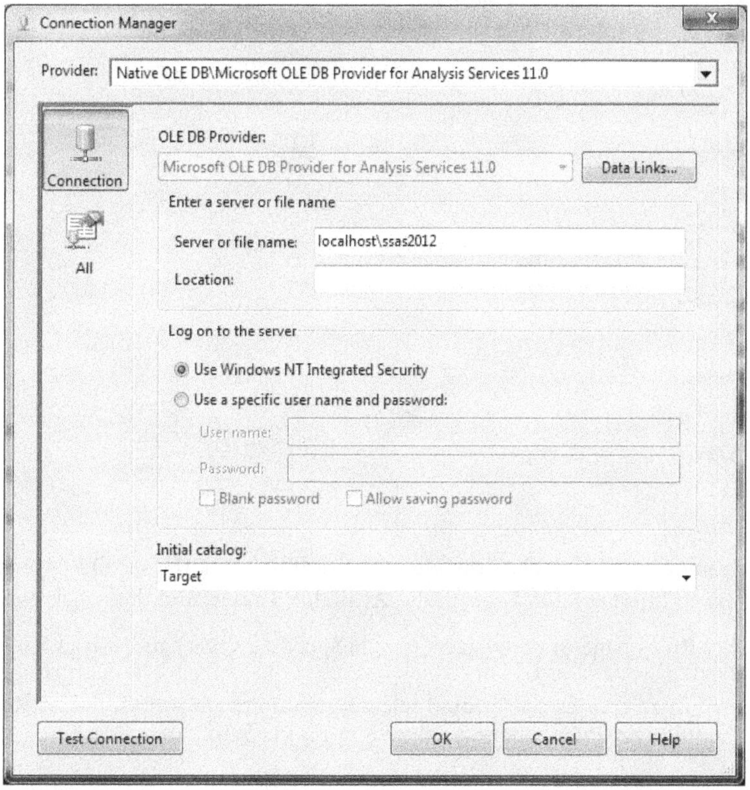

FIGURE 9-66

14. Click OK to close the Connection Manager dialog. Select the created data source for the Target database; then click Next. On the Impersonation Information page, select Inherit and click Next. Accept the default name provided by the Data Source Wizard, and click Finish.

15. It is nearly time to create the remote partition; but first you need to make room for one by deleting an existing partition. Sacrifice one of the Internet Sales partitions by opening the Adventure Works cube and clicking the Partitions tab; then click the double down arrows next to Internet Sales to open the section for the Internet Sales measure group. To delete the Internet_Sales_2005 partition, right-click the partition, and click Delete, as shown in Figure 9-67.

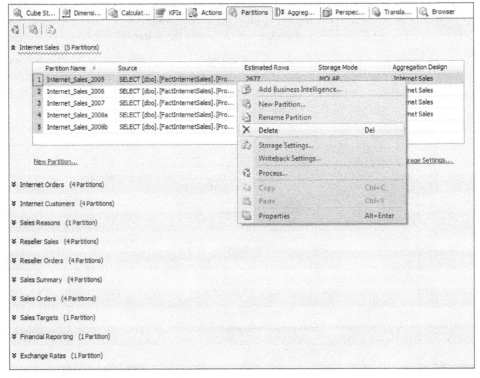

FIGURE 9-67

16. To build the remote partition, click the New Partition link. On the second page, click the check box next to Internet Sales Facts under Available Tables, and then click Next.

17. On the Restrict Rows page of the wizard, enable Specify a Query to Restrict Rows.

    The Partition Wizard creates a relational select query up to the WHERE clause. Replace the query with the following SQL query, as shown in Figure 9-68, and click Next.

```
SELECT
[dbo].[FactInternetSales].[ProductKey],
```

```
[dbo].[FactInternetSales].[OrderDateKey],
[dbo].[FactInternetSales].[DueDateKey],
[dbo].[FactInternetSales].[ShipDateKey],
[dbo].[FactInternetSales].[CustomerKey],
[dbo].[FactInternetSales].[PromotionKey],
[dbo].[FactInternetSales].[CurrencyKey],
[dbo].[FactInternetSales].[SalesTerritoryKey],
[dbo].[FactInternetSales].[SalesOrderNumber],
[dbo].[FactInternetSales].[SalesOrderLineNumber],
[dbo].[FactInternetSales].[RevisionNumber],
[dbo].[FactInternetSales].[OrderQuantity],
[dbo].[FactInternetSales].[UnitPrice],
[dbo].[FactInternetSales].[ExtendedAmount],
[dbo].[FactInternetSales].[UnitPriceDiscountPct],
[dbo].[FactInternetSales].[DiscountAmount],
[dbo].[FactInternetSales].[ProductStandardCost],
[dbo].[FactInternetSales].[TotalProductCost],
[dbo].[FactInternetSales].[SalesAmount],
[dbo].[FactInternetSales].[TaxAmt],
[dbo].[FactInternetSales].[Freight],
[dbo].[FactInternetSales].[CarrierTrackingNumber],
[dbo].[FactInternetSales].[CustomerPONumber]
FROM [dbo].[FactInternetSales]
WHERE OrderDateKey <= '20051231'
```

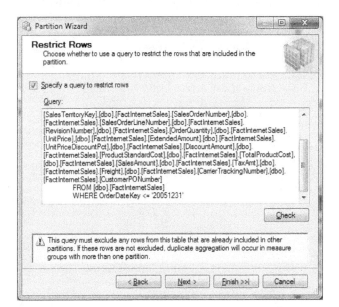

FIGURE 9-68

18. In the Processing and Storage Locations page, select the option Remote Analysis Services Data Source, select the data source Target, as shown in Figure 9-69, and click Next.

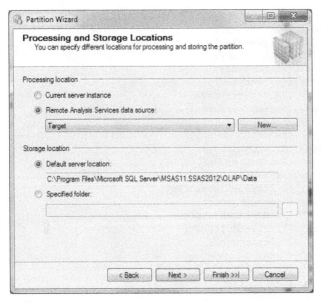

FIGURE 9-69

19. Select the Design Aggregations Later radio button, name the partition **Internet_Sales_2005,** as shown in Figure 9-70, and click Finish.

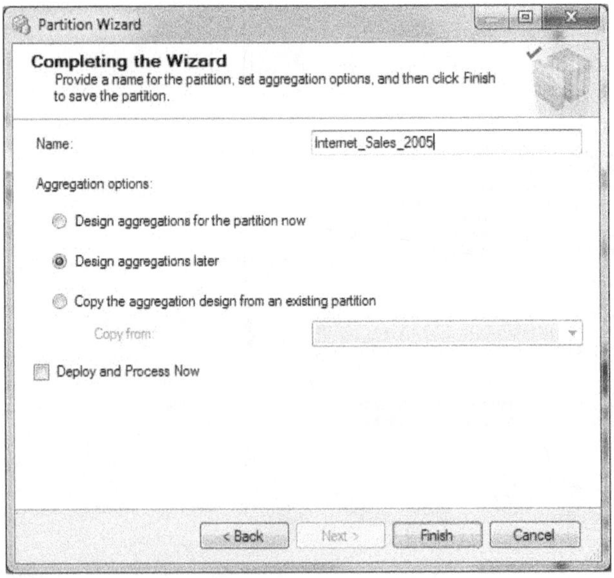

FIGURE 9-70

20. Open the Internet Sales Order Details dimension, and change the storage mode from ROLAP to MOLAP in the Properties window.

IMPORTANT SECURITY INFORMATION FOR REMOTE PARTITIONS

Choose the Impersonation mode to be Inherit for the Data Sources within the master and subordinate databases (instances). By choosing Inherit, at the time of processing, Analysis Services instances use the service's start-up account while connecting to Analysis Services 11.0 databases. If your server start-up account for both instances is a Windows domain (user) account, you would have appropriate permissions to access the databases (so long as that start-up account has admin permissions). However, if both instances were installed with server start-up accounts as Local System, you might encounter an access permissions error when the master database tries to connect to the subordinate. This is because connections to named instances of Analysis Services are routed via SQL Browser, and by default the server start-up account for SQL Browser is Network Service. If your installation has the SQL Browser server start-up account as Network Service and the Analysis Services instances server start-up account is Local System, change the server start-up account of SQL Browser and the two Analysis Services instances to a Windows domain account using SQL Server Configuration Manager. The Configuration Manager can be launched from Start\All programs\Microsoft SQL Server 2012\ Configuration Tools\SQL Server Configuration Manager.

---

21. To populate the partition on the remote machine, change the deployment properties by right-clicking the Adventure Works DW Multidimensional project name and selecting Properties. Select Deployment on the Property page, and change Processing Option to Do Not Process and Deployment mode to Deploy All. Deploy the changes to your Analysis Services instance. Right-click the cube Adventure Works in the Solution Explorer, and select Process. If asked to deploy the project, select No. In the Process dialog, click Run. After processing is complete, you can query data from the remote partitions.

When the Adventure Works DW Multidimensional database has been processed, you can see the remote partitions quite clearly in the data folder on the remote server after processing, as shown in Figure 9-71. And if it doesn't work for you the first time (you get errors back from your Analysis Services instance), don't worry; there are a lot of steps and therefore lots of opportunities to get things messed up. Most likely though, there are security errors; be sure to verify you have all the correct Firewall settings and Impersonation settings. You can change Impersonation settings in a secondary tab in the Data Source Wizard.

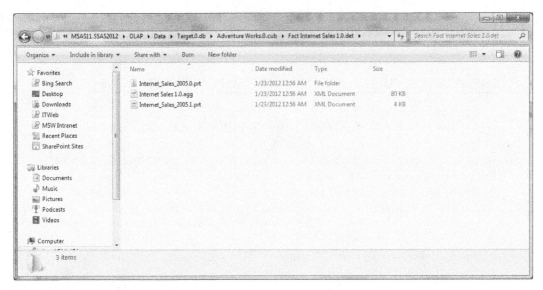

FIGURE 9-71

Storage Modes and Storage Settings

In Analysis Services, the storage and processing schemes are linked through the setting of caching options. Caching is a way to increase query response time by keeping the data used most often on a local disk. Where you store partition data is just one part of the storage picture; the mode in which you store it is the other. The storage modes used with Analysis Services solutions include MOLAP (Multidimensional OLAP), ROLAP (Relational OLAP), and HOLAP (Hybrid OLAP). These storage types were discussed in some detail way in Chapter 1, so this section contains only a brief review. The main difference between these storage modes concerns where the data and/or aggregated fact data is stored. MOLAP is the traditional storage mode for OLAP servers and involves keeping both data and aggregations on the server. This results in fast query response times, but it is not as scalable as other solutions. ROLAP is the storage mode in which the data is left in the relational database. Aggregated or summary data is also stored in the relational database. The key advantage here is that ROLAP scales as well as your relational hardware/software will support, but typically results in slower queries. The HOLAP storage mode theoretically combines the best features of MOLAP and ROLAP, but is not recommended in practice because the difference in query performance between queries that involve aggregations and those that require queries to the source data is so great that users typically find this disconcerting. In HOLAP, the data in the relational database is not duplicated while the aggregated or summary data is stored on the Analysis Server in a proprietary format; queries that can be resolved in the Analysis Server are, and those that cannot are redirected to the relational backend.

MOLAP is generally the preferred mode due to the performance gains and efficiency in its use of storage space. If you need to analyze real-time data, ROLAP is probably more appropriate. ROLAP is also a better option when you have a large data warehouse and you do not want to duplicate the data. Each partition can have its own storage mode, which you specify on the Partitions tab of the Cube Designer in SSDT. Just click the Storage Settings link as shown in Figure 9-72.

| | Cube Structure | Dimension Usage | Calculations | KPIs | Actions | Partitions | Aggregations | Perspectives | Translations | Browser |

Internet Sales (5 Partitions)

	Partition Name	Source	Estimated Rows	Storage Mode	Aggregation Design
1	Internet_Sales_2005	SELECT [dbo].[FactInternetSales].[ProductKey],...	0	MOLAP	
2	Internet_Sales_2006	SELECT [dbo].[FactInternetSales].[ProductKey],...	32265	MOLAP	Internet Sales
3	Internet_Sales_2007	SELECT [dbo].[FactInternetSales].[ProductKey],...	32265	MOLAP	Internet Sales
4	Internet_Sales_2008a	SELECT [dbo].[FactInternetSales].[ProductKey],...	1013	MOLAP	Internet Sales
5	Internet_Sales_2008b	SELECT [dbo].[FactInternetSales].[ProductKey],...	0	MOLAP	

New Partition....   Storage Settings...

FIGURE 9-72

When you click Storage Settings, the dialog displays the Partition Storage Setting configuration screen from the Partition Wizard (see Figure 9-73). Typically, for most partitions you would have the storage setting as MOLAP for optimal performance. In certain instances you might want to see real-time data with certain acceptable latency in loading the data into your multidimensional BISM. The various options from Real-time ROLAP to MOLAP are a mechanism that gives you control over the latency, processing frequency as well as storage mode. You learn more about some of the settings and under which scenarios these might be useful in the Real-Time Cubes section in this chapter.

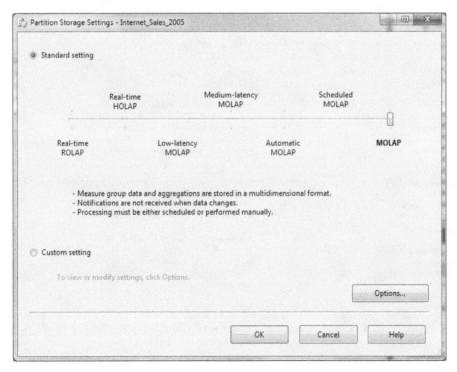

FIGURE 9-73

Building Aggregations

Aggregations make querying OLAP systems fast. An *aggregation* is nothing more than a precalculated summary of a specific partition of data. Many partitions may share the same aggregation design or blueprint, but the actual aggregations that are precomputed and written to disk are specific to a given a partition. The collection of all aggregations, typically in the tens up to low hundreds, is what is meant when referring to the aggregation strategy or aggregation level for a given partition or set of partitions.

In Analysis Services 2012, the Cube Designer has a tab for designing aggregations, as shown in Figure 9-74. The aggregation designer has two views: a standard view (Figure 9-74) that displays measure groups and aggregation designs and an advanced view (Figure 9-75) that shows the individual aggregations of a given aggregation design, in a given measure group.

Aggregation designs are essentially blueprints for aggregations within a measure group and are intended to be shared among multiple partitions. The concept of aggregation designs, though first introduced in Analysis Services 2005, was not something that the user interface displayed explicitly until Analysis Services 2008. One of the motivations for exposing aggregation designs in the Analysis Services 2008 user interface was to avoid the bad practice to create too many aggregation designs! In practice, you may have a need for multiple aggregation designs to differentiate highly queried partitions from those less often queried, but it would be rare to need more than three.

	Aggregations	Estimated Partiti...	Partitions
⊟ 〰 Internet Sales (1 Aggregation Design)			
⬚ Internet Sales	54	32265	Internet_Sales_2008a, Internet_Sales_2006, Internet_Sales_2007
⬚ Unassigned Aggregation Design	-	-	Internet_Sales_2008b, Internet_Sales_2005
⊟ 〰 Internet Orders (0 Aggregation Designs)			
⬚ Unassigned Aggregation Design	-	-	Internet_Orders_2005, Internet_Orders_2006, Internet_Orders_2007, ...
⊟ 〰 Internet Customers (0 Aggregation Designs)			
⬚ Unassigned Aggregation Design	-	-	Customers_2005, Customers_2006, Customers_2007, ...
⊟ 〰 Sales Reasons (0 Aggregation Designs)			
⬚ Unassigned Aggregation Design	-	-	Internet_Sales_Reasons
⊟ 〰 Reseller Sales (1 Aggregation Design)			
⬚ Reseller Sales	34	26758	Reseller_Sales_2005, Reseller_Sales_2006, Reseller_Sales_2007, ...
⊟ 〰 Reseller Orders (0 Aggregation Designs)			
⬚ Unassigned Aggregation Design	-	-	Reseller_Orders_2005, Reseller_Orders_2006, Reseller_Orders_2007, ...
⊟ 〰 Sales Summary (1 Aggregation Design)			
⬚ Sales Summary	48	51201	Total_Sales_2005, Total_Sales_2006, Total_Sales_2007, ...
⊟ 〰 Sales Orders (0 Aggregation Designs)			
⬚ Unassigned Aggregation Design	-	-	Total_Orders_2005, Total_Orders_2006, Total_Orders_2007, ...
⊟ 〰 Sales Targets (1 Aggregation Design)			
⬚ Sales Targets	4	163	Sales_Quotas
⊟ 〰 Financial Reporting (0 Aggregation Designs)			
⬚ Unassigned Aggregation Design	-	-	Finance
⊟ 〰 Exchange Rates (1 Aggregation Design)			
⬚ Exchange Rates	2	14264	Currency_Rates

FIGURE 9-74

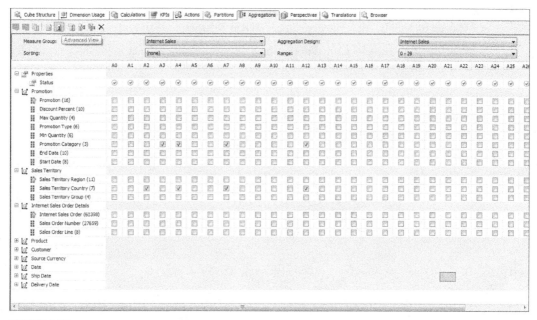

FIGURE 9-75

The standard view is what most people should use most of the time. This view enables launching the aggregation wizards, changing a partition's aggregation design, assigning aggregation designs to additional partitions, and getting an overall picture of how the aggregations look within a cube. The advanced view of the aggregation designer enables viewing, editing, and creating both aggregation designs and aggregations by hand. Use this view only when you need either particular attributes included in one or more aggregations or particular aggregations defined when the wizards are not enabling this. In the advanced view, if you create aggregations that may not be beneficial for query performance due to redundant attributes in a dimension, you see a warning provided by the designer, as shown in Figure 9-76. The designer warns you to look further into your aggregation design and make sure this is essential. This is primarily to help the Cube Designer to design the cube with performance as a key design principle.

To start the Aggregation Design Wizard, in the standard view of the Aggregations tab, click Design Aggregations. This wizard helps you to create aggregations for each partition, using statistical analysis of the meta data combined with custom heuristics to improve overall query performance independent of usage data. You learn Aggregation design and benefits in detail in Chapter 10. Follow these steps to understand the Aggregation Design Wizard outcome:

1. Select the Internet Sales measure group, and start the Aggregation Design Wizard using the first icon in the standard view of the Aggregations tab in the Cube Designer.

2. In the Select Partitions to Modify page, select all the partitions and click Next.

3. Select the defaults on the Review Aggregation Usage page, and select Next.

4. In the Specify Object Counts page, click the Count button to get the counts for attribute members, and click Next. These counts are used by an algorithm to create the optimal aggregation design.

5. On the Set Aggregation Options page, you can specify various options to design aggregations for the chosen partitions. Click the Performance Gain Reaches 30% option, and click Start.

6. The performance benefits gained are graphically compared to the storage space required to store the aggregations, as shown in Figure 9-77, where you can see that the Performance Gain is set to 30 percent. A good starting target should be approximately 25 percent to 30 percent, but you learn about the Usage-Based Optimization Wizard in Chapter 10 for fine-tuning performance gains even further using actual usage data. Click Cancel in the Aggregation Design Wizard.

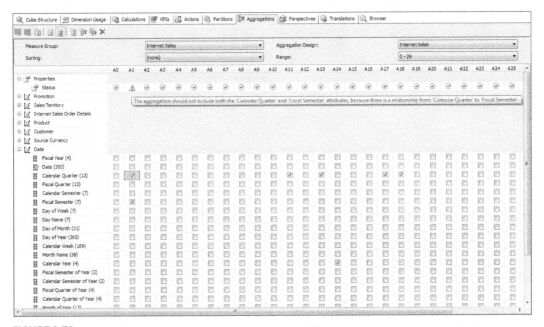

FIGURE 9-76

You can validate that the aggregations were defined by the wizard by expanding the relevant measure group in the Aggregations tab, locating the row corresponding to the aggregation design, and clicking the button in the cell corresponding to the Partitions column or reviewing the Aggregation Design column for each partition in the Partitions tab, as shown in Figure 9-72. You do need to deploy the aggregations created by the wizard to your Analysis Services instance to make sure the aggregations are processed and available for querying. To validate that the aggregations defined by the wizard are useful, you need to trace the query execution using SQL Server Profiler, which you learn how to do in Chapter 11.

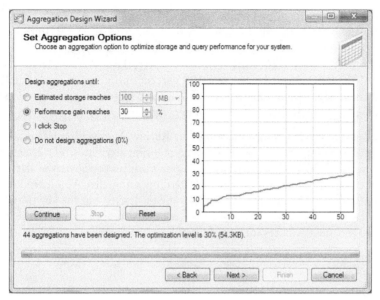

FIGURE 9-77

The Aggregation Design Process

You can design aggregations in three ways:

➤ **Use the Aggregation Design Wizard:** This wizard uses built-in heuristics combined with statistical techniques to determine candidate aggregations based on database meta data. No usage information is required here. The only requirement is that you can successfully deploy (not process) the database to a server.

➤ **Use the Usage-Based Optimization (UBO) Wizard:** As the name implies, this wizard takes the queries recorded in the query log as the primary input and reconciles these with database meta data to generate candidate aggregations.

➤ **Manually design aggregations using the Advanced View of the Aggregation Designer:** This is an inherently risky and error-prone option that should be used only by advanced users. As the name implies, this method requires you to work at the level of individual aggregations and make decisions regarding which attributes will be included.

All three methods are of course valid, but there are recommendations for how and when to use each method. Generally speaking, the safest and best starting point in the absence of usage data is to run the Aggregation Design Wizard, selecting an optimization level of between 25 and 30 percent. This can provide you with a baseline set of aggregations while you build your query log. Another option is to populate the query log if you are confident that you have a representative query set. In this case, you would skip the Aggregation Design Wizard and go straight to the Usage-Based Optimization (UBO) Wizard. For reasons discussed in the UBO section in this chapter, the recommendation when running the Analysis Services 2012 UBO Wizard is to use a 100 percent optimization level. Finally, advanced users with detailed knowledge of query patterns, attribute and fact sizes, and a good feeling for sparseness levels, can manually design the initial set of aggregations.

When using the Aggregation Design Wizard, you can leverage the Review Aggregation Usage screen (see Figure 9-78), to lower or raise the importance level of cube dimension attributes. The effect of this property is to control the way in which the aggregation design algorithm considers the attribute (raise or lower importance), or, optionally, to exclude the attribute altogether. You learn how the algorithm deals with attributes and what the various settings mean shortly, but the key initial takeaway is that you should view the functionality of this screen as a way to both reduce the search space of the algorithm and give certain attributes increased weighting.

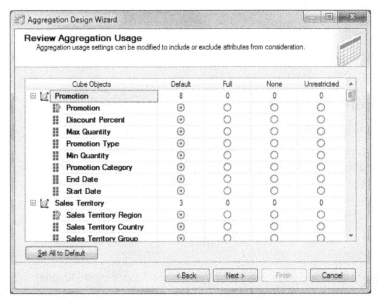

FIGURE 9-78

By default, all cube attributes have their aggregation usage property value set to Default, as you might expect. Before modifying this property, you need to understand each of the respective values:

➤   **Full:** Every aggregation for the cube must include this attribute or a related attribute that is lower in the attribute chain. For example, you have a date dimension with the following chain of related attributes: Date, Month, and Quarter. If you specify the Aggregation Usage for Quarter to be Full, Analysis Services may create an aggregation that includes Month as opposed to Quarter, given that Month is related to Quarter and can be used to derive Quarter totals.

➤   **None:** No aggregation for the cube may include this attribute. This is a good value to set when you know the attribute in question is unlikely to be queried by end users.

➤ **Unrestricted:** No restrictions are placed on the aggregation designer. However, the attribute must still be evaluated to determine whether it is a valuable aggregation candidate. This is a good middle ground between Default and Full and should generally be used when application of the default rule does not result in a commonly queried attribute to be considered.

➤ **Default:** The designer applies a default rule based on the type of attribute and dimension.

Following is the set of rules that determines how the value Default is interpreted by the wizards. In general, the wizard is highly conservative about which attributes are considered for aggregation when the aggregation usage is set to default.

➤ **Default Constraint 1:** Unrestricted for the Granularity and All Attributes: For the dimension attribute that is the measure group granularity attribute and the All attribute, apply Unrestricted. The granularity attribute is the same as the dimension's key attribute as long as the measure group joins to a dimension using the primary key attribute.

➤ **Default Constraint 2:** None for Special Dimension Types: For all attributes (except All) in many-to-many, nonmaterialized reference dimensions, linked, and data mining dimensions, use None. The wizard simply removes these dimension types from the UI. The designer, in turn, will do the same.

➤ **Default Constraint 3:** Unrestricted for Natural Hierarchies: For all user hierarchies, apply a special scanning process to identify the attributes in natural hierarchies. A natural hierarchy is a user hierarchy where all attributes participating in the hierarchy contain attribute relationships at every level of the hierarchy (hierarchies are discussed in more detail in Chapter 10). To identify the natural hierarchies, Analysis Services scans each user hierarchy, starting at the top level and then moving down through the hierarchy to the bottom level. For each level, it checks whether the attribute of the current level is linked to the attribute of the next level via a direct or indirect attribute relationship. For every attribute that passes the natural hierarchy test, apply Unrestricted, except for nonaggregatable attributes, which are set to Full.

➤ **Default Constraint 4:** None for Everything Else: For all other dimension attributes, apply None.

Now that you know what the various values of the Aggregation Usage mean, you can correctly modify the setting to obtain better quality aggregations when designing aggregations using the Aggregation Design Wizard. This property does not apply (it's ignored) when running the Usage-Based Optimization Wizard. The Review Aggregation Usage screen displays only dimensions eligible to participate in the aggregation usage process. Changes made in this screen overwrite the cube attribute's Aggregation Usage property. When an attribute is going to be considered, the text of the name displays in bold; this applies to Default, Unrestricted, and Full settings. In addition, the first time the Full value is selected, a pop-up message appears warning that this value should be used sparingly. You may ask why the UI goes to such lengths to call out this scenario. The reason for this is that if a large (high cardinality) attribute is selected and multiple attributes have their values set to Full, every single potential aggregation may be thrown out due to excessive size. What would result in such cases is fewer or even no aggregations being designed because the wizard automatically discards any aggregations greater than 30 percent of the size of the partition tables. Aggregation design is also discussed in Chapter 10 because it is critical to optimal cube design to get the best query performance.

Usage-Based Optimization

The Usage-Based Optimization (UBO) Wizard can be launched using the second icon on the Aggregations tab of the Cube Designer in SSDT. With the help of the UBO Wizard in Analysis Services 2012, you have the option to create a new aggregation design or append the results of a UBO pass to an existing aggregation design in the final page of the UBO Wizard (see Figure 9-79). The UI automatically strips out any duplicates when doing the merge, but logically equivalent aggregations (those that essentially cover the same or similar cube space) will not be detected. In practice, this means that you must be careful not to over-aggregate via this option. So, how do you know when you've over-aggregated? Having several hundred aggregations or more is a good initial indication. Another indication, which is more common in practice, has to do with the inability to process your data in the allotted window of time. Remember, aggregations must be computed in memory and subsequently written to disk during processing, so you need to validate the impact on processing as well as query performance.

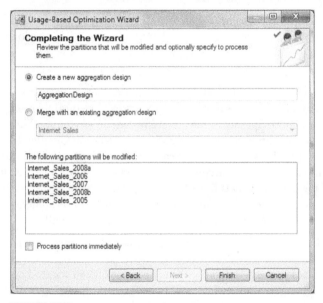

FIGURE 9-79

The UBO algorithm focuses exclusively on the cube space as described by the query log. The net effect of this is to produce more effective aggregations in less time. In internal product team testing, great improvements have been made for three key dimensions of performance: time to converge (which is the time it takes to design aggregations in the UI), time to process, and query performance.

The algorithm changes in Analysis Services 2012 have necessitated a few UI tweaks. First, all attributes now need to be counted, and the UI can accordingly enforce this. Second, 100 percent optimization is the recommend setting for optimization level, and the defaults in the UI have been modified accordingly. This setting ensures that all possible aggregations are considered and typically lead to a better end result. If time and/or space considerations dictate the need for fewer aggregations, you can always edit the aggregation design in the new aggregation editor and delete any aggregations you find to be less useful.

Designing aggregations using UBO is discussed in the context of designing high-performing cubes in Chapter 10.

REAL-TIME CUBES

What does real time mean to you or your business? Does it mean the ability to query the cube at any time? Does it mean you have the most up-to-date data in your cube? If you think of most up-to-date data, what does that mean to you? Perhaps it means something like the previous quarter's data or previous month's data, or perhaps it is weekly or daily data. There are cases in which even seconds count, as with the stock-related example. The question of how soon the data needs to be available in the multidimensional BISM is what you need to think about when you design a real-time cube. The daily transactional data in most retail companies arrives at the data warehouse nightly or on a weekly basis. Typically, these companies have a nightly job that loads the new data into their cube through an incremental process.

If your company is multinational, the concept of a nightly job (which is typically considered a batch process) is not nightly at all — due to the many time zones involved. Assume your company had offices in the United States and you were loading new data during the night. If your company expanded to include data-generating offices in Asia and those employees needed to access the cubes, you would need to make sure the multidimensional BISM was available for querying throughout the day and night while giving consistently correct data. Some companies can find the right sweet spot of time needed to upload the data while users do not access the cube and do the data load then. What if your transactional data arrives at regular intervals during the day and the end users of the cube need access to the data instantaneously? Then you must design a special way to meet the needs of your users. SSAS 2012 enables you to address these sorts of challenges. You simply need to choose the right method based on your requirements.

By now you are familiar with MOLAP, HOLAP, and ROLAP storage modes; they can be crossed with varying methods of data update for both fact and dimension data through the Storage setting. With the right storage setting chosen, you can count on getting the real-time data with MOLAP performance through the use of cache technology. By specifying the right storage mode option with appropriate latency that is acceptable to your end-users, you can achieve appropriate real-time data that your users need. This section provides you with some thoughts on which approach to take in a case and why, with three general scenarios to designing real-time cubes. They are a long latency scenario for those times when quick updates are not required; an average latency scenario for those periodic, non-time-critical updates; and finally, a short latency scenario for the most demanding of users.

Long Latency Scenario

Assume you own a small company that is selling a key set of products that is essentially static in nature; the base list of products just doesn't change. New products may be added to the list, but the original set of products remains the same. In this scenario, several of your products are sold each day, and the sales data arrives at your data warehouse sometime after normal business hours. Further, your company is headquartered in the United States. The business analysts on your team want to see sales data no later than the next working day following the actual sale. In this scenario, assume incremental processing of your cube takes a relatively small amount of time (just 1–2 hours), which can be completed before the start of the next business day. Also, assume that data updates (information about new products added into the system) in your relational databases arrive within a reasonable time.

The traditional approach to solving the outlined scenario would be to have the dimension storage as MOLAP and do an incremental update of dimensions after the relational data update is completed. This approach is computation-intensive and is a fairly costly operation. Following the dimension data update, an incremental process of the relevant measure groups is required, and when that completes, the consumers of the cube can browse the results. This approach has advantages. Indeed, this approach is good whenever your relational data updates occur regularly at a specific time interval and you have sufficient time to update the cubes. Several existing Analysis Services users in the retail space use this solution. Data typically arrives during the night, and the cubes are processed nightly for use the next business day.

As with the traditional approach, you can do an incremental process of dimensions and measure groups. Or for the sake of completeness and given the time, you could even do a full process of the entire cube. Again, these things typically take place during the night, so time is not often a constraint. You could use SQL Server 2012 Integration Services to create a package to do this job (see this example in Chapter 13). Alternatively, you can set the right storage setting options. Two basic methods (with multiple variations) within storage settings can be used to initiate data updates: the query-based method and the time-based method. The method you choose depends on your needs.

Caching After Data Change

One of the solutions for the long latency scenario is to set caching on your multidimensional BISM to kick in as soon as the data changes using the option Scheduled MOLAP. For the Scheduled MOLAP option, you need to specify a query to be run at scheduled time intervals to determine if there has been a change to the source data. Here is how it works: The first time Analysis Services sends the specified query to the relational data source, it collects and stores the response. That stored response provides a baseline against which subsequent query results can be compared. When a subsequent query returns a result set that does not match the baseline, it is presumed there has been a data update, and the caching starts the process of incremental update. Depending on the other caching settings such as latency, the cache will be updated. The latency setting tells Analysis Services how long to wait between cache updates. This is what provides that real-time appearance to the end user.

Figure 9-80 shows the caching option where you specify a polling query that detects the change in source data. This could be as simple as a count of rows in the relational table or as complex as a hash value of the entire result set. For the long latency scenario, you need to click the Enable Incremental Updates option so that dimension and partitions are processed incrementally only with the data that has been added. If this option is enabled, Analysis Services processes the dimension or partition object by sending a Process Add statement. If you do not specify this option, Analysis Services automatically sends a Process Update statement to the dimension or the cube partitions. Process updates on dimensions could be expensive based on the size of the dimensions and the partitions and aggregations built for the partitions. For trade-offs on which processing option (Process Update or Process Add) would be good for your cube, refer to Chapter 10. After specifying the polling query, you need to specify the processing query that can retrieve appropriate data from the relational data source for processing.

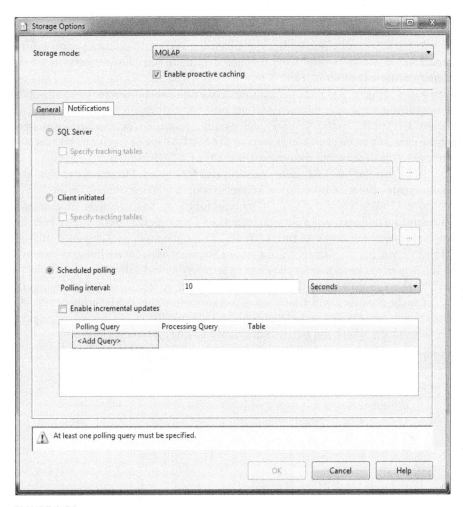

FIGURE 9-80

Here is a handy proactive caching technique that you can apply to dimensions, which can optimize your incremental processing query. First, specify the polling query. The results of the polling query can then be used as parameters to the incremental processing query. For example, if you have SELECT max(product_id) from Products; say initially it returns 100; then 50 products are added. When the polling query is subsequently run, you would get 150. Then use these two parameters, illustrated by question marks in the following code, to create the incremental processing query:

```
SELECT * from Products where product_id >COALESCE(?,0) And
product_id <=COALESCE(?,-1)
```

In this way, the processing query returns only those rows that were added since the last data change. This technique can be a timesaver if your Products table is the size of large retailers such as Wal-Mart's, Target's, or Amazon.com's.

Caching Using Timed Updates

The second method to proactive cache is to update the dimension and partition data periodically. Though this approach could hardly be considered sophisticated, there is no doubt it gets the job done and doesn't take much in the way of setup. Here is how it works: You set caching to update any new source data and itself (the cache) at a predetermined time. For example, if you want to set the update at 24 hours since last process, you set a proactive caching property that ensures the MOLAP cache is rebuilt every 24 hours. In the long latency scenario, you would typically not set the latency property because you want the new data to be available as soon as the MOLAP cache is rebuilt. You specify the option of when to rebuild the cache using the option Update the Cache Periodically, as shown in Figure 9-81. This option ensures that the MOLAP cache is rebuilt every 24 hours. However, you should be aware that the cache update occurs 24 hours after the previous update. For example, on the first day if the processing started at 12 midnight and it took 30 minutes for the cache to be updated, then on the second day the cache update will start at 12:30 a.m. instead of 12 midnight. It would have been nice to have the update cache happen at the same time each day. This option will probably be available in future releases. However, you can implement this functionality using SQL Server Integration Services (refer to Chapter 13). You might need to reset the caching property periodically to keep it aligned with your business needs so that the most up-to-date data is available for your end users. The configuration used for updating the cache periodically is also referred to as Scheduled MOLAP because the cache update is scheduled. If you click OK in the dialog, as shown in Figure 9-81, you will be in the partition's Partition Properties pane where you see the Scheduled MOLAP option.

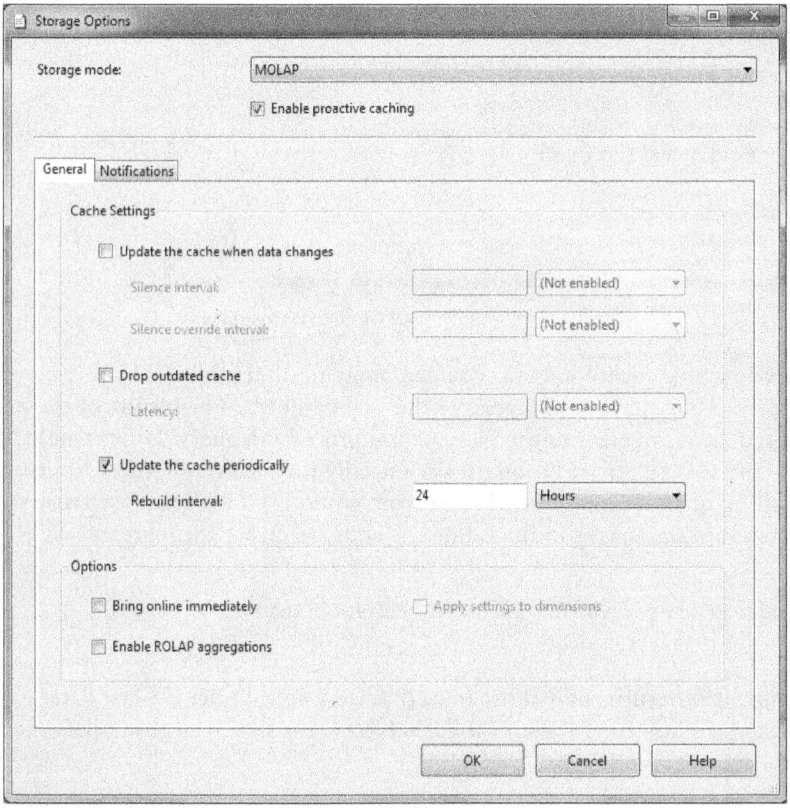

FIGURE 9-81

Average Latency Scenario

For the average latency scenario, assume you run a large retail business intelligence implementation with several hundred product-related data changes being added overnight, every night. These additions come in the form of stocking and pricing changes. Actual sales information arrives in your data warehouse periodically, and your users want to see the data under reasonable real-time conditions. For this case, assume updates are available every 2 hours or so and your cube typically takes about 1 hour to process. However, your users are willing to see old data for up to 4 hours. Assume the data partition is not large (say, less than 5GB) for this scenario.

Caching with MOLAP Storage Option

Assume you have built the cube, and its dimensions are updated nightly using incremental processing. Incremental processing is good whenever you want the current dimensions to be used by customers because incremental processing can take place in the background and not prevent customers from querying the data.

The case for which it makes sense to use caching with the MOLAP storage option is when you need to update the sales information (or other information) into the measure groups on a periodic basis so that users see near real-time data without any performance degradation. In this case, the data arrives in your data warehouse in the form of a bulk load from your relational transactional database. Further, assume that incremental processing of your cube is faster than the time required for a bulk load to your data warehouse. You can set up storage settings for the average latency scenario to be Medium-Latency MOLAP, as shown in Figure 9-82, so that as soon as a notification arrives, Analysis Services automatically starts building the new MOLAP cache. Because your users are willing to wait to get the new data for up to 4 hours, the caching property called latency is set to 4 hours. If the new MOLAP cache is not built within 4 hours of the last data change, Analysis Services switches to ROLAP mode to retrieve data from the relational data source. As soon as the build of the new MOLAP cache is complete, Analysis Services serves the users from the new MOLAP cache. Typically in this scenario you would want to specify the latency time interval to be much higher than the incremental processing time for the partitions. If the incremental processing takes much longer than the latency, you might experience occasional degradation in performance because the existing MOLAP cache in Analysis Services is outdated, and Analysis Services needs to fetch the results from the relational data source.

Latency simply refers to the amount of time you want the system to wait before unceremoniously dumping an existing MOLAP cache used to serve users. The SilenceInterval property indicates that no less than the specified period must elapse before initiating the rebuilding of a MOLAP cache upon data change. The SilenceOverrideInterval property is a little trickier to get your head around but by no means daunting. If SilenceInterval is reset due to frequent data changes, the MOLAP cache is never rebuilt fully and dumped often whenever data changes. There is some limit to your patience because users always see performance degradation from the time Analysis Services switches to fetching the data from the relational data source after the specified latency time. To overcome this issue, the SilenceOverrideInterval property ensures that it stops resetting the silence interval for future data changes until the existing MOLAP cache is rebuilt fully.

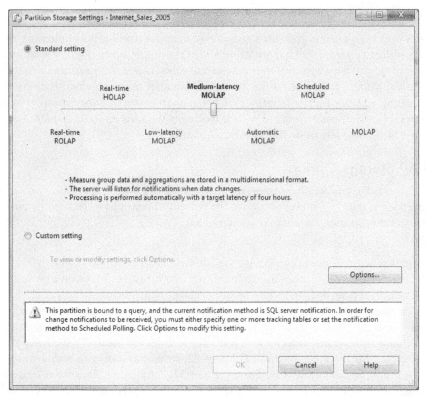

FIGURE 9-82

Normally you know how frequently updates occur to your relational data source. Based on that information you can specify the SilenceInterval. On certain occasions there might be frequent data changes that result in the Silence Interval timer being reset, and this can potentially lead to not rebuilding the MOLAP cache. That's when SilenceOverrideInterval comes in handy. Think of SilenceOverrideInterval as simply your way to say, I don't care if the update notifications keep coming, I want to do an update no longer than, say, every 60 seconds. So, even though SilenceInterval keeps on ticking away the seconds, SilenceOverrideInterval overrides it if SilenceInterval overstays its welcome — and that is just what happens in Figure 9-83. You can see how SilenceOverrideInterval (SO) times out and a rebuild of the MOLAP cache is kicked off. Typically, if the SilenceInterval is specified in the order of seconds, your SilenceInterval override would be specified in minutes so that your MOLAP cache is not outdated too long. Figure 9-83 shows a graphical timeline representation of events occurring due to proactive caching being enabled but is demonstrated using smaller time intervals for SilenceInterval and SilenceOverrideInterval rather than typical values. After the cache is rebuilt, Analysis Services handles the normal process of proactive caching using the SilenceInterval during future notifications.

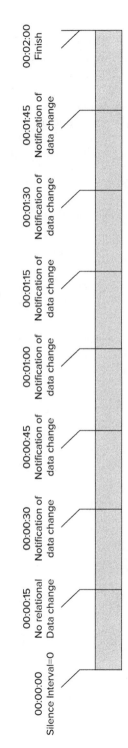
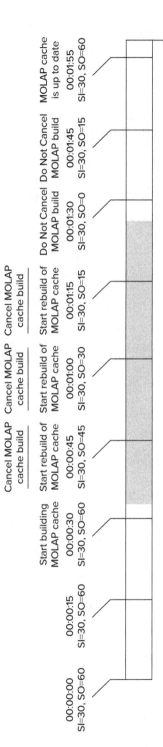

FIGURE 9-83

For the average latency scenario example explained here, you should customize the medium-latency MOLAP default settings so that you set the Silence interval, Silence Override Interval, and Latency as shown in Figure 9-84. Silence interval is set to 10 seconds so that the MOLAP cache rebuilding starts 10 seconds after the data update. The processing of the partition takes approximately 2 hours. If multiple data updates are within the first 2 hours, make sure the Silence override interval kicks in and stops frequent cache update attempts; by the time of the 4-hour time limit (Latency) you have a new MOLAP cache ready for users to query. There might be some times in which you have frequent data updates on the relational database, and your MOLAP rebuilding has not completed yet but latency has expired. During that time all requests will be served by retrieving results from the relational data source. You need to ensure this time period is as small as possible so that users perceive the data is real time and with good performance (due to MOLAP cache).

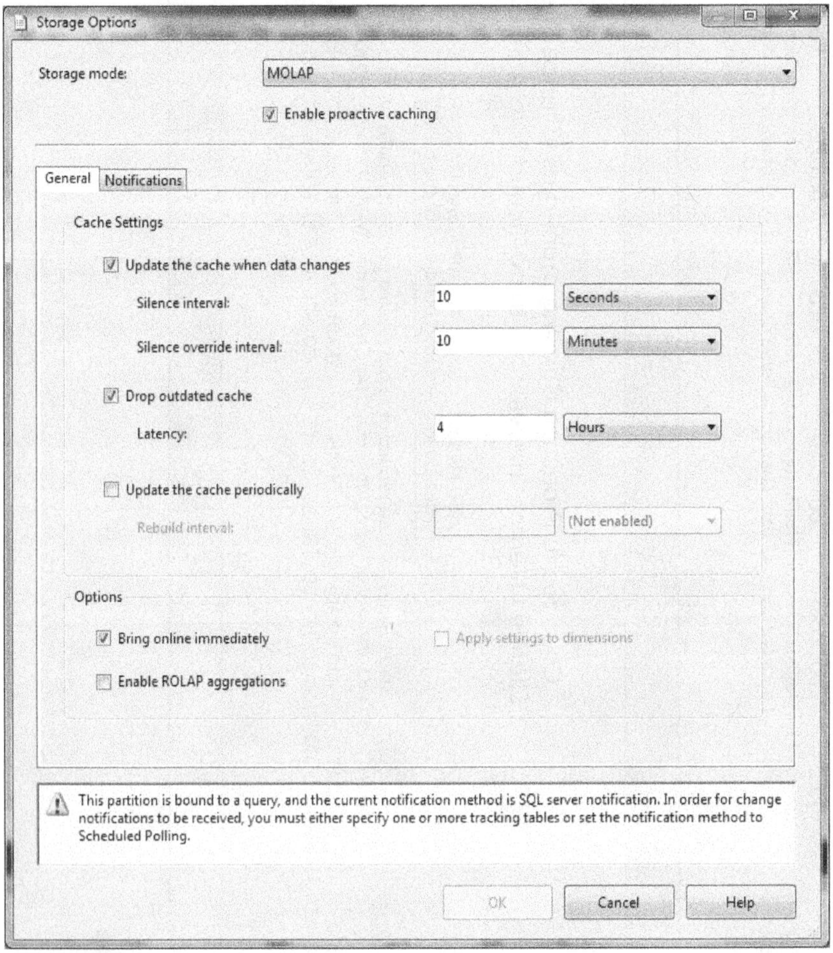

FIGURE 9-84

To recap, Analysis Services serves data to users with the help of a cache.

➤ If the data in the relational data warehouse changes, the cache needs to be updated (that is, rebuilt). It takes some amount of time to rebuild the cache.

➤ Latency is a proactive caching property that allows you to control serving your customers from an old MOLAP cache for a certain period of time, or to instantaneously serve the customers with the latest data.

➤ If your users are concerned about getting the most up-to-date data, you would set the property called Latency to zero. This informs Analysis Services that users are interested in the latest data, and the existing MOLAP cache needs to be cleared.

➤ Because the new MOLAP cache might take some time to be rebuilt, you want to keep the results coming to the users. During the time the MOLAP cache is rebuilt, Analysis Services fetches the data from the relational data warehouse to accomplish this.

➤ Even though you do get the most up-to-date data, you might see slight performance degradation because Analysis Services needs to retrieve the data from the relational data warehouse.

As soon as the MOLAP cache is rebuilt, Analysis Services starts serving the customers with the new MOLAP cache, and you start seeing your original query response times. If you want the users to continue using the existing cache while a new cache is generated based on new data, you can specify the time that it would take for rebuilding the MOLAP cache as latency. For example, if it takes 15 minutes to rebuild your MOLAP cache, you can specify the latency as 15 minutes. By specifying this, the current users would receive slightly old data for 15 minutes but at the MOLAP performance level. As soon as the MOLAP cache is rebuilt, Analysis Services starts serving all the customers using the new MOLAP cache, and they would instantaneously see the new data. The trade-off here is how current the data is versus query performance. This is a key configuration that you expect many users to use if they want to see near real-time data but with MOLAP performance. In this scenario, customers need to be willing to wait for a certain period of time for data to be propagated through the multidimensional BISM.

This solution for dimensions (changes to existing dimension members) is not recommended because occasionally you might end up in a state in which you would need to query the data from the relational data source. This is feasible, but when the dimension storage mode switches from MOLAP to ROLAP, it is considered a structural change by Analysis Services, which means that the partitions must be rebuilt. This can potentially have a significant performance impact, and clients might need to reconnect to query the multidimensional BISM. However, if your business needs demand this and your users always establish a new connection to send queries, you can still use the settings for dimensions.

No Latency Scenario

In this short latency scenario, you are in charge of an e-commerce site that provides customers' links to the most up-to-date products on the web, which when sold, provide you with a commission. Your Internet affiliates add additional products to your catalog electronically, and at this point you are at 2.3 million product SKUs and the number is rising. Meanwhile, your partition data changes frequently, and you have large numbers of members in the product dimensions. What does a BI application developer do?

Real-Time ROLAP Storage Option

The recommended solution here would be to set up the measure group and dimension data (which are frequently changing) to use ROLAP storage mode so that data is automatically retrieved from the relational data store as needed by the user. Working in this way does not come without a price. Indeed, although it is definitely a useful storage mode, the query performance of ROLAP mode is much slower than that of the MOLAP mode. In general, use a MOLAP solution for large dimensions, but if your dimension members constantly change and these changes need to be reflected immediately to end users, ROLAP would be a better option. This is because the data is retrieved directly from your relational data source, which often requires over-the-net communication. Yes; you could go with HOLAP, but performance depends largely on your aggregated data and how frequently it is impacted due to changes in the data.

Just setting the storage mode to ROLAP is not sufficient. Analysis Services caches data, and if there is a change in your relational data warehouse, this might need to be immediately reflected in your users' queries. If you definitely need real time, as in zero latency updates, you need to specify Real-Time ROLAP, which amounts to setting up proactive caching on ROLAP partitions or dimensions. Under this configuration, on a change in the source data, Analysis Services immediately drops the cache and gets the data from the relational data warehouse. Figure 9-85 shows the selection for Real-Time ROLAP on the Storage Settings dialog. If you click the Options button, you can see the proactive caching properties set up so that latency is 0 and you bring the new data online immediately, as shown in Figure 9-86.

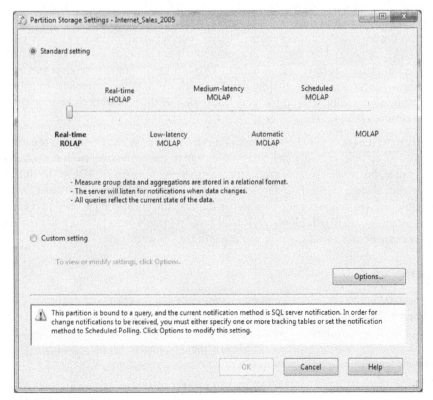

FIGURE 9-85

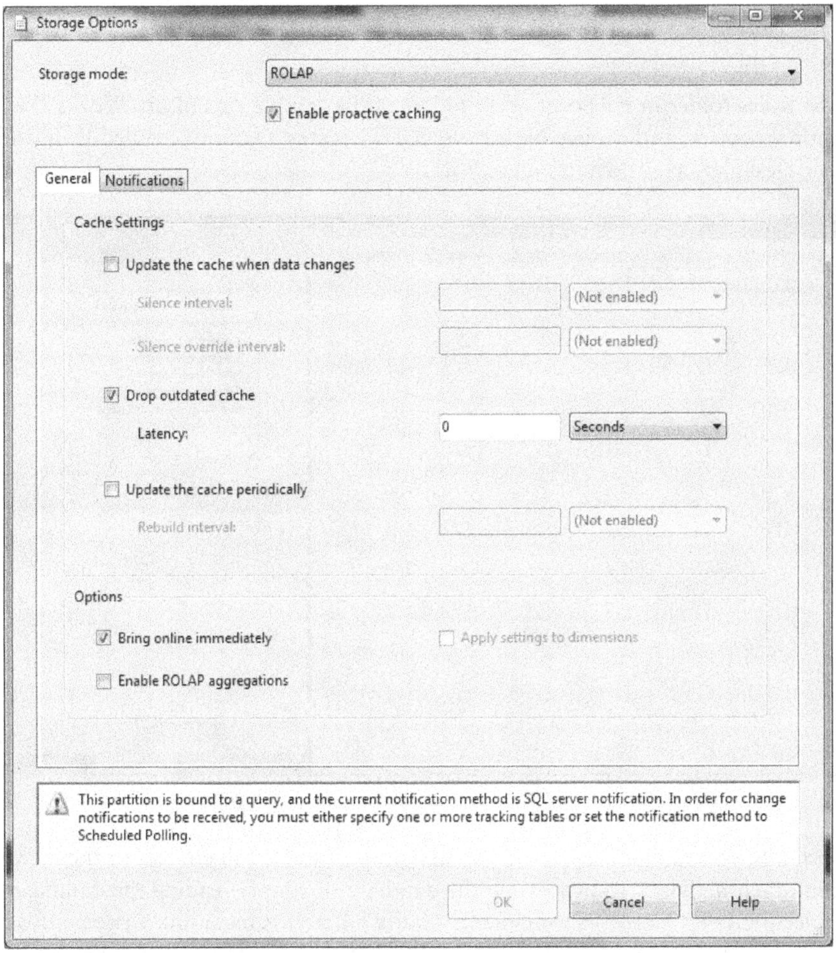

FIGURE 9-86

DEFINING SECURITY

Now that you know how to create and enhance a cube to meet your business needs, you also need to know how to provide the right level of access to end users. Many people consider security to be a management task that should be assigned to the administrators. However, your solution might require Analysis Services to perform fine-grain security checks, which can adversely impact calculations. Hence, the cube developer should be actively involved in defining and testing security to verify that users see the right data and experience good query performance.

Analysis Services provides you with fine-grain security settings to control access to meta data and data. You can also grant permissions to certain users who need the ability to process a database, but who do not need full control of the database. You can choose to secure data at the cube level, the dimension level, or the cell level. Because security is an important topic for you to understand, especially for dimension and cell security, Chapter 14 provides a complete example of a security definition. In this section, you learn the basic steps involved in granting write access permissions to a cube and its dimensions. The following steps can help you better understand how access permissions can be applied to your cubes and dimensions:

1. Right-click the Roles folder in the Solution Explorer of the sample Adventure Works DW Multidimensional project, and choose New Role. SSDT creates a new role called Role and opens the Role Designer, as shown in Figure 9-87.

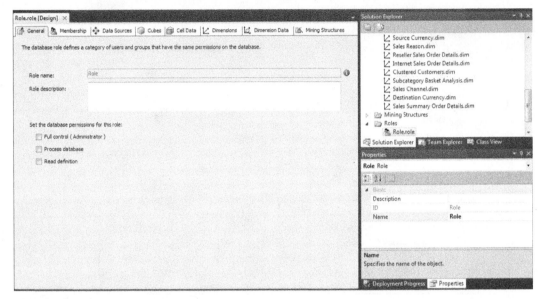

FIGURE 9-87

2. On the General tab, you can give members you assign to this role full control of the database, or you can limit their activities to processing the database or simply reading the database definitions. Selecting Full Control automatically grants full access including write permissions to change the objects within the current database. The Process Database option grants access to the users so that they can read the meta data about database objects and process the objects. Users who have Process Database control cannot make changes to dimensions and cubes or even data within these. Read Definition enables the users to read meta data of the objects within the database; however, it does not give you access to the data. Select the option that is best-suited for your users, and provide some description for the current role in the Role description box.

3. Click the Membership tab. On the Membership tab, you can add the list of users for whom you want the specific access you have selected. Analysis Services accepts all domain users or machine users in this dialog. Analysis Services verifies that the user entered is a valid user and then stores the ID of the user within the database. Add a local machine user or a domain user in your company to the membership list, and then click the Data Sources tab.

4. Figure 9-88 shows the Data Sources tab, which you use to restrict users from accessing the cube's data sources. By default, access to data sources is set to None. Typically, access to

data sources might be needed in data mining scenarios in which you might query the relational source data for prediction. Enabling the Read Definition option allows the users to retrieve information such as database name, tables, views, and so on of the data source.

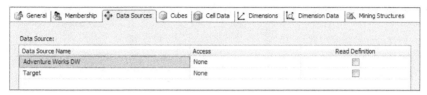

FIGURE 9-88

5. The Cubes tab is shown in Figure 9-89. Here you have the option to grant access to specific cubes. By default, users have no access to any cube in a database to ensure that developers or administrators do not accidentally provide cube access to users who are not supposed to have access. You have the option to provide read access only or read/write access to each cube in the database. You can also see there is the option of Local Cube/Drillthrough Access. These options enable you to specifically grant users the ability to create local cubes or drill through to more detailed data. In addition, you can limit access to Drillthrough only or to Drillthrough and Local Cube. Local cubes are typically created from Excel so that small versions of cubes can be shared with other users. Local cubes are also called offline cubes. The Process option enables you to grant users the ability to process selected cubes. Select Read/Write access to the Adventure Works cube, and then click the Dimensions tab.

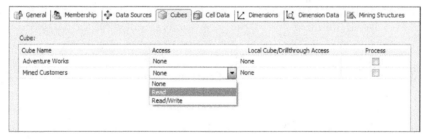

FIGURE 9-89

6. On the Dimensions tab, you have the option to control which database dimensions or cube dimensions a user can access if they've already been granted access to the cube. Figure 9-90 shows how you can define security for the database dimensions or the cube dimensions of the Adventure Works cube. If you select the All database dimensions option, you see all the dimensions listed with three columns in which you specify the type of access, Read Definition access, and Process capabilities. The Process column is used to provide process permission to specific dimensions. By default, Read access is applied to all the dimensions, but you can change the access type to Read/Write for any dimension. If you allow the Read/Write option, the users have the ability to alter the dimension structure or data. The Read Definition access allows users to query for certain properties of the dimension such as count of hierarchies, members, and levels in the dimension.

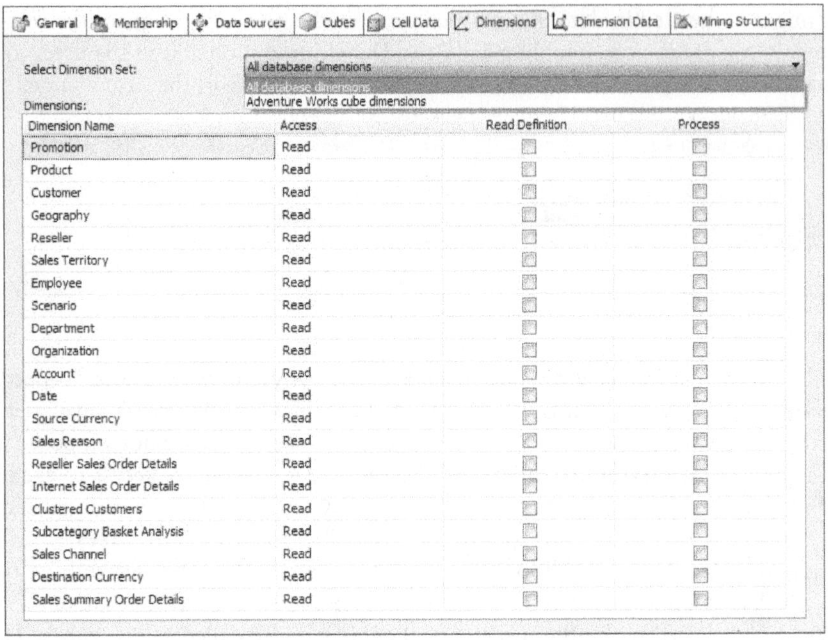

FIGURE 9-90

If you select the cube dimensions option from the Select Dimension Set drop-down, you see two columns called Inherit and Access for each of the dimensions, as shown in Figure 9-91. By default, the Inherit column is selected, meaning that all the permissions specified for the database dimension are inherited by the cube dimension. You do have the option to override the database dimension access permissions. For example, you might provide Read access to all the database dimensions, Inherit for all the cube dimensions, and then Read/Write permissions on a specific dimension so that you allow certain users to write back data to the dimension or alter dimension structure. To override the database dimension permission access, you need to deselect the Inherit option and then select the Read/Write option from the Access column.

As you can see, the role of designer lets you easily specify the right access permissions to the dimensions and cubes within an Analysis Services database. If you have provided access only to the Adventure Works cube, but not to the Mined Customers cube, then when you connect to Analysis Services through SQL Server Management Studio as one of the users listed in the role's membership, you do not see the Mined Customers cube. On the other hand, if you assign a user to two roles, with one role granting access to the Adventure Works cube and the other role granting access to the Mined Customers cube, the user can see both cubes because role permissions are additive. In SSDT, you can test the effect of security, including membership in multiple roles, by browsing the cube under a specific role or a user. If you try to browse a cube for which the current user or role has not been granted permissions, you get an error message that says you do not have access to the cube.

In this section, you have learned how to define access permissions (read or write permissions) for cubes and dimensions. This ensures correct access restriction to a specific cube or a dimension as a whole to certain users querying the database. Some business scenarios call for restricted access to just a part of the dimension or cube. For example, if you are a sales manager in a chain of retail stores, you might be given access to only view sales information specific to your store. Defining the right security for dimension and cell data is best learned through a scenario; you can find more about restricting data access to users in Chapter 14. As for mining models, the Mining Structures tab enables you to define security for mining models, which is not covered in this book.

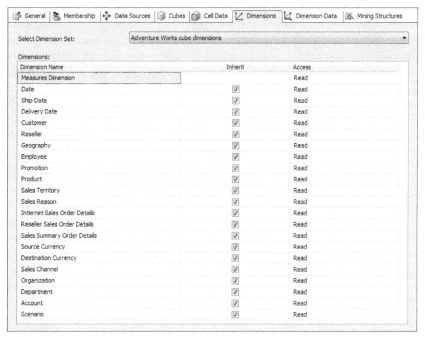

FIGURE 9-91

CELL WRITEBACK

The ability to create "hypothetical" what-if scenarios is central to business intelligence because it enables the executive to explore contingencies associated with the financial landscape. In this way, the executive can seek out the profit maximizing potential of the firm while minimizing risk and generally mitigating threats. Because these concepts are so much better explained by way of example, following are two specific examples to help you understand what is meant by what-if scenarios.

In the first example, a company president considers her options for resource allocation for the coming fiscal year. Her BI team has astutely developed a multidimensional BISM that calculates key business drivers for the company. Because the user can write back new values into those seed measures, new configurations of company resource allocation can be tried and the results assessed. The key business metrics will be recalculated due to new values entered into the system. The sorts of questions that can be "asked" of the system through the use of these simulations depend on how many measures are designed to act as seed values. Typical questions include, "What if we increase our advertising budget for the next fiscal year?," "What if we charge more (or less) for our product?," and "What if we take on more debt to expand production facilities and therefore enhance manufacturing capacity?" Not just any question can be asked of the system. Only those questions that have the required measures available for use as seed values and underlying calculations or KPIs in support of cascading correct changes can provide meaningful results.

The second example considers the needs of a bank. The vice president is considering strategies for the coming year for appropriate risk distribution for commercial loan application acceptance. The bank has good metrics from which to base calculations on successful loan repayments versus defaults, and those metrics have been entered into the relevant cubes. If banks are anything like most bureaucratic organizations, they likely have regulations that mandate certain minimum distributions of loans to different risk categories. For example, in the interest of economic development and creating new active bank customers in the future, a certain percentage of high-risk loans should be accepted. The vice president is most likely looking to give loans to maximize income from loans for the bank. With a fund of $500 million from which to make loans, the president can consider the manipulation of multiple seed values such as interest rates and risk acceptance percentages. In the end, some optimal state will emerge, such as allocating $100 million to low-risk businesses, $250 million for moderate-risk businesses, and $150 million to high-risk businesses.

In financial applications (corporate plan, budget, and forecast systems), most of the time the multidimensional BISM is applied as a data-gathering and analysis business model to gather data input from all departments, and perform many what-if analyses for future business decisions. When the analysts make a final decision, the data values need to be updated in the cube for appropriate actions to be taken. For example, the budget for a department might get allocated based on the current year's revenue, and that department would need to plan the next fiscal year's financial plans based on the allocated budget. If the executives have made a forecast to achieve specific revenue for the next year, other business decisions need to be propagated to the people in the corporate food chain appropriately. For example, if the sales target for the organization were to have 500 million dollars (10% growth over the current year), the business goals or commitments for the individual sales employees need to be appropriately set to reach the organization goal.

In this section you learned how to effectively use Analysis Services to provide what-if scenarios to top executives and to update the cube data so that it can be appropriately propagated to the entire organization. Updating the data in an Analysis Services cube is referred to as cell writeback because you update the cell values in the cube space.

You are aware that a cube contains one or more measure groups. When a cube is write-enabled, it means that one or more measure groups in the cube are enabled for writeback of data. Each measure group contains one or more partitions. The data from the relational data source is read and stored within partitions by Analysis Services. To writeback cell data within the cube, you need to have a new partition called the writeback partition for each measure group you want to enable for writeback of data. Any data (measure values) that is updated in the cube space will be entered into this writeback partition. Similar to a regular partition, the writeback partition points to a table in a relational data source. However, unlike regular partitions, Analysis Services populates the rows of this table based on writeback operations performed on the cube. This data can reside within the same relational data source used by the cube or in a different relational database.

Cell Writeback Prerequisites

When data is written back to the cells of a cube, Analysis Services stores appropriate information in a relational database table. Therefore, you do need to define a connection to a relational data source. This data source can be the one where you load data into the cube, or it can be a different relational data source as well. In addition you have the option to specify if the Writeback partitions needs to be MOLAP or ROLAP, as shown in Figure 9-92.

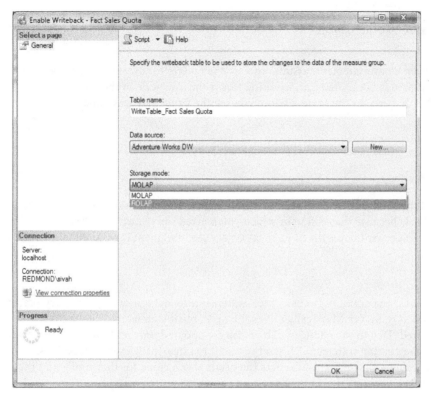

FIGURE 9-92

At the time of processing the cube or measure group, Analysis Services first checks if a writeback partition has been specified. If a writeback partition is specified, it then goes to the relational data source to identify if the writeback partition exists. If not, Analysis Services creates a table to hold the writeback data.

Writeback Statement

To perform data writeback, Analysis Services provides the UPDATE CUBE statement to help with updating the cell values in a cube. The syntax of the update statement is as follows:

```
UPDATE CUBE <CubeName>
SET <Tuple Expression> = Numeric or String value
[ALLOCATION TYPE clause]
```

The UPDATE CUBE syntax is straightforward: You specify the coordinates in the cube to update the new values. The ALLOCATION TYPE clause is an optional clause by which you can specify the nature of the allocation. You have the option to write back to a single cell or multiple cells depending on where you write the data. An example of a writeback command is shown here:

```
UPDATE CUBE [Adventure Works DW Multidimensional]
SET ( [Employee].[Manager].&[291],
[Date].[Calendar].[Calendar Quarter].&[2008]&[3] ,
[Measures].[Sales Amount Quota]
) = 1000
```

In the preceding UPDATE CUBE statement, assume you set the budget for an employee to be 1000. Also assume this employee is not a manager, meaning this is the leaf node in the dimension. If you send the following MDX query in the same session, you see the value that was allocated: 1000.

```
SELECT {
[Employee].[Employees].&[291] } ON 1 ,
[Date].[Calendar].[Calendar Quarter].&[2008]&[3] ON 0
FROM
[Adventure Works]
```

However, if you send the same MDX statement on a new connection or session, you do not see the writeback results. This is because the session in which you started the UPDATE CUBE statement has not been committed. To persist the results of your UPDATE CUBE statement in your cube, you need to send a COMMIT command:

```
COMMIT
```

COMMIT is a short form for the COMMIT TRANSACTION statement. By default, when you start executing new queries within SQL Server Management Studio, an implicit statement called BEGIN TRANSACTION is executed. Due to the changes, cell values get updated only after you call the COMMIT TRANSACTION or just the COMMIT statement. When the COMMIT statement is executed, Analysis Services gets the new value to be written, subtracts the original cell value for that tuple, and then writes back the difference in the partition that has been set up for writeback.

One interesting thing to note is you can still do what-if analysis on a cube, even if the cube is not enabled for writeback. The changed measure cannot be committed back to the server if the cube doesn't have a writeback partition. However, you can still do a BEGIN TRANSACTION, update cell values, and send MDX queries to view the results of the measure (cell value) change, and then simply ROLLBACK TRANSACTION when you're finished.

When you send an UPDATE CUBE statement to perform cell writeback and the cell update is committed to a writeback partition in MOLAP mode, Analysis Services performs the following steps:

1. Begin SQL transaction
2. Update SQL
3. Incremental the process from cache
4. Commit lock
   a. Commit SQL transaction
   b. Commit incremental process
5. End commit lock

Update Nonleaf Cell Value Using Allocation

The previous section demonstrated how to update budget data for an employee who is a leaf member in the dimension and does not have any reports under him. A leaf-level cell in Analysis Services means all dimension members of that cell are on the granularity level. If you have another dimension, you must include a member from that dimension for the granularity attribute. However, in many cases, a user might want to input a number at a higher-level granularity and allocate down to the leaf-level members via different rules. For instance, a user can input an entire year's budget and allocate to each quarter by last year's sales. In this section, you allocate the budget for a manager with multiple level of reports and the options by which you can specify how the assigned budget needs to be cascaded down to all the employees in an organization.

Analysis Services provides three ways to allocate/update values for nonleaf-level cells. Because the actual data allocated cannot be held directly in a nonleaf cell within Analysis Services, the data needs to be propagated to the leaf-level cells. The most obvious and easiest way to allocate in this way is to allocate the value equally to all the leaf-level cells.

Equal Allocation

Consider the scenario in which an employee is allocated $1,000, and this needs to be propagated to the employee and all their direct reports because the employee also needs to be included as part of the budget allocation. As shown with the update statement syntax, you have an optional allocation clause. To allocate this value equally to her direct reports, you need to specify the keyword USE_EQUAL_ALLOCATION. The following UPDATE CUBE statement updates the budget value for the employee by equally allocating the value to her direct reports:

```
UPDATE CUBE [Adventure Works DW Multidimensional]
SET (
[Employee].[Manager].&[290]
,
[Date].[Calendar].[Calendar Quarter].&[2008]&[3] ,
[Measures].[Sales Amount Quota]
) = 1000
USE_EQUAL_ALLOCATION
```

If you did not specify the allocation clause to be USE_EQUAL_ALLOCATION, Analysis Services assumes that the data allocated needs to be equally distributed to all the children. Therefore, the following UPDATE CUBE statement also results in the same results, as shown in the previous table:

```
UPDATE CUBE [Adventure Works]
SET (
[Employee].[Employees].&[290]
,
[Date].[Calendar].[Calendar Quarter].&[2008]&[3]
,
[Measures].[Sales Amount Quota]
) = 1000
```

You can now query the values for all employees whose Unique name is [Employee].[Manager].&[290], and you can see that the value is equally allocated among the employee and all the reports in the employee's organization.

Weighted Allocation

In a little more complex scenario, allocation of budgets depends on the size of the organization or the revenue generated by the person (or group) in the previous year. A common form of allocation in the real world is to allocate values based on rates calculated by using the last period's budget rate plus some percentage increase to determine this period's value, or to just use last year's sales to allocate this year's budget. Analysis Services provides a way to write back data to leaf levels using various proportions; therefore, such an allocation is called a *weighted allocation*.

Consider a case in which an employee gets a $1,000 budget and wants to allocate it to her direct reports and herself based on the ratio calculated from the previous quarter. Now, how do you go about forming an UPDATE CUBE statement that can accomplish this? First, break it down and build the MDX.

You know that the UPDATE CUBE statement to allocate for the employee is

```
UPDATE CUBE [Adventure Works]
SET (
[Employee].[Employees].&[290],
[Date].[Calendar].[Calendar Quarter].&[2008]&[3],
[Measures].[Sales Amount Quota]
) = 1000
```

Next, you need to add the allocation clause. For weighted or ratio allocation you need to use the keyword USE_WEIGHTED_ALLOCATION BY, which gets added at the end of the preceding statement. Following the USE_WEIGHTED_ALLOCATION BY you need to specify a ratio or weight that derives the rate based on the previous quarter. The following MDX expression calculates the ratio of budget for the previous quarter for all the employees reporting to the employee with Unique Name [Employee].[Employees].&[290].

```
([Date].[Calendar].[Calendar Quarter].&[2008]&[2], [Employee].[Employees]
.currentmember)/
([Employee].[Employees].&[290],[Date].[Calendar].[Calendar Quarter].&[2008]&[2])
```

The first part of the MDX expression takes the current member in the context of the query, which is one of the direct reports of the employee and her budget value in the second quarter of 2008. The second part of the MDX query provides the budget value for the employee for the second quarter of 2008. Because the value for the employee is the aggregated value of all her reports, you get a ratio of each employee's budget as compared to the overall budget allocated to the employee in the second quarter of 2008.

Combining all the sections of the MDX you have seen, you have the following MDX query to allocate the budget to the employee's team based on a ratio of the previous quarter:

```
UPDATE CUBE [Adventure Works]
SET (
[Employee].[Employees].&[290]
,
[Date].[Calendar].[Calendar Quarter].&[2008]&[3]
,
[Measures].[Sales Amount Quota]
) = 1000
```

```
USE_EQUAL_ALLOCATION
([Date].[Calendar].[Calendar Quarter].&[2008]&[2], [Employee].[Employees]
.currentmember)/
([Employee].[Employees].&[290],[Date].[Calendar].[Calendar Quarter].&[2008]&[2])
```

Incremental Allocation

The third scenario is where a cell has an existing value and you want to update that value and have the incremental change allocated down. This allocation of the incremental change can be done based on either equal or weighted allocation. Consider an organization that receives funding from multiple sources and these funds need to be allocated to subdivisions one by one. Further, you do not want to overwrite the previous data. Before you learn about incremental allocation, delete the writeback table in the relational data source, and reprocess the database.

Assume a manager obtained funding in the amount of $1,000 in support of the project he is working on. Now assume his manager allocates this budget directly to the employee for quarter 3 of 2008. Send the following update statement to allocate the budget to the employee.

```
UPDATE CUBE [Adventure Works]
SET (
[Employee].[Employees].&[291]
, [Date].[Calendar].[Calendar Quarter].&[2008]&[3]
, [Measures].[Sales Amount Quota]
) = 1000
```

Now assume his manager gets funding in the amount of $2,000 for the entire group and wants to allocate this equally to all her direct reports. She obviously does not want to overwrite the existing budget value allocated for the employee. Analysis Services provides a way to allocate this new budget amount to the leaf-level cells either through equal or through weighted allocation. The allocation clause keyword that needs to be used is USE_EQUAL_INCREMENT or USE_WEIGHTED_INCREMENT along with the weight, as shown in the weighted allocation example.

```
UPDATE CUBE [Adventure Works]
SET (
[Employee].[Employees].&[290]
, [Date].[Calendar].[Calendar Quarter].&[2008]&[3]
, [Measures].[Sales Amount Quota]
) = 2000 use_equal_increment
```

Try the various writeback examples previously shown with a simple cube to understand the concepts, and then solve your organization's needs appropriately.

Cautions

You should be aware of some things while updating cell values using the update statement. Assume you have a reasonably sized cube with several dimensions that each contain several attributes. Due to multidimensionality, every cell is referred to by a coordinate for every attribute hierarchy in every dimension. If you do an allocation using the update statement that includes only a few dimensions' granularity attributes, Analysis Services tries to equally distribute the value allocated to a cell in the cube to all the leaf-level cells (across all the hierarchies in each dimension). Therefore, if you do an update on a cell referred to by the topmost-level on certain dimensions, the update to leaf levels can be quite expensive because Analysis Services needs to equally distribute the value across all members of all dimensions. This can happen easily because the default member for hierarchies not included in an update statement is usually a top-level member such as an All member. Such an update of several non-leaf members can result in a huge number of rows being entered into the writeback table. Whenever possible, make sure you do the writeback to the appropriate level intended. This is a warning about data expansion.

To understand the data expansion problem better, consider the following example of updating Amy Alberts' budget for the year 2003, which is referred to by the tuple (`[WB Employee]`.`[Manager]`.`&[290]`, `[Date]`.`[Calendar]`.`[Calendar Quarter]`.`&[2008]`&`[3]`). This updates all the leaf-level members, which is the product of all the members reporting to Amy Alberts and all the quarters in 2003. This update results in changes to 16 cells at the leaf level. Imagine dimensions that have hundreds or even thousands of members. As with a Product dimension, a simple mistake of updating at the topmost level can cascade out with millions of leaf-level cells being updated — and you see millions of rows in the writeback table. To mitigate this problem you need to identify meaningful leaf-level cells and then write back to just those specific cells.

AMO WARNINGS

Analysis Services Management Object (AMO) Warnings is the name given to a set of best practices built into the Analysis Services object model and exposed by the design tools. There's a lot of history behind this feature. When working on the 2005 release of SQL Server Analysis Services, the notion of real-time designer validations of errors was introduced. These validations were surfaced via red squiggly lines under the offending object. The validations proved to be a benefit to cube designers because they allowed for a tight temporal correlation between an action and the result of that action. Practically speaking, it's much easier to correct errors as they happen, while the action that triggered the error is still fresh in your mind, rather than doing it infrequently (such as on build or deploy) and then needing to remember what you were thinking when you made the change that caused the error and to parse through potentially many such errors.

All of this formed the backdrop of the AMO Warnings feature. After the release of SSAS 2005, it became clear that the product was complex, with an open-ended and sometimes overly optimistic set of tools, and dispersed best practices (blogs, forums, whitepapers, and so on) that were not immediately obvious to the average user. To this end, work was done to pull together the most important best design practices (you learn the best practices in Chapter 10) and place this information in the product via warnings, which unlike errors would not prevent deployment and could therefore be dismissed and/or ignored. The goal was to provide a path of success through the product that was built in (and thus minimize the need to search blogs, forums, whitepapers, and so on), obvious, efficient (real/design time rather than after deployment), and unobtrusive (no pop-ups or anything else that might result in blockage of workflow).

The mechanism to expose the warnings is via blue squiggly lines that, like their red counterparts, surface tooltips on hover. On build, any warnings display in the error list. More than 50 such warnings are in the product. Over time, expect this list to grow and change in response to customer and community feedback.

Design Experience

If you open the AnalysisServicesMultidimensionalTutorial project provided online for Chapter 9 and open the Dim Date dimension, you see two warnings, as shown in Figure 9-94. Like errors, most of the OLAP designers now check (on every change, otherwise periodically) with AMO to validate the structure of the object in question. The existing VALIDATE method was simply extended to enable receiving warning information as well.

As mentioned, hovering over a given warning surfaces the textual description (see Figure 9-93). In addition, each AMO Warning has a dedicated help topic that can be queried when more information is needed about the warning in question.

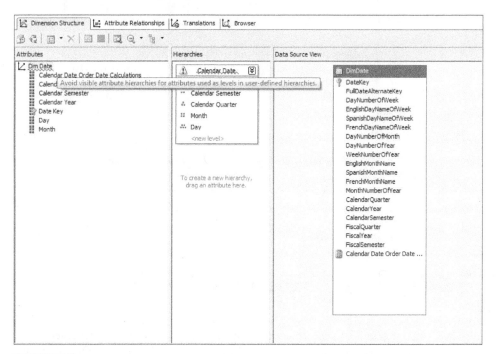

FIGURE 9-93

Dismissing Warnings

Figure 9-94 shows the integration with the Error List window as well as the Dismiss Warning dialog. The Error List window shows the list of AMO Warnings when you build your Analysis Services project. You can right-click a specific warning and click Dismiss to remove warning from future project builds. Each warning can be individually dismissed via the Dismiss Warning dialog, which is invoked from the Error List. In addition, a comment can be specified, which is especially useful if you work in a team environment. You are dismissing only a single instance of a single warning via this dialog. For example, there is a warning about not setting the Unknown Member property of a dimension to None. This warning is then shown for every dimension that violates the best practice. Using the Dismiss Warning dialog, you can handle each dimension on a case-by-case basis.

To dismiss a given warning globally (in other words, turn it off), you need to deselect the warning in the database editor (more on this in the next section).

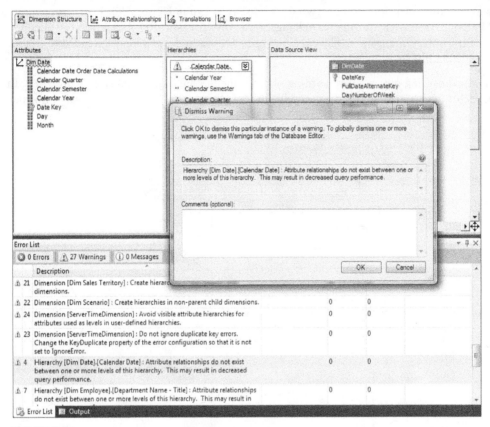

FIGURE 9-94

Where do dismissed warnings go? This information is not lost. Dismissed warnings, whether individual or global, are recorded as database annotations and displayed in the database editor. One of the main benefits of this approach is that the information is not user-specific and can be viewed by anyone who opens the project. As you learn in a moment, dismissed warnings can also be re-enabled.

Warnings Designer

Figure 9-95 shows the Warnings tab in Analysis Services 2012. You can access this editor by right-clicking the Analysis Services project name and selecting Edit Database. The designer consists of two grids: The top grid contains the available warning rules. The lower grid contains any individually dismissed warnings.

FIGURE 9-95

Warning rules are grouped by area:

- ➤ Cube Design
- ➤ Data Source Design
- ➤ Database Design
- ➤ Dimension Design
- ➤ Partition and Aggregation Design

Warning rules also have a notion of importance, with three such levels: High, Medium, and Low. Warnings rules can be turned off using the top grid. As with the Dismiss Warning dialog, a comment may optionally be specified for the benefit of teammates or even if only to jog your memory down the line.

Individually dismissed warnings are displayed in the lower grid. There is also a button to re-enable warnings should you find that you've changed your mind. Generally speaking, it's strongly recommended to heed the high importance warnings. Medium importance warnings vary (in reality there's a spectrum here), but those should be carefully considered as well. The low importance warnings are obviously less important and less of an issue to dismiss.

SUMMARY

Okay Neo, crawl up out of the rabbit hole; you have reached the conclusion of this chapter. And what a profound trip that was! This chapter has hopefully provided you with amazing new tools for your BI repertoire. Consider yourself admitted to the knowledgeable inner-circle of BI professionals because you know that you can add measure groups from any accessible cube to your own cube without the use of SQL Server. This one change encapsulates a lot of power, and you are going to have fun discovering that power. Similarly, with remote partitions there is that compelling scalability factor that kicks in; it's great! The Cube Wizard has two templates to choose from. After the cube has been created, you would need to populate the tables with appropriate data before processing the cube. You can explore this option from the Cube Wizard by selecting the build method Build a Cube Without a Data Source.

You've also learned about partition and aggregation design, including the enhancements made to the new UBO algorithm and dedicated aggregation designer. These aggregation tools in Analysis Services 2012 enable better initial aggregation designs, better usage-driven aggregations than in prior versions, and the ability to gain insight and even modify individual aggregations. You learned about various techniques and options to design the right real-time cube for your organization using the storage settings. In addition you learned about cell writeback and how this can help with what-if analysis in your cube or actually performing writeback to the cube. AMO Warnings in Analysis Services 2012 help with best practices in designing your multidimensional BISM. With the inclusion of these best practices, even novice cube builders can build optimized, well-performing databases!

Much of this chapter was dedicated to cube enhancements, which fall directly to the bottom line of providing business information; using actions and KPIs both can enhance any digital dashboard you might create. When you start building custom front ends for consumption of your business intelligence applications, such as the now ubiquitous dashboards, which reflect current business operations, there are cases in which you must write your own application for filtering based on real-time data. In the next chapter you see more detailed best practices in designing your cube with performance as a key criteria.

10

Designing Mulitdimensional BISM for Performance

WHAT'S IN THIS CHAPTER?

➤ Fine-tuning your dimensions

➤ Fine-tuning your cube

➤ Optimizing processing performance

➤ Designing aggregations

➤ Managing aggregations

➤ Scalability optimizations

As any good English dictionary can tell you, *performance* has several possible meanings. In computer science, performance most often refers to the functioning efficiency of software and can relate to both speed and scalability. Established standards and benchmarks measure and compare the performance of products and services. Why care about performance? Well, consider your job performance; assuming you are an employee, your job review, salary raise, and bonus hinge on how well you do your job. To get the best work out of you, your manager needs to know what your interests are, what motivates you, and then assign appropriate tasks. Your manager rewards you for your performance — usually in the currency you like most, cash.

It follows that if you are a data warehouse designer using Analysis Services, you need to know how to get the best performance from the system to satisfy the customers. Just like your boss can push certain buttons to motivate you, Analysis Services provides various parameters that you can set to achieve maximum performance. For server products such as Analysis Services, you can attribute performance results to how well server properties are tuned in the context of speed and scalability requirements.

Various factors influence the performance of an application. SQL Server's performance depends not only on the system (processors, memory, and disk speed) but also on the operating system's configuration and the properties of the application that can be fine-tuned. Figure 10-1 shows a typical server scalability graph. The query throughput lines show the server throughput (queries served per minute) as more users use the system concurrently for two different hardware configurations. For Hardware 1, up to approximately 50 users, the server throughput increases linearly. That means the server has sufficient resources to support 50 concurrent users. Then after approximately 50 users, the throughput starts to flatten out. In the 50-to-100 user range, the server doesn't have enough resources (CPU, memory, or disk) to serve requests of all concurrent users. In this circumstance, some user requests would be queued in the system request queue to keep the system from slowing down all the user requests. At approximately 100 users, the system runs at maximum capacity. The curve flattens off at high loads because internally the server executes only a few queries concurrently and queues the rest. This is so that with many outstanding queries, new users can still get reasonable response times while connecting to the server and executing nonquery commands.

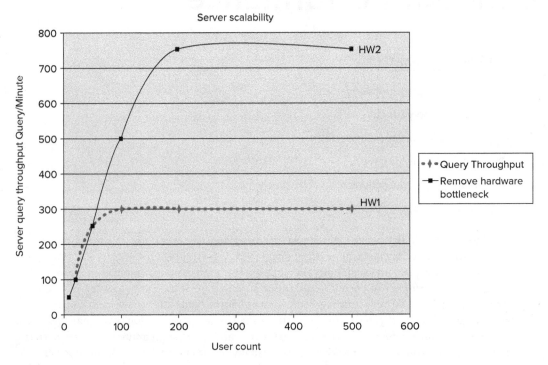

FIGURE 10-1

From the perspective of a user, when a server is under an extreme load with many outstanding queries, some of the execution time is spent waiting in the queue, and some time is spent actually working on the query. You might compare it to waiting in line for food in a crowded baseball stadium. When the load is high, the wait time can easily exceed the time to actually do the task. Hardware 2 has better resources (CPUs, memory, network) compared to Hardware 1. Therefore, if you run the server on Hardware 2, you obviously get a better throughput because the saturation to maximum users occurs at approximately 200 users.

If you have a well-architected server, Figure 10-2 shows the average query response under load. The average response time starts to increase, and eventually the average response time increases linearly. If your system needs to support only 10 to 50 members, you don't need to do anything. But if your system needs to support 100+ users, you need to identify the system bottlenecks. Typically, servers expose performance monitoring counters to expose internal values. You can use the task manager and performance counters to identify bottlenecks; whether the system is CPU-bound (the Server CPU is pegged at 100%), memory-bound (memory usage is constantly maxed out), or disk-bound (reads/writes to disk). By removing the system hardware bottleneck and adding more CPU or memory to the server, you should get performance improvements and support more concurrent users, as shown in Figure 10-2 for Hardware 2.

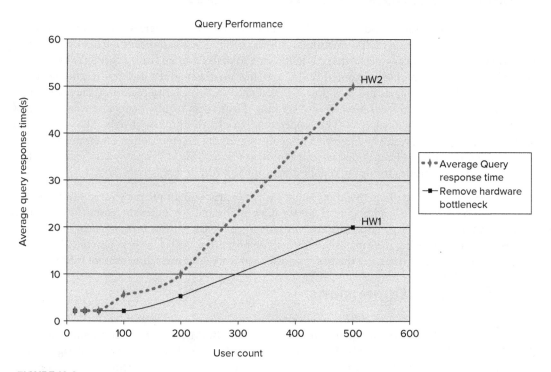

FIGURE 10-2

Assume HW1 is obtained by adding more CPU and/or memory to HW2. Although you expect to see the general shape of the curves described in the figures, the limits will be different for your hardware, your cube design, the queries your users execute, and the frequency with which queries are executed. For Analysis Services, in a typical query scenario, CPU, memory, and disk read speed can all be potential bottlenecks for your system. In a cube or dimension processing scenario, CPU, memory, disk writing speed, network speed and SQL query performance between the relational source and Analysis Services can all be candidate areas for system optimization work.

Analysis Services performance has three main areas: database design and processing, querying, and configuring Analysis Services (setting properties). The first involves design optimization to facilitate the optimized processing of dimensions and cubes. The second relates to optimization to speed up MDX queries or Analysis Services configuration properties of features, which you learn about in Chapter 11. The third involves fine-tuning Analysis Services or appropriate hardware acquisition based on requirements. Does performance imply both scalability and optimization of Analysis Services? Depending on whom you ask, one or both are true. The bottom line is that you need best query performance for your OLAP cubes. That is true regardless of size, and however you can get it that doesn't involve the violation of federal or state laws is fine. In the next section you learn some of the design techniques that can help to improve your Analysis Services performance.

OPTIMIZING MULTIDIMENSIONAL BISM DESIGN

You learned to create the multidimensional BISM and refine it in Chapters 4 through 9. The data modeling completed during multidimensional BISM creation has a significant impact on both query performance and processing performance, so it is not something to be rushed through. Even before starting to build your multidimensional BISM, you must understand the business requirements of the system under assembly as much as possible. You need to have clarity regarding the goal of the system, and that, in turn, feeds directly into creating the analysis requirements and what potential queries the system needs to support. That understanding can also provide insight into what dimension attributes the user won't be interested in analyzing. Based on your design requirements, certain attributes do not need to be included in your multidimensional BISM design or can be fine-tuned with dimension properties for optimal multidimensional BISM design.

Every dimension, and attribute in a dimension, demands processing time for your multidimensional BISM. In addition, because adding unnecessary dimensions and attributes increases the cube space, it can also slow the query performance. In this section you learn various techniques to optimize your dimension and cube using the dimension or attribute properties as well as best practices for designing your cube so that you can get the best performance from your multidimensional BISM.

Fine-Tuning Your Dimensions

In Analysis Services 2005 and 2008, dimensions can contain several hierarchies. Including unnecessary attributes and hierarchies in your multidimensional BISM can cause performance impact. Therefore, the Dimension and Cube Wizards in Analysis Services 2012 guide you to design your dimensions and cubes with performance in mind, and you must be more specific about which dimension attributes you want to include in the multidimensional model. The design tools also enable you to visualize the relationships between the attributes that you need and thus help you build a better dimensional model.

In this section you learn various techniques that guide you regarding how to design the right dimension suited to your business needs and get the optimal performance acceptable for your business.

Choosing the Right Key Attribute

Each dimension needs to have a *key attribute*. The key attribute helps to identify each dimension member uniquely and in most cases is used as the granularity attribute when the dimension is added to be part of a cube. The relational dimensional tables typically have a column defined as the primary key which is automatically inferred as the key attribute by the Dimension Wizard. In certain relational databases, the relationships between the fact and dimension tables using the primary and foreign keys might not be defined, and therefore the DSV Wizard cannot automatically infer the relationship and show this in the DSV. In such cases you need to define the relationships between the tables in your DSV. Choosing the key attribute can actually impact processing and query performance. If you know that you have two columns in the dimension table that each uniquely identifies a row in the table and if they are of different data types, such as integer and string, try to choose the column that is an integer. Key attributes of integer data types occupy less storage and are faster to retrieve than those of type string because the number of bytes used to store string types is typically larger than that for integer data types. In addition, if you have a choice to choose a single column as a key attribute as compared to choosing multiple columns in the table, choose the single column as the key column. If you are already aware of these techniques and have designed your database accordingly, it's great. Some might think that all they need is just more disks — disk space is quite cheap to buy, and disks are much faster than before — and some might think a few bytes might not make a big difference. However, imagine your dimension has millions of members — no matter how much disk space you have, accessing each member during queries takes time.

The fastest processing time of fact-table partitions occurs when the fact table has integer foreign keys for the dimension, and the dimension contains the integer key as an attribute (perhaps hidden). This enables the SQL query sent by Analysis Services during processing to be efficient in query performance. Several international major customers with large data warehouses use composite keys with long strings. Each of these companies had a data warehouse before they started using Analysis Services and consider a change prohibitively expensive. Their design works, and their business benefits from using Analysis Services. But their time window for processing fact-table partitions would be much smaller if they had used integer keys.

To summarize, always consider integer attributes to be chosen as key attributes and having single columns as the key attribute instead of composite keys.

Avoiding Unnecessary Attributes

Because Analysis Services supports attribute hierarchies, you can create many attributes that enable users to analyze their data along those attributes. However, if you create too many attributes that are never used in customer queries, it wastes system data storage slowing both processing and query performance. Look at each dimension in detail and eliminate attributes that users never query. Although your dimension tables might contain several columns, it is usually not necessary to convert every column in the dimension tables to attribute hierarchies in the dimension. You can see an example in the Adventure Works DW project's Customer dimension. Figure 10-3 shows the Customer dimension, where you can see the list of columns in the DSV and compare it against the list of attribute hierarchies included within the dimension.

You can see that the Customer relational table contains several columns. However, the Customer dimension includes only a subset of those columns that are essential for data analysis as attribute hierarchies. For example, the column Title in the Customer table is not used in data analysis and is not included as an attribute in the Customer dimension.

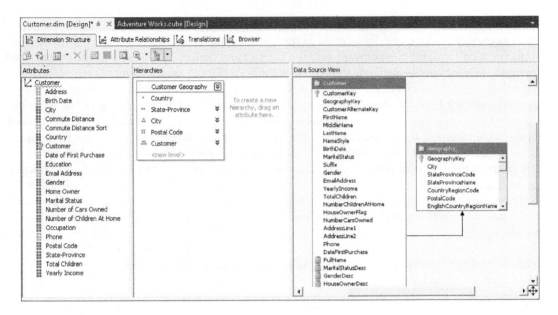

FIGURE 10-3

Turning Off Optimization for Rarely Used Attributes

Although some attributes in a dimension are used for data analysis, they might be needed only on rare occasions. For example, you might query an employee's ZIP code or phone number infrequently for analysis. By default, Analysis Services creates indexes for each attribute, assuming the attribute hierarchy will be used often in queries. By turning off attributes' optimization via their

AttributeHierarchyOptimizedState, you can save processing time and resources by not creating indexes for such attributes. A query involving any NotOptimized attribute will be slower; however, because it is rarely used, it won't hurt most of your users' query performance.

Most often you will have certain attributes that are used as member properties. We recommend you set the AttributeHierarchyOptimizedState for member property attributes as well as attributes that might be used infrequently during querying to be NotOptimized for those attributes that are not involved in queries. The improvement for data storage and processing time would justify this choice. The AttributeHierarchyOptimizedState is a property for each attribute. If you click an attribute you see this property under the Advanced section in the Properties window. Figure 10-4 shows the

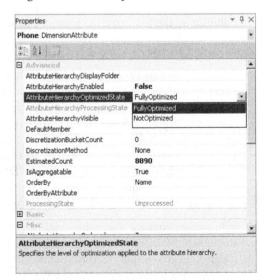

FIGURE 10-4

AttributeHierarchyOptimizedState property. To turn off the property for an attribute in the dimension, change the value from FullyOptimized to NotOptimized.

Turning Off AttributeHierarchy for Member Properties

Some attributes are not relevant to data analysis, which means user queries never pivot on those attributes. Still, it is useful to display and use those attributes as member properties. Consider the birth date attribute; although customer queries may never break down fact data by birth date, the customer birth date might display next to customer names in reports, perhaps as a sorting criteria for listing customers. You can turn off the AttributeHierarchyEnabled property for birth date to tell Analysis Services not to build an attribute hierarchy for this attribute, but keep it as a member property. This reduces the time and space needed for dimension processing.

It also has the benefit to reduce the cube space that the server must work with. Internally, the server maintains cell coordinates that include all the browsable attributes in the cube. The size of these cell coordinates impacts the performance of calculations as well as the memory usage during query execution. By disabling attribute hierarchies, the size and complexity of cell coordinates is reduced, which has a positive impact on query performance.

Figure 10-5 shows the AttributeHierarchyEnabled property for a dimension attribute. If this property is set to False for an attribute, you cannot browse the hierarchy. Rather, you can query the attribute members as member properties.

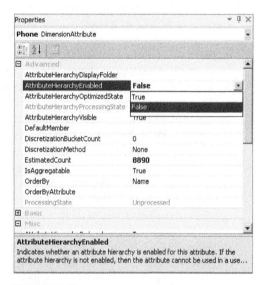

FIGURE 10-5

Defining Relationships between Attributes

If attributes within a dimension are related by a one-to-many relationship, establish that relationship in the Dimension Designer. For example, in a geography dimension you typically have Country, State, and City attributes and know that there is a one-to-many relationship between these attributes. Define these relationships in the Dimension Designer for improved processing and query performance. If you create user hierarchies within a dimension, and if the user hierarchies have multiple levels and there is a natural relationship between these attributes, define these relationships. Often when user hierarchies are created, they are used in queries, and defining the natural relationships helps significantly in query performance. The attribute relationship helps the server build efficient indexes, which benefit query performance along the user hierarchies significantly. To understand this issue, you first need to learn about natural and unnatural hierarchies.

All attributes within a dimension are related to the key attribute because the key attribute is unique, and by definition a key has a one-to-many relationship with all the attributes. As for the natural hierarchy, consider the multilevel hierarchy Full Name ⇨ Postal Code ⇨ City ⇨ State-Province ⇨ Country, as shown in Figure 10-6. A hierarchy is called a natural hierarchy if there is a one-to-many relationship between every pair of attributes from successive levels of a user hierarchy. Figure 10-6 shows the relationship between attributes of various levels established in the Dimension Designer;

the Customer attribute (called FullName in the multilevel hierarchy) has a relationship with Postal Code, Postal Code has an attribute relationship with City, City has an attribute relationship with State-Province, and State-Province has an attribute relationship with Country. Essentially, a chain of relationships from the bottom-level attribute to the top-level attribute is created. Such a hierarchy is called a natural hierarchy.

In a natural hierarchy, the attribute at a given level maintains a many-to-one relationship with an attribute directly above it. The many-to-one relationship is defined by the attribute relationship, as shown in Figure 10-6, and the server builds indexes for fast navigations. A natural hierarchy for which indexes are created during processing time is referred to as a materialized hierarchy. For the customer hierarchy example shown in Figure 10-6, indexes for State-Province to Country, City to State-Province, and so on are built and stored in the server. Analysis Services uses those indexes to accelerate query performance; it can easily find all states in the USA because the query can be directly resolved from the State-Province to Country index. Also, if the data cache or aggregated data stored in Analysis Services has data for State-Province, Analysis Services can use the same index to quickly get an aggregate value for Country.

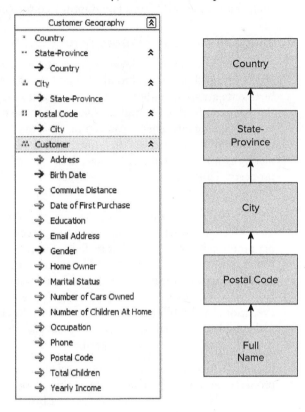

FIGURE 10-6

Defined relationships not only help during query performance, but also during processing. Analysis Services processes the key attribute of the dimension after processing all the remaining attributes. If no relationships are defined, then at the time of processing the server needs to retrieve the keys for all the attributes while processing the key attribute. This increases the processing time of the key attribute and the dimensions. If you have defined the natural relationships between attributes, the cost of looking up the keys of the related attributes is distributed across the attributes in the dimension. This reduces the cost of key attribute processing, which otherwise has to look up the keys for fewer attributes, thereby reducing the overall dimension processing time. You can see significant differences in processing times for large dimensions that have hundreds of attributes. For some large dimensions (>10 million members and >100 attributes) you might reach the physical processing limits of a 32-bit environment and might need to move to 64-bit servers. Establishing relationships (as discussed) combined with other dimension optimizations (also discussed) can facilitate processing for large dimensions on a 32-bit platform.

For an unnatural hierarchy, only the key attribute has an attribute relationship to all other attributes, so the relationship resembles Figure 10-7. The system builds indexes only along attribute relationships and builds one-to-many indexes for Country to Customer, State-Province to Customer, City to Customer, and Zip Code to Customer. When you create a user hierarchy such as Customer ZipCode ⇨ City ⇨ StateProvince ⇨ Country, no additional indexes are created.

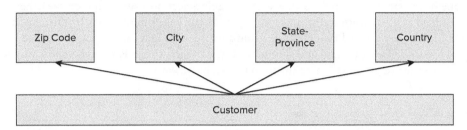

FIGURE 10-7

Unnatural hierarchies need to be materialized (identifying navigation paths for members from one level to the next level and data corresponding to members in a level need to be aggregated from the members at the lowest level) during query time and result in slow query performance. For example, to resolve a simple [USA]. Children MDX expression that requests for all the states of the country USA, the server must use the Country ⇨ Customer relationship to find all customers in the USA and then use the Customer ⇨ State Province relationship to find all states for those customers in the USA. If there are millions of customers in the USA, the query traverses the millions of records, thereby resulting in slow performance. In addition, if the server has cached values or precalculated aggregations for State-Province, the cache cannot be used to resolve a country query because no direct relationships exist between Country and State-Province.

You should specify one-to-many relationships whenever possible. Not only can it help significantly for query performance, but it also can save storage space. For the Country to Customer index in the unnatural hierarchy example, every customer member in the USA can have an entry in the index. However, by moving the relationship to State-Province to Country, you need only 50 entries for that index. In Analysis Services 2012, you can use the Attribute Relationship tab in the dimension editor to visualize and manage the attribute relationships. To establish the attribute relationship, as shown in Figure 10-8, drag a relationship from each attribute to the related attribute. For example, click State-Province, and drag it to the Country attribute.

Fine-Tuning Your Cube

You have seen some of the design techniques for your multidimensional BISM that can help you achieve improved dimension processing and query performance. Similarly, certain design optimizations within the cube can also help you to achieve better performance during processing or querying. This section discusses cube optimization design techniques.

Fact Table ⇨ Measure Groups or Partitions

When you run the Cube Wizard on a DSV containing multiple fact tables, the wizard creates a separate measure group for each fact table identified. However, such a multidimensional BISM may or may not be the right design for your business analysis. For example, if you have two fact tables, salesfact2011 and salesfact2012, which have the sales information of your business for the years 2011 and 2012 (containing identical columns), the Cube Wizard creates two measure groups. However, for your purposes these should actually be modeled within the same measure group as two partitions so that appropriate data can be rolled up. If you create the cube using the Cube Wizard, select one of the fact tables on the Cube Wizard Table Selection page, and then the other fact table can be added as a partition to the measure group. If you select both tables by mistake and the Cube Wizard has already created two measure groups for the two fact tables, you can delete one of them from the Cube Designer and add that table as a partition in the Partitions tab. A way to think about this is a measure group contains the union of all partitions.

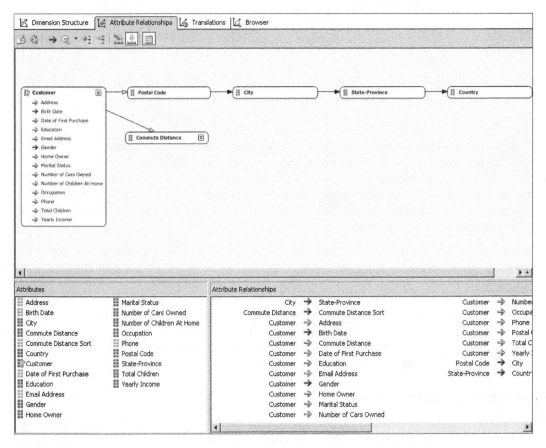

FIGURE 10-8

You can have fact data spread across multiple tables. For business reasons it might make sense to have all the fact data within the same measure group. Consider a measure group as an entity within your multidimensional BISM that represents a set of measures grouped logically for business reasons; or in Analysis Services terms, share the same dimensionality and granularity. Therefore, even if you have fact data spread across multiple tables and for business reasons, you actually need to combine the data; make sure you have the fact data (measures) added within a single measure group. You can join the fact tables containing measures into a single view within the DSV and create a measure group from that, or you can add measures from either of the fact tables within a single measure group using the Cube Designer.

Optimizing Reference Dimensions

If your multidimensional BISM contains reference dimensions, you need to be aware of making optimizations for the reference dimensions. If you query a reference dimension that is not optimized, you might not get the best query performance. Figure 10-9 shows the relationship definition for a reference dimension. You have a small check box called Materialize. You learned in Chapter 8 about reference dimensions and materializing them. To recap, materializing the reference dimensions ensures that the reference dimension keys are materialized into the partition fact records. After you materialize the reference dimensions, Analysis Services views those reference dimensions as regular dimensions. This helps to improve the query performance. An unmaterialized reference dimension requires dynamic lookups at query time to join between the partition records and the reference dimension through the intermediate dimension.

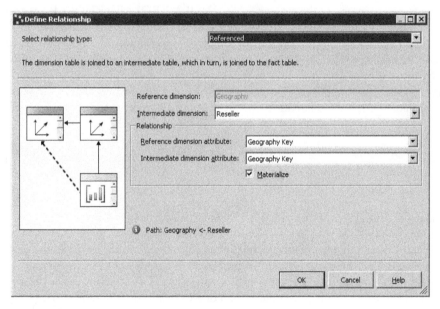

FIGURE 10-9

Also, materializing a reference dimension is the only way to create a chain of two or more dimensions as reference dimensions that include intermediate reference dimensions.

Many-to-Many Dimensions

One of the modeling features available in Analysis Services 2012 is called many-to-many dimensions. The Sales Reason dimension is used as a many-to-many dimension in the Adventure Works sample multidimensional BISM. It expresses the notion that a single sale in the Internet Sales measure group may be caused by multiple Sales Reason members. When analyzing what the reasons are for a sale, you want each sale to be counted for each applicable reason. This means that a single record is added more than once to the result. In SQL terminology, think of this as somewhat similar to a join between two fact tables based on the common dimension tables.

This feature is powerful for the modeling capabilities it provides to the designer of a multidimensional BISM. However, you must use it with care due to the performance implications. Queries that involve a many-to-many dimension are apt to be much slower than regular queries. There is a significant price to be paid to query two measure groups and dynamically perform a join between them based on the shared dimensions. A general guideline to follow is to avoid many-to-many dimensions in which the intermediate measure group contains more than one million records.

Some techniques exist for optimizing for many-to-many dimensions. For example, building good aggregations on the appropriate measure groups can help performance. A white paper published by Microsoft called "Analysis Services Many-to-Many Dimensions: Query Performance Optimization Techniques" describes this in more detail, as well as some advanced optimization techniques that may be adopted to help improve performance when many-to-many dimensions are necessary.

Partitions

Partitions store cube fact data in one of the storage modes: MOLAP, ROLAP, or HOLAP. By dividing the data in fact tables into multiple partitions, you can take advantage of parallelism, which can reduce the processing time for the cube and get improved query performance. Assume you have fact data for various months since the year 2008, which is part of a specific measure group. The following table shows a partition scheme that uses time to partition the fact data. Partitions 1–3 include data for past years, and they do not change. Partition 4 includes data for past months in the year 2011, which also does not change. Only Partition 5, which contains current month data, changes daily.

PARTITION 1	PARTITION 2	PARTITION 3	PARTITION 4	PARTITION 5
2008	2009	2010	2011	CurrentMonth

Assume the fact data is in a single fact table called Yearly Sales, and you have a measure group within your multidimensional BISM that has been created from this fact table. By default, the Cube Wizard creates a single partition that points to the relational table Yearly Sales. By dividing the data into multiple partitions, all the partitions can be processed in parallel, which use the processor and memory resources of your machine more efficiently. Analysis Services 2012 processes objects in parallel by default. If the server machine has more than one CPU and sufficient memory, parallel processing reduces total process time as compared to a machine with a single CPU. Analysis Services analyzes each request and splits them into many smaller units when possible that can be processed in parallel to accomplish the tasks. It then schedules them to be executed on multiple threads. Therefore, if you have multiple processors or cores on your machine, you get the benefit of parallelism.

During query time, if cubes contain several partitions, Analysis Services can scan those partitions in parallel, and queries can return results quickly because the server has multiple jobs running in parallel, each one scanning a partition. In addition to that, when you divide the data into multiple partitions based on a specific dimension member, Analysis Services 2012, by default, retrieves data only from relevant partitions needed for the query if the cube is of storage type MOLAP. For example, if a query requests data for 2008, Analysis Services queries only the data from the partition containing 2008 data.

To create multiple partitions, you can create multiple tables in the relational database and then create the partitions. Alternatively, you can create named queries within your DSV that correspond to your wanted partition strategy. Or you can simply define the SQL query for the partition when you create it.

The second benefit of creating partitions in an environment in which most of the data does not change is that you need to process only the current partition, which has new data added or modified. You need to process only the CurrentMonth partition in the partition scheme to refresh the latest data changes within your multidimensional BISM. The data volume to process is reduced, load on the relational source and the network is reduced, and the process time significantly decreases compared to processing the entire multidimensional BISM. This also helps reduce the load on the relational source.

The third benefit of partitioning data is that you can set up different storage modes for each partition. In business scenarios in which a certain amount of data does not change and the data volume is huge, it is better to use MOLAP to increase query performance. In addition, if you need real-time access to your data for analysis, you can create a small partition with the current month's data and set the storage mode for that partition as ROLAP. Analysis Services retrieves the data from the appropriate partitions and provides you with the aggregated real-time data for your business analysis.

Another benefit to partition data is that you can create different aggregations (precalculated data cache for improved query performance) for maximum benefit. Creating aggregations for your multidimensional BISM is covered in detail later in this chapter. You can design heavy aggregations for those partitions that are queried most (the current year data) to maximize query performance and create fewer aggregations for old data that is queried less to save the server storage. Creating such aggregations not only saves storage space, but also reduces processing times if the entire multidimensional BISM is processed.

Finally, refreshing the data within a partition is much faster than refreshing the entire multidimensional BISM. You do not need to apply incremental processing on all the partitions. You just must do incremental processing on the partition whose data needs to be updated. During incremental processing of the current partition, a temporary partition is created and then merged into the existing partition, which could possibly result in data fragmentation. By fully reprocessing the partition, the server re-sorts the data for optimized query performance.

Merging Partitions

If you have multiple partitions where data is used sparsely, merge the partitions so that data from each partition does not get aggregated every time a query is issued. Assume you have your measure group data partitioned by month for the year 2008. If every user's query is asking for the entire year's data, Analysis Services needs to retrieve the data from all the partitions and aggregate data within the server. Having too many partitions could hurt query performance because the server needs to scan those partitions and aggregate data from them. Instead you can merge the data from all the partitions to form a single partition. Queries referring to 2008 henceforth touch a single partition. If you have aggregations created at the year level, your queries can be instantaneous.

A common scenario for many Analysis Services users is to partition by time and have a weekly or monthly schedule to update the cube. This typically involves merging the most recent partition into the year-to-date partition and creating a new partition for the next period. Sometimes SSIS (SQL Server Integration Services, which you learn about in Chapter 13) is used to control the flow of operations. This is another scenario in which data from existing partitions needs to be merged.

Consider the example reviewed in the "Partitions" section, where data was partitioned by time. If you want to merge the partitions to a single partition because queries are infrequent, you can do so using SQL Server Management Studio (SSMS) by following these steps:

1. Deploy the sample Adventure Works DW enterprise project sample available from www.codeplex.com. The Adventure Works cube contains several measure groups. Connect to the Adventure Works DW database using SSMS.

2. Navigate through the cube and notice the four partitions under the Internet Sales measure group, as shown in Figure 10-10.

FIGURE 10-10

3. Right-click the Internet_Sales_2007 partition, and select Merge Partitions. Assume you want to merge the 2008 data into this partition.

4. In the Merge Partition dialog, select Internet_Sales_2008, as shown in Figure 10-11, and click OK. You are done! You have now successfully merged 2008 partition data into the 2007 partition.

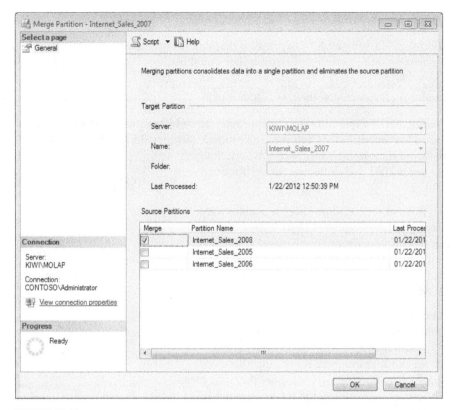

FIGURE 10-11

5. In the SSMS object browser, refresh the measure group object. The partition of Internet_Sales_2008 is gone because it was just merged to the Internet_Sales_2007 partition. You can see this in Figure 10-12. You can still query the data for 2008 and 2007 as before. The cube still contains the same data, and all queries still return the same result. It is important to remember that the Where clause for the Internet_Sales_2007 is not updated during the merge of the partition, which could result in "missing" data if the Where clause is not properly updated.

Your multidimensional BISM should have several partitions for each of your measure groups, especially the ones that contain a large volume of fact data. Investigate the queries sent to your multidimensional BISM to identify the requirements of your business users. One mechanism to identify the queries sent to Analysis Services is SQL Server Profiler. You learn about profiling Analysis Services using SQL Server Profiler in Chapter 11. Most measure groups partitioned are data that map to time. This is the most logical and common scenario for most businesses. If after analyzing the queries, you see that your user queries are targeted to specific partitions, and the remaining partitions are infrequently queried or queries to those partitions retrieve data at a higher grain, merge such partitions.

Partition Slices

The partition slice is a simple MDX expression that defines what parts of the cube are present in a particular partition. For example, a partition slice could be

```
{ [Date].[Calendar Year].&[2005], [Date].[Calendar Year].&[2006] }*
{ [Product].[Product Categories].[Category].&[1] }
```

In the preceding MDX expression the member referred to by the unique name `[Product].[Product Categories].[Category].&[1]` refers to the product category Bikes. Therefore the entire MDX expression would indicate that this partition contains only data for the years 2005 and 2006 and for the Product Category Bikes.

What is the value of the partition slice? It enables the server to detect which partitions can be simply ignored for a query. If a query is querying the months January, February, and March in the year 2007, a partition with a slice defined on the years 2005 and 2006 doesn't even need to be scanned.

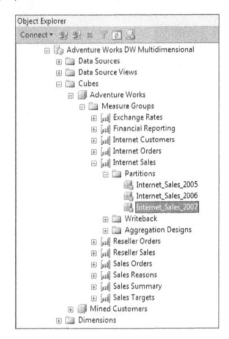

For MOLAP partitions, the server can automatically infer single-member attribute slices. For example, a partition with data for only the year 2005 would automatically have a slice for the Year attribute for the member 2005. However, if the partition has data for more than one member as in the preceding example, the server does not infer this slice and should be set explicitly on the partition using the Slice property. The Slice property does not restrict the data returned by partition query. For MOLAP partitions, the server will validate this property and if there are additional rows for different years included at the time of processing then the server will fail the processing operation.

FIGURE 10-12

Partition Slices and ROLAP

The partition slice can be even more important when there are ROLAP partitions in the multidimensional BISM. The server cannot even infer single-member slices on attributes for those partitions and is required to send a SQL query for every ROLAP partition unless the DBA can help by specifying good partition slices.

Assume a large-scale multidimensional BISM containing several partitions where all the partitions are ROLAP. In such a scenario, when a query comes in requesting data, Analysis Services sends relational queries to each partition with appropriate conditions to retrieve the data. Analysis Services then aggregates the data retrieved from the different partitions and sends the results to the end user. However, generating the queries for each partition, establishing a connection to the data source, and then retrieving results is an operation that takes a certain amount of time. If the Slice property is not specified, by default, Analysis Services assumes data can be contained in that partition for any MDX query.

A Partition Slice Example

Assume you have partitioned the data by time, five partitions for five years. Typically, most of the queries involve only the current year. In this case there is no need to send five queries, of which four will return no data. By setting the slice property indicating that the 2005 partition contains data for year 2005, the 2006 partition contains data for year 2006, and so on, you provide a hint to Analysis Services so that it can optimize the relational queries sent. The Slice property for a partition can be set in SSDT or SSMS. For example, if you need to set a specific partition's data for year 2007, you can provide the MDX expression for 2007 as [Date].[Calendar].[Calendar Year].&[2007]. By default, the value for the slice property is set to null, which indicates to Analysis Services that this specific partition can contain data for all the queries. The following steps show how to set the slice property.

1. Open the Adventure Works DW sample project shipped with SQL Server 2012. Deploy the sample Adventure Works DW project and ensure the database is processed. Connect to the Adventure Works DW database using SSMS.

2. Navigate to the Internet Sales Measure Group and double click on each partition to open the partition properties dialog. See Figure 10-13.

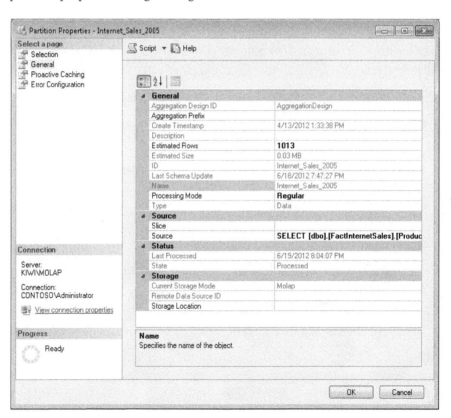

FIGURE 10-13

3. Select the Proactive Caching page.

4. Click Custom Settings and then click the Options button to launch the Storage Options dialog.

5. In the Storage Options dialog, select HOLAP from the Storage Mode drop-down list box and ensure the Enable proactive caching check box is not checked and click OK.

6. Click OK again to close the Partition Properties dialog.

7. Repeat 1-6 for each partition.

8. Reprocess the partitions.

9. Start SQL Server Profiler and run the following MDX query:

```
Select {[Measures].[Internet Sales Amount]}
on 0,
{[Product].[Product Categories].[Category].members}
on 1
FROM
[Adventure Works]
WHERE
{[Date].[Calendar].[Calendar Year].&[2005]})
```

10. Click the ellipsis next to the Slice property. This launches the MDX editor, as shown in Figure 10-14.

FIGURE 10-14

11. Navigate through the Date dimension and select the member [Date].[Calendar] .[Calendar Year].&[2005]. When you double-click this member, the MDX expression corresponding to it appears in the text box. Click Check to verify the MDX syntax, and then click OK.

12. Similar to step 5, specify the slice property for the remaining partitions Internet_Sales_2006, Internet_Sales_2007, and Internet_Sales_2008 with corresponding members in the Date dimension for the years 2006, 2007, and 2008.

13. If you use MOLAP partitions, you need to reprocess them after making these changes.

You have now successfully defined the slice for all the partitions in the Internet_Sales measure group of the Adventure Works cube. To verify that Analysis Services can use the slice information, you can send an MDX query that retrieves measures from the Internet_Sales measure group containing specific members from the [Date].[Calendar] hierarchy, such as year 2005. If you trace the queries sent to the SQL Server using SQL Server Profiler without setting the slice information, you see that Analysis Services sends four queries to the relational server. After setting the slice information, you can see that exactly one query is sent to the SQL Server.

An important factor is that Analysis Services does not validate your slice information for ROLAP partitions. Analysis Services just honors the slice property you have set, assuming you have the in-depth knowledge of your data. If you set an incorrect slice on a partition, you get incorrect query results. For example, if you set the slice for partition Internet_Sales_2006 with a time member corresponding to 2005, a query requesting data for year 2006 can result in no data (assuming slice information is set for the remaining partitions correctly). The slice property is a directive to Analysis Services, and you need to be careful about setting the correct slice. Because Analysis Services is aware of the slice information for MOLAP partitions, if you set an incorrect slice for a specific partition and try to process the partition, the processing results in errors. Each row processed is validated against the slice, and processing fails if it does not fit within the space defined for the partition.

Distinct Count Partitioning

Distinct count measure groups have some special behaviors worth mentioning from a performance standpoint. Each distinct count partition processed is ordered by the distinct count measure column. For example, the Internet Order Count measure in the Internet Orders measure group in Adventure Works DW is processed using a SQL query:

```
SELECT
   [dbo_FactInternetSales].[SalesOrderNumber] AS
   [dbo_FactInternetSalesSalesOrderNumber0_0],
   [dbo_FactInternetSales].[PromotionKey] AS
   [dbo_FactInternetSalesPromotionKey0_1],
   ...
FROM
   facttable AS [dbo_FactInternetSales]
ORDER BY
   [dbo_FactInternetSales].[SalesOrderNumber] ASC
```

As you can see, an ORDER BY clause in the SQL query enforces that the fact records stored in the Analysis Services partition files are ordered by the values of the distinct count measure. This is important for two reasons.

First, it impacts the cost of processing. The ORDER BY clause can make the SQL query take much longer to execute, and you may find it possible and valuable to build indexes in the relational database to optimize the SQL query performance.

Second, the partitioning strategy in Analysis Services is also impacted by this, albeit somewhat indirectly. For example, take a partitioning strategy in which 12 partitions are based on the Month attribute in the Date dimension. This is generally a reasonable approach for partitioning. However, when a query hits a distinct count measure group asking for the total across all months, the server must scan all the partitions in a relatively inefficient manner. It must synchronize the records scanned across all the partitions to match up the records that have the same measure value, such that all these records will be counted for the total value.

An alternative strategy is to partition based on the Distinct Count column value. For the Internet Order Count measure group, this would be the Sales Order Number column. The benefit of this type of partitioning scheme is that the partitions now have distinct ranges for the distinct count measure values. (No two partitions have data for the same measure value.) The server detects this and can avoid the synchronization and can scan all the partitions in parallel. Essentially, it now knows that the same Sales Order Number can never be in any of the other partitions, so it can simply count the records in the current partition to determine the distinct count.

An extended variation of this is to partition by the distinct count measure and also by one or more dimensions. In this case, you get the benefit to avoid partition scans for partitions that don't match the current slice in the query. (For example, queries to the year 2008 don't need to scan partitions for years 2005, 2006, and 2007.) You also get some benefit of better parallelism because the server groups partitions together for the synchronization that have overlapping distinct count ranges. Therefore, the partitions that have disjointed ranges can be queried in parallel and have reduced overhead.

For example, say that you define partitions like this:

```
P1: Year 2005 and       0 < Sales Order Number < 10000
P2: Year 2005 and   10000 < Sales Order Number < 20000
...
P10: Year 2005 and 90000 < Sales Order Number

P11: Year 2006 and       0 < Sales Order Number < 10000
...
```

Now all the partitions for each year can be scanned independently because their ranges are disjointed. If a query crosses years (for example, All Years), the partitions that have the same ranges will be grouped together but the groups can operate independently of each other, which improves performance.

Microsoft has published a white paper for distinct count optimization that is available at www.microsoft.com/download/en/details.aspx?displaylang=en&id=891.

In this section, you learned various design techniques that can help you to optimize your multi-dimensional BISM for better performance during processing and querying. In the next section you learn about other optimizations that help you reduce processing time.

OPTIMIZING FOR PROCESSING

To understand how to improve multidimensional BISM processing performance, you first need to understand the processing operation of Analysis Services. Analysis Services 2012 supports ROLAP and MOLAP storage modes for dimensions and ROLAP, MOLAP, and HOLAP storage modes for partitions. Assume the data source is a relational database. Figure 10-15 shows the architecture of a regular processing operation when the storage mode for the dimensions and cubes is MOLAP. Analysis Services sends separate relational queries to the retrieve dimension and fact data. The relational data source executes the query and sends the records to Analysis Services. Analysis Services reads the records from the relational data source and stores it in a proprietary format for fast data access. During dimension processing Analysis Services sends separate queries to process each attribute of the dimension. Members from each attribute are stored and indexed by Key and Name for fast data access. The related properties to the attribute are also indexed. If an attribute has a related attribute defined, the related attribute needs to be processed first before the attribute. Analysis Services processes attributes in parallel based on resource availability, parallelism specified, and dependencies. The key attribute of the dimension is the last attribute processed because all the attributes are either directly or indirectly related to the key attribute. While processing the partitions Analysis Services reads fact data from the relational data source and stores it in proprietary format. Analysis Services then creates indexes to access the data efficiently. If aggregations are designed for the partitions, then aggregations are built followed by indexes.

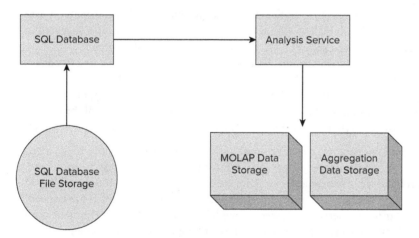

FIGURE 10-15

If the storage type is ROLAP, Analysis Services needs to store only the meta data in Analysis Services. There is no data transfer between the relational data source and the Analysis Services database, and there is no actual data storage on the Analysis Services side. Therefore, ROLAP processing is faster. Use of the ROLAP storage format does impose a performance penalty at query time; queries will be slower when compared to MOLAP. This is because at query time data needs to be retrieved from the data source, aggregated within Analysis Services, and then results returned to the end user.

When the storage type is HOLAP, the source data resides in the data source while aggregations are calculated and stored on Analysis Services. HOLAP storage is typically used only when you primarily have space constraints on replicating the data on Analysis Services. HOLAP storage mode doesn't save much processing time as compared to MOLAP. Because of the performance advantage of MOLAP data storage, use MOLAP storage for Analysis Services databases instead of HOLAP. For small and active partitions (current period data) where data cannot be allowed to be stale use of ROLAP storage mode in combination with the Real-Time Proactive Caching feature to get the most recent data.

You can have users querying the cube when you initiate processing. Analysis Services uses locks inside transactions to ensure atomic changes and consistent views of data. The lock is referred to as a database (DB) commit lock. Usually everything works, and you do not need to know about the DB commit lock. However, for sophisticated usage scenarios, understanding this process can help explain system behavior that might otherwise seem anomalous. This can also help you to perform processing operations based on the load on the system.

During a query, the server takes a read DB commit lock. This ensures the database will not be deleted or modified during the query. During processing, a new version of the object (dimension, fact-table partition, and so on) is created. The original version on disk is not immediately overwritten though; a shadow copy is created. When the new version has been successfully created, within the process transaction, a write DB commit lock is acquired. Then the new files automatically replace the old files, and the lock is released. The duration over which the lock is held is typically small, perhaps less than 1 second. However, acquiring this lock requires waiting for current lock holders to relinquish their locks. Thus a long-running query can block the completion of a processing command.

The `ForceCommitTimeout` server property specifies the period of time a process command must wait to acquire the DB commit lock. The default is 30000 milliseconds (30 seconds) and is specified in the configuration file `\Program Files\Microsoft SQL Server\<MSSQL.x>\OLAP\Config \msmdsrv.ini`. After the timeout, all transactions holding database read locks will be forced to fail. For the English version of Analysis Services, the error message returned is The Operation Has Been Cancelled. There are other scenarios under which this message will also be returned, but this is one cause to keep in mind when troubleshooting. Typically, the holder of the read lock will be one or more long-running queries, and for the system as a whole, forcing them to fail is probably the better choice.

Lock chains can result when long-running queries coexist with processing commands. While a process command is waiting for a long-running query, new queries must wait for the processing command to complete. Although the request for a new read lock is compatible with existing granted read locks, granting the new request could lead to starvation of the processing command, so locks are queued. The resulting behavior can appear to be a server hang, even though it is not. You can see this behavior if you try to connect to Analysis Services using SSMS when you have a long-running query along with a processing command waiting for the long-running query to complete. This is because SSMS sets a default database that requires a read DB commit lock. Following is a list of events creating a lock chain:

1. Long-running query acquires and holds read DB commit lock
2. Process command completes and waits to acquire write DB commit lock
3. New query waits to acquire read DB commit lock

Having learned the basic trade-offs to process time and query performance benefits for the various storage modes supported by Analysis Services, next look at some of the techniques that help in optimizing processing.

Creating Partitions to Speed Up Processing

You might expect Analysis Services to be installed on a multiprocessor machine to take advantage of multiple processors and have better performance. When a fact table is partitioned into multiple partitions within a measure group, due to the inherent parallelism in Analysis Services, the partitions are processed in parallel. You can also specify the parallelism to be used by Analysis Services through the processing option as discussed in Chapter 7. Therefore, having multiple partitions reduces the processing time for the measure group as compared to a single partition.

As discussed in the design optimization section, creating partitions can significantly improve processing performance during the typical daily, weekly, or monthly updates. Most often the partition corresponding to the most recent time period needs to be updated. Because a small subset of the data (most recent partition) is processed, you speed up the processing time for the entire measure group.

Create multiple partitions for the measure groups whenever you have large volumes of data. The size and number of partitions need to be determined based on these factors:

➤ Your multidimensional BISM

➤ How frequently data is loaded or modified into the BISM

➤ How the data is retrieved by end users during querying

➤ The machine configurations

The SQL Server 2008 R2 Operations guide white paper from Microsoft mentions that the large partitions' size (>20 million rows) show a negligible performance difference as compared to the small partitions' size. Determine the partitions' size based on your BISM usage. In general, if you do have partitions and you periodically do incremental processing partitions, perform full processing of the partitions to improve performance.

Creating too many partitions can potentially hurt processing performance. Analysis Services processes objects in parallel based on your system resources. If all the partitions are processed in parallel, they can compete for resources. Furthermore, the relational data source can also slow down processing performance if Analysis Services sends requests to retrieve data for all the partitions. Analysis Services enables you to control the number of objects to be processed in parallel (described in the section "Parallelism During Processing" in this chapter). Make sure you design the right number of partitions based on user queries and process with a certain degree of parallelism.

Microsoft has published a white paper called SQL Server 2008 R2 Analysis Services Operations Guide that is available at `http://msdn.microsoft.com/en-us/library/hh226085.aspx`.

Choosing Small and Appropriate Data Types and Sizes

Choosing integers as keys for your tables helps improve processing and query performance. Using integer keys (rather than strings or composite keys) results in faster processing time due to decreased size, decreased network usage, and the handling of keys internal to the relational data source, and Analysis Services can be done with simple native machine instructions. Analysis Services looks up the keys of dimension members while processing dimensions and cubes. The key lookup routines used by Analysis Services can run tens or hundreds of times faster for integer data types compared to other data types used as the key. In general, set appropriate keys and or consider a design using integer surrogate keys in the relational data source in advance of building your multidimensional BISM.

SQL Server and Analysis Services Installations

When you install SQL Server 2012, you can have SQL Server and Analysis Services installed on the same machine or a different machine. You might want to consider some trade-offs for processing when you have multidimensional BISM retrieving data from the SQL Server. If you have both installations on the same machine, SQL Server and Analysis Services may compete for resources. You need to make sure you have sufficient processors and memory configurations on your system. Whenever your Analysis Services dimensions are large (millions of members) there will be an impact on processing speed. If SQL Server and Analysis Services compete for memory, you might have significant paging of data to disk, which could slow down operations dramatically.

For 32-bit versions of Windows turn on the /3GB flag. By default, each process running in Windows can access a maximum of 2GB. By turning on the /3GB flag, you allow the Analysis Services process to access up to 3GB of addressable space. This increases the accessible memory and facilitates large dimension processing and aggregation building. To enable the /3GB option, open your boot.ini file on your system drive, and add the /3GB option as shown here, and then reboot the machine:

```
multi(0)disk(0)rdisk(0)partition(2)\WINNT="????" /3GB
```

In addition to turning on the /3GB option on a 32-bit machine, consider using a machine with a large amount of memory (for example, 8GB) whenever you have SQL Server and Analysis Services installations on the same machine and your multidimensional BISMs have large dimensions (on the order of millions of members). The additional memory on the 32-bit machine can be accessed by SQL Server 2012 through Address Windowing Extensions (AWE). Therefore, adding the additional memory helps ensure that both servers have sufficient memory resources to provide good performance. Another option is to use SQL Server and Analysis Services on 64-bit machines with larger memory.

If you do install SQL Server and Analysis Services on separate machines, they do not compete for resources, but you need to make sure you have a good high-speed network connection between the servers, such as gigabit Ethernet or fiber channel. Having good network connectivity helps reduce the network transfer time for queries returning large volumes of data. To stay legal, check your licensing agreement for installing SQL Server and Analysis Services on separate machines.

Optimizing a Relational Data Source

When you read fact table data in Analysis Services 2012, you send the fact table scan query without joining dimension tables during MOLAP partition processing. Analysis Services 2012 sends a table scan query similar to the following to get the fact data without the join:

```
SELECT [dbo_WB_Fact].[BudgetExpenseAmount] AS
[dbo_WB_FactBudgetExpenseAmount0_0], [dbo_WB_Fact].[EmployeeKey] AS
[dbo_WB_FactEmployeeKey0_1], [dbo_WB_Fact].[quarterkey] AS
[dbo_WB_Factquarterkey0_2]           FROM [dbo].[WB_Fact] AS [dbo_WB_Fact]
```

This query is a pure table scan query for the whole partition. It is unnecessary to put an index on the fact table because there are no joins involved with the dimension table.

However, if you do have ROLAP partitions set up, have appropriate indexes created on your relational database so that queries sent to the relational data source at query time return results faster because those can involve joins to dimension tables. If you trace the operations of Analysis Services with the help of SQL Server Profiler, you can identify the queries sent to your relational server. Set up efficient indexes for the queries targeted to your relational server for best performance when querying ROLAP partitions.

Dimension processing may also benefit from indexes in some cases. The queries generated by Analysis Services for each attribute look something like this:

```
SELECT DISTINCT
[dbo_DimProductCategory].[ProductCategoryKey] AS
        [dbo_DimProductCategoryProductCategoryKey0_0],
[dbo_DimProductCategory].[EnglishProductCategoryName] AS
         [dbo_DimProductCategoryEnglishProductCategoryName0_1],
[dbo_DimProductCategory].[SpanishProductCategoryName] AS
         [dbo_DimProductCategorySpanishProductCategoryName0_2],
[dbo_DimProductCategory].[FrenchProductCategoryName] AS
         [dbo_DimProductCategoryFrenchProductCategoryName0_3]
FROM [dbo].[DimProductCategory] AS [dbo_DimProductCategory]
```

For the key attribute, all the key columns of the related attributes can also be included in the list of columns. The DISTINCT clause can sometimes be an expensive operation for the relational database, and indexes on the dimension table may be worth considering. This is usually not an issue for typical dimensions and is worth considering only if it appears that a dimension takes unusually long to process.

Avoiding Excessive Aggregation Design

Aggregation design is a way to define aggregated data that needs to be created during processing of partitions. You learn more about aggregations in the "Designing Aggregations" section later in this chapter. If you have the right aggregations created, it helps in query performance. However, having excessive aggregations for partitions the processing time of the partitions. Analysis Services may need additional temporary files during the process and need to write more data onto the disk for each partition. As a general rule of thumb, create aggregations to improve performance by 10–30 percent. If you do need additional query performance improvements, use a usage-based aggregation design to create targeted aggregations based on the requests sent by the users accessing the cubes. You also have the choice to use different aggregations for each partition, which can help to remove unwanted aggregations for certain partitions and speed up cube processing time. Consider designing more aggregations on heavily queried partitions and using fewer aggregations for partitions rarely used. This may seem like a fairly obvious guideline, but it does have a management overhead because creation and management of partitions now needs to take into consideration multiple candidate aggregation designs.

Using Incremental Processing When Appropriate

Often, data changes in the relational data source. These changes could be due to new rows being added to existing tables or updates on existing rows. If you have set up the storage mode for dimensions and partitions as ROLAP, you can retrieve the data from the relational data source for queries sent by users. In situations in which the result set has been cached on Analysis Services due to a previous query, Analysis Services does not fetch data from the relational database by default. You can force Analysis Services to always fetch data from the relational data source by using ROLAP. However, if the storage mode for all your cubes and dimensions is MOLAP, Analysis Services serves queries only from the processed MOLAP data that resides on Analysis Services. Future updates to relational tables are not available to end users unless you update the MOLAP data on Analysis Services.

You have several ways to update the data on Analysis Services. You can do a full process of the corresponding dimensions and cubes that need to be refreshed due to changes in the corresponding relational tables. Several processing options are available, however, to optimize your processing needs. Process Incremental and Process Add are options that help you process the dimensions and partitions so that they are updated with the new data on the relational data source as necessary. Not all the data in the partitions or dimensions is updated during these operations; only data that changed since the last round of processing is refreshed.

During an incremental process of partitions, Analysis Services retrieves the new data from the relational data source and adds it to a temporary partition. Aggregations are then created for this new data, and finally the temporary partition is merged to the existing partition. As soon as the data merges, it is available for querying, and you see the new data reflected in user queries. Because Analysis Services retrieves only the new data added to relational tables, the incremental processing option for partitions helps you to process the partition quickly as compared to full process. However, if your partition is to be processed frequently due to data changes in the relational data source, do a full process on that partition periodically (not often), because full processing has a better layout of data on disk and results in some performance benefits similar to the defragment technique in file storage.

Dimensions can be incrementally processed using the `ProcessIncremental` or `ProcessAdd` options. `ProcessIncremental` retrieves the data from the relational data source, compares the data to existing dimension members on Analysis Services, and then makes updates to existing dimension members if there are any changes. If there are new members, they are added to the dimension, and this does not affect the partitions. However, if the dimension members are updated such that the relationship between attributes has changed (an employee's marital status changed from single to married), then the aggregations for the corresponding partitions will be dropped. The cube is still available for querying, but it can impact the performance of the queries that were using the dropped aggregations. `ProcessIncremental` takes more time than full process of the same dimension because Analysis Services does the additional work to check for updates for existing members; however, it provides you with the flexibility to have the dimension available for querying and the cube does not need to be reprocessed. This option enables you to add new dimension members that have been added in the relational data source to existing processed dimensions. Use the `ProcessAdd` option for dimensions whenever you have new members added to the corresponding dimension tables in the relational data source. `ProcessAdd` for dimensions is useful in cases in which new products are added to the products table on a periodic basis. You need to specify relational queries to the data source that return the new rows that have been added since the last dimension update. The query to retrieve new data along with the data source and Data Source View elements is to be specified in the DDL along with the `ProcessAdd` called out of line binding. The following is an example of using DDL using `ProcessAdd` with out-of-line binding:

```
<Batch xmlns="http://schemas.microsoft.com/analysisservices/2003/engine">
  <Parallel>
    <Process xmlns="http://schemas.microsoft.com/analysisservices/2003/engine">
```

```
<Object>
 <DatabaseID>Adventure Works DW </DatabaseID>
 <DimensionID>Dim Customer</DimensionID>
</Object>
<Type>ProcessAdd</Type>
<DataSourceView>
 <ID>Adventure Works DW</ID>
 <Name>Adventure Works DW</Name>
 <DataSourceID>Adventure Works DW</DataSourceID>
 <Schema>
  <xs:schema id="Adventure_x0020_Works_x0020_DW 2012" xmlns=""
      xmlns:xs="http://www.w3.org/2001/XMLSchema" xmlns:msdata=
      "urn:schemas-microsoft-com:xml-msdata" xmlns:msprop="urn:schemas-
      microsoft-com:xml-msprop">
  <xs:element name="Adventure_x0020_Works_x0020_DW 2012"
      msdata:IsDataSet="true" msdata:UseCurrentLocale="true">
   <xs:complexType>
    <xs:choice minOccurs="0" maxOccurs="unbounded">
     <xs:element name="dbo_DimProduct" msprop:FriendlyName="DimProduct"
         msprop:DbSchemaName="dbo" msprop:DbTableName="DimProduct"
          msprop:QueryDefiniton ="SELECT
        * FROM DimProduct WHERE ProductKey &gt; 600"
          msprop:DbTableName="DimProduct"
          msprop:IsLogical="True"
          msprop:TableType="View">
     <xs:complexType>
      ... //Details of columns returned
     </xs:complexType>
    </xs:element>
   </xs:choice>
  </xs:complexType>
 </xs:element>
 </xs:schema>
 </Schema>
 </DataSourceView>
 </Process>
 </Parallel>
</Batch>
```

Parallelism during Processing

Analysis Services 2012 has the processing behavior of using max parallelism to process independent components by default. If you have 16 partitions, all 16 partitions are processed in parallel. Having too much parallelism can actually hurt performance through context switching and disk thrashing; happily, Analysis Services provides you with several options to control the amount of parallelism used for processing. Based on the complexity of the cube and the set of aggregations, you should have two to three objects processed per CPU.

You can control the amount of parallelism by changing certain server properties. For processing, the main server property impacting processing performance is CoordinatorExecutionMode. The server properties can be changed using the properties dialog from SQL Server Management Studio or in the config file msmsdsrv.ini located in the %System Drive%\Program Files\Microsoft SQL

Server\MSSQL.x\OLAP\Config folder. The CoordinatorExecutionMode server property sets the maximum parallelism allowed for a specific job, such as processing that needs to be executed on the server at a specific time. This property can have a positive or negative value. If the value is positive, the actual value is used, and if the value is negative, it is multiplied by the number of processors, and the absolute value of the result is used. For example, the default Analysis Services 2012 value is –4, which on a 4-processor machine indicates that the maximum parallelism to be used on the machine is 16 for each request. By setting this property you can avoid the server overloading with processing operations, perhaps to allow some resources for queries.

Another property, ThreadPool\Process\MaxThreads, specifies the maximum number of threads in the processing thread pool. We do not use this as a way to limit concurrency because internally the server often executes tasks by queuing other tasks and waiting for completion. The server is designed to be smart enough to know that more threads are needed to avoid deadlocking by exceeding MaxThreads.

When all the objects within a database are processed in parallel, Analysis Services sends queries to the data source for dimension and partition processing. Sometimes having too many connections and queries to the data source can increase processing time. You can limit the number of connections Analysis Services establishes with the data source. You can limit concurrent connections using the Data Source property Maximum Number of Connections. You can alter this value from SQL Management Studio. See Figure 10-16.

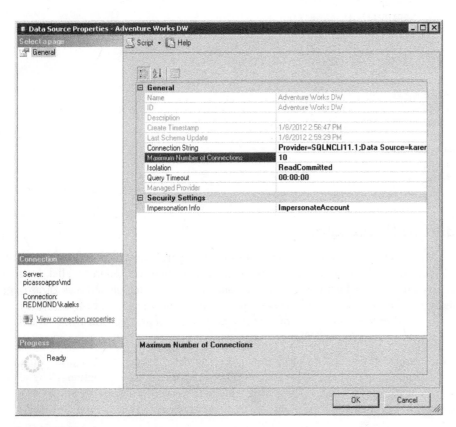

FIGURE 10-16

You can specify the amount of parallelism for a specific processing operation along with the processing command. Follow these steps to restrict the parallelism in the Processing dialog while processing a database:

1. Open the sample Adventure Works DW project, and deploy it to the Analysis Services instance.

2. Open SSMS, and connect to the Analysis Services instance.

3. Navigate to the Internet_Sales measure group for the Adventure Works cube in the Object Browser window.

4. Right-click the measure group, and choose Process to open the Process dialog shown in Figure 10-17.

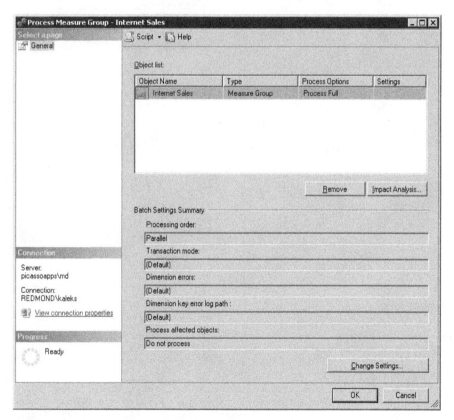

FIGURE 10-17

5. Click the Change Settings button to open the Settings dialog.

6. The Change Settings dialog shown in Figure 10-18 enables you specify the amount of parallelism while processing the current object. Select the value 8, as shown in the figure, and click OK.

7. You learned in Chapter 7 that you can process the objects on an Analysis Services instance using the dialogs or through scripts. The Process dialog has the option to script the current settings to process the Internet_Sales measure group into XMLA. Click the Script button in the Process dialog (refer to Figure 10-17). A processing script is now opened within SSMS, as shown below. You could also use SQL Server Profiler to view the process command received by the server.

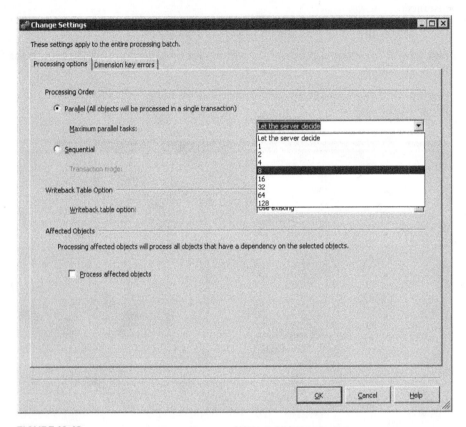

FIGURE 10-18

```
<Batch xmlns="http://schemas.microsoft.com/analysisservices/2003/engine">
  <Parallel MaxParallel="8">
    <Process xmlns:xsd="http://www.w3.org/2001/XMLSchema"
xmlns:xsi="http://www.w3.org/2001/XMLSchema-instance"
xmlns:ddl2="http://schemas.microsoft.com/analysisservices/2003/engine/2"
xmlns:ddl2_2="http://schemas.microsoft.com/analysisservices/2003/engine/2/2"
xmlns:ddl100_100="http://schemas.microsoft.com/analysisservices/2008/engine/100/100"
xmlns:ddl200="http://schemas.microsoft.com/analysisservices/2010/engine/200"
xmlns:ddl200_200="http://schemas.microsoft.com/analysisservices/2010/engine/200/200"
xmlns:ddl300="http://schemas.microsoft.com/analysisservices/2011/engine/300"
xmlns:ddl300_300="http://schemas.microsoft.com/analysisservices/2011/engine/300/300">
      <Object>
        <DatabaseID>Adventure Works DW</DatabaseID>
        <CubeID>Adventure Works</CubeID>
        <MeasureGroupID>Fact Internet Sales 1</MeasureGroupID>
```

```
        </Object>
        <Type>ProcessFull</Type>
        <WriteBackTableCreation>UseExisting</WriteBackTableCreation>
      </Process>
    </Parallel>
  </Batch>
```

In the processing script you can see the option MaxParallel=8, which instructs the Analysis Services instance to process a maximum of eight objects in parallel.

Identifying Resource Bottlenecks

Analysis Services processing and query performance requires well-configured hardware resources for best results. Processing performance requires sufficient memory, CPU speed, and good hard disk I/O speed. These three play a significant role in getting the best performance. Analysis Services enables you to monitor resources used during operations of the server by way of PerfMon counters. There are specific PerfMon counters that show the memory utilization on the Analysis Services instance. You can monitor the server behavior during the processing operation via PerfMon counters of the objects \\<*machinename*>\Processor, \\<*machinename*>\Memory, \\<*machin-ename*>\PhysicalDisk, and specific counters provided by Analysis Services \\<*machinename*>\ MSAS11: Processing, \\<*machinename*>\MSAS11: ProcIndexes, \\<*machinename*>\MSAS11: ProcAggregations, and \\<*machinename*>\ProcIndexes. For named instances of Analysis Services, the PerfMon counters have names in the format of \\<*machinename*>\MSOLAP$<*instanc ename*>\<*countername*>. After identifying the bottlenecks of the system, you can take appropriate action to relieve the server performance hot spots.

Some simple hardware additions, such as increasing server memory, adding more CPU, or using fast writing disks can potentially improve the system processing performance. As mentioned earlier, if you have memory over 3GB for a 32-bit machine, you might consider using the /3GB flag to allow Analysis Services to use memory over the 3-GB limit. If memory is the main bottleneck, consider using 64-bit machines to increase the performance and capacity of your system, especially for cubes with large dimensions (10> million dimension members).

In certain cases in which the number of partitions is in the order of hundreds, processing partitions in parallel on a 32-bit machine can result in partitions competing among themselves for memory resources. In such circumstances, processing can result in errors that say the system does not have sufficient memory. You can split the processing of the partitions by one of the following techniques:

1. Process fewer partitions at a time, and stagger them to complete processing of all the partitions.

2. Use one of the techniques mentioned in the "Parallelism During Processing" section.

3. Instead of doing a full process of the partitions, which includes processing data, indexes, and aggregations, split the processing as Process Data first for all partitions followed by Process Indexes.

4. If you run on 64-bit hardware and you have a lot of memory at your disposal, you could change the settings for the OLAP\Memory\LowMemoryLimit and TotalMemoryLimit. These settings default to 65 percent and 80 percent of available memory. On a machine with large

amounts of available memory, you could increase these if other processes on the server do not need significant amounts of memory. This would allow Analysis Services to make use of more memory during processing and queries.

DESIGNING AGGREGATIONS

The power of Analysis Services is its capability to provide fast query response time for decision makers who need to analyze data, draw conclusions, and make appropriate changes in business. As per The OLAP Report (http://www.olapreport.com), OLAP is defined as Fast Analysis of Shared Multidimensional Information (FASMI). The word fast means that the system can deliver results to users within 5 seconds, with a few complex queries that may take more than 20 seconds. Most of the business users use business client tools that graphically represent that data from Analysis Services for easy interpretation and understanding. As an end user you would expect to see the data quickly to analyze and make decisions. (The OLAP Report cites users typically wait for only 30 seconds as per an independent study in the Netherlands.) Some of the common operations the client tools offer are drill down, drill up, and compare data year over year. Users do not have the time to wait hours for a response. Therefore, the queries sent to Analysis Services need to return data within seconds, at most in minutes. The query performance is pivotal to a successful Business Intelligence project deployment. A system that has good performance can bring great business value to your system and company.

Even though Analysis Services supports storage modes MOLAP, ROLAP, and HOLAP, you obtain the best performance when your multidimensional BISM storage mode is MOLAP. When you choose MOLAP storage, Analysis Services 2012 stores the dimension data and fact data in its own efficient, compact, and multidimensional structure format. Fact data is compressed, and the size is approximately 10–30 percent of the size in the relational database. In addition to its own efficient and compact data store, Analysis Services builds specialized dimension attribute indexes for efficient data retrieval. The data is stored specifically in a multidimensional structure to best serve MDX query needs. If you use the ROLAP or HOLAP storage modes, queries to Analysis Services might need to fetch data from the relational data source at query time. Retrieving data from the relational data sources significantly slows your query performance because you incur relational query processing time — the time needed to fetch the data over the network and then finally aggregating the data within Analysis Services.

Analysis Services 2012 tries to achieve the best of the OLAP and relational worlds. OLAP queries typically request-aggregated data. For example, if you have sales information for products each day, a typical OLAP query might be to get the aggregated sales for the month or quarter or year. In such circumstances, every day's sales data needs to be aggregated for the entire year. If the users request aggregated data on a single dimension, you can do a simple sum in the relational database. However, OLAP queries are typically multidimensional queries, which need aggregated data across multiple dimensions with complex business logic calculations applied to each dimension. To improve the query performance, Analysis Services enables you to specify the multidimensional intersections for which data needs to be pre-aggregated so that queries requesting such data can be served instantaneously. Assume you have a database with a dimension called Products having a multilevel hierarchy Product Category ⇨ Product Sub Category ⇨ Product Name; a Time dimension having the hierarchy Year ⇨ Quarter ⇨ Month ⇨ Date; and a Geography dimension having a hierarchy Country ⇨ State ⇨ County ⇨ City. Fact data is typically at the lowest levels — sales of a specific product on a specific date at a specific city. For analysis you would request aggregated data of Sales at a city for a month for various product categories. You can have pre-aggregated data for the cross product of various levels in each hierarchy such as Quarter, State, and Year. To create the pre-aggregated data, you need to specify the dimensions for which Analysis Services needs to precalculate the data. The precalculated data along with definitions are referred to as aggregations.

Understanding Aggregations

Analysis Services 2012 enables you to build precalculated subtotals for each partition of your cubes and store them in either an OLAP data store or relational database based on the storage modes chosen for the partitions. Because most OLAP queries typically request aggregated data at various levels of dimension hierarchies, storing pre-aggregated data can help to get the results to end users quickly. When you query for data at higher levels of hierarchies (other than the granularity level, which is the level at which fact data is available), the server can directly fetch those aggregate numbers instead of bringing all related detailed fact data and aggregating them within the engine. In this section you learn to create aggregations for cubes using the Adventure Works DW sample database.

Using Adventure Works dimensions as an example, assume you have a measure group using the Date, Product, and Customer dimensions, and each dimension has hierarchies and levels, as shown in the following table. Assume the granularity attribute for the dimensions Date, Products, and Customer are Date, Product Name, and Full Name, respectively. If you query the data for [Date] .[2008].[Q3] and if there is no aggregated data stored in your OLAP database, the server needs to retrieve the lowest-level fact data for all dates in Quarter Q3 of year 2008 for all products and all the customers. This can result in a large data scan on the OLAP fact data, followed by the server aggregating the data and returning the results to you.

DATE DIMENSION		PRODUCT DIMENSION		CUSTOMER DIMENSION	
Year	4	Category	4	Country	6
Semester	8	Subcategory	37	State-Province	71
Quarter	16	Product Name	395	City	587
Month	48			Postal Code	646
Date	1461			Full Name	18484

Analysis Services 2012 provides wizards that help define the combinations of hierarchy members for which aggregated data needs to be created, either by analyzing the statistics of members at each level and based on the queries requested by users. After the aggregations are defined, you need to process the partitions so that Analysis Services creates the pre-aggregated data and stores them in the OLAP data store. In addition to the pre-aggregated data, Analysis Services also creates indexes to access the aggregated data, which speeds up data retrieval. Reviewing the preceding example, if the server has aggregations for levels Quarter, Subcategory, and State-Province of the user hierarchies in Date, Product, and Customer dimensions, respectively, then a query for Quarter Q3 of year 2008 can be fulfilled right away from the aggregation. In this case, a fact scan is not needed, and you receive the results more quickly because the amount of data that must be scanned is significantly smaller. Furthermore, queries requesting data for the levels above Quarter, Subcategory, and State-Province also benefit from the aggregation. For example, if you query for Year, Subcategory, and State-Province, the server needs to get only the data for Quarter from the existing aggregations and aggregate a much smaller data set than a huge fact table scan. Thus, aggregations help to improve the query performance time of your MDX queries.

Storing aggregation values in the Analysis Services database is a typical trade-off of database size and performance. Aggregation values take disk space and benefit from query performance for queries sent to the server. In addition to that, the time to build aggregations during processing can also play an important role in performance for when the multidimensional BISM is available. In the example discussed in the preceding paragraph, if you count the permutations of all levels in the three dimensions, you see there are 74 combinations ($5 \times 3 \times 5$) -1[fact table] = 74) to build aggregations. You might immediately have the following questions:

➤ Do I need to build aggregations for all the combinations? Will that be useful?

➤ Can I build a subset of the aggregations?

➤ What parameters affect the choice of Analysis Services for aggregation design?

➤ How much disk space can these aggregations take?

➤ What percentage of optimization can I get based on the aggregations designed?

The estimated dimension that members count of all the hierarchies in a dimension is an important metric to calculate the cost of storage for aggregations. For example, aggregation (Month, Product Name, Postal Code) potentially results in 12 million ($48 \times 395 \times 646 = 12,248,160$) cells to compute and store. However, not every cell has data just as the fact data doesn't have all combinations for every dimension key. Because Analysis Services stores only data for coordinates that have fact values, the equation needs to be adjusted to consider the partition fact count. Analysis Services assumes the data is of uniform distribution and uses an algorithm to calculate the estimated aggregation cells for a specific aggregation. Analysis Services, by default, selects attributes from cube dimensions to be considered for aggregation. Analysis Services estimates the aggregation size and the benefit due to the aggregation for various combinations of attributes. Based on the aggregation disk size or percentage of optimization chosen by the user, Analysis Services stops iteration of calculating the optimized aggregation designs as soon as one of the criteria is met.

For query benefits, the lower the aggregation design, the more useful the aggregation because all higher-level queries can benefit from the aggregation. However, the lower the aggregation design, the bigger the size of the aggregation data store and the longer the aggregation build time. It does not make sense to have aggregated cells with a size close to the fact size; it won't save any disk scan time because the server reads almost the same amount of data from the disk. Therefore, building too many aggregations actually does not benefit query performance and sometimes might actually hurt it. Analysis Services, however, enables you to create aggregations up to 100 percent. As previously mentioned, you should have aggregations where the estimated size is between 10 and 30 percent of the fact table size.

Creating Aggregations

Analysis Services enables you to specify the percentage of aggregation of the disk space to be used for creating aggregations. Analysis Services uses a complex algorithm to estimate the best aggregations based on the number of fact table and dimension members that provide you with the maximum benefit. The following steps show how to design aggregations for the Adventure Works sample Internet Sales partitions:

1. Open the Adventure Works DW sample project in SSDT.

2. Open the Adventure Works cube, and switch to the Aggregations tab.

3. Right-click the Internet Sales measure group, and select Design Aggregations, as shown in Figure 10-19.

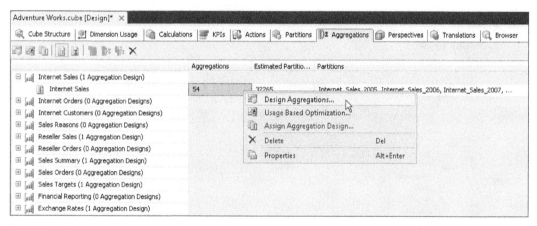

FIGURE 10-19

4. You are now in the Aggregation Design Wizard, as shown in Figure 10-20. Select the Internet_Sales_2005 partition, and click Next.

5. The Review Aggregation Usage page, as shown in Figure 10-21, enables you to control which attributes in each dimension should be considered for the aggregation design. Marking an attribute as Full means that all aggregations include the members of the attribute. Marking an attribute as None means that no aggregation includes that attribute. The setting of Unrestricted enables the server to decide according to the heuristic-based algorithm. The setting of Default means that certain attributes default to None (such as attributes that do not participate in a user hierarchy), whereas others are Unrestricted. Click Next.

FIGURE 10-20

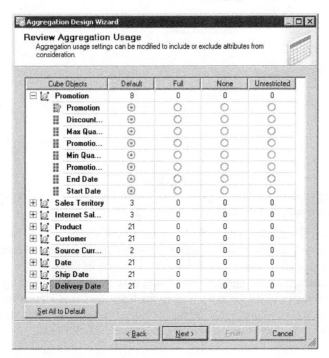

FIGURE 10-21

6. The Specify Object Counts page enables you to retrieve the count of dimension members relevant to the current partition and the count of fact table rows, as shown in Figure 10-22. At the top of the grid is the fact table count; Estimated Count is the total number of fact table rows for all partitions in the current measure group. The Partition Count contains the count of fact table rows for the current partition. This page also enables you to override the values for the current partition. Click the Count button. Analysis Services retrieves the count of dimension members and the partition by sending queries to the relational database. Estimated Count is the count for the entire measure group, and the Partition Count has the values for the current partition. If the values of the current partition have different values in your production environment, you can enter the new counts in the Partition Count column. The count specified in the Object Counts page is used to calculate appropriate weights to design aggregations. Therefore, make sure you provide the right counts; otherwise, you might end up with a suboptimal aggregation design.

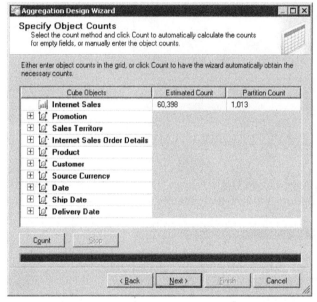

FIGURE 10-22

7. If you expand the Customer dimension, all the attributes being considered for aggregation design display along with the estimated count of members, as shown in Figure 10-23. You should be aware that the attributes of the Customer dimension that are not considered for aggregation design are not shown in this wizard. For the Partition Count column, because the fact table includes only the granularity attribute (the customer key), that count is also available for Analysis Services to determine the aggregation design. You have the option to include or exclude attributes for consideration for aggregation design. By default, Analysis Services includes the key attributes for consideration during aggregation design. All the attributes that are levels of natural hierarchies are considered for aggregation design. If a user hierarchy is unnatural, the topmost level is considered for aggregation design. The remaining levels of the unnatural hierarchy from the topmost level are included for consideration if there is a one-to-many relationship from that level to the next level. As soon as there is no relationship between successive levels, the remaining levels below that level of the unnatural hierarchy are not considered during aggregation design. Click the Next button.

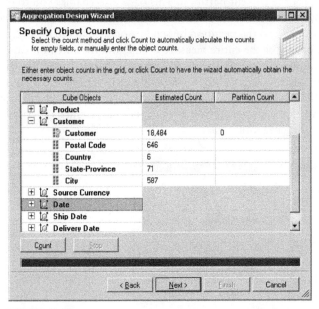

FIGURE 10-23

8. You are now on the Set Aggregation Options page, as shown in Figure 10-24. The engine gives you four possible options for how to design the aggregations:

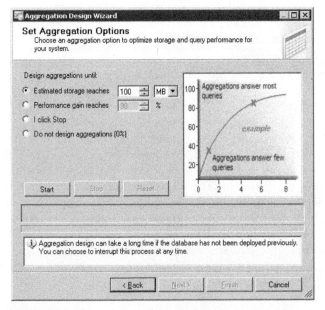

FIGURE 10-24

➤ **Setting the storage limit for estimated aggregation data:** The system looks for the aggregation combinations whose total estimated size is within the user-specified limit.

➤ **Performance gain setting:** You can choose a percentage of performance gain. The system uses the cost and performance gain algorithms to search for the best combinations that fulfill the performance gain metric. The lower the percentage, the fewer aggregations built and the fewer queries answered through precalculation. Begin with 30-percent aggregation performance gain for most cubes.

➤ **User click-stop option:** The system starts to analyze the aggregation design and design aggregations. The server stops searching for more aggregations when the user click-stops or the performance gain reaches 100 percent.

➤ **Do not design aggregations (0%):** The server cannot design any aggregations for the current partition.

9. Choose the second option, Performance Gain Reaches, and set the number to 30 percent. Click the Start button to design the aggregation.

10. The server starts to analyze the aggregation design and sends feedback on the aggregations generated. The feedback is shown graphically on the Set Aggregation Options page, as shown in Figure 10-25. The X-axis of the graph contains the amount of storage used and the Y-axis of the graph shows the percentage of performance gain. The status bar shows the number of aggregations that have been created during that time. When the performance gain reaches the percentage you have specified (30%), the server stops designing further aggregations. You can see 27 aggregations have been created for 30 percent performance gain and the estimated storage is 30.6KB. Click the Next button.

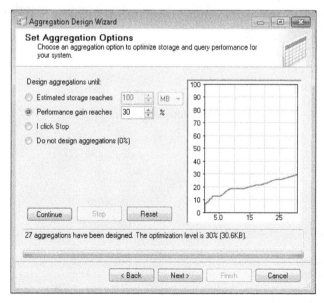

FIGURE 10-25

11. In the final page of the Aggregation Design Wizard, you have two choices to either deploy and process the partition or save the aggregation design and process later. Choose Deploy and Process Now. Then click Run to Process the partition.

You have now successfully created aggregations for the partition Internet_Sales_2005 using the Aggregation Design Wizard. To find out what partition aggregations have been created for this partition, you can either deploy the project followed by scripting from SSMS or open the file Adventure Works.partitions in your current project's directory in an XML editor. If you look at the partition Internet_Sales_2005 you can find the following definition, which indicates that the partition has an aggregation design defined, and the aggregation design used has the ID AggregationDesign:

```
<Partition>
 <ID>Internet_Sales_2005</ID>
 <Name>Internet_Sales_2005</Name>
 <CreatedTimestamp>0001-01-01T08:00:00Z</CreatedTimestamp>
 <LastSchemaUpdate>0001-01-01T08:00:00Z</LastSchemaUpdate>
 ........
 <EstimatedRows>1013</EstimatedRows>
 <AggregationDesignID>AggregationDesign</AggregationDesignID>
</Partition>
```

You can find the aggregation designed by the server in the AggregationDesign section for the measure group Internet Sales. Following is a section of the definition for the aggregation that has been designed. Each aggregation design can have one or more aggregations defined. The dimension section within Aggregations includes the estimated counts for dimension attributes. In the aggregation section, it lists the detailed aggregation design for each aggregation. The definitions for each aggregation contain the combination of the hierarchies to be included for aggregating the data. If a hierarchy has not been specified in the aggregation design, by default it is implied that the top-level member or the default member of that hierarchy is included.

```
    <AggregationDesigns>
     <AggregationDesign>
<ID>AggregationDesign</ID>
<Name>AggregationDesign</Name>
<CreatedTimestamp>2008-08-24T05:08:31Z</CreatedTimestamp>
<LastSchemaUpdate>2008-08-24T05:08:31Z</LastSchemaUpdate>

<EstimatedRows>1013</EstimatedRows>
<Dimensions>
......
 </Dimensions>

  <Aggregations>
        <Aggregation>
         <ID>Aggregation 0</ID>
         <Name>Aggregation 0</Name>
         <Dimensions>
          <Dimension>
           <CubeDimensionID>Dim Promotion</CubeDimensionID>
          </Dimension>
```

```
        <Dimension>
          <CubeDimensionID>Dim Sales Territory</CubeDimensionID>
        </Dimension>
        <Dimension>
          <CubeDimensionID>Internet Sales Order
              Details</CubeDimensionID>
        </Dimension>
        <Dimension>
          <CubeDimensionID>Dim Product</CubeDimensionID>
          <Attributes>
            <Attribute>
              <AttributeID>Safety Stock Level</AttributeID>
            </Attribute>
          </Attributes>
        </Dimension>
        <Dimension>
          <CubeDimensionID>Dim Customer</CubeDimensionID>
        </Dimension>
        <Dimension>
          <CubeDimensionID>Dim Currency</CubeDimensionID>
        </Dimension>
        <Dimension>
          <CubeDimensionID>Destination Currency</CubeDimensionID>
        </Dimension>
        <Dimension>
          <CubeDimensionID>Order Date Key - Dim Time</CubeDimensionID>
        </Dimension>
        <Dimension>
          <CubeDimensionID>Ship Date Key - Dim Time</CubeDimensionID>
        </Dimension>
        <Dimension>
          <CubeDimensionID>Due Date Key - Dim Time</CubeDimensionID>
        </Dimension>
        <Dimension>
          <CubeDimensionID>Sales Reason</CubeDimensionID>
        </Dimension>
      </Dimensions>
    </Aggregation>
......
    </Aggregations>
  </AggregationDesigns>
</AggregationDesign>
```

Applying Aggregation Design

You have so far designed aggregations for a single partition. If all your partitions contain the same fact table data and characteristics in terms of dimension member distributions, you can design the same aggregations. You can select a group of partitions in the SQL Server Data Tools (SSDT) and then select Design Aggregations to design the same aggregation. Alternatively, Analysis Services 2012 enables you to apply an existing aggregation of a partition to other partitions in the same measure group. However, if you have some partitions that include fact records for an entire year and one partition holding current or last month's data, you may want to design separate aggregations to have the most optimal performance. To design the same aggregations for a group of partitions from SSDT, follow these steps:

1. Open the Adventure Works cube of the sample project in SSDT, and switch to the Aggregations tab.

2. Right-click the Internet Sales measure group, and choose Design Aggregations, as shown in Figure 10-26 to bring up the design aggregation window.

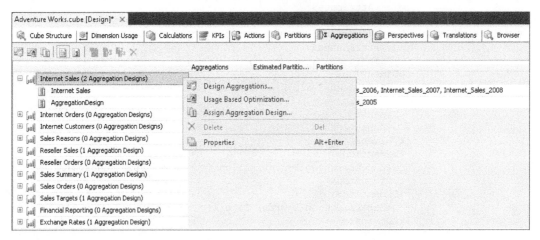

FIGURE 10-26

3. Select all the partitions for which you want the same aggregation design to be applied in the Specify Partitions to Modify page. Go through the same steps to design aggregations for the first partition. The wizard automatically copies the aggregation design to other partitions.

To assign an existing aggregation design to other partitions, perform the following steps:

1. Launch SSDT, and connect to your Analysis Services instance.

2. Navigate to the Adventure Works cube in the Object Explorer.

3. In the Measure Groups folder, open the Internet Sales measure group, and open the Partitions folder.

4. Right-click the Internet_Sales_2005 partition, and select Assign Aggregation Design, as shown in Figure 10-27.

5. You now see the Assign Aggregation Design Wizard. You can choose to assign any existing aggregation design to one or many partitions in this measure group. Select the partition for which you want to apply the same aggregation design, as shown in Figure 10-28, and click OK.

FIGURE 10-27

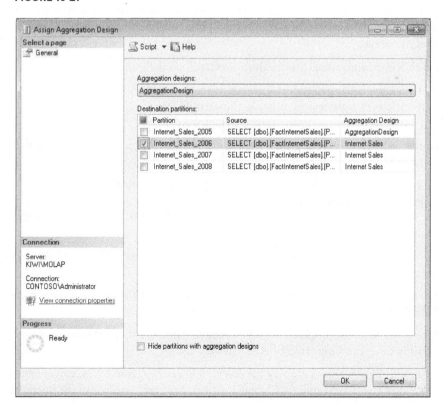

FIGURE 10-28

You can see each partition and which aggregation design (if any) is currently assigned to it. By selecting the available aggregation designs from the drop-down, you can assign a new aggregation design to one or more of the partitions. This example shows how to apply aggregation design from SSMS. You can do the same steps outlined to applying aggregation design from the Aggregations tab of the Cube Designer in SSDT. You need to process all the modified partitions using the ProcessIndexes option so that Analysis Services creates the aggregated data. You can later send a query that requests data for a specific level and analyze its performance. If aggregations have been built for the cells that have been requested, Analysis Services serves the query from the aggregations. Based on the size of your cube and aggregations designed, you can notice performance gain for queries touching the aggregations. Finally, you can use SQL Server Profiler to see if specific aggregations are getting hit (see Chapter 11).

Usage-Based Aggregation Design

In addition to the Aggregation Design Wizard, Analysis Services supports aggregation design based on the user queries sent to Analysis Services. Designing aggregations based on user queries is called usage-based optimization because aggregations are designed based on users' requests, making sure performance gains are achieved for those specific queries. For Analysis Services to analyze the queries and design aggregations, the queries served by Analysis Services need to be logged at a specific location. Analysis Services provides a way to log the queries in a relational table with specific parameters. Because this aggregation design technique is dependent on the usage pattern, it is more likely that Analysis Services can create more useful aggregations to increase performance of future queries. To create the user-based aggregation design, you first need to enable Analysis Services to log the queries sent to the server. Follow these steps to enable query logging and design aggregations based on a set of queries:

1. Launch SSMS, and connect to Analysis Services.

2. Right-click the Analysis Services instance connected, and choose Properties. You see the Analysis Server Properties window, as shown in Figure 10-29.

3. Set the Log\QueryLog\QueryLogConnectionString property so that it has a connection string pointing to a relational database where queries can be logged. To do so, click the ellipsis (...) to launch the connection string dialog.

4. You see the Connection Manager dialog, as shown in Figure 10-30, which you have used to specify data sources. Specify the connection details to your SQL Server that contains the sample relational database Adventure Works DW. Click OK after you specify the connection details.

5. The connection string will be copied as the value for the server property Log\QueryLog \QueryLogConnectionString.

6. Define the server property Log\QueryLog\QueryLogTableName with a table name OLAPQueryLog.

7. Make sure the server property Log\QueryLog\CreateQueryLogTable is set to true so that the query log table can be created by Analysis Services.

8. By default, the server logs a query for every 10 queries executed. You can change Log\ QueryLog\QueryLogSampling. Change it to 1 to log every query into the query log table.

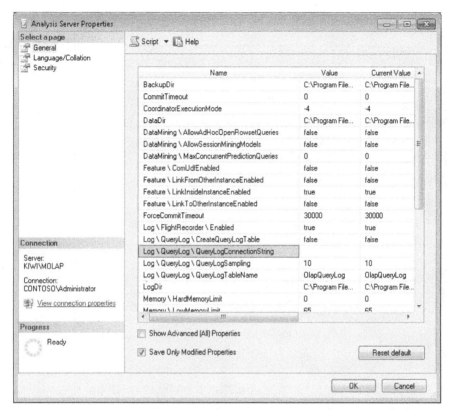

FIGURE 10-29

9. Click OK to save the server properties.

10. Restart Analysis Services so that the new properties are set for Analysis Services and the query log table can be created on the relational database.

11. Connect to SQL Server and open Adventure Works DW; an OLAPQueryLog table has been created. The table definition is shown here:

```
CREATE TABLE [dbo].[OlapQueryLog](
     [MSOLAP_Database] [nvarchar](255) NULL,
     [MSOLAP_ObjectPath] [nvarchar](4000) NULL,
     [MSOLAP_User] [nvarchar](255) NULL,
     [Dataset] [nvarchar](4000) NULL,
     [StartTime] [datetime] NULL,
     [Duration] [bigint] NULL
)
```

12. In SQL Server Management Studio, connect to your Analysis Services instance.

13. Right-click the Adventure Works cube and select Browse. Drag and drop measures into the data grid and drag and drop several dimensions. Perform some drill up and drill down to log some MDX queries into the query log.

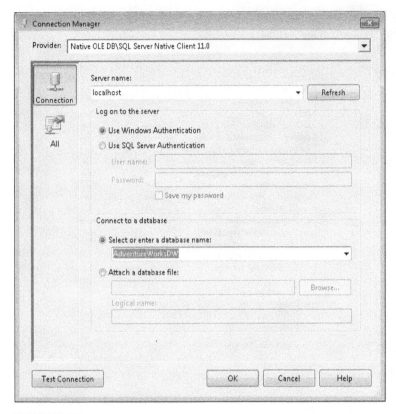

FIGURE 10-30

14. Open a relational query window in SQL Server Management Studio and send the following query:

```
SELECT [MSOLAP_Database]
    , [MSOLAP_ObjectPath]
    , [MSOLAP_User]
    , [Dataset]
    , [StartTime]
    , [Duration]
FROM [Adventure Works DW].[dbo].[OlapQueryLog]
```

Many records are logged in the OLAPQueryLog table. Analysis Services logs the username, timestamp, database name, cube name (object path), duration and the subcubes that are hit during the MDX query. The subcube definition is a sequence of 0s and 1s, which indicate which hierarchies are involved in the query.

15. In the Object Browser, right-click the Internet_Sales_2005 partition, and choose Usage Based Optimization, as shown in Figure 10-31.

16. You see the Usage-Based Optimization Wizard. Click Next in the welcome screen. Choose Internet_Sales_2005 to modify aggregation settings, as shown in Figure 10-32, and click Next.

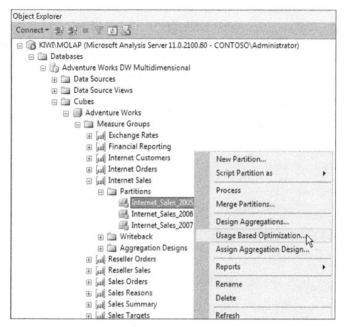

FIGURE 10-31

FIGURE 10-32

17. In the Specify Query Criteria dialog, you can select the queries based on time, users, or frequency and request those queries to be used for aggregation design, as shown in Figure 10-33. In addition to that, this dialog also provides statistics of the queries that have been logged. You can specify a beginning and ending date to get specific queries running in a certain time period, or choose specific queries for a particular user or users, or the user can choose the most frequent percentage of queries. Select all the queries logged so far to design aggregations. Do not make any selection in the Specify Query Criteria dialog, and click Next.

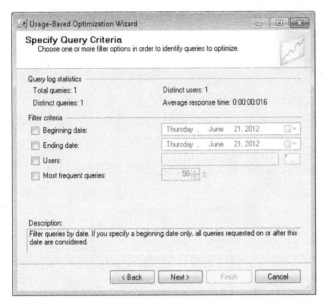

FIGURE 10-33

18. In the query list window (see Figure 10-34), Analysis Services provides information for all the queries requested by the users. Select all the queries, and click Next.

19. You now see the Review Aggregation Usage dialog that you saw during aggregation design. Click Next.

20. In the Specify Object Counts dialog, you do not need to update object counts because you did this during aggregation design. Click Next to proceed to the Aggregations Options page.

21. In the set design aggregation options, choose 30 percent performance gain, and click Start to request aggregations be designed based on the queries selected. At this moment, Analysis Services explores the various aggregations that would benefit from improving the performance gain for the selected queries. If a specific aggregation would benefit a specific query, that aggregation is allocated more weight so that that aggregation can be chosen from all possible aggregations. Analysis Services does a breadth-first search to explore the search space. Hence, if you have a cube that has a large dimensionality, sometimes you might explore aggregations at a low level (closer to the key) due to the queries and performance optimization that you have chosen. Look at the aggregations getting created in the script, and if you are interested in a specific aggregation being created, you can specify a higher performance gain (>30%) that forces Analysis Services to expand the search space to deeper levels. Typically, while designing aggregations are based on query usage using the UBO, specify 70–80 percent performance gain. Click Next after the aggregations have been designed.

FIGURE 10-34

22. In the Completing the Wizard dialog, you can either create a new aggregation design or merge the created aggregations within existing aggregation designs. Select the option to create a new aggregation design, and select the Process Partitions Immediately check box, as shown in Figure 10-35; click Finish. The new aggregations will be created and applied to the Internet_Sales_2005 partition.

FIGURE 10-35

If you have existing aggregations at the start of design usage-based aggregation, Analysis Services doesn't take that existing aggregation design into consideration. You can design custom aggregations using the Aggregation Design tab to visualize, create, and manage aggregation designs. This user interface is explained later in this chapter in the "Managing Aggregation Designs" section. Alternatively, you can design your own aggregations using a custom AMO program.

Aggregation Design Options

So far you have learned to design aggregations using the Aggregation Design Wizard and the Usage-Based Optimization Wizard. In both wizards you have seen that some of the dimension attributes are considered by Analysis Services for aggregations and some are not. The Aggregation Design Wizard considers certain attributes when designing aggregations based on the design of the attributes (as part of natural hierarchies), as well as the properties of the dimensions and cube dimensions. In addition to that, the user can give hints to tell the aggregation designer to consider, include, or exclude hierarchies while designing aggregations.

Designing Efficient Aggregations Using Hints

The aggregation design algorithm uses the partition fact data count and dimension-level member count to estimate the cost of aggregation design. Having an accurate fact data count and dimension-level member count is crucial for Analysis Services to find the aggregation designs that would yield the best performance. The fact table row count and level member count are metrics counted once at design time, stored in the Analysis Services meta data, and never changed afterward. Therefore, the user must update the member counts and fact table counts for changing dimensions and increasing rows in fact tables. You can click the Count button in the Specify Object Counts window to get the newest counts for various objects.

Typically, partitions contain only a specific slice of the fact data. The member count for dimension attributes and the partition are by default the same. In the Aggregation Design Wizard it is a good practice for you to provide Analysis Services with the hint of accurate member count in the Partition Count column. In the Adventure Works DW sample, partitions contain data for each year, so enter a value of 1 in the Fiscal Year column, as shown in Figure 10-36. This helps Analysis Services use the value 1 instead of 4 (which is the total number of years that contain partition data) to calculate the cost of the aggregation while including the Fiscal Year attribute. The member count for other dimension attributes, such as Fiscal Week of Year, Fiscal Quarter of Year, and Fiscal Semester of Year, should also be adjusted to correctly calculate the cost of the aggregation for those dimension attributes.

Relationships between Attributes

All the attributes within a dimension are related to the key attribute because there is a one-to-many relationship. When you establish a relationship between two attributes within a dimension, you can specify the type of relationship between these attributes. Two types of relationships are allowed in Analysis Services 2012, Rigid and Flexible, and they refer to the dimension attribute relationship changeability. Rigid relationships mean that there will be no change in the data value for this relationship. For example, if you have the relationship between City and State set to be rigid, it indicates that a specific city always belongs to only one state, and the initial value never changes over time.

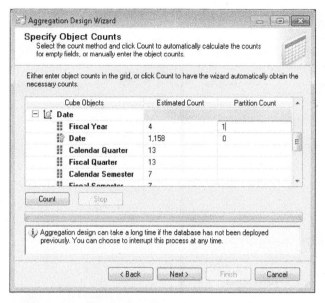

FIGURE 10-36

Flexible relationships, however, mean that the values of the relationship can change over time. By default, all the relationships between the attributes and the key attributes of the dimension are flexible. The relationship type determines how Analysis Services treats partition aggregation data when you choose to perform an incremental process of the dimension. Assume a relationship between two attributes has been specified as rigid and the value changes for the attribute nonetheless. When an incremental process of the dimension is initiated, Analysis Services presents an error that the data has changed for an attribute whose relationship has been specified as rigid.

You can set the relationship type between attributes in SSDT by doing the following:

1. Open the sample Adventure Works DW Analysis Services project.

2. Open the Customer dimension by double-clicking that dimension in Solution Explorer.

3. In the Attribute Relationships pane, click one of the relationships to the key attribute Customer such as Phone.

4. Look at the Properties window for the Customer-Phone relationship, and you see a Relationship Type property, as shown in Figure 10-37, which has the values Flexible and Rigid.

5. Click the relationship between the Country attribute and the State-Province attribute, as shown in Figure 10-38. In the Properties window you can find that its relationship type is set as Rigid because a state's country won't change over time. On the other hand, click the customer address relationship, and you see it is set to Flexible because a customer's address can change over time.

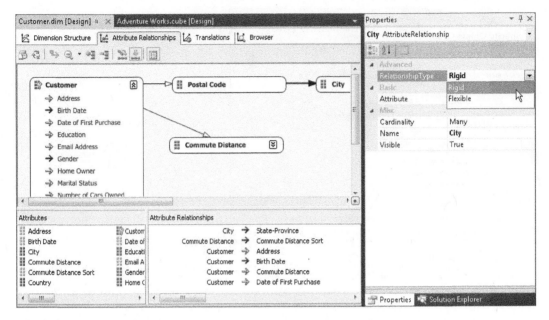

FIGURE 10-37

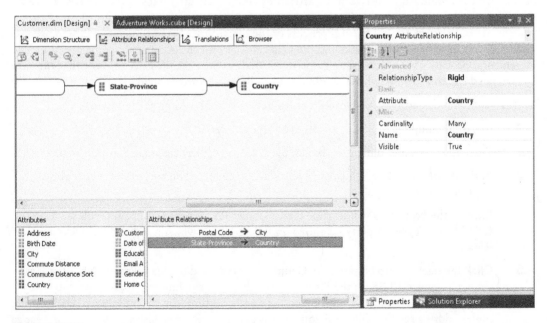

FIGURE 10-38

The aggregation design algorithm bases the aggregation designed on the type of relationships between the attributes it uses, enabling you to classify aggregations as rigid or flexible.

Rigid aggregations are aggregations that include attributes that have a rigid relationship with the granularity attribute. The aggregation created in the previous section that included Customer. Country, and all other dimensions where the other dimensions included the top level, is an example of rigid aggregation. Flexible aggregations are aggregations built on one or more attributes with a flexible relationship with the granularity attribute. An example of a flexible aggregation is an aggregation that uses the Customer.Address attribute.

Rigid aggregations are updated when partitions are incrementally processed. If attributes that are part of rigid aggregations are incrementally processed, existing aggregations are not dropped. Analysis Services keeps the old aggregation data as such and creates a temporary aggregation store for the newly coming data. Finally, Analysis Services merges the temporary aggregation store with the old aggregation data within a transaction. Old aggregation can still be available for query access when aggregations are processed. The aggregated data gets rebuilt only when the user chooses to do ProcessFull on the partition or cube.

Flexible aggregations are fully rebuilt whenever a cube and partition is incrementally processed. When attributes that are part of a flexible aggregation are incrementally processed, Analysis Services drops all the flexible aggregations because the old aggregation data is not valid anymore due to dimension member changes. After dropping the flexible aggregations, Analysis Services recalculates those dropped aggregations. If you choose the option to create aggregations lazily (ProcessingMode property of a dimension), flexible aggregations are recalculated as a background task. Users can still query without aggregations; however, you might see that the queries are slow. When the aggregations are rebuilt, future queries will be fast.

Properties Controlling Attributes and Aggregation Design

In addition to the dimension member count and partition member count, Analysis Services enables you to fine-tune the aggregation design via an AllMemberAggregationUsage property for cube dimensions and an AggregationUsage property for cube dimension attributes. Various values of these properties provide hints to the Aggregation Design Wizard to consider and include the attribute or dimension while designing aggregations. The following steps show you how to set the various values for these properties in SSDT:

1. Open the Adventure Works DW Analysis Services sample project.

2. Open the Adventure Works cube.

3. Click the cube dimension Customer in the Cube Designer. You can see the associated properties in the Properties pane, as shown in Figure 10-39.

4. You see the AllMemberAggregationUsage property, which enables you to either include or exclude the All member of the dimension while creating aggregations. Based on the value set for this property, the Aggregation Design Wizard considers this dimension while performing the design task. Following are four choices for the AllMemberAggregationUsage property:

   ➤ **Full:** Always include the All member while creating aggregations.

   ➤ **None:** Never include the All member while creating aggregations.

➤ **Unrestricted:** Let Analysis Services consider the dimension during aggregation design, and it can choose to build or not build aggregation for the All members of each dimension attribute.

➤ **Default:** Same as unrestricted.

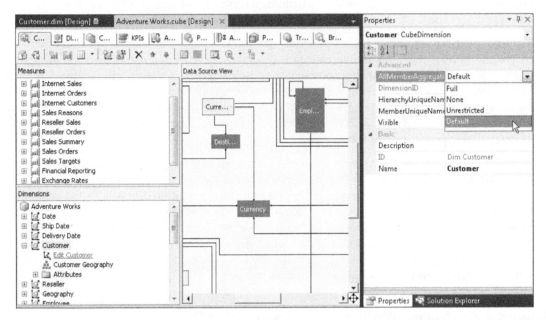

FIGURE 10-39

If most of your users query the All member of this dimension, change the AllMemberAggregationUsage property to Full. This ensures that aggregations include the All member and that your user queries hit and benefit from the aggregations. If most of your users query this dimension at the detail level, set it to None to avoid aggregation at the All level. The only time avoiding aggregation at the All level is a good idea is if you can guarantee that the All member will never be used. If you are not sure about the All member usage, then leave it to Default (which also means Unrestricted).

 Set AllMemberAggregationUsage property to Full or None if the user uses All aggregation or if the user uses detail.

5. Leave the setting for the customer dimension as Default, and expand the cube dimension Customer. Under the Attributes folder click the Country attribute, as shown in Figure 10-40.

6. Click any of the cube dimension attributes. If you look at the Properties window, you see the AggregationUsage property, as shown in Figure 10-40. Similar to AllMemberAggregationUsage, the AggregationUsage property also has four possible values. They are Full, None, Unrestricted, and Default. These properties once again instruct the aggregation design algorithm to appropriately include or exclude a dimension attribute while designing aggregations. The meanings of the values are as follows:

➤ **Full:** Always include this attribute in any of the aggregation designs considered while designing aggregations.

➤ **None:** Never include this attribute in any of the aggregation designs considered while designing aggregations.

➤ **Unrestricted:** Analysis Services might consider this attribute during aggregation design as any other attribute.

➤ **Default:** Same as unrestricted.

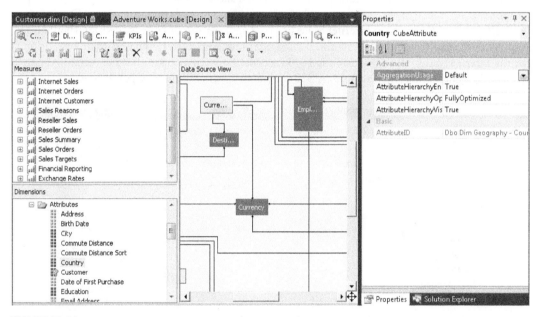

FIGURE 10-40

If most of your users query the data by customer country, you can change the country attribute's AggregationUsage to Full. You should set the value of AggregationUsage to Full only for attributes that have a small number of members and you know that all the queries used by the users do touch these members. However, if you know your users rarely break down numbers for one attribute, you can turn it off by setting the property to None. You need to analyze your user's MDX queries using SQL Server Profiler and then set the appropriate values for these properties for various dimensions and attributes. If you have made an incorrect setting to the aggregation usage property and see that some queries for which you wanted aggregations to be created are not getting created, you need to review and update the properties and then run aggregation design or usage-based optimizations.

Yes, query performance can be improved by designing aggregations and fine-tuning. However, your users might be generating MDX queries that are not optimal. In the next chapter you will see a few ways to optimize MDX queries.

MANAGING AGGREGATION DESIGNS

The development environment in Analysis Services has a tab in the cube editor called Aggregations. This viewer/editor enables you to better understand the aggregation designs in your cube and helps you to modify and apply them to partitions in a powerful way.

Look at an example with a sample Adventure Works DW Analysis Services project. In Figure 10-41, you can see the Aggregations design tab, which shows a list of all the measure groups and a high-level summary of the aggregation designs that apply to each measure group. For example, you can see that the partition Internet Sales has two aggregation designs (called Internet Sales and AggregationDesign), which have 54 and 28 aggregations, respectively. The estimated partition size for the Internet_Sales_2005 partition is 1013 records. You can also see that the estimated partition size for the aggregation Internet Sales is 32265, which covers all the four partitions.

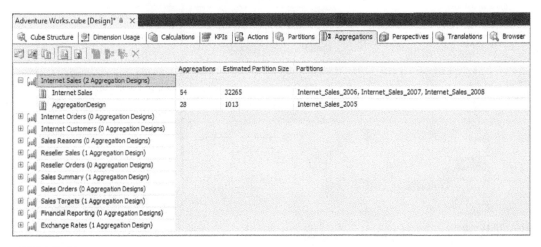

FIGURE 10-41

The other partitions shown under the AggregationDesign section have other aggregation designs assigned to them. Old aggregation designs can now be deleted in this viewer, or they can be revived by easily assigning aggregation designs to partitions via the Assign Aggregation Design button.

There are also convenient toolbar options for designing new aggregations using the Aggregation Design Wizard and the Usage-Based Aggregation Design Wizard.

One of the great features of this tab is visible when you switch to the Advanced view. In this view, you can select a measure group and aggregation and examine exactly which attributes have granularity defined in each aggregation. Figure 10-42 shows what this looks like.

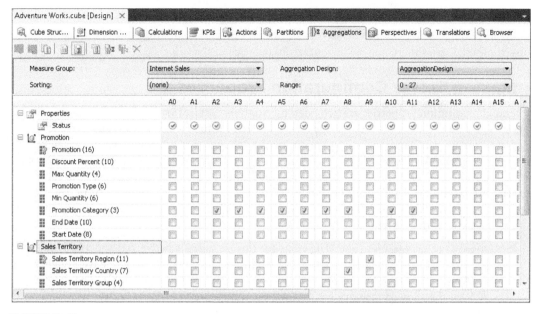

FIGURE 10-42

As you can see in the figure, each aggregation in the design shows up across the top (titled A0, A1, A2, and so on), and for each aggregation you can examine which dimension attributes have granularity by examining the check boxes in the grid. This view shows what your aggregation design looks like, and at the same time it enables you to modify it by checking and unchecking the intersection of attribute and aggregation.

This view also enables you to manually customize an aggregation design by adding and deleting aggregations. By right-clicking the Status for an aggregation, you can delete it or copy it to a new aggregation or just create an empty aggregation, which you can then customize as needed.

The aggregation design viewer/editor is a powerful tool. It provides a much greater understanding of the aggregations that have been designed and enables you to customize them based on your knowledge of long-term query patterns and your partitioning strategy.

SCALABILITY OPTIMIZATIONS

Scalability with Analysis Services indicates how well Analysis Services handles increases for dimension sizes, number of dimensions, size of the cube, number of databases, and number of concurrent users — all of which affect server behavior. Analysis Services provides several scalability-related values, such as handling a large number of partitions or a dimension with a large number of members (>5 million). In this section you learn about optimizations relevant specifically to scalability of Analysis Services.

For Analysis Services 2012 you can control the number of queries executed concurrently with the advanced configuration property ThreadPool\Query\MaxThreads. The default value 0 (server decides based on the machine configuration) works well for most scenarios, but on a machine with many processors, it may need to be increased, or for scenarios combining short-running queries with long-running queries there may be benefits from decreasing the value.

Configuring Server Configuration Properties

Several configuration properties are provided by Analysis Services with which to fine-tune the server. The default values for these properties have been set for the most common scenarios. However, for specific requirements you might need to change these settings to achieve the best performance from Analysis Services. In general, Microsoft recommends you change configuration settings only when working with Microsoft product support. Documentation of all the supported server configuration properties has been released by Microsoft; you can find it at Microsoft's TechNet at `http://technet.microsoft.com/en-us/library/ms174556.aspx`. Following is information on some of the configuration properties:

➤ `Memory\TotalMemoryLimit`: The value for this property is between 0 and 100 because it is a percentage of the available memory. On a 4GB memory machine if you have not enabled the `/3GB` switch, the `msmdsrv.exe` process has a maximum of 2GB available. The default value is 80% of the allowed memory for Analysis Services server.

➤ `Memory\LowMemoryLimit`: Analysis Services contains a cleaner thread, which reclaims memory from jobs that are idle or have lower priority. The cleaner thread constantly wakes up and reclaims memory based on the `LowMemoryLimit`. The default value is 65 percent. As soon as the low memory limit crosses the threshold value that the server considers important, the cleaner thread requests existing jobs to shrink memory and starts to reclaim the memory. In certain instances while processing multiple partitions in parallel, the cleaner thread might not be fast enough to wake up and reclaim memory. Due to this existing processing, jobs could fail. By lowering the `LowMemoryLimit`, you can make sure the cleaner thread starts to reclaim memory earlier and therefore all the processing jobs will complete.

➤ `CoordinatorExecutionMode`: This property is used for parallelism of jobs and takes a negative or positive value. The value indicates the number of coordinator jobs that can be in parallel at a given point in time. If the value is negative, the number is multiplied by the number of processors on the machine. Having a high value can deteriorate performance because multiple threads are competing for resources. The default value is –4.

➤ `ThreadPool\Query`: This node contains several properties such as the minimum and maximum number of threads to be allocated for a query and the priority for these threads. The `MinThreads` property indicates the minimum number of threads that stay available for query execution, and the `MaxThreads` property indicates the maximum number of threads that may be available to execute queries. This thread pool sometimes also executes other tasks that may be long running (for example, proactive caching), and you may need to increase this limit for a greater concurrency of queries.

➤ `ThreadPool\Process`: Similar to `ThreadPool\Query`, this node contains the same subproperties. However, the properties are applicable for each processing operation.

➤ `ThreadPool\IOProcess`: These properties are new to Analysis Services 2012 and are related to scanning of storage engine data.

➤ Query\DefaultDrillthroughMaxRows: While performing drill-through on a specific cell, the number of resulting rows can be large. This impacts the performance of drill-through. Most often users might look for the top 100 rows. While defining drill-through you can specify the number of rows to be returned. However, if that option is not specified in the drill-through statement, the value specified for this property is used to restrict the number of rows returned.

Scaling Out

If your cube contains a large number of partitions (thousands of partitions), queries retrieving data from all the partitions might be slow. This is because Analysis Services needs to read the data from all the partitions and then needs to aggregate the data. For efficient data reads you need to have high-speed disks optimized for reads. The aggregation of the data from various partitions is a CPU-intensive operation; you can certainly increase the number of processors on the machine to reduce latency. Another alternative provided by Analysis Services is to make the partitions remote so that multiple Analysis Services are involved in reading data from various partitions. This scale-out solution helps in distributing the read and data aggregation on multiple Analysis Services and thereby reduces the overall query time. You do have the master Analysis Services, which still needs to gather the data from various slave machines and then aggregate the final data to the end user. We recommend you perform cost benefit analysis in which you calculate the total costs of all the Analysis Services machines and the benefit you would be getting from it — all before implementing a solution using remote partitions.

One of the features in Analysis Services 2012 is the ability to attach and detach a read-only database. This lets you have several servers that share a common storage attached network (SAN). The SAN hosts a read-only database that is attached to all the servers. A standard Windows Network Load Balancing (NLB) solution then enables you to scale out active users over the different servers. The advantage of this solution is that the data is maintained just once on the SAN, and a good SAN provides good I/O performance that justifies having multiple servers sharing it as a resource. However, when the read-only database needs to be updated, the servers must be drained of their users before the database is detached, refreshed, and then attached again by the servers. You learn more about the read-only database and scale-out strategy in terms of improving query performance in Chapter 11.

This type of solution can also be applied without using the Read-Only feature. However, it would require the databases to be distributed and managed manually.

Scaling Up

For large databases where the queries are data-intensive or the load on the system is heavy with several users, you need to consider adding additional CPUs. Typically, commodity machines for servers are four processors. Based on your system load, consider increasing the number of processors. Your system might be bottlenecked by memory as well. Assuming you have a system with 4GB (maximum on a 32-bit machine), by default each process can access up to 2GB of memory. Change the boot.ini file to enable the /3GB option so that Analysis Services can utilize maximum memory on the system. If your database is large (dimensions having greater than 10 million members) and the user load on your system high, consider moving to a 64-bit system and adding additional processors and memory.

Handling Large Dimensions

Certain Analysis Services databases can contain large dimensions. Analysis Services 2012 handles loading large dimensions by loading parts of dimensions that are requested. Based on experience working with certain customers with large, MOLAP dimensions, the authors have identified that you might reach the 32-bit system limit if you have dimensions containing memory in the range of approximately 10 to 15 million members along with several hundred attributes in the dimensions. Typically, when you have customer or product dimensions along with various properties of the customer, you can encounter processing issues due to unavailability of system resources. You can certainly tweak certain server configuration properties to get the maximum from Analysis Services. However, move to 64-bit systems if you have dimensions with more than 10 million members. Another suggestion is to have large dimensions like ROLAP dimensions. Consider the alternatives mentioned in this section while handling large dimensions.

SUMMARY

After reading this chapter, on hearing the word *performance*, your head should swell with visions of highly performing, scalable systems, each optimized to fulfill its designated mission — never again will this word simply evoke images of entertainment provided by a theatrical group! To build a system that scales up and performs well, you must consider high- and low-level issues. At the high level, aggregation design forms the foundation for an optimally performing OLAP system; take the time to analyze the requirements of the application to get this step right. Another high-level consideration is the type of storage you choose for your system, be it MOLAP, HOLAP, or ROLAP. At lower levels there are many ways to optimize design, such as avoiding the use of unnecessary attributes that are never used in customer queries. They can waste precious system data storage and slow down both processing performance and query performance. You learned other lower-level issues, about natural and unnatural hierarchies, and about how you should specify one-to-many relationships whenever possible for better query performance and reduced system data space requirements. You even dove down deep into tuning the Analysis Services instance by changing certain server properties. Finally, you learned how aggregations can be created and how they help to achieve better query performance. You can now exploit all the best practices provided in this chapter and design your OLAP databases optimally based on your business needs. In the next chapter you learn how an MDX query executes within the Analysis Services and how to analyze bottlenecks and optimize your MDX queries to achieve better query performance.

11

Optimizing Query Performance

WHAT'S IN THIS CHAPTER?

➤ The calculation model

➤ Query execution architecture

➤ Performance analysis and tuning tools

➤ Analyzing and solving query performance issues

➤ Query optimization techniques

➤ Scale out with read-only databases

➤ Writeback query performance

The power of Analysis Services lies in its capability to provide fast query response time for decision makers who need to analyze data, draw conclusions, and make appropriate changes in their business. The OLAP Report defines OLAP as Fast Analysis of Shared Multidimensional Information (`www.olapreport.com/fasmi.htm`). The word "fast" in this context means that the system can deliver results to users in less than 5 seconds (with a few highly complex queries taking more than 20 seconds). You can also expect that most business decision makers use client tools that graphically represent the data from Analysis Services for easy interpretation and understanding. As an end user, you expect to see the data quickly to analyze and make decisions.

Queries sent to Analysis Services need to return data within seconds and query performance is pivotal to a successful Business Intelligence (BI) project deployment. A system that has good performance can bring great business value to your company. However, you should be aware there can be queries to Analysis Services that can take more than a few minutes. Typically, such queries are issued via overnight reporting systems.

HOW OLAP ENHANCES PERFORMANCE

Analysis Services supports three storage modes: MOLAP, ROLAP, and HOLAP. You can usually obtain the best performance when your multidimensional BISM storage mode is MOLAP. When you choose MOLAP storage, Analysis Services 2012 stores the dimension data and fact data in its own efficient, compact multidimensional structure format. Fact data is compressed and its size is approximately 10 to 30 percent of the size as when stored in a relational database. In addition to its own efficient and compact data store, Analysis Services builds specialized dimension attribute indices for efficient data retrieval. The data is stored specifically in a multidimensional structure to best serve MDX query needs. If you use the ROLAP or HOLAP storage modes, queries to Analysis Services might need to fetch data from the relational data source at query time. Retrieving data from the relational data sources can significantly slow your query performance because you incur relational query processing time, the time needed to fetch the data over the network, and finally the time it takes to aggregate the data within Analysis Services.

Queries to Analysis Services 2012 multidimensional BISM typically request aggregated data. For example, you may store daily sales information for products. Typical OLAP queries request aggregated sales by month, quarter, or year. In such circumstances, every day's sales data must be aggregated for the period requested by the query, for example the entire year. If users request aggregated data on a single dimension, you can to do a simple sum in the relational database. However, OLAP queries are typically multidimensional and need aggregated data across multiple dimensions with complex business logic calculations applied to each dimension. To improve query performance, Analysis Services enables you to specify aggregations, which you learned about in Chapter 10. In addition to aggregations, you learned several design techniques in that chapter to optimize your multidimensional BISM to get the best performance from your Analysis Services database. After creating your multidimensional BISM design to satisfy your business needs, you might still encounter performance issues at query time. In this chapter you learn about the various components of Analysis Services that work together to execute MDX queries. You also learn how to analyze Analysis Services query performance issues as well as techniques and best practices for improving query performance.

THE CALCULATION MODEL

Before looking at the overall Analysis Services query execution architecture, recap what you learned about the calculation model of Analysis Services in previous chapters of this book. When using the MOLAP storage mode, the data that comprises the cube is retrieved from a relational database and stored in SSAS's proprietary format. The data will be aggregated by the SSAS engine based on the MDX query. SSAS provides a way to precalculate aggregated data. This helps speed the retrieval of query results for MDX queries that can be satisfied with these precalculated aggregations. Most of the calculations that apply specific business logic in the multidimensional BISM are written in MDX Scripts, objects within your Analysis Services 2012 database that provide a procedural way to define calculations. SSAS features such as unary operators and custom rollups also help to define MDX calculations needed within your UDM. The cube editor in SQL Server Data Tools provides a way to debug the calculations defined in your MDX Scripts. However, there is complex calculation logic within the SSAS engine that defines how the calculations are applied to a specific cell. Each cell within the cube is either a value from your relational database or a calculation.

Figure 11-1 shows cells with sales corresponding to various months in the year and cities in the states of Washington and California. The members of the axes and the cell values calculated from the relational backend are shown in one color. You can see that some cells have a dash (–), indicating that no value was available for that specific cell from the relational backend. The remaining cells contain aggregated data and are shown in a darker color. For example, cells corresponding to Seattle and the months April, May, and June were all retrieved from the relational backend table. However, the cell value for the Q2 quarter and Seattle is aggregated from the sales for Seattle for the months of April, May, and June.

	All	WA	Seattle	Redmond	CA	Los Angeles	San Francisco	San Diego
All	1237	475	176	299	762	148	149	465
Q1	367	110	44	66	257	53	32	172
Jan	148	55	12	43	93	10	-	83
Feb	164	32	32	-	132	25	32	75
Mar	55	23	-	23	32	18	-	14
Q2	360	17	65	113	182	28	65	89
Apr	55	23	23	-	32	9	23	-
May	135	73	19	54	62	19	19	24
Jun	170	82	23	59	88	-	23	65
Q3	235	122	11	111	113	11	17	85
Jul	24	12	-	12	12	-	-	12
Aug	42	34	-	34	8	-	-	8
Sep	169	76	11	65	93	11	17	65
Q4	275	65	56	9	210	56	35	119
Oct	133	24	21	3	109	21	-	88
Nov	100	23	23	-	77	23	23	31
Dec	42	18	12	6	24	12	12	-

FIGURE 11-1

You can have several MDX calculations defined for a specific cell. The value for a cell that contains multiple MDX calculations is the value of the last calculation applied to the cell. In addition to MDX Scripts, calculations can also be defined for sessions or queries. Those concepts are discussed in previous chapters. The remainder of this section offers a quick review of calculations in Analysis Services before you look at the details of the MDX query execution architecture.

MDX Scripts

You can define calculations in multiple ways using Analysis Services 2012 by mostly using the MDX Script, which is a centralized calculation store for the cube. Dimension calculations such as unary operators and custom rollups are a part of the dimension, which you can define using attribute properties. You can define these calculations via an MDX Script, consider using the support for defining them via dimension attribute properties to achieve better performance. Each cube in Analysis

Services 2012 contains a single MDX Script. SQL Server Data Tools (SSDT) exposes the MDX Script object to editing and debugging via the Calculations tab, as shown in Figure 11-2. MDX Script provides a procedural execution model and easier debugging of calculations. The commands in the script are executed in the order they have been defined. In Chapter 3 you learned about the Pass Value (also called Pass Order), which refers to stages of calculations applied to the cube when there are multiple calculations such as custom rollup, unary operators, and assignment statements applied to the cells of a cube. In Analysis Services 2012, a new Pass Value is created for each MDX calculation defined in the MDX Script to avoid infinite recursion. The creation of a new Pass Value for each cell calculation also eliminates the need for Solve Order. (Solve Order can help to determine the order of calculations within a single Pass in SQL Server Analysis Services 2000, which has been deprecated since SSAS 2005.)

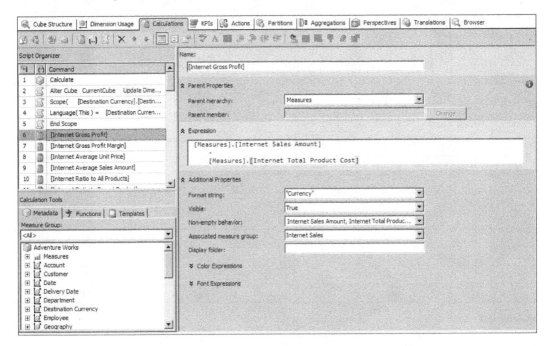

FIGURE 11-2

The single view of the calculations via the MDX Script simplifies the maintenance of your MDX calculations as well as debugging. As part of your multidimensional BISM development, you can use source code control and check in various versions of your Analysis Services project. This helps you track the history of changes to your project and also aids in maintenance. Because the calculations are part of the Analysis Services project, you automatically get version control of the calculation changes.

 You should periodically check in the changes made to your Analysis Services project similar to what you would do for a C# or a C++ project.

The first and foremost command in an MDX Script is the CALCULATE command. The CALCULATE command populates each cell in the cube along with aggregated data from the *fact-level data* (also called *leaf-level data*). Without the CALCULATE command, the cube contains only the fact level data. The syntax of the CALCULATE command is

```
CALCULATE   [<subcube>];
```

If the `<subcube>` argument is not specified, the current cube is used. The CALCULATE command is automatically added by the Cube Wizard when you create a cube in SQL Server Data Tools. SSDT typically adds the CALCULATE statement at the beginning of the MDX Script, resulting in the default aggregation behavior for the measures, which you see in previous versions of SQL Server Analysis Services. When Analysis Services evaluates the cells, it first loads the fact data into the cube's cell values. Then it does the default aggregation of the nonleaf cell values. Finally, the MDX calculations as defined by the Analysis Services rules are applied to determine the final values of the cells in the cube. The assignment calculations in the MDX Script are evaluated using the Pass Value, which gets incremented for each MDX Script assignment. The CALCULATE statement does not have any effect on calculated members defined in the MDX Script.

Scope and Assignments

Analysis Services 2012 supports multiple ways to define cell calculations. Each cell can have one or more calculations defined for it. Unary operators, custom rollups, and Assignments are three ways you can define cell calculations while designing a cube. In addition, you can define calculations as part of sessions (session calculations) or queries (query calculations). Unary operators and custom rollups are defined as part of dimension creation using the dimensions' attribute properties, and Assignments are statements that define cell calculations and are defined in the MDX Script.

Assignments are typically enclosed within a Scope statement, which helps define calculations on a subcube. Following is the syntax for the Scope and Assignment statement (=) that you learned about in Chapter 3. You can have one or more assignments within each Scope statement. In addition, you can have nested scopes. Scopes by default inherit the parent scope; however, you can override this. For example, you can have a parent scope of Customers.USA, which scopes to all customers in the country USA. You can have a nested scope of Customers.Canada, which overrides the parent and changes the scope to customers in Canada.

```
Scope(<subcube>);
    <subcube1 definition> = expression; [Example: this = 1000;]
    ...
End Scope;
```

Analysis Services restricts the cube space as defined by the Scope statement. Then the assignment statement is evaluated for all the cells within the specified subcube1 definition. The term this is a special keyword that denotes the assignment to be evaluated on the default measure of the subcube defined within the Scope statement. You can have multiple assignment statements that overwrite a specific cell within the same Scope statement.

Dimension Attribute Calculations

You learned about the Custom Rollup and Unary Operators features in Analysis Services 2012 in Chapter 8. These features help define how to aggregate data to parent members or other members in the hierarchy. Analysis Services uses special rules while aggregating data when performing cell calculations in MDX Scripts. In general, you can assume that the last cell calculation is the one that is the final cell value. This behavior is referred to as Latest Wins. In addition, instances exist in which a calculation called as the closest calculation for the cell aggregated is the final value; this is called Closest Wins. Richard Tkachuk, program manager from Microsoft, has written a whitepaper ("Introduction to MDX Scripting in Microsoft SQL Server 2005") that demonstrates examples of Latest Wins and Closest Wins (http://msdn.microsoft.com/en-US/library/ms345116(v=SQL.90).aspx).

Session and Query Calculations

Analysis Services enables you to specify cell calculations in session, query, or global scopes. Following are examples that show how a cell calculation is defined at query, session, or global scopes, respectively:

```
WITH CELL CALCULATION [SalesQuota2007]
FOR '( [Date].[Fiscal Year].&[2007],
     [Date].[Fiscal].[Month].MEMBERS,
     [Measures].[Sales Amount Quota] )'
AS '( PARALLELPERIOD( [Date].[Fiscal].[Fiscal Year], 1,
     [Date].[Fiscal].CurrentMember), [Measures].[Sales Amount] ) * 2'
SELECT { [Measures].[Sales Amount Quota],
     [Measures].[Sales Amount] } ON COLUMNS,
DESCENDANTS( { [Date].[Fiscal].[Fiscal Year].&[2006],
     [Date].[Fiscal].[Fiscal Year].&[2007] }, 3, SELF ) ON ROWS
FROM [Adventure Works]

CREATE CELL CALCULATION [Adventure Works].[SalesQuota2007]
FOR '([Date].[Fiscal].[Month].MEMBERS,[Measures].[Sales Amount Quota]
     )'
AS '(PARALLELPERIOD ( [Date].[Fiscal].[Fiscal Year],
1,[Date].[Fiscal].CurrentMember),[Measures].[Sales Amount])*2',
CONDITION = '[Date].[Fiscal Year].CurrentMember IS
[Date].[Fiscal Year].&[2007]'

SCOPE([Date].[Fiscal Year].&[2007],
     [Date].[Fiscal].[Month].MEMBERS,
     [Measures].[Sales Amount Quota]);

     THIS = (ParallelPeriod( [Date].[Fiscal].[Fiscal Year],
          1,[Date].[Fiscal].CurrentMember),[Measures].[Sales Amount])*2;

END SCOPE;
```

Having calculations at appropriate scopes is based on the requirements of your cube and the client tools used to interact with the cube. Analysis Services 2012 has specific optimizations that cache the results of calculations at each scope. When a query is evaluated, Analysis Services 2012 first tries to retrieve the results from the query scope. If this is not possible, it looks at the session scope and finally at the global scope. This is a specific optimization implemented in Analysis Services to help improve query performance; however, some calculations may not be cached (such as calculations that include locale-related information).

Having reviewed the calculation model of Analysis Services, now look at the architecture and the steps involved when executing an MDX query.

QUERY EXECUTION ARCHITECTURE

Microsoft SQL Server Analysis Services 2012 consists of server and tools components that enable you to create databases and manage them. The server components are a set of binaries that comprise the Analysis Services service. SSDT, SQL Server Management Studio (SSMS), Profiler, and a few additional binaries constitute the tools components. The multidimensional databases are stored on the server, which is also referred to as the SSAS engine. SSAS clients communicate to the SSAS engine via XML for Analysis (XMLA), a standardized application programming interface for online analytical processing (OLAP). The XMLA API has two main methods, Discover and Execute. Discover enables callers to request meta data and data from the databases. Execute enables callers to send commands such as Create, Alter, and Process, which create and update the multidimensional database or MDX queries. MDX query results can be retrieved in multidimensional or tabular format by the client. The Create, Alter, Delete, and Process statements are part of the Data Definition Language (DDL). SSAS provides a set of object models that abstract XMLA and make it easy for developers to build applications that can communicate with the SSAS engine.

Analysis Services Engine Components

Figure 11-3 shows the Analysis Services query execution architecture. Five major components constitute the Analysis Services server: Infrastructure, Metadata Manager, Data Mining, Storage Engine, and Formula Engine, which are detailed in the following list.

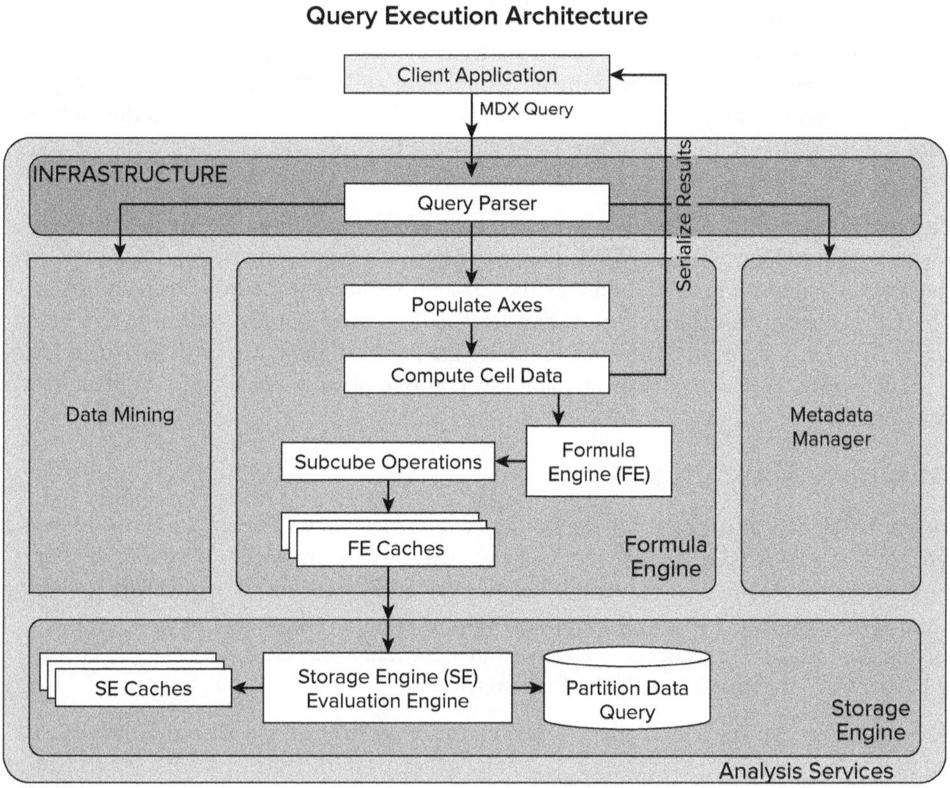

FIGURE 11-3

➤ **Infrastructure:** Handles operations such as accepting requests from clients, distributing the requests to the appropriate components, scheduling the jobs, and memory management. Parsing and validating the XMLA requests are also part of this component, as well as providing the support for retrieving data from external data sources. Consider this component as being the main interface for the client and also providing appropriate infrastructure to support the operation of the remaining components.

➤ **Metadata Manager:** Handles the DDL statements that operate on the multidimensional database objects. DDL statements such as Create, Alter, Delete, and Process are directed from the infrastructure component to the Metadata Manager. This component also implements the transaction handling for all Analysis Services objects. When processing statements are issued, it coordinates with the storage engine or data mining component and the infrastructure to retrieve data from the relational data sources and store them in an optimized storage format within Analysis Services.

➤ **Data Mining:** (You learn about data mining in Chapter 12.) Serves all Data Mining requests and coordinates with the infrastructure and Metadata Manager at the time of processing data mining models. If there are OLAP mining models, the data mining component sends queries to the storage engine and formula engine components to retrieve appropriate data from the cube. This component handles Discover and DMX queries sent to the data mining models.

➤ **Storage Engine:** One of the core components of an OLAP database, which populates the multidimensional database with data from relational databases and optimally stores them on disk. It also optimizes the storage for dimension and cube data and builds relevant indices to aid in fast and efficient retrieval of the data from the disk. Typically, you see approximately a 10:1 compression ratio between the relational data and the OLAP data. The storage engine component provides internal interfaces to the formula engine component so that subcubes of data can be retrieved; these can then be used by the formula engine for efficient retrieval and aggregation of the data to satisfy MDX query requests.

➤ **Formula Engine:** The MDX Query Processor, also referred to as Formula Engine, determines the execution strategy for each MDX query. The Formula Engine can be considered the most important component for MDX queries and calculations because the query evaluation and computation is done by this component. It translates each query into a sequence of requests to the Storage Engine to access the data and computes the results of the query based on any calculations defined in the multidimensional database. It also implements caching for optimal query performance.

Stages of Query Execution

A query is sent from a client to the Analysis Services engine, as shown in Figure 11-3. The Analysis Services engine first parses the client request and routes it to the Data Mining Engine, the Formula Engine, or the Metadata Manager. Figure 11-3 shows the query execution architecture for serving Discover and MDX queries. Query evaluation has several key steps: parsing the query, populating and serializing the axes, computing the cell data, and serializing the results back to the client. The following list provides more detail of each of the steps:

➤ **Parsing the query:** The MDX query is first analyzed by the query parser and then passed on to the Formula Engine. If there is a syntactical error in the query, the parser returns an appropriate error message to the client.

➤ **Populating the axes:** The Formula Engine evaluates the members of the axes of the MDX query. After this has been done, the details of the axes are populated.

➤ **Serializing the axes:** After the axes are evaluated and populated, Analysis Services sends details of the cube being queried back to the client, including the hierarchies and levels of the cube dimensions. Then the axes information, which includes the tuples and members that form the axes, are serialized. Some dimension properties of the members such as caption, unique name, and level name are sent to the client by default. If additional properties are requested in the MDX query, they will be included as well.

➤ **Evaluating the cell data:** After the axes data has been populated, the Analysis Services engine understands which cell coordinates need to be evaluated. The Formula Engine (FE) first tries to retrieve the results from the FE cache. If the query cannot be retrieved from the FE cache, appropriate internal queries are sent to the Storage Engine (SE). The SE has its own cache. The SE determines if the query can be satisfied from the SE cache. If the query results are not available in the SE cache, results are retrieved from partition data on the disk, stored in the SE cache, and sent to the FE. The FE then performs the calculations needed to satisfy the query and is then ready to send the results back to the client.

➤ **Serializing the cells:** After the results are available, they are sent back to the client. The results are sent in the XMLA format.

Query Evaluation Modes

Now that you understand the various stages of MDX query evaluation, look at the two query evaluation modes in Analysis Services 2012: cell-by-cell mode and subspace computation.

Cell-by-Cell Mode

When an MDX query has been parsed, it is evaluated to see if the query can use the subspace computation mode. (The factors that determine whether the query can use the subspace computation mode are addressed in the next section.) If the query cannot be evaluated in the subspace computation mode, it is evaluated in the cell-by-cell mode.

Query evaluation can include several thousand or even millions of cells, and thus evaluating every cell, which happens in the cell-by-cell mode, is typically slower than the subspace computation mode. The following example, an MDX query against the sample Adventure Works DW can help you see how cell-by-cell mode works:

```
WITH MEMBER Measures.ContributionToParent AS
([Measures].[Internet Sales Amount]/
            ([Measures].[Internet Sales Amount],
             [Customer].[Customer Geography].CurrentMember.Parent)),
FORMAT_STRING="Percent"
SELECT {[Product].[Product Categories].[Category].MEMBERS} ON 1,
[Customer].[Customer Geography].[Country].MEMBERS ON 0
FROM [Adventure Works]
WHERE (Measures.ContributionToParent)
```

The preceding MDX query contains a calculated member that calculates the contribution of `[Internet Sales Amount]` from each country for each product. If you execute this query in the SSMS MDX query editor, you see the results, as shown in Figure 11-4.

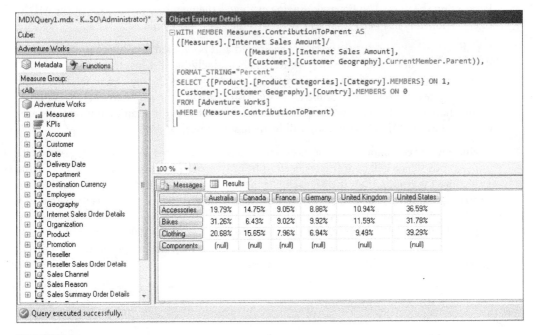

FIGURE 11-4

You can see six countries and four products in the results. If you aggregate the percentage for each product across all countries you get 100 percent. After the axes information is populated, Analysis Services needs to calculate the values for 24 cells. The cell-by-cell mode in Analysis Services would use the following steps to resolve the query:

1. Evaluate the measure [Internet Sales Amount] for a cell.

2. Evaluate the [Internet Sales Amount] for the member [Customer].[Customer Geography].[All Customers] for that cell.

3. Evaluate the measure ContributionToParent, which is the calculated member in the MDX query for that cell.

4. Repeat steps 1, 2, and 3 for each cell including cells that have null values.

Figure 11-5 shows the results of steps 1 and 2 for all the cells.

In this example you can see that the evaluation of step 2 needs to be done only once. In addition, the cells for which [Internet Sales Amount] is null don't need to be calculated because the calculated measure ContributionToParent for null values will be null. When millions of cells exist, evaluation of every cell can take a considerable amount of time. The next evaluation mode, subspace computation, helps optimize query evaluation.

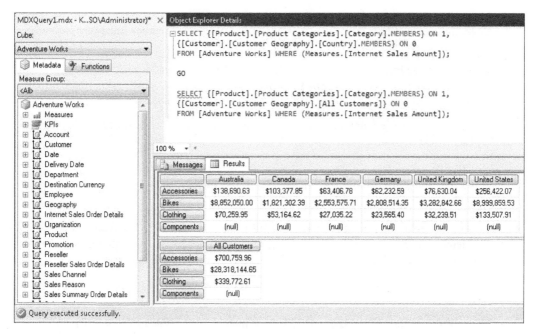

FIGURE 11-5

Subspace Computation

The Analysis Services cube space is typically sparse. This means that only some of the cells in the dimensional space have values. The remaining cell values are null. The goal of the subspace computation query evaluation mode is to evaluate MDX expressions only when they need to be evaluated. For example, if a cell value is null, an MDX expression using that value results in a null value and therefore doesn't need to be evaluated. Subspace computation can reduce cell evaluation time by orders of magnitude, depending on the sparseness of the cube. Some queries that run in minutes using cell-by-cell mode are evaluated within seconds using subspace computation mode. Subspace computation was first introduced in Analysis Services 2005 Service Pack 2 for a limited number of scenarios and extended in each subsequent major product release. In Analysis Services 2012, subspace computation mode has been enhanced to cover a wider scope of MDX evaluations and automatic query optimizations.

The subspace computation mode can be taken by Analysis Services only under specific conditions. Some of the important conditions where Analysis Services will use the subspace computation mode are given here:

➤ Basic operations that involve arithmetic operators (*, /,+, −), and relational operators (<, >, <=, >=, =).

➤ Static references to members and tuples as well as constant scalars such as NULL.

➤ Scalar operations using functions IS, MemberValue, Properties, Name, IIF, IsNonEmpty, Case, IsLeaf, IsSiblings, CalculationPassValue, and member functions such as PrevMember, NextMember, Lag, Lead, FirstChild, LastChild, Ancestor, and so on.

➤ Basic Aggregate functions such as Sum, Min, Max, and Aggregate on static sets; as well as sets built using functions PeriodsToDate, YTD, QTD, MTD, Crossjoin, Cousin, Descendants, Children, Hierarchize, and Members.

➤ The CurrentMember function (only on the Measures dimension) and basic unary operators and semi-additive measures.

Some examples where subspace computation mode will not be chosen include named sets when used with Aggregate functions, dynamic operations (for example: [Date].[Fiscal].Lag([Measures] .[Count])), and when encountering recursion.

For example, consider the simple MDX query from the previous section. The MDX query is first analyzed to determine if it can be evaluated using the subspace computation mode. Because the answer is yes, Analysis Services uses the following steps to evaluate the query:

1. Retrieve non-null values of the [Internet Sales Amount] measure for the query results space.

2. Retrieve the [Internet Sales Amount] for member [Customer].[Customer Geography].[All Customers] once.

3. Evaluate the ContributionToParent measure for the non-null values retrieved.

Figure 11-6 provides a graphical illustration comparing the cell-by-cell and subspace computation modes. Assume the machine in the diagram is the Analysis Services engine. The figure on the left shows the cell-by-cell mode, where all the cells are evaluated. The figure on the right shows that the cells that have non-null values (highlighted by darker color) are first identified via storage engine requests and then evaluation is done only for those cells. When Analysis Services serializes the results back to the client, it includes only the cell values that contain data. The remaining cell values are assumed to be null. Figure 11-7 shows this with an MDX query. This MDX query should return 24 cells with cell ordinals 0 to 23. However, this returns only 18 cell values because the cell values corresponding to the product member Components ([Product].[Product Categories] .[Category].&[2]) are null. The client object models provided by Analysis Services 2012 interpret the results returned from the Analysis Services engine and populate the missing cells with null values for the client accessing the data.

Analysis Services has two NON EMPTY code paths that would eliminate null cell values: Naïve NON EMPTY and Express NON EMPTY. The Naïve NON EMPTY code path was used in the cell-by-cell mode, and the Express NON EMPTY path was used to identify the tuples that contained data. However, in Analysis Services 2005 and subsequent releases, Express NON EMPTY was restricted to measures that did not have calculations or where NON_EMPTY_BEHAVIOR (discussed in the "Query Optimization Techniques" section later in this chapter) was specified. Analysis Services 2012 Express NON EMPTY has been enhanced to support measures with calculations (except for recursive or complex overlapping calculations). Now that you've learned more about the Analysis Services query execution architecture and query evaluation modes, look into analyzing performance bottlenecks and fine-tuning them.

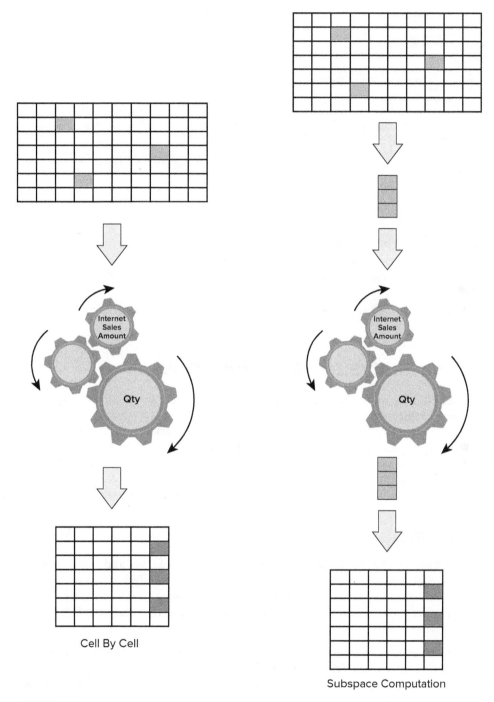

Cell By Cell

Subspace Computation

FIGURE 11-6

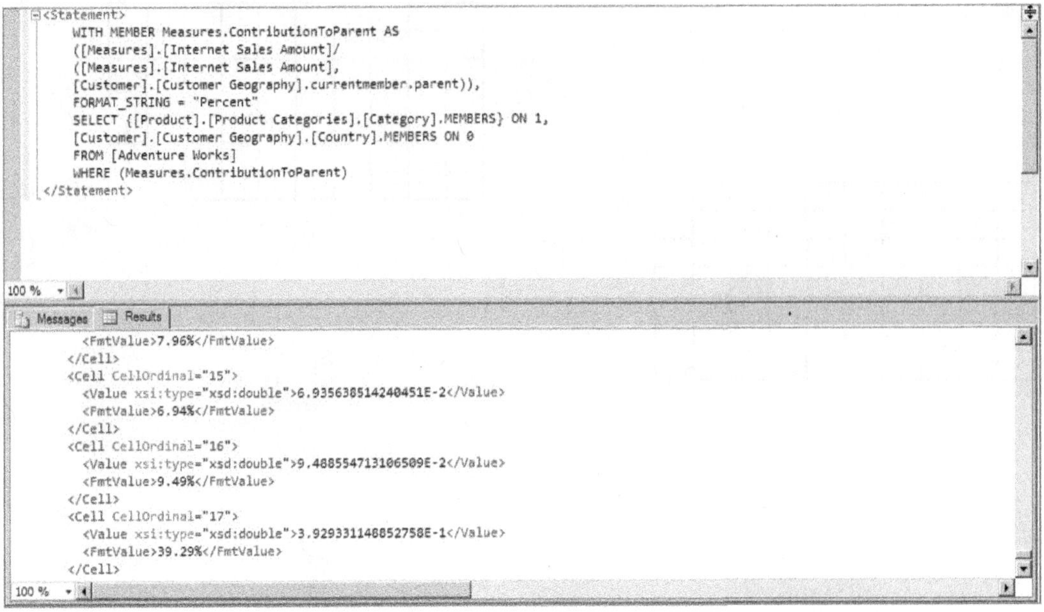

```
<Statement>
    WITH MEMBER Measures.ContributionToParent AS
    ([Measures].[Internet Sales Amount]/
    ([Measures].[Internet Sales Amount],
    [Customer].[Customer Geography].currentmember.parent)),
    FORMAT_STRING = "Percent"
    SELECT {[Product].[Product Categories].[Category].MEMBERS} ON 1,
    [Customer].[Customer Geography].[Country].MEMBERS ON 0
    FROM [Adventure Works]
    WHERE (Measures.ContributionToParent)
</Statement>
```

100 %

Messages   Results

```
        <FmtValue>7.96%</FmtValue>
    </Cell>
    <Cell CellOrdinal="15">
        <Value xsi:type="xsd:double">6.935630514240451E-2</Value>
        <FmtValue>6.94%</FmtValue>
    </Cell>
    <Cell CellOrdinal="16">
        <Value xsi:type="xsd:double">9.488554713106509E-2</Value>
        <FmtValue>9.49%</FmtValue>
    </Cell>
    <Cell CellOrdinal="17">
        <Value xsi:type="xsd:double">3.929331148852758E-1</Value>
        <FmtValue>39.29%</FmtValue>
    </Cell>
```

100 %

FIGURE 11-7

PERFORMANCE ANALYSIS AND TUNING TOOLS

Analysis Services 2012 includes significant enhancements targeted at getting the best query performance. Improvements include tools to help in designing cubes, subspace computation optimization, caching enhancements, and improved writeback query performance. (You learn about this in the "Writeback Query Performance" section later in this chapter.) You might still have queries that are not performing as expected, however, due to cube design or the way MDX has been written. To analyze and improve your query performance, you can use tools to help you analyze the performance of your queries and then tune them to get the best performance from Analysis Services 2012.

SQL Server Profiler

SQL Server Profiler is a tool that can trace operations on the SQL Server and Analysis Services database engines. SQL Server Profiler is the primary performance analysis tool used to debug performance bottlenecks in SQL Server (including Analysis Services). The capability to trace Analysis Services operations through SQL Server Profiler was first introduced in SQL Server 2005.

Analysis Services exposes the commands sent to it as well as internal operations that occur within the server through *events*. Some examples of these events are Command Begin, Command End, Query Begin, and Query End. Each event has properties associated with it such as start time, end time, and the user sending the query. These properties appear as columns in the tool. SQL Server Profiler requests these events and their properties through trace commands to the server. Analysis Services periodically sends the events to the clients who have subscribed to a trace. SQL Server Profiler shows the events and event column values in a grid. Only Analysis Services administrators can trace Analysis Services events. To learn how to use the Profiler, follow these steps:

1. Make sure you are an administrator on the Analysis Services server you want to profile. You can connect to Analysis Services through SSMS and use the Analysis Services Server Properties dialog to add users as administrators of Analysis Services.

2. From the Start menu, launch SQL Server Profiler: All Programs ⇨ Microsoft SQL Server 2012 ⇨ Performance Tools ⇨ SQL Server Profiler.

3. The SQL Server Profiler application appears. Create a new trace by selecting File ⇨ New Trace.

4. In the Connect to Server dialog, as shown in Figure 11-8, select Analysis Services as the Server Type, and enter the name of your Analysis Services instance. Click Connect.

FIGURE 11-8

5. In the Trace Properties dialog, enter the Trace Name, for example **FirstTrace**. SQL Server Profiler provides three trace templates with preselected events to trace. Select the Standard template, as shown in Figure 11-9.

6. To see the events selected in the standard template, click the Events Selection tab. You see the event columns that have been selected, as shown in Figure 11-10. This page shows only the events that have properties that have been selected. To see all the events and event properties supported by Analysis Services, check the Show All Events and Show All Columns check boxes, respectively. Familiarize yourself with the various events, and click Run.

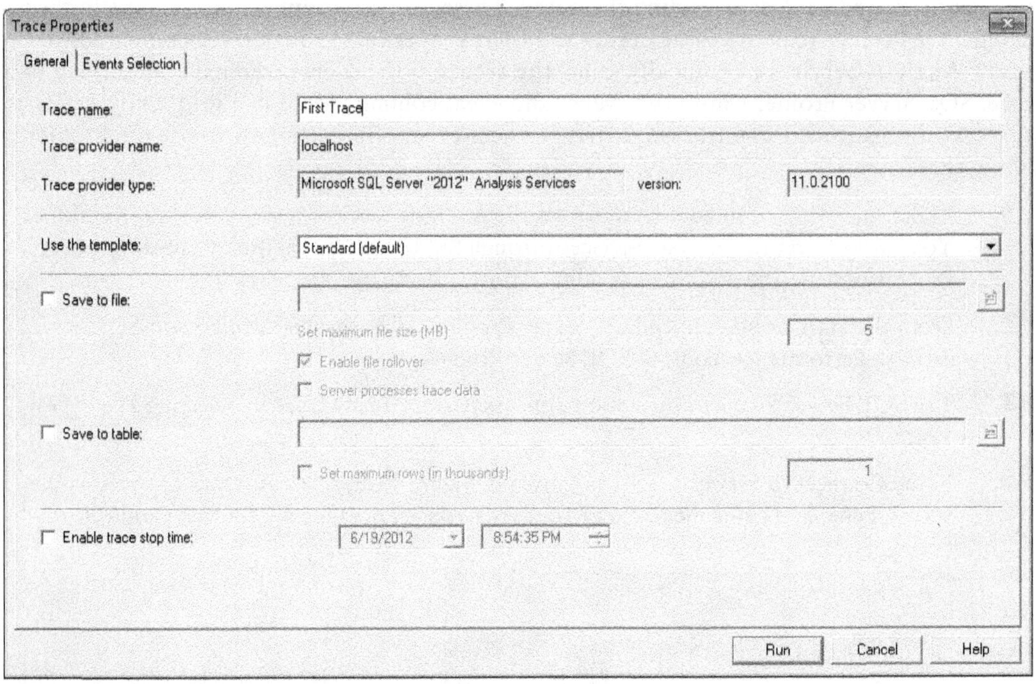

FIGURE 11-9

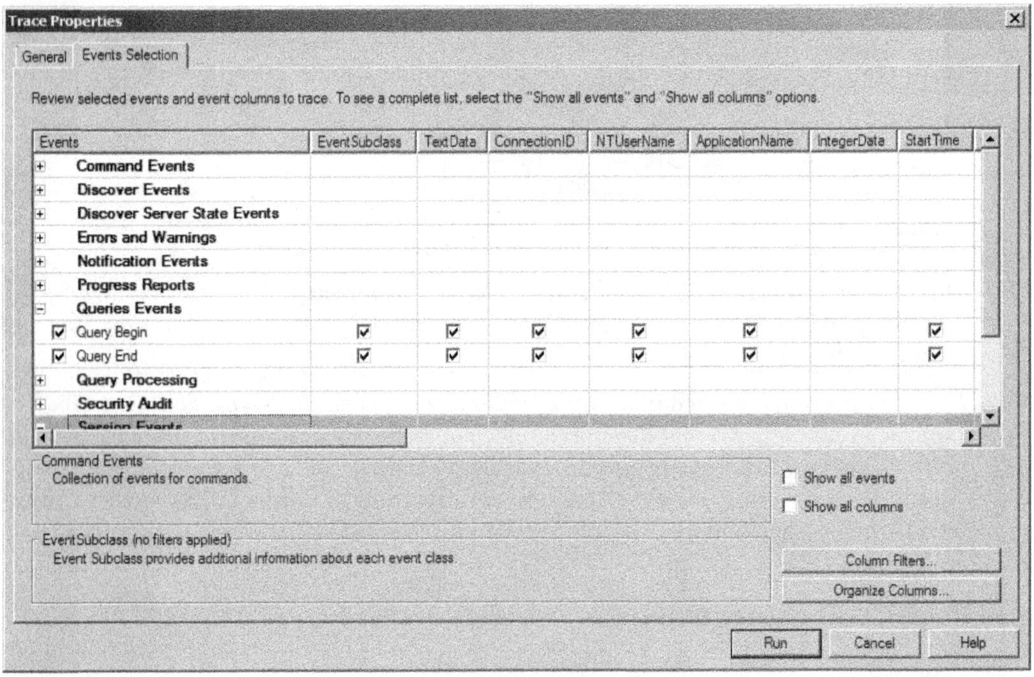

FIGURE 11-10

7. You can see the various event property columns within Profiler. To see processing operations events, open the Adventure Works DW sample project, and deploy it to the Analysis Services instance. You see the events that happen during processing, including the processing duration of each object, as shown in Figure 11-11. The SQL Server Profiler gives you useful information such as the time it takes to process each dimension, the partition processing time, and the overall processing time of the entire database.

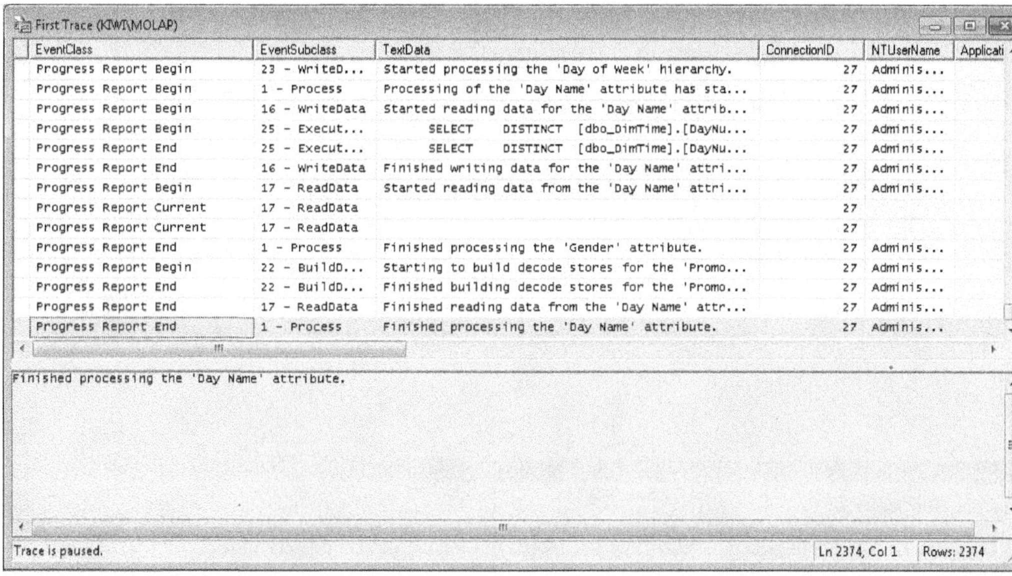

FIGURE 11-11

After the processing has completed for the Adventure Works cube, send the following MDX query using SQL Server Management Studio:

```
SELECT {[Measures].[Sales Amount],[Measures].[Gross Profit]} ON 0,
[Customer].[Customer Geography].MEMBERS ON 1
FROM [Adventure Works]
```

You can see the Query events in the SQL Server Profiler, as shown in Figure 11-12. You can see the duration of each event in the Profiler trace (not shown in Figure 11-12). One piece of information that is interesting is the subcubes accessed by this query and how long each subcube query took. The subcube events indicate the requests of the storage engine to retrieve data from disk. You can utilize this subcube information to build custom aggregations to optimize query performance.

Assume you built aggregations using a usage-based optimization wizard. You would like to find out if the aggregations are utilized. Analysis Services provides events that help you identify if the aggregations are hit. Create a new Trace and switch to the Events Selection tab. Check the box next to Show All Events. Expand the events under the Query Processing event group. You can see the events related to query processing provided by Analysis Services, as shown in Figure 11-13.

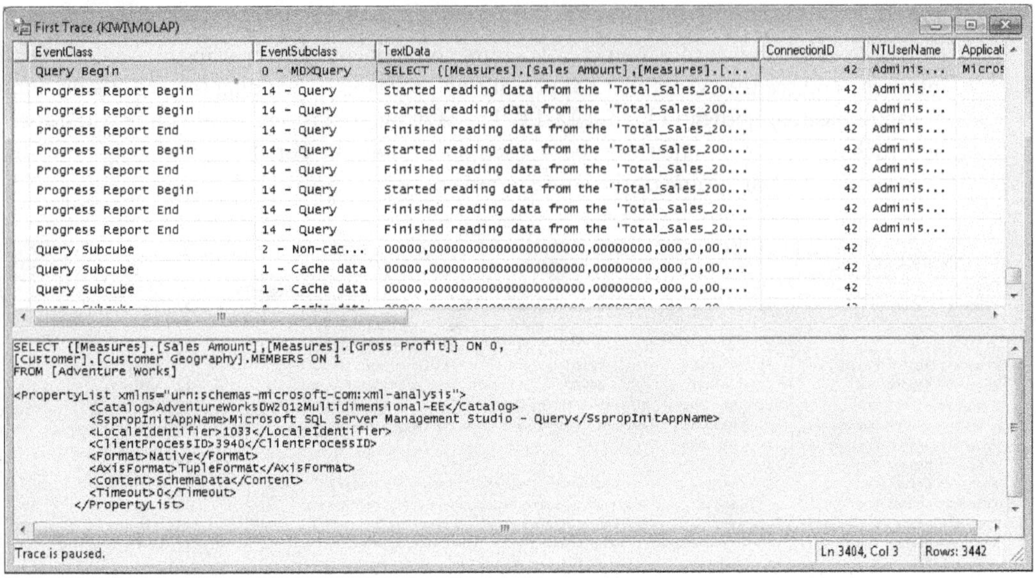

FIGURE 11-12

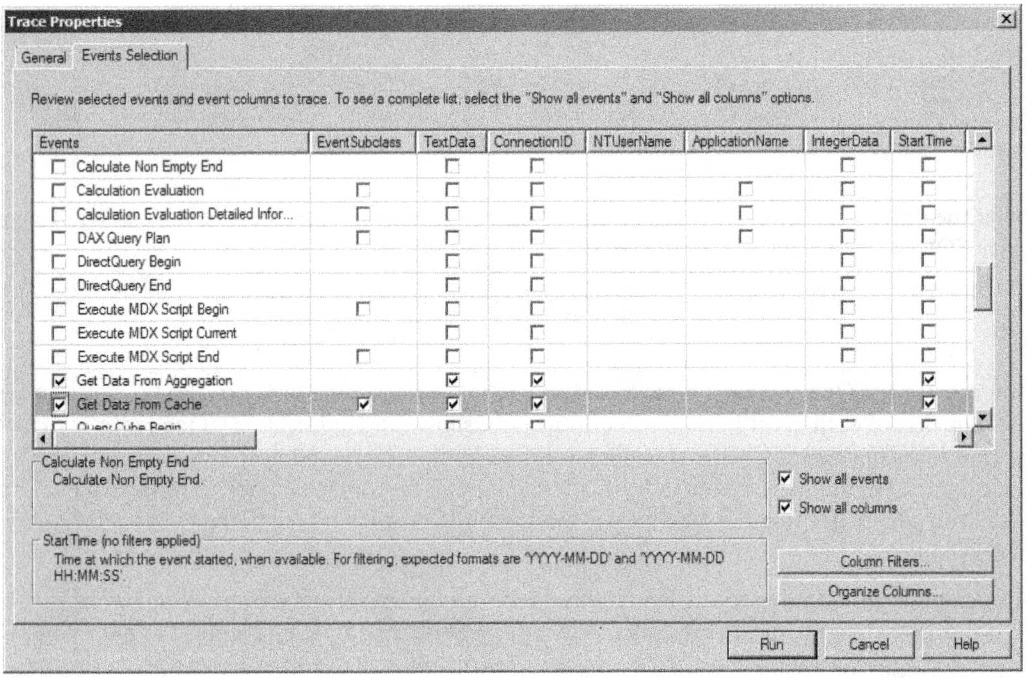

FIGURE 11-13

If you select the events under Query Processing and monitor the trace events, you can obtain information such as if the Non Empty code path is utilized, if the MDX Script is evaluated, and if data is retrieved from Aggregations (Get Data from Aggregation event) or from the existing cache (Get Data from Cache event). These events help you identify more details about the queries sent by the users as well as their duration. You can later analyze the MDX queries, build usage-based optimization aggregations for long-running queries, enhance your aggregations using the new Aggregation Designer (which is discussed in Chapter 9), or try to optimize the long-running MDX queries (which is discussed in the "Query Optimization Techniques" section later in this chapter). You do need to know a little bit about the internals of the server to fine-tune it. The ability to trace Analysis Services activity through SQL Server Profiler can help with that, so try it out.

Analysis Services Trace Events

The SQL Server Extended Event architecture is a great way to leverage the events engine in SQL Server to capture event information from Analysis Services. SQL Server Analysis Services 2012 provides event tracing capability through SQL Server Extended Events. You can start and stop the trace of events in SQL Server Analysis Services using an XMLA command.

Following is an example XMLA command to start an event, which is provided in the MSDN documentation at http://msdn.microsoft.com/en-us/library/gg492139(v=SQL.110).aspx.

```
<Execute …>
   <Command>
      <Batch …>
         <Create …>
            <ObjectDefinition>
               <Trace>
                  <ID>trace_id</ID>
                  <Name>trace_name</Name>
                  <ddl300_300:XEvent>
                     <event_session …>
                        <event package="AS" name="AS_event">
                           <action package="PACKAGE0" …/>
                        </event>
                        <target package="PACKAGE0" name="asynchronous_file_target">
                           <parameter name="filename" value="data_filename.xel"/>
                           <parameter name="metadatafile"
                            value="metadata_filename.xem"/>
                        </target>
                     </event_session>
                  </ddl300_300:XEvent>
               </Trace>
            </ObjectDefinition>
         </Create>
      </Batch>
   </Command>
   <Properties></Properties>
</Execute>
```

You need to specify a trace ID, trace name, and then parameters for tracing with the events you want to trace such as Command Events, Discover Events, Query Events, or Query Processing events.

The various events supported are available at MSDN documentation at `http://msdn.microsoft`
`.com/en-us/library/ms174867(v=SQL.110).aspx`. To analyze your query performance, you can
use the event tracing on your server with Query Processing and Queries events and later analyze the
log to understand the performance bottleneck area.

Performance Monitor

Analysis Services provides several performance monitoring counters that help you understand
internal operations of your Analysis Services server, as well as help in debugging and troubleshooting performance issues. You need to be an administrator on the Analysis Services server to utilize
PerfMon, a tool that enables you observe and analyze the Analysis Services 2012 performance counter
values. The following steps walk you through working with Analysis Services performance counters:

1. Click Start and type **perfmon**, as shown in Figure 11-14, and select perfmon.exe from the
    Programs list.

FIGURE 11-14

2. You see the Reliability and Performance Monitor application. Select the Performance
    Monitor page, as shown in Figure 11-15.

3. Right-click the page and select Add Counters. You see the groups of Analysis Services
    performance counters, as shown in Figure 11-16. You can expand a specific group to see the
    list of counters in that group.

4. Select the MSAS11 :MDX category of performance counters, and click Add to include these
    counters.

5. Click OK in the Add Counters dialog.

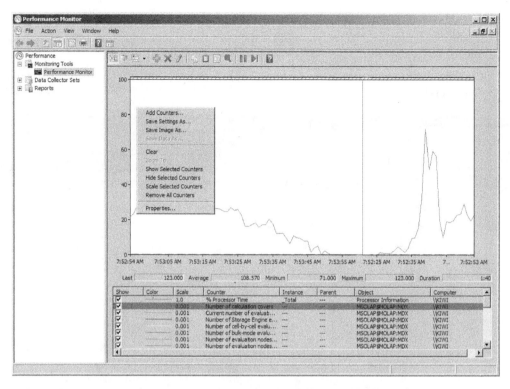

FIGURE 11-15

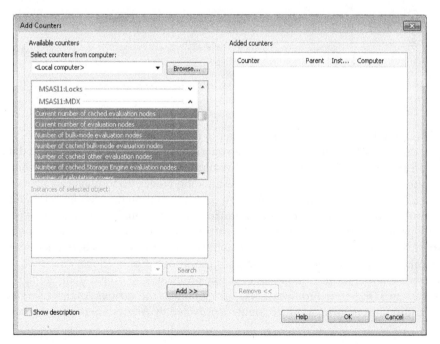

FIGURE 11-16

The MDX counters are added to the Performance Monitor page, as shown in Figure 11-17. If you click a specific counter, you can see the line view of that value over time. It is easier to understand and analyze the counters using their raw numbers.

6. Click the down arrow next to the Change Graph Type icon, and select Report, as shown in Figure 11-17.

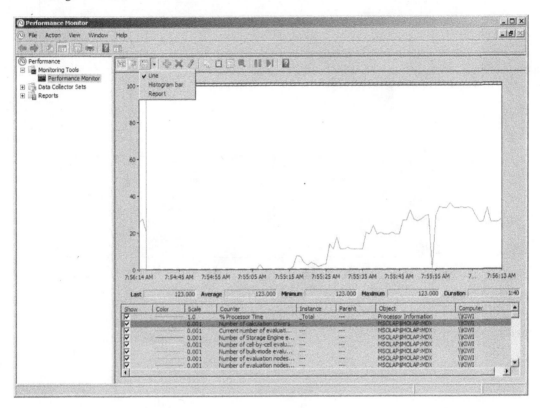

FIGURE 11-17

You see the list of MDX counters along with their values in a report format, as shown in Figure 11-18. If you execute MDX queries from SSMS you should see these values getting updated. For example, you can see the Number of Bulk-Mode Evaluation Nodes (nodes during subspace computation evaluation) and Number of Cell-by-Cell Evaluation Nodes performance counters for a specific query to understand if the query uses the subspace computation or a cell-by-cell evaluation mode. This can help you to understand and optimize your MDX query. It is important to remember that these performance counters are for the entire server, so your MDX queries should be tested in isolation. Similar to MDX performance counters, there are Analysis Services performance counters in other categories such as Processing, Aggregations, Connections, and so on. These counters are valuable when you troubleshoot specific problems and do not understand or resolve the problem using SQL Server Profiler traces. Take a look at the various Analysis Services counter groups. In addition to the performance counters provided by Analysis Services, you can also look at other performance counters such as processors, memory, and disk I/O on your computer system to understand and troubleshoot relevant issues such as long-running queries, which are CPU-intensive or memory/disk-intensive.

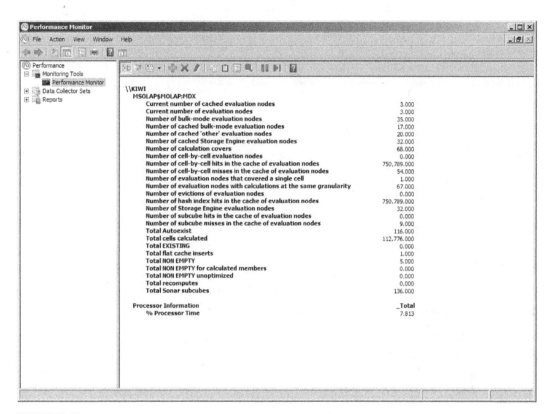

FIGURE 11-18

Task Manager

You might have used the Task Manager on your computer to look at the percentage of CPU time or memory consumed by a process. You can get the same information for Analysis Services using the Task Manager, as shown in Figure 11-19. The process msmdsrv.exe is the Analysis Services 2012 process. If you have multiple instances of Analysis Services installed, you see multiple instances of msmdsrv.exe in Task Manager. You can also see the various instances of Analysis Services on your machine using the Services tab in Task Manager. The Task Manager gives you a quick way to understand if your Analysis Services server is CPU-intensive or its memory usage is growing when you have executed a long-running query.

SQL Server Profiler, Performance Monitoring counters, and Task Manager help you analyze and troubleshoot issues with your Analysis Services. SQL Server Management Studio and SQL Server Data Tools are tools that help you tune your Analysis Services instance.

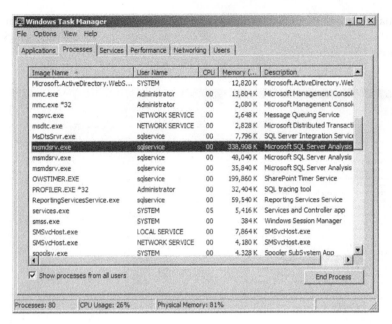

FIGURE 11-19

SQL Server Management Studio

You can use SSMS to execute your MDX queries and get the query execution time or look at the query results. You can also use it with the Profiler to troubleshoot specific query issues. In addition, you can also use SSMS for debugging processing issues or tuning your Analysis Services server processing options. SSMS also helps you define aggregations to help speed up query performance. Other important uses of SSMS are changing your Analysis Services server properties, fine-tuning engine behavior, and restarting your Analysis Services service if needed.

SQL Server Data Tools

You can use SSDT to refine your cube and dimension design based on the troubleshooting you have done using other tools. In addition, SSDT helps you build custom aggregations and make use of usage-based optimization, which helps you improve query performance.

Server Properties

You learned specific Analysis Services server properties in Chapter 10 for improving performance in the context of designing the cube and processing it. Some of the server properties such as memory limit and ThreadPool also help with query performance. In SQL Server Analysis Services 2012, you have the ability to configure a few additional properties to help in query performance on machines with NUMA architecture. These properties are added to help configure your system appropriately based on your cube and workload. The server properties provided here are expected to help improve query performance when you have cubes with a large number of partitions and multiple users querying the cube where the queries touch the partitions most of the time.

➤ `\ThreadPool\IOProcess\GroupAffinity`: On NUMA node systems this property helps to set the affinity mask for the SSAS IOProcess thread pool for specific processor groups. The IOProcess thread pool helps in querying the partitions data. This property thereby helps with partition data being localized to a specific NUMA node. By default, all the processors of the NUMA node are enabled for utilization by Analysis Services.

➤ `\FileStore\RandomFileAccessMode`: This property helps Analysis Services with reading the files (specifically partition data) in Random Access Mode. In Random Access Mode, Windows bypasses page mapping operations that read data from disk into the system cache. This lowers contention on the cache.

➤ `\Feature\ResourceMonitoringEnabled`: This flag helps turn off resource monitoring on high-end systems to get improved throughput. However, certain DMVs do not report accurate data when Resource Monitoring is turned off.

Based on the cube and the multiuser query workload, the query performance you obtain for your users might vary. Do an evaluation of your workload with these properties in your test environment before applying these in production.

ANALYZING QUERY PERFORMANCE ISSUES

Analysis Services 2012 has significant query optimization features. However, some factors can affect query performance such as the complexity of the cube's design, aggregations, server configuration properties, hardware resources, and so on. Before you start analyzing query performance, you need to understand where time is spent during the overall execution. You already learned that about two major components, Formula Engine (FE) and Storage Engine (SE), where the majority of the execution time is spent. The time spent in the infrastructure component is negligible; therefore, you can arrive at the following equation:

```
MDX Query execution time = Formula Engine time + Storage Engine time
```

In the "SQL Server Profiler" section earlier in the chapter, you learned that query subcube events indicate requests to the SE. Therefore, the SE time is the duration of time spent for all the query subcube events. You can obtain the overall query execution time for the query from the SQL Server Profiler trace. The time spent by the query in the FE component is equal to the difference of the total execution time minus the SE time. These relationships are expressed in the following equations:

```
Storage Engine time = Time needed to evaluate all query subcube events
```

```
Formula Engine time = Total query execution time - Storage Engine time
```

Assuming you want to analyze and optimize your query execution time, you must focus your efforts on the following recommendations:

➤ If the SE time is greater than 30 percent of the total execution time, look at optimizing it.

➤ If the SE time is less than 30 percent of the total execution time, look at optimizing the FE.

➤ If both FE and SE times are greater than 30 percent of the total execution time, look at optimizing both areas.

Understanding FE and SE Characteristics

The FE performs the evaluation of the results and sends the results back to the client. This component is mostly single-threaded and CPU-intensive because it might have to iterate over millions of cells to perform calculations. If you observe, using Task Manager, that Analysis Services consumes 100 percent of one of the processors during a query evaluation, you can assume that the time is spent in the FE. The FE has little disk utilization.

The SE retrieves data for subcubes from the SE cache or from disk when requested by the FE. Partition and dimension data is stored as segments that can be read in parallel. Therefore, the SE component is heavily multithreaded to maximize the hardware resources and perform I/O operations in parallel. The SE is CPU- and disk-intensive. If you see all the processors of your machine utilized and heavy disk usage (using Task Manager or performance counters), you can be confident that the query is spending time in the SE component.

When analyzing query performance, one important thing you need to be aware of is predictability. Analysis Services caches data in the SE and FE components. In addition, you have caching done by the operating system for disk I/O and the multiuser environment that play a critical factor in query performance. Therefore, executing the same MDX query a second time can result in improved performance due to caching in Analysis Services. The recommended approach is to investigate query performance in single-user mode. In addition, Analysis Services has the Clear Cache command that clears all the Analysis Services caches. This improves the predictability of query execution when you investigate performance issues. The syntax for the Clear Cache statement is shown in the following code. You need to pass the database ID as input to the statement to clear the caches of a specific database.

```
<ClearCache xmlns="http://schemas.microsoft.com/analysisservices/2003/engine">
  <Object>
    <DatabaseID>MyDatabaseID</DatabaseID>
  </Object>
</ClearCache>
```

Operating system file caching can also impact query performance. To get repeatable results, you can shut down and restart the Analysis Services service or even the entire machine if needed. In most cases you should get repeatable results using the Clear Cache statement.

Common Solutions for Slow Queries

MDX query execution time is the sum of the time spent in the FE and SE components. The issues causing queries to be slow can be classified into three main categories: large SE requests, multiple SE requests, and FE-intensive queries.

Large Storage Engine Requests

As you learned earlier, query evaluation plans are decided by the FE. A large SE request translates to a subcube query that takes a long time. This means the majority of the query execution time is spent getting results for a single SE request. An SE request can take a long time due to factors such as having a large partition, no aggregations, or aggregations getting missed. You need to follow the best practices mentioned in Chapter 10 to design the right cube, including defining effective attribute relationships, adopting an effective partitioning scheme, and designing aggregations using Aggregation Designer or usage-based optimization. These can help resolve the issue of an MDX query being slow due to a large storage engine request.

Several Storage Engine Requests

If you see several subcube query events in the SQL Server Profiler when you execute an MDX query repeatedly, it means that the SE caches are missed each time; therefore the SE component must retrieve data from the disk. Retrieving data from disk is an expensive operation compared to getting the data from the SE caches. The EventSubclass property of the Query Subcube Verbose event shows whether the query is retrieved from cache or noncache data. If the query is retrieved from noncache data, the data is retrieved from the disk. Analysis Services 2012 provides you a way to forcibly cache the data in SE component using the Create Cache statement. The syntax of the statement is

```
CREATE CACHE FOR <CubeName> AS <MDX Expression>
```

The Create Cache statement applies to a specific cube. This is extremely useful in cases in which you are aware of long-running queries due to several storage engine requests. You can "warm up" the Analysis Services SE cache using this statement, which can help improve performance of MDX queries using this cache.

Formula Engine-Intensive Query

The FE component is single threaded. Therefore, if an MDX query contains intensive calculations, it could spend a significant amount of its execution time in the FE component. You should identify an FE-intensive query using Task Manager. Look for msmdsrv.exe pegging one CPU on your machine at 100 percent. One of the critical factors in getting the best performance from your MDX query is to make sure your query uses the subspace computation code path. Looking at MDX performance counters and SQL Server Profiler traces should help you identify if your queries are not using subspace computation. In addition, other MDX query optimization techniques can help you reduce the time spent in the FE component, which you learn about in the next section.

Figure 11-20 provides a summary of the three categories of problems that can contribute to slow MDX queries and what techniques to investigate to improve query performance.

Scenario	Large SE Request	Several SE Requests	FE-Intensive Query	
Solution	Partitioning, aggregations	CREATE CACHE	Cell-by-cell → Subspace	Optimizations: Auto-exists, Scope, MemberValue ...

FIGURE 11-20

QUERY OPTIMIZATION TECHNIQUES

As you learned in this chapter, several factors such as cube design, Analysis Services caching, and hardware can impact MDX query execution time. One of the important factors to achieve the best MDX query execution time is the efficiency of your MDX. Using the right MDX query optimization technique is not simple and involves a deeper understanding of your cube and MDX. In this section you learn some of the important techniques that can help you optimize your MDX queries.

Using NON EMPTY on Axes

Most cubes are quite sparse; many of the cells in the cube space do not have a value associated with them. For example, in the Adventure Works DW sample Analysis Services database, if every coordinate of the Internet Sales measure group has data and only the key attribute in each dimension, the total number of cells with data would be the following:

(Date) 1,189 * Date (Ship Date) 1,189 * Date (Delivery Date) 1,189 * Customer (18,485) * Promotion (17) * Product (398) * Sales Territory (12) * Sales Reason (11) * Source Currency (106) * Destination Currency (15) * Internet Sales Order Details (60,399)

which is $2.66 * 10^{27}$ cells. This result increases when additional attributes are added from each dimension. Although most of the cells do not have any business meaning associated with them — for example, if the delivery date is ahead of the order date — they belong to cube space and can be queried by the users. Querying such cells results in an empty value, which indicates that data is not available for that cell's coordinates.

The fact table rows represent the leaf-level cells for a cube. The fact table row count is much less than possible cube space. The Analysis Services engine has many optimizations for improving query performance by limiting the search space. The basic rule is that if a cube doesn't have calculations (such as calculated scripts, custom rollup, and custom members), the nonempty space of the cube is defined by fact table cells and their aggregations. Analysis Services enable users to write effective, optimized MDX queries to prevent empty cells from being returned. This is because those empty cells simply do not add value for business analysis. By limiting the search space, Analysis Services can find the results much more quickly.

Analysis Services 2012 supports many ways for users to eliminate cells containing empty values in a query. The keyword NON EMPTY eliminates members along an axis whose cells are empty. The NON EMPTY keyword is used at the beginning of the axis statement in an MDX query as shown here:

```
SELECT Measures.Members on COLUMNS,
NON EMPTY Dimension.Hierarchy.Members on ROWS
From <CubeName>
```

You can use the NON EMPTY keyword on rows or columns (or any axis). In most cases, only results with nonempty cells are meaningful for end users. Therefore, most Analysis Services 2012 client tools generate MDX queries with the NON EMPTY keyword. We use the NON EMPTY keyword in your MDX cell set and row set queries whenever possible. Not only can it limit the size of the returned cell set, but also additional optimizations are applied when you do this that speed up your query execution time.

Following is an MDX query without the NON EMPTY keyword. Execute this query using SQL Server Management Studio against a deployed sample Adventure Works project.

```
SELECT [Customer].[Customer Geography].[Customer].members *
    Descendants([Product].[Product Categories].[Category].&[3],[Product].
    [Product Categories].[Product Name]) ON 1,
    {[Measures].[Internet Sales Amount]} ON 0
FROM [Adventure Works]
```

The query returns 18,485 cells. Now change the query to include the NON EMPTY keyword on both axes as shown here, and execute the new query in SQL Server Management Studio:

```
SELECT NON EMPTY [Customer].[Customer Geography].[Customer].members *
    Descendants([Product].[Product Categories].[Category].&[3],[Product].
```

```
        [Product Categories].[Product Name]) ON 1,
        {[Measures].[Internet Sales Amount]} ON 0
    FROM [Adventure Works]
```

This query, which includes the NON EMPTY keyword, returns just 6,853 cells, which is a reduced number of cells to evaluate. The execution time for the query with NON EMPTY is lower than that of the query without NON EMPTY. Follow these steps to observe the performance:

1. Connect to the sample Adventure Works DW Analysis Services database.

2. Start SQL Server Profiler.

3. Create a New Trace with Query Begin and Query End events selected.

4. Send the Clear Cache statement.

5. Send the query without NON EMPTY.

6. Send the Clear Cache statement.

7. Send the MDX query with NON EMPTY.

8. Observe the Duration column to see the performance difference between the two queries.

You can see the performance difference in duration times between the two queries, as shown in Figure 11-21. This example highlights the benefit of eliminating empty cells using NON EMPTY.

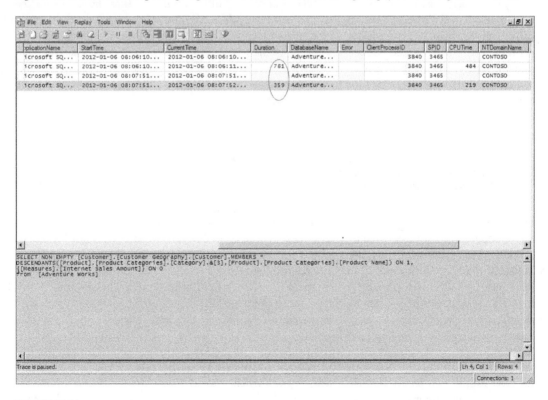

FIGURE 11-21

Using NON EMPTY for Filtering and Sorting

Many users apply filter conditions on a set or try to evaluate the top N members of a set based on certain conditions using the Filter and TopCount functions, respectively. In most cases, only non-empty members are needed in the results of the Filter and TopCount functions. You can improve the performance dramatically by first using NON EMPTY() to retrieve nonempty sets, followed by the Filter, Sort, or TopCount functions on the smaller set. In the Adventure Works sample, for example, if you want to get the top ten Customer/Product combinations to start a marketing campaign, your query should look like the following:

```
SELECT
TopCount([Customer].[Customer Geography].[Customer].members*
    [Product].[Product Categories].[Product].members, 10 ,
    [Measures].[Internet Sales Amount]) ON ROWS ,
    [Measures].[Internet Sales Amount] ON COLUMNS
FROM [Adventure Works]
```

This query contains a cross-join of customers and products (shown by the following expression). Whenever a cross-join is applied, the server sorts the result based on the order of the hierarchies.

```
([Customer].[Customer Geography].[Customer].members*[Product].
    [Product Categories].[Product].members)
```

The cross-join of the customer and product dimension results in 18,484 * 397 = 7,338,148 cells. Analysis Services now evaluates the top 10 cells out of the 7 million cells to return the results for the preceding query. This query took approximately 48 seconds on the machine used to run the query and consumed 1 CPU at 100 percent during the entire execution. Most of the cells of the cross-join were actually empty cells that did not need to be part of the result of the cross-join. Not only did the server take the time in sorting these cells, but it also had to iterate through the 7 million cells to determine the top 10. The following query uses the NONEMPTYCROSSJOIN function, which eliminates the empty cells:

```
SELECT
TopCount(NONEMPTYCROSSJOIN(
    [Customer].[Customer Geography].[Customer].members*
    [Product].[Product Categories].[Product].members,
    {[Measures].[Internet Sales Amount]},1),10,
    [Measures].[Internet Sales Amount]) ON ROWS ,
    [Measures].[Internet Sales Amount] ON COLUMNS
FROM [Adventure Works]
```

In this query, the NONEMPTYCROSSJOIN function first eliminates all empty cells, and therefore the TopCount function had a smaller set of cells to work on. The query took 3 seconds on the same machine used in the previous example because of the optimization provided by using the NONEMPTYCROSSJOIN function. Only cells containing fact data were sorted, and the top 10 values were returned. The performance improvement is dramatic (can be observed in SSMS or in the SQL Server Profiler duration column) and both queries returned the exact same results. The rule of thumb is that the fewer tuples or cells involved in calculations, the better the query performance. Because Analysis Services has an efficient algorithm to get nonempty sets, you should use NON EMPTY whenever it is applicable and appropriate for your business requirements. You can use the NONEMPTYCROSSJOIN function whenever you are aware that a real measure will be used by the server for Non-Empty evaluation, but use it with caution when you have calculated measures because certain optimization may not be available for all calculated measures. You can also use the HAVING clause, which eliminates cells with null values.

Using SCOPE Versus IIF and CASE

Earlier in this chapter, you learned about the SCOPE, IIF, and CASE statements. Using SCOPE helps improve query performance when evaluating cells compared to the IIF and CASE statements. When using SCOPE, calculations get applied only to the subcube, compared to other calculations, which get evaluated for the entire cube space. In addition, SCOPE statements are evaluated once statically, compared to IIF/CASE, which are evaluated dynamically. These two factors contribute to improving query performance when using SCOPE. The following code is an example of an MDX expression that is translated from IIF to SCOPE:

```
CREATE MEMBER Measures.[Sales Amount] AS
  IIF([Destination Currency].CurrentMember IS Currency.USD,
  Measures.[Internet Sales Amount], Measures.[Internet Sales Amount] *
  Measures.AverageRate);

CREATE MEMBER Measures.[Sales Amount] AS Null;
SCOPE(Measures.[Sales], [Destination Currency].Members);
  THIS = Measures.[Internet Sales Amount] * Measures.AverageRate;
  SCOPE(Currency.USA);
    THIS = Measures.[Internet Sales Amount];
  END SCOPE;
END SCOPE;
```

Auto Exists Versus Properties

When you include attributes and hierarchies within a dimension in a query, Analysis Services returns only the relevant members. For example, take the following MDX query:

```
SELECT [Measures].[Internet Sales Amount] ON 0,
  [Customer].[City].&[Seattle]&[WA] * [Customer].[State-Province].MEMBERS ON 1
FROM [Direct Sales]
```

This query returns only results for (Seattle, Washington) and (Seattle, All Customers). It does not return the complete cross product of Seattle and all the States in the Customer.[State-Province] hierarchy. This behavior is called *auto exists* and helps improve performance. Therefore, you should use Exists or CrossJoin functions instead of using the Properties function in your MDX expression. The following code is an example of how you can rewrite your MDX expressions that use the Properties function:

```
Filter(Customer.Members,
  Customer.CurrentMember.Properties("Gender") = "Male")

Exists(Customer.Members, Gender.[Male])
```

Member Value Versus Properties

Analysis Services 2012 has an attribute member property called Value Column. When defined, this is helpful to retrieve the values in a typed format. For example, if you have the yearly income of a customer, you can retrieve its value as an integer rather than as a string and then converting it using one of the VBA functions. Following is an example of how to use the MemberValue MDX function to retrieve the Value Column:

```
Create Set [Adventure Works].RichCustomers As
  Filter(Customer.Customer.Members,
```

```
    CInt(Customer.CustomerCurrentMember.Properties("Yearly Income"))
    > 100000);

Create Set [Adventure Works].RichCustomers As
    Filter(Customer.Customer.Members,
    Customer.Salary.MemberValue > 100000);
```

In this example, the first expression creates a set of customers whose Yearly Income is greater than 100000 using the `Properties` MDX function, which retrieves the member property. The return type for the `MemberProperty` function is a string, and you need to use the `CInt` VBA function to convert this to an integer value before you compare it with 100000. The preceding example is provided for illustration purposes only. The actual data in the sample Adventure Works DW in the Yearly Income is a range represented as string. Try the preceding illustration on a large database with appropriate data to see the benefits. When you have a large number of customers, converting strings to integers becomes expensive. The second MDX expression uses the `MemberValue` MDX function to retrieve the value directly as an integer.

Move Simple Calculations to Data Source View

If there are simple static calculations, such as converting based on exchange rates, these calculations can be changed to calculated columns in the Data Source View (DSV). Analysis Services does these calculations at processing time and stores the values in the cube rather than calculating these expressions during query execution time. These simple calculations should be fast in Analysis Services 2012, and you may not observe the performance hit. However, as a general best practice, move them to DSV.

Features Versus MDX Scripts

Analysis Services 2012 provides features such as many-to-many dimensions, measure expressions, unary operators, custom rollup, and semi-additive measures. You have learned about these features and how and when to use them during the course of this book. Almost all these features can be defined as MDX expressions in MDX Script. Design your cubes using built-in features rather than defining the equivalent functionality as MDX expressions in MDX Script. The built-in features provide better performance for most scenarios. If you do find a specific feature causing query performance degradation, you can revisit implementing the functionality in MDX Scripts.

You have looked at some of the common problems the Analysis Services team has observed while investigating customer performance issues and how to solve them in this section. There are additional MDX optimizations that you can perform. Look at the following resources for additional information on MDX optimizations:

➤ *MDX Solutions: With Microsoft SQL Server Analysis Services*, 2nd edition by George Spofford et al., (Wiley, 2006).

➤ The SQL Customer Advisory Team: www.sqlcat.com.

➤ Chris Webb's BI Blog: http://cwebbbi.wordpress.com/.

SCALE OUT WITH READ-ONLY DATABASE

After performing all these query optimization techniques, you might still find query performance degradation when multiple users connect to your Analysis Services instance and actively query the database. This is one of the problems Analysis Services customers face when the customer load on a specific database increases. You can try to use larger machines with more CPUs if memory or CPU is the bottleneck. You can also move to 64-bit machines if you are currently using 32-bit hardware. Of course, as you scale up, the cost of your machines will become higher. Analysis Services 2012 provides the read-only database feature, which is discussed in Chapter 7. If your customer needs are only to improve query performance and your customers are performing only read-only queries (no updates, no writeback), you can use the read-only database feature and create a scale out strategy, as shown in Figure 11-21, to improve query performance for this type of multiuser scenario.

You need multiple Analysis Services 2012 servers configured to read from a single database on a shared storage area network (SAN) to form Scalable Shared Databases that can be queried by multiple users. These servers must be load balanced using a network load balancer, as shown in Figure 11-22. You need a separate isolated machine for processing the database when there are data updates. After the database has been processed, you can detach the database and copy it to your SAN. You can then use XMLA scripts to attach the database to the Analysis Services query servers in read-only mode. All the query servers need an identical copy of the database and need to serve multiple users. This scale out strategy can help you improve query performance for this type of multiple user scenario.

Scalable Shared Databases

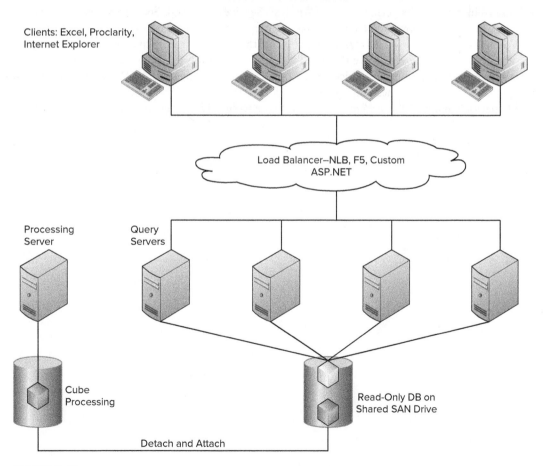

FIGURE 11-22

WRITEBACK QUERY PERFORMANCE

SQL Server Analysis Services 2012 has several performance optimizations to improve writeback query performance. In addition, in Analysis Services 2012 you can obtain improved writeback performance by enabling the MOLAP storage option when you enable writeback. When you perform cell writeback, Analysis Services writes data back to the relational table specified. In addition, the MOLAP partition associated with the writeback partition is reprocessed automatically. Because of this, all queries using the writeback partition can retrieve the data from the MOLAP storage rather than fetching the data from the relational table and then aggregating the data. Therefore, using MOLAP storage for the writeback partition helps to improve query performance. Set MOLAP storage mode for the writeback partition when you enable the cube for cell writeback.

SUMMARY

In this chapter you first learned about the calculation model in Analysis Services, followed by the query execution architecture of Analysis Services. You learned about the various tools that you can use to investigate the performance of Analysis Services. The SQL Server Profiler and PerfMon counters in particular are valuable tools that can help you investigate performance bottlenecks. You then learned about various classes of problems that can contribute to slow queries, along with recommendations on how to solve these problems. Finally, you learned about important query optimization techniques and best practices that can help you fine-tune your MDX queries. After reading Chapters 10 and 11, upon hearing the word *performance*, your head should swell with visions of highly performing, scalable systems, each optimized to fulfill its designated mission!

12

Data Mining, Multidimensional BISM, and Data Mining Add-ins for Office 2010

WHAT'S IN THIS CHAPTER?

➤ Understanding the data mining process

➤ Data mining applications in the real world

➤ Solving business problems with data mining algorithms in SQL Server Analysis Services 2012

➤ Working with relational and OLAP mining models

➤ Using data mining with Office 2010

Not everyone is well versed in the area of data mining, so this chapter starts with what data mining is and what you can do with it. *Data mining* is the process of applying algorithms to data sets with the goal to expose patterns in the data that would not otherwise be noticed. The reason such patterns would not otherwise be noticed owes to the complexity and volume of data within which the patterns are embedded. Another, less academic way to look at data mining is as a technology that you can use to answer questions like the following:

➤ When customers visit our corporate web site, what paths are they most likely to take when navigating through the site?

➤ When a $10 credit card transaction is processed at a gas station immediately followed by a $600 purchase on the same account from an electronics store in a different ZIP code, should a red flag be raised?

➤ For optimal sales revenue generation in a grocery store, which products should be placed in close proximity to one another?

➤ What additional products can we recommend to our online shoppers that can help increase our revenue?

To address these types of questions, and many others, you can turn to data mining technology. In this chapter, you learn about data mining and how it helps you answer questions by creating and using data mining models and applications. You will understand the data mining algorithms supported by SQL Server Analysis Services 2012 and how you can use them. You learn two data mining algorithms in depth and learn to create data mining models in SSAS from relational data sources (relational mining models) as well as from cubes, which are part of the multidimensional Business Intelligence Semantic Model (BISM multidinensional). In addition, you learn how to use Microsoft SQL Server 2012 Data Mining Add-ins for Office 2010 to analyze and visualize data in Office 2010.

THE DATA MINING PROCESS

Wherever you look, people and businesses collect data, in some cases without even an obvious immediate purpose. Companies collect data for many reasons, including accounting, reporting, and marketing. Those companies with swelling data stores have executives with many more questions than answers; in this book, you have seen how executives can use BISM multidimensional-based analysis to find the answers they need. This is typically a process in which you know what you are looking for and can extract that information from your BISM multidimensional. However, there might be additional information in your data that can help you make important business decisions that you are not aware of because you don't know what to look for. Data mining is the process of extracting interesting information from your data such as trends, clusters, and other patterns that can help you understand your data better. You can accomplish data mining through the use of statistical methods, as well as machine learning algorithms. The ultimate purpose of data mining is the discovery of subtle relationships between data items. It can also entail the creation of predictive models. When data mining is successfully applied, rules and patterns previously unknown and potentially useful emerge from heaps of data.

You don't need a vintage coal-mining helmet with a lamp to begin the data mining process. (But if you feel more comfortable wearing one, you can likely find one on eBay.) What actually is required is a problem to solve with a good understanding of the problem space; this isn't just an exploratory adventure. The main requirement is having the appropriate hardware to store the data to be analyzed and the analysis results. Then, you need off-the-shelf data mining software or, if you are particularly knowledgeable, you can write your own software. For hardware, you need a machine for storing the data (typically relational databases that can store gigabytes or terabytes of data) and a machine to develop and run your data mining application on. Although those are normally two different machines, these functions can all reside on a single machine. You learn about data mining software in terms of data mining algorithms, the infrastructure to use them, and data visualization tools for use in evaluating the results such as the SQL Server 2012 Data Mining Add-ins for Office 2010. When you have the software and the required hardware, you need a good understanding of the data you are about to mine as well as the problem you are trying to solve. This is a critical prerequisite to have before you start using the software to perform data mining. You learn more about understanding the problem space and data in subsequent sections. Having the hardware and right software set up is a necessary precursor to the data mining process.

When you have the hardware and software requirements satisfied, you then get into the process of building a model or representation of your data, which helps you visualize and understand information in your data better. Over time, through systematic efforts and by trial and error, several methodologies and guidelines emerge. Figure 12-1 shows the typical process of data mining divided into five steps. First and foremost, you need to understand the domain area and what your business needs. Then, you might run some initial statistics on the data to understand it better. After understanding the data, you create mining models and train them with input data. You need to analyze the mining models and validate the results from the models. After you build mining models to suit your business needs, you deploy the models to your production system. Your end users can consume the results directly from the model or through applications that use content from the model. You might need to go through this data mining life cycle periodically to meet the changing needs of your business or data or both.

Topic Area Understanding

The last section stated that before data miners begin to mine data, they first need to understand the data and the problem space. Problem type and scope vary dramatically by subject area; from retail business, sales forecasts, and inventory management to logistics. Outside the realm of business, there are data-mining-relevant science questions such as, "Some star has luminosity L, radiates brightly in the ultraviolet spectrum, and appears to have a small surface area. How hot is it likely to be?" If you have a reasonably sized database from which to train initially — more on what that means later — predictive data mining could uncover that the hotter the star, the shorter the wavelength peak in the star's spectrum and that the hottest stars peak in the ultraviolet area of the spectrum. You do need to have an idea about the topic or subject area and the problem you want to solve to identify nonintuitive relationships and patterns using data mining as a tool.

To accomplish the goal of your data mining project, you must understand what business you're in; moreover, what success means for your business in quantitative terms. To "understand the business," you have to sometimes ask hard questions like does your company sell sugar water with flavoring? Or does it actually sell an imagined lifestyle of fun, action, and perpetual happiness through the marketing of sugar water? What metrics can you use to measure gradients of success? For example, volumes of sales, market share ownership, or customer feedback scores? You as the person to mine your company's data or as a data mining consultant at a customer's site need to know as much information as possible about the customer and what the customer wants to achieve so that you can interpret the data mining results and make good recommendations. The bottom line is that the company wants to improve profits. That can be accomplished by targeting the best sellers, adding value for customers (in the form of making suggestions based on customer usage patterns or detecting fraud against the customer's credit cards), and loss reduction (by identifying processes that drain the business of funds unnecessarily).

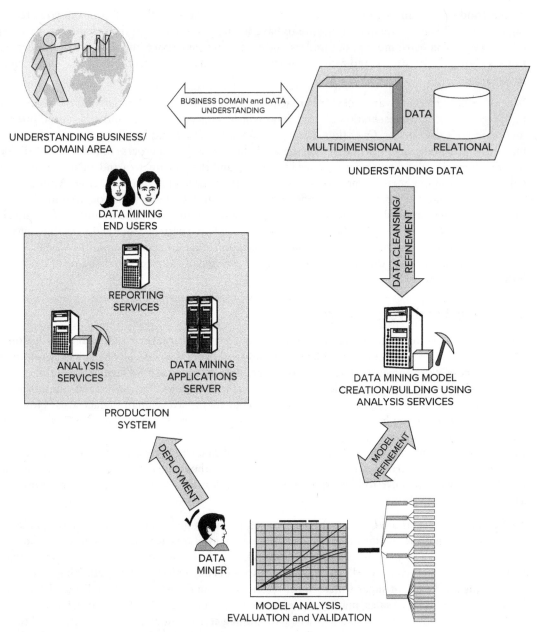

FIGURE 12-1

Data: Understand It, Configure It

First, you must know how to collect data from disparate sources and then ensure the data description scheme (metadata) is integrated, consistent, and makes sense for all the data to be used. It is a good idea at this point, though not required, to explore the data by creating distributions and running simple statistical tests. It is critical that the data be clean and free of type mismatches;

otherwise, the algorithms might not extract important information or, if they do, they might yield erroneous results. You might take other preparatory actions; for example, you might want to construct *derived attributes*, which are also called *computed attributes* or *calculated columns*. To verify the accuracy of the data mining algorithm's results, the source data is often divided into training and testing data. You should split your source data as follows: two-thirds for training purposes and the remaining one-third for testing and verification of results.

Understanding the data also involves understanding attributes of the data. For example, if you look at customer data, then name, gender, age, income, children, and so on are possible attributes of the customer. You need to have a good understanding of the values of the attributes that best represent attributes to the data mining model you are about to create. For example, gender of a customer can typically have values Male, Female, or Unknown. Only three possible values exist for the attribute gender. If you look at the income of the customer, though, the income can have a wide variance, such as zero to millions of dollars. These attributes need to be modeled appropriately for the chosen data mining algorithm to get the best results. The gender attribute would typically be modeled as a discrete attribute, which means a fixed number of values, whereas the income would typically be modeled as continuous because there is a wide variation of the values for income. Understanding your data is critical.

Choose the Right Algorithm

When you have a good understanding of your business and matching your needs to the data, you then need to choose the right data mining algorithm. A *data mining algorithm* is a technique or method by which data is analyzed and represented as patterns or rules, which are typically called *data mining models*. Choosing the right algorithm is not always easy. There might be several data mining algorithms that can solve your business problem. First, identify the algorithms that can solve your problem. The data mining model created by the algorithm is later analyzed to detect patterns or predict values for new data. Now, if you are aware of each data mining algorithm in depth, you can potentially pick the right one. If not, identify the algorithms that can potentially solve your problem and analyze results from each algorithm. Later in this chapter, you learn about various algorithms supported by SQL Server Analysis Services 2012 and what class of problems they can solve. Fine-tune the models of various algorithms, and pick the most efficient one that provides you the maximum satisfaction for your business needs. You can use several techniques to compare the results of several mining models, such as lift versus profit chart. (You learn about these in the "Working with Mining Models" section later in this chapter.) After you compare and identify the right model, you can use the specific algorithm for more detailed analysis.

Train, Analyze, and Predict

With the data mining algorithm in hand, you now need to choose the data set to identify and analyze interesting information for your business. You can use data mining not only to analyze existing data, but also to predict characteristics of new data. Typically, the data set to be analyzed will be divided into two sets — a training set and a validation set — usually in the ratio 70%:30%. The training data set is fed as input to the data mining algorithm. The algorithm analyzes the data and creates an object called a data mining model, which represents characteristics of the data set to be analyzed. You need to identify the right training data set to best represent your data. You also need to consider training data size because that directly impacts training time. Training of a model is also referred to as *model building* or *processing of a model* in this book. After you determine the training data set, you train the model with the chosen algorithm. When you have the trained model, you can analyze it and have a better understanding of the training data set to see if that provides you useful information for your business.

Prediction is the process of anticipating a value or values of a data set based on the characteristics of the data set. For example, if you own a store and create a mining model of all your customers, you might classify them as Platinum, Gold, Silver, or Bronze membership based on several factors, such as salary, revenue they bring to your store, number of household members, and so on. Now, if a new member shops at your store, you might predict his membership based on salary, household members, and other factors. When you have this information, you can send membership-relevant promotional coupons to the member to increase your sales. One of the features in SQL Server Analysis Services 2012 is structured columns drillthrough. This feature enables the addition of informational data such as e-mail, address, and phone number into the mining structure that you do not want to consider when building the mining model, but do want to return when you query the data mining structure.

In addition to analyzing your data using a mining model, you can perform predictions for new data sets by simply providing the new data set as input to the model and retrieving the prediction results To determine the accuracy of the model, you could use the validation data set, predict values for the validation set, and compare the actual values with the predicted values. Based on the number of accurate predictions, you can know how good the model is. If the model is not providing prediction results as per your expectations, you might tweak it by changing properties of the data mining algorithm, choosing the right attributes as inputs, or choosing a different mining algorithm. You might need to periodically maintain the model based on additional information available to you — in this way, your model is trained well with the most up-to-date information and should yield optimal results.

REAL-WORLD APPLICATIONS

Mapping theory to the real world is not always the most intuitive process imaginable. Several successful data mining applications have been deployed across various sectors. In this section, you learn examples of real-world applications that use data mining technology. These applications can help you understand data mining and its use.

Fraud Detection

Have you ever received a call from your credit card company asking whether you made a specific credit card purchase? Do you know why you received the call? Chances are good that it was due to an anomaly detected in your credit card usage as part of the company's fraud detection effort. Typically, customer usage patterns on credit cards are quite consistent. When a credit card is stolen, the usage pattern changes drastically. In spite of increasingly advanced theft protection schemes, credit card companies still lose a lot of money due to theft. Because credit card fraud is approximately 10% higher on the Internet than off, Visa introduced Cardholder Information Security Processing (CISP) in 2000, and MasterCard followed with its Site Data Protection Service (SDPS) in 2001. The CISP and SDPS help only in securing and validating the data and do not actually prevent the use of stolen credit cards. To detect anomalies and act immediately, credit card companies are now using data mining to detect unusual usage patterns of credit cards; and when such a pattern is detected, the customer is called to verify the legitimacy of certain purchases.

Increasing Profits in Retail

Following is an example almost everyone can relate to. Have you shopped at Amazon.com and seen a suggestion pop up that read something like this: "Customers who bought this book also bought the following" and then some list of pertinent books follows? Do you know how it does this? This is typically accomplished with the use of a data mining algorithm called *association rules*. To boost sales, companies like Amazon.com use this algorithm to analyze the sales information of many customers. Based on your book buying behavior, Amazon.com uses the algorithm to predict what other books you would likely be interested in. From the list of books provided by the algorithm, it typically chooses the top five books that have the highest likelihood of being purchased by the customer — then it suggests those books. Another example of where just such an algorithm is used is in the area of DVD rentals. If you have subscribed to Netflix for streaming movies via your favorite game console, you can see movie recommendations based on the movies you have watched recently. The Data Mining Add-ins for Office 2010 that you learn about later in this chapter have a Table Analytics tool for Market Basket Analysis, which is an example of this type of application.

Data Mining in the NBA

As many of you sports fans know, NBA coaches need to analyze opponent teams and adopt appropriate strategies for winning future games. Typically, the coach looks for key players on the opposing team and appropriately matches up his own players to counter the opposing team's strengths and expose their weaknesses. Relevant information can be gleaned from past games that have been analyzed and other sources. The NBA is fast paced, and coaches need to adapt based on current game situations. For this purpose, they need to analyze information every quarter and often in real time.

NBA coaching staffs collect information on players and points scored during a game and feed it into a data mining software application called Advanced Scout. With the help of this software, coaches can analyze patterns — when the opponent scored the most points, who was guarding the highest point scorer on the opposing team, where the shots were taken, and so on. With such information readily available, coaches can adapt to the situation and make decisions to help their team win.

Yes, but how was Advanced Scout helpful, you ask? When the Orlando Magic was devastated in the first two games of the 1997 season finals, which was against the second-seed Miami Heat, the team's fans began to hang their heads in shame. Advanced Scout showed the Orlando Magic coaches something that none of them had previously recognized. When Brian Shaw and Darrell Armstrong were in the game, something was sparked within their teammate Penny Hardaway — the Magic's leading scorer at that time. Armstrong was provided more play time and, hence, Hardaway was far more effective. The Orlando Magic went on to win the next two games and nearly caused the upset of the year. Fans everywhere rallied around the team, and naysayers quickly replaced their doubts with season-ticket purchases for the following year.

Data Mining in Call Centers

Companies spend a lot of money on call center operations to meet customer needs. Customers use a toll-free number provided by the company, and the company pays for each call based on the duration of the call. Typically, most calls target a few specific questions. For example, if the documentation for product setup was not sufficient, the call center might get calls with the same question or related questions on getting the product set up and configured properly.

Often, the information obtained from customers is entered into the computer system for further analysis. With the help of Text Mining, the customers' questions can be analyzed and categorized. This type of analysis can identify a set of questions that are due to a specific problem. Companies can use this information to create a FAQ site where they can post answers on how to solve the specific problem. Making the FAQ available to provide answers to common problems helps the company and its customers have a faster turnaround, saving both time and money. In addition to this, the call center operators can be trained to use the information provided by Text Mining to easily nail down a solution to the problem posed by the customer. The duration of each call is reduced, thereby saving valuable cash for the company.

DATA MINING ALGORITHMS IN SQL SERVER ANALYSIS SERVICES 2012

SQL Server Analysis Services 2012 provides you with nine data mining algorithms that you can use to solve various business problems. These algorithms can be broadly classified into five categories based on the nature of the business problem they can be applied to:

➤ Classification

➤ Regression

➤ Segmentation

➤ Sequence analysis

➤ Association

Classification data mining algorithms help solve business problems such as identifying the type of membership (Platinum, Gold, Silver, Bronze) a new customer should receive or whether the requested loan can be approved for customers based on their attributes. Classification algorithms predict one or more discrete variables based on the attributes of the input data. Discrete variables are variables that contain a limited set of values. Some examples of discrete variables are gender, number of children in a house, and number of cars owned by a customer.

Regression algorithms are similar to classification algorithms; instead of predicting discrete attributes, however, they predict one or more continuous variables. Continuous variables are variables that can have many values. Examples of continuous variables are yearly income, age of a person, and commute distance to work. Algorithms belonging to the regression category should be provided with at least one input attribute that is of type *continuous*. For example, assume you want to predict the sale price of your house, a continuous value, and determine the profit you would make by selling the house. The price of the house would depend on several factors, such as square feet area (another continuous value), ZIP code, and house type (single family, condo, or town home), which are discrete variables. Hence, regression algorithms are primarily suited for business problems where you have at least one continuous attribute as input and one or more attributes that are predictable.

Segmentation algorithms are probably the most widely used algorithms. Segmentation is the process of creating segments or groups of items based on the input attributes. Customer segmentation is one of the most common business applications, where stores and companies segment their customers based on the various input attributes. One of the most common uses of segmentation is to perform targeted mailing campaigns to those customers who are likely to make purchases. This reduces cost when compared with sending mail to all customers, thereby maximizing the profit for the company.

Sequence analysis algorithms analyze and group input data based on a certain sequence of operations. For example, if you want to analyze the navigation patterns of Internet users (sequence and order of pages visited by a user on the Internet) and group them based on their navigations, you can use sequence analysis algorithms. Based on the sequence of pages visited, you can identify interests of people and provide appropriate information to the users as a service or show advertisements relevant to the users' preferences to increase sales of specific products. For example, if you navigate through pages of baby products at www.amazon.com, subsequent visits to Amazon.com pages might result in baby product-related advertisements. Similarly, sequence analysis is also used in genomic science to group a sequence of genes with similar sequences.

Association data mining algorithms help you to identify associations in the data set. Typically these algorithms are used for performing market-basket analysis in which associations between various products purchased together are analyzed. Based on the analysis, associations between various products are identified, and these help in the cross-selling of products together to boost sales. One famous data mining example highlights associations — customers buying diapers also bought beer, and the purchases occurred on Thursday and Friday. One of the reasons is that diapers often need replenishing, and women request their husbands or significant others to buy them. Men often buy over the weekend, and therefore, these purchases were made together. Based on this association, supermarkets can have diapers and beer stocked adjacently, which helps boost the sales of beer.

Following are brief descriptions of the nine data mining algorithms supported in Analysis Services 2012. The description give you an overview of the algorithm and scenarios and where they can be used. Refer to SQL Server Analysis Services 2012 documentation for details such as algorithm properties, their values, and various content types supported by the algorithm for input and predictable columns. Following these descriptions, you learn two data mining algorithms in detail by creating mining models using the data mining wizards.

Microsoft Decision Trees

Microsoft Decision Trees is a classification algorithm used for predictive modeling and analysis. A *classification algorithm* is an algorithm that selects the best possible outcome for the input data from a set of possible outcomes. A data set called the *training data* that contains several attributes is provided as input to the algorithm. Usage of the attributes as either input or predictable is also provided to the algorithm. The classification algorithm analyzes the attributes of the input data and arrives at a distribution, which includes a combination of input attributes and their values that result in the value of the predictable column. Microsoft Decision Trees is helpful in predicting both discrete and continuous attributes. If the data type of the predictable attribute is continuous, the algorithm is called Microsoft Regression Trees, and there are additional properties to control the behavior of the regression analysis.

Microsoft Naïve Bayes

Naïve Bayes is another classification algorithm available in Analysis Services 2012 used for predictive analysis. The Naïve Bayes algorithm calculates the value of the predictable attribute based on the probabilities of the input attribute in the training data set. Naïve Bayes helps you predict the outcome of the predictable attribute quickly because it assumes the input attribute is independent. Compared to the other data mining algorithms in Analysis Services 2012, Naïve Bayes is computationally less intense for model creation.

Microsoft Clustering

The Microsoft Clustering algorithm is a segmentation algorithm that helps in grouping the sample data set into segments based on characteristics of the data. The clustering algorithm helps identify relationships that exist within a specific data set. A typical example would be grouping store customers based on their characteristic purchasing patterns. Based on this information, you can classify the importance of certain customers to your bottom line. The Microsoft Clustering algorithm is unique because it is a scalable algorithm that is not constrained by the size of the data set. Unlike the decision trees or naïve Bayes algorithms, the Microsoft Clustering algorithm does not require you to specify a predictable attribute for building the model.

Microsoft Sequence Clustering

As the name indicates, the Sequence Clustering algorithm groups sequences in the sample data. Similar to the clustering algorithm, the sequence clustering algorithm groups the data sets but based on the sequences instead of the attributes of the customers. An example of where sequence clustering would be used is to group the customers based on the navigation paths of the web site they have visited. Based on the sequence, the customer can be prompted to go to a web page that would be of interest.

Microsoft Association Rules

The Microsoft Association algorithm is an algorithm that typically identifies associations or relationships between products that are purchased. If you have shopped at Amazon.com, you have likely noticed information such as "people who have purchased item one have also purchased item two." Identifying the association between products purchased is called market basket analysis. The algorithm analyzes products in a customer's shopping basket and predicts other products the customer is likely to buy. That prediction is based on purchase co-occurrence of similar products by other customers. This algorithm is often used for cross-selling through product placement in the store.

Microsoft Neural Network

The Microsoft Neural Network algorithm is a classification algorithm similar to Microsoft Decision Trees. It calculates probabilities for each value of the predictable attribute, but it does so by creating internal classification and regression models that are iteratively improved based on the actual value. The algorithm has three layers (the input layer, an optional hidden layer, and an output layer) used to improve the prediction results. The actual value of a training case is compared to the predictable value, and the error difference is fed back within the algorithm to improve the prediction results. Similar to the decision trees algorithm, the Neural Network algorithm is used for predicting discrete and continuous attributes. One of the main advantages of neural networks over the decision trees algorithm is that neural networks can handle complex as well as a large amount of training data much more efficiently.

Microsoft Time Series

The Microsoft Time Series algorithm is used in predictive analysis but is different from other predictive algorithms in Analysis Services 2012 because during a prediction, it does not take input columns to predict the predictable column value. Rather, it identifies trends in the input data and predicts future values based on those trends. A typical application of a time series algorithm is to predict the sales of a specific product based on the sales trend of the product in the past, along with the sales trend of a related product. Another example would be to predict stock prices of a company based on the stock price of another company.

An Analysis Services 2012 Time Series algorithm is used for predicting continuous attributes. Analysis Services 2005 supported a time series algorithm called Auto Regression Trees with Cross Predict (ARTxp). In addition to that, SSAS 2008 introduced another time series algorithm called ARIMA (Auto-Regressive Integrated Moving Average). Therefore, a time series analysis scenario can be modeled by using the ARTxp algorithm, using the ARIMA algorithm, or simultaneously using both algorithms. In the last case, the future predictions are a blend of the values predicted by both algorithms. For the time series algorithms, the DMX language was extended with statements accepting prediction join syntax for time series that allow new data to be appended to the data used for training and to obtain future predictions using the new extended data. You can use this approach to split the training data into two groups, D1 and D2. You can first create a model using D1 and then use the join syntax in DMX to append D2 to obtain future predictions.

Microsoft Linear Regression

Microsoft Linear Regression is a special case of a Microsoft Decision Trees algorithm in which you set an algorithm property so that the algorithm never creates a split and thereby ends up with a linear regression. The algorithm property MINIMUM_LEAF_CASES for the Microsoft Decision Tree will be set to a value greater than the number of input cases used to train the model. Typically, you use the linear regression algorithm when you want to find the relationship between two continuous columns. The algorithm finds the equation of a line that best fits data representing the relationship between the input columns. The Microsoft Linear Regression algorithm supports only input columns that have certain content types. The content type typically used is continuous. The algorithm does not support the content types discrete or discretized. For more details on the content types supported by the algorithm, refer to product documentation.

Microsoft Logistic Regression

The Microsoft Logistic Regression is a variation of the Microsoft Neural Networks algorithm in which the hidden layer is not present. The simplest form of logistic regression is to predict a column that has two states. The input columns can contain many states and can be of different content types (discrete, continuous, discretized, and so on). You can certainly model such a predictable column using linear regression, but the linear regression might not restrict the values to the minimum and maximum values of the column. Logistic regression can restrict the output values for the predictable column to the minimum and maximum values with the help of an S-shaped curve instead of the linear line, which would have been created by a linear regression. In addition, logistic regression can predict columns of content type discrete or discretized and can take input columns that are content type discrete or discretized.

WORKING WITH MINING MODELS

SQL Server Analysis Services 2012 provides two types of mining models: the relational mining model and the OLAP mining model. Relational mining models are created directly from the relational data source, and OLAP Mining models are created from an existing cube or part of a cube. Use of the nine types of data mining algorithms is made within the context of the relational or OLAP mining models. In this chapter, you learn both these models by creating mining models using a few algorithms and analyzing the results.

Relational Mining Model

The AdventureWorksDW sample relational database has specific patterns that you can use to demonstrate the various algorithms available in Analysis Services 2012. In this section, you learn how to create and analyze a decision tree model and a clustering model. Obviously, you need to create a new mining model to explore and analyze the information. When you build a mining model, Analysis Services 2012 retrieves data from the data source and stores it in a proprietary format. Building several mining models from the same data set can result in redundant data stored in Analysis Services 2012. To share data across several mining models, Analysis Services 2012 stores the information about the data that can be shared across several mining models in an object called a Mining Structure. Internally, the information read from relational data sources is stored in a cube to efficiently retrieve the data during mining model creation. The Mining Structure stores data type of attributes, the corresponding column in the data source, and enables you to modify the certain data mining properties that are common across all your mining models.

Have you received coupons in the mail? If you have a postal address, you have. Retail companies used to send coupons to all customers and even some people who weren't customers. That was expensive and of less than optimal efficiency. To minimize cost and maximize profit, companies now use data mining to select targets for coupon or other special postal distributions. Based on certain attributes, retail companies can classify customers into groups (for example; Gold, Silver, or Bronze membership). By doing this, they clearly identify unique characteristics of the group. From there, targeted mailing to those groups can be made instead of mailing to every address on file. This practice saves marketing money for companies and results in a better probability of making sales.

The following steps show you how to solve the targeted mailing type problem by creating a relational mining model on top of the vTargetMail view in the AdventureWorksDW relational database. To create a relational mining model, you first need a data source view containing the tables on top of which you want to build a mining model.

1. Create a new Analysis Services Multidimensional and Data Mining Project named DM2012Tutorial.

2. Create a data source Adventure Works to the AdventureWorksDW relational database.

3. Create a DSV called Adventure Works that includes the vTargetMail view from the AdventureWorksDW data source.

    vTargetMail is a view that retrieves information from several tables in the AdventureWorksDW database. The vTargetMail view contains information about customers who buy bicycles. Based on the information in the view, you can identify potential customers who are likely to buy bicycles. The vTargetMail view has been specifically designed to contain patterns that can be identified by the data mining algorithms. As the name of the view indicates, vTarget-Mail demonstrates the usefulness of the data mining in which the customers can be categorized based on their attributes, and targeted mails with discounts or attractions can be sent only to customers who are likely to buy bicycles.

4. To create a relational mining model, right-click the Mining Structures folder in the Solution Explorer, and select New Mining Structure, as shown in Figure 12-2, to launch the Data Mining Wizard that helps you to create data mining structures and models.

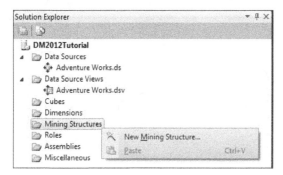

FIGURE 12-2

5. The welcome page provides information about the Data Mining Wizard. Click the Next button.

You can now see the Select the Definition Method page, which enables you to create a mining model from a relational data source or from a cube.

6. Select the From Existing Relational Database or Data Warehouse radio button, as shown in Figure 12-3, and click Next.

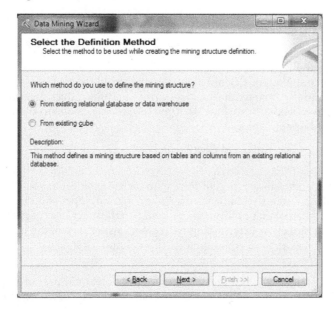

FIGURE 12-3

On the Create the Data Mining Structure page, you can select the data mining technique to use for modeling. If you click the drop-down list box, you can see all the available algorithms, as shown in Figure 12-4. Analysis Services also provides you the option to add your own data mining technique. If you have added a custom data mining technique and exposed it, you can see your data mining technique in this drop-down list box.

7. Select Microsoft Decision Trees, and click Next.

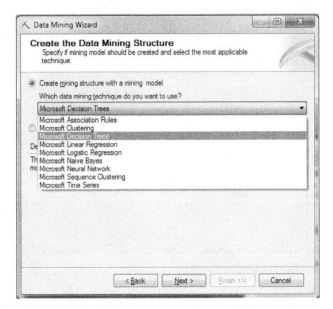

FIGURE 12-4

8. On the Select Data Source View page, select Adventure Works that contains vTargetMail (the DSV you created in step 3) and click Next.

The Specify Table Types page enables you to select the tables upon which you create a mining model. The Specify Table Types page, as shown in Figure 12-5, shows two selections: Case (the primary table) and Nested. Certain algorithms are used for problems such as market-basket analysis and the need to analyze data across multiple tables. In such cases, you need to select certain tables as Nested tables. Typically, there is a one-to-many relationship between the case and nested tables.

9. Select the vTargetMail as a Case table, and click Next.

On the Specify the Training Data page of the wizard, you select the columns from the source tables that are to be used in creation of mining models. In addition, you need to specify whether a specific column should be used as a key column, input column, or predictable column. If you specify a column as an input column, Analysis Services uses this column as an input to the mining model for determining patterns. If a specific column is marked as predictable, Analysis Services enables you to predict this column for a new data set based on the existing model if the input columns for the new data set are provided.

In the current data set, you want to predict if a customer is a potential buyer of bikes. The column BikeBuyer determines if an existing customer bought bikes before. Therefore, you need to mark this column as a predictable column. When you have marked this column as predictable, you need to identify the potential factors that can influence a customer who buys bikes. If you think certain factors can influence a customer to buy bikes, select those columns as input columns. The wizard provides you a way to recommend columns as input columns by analyzing a sample data set.

FIGURE 12-5

10. Select the BikeBuyer column as predictable by enabling the check box, as shown in Figure 12-6.

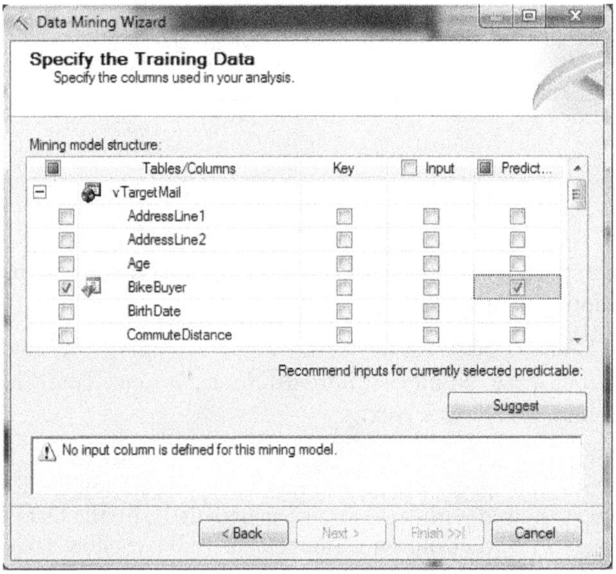

FIGURE 12-6

11. Click the Suggest button.

The wizard analyzes a sample of the data set and provides you the list of columns related to the selected predictable attribute BikeBuyer, as shown in Figure 12-7. The score column indicates how close an attribute is related to the BikeBuyer column; a higher number indicates a stronger relationship. Stronger relationship can mean that a specific column can influence the chosen predictable column. Based on the score, the wizard auto-selects certain columns as input columns. You can deselect these attributes or select additional attributes that you think might influence a customer's decision on buying bikes.

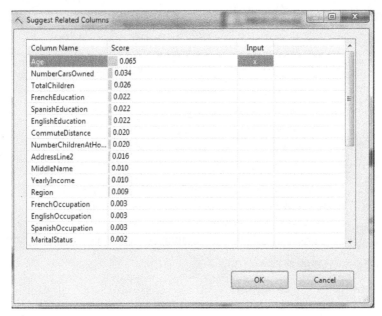

FIGURE 12-7

12. Click OK to Continue.

13. The selections you made in the Suggest Related Columns page now display in the Specify the Training Data page, as shown in Figure 12-8.

14. Select the columns Age, CommuteDistance, EnglishEducation, Gender, HouseOwnerFlag, MaritalStatus, NumberCarsOwned, NumberChildrenAtHome, Region, TotalChildren, and YearlyIncome as input columns, and click Next.

The selected columns along with their content types and data types are shown in the Specify Columns' Content and Data Type page. The relational data type of a column is mapped to the corresponding data type used within Analysis Services 2012 by the Data Mining Wizard. As shown in Figure 12-9, the column Content Type indicates how each selected column will be used by Analysis Services when creating the mining model. You learn more about these content types when refining this model.

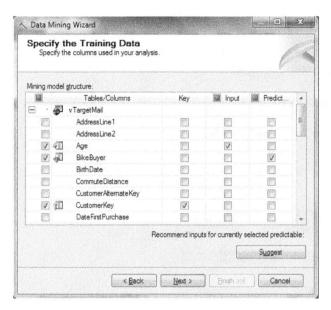

FIGURE 12-8

FIGURE 12-9

15.   Make all of the Continuous content types Discrete except Yearly Income, and click Next.

In SSAS 2012, the ability to specify some percentage of your data for testing the model is built into the product. The Create Testing Set page shown in Figure 12-10 enables you to specify the percentage of data to hold back and also the maximum number of cases in the testing data set. You can specify both options to restrict the testing data used for verifying model accuracy.

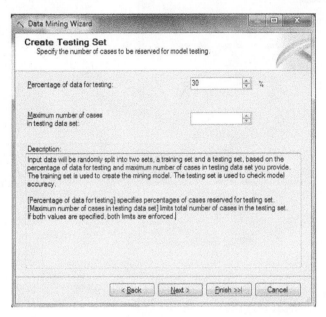

FIGURE 12-10

16. In the Create Testing Set page, accept the default value of 30% for the percentage of data for testing, and click Next.

17. Because all mining models are contained within a mining structure, Analysis Services automatically creates a mining structure with the same name as the mining model. However, you can use different names for the mining structure and the mining model in the completion page. Specify Targeted Mailing for the mining structure name and TM Decision Tree for the model.

You also have the option to allow drillthrough while analyzing a mining model to understand the training data corresponding to a specific node, which gives you the ability to see additional details.

18. Enable the Allow Drill Through option, and click Finish to create the mining model.

The mining structure object can be seen in the mining structure editor, as shown in Figure 12-11. The mining structure editor contains five views: Mining Structure, Mining Models, Mining Model Viewer, Mining Accuracy Chart, and Mining Model Prediction. By default, you will be in the Mining Structure tab. The mining structure view contains two panes. The Data Source View pane shows the tables used by the mining structure and allows you to perform the operations available within a DSV. The pane on the left shows the columns of the mining structure in a tree view. You can delete existing columns or add columns to the mining structure by dragging and dropping them from the DSV. The properties of a column can be edited in the properties pane when the column is selected.

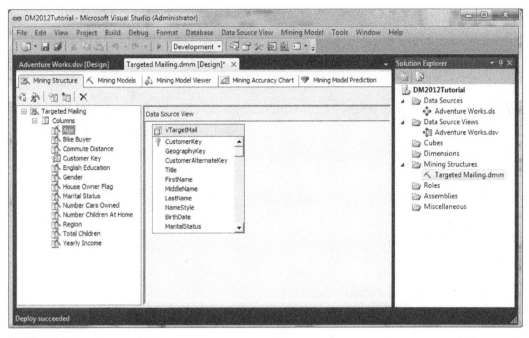

FIGURE 12-11

Figure 12-12 shows the Mining Models view. The Mining Models view shows the mining models in the current mining structure. You can have one or more mining models within each mining structure. The columns of the mining structure are by default inherited as columns of a mining model. Each column of a mining structure can be used for a specific purpose in a mining model. A column can be used as input to the mining model, used as a predictable column, used for both input and as a predictable column, or not be used by the mining model at all. These four usages are represented as Input, Predict Only, Predict, and Ignore, respectively, in the Mining Models view. These usages can be selected from the drop-down list box corresponding to a column in a mining model. You can add additional mining models within a mining structure by right-clicking in the Mining Models view and selecting New Mining Model.

The mining structure editor is used to make refinements to the mining model created by the Data Mining Wizard. You learn to make refinements in the mining structure editor by making a few refinements to the decision tree mining model you have created. You make two refinements: Change the content type for column Age and the usage of the Bike Buyer column. Age is a unique attribute that can be viewed as discrete because the value is recorded as an integer between 0 and 100. If you have ever participated in market surveys, you know they generally ask your age within a specific range rather than your exact age. Most adults do not like to admit their age publicly, especially in the later years, so if you are extremely reticent to mention your age, be worried. Be very worried. In this example, you model Age as a set of ranges rather than a discrete value. This content type is called Discretized. Discretized means that the values split across N number of ranges and any value of Age is assigned the new value based on the range. The number of ranges is controlled by the property DiscretizationBucketCount. Based on the value set for DiscretizationBucketCount property, Analysis Services 2012 can identify the right ranges based on the minimum and maximum values of Age.

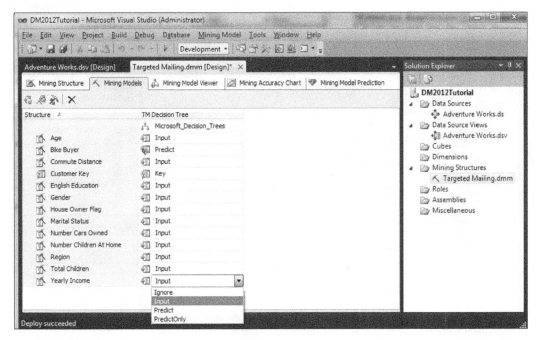

FIGURE 12-12

19. In the Mining Models view, select Age in the Structure column. You can see the properties for the Age column in the Properties window, as shown in Figure 12-13.

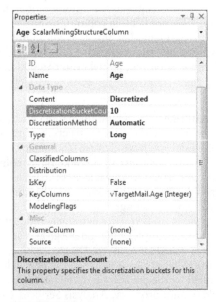

FIGURE 12-13

20. Change the Content property from Discrete to Discretized, and set the DiscretizationBucketCount property to 10.

21. Change the usage of Bike Buyer column to Predict.

The Usage of the column Bike Buyer was initially set to Predict Only because this is what you selected in the wizard. The value Predict means that the Bike Buyer attribute will be used as an input as well as an output to the mining model. By choosing the Bike Buyer as an input column, you can provide additional information to the mining model algorithm so that the model accurately represents the input data. You have now completed all the refinements to the decision tree mining model, and it is ready to be deployed on your SSAS instance.

22. Right-click the project name DM2012Tutorial from Solution Explorer, change the Deployment Server in Property Pages, and click OK.

23. Press the F5 button to deploy the mining model.

SQL Server Data Tools (SSDT) sends the definition of the entire project you created to the server along with a process request. When the database is processed, SSDT switches the view to the Mining Model Viewer, as shown in Figure 12-14. The decision trees algorithm identifies the factors influencing customers to buy bikes and splits customers based on those factors. It stores those factors within the model. The Mining Model Viewer represents the contents of the mining model in the form of a tree view. The root of the tree starts with a single node that represents all the customers. Each node shows the percentage of customers (shown by the horizontal bar within the node) who have bought bikes based on the input set. Each node is split into multiple nodes based on the next most important factor that determines why a customer has bought a bike. The tree contains nodes at several levels from 1 to N based on the number of splits determined by the decision tree algorithm. Each node in the tree is associated with a specific level in the tree. The root node is at level 1, which is the topmost level. The depth of the tree is measured by the number of splits or levels of the tree. In the Mining Model Viewer, you can select the depth of the tree to view using the Show Level slider above the tree view. Figure 12-14 shows nodes with horizontal bars that are shaded with two colors: red and blue. The Mining Legend window shows the legend for the colors in the horizontal bars of a node. If the Mining Legend window is not visible, you could right-click in the Mining Model Viewer, and select Show Legend.

The Mining Legend window in Figure 12-14 shows that blue (Value = 0) indicates customers who are not bike buyers, red (Value = 1) indicates the customers who have bought bikes, and white indicates customers for whom the BikeBuyer value is missing. The split from a node at one level to nodes in the next level is based on a condition determined by an input column that influences the predictable attribute, which is shown within the node, such as Region = North America.

In the sample that you are analyzing, the most important factor that determines a customer buying a bike is the number of cars owned by the customer. The root node is split into five nodes based on the values for the number of cars owned (zero to four); three of these nodes are shown in Figure 12-14. If you click the node with Number Cars Owned = 2, you can see that 39.47% of such customers are likely to be bike buyers. The next most important influencing factor when the number of cars owned is 2 is the customer's Region. You can traverse the tree from each node to identify the conditions that are likely to affect customers' decision to buy a bike. Based on the information available in the mining model, you can not only understand factors influencing the customers' decisions to buy bikes, but also predict if customers are potential bike buyers based on their properties. After you identify potential customers, you can send targeted mails to customers who are potential buyers rather than all customers.

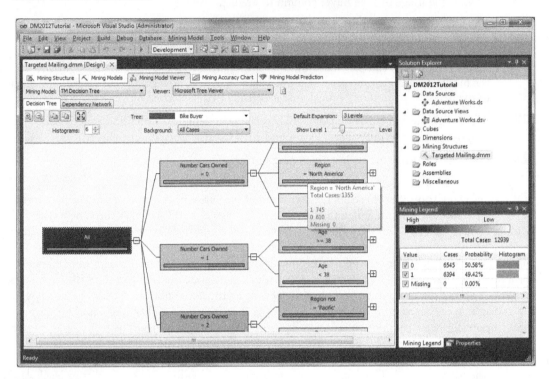

FIGURE 12-14

When created, can your model predict accurately? If so, how accurate is it? How much trust can you place in the results of the model? To answer these questions, the data mining editor has a view called the Mining Accuracy Chart, as shown in Figure 12-15. The Mining Accuracy Chart view contains four sub-views or sub-tabs that help you validate model accuracy. These are Input Selection, Lift Chart, Classification Matrix, and Cross Validation. The Input Selection view provides you three panes.

The first pane enables you to select certain predictable attributes and specific values to use in Lift Chart comparison. In this example, you have only the Bike Buyer column as predictable. You can choose a specific value 0 or 1 for the Bike Buyer to analyze the accuracy for specific values if needed. The second pane provides a way to specify an input data set to validate the mining model (refer to Figure 12-15). You can use the test cases in mining model or test cases in mining structure based on the data you have held back while creating the model. The third option enables you to specify an entirely new data set. If you select the third option, you can see a button that enables you to map the columns from a new data set to the columns of the mining model. If you select a new data set to validate against, you can use the third pane to specify a filter condition using the Open Filter Editor button in the Filter pane. This editor allows you to specify conditions to restrict the data set or enter your own query to restrict the data set.

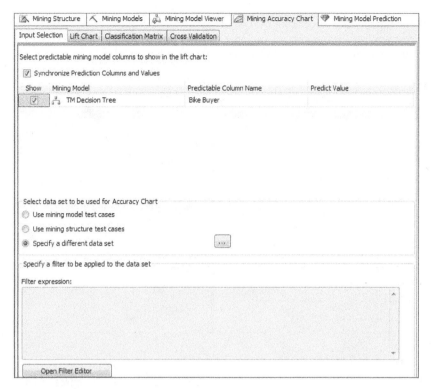

FIGURE 12-15

You can use the mining model to predict the bike buyer value for each customer. If the predicted value is the same as the actual value in the validation data set you have chosen, the model has predicted the value correctly. If not, the model has inaccurately predicted the Bike Buyer value for the customer.

To analyze the accuracy of the mining model, do the following:

1. In the Mining Accuracy Chart view, select Use Mining Model Test Cases.

Analysis Services knows the original data source that was selected and the input data set that was held back to validate the accuracy of the mining model. SSAS provides two ways to analyze the validity of the model. One is to show the results graphically, and the other is to show the actual numbers. To see the validity of the model graphically, select the Lift Chart sub-tab of the Mining Accuracy Chart view. You can see the graph shown in Figure 12-16. The X-axis shows the percentage of data set used for prediction, and the Y-axis shows the percentage of prediction correctness. You can see a legend window providing details on the two lines. If you create a perfect model that predicts correctly, the percentage correctness is always 100%. This is represented by a blue line in the graph (the 45-degree line in Figure 12-16). In the current model, the predictable attribute value can have only one of the two values: 0 or 1. Obviously, you would want a model that predicts values close to that of an ideal model. This graph gives you a visual way to easily compare the prediction correctness of the model as compared to the ideal model. The prediction correctness percentage of the model is shown with a red line. You can see from Figure 12-16 that the prediction correctness of the model does not match that of the ideal model, but it is reasonably good because the prediction results are correct for 73% (population correct % for 100% of overall population) of the overall data set, as shown in the Mining Legend.

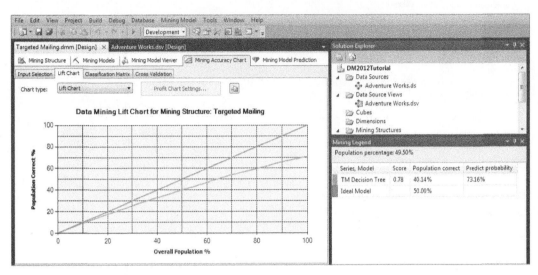

FIGURE 12-16

This is all well and good, but how is the lift chart calculated and visually represented? Analysis Services 2012 predicts the bike buyer attribute for every row in the input table. Each prediction also has a value called predict probability that provides a confidence value associated with the prediction. If you have a predict probability of 1.0, it means that the model believes the predicted value is always correct. If the predict probability for an input is 0.90, that means there is a 90% probability the predicted value is correct. After predicting the values for all the input rows, the results are ordered based on the predict probability. Then the predicted results are compared with the original values to calculate the prediction correctness percentage, and they are plotted on a graph. This can be seen in the graph (refer to Figure 12-16), where the lines indicating the current model and ideal model are nearly identical up to 10% of the population. The mining legend shows the score, population correct percentage, and predicts probability values for a specific population selection. The population percentage is 49.50%, which is indicated by a darker vertical line (refer to Figure 12-16). You can select a different population percentage by clicking the mouse on a specific population. When 100% of the data set is considered, the decision tree mining model can predict correct values for 71% of the data set correctly. For an ideal model, this prediction value is 100%. The score for a model helps you to compare multiple models within a mining structure. The value is between 0 and 1 and shows the effectiveness of one model versus another model. A higher score value means the model is more efficient.

Two types of charts are provided by the Mining Accuracy Chart viewer to help in analysis of the mining model. You have just seen the lift chart. The second chart is called the profit chart. The profit chart helps you analyze the potential profit your business would make based on four input parameters: number of samples, fixed cost incurred, cost per each row, and profit gained due to prediction. You can see the benefit of the profit chart only when there is a significant cost involved per sample.

2. Select the chart type Profit Chart in the drop-down list box.

3. In the Profit Chart settings dialog, specify the Individual cost as 11 to indicate the cost of mailing a customer.

4. Leave the remaining values set to their defaults, and click OK.

You now see the profit chart, as shown in Figure 12-17.

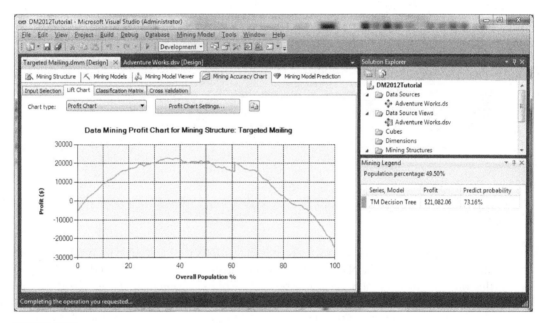

FIGURE 12-17

Analysis Services 2012 predicts the bike buyer value and calculates profit based on the profit chart settings you have provided. Similar to the lift chart, you can move the gray vertical line. The mining legend shows the profit and predicts probability values for the corresponding population percentage selected by the gray vertical line, as shown in Figure 12-17. Similar to the lift chart, the predicted values are sorted based on prediction probability and then plotted on the graph. Therefore, the lower values of overall population percentage have higher prediction probability values. As you can see from the profit chart, the profit increases with an increase in the sample size, reaches a maximum profit, and then drops down. If you send mail to the entire population, you are likely expected to incur a loss of approximately $25,469. You definitely want to get the maximum profit. The maximum profit you can obtain for the specified lift chart parameters is approximately $22,833 when you mail to about 35% of the population. To maximize your profit, you need to send mails only to customers who have a prediction probability greater than the prediction probability corresponding to the population percentage that has maximum profit. Thus, the profit chart helps improve the profit of a business by saving the cost that would have been incurred for mailing to customers who are not potential buyers.

The third sub-view in the Mining Accuracy chart view is called the Classification Matrix. Figure 12-18 shows the classification matrix of the decision tree model on vTargetMail. The classification matrix shows the original and predicted values for the predict attribute. In the decision tree model, the predictable values for bike buyer are 0 or 1. The matrix shows the actual and predicted values for all the specified input rows. Figure 12-18 shows that the columns indicate the actual values, whereas the rows indicate the predicted value. There are 2,759 input rows that have the Bike buyer value 0. Of these, the model predicted 1968 of them to be the correct value 0, whereas it predicted the remaining 791 rows incorrectly to value 1. Similarly, the model predicted 1947 of 2,786 input rows correctly to have a value of 1. The prediction values might be slightly different based on your machine. This matrix provides you an overview of how good the predicted values are as compared to the actual values in a matrix format.

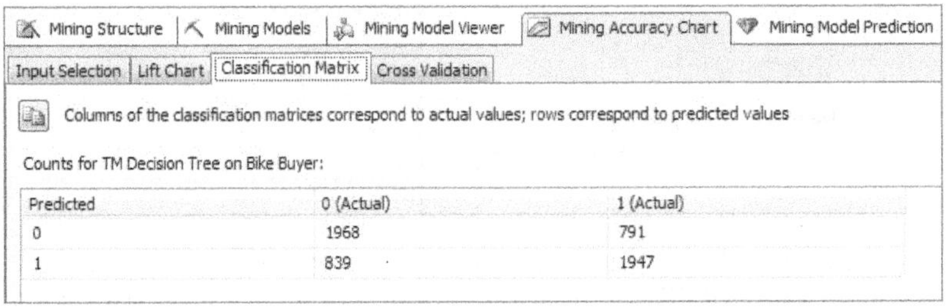

Mining Structure	Mining Models	Mining Model Viewer	Mining Accuracy Chart	Mining Model Prediction

Input Selection	Lift Chart	Classification Matrix	Cross Validation

Columns of the classification matrices correspond to actual values; rows correspond to predicted values

Counts for TM Decision Tree on Bike Buyer:

Predicted	0 (Actual)	1 (Actual)
0	1968	791
1	839	1947

FIGURE 12-18

The last sub-view in the Mining Accuracy Chart is the Cross Validation sub-tab. Analysis Services 2012 enables you to validate the chosen mining models using cross-validation methods. It does this by splitting the training data set into a specified number of folds. (Fold count is a value that you input in the Cross Validation tab, as shown in Figure 12-19.) Folds are also called partitions. After the data set is split into multiple partitions, Analysis Services creates a mining model for each partition. The training data set corresponding to a mining model for a specific partition is the data set from all the remaining partitions other than the current partition. Analysis Services then evaluates the accuracy of the model using the data set in the current partition. The result will be the quality of the model measured on a fold of the input dataset as captured by the following measures: for discrete attributes, the number of false and true classifications, log score, lift, and root mean square error; for continuous attributes, root mean square error, mean absolute error and log score; for clustering model, the case likelihood measure. The last page in the Mining Accuracy Chart view helps in using the cross-validation feature and analyzing the effectiveness of model. Follow these steps to perform cross validation.

1. Switch to the Cross Validation page in the Mining Accuracy Chart view.

2. Set Fold Count to 4.

3. Set Max Cases to 3000.

4. Click the Get Results button.

You now see the results of the cross validation, as shown in Figure 12-19. This view enables you to analyze the results of the cross validation done comparing the data set against the mining model. Refer to Figure 12-19 to see the decision tree model; you can see the first two tables indicating the accuracy of the overall model. The key factors to consider here are the average percentage of values in which the mining model predicts accurately as well as the standard deviation. Ideally, you want the Value column as close as possible to the partition size with a low standard deviation. Please be aware that the cross-validation results for various mining model algorithms are different and need to be interpreted appropriately.

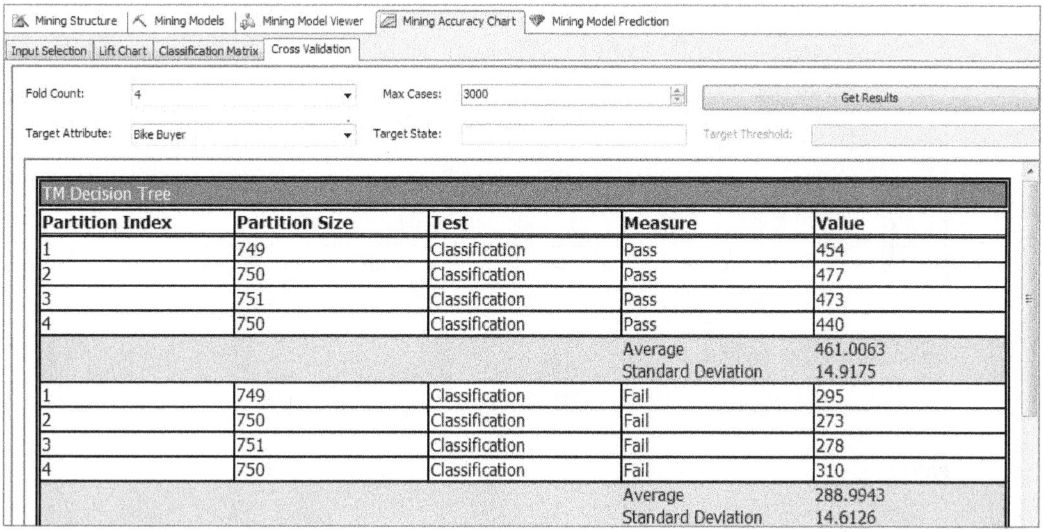

Partition Index	Partition Size	Test	Measure	Value
1	749	Classification	Pass	454
2	750	Classification	Pass	477
3	751	Classification	Pass	473
4	750	Classification	Pass	440
			Average	461.0063
			Standard Deviation	14.9175
1	749	Classification	Fail	295
2	750	Classification	Fail	273
3	751	Classification	Fail	278
4	750	Classification	Fail	310
			Average	288.9943
			Standard Deviation	14.6126

FIGURE 12-19

Having seen the accuracy of the model created by Analysis Services 2012, you can meaningfully start predicting the values using the model. The Mining Model Prediction view helps you perform predictions and save the results. Figure 12-20 shows the Mining Model Prediction view. Similar to the Mining Accuracy Chart view, you can specify the case table that contains the input data for which you want to perform a prediction. Follow these steps to understand how to predict whether new customers are bike buyers:

1. In the Select Input Table(s) section of the Mining Model Prediction view, click the Select Case Table button. In the Select Table dialog that appears, select the source table vTargetMail with which you can now predict the bike buyer value.

    You can select columns from the input table and certain data mining prediction functions or custom expressions on the predicted values to retrieve results such as the top 10% of the customers or top 10 customers. The columns from the input table or applying certain data mining prediction functions can be selected in the lower half of the window pane, as shown in Figure 12-20.

2. Select the CustomerKey, FirstName, LastName, and EmailAddress columns from the input table vTargetMail, as shown in Figure 12-20.

3. Select the Bike Buyer predictable column from the mining model vTargetMail, as shown in Figure 12-20.

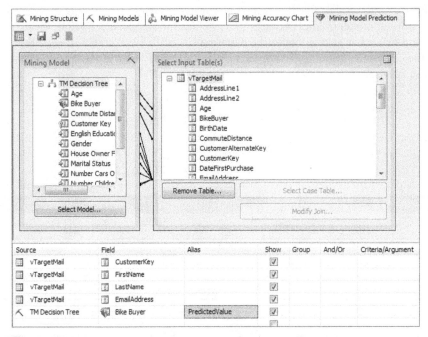

FIGURE 12-20

4. Click the Switch to Query Result View button (leftmost button on the Mining Model Prediction view toolbar) as shown in Figure 12-21 to see the prediction results.

You see the results of the prediction, as shown in Figure 12-21. You can specify constraints to the predicted value such as predicted value = 1 so that the results view shows only customers who are likely to buy bikes.

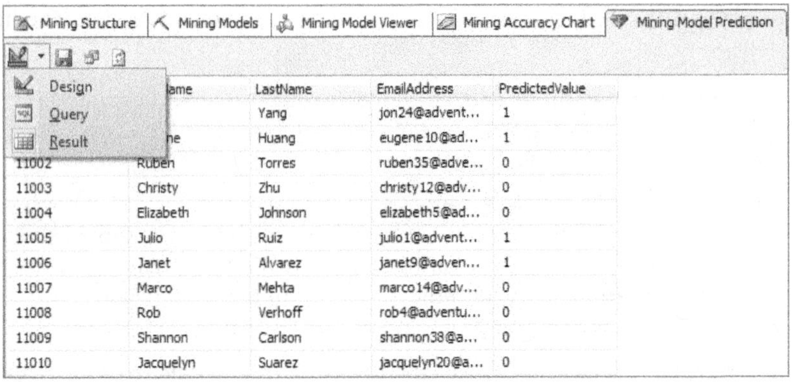

	Name	LastName	EmailAddress	PredictedValue
Design		Yang	jon24@advent...	1
Query	he	Huang	eugene10@ad...	1
Result				
11002	Ruben	Torres	ruben35@adve...	0
11003	Christy	Zhu	christy12@adv...	0
11004	Elizabeth	Johnson	elizabeth5@ad...	0
11005	Julio	Ruiz	julio1@advent...	1
11006	Janet	Alvarez	janet9@adven...	1
11007	Marco	Mehta	marco14@adv...	0
11008	Rob	Verhoff	rob4@adventu...	0
11009	Shannon	Carlson	shannon38@a...	0
11010	Jacquelyn	Suarez	jacquelyn20@a...	0

FIGURE 12-21

You can predict the bike buyer value for the input case table using the designer. The designer creates a query that retrieves the predicted data from SSAS. The query language used to retrieve predicted results from mining models is called Data Mining Extensions (DMX). The DMX language is specified in the OLEDB for Data Mining specification. The DMX language is similar to SQL and contains statements for data definition and data manipulation. The data definition language includes statements for model creation, and the data manipulation language contains statements for training the model, which includes inserting data into the model and retrieving prediction results from it. Just as the SQL language has a SELECT statement to retrieve data from a relational database, DMX has a SELECT statement to retrieve data from mining models. The DMX SELECT statement has several variations based on the nature of the results retrieved. For detailed information on the data definition language and data manipulation language of DMX, refer to the Analysis Services 2012 documentation.

Click the drop-down arrow of the button that you used to switch between Design and Result view (refer to Figure 12-21) and select the Query option. You can see the following DMX query, which was generated to retrieve prediction results.

```
SELECT
  t.[CustomerKey],
  t.[FirstName],
  t.[LastName],
  t.[EmailAddress],
  ([v Target Mail].[Bike Buyer]) as [PredictedValue]
From
  [TM Decision Tree]
PREDICTION JOIN
  OPENQUERY([Adventure Works],
    'SELECT
      [CustomerKey],
      [FirstName],
      [LastName],
      [EmailAddress],
      [MaritalStatus],
      [Gender],
      [YearlyIncome],
      [TotalChildren],
      [NumberChildrenAtHome],
      [EnglishEducation],
      [HouseOwnerFlag],
      [NumberCarsOwned],
      [CommuteDistance],
      [Region],
      [Age],
      [BikeBuyer]
    FROM
      [dbo].[vTargetMail]
    ') AS t
  ON
    [TM Decision Tree].[Marital Status] = t.[MaritalStatus] AND
    [TM Decision Tree].[Gender] = t.[Gender] AND
    [TM Decision Tree].[Yearly Income] = t.[YearlyIncome] AND
    [TM Decision Tree].[Total Children] = t.[TotalChildren] AND
    [TM Decision Tree].[Number Children At Home] = t.[NumberChildrenAtHome] AND
```

```
[TM Decision Tree].[English Education] = t.[EnglishEducation] AND
[TM Decision Tree].[House Owner Flag] = t.[HouseOwnerFlag] AND
[TM Decision Tree].[Number Cars Owned] = t.[NumberCarsOwned] AND
[TM Decision Tree].[Commute Distance] = t.[CommuteDistance] AND
[v Target Mail].[Region] = t.[Region] AND
[v Target Mail].[Age] = t.[Age] AND
[v Target Mail].[Bike Buyer] = t.[BikeBuyer]
```

The preceding prediction query is one of the variations of the DMX SELECT query that has the following syntax:

```
SELECT [FLATTENED] [TOP <n>] <select expression list>
FROM <model> | <sub select> [NATURAL]
PREDICTION JOIN  <source data query>
[ON <join mapping list>]
[WHERE <condition expression>]
[ORDER BY <expression> [DESC|ASC]]
```

The input data for a prediction is specified after the keywords PREDICTION JOIN. The <select expression list> contains the columns to be retrieved as part of the results and includes columns from the input/case table and the predicted columns, which are specified after the SELECT keyword. The mining model used for prediction is specified after the FROM keyword. The mapping of columns from input data set to the mining model attributes is specified in the ON clause, as seen in the preceding prediction query. The prediction query retrieves four columns from the input table along with the predicted column for each input row. Similar to executing MDX queries from SQL Server Management Studio, you can execute the preceding DMX query. You have seen only a simple DMX query in this example. Analysis Services 2012 tools help you build DMX queries graphically, but if you are the kind of person who wants to write your DMX, this query will be a good start. You can learn more about DMX and writing prediction queries from the Analysis Services documentation and book.

You can create multiple mining models within the same mining structure, and they can use either the same or a different mining algorithm. You would typically want to create a new mining model with the same algorithm if you want to see the accuracy of the existing mining model with a slight change in properties of the columns, such as disabling certain input columns or changing columns from PredictOnly to Predict. Alternatively, you can create a new mining model with a different mining algorithm and have the same attributes. A typical example would be to create a clustering or use the Naïve Bayes algorithm on a data set for which you have created a decision tree model. Next, you learn to create a clustering algorithm on the same data set and analyze the results. Follow these steps to create a new clustering algorithm:

1. Switch to the Mining Models view in the Mining Structure editor.

2. Right-click anywhere within the mining pane, and select New Mining Model, as shown in Figure 12-22.

3. Enter **TM Clustering** as the Model Name in the New Mining Model dialog, as shown in Figure 12-23.

4. From the Algorithm name drop-down list, select Microsoft Clustering, and click OK.

A new mining model is created with the name TM Clustering in the Mining Models view, as shown in Figure 12-24.

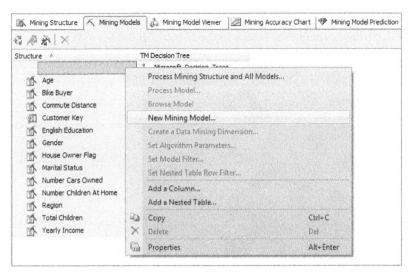

FIGURE 12-22

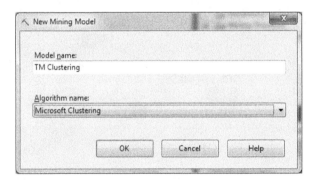

FIGURE 12-23

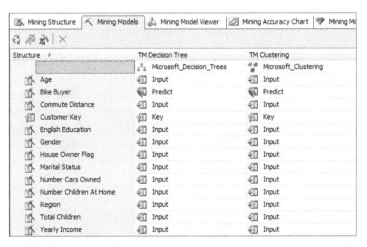

FIGURE 12-24

5. Deploy the project.

6. After the deployment completes, switch to the Mining Model Viewer.

7. Click the Mining Model drop-down list, and select TM Clustering, the name of the clustering mining model you created (Figure 12-25).

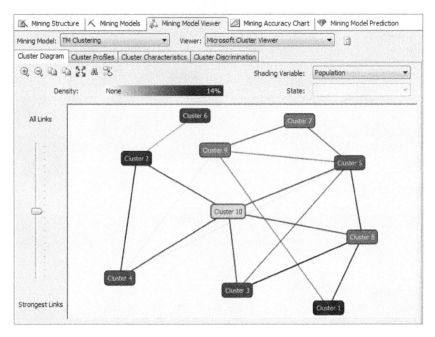

FIGURE 12-25

You now see the clustering mining model represented as several nodes with lines between these nodes, as shown in Figure 12-25. By default, the clustering mining model groups the customers into ten different clusters. The number of clusters generated can be changed from a property for the cluster mining model. Each cluster is shown as a node in the cluster viewer. The shade of the node is dependent upon the shading variable column and a specific state of the column that is shown in the viewer. Darker shading on the node indicates that the cluster favors a specific input column and vice versa. If there is a relationship (that is, similarity) between two clusters, that is indicated by a line connecting the two nodes. Similar to the shade of the color node, if the relationship is stronger between two nodes, it is indicated via a darker line such as the relationship between Cluster 3 and Cluster 8. You can move the slider on the left of the cluster diagram from All Links to Strongest Links. As you do this, you can see the weaker relationships between the clusters are not displayed. You can change the cluster name by right-clicking the cluster and selecting Rename. The cluster diagram helps you get an overall picture of the clusters, how the cluster is affected based on a specific column of the model used as the shading variable, as well as the relationships between clusters.

In Figure 12-25, the chosen column is Population. Population is the name used in the Mining Model Viewer for the entire data set used for training the mining model. You can select wanted input columns of the mining model from the drop-down for Shading Variable to see the effect of the column on the various clusters. When you choose a specific shading variable column, you need to choose one of the states of the column to be used as the shading variable for the clusters.

For example, if you choose the shading variable as Age, you have several options for the State, such as missing value, < 39, >=87, and so on, as shown in Figure 12-26. You can see that Cluster 6 has a darker shade, indicating that cluster is predominantly populated with customers whose age is <39. Overall, the Cluster Diagram page enables you to analyze the various clusters, their characteristics, and relationships between clusters based on a specific column value, which enables you to get a quick grasp of the cluster's characteristics.

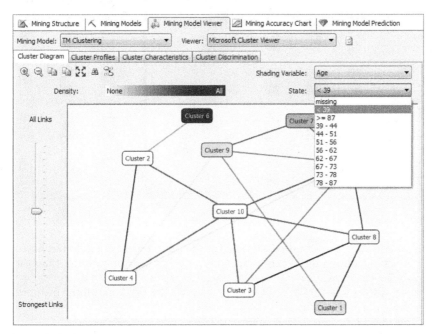

FIGURE 12-26

When you have a good overview of the clusters from the Cluster Diagram view, the next step is to learn more about each cluster along with the distributions of various values for each column.

1. Click the Cluster Profiles tab to learn more details about each cluster and various values for each column.

   The Cluster Profiles view shows the relationship between the mining columns of the model and the clusters in a matrix format, as shown in Figure 12-27. The intersection cell of a specific column and a cluster shows a histogram bar of the various values of the column that are part of the cluster. The size of each bar reflects the number of items used to train the model. If you hover over the histogram, you can see the size of each bar (refer to Figure 12-27). The number of histogram bars shown is controlled by the value set for histogram bars. The histogram bars are sorted based on the size, and the first N bars (where N is the value set for Histogram bars) display. For example, for the age attribute, 1 groups display in the legend. Because the histogram bars value is 4, the cluster viewer picks up the four most important buckets of the column age and shows how this column contributes toward the profile of a specific cluster.

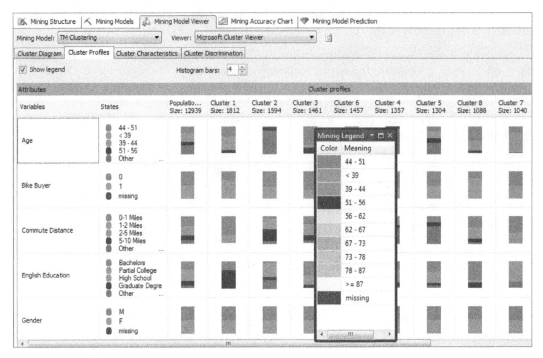

FIGURE 12-27

Each column has a histogram bar called Missing for the input records that do not have any value specified for that column during training. Columns that have more states than the number of states shown in the view (number of states shown is controlled by the value set for Histogram bars) have a bucket called Other that shows the value for all the histogram states that are not shown explicitly.

2. Click the Cluster Characteristics tab to see the characteristics of a single cluster and how the various states of the input columns make up the cluster.

On this page, you see the cluster characteristics of the entire data set, as shown in Figure 12-28. You can view the characteristics of a specific cluster by selecting the cluster name from the drop-down list for Cluster. The probability associated with a specific value for an input column such as Number Cars Owned = 0 is calculated based on the number of input records having that specific value. The probability column shows the calculated probability for an input variable for the chosen cluster. If you hover over the bar in the probability column, you can see the corresponding probability value (refer to Figure 12-28).

After clusters are formed, one of the typical operations that you would want to do is compare the characteristics of two clusters to have a better understanding of each cluster; especially related clusters. The Mining Model Viewer provides a way to explore these differences between clusters.

3. Click the Cluster Discrimination tab.

You can see the characteristics of Cluster 1 and the complement of Cluster 1. Using the cluster diagram, you can see that the strongest relationship for the entire data set is between Cluster 3 and Cluster 8.

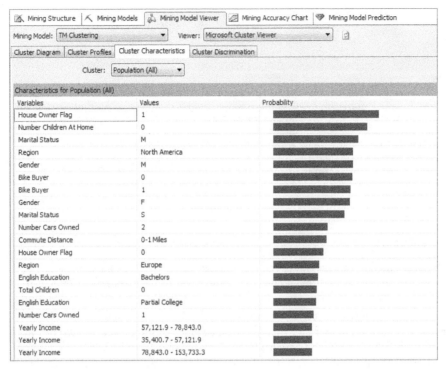

FIGURE 12-28

4. To compare the differences between these clusters, from the drop-down list next to Cluster 1 and Cluster 2, select Cluster 3 and Cluster 8, as shown in Figure 12-29.

The strongest clusters on your machine might be different. Review the cluster diagram and choose the strongest clusters for comparing differences.

On the Cluster Characteristics page (refer to Figure 12-28), you can see the characteristics of a single cluster. On the Cluster Discrimination page, you can see the states of an input column that favor one cluster over another. The states of the input columns indicate the differences between the two clusters and are ordered based on the importance of the difference the column contributes toward the clusters. The two columns on the right indicate which cluster the specific column value favors, and the length indicates how strong the value is that influences the cluster (refer to Figure 12-29). For example, from the figure, you can see that when customers have no child or have no child at home, Cluster 8 is favored, and when customers have a total of 4 children, Cluster 3 is favored. Similarly, you can review the other input columns' states to get a better understanding of the clusters' relationships.

You can also create new mining models using the Data Mining Wizard. However, when you create a new mining model with the wizard, the wizard automatically creates a new mining structure and then creates the mining model within this mining structure. Whenever you need to create multiple mining models for comparison, create the first model using the wizard and the remaining models within the same mining structure using the Mining Structure editor. The Data Mining Wizard is self-explanatory, and you can explore the creation of other mining models such as Microsoft Sequence Clustering, Microsoft Regression Trees, Neural Networks, and Sequence clustering using the data sets available in the AdventureWorksDW sample relational database.

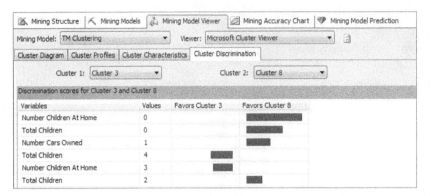

FIGURE 12-29

OLAP Mining Models

Certain types of business problems necessitate the use of aggregated data for analysis instead of individual input rows. For example, assume a customer buys several products from various stores. You might want to segment the customers not only by their individual attributes, but also by the total amount they have spent in the stores. The mining model requires aggregated sales from the various purchases made by the customer and includes that amount as an input attribute to the clustering mining model. You can certainly add such a column to the customer table using a named query, but if the sales information table has billions of records, the aggregation of the relational data source will be slow. You should also consider maintainability of the mining model because you might want to process it on a periodic basis. There is a better solution than aggregating the data at the relational data source level. What better way to aggregate data than by creating a cube?

Because Analysis Services helps you create cubes as well as mining models, it provides a way to create mining models from cubes. Such mining models are called OLAP mining models because the data source for the mining models is a cube, and cubes contain OLAP data. Analysis Services 2012 also provides the functionality to create new cubes that include content from the created mining model along with the original cube data, which provides you the power and flexibility to analyze the cubes based on patterns discovered by the mining model. Such an analysis can help you understand your data better and make better business decisions. You create and analyze cubes containing mining model content in this section. You use the AnalysisServicesMultidimensionalTutorial you created earlier to create OLAP Mining Models in this chapter. When you download the samples for this book, the AnalysisServices2012Tutorial project is under the Chapter12 folder. To create an OLAP mining model, do the following:

1.   Open the AnalysisServicesMultidimensionalTutorial project.

2.   Deploy the entire project to your Analysis Services instance.

3.   In Solution Explorer, right-click the Mining Structures folder, and select New Mining Structure to launch the Data Mining Wizard.

4.   Click the Next button on the welcome screen.

5.   On the Select the Definition Method page of the Data Mining Wizard, select the option From Existing Cube, as shown in Figure 12-30, and click Next.

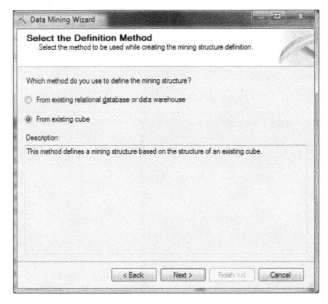

FIGURE 12-30

6. In the algorithm selection page, select the Microsoft Clustering algorithm, as shown in Figure 12-31, and click Next.

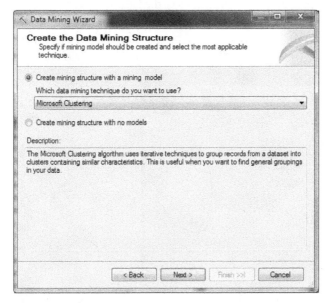

FIGURE 12-31

You are now on the Select the Source Cube Dimension page, as shown in Figure 12-32. This page lists the cube dimensions within the database upon which you can create a mining model. You need to select the cube dimension that will be used as the case table for creating the mining model.

7. From the Adventure Works DW cube, select the cube dimension Dim Customer, and click Next.

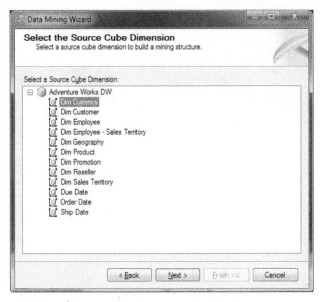

FIGURE 12-32

8. On the Select the Case Key page of the wizard, select the Customer attribute (the key of the Dim Customer dimension) to be the key for the mining structure, as shown in Figure 12-33, and click Next.

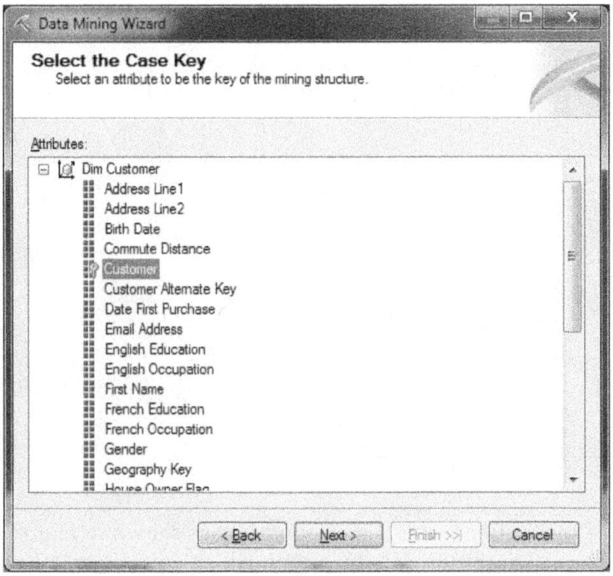

FIGURE 12-33

The Customer attribute you selected in the Select the Case Key page will be used as the key for the mining model. On the Select Case Level Columns page, you need to select all the attributes that will be part of the mining model. Attributes that will be used as input or predictable should be selected on this page.

9. Select the cube dimension attributes Commute Distance, Education, Occupation, Gender, House Owner Flag, Marital Status, Number Cars Owned, Number Children At Home, Total Children, and Yearly Income. Also, select the facts Internet Order Quantity and Internet Sales Amount from the measure group Fact Internet Sales, as shown in Figure 12-34, and click Next.

FIGURE 12-34

10. On the Specify Mining Model Column Usage page, select the Sales Amount as predictable, as shown in Figure 12-35, and click Next.

On the Specify Columns' Content and Data Type page, you can change the data type and content type for each attribute if needed. Both the content type and data type play an important role in the creation or training of the mining model.

11. Accept the defaults on the Specify Columns Content and Data Type page, and click Next.

You are now on the Slice Source Cube page. This page enables you to slice the cube and build the mining model based only on a specific part of the cube. You can specify the constraints for slicing the cube on this page similar to specifying filter conditions in the cube browser. You have the option to filter on dimensions other than the Dim Customer dimension, such as specific dates for Order Date or specific categories or products.

12. Accept the default (no slicing on the cube) on the Slice Source Cube page, as shown in Figure 12-36, by clicking Next.

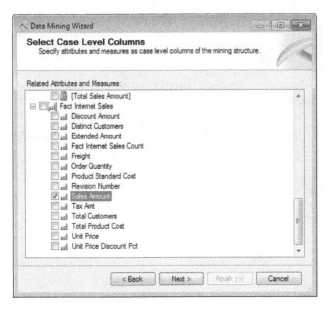

FIGURE 12-35

FIGURE 12-36

13. On the Create Testing Set page, select the defaults, as shown in Figure 12-37, and click Next.

14. On the final page, specify the name for the mining structure as OLAPMiningStructure and for the mining Model as CustomerOLAPMiningModel, as shown in Figure 12-38.

15. Click the check boxes for Create Mining Model Dimension, Create Cube Using Mining Model Dimension, and Allow Drill Through (refer to Figure 12-38) and click Finish.

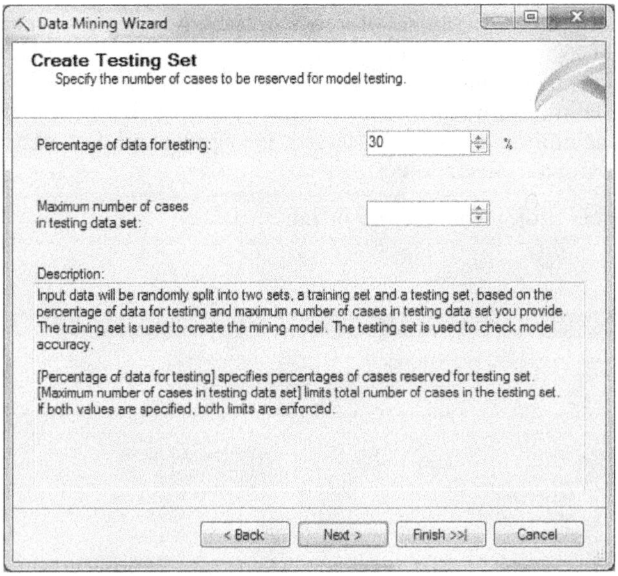

FIGURE 12-37

You can analyze the mining model separately using the mining model viewer, but Analysis Services 2012 takes it one step further by enabling you to create a cube that includes the results of the mining model. In Analysis Services 2012, you can create a dimension from the results of the mining model and add this to the existing cube. The Mining Structure Wizard facilitates the creation of the new cube that includes the existing cube and results of the mining model.

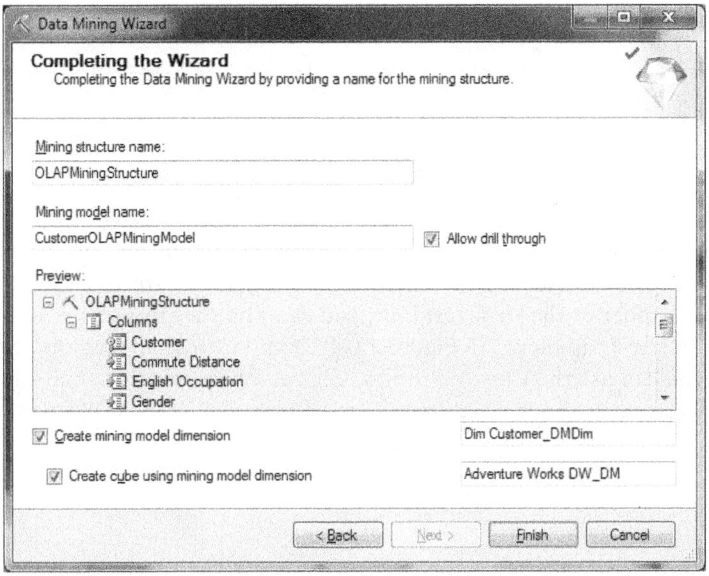

FIGURE 12-38

The OLAP Mining Model is created, and you now see it in the Mining Structure editor, as shown in Figure 12-39. The input columns of the data mining structure are mapped to the corresponding cube dimension and measure group of the cube, which is indicated by the line connecting the case level columns and fact Internet sales within the DSV pane of the Mining Structure editor. When the mining model is processed, the aggregated data of the measures is used instead of the individual transactions.

16. Deploy the Analysis Services project to the SSAS instance.

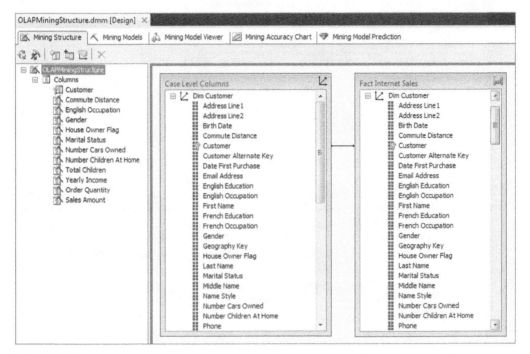

FIGURE 12-39

When processing is complete, switch to the Mining Model Viewer, where you can see the various clusters created based on the chosen attributes from the cube. There are 10 clusters created by default. If you move the slider to the strongest link, you can find the strongest relationship between Cluster 5 and Cluster 8, as shown in Figure 12-40. Similar to analyzing the relational mining model clusters, you can use the Cluster Profiles, Cluster Characteristics, and Cluster Discrimination tabs to learn more about the clusters created from the cube. Explore the OLAP cluster mining model.

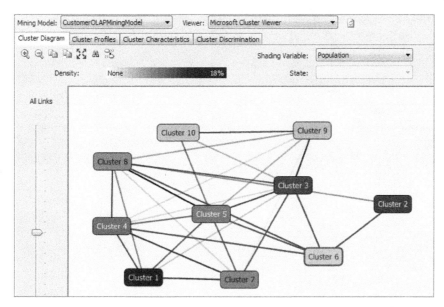

FIGURE 12-40

Analyzing the Cube with a Data Mining Dimension

When you created the OLAP Mining Model, you selected the creation of a data mining dimension and a cube in the Data Mining Wizard. To create a new dimension and cube, you need a DSV. Therefore, a DSV that includes a query to the OLAP mining model to retrieve the data from the mining model was created by the wizard. You can see a DSV called Dim Customer_DMDSV created in the DSV folder in the Solution Explorer. Also, you see a dimension called [Dim Customer_DMDim] that includes attributes from the data mining model that was created. Finally, a cube called [Adventure Works DW_DM] was created that includes all the cube dimensions and measure groups of the Adventure Works DW cube and also the newly created data mining dimension [Dim Customer_DMDim]. In Chapter 9, you learned about the data mining relationship between a dimension and cube. The data mining relationship is defined between a dimension derived from a data mining model and a cube that contains it. The cube [Adventure Works DW_DM] that was created by the Data Mining Wizard includes a data mining dimension. If you open the Dimension Usage tab of the [Adventure Works DW_DM] cube, you can see a data mining relationship, as shown in Figure 12-41.

You can browse the [Adventure Works DW_DM] cube along with the data mining dimension to analyze the Internet sales you have obtained from various clusters, as shown in Figure 12-42. How is this information useful? You can perform an analysis of the current sales with various clusters and then perform a comparison of sales after the targeted mailing to analyze the sales and identify the effectiveness of the targeted mailing. Analysis Services thereby provides an integrated environment for creating mining models and cubes that help you with effective business analysis.

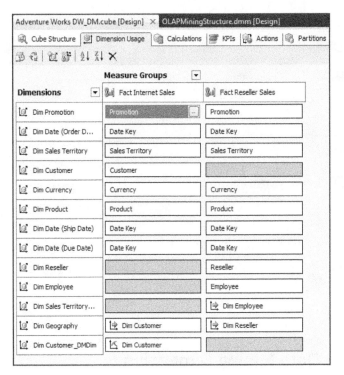

FIGURE 12-41

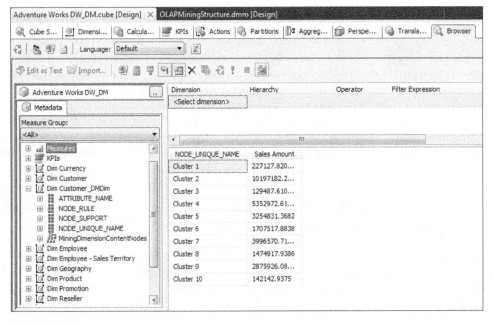

FIGURE 12-42

USING DATA MINING WITH OFFICE 2010

Traditionally, data mining has been considered a specialized area, and you need to have an in-depth understanding of the data mining algorithm to create and analyze data mining models and to recognize interesting patterns in the data set. You still need to understand data mining to effectively replicate the mining models using SSDT. SQL Server 2012, however, aims to make data mining available to end users in an intuitive way that helps them to analyze the data without having to understand data mining.

The Microsoft SQL Server 2012 Data Mining Add-ins for Office 2010 is a redistribution package available for download from www.microsoft.com as part of the SQL Server 2012 release. It requires Microsoft .Net Framework 4.0 and supports both x86 bit and amd64 bit in Office 2010. Three components are part of this add-in: Table Analytics, Data Mining Client, and Visualization. Table Analytics and Data Mining Client are add-ins for Excel, and Visualization is a Visio template you can use to effectively visualize and present data mining.

The add-ins by themselves are not sufficient to perform the analysis. You also need SQL Server Analysis Services 2008 R2 or a later version to perform the analysis of the data at the backend. SQL Server Analysis Services (SSAS) could be on the same or a remote machine. When you have access to SSAS and have the add-ins installed, you are ready to analyze data in an Excel spreadsheet.

The first step is to download and install the add-in from http://www.microsoft.com/download/en/details.aspx?id=29061. Next, configure your SSAS instance to enable creation of temporary mining models. Perform the following steps to configure your SSAS:

1. Click Start, and click the Server Configuration utility from All Programs ⇨ Microsoft SQL Server 2012 Data Mining Add-ins.

2. Click Next on the welcome screen.

3. Enter your SSAS instance name in the Server box, and click Next to view the Allow Creation of Temporary Mining Models page.

4. Ensure the check box that enables session mining models is enabled (checked) and click Next.

5. On the Create Database for Add-in Users page, you have the option to create a new database or use an existing database that can be used by the data mining add-in users to create temporary and permanent mining models. The wizard connects to your SSAS instance and retrieves the list of databases.

6. Select the default Create New Database with the database name DMAddinsDB. On the final page of the wizard, you can add all the end users who would be using the Microsoft SQL Server 2012 Data Mining Add-ins for Office 2010, as shown in Figure 12-43. All these users need to have full database permissions on the chosen database. By default, the wizard adds the user running the wizard as the database admin of the database.

7. Enter any users that need to use the Microsoft SQL Server 2012 Data Mining Add-ins for Office 2010, and click Finish.

After you click the Finish button, the wizard connects to the SSAS instance, configures the instance to enable the session mining model by changing the appropriate server property, creates the database

DMAddinDB, and adds permissions to the users specified. You can see each action taken by the wizard along with the status on the confirmation page.

FIGURE 12-43

You have now made the necessary configuration to your SSAS instance that allows you to use the Data Mining Add-ins. As mentioned earlier, the add-ins have three components: Table Analytics, Data Mining Client, and the Visio template. In the next section, you learn about Table Analytics.

Table Analytics

Table Analytics, one of the Microsoft SQL Server 2012 Data Mining Add-ins for Office 2010, helps you to analyze the tables within Excel spreadsheets. You can use the shipped sample Excel spreadsheet DMAddins_SampleData.xlsx to learn about the Table Analytics component. To start using Table Analytics, follow these steps:

1. Open the sample spreadsheet DMAddins_SampleData.xlsx by clicking Start All Programs ➪ Microsoft SQL Server 2012 DM Add-ins ➪ Sample Excel Data.

   The spreadsheet has nine sheets that contain sample data to highlight various features of the Data Mining Add-ins.

2. Click the sheet named Table Analysis Tools Sample.

3. On the sheet, click one of the cells in the table. You see additional tabs in the Excel Ribbon called Analyze and Design.

4. Click the Analyze Ribbon.

You see the various Table Analytics features from the Table Analytics Tools add-in as icons shown in Figure 12-44. Each icon is used to perform specific tasks on your table to provide results from which you can potentially take meaningful actions. On the SQL Server 2012 Analysis Services server selected when you configured the add-ins, it creates a mining model and performs predictions using data mining algorithms supported by SQL Server 2012. For the end user who does not have knowledge of data mining, this is presented in simple, easy-to-understand names that intuitively suggest the outcome of the icon. For example, you can use the Analyze Key Influencers icon to identify the key columns of the table in Excel that contribute to influencing the data. You first need to establish a connection to the SSAS instance to use the various options in the Analyze Ribbon.

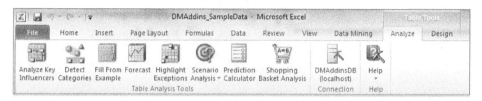

FIGURE 12-44

5. Click the Connection icon.

6. In the Analysis Services Connections dialog that appears, click New.

7. In the Connect to Analysis Services dialog, enter your SSAS instance name; then click the Catalog name drop-down list and select DMAddinsDB. Click OK to close the New Connection dialog.

The Connect to Analysis Services dialog combines the SSAS instance name and the catalog name as the default-friendly name and enables you to change it. A new connection to your SSAS instance is created under the Current Connection in the Analysis Services Connections dialog, whereas additional connections are shown under a separate group called Other Connections. You can manage and test connections in this dialog.

8. Click the Close button in the Analysis Services Connections dialog.

Now that you have established a connection to your Analysis Services database, next look at the various table analytics features.

Analyze Key Influencers

Analyze Key Influencers helps to analyze data in a column that holds significant interest or business value to see what factors are important in indicating or differentiating values. For example, from the data in the Table Analysis Tools Sample sheet, you can identify the factors (columns) that indicate whether a person is married or single. In this example, you use Analyze Key Influencers to determine what factors indicate whether people purchased a bicycle:

1. After clicking a cell in the table, click the Analyze Key Influencers icon (refer to Figure 12-44).

2. In the Analyze Key Influencers dialog, select the Purchased Bike column.

3. Click the link Choose Columns To Be Used for Analysis.

4. In the Advanced Columns Selection dialog, select each column except ID, as shown in Figure 12-45, and click OK.

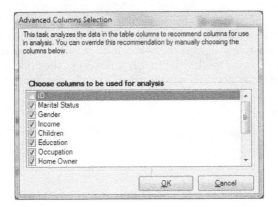

FIGURE 12-45

5. Click Run to start the analysis.

The wizard provides status on the operations performed in a status window. The wizard first reads the table data, creates a data mining model on your SSAS instance, and then retrieves the results of the mining model and displays them in a new spreadsheet. In this example, the wizard creates a worksheet called Influencers for Purchased Bike to show the key influencing columns that determine if a person buys a bike.

The column chosen to analyze key influencers can contain several values. A discrimination report is extremely valuable in this case because it indicates the various values of the columns and the influencing values of other columns and helps you to compare any two values. In this example, the Purchase Bike column has only two values, Yes and No. The Analyze Key Influencers Wizard upon creating the new spreadsheet shows a dialog to add the discrimination report to your new spreadsheet.

6. In the Discrimination Based on Key Influencers dialog box, click Add Report, and then click Close.

You should see the discrimination report for the Yes and No values of the Purchased Bike column added to the Influencers for Purchased Bike spreadsheet (refer to Figure 12-46). Now analyze the results provided by the dialog.

The first report, the key influencer report, shows influencers for all values of the column Purchased Bike. In this case, you can clearly see that people in the data set who are married, own two cars, and live in North America tend not to purchase bikes, whereas single people with zero or one car who live in the Pacific region do. The length of the bar in the Relative Impact column indicates the importance of this particular factor in indicating the specified value. In this case, you can see that not owning a car, for example, is much more important than marital status or region in indicating whether people have bought a bike.

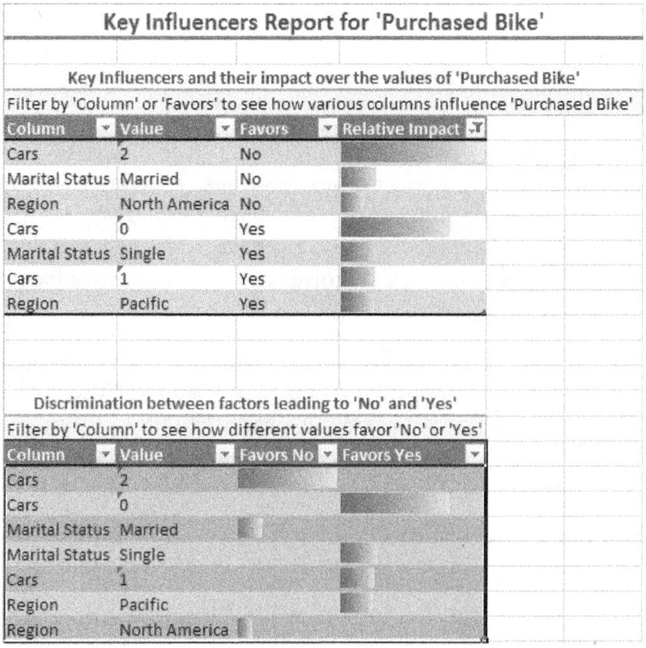

Key Influencers Report for 'Purchased Bike'			
Key Influencers and their impact over the values of 'Purchased Bike'			
Filter by 'Column' or 'Favors' to see how various columns influence 'Purchased Bike'			
Column	Value	Favors	Relative Impact
Cars	2	No	
Marital Status	Married	No	
Region	North America	No	
Cars	0	Yes	
Marital Status	Single	Yes	
Cars	1	Yes	
Region	Pacific	Yes	

Discrimination between factors leading to 'No' and 'Yes'			
Filter by 'Column' to see how different values favor 'No' or 'Yes'			
Column	Value	Favors No	Favors Yes
Cars	2		
Cars	0		
Marital Status	Married		
Marital Status	Single		
Cars	1		
Region	Pacific		
Region	North America		

FIGURE 12-46

You can filter for specific values in each column of your report to analyze specific data. This is especially useful when you have several rows in your report and you want to analyze the effect of specific values on the column analyzed.

The discrimination report is similar to a key influencer report except that it shows clearly the distinction in factors that influence one value over another. The factors are ordered by their importance. This report is generally more useful when the column you analyze has more than two values; however, even with this example, you can see that being married is a stronger influencer of not being a bicycle purchaser in the data set than being from the Pacific influences being a purchaser.

When your analysis is complete, you can share your results with any of your end users or SharePoint users via Excel Services by sharing or posting (Publish Option) your workbook.

Because this is done by end users, the Table Analytics add-in does not use words specific to data mining. The Key Influencer Wizard uses the Naïve Bayes data mining algorithm to predict the columns that are key influencers. If you know about data mining and want to know what commands are sent to an SSAS instance, you can click the Trace icon from the Connection section at the far right of the Data Mining tab on the Ribbon.

The Trace icon helps you view and analyze the sequence of commands sent by the Data Mining add-in to your SSAS instance. After clicking it, you see the SQL Server Data Mining Tracer dialog, which shows the command to create the Naïve Bayes algorithm. Now review the next icon, Detect Categories.

Detect Categories

Data is gathered periodically for your personal or business needs. You can analyze the data based on individual columns or a combination of columns with ease. However, there are just too many combinations to analyze to take meaningful action. Categorization is a way to group similar entities. You can then analyze each category to understand and interpret the data, which is easier than analyzing based on combinations of columns and their values. The Categories icon helps you group the data in the spreadsheet using data mining, which then enables you to analyze your data efficiently. In this example, you group people with similar characteristics using the data set in the Table Analytics Tools Sample spreadsheet. Categories help you to reduce paralysis by analysis.

Detect Categories analyzes your data to see which rows are similar to each other by examining all the column values for each row. It then creates a report to assist you to understand the categories found and labels each row as to which category it belongs to. You also have the option to add an additional column within the spreadsheet to indicate the category, which makes it easier to analyze a specific category.

1. Switch to the Table Analysis Tools Sample spreadsheet.

2. In the Analyze tab, click the Detect Categories icon at the left end of the tab.

   You can see the Detect Categories dialog where you can select the columns that you want to use to categorize the data set. Columns that uniquely identify each row in the table, such as the ID column, are not useful for data categorization because these identifiers are normally used as a key to access the data and rarely have any categorical meaning to the outside world. Therefore, don't include any column that can serve as unique identifiers, such as IDs, phone numbers, and addresses. By default, the dialog identifies the identifier column ID and does not include the column in the selection. You have the option to create a specific number of categories and have the default option Auto-detect where SSAS can detect the right number of categories. You also have a check box to add a new column within the spreadsheet and add the category name so that you can use this column for further analyzing the data.

3. Choose the defaults in the Detect Categories dialog, and click Run. Detect Categories takes the data and sends a request to SSAS to create a cluster session mining model. The dialog later queries information from the created cluster data mining model to create a new spreadsheet called Categories Report, as shown in Figure 12-47. This report has three parts: a category list showing the size of each category that you can use to relabel the categories, a table containing descriptions of the categories, and a pivot chart enabling you to analyze how column values are distributed among the categories. In addition to this, the Detect Categories dialog adds a column to the original table indicating the category of each row, as shown in Figure 12-48.

In this example, you see that Detect Categories has identified seven distinct categories of people in the data set, with the largest group having 189 members and the smallest having 108 members, as shown in the category list report. You can switch to the Table Analytics Tools Sample sheet to see which row of data belongs to which category based on the Category column (refer to Figure 12-48). Now, you can filter the rows for a single category. You could rename a category in the Categories report. The new name is automatically reflected in the Category column in the original data sheet.

7 categories were detected

To rename a category, edit the 'Category Name' below.

('Category Name' changes are visible in the 'Category' column of the source Excel table)

Category Name	Row Count
Category 1	189
Category 2	141
Category 3	158
Category 4	149
Category 5	126
Category 6	129
Category 7	108

Category Characteristics

Filter the table by 'Category' to see the characteristics of different categories.

Category	Column	Value	Relative Importance
Category 1	Income	Very Low:< 39050	
Category 1	Region	Europe	
Category 1	Occupation	Manual	
Category 1	Occupation	Clerical	
Category 1	Commute Distance	0-1 Miles	
Category 1	Cars	0	
Category 1	Children	2	
Category 1	Children	1	
Category 1	Education	Partial High School	
Category 1	Education	High School	
Category 1	Children	3	

FIGURE 12-47

Sample data for Analyze Key Influencers, Detect Categories, Highlight Exceptions and Scenario Analysis

ID	Marital Status	Gender	Income	Children	Education	Occupation	Home Owner	Cars	Commute Distance	Region	Age	Purchased Bike	Category
12496	Married	Female	40000	1	Bachelors	Skilled Manual	Yes	0	0-1 Miles	Europe	42	No	Category 2
24107	Married	Male	30000	3	Partial College	Clerical	Yes	1	0-1 Miles	Europe	43	No	Category 1
14177	Married	Male	80000	5	Partial College	Professional	No	2	2-5 Miles	Europe	60	No	Category 5
24381	Single	Male	70000	0	Bachelors	Professional	Yes	1	5-10 Miles	Pacific	41	Yes	Category 5
25597	Single	Male	30000	0	Bachelors	Clerical	No	0	0-1 Miles	Europe	36	Yes	Category 1
13507	Married	Female	10000	2	Partial College	Manual	Yes	0	1-2 Miles	Europe	50	No	Category 1
27974	Single	Male	160000	2	High School	Management	Yes	4	0-1 Miles	Pacific	33	Yes	Category 7
19364	Married	Male	40000	1	Bachelors	Skilled Manual	Yes	0	0-1 Miles	Europe	43	Yes	Category 2
22155	Married	Male	20000	2	Partial High School	Clerical	Yes	2	5-10 Miles	Pacific	58	No	Category 1
19280	Married	Male	20000	2	Partial College	Manual	Yes	1	0-1 Miles	Europe	48	Yes	Category 1

FIGURE 12-48

The Category Characteristics report shows factors that are important in describing each category. By default, it displays only factors for the first category, Category 1 (refer to Figure 12-47). Analyzing Category 1, you can see the category is composed of manual or clerical workers in Europe with low incomes. Many other factors are also listed for Category 1 but much less important according to the relative importance bars. Now look at characteristics of Category 2.

1. Click the filter next to the Category column (as shown in Figure 12-49).

2. Select Category 2, deselect Category 1, and click OK.

FIGURE 12-49

Analyzing people in Category 2, you see that it is composed of people who do not have a car, but do have a bike. In addition, these people have a graduate degree but earn less and live close to their work, which is indicated by their commute distance. You can rename Category 2 as LowIncomeGraduates by clicking the Category 2 cell in the Category Name report and typing in the new name.

The third part of the Categories report is the Category Profile report. This report shows the distribution of column values across all the categories. The report uses a pivot chart to show the distribution. By default, the report shows the first column ordered alphanumerically, in this case by age.

You can choose a different column to analyze values across all categories by doing the following:

1. Click the report to enable the PivotTable Field List.

2. Click the filter next to the Column field, deselect Age, select the Income field, as shown in Figure 12-50, and click OK.

You see the distribution of the Income field, as shown in Figure 12-50. You can see that Category 1 has the maximum number of people with the lowest income, and Category 7 has the maximum number of people in the high income bracket. You can select more than one column; however, it can quickly become confusing with too many distributions at the same time, so analyze the categories one column at a time.

When you finish your analysis, you can share the results with any Excel or SharePoint users via Excel Services by sharing or posting your workbook. Viewing or manipulating the results does not require DM Add-ins.

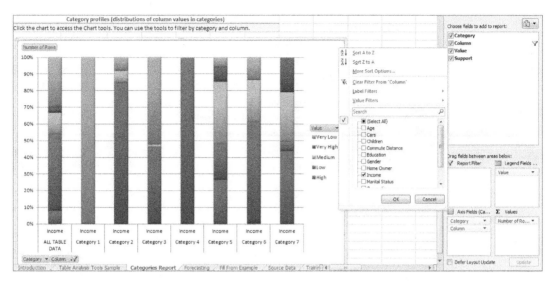

FIGURE 12-50

Fill from Example

Excel has always had this terrific feature of understanding patterns and extending them. For instance, after entering 2, 4, and 6 in adjacent cells in the same column, you can select the three cells, click and drag (or double-click the bottom right of the selection), and Excel enters 8, 10, 12, and so on, on your behalf. Fill from Example takes a similar approach. Based on the entered values and implicated patterns, Fill from Example can predict and fill in values for all other unfilled rows in a specific column. For this example, you use Fill from Example to identify if a person is a highly valued customer:

1. Switch to the Fill from Example sheet in the workbook. You can see the column called High Value Customer, which shows a few rows that have the values Yes or No.

2. Click one of the cells in the table, click the Analyze tab, and then click the Fill from Example icon.

3. The Fill from Example Wizard displays a column that it detects as potentially needing to be filled. In this example, the wizard has selected the High Value Customer column by default because it has detected that this column has only a few values and the remaining values are not filled in. The Choose Columns To Be Used for Analysis link enables you to add more columns.

4. Select the default values in this dialog, and click Run.

The wizard now creates a mining structure with the columns, inserts the values into the mining structure, and then creates a logistic regression mining model. After the mining model is created, the wizard creates a new spreadsheet called Pattern Report for 'High Value Customer', as shown in Figure 12-51. In addition, the wizard creates a new column in the original data sheet called High Value Customer_Extended and fills in the predicted values for each row using the mining model.

In this example, you can see how each column in the table influences if a customer is a highly valued customer. (The Favors column value is Yes.) In addition to having the information on whether a column impacts the value, you also see to what extent the column influences the value by the length of the bar shown in the Relative Impact column.

Pattern Report for 'High Value Customer'			
Key Influencers and their impact over the values of 'High Value Customer'			
Filter by 'Column' or 'Favors' to see how various columns influence 'High Value Customer'			
Column	Value	Favors	Relative Impact
Region	Pacific	No	
Commute Distance	5-10 Miles	No	
Gender	Female	No	
Education	Partial High School	No	
Education	Bachelors	No	
Commute Distance	1-2 Miles	No	
Occupation	Professional	No	
Commute Distance	2-5 Miles	Yes	
Children	5	Yes	
Region	Europe	Yes	
Home Owner	No	Yes	
Education	Partial College	Yes	
Children	3	Yes	
Cars	2	Yes	

FIGURE 12-51

Fill from Example is useful in scenarios in which you have some missing data for certain columns due to data entry errors or someone accidentally deleting it. Based on the other information in the table, you would have a high probability to get the right value using Fill from Example.

Forecast

The Forecast tool enables you to extend a series of data using the predictive power of SSAS. The data series must be in columns for the tool to work. If your data is in rows, you must first pivot the data before running the Forecast tool. You can pivot your data by copying it and selecting Paste Special and choosing the Transpose option.

Practice using the Forecast tool using the sample data in the spreadsheet provided in the DMAddins_SampleData:

1. Click the Forecasting worksheet, and click one of the cells in the table.

2. Click the Analyze tab to see the Excel Ribbon, and then click the Forecast icon.

The Forecast dialog enables you to select the columns to forecast. The dialog has automatically detected that Year is a column that indicates time and has deselected that column for prediction. You need to select the column to be used as a time slice. In addition, you can indicate the number of time units to forecast for. Optionally, you can select the periodicity of the data if the data is available on a daily or an hourly basis, which provides more information to the dialog and enables better forecasting.

3. Select the Year_Month column for the timestamp option.

4. Make sure the remaining default values are chosen for the number of time units and periodicity of the data, as shown in Figure 12-52, and click Run.

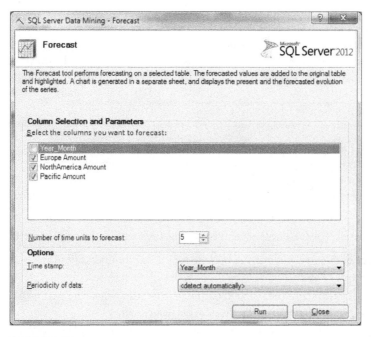

FIGURE 12-52

The Forecast dialog gets all the inputs and sends them to your SSAS 2012 instance to create a time series mining model using the data provided. After the analysis is complete, Forecast creates a new spreadsheet containing the original data with the forecasted results highlighted by dotted lines, as shown in Figure 12-53, and appends forecasted values at the bottom of the original data set.

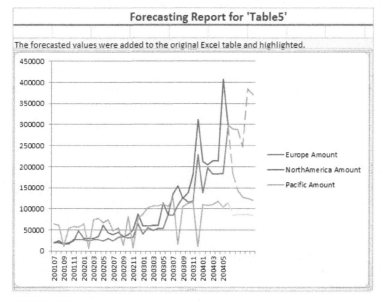

FIGURE 12-53

This information is forecasted by the mining model based on the data for the previous year and months. You should be aware that in some cases, the Forecast tool returns fewer results than requested. This occurs when Analysis Services determines that it can no longer produce viable predictions and therefore stops. This behavior is entirely determined by the data itself and cannot be modified. When your analysis is complete, you can use the forecasting results to take appropriate business actions.

Highlight Exceptions

Assume you have data that you have received as an Excel spreadsheet that has been entered manually by several users. You may want to find if there are exceptions or anomalies in the data entry. The Highlight Exceptions tool can help you in such a scenario. In this example, assume the income of one of the customers was entered incorrectly to see if the tool can detect the exception:

1. Switch to the Table Analysis Tools Sample spreadsheet, and click one of the cells in the table.

2. To simulate an incorrect data entry, change the Income for the ID number 27974 from 160000 to 1600, as shown in Figure 12-54.

FIGURE 12-54

3 Click the Analyze tab, and then click the Highlight Exceptions icon. The Highlight Exceptions dialog allows you to select the column you suspect might have exceptions. By default, the dialog excludes a column that it detects as a unique identifier.

4. Accept the default selection suggested in the dialog, and click Run. The Highlight Exceptions tool creates a clustering algorithm on the provided data set and then predicts the values to identify if exceptions exist. The dialog creates a new worksheet called Table2 Outliers. This worksheet shows the threshold for detecting exceptions. The default value chosen is 75%. In addition to that, it shows each column and how many exceptions were identified for each column.

5. Increase the exception threshold from 75% to 95%. You now see that the Table2 Outliers worksheet shows only two exceptions, one in Income and one in Age, as shown in Figure 12-55.

6. Switch to the Table Analysis Tools Sample worksheet. You see that the row for customer ID 27974 where you changed the income from 160000 to 1600 in step 4 is highlighted.

7. Change the income for the customer with ID 27974 to the original amount of **160000**. You now see that the Highlight Exceptions tool automatically detects that the value is within the range of what was expected based on the clusters that were created. Therefore, the background highlight for this row is now removed. If you switch to the Table2 Outliers worksheet, you see that the Income column is no longer considered to be an exception because the Outliers column is set to zero.

Highlight Exceptions Report for Table2

The outlier cells are highlighted in the original table.

Exception threshold (more or fewer exceptions) 95

Column	Outliers
Marital Status	0
Gender	0
Income	1
Children	0
Education	0
Occupation	0
Home Owner	0
Cars	0
Commute Distance	0
Region	0
Age	1
Purchased Bike	0
Total	2

FIGURE 12-55

Shopping Basket Analysis

The Shopping Basket Analysis tool helps you to explore cross-selling opportunities. Assume you have a table with transaction data that contains the products sold within a transaction. The Shopping Basket Analysis tool helps you to identify the products that have been bought together. SSAS 2012 provides a separate data set that contains four columns: the transaction ID, category, name, and price of the product to help you understand shopping-basket analysis. The transaction ID column contains several entries for certain transactions because customers bought multiple products in the same transaction.

1. Click the worksheet Associate. You see that the first two entries in the table have the same transaction ID, SO61269.
2. Click one of the cells in the table.
3. Click the Analyze tab in Table Tools, and then click the Shopping Basket Analysis icon.

   The Shopping Basket Analysis tool first analyzes the table to identify the likely column that indicates the transaction number. You can see in the Shopping Basket Analysis dialog shown in Figure 12-56 that the tool has identified the Order Number column as the transaction ID. It has identified the Category column as the Item and the Product Price column as the Item Value.

   The Shopping Basket Analysis tool uses the Microsoft Association algorithm to perform the analysis on the table. You can specify advanced settings for the algorithm by clicking the Advanced link.

4. Select the defaults suggested by the dialog, and click Run. The Shopping Basket Analysis dialog creates an Association mining model on your SSAS instance, analyzes the results, and then creates two spreadsheets called Shopping Basket Related Items and Shopping Basket Recommendations. The Shopping Basket Bundled Items sheet shown in Figure 12-57 provides you with an aggregate view of the number of products, the product names, the number

of each type of bundled sale, along with the information on average sales per transaction and the overall value of the products.

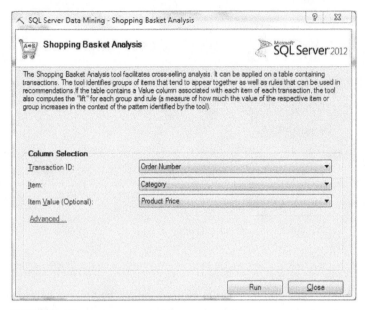

FIGURE 12-56

In this example, you choose the Category column as the Item; therefore, the overall value of the bundle is the aggregation of all the products in the categories selected. For example, you see that the overall value of the bundle of the products in Road Bikes and Helmets (refer to the first row in Figure 12-57) is quite large as compared to the average sales. You can format the sales amounts as currencies using Excel's Format Cells option to have better readability, which eventually aids you in your analysis. You can use this sheet to analyze the list of products that customers purchase together. This can provide you with an indication of the items to bundle and promote to customers.

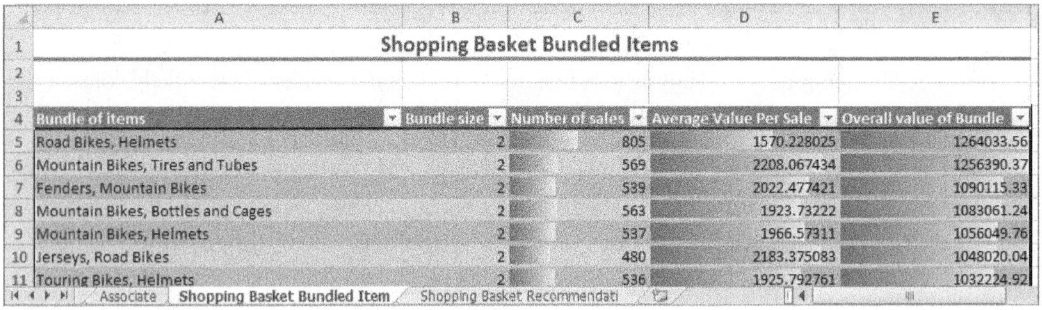

	A	B	C	D	E
1			Shopping Basket Bundled Items		
2					
3					
4	Bundle of items	Bundle size	Number of sales	Average Value Per Sale	Overall value of Bundle
5	Road Bikes, Helmets	2	805	1570.228025	1264033.56
6	Mountain Bikes, Tires and Tubes	2	569	2208.067434	1256390.37
7	Fenders, Mountain Bikes	2	539	2022.477421	1090115.33
8	Mountain Bikes, Bottles and Cages	2	563	1923.73222	1083061.24
9	Mountain Bikes, Helmets	2	537	1966.57311	1056049.76
10	Jerseys, Road Bikes	2	480	2183.375083	1048020.04
11	Touring Bikes, Helmets	2	536	1925.792761	1032224.92

Associate / **Shopping Basket Bundled Item** / Shopping Basket Recommendati

FIGURE 12-57

The Shopping Basket Recommendations spreadsheet provides you with suggestions of what items to recommend, the probability of customers buying the additional recommended items, and what your overall increase in sales would be due to these recommendations.

5. Switch to the Shopping Basket Recommendations worksheet.

6. Select the columns Average Value of Recommendation and Overall Value of Linked Sales.

7. Under Cells on the Home Ribbon, select the drop-down Format menu.

8. In the Format Cells dialog, select Currency as the Category, and click OK. You now see the columns' Average Value of Recommendation and Overall Value of Linked Sales formatted as currencies (see Figure 12-58). This worksheet helps you to understand the average gain you will have based on the recommendation. Assume you recommend Tires and Tubes for customers purchasing Bike Stands. Approximately 80% of the customers are likely to buy your recommendation as indicated by the % of Linked Sales column. The average value/ increase in revenue due to your recommendation is $243 as indicated by the Average Value of Recommendation column. This worksheet can help you to understand the percentage of customers that might buy certain products if you recommend them and what additional revenue you would make due to this recommendation.

	A	B	C	D	E	F	G
1		Shopping Basket Recommendations					
2							
3							
4	Selected Item	Recommendation	Sales of Selected Items	Linked Sales	% of linked sales	Average value of recommendation	Overall value of linked sales
5	Fenders	Mountain Bikes	1238	539	43.54 %	$870.98	$1,078,268.11
6	Cleaners	Tires and Tubes	525	259	49.33 %	$182.32	$95,717.86
7	Helmets	Tires and Tubes	3794	1617	42.62 %	$9.42	$35,732.95
8	Bike Stands	Tires and Tubes	130	103	79.23 %	$243.20	$31,615.63
9	Bike Racks	Tires and Tubes	191	94	49.21 %	$158.78	$30,327.60
10	Gloves	Helmets	849	352	41.46 %	$22.38	$19,004.48
11	Hydration Packs	Bottles and Cages	428	191	44.63 %	$3.86	$1,652.09

FIGURE 12-58

Scenario Analysis

The Scenario Analysis tool enables you to understand what factors (columns) would help in influencing a change in specific columns. For example, if you want to convert a bike buyer from No to Yes, what should be the income? This tool helps in scenarios in which there are multiple parameters you can change to achieve a desired goal. For example, you might want to increase your revenue by 10% for certain products. You can probably allocate a certain amount in promotions, and you can decide whether to invest the promotions in television advertisements or advertisements in papers, online coupons, and so on and decide what factor or combination of factors might provide you with the maximum benefit. The Prediction Calculator tool enables you to detect patterns in various columns of the table to predict a specific value in one of the columns.

In this section, you learned about various tools available to you to analyze data in your Excel spreadsheets using the Data Mining Add-ins.

Data Mining Tools

Table Analytics is aimed at end users who might not have knowledge of data mining. whereas some end users might have in-depth knowledge of data mining and would like to create their own data mining models on the data in an Excel spreadsheet.

In this section, you learn to create, refine, and view a data mining model on data in an Excel spreadsheet using the Data Mining Tools add-ins that are part of the Microsoft SQL Server 2012 Data Mining Add-ins for Office 2010. You learn to create a classification mining model using the sample data set that has been provided as part of the DMAddins_SampleData.xlsx document. You first need to select the Source Data worksheet and then select the Data Mining tab. You then see the Data Mining Ribbon, which supports the same features you have seen in SSDT.

Similar to the Table Analytics Tools add-in, you first need to connect to your SSAS instance. After establishing the connection, you need to select the data set to analyze. The Data Mining tools provide you with the option of not only analyzing data within an Excel spreadsheet, but also analyzing data from external data sources.

Click the Classify icon under the Data Modeling group of the Ribbon to launch the Classify Wizard. Click Next on the Getting Started with the Classify Data Wizard dialog. The Select Source Data page provides three options for selecting data: from a table, from a data range, or from an Analysis Services data source.

By default, the dialog selects the table in the current worksheet as the data source to be used. You can use the drop-down list to select a table from a different worksheet.

The second option is to select a data range, where you can either type the range descriptor in the text box or click the Range tool to make your selection. When using data in a table or range with the Data Mining Client, with the exception of the data preparation tools, your Excel data is remoted to the Analysis Services instance where the data mining work is performed. The data preparation tools perform their work on the client and therefore do not remote the data.

The third option is the External Data Source, which allows you to either choose existing external data sources or create new ones.

Now, after connecting to Analysis Services and selecting expected data sets using one of above options, you are ready to start using the Data Mining Client for Excel. You should be aware that the Analysis Services Data Source option is not available for all tools, in which case it will not be presented as an option. Now go through the various steps you need to take to analyze the data, build a model, and understand the results.

Explore Data Wizard

The first step to understanding any data set is to explore and identify statistical information in the data that can help you with further analysis. The Explore Data Wizard enables you to see histograms of numeric and nonnumeric data in your worksheet and to group numeric data into equal-sized buckets.

1. Open the sample spreadsheet DMAddins_SampleData.xlsx.

2. In the Data Preparation section of the Data Mining tab, click the Explore Data icon. (See Figure 12-59.)

Review the content on the Getting Started page of Explore Data, and click Next. On the Select Source Data page, you can choose to explore data in either a table or an Excel Range. Explore Data does not work with data from an external data source. If you want to explore data from a database, you first need to import the data into your Excel workbook. Because the data from an external data source can be large, you may have to get a sample data set to perform the exploration. The Sample Data Wizard provides the functionality to extract a sample of database data into Excel.

FIGURE 12-59

3. Select 'Source Data'!'Source Data' in the Source Data dialog box, and click Next.

On the Select Column page, the grid shows data samples. You need to choose a specific column of interest by either selecting from the Select Column drop-down list or clicking the header or cell of the column. The column chosen is highlighted, as shown in Figure 12-60.

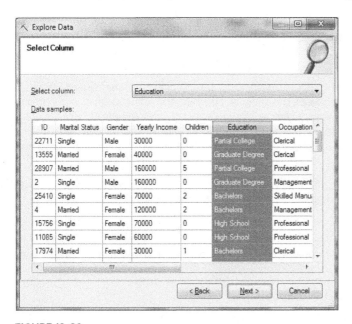

FIGURE 12-60

4. Choose the Education column, which has nonnumeric and discrete values. You can see the histograms for the Education column in the Explore Data dialog (see Figure 12-61). The histogram shows the count of the distinct values in the entire table for the chosen column in descending order.

5. Click Back to return to the Select Column page, select the Yearly Income column, then click Next.

6. Click Copy to copy a bitmap of the chart to the clipboard, and click Finish to exit the wizard.

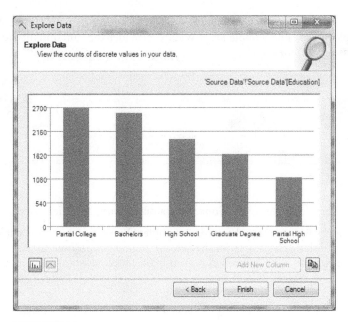

FIGURE 12-61

The Explore Data Wizard groups the numeric data into buckets of equal ranges; the default is 8 buckets. You can toggle between the View as Discrete and View as Numeric buttons that are available at the lower-left corner to change how the data is viewed. These buttons are available whenever you explore a column with numeric or mixed numeric and nonnumeric data. If you want to use the bucketed data as a column in the worksheet for further analysis, you can click the Add New Column button, which inserts a column with the appropriate ranges next to your original column.

7. Click Finish in the Explore Data dialog after you have explored all the columns.

The Explore Data Wizard provides a simple interface for viewing histograms of your nonnumeric and numeric data. It also enables you to add bucketed columns and histogram views to your workbook. You can see the flexibility and options provided by the Explore Data Wizard to make your analysis more efficient.

Clean Data: Outliers and Re-label Wizards

After you do an initial analysis of your data, the next step is to determine if the data is clean. Often, the data might have unknown values that might not add useful information, or there might be outliers that you do not want to be considered for analysis. You would need to clean such data to have a good mining model. Data mining model creation typically requires that the data within a column be consistent. Each distinct value in a column has a unique meaning, and therefore, each column should be checked to ensure that there aren't multiple values with the same connotation. For example, if you have a marital status column with values Married and Currently Married, a data mining algorithm would treat these values as different. You can use the Re-label Wizard to quickly correct such inconsistencies in a column. Another typical scenario is when many different values are in a column that can be summarized into fewer values. For example, the Marital Status column could have the values Single, Married, Divorced, and Widowed, among others, whereas you might be interested in categorizing people as currently married or single.

The Clean Data group provides two wizards called Outliers and Re-label. The Outliers Wizard helps you to detect outlier values in a specific column and remove them, whereas the Re-label Wizard enables you to easily change data within a column to your wanted value. To understand these wizards, first make a few changes in the table you are using. To start, change the cells F4 and F13 to Some College in the Source Data worksheet.

There are several ways to detect duplicate meaning values which are entered differently in the Excel worksheet. One method is to drop down the filter control on a column header. Doing this on the Education column, you can see Partial College and Some College, which have the same meaning. You can now use the Clean Data Re-label Wizard to quickly correct these issues.

1. Launch the Re-label Wizard by clicking Clean Data on the Data Mining Ribbon and selecting Re-label.

2. Read the Start page of the Re-label Wizard, and click Next.

3. In the Select Source Data page, use the default Source Data table selection, and click Next.

4. On the Select Column page, select the Education column, and click Next.

   You see the various values in the Education column along with the count of rows that have those values. You can provide the new labels to existing labels in this dialog.

5. On the Re-label Data page, select Partial College as the new label for Some College, as shown in Figure 12-62, and click Next.

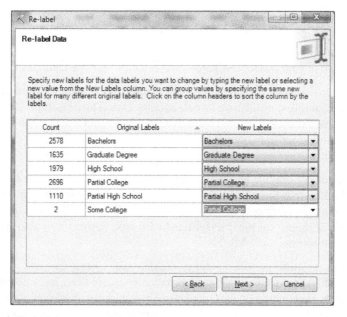

FIGURE 12-62

The Select Destination page provides you with three options for applying the new values chosen. The first option is to add a new column to the current worksheet. The second option is to copy sheet data with changes to a new worksheet. The third option is to change data in place. Be aware that the actions performed by the Re-label Wizard cannot be reverted. This is extremely important for option three. Therefore, you should use option one or two to be safe.

6. Select option two to create a new worksheet, and click Finish. You should see the wizard has added a new column Education2 next to the column Education, and set the values for cells G4 and G13 to Partial College.

Now, you can further consolidate the various Education values to two values, Has Bachelors and No Bachelors, indicating whether a customer has a college degree.

The Re-label Data Wizard provides a convenient interface for making comprehensive changes across the values of a column in your worksheet. It can be used to consolidate values, to ensure consistency, or for many other purposes in which you need to quickly view and modify all the values in a column. Now that you have learned to clean the data before creating mining models, next you learn why you need to partition the data set and how you can do that within the Data Mining Client.

Sample Data Wizard

You learned in the "Data: Understand It, Configure It" section earlier in this chapter that one of the key processes to build the data mining model is to split the input data set into training and testing data. The Sample Data Wizard enables you to do that. The wizard also helps to sample data from a larger data set in an Excel sheet or in an external database, and create samples that balance distributions of a target variable. By validating your models against a testing set, you can estimate how well your model performs against new data. This is particularly important for Classification and Estimation tasks.

1. Click the Sample Data icon in the Data Preparation group on the Data Mining Ribbon. Click Next.

2. In the Select Source Data page, select the Table 'Source Data'!'Source Data', and click Next.

3. The sampling page provides you with two options for splitting the data set training and testing sets: Random Sampling or Oversample to Balance Data Distributions. The over-sampling is needed when the distribution in the data set is not uniform. You need the right distribution in the training set to make the model effective. Select the Random Sampling option, and click Next.

4. You can perform random sampling either as a percentage of the data set or by specifying a row count. On the Random Sampling Options page, you can sample the data for training, and conversely, how much is left over for testing. The default split of 70% training and 30% testing is a good rule of thumb for most Excel-sized data sets, but you may also split differently. Keep the default setting, and click Next.

5. The Finish page enables you to provide names to the new worksheets that will be created by the Sample Data Wizard. You have the option to create a new sheet for unselected data. Specify the Selected set sheet name as Training Data Sheet and the unselected data to be moved to Testing Data Sheet, and click Finish. The Sample Data Wizard now samples the data and creates two new sheets called Training Data Sheet and Testing Data Sheet.

The Sample Data Wizard provides a convenient interface for the necessary data preparation step of splitting your data into two sets, one for training a mining model and another for validating models that you have created.

Classification Model

After you have cleaned the data and partitioned it into training and testing data sets, you are ready to start building the mining model. In this section, you create a classification mining model. The Classify icon uses the decision tree data mining algorithm to create the appropriate nodes and splits. You can then predict values for new data sets based on the mining model created.

Model Creation

To create your classification model, follow these steps:

1. Switch to the Training Data Sheet that was created by the Sample Data Wizard. Click the Data Mining tab.

2. Click the Classify in the Data Modeling group, and click Next.

3. Select the default Table selection on the Select Source Data page, and click Next.

   The Classification page enables you to choose the column to analyze or predict and the input columns. You can launch the Parameter dialog via the Parameters button to specify parameters for the decision tree algorithm, such as score method, split method, and support.

4. Select BikeBuyer as the column to analyze.

5. Select all the remaining columns as input columns except the ID, as shown in Figure 12-63, and click Next.

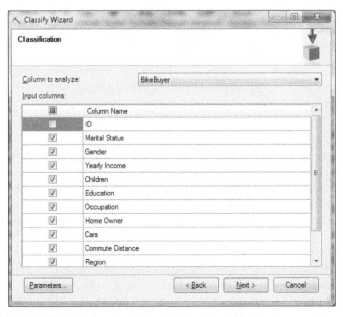

FIGURE 12-63

6. Specify the percentage of data for testing as 0 because you have already partitioned the original data set into training and testing data. Click Next.

7. The Finish page enables you to specify names and add descriptions for the mining structure and mining model. It also provides the options to create the model as a temporary model and enable drillthrough to the source data similar to the SSDT Decision Tree Wizard. Select the defaults for the mining structure and mining model names and keep drillthrough as enabled, as shown in Figure 12-64, and click Finish.

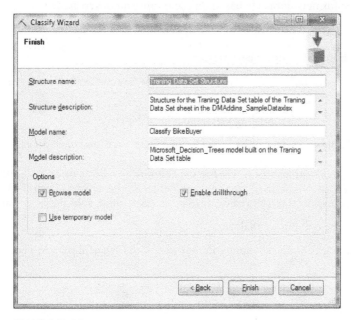

FIGURE 12-64

The Classify Wizard now creates the mining structure and the mining model based on options provided and reads the data from the worksheet to train the model.

Browse the Model

When the model has been trained, the Classify Wizard launches the mining model browser, as shown in Figure 12-65. You can also launch this browser from the Browse icon in the Model Usage group and select the model you want to browse from the connected SSAS database. The Decision Tree view shows all the nodes and splits of the mining model that was created from the table in the Training Data Sheet. You can click each node to see the percentage of customers with a specific characteristic who are likely to buy bikes. The decision tree indicates that the most important factor for customers who buy bikes is the customer's age. The mining model has split the customers into four nodes based on their age. The Mining Legend displays the percentage of customers in a specific node and the likelihood of them buying bikes. For example, when you click the node Age >= 33 and Age < 41, you see that 15.80% of customers in this group buy bikes. You can identify potential customers based on the information in the mining models and use that information to send out targeted mails to customers who are likely to buy bikes instead of sending the mail to all customers.

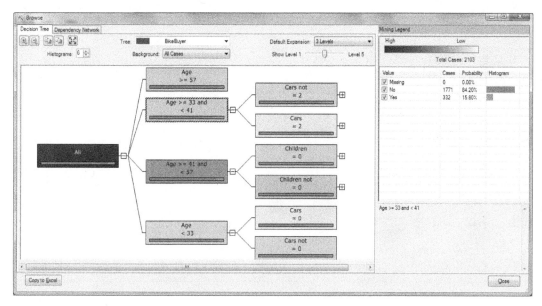

FIGURE 12-65

The Browse dialog has a Dependency Network tab, which shows the dependencies between various columns and the analyzed column Bike Buyer, as shown in Figure 12-66. The decision tree mining model has identified that the columns Cars, Age, Marital Status, and Children are the columns that influence the Bike Buyer column. By default, the slider on the left is at All Links. If you move the slider down to the bottom, you can see that the strongest influencing column for bike buyers is Age, which you identified in the Decision Tree view.

If you want to share this data with some end users but do not want to grant them access to SSAS instance, you can share the graphs via the Copy to Excel button.

Model Accuracy

You have created a decision tree mining model using 70% of the table data from the Training Data Sheet and browsed the model to understand the results from the mining model. Now, you need to identify how good the mining model is in predicting bike buyers using the 30% of the data that you originally partitioned in the Testing Data Sheet.

1. Click the Testing Data Sheet worksheet, and click the Data Mining Tools tab.

2. In the Accuracy and Validation group, click the Accuracy Chart icon.

3. On the Getting Started page, click Next.

4. In the SelectStructure or Model dialog, select the Classify Bike Buyer mining model, as shown in Figure 12-67, and click Next.

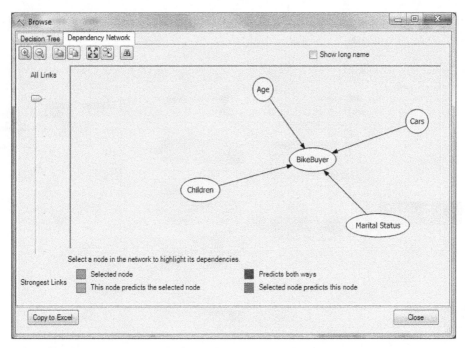

FIGURE 12-66

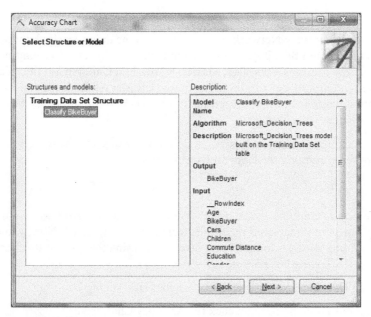

FIGURE 12-67

5. On the Specify Column to Predict and Value to Predict page, make sure you have BikeBuyer as the column to predict and Yes as the value to predict, as shown in Figure 12-68, and click Next.

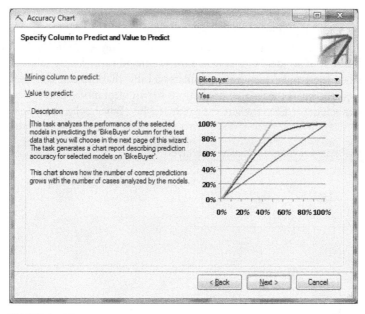

FIGURE 12-68

6. On the Select Source Data page, select the 'Testing Data Sheet'!'Testing Data Sheet' from the table drop-down box, and click Next.

7. On the Specify Relationship page, the relationship between the columns in the mining model and the columns in the Testing Data Sheet are shown by default. Accept the default, as shown in Figure 12-69, and click Finish.

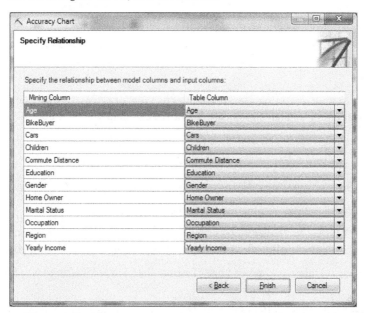

FIGURE 12-69

The Accuracy Chart Wizard predicts the rows in the Test Data Sheet that should contain the value Yes and compares the results to that of an ideal model. The result of the wizard is a new spreadsheet, as shown in Figure 12-70. You can see graphical information comparing the decision tree mining model you have created to that of an ideal model where the predicted value for the BikeBuyer column is expected to be Yes. Below the graph, the wizard populates a table that indicates the percentile of the population and the percentage of the correct predictions for an ideal model and the current model. You should create another Accuracy Chart where the predicted BikeBuyer column value is No.

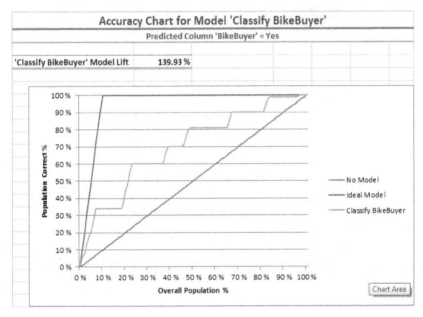

FIGURE 12-70

Classification Matrix

You might be interested in understanding the overall effectiveness of the matrix for the values Yes and No for the BikeBuyer column. The Classification Matrix can help you as it does in SSDT.

1. Switch to the Testing Data Sheet, and click the Data Mining Tools tab.

2. In the Accuracy and Validation group, click the Classification Matrix icon.

3. On the Getting Started page, click Next.

4. Select the Classify Bike Buyer mining model, and click Next.

5. On the Specify Columns to Predict page, you have the option to provide the results as a percentage or as a count. Select the defaults, as shown in Figure 12-71, and click Next.

6. On the Select Source Data page, select table 'Testing Data Sheet'!'Testing Data Sheet', and click Next.

7. Accept the default selection on the Specify Relationship page, and click Finish.

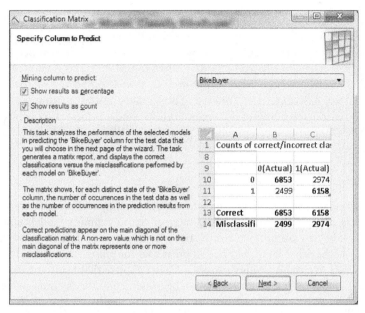

FIGURE 12-71

The wizard creates a Classification Matrix sheet that predicts the values for Yes and No and compares the values with the actual values, as shown in Figure 12-72. This matrix gives you a good understanding of how effective the mining model is in predicting whether a customer will buy a bike.

	A	B	C	D	E
1	**Counts of correct/incorrect classification for model 'Classify BikeBuyer'**				
2	Predicted Column 'BikeBuyer'				
3	Columns correspond to actual values				
4	Rows correspond to predicted values				
5					
6	Model name:	Classify BikeBuyer	Classify BikeBuyer		
7	Total correct:	89.87 %	2696		
8	Total misclassified:	10.13 %	304		
9					
10	Results as Percentages for Model 'Classify BikeBuyer'				
11		No(Actual)	Yes(Actual)		
12	No	100.00 %	100.00 %		
13	Yes	0.00 %	0.00 %		
14					
15	Correct	100.00 %	0.00 %		
16	Misclassified	0.00 %	100.00 %		
17					
18	Results as Counts for Model 'Classify BikeBuyer'				
19		No(Actual)	Yes(Actual)		
20	No	2696	304		
21	Yes	0	0		
22					
23	Correct	2696	0		
24	Misclassified	0	304		

Testing Data / **Classification Matrix** / New Customers / Associate

FIGURE 12-72

In this section, you have learned the usefulness of the Data Mining Client add-ins. You learned to explore data within an Excel spreadsheet, clean the data, and partition the data. Then, you created a classification mining model, analyzed the results by browsing the model, and determined if the mining model is predicting values effectively using the Classification Matrix and Accuracy Chart. Similar to the classification model, you can create other mining models supported by the Data Mining Tools: Estimate, Cluster, Associate, and Forecast. You should explore creating these models using the sample data. You also have a way to document mining model information using the Document Model Wizard. The Data Mining Client add-in gives a friendly interface to harness the full power of data mining features in SSAS 2012.

Visio Add-in

Typically, you might expect IT professionals or IWs to create and analyze mining models and present the results to decision-makers. SSDT and Data Mining Add-ins support creating mining models and analyzing and interpreting the result but do not provide an effective way to present information to the decision-makers. Microsoft Visio, on the other hand, has been a great tool for presentations that use diagrams and figures. Therefore, Data Mining Add-ins provides a Visio template that helps you to create, edit, and enhance data mining model representations that can be presented to the decision-makers.

To learn about Visio templates, you can download and deploy the Adventure Works 2012 Analysis Services project sample available from www.wrox.com. Next, click Start ➪ All Programs ➪ Microsoft SQL Server DM Add-ins ➪ Data Mining Visio template. You see a new Visio document with the Data Mining Shapes template open showing three shapes: Dependency Network, Cluster, and Decision Tree. These objects help you to view the mining models on your SSAS instance.

The Decision Tree Shape

The Decision Tree Shape helps you to view decision and regression tree mining models from your SSAS 2008 R2 or later version. To use this shape, follow these steps:

1. Drag and drop the Decision Tree Shape icon from the template onto the Visio document drawing surface to launch the Decision Tree Visio Shape Wizard. The Select a Data Source dialog that appears enables you to choose a connection to SSAS instance.

2. In the Select a Data Source dialog, click the New button.

3. In the Connect to Analysis Services dialog, specify your SSAS instance name, select the Adventure Works DW Multidimensional sample database you have deployed, and click OK.

4. In the Select a Data Source dialog, select the Analysis Services connection, and click Next. The wizard now requests for all the mining models on your SSAS instance to filter the ones that can be viewed by the Decision Tree Shape Wizard and show them for your selection.

5. On the Select a Mining Model page, select the TM Decision Tree model, and click Next.

   The wizard now requests that you select a decision tree along with the depth of the tree you want to view. You could change the default level, 3, but increasing this number may cause the resulting decision tree diagram to become more complex and harder to interpret. However, you have the flexibility to show subsections of the trees or move certain sections to a new page. You have the option to change the values of the predicted values for display using the Select Decision Tree page as well as the option to choose different colors.

6.   Change the value of 1 to Yes and 0 to No, as shown in Figure 12-73, and click Finish. The wizard now retrieves the decision tree mining model information and draws a decision tree diagram on the Visio page. The wizard shows the status page of all the operations performed.

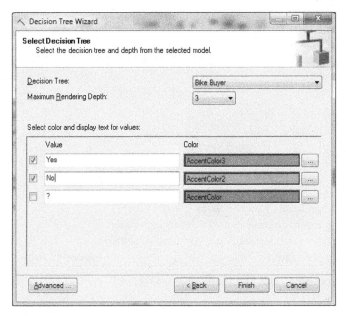

FIGURE 12-73

7.   Click Close on the Confirmation of Decision Tree Rendering Wizard page.

You can see the entire decision tree with all the nodes along with the splits, as shown in Figure 12-74. You can zoom in to a specific node, for example, Number Cars Owned = 0, as shown in Figure 12-75. You can see the node is being split on Region into three nodes with values North America, Pacific, and Europe. Each of the nodes shows the percentage of customers likely to buy bikes along with the values Yes or No. The decision tree diagram helps you view the mining model better as well as add any Visio annotation for the presentation's purpose.

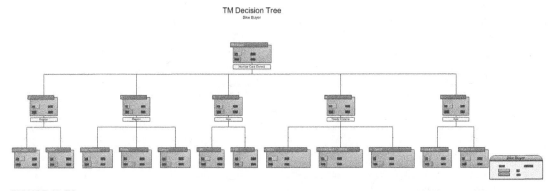

FIGURE 12-74

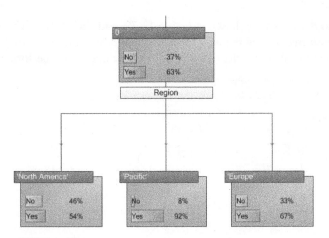

FIGURE 12-75

You can also see the Data Mining toolbar on the Visio Ribbon on the Add-ins tab. The Data Mining toolbar shows context-dependent icons based on the model. It contains Layout, Resize Page, and Description for the decision tree, as shown in Figure 12-76.

FIGURE 12-76

1. Click the node that has a split on Region (as shown in Figure 12-75).

2. Click the Description icon in the Data Mining toolbar.

You can see a more detailed description of the node, as shown in Figure 12-77. The description indicates that this is a node due to the split of Number of Cars Owned = 0 from the root node with support value 4238, that is, the number of total customers who have 0 cars. Within these customers, the people who buy bikes are shown with the State = Yes along with support and Probability information. The description helps you to understand a specific node better. Click Close.

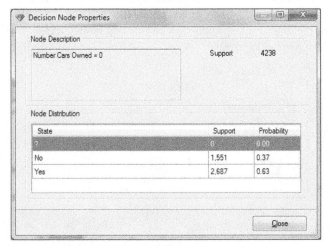

FIGURE 12-77

3. The decision tree shown on the Visio page can contain a lot of nodes that make the analysis or viewing of the nodes a bit challenging. Therefore, the data mining template provides you operations to move subsections efficiently.

4. Select the node where the value for Number Cars Owned is 1, right-click, and select Collapse Child Nodes, as shown in Figure 12-78.

FIGURE 12-78

5. Repeat the previous step for the nodes with the value of Number Cars Owned equal to 0, 2, 3, and 4.

6. Click the Layout icon in the Data Mining toolbar. You should now see all the collapsed nodes. The collapsed nodes are indicated with a shadow behind the actual node.

In addition to collapsing the nodes, you can also move the children of a specific node to a separate page to isolate the specific node and do a better analysis.

7. Right-click the node that has Number Cars Owned = 2, and select Move Children to New Page. You see a link created from the main page to a new page indicating that the child nodes are continued on page 2.

8. Double-click the link Continued Page 2. You now go to page 2, which has the children of the node Number Cars Owned = 2. In addition to that, the legend is also included on page 2. You can now add appropriate annotation specific to customers having two cars and present the information.

You can now save the Visio document with your annotations and send them to people interested in the results. The end users do not need Data Mining Add-ins to view the results. Alternatively, you can publish the Visio page on a web site for others to view it.

1. Click the File menu, Save to SharePoint, and then Save As.

2. In the Save As dialog, enter DTModel.htm, and click Save.

Visio saves the Visio pages as a web page and launches the web page within Internet Explorer. Based on your security settings, you might be prompted to enable ActiveX controls. Right-click the warning, and select the Allow Blocked Content control to enable ActiveX controls. You see the mining model published as a web page. You can navigate between the various Visio pages.

You have learned to view decision tree mining models within Visio using the Decision Tree Shape Wizard as well as options to efficiently view and present information in Visio and publish the pages as a web page. In the next two sections, you learn about viewing additional mining models supported by SSAS using the Cluster Shape Wizard and the Dependency Network Shape Wizard.

The Cluster Shape Wizard

The Cluster Shape Wizard helps you to analyze and present the cluster mining models using Visio. The wizard enables you to customize the shape, size, and profiles of each cluster shown in the Visio page.

1.   Click the Insert menu, and select New Page.

2.   Drag and drop the Cluster Shape icon to the new page.

3.   Read the information on the Cluster Visio Shape Wizard introduction page, and click Next.

4.   On the Select a Data Source page, select the Adventure Works DW Multidimensional connection, and click Next.

> The Cluster Shape Wizard retrieves all the mining models from your chosen Adventure Works database, filters the cluster mining models, and shows them to you along with the details of the mining models such as name, algorithm, and input and output columns.

5.   Select the targeted mailing TM Clustering model, and click Next.

> The Options for Cluster Diagram dialog provides you with three options:

> ➤ **Show Cluster Shapes Only:** Draws a simple cluster shape. The default shape is oval, as shown in Figure 12-79. The relationships between clusters are shown by lines with no other details. This is useful for a large number of clusters.

FIGURE 12-79

> ➤ **Show Clusters with Characteristics Chart:** Show the list of characteristics with the percentage representing the likelihood that the characteristic will appear in the cluster, as shown in Figure 12-80.

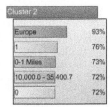

FIGURE 12-80

➤ **Show Clusters with Discrimination Chart:** Enables you to compare attributes between clusters. The attributes are now displayed in the order of their importance when discriminating between clusters, as shown in Figure 12-81. The size of the bars shows how strongly the attributes favor the characteristic.

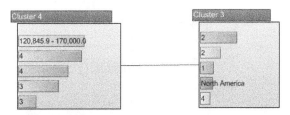

FIGURE 12-81

The number of rows in the chart helps you to specify the number of rows of attributes to show in the cluster diagram for options two and three. Default displays the top five characteristics in each cluster.

The Advanced button enables you to choose additional options for Font, Fill, and Line colors as well as choosing various shapes to represent clusters, as shown in Figure 12-82. You also have the option to preview the cluster within this dialog.

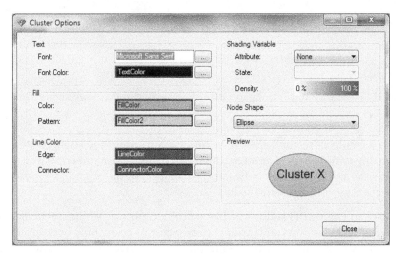

FIGURE 12-82

6. Select the Show Cluster Shapes Only option in the Options for Cluster Diagram dialog as mentioned in the previous step, and click Finish. The Cluster Shape Wizard now retrieves the details of the mining model chosen and renders the diagram within the Visio page. The wizard also shows a dialog with various options taken during this rendering process.

7. Click Close as soon as the diagram has been rendered.

You see the cluster diagram on the Visio page, as shown in Figure 12-83. You can see the Data Mining toolbar has three more options as compared to a Decision Tree dialog: Edge Strength, Slider, and Shading.

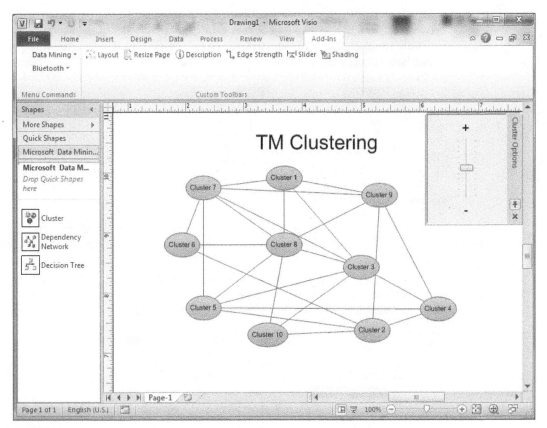

FIGURE 12-83

The Edge Strength is a toggle icon that helps you to turn on or turn off the strength label of the relationship between any two clusters. The strength is represented as a number between 0 and 100, where 0 indicates no relationship and 100 indicates the members of the clusters are closely related. Figure 12-84 shows the Edge Strength is turned on.

The Slider icon is used to enable the slider window (see the right side of Figure 12-84) if it is closed. The slider window helps you to identify the strongest relationships between various clusters. By default, the slider window is in the middle. If you move the slider toward the plus sign, you can see only the strongest link, and if you move the slider to the minus sign, you see all the links. For this example, move the slider close to the plus sign to show only the strongest link, which is the one between Cluster 3 and Cluster 4. Displaying the cluster characteristics or cluster discrimination information from the node context menu could help you analyze the clusters better.

The Shading icon in the Data Mining toolbar is used only when you have the clusters represented as shapes without the cluster characteristics or discrimination information. When you click the Shading icon, you see the shading window within the Visio page, which is shown on the top of Figure 12-85. The shading helps you to easily identify visually which clusters are favored by a specific attribute and state.

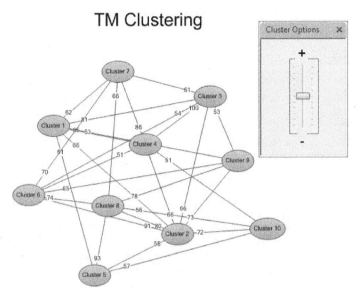

FIGURE 12-84

Figure 12-85 shows the cluster diagram with shading applied for the English Education attribute with the state Graduate Degree. A darker shading indicates that there are large numbers of customers in a specific cluster. You can easily observe that Cluster 1 has the maximum number of graduates as compared with other clusters. You should try various shading options.

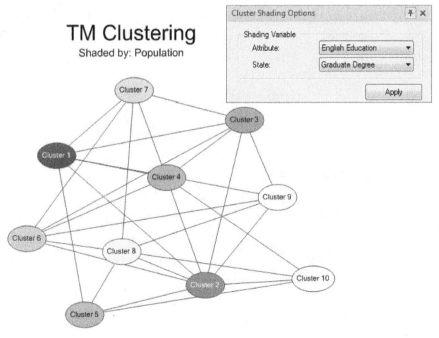

FIGURE 12-85

When you are using shapes for a cluster, you have the option to select any image to display a cluster. This can be done by right-clicking the cluster and selecting Custom Shape.

The Dependency Shape Wizard

The Dependency Shape Wizard helps you to visualize Naïve Bayes, decision trees, and association rule mining models supported in SSAS. In this example, you view an association mining model.

1. From the Visio Ribbon, insert Blank Page.

2. Drag and drop the Dependency Network shape onto the new page.

3. On the welcome page, click Next.

4. In the Select a Data Source dialog, select Adventure Works DW Multidimensional as the current connection.

> The wizard now retrieves all the mining models within the chosen database. It then filters the mining models that can be rendered by the Dependency Network Shape Wizard and shows them on the Select a Mining Model page. The mining models are listed along with the mining structure, whereas details are listed in the Properties pane.

5. Select the Association mining model, and click Next.

> The Select Nodes to Render page helps you to choose a specific number of nodes to be rendered based on certain selection criteria. You can either choose a number of nodes to be fetched or optionally provide wildcard searches based on the node names. For example, typing the word **Cage** into the text box results in retrieval of nodes Mountain Bottle Cage and Road Bottle Cage in the chosen mining model.

6. Choose the default five nodes, and click the green arrow button to retrieve the nodes. You see five nodes retrieved and shown in the Query results pane. You have the option to specify which nodes you want to be rendered by the wizard on the Visio page by using the check boxes.

> The Dependency Network Shape Wizard also has an Advanced button to help you specify and preview various Name Styles for each node, as shown in Figure 12-86.

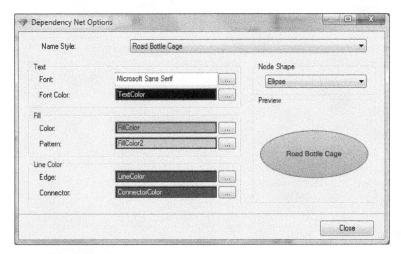

FIGURE 12-86

7. Click Finish on the Select Nodes to Render page with the five nodes that have been retrieved. The Dependency Network Shape Wizard retrieves the nodes and their properties and renders the dependency network on the Visio page. The sequence of steps taken by the wizard is shown on the confirmation page.

8. Click Close on the Confirmation of Dependency Network Rendering Wizard page. You can see the dependency network with five nodes rendered in the Visio page, as shown in Figure 12-87. The Data Mining toolbar's icons Layout, Re-size page, Edge Strength, and Slider have the same functionality as the ones you learned for the Cluster Shape Wizard. In the dependency network, you see the slider by default is closer to the minus sign to show all dependency links.

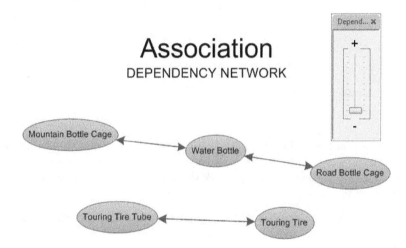

FIGURE 12-87

9. Click the Edge Strength to see the strengths between the nodes. The edges between the nodes have a bidirectional arrow unlike the cluster diagram, which didn't have any directions. The arrows indicate the strength of the relationship from one node to another node. As soon as the edge strengths are enabled, you see the values. The dependency network shows that someone buying Touring Tire Tubes is 100% likely to buy Touring Tires, whereas if they buy Touring Tires, they will probably buy Touring Tire Tubes 55% of the time. Therefore, the dependency network diagram enables you to visualize the association mining model information that identifies items purchased together so that you can use this information to cross-sell products to customers to increase your overall revenue.

The Node context menu provides several options to improve visualization of the dependency network, including highlight dependent items, highlight items that the current node depends on, and move certain nodes to a new page.

In addition, you can add additional nodes to the Visio page via the context menu or toolbar. Select the node Touring Tire Tube, right-click and select Add Related Items. In the Select Nodes to Render dialog, click the green arrow to retrieve the nodes related to Touring Tire Tube. You see two additional nodes retrieved, as shown in Figure 12-88.

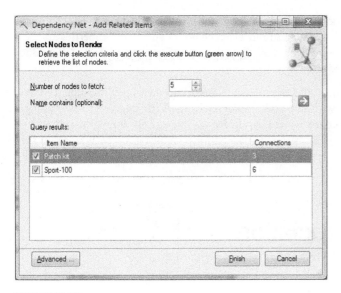

FIGURE 12-88

Click Finish to add the new nodes to the existing Visio page. You see the new nodes along with existing nodes. You can change the shape of a specific node, new nodes being added, or all nodes using the options provided by the dependency network shape or add annotation to your diagram to have appropriate recommendations.

You have successfully learned to create Visio diagrams that represent the SSAS mining models.

SUMMARY

In this chapter, you learned about data mining, what it is used for, what specific algorithms are available for use in SSAS 2012, and different tools. If you are now a step or two closer to an answer to the question, "How does it help my business?" you're doing great.

After understanding the data mining algorithms supported by SSAS 2012, you drilled down on two step-by-step developing Microsoft Decision Trees and Microsoft Clustering models using data from a relational data source. You also learned about OLAP mining models, where you essentially built a model on top of a cube. With the OLAP mining model, you segmented the customers based on Internet Sales, and you used the results of that mining model within a cube.

Aside from those off-the-shelf algorithms, SSAS 2012 provides a way to plug in your own data mining algorithm and data visualization capability (viewer). For details on this, refer to the SSAS 2012 product documentation. You use the plug-in architecture provided by SSAS 2012 and implement certain interfaces so that the server can use the results coming out of the algorithm you created. After you have implemented your algorithm, you can expose it using the SSAS server properties.

SSAS aims at providing Business Intelligence for everyone. Aligned with this goal, SQL Server 2012 provides Data Mining add-ins for Office 2010 in addition to the above tools. You first learned about the various features of Table Analytics tools that help you to analyze tabular data in your Excel spreadsheets. If you recall, the features in Table Analytics were more intuitive operations on your spreadsheet and didn't use any specific data mining terms. After the Table Analytics, you learned the Data Mining tools that help you to create and visualize data mining models on tabular data in Excel or even from external data sources. Finally, you learned to visualize mining models using Visio 2010 and the ability to add annotation to your mining models so that you can present them efficiently to the business decision-makers.

This chapter has provided you with the ability to use the Table Analytics and the Visio templates effectively along with an introduction to the Data Mining Tools add-in. For an in-depth understanding of Microsoft SQL Server Data Mining Add-ins for Office and all the algorithms in Data Mining Tools in SQL Server Analysis Services, refer to the book *Data Mining with Microsoft SQL Server 2008* by Jamie MacLennan, ZhaoHui Tang, and Bogdan Crivat (Wiley, 2008).

In the next chapter, you learn about SQL Server Integration Services 2012 (SSIS), its integration with SSAS 2012, and how the tasks and transforms in SSIS help you to perform certain SSAS operations effectively.

13

SQL Integration Services and SQL Server Reporting Services with Multidimensional BISM Models

WHAT'S IN THIS CHAPTER?

➤ Introduction to SQL Server Integration Services

➤ Creating an Integration Services package

➤ Automating exection of SSIS packages

➤ Monitoring SSIS package execution

➤ Introduction to Reporting Services

➤ Report Designer and Report Builder

➤ Report Server

➤ Creating a report on a relational database

➤ Creating a report on a multidimensional model

SQL Server Integration Services (SSIS) performs Extract, Transform, and Load (ETL) tasks. SSIS is used for data integration of heterogeneous data sources to one or more destinations with the capability to apply transformations on the data based on business requirements. Integration Services is not just about integrating data from and into databases; it helps you to perform operations on files ranging from simple file search operations on disk to transferring files using FTP. It also enables you to write managed code and execute it as a script, and define and automate your complex business processes as routine or scheduled tasks. SSIS helps developers to develop their ETL tasks as packages using SQL Server Data Tools (SSDT) and manage them efficiently. Finally, the SSIS extensible object model enables developers to build their own custom tasks and transform components that can be added to the SSIS platform.

SQL Server 2012 Integration Services introduces new capabilities for improving the experience of SSIS developers and administrators in building and maintaining their SSIS packages. New SSIS developers can now make use of the new capabilities in the SSIS package designer in SSDT to ramp up the learning process of using SSIS. Seasoned SSIS developers can now increase their productivity and make use of new tasks and transformation that have been introduced in SQL Server 2012.

SQL Server Reporting Services is a server-based report generation environment that can deliver both interactive and printed reports. Starting with its introduction, it has been an award-winning product, winning, for example, the 2004 Intelligent Enterprise Reader's Choice award for ad-hoc query and reporting. Reporting Services 2005, in addition to providing several Reporting Services features, provided a tighter integration with Analysis Services with the ability to build reports easily using MDX and DMX query designers. The Reporting Services 2008 server has been re-architected for scalability. Reporting Services 2008, 2008 R2, and 2012 (in so-called native mode) are not hosted inside IIS. The report server web server is, rather, based on components that provide high scalability for the database server. As part of the re-architecture in 2008, the Reporting Services service component is also streamlined so that rendering, Web Service enablement, and background processing (scheduling, subscriptions, delivery, and others) scale in proportion because they use a common memory management and application domain management substrate.

More important, Reporting Services has become a critical part of many business intelligence (BI) solutions. With SQL Server Reporting Services 2012, you can not only create tabular and matrix reports, but also you can add many additional types of visualizations (such as maps, gauges, and charts such as Gantt charts, Radar, and so on) to regular tabular reports that show the results in a much more appealing and easy-to-understand fashion. Microsoft ISVs and partners integrate seamlessly with Reporting Services to provide additional enhancements beyond those described here.

Finally, Reporting Services 2012 in its SharePoint Integrated mode introduces Power View, a new reporting tool targeted at data consumers so that they can visually explore their data and answer ad-hoc questions with ease. Power View is for end users and complements the existing set of report design tools in SSDT and Report Builder for IT professionals, BI developers, and power users. Power View is optimized for ad-hoc, interactively exploring data and presenting. It connects directly to BI Semantic Models in Analysis Services tabular and PowerPivot workbooks.

Report Designer in SSDT and Report Builder as a standalone application are optimized for operational and pixel-perfect report design scenarios. Using the Report Designer, you can design reports from relational as well as multidimensional databases, and if wanted or necessary, provide fine-grained control over calculations, layout, and visual representation.

This chapter provides an overview of SSIS and SSRS, and their key features in SQL Server 2012. Chapters 22 and 23 cover using Power View in Reporting Services with tabular models. In this chapter, you see how SSIS and SSRS integrate with SQL Server Analysis Services multidimensional business intelligence semantic models (BISM) to help provide an integrated end-to-end experience for developers and administrators to build and manage their BI warehousing solutions efficiently for their organizations.

SQL SERVER INTEGRATION SERVICES

An Enterprise Data Warehouse (EDW) is a data warehouse that serves an entire company rather than having individual data marts for each organization. Businesses use a single data warehouse to provide "one version of the truth" for many users. You can build EDWs in several ways. Because most companies generally have individual data marts, creating an EDW typically includes extracting data from multiple operational data sources of various kinds (database servers, FTP, files, and Excel files), transforming them to match the warehouse schema, and loading them into tables.

SQL Server Integration Services is designed to help in building the EDW. Data is almost never clean or formatted quite the way you would like, and the data almost always comes from heterogeneous data sources. Integration Services is important to the BI professional because it is simple to use and provides powerful capabilities to ensure that the data that lands in the EDW is clean and accurate. Although there are multiple ways to perform data integration, Integration Services adds a new dimension to that equation! It provides the functionality to do a specific operation via different methods, and you can choose the one that is most convenient for you.

SQL Server Integration Services (SSIS) 2012 provides a developer the ability to create SSIS packages using SSDTs. When the packages are developed by SSIS developers, these can be handed to administrators, and SSIS 2012 provides them the ability to deploy SSIS packages or projects, and to execute and manage the packages efficiently within a SQL Server instance. In addition to these, SSIS 2012 provides you with efficient tools by which the database administrator can monitor and debug execution of the SSIS packages. In this chapter, you learn to create SSIS packages, specifically packages that help developers with specific tasks such as data load on your existing SSAS databases.

Creating an Integration Services Project

To populate data warehouses and data marts, the ETL developer requires clean data. Integration Services provides capabilities for sorting, merging, and transforming the data. Different data representations from various source systems might cause difficulties during data integration. There is a strong business need to have a standard format and merge the relevant data. Because there are many transforms available in Integration Services, there is no lack of possibilities you can use to make your data conform to whatever format and design you want it to take.

An Integration Services package describes the data integration logic and how data flows from the different data sources to the destination. It contains one control flow and several data flows.

The data movement, handling of exceptions, logging, and dependencies can be complex; you can use the Control Flow to model the logical flow of different tasks. In a Control Flow, precedence constraints determine the flow of one task to another task. For example, a Control Flow can describe how failure of some tasks causes the termination of the whole package, whereas failure for another task might mean nothing more than a speed bump and the processing should continue. One capability of interest for the tasks is that the product enables you to have multiple tasks in the designer that can be executed in parallel. Examples of commonly used tasks are the Send Mail task, which is used to notify the administrator of job status and the Bulk Insert task, which is used to insert data from flat files into tables at high speed.

You can use the Data Flow task for handling the extraction, transformation, and loading of the data to the data warehouse. In a Data Flow task, an ETL developer can make use of different source and destination components to connect to the data sources and destinations. Integration Services provides a rich set of high-performance connectivity options. In addition, the ETL developer can make use of the rich set of transformations available in the Data Flow task for transforming data. In SQL Server 2012, new transformation such as DQS Cleansing are introduced to provide the ability to clean the data using capabilities introduced in SQL Server Data Quality Services (DQS). DQS provide the ability to cleanse data using an existing DQS knowledge base, or referencing external providers.

An Integration Services Project contains one or more Integration Services packages. In SQL Server 2012, you can perform a build of the Integration Services project and obtain an Integration Services Project Deployment File (with an .ispac extension). The Integration Services Project Deployment File is used as the unit of deployment to the Integration Services catalog. The SSIS catalog refers to a database on the instance where SSIS is installed and is used for storing the SSIS packages, as well as provides a set of public views and stored procedures for interacting with the deployment packages. On a SQL Server instance, the Integration Services catalog corresponds to a user database, called SSISDB. One of the advantages of having a single unit of deployment as an Integration Services Project is that it provides the ability to have all the packages and dependencies in a self-contained deployment file. For example, in a project, a parent package can make use of several Execute Package Tasks. Each of these Execute Package Tasks can refer to packages that have been deployed to different package locations (for example, MSDB, file system). Prior to SQL Server 2012, an ETL developer ensured that the packages and its dependent packages were deployed. SQL Server 2012 Integration Services enables the ETL developer to refer to packages in the same project via a project reference in the Execute Package Task.

SQL Server 2012 Integration Services introduces two deployment models for the Integration Services project: Package Deployment Model and Project Deployment Model. The Package Deployment Model supports deployments to traditional package locations (for example, an msdb database in SQL Server or the file system). The Project Deployment is designed for deployment to the SSIS catalog. When SSIS developers use the Project Deployment, which is the default when a new project is created, they can take advantage of the new capabilities introduced in SQL Server 2012. These include (a) the ability to define parameters for the project and packages (developers and administrators can provide values for the parameters, depending on the execution context in which the packages are executed) and (b) the ability to refer to the packages in the same project using the Execute Package Task (EPT).

In this chapter, you see examples of SQL Server Integration Services tasks and transforms that help you to manage your SQL Server Analysis Services efficiently. Refer to *Professional Microsoft SQL Server 2012 Integration Services* by Brian Knight et al. (Wiley, 2012).

Creating Integration Services Packages for Analysis Services Operations

Using Integration Services is convenient and improves administration productivity by executing administrative tasks on a periodic basis on Analysis Services. Integration Services provides several tasks and transforms specifically designed for integration with Analysis Services to help you to build packages in the SSDT you have been working with in Analysis Services 2012.

The Execute DDL Task

The Execute DDL task is used for sending a DDL script to Analysis Services. This task is typically used to accomplish administrative tasks such as backup, restore, or sync operations that need to be performed on a periodic basis. You can also use this task to send process statements to Analysis Services for processing Analysis Services objects or include this task along with other Integration Services tasks to create a more generalized package; for example, dynamically create a new partition in a cube by analyzing the fact data — and then processing that partition. To create a package that backs up your Analysis Services database on a periodic basis, do the following:

1. Open SSDT and load the AnalysisServicesMultidimensionalTutorial project sample for this chapter available for download on this book's web site at www.wrox.com.

2. After you load it, go ahead and deploy the project. This specific project has some additions to the ones you have created earlier, so make sure the full project is deployed.

3. While still in SSDT, create a new Integration Services project named IntegrationServicesTutorial by selecting File ➪ New ➪ Project and selecting the Integration Services Project template. You are now in the Integration Services project, as shown in Figure 13-1.

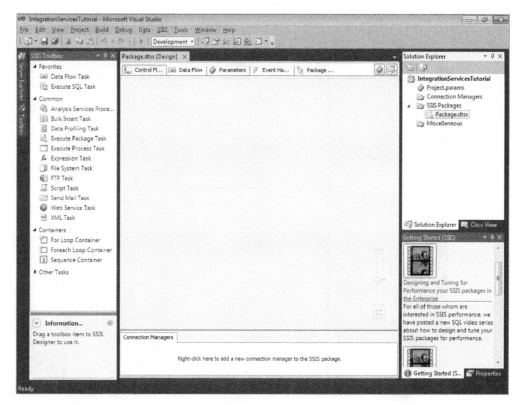

FIGURE 13-1

By default, when a new project is created, the Integration Services project uses the Project Deployment Model. The Solution Explorer window shows the following: Project.params, Connection Managers, a folder for SSIS packages, and a Miscellaneous folder (refer to

Figure 13-1). Both Project.params and Connection Managers are new features introduced in SQL Server 2012. Project.params defines parameters used by all the packages in the same project. For example, when the value for a project parameter changes, the value can be used by any packages that use the parameter. The Connection Managers folder contains shared connection managers that can be used by all the packages in the same project.

It is important to familiarize yourself with the design surface and the various other windows in SSIS. All the connections used in your SSIS package are shown in the Connection Managers window, thereby providing a consolidated view. If you right-click in the Connection Managers window, you can see the various types of connections that SSIS supports. The main window, which is a graphical designer, is used to create SSIS packages. The SSIS Design window has four views: Control Flow, Data Flow, Event Handlers, and Package Explorer. You explore the use of these views in this chapter.

All the tasks and transforms provided by SSIS are represented within the Toolbox window. To see the Toolbox window, click the SSIS Toolbox in the SSIS drop-down menu. The Toolbox window can be docked by clicking the pin icon, as shown in Figure 13-2.

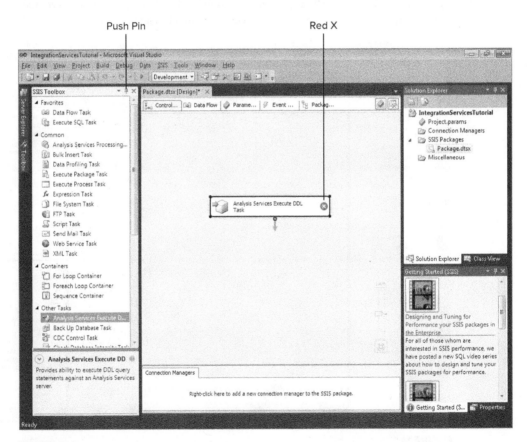

FIGURE 13-2

4.   Drag and drop the SQL Server Analysis Services Execute DDL task to the Control Flow tab. You now see the task in the window (refer to Figure 13-2).

The SSIS designer in SSDT completes a validation on every task and transform in your package. Each task has a certain set of required properties and some optional properties. If the required properties are not specified, you see a red "x" mark within the task. If the optional properties are not defined, you see a yellow "x" mark within the task. If any of the tasks or transforms within your package have a red "x" mark, that indicates that there is an error in your package and you cannot run the package without resolving the error. The Execute DDL task needs the connection details to Analysis Services and the DDL to execute. Because these properties have not been defined when you drag and drop the task in your editor, you see a red "x" mark (refer to Figure 13-2).

5. One of the properties for the Execute DDL task is to specify the connection details to an Analysis Services database. To create a connection to the AnalysisServicesMultidimensionalTutorial database, right-click the Connection Managers window. You can see all the various types of connections SSIS supports, as shown in Figure 13-3. Select New Analysis Services Connection.

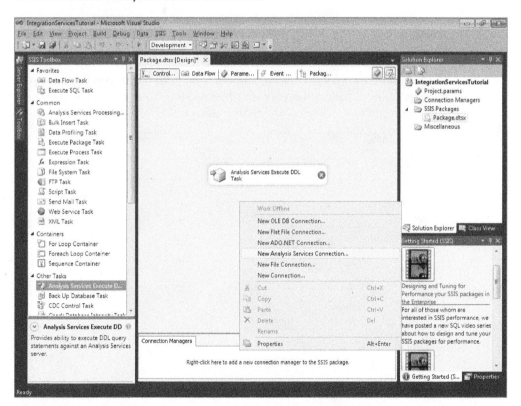

FIGURE 13-3

The Add Analysis Services Connection Manager dialog is launched as shown in Figure 13-4. You have the option to establish a connection to an Analysis Services database or to an Analysis Services project within your solution. SSDT supports having multiple projects within the same solution. This means that you can have Analysis Services and Integration Services projects within the same solution. If you build an SSIS package for the Analysis Services project within the same solution, you would choose the second option.

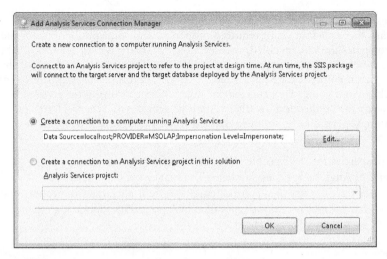

FIGURE 13-4

6. Select the first option (refer to Figure 13-4) and click Edit.

7. In the Connection Manager dialog, you can specify the connection details to your Analysis Services database such as Server or file name and the Initial catalog, as shown in Figure 13-5. After you have specified the connection details, click OK to complete both dialogs.

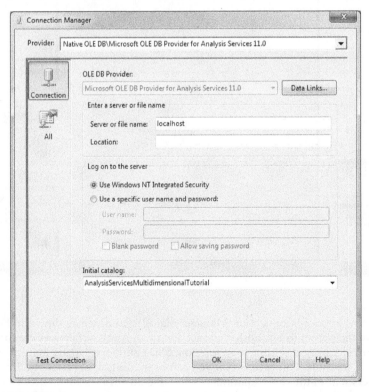

FIGURE 13-5

8. To specify properties needed by the Execute DDL task, double-click the Execute DDL task object within the designer. You see the Execute DDL Task Editor, as shown in Figure 13-6. Click the DDL option.

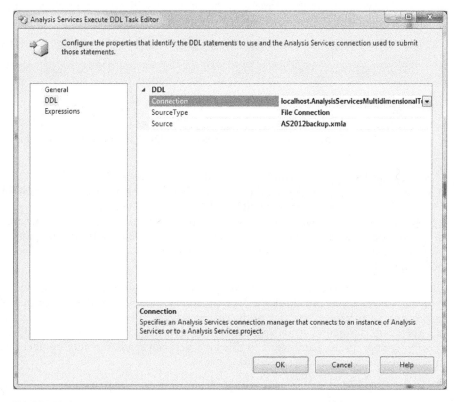

FIGURE 13-6

9. From the drop-down list for Connection, you can either create a new connection or select an existing connection. Select the Analysis Services connection you established in step 7. Following are three ways to specify the DDL to be executed:

➤ **Enter the DDL in a text box**: Whenever you know that your DDL is static and will not change, you can use this option.

➤ **Specify a connection to the file**: This option is used whenever you have a file containing the DDL. This file can be static or dynamic in the sense that the DDL contents can be changed by another operation, such as a different SSIS task or an external program.

➤ **Specify the DDL using a variable in the SSIS package where the value of the variable is the actual DDL**: Use this option whenever the results from one task need to be used as an input to another task. The variable can be initialized during package execution, or the task setting the value for the variable needs to be executed before the Execute DDL task in the control flow.

10. Select the source type as File Connection. Select the drop-down list under Source, and select New Connection. In the File Connection Manager dialog, select the DDL file AS2012backup .xmla provided under the Chapter 13 directory of the downloaded sample from the web site. The following shows the contents of the DDL. This DDL will take a backup of the AnalysisServicesMultidimensionalTutorial database.

```
<Backup xmlns="http://schemas.microsoft.com/analysisservices/2003/engine">
  <Object>
    <DatabaseID>AnalysisServicesMultidimensionalTutorial</DatabaseID>
  </Object>
  <File>AnalysisServices2012Tutorial.abf</File>
</Backup>
```

11. After you specify all the properties for the Execute DDL Task Editor (refer to Figure 13-6) click OK.

If you run the SSIS package you have created, a backup of the AnalysisServicesMultidimensionalTutorial database will be created in Program Files\ Microsoft SQL Server\MSAS10.MSSQLSERVER\OLAP\Backup. The backup is usually an operation scheduled for when the load on Analysis Services is minimal. Many companies do backup operations on a nightly basis, but if you are a multinational company or have customers using the database across the globe, you must factor in your customers' needs and perform the backup at an appropriate time.

Regardless of when the package runs, you need to know whether the operation succeeded or failed. Obviously, you can check the logs on Analysis Services or the logs of the SSIS package, but as an administrator, one of the easiest ways is to send an e-mail about the results of the operation. To facilitate this operation, SSIS provides a task called the Send Mail task. By specifying appropriate parameters to this task, you can send an e-mail upon completion of a specific task or an entire SSIS package.

12. To add the Send Mail task to your SSIS package, drag and drop two instances of the Send Mail task to your designer.

Use one task to send an e-mail when the Execute DDL task succeeds and the other one to send mail when the Execute DDL task fails. Now that you have two Send Mail tasks in the Control Flow pane, it is time to connect the Execute DDL task to the Send Mail tasks.

13. You can connect tasks in a control flow by clicking the originating object (a downward-facing green arrow appears) and dragging the arrow end to the target object. Do that for the first Send Mail task.

14. For the second Send Mail task, just click the Execute DDL task again, and you see another green arrow appear as an output of the item. Drag the green arrow and connect it to the next Send Mail task. Your package should look like the one shown in Figure 13-7.

The connecting line represents precedence constraint functionality; if you double-click the green line, the Precedence Constraint Editor appears. The green lines indicate success, and whenever the Execute DDL task completes successfully, execution continues with the task connected on the success line.

15. To configure the second mail task to send e-mail on failure, double-click the connecting line.

You should see the Precedence Constraint Editor, as shown in Figure 13-8. The connecting line between the two tasks has several properties evaluated after the completion of the source task. You can specify an expression and constraint that can be evaluated after the completion of the task. The value property of the connecting line helps you to choose the constraint and determines whether the control transfers to the next task. The three options for the value property are Success, Failure, and Completion. Change the value from Success to Failure. You can also configure the precedence control by right-clicking the connecting line between two tasks and selecting Success, Failure, or Completion.

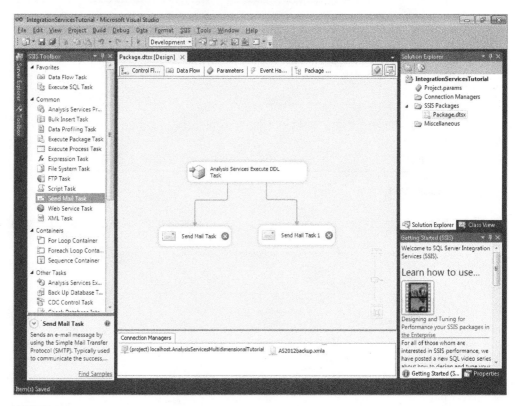

FIGURE 13-7

16. Click OK after you complete specifying the constraint value to Failure (refer to Figure 13-8).

17. You need to specify the mail server and details of the mail content in the properties of the Send Mail task. Double-click the Send Mail task to configure the properties of the task. Figure 13-9 shows the Send Mail Task Editor. Specify the details of the mail server by clicking the drop-down list of the SmtpConnection property. Your company should have an SMTP server. Contact your IT administrator to get details on the name of your SMTP server. Specify the e-mail address from which you want this mail to be sent, the people who need to receive the status of this package execution, and the content of the mail (refer to Figure 13-9). Based on the Send Mail task you have chosen, provide the appropriate subject and message source. Refer to Figure 13-9 to see the contents of the Send Mail task that will be executed on successful completion of the Execute DDL task created in a previous step.

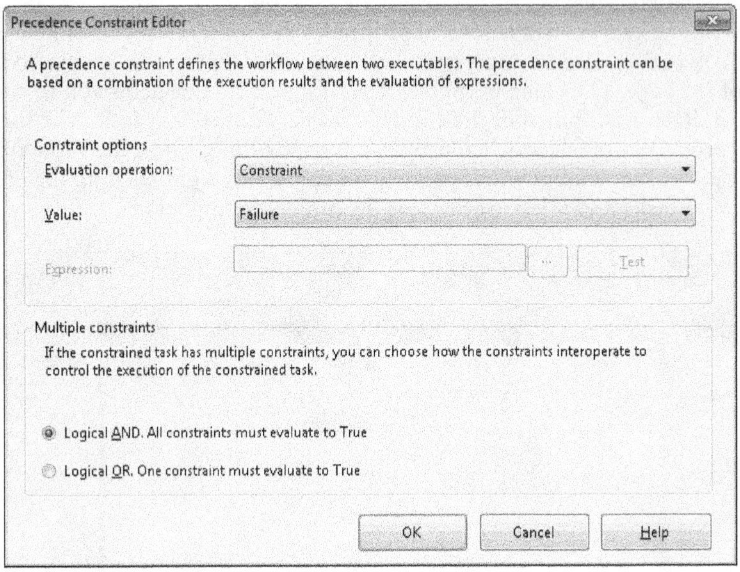

FIGURE 13-8

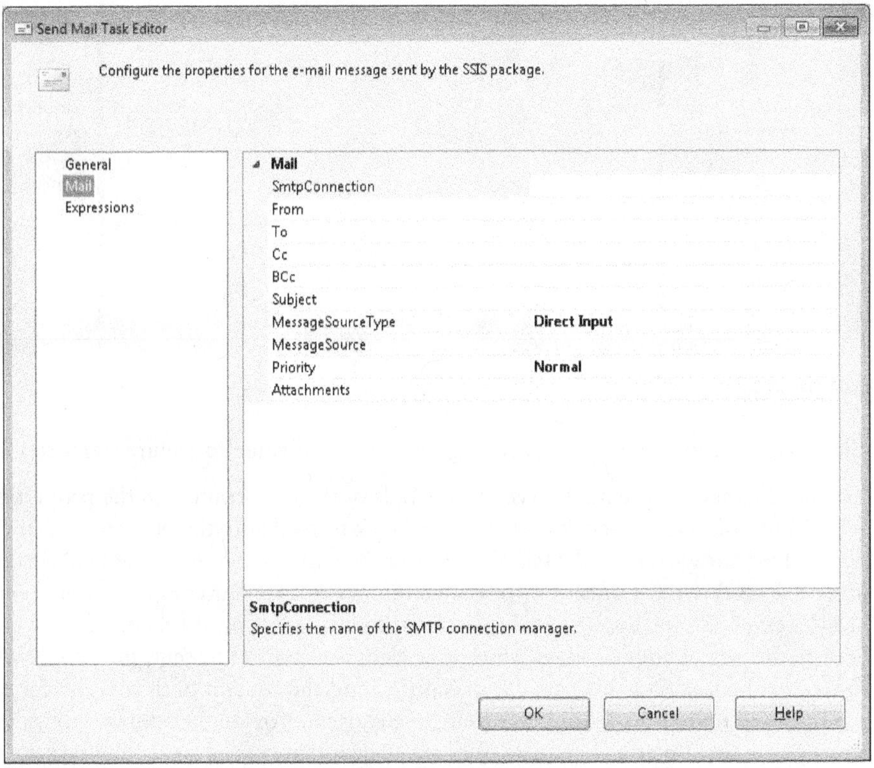

FIGURE 13-9

18. Make sure the second Send Mail task properties are appropriately changed to reflect the failure of the backup of the Analysis Services database.

19. Rename the Send Mail tasks as Send Mail Success and Send Mail Failure by changing the name of the tasks, as shown in Figure 13-10. Appropriate naming makes the SSIS package easily readable and can be interpreted immediately by another person working on this task.

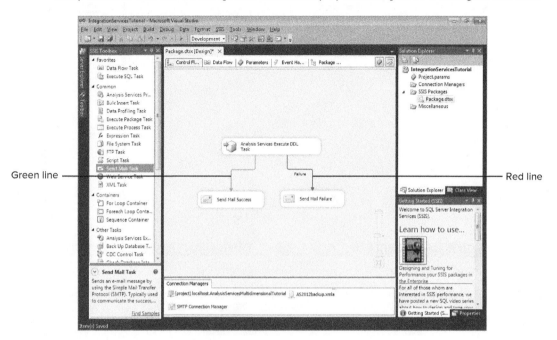

FIGURE 13-10

20. The SSIS package is now ready for execution. You can select Debug Start, press the F5 key, or right-click the package name and select Deploy.

SSDT now starts the execution of the SSIS package. SSDT operates in the debugging environment, similar to debugging a program. You first see the SQL Server Analysis Services Execute DDL task with a yellow icon at the top-right corner of the task, as shown in Figure 13-11, which indicates that the task is currently under execution. If the task completed successfully, the top-right corner of the task shows a green tick, as show in Figure 13-12. If the task fails, the status is shown in red. You do have the ability to insert break points and analyze variables used within tasks or transforms in the debug environment. When the entire package is completed, status on each of the tasks is shown; that is, the two tasks are shown in green having completed successfully.

21. In the debug environment you can see detailed information for each task and the time taken by the task for completion in the Progress window. You can switch to the Progress window when the package is executed. The Progress window updates when the control moves from one task to another. Figure 13-13 shows the progress report of the execution of the task. You can see that the DDL Execute task, which took a backup of an Analysis Services database, completed successfully.

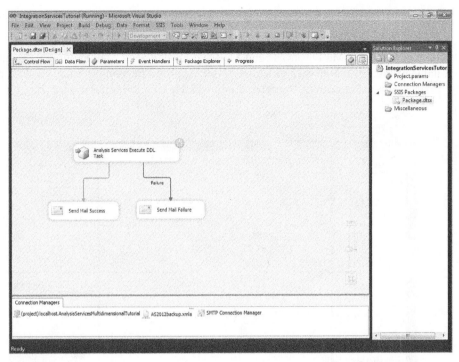

FIGURE 13-11

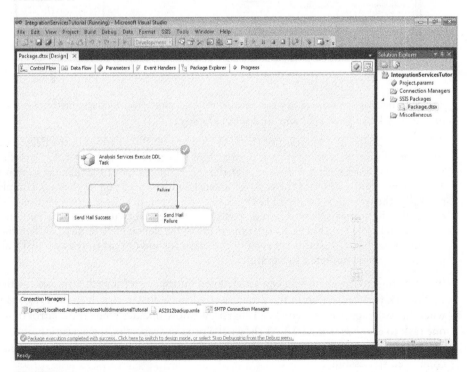

FIGURE 13-12

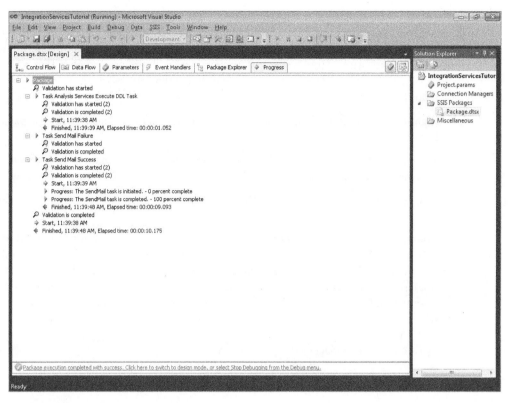

FIGURE 13-13

Processing an Analysis Services Object

SSIS provides a task for processing Analysis Services objects. You can process an entire Analysis Services database or choose a specific dimension, cube, or even partitions for processing using the SSIS task called the SQL Server Analysis Services Processing task.

The Analysis Services Processing task is useful whenever you have changes in your relational data that need to get propagated to the cube. Often, retail companies have new products added to their catalog every day, and the products table gets updated with the new products or changes in existing products as a daily batch process. Also, the daily sales data gets updated in the relational database as a nightly batch process. To propagate these changes to the cube for analysis, the dimensions and cubes need to be processed unless you have set the storage mode as ROLAP for dimensions and cubes or have set up proactive caching on your dimensions and partitions.

Several considerations are involved in determining frequency of processing. Should cubes be processed on a daily, weekly, or monthly basis? The decision to process the Analysis Services objects is typically based upon the size of the dimensions and cubes, how often data changes on the relational database, and the frequency with which business analysts analyze the cube data. In most cases, there are additions to the products table rather than updates, and hence an incremental process of the products table might be sufficient. If your fact table gets updated with daily transactional data in the same table, you have the option to create new partitions in the cube on a daily or weekly basis or doing a full process of the cube.

The Microsoft performance guide for Analysis Services suggests you have a new partition based on various factors from processing, manageability, aggregations, and query performance. We recommend you decide on the right partition size based on your cube design needs to achieve optimal performance for your users. How you partition your data is based on decisions that relate to your business needs. To create an Integration Services package that processes an Analysis Services Sales partition, do the following:

1. Right-click the SSIS Packages folder, and select New SSIS Package. Name the package PartitionProcessing.

2. Similar to what you did in the Backup package earlier in this chapter, create a connection to the AnalysisServices2012Tutorial database in the Connection Managers window.

3. Drag and drop the SQL Server Analysis Services Processing task and two Send Mail tasks into the SSIS designer.

4. Configure one of the Send Mail tasks for success and another one for failure. Make the connections from the Analysis Services Processing task to Send Mail tasks similar to the Analysis Services Backup package you created in the previous example. Double-click the SQL Server Analysis Services Processing task. This launches the Analysis Services Processing Task Editor, as shown in Figure 13-14. This dialog is similar to the Processing dialog of Analysis Services, which you learned about in previous chapters.

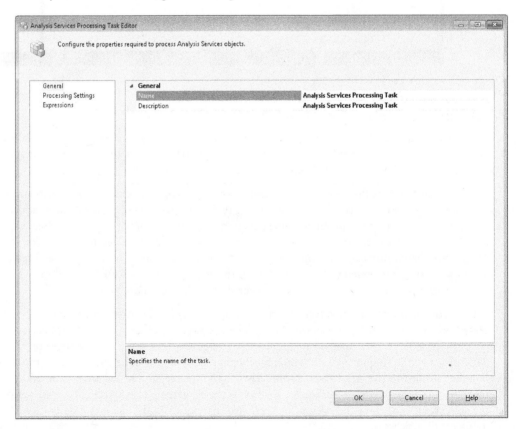

FIGURE 13-14

If you click the Change Settings button, the Change Settings dialog pops up, as shown in Figure 13-15. The Change Settings dialog enables you to process the selected Analysis Services objects sequentially or in parallel. You can use the Dimension Key Errors tab to configure the processing options so that appropriate actions are taken when errors are encountered during the processing operation. The selected option applies to all the Analysis Services objects chosen in the Analysis Services Processing Task Editor.

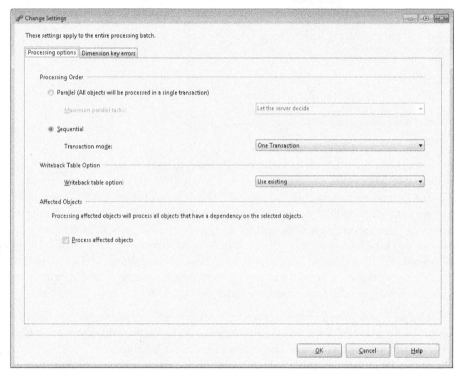

FIGURE 13-15

5. To add Analysis Services objects for processing, click the Add button on the Analysis Services Processing Task Editor (refer to Figure 13-14). The Add SQL Server Analysis Services Object enables you to choose the object you want to process. Select the Fact Internet Sales partition, as shown in Figure 13-16, and click OK. Click OK again to accept the modifications in the Analysis Services Processing Task Editor dialog.

6. Press the F5 button on your keyboard to deploy the SSIS processing package and make sure it executes correctly. If everything has been specified correctly, you see successful completion of the SQL Server Analysis Services Processing task and the Send Mail Success tasks — also, these tasks show a green tick at the top-right corner of each task. This indicates the successful execution of the tasks. You must have the appropriate privileges on the Analysis Services instance to perform these operations.

Loading Data into an Analysis Services Partition

Typically, the data from the transactional source database (production system) is extracted, staged to some intermediate storage, and then undergoes transformations before being stored in a data warehouse (flat file or relational format). This data then needs to be propagated to the cube for analysis.

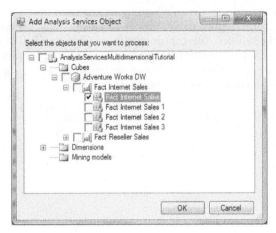

FIGURE 13-16

Analysis Services has the capability to read data from various data sources, from flat files to various relational databases. One way to add new fact data to the cube is to create new partitions that read data from the data sources. You can use SSIS's Script task to create a new DDL, execute the DDL using the Execute DDL task, and then process the partition using the Analysis Services Processing task. You can create a package that integrates all these tasks. Even though you can utilize these tasks to load fact data, it is not easy to load new dimension data to an existing dimension table. Therefore, SSIS provides an easy way to load new fact and dimension data into your current cube using SSIS transforms. The two transforms that help in loading such data are the Partition Processing transform and the Dimension Processing transform.

Many large retail stores still use flat files to extract data from the transactional systems. Your company probably does the same. Often, the columns in the flat files do not contain clean data. During the staging process, you clean the data and format it with appropriate IDs that match your cube to load the data into your cube. SSIS provides transformations to do lookups, get the correct IDs, clean the data on-the-fly, and then load the data into your cube. In the following example, you work with clean data that needs to be loaded from a flat file into one of the partitions of the AnalysisServices2012Tutorial cube:

1. Create a new SSIS package under the SSIS Packages folder, and name it PipelineDataLoad.

2. The SSIS task that helps you to read data, perform transforms, and then push the data into a destination is called the Data Flow task. Drag and drop the Data Flow task into your SSIS editor, as shown in Figure 13-17, and name it Data Flow Partition Load.

    Double-click the Data Flow task. You are now in the Data Flow view. The Toolbox window shows you the SSIS transforms available for use in the Data Flow view. The data flow transforms are categorized into three main areas, namely, data flow sources, data flow transformations, and data flow destinations. Data to be loaded into the partition of the AnalysisServicesMultidimensionalTutorial cube is provided as a flat file in the Chapter 13 samples folder named AdventureWorksPartition3Data.txt. To retrieve this data, you need to use the Flat File Source transform. This data needs to be pushed to the partition in the AnalysisServicesMultidimensionalTutorial cube. Therefore, you need a Partition Processing destination.

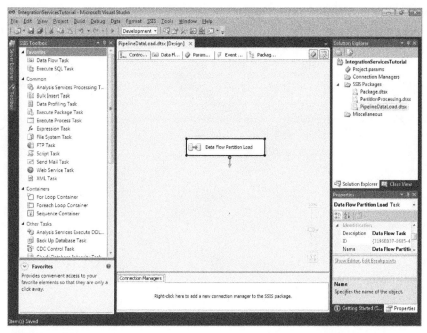

FIGURE 13-17

3. Drag and drop the Flat File Source and Partition Processing destination from the Toolbox to the Data Flow Editor and join them through the connector, as shown in Figure 13-18.

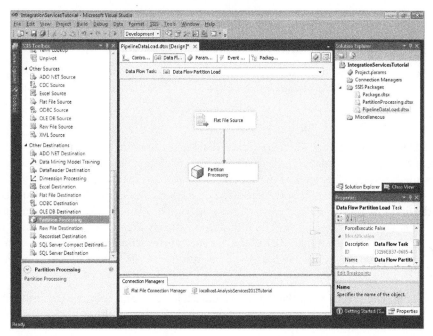

FIGURE 13-18

4. Double-click the Flat File Source transform to specify the connection to the flat file. You are now in the Flat File Source Editor, as shown in Figure 13-19. You need to specify the flat file using the Flat File Connection Manager. Click the New button.

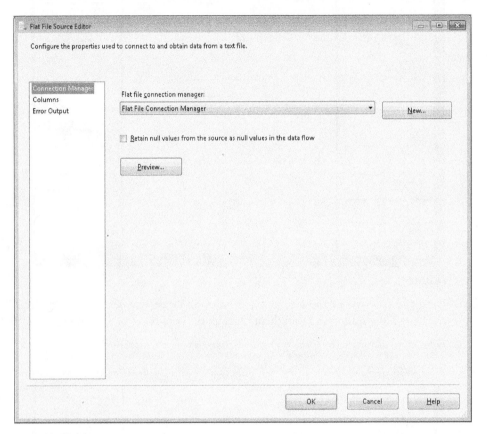

FIGURE 13-19

5. The Flat File Connection Manager Editor dialog, as shown in Figure 13-20, now pops up. Click the Browse button, and select the flat file AdventureWorksPartition3Data.txt, which is available in the Chapter 13 samples that you can download from the book web site. The dialog now parses the data in the flat file. You have the option to skip rows from the flat file if the first row or the first few rows indicate column headers. Click the Column Names in the First Data Row check box. You also need to specify the type of delimiter used in the flat file to separate the columns. Click Columns and set the delimiter as Tab, as shown in Figure 13-21. To see if the dialog can read the data from the flat file correctly based on the delimiter, click the columns property.

6. You now see the data from the flat file organized as rows and columns (refer to Figure 13-21). After you confirm that the dialog can read the data in the flat file, click OK.

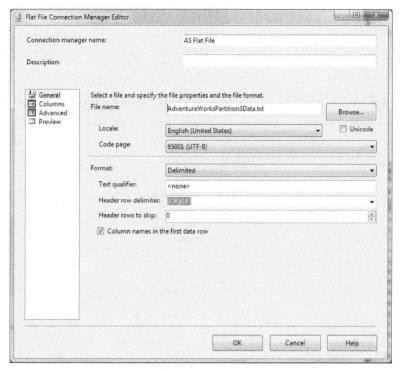

FIGURE 13-20

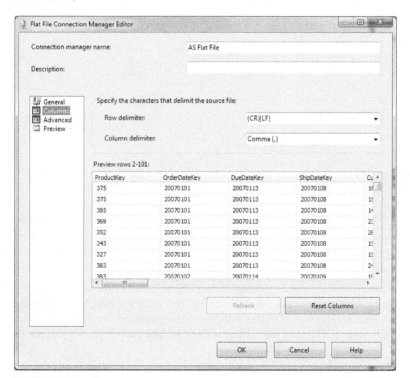

FIGURE 13-21

7. In the Flat File Source Editor dialog, click Columns, as shown in Figure 13-22. By default, SSIS uses the column names to be the output column names. You can change the output column names in this dialog by editing the appropriate row. Leave the default names suggested by SSIS, and click OK.

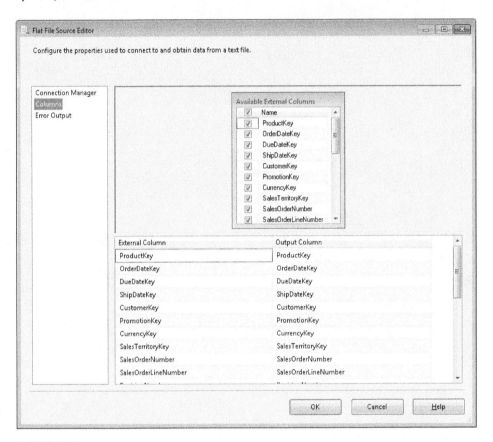

FIGURE 13-22

8. After configuring the flat file source, you need to specify the partition into which this data needs to be loaded. Double-click the Partition Processing transform in the Data Flow Editor. You can now see the Partition Processing Destination Editor, as shown in Figure 13-23. Similar to the first two SSIS packages, you need to specify the connection to the database. Click the New button to specify the connection to the AnalysisServicesMultidimensionalTutorial database. You now see the cubes and partitions within the database.

You now need to select the partition under which the data needs to be loaded and specify the processing method that needs to be applied. If the data is new, you typically need to use the Add (Incremental) option that processes the partition incrementally. Processing the partition incrementally means that the new data will be incrementally added to the cube while the current data is available for querying. After the new data has been processed, the data is committed, and it is available for querying. The incremental processing method's primary functionality is to serve the customer's queries even when the new data is added to the partition. In addition, you get the performance benefit of only adding the new rows to the partitions rather than reprocessing the entire partition. Analysis Services can accomplish this by cloning the existing version of the partition and adding data to that. When the entire data has been processed in the new version of the partition, and when the original partition is free from any query locks, Analysis Services switches the versions, and the new version containing the entire data set is now available for querying.

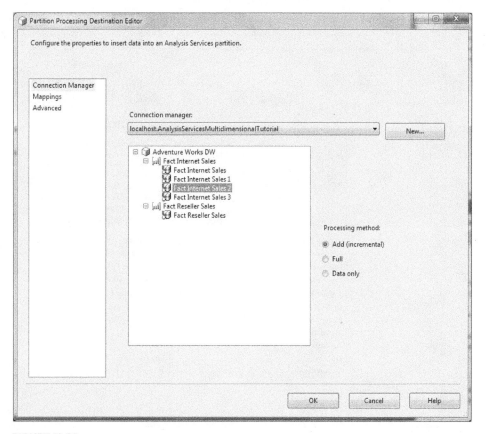

FIGURE 13-23

9. Select Fact Internet Sales 2 as the partition to add the data and Add (incremental) as the processing method (refer to Figure 13-23).

A more typical package using the Partition Processing transform contains several lookup transforms to map the incoming dimension columns to the right ID in the dimensions of the multidimensional database. When the correct IDs for each dimension are obtained, retrieved dimension ID columns are mapped to the partition processing columns to load the data.

10. Click Mappings, as shown in Figure 13-24, to specify the right mappings from the columns from the flat file to the columns in the partition. The columns in the flat file have been specified to be the same names as the ones in the cube. Therefore, it is easy to map each column directly (as shown in Figure 13-24). Make sure you mark all the columns correctly on this page. You can ignore the Dim Geography.Dim Geography destination column because Dim Geography is a reference dimension; therefore, the key for this dimension does not exist in the fact table. Click OK after completing all the mappings in the Partition Processing Destination Editor.

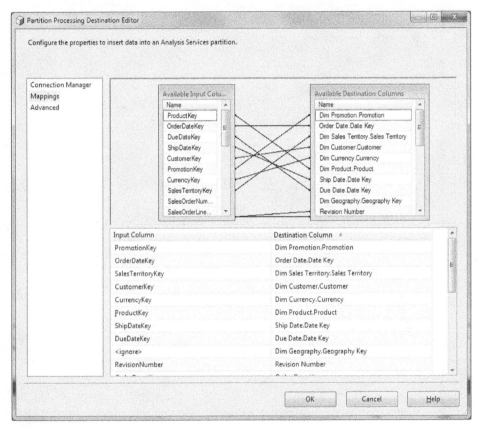

FIGURE 13-24

11. You have completed all the necessary settings in the SSIS package to load data into a partition. Press F5 to test the execution of your SSIS package. You see that the top-right corner of the Flat File Source and Partition Processing has a yellow icon, indicating that the SSIS package is being executed. Along the connector line between the two transforms Flat File Source and Partition Processing, you can notice the number of rows being processed, as shown in Figure 13-25.

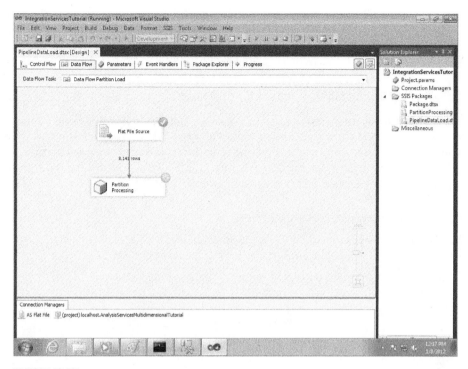

FIGURE 13-25

Refer to Figure 13-25 to see a snapshot of the SSIS package execution. After all the data has been loaded without errors, you see a green tick at the top-right corner of the Flat File Source and Partition Processing indicating successful completion of the package. During this SSIS operation that does incremental processing, Analysis Services creates a new temporary partition, loads the data from the flat file, and then merges the partition to Fact Internet Sales 2 partition. There is a potential bug in Analysis Services 2012 that causes the partition processing to fail because the data source of the partition and the flat file are not the same. You can find an update on the book's web site for this sample. To understand partition processing, load the flat file data to a relational database, change the source from flat file source to OLE DB source, and retrieve the same data from the new table.

In the preceding data load example, there was one-to-one mapping between the columns in the flat file and the measures and granularity attributes of the partitions, except for the reference dimension granularity attribute DimGeography. This was possible because all the measures in the partition directly mapped to the columns in the flat file. Assume you have a fact data column that was used twice in a measure group as two measures: one with Sum as the aggregation function and another as Count or Distinct Count as aggregation functions. Such a scenario is common. In this scenario, you cannot map the corresponding column from the flat file to the two measures because the SSIS Partition Processing transform disallows a column from the source (in this example, the flat file) to be mapped to multiple destination columns that are part of the partition. If you ignore mappings even for a single destination column that is part of the partition, your data load will fail. You would need to either have additional columns in the source so that you can map those to the corresponding columns in the partition, or use the SSIS transform Copy Column to duplicate existing columns to serve as input to the Partition Processing transform. Modify the AdventureWorks2012Tutorial database to have a distinct count measure in the Internet Sales partition, and then create an SSIS package with the Copy Column transform between the Flat File Data Source and Partition Processing transforms to map the column from the flat file to the distinct count measure.

You have successfully learned to create SSIS packages for performing administrative tasks on Analysis Services such as backup and processing. You can perform other administrative tasks such as synchronization, restore, and so on using the tasks and transforms provided by SSIS. In addition to providing tasks and transforms for OLAP features, SSIS also provides tasks and transforms for data mining, which you learn about in the next section.

Deploying the Integration Services Project

In SSIS 2012, if the project uses the Project Deployment Model (which is the default), you can build the project to produce an Integration Services Project Deployment File:

1. Right-click the project, and select Build, as shown in Figure 13-26.

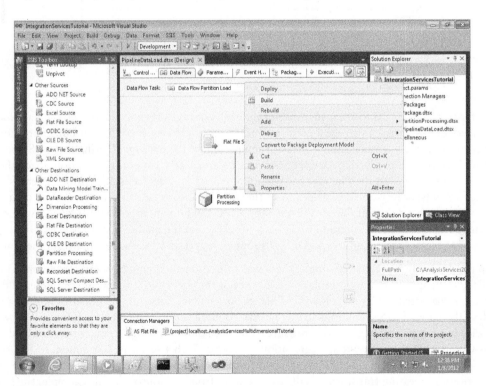

FIGURE 13-26

In the `bin\Development` directory, you can find a file called `IntegrationServicesTutorial.ispac`. The `.ispac` extension refers to the Integration

Services Project Deployment File, which is the unit of deployment to the SSIS catalog created on a SQL Server instance. You are now ready to deploy the SSIS project to the SSIS catalog. In SSIS 2012, the SSIS catalog is a centralized database for storing packages and the SSIS project. The SSIS catalog corresponds to a database, called SSISDB, on the SQL Server instance in which it is installed. By having all the packages stored in a centralized user database, it makes it easier for the administrator to manage all the packages in the organization. In addition, when packages (stored in the SSIS catalog) are executed, SSIS 2012 provides new capabilities that make it easier to troubleshoot package executions.

The unit of deployment to the SSIS catalog is an SSIS project. Because the SSIS project is a self-contained unit of deployment, it ensures that all the packages and its dependent packages are deployed and managed together. When the project is deployed, information about the SSIS project is extracted during deployment and stored in the SSIS catalog.

To deploy the SSIS project, do the following:

2. Right-click the project and choose Deploy, as shown in Figure 13-27.

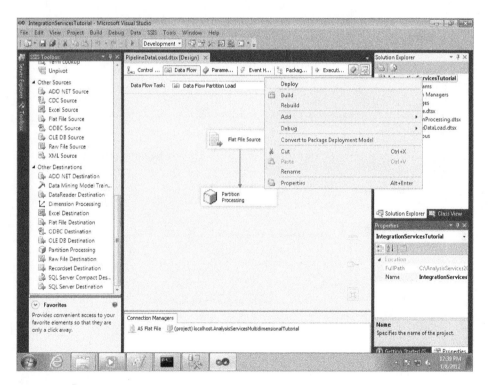

FIGURE 13-27

3. This launches the Deployment Wizard, as shown in Figure 13-28.

4. Click Next. This allows you to specify the SSIS project deployment file to be deployed. By default, it refers to the current SSIS project, as shown in Figure 13-29.

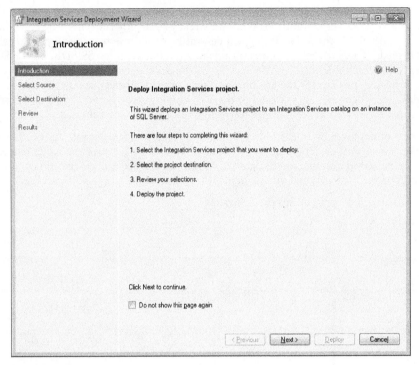

FIGURE 13-28

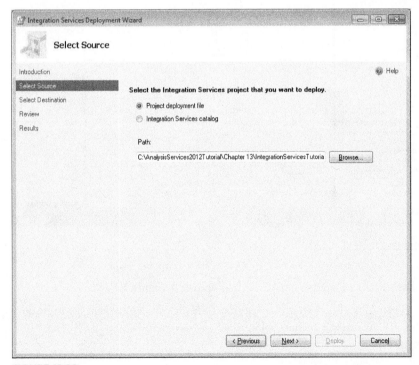

FIGURE 13-29

5. Specify the server name, and click Browse, as shown in Figure 13-30.

6. Choose the folder that you want to deploy the project. If no folders exist, click New Folder. This will create a new folder, as shown in Figure 13-31.

FIGURE 13-30

FIGURE 13-31

7. After the path is specified, click Next to display the screen shown in Figure 13-32.

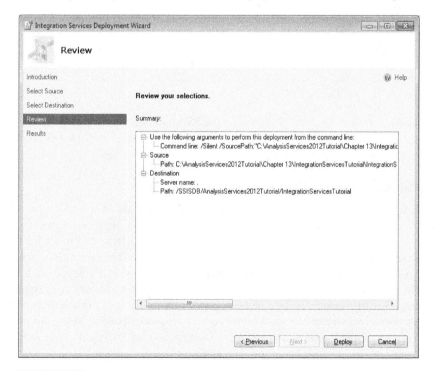

FIGURE 13-32

8. The screen shows a summary of the deployment. Review it, and click Deploy to start the deployment.

9. Refer to Figure 13-33 to see the project being deployed. If deployment is successful, you see that the result for Deploying Project shows Passed, as shown in Figure 13-34.

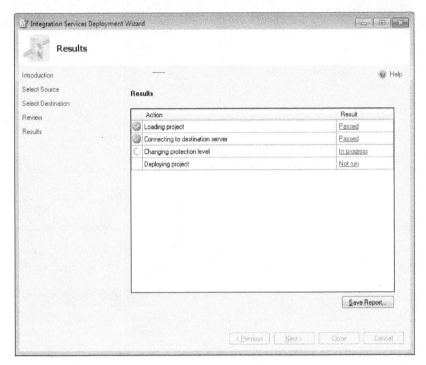

FIGURE 13-33

10. After the SSIS project has been deployed to the SSIS catalog, you can use SQL Server Management Studio (SSMS) to manage, configure, and execute the packages contained in the project, as shown in Figure 13-35.

Integration Services Tasks for Data Mining

SSIS 2012 provides tasks and transforms specifically targeted for Data Mining objects in Analysis Services 2012. With the Data Mining Query task, you can query mining models and store the results in a destination such as a relational database. One of the common uses of such a task is to predict a list of customers for a targeted marketing campaign. If the company wants to offer promotional discounts to targeted customers every month, it would predict if a new customer is valuable based on the customers' attributes, calculate an appropriate discount, and mail them a coupon. The Data Mining Query transform is used when you want to manipulate the source data to the mining model or the output of the mining model in a better format. For examples and illustrations of Integration Services Tasks for Data Mining, refer to *Professional Microsoft SQL Server 2012 Integration Services* by Brian Knight et al. (Wiley, 2012).

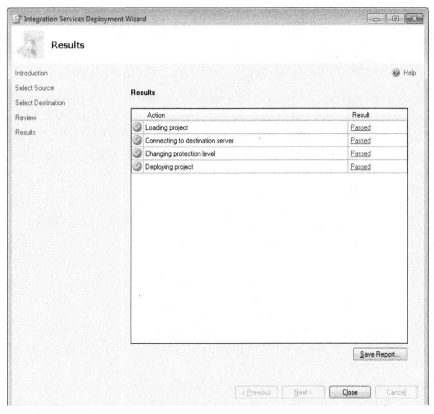

FIGURE 13-34

FIGURE 13-35

Automating Execution of SSIS Packages

Integration Services works on a slightly different model compared to Analysis Services. With Analysis Services, you deploy projects to the server. There are several ways to automate the execution of SSIS packages. In SQL Server 2012, if you make use of the Legacy Deployment Model during development and deployment, you can schedule the execution of packages deployed to SQL Server, through the file system, or using the SSIS Package Store (which is a variant of the file system solution). In SQL Server 2012, you can develop a SSIS project. The SSIS project contains one or more SSIS packages. The SSIS project is then deployed to a SSIS catalog. Therefore, you can also schedule the execution of packages that have been deployed to the SSIS catalog using SQL Agent. In this chapter, you look at both the file system approach and the SSIS catalog approach.

Start with the file system approach. Specifically, from SSDT (using the Legacy Deployment Model), you save a package in the form of an XML file (a .dtsx file). You can see the source for a .dtsx by right-clicking a package in Solution Explorer and selecting View Code. After you check that out, do the following:

1. In SSDT Solution Explorer, click one of your working packages and select File ➪ Save *<file-name>* As, and give the file a descriptive name. In this way, you save an XML version of the package to the file system.

2. Next, open up SSMS and connect to Integration Services; open it in Object Explorer, and right-click Stored Packages. At this point, you can select Import Package, as shown in Figure 13-36.

3. The Import Package dialog appears and you should change Package Location from SQL Server to File System. Then click the button associated with Package Path to specify the dtsx file you want. If you just click the Package Name textbox, it fills in the package name for you. At this point, the dialog should look something like Figure 13-37.

FIGURE 13-36

With the package in the Stored Packages area, you can easily run it by right-clicking the package name and selecting Run Package. What you need to do, however, is schedule to have your package run on a regular basis so that you don't need to think about it. You can accomplish scheduling SSIS packages to be run periodically by using the SQL Server Agent. The Agent is its own process, which you can access by opening a connection to the Database Engine, as shown in Figure 13-38.

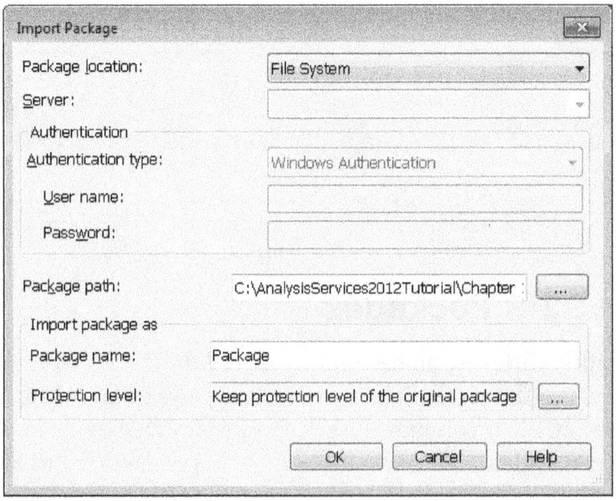

FIGURE 13-37

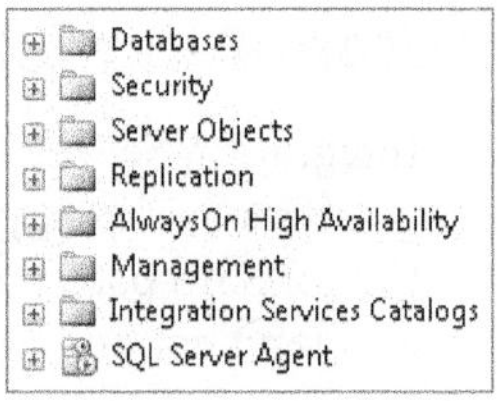

FIGURE 13-38

4. To create a scheduled job, right-click the Jobs folder, and select New Job. Give it an appropriate name and description, as shown in Figure 13-39.

5. On the Select a Page pane at the top, click Steps. Click the New button that appears at the bottom of the dialog. On the New Job Step page, name your step SSAS Processing and under Type (type of operation) select SQL Server Integration Services Package, as shown in Figure 13-40.

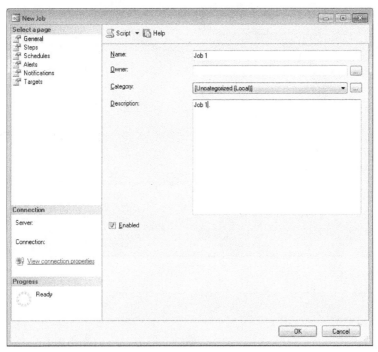

FIGURE 13-39

6. For the Package Source, you need to select File System (because you will use the dtsx previously saved to the file system).

7. Click the ellipsis button for Package, and select the package you saved before. At this time, your New Job Step dialog should look something like Figure 13-40. Click OK to continue; when you are asked if the On Success action is intended, click Yes.

8. On the Select a Page pane at the top right, click Schedules and then the New button that appears at the bottom of the dialog. The dialog that comes up now is the New Job Schedule dialog; it is here that you can schedule your package to be run on a recurring basis. For illustrative purposes, select Schedule Type: One Time. Select today's date with a time of 5 minutes from now. After you enter the details, your job scheduler dialog should resemble Figure 13-41.

9. Click OK in the New Job Schedule dialog.

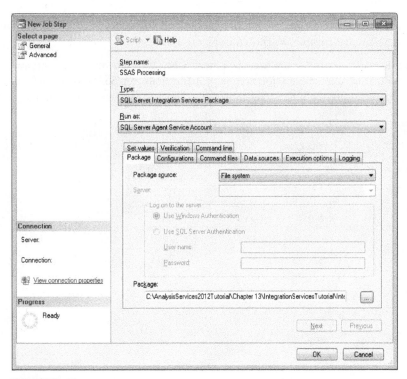

FIGURE 13-40

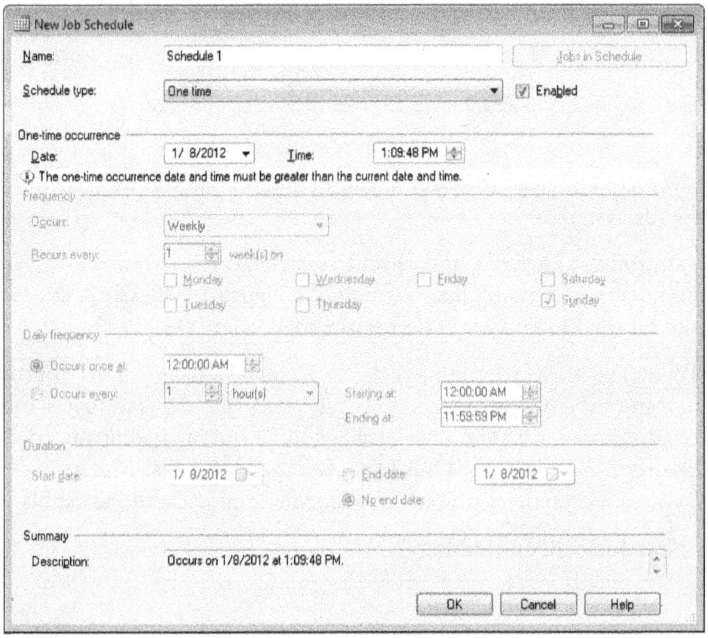

FIGURE 13-41

To see the job kicked off as scheduled, double-click the Job Activity Monitor icon, which is under the SQL Server Agent Folder in SSMS's Object Explorer. When your job starts, you see the Status change to Executing, as shown in Figure 13-42.

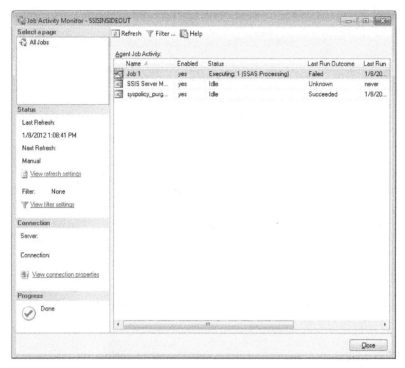

FIGURE 13-42

Hopefully, you can see the power of this approach — the ability to create packages chock-full of administrative functions to manage your instance of Analysis Services, all scheduled to run on a recurring basis and send e-mails based on success or failure. This is great stuff, especially for users who want to automate as much as possible and utilize their remaining time to learn and implement new things! You have gained sufficient knowledge of SSIS by now that you can create Analysis Services SSIS packages and schedule them. Make a habit to use SSIS when applicable for your business.

The SSIS tasks and transforms for SSAS 2012 were available in SQL Server 2005. There are enhancements made in SSIS such as data flow performance that can benefit your SSIS packages. For an in-depth understanding of SSIS 2012 features and enhancements, read *Professional Microsoft SQL Server 2012 Integration Services* by Brian Knight et al. (Wiley, 2012).

Next, you see how to schedule the execution of packages that have been deployed to the SSIS catalog.

1. To create a scheduled job, right-click the Jobs folder, and select New Job. Give it an appropriate name and description, as shown in Figure 13-43.

2. On the Select a Page pane at the top, click Steps. Click the New button that appears at the bottom of the dialog. On the New Job Step page, name your step SSAS Processing and under Type (type of operation) select SQL Server Integration Services Package, as shown in Figure 13-44.

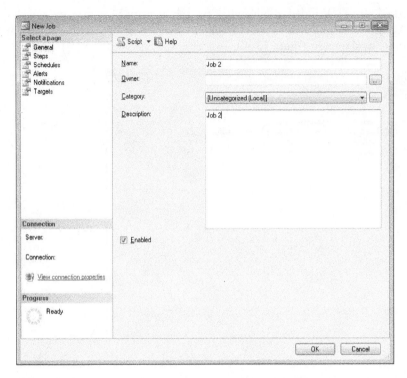

FIGURE 13-43

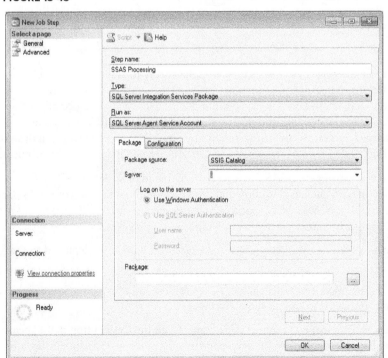

FIGURE 13-44

3. For the Package Source, you need to select SSIS catalog.

4. Click the ellipsis button for Package, and select the project that you have deployed to the SSIS catalog, as shown in Figure 13-45.

FIGURE 13-45

5. At this time, your New Job Step dialog should look something like the one in Figure 13-46. Click OK to continue.

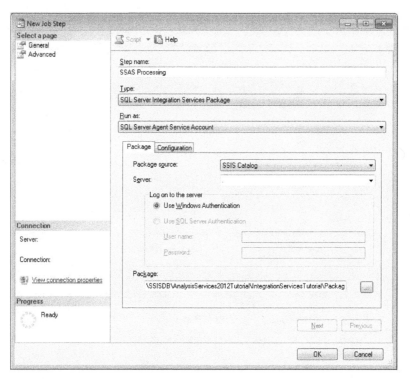

FIGURE 13-46

6. You can make use of the same steps described earlier to create a schedule for the execution.

Monitoring SSIS Package Executions

SSIS 2012 provides troubleshooting features to make it easier for administrators to identify the cause of package failures and identify performance issues. Using SSMS, administrators can launch the Integration Services Dashboard to get an overview of all the packages that have been executed in the past 24 hours. Figure 13-47 shows how the dashboard can be launched in SSMS. Figure 13-48 shows the information presented in the dashboard. The information shown includes package, connection, and detailed information for all the package executions that have happened in the past 24 hours.

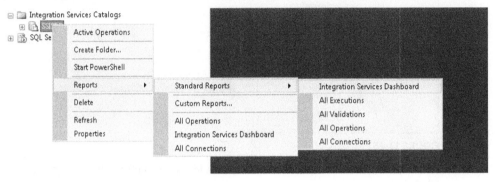

FIGURE 13-47

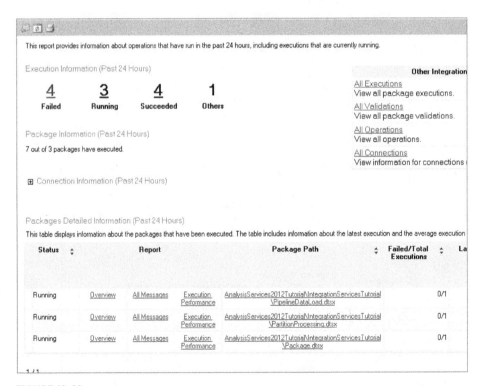

FIGURE 13-48

An administrator can click the hyperlinks for an execution to obtain more details about the execution. If an execution failed, the administrator can zoom in to the details to see the messages produced during the execution.

SQL SERVER REPORTING SERVICES

Chapters 23 and 24 cover using Power View in Reporting Services with tabular models in detail. This section focuses on so-called operational reports with pixel-perfect design requirements. Before you learn the techniques briefly mentioned here, you should understand the life cycle of reporting to deliver a key aspect of BI functionality. The life cycle consists of the following:

➤ Report Authoring

➤ Report Management

➤ Report Delivery

You learned about the basics of BI tasks for organization in Chapter 1. Report Authoring is the process to design the formats, identify needed parameters, and create the reports as needed by end users. Report Management deals with controlling who can view the reports and when to refresh the reports. Report Delivery deals with the techniques of how to alert or deliver reports to end users.

In the remainder of this chapter, you learn how to create a report on top of a relational database, deploy that report to the reports server, and then browse it locally or over your corporate network or the Internet. You learn to create a report using an Analysis Services database from the Report Wizard and further enhance your Analysis Services reporting skills by creating calculated members and using specific properties within a report. You also learn to create charts in reports for better visual representation of data, how to manage reports from the Reports Server front end, and finally, how to build ad-hoc reports from a multidimensional Analysis Services database using Report Builder.

Report Designer, Report Builder

Use Report Designer in SQL Server Data Tools and Report Builder to design a report that includes the data definition and layout for a report. The data definition requires specification of one or more data sources, or alternatively reuses so-called shared datasets already published on a report server.

Data sources supported include anything accessible through the list of Providers shown in the Data Link Properties dialog (what you're used to seeing when creating data sources for other purposes). For the extraction of specific data, query builders facilitate the query building process. This is built into SQL Server Data Tools and hosts a similar look and feel to Analysis Services and Integration Services projects. These tools enable the creation of tabular and matrix-based reports using a common infrastructure called tablix data region. You learn about tabular and matrix reports through examples in this chapter. Tablix supports capabilities of tabular and matrix report layouts. It also enhances the Reporting Services 2005 matrix feature to provide parallel (adjacent) row/column support and dynamic nesting of column groups and parallel (adjacent) row groups for the Reporting Services 2005 tabular feature. In addition, map visualizations, gauges, and chart types such as Histogram and Radar are also supported in Reporting Services 2012. You can customize your report to span multiple pages based on conditionals and grouping; this capability supports readability as does the judicious use of fonts and colors. Less is often more for things such as fonts and colors; the fewer variations displayed in a report, the more meaningful are those that are used. Interactivity can be provided by defining actions on clickable cells in the reports. After you define your report, it can be previewed within the designer; when you are pleased with the layout, you can deploy the report to a report server.

Report Definition Language

Report Definition Language (RDL) is an XML-based language used to specify all the characteristics that make up a report. RDL is created using Report Designer and manifests itself when a report is processed and viewed. When you create your report, all the definitions are in this form of XML. It is this definition that is deployed onto the server. If you are a reporting whiz, you might take to editing RDL files easily; all of the element definitions and appropriate XML Diagrams are described in Books On-Line. The following table shows some sample report definition XML elements from Books On-Line.

ELEMENT	PARENT	DESCRIPTION
Axis	CategoryAxis, ValueAxis	Defines properties for labels, titles, and gridlines on an axis
DataCollectionName	Grouping	Contains the name of the data element of the collection containing all instances of the group in a report rendered using a data rendering extension, such as the XML rendering extension
Parameters	Drillthrough, Subreport	Contains a list of parameters to pass to the report or control
Visible	Axis, DataLabel, Legend	Indicates whether the item is displayed in the chart

Report Wizard

The Report Wizard provides time-saving functionality that simplifies the creation of the most basic reports; actually, you can get as sophisticated as you like in terms of query building because graphical query builders are available in the wizard. Of course, you also have the option to create reports without use of the Report Wizard.

Report Server

As the name suggests; the Report Server "serves" reports to users. The report server operates in two modes:

➤ **Native mode:** The report server provides a built-in web portal called Report Manager for viewing, exporting, and managing reports. The manageability of the Report Server is provided through a web interface as well as through SQL Server Management Studio (SSMS).

➤ **SharePoint Integrated mode:** The report server is installed as a SharePoint shared service into an existing SharePoint farm. Management of the server is done through SharePoint Central Admin as for other SharePoint services. Reports are viewed directly in SharePoint utilizing a Reporting Services web part.

Chapters 23 and 24 cover SharePoint Integrated mode in more detail.

Some of the management tasks on Report Server include credentials definition, which is needed by Report Server to retrieve data from the data source, to provide appropriate access to the reports for end users, and to define a report execution schedule. You can cache the results of a report on Report Server, which is handy when the report takes a long time to run.

Creating a Report on a Relational Database

You can use the Report Builder to design reports based on a relational database. It provides the functionality to retrieve data from various data sources, design the actual report, and finally, deploy it.

The Report Builder also enables you to preview the report before you deploy to the Report Server to share it with other users. In this section, you design a report on Sales of products from the relational AdventureWorksDW database. To design this report, perform the following steps:

1. Launch Report Builder.

2. In the Getting Started wizard, select Table or Matrix Wizard, as shown in Figure 13-49.

3. In the New Table or Matrix Wizard page, select creating a new dataset, and click Next.

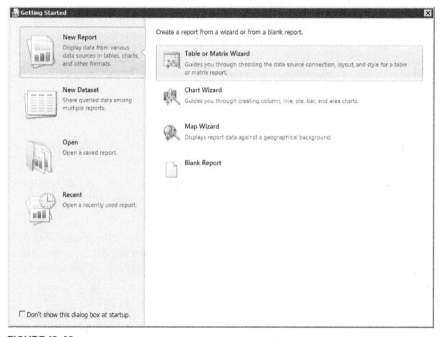

FIGURE 13-49

Alternatively, if you are connected with Report Builder to a report server that has shared datasets already published, you could simply connect to an existing shared dataset and use it in your report. For this tutorial, however, you go through the process to create a data source connection and a new (embedded) dataset in the report.

4.   On the Choose a Connection to a Data Source page, click New to define a new data source. This opens the Data Source Properties dialog.

5.   On the Data Source Properties dialog, the default data source type is Microsoft SQL Server. Click the Build button to open the Connection Properties dialog. In this example, you create a report based on the AdventureWorksDW relational database. On the Connection Properties dialog, specify the connection details, as shown in Figure 13-50.

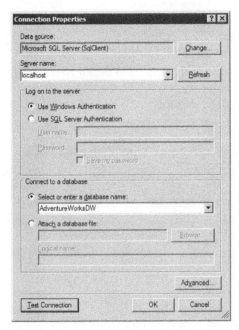

FIGURE 13-50

6.   Click OK after you test the connection to the data source using the Test Connection button. You are on the Data Source Properties dialog, with the connection string filled in, as shown in Figure 13-51.

7.   Click Next, select this newly created data source connection called DataSource1, and click Next again to get to the query design page; here, you form the query to retrieve data from the relational data source using a query builder. On the left side of the query builder, you can explore tables, views, and stored procedures of the underlying database. Select the FactInternetSales, DimDate, DimProduct, and DimProductSubcategory tables, as shown in Figure 13-52.

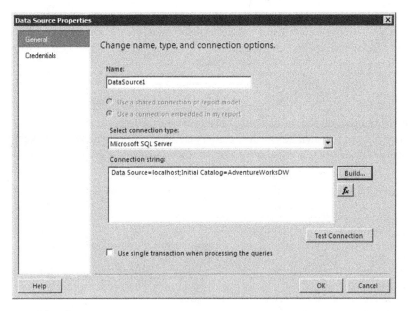

FIGURE 13-51

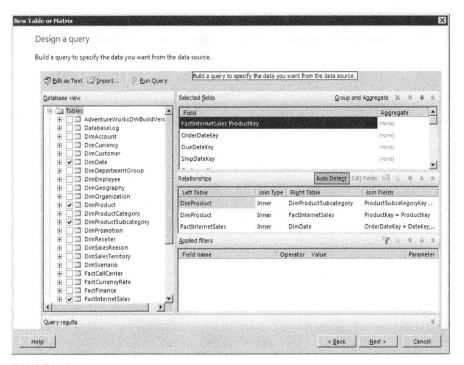

FIGURE 13-52

8. The query builder automatically retrieves the relationships between tables from the database and shows them in the Relationships section of the query designer. (Click the blue chevron icon for the Relationships section to expand.)

By default, all table columns are selected, but you can expand tables in the Database View and deselect columns. The designer in the Query pane creates appropriate SQL queries.

9. In the query builder, click Edit as Text. This mode enables you to directly type in a query. Enter the SQL query shown below in the query designer, and then click the exclamation ("!") icon to validate and execute the query. You should see sales information, as shown in Figure 13-53.

```
SELECT DimDate.CalendarYear, SUM(FactInternetSales.SalesAmount) AS TotalSales,
    DimProduct.EnglishProductName,
    DimProductSubcategory.EnglishProductSubcategoryName
FROM  FactInternetSales INNER JOIN
    DimProduct ON FactInternetSales.ProductKey = DimProduct.ProductKey
    INNER JOIN
    DimDate ON FactInternetSales.OrderDateKey = DimDate.DateKey INNER JOIN
    DimProductSubcategory ON DimProduct.ProductSubcategoryKey =
    DimProductSubcategory.ProductSubcategoryKey
GROUP BY DimDate.CalendarYear,
    DimProduct.EnglishProductName,
    DimProductSubcategory.EnglishProductSubcategoryName
```

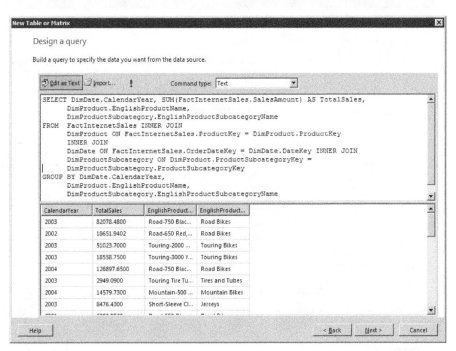

FIGURE 13-53

10. Click Next, which enables you to select how you want to lay out fields in your report. The report layout can be specified by dragging fields into the areas for Column Groups, Row Groups, and Values. In a tabular layout, the report contains the values in the row column format similar to the relational tables. The columns have a header corresponding to the column and each row contains the values.

In a matrix layout, there are groups with headers for rows and columns, and each cell in the report corresponds to a specific row and column. For example, you can have Time on rows and Cities on columns, and the cells will indicate the sales amount of a product or a store for a given time and a city.

Select the report layout, as shown in Figure 13-54. Specifically, select the CalendarYear field and add it as a row group. Rows can be grouped based on a specific field. For example, sales of various sizes of televisions in a store can be grouped under a category called TVs. In this example, you group the sales of products based on the subcategory name. Grouping helps you to organize reports for enhanced readability. Select the EnglishProductSubCategoryName, and add it under the row group section. Add EnglishProductName as the final row group. The field values in the group are shown once in the report. Finally, select the TotalSales field, and drag it to the Values section, which aggregates Sales by Product. Click Next.

11. On the Choose the Layout page, select a Stepped Layout, and select Expand/Collapse Groups (to enable drill-down), as shown in Figure 13-55. Stepped and block report styles are quite similar; they differ only due to the values housed in a block. If you click the options, you can judge the visual impact of the final report.

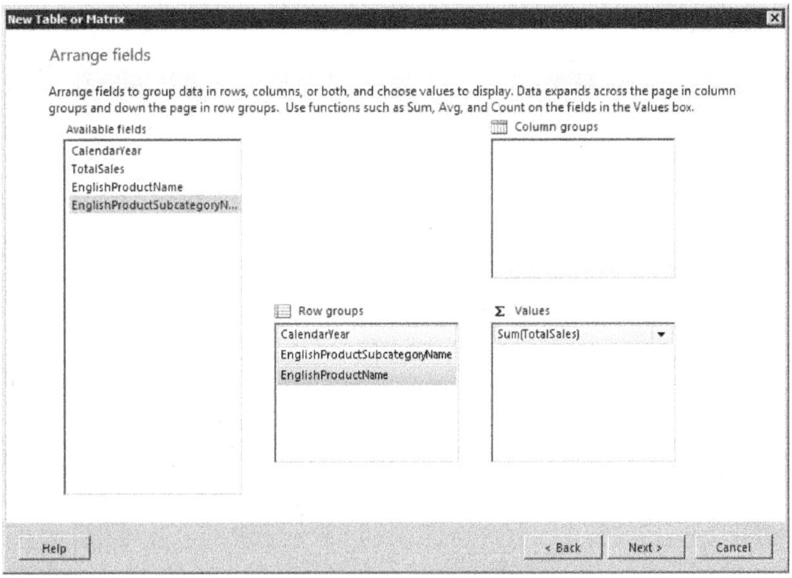

FIGURE 13-54

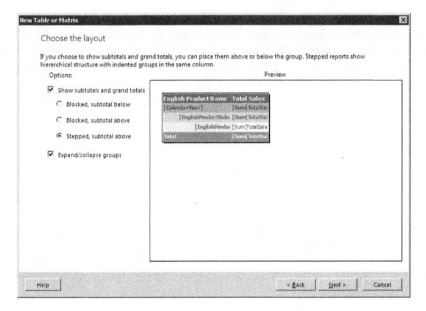

FIGURE 13-55

12. The next page of the wizard provides you with the option to choose predefined report styles or templates. When you select the specific option, you can see a preview of the style within the pane on the right side. Figure 13-56 shows the Ocean style. Select the template of your choice, and click Finish.

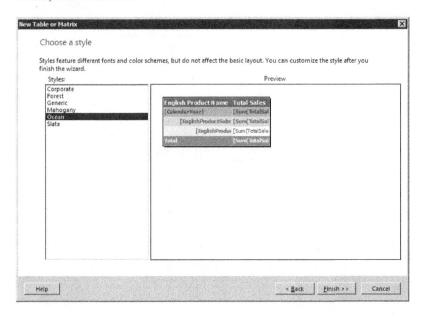

FIGURE 13-56

13. The wizard creates the report structures, and you can now be in the Report Builder design mode, as shown in Figure 13-57. Report Builder has two modes: Design and Preview. The Design pane helps you create and edit data sources to modify your queries and design your report. The Preview pane helps you to preview the report within the Report Designer with your current credentials. The list of report items available to build your report is on the Ribbon of Report Builder. If you do not have the Properties window showing, you can enable it using the View tab and selecting Properties.

14. Now that you have created the report, you no doubt want to see a preview. Click the Home tab and select Run to view the report you have created. Figure 13-58 shows the preview of the report you have created. Within each year group, you can see the product subcategories along with the sales information. Because the report is grouped and you selected the drill-down option, the default view of the report does not show all the details. You can click the + sign associated with a product subcategory to see the details of the total sales of that product category. In Figure 13-58, the year 2001 is expanded, as well as the first product subcategory for Mountain Bikes.

You have now successfully created a simple report from a relational data source using Reporting Services 2008 and previewed the results of your report. You can design modifications to your report to change alignment, color, and other properties.

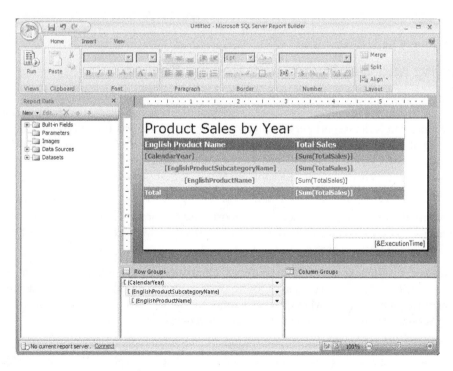

FIGURE 13-57

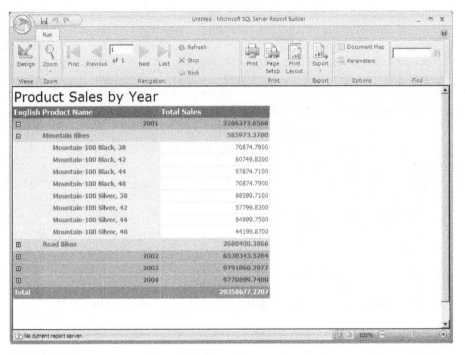

FIGURE 13-58

Connecting and Deploying to a Report Server

Using Report Builder, you have learned to design and preview the reports. However, when other end users need to access the reports, you need to deploy the reports to a centralized location. This centralized location is the Report Server, which can render the reports for end users. Access to the functionality of the Report Server is provided through the Report Server Web Service, which uses Simple Object Access Protocol (SOAP) over HTTP and exposes interfaces for report execution and report management. When you install Reporting Services, SQL Server 2012 setup configures a web interface to the Report Server.

You can access Report Manager to view your reports and perform management operations through http://*<machinename>*/reports. The report server web site is accessible through http://*<machinename>*/reportserver.

Reporting Services provides a configuration tool that enables you to configure Reporting Services to run on a specific port of choice. In addition to this interface, you can perform management operations through SQL Server Management Studio. In this section, you learn to configure your Reporting Services server and then deploy and access reports.

1. Open your web browser and connect to http://localhost/reportserver. If you encounter an error reaching your Report Server, launch Start ⇨ All Programs ⇨ SQL Server 2012 ⇨ Configuration Tools ⇨ Reporting Services Configuration Manager. When asked to run in administrator mode, click Continue.

2. In the Reporting Services Configuration Connection dialog (see Figure 13-59), enter the instance of your Reporting Services server, click Find, and then click Connect.

FIGURE 13-59

3. Click the Web Service URL configuration, specify TCP Port 80, and click the Apply button. If port 80 is not available, try port 8080. The remaining steps assume port 80 is available, but you can replace 80 with another port number.

You can now see the URL specified for your Report Server, as shown in Figure 13-60.

4. Click the Report Manager URL and then the Advanced button.

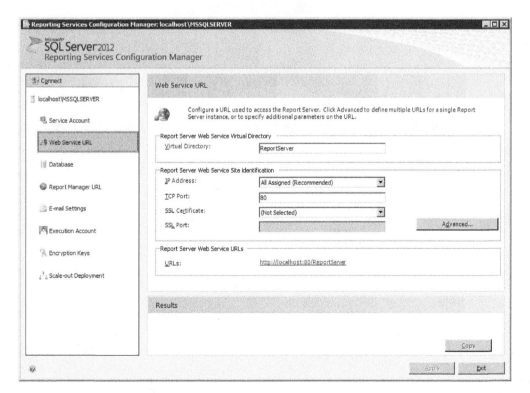

FIGURE 13-60

5. In the Advanced Multiple Web Site Configuration dialog (Figure 13-61), click the Add button, and specify the TCP Port as 80 in the Add Report Manager HTTP URL dialog. You should finally have an entry with TCP port 80, as shown in Figure 13-61. Click OK. Click the Apply button to configure the Report Manager URL, and click Exit.

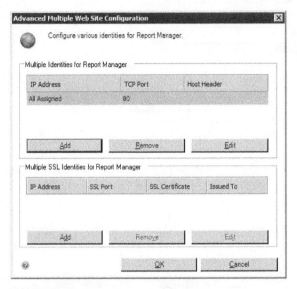

FIGURE 13-61

6. Open your web browser in administrator mode and connect to `http://localhost:80/Reports`. You should see the Home page of your Reporting Services server, as shown in Figure 13-62.

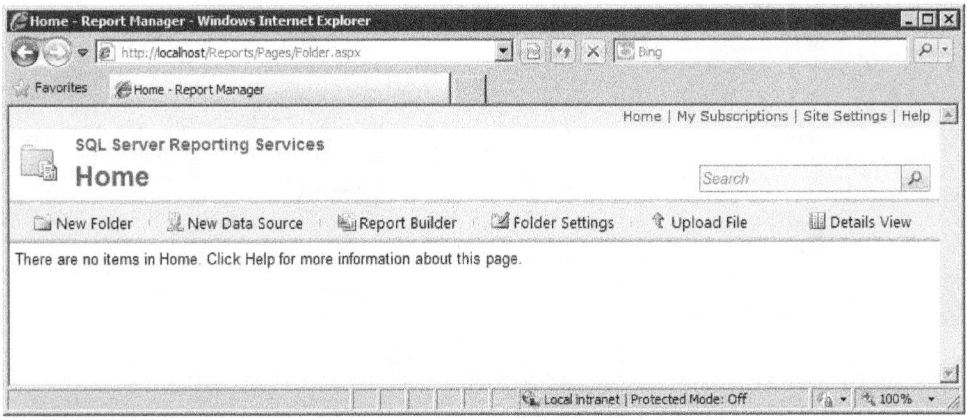

FIGURE 13-62

7.   Click the Site Settings tab, select Security, create a new role, and add your account as a System Administrator.

8.   You are now ready to deploy your reports to your Reporting Services server. To deploy the reports you designed in the previous section, you need to set the location of your Report Server. In Report Builder, you can accomplish this while in Design mode by clicking the Connect link in the status line, as shown in Figure 13-63.

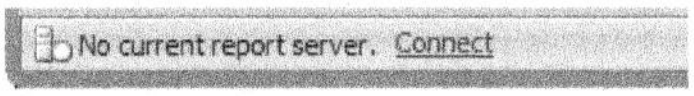

FIGURE 13-63

9.   Specify `http://localhost:80/reportserver` as the target report server, as shown in Figure 13-64. Click OK, Report Builder connects to the report server, and the status line updates, as shown in Figure 13-65.

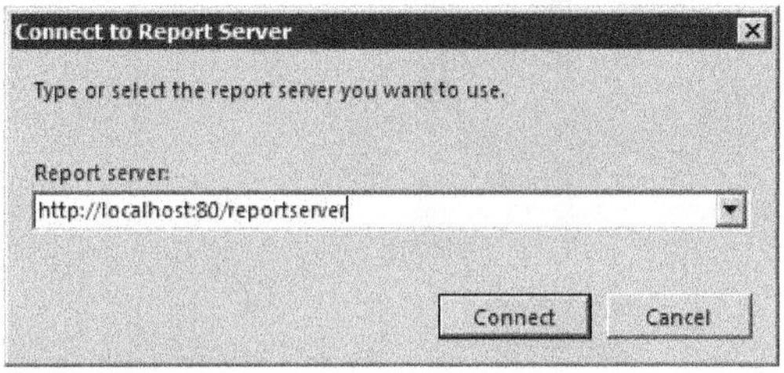

Connect to Report Server

Type or select the report server you want to use.

Report server:

`http://localhost:80/reportserver`

Connect   Cancel

FIGURE 13-64

Current report server http://localhost:80/reportserver Disconnect

FIGURE 13-65

10.   In Report Builder, click the Application icon in the top-left corner, select Save, and specify SalesAnalysis.rdl as the report name.

11.   To make sure your reports can be accessed, open Internet Explorer, and go to `http://localhost/reports`. You see the report was saved directly in the Home folder. When you select SalesAnalysis, the report server renders the report, and you see the report, as shown in Figure 13-66. Reporting Services enables you to export the report in various formats. If you want to export this report, select the format such as PDF, Excel, Word, CSV, and so on, and then click Export.

You can now publish your first report using data from a relational database to the report server. In the next section, you learn to use data from a multidimensional database in reports.

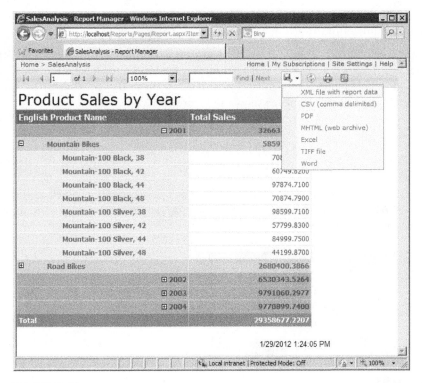

FIGURE 13-66

Creating a Report on a Multidimensional Model

So far, you have seen some capabilities provided by Reporting Services 2012 and how it can facilitate the creation of reports from a relational database. In earlier sections of this chapter, you learned about the tight integration of Analysis Services with Integration Services that helps you load data into Analysis Services and perform administrative operations. By adding to those functions, Reporting Services provides you with the ability to create reports from a BI semantic model by which Microsoft's SQL Server 2012 provides a truly end-to-end BI solution. Designing reports from Analysis Services 2012 databases is actually similar to designing reports from a relational database using Reporting Services.

The MDX query designer in Report Designer in SSDT as well as in Report Builder enables you to retrieve data from any BI semantic model through the technique of drag and drop, without you actually needing to understand and write MDX queries. Assuming you have worked through this whole book, you already know some MDX. You have the option to write your own MDX query in the query designer, but your MDX query should have only two axes and be in a specific format of having measures on columns and dimension members in rows.

Aside from the query designer, additional integration areas are in Reporting Services specifically for Analysis Services data sources. For example, you can send a list of country names as a parameter to an MDX query; this enhances what you can accomplish to build dynamic reports. The ability to retrieve intrinsic properties is available for dimension members such as unique name, parent unique name, and so on, and cell properties such as background color. Furthermore, Reporting Services takes advantage of aggregated data provided by Analysis Services. This helps increase the performance of report processing — especially when there is a large amount of source detail-level data (such as sales per store) and the report includes aggregations based on that (such as sales per region). This is more important when the aggregation of member values to their parent is semi-additive in nature, such as with the Account dimension, which you learned about in Chapter 8.

Designing Your Analysis Services Report

In this section, you create a sales report from the UDM for the AdventureWorks2008Tutorial using the Report Wizard. You later refine the report based on certain requirements surprisingly imposed by your boss at the last moment. At the end of this section, you will be familiar with creating specialized reports on a UDM. The following steps can help you to build reports from Analysis Services by establishing a connection to Analysis Services, building the MDX query, and previewing the report. Follow the steps to create your Analysis Services reports:

1. Open the AdventureWorksDWTutorial from the book's website (www.wrox.com) and deploy it to your Analysis Services server instance.

2. Start Report Builder. In the Getting Started wizard, select the Table or Matrix Wizard, select creating a new dataset, and click Next.

3. On the Choose a Connection to a Data Source page, click New to define a new data source. This opens the Data Source Properties dialog.

4. On the Data Source Properties dialog, set the data source type to Microsoft SQL Server Analysis Services.

    Click the Build button to open the Connection Properties dialog. Enter the machine name of your Analysis Services server instance, and select the AdventureWorksDW multidimensional database, as shown in Figure 13-67.

    Click OK after you test the connection to the data source using the Test Connection button.

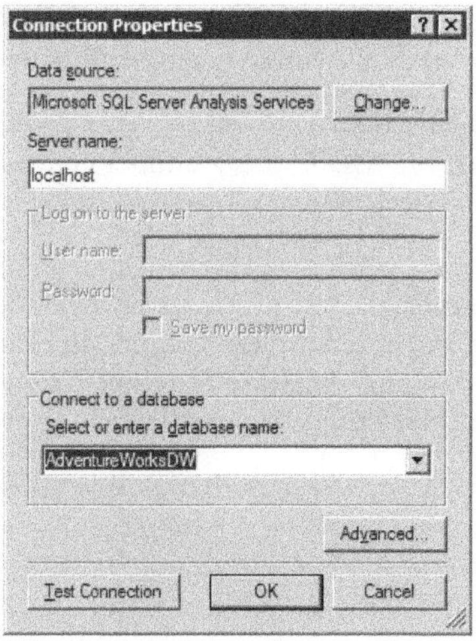

FIGURE 13-67

5. You are now on the Data Source Properties dialog, with the connection string filled in, as shown in Figure 13-68.

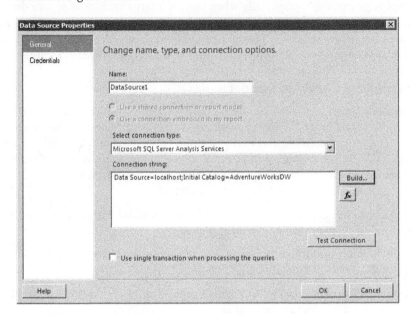

FIGURE 13-68

6. Click Next, select this newly created data source connection called DataSource1, and click Next again to get to the query design page. Because the data source is connected to Analysis Services, it automatically starts the MDX query builder, as shown in Figure 13-69. The MDX query builder contains a Metadata pane where you can select a specific cube from the database to see the measures and dimensions of the cube. There is a pane in which you can specify calculated members that are within the scope of the query sent to your Analysis Services instance. There is a Filter pane to restrict data, and finally, there is a Data pane where you can drag and drop the dimensions and measures that you want to include in your report.

7. Drag and drop the measure Sales Amount in the Fact Internet Sales measure group from the Metadata pane to the Data pane. At this moment, the MDX query builder creates the MDX query to retrieve the selected measure from the Analysis Services instance and shows the results in the Data pane.

Using the Report Wizard, create a report of Internet sales of products in the United States along with the customer's gender information. Drag and drop the Gender attribute hierarchy from the customer's Demographic dimension and the State Province Name attribute hierarchy from the customer's Geography dimension, which indicates the customer's geographical location. You now see a results set in the Data pane. Because the database contains Internet sales information from various countries, you see the data for all the provinces of various countries.

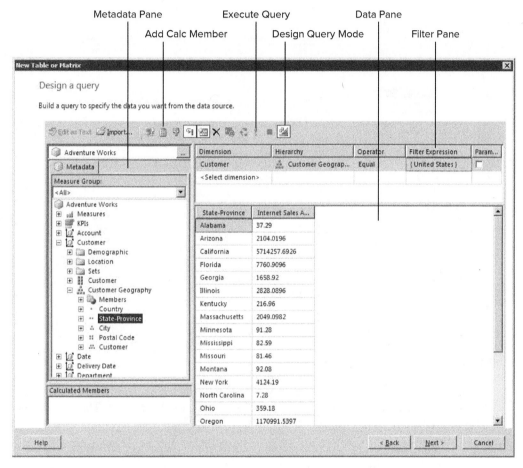

FIGURE 13-69

8. To restrict the data to the provinces in the United States, drag and drop the Customer Geography attribute to the Filter pane. Click the filter expression field in the filter area, and select United States by selecting the United States member from the pop-up list. You see the Sales Amount for the Internet Sales measure group from various provinces within the United States along with the gender of the customer, as shown in Figure 13-70.

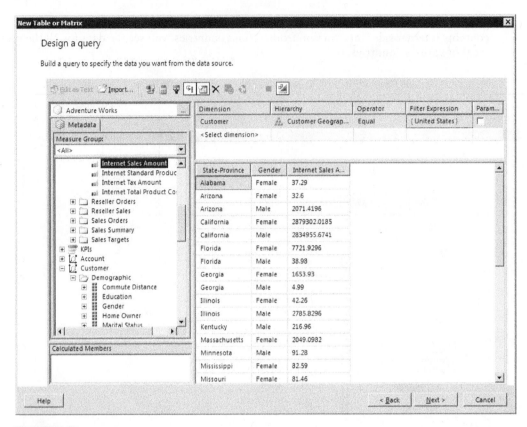

FIGURE 13-70

9. You can see the underlying MDX query generated by switching from the graphical design view to the MDX query view by clicking the Design Query Mode icon. The result is shown in Figure 13-71.

➤ The MDX query generated by the query builder (which you can happily ignore if so inclined) follows:

```
SELECT NON EMPTY {[Measures].[Internet Sales Amount]} ON COLUMNS,
NON EMPTY {([Customer].[Customer Geography].[State-Province].ALLMEMBERS
 * [Customer].[Gender].[Gender].ALLMEMBERS )}
DIMENSION PROPERTIES MEMBER_CAPTION, MEMBER_UNIQUE_NAME ON ROWS
FROM (
  SELECT ({[Customer].[Customer Geography].[Country].&[United States]})
    ON COLUMNS
  FROM [Adventure Works])
CELL PROPERTIES VALUE, BACK_COLOR, FORE_COLOR, FORMATTED_VALUE,
FORMAT_STRING, FONT_NAME, FONT_SIZE, FONT_FLAGS
```

➤ The query generated by the MDX query builder within Report Designer is an MDX subselect query. The preceding query contains two MDX select queries. The inner SELECT query restricts the cube space based on the member [Customer

Geography].[Country].&[United States], and the outer SELECT query retrieves the data within the cube space provided by the inner SELECT query.

➤ One important thing you should be aware of in the MDX query builder is that if you switch from the design view to the MDX view and make changes, at that point, you are at risk of losing the original configuration built in the design view if you then return to the design view. Therefore, that particular action is not recommended — if you want to return to the design view. In the design view, as you drag and drop fields, the automatically generated MDX query is executed immediately and displays the results. If you know that your query is going to retrieve a large result set, you can turn off the auto-execute query mode using the icon in the toolbar or by right-clicking in the Result pane and deselecting auto-execute mode. If you are an MDX expert, you might actually prefer to use the MDX view. In such a circumstance, switch to the MDX view, type in your MDX query, and then click Execute to ensure your query is correct and returns results expected by you. Click OK after you select the fields you need for the query.

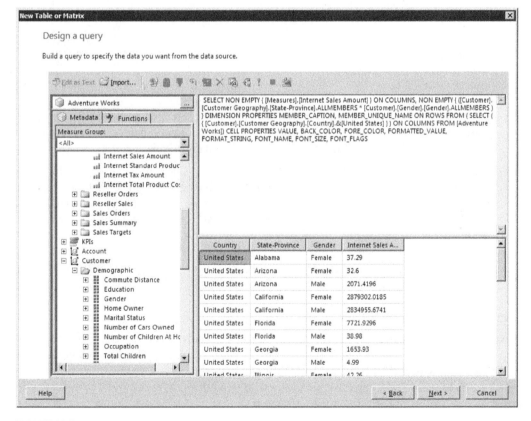

FIGURE 13-71

10. With the MDX query shown on the Design Query page, click the Next button.

11. The Arrange Fields page shows the fields you selected in the MDX query builder. In this report, you group the sales of customers based on the provinces. Therefore, drag

State_Province and Gender to Row Groups. Drag Internet_Sales_Amount to Values, as shown in Figure 13-72. Click Next.

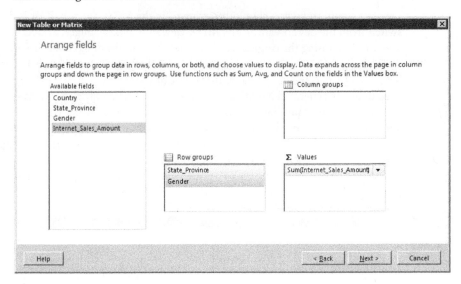

FIGURE 13-72

12. Similar to the relational report you created earlier, select Stepped layout on the next page. Select the option to have subtotals displayed as well as enable expand/collapse (drilldown) on this page, and click Next. Select the Ocean theme and click Finish.

13. You are now in the Design view of the Report Designer. Click the various items in the layout such as the table and the grouping row within the table based on the State Province, and look at their properties to have a brief overview of how the wizard created your layout. You can also change the report title and table headers, and resize columns. Select the Internet Sales Amount column, and in the ribbon, select the "$" icon to apply currency formatting for that table column. After you tweak the layout, you want to see the behavior of the report before you deploy it onto your Report Server. To preview your report, select the Home tab, and click Run. You can now see a report, as shown in Figure 13-73.

Enhancing Your Analysis Services Report

You have successfully created your first report on top of an Analysis Services database. This is a basic report. The report you created in the previous section includes only the Sales Amount information for the states within the United States and the genders of various customers. In this section, you enhance your report by including the countries, and instead of sales information, you create a report that shows sales profits of each state for various years.

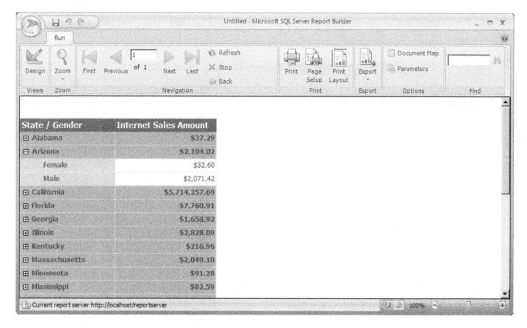

FIGURE 13-73

First, you need to change the query that retrieves the results from your Analysis Service instance. To change the MDX query, switch from the Preview pane to the Design pane. Because your new report needs to include the profit, you need to create a measure that calculates the profit. The AdventureWorksDW cube contains measures for Internet and Reseller sales along with the cost of the products sold over Internet and Reseller sales. You need to create calculated members in the cube to aggregate the data and then calculate the profit. Instead of creating these calculated measures within the cube, you can create calculated measures in an MDX query using the WITH MEMBER clause, which was introduced in Chapter 3 of this book. You can edit the dataset to launch the MDX query designer. The MDX query designer enables you to graphically specify these calculated members instead of writing the full MDX query. Creating the calculated members using the designer enables you to still work in the design mode. Follow these steps to enhance your report:

1. Right-click the DataSet1 in the Report Data pane, and select Query, as shown in Figure 13-74. You are now in the MDX Query Editor.

2. To create a calculated measure Total Sales Amount, click the calculator icon, or right-click in the Calculated Members pane (shown in Figure 13-69) and select New. The Calculated Member Builder dialog, as shown in Figure 13-75, launches.

3. Type **Total Sales Amount** in the Name text box for the calculated measure. Drag and drop the Sales Amounts from Fact Internet Sales and Fact Reseller Sales measure groups from the Metadata pane, and add a plus (+)

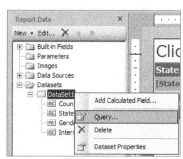

FIGURE 13-74

sign between these measures, as shown in Figure 13-75. Click OK to create the calculated measure.

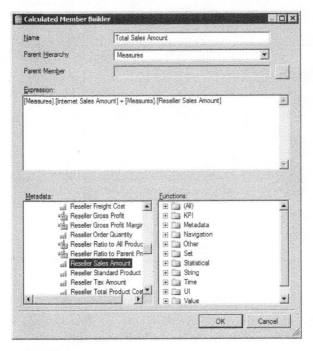

FIGURE 13-75

4. Create a calculated measure called Product Cost as the sum of the Total Product Cost measures from the Internet Sales and Reseller Sales measure groups.

5. Create a calculated measure called Total Profit, which is the difference between the numerical values in the calculated measures Total Sales Amount and Product Cost. You can now see the three calculated measures in the Calculated Members pane of the query builder, as shown in Figure 13-76.

6. Remove the Internet Sales Amount measure from the Result pane by dragging and dropping the field from Result pane to the Metadata pane or by selecting the field, right-clicking, and selecting Remove.

7. Remove the field Gender from the Data pane.

8. Verify that no filters are specified in the Filter pane. If there is a filter based on country name, remove it.

9. Drag and drop the calculated member Total Profit from the Calculated Members pane to the Result pane. Add the attribute hierarchy Country from the Geography dimension and Calendar Year hierarchy from the Date dimension to the data field, as shown in Figure 13-76.

10. The Result pane now shows the profit for various countries and provinces for all the years. Now, you have all the data required for enhancing your report. Click OK in the Query Designer dialog. The Report pane now contains the fields State_Province, Country,

Calendar_Year, and Total_Profit, as shown in Figure 13-77. You can now redesign the report using these fields.

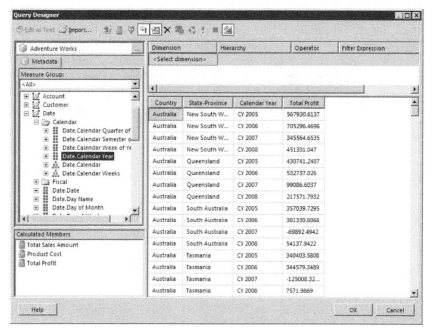

FIGURE 13-76

11. The Design pane still contains the table that was used for the first report you created. Select the existing table object, right-click, and select Delete to delete the table. After you delete the table, you can notice that the grouping within the RowGroups is also removed.

12. In your report, you need the profits of each country to be seen on different pages. To design such a report, you need a report item called List in your Report Designer layout. Click the Insert tab and select the List item. This changes the mouse cursor and enables you to position the new List report item below the title of the report, as shown in Figure 13-78.

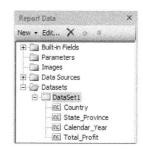

FIGURE 13-77

13. Drag and drop the Country field into the list area, and center it. You want a report with the state-provinces grouped within the same country, and each country has its own page. To do this, right-click within the Row Groups area, and select Group Properties, as shown in Figure 13-79.

14. In the Group Properties dialog on the General tab, change the name of the Group to CountryGroup, and select the Country field, as shown in Figure 13-80.

15. Select the Page Breaks tab, and select the check box for Between Each Instance of a Group, as shown in Figure 13-81; click OK.

16. Go to the Insert tab, select Table ⇨ Insert Table. This changes the mouse cursor and enables you to insert a new table within the existing List report item.

17. You see a new empty table with three columns and two rows. Delete the left-most column in the table. Your table should now have two columns. Drag and drop the Calendar_Year field to the first column in the Data area. You see the Header row is automatically populated with the name Calendar Year.

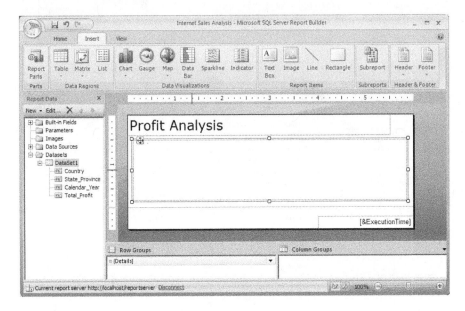

FIGURE 13-78

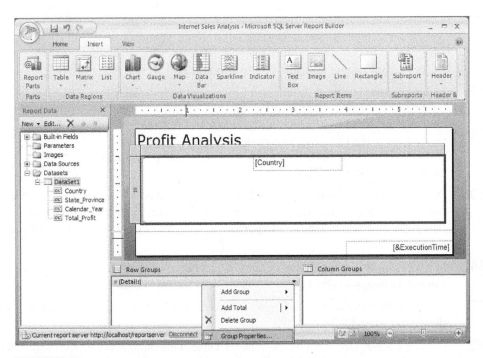

FIGURE 13-79

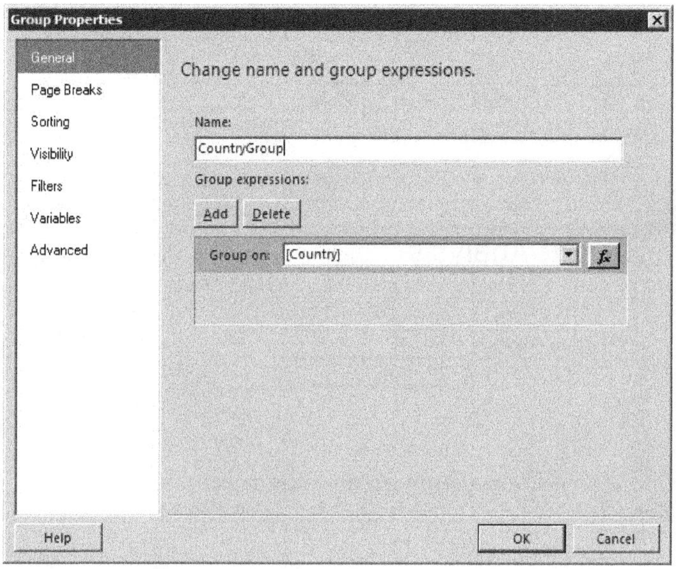

FIGURE 13-80

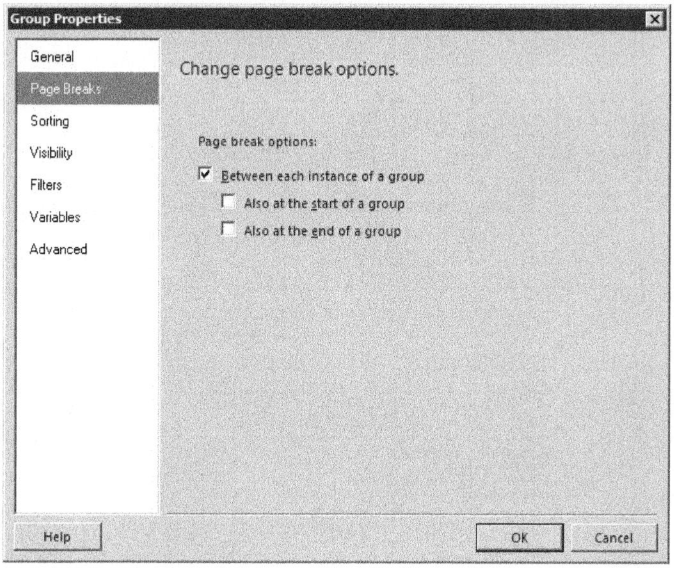

FIGURE 13-81

Aside from drag and drop, you can also hover with the mouse over a table cell, select the field icon, and pick a field directly, such as the Total_Profit field for the second table column, as shown in Figure 13-82.

18. Select the table. Right-click the Row Groups area, and select Add Group ➪ Parent Group, as shown in Figure 13-83.

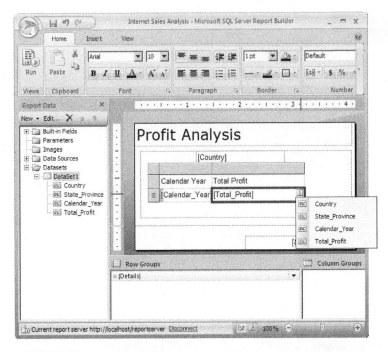

FIGURE 13-82

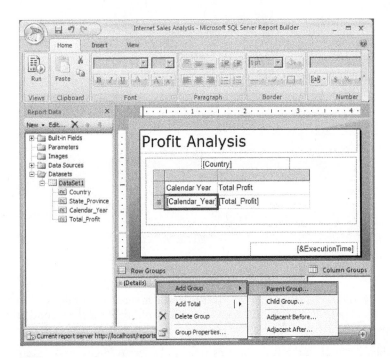

FIGURE 13-83

19. In the Tablix Group dialog, select State_Province in the field next to the Group By radio button. Select the check boxes for Add group header and Add group footer, and click OK.

20. You now see a new row and a new column added to the table. The new column has the field State_Province included in the cell with a header named State Province, as shown in Figure 13-84.

21. Click the last cell of the Total Profit column. You see a small table icon, as shown in Figure 13-84. Click that table, and select Total_Profit. The designer now adds Sum(Total_Profit) as the expression for the cell.

Select the Total Profit column of the table, go to the Home tab, and click the "$" icon to apply currency formatting.

22. Click the Preview tab to see the initial version of the report you have designed. You should see a report, as shown in Figure 13-85. The report shows the profit report for a specific country on a single page, which includes the states within the country along with profits for each year. The report also shows the aggregated profit for each state. You can switch to the profit report for the next country by selecting the next page or entering a specific page number, as shown in Figure 13-85.

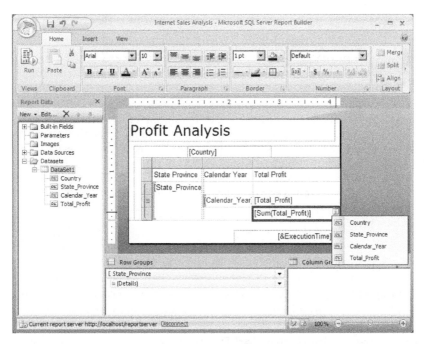

FIGURE 13-84

23. One of the key things in reports involving profit is the ability to easily distinguish the amount of profit. Typically in ledgers, positive amounts are shown in black, and negative amounts are shown in red. In this report, you can modify the profit to be shown in green or red depending upon the profit amount.

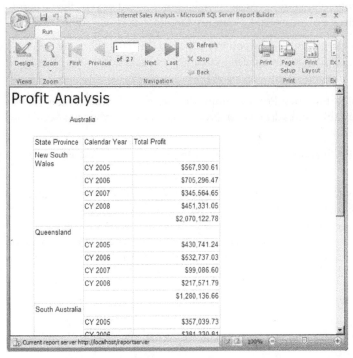

FIGURE 13-85

To specify appropriate colors to be displayed for profit, select the cell corresponding to the profit in the Design mode. Right-click the cell, and open the textbox properties. In the Textbox Properties dialog, go to the Font page, and click the Fx button next to the Color value. The Expression editor dialog for specifying the color opens. You can use VBA functions as part of the expressions. To check if the profit amount is positive or negative, use the VBA function IIF. Set the expression for Color to check if the value for profit is greater than zero. If yes, the function returns the color green, or else the color red. After you specify the expression, your expression window should look like Figure 13-86. Click OK.

24. If you preview the report after setting the colors and go to the page to view the Total_Profit for United States, you see that states such as Alabama showed profits and losses over different years. You have seen some of the enhancements that can be made to your UDM reports using the Report Designer. Next, you look at some of the extensions in Reporting Services that have been specifically added to have a tighter integration with Analysis Services.

Enhancing Your Report Using Extended Properties

The dimension members and cells in Analysis Services have certain specific properties associated with them. These properties can be retrieved from the Analysis Server along with the query result. Dimension and cell properties from Analysis Services get mapped to field properties in Reporting Services. These are called predefined properties and are accessed within reports as `Fields!FieldName.PropertyName`.

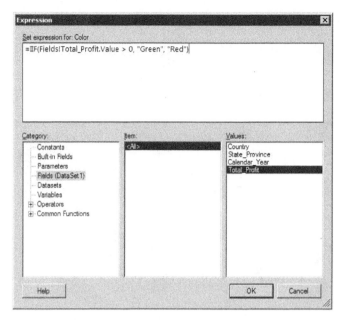

FIGURE 13-86

Predefined properties in Reporting Services are Value, UniqueName, IsMissing, BackgroundColor, Color, FontFamily, FontSize, FontWeight, FontStyle, TextDecoration, FormattedValue, LevelNumber, and ParentUniqueName. Extended properties are additional properties returned from Analysis Services. Because these properties are not returned as fields, you cannot drag and drop from the field list to your report layout. Reporting Services provides functionality to access these values in a unique way and include them in the report. You can access the extended properties in one of the following formats:

➤ Fields!FieldName!PropertyName

➤ Fields!FieldName("PropertyName")

➤ Fields!FieldName.Properties("PropertyName")

To see an example of how extended properties can be used in your reports, you can now enhance the report in the previous section by using the extended property FormattedValue that is returned by Analysis Services for the measure Total Profit.

1. In the Report Designer, switch to the Design mode.

2. Select DataSet1, right-click, and select Query to launch the MDX query designer.

3. Select the calculated member Total Profit, right-click, and select Edit.

4. Add the text **,FORMAT_STRING = "Currency"**, as shown in Figure 13-87, in the Calculated Member Builder dialog, and click OK. You might see a Parser error, which is a bug. If you see an error, click OK to ignore the error message. Switch to the MDX window mode in the Query editor, and re-execute the MDX query. Click OK in the MDX Query Editor dialog.

FIGURE 13-87

5. In the table report item, select the Total_Profit cell, right-click, and select Expression.

6. In the Expression editor, change the expression of the cell from using Value to FormattedValue, as shown in Figure 13-88, and click OK.

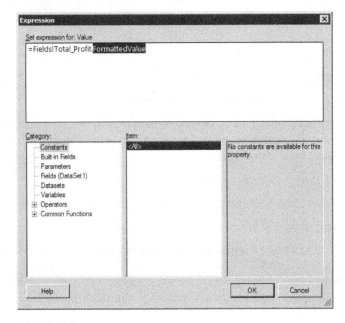

FIGURE 13-88

7. Save the report and run the report in preview. You see a report where the profit values are formatted based on the currency format and the values are retrieved from Analysis Services, as shown in Figure 13-89.

You can also retrieve extended properties for dimension members and for cells that are not part of the predefined reporting services properties.

Custom Aggregates

When you create reports that contain groups, most likely you have subtotals for the group members. For example, if you have sales for various years and products, you might want to view the sales for each year. Therefore, each year needs to be aggregated. Reporting Services provides you with a set of aggregation functions such as sum, count, distinct count, and so on. For a detailed list of the aggregation functions supported by Reporting Services 2012, refer to the product's documentation. In addition to these built-in aggregate functions, Reporting Services supports custom aggregates supported by data providers. If a data provider such as Analysis Services supports custom aggregates, Reporting Services has the capability to retrieve that data for the aggregate rows by the aggregate function called Aggregate. Custom aggregates are also referred to as server aggregates.

An example of a custom aggregate in Analysis Services 2012 is semi-additive measures. They use aggregate functions such as `ByAccount`, `FirstNonEmpty`, `LastNonEmpty`, `FirstChild`, `LastChild`, `AverageofChildren`, or `None`. Other examples of Analysis Services custom aggregates include cell values controlled by custom rollups or parent-child hierarchies, or custom aggregates specified in MDX scripts.

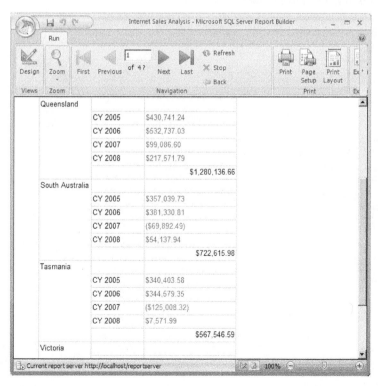

FIGURE 13-89

Some of the custom aggregate functions supported by Analysis Services are also supported by Reporting Services. However, use custom aggregates for improved performance; in this way, Reporting Services does not need to calculate the aggregate from the underlying data, but instead retrieves it directly from Analysis Services. In this section, you create a report that uses custom aggregate functions to retrieve semi-additive measures from Analysis Services 2012. Follow these steps to generate a custom aggregate report:

1. In Report Builder, create a new Blank Report using the Start menu.

2. In the Report Data pane, select the drop-down, and create a new Data Source.

3. Create an Analysis Services connection to the AdventureWorksDW database, test the connection, and click OK.

4. In the Report Data pane, select the drop-down, and create a new DataSet.

5. In the Dataset Properties dialog, click the Query Designer button to launch the MDX Query Editor.

6. Select the measure Internet Average Unit Price in the Internet Sales measure of the cube Adventure Works DW, which is a semi-additive measure with the aggregate function FirstNonEmpty. Drag and drop this measure from the Metadata pane to the Result pane. Drag and drop the hierarchy Product from the Product dimension. Your Result pane should now include columns: three levels of the Products hierarchy (Category, Subcategory, and Product), and the measure Internet Average Unit Price, as shown in Figure 13-90. Click OK in the Query Designer and the Dataset Properties dialog.

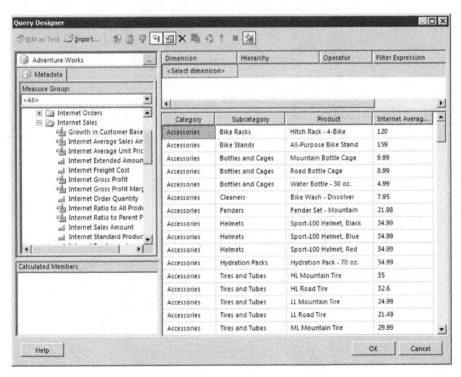

FIGURE 13-90

7. Add a table report item, using the Insert Ribbon tab.

8. Drag and drop Product and Internet_Average_Unit_Price to two columns in the table; delete the third column in the table.

9. Right-click the Details in the Row Groups pane, and select Add Group ⇨ Parent Group.

10. In the Tablix group dialog, select the Category field for the Group By radio button, and enable the check box for Add Group Header.

11. You see a new column and row created. The column field has the expression for the field Category with the header text Category.

12. In the group header cell corresponding to the aggregate of the Internet_Average_Unit_Price column, select the field Internet_Average_Unit_Price. Generally, Report Builder automatically adds the expression Sum(Internet_Average_Unit_Price) as a default aggregation function.

13. Select the cell showing the aggregate value Sum(Internet_Average_Unit_Price), right-click, and select Expression.

14. In the Expression dialog, enter the following expression:

```
=Aggregate(Fields! Internet_Average_Unit_Price.Value)
```

15. Save the report, and in the Home tab, select to run the report. You now see the aggregate of categories is not a sum of all the products, as shown in Figure 13-91. The unit price calculated aggregate is now retrieved directly from Analysis Services rather than being calculated by Reporting Services.

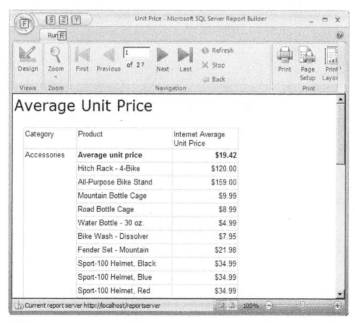

FIGURE 13-91

16. When you change the aggregation function on the table textbox from Sum to Aggregate, Report Builder changes the MDX query automatically to retrieve appropriate results from the Analysis Services instance. You can verify this in the MDX Query Editor. Right-click the DataSet1, and select Query. Click Execute Query to see the results of the modified MDX query. You see additional rows with (null) values for various Subcategories and Categories, as shown in Figure 13-92. Reporting Services detects the rows with null values for Product Name as the aggregate rows and uses this information to render the report.

Custom aggregates, as mentioned earlier, are useful to create reports that need the aggregated data from Analysis Services. You definitely need to use custom aggregates when the aggregate function is not supported by Reporting Services. In addition to that, use custom aggregates whenever you need aggregated data from Analysis Services because you can see performance benefits, especially when the report retrieves a large set of members from Analysis Services.

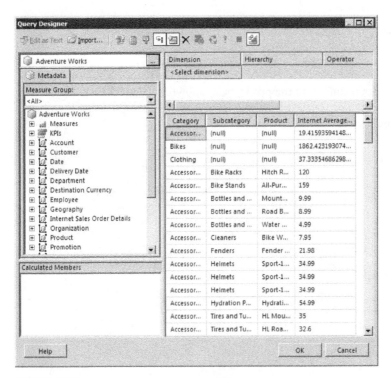

FIGURE 13-92

SUMMARY

Integration Services provides the mechanism for automated tasks ranging from data cleansing to data split to data merging. In this chapter, you learned that a package must have a control flow and may also have data flows; the control flow is represented by tasks and containers, which are connected by precedence constraints. These precedence constraints determine the fate of a control flow after each step is completed. The precedence constraint can be an expression that leads to a success or failure condition, or the constraint can be set to "completion" without further consideration for continued control flow. Finally, you learned how to import packages into Integration Services using SSMS and create scheduled jobs of packages using SQL Server Agent.

In the previous chapter's summary, you were promised a wonderful synergy between Integration Services and Analysis Services and in the sections from "Creating Integration Services Packages for Analysis Services Operations" to "Automating Execution of SSIS Packages," you got it!

This chapter also introduced you to Reporting Services, creating reports with Report Builder from relational databases, and Analysis Services databases. You learned some of the key features in Report Builder with Analysis Services such as drag-and-drop-based query generation, custom aggregates, and retrieving extended properties for dimension members and cells.

Using the new Power View capabilities introduced in Reporting Services 2012 is covered in dedicated Chapters 23 and 24 of this book. If you need an in-depth understanding of Reporting Services 2012, read *Professional Microsoft SQL Server 2012 Reporting Services* by Paul Turley et al. (Wrox, 2012).

14

Securing Multidimensional BISM

WHAT'S IN THIS CHAPTER?

➤   Securing source data

➤   Securing dimension data

➤   Securing cube data

Your data has value, and as with any item of value, you must protect it from outside threats. Security is an extremely important consideration in the area of business intelligence. Think about it — the keys to your company's profitability can be surfaced through your data and analytical applications. Just as you secure your personal belongings in a safe place, such as a safe deposit box, and appropriately provide access to authorized people, you must secure your corporate data and applications. Analysis Services provides you with ways to protect your data so that you can restrict access to only those users who are authorized.

The environment within which you work has a significant impact on the security precautions you should take. In general, if a server runs within the confines of a firewall, it helps to mitigate the external threats posed and provide increased protection. Disabling unused services or features that can potentially be exploited by hackers is yet another way to reduce risk. Running servers under least-privilege accounts such as the network service account also helps ensure your system cannot be compromised. Analysis Services provides you with the ability to enable or disable features such as stored procedures or ad-hoc queries, which thereby reduces the product areas likely to have security attacks and also run under least-privilege accounts on the system, as shown in Chapter 7. In addition to these techniques, you learned about additional core security features in Analysis Services that restrict access to unauthorized users in Chapter 9.

In this chapter you learn about the security features in Analysis Services that enable the administrator to define access permissions, such as read or write to objects in Analysis Services, followed by restricting access to sensitive data only to those who are allowed to access the data. You can restrict access to cube and dimension data by specifying MDX expressions that define if a dimension member or cell data referenced by a tuple can be viewed by the user.

What better way to learn how to restrict access to the data than a real-world scenario? You learn the functionality of restricting dimension and cell data by means of scenarios targeted for these features.

SECURING YOUR SOURCE DATA

You need to ensure that your source data is not compromised through Analysis Services. Analysis Services 2012 provides you with several authentication mechanisms to ensure your source data is retrieved securely by Analysis Services. To retrieve data either at processing time or at query time, an Analysis Services instance needs to connect to data sources based on the storage options (MOLAP, ROLAP, or HOLAP) specified for the dimensions and cubes within the database. To connect to the relational data source and retrieve the data, the Analysis Services instance needs appropriate credentials.

As with prior versions of Analysis Services, when you establish a connection to the data source, you can specify an authentication mechanism provided to that specific data source. For example, if you choose Microsoft's SQL Server, you have the choice of either Windows Authentication or SQL Server Authentication, as shown in Figure 14-1. Instead of connecting to the data source as the service startup account, Analysis Services 2012 provides four options to connect to data sources, as shown in Figure 14-2. After a data source has been created, you can then specify the credentials under which you want the Analysis Services instance to retrieve data. The Impersonation Information tab on the Data Source Designer page, as shown in Figure 14-2, provides you with the flexibility to specify the impersonation option suited to your database. Whenever the Analysis Services 2012 instance connects to the data source, Analysis Services uses the impersonation information specified in the data source.

If you choose the Use the service account option, Analysis Services 2012 impersonates the Windows account used as the services startup account for the SQL Server Analysis Services instance to connect to the specified data source. When you choose the option Use a Specific Windows username and password, you need to specify a valid Windows credential account username and password. The Windows username is specified as *domainname\username*. With the Use a specific Windows username and password option, you can have different Windows accounts having access to various data sources within a single database or across Analysis Services databases. If a specific account has access in the data source, that account can just be specified on the Impersonation tab, and you do not need to provide data source access to the service startup account of Analysis Services.

Use the Use a specific Windows username and password option with Analysis Services running under a low-privilege account to have a more secure environment. However, whenever the password of the Windows account expires, you need to update the passwords in data sources, which you can do via SQL Server Management Studio if you have permissions to administer the database, or through a custom AMO program if needed. The third option in the Impersonation Information page is Use the credentials of the current user. Select this option primarily it to issue open rowset queries, which are used during data-mining querying and for processing objects that have out-of-line bindings. (The object to be processed retrieves data through a query or a table dynamically at the time of processing through the process command.) The last impersonation option is Inherit. When you select the Inherit impersonation, the impersonation information is obtained from the impersonation information specified for the entire database object that also has the same four options. If the impersonation information is Inherit, even for the database object, the service startup account is used for impersonation while retrieving data for processing Analysis Services objects, server synchronization, and ROLAP queries, and the Use the credentials of the current user option is used for data mining open rowset queries and out-of-line binding data sources.

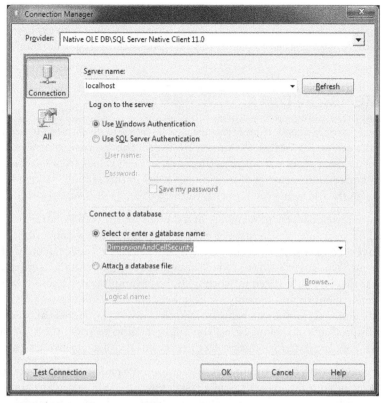

FIGURE 14-1

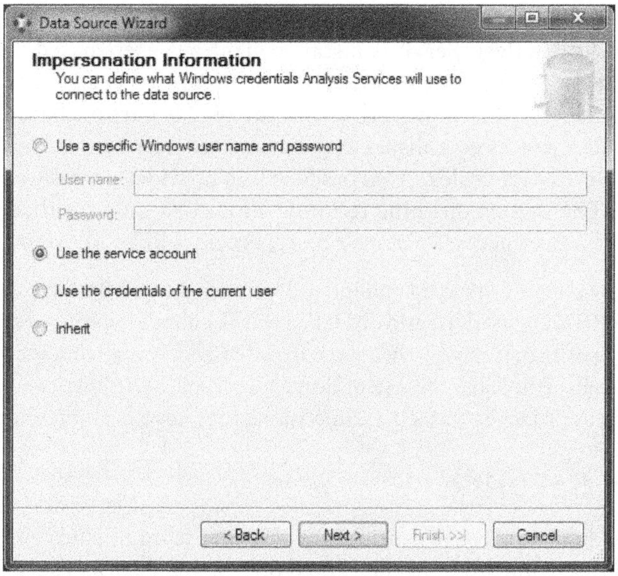

FIGURE 14-2

You have learned the various impersonation modes that can be set on data source objects in Analysis Services 2012 databases along with the recommended option to ensure that source data exposed through Analysis Services is secure. You next learn to secure your dimension and cube data appropriately for your end users.

SECURING YOUR DIMENSION DATA

Often in business you must restrict data access from certain sets of users. You might need to restrict members and their children of a dimension or just cell values. Restricting access to members of a dimension from users is called *dimension security*. Restricting access to cell values from users is called *cell security*. You learn more about securing dimension members in this section, followed by restricting access to cell values in the following section with the help of a business scenario.

Dimension security helps you to restrict access to members of a dimension for your Analysis Services database users based on your business needs. For example, you can have a dimension named Account that could have members such as accounts payable, accounts receivable, and materials inventory for your company. You might want to restrict user access so that certain users can see only the account types that they are authorized to work with. For example, the personnel working in the accounts payable department should see only the members under accounts payable and should not see all the accounts under accounts receivable or materials inventory. Here is another example: If your company sells products in various cities, you might want to restrict access for sales employees so that they can see only the data for which they are responsible on a city-by-city basis.

Analysis Services provides security restrictions on objects using an object called "role," (refer to Chapter 9). You can define roles in your database and then restrict permissions to certain dimension members or cells of the cube based on those roles. There are several techniques to model security based on the user, and you learn those techniques in this section. A user or a group of users is typically part of a specific role, and all the users in a role have the same level of security. A user can be part of one or more roles. An Analysis Services instance identifies users based on their Windows login credentials. When a user connects to an Analysis Services instance, the server iterates through various roles within the server to determine the roles the user is part of. Based on the list of roles a user belongs to, Analysis Services establishes appropriate security restrictions specified in those roles. If a user is part of multiple roles, Analysis Services provides access to a union of all the roles the user is part of. The important thing to know about this union is that if two roles give contradicting indications for user access of some object, access will be allowed.

If you have a group of users whose security constraints keep changing dynamically, you do have design alternatives by which you can specify security dynamically. That this is called *dynamic security* should come as no surprise. Analysis Services provides you with the capability to appropriately model and secure your data for your business needs. You learn the use of dimension security in the following business scenario; you also see the various approaches to secure dimensions that have been mentioned.

A Scenario Using Dimension Security

Business Problem definition: You are the data warehouse designer for the sales team in your company. You have sales representatives in certain states in the United States, and each sales representative is responsible for sales within that state. The sales representatives report to regional managers who might also be responsible for sales in a state, and the regional managers report to the

U.S. sales manager. The sales representatives can see the sales information for their state. The managers can see the sales information specific to them, as well as the data of the sales representatives reporting to them. You need to design a sales cube so that all the preceding security restrictions are applied to the users when they browse the cube.

Download the data specifically generated for this scenario from the download files for this chapter on www.wrox.com to help you understand the various design techniques that you can apply. This data set contains a list of employees in a company along with several months' worth of sales data; there is also a geography table that contains a list of states. Follow these instructions to restore the relational database from which you can create a cube:

1. Copy the file `DimensionandCellSecurity.bak` from this chapter's code download files to the backup folder of your Microsoft SQL Server 2012. For your SQL Server instance, this is at `<drive>:\Program Files\Microsoft SQL Server\MSSQL11.<instancename>\MSSQL\Backup`.

2. Connect to the relational SQL Server 2012 using SQL Server Management Studio. Right-click the Databases folder and select Restore. You see the SQL Server Restore dialog, as shown in Figure 14-3.

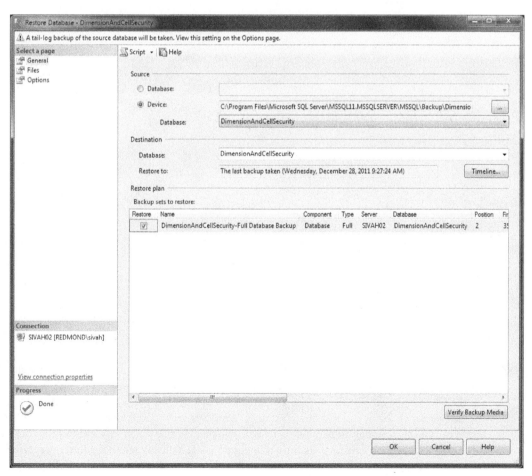

FIGURE 14-3

3. Select the From Device option. Click the ... [ellipsis] button, and specify the entire path to the relational database backup. You now see the various databases within the backup file listed below Select the Backup sets to restore.

4. Select the database DimensionAndCellSecurity-Full Database Backup to restore, as shown in Figure 14-3.

5. Select the To Database drop-down box, and select DimensionAndCellSecurity, as shown in Figure 14-3.

6. Click the Files page in the Restore Database dialog and make sure the paths for restoring the backup for the database and log files are specified correctly, as shown in Figure 14-4. After you verify this, click OK. The database will be successfully restored on your machine.

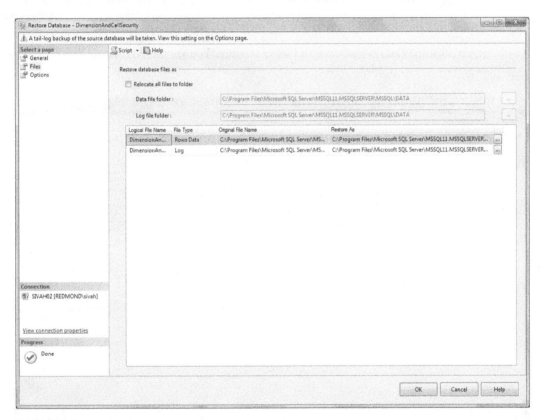

FIGURE 14-4

7. To demonstrate the dimension and cell security, you need users on a domain. To keep it simple, create local users on your current machine. Run the batch file `adduserscript.bat` provided in the Chapter 14 download samples available at www.wrox.com. If you use the Windows 7, Windows Server 2008 R2, Windows Vista, or Windows Server 2008 operating systems, you need to run this script as an administrator by right-clicking this script in Windows Explorer and selecting Run as Administrator, as shown in Figure 14-5. You can see that 15 users are added to your machine on your computer's computer management console, as shown in Figure 14-6.

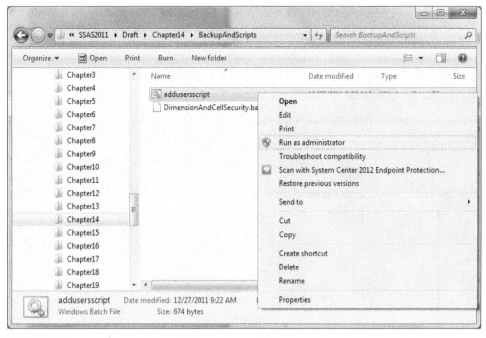

FIGURE 14-5

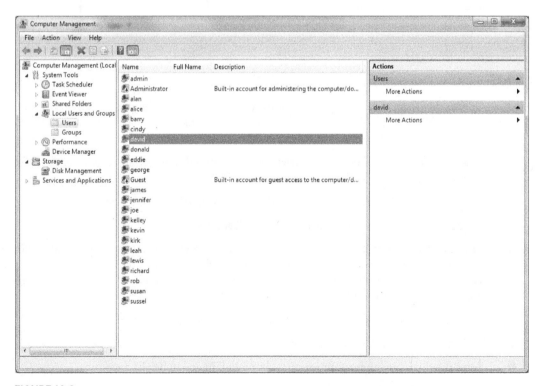

FIGURE 14-6

Some of the recommended solutions need to detect the username along with domain name. The Employee table within the DimensionAndCellSecurity database has two columns called Employee Login and Manager Login. You created the login names for the users in the Employee table in step 5. You need to update the domain name in these columns to your machine name.

8. To get the machine name of your system, open a command prompt, and type **hostname**.

9. Open the Employee table by right-clicking it in SQL Server Management Studio and selecting Edit Top 200 Rows. You now have all the rows of the Employee table, as shown in Figure 14-7.

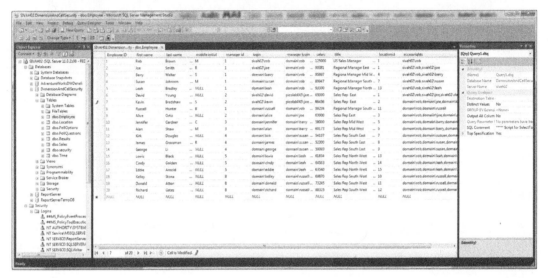

FIGURE 14-7

10. Update the Login, Manager Login, and Access Rights columns by replacing domain with your machine name. (You can see that some of the logins and manager logins for a few rows are updated with domain name as sivah02.)

You are now ready to create a cube and restrict users to view sales information only for the states for which they are allowed to see the information.

1. Create an Analysis Services project called DimensionAndCellSecurity-Scenario1.

2. Create a data source to the DimensionAndCellSecurity relational database you restored.

3. Create a Data Source View using the data source to the DimensionAndCellSecurity database, and select the tables Employees, Location, Time, and Sales. Select the columns in each table as shown in Figure 14-8, right-click, and select Select Logical Primary key. Create the relationships between the tables shown in Figure 14-8.

4. Right-click the Employee table and select New Named Calculation.

5. Enter **Full Name** as the column Name.

6. Enter the following expression for the column Full Name under Expression:

[first name] + ' ' + [last name]

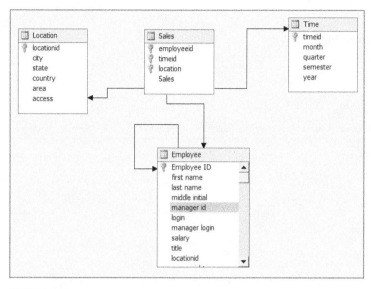

FIGURE 14-8

7. Create a multidimensional BISM using the Cube Wizard by selecting the Sales table as Measure Group table, and select the defaults in the other dialogs of the Cube Wizard. The Cube Wizard creates the three dimensions: Location, Employee, and Time.

8. Open the Location dimension by double-clicking the Location.dim dimension object.

9. Add the columns Access, Area, City, Country, and State as attributes within the Location dimension by dragging and dropping the columns from the Dimension Designer's Data Source View pane to the Attributes pane.

10. Create a user hierarchy Geography with levels Country, Area, State, and City, as shown in Figure 14-9.

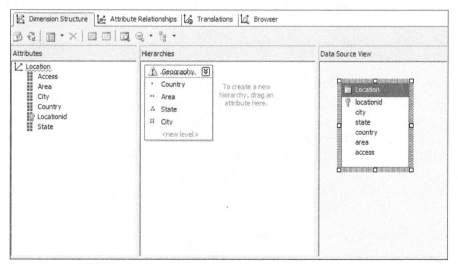

FIGURE 14-9

11. Create attribute relationships between the various attributes of the Location dimension, as shown in Figure 14-10.

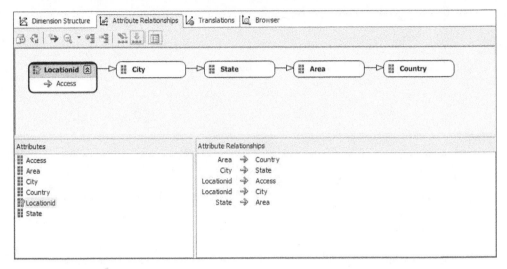

FIGURE 14-10

12. Open the Time dimension by double-clicking the `Time.dim` dimension.

13. In the Properties window of SSDT, set the Dimension Property Type for the Time dimension to Time.

14. Add the columns Month, Quarter, Semester, and Year as attributes by dragging and dropping the columns from the Dimension Editor's Data Source View pane to the Attributes pane.

15. Create a user hierarchy with levels Year, Semester, Quarter, and Month, as shown in Figure 14-11.

16. Create the attribute relationship between the attributes of the Time dimension, as shown in Figure 14-12.

17. Open the Employee dimension by double-clicking the `Employee.dim` object.

18. Add the columns Full Name, LocationId, Login, Manager Login, Salary, and Title as attributes of the Employee dimension. From the Dimension Editor of the Employee dimension, you see that the dimension contains a parent-child hierarchy. The manager-employee relationship in the Employee dimension is modeled as a parent-child hierarchy.

19. Select the key attribute Employee ID. Change the Name Column Property for the key attribute to Full Name. This step enables you to see the employee's name while browsing the parent-child hierarchy.

20. Select the parent attribute Manager ID, and rename the attribute to Employees.

21. Deploy the cube to your Analysis Services instance.

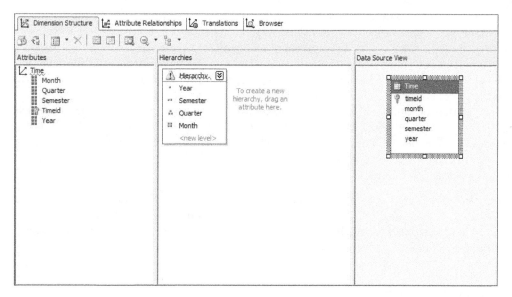

FIGURE 14-11

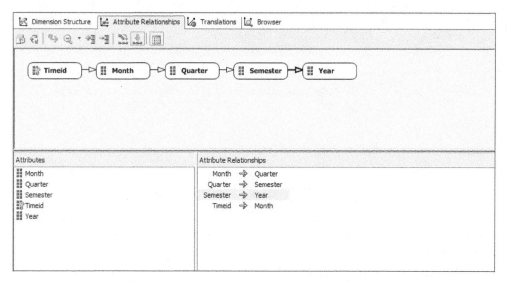

FIGURE 14-12

After you create your multidimensional BISM, the next step is to define security to restrict the data seen from the users based on their location. The roles object in Analysis Services enables you to restrict data access based on the login of a user. The roles object contains a collection called membership (refer to Chapter 9). You can add a user or a group of users to this membership collection. The security restrictions applied in this role will be applied to all the users in the membership collection. In this business problem you need to limit access to the sales representatives so that they can see only the sales information relevant to their state or their direct reports. You learn several solutions to restrict the dimension member access along with their merits and demerits.

Restricting a user to see only certain members of the dimension Location automatically restricts the user from seeing the sales information for that location. Location is a dimension and applying security or restrictions to users to certain members of a dimension is therefore called *dimension security*. If a user is part of more than one role, Analysis Services restricts the user to just a union of the roles the user is a member of. For example, if a user is a member of Role1 where you have restricted the users to see the location New York, and the user is also a member of Role2 where you have restricted the users of Role2 to the location New Jersey, the user can see both these locations when he connects to Analysis Services. If Role1 had security restrictions for a user that did not allow you to see the dimension member New York, but Role2 had security restrictions that allowed you to see the member New York, then Analysis Services would allow the user to access and retrieve the dimension member New York.

Now you can see the various design techniques for role definitions and what the trade-offs are for those design techniques. Some of the techniques mentioned in the following sections are from the dynamic security presentations by Dave Wickert, program manager, Microsoft Corporation. These design techniques have been modified for Analysis Services 2012.

The User-Role Approach

One approach is to restrict location access by defining the list of locations a user can see. To do this you need to create a role for each user and define the restrictions so that a user can have access only to members of specific states. In the following example you create roles for the users David and Robert. The following instructions show how to solve the problem of definition by creating roles for each user:

1. To create a new role for the Sales multidimensional BISM, right-click the Roles folder, and select New Role. A new role is created with the name Role, and you now see the Role Designer.

2. Right-click the Role.role in Solution Explorer, and rename it **David.role**.

3. You will be prompted with a dialog box asking you if the object name needs to be changed. Click Yes. The Role Designer has several views, as shown in Figure 14-13. In the General view you can define administrative tasks on the cube, such as process permissions or permission to read definitions of the objects in the database. You can also give full control at the database level, which means the users have full control to edit objects within this database.

4. Click the Membership tab in the Role Designer.

5. Click the Add button to add a user to this role, and add the user David. You have already created a user account on your machine for David earlier in this section. David's login account will be *<machinename>*\David, where *machinename* is the name of the machine you are working on. When you click the Add button, you see a dialog where you can enter the *domainname\loginname*. Enter your machine name followed by **\David** in this dialog, as shown in Figure 14-14, and click OK.

    You now see that the user David has been added to the role Role, as shown in Figure 14-15.

    The next step is to provide access to the cubes and dimensions in the database.

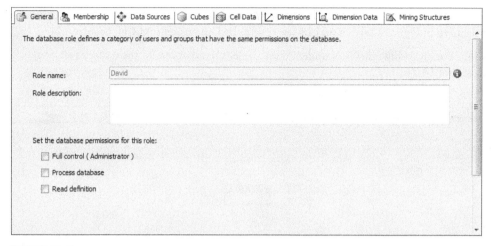

FIGURE 14-13

FIGURE 14-14

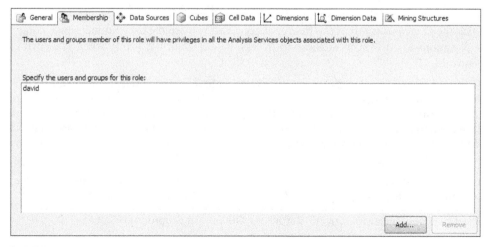

FIGURE 14-15

6. Click the Cubes tab in the Role Designer. You now see the list of cubes within the database, as shown in Figure 14-16. You can see your cube Dimension and Cell Security.

7. From the drop-down list box under Access, select Read access to the cube, as shown in Figure 14-16.

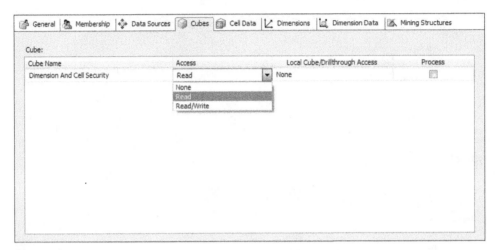

FIGURE 14-16

By selecting the access type Read, you allow users or groups with the role of David to read the data from the cube Dimension and Cell Security. In addition to providing access to the cube, you can also provide access to the users to drill-through to detail data or to process the cube in this pane. By default, when you provide access to the cube for the users of the role, they do not get drill-through to fact data or the ability to process the cube unless these security permissions are explicitly enabled. Leave the Local Cube/Drillthrough Access option to None. After providing access to the cube, you can provide access to the database dimensions as well as the cube dimensions in the Dimensions View.

8. Click the Dimensions tab of the Role Designer, and you see the list of dimensions along with options to provide permissions to Access, Read Definition, and Process, as shown in Figure 14-17.

To provide permissions to a dimension in the database, you can select the Read or Read/ Write option in the Access column in the Dimension tab of the Role Designer. By default, access to the dimension is set to Read. If you select the Read Definition check box, users have the ability to send discover statements to see the metadata information associated with the dimension. You can provide permissions to process a dimension by selecting the check box for the specific dimension.

9. You can provide access to specific dimension members of the database by using the Dimension Data tab in the Role Designer. Click the Dimension Data tab of the Role Designer.

10. Select the cube dimension Location from the Dimension drop-down list box.

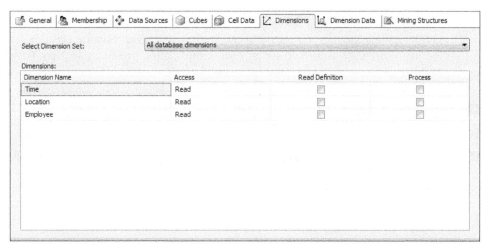

FIGURE 14-17

11. From the Attribute Hierarchy drop-down list box, select City. The Dimension drop-down enables you to choose the database dimensions in the database. The default view shows the first dimension in the database. When you select a specific dimension, the list of attribute hierarchies is shown as a drop-down list by Attribute Hierarchy, as shown in Figure 14-18.

| General | Membership | Data Sources | Cubes | Cell Data | Dimensions | Dimension Data | Mining Structures |

Dimension: DimensionAndCellSecurity-Scenario1.Location

Basic   Advanced

Attribute Hierarchy: City

○ Select all members

   Manually deselect members to deny. New members added to the top level will be allowed.

☐ ☑ All
   ☑ Atlanta
   ☑ Boise
   ☑ Boston
   ☑ Chicago
   ☑ Columbia
   ☑ Madison
   ☑ Montgomery
   ☑ New York
   ☑ Philedelphia
   ☑ Phoenix
   ☑ Portland
   ☑ Reno
   ☑ Sacramento
   ☑ Seattle
   ☑ St. Louis

○ Deselect all members

   Manually select members to allow. New members added to the top level will be denied.

Allows access to all members currently in the dimension, and allows access to members that are added to the topmost level after the role is defined. To deny access to any member currently in the dimension, clear the corresponding check box.

FIGURE 14-18

12. Click the Dimension Data tab to restrict the members that can be seen by the current role. In this example assume you restrict access to the user David. Because David is responsible for New York City, he should see only sales information pertaining to New York City. To specify this you need to select the dimension Location from the Dimension drop-down list, as shown in the next few steps.

13. Select the radio button Select all members.

14. Select the attribute hierarchy City from the Attribute Hierarchy drop-down list.

15. Deselect all the members except New York, as shown in Figure 14-19. The selection of the city New York restricts the users of the role from seeing other cities when they access the dimension Location. If you have complex business logic concerning access to members of a hierarchy, you can implement your logic using MDX expressions on the Advanced tab.

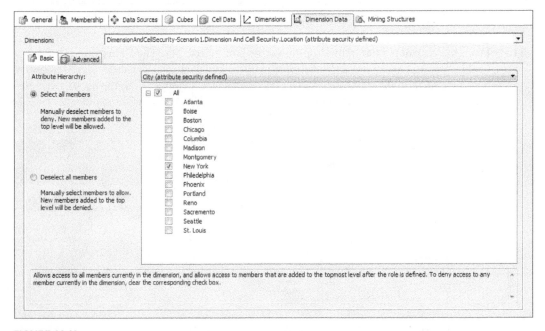

FIGURE 14-19

If you click the Advanced tab, you see three sections: Allowed member set, Denied member set, and Default member, as shown in Figure 14-20. You can see that the Denied member set shows all the members of the City hierarchy, except New York, that were not selected on the Basic tab. Analysis Services interprets all members not in the Denied member set (New York in this scenario) to automatically be included in the Allowed member set. This is the reason why you do not see the member New York in the Allowed member set. You can include your business logic to select the members that are to be allowed or denied for this specific role. The MDX expressions should result in a set of members of the current hierarchy in the Allowed member set and Denied member set. The result of the MDX expression specified in the Default member pane should be a single member from the current hierarchy.

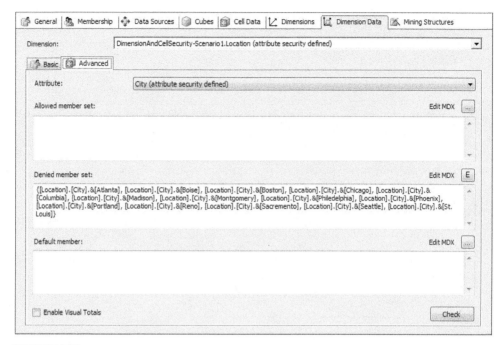

FIGURE 14-20

 An empty set for the Allowed member set (refer to Figure 14-20) indicates all the members of the current role have access to the members of the current hierarchy. An empty set in the Denied member set indicates there are no restrictions applied. {} is not the same as an empty set. Having {} in the Allowed member set simply disallows the role members to see any other member.

16. Similar to restricting access to New York City using the Basic tab in the Dimension data, you can restrict access for the attribute hierarchies Area, State, Country, and LocationId to the members East, New York State, USA, and 1, respectively, so that the user David can see only members relevant to New York City.

Having defined the dimension security, you need to test the security you have defined for user David.

17. Deploy the entire project to your Analysis Services instance.

18. Open the Dimension Security cube, and switch to the Browser pane.

By default, if you select Sales and the hierarchy Geography, you can see the sales information for all the cities.

19. Click the Change User icon, as shown in Figure 14-21.

FIGURE 14-21

20. You now have a dialog where you can select the role you have created. Select the role David, as shown in Figure 14-22, and click OK.

FIGURE 14-22

21. Drag and drop the sales measure and the Geography hierarchy of the Location dimension into the Cube Browser, as shown in Figure 14-23.

As you can see, the user David can see only results for the member New York; his access to the sales information is restricted to that and the totals. You can also analyze the data along with the totals in Excel. Follow these steps to see the information in Excel pivot tables.

22. On the Cube Browser tab, click the Excel icon.

23. In the Microsoft Excel Security Notice dialog, click Enable.

24. Click the Sales measure and the Geography hierarchy in the Location dimension. You can now see the Sales amount for USA.

25. Select USA on Row Labels as shown in Figure 14-24, right-click and select Expand/Collapse ⇨ Expand to "City."

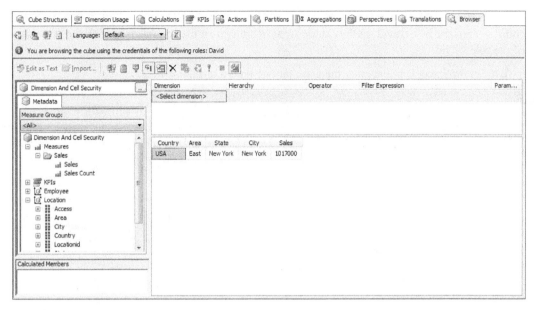

FIGURE 14-23

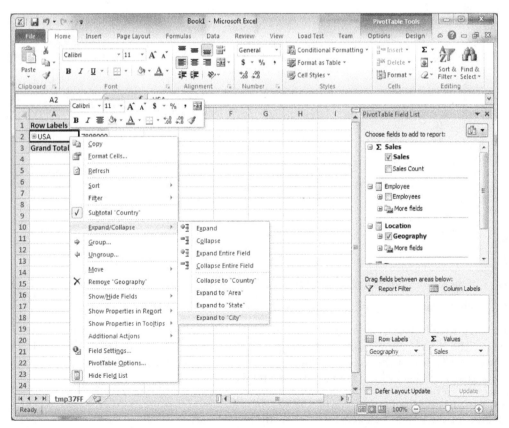

FIGURE 14-24

You now see the sales amounts for each state and city. To see the security enabled, you need to connect with the role David. Follow these steps to simulate a user connecting with the permissions of the role David.

1. In the Excel Ribbon, click the Data tab, as shown in Figure 14-25.

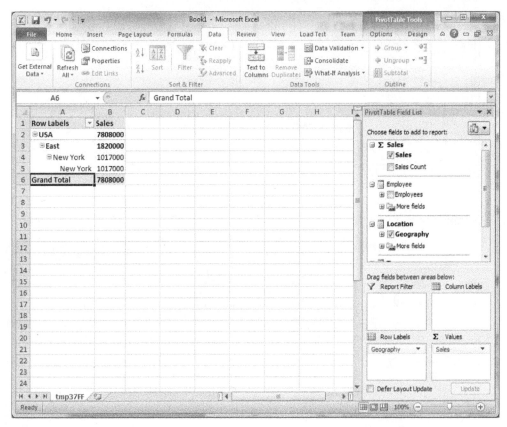

FIGURE 14-25

2. On the Connections group, click Properties.

3. In the Connection Properties dialog, switch to the Definition tab.

4. In the Connection string: box, append; Role=David and click OK.

5. When prompted to save the connection information, click Yes.

Connecting with Role=David instructs Analysis Services to simulate a user connecting to the database who has the permissions of the role David. You see the data restricted to New York. However, the Totals for the Area and Country do not match the value for city New York. This is because sales for other cities are included in the totals.

You can define security permissions on roles so that the totals returned by Analysis Services are calculated for the visible members rather than all the members in the dimension.

1. Open the role David, and switch to the Dimension Data tab.

2. Select the cube dimension Location and the attribute hierarchy Area.

3. Switch to the Advanced tab within Dimension Data tab and enable the check box Enable Visual Totals, as shown in Figure 14-26.

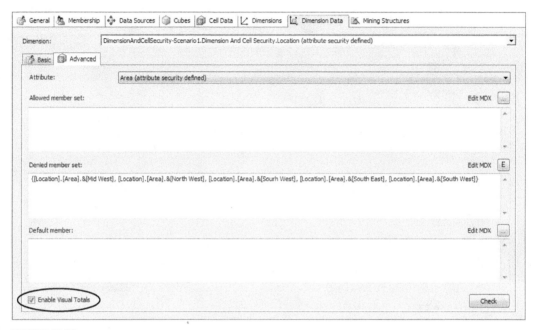

FIGURE 14-26

4. Enable the check box for the attribute hierarchies City, Location, State and Country, and deploy the project to your Analysis Services instance so that new security definitions are updated on the server.

5. Switch back to the Cube Browser, and reconnect to the SSAS instance.

6. Launch Excel, and add Role=David to the connection string in the Connection Properties dialog in Excel.

   You see that user David can see the sales information for the city New York and all the totals now match the sales of the city New York, as shown in Figure 14-27. By enabling visual totals in dimension security, you have ensured that the role David can see only aggregated data for cities that can be accessed by users of the role David.

   Similar to what you did for David, you need to define appropriate security for all the users in the organization to access data from the cube. The goal in this scenario is to define dimension security to restrict the regional sales managers to seeing only the results for the cities of just their direct reports, while the U.S. sales manager can see the entire set of cities. Just as you specified security on the Location dimension for the role David, you should repeat the process to create a role for each user and provide access to the cities that can be accessed by the user. In this way you can restrict data access to users of the cube using the dimension security feature of Analysis Services.

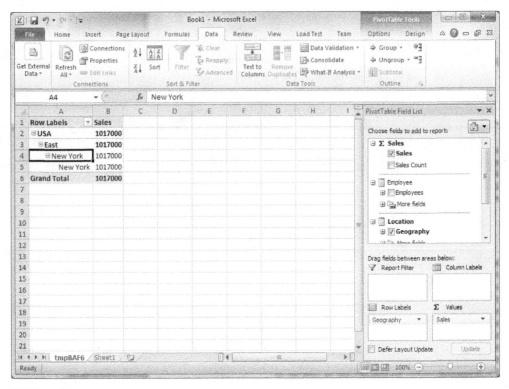

FIGURE 14-27

7. To restrict the user David to only see sales data relevant to him, you can restrict him from seeing other employee members in the Employee dimension. The Employee dimension has a parent-child hierarchy called Employees. Switch to the Dimension Data tab.

8. Select the Employee cube dimension and the attribute hierarchy Employees.

9. Select the member David Young and the members Joe Smith and Rob Brown (who are managers of David Young). Also, select All from the Employees hierarchy, as shown in Figure 14-28. You have now restricted the user David to have appropriate permissions on the Employee dimension.

The members of role David can see only the dimension member David and its parents under the parent-child hierarchy Employees. To make sure David truly can see only data relevant to himself, verify it again using the Cube Browser, as in the next few steps.

10. Save and deploy the project to your Analysis Services instance.

11. Switch to the Cube Browser.

12. Change the user to simulate David by selecting the role David.

13. In the Cube Browser, drag and drop the measure Sales amount.

14. Drag and drop the Location Geography hierarchy from the metadata browser to the data area in the Cube Browser.

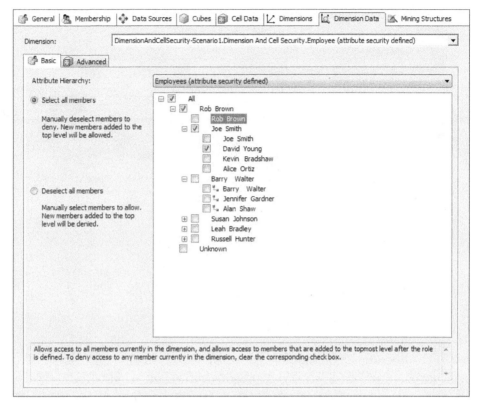

FIGURE 14-28

15. Drag and drop the Employee Employees hierarchy from the metadata browser to the data area in the Cube Browser, as shown in Figure 14-29. You can now see only the user David. However, you can see that the users of role David can also see the totals of David's managers Joe Smith and Rob Brown (refer to Figure 14-29). This is due to the security definition that is unique to parent-child hierarchies. To make sure David sees only the sales amount sold by him, you can enable Visual Totals on the Advanced tab.

Each hierarchy has a default member that can be specified using the properties of the hierarchy or by using an MDX script. When you define dimension security, the default member of a hierarchy might be restricted to the users of a role. Therefore, the Role Designer enables you to specify the default member for hierarchies in a dimension for a specific role. To specify the default member for a hierarchy, you can either enter the member name in the Default Member pane or use the Edit MDX button. Follow the next steps to specify the default member.

1. Switch to the Role Designer for David.

2. In the Dimension Data tab of the Role Designer, click the Advanced tab.

3. Select the Location cube dimension and the State hierarchy.

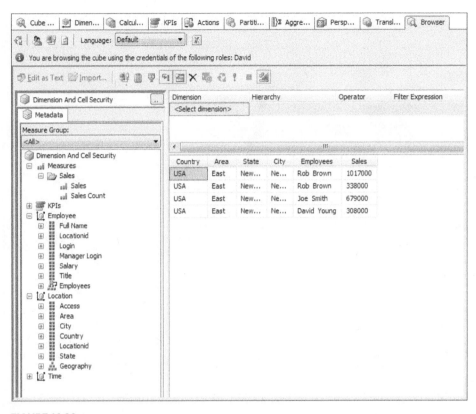

FIGURE 14-29

4. Click the Edit MDX button for the Default member pane to launch the MDX Builder dialog, shown in Figure 14-30.

5. Double-click the member you want to set as the default member for the hierarchy chosen: New York for the hierarchy State in the Location dimension. You see the unique name of the member in the Expression pane (refer to Figure 14-30).

6. Click Check to make sure your chosen MDX expression is correct.

7. Click OK. You can see the default member expression is the Role Designer.

8. Specify the default member for the remaining hierarchies for which you have applied dimension security: New York for the City attribute, East for the Area attribute, 1 for LocationId, and David Young for the Employees attribute in the Employee dimension.

9. Specify default members for the cube dimension hierarchies State, City, and Area in the dimension Location and the Employees hierarchy in the dimension Employee.

10. Deploy the changes to your Analysis Services instance.

FIGURE 14-30

To verify your default member setting, you can run SQL Server Management Studio as a specific user who is part of the role you have created.

1. Open a command prompt on your machine.

2. Type **runas /user:<yourmachinename>\david ssms.exe,** as shown in Figure 14-31.

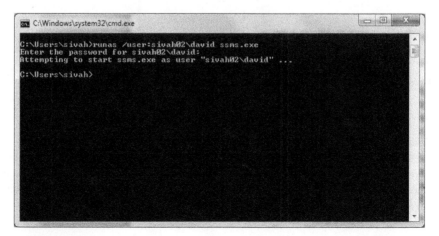

FIGURE 14-31

3. When prompted for a password, enter the password for david: **divad*123!**

You now see the SQL Server Management Studio launched under the user david.

4. Open the MDX query editor in SQL Server Management Studio using the MDX icon or File ⇨ New ⇨ Analysis Services MDX Query.

5. Select the DimensionAndCellSecurity database.

6. Send the following MDX query by substituting for dimension, hierarchy, and cube name, and you should see the results for the default member, as shown in Figure 14-32.

```
SELECT
<Dimension>.<Hierarchy>.Defaultmember on 0
From <CubeName>
```

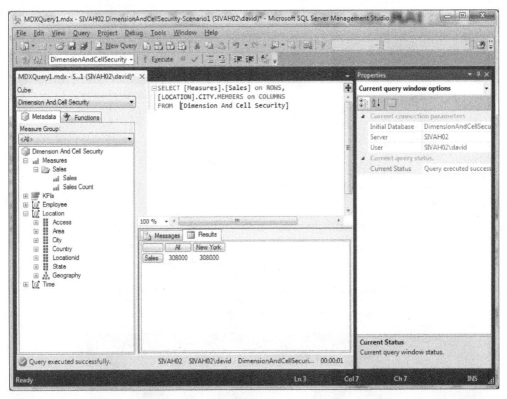

FIGURE 14-32

If a user belongs to more than one role, the default member for the first role in the roles collection is chosen as the default member for the hierarchy. The user-role approach is suited to business scenarios in which you have a limited set of users and their security permissions do not change frequently. Typically, when the permissions for users are static, this approach is sufficient to suit your business needs and is easy to implement and maintain.

The Access-Role Approach

In the user-role approach, you solved the business problem of restricting data access for certain employees in the company. You created a role for each employee in the company and provided appropriate restrictions. Under that design, if new employees join the company, the administrator of the cube needs to create a new role for every new salesperson and appropriately provide the restrictions. Similarly, if employees leave or change roles, such as a salesperson promoted to sales manager, you must appropriately update the dimension security within the cube. You can choose from two design alternatives to accommodate changes of this nature: to create a role for each city where employees get the permissions, or to create roles based on Windows users groups where the users are added or removed to the Windows groups.

You can create roles based on cities rather than the users. In this design alternative, you add all the users who have the right to access specific cities to the role of a specific city. If your company has 100 employees selling into 10 different cities, you would create 10 roles and assign users to those roles — as opposed to creating 100 roles with cities assigned to each. This design leaves open the question of how to go about restricting the employee name in the Employee dimension. Assuming the employees have an account of the format <domain name>\<login name>, you can restrict employee access by using an MDX expression that uses the MDX function USERNAME as shown here:

```
FILTER(employee.[employees].MEMBERS,
INSTR(employee.[employees].CURRENTMEMBER.NAME,
RIGHT(USERNAME,len(USERNAME)- instr(USERNAME,"\"))))
```

In this dimension security scenario, the logins of each employee match the first name of the employee. The employee's parent-child hierarchy in the Employee dimension has been modeled in a way that the employee's full name is the named column for the hierarchy. Therefore, while browsing the Employees hierarchy, you see the full name of the users. If you check the name in the login and match it with the appropriate employee name, you automatically get the employee member for the user who has logged in. The preceding MDX expression completes the operation to identify the employee member for the corresponding login using the MDX function username. The username MDX function returns the <domainname>\<loginname>. Finally, the third line in the MDX expression extracts the loginname. This loginname is used in the condition of the Filter MDX function to iterate through all the members of the employees hierarchy and extract the member(s) where the employee name contains the login name.

To extract the login name from the employee name, the VBA function Instr is used. The result of the MDX expression is the correct employee member name. Most companies do not have login names that match exactly to the first name or last name of the employees. In such a case you would need to form a complex MDX expression that can return the correct employee member for the Allowed set. You see an example of a complex MDX expression in the "Securing Your Cube Data" section.

To test the preceding solution, you can go to the Cube Browser and bring up the user of interest, as shown in Figure 14-33. Analysis Services now impersonates the user account specified in the Other user option to access the cube data. Security restrictions are applied to the user based on the roles that user is part of. You can now browse the dimensions and cell values in the Cube Browser to ensure your security restrictions were applied correctly. You do need to be aware that the Other user option is supported by Analysis Services only on a valid domain account and not a local machine account.

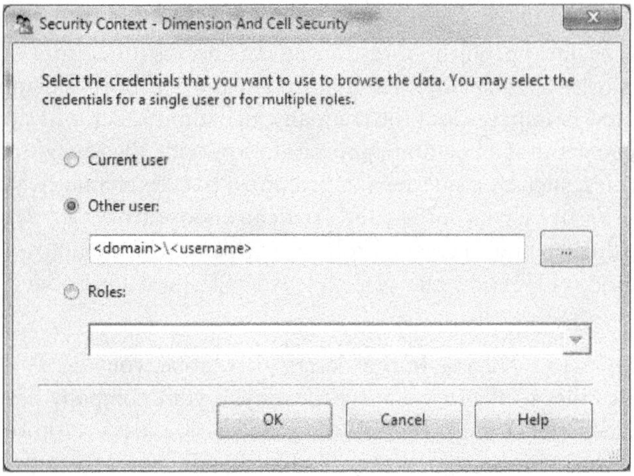

FIGURE 14-33

If your business needs are such that data access restrictions for users are reasonably static but the number of users is large as compared to the data members in the dimension, the access-role approach might be better suited for your business problem. If your business needs are such that the security restrictions of users change due to modification of roles or location, you need a solution in which you can dynamically add or remove users. We recommend the approach to create Windows user groups and add the users to those Windows groups. The Windows groups will actually be added to the membership of a role rather than the users themselves. For the current scenario, you would create a Windows group for each city. If the employees move from one location to another, they can easily be removed or added to the appropriate city group. In this way, you do not need to make changes to the roles in Analysis Services. This solution is feasible because Analysis Services leverages Windows authentication to authenticate users, users' permissions keep changing through Windows security groups, and Analysis Services can handle the security restrictions dynamically. This solution is suited for an enterprise where multiple applications connecting to Analysis Services can use this. However, in this technique you still need to maintain a role for each Windows group. Therefore, your Analysis Services database can potentially have several roles that are equivalent to the number of members in the dimension. If you want to have only one role that provides you with the ability to restrict data for all users dynamically, you have three different techniques, which are explained in subsequent sections. Restricting dimension data access using one role for several users whose data access permissions change periodically is called *dynamic dimension security*.

The Member Property Approach

One of the ways to provide access to locations for employees is to have a column in the relational data source that contains the list of employees who have access to that location. When you need to modify user access to a location, you can either restrict them or provide access by updating the list of users who have access in the relational column. You might wonder how this translates into defining the security in Analysis Services dynamically — when a list in the relational data source must be maintained. Actually, it is quite simple with the help of an MDX expression.

You need to make sure the relational column in the dimension table is added as an attribute hierarchy in the dimension. You do not necessarily need to browse this attribute, but you need to make this attribute a member property for the Attribute hierarchies for which you need to apply dimension security.

1. Launch SQL Server Management Studio, and connect to your relational database server.

2. Open the relational table called Location in the DimensionAndCellSecurity database from within SQL Server Management Studio.

3. Replace all instances of the name domain\<username> in the Access column to your local machine name\<username> and save the changes.

4. Open the Analysis Services project DimensionAndCellSecurity you created in this chapter.

5. Open the Location dimension.

6. Specify the Access attribute as a member property for the attribute City by dragging and dropping the City attribute onto the Access attribute in the Attribute Relationships tab of the Dimension Editor.

7. Your Attribute Relationships pane of the Dimension Editor for the Location dimension should look like Figure 14-34.

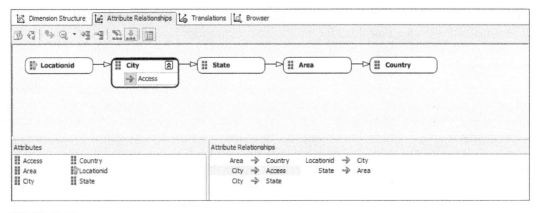

FIGURE 14-34

8. Create the MDX expression in a single role that defines dynamic security for all the users. Again, you need the MDX function username. Start by creating a new role.

9. Add all the users who need access to the cube to the membership collection of the role.

10. After you provide read access to the cube and the dimensions, go to the Advanced tab of the Dimension Data pane. Select the dimension Location and hierarchy City. Enter the following MDX expression for the Allowed set:

```
Filter(Location.City.City.members,
Instr(Location.City.currentmember.properties('Access'),
USERNAME))
```

This expression filters the list of cities that can be accessed by the current user. Member property Access for each city is checked to see if the current user has access using the VBA function `Instr`. The expression `Location.City.currentmember.properties('Access')` returns a string that contains the login names of all the users who have access to the current city. The `username` function returns the string containing the login name of the current user. The `Instr` VBA function searches for the occurrence of the current user in the member property attribute Access of the City attribute. If there is a match, the `Instr` function returns a positive number, and the `Filter` expression uses that as an indication the condition is true; therefore, the current city can be accessed by the current user. Thus, the `Filter` function can retrieve a set of cities that can be viewed by the current user.

You can have additional columns that contain the users who have access to State, Area, and Country. Similar to step 6 you can use these columns to create additional attributes to the dimension and make them as member properties to the corresponding attributes State, Area, and Country. If you use the same access column for more than one attribute, you can see redundant relationships in the Attribute Relationships designer along with the warnings, which you can ignore. By default, the access attribute is a member property of the key attribute LocationId. If you do not want your users to browse this attribute, you can disable the attribute hierarchy Access by changing its `AttributeHierarchyEnabled` property to false. You also need to specify the MDX expressions for the attributes State, Area, and Country, respectively, in the Location dimension in the Dimension Data tab to restrict the access to the right users. Add appropriate columns in the relational database and set up the security restrictions for the attributes State, Area, and Country.

The Analysis Services project modeling the business problem using the member property approach is provided with the code download for this chapter and is called DimensionAndCellSecurity-Scenario2. You can test the preceding expression by deploying the current role to the Analysis Services instance and then browsing the cube using a specific user (refer to Figure 14-33).

The member property approach is one of the three dynamic security approaches recommended in this chapter. This is easy to implement, and the cost of maintenance (updates of permissions to users in the relational table) is typically low because only a few columns get updated for security changes. One of the advantages of the member property approach over the previous approaches is that you have a single role to maintain. However, the important trade-off in this approach is that whenever you change the security restrictions for the users, the dimension needs to be processed to reflect the changes in the database, thereby restricting the right dimension members. Based on your business requirements you can allow proactive caching on the dimension so that the dimension is processed automatically without intervention from an admin. If your dimension has a large number of members and if you need security changes to be in effect immediately, you might have performance implications because Analysis Services would need to use the dimension in ROLAP mode until the time the MOLAP cache gets updated. Based on the size of the dimension members and your business need, you can choose to implement this approach.

The Security Measure Group Approach

In this approach, dimension security is modeled using a fact table. A relational table can hold the access permissions of users for the dimension members. If a user has permission for a specific location, this is indicated by a row containing the username, the location, and another column containing a value 1, which indicates the user has permissions to the location. A value of 0 indicates that the user does not have permissions. Ah, something simple! Now you want to learn this approach, right?

The fact table containing the dimension security restrictions is added as a measure group to the existing cube. The relational column that contains the value of 0 or 1 is the measure that can be used for modeling dimension security. An MDX expression using the measure from the security measure group can restrict the dimension members to authorized users. Follow these steps to model the measure group approach for restricting access to users:

1. Use the Analysis Services project you used in any of the approaches discussed earlier, and delete all existing roles.

2. In the DSV designer, right-click and select Add/Remove Tables. Select the security table and click OK.

3. Mark the employeeid and locationid as key for the security table, and make appropriate joins to the dimension and Employee tables in the DSV, as shown in Figure 14-35.

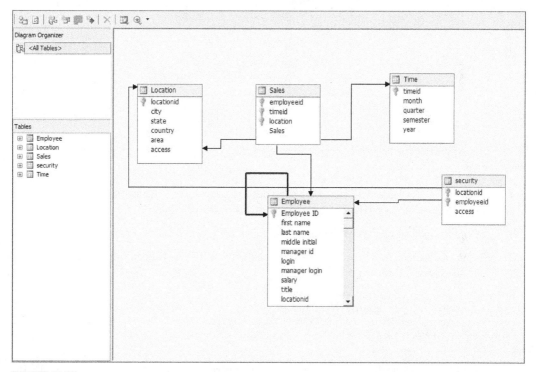

FIGURE 14-35

4. Open the cube DimensionAndCellSecurity, and click the Cube Structure tab.

5. Right-click the cube name in the Measures pane, and select New Measure Group.

6. Select the security table from the DSV. The Analysis Services cube designer automatically adds a new measure group called Security and creates two new measures, as shown in Figure 14-36. The Analysis Services tools automatically define the right relationships between the existing dimensions based on the joins specified in the DSV. If you click the Dimension Usage tab, you see the details of the dimension types and the granularity attributes. Deploy the new cube structure to your Analysis Services instance.

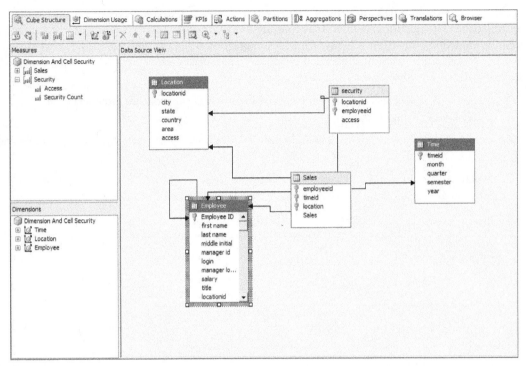

FIGURE 14-36

7. Create a new role, add all the users who need to access the Dimension Security cube, and provide read access to the cube and dimensions in the database.

8. In the Role Designer, go to the Dimension Data tab, and select the Advanced option.

9. Select the dimension Location and hierarchy City. In the Advanced tab, enter the following MDX expression for the Allowed set:

```
FILTER(Location.city.city.MEMBERS,
(FILTER(Employee.Employees.MEMBERS,
instr(Employee.Employees.CURRENTMEMBER.NAME,
right(USERNAME,len(USERNAME)- instr(USERNAME,"\")))).ITEM(0),
measures.access)=1)
```

In this expression, the login of the current user is retrieved using the username MDX function. The inner filter expression iterates through all the members of the Employee dimension and retrieves the set of members who have the same name as the login name. Because there is a one-to-one relationship between users and logins, the inner filter condition results in a set with one member. The returned set cannot be used directly to form a tuple in the conditional expression. There are several ways to form the condition expression using the outer filter function to retrieve the list of cities accessible by the current user. In the preceding MDX expression, you can retrieve a single tuple of the inner filter function using .ITEM(0). You then must check if the current user has access to the location. To do so, the outer filter function is used, which checks for a value of 1 for each tuple. The resulting set from the outer filter function is the set of cities for which the current user has access. Thus, you form an MDX expression that secures the location for each user.

10. Similar to the MDX expression used in step 9, form an MDX expression with the remaining attribute hierarchies Area, Location, State, and Country in the Location dimension, and set the allowed member set for each hierarchy.

11. Restrict the access to members of the Employee dimension, using the following MDX expression, which uses the login of the user and restricts access to members in the Employees parent-child hierarchy in the Employee dimension.

```
FILTER(Employee.Employees.MEMBERS,
instr(Employee.Employees.CURRENTMEMBER.NAME,
right(USERNAME,len(USERNAME)- instr(USERNAME,"\"))))
```

12. Deploy the project to the Analysis Services instance.

The Analysis Services project modeling dimension security scenario using a fact table is provided under this chapter's 14 download samples and is called DimensionAndCellSecurity-Scenario3. Using the Cube Browser's change user option, you can verify the dimension security restrictions you have applied in the measure group approach. However, as mentioned earlier, you need to use a valid domain account rather than a machine account.

The security measure group approach is an extension of the member property approach. Similar to the member property approach, you can implement this approach quickly and maintenance is also low cost. You do need to process the security measure group whenever there are security changes, and you need the security permissions to take effect immediately. This approach has a lower performance impact as compared to the member property approach because only the specific measure group needs to be updated. For automatic updates you can set up proactive caching on the security measure group. If you have proactive caching set on this measure group, retrieving the data from this measure group would be fast, even if you have a large number of members in the dimension for which security has been updated. After the security information is cached on Analysis Services, you do not have a dependency on the relational data source.

The External Function Approach

The member property approach and the secure measure group approach require appropriate dimensions and measure group processing to keep abreast of changes. You can certainly set up proactive caching on the dimension and measure group so that changes to security are immediately reflected. However, processing does involve some cost. The external function approach alleviates the problems of processing and ensures that only the most up-to-date security restrictions are applied to the users.

In the external function approach, you write a UDF or a .NET stored procedure that can retrieve the list of locations the current user is authorized to access. For example, the stored procedure can return the list of cities or states or areas that a specific user can access as an MDX set. This set is then defined in the Allowed member set as the dimension security restrictions for the current user. Analysis Services exposes the security permissions for .NET stored procedures, which restricts the stored procedures access on specific resources such as accessing a network or creating a new file. The security permission provides an extra level of code security so that your Analysis Services is more reliable. There are no such security permissions that can be defined for COM UDFs, and you need to trust that the programmer has written good quality code. In addition you have the option to use the ADOMD server object model in your .NET stored procedure to perform custom business logic, which is not available if you code a COM UDF. You still need to maintain a relational table that provides information on a user's access to locations via a column.

In this example you use the security table that was used in the measure group approach. Because the security table contains only IDs of employees and location, you need to make joins to Employee and Location tables in the relational database to retrieve the right location members. However, you can create a new table that has the list of locations for employees based on the login information. Such a table should probably have the columns Login Name, City, State, Country, Location ID, and access where the column access has values 1 or 0 that indicate if the user has access to the specified location.

The .NET stored procedure either needs to return a string that contains the list of locations or an MDX set of locations. The string needs to contain the unique name of the locations separated by a comma so that you can be converted to a set using the StrToSet MDX function. This function in a .NET stored procedure or a UDF enables you to get an MDX set of members that need to be allowed or denied for the users of the current role. Your .NET stored procedure alternatively can return an MDX set using the ADOMD server object model that can be directly used in the Allowed members or Denied member sets for dimension security restrictions. To create the set of members, your .NET stored procedure needs to identify the member(s) from Analysis Services based on the security restrictions defined in the relational database.

In this dimension security you create a .NET stored procedure that returns a string containing the unique names of the locations accessible for the current user. The stored procedure can take two arguments, login and location, which are strings. For the login of the current user, you can directly pass the MDX function username. The location argument is the column name of the attribute hierarchy for which you need to retrieve the list of members accessible by the current user. Following is the pseudo-code for translation into a function in your favorite .NET language:

```
Public string getAllowedSet(string login, string location)
{
        1. Connect to your relational data source database
        2. Form the SQL query using the login and location to retrieve
           the members that can be accessed by the users
        3. Iterate through the result set and form the output string so that the
           members are returned in the unique name format.
}
```

The stored procedure first needs to connect to the relational database and send the following query:

```
select <location>
from employee, location, [security]
where employee.[login] = '<login>' and
employee.[employee id] = [security].employeeid and
location.locationid = [security].locationid
```

The words within <> are the parameters passed to the stored procedure. There is a potential for SQL injection attacks with the above query. You can use a parameterized SQL query, which can help you to prevent a breach of security. The stored procedure retrieves the results from the query and forms the output string, which needs to be in the following format:

```
{[Location].<location>.<location>.&[<resultvalue1>],
[Location].<location>.<location>.&[<resultvalue2>],
[Location].<location>.<location>.&[<resultvalue3>],...}
```

The unique name for a member is represented as [Dimension].<Hierarchy>.<Level>.&[Member Name]. For attribute hierarchies the Hierarchy name and Level name will be the same. If the key column and named column for an attribute hierarchy are the same, the member in an attribute hierarchy can be referenced as [Dimension].[AttributeHierarchyName][AttributeHierarchyName] .&[MemberName]. Follow the same approach to build a string that represents the set of members for the members of a hierarchy in the Location dimension. The values resultvalue1, resultvalue2, and so on are the results from the SQL query, which you need to iterate to form the output of the function. You need to add appropriate error handling to your stored procedure. After you compile your stored procedure, add the stored procedure to the assembly collection of the database with the appropriate impersonation mode and permission set. This stored procedure requires an external access permission because it needs to access an external resource (the relational database).

Create a new role, and add all the employees' logins to the membership collection. Then specify read access to the cube and dimensions. Assuming the name of the assembly that contains the `getAllowedSet` function is `SecurityMemberSet`, specify the following MDX expression for the Allowed member set:

```
StrtoSet(SecurityMemberSet.SecurityMemberSet.getAllowedSet(USERNAME, "City"))
```

Test the security restriction using the Cube Browser, and change to one of the local users to verify the current user can see only the locations for which he has been given access.

The external function approach provides maximum flexibility for design approaches. Also, you do not have the overhead of processing a measure group or dimension whenever changes to security restrictions occur. Security restrictions are always immediate because they are queried directly from the relational database each time; therefore, you need to make sure the relational server is up and running all the time. Implementing this involves some amount of coding and proper error handling, but it should be worth spending the time upfront to implement this type of solution.

SECURING YOUR CUBE DATA

Restricting user access to certain cell values of the cube is referred to as *cell security*. For example, for confidential information such as employee salaries, you can allow your employees to browse information about other employees such as the number of years in the company, title, phone number, address, and login information but restrict salary information. Because you want the information viewable by the person's manager, you need to control access at the cell value level rather than for whole dimension members.

Similar to dimension security, Analysis Services enables you to specify permission to cells using the roles. Access to cell values in a cube is restricted through an MDX expression that can be defined similar to dimension security. The MDX expression needs to evaluate to true or false. You can specify read-and-write permissions for cells in a cube. When a query is sent to the Analysis Services instance, the cells that are part of that query result are evaluated and returned. Whenever a cell is evaluated, Analysis Services checks the permissions set for the cell. If the permission is set, it evaluates the condition to see if the user has access to the cell. If the user is allowed to view the cell, that cell value would be returned as part of the result. If the user does not have access to that specific cell, an appropriate message is returned to the user.

Scenario Using Cell Security

Business Scenario definition: You are the director of the company and you want to take a satisfaction survey or poll of your employees. Employees can view only results of the survey they have filled in. However, managers can view the aggregated results of the poll only if they have more than two direct reports. Managers cannot see individual responses of their direct reports because this is a confidential survey. As an administrator you need to implement a multidimensional BISM in Analysis Services 2012 so that you give appropriate security restrictions to the users to see the results.

You use the same Dimension And Cell Security relational database as you used in the previous scenarios in this chapter. This database contains tables that have the questions of the poll and the results from the employees. The following steps show how to create the right multidimensional BISM and then apply cell security restrictions for the employees:

1. Create a new Analysis Services multidimensional and data mining project. Create a data source to the relational database Dimension And Cell Security relational data source.

2. Create a data source view that includes all the tables from the data source except the security table.

3. Create the joins between the tables, as shown in Figure 14-37.

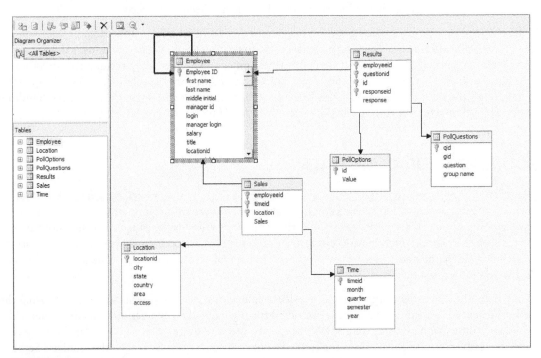

FIGURE 14-37

4. Create a calculated column in the Employee table called Full Name with the following expression:

```
[first name] + ' ' + [last name]
```

5. Browse the tables Poll Questions, Poll Options, and Results so that you get a good understanding of the scenario. There are 25 poll questions with responses from each employee stored in the Results table.

6. Create a cube using the Cube Wizard by selecting the Sales and Results tables as Measure Group tables, and select the defaults in the other dialogs of the Cube Wizard.

7. The Cube Wizard creates the dimensions Location, Employee, Time, Poll Questions, and Poll Options. You now have the cube, as shown in Figure 14-38.

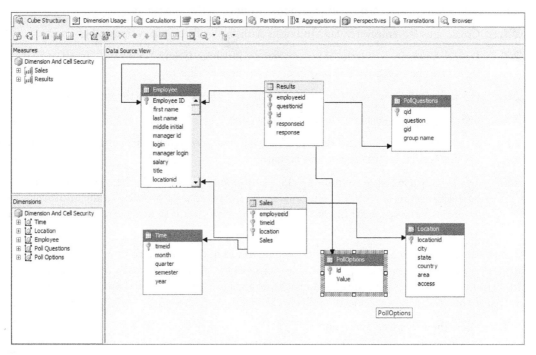

FIGURE 14-38

8. Open the Location dimension by double-clicking the Location.dim dimension object.

9. Add the columns Area, City, Country, and State as attributes within the Location dimension by dragging and dropping the columns from the Dimension Designer's Data Source View pane to the Attributes pane.

10. Create a user hierarchy with levels Country, Area, State, and City named Geography.

11. Define attribute relationships between the attributes City, State, Area, and Country.

12. Open the Employee dimension.

13. Specify the name column for the Employee ID attribute to point to the Full Name column.

14. Rename the Manager ID attribute to Employees.

15. Add the attributes Login, Manager Login, Salary, and Title to the Employee dimension.

16. Open the Time dimension.

17. Change the dimension type of the Time dimension from Regular to Time by changing the Type property.

18. Add the attributes Year, Semester, Quarter, and Month.

19. Create a user hierarchy called Time with the levels Year, Semester, Quarter, and Month.

20. Define the attribute relationship between the attributes in the Time dimension.

21. Open the Poll Questions dimension.

22. Add Group Name, GID, and Question attributes to the dimension.

23. Create a user hierarchy called Questions with the levels Group Name and Question.

24. Define the attribute relationship between the attribute Group Name and Question because there is a one-to-many relationship between these attributes.

25. Open the Poll Options dimension, and add the Value attribute to the dimension.

26. Switch to the Dimension and Cell Security cube.

27. Delete the Sales Count and Results Count measures created by the Cube Wizard because they are not needed for analysis in this scenario.

28. The response measure contains a value corresponding to whether the employee agrees or disagrees to the question. Make the `AggregationFunction` (a property of the measure) for the response measure Count instead of Sum because you want to analyze how many users agreed or disagreed to the poll questions.

In this cell security scenario, managers are also involved in the survey. You need a way to distinguish the responses of the manager to the responses of the aggregated results of her direct reports. To distinguish the results of a specific manager, change the property `MembersWithDataCaption` for the parent hierarchy, as shown in the following steps.

1. Open the Employee dimension.

2. Set the `MembersWithDataCaption` property of the parent attribute Employees to (* data), as shown in Figure 14-39.

3. Having created the cube, you now need to define security restrictions for the cells as per the business requirement. Similar to dimension security, create a new role in the database, add all the employees to the membership collection, and provide read access to the cube and the dimensions in the database.

4. Click the Cell Data tab. Click the drop-down list box for the Cube, and select the cube Dimension And Cell Security, as shown in Figure 14-40.

The three panes shown in Figure 14-40 help you define the MDX expression for securing the cells. The MDX expression specified here needs to evaluate to either true or false, and this expression gets evaluated for each cell. You need to be careful in specifying the right MDX expression so that you secure the cell values correctly. You can define read permission, read-contingent permission, and read/write permission to the cells. The read and read/write permissions are intuitive as to what the behavior is. If the MDX expression evaluates to true, either read or read/write access for that specific cell is provided to the current user accessing the cell. If an expression is specified for read-contingent permission, the cells specified as viewable by the MDX expression are viewable under two conditions. If those cells are not derived from other cells, they are viewable based on the MDX expression. If those cells are derived from other cells in the cube, those cells are viewable only if that cell and all the cells from which it is derived are viewable.

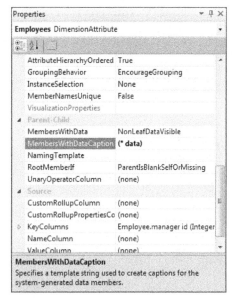

FIGURE 14-39

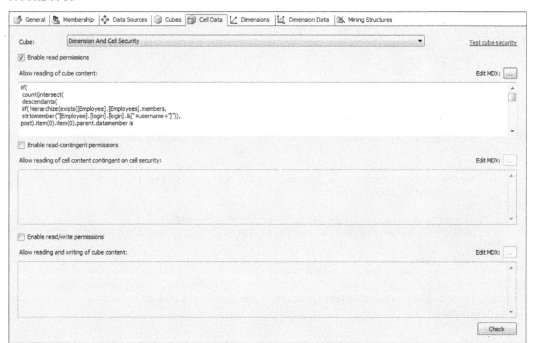

FIGURE 14-40

Following is the MDX expression that needs to be entered in the Enable read permissions pane to meet the business requirement of allowing employees to view their individual responses and managers to see the aggregated response of the poll questions if they have more than two direct reports. In the dimension security section, you can demonstrate a complex MDX expression to retrieve the employee name based on the login. The following MDX expression is a generic MDX expression and does not depend on the login name to be the user's name:

```
iif(
count(intersect(
descendants(
iif( hierarchize(exists([Employee].[Employees].members,
strtomember("[Employee].[login].[login].&["+username+"]")),
post).item(0).item(0).parent.datamember is

hierarchize(exists([Employee].[Employees].members,
strtomember("[Employee].[login].[login].&["+username+"]")), post).item(0).item(0),

hierarchize(exists([Employee].[Employees].members,
strtomember("[Employee].[login].[login].&["+username+"]")),
post).item(0).item(0).parent,

hierarchize(exists([Employee].[Employees].members,
strtomember("[Employee].[login].[login].&["+username+"]")), post).item(0).item(0))

).item(0)
, employee.employees.currentmember)) > 2    // Condition Check


 (count(employee.employees.currentmember.children) > 2
 and
 count(intersect(
descendants(
iif( hierarchize(exists([Employee].[Employees].members,
strtomember("[Employee].[login].[login].&["+username+"]")),
post).item(0).item(0).parent.datamember is

hierarchize(exists([Employee].[Employees].members,
strtomember("[Employee].[login].[login].&["+username+"]")), post).item(0).item(0),

hierarchize(exists([Employee].[Employees].members,
strtomember("[Employee].[login].[login].&["+username+"]")),
post).item(0).item(0).parent,

hierarchize(exists([Employee].[Employees].members,
strtomember("[Employee].[login].[login].&["+username+"]")), post).item(0).item(0))

).item(0)
, employee.employees.currentmember))

    > 0 ) or  (strcomp(employee.employees.currentmember.properties("login"),
username) =0),
 // Value 1
```

```
( count(intersect(
descendants(
iif( hierarchize(exists([Employee].[Employees].members,
strtomember("[Employee].[login].[login].&["+username+"]")),
post).item(0).item(0).parent.datamember is

hierarchize(exists([Employee].[Employees].members,
strtomember("[Employee].[login].[login].&["+username+"]")), post).item(0).item(0),

hierarchize(exists([Employee].[Employees].members,
strtomember("[Employee].[login].[login].&["+username+"]")),
post).item(0).item(0).parent,

hierarchize(exists([Employee].[Employees].members,
strtomember("[Employee].[login].[login].&["+username+"]")), post).item(0).item(0))

).item(0)
, employee.employees.currentmember))

    > 0 ) or (strcomp(employee.employees.currentmember.properties("login"),
username) =0)
) // Value 2
```

5.   Enter the preceding MDX expression to the Allow Reading of Cube Content pane in the Cell
      Security tab of the Roles editor.

Now, take a look at how this MDX expression helps to define the intended cell security. You can
break up the MDX expression into three different parts for easier understanding. First, the MDX
expression checks if the current user logged in is a manager. If the user is a manager with more than
two direct reports, then value 1 expression is evaluated. If the user is a regular employee, then value
2 expression is evaluated. This is done using the IIF statement. The following MDX expression
identifies if the current user is a manager with more than two direct reports:

```
count(intersect(
descendants(
// Check if current employee is a manager
iif( hierarchize(exists([Employee].[Employees].members,
strtomember("[Employee].[login].[login].&["+username+"]")),
post).item(0).item(0).parent.datamember is

hierarchize(exists([Employee].[Employees].members,
strtomember("[Employee].[login].[login].&["+username+"]")), post).item(0).item(0),
// End of check if current employee is manager

hierarchize(exists([Employee].[Employees].members,
strtomember("[Employee].[login].[login].&["+username+"]")),
post).item(0).item(0).parent,

hierarchize(exists([Employee].[Employees].members,
strtomember("[Employee].[login].[login].&["+username+"]")), post).item(0).item(0))
).item(0)
, employee.employee.currentmember)) > 2
```

The username function is used to retrieve the current user's login. With the help of the StrToMember function and appropriate string concatenation, the corresponding member in the Login hierarchy is identified. The MDX function Exists can identify the intersection of the Employee hierarchy with the member in the Login hierarchy for the current user. The result of the Exists function is a set that contains the employee's name and all his parents. To retrieve the employee's name, use the Hierarchize MDX function with the parameter Post so that all the members in the set are ordered in a hierarchical order so that the employee name is the first item in the set. Then retrieve the first item of the set using .ITEM(0).ITEM(0) to retrieve the employee's name. In a parent-child hierarchy, if a member is a parent and also has data values (manager having sales quotas), the same employee name is used to represent the real member as the one that has the aggregated values. However, these employee names will be at different levels in the parent-child hierarchy, which helps in distinguishing its own data value from the aggregated value for that member. This is shown in Figure 14-41 for the employee Rob Brown.

To check whether the current member is a manager, use the .parent.datamember function and compare it against another MDX expression that just gives the employee name. This MDX expression for evaluating if the current user is a manager is enclosed within comments in the preceding MDX expression.

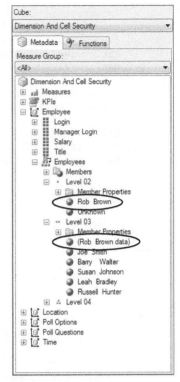

FIGURE 14-41

Based on the evaluation, the correct employee name is identified, and you check whether the employee has more than two direct reports using the MDX function Descendants.

After a member has been identified as a manager having more than two direct reports, the IIF function chooses the following expression as the expression for evaluation:

```
(count(employee.employees.currentmember.children) > 2  // Check 1
and
count(intersect(
descendants(
iif( hierarchize(exists([Employee].[Employees].members,
strtomember("[Employee].[login].[login].&["+username+"]")),
post).item(0).item(0).parent.datamember is

hierarchize(exists([Employee].[Employees].members,
strtomember("[Employee].[login].[login].&["+username+"]")), post).item(0).item(0),

hierarchize(exists([Employee].[Employees].members,
strtomember("[Employee].[login].[login].&["+username+"]")),
post).item(0).item(0).parent,

hierarchize(exists([Employee].[Employees].members,
strtomember("[Employee].[login].[login].&["+username+"]")),
```

```
post).item(0).item(0))).item(0)

, employee.employees.currentmember))
    > 0 )  // Check 2
or
(strcomp(employee.employees.currentmember.properties("login"),username) =0)//
Check 3
```

In this expression two checks are performed to give access to the cells for the employee. The first conditional check (Check 1 AND Check 2) is for providing access to the aggregated cell for the managers, which involves checking if the employee corresponding to the current cell has more than two direct reports followed by the second condition (Check 3), which is an OR condition to enable access to the cells of the employee. The second check (Check 3) is a simple check to match the employee with the login name because login is a member property for the employee attribute. The first condition has two conditional checks, Check 1 and Check 2, which are combined by a logical AND. By default, parent members can see the cell values of their descendants (Check 2). To make sure individual cell values are not seen by managers, rather just the aggregated cell values can be seen, the additional conditional check (Check 1) is done in the preceding expression.

If the first argument of the IIF function evaluates to false, the result of the third argument of the IIF function is the result of the function. The third argument is basically the MDX expression to enable regular employees or managers with less than or equal to two direct reports to see their individual responses of the poll.

You may have grasped the entire MDX cell security expression that solves the business problem by now. You can verify the results of your expression using the Cube Browser and choosing a specific user or by sending queries from SQL Server Management Studio as a specific user. Launch SQL Server Management Studio using the Run As command with the user Rob. Send the following query to an instance of Analysis Services:

```
SELECT [Measures].[Response] ON 0,
{DESCENDANTS([Employee].[Employees].[Level 02].&[1])}*
[Poll Options].[Value].MEMBERS ON 1
FROM [Dimension And Cell Security]
```

You will see results for the query with certain cell values showing #N/A, as shown in Figure 14-42.

If you click the cell with #N/A you see a message that the cell has been secured, as shown in Figure 14-43. You have now successfully solved the business problem of securing the poll results so that managers can see only the aggregated results if they have more than two direct reports.

Writing an MDX expression like the one shown in this example is not trivial. Even an expert MDX developer might make some mistakes. You should execute sections of your MDX expression as MDX queries or create MDX expressions as calculated members (especially where the MDX expression contains .currentmember), and then ensure the results of the MDX expressions are correct. After you validate your MDX expressions, you can successfully define cell security and verify that cell security is applied correctly.

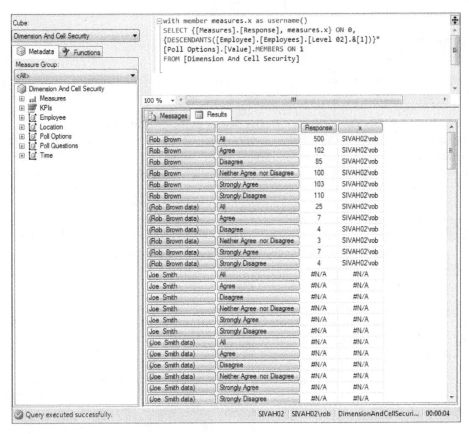

FIGURE 14-42

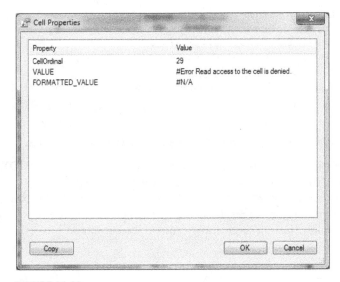

FIGURE 14-43

SUMMARY

Just because you're paranoid doesn't mean they're not out to get you! That should be your mantra as you ponder the possibilities in the security space. In this chapter, you have seen many possible approaches to keeping your data secure. You learned about applying permissions to your relational data sources to help keep them secure, and about how you can restrict access to data in your Analysis Services databases using one of two types of restriction: dimension security and cell security. You learned the techniques to apply dimension security, such as how to define roles and how to manage security in a dynamic business environment. Further, you learned about the relevant design choices and how you can implement them in a business scenario. Specifically, you learned five different approaches to secure dimension data using the user-role approach, the access-role approach, the member property approach, the security measure group approach, and the external function approach. You learned how to apply cell security to restrict data at the cell level for certain defined roles at your company using the poll results scenario. That technique can prevent members of the targeted roles from seeing confidential information. With all that information and the samples demonstrated in this chapter, you should have a good grasp of the techniques and challenges associated with security in SQL Server Analysis Services 2012. This chapter concludes the section on advanced topics for creating and deploying multidimensional BISM. In the next part of the book ("PowerPivot and Tabular BISM") you start with a chapter about building self-service business intelligence applications with PowerPivot for Excel and then create tabular BISM on an Analysis Services server.

PART IV
PowerPivot and Tabular BISM

15

Self-Service Business Intelligence and Introduction to PowerPivot

WHAT'S IN THIS CHAPTER?

➤   Reviewing SQL Server 2012

➤   Understanding self-service business intelligence

➤   Getting to know PowerPivot

➤   Looking at PowerPivot applications (Excel and SharePoint)

➤   Understanding the VertiPaq engine

Released as part of SQL Server 2008 R2, PowerPivot is Microsoft's entry into self-service business intelligence (SSBI). Although PowerPivot was built specifically for SSBI (more on this later in this chapter), as you read in future chapters, it is the cornerstone for the ability to easily shift from self-service to IT-managed (or corporate) BI. This enables IT to focus on 70% of the users and gives power users the ability to explore and understand the data surrounding the analysis. By integrating with Microsoft Office (specifically Excel and SharePoint), it provides users with friendly and familiar tools for deeper data exploration.

This chapter provides you with a clear idea of the "what and why" of PowerPivot. It provides an overview of PowerPivot, but not an exhaustive list of PowerPivot features. Most of the features available in PowerPivot are available while creating Tabular BISM, which you learn about in detail in subsequent chapters. For more information about PowerPivot, read *Professional Microsoft PowerPivot for Excel and SharePoint* (Wrox, 2010. ISBN: 978-0-470-58737-9).

SQL SERVER 2012

PowerPivot was originally included in the R2 release of SQL Server 2008 and it has been enhanced with SQL Server 2012. SQL Server 2012 includes major new functionality, such as the following:

➤ Greater uptime, better hardware utilization and productivity with new features such as SQL Server AlwaysOn and reduced OS patching with new support for Windows Server Core.

➤ Boost data warehousing queries up to 10x for star join type queries with the new Columnstore Index, and accelerate performance of I/O-intensive workloads by cutting data volumes by 50–60% with enhanced backup and data compression capabilities.

➤ Enhance organizational security and compliance through enrichments in encryption and certification controls. Better separation duties and expanded audit has made SQL Server the most secure of any of the major database platforms.

 For information about the strength of SQL Server's security record, read what the National Institute of Standards and Technology has to say about SQL Server from 2002–2010 at `http://itic-corp.com/blog/2010/09/sql-server-most-secure-database-oracle-least-secure-database-since-2002/`.

➤ Have peace of mind with your SQL Server system with more product enhancements, no-fee tools, a trusted partner ecosystem, and premier services.

➤ Empower end users with new insights through rapid data exploration and visualization with an enhanced PowerPivot, and amazing interactive data visualization with Power View.

➤ Enable users with SSBI while gaining better monitoring and management capabilities for IT using PowerPivot for SharePoint, ease of administration through SharePoint, and SQL Azure Reporting.

➤ Deliver credible consistent data to the right users across the organization with one single BI Semantic Model, seamlessly integrate data with Integration Services, cleanse data with Data Quality Services, and efficiently manage data through Master Data Services.

➤ Provide scalable analytics and data warehousing through options including optimized Fast Track configurations, functionality such as Remote BLOB Storage and scaling to 15,000 partitions, scaling OLAP to tens of terabytes, and Parallel Data Warehouse.

➤ Scale on Demand with flexible and hybrid deployment options from server to cloud, including features such as Contained Databases and SQL Azure Federations.

➤ Deploy prepackaged appliances and reference architectures in a matter of days.

Although SQL Server 2012 includes enhancements to PowerPivot and the underlying VertiPaq engine, it also includes many other enhancements to help you "extend any data, anywhere."

SELF-SERVICE BUSINESS INTELLIGENCE

As it is a relatively new paradigm, the definition of SSBI changes depending on whom you ask. It has yet to be around long enough to have an applied standard such as traditional BI, data warehousing, or OLTP. But there are some generally agreed upon principles and concepts based on traditional BI practices (often referred to as *Corporate BI*). The state of Corporate BI can be described as follows:

➤ To build your customized BI applications, you had to be a BI developer with highly specialized skills or have enough resources to hire one.

➤ After the BI application was built and deployed, it often was difficult to modify or update based on evolving customer requirements and business scenarios.

➤ If you were part of the systems engineering team responsible for BI applications, you most likely had to maintain every BI application with its own unique set of instructions — including configuration, deployment, operations, and maintenance.

➤ An analyst needing to use this data to make important business decisions often did so in an ad hoc fashion. Often it was in the form of spreadsheets and files mashed together in a haphazard fashion. The business domain knowledge was not maintained by IT but was locked away in the hidden formulas in the corporate ecosystem.

➤ Often this analytical data would be disconnected from the original source and hard to reproduce or reconnect.

➤ Even if the source were known, the data would often be replicated and modified based on some other person's requirements. Multiple copies of the same set of data would be available — the "true" analysis would become difficult or impossible to identify.

➤ No one would have control of these replicated copies, so there would be no way to ensure confidentiality and compliance of the data.

In the world of Microsoft's vision of SSBI — or managed self-service business intelligence in the form of PowerPivot:

➤ Anyone can easily build their own SSBI application using one of the most common and powerful analytics tools: Microsoft Excel.

➤ SSBI applications are easy to update and modify. This can be done by any authorized person, even if that person is not a BI application developer.

➤ Although there may be many PowerPivot applications, the deployment and management of these BI applications is the same to systems engineering. In addition, they now have a set of tools to track usage, administer security, and deploy new hardware in response to system needs.

➤ Refreshing your BI application is easy because your analytical data remains connected to its source, and the system can automatically refresh the application.

➤ You can easily share data through a web browser in a controlled fashion.

Microsoft's previous tagline for its BI products was "business intelligence for the masses." With PowerPivot, the tagline can now be expanded to "business intelligence for the masses, by the masses."

POWERPIVOT: MICROSOFT'S IMPLEMENTATION OF SSBI

PowerPivot is made up of two separate components:

> **PowerPivot for Excel:** This is an Excel add-in that enhances the capabilities of Excel by enabling business analysts and Excel power users to create and edit PowerPivot applications. This add-in helps integrate data from multiple data sources, enhance the model with simple BI semantics, and create a PowerPivot application using Excel and PowerPivot — all within the Excel workbook. PowerPivot for Excel, shipped with SQL Server 2012, supports Excel 2010.

> **PowerPivot for SharePoint:** PowerPivot for SharePoint extends Microsoft SharePoint to include the capabilities to share and manage the PowerPivot applications that are created with PowerPivot for Excel.

The next section describes what a PowerPivot application looks like.

PowerPivot Applications

You launch PowerPivot using the PowerPivot Window button in the PowerPivot ribbon. At first glance, PowerPivot applications look just like Excel workbooks. And that they are, but they also include something more — PowerPivot data and metadata embedded in the workbook itself. This enables a PowerPivot workbook to contain more functionality. For example, PowerPivot workbooks can contain tables that are much bigger than Excel tables. Excel tables (in Office 2010) can contain 1 million rows per Excel sheet. A PowerPivot workbook, shown in Figure 15-1, can contain tens or even hundreds of millions of rows of data.

The PowerPivot data within this workbook is composed of the previously noted tables. These tables can be joined together and then used as the source data for Excel PivotTables and PivotCharts for analysis and reporting.

PowerPivot applications can be shared among stakeholders, co-workers, management — anyone who wants to view or interact with them. To do this, you publish your PowerPivot workbook to Microsoft SharePoint. People can then browse and interact with your application using either the Excel client or a web browser. You can also set up PowerPivot to automatically refresh your application from the source data on a regular schedule.

To summarize, you can think of a PowerPivot application as an Excel workbook "on steroids." It gives you all the power of Excel, plus the greater analytical capability necessary to deliver true SSBI.

Now, take a look at the two components that make PowerPivot applications possible.

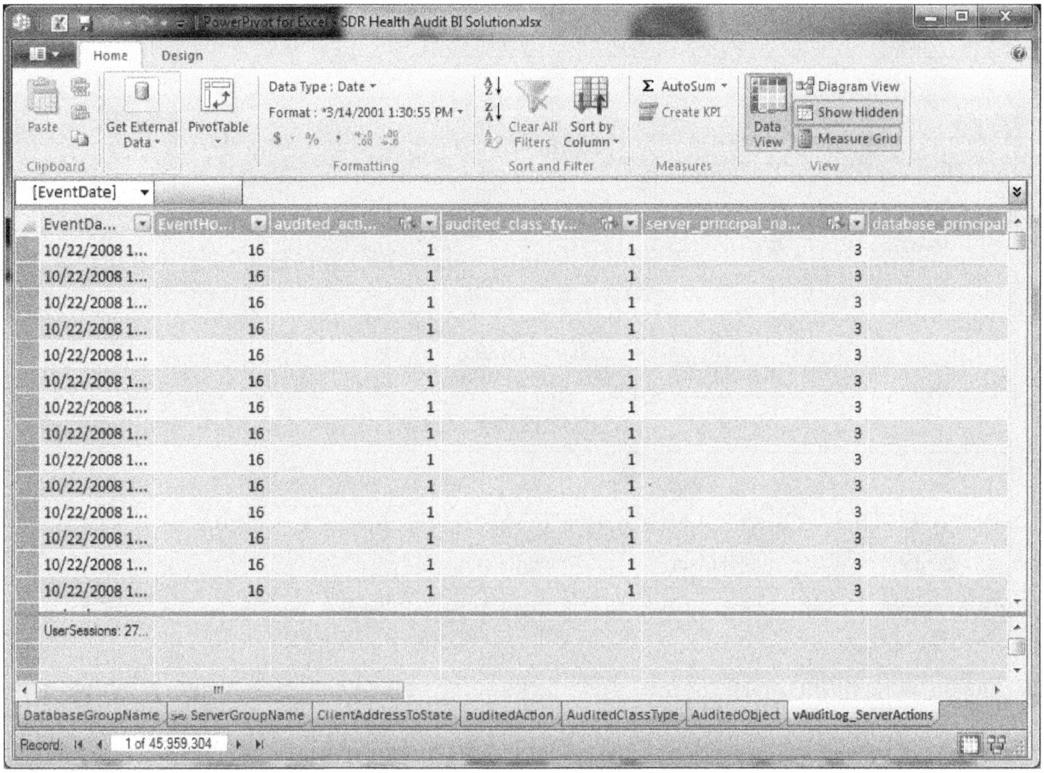

FIGURE 15-1

PowerPivot for Excel

PowerPivot for Excel is the tool you use to create and edit PowerPivot applications. One of the key benefits is its ability to make it easier to integrate disparate external data sources, auto-create (or assist-create) relationships, and augment with custom calculations so that you can perform even more powerful analysis using familiar PivotTables and PivotCharts. PowerPivot for Excel is implemented as a managed Excel add-in that provides the user interface for working with PowerPivot data. Figure 15-2 shows the architecture of PowerPivot for Excel.

Embedded within PowerPivot for Excel is the VertiPaq engine, a local, in-process version of the Analysis Services tabular engine or Analysis Services engine in VertiPaq mode (which is discussed later in this chapter). The PowerPivot for Excel add-in communicates with the VertiPaq engine via the traditional Analysis Services interfaces Analysis Management Objects (AMO) and ActiveX Data Objects Multi-Dimensional (ADOMD.NET). The add-in communicates with Excel via its object model using the Visual Studio Tools for Office (VSTO) managed interface. Excel communicates with the in-process VertiPaq engine via the Analysis Services OLE DB Provider.

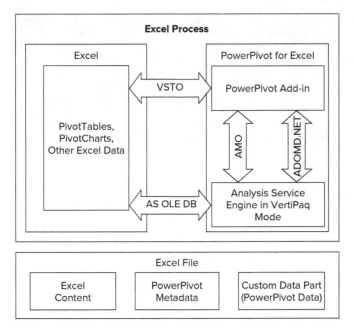

FIGURE 15-2

When you work with PowerPivot for Excel, the PowerPivot data resides in memory. But when you save your workbook, PowerPivot stores its data and metadata inside the Excel file. The in-memory database will be stored in a section of the file called the Custom Data Part (CDP). The writing of the CDP is done through a public interface in Excel 2010. It enables applications to write and retrieve their own data inside an Excel file.

PowerPivot for Excel can also store metadata and workbook settings in XML streams inside the Excel file. This saved metadata enables PowerPivot to attempt to reconstruct a workbook's data model if the CDP data becomes corrupted. If the structure is successfully recovered, you may refresh the workbook's external data and recover the contents of the workbook.

Altogether, the PowerPivot add-in and the VertiPaq engine work with Excel PivotTables and PivotCharts to provide powerful self-service BI analytics.

Microsoft makes it as easy as possible to start with PowerPivot, so it makes this part of PowerPivot available as a free download on the Web. PowerPivot for Excel has the following prerequisites:

➤ **.NET 4.0 SP1:** If you install on an older operating system such as Windows XP or Windows Vista, you need to install .NET 3.5 SP1. Install this before installing Office 2010.

➤ **Platform update for Windows Vista/Windows Server 2008:** PowerPivot for Excel requires this component if you run on the Windows Vista or Windows Server 2008 operating system. You can find more information about this prerequisite at http://support.microsoft.com/kb/971644.

> ➤ This component is installed via Windows Update; it is an important rather than a critical update. If you have set up Windows Update to install only critical updates, you may miss this.

➤ **Excel 2010 plus Office Shared Features:** PowerPivot for Excel requires Excel 2010. It cannot install on earlier versions of Excel. Also, the architecture of PowerPivot for Excel must match the architecture of Excel itself. If you have 32-bit Excel installed, you must install the 32-bit version of PowerPivot for Excel. If you have 64-bit Excel installed, you must install the 64-bit version of PowerPivot for Excel.

> ➤ When installing Office 2010, you must also install the Office Shared Features item along with Excel. This is because PowerPivot for Excel is a Visual Studio Tools for Office (VSTO) add-in and requires the VSTO runtime to work. Office Shared Features can install the VSTO runtime. If you install Excel without Office Shared Features, you must uninstall Excel and then reinstall including Office Shared Features.

➤ **Visual Studio 2010 Tools for Office Runtime:** PowerPivot for Excel relies on the updated Visual Studio 2010 Tools for Office.

➤ **Drivers for connecting to non-Microsoft data sources:** If you want to import data from data sources other than Microsoft data sources that are included with PowerPivot (such as HIVE/ Hadoop, Oracle, Teradata, or DB2), you must acquire and install those drivers and any related client components yourself. They are not included with PowerPivot for Excel.

The operating system requirements for PowerPivot for Excel are noted in the following table.

OPERATING SYSTEM	REQUIREMENT
Windows XP	SP3 or greater, 32-bit only
Windows Server 2003 R2	32-bit or WOW64 mode on 64-bit
Windows Vista	SP2 or greater
Windows Server 2008	SP2 or greater
Windows 7	No special requirements
Windows Server 2008 R2	No special requirements

Launch Excel upon installing the necessary prerequisites and PowerPivot for Excel. The first time you launch Excel after installing PowerPivot for Excel, you see a dialog asking for confirmation that you want to install the add-in; accept this dialog, and PowerPivot for Excel loads. The Excel toolbar now has one new tab called PowerPivot, as shown in Figure 15-3. This tab is your entry point into PowerPivot for Excel.

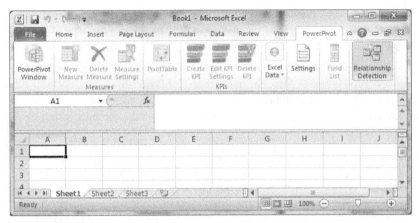

FIGURE 15-3

If you click the PowerPivot Window button on the left side of the ribbon, the PowerPivot window appears, as shown in Figure 15-4.

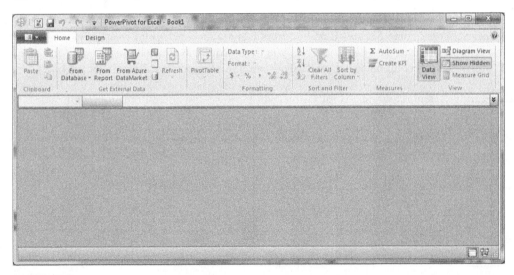

FIGURE 15-4

This is the window into your PowerPivot data, where you can import and work with analytical data in your PowerPivot application. It is here where you launch the Import Wizard, the tool that enables you to import data from various data sources. These data sources include the following:

➤ Various relational data sources including SQL Server, SQL Server Parallel Data Warehouse, Oracle, Teradata, and others where you can connect via OLE DB/ODBC (such as HIVE)

➤ Data from Analysis Services and other PowerPivot workbooks

➤ File-based data from Microsoft Access, Microsoft Excel, and delimited text files

➤ Data feeds, which are syndicated sources of data that can be updated in a manner similar to RSS or Atom, including SharePoint 2010 lists and SQL Server Reporting Services reports (for SQL Server 2008 R2 and SQL Server 2012)

Data recognized as tabular can be pasted directly from the Windows clipboard into PowerPivot as well. If the source of this pasted data is your Excel workbook table, you can link it so that subsequent changes to the Excel table result in the PowerPivot table being updated as well. Both pasted and linked tables require that the data you are referencing in Excel is in a table format (use the Format as Table option on your tables). Note that neither pasted nor linked tables can be updated (via data refresh) using PowerPivot for SharePoint.

 For more information on assembling data within PowerPivot, refer to Chapter 3 of Professional Microsoft PowerPivot for Excel and SharePoint.

Data imported into a PowerPivot workbook is stored inside the workbook itself (refer to Figure 15-2). PowerPivot can do this because of a new feature in Excel 2010 that enables external applications (such as Excel add-ins) to store custom data inside the Excel workbook. This is one of several reasons that PowerPivot requires Office 2010.

WHY POWERPIVOT REQUIRES OFFICE 2010

The requirement to use Office 2010 is based on the following specific features:

➤ **The capability to embed custom data inside an Excel 2010 workbook file:** This enables PowerPivot data to be included in the PowerPivot workbook, as noted in the blog post "For Excel PowerPivot, the database is IN the workbook" at `http://powerpivottwins.com/2009/11/07/for-excel-powerpivot-the-database-is-in-the-workbook/`.

➤ **Slicers:** Slicers are a new type of control in Excel 2010 that make it much easier to filter analytical data in PivotTables and PivotCharts. PowerPivot for Excel includes more enhancements to slicers than what is available in Excel without PowerPivot.

➤ **The shared service support in SharePoint 2010:** SharePoint 2010 has defined extensibility points that enable third-party applications to plug into the SharePoint infrastructure in a well-defined way that wasn't available in previous versions of SharePoint. In essence, it enables third-party applications to integrate with SharePoint in a way similar to how Excel Services or SharePoint Search integrate into SharePoint.

➤ **Specific events that PowerPivot listens to:** PowerPivot listens to specific events to ensure consistency of data between the field list in Excel and Excel data updates.

An important aspect of Office 2010 that PowerPivot benefits from is the availability of a 64-bit version. Because PowerPivot works with its data in memory, the increased memory address space available to a 64-bit application is a benefit when your analysis data is large.

After data is imported into PowerPivot, it appears in the PowerPivot window as tables, as shown in Figure 15-5.

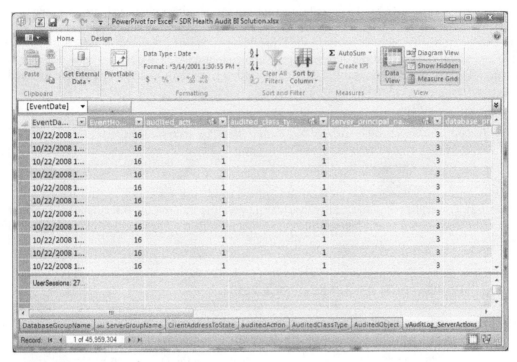

FIGURE 15-5

Tables in the PowerPivot window appear similar to worksheets in an Excel workbook, except that the former only shows the cells that include data. Also, every table has its own sheet. In PowerPivot, the basic unit you work with is the table.

Functional Differences between PowerPivot and Excel

The major functional differences between PowerPivot and Excel include:

➤ Automatically build (or easily build) relationships

➤ PowerPivot can handle larger volumes of data than Excel (and includes an optimized storage and retrieval mechanism for this data)

➤ Includes DAX language to manipulate data by columns

One of the more powerful usability features of PowerPivot is its ability to automatically discover relationships within PowerPivot tables (instead of using VLOOKUP in Excel). When a user drags and drops fields from the PowerPivot Field List, this automatically triggers an internal event to determine if there are any required relationships between the existing tables. For example, Figure 15-6 shows the domain_name field from the ServerPrincipalName table dropped into the Row Labels dialog. Because there are no existing relationships between the ServerPrincipalName table and other tables within the model, PowerPivot then informs the user that a relationship may be needed, as noted within the PowerPivot Field List.

Once the user clicks the Create button, PowerPivot itself will attempt to create a relationship between the ServerPrincipalName table and the other active tables within the model. Because the VertiPaq engine is an in-memory database, it becomes easier for PowerPivot to automatically detect relationships because all of the data is already available in memory. To determine if a relationship exists, it will not only look at the similarity of the column names, but more importantly it will also look at the similarity of the data within the columns. If it cannot find a relationship, the Relationship dialog will indicate that and you can manually create a relationship using the Manage Relationship dialog. If it is successful, as noted in Figure 15-7, the Relationship dialog will indicate the successful detection and creation of the relationship. The user needs only to click on Close (in the Relationship dialog) and the worksheet will automatically refresh, reflecting the new model relationship.

FIGURE 15-6

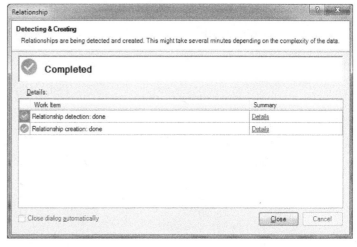

FIGURE 15-7

Another major difference between PowerPivot and Excel is the sheer amount of data that can be included in a single table. In later versions of Excel, the number of rows that can be included in a table was increased to 1 million. Although this may seem like a lot, in the BI world, a table with 1 million rows of data is considered relatively small. PowerPivot enables you to have tables that include tens or even hundreds of millions of rows of data. PowerPivot includes optimized storage and retrieval of data (as noted earlier in this chapter) to ensure fast performance against all this data. In subsequent chapters, we review the managed version of the VertiPaq engine (i.e. stand-alone Analysis Services tabular). With its partitioning feature, it can handle billions of rows of data.

Data Analysis eXpressions (DAX) is referenced in Chapters 18 and 19 of this book. This is a powerful functional language that, at its most basic, is a superset of the existing Excel macro functionality and/or calculated cells, with the primary difference being that DAX performs a calculation on an entire column as opposed to an individual cell. In addition to using DAX to define calculated measures, it can also be used to do simple transforms against the data stored within PowerPivot directly (i.e. calculated columns).

For more information on enriching data within PowerPivot, refer to Chapter 4 of Professional Microsoft PowerPivot for Excel and SharePoint.

NEW FEATURES IN POWERPIVOT V2

The following is a list of the new features included in PowerPivot V2 as part of the SQL Server 2012 release.

➤ Hierarchies

➤ KPI

➤ Drillthrough

➤ Measure grid

➤ Diagram view

➤ Measure formatting persisting

➤ Perspectives

➤ Date table and calculations

➤ DAX as a query language (not just calculated measures and columns)

➤ Multiple relationships

➤ Power View Reporting Properties

➤ Sort by other column

➤ BLOB support

➤ Change data type of calculated columns

Most of these features are covered in Chapters 16 or 17 in this book.

Because PowerPivot is a part of Excel, and PowerPivot workbooks are Excel workbooks, you can leverage all the capabilities of Excel itself to do your analysis and reporting. Features such as PivotTables, PivotCharts, named sets, conditional formatting, and others are all available as you work with PowerPivot data.

With all of the features just discussed working in concert with existing Excel functionality, PowerPivot provides the user with a powerful BI tool for self-service analysis. For example, Figure 15-8 is a screenshot of the SDR Healthcare Audit application. It includes usage of Excel conditional formatting and slicers (introduced in Excel 2010 as part of needed functionality for PowerPivot) against a 45-million-row data set. The slicers are particularly powerful in their ability to interact with multiple PivotTable and PivotChart objects on the same worksheet.

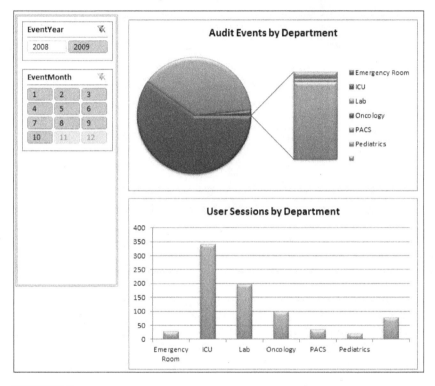

FIGURE 15-8

As noted in Figure 15-9, by clicking on the EventYear of 2008, in addition to the changes to the two audit charts, the values within the EventMonth slicers are reorganized and greyed out. The greyed out values represent the values that do not have any data in them.

 For more information on self-service analysis and the SDR Healthcare Audit application, refer to Chapter 5 of Professional Microsoft PowerPivot for Excel and SharePoint.

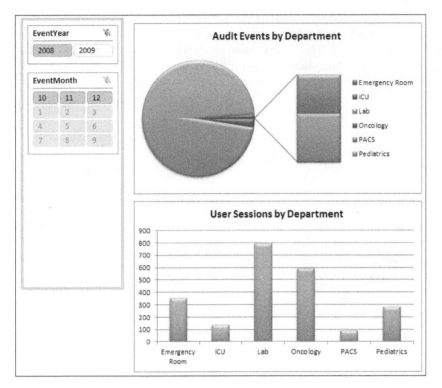

FIGURE 15-9

After you build your PowerPivot application and you're happy with the capabilities it gives you to analyze your data and present it in an insightful way, you probably want to share it with others. This is where PowerPivot for SharePoint comes in.

PowerPivot for SharePoint

PowerPivot for SharePoint installs on top of SharePoint 2010 and adds services and functionality to SharePoint to make PowerPivot workbooks first-class citizens of the SharePoint system. If you think of PowerPivot for Excel as the tool for creating and editing PowerPivot applications, PowerPivot for SharePoint is the tool that enables collaboration, sharing, and reporting. In addition, with Excel Services, PowerPivot for SharePoint provides a "thin-client" capability for PowerPivot applications.

Because of the nature of SharePoint itself, installing PowerPivot for SharePoint is more complex than installing PowerPivot for Excel. Chapter 21 presents these details. For now, take a high-level look at the parts of PowerPivot for SharePoint so that you can get an idea of what it looks like and what it does.

PowerPivot for SharePoint consists of two main components that give SharePoint the capability to host PowerPivot applications. These two components are the *PowerPivot System Service* (the *PowerPivot Service* for short) and the *Analysis Services Service in VertiPaq mode* (or the *Analysis*

Services Service). PowerPivot for SharePoint also includes a Web Service component that enables applications to connect to PowerPivot workbook data from outside the farm.

Figure 15-10 shows an overview of the components that make up the PowerPivot for SharePoint system.

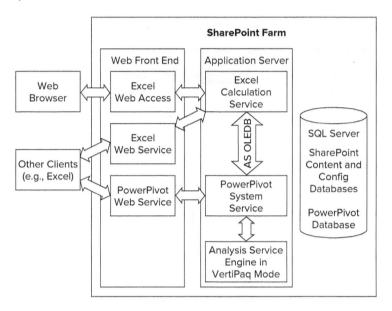

FIGURE 15-10

On the backend, PowerPivot for SharePoint includes one or more instances of the Analysis Services Service. These service instances are analogous to the traditional Analysis Services servers, although these services are under the control of the PowerPivot System Service. The PowerPivot System Service mediates the requests to load and work with the data in PowerPivot workbooks.

PowerPivot for SharePoint can load balance those requests among a pool of one or more Analysis Services Servers. If more requests come in than there are servers that can handle them, PowerPivot for SharePoint unloads the oldest unused workbooks in favor of the newest requests. When PowerPivot for SharePoint loads a workbook, it opens the workbook file (which, you will remember, contains the PowerPivot data store), extracts the PowerPivot data from the file, and sends it to an Analysis Services server that loads it as an in-memory analytical database. It also connects that server instance as an external data source to the corresponding published workbook. If more than one user requests a read-only copy of the same workbook, only one copy loads, and the multiple workbooks connect to that same single instance. This is just one of the ways that PowerPivot for SharePoint provides scalability for your SSBI applications.

To maintain state and metadata, PowerPivot can connect to a database on the SharePoint farm's SQL Server (refer to Figure 15-10).

PowerPivot for SharePoint also provides automatic data refresh from the source data of the workbook. Workbook owners can schedule this data refresh to happen at a periodic interval, or invoke a one-time refresh. When the time arrives to refresh the workbook, PowerPivot loads the data and tells the Analysis Services Service to reprocess it with the latest version of the source data. When the data refresh finishes, the workbook is saved so that the next time a user asks for the workbook, it contains up-to-date data. Figure 15-11 shows the web page that enables scheduling of automatic data refresh.

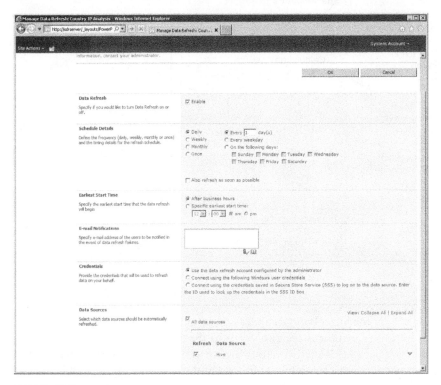

FIGURE 15-11

Although PowerPivot for SharePoint has a lot of moving parts, the goal was to make the management of it easy. To do that, PowerPivot for SharePoint does extensive logging to SharePoint's Unified Logging Services (ULS) log. Becoming proficient at understanding ULS logs can give you a leg up to successfully manage and administer PowerPivot for SharePoint. Chapter 21 provides more detail on this.

To simplify application management, the PowerPivot Management Dashboard (as shown in Figure 15-12) enables SharePoint administrators to understand usage patterns of PowerPivot applications that live in their SharePoint farm. For example, high usage of a particular application may indicate that it is ready to be built out into a full-blown corporate BI application. For more information, see Chapter 21 in this book, and the online white paper "Customizing the PowerPivot Management Dashboard," available at http://bit.ly/9C9yKd.

Another feature of PowerPivot for SharePoint is the *PowerPivot Gallery* providing richer views of the document library. Figure 15-13 shows the default view and Figure 15-14 shows the carousel view of the same gallery.

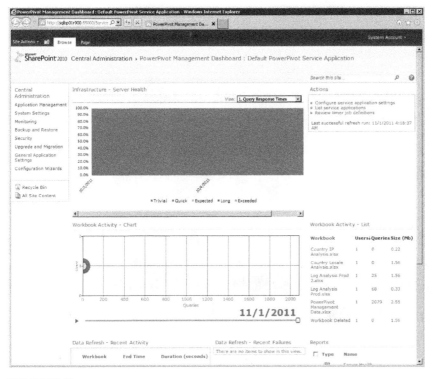

FIGURE 15-12

FIGURE 15-13

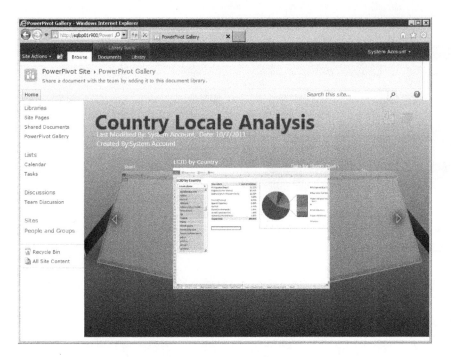

FIGURE 15-14

POWERPIVOT AND THE NEXT STAGE OF CORPORATE BI

What happens to corporate business intelligence (corporate BI) after PowerPivot? The short answer is, "Not much will change." PowerPivot was not designed to replace corporate BI. It was designed to add to it and bring the power of BI to people who don't have it today. It augments rather than replaces previous BI tools and techniques.

As you read the next chapters, you see how the *Analysis Services in VertiPaq mode* becomes *Analysis Services Tabular mode* as part of the SQL Server 2012 release. It is a stand-alone server that provides IT with the tools and development environment to maintain these tabular models. But because PowerPivot and Analysis Services Tabular mode use the same underlying VertiPaq engine, migration of your PowerPivot model to a stand-alone service is easy and straightforward. This allow for a clearer separation of duties between the IW/Analyst designing the business model and the DBA/Systems Engineer deploying, configuring, and maintaining the underlying IT infrastructure.

The Analysis Services Engine in VertiPaq Mode

A common component of both PowerPivot for Excel and PowerPivot for SharePoint is the *VertiPaq in-memory engine*. VertiPaq is actually a new mode of the Analysis Services server engine and has a number of innovative new features. Just as SSBI is an extension (not a replacement) of corporate BI (see the sidebar, "PowerPivot and the Next Stage of Corporate BI"), the Analysis Services engine in VertiPaq mode (or Analysis Services Tabular mode) is an extension of (rather than a replacement for) Analysis Services Multidimensional mode. Both modes are made up of two main components: the calculation engine and the storage engine.

The *calculation engine* is responsible for all calculations, including both *data analysis expressions (DAX)* language (for tabular mode) and *Multidimensional Expressions (MDX)* — primarily for multidimensional mode, although tabular understands and returns results for MDX queries. This allows traditional Analysis Services client applications (such as Excel) to work without modification against PowerPivot data.

The *storage engine* component of the Analysis Services engine is responsible for the importing of data from external data sources, as well as the efficient storage and retrieval of data in response to requests from the calculation engine. The key difference between the two modes is where the data is stored when it is operated on.

In multidimensional mode, the data is stored on disk. This is the traditional mode of most typical database engines. It made sense that this was the only mode of storage when RAM was expensive and disk storage was relatively cheap. Relying on the normal amount of RAM in a typical system to hold all the data in large databases wasn't feasible in those days, especially for analytical data, where analysis is usually based on calculations against large data sets.

In today's world, this is changing. RAM in large quantities has become cheap relative to where it was even just a few years ago. Now, having enough RAM to store large quantities of data in typical machines is much more feasible — especially when optimized compression algorithms are applied. When you can consider doing this, different capabilities become available. First, accessing data from RAM is much faster (orders of magnitude faster) than accessing data from disk. This allows higher performance when working with data than was possible before.

In the BI world, performance is king. Interacting with your data (that is, slicing and dicing in an ad-hoc manner as ideas flow and questions about the data arise) is a big part of the power of BI. Because of this, disk-based BI servers would do things like pre-aggregate data in anticipation of the way analysts would want to slice and dice it. If calculations could be done fast enough, though, all that pre-aggregation, with its attendant processing and storage requirements, would not be necessary. This is one of the big advantages of an engine that works with data in memory.

Although RAM has become much cheaper and more plentiful, it is still more costly than disk storage. And there is a limit on the amount of RAM that systems can have. Clearly, you still must be cognizant of the amount of RAM you need and optimize your usage of it.

Because of this, the tabular mode also includes patented compression technology that is made possible by implementing a *column-oriented store*. This means that, unlike traditional database storage engines that store data by rows, tabular mode stores data by columns. This allows much more effective compression of the data. VertiPaq compression rates depend on the nature of the data stored. Compression rates greater than 10:1 are common, but depend on the number of tables and columns, the data types, and the actual values.

Another goal of SSBI is to make building analytical applications much simpler than building analytical applications using corporate BI tools. With that in mind, the VertiPaq engine implements the new DAX expression language that allows SSBI practitioners to create calculations in a manner close to working with Excel formulas.

Although DAX expressions are designed to be similar to Excel formulas, they are different in a fundamental way. DAX is not designed to operate on single cells of data. It is designed to work on groups of data (such as tables and columns) simultaneously. This is key to the way that BI analysis is done. So, when you write a DAX expression for a calculated column of a table, that expression can apply to that entire column for every row in the table. You learn much more about DAX in later chapters of this book.

INSIDE POWERPIVOT

PowerPivot was born from two 2006 Think Week papers by Amir Netz, who was at that time the Microsoft Business Intelligence partner-level architect. (As of the writing of this book, Netz has been made a Microsoft Distinguished Engineer.)

Think Weeks were dedicated periods of time that Bill Gates, when he was head of Microsoft, would take to immerse himself in reading and thinking about new trends and concepts that could impact the future direction of Microsoft. Microsoft employees were encouraged to write papers that would be a part of Gates's Think Week reading. Compelling Think Week papers could lead to allocation of resources to make new products and technologies happen. With the papers that led to PowerPivot, this was the case.

The first paper was about the concept of a BI *sandbox* — a product that would allow much easier BI application creation in a defined and controlled space that would include a relational database, a multidimensional database, and a report generator. Although some of what was in that paper changed as PowerPivot grew (for example, the initial thought was that Microsoft Access would be the PowerPivot client), many of the ideas remain and at the core of PowerPivot today.

The second Think Week paper proposed an in-memory BI engine that took advantage of the emerging trends in computer hardware (such as falling RAM prices and multicore processors) that would allow such an in-memory engine to be both possible and practical. The capabilities that such an engine would make possible included some of the features in the previous paper.

Both papers were well received and a small incubation team was formed to explore the possibility of building a product incorporating the ideas in the papers. At the time, the project was called the Sandbox Project after the title of the first of the Think Week papers. This incubation team spent the second half of the SQL Server 2008 product cycle putting together specifications, designs, and plans under the code name Gemini. Toward the end of the 2008 product cycle, the go-ahead was given to turn the project into a product, and the rest is history.

SUMMARY

This chapter examined the attributes of SSBI and Microsoft's vision for SSBI. It discussed Microsoft's SSBI product, PowerPivot, and described its components and features, with an overview of the features in PowerPivot for Excel and PowerPivot for SharePoint. It also provided an example of using PowerPivot from end to end.

To take your BI model to the next stage, Chapter 16 discusses how you can use the VertiPaq engine technology by creating Analysis Services tabular projects. SQL Server 2012 also provides the functionality to import the PowerPivot model as an Analysis Services tabular project.

16

A First Look at Tabular BISM

WHAT'S IN THIS CHAPTER?

➤ Understanding BISM tabular mode

➤ Setting workspace and deployment servers

➤ Importing data into your tabular model

➤ Working with your model in the tabular designer

➤ Adding relationships and calculations to your model

➤ Browsing and deploying your tabular model

➤ Administering tabular instances in SSMS

In Chapter 1 you learned about the Microsoft Business Intelligence Semantic Model (BISM). You learned that it was made up of two components: multidimensional mode BISM and tabular mode BISM. Tabular mode BISM is a new business intelligence (BI) approach first implemented in the initial release of PowerPivot in SQL Server 2008 R2. Previous chapters discussed the details of many aspects of the multidimensional side of the Business Intelligence Semantic Model and Chapter 15 provided a brief overview of PowerPivot, including the new features in the SQL Server 2012 version. This chapter takes a first look at the tabular side of the Business Intelligence Semantic Model outside the scope of PowerPivot. This functionality is new in Analysis Services 2012.

After the Analysis Services team shipped Analysis Services 2008 R2 and PowerPivot, they started planning the next release of the product that would ship with SQL Server 2012. They received a lot of positive feedback on PowerPivot and started to think about how they could make the PowerPivot model available to corporate BI developers. Initially, the team wasn't sure about how to do that. They considered the different approaches they could take and boiled them down to two: 1) Continuing to evolve PowerPivot, in which case the development tool for tabular models would be Excel, or 2) Host the development environment in Visual Studio as they had done with the multidimensional approach.

After talking with several members of the BI developer community, the team found that the preference from customers was to provide tools hosted in Visual Studio to do development of tabular model BI applications. Reasons cited for preferring that approach included the following:

➤ Familiar user interface

➤ Support for developer-oriented features such as source code control support and the ability to include projects in Visual Studio solutions

➤ Not wanting to deal with the models inside Excel workbooks

The Analysis Services team listened to that feedback and implemented support for tabular projects in Visual Studio. In SQL Server 2012 you can work with tabular projects and databases using the same tools you know from the multidimensional world: SQL Server Data Tools (formerly known as Business Intelligence Development Studio) for development and SQL Server Management Studio for management tasks.

This chapter walks you through creating a simple tabular model based on the familiar AdventureWorksDW relational database. Chapter 17 goes into more advanced aspects of tabular projects.

TABULAR MODE PROJECTS IN SSDT

To build tabular projects, you need to have a tabular instance of Analysis Services to interact with while you build and work with your model. A single instance of Analysis Services cannot support both multidimensional and tabular modes. Also, there is no equivalent to the project mode as there is in the BISM multidimensional mode, where you can build your complete model without interacting at all with the Analysis Services instance. As such, the typical development model involves having a tabular instance of Analysis Services running on the same machine as your development environment. This instance is referred to as the workspace server. You can set your development environment to use a remote server as the workspace server, but because you interact with it frequently during the development process, it can be more efficient to have the workspace server be a local instance. On the other hand, if you have large data volumes that you need to work against when building your model, you can use a remote workspace server, albeit with some loss of performance in the modeling experience.

Setting Up a Tabular Instance of Analysis Services 2012

Installing a tabular instance is similar to installing a multidimensional instance, which is described in Chapter 2. The difference is that when you reach the Analysis Services Configuration page in the Setup Wizard, you need to change the Server Mode setting from the default of Multidimensional and Data Mining Mode to Tabular Mode, as shown in Figure 16-1. This causes SQL Server Setup to configure your Analysis Services instance to be a tabular mode instance.

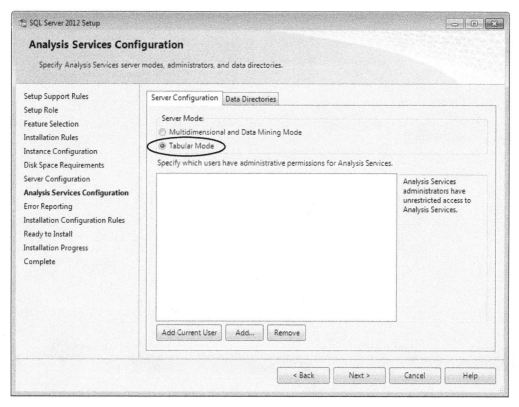

FIGURE 16-1

CREATING A TABULAR PROJECT USING SQL SERVER DATA TOOLS

When you have SQL Server Data Tools and a tabular mode instance of Analysis Services 2012 installed, you are ready to create your project. In Analysis Services 2012 there are three project types related to tabular mode (seen in Figure 16-2):

➤ **Import from Server (Tabular):** This project type creates a new tabular project by copying the metadata of an existing Analysis Services tabular database.

➤ **Import from PowerPivot:** This project type creates a new tabular project by copying the model from an existing PowerPivot workbook. To successfully import from a PowerPivot workbook, the Analysis Services workspace server instance service account must have access to the PowerPivot workbook. Also, if your workspace server is a remote server, only the model metadata will be imported. If your workspace server is a local instance, both data and metadata are imported.

➤ **Analysis Services Tabular Project:** This project type creates a new empty tabular project.

FIGURE 16-2

In this part of the book you create a new Analysis Services tabular project, building the model from scratch to learn how to create and use the features of tabular mode. Follow these steps to create a new Analysis Services tabular project.

1. From the SQL Server Data Tools main menu, select File ⇨ New ⇨ Project.

2. In the Installed Templates section of the New Project dialog, select Business Intelligence.

3. In the list of Business Intelligence project types, choose Analysis Services Tabular Project, as shown in Figure 16-2.

4. In the Name field, enter **AnalysisServicesTabularTutorial**.

5. In the Location field, enter the path of the directory where you want to create the project.

6. Click OK to create the project.

Workspace Server and Deployment Server

If the Analysis Services tools cannot find an existing workspace server, a dialog appears that enables you to enter a workspace server name, as shown in Figure 16-3.

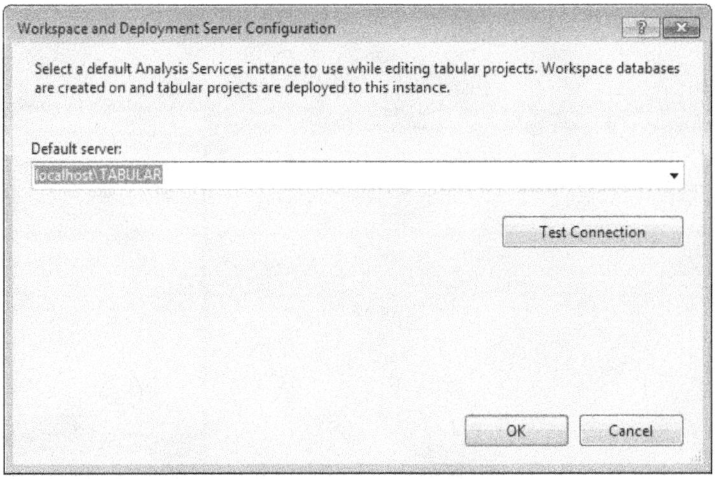

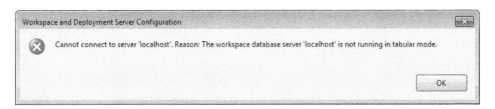

FIGURE 16-3

Enter the name of the Analysis Services tabular instance that you want to use as your workspace server into the Default Server field of the dialog. You can click the Test Connection button to make sure SSDT can connect to the instance you specify. This can be helpful also in confirming that the instance you choose is a tabular instance. If you choose an Analysis Services multidimensional instance and click the Test Connection button, you get an informative message telling you the server is not running in tabular mode, as shown in Figure 16-4.

Once you have selected your Analysis Services tabular instance, click the OK button to set the default workspace and deployment servers.

FIGURE 16-4

When you click OK, the default workspace server and deployment server settings are set to the server you specify. You can change both of these settings independently through the Tools ➪ Options dialog. These options are described in the "Modeling and Deploying" section later in this chapter.

Once you click OK and have a valid workspace server, SQL Server Data Tools (SSDT) creates a new empty tabular project and opens the blank model in the designer, as shown in Figure 16-5.

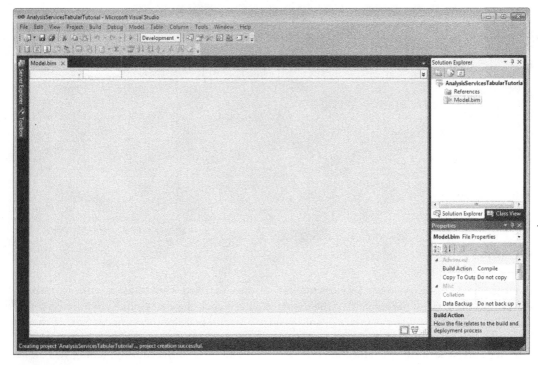

FIGURE 16-5

One thing to notice about tabular projects, in contrast to multidimensional projects, is apparent if you look at the Solution Explorer. Whereas multidimensional models contain one file for each major object in your project, tabular models store everything in a single file with the .bim extension. This is one clue that tabular models are much simpler than multidimensional models. You can also notice this simplicity as you build your initial tabular project in this and the following chapter. To start building your model, you need data to work with, so next you import the data that you build your model on top of.

IMPORTING DATA

The tabular mode supports importing data from various data sources. Almost anything you can import into a PowerPivot workbook can be imported into a tabular model. This includes data from relational data sources, Analysis Services databases, data feeds such as those from the Azure Data Market (which are not supported in multidimensional mode), and text files. One thing to note, however, is that certain non-server–based data source types, such as text files and Excel workbooks, can be problematic to update on the server compared to PowerPivot. You need to make sure that the proper drivers and other client components are available to the Analysis Services instance.

For this first tabular project, you import data from the same SQL Server database that you used for the multidimensional tutorial you started in Chapter 2. Follow these steps to import data from the AdventureWorksDW relational database into your model.

1. From the main menu select Model ➪ Import from Data Source. The Table Import Wizard appears.

2. In the list of data source types in the Connect to a Data Source page, select Microsoft SQL Server, and click Next.

3. In the Connect to a Microsoft SQL Server Database page, enter the name of the server with the AdventureWorksDW relational database in the Server Name field.

4. In the Database Name field's drop-down list, select AdventureWorksDW, and click Next.

   The Impersonation Information page appears. This page allows you to specify the credentials that will be used by the Analysis Services server to connect to the relational source database when it needs to refresh the source data.

5. Select Specific Windows username and password, and enter Windows logon credentials that have permissions to access the source database. Click Next.

6. In the Choose How to Import the Data page, choose the first selection, Select from a list of tables and views to choose the data to import. Click Next.

7. In the Select Tables and Views page, check the following tables:

   - ➤ DimCustomer
   - ➤ DimDate
   - ➤ DimProduct
   - ➤ DimProductCategory
   - ➤ DimProductSubcategory
   - ➤ FactInternetSales

   The tabular model differs from the traditional multidimensional model in several ways. One important and visible way is that the model is based on tables and relationships rather than facts and dimensions. For your tabular project, you need to give your imported tables friendly names that don't include the "Dim" and "Fact" prefixes.

8. Select the Friendly Name column, and remove the "Dim" and "Fact" prefixes from each table's friendly name, as shown in Figure 16-6, and click Finish to import the selected tables.

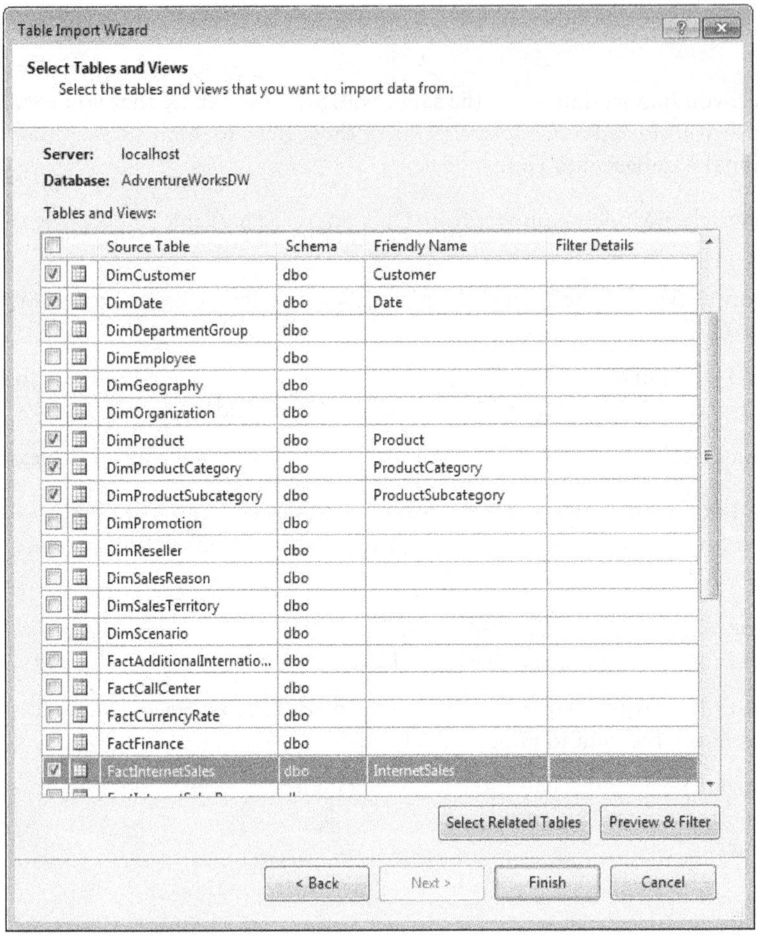

FIGURE 16-6

THE TABULAR DESIGNER

Now that your initial source data has been imported, you can start to build your model. Before you do that, though, take a look at some of the features of the tabular designer.

Figure 16-7 shows the tabular designer after the import completed. If you are familiar with PowerPivot for Excel, which you learned about in Chapter 15, you can notice that the tabular designer in SSDT looks similar. That's because the tabular designer is using the same components that PowerPivot for Excel uses, just hosted inside Visual Studio rather than Excel. Following are several advantages to this:

Tabular Designer Toolbar

Tabular Designer Menus

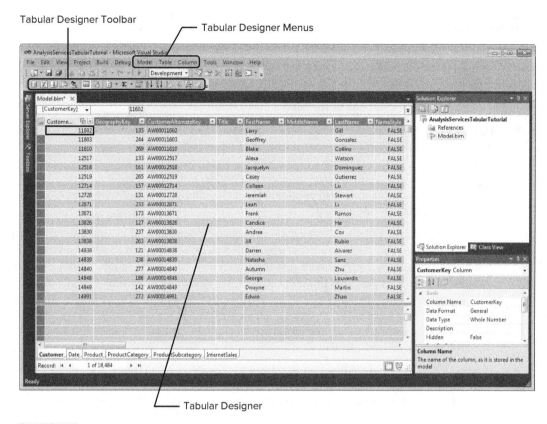

Tabular Designer

FIGURE 16-7

➤ A common modeling experience for both PowerPivot and SSDT. If you know how to work with tabular models in PowerPivot, you know how to work with tabular models in SSDT.

➤ Because the components are shared, any improvements made to the designer on either side can be immediately available in both places. This actually is the case in SQL Server 2012; some of the features added specifically for tabular models in SSDT, such as support for hierarchies and KPIs, show up in the new release of PowerPivot without needing to implement them in two places.

➤ From a standpoint of implementation by the Analysis Services team, they can put more effort into adding features to the designer rather than spending time implementing a totally new designer.

When the tabular designer is active, new menu items Model, Table, and Column appear in the main SSDT menu, and a tabular designer toolbar also appears (refer to Figure 16-7). Now explore the tabular designer menus to see what commands are available in the tabular designer.

The Model Menu

The Model menu contains commands that apply to the model that you are currently working on — that is, they apply to the whole project. Figure 16-8 shows the contents of the Model menu.

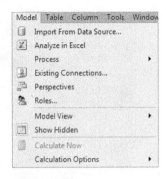

FIGURE 16-8

The following are brief descriptions of the Model menu commands:

➤ **Import From Data Source:** You just saw this command when you imported data into your model in the previous section. Generally, this is the first thing you do after you create your project. You can also use it to import data at any time. This command is also available from the tabular designer toolbar.

➤ **Analyze in Excel:** In addition to seeing your model as it appears in the tabular designer, it can be helpful to use your model in a client application to do actual analysis actions with it. This command opens Excel with a PivotTable connected to your tabular model. You need Excel installed on your computer for this command to work. Having PowerPivot installed is not a requirement and in Excel you will see your tabular model as an Analysis Services data source. (This means that, for example, even if you have PowerPivot installed, you will see the Excel PivotTable field list rather than the PowerPivot field list.) This command is also available from the tabular designer toolbar.

➤ **Process:** This command enables you to refresh the data and calculations in all or part of your model with the current contents of the source data. You can process the entire model, the currently selected table, or a single partition in the current table. This command is also available from the tabular designer toolbar.

➤ **Existing Connections:** This command brings up the Existing Connections dialog, which enables you to interact with all the data connections that are part of the model. From this dialog you can import more data from an existing connection, edit an existing connection's properties, refresh the source data for a single connection, or delete a connection. This command is also available from the tabular designer toolbar.

➤ **Perspectives:** This command brings up the Perspectives dialog, which enables you to add or change the perspectives defined in the model. You learn more about perspectives in tabular mode in Chapter 17. This command is also available from the tabular designer toolbar.

➤ **Roles:** This command brings up the Role Manager dialog that enables you to define and modify the roles in the model. You learn more about roles in tabular mode in Chapter 17. This command is also available from the tabular designer toolbar.

➤ **Model View:** The default view of a model in the tabular designer is Data View, where you can see a single table at a time and switch between them using tabs at the bottom of the designer window (refer to Figure 16-7). There is another view in the designer that can show you all the tables in your model and the relationships between them called the Diagram View, as shown in Figure 16-9. You can toggle between the two views using the two icons at the bottom right of the designer.

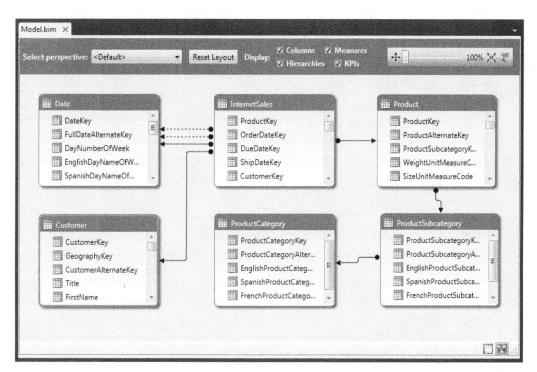

FIGURE 16-9

Diagram View doesn't show the actual data in the tables, but it allows you to visualize the entire model, showing all the tables and the relationships between them. Some operations are more intuitive in the Diagram view, and some can only be done using the Diagram View. For example, you can only create hierarchies in your tabular model using the Diagram View.

Diagram view allows you to choose which perspective to work with in the designer using the Select perspective drop-down in the toolbar at the top of the designer. There are also check boxes that enable you to choose which types of objects to view: Columns, Measures, Hierarchies, and/or KPIs. You see and use the Diagram View of the designer in Chapter 17.

➤ **Show Hidden:** This command toggles whether hidden elements are shown in the designer.

➤ **Calculation Options, Calculate Now:** These commands control the calculation mode of the designer. In automatic calculation mode, calculations are updated automatically whenever the data changes. This can have performance implications for large models. In automatic mode, the Calculate Now command is disabled.

You can use the Calculation Options menu item to change to manual calculation mode. In manual mode, the Calculate Now command is enabled, and calculations update only when you invoke the Calculate Now command.

Working with Tables in the Designer

Figure 16-10 shows the commands available from the Table menu at the top of the designer. Commands invoked from this menu affect the table that is currently selected in the designer.

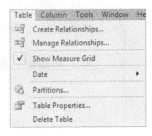

FIGURE 16-10

➤ **Create Relationships, Manage Relationships:** These commands enable you to work with relationships. You learn about relationships in tabular mode in the next section of this chapter.

➤ **Show Measure Grid:** This command toggles the display of the measure grid for the current table. You learn about measures and the measure grid later in this chapter. This command is also available from the tabular designer toolbar.

➤ **Date:** The two commands under this menu item enable you to mark the currently selected table as a date table. When a table is marked as a date table, special date filtering functionality in Excel is enabled on columns that are joined to the date table. In addition, marking your date table as a date table allows DAX time intelligence functions to work on columns of tables joined to the date table even if the join is not through a column of type datetime (this is a new feature in Analysis Services 2012).

➤ **Partitions:** This command brings up the Partition Manager dialog. You learn about partitions in tabular mode in Chapter 17. This command is also available from the tabular designer toolbar.

➤ **Table Properties:** This command invokes the Edit Table Properties dialog, which enables you to change the definition of the currently selected table.

➤ **Delete Table:** This command deletes the currently selected table.

In addition to the commands available on the Table menu at the top of the designer, you can also perform actions and set various properties on tables in your model from the context menu of the table's tab at the bottom of the designer and from the properties window.

Figure 16-11 shows the commands available when you right-click on the table's tab at the bottom of the designer.

Two of these commands, Delete and Show Measure Grid, are also available from the Table menu at the top of the designer. The other commands are described next.

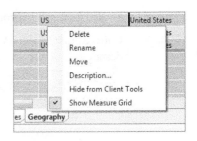

FIGURE 16-11

➤ **Rename:** This command lets you rename the table.

➤ **Move:** This command enables you to reorder the table's tab at the bottom of the designer.

➤ **Description:** This command invokes the Table Description dialog, which allows you to add a description for the table. The description of the table is available to client tools connecting to the tabular model.

➤ **Hide From Client Tools:** This command allows you to mark the table as hidden. This setting is available to client tools connecting to the model and can be used to indicate that client tools should not show the table to users.

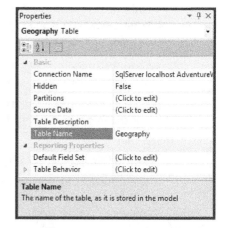

Other properties of tables can be viewed and edited in the Properties window of SSDT. To see these properties, click on the table's tab at the bottom of the designer window (in Data View) or select the table (in Diagram View). The properties of a table are shown in Figure 16-12.

FIGURE 16-12

➤ **Connection Name:** This property indicates the data source connection of the table. If you select this property and click the Ellipsis button at the far right of the property row you see the Edit Connection dialog (shown in Figure 16-13). In this dialog you can see and edit the properties of the connection.

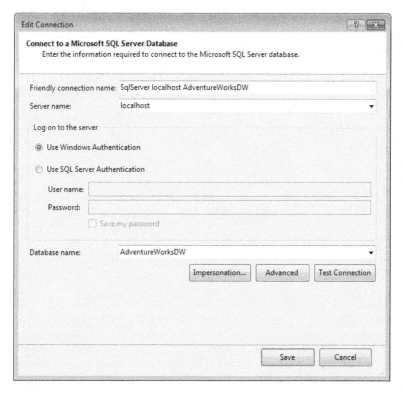

FIGURE 16-13

➤ **Hidden:** This property marks the table as hidden. It is the same property set by the Hide From Client Tools command in the context menu of the tables tab at the bottom of the designer.

➤ **Partitions:** This property enables you to work with the Partitions dialog. It is the same as selecting the Partitions command from the Table menu at the top of the designer.

➤ **Source Data:** This property enables you to work with the Edit Table Properties dialog. It is the same as selecting Table Properties from the Table menu at the top of the designer.

➤ **Table Description:** This property is the description of the table.

➤ **Table Name:** This property is the name of the table.

The two properties in the Reporting Properties section of the Properties window set values that affect how tables appear and behave in Power View reports. You learn more about working with tabular models in Power View in Chapters 23 and 24.

➤ **Default Field Set:** This property enables you to work with the Default Field Set dialog shown in Figure 16-14. The default field set is a collection of columns and measures that are automatically added to a Power View report when the table is selected in the Power View report field list.

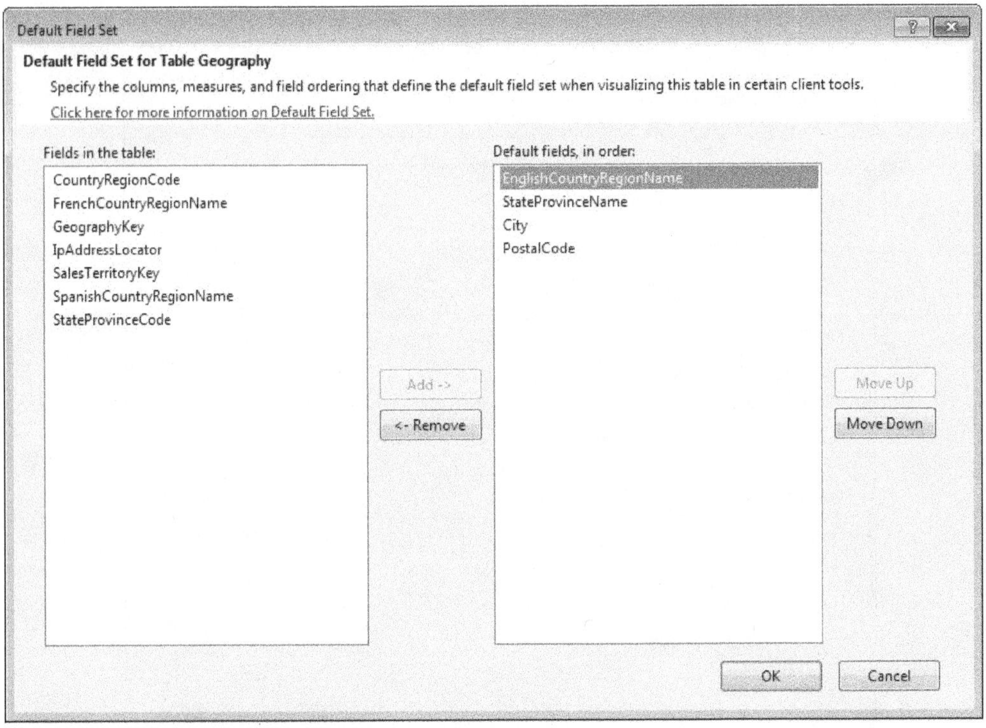

FIGURE 16-14

➤ **Table Behavior:** This property enables you to work with the Table Behavior dialog shown in Figure 16-15. The Table Behavior dialog allows you to set a number of properties that define the table behavior in Power View reports.

    ➤ **Row Identifier:** This field allows you to specify the single column in the table that will act as the unique identifier for the row. This setting affects grouping behavior in Power View reports. The data values in this column must be unique and they must not contain any null values. Also, the Row Identifier property cannot be set on tables marked as date tables. Setting this property will enable the other properties in the dialog.

    ➤ **Keep Unique Rows:** This field allows you to indicate columns in the table that should be treated as unique even if the values in the column contain duplicates. For example, you might have two different cities with the same name in a given country and you don't want their data values to be combined. Duplicate names in columns with this field set will appear multiple times in the report.

    ➤ **Default Label:** This field allows you to indicate a column that will be shown as the label in the navigation strip of the report.

    ➤ **Default Image:** This field allows you to indicate a column that contains or refers to an image that will appear in the navigation strip of a tile report or at the front of a card in the report.

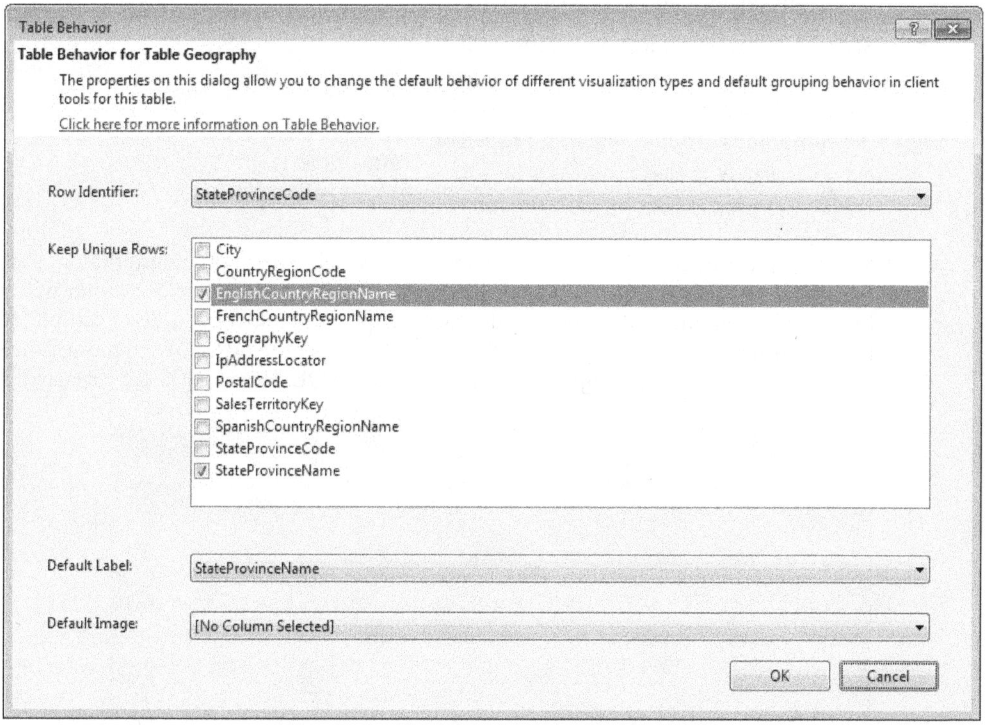

FIGURE 16-15

Working with Columns in the Designer

The Column menu at the top of the designer contains commands that pertain to a single selected column, as shown in Figure 16-16.

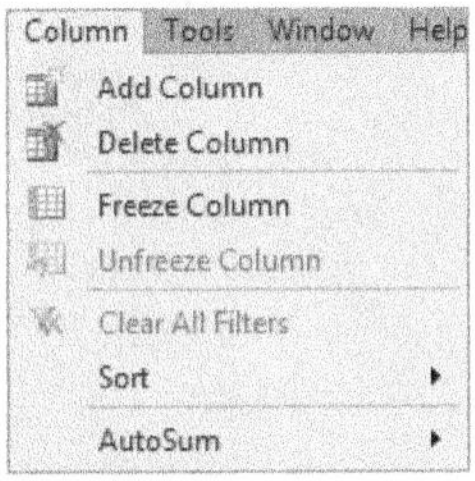

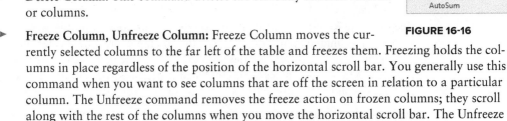

➤ **Add Column:** This command enables you to add a calculated column to the table. You learn about calculated columns later in this chapter.

➤ **Delete Column:** This command deletes the currently selected column or columns.

FIGURE 16-16

➤ **Freeze Column, Unfreeze Column:** Freeze Column moves the currently selected columns to the far left of the table and freezes them. Freezing holds the columns in place regardless of the position of the horizontal scroll bar. You generally use this command when you want to see columns that are off the screen in relation to a particular column. The Unfreeze command removes the freeze action on frozen columns; they scroll along with the rest of the columns when you move the horizontal scroll bar. The Unfreeze Column command does not move the columns back to their original positions.

➤ **Clear All Filters:** This command clears all existing filters on the currently selected column(s). This command is also available from the tabular designer toolbar.

➤ **Sort:** The Sort menu item contains various commands that affect sorting of the table as shown in Figure 16-17. Most of the commands on this submenu are self-explanatory. One that requires a bit more explanation is the Sort by Column item.

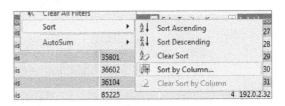

FIGURE 16-17

Selecting the Sort by Column menu item brings up the Sort by Column dialog, shown in Figure 16-18. This dialog allows you to specify that the values in the column will be ordered by the values in another column in the same table. This allows you, for example, to sort a column of month names by another column that contains the order of the months in a year. This was a highly requested feature not available in the SQL Server 2008 R2 release of PowerPivot.

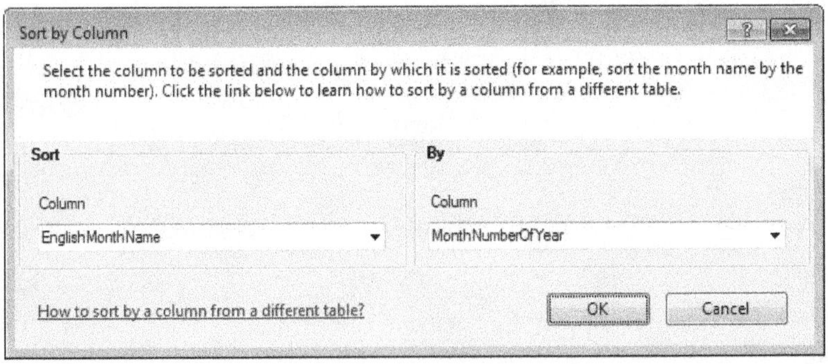

FIGURE 16-18

The commands under this menu item are also available from the tabular designer toolbar.

➤ **AutoSum:** AutoSum enables you to create a measure using common aggregation functions over the data in the currently selected column. AutoSum is covered later in this chapter in the Measures section. This command is also available from the tabular designer toolbar.

When working with your model in the tabular designer it can be helpful to sort and filter the data you are working with. You can sort and filter the data in a table based on data in a column by clicking on the button on the right side of the column header. This will show the sort and filter drop-down shown in Figure 16-19. In the drop-down you can choose a sort order and specify values that you can filter the table's data by. Note that settings in the drop-down affect the data as shown in the designer — they do not restrict data in the model itself.

Additional column-related commands are available in the designer's context menu when you right-click with a column selected (see Figure 16-20).

FIGURE 16-19

FIGURE 16-20

➤ **Create Relationship:** This menu item brings up the Create Relationship dialog. This dialog allows you to create relationships between the tables in your model. You learn about relationships in the tabular designer in the next section of this chapter.

➤ **Navigate to Related Table:** This menu item enables you to switch the active table to the table that contains the column that is related to this column with a relationship. This command only works from the "related lookup" side of the relationship.

➤ **Copy:** This menu item will copy the contents of the selected column into the Windows clipboard.

➤ **Insert Column:** Enables you to add a new calculated column at the position of the currently selected column.

➤ **Delete Columns:** Deletes the currently selected columns from the table.

➤ **Rename Column:** Enables you to rename the currently selected column.

➤ **Freeze Columns, Unfreeze All Columns:** These commands are the same as the Freeze Column and Unfreeze Column commands in the Column menu at the top of the designer.

➤ **Hide from Client Tools:** This command is similar to the Hide from Client Tools command you saw in the previous section of this chapter. The difference is that it operates on a single column instead of the entire table.

➤ **Column Width:** Enables you to specify the width of the currently selected column.

➤ **Filter:** This menu item has a subitem that enables you to remove any filters set on the currently selected column.

➤ **Description:** Brings up the Column Description dialog where you can specify a description for the column. The description of the column is available to client tools connecting to the tabular model.

Figure 16-21 shows the properties that are available in the properties window when a column is selected. In the Basic group, you see some properties (Column Name, Description, Hidden, Sort By Column) that you have learned about already. The remaining Basic properties are described now.

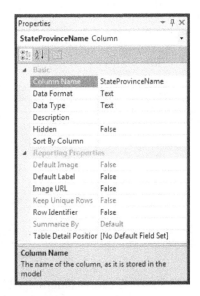

FIGURE 16-21

➤ **Data Type:** This property is the data type of the column. By default, the tabular designer will match the data type of the source data to the closest match among the data types supported by Analysis Services. In some cases, that might not be the best choice. For example, a column might have the data type Text in the source data, but you know that the column will only contain numbers. In that case you may want to change the data type of the column to a numeric type since you can get a performance improvement by doing so. If you choose the Currency data type, the Decimal Places and Show Thousands Separator properties will appear in the Properties window, enabling you to set how currency values will be displayed.

➤ **Data Format:** Each data type supported by Analysis Services has a set of formats that can be applied to it that determine how the values in the column will be displayed. This property allows you to view and change the format.

In the Reporting Properties section of the Properties window you can view and set the values of properties used by Power View to work with your tabular model.

➤ **Default Image:** Identifies the column as containing the image that represents each row in the table. The data type of the column must be one that can contain or refer to an image. Only one column in a table can have the Default Image property set to True.

➤ **Default Label:** Identifies the column as containing the defining label for each row in the table. Only one column in a table can have the Default Label property set to True.

➤ **Image URL:** Identifies the column as containing a URL that refers to an image file. Only Text columns can have this property set to True.

➤ **Keep Unique Rows:** The behavior of this property was described earlier in this chapter in the Keep Unique Rows bullet in the "Working with Tables in the Designer" section.

➤ **Row Identifier:** Identifies the column as the identity column for the table. Values in this column must be unique and cannot contain null values. Only one column in a table can have this property set to True.

➤ **Summarize By:** Enables you to set the default aggregation function for this column.

➤ **Table Detail Position:** If the column is a member of the Default Field Set (see the Default Field Set subsection of the "Working with Tables in the Designer" section earlier in this chapter), this property indicates the column's place in the order of the default field set.

After that overview of the Analysis Services tabular designer, you next look at various modeling actions available in the designer.

RELATIONSHIPS

The tabular model is relational as opposed to multidimensional in nature. This makes for a simpler modeling approach that involves tables and relationships rather than facts, dimensions, and cubes. The key to the power of the tabular model is relationships between tables. The Table Import Wizard understands the relationships present in the source data and creates relationships in your model based on the relationships defined in the source data. In addition, the tabular designer provides ways to add relationships.

If you work in the Data View, the designer indicates columns that participate in relationships with a glyph in the column header, as shown in Figure 16-22.

The diagram view provides a richer environment for working with relationships than the data view. You can see all the relationships in your model simultaneously. You can also work with them in a graphical way. For example, you can create relationships by dragging and dropping from one column to the other. Follow these instructions to add a new column to the model and manually create a relationship between it and an existing table.

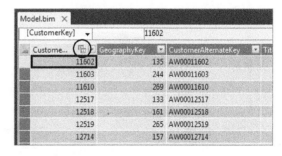

FIGURE 16-22

1. From the Model menu item, select Existing Connections. The Existing Connections dialog opens.

2. Click the Open button.

3. If a dialog appears asking for credentials, enter the credentials to re-open the connection to the relational data source. The Choose How to Import the Data page appears. Click Next.

4. In the Select Tables and Views page, select the DimGeography table. Rename the Friendly Name for the table to **Geography**.

5. Click Finish.

The Geography table is now added to the model, as shown in Figure 16-23. If you view the model in Diagram View, you can see the newly added table, and you can also see that it is not connected to any other table in the model.

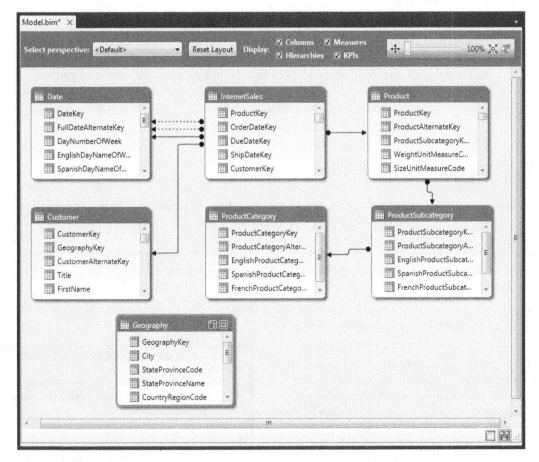

FIGURE 16-23

6. To create a relationship between the newly added Geography table and the Customer table, click and drag the GeographyKey field in the Customer table, and drop it onto the GeographyKey field in the Geography table as shown in Figure 16-24.

When you release the mouse, the designer creates a relationship between the two fields that you dragged and dropped.

Alternatively, you can use the Create Relationships dialog available from the Table menu.

Relationships are a key part of the tabular model. The calculations that you create with DAX can make use of relationships to allow calculations that involve columns in different tables. Understanding when and how to create relationships in your model can help you realize your goals in analyzing your business data.

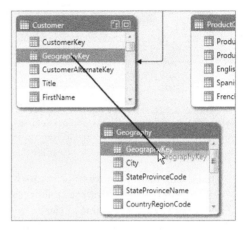

FIGURE 16-24

ADDING CALCULATIONS TO YOUR TABULAR MODEL

Another important tabular mode capability is the ability to create calculations using the Data Analysis eXpressions (DAX) query language in your model. DAX calculations can be added to your model in two ways. The first, calculated columns, allows you to add expressions that define a new column in an existing table. You can refer to columns in the same table in your calculation, and Analysis Services tabular can use the value of the column in the current row as the calculation being evaluated. Another way to add calculations to your model is through *measures*, which are calculations that are not done within the context of a table row. Rather, they are evaluated in the contents of the particular cell whose value they are being asked to provide.

You learn more details about DAX, calculated columns, and measures in Chapters 18 and 19. For this walkthrough, though, you see how to work with DAX in SSDT. To accomplish this, you add some simple calculated columns to your model in the next section and see how measures work along with the AutoSum function of the designer in the following section on measures.

Calculated Columns

Calculated columns come in handy when you need particular data values in your tables but those values are not in the data that you have imported. It could be that you want to format data to display in a certain way in your client application, or you may want to analyze a value that could be calculated from data values in the table; or you may need a calculated column for some other purpose. The following steps show how to add calculated columns into your model.

1. Switch to the Data View in the tabular designer, and select the Date table.

2. From the main menu, select Column ➪ Add Column.

The far-right column in the table grid is selected, and the formula bar (located above the table data) goes into editing mode, as shown in Figure 16-25.

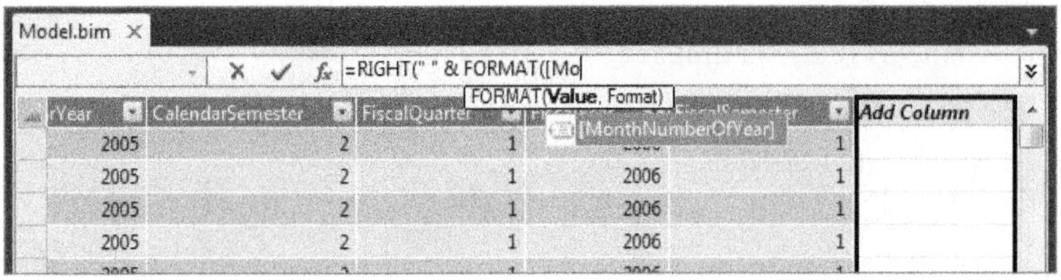

FIGURE 16-25

In editing mode, the formula bar provides help in the form of autocomplete, tooltips that show the arguments expected for the function you enter, and the ability to click on a column in the table to enter that table's name at the current point in the formula. In addition, you can click the Insert Function (*fx*) button at the left of the formula bar to select a DAX function name to insert into the formula.

3. Enter the following DAX expression and press Enter:

```
=RIGHT(" " & Format([MonthNumberOfYear],"#0"),2) & " - " & [EnglishMonthName]
```

4. Select the newly created column, right-click it, and select Rename column. Enter **DateHeader** for the new column name.

5. Select the Internet Sales table, and on the main menu select Column ⇨ Add Column.

6. Enter the following DAX expression as the definition of the new calculated column and press Enter:

```
=[SalesAmount] - [TotalProductCost]
```

7. Rename the new column to **Profit**.

You now know how to create calculated columns in the tabular designer. The columns you added are now available in client tools the same as any column that came from the source data. In this way calculated columns enable you to customize the data for your model beyond the data that you imported. This is a powerful capability of the tabular mode.

Measures

Measures, like calculated columns, are defined by a DAX expression. Unlike calculated columns they can't refer to a particular column as a value unless an aggregation function has been applied to the column name. The values for measures are calculated at the time they are evaluated in the context that the value is being asked for. You learn more about measures in the two DAX chapters, 18 and 19. For now the goal is to familiarize you with how you work with measures in the designer by using another feature of the tabular designer, AutoSum.

In the tabular designer, you work with measures in an area of the designer called the Measure Grid. The Measure Grid is the grid area below the splitter bar in the lower half of the Data View grid, as shown in Figure 16-26.

ShipDateKey	CustomerKey	PromotionKey	CurrencyKey	SalesTerritoryKey	SalesOrderNumber	SalesO
3	20070808	14870	1	100	4	SO51900
4	20070809	15319	1	100	4	SO51948
6	20070811	16384	1	100	4	SO52043
6	20070811	15476	1	100	4	SO52045
7	20070812	15861	1	100	4	SO52094
9	20070814	26017	1	100	4	SO52175
9	20070814	14761	1	100	4	SO52190
0	20070815	22038	1	100	4	SO52232
0	20070815	22163	1	100	4	SO52234
0	20070815	16018	1	100	4	SO52245
1	20070816	25839	1	100	4	SO52301
1	20070816	11260	1	100	4	SO52314
2	20070817	23695	1	100	4	SO52342
3	20070818	15198	1	100	4	SO52387
5	20070820	15414	1	100	4	SO52499
5	20070820	15469	1	100	4	SO52500
6	20070821	14901	1	100	4	SO52545
7	20070822	17369	1	100	4	SO52593
8	20070823	24930	1	100	4	SO52627

Customer | Date | Product | ProductCategory | ProductSubcategory | InternetSales | Geography

Record: 1 of 60,398

The Measure Grid

FIGURE 16-26

Follow these steps to create a measure in your model using the AutoSum feature.

1. In the Data View, select the InternetSales table to make it the active table.

2. If the measure grid is not visible, right-click the InternetSales tab to show the context menu, and select Show Measure Grid, as shown in Figure 16-27.

3. Select the SalesOrderNumber column.

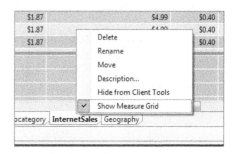

FIGURE 16-27

4. Click the right edge of the AutoSum button on the toolbar and select DistinctCount, as shown in Figure 16-28.

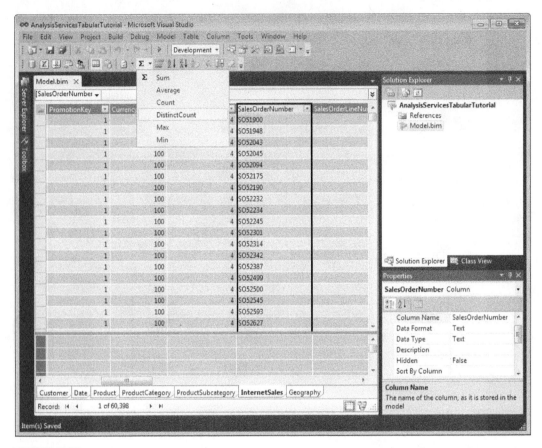

FIGURE 16-28

5. In the Properties window, change the Measure Name property to **DistinctSalesOrders**.

At this point, your newly created measure should appear as in Figure 16-29. With the measure selected in the Measure Grid, the formula bar shows the formula that defines the measure, but in the measure grid you see the value that the formula produces.

6. In the upper portion of the Data View, select the Sales Amount column of the Internet Sales table.

7. From the AutoSum button's drop-down, select Sum.

8. In the Properties window, change the newly created measure name from Sum of SalesAmount to **InternetSalesAmount**.

You have now used the AutoSum function to create two measures. As you learn more about DAX you can create your own DAX measures to do more sophisticated data analysis.

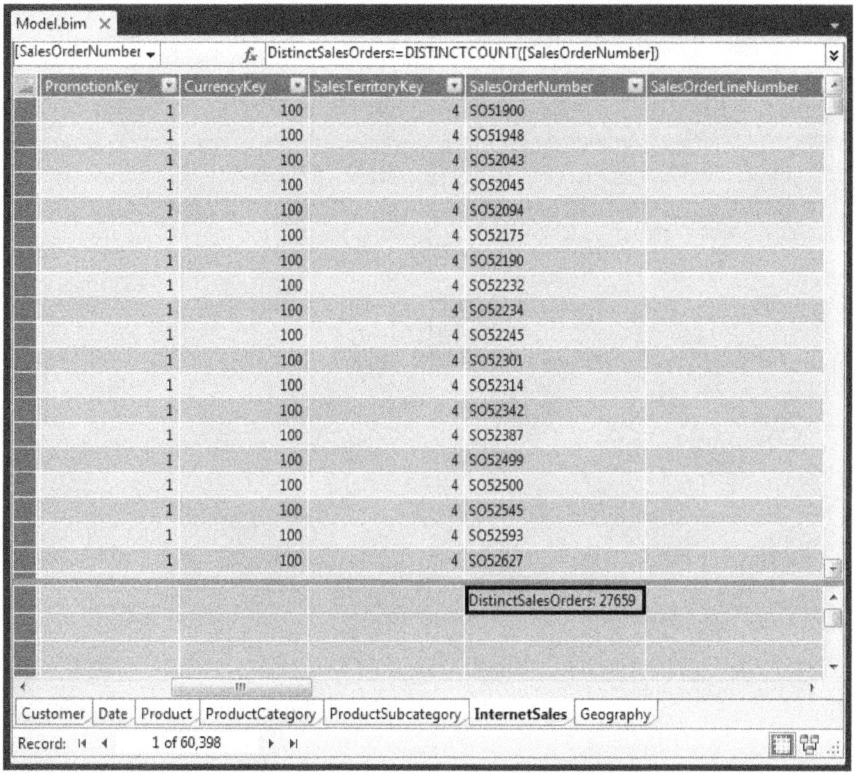

FIGURE 16-29

BROWSING THE MODEL

As you work with your tabular model, you may want to work with it in a client tool to verify your model. To accommodate that, the tabular designer has a command that allows you to open Excel with a PivotTable connected to your tabular model. Of course, it relies on Excel being installed on the computer that you build your model on. When you invoke the Analyze in Excel function, either from the Model menu or the tabular designer toolbar, you see a dialog, as shown in Figure 16-30, which enables you to set some parameters on how the model appears to Excel.

In this dialog you can browse the model as the current user, a specific Windows user (you will be asked to provide credentials), or as a particular role. (You learn about roles in tabular mode in the next chapter.) For now, select Current Windows User, and click OK. Figure 16-31 shows Excel opened with a PivotTable connected to the current model. The measures that you defined in the previous section are available as values for analysis.

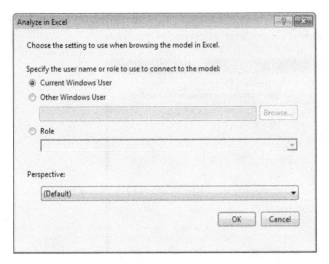

FIGURE 16-30

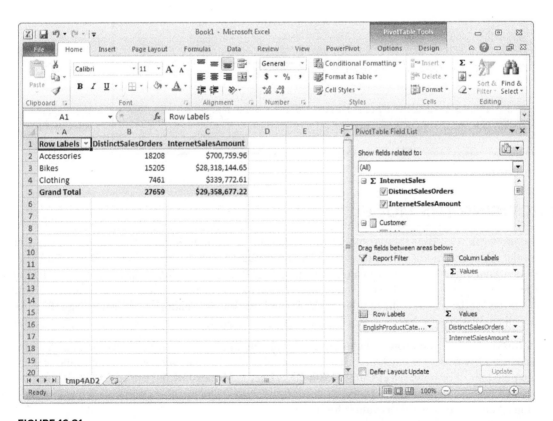

FIGURE 16-31

MODELING AND DEPLOYING

While you were working on your model, the tabular designer was talking to the workspace database. You can think of the workspace database as a private database backing the model while you work with it in SSDT.

You can set various properties of your workspace database in the SSDT Tools ⇨ Options ⇨ Analysis Services ⇨ Data Modeling page, as shown in Figure 16-32.

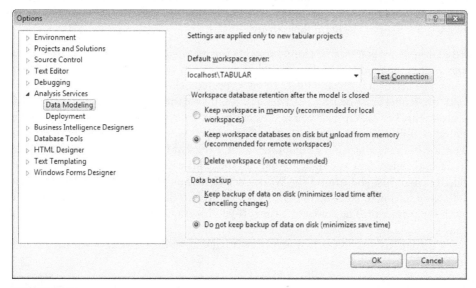

FIGURE 16-32

The Default workspace server setting is self-explanatory. It enables you to specify the Analysis Services instance that the designer uses to create the workspace database. This must be a tabular Analysis Services instance, or you get an error when you try to use it.

The Workspace database retention after the model is closed setting lets you specify what happens with the workspace database when you close the model. Following are three options:

➤ **Keep workspace in memory:** If you remember, the tabular model is built on the in-memory Vertipaq technology. This option keeps the Vertipaq database loaded after you close the model. The advantage is that when you reopen the model you are ready to go as soon as possible. The downside is that your model consumes memory when you are not using it. Use this option if sufficient memory is available and you work with the database frequently.

➤ **Keep workspace database on disk but unload from memory:** This option detaches the database from the workspace database server but keeps the detached data in a file on disk. When you open the model again with this setting, you must pay the time cost of re-attaching the database and loading it into memory. Use this option if you work on the model periodically and you don't want to pay the price in memory to keep the workspace database loaded.

➤ **Delete workspace:** This option does not store the contents of the workspace database anywhere when you close your model. The downside of this approach is that the database must be re-created when you want to open it up to work on it again. For large models, re-creating the database can be expensive. This option is not generally recommended, but it could be a last resort if both memory and disk are at a premium and you don't mind waiting for the database to be re-created when you open your model.

The last option you can set in the Tools ➪ Options ➪ Analysis Services ➪ Data Modeling page is the Data backup setting. This setting determines whether a database backup is taken on project close and that backup is restored on project open or not. Some background on the internals of how tabular projects work is necessary to explain this setting.

The .bim file that you see in Solution Explorer contains the *metadata* of the tabular model. It does not contain the *data* in the model. The data is held in memory by the server and is modified by the modeling actions you perform in the designer. To get expected behavior in your project, the metadata and data of the model must be in sync. This will usually be the case but they can get out of sync in some situations. For example, if you make changes in your model and then close without saving, the metadata will reflect the state of the project when it was last saved. The data, however, will reflect the state of the last modeling commands that were sent to the server. If you reopen the project in this case, the metadata and data are out of sync. This can lead to cryptic error messages and confusion. To avoid this, you can set the Workspace Retention setting to delete the workspace and the Data Backup setting to back up to disk. Now, on project close, the data will be backed up and in sync with the metadata. The tradeoff is time. If you have a large amount of data in your database the amount of time taken for backup and restore may be prohibitively expensive and you may want to not back up data to disk. Note that you cannot back up to disk if your workspace database is on a remote server.

After you have your model to the point where you want to share it with others and allow them to connect to it and use it to do their data analysis, you deploy it. Usually you deploy it to a server that isn't the local machine. You can specify the deployment server in the Tools ➪ Options ➪ Analysis Services ➪ Deployment page. This is a simpler page than the Data Modeling page. Only one setting is possible: the Default Deployment Server. There is also a button that lets you test the connection to make sure SSDT can talk to it.

These settings in the Tools ➪ Options dialog pages set the default values for these properties. You can override these defaults for a specific project by setting properties in the project. To set the deployment server properties for a project, right-click the project node in Solution Explorer and select Properties on the context menu. Here, you can set the deployment server the project uses.

To change the workspace server and related properties used by the designer, select the .bim file node in Solution Explorer, and look at the properties window. You can see the workspace database property value and view and set the Data Backup property, the Workspace Retention property, and the Workspace Server property, as shown in Figure 16-33.

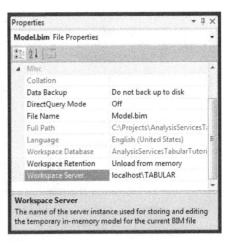

FIGURE 16-33

ADMINISTERING YOUR TABULAR MODEL USING SSMS

You can use SQL Server Management Studio (SSMS) to administer Analysis Services tabular instances. In SQL Server 2012, SSMS recognizes tabular instances and shows tabular databases differently than multidimensional databases in Object Explorer as seen in Figure 16-34.

Tabular databases only have three different object types in SSMS: Connections, Tables, and Roles.

If you click on the Databases folder, you see the commands shown in Figure 16-35.

You can use these commands to perform normal administrative tasks on your tabular server, such as restore a database from a backup file, attach a detached database, and synchronize the data and metadata of two databases on different servers. These commands are similar to the ones you use to administer multidimensional Analysis Services databases.

At the individual database level, you can use SSMS to perform normal administrative tasks on your specific tabular databases, such as Process, Backup, and Detach, as shown in Figure 16-36. Some of the commands available from the Databases node of the Object Explorer, such as attach and restore, are also available on this menu.

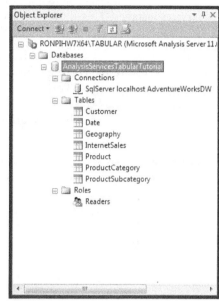

FIGURE 16-34

FIGURE 16-35

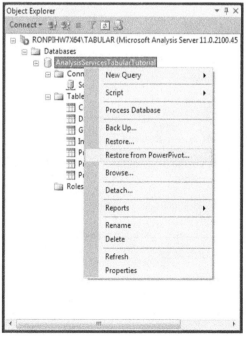

FIGURE 16-36

One interesting command available on both nodes' context menus is Restore from PowerPivot. This command allows you to take a PowerPivot workbook and deploy it to a tabular Analysis Services instance. This allows scenarios such as scaling up an organization's popular PowerPivot workbook into a tabular model that lives on a server.

When you restore from a PowerPivot workbook, Analysis Services will extract the model embedded in the workbook and create a tabular model based on it. This is very similar to what happens when you use the Import from PowerPivot project type in SSDT, as you saw in the "Creating a Tabular Project Using SQL Server Data Tools" section earlier in this chapter. The same caveat applies here with respect to the workbook location: the Analysis Services tabular instance's service account must be able to access the PowerPivot workbook.

Connection objects allow you to script and refresh connections to external data sources in the database. You can also view the properties of a connection as shown in Figure 16-37.

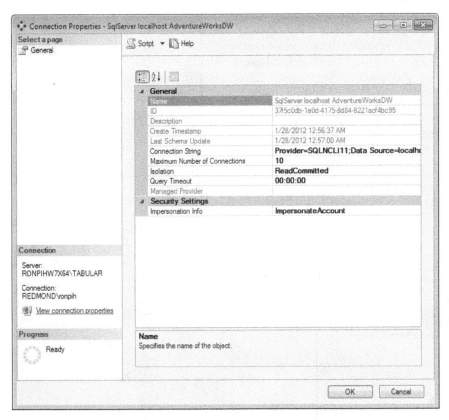

FIGURE 16-37

Actions available from table objects in SSMS include sending processing commands and working with partitions. The Process Table(s) menu item brings up the Process Table(s) dialog (see Figure 16-38) that enables you to process one or more tables in the tabular database. The Partitions menu item brings up the Partitions dialog that allows you to work with the partitions in your table. Working with partitions will be covered in detail in the next chapter.

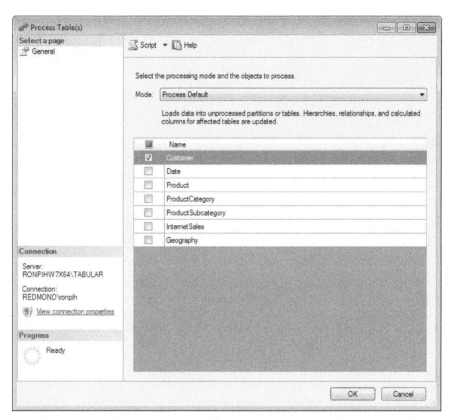

FIGURE 16-38

The Roles folder allows you to add new roles to a tabular database. Inside the folder you can see all the roles already defined for the database. You can modify existing Role objects by right-clicking on the role and selecting properties. This shows the Role Properties dialog, shown in Figure 16-39. Roles and security in tabular projects are discussed in the next chapter.

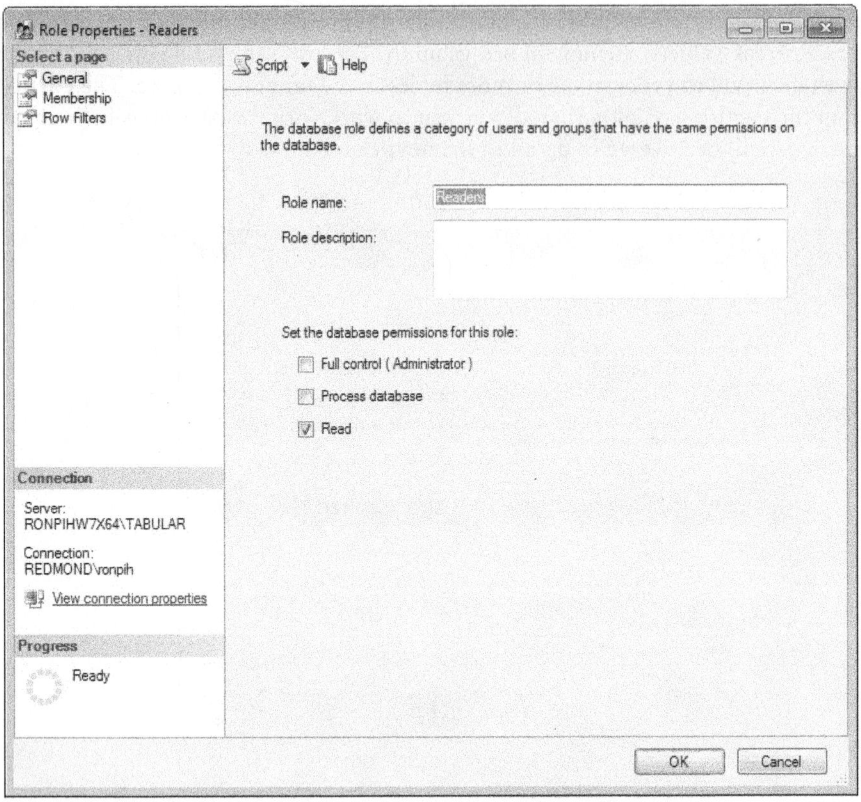

FIGURE 16-39

SUMMARY

In this chapter you got your first taste of working with an Analysis Services tabular model. You learned about all the commands available in the tabular designer and the two main model views: Data View and Diagram View. You walked through a simple scenario that showed the main components that make up a tabular model and saw how to administer your tabular instance using SSMS.

In Chapter 17 you learn more about the advanced features of the tabular model. You learn how to enhance your tabular models with new features that were highly requested in SQL Server 2008 R2 PowerPivot, including Heriarchies, KPIs, and Row-level Security. You learn about how to work with Perspectives, a helpful feature that allows you to view and work with a subset of the objects in your tabular model. You also learn how to work with Partitions, which help in updating really large tables, and Direct Query mode, which allows your model to query data directly from the underlying source data for results that include the most current data available. Chapters 18 and 19 are about DAX, the query language of the tabular mode. Exciting stuff!

17

Enhancing Your Tabular BISM

WHAT'S IN THIS CHAPTER?

- ➤ Sourcing data for your model
- ➤ Understanding operations to enhance your model
- ➤ Enhancing with hierarchies and parent/child hierarchies
- ➤ Enhancing measures with distinct count and semi-additive measures
- ➤ Creating KPIs
- ➤ Creating perspectives
- ➤ Creating partitions
- ➤ Creating and applying security roles

In Chapter 16, you learned how to create a simple tabular project using the developer IDE Visual Studio 2010. This chapter walks you through the more advanced aspects of tabular projects; you enhance the tabular project you created in Chapter 16.

SOURCING DATA FOR YOUR MODEL

The Analysis Services tabular model supports working with a diverse range of data sources through the use of installed providers. Many common data sources such as SQL Server, Oracle, Teradata, Informix, Sybase, IBM DB2, and other ODBC-compliant databases are supported using the appropriate provider. In fact, the tabular model not only supports all of the same sources as the multidimensional model, but it supports additional sources which were previously not supported.

Common sources of data that are supported by the tabular model include:

➤ Text files

➤ Microsoft Excel spreadsheets

➤ Microsoft Access databases

➤ OData feeds (Reporting Services, Azure DataMarket, other)

➤ Analysis Services cubes

These new sources of data provide the tabular model with a robust set of options for pulling data together without the need to preload the data into a SQL Server or other relational database.

REFINING YOUR TABULAR MODEL

While a simple model like the one created in Chapter 16 may suit your business needs, many times you will find it is necessary to either change or refine the model to make it more accessible or to address a new requirement. The truth is that change is inevitable. This section walks you through the steps necessary to change or refine your model.

Changing the Model

As business requirements evolve it can become necessary to add, update, delete, or sometimes hide tables, columns, and measures within the tabular model. Making these types of model changes boils down to adding a new data source or modifying an existing data source, updating the table properties, or deleting or hiding the object from the Diagram Model View.

Adding a New Table

To create a new table within a tabular model, you need to either add a new data source or modify one of the existing data sources. This section walks you through modifying the existing connection to add a new table that will be used later in this chapter.

1. From the Model menu, select Existing Connections (Model ➾ Existing Connections...).

2. Select the AdventureWorksDW connection and click Open.

3. Choose the Write a query that will specify the data to import option and click the Next button.

4. Change the Friendly Query Name to Model Measures and use the following SQL Statement as the source select, as shown in Figure 17-1:

   ```
   SELECT 0 AS NullColumn
   ```

5. Click Finish to add the new table and then click Close. Don't forget to save your model.

FIGURE 17-1

Modifying an Existing Table

Occasionally it can be necessary to modify the column set of a table within the model. To modify an existing table, you edit the properties of the table by either altering the selected columns from the source or modifying the underlying SQL statement. In the following steps, you modify an existing table within the model.

1. Starting from the Model Diagram View (Model ➪ Model View ➪ Diagram View), select the Employee table.

2. From the Table menu, select the Table Properties option (Table ➪ Table Properties...).

3. Change the Edit Table Properties to use the Query Editor by changing the Switch to prompt to Query Editor.

4. Update the SQL Statement as shown in Figure 17-2 by adding the following column definition to the existing statement:

```
[dbo].[DimEmployee].[FirstName] + ' ' + [dbo].[DimEmployee].[LastName] AS FullName
```

5. Click Validate to ensure the new statement is valid and then OK to finish modifying the table. Save the model when you have finished.

FIGURE 17-2

Hiding and Deleting Tables, Columns, and Measures

In cases where foreign key columns are needed for relationships between tables, it is often desirable to hide the foreign key column from the client to force the use of a hierarchy. Many other scenarios exist as well in which a column should be present in the model but not available to the client. Handling this situation within the tabular model is accomplished using the Hide from Client Tools function.

The Hide from Client Tools function can be used on tables, columns, and measures and is accessible by right-clicking the model object and choosing the Hide from Client Tools option.

In the same manner which tables, columns, and measures are hidden, you can also clean up unwanted objects within the model by removing them. From either model view, with the object selected, right-click on the object you wish to remove and select the Delete option. You will be prompted to confirm your choice before the model is affected. Note that when removing tables, any associated measures will also be removed.

Creating a Date Table

A prerequisite for not only using the DAX time intelligence function but also for getting the expected behavior when working with your model using either Microsoft Excel or PowerPivot is a correctly configured date table. The following steps walk you through creating and configuring a date table for your tabular model.

1. Start by adding the date table to the tabular model as described earlier in this chapter. For this exercise you add a second copy of the DimDate table using a unique friendly name to differentiate it.

2. With your new date table selected, click the Table menu. Next select the Date option and then choose the Mark as Date Table option.

3. You will be prompted to choose the column that represents the unique key for the table. This unique key will be used when building relationships. If you used the DimDate table, select the DateKey column and click OK to configure the table as a date table. Save your model when complete.

Creating and Managing Relationships

Although relationships were covered in Chapter 16, be aware that relationships can be created and managed from the Diagram Model View (Model ⇨ Model View ⇨ Diagram View). Creating a new relationship is as simple as dragging a column from its table to its related column. If a relationship is created incorrectly, you can also edit the relationship mapping by right-clicking the relationship arrow and choosing Edit Relationship. Likewise, if you wish to disable a relationship, you can make it inactive by choosing the Make Inactive option.

Column Operations

The Analysis Services tabular model allows you to perform common operations such as filtering and sorting column operations, which helps during the course of data analysis. You can also configure additional column operations like controlling how a column is summarized in client tools and forcing the column to sort on a related column.

Filtering and Sorting

Key operations for any tool used to analyze data are filtering and sorting. The tabular model supports both capabilities in the same manner as those found in PowerPivot.

To sort a table in the tabular model, start in the Data Model View (Model ⇨ Model View ⇨ Data View). A drop-down selection (see Figure 17-3) is available on each column, which provides options such as Sort A to Z and Sort Z to A. The options that are presented for each column are based on the column data type. For a column of Date data type, you will see Sort Oldest to Newest and Sort Newest to Oldest. For a column of numeric data type you will see Sort Smallest to Largest and Sort Largest to Smallest.

FIGURE 17-3

The capability to filter column values is available in the tabular model in the same drop-down selection mentioned previously. The filtering operation is handled by the xVelocity engine using a style of SQL queries called *tabular queries*. As with sorting, the column filters that are available are data type specific.

Textual filters can consist of equal to and not equal to or a custom filter which allows you to combine two filter expressions using a logical and/or. The custom filter is available for all data types (see Figure 17-4). Numeric filters have the same capabilities as textual filters and include the ability to do value-based comparisons (greater than, less than, between, and so on.) Finally, the date filters offer an array of choices that include the more standard equality- and value-based comparisons as well as more specialized contextual filters that allow for filtering dates based on values of Today, Tomorrow, Yesterday, Next Week, Quarter, Year, and Year to Date.

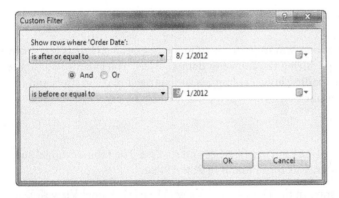

FIGURE 17-4

Behind the scenes, when a sorting or filtering operation is requested, a tabular query is generated and sent to the xVelocity engine. The syntax for a tabular query is as follows:

```
SELECT
[SKIP <integer argument>]
```

```
[TOP <integer argument>]
<list_of_columns> | COUNT(*)
FROM <object>
[NATURAL JOIN <object>][NATURAL JOIN <object>...]
[WHERE <search_condition>]
ORDER BY [<column> [ASC | DESC],] <$Row_Num> [ASC]
```

In addition to providing the sorting and filtering capabilities using the search condition and order by clauses, the tabular query syntax provides the option to skip a specified number of rows or the ability to retrieve the first N rows. When a table is imported into the tabular model, a column called RowNumber is generated and added to it. This column is not directly available in the model, but is used to retrieve data efficiently from the xVelocity engine.

Configuring for PowerPivot and Power View

If you intend to use your tabular model as a data model for either PowerPivot or Power View reports, you can predefine the list of columns and measures that are added for the report author as well as configure the grouping behavior of your model. The following table contains a list of properties that control both the grouping behavior and the field set for your model.

PROPERTY NAME	DESCRIPTION
Row Identifier	Used only in Power View. Identifies the column within the table that has the unique value that can be used as the grouping key.
Keep Unique Rows	Used only in Power View. Allows you to specify columns that should be treated as unique even when duplicates are present. A common example of this is first and last name columns in a customer or employee table.
Default Label	Used only in Power View. A column, such as a customer or employee name, that is used as the display name for a given row of data.
Default Image	Used only in Power View. A column containing an image for a given row.
Default Field Set	A pre-selected list of columns and measures that will be added automatically to either the PowerPivot workbook or Power View report canvas.

ENHANCING YOUR MODEL WITH HIERARCHIES

An important shortfall with PowerPivot/SQL Server 2008 R2 was the lack of hierarchies. Hierarchies, however, are a fundamental concept in Analysis Services multidimensional because to perform their tasks, all query and processing functionality fundamentally rely on how hierarchies are structured. Yet, hierarchies were not structurally necessary within PowerPivot because it relies on the VertiPaq engine or the Analysis Services tabular.

To query data, even in tabular mode, you must group columns in arranged levels — hierarchies — making the data easier to navigate and understand. A good fundamental example of this is a [date] hierarchy such as [Year] ⇨ [Month] ⇨ [Day].

This section walks you through the steps to create various types of hierarchies including date, geography, and product hierarchies. These hierarchies were chosen because they are common throughout many BI solutions.

Creating a Date Hierarchy

In almost any BI solution, it is important to create date hierarchies because you will be examining your data over some time period. To do this, you create two common date hierarchies — one by Year, Quarter, Month, and Date (YQMD) and another one by Year, Week, and Date (YWD).

The YQMD is a popular date hierarchy because most analysis will be broken down in terms of days and months. Using a specific example, Valentine's Day is a popular day for the purchase of flowers and chocolates, hence the days leading up to February 14th (and for that matter, the month of February) will have higher chocolate and flower sales when compared to other months. As for the YWD hierarchy, it is commonly used when you want to look at week-over-week sales figures. For example, the weeks before the Super Bowl, Thanksgiving, and Christmas have higher electronic sales than summer weeks.

To better understand these trends, it's necessary to at minimum create these date hierarchies as your starting point. You may need other hierarchies such as ones derived from a fiscal calendar, but the steps to create those hierarchies will be similar to the ones provided below.

As a quick reminder, most of the tasks below will be done through the Model Diagram View (Model ⇨ Model View ⇨ Diagram View). To create a date hierarchy, open the Adventure Works 2012 Tabular Model Project, go to the Date table in the model designer, and initially create a YQMD (Year ⇨ Quarter ⇨ Month ⇨ Day) hierarchy by following these steps:

1. Right-click the Date table, and click Create Hierarchy, as shown in Figure 17-5. This creates a new hierarchy within the Date table called "Hierarchy1" with a hierarchy icon instead of a column icon.

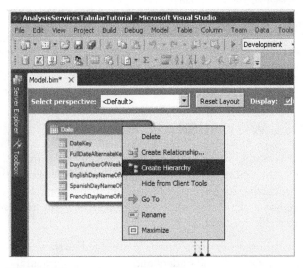

FIGURE 17-5

2. Rename the hierarchy you just created to YQMD for Year, Quarter, Month, and Date. To do this, either you can rename the "Hierarchy1" that is highlighted in the Date table or you can rename the name property located in the Properties dialog in the lower right, as seen in Figure 17-6.

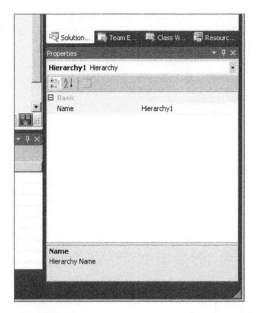

FIGURE 17-6

3. Add the following columns in the following order and rename them:

COLUMN FROM DATE TABLE	RENAME IT TO
Calendar Year	Year
Calendar Quarter	Quarter
English Month Name	Month
Day Number of Month	Day

To make this easier, you can click the Maximize icon (on the top right of the Date table within the Diagram View) so it's easier to drag and drop the various columns in your hierarchy, as seen in Figure 17-7.

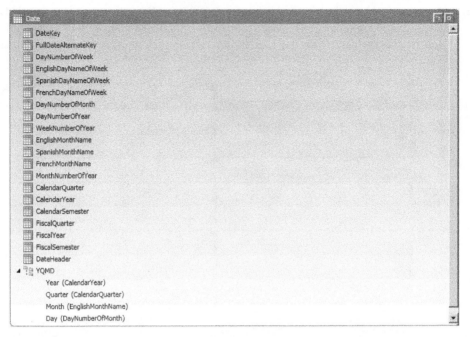

FIGURE 17-7

4. Using the same Date table, repeat the previous steps for a Week-Day (or YWD) hierarchy, adding the columns in the following table. The resulting hierarchy can be seen in Figure 17-8.

FIGURE 17-8

COLUMN FROM DATE TABLE	RENAME IT TO
Calendar Year	Year
Week Number of Year	Week
Day Number of Week	Weekday

5. Using the same Date table, repeat steps 1 through 4 for a Fiscal hierarchy, adding the columns in the following table. The resulting hierarchy can be seen in Figure 17-9.

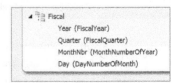

FIGURE 17-9

COLUMN FROM DATE TABLE	RENAME IT TO
Fiscal Year	Year
Fiscal Quarter	Quarter

COLUMN FROM DATE TABLE	RENAME IT TO
Month Number of Year	MonthNbr
Day Number of Month	Day

6. Click File and then Save to finish your model.

Making Use of Time Intelligence Functions

One of the more powerful features included in PowerPivot V2/SQL Server 2012 Tabular is the ability to use Time Intelligence functions. These functions allow you to pivot and slice your calculations by time. For example, to compare the current month with the previous month, you can use the PREVIOUSMONTH function to automatically determine the previous month based on the current day or month. More information is available in Chapters 18 and 19 on DAX.

In the previous version of PowerPivot (i.e., SQL Server 2008 R2), the golden rules for creating time intelligence functions were:

➤ Never use the datetime column from the fact table in time functions.

➤ Always create a separate Date table.

➤ Make sure your Date table has a continuous date range.

➤ Create relationships between fact tables and a Date table.

➤ Make sure that the relationships are based on a datetime column (*not* on an artificial key column).

➤ The datetime column in the Date table should be at the day granularity (i.e., not hours, minutes, or seconds).

The fifth bullet is the key here in that the relationship between the Date table and the fact table had to be done by a datetime column key. This can be rather inflexible in that many data warehouse designs involve joining a fact table and a Date table with an integer key value. Even more disconcerting is that if you did not follow these rules, your time-based calculations may result in incorrect calculations! Frederick Vandeputte provides a great explanation of how the wrong results may appear in his slideshare "Building your first Analysis Services Tabular BI Semantic model with SQL Server 2012" (http://slidesha.re/GAFga1).

As part of SQL Server 2012, this aberration has been solved by providing the Mark as Date functionality. By declaring a separate table as the Date table, the time intelligence functions will work correctly no matter how the relationship between the fact and Date tables is defined.

To mark a Date table, follow these steps:

1. Go to your Analysis Services Tabular model and choose your Date table (in the sample BISM model, it is the table tab called [Date]). If you review the date information within the [Date] table, you will notice that the DateKey is an integer value used to join the fact table and the dimension table. Meanwhile, the Date column contains the actual date values (e.g., 7/1/2005, etc.)

2.   As shown in Figure 17-10, select Table ⇨ Date ⇨ Mark as Date Table.

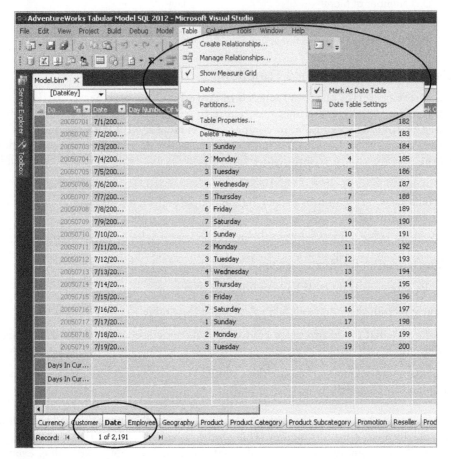

FIGURE 17-10

This will prompt the Mark as Date Table dialog shown in Figure 17-11.

3.   Choose the column within the Date table that contains the Date values — in this case, this is the Date column.

Now that you have configured your Date table within your BISM model, your time intelligence functions will automatically work for any value that joins to this Date table. In summary, for SQL Server 2012, the "golden rules" for time intelligence functions are now:

➤   Never use the Datetime column from the fact table in time functions.

➤   Always create a separate Date table.

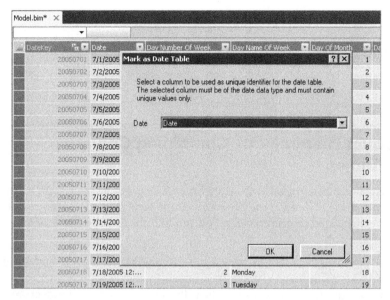

FIGURE 17-11

➤ Make sure your Date table has a continuous date range.

➤ Create relationships between fact tables and a Date table.

➤ The Datetime column in the Date table should be at a granularity of days (not hours, minutes, or seconds).

➤ Apply the Mark as Date table tag to your Date table to ensure time intelligence functions will work correctly.

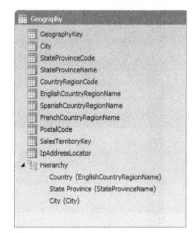

For more information, you can also review Kasper de Jonge's PowerPivot Blog on PowerPivot CTP3: "What is new for Time Intelligence functions" (http://bit.ly/qir0eg) or Frederik Vandeputte's blog post: "PowerPivot Nuggets - Part 5 - Mark As Date Table" (http://bit.ly/qpSYdb).

Creating a Geography Hierarchy

You can apply this same logic to all information where it becomes easier to navigate by using hierarchies. The following table shows the column mapping and view (Figure 17-12) of the geography hierarchy.

FIGURE 17-12

COLUMN FROM GEOGRAPHY TABLE	RENAME IT TO
English Country Region Name	Country
State Province Name	State Province
City	City

Creating a Product Hierarchy by Combining Columns from Different Tables

The product hierarchy involves more work to create because it spans three separate but related tables. These tables can also be found in the Model Diagram View (Model ➪ Model View ➪ Diagram View) of the associated tutorial project. You can find the three product tables in question in Figure 17-13.

To create a hierarchy involving Product Category (EnglishProductCategoryName) ➪ Product Subcategory (EnglishProductSubcategoryName) ➪ Product (EnglishProductName), you need to relate columns between three different tables (Product, ProductSubcategory, ProductCategory). This is shown in Figure 17-14.

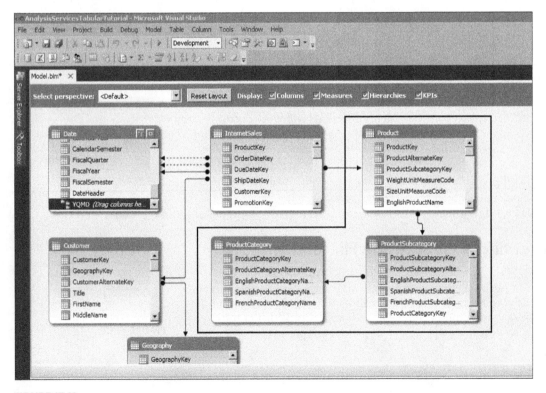

FIGURE 17-13

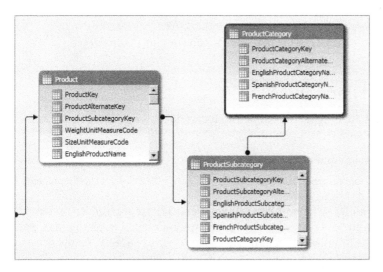

FIGURE 17-14

To relate the columns between the three tables, you will first need to open the Data View (Model ⇨ Model View ⇨ Data View) and apply the RELATED DAX function. This creates related columns within the Product table to the ProductCategory and ProductSubcategory tables so that you can create the hierarchy spanning three tables as noted in Figure 17-11. Follow these steps:

1. Go to the Product table and click Add Column.

2. To add the Subcategory information, add the DAX formula:

   `=RELATED(ProductSubcategory[EnglishProductSubcategoryName]).`

3. Rename the column from CalculatedColumn1 to EnglishProductSubCategoryName.

4. To add the category information, add the DAX formula:

   `=RELATED(ProductCategory[EnglishProductCategoryName]).`

5. Rename the column from CalculatedColumn1 to EnglishProductCategoryName.

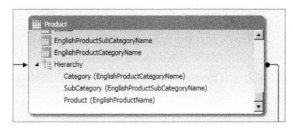

Now, you are set to create your Product Hierarchy as noted in Figure 17-15. Go to the Model view and create your hierarchy as defined in the following table.

FIGURE 17-15

COLUMN FROM PRODUCT TABLE	RENAME IT TO
English Product Category Name	Category
English Product Subcategory Name	Subcategory
English Product Name	Product

For more information, you can also reference SQL Server 2012 ⇨ Analysis Services Tutorials ⇨ Create Hierarchies at: `http://msdn.microsoft.com/en-us/library/hh231692%28v=SQL.110%29.aspx`.

Creating Parent/Child Hierarchies

Parent/Child hierarchies involve creating relationships and hierarchies so that one column references another column in the same table.

Enter the following DAX expression and press Enter:

```
=RIGHT("\" " & Format([MonthNumberOfYear],"#0"),2) & " - " & [EnglishMonthName]
```

For more information, you can also refer to "PowerPivot Denali: Parent child using DAX" at `http://www.powerpivotblog.nl/powerpivot-denali-parent-child-using-dax` and "Parent/Child Hierarchies in Tabular with Denali" at `http://sqlblog.com/blogs/alberto_ferrari/archive/2011/07/19/parent-child-hierarchies-in-tabular-with-denali.aspx`.

ENHANCING MEASURES

As discussed in Chapter 16, measures are defined by a DAX expression. The values for measures are calculated at the time they are evaluated in the context that the value is being asked for. You learn more about measures in the two DAX chapters: Chapters 18 and 19. For now, become familiar with how to build a distinct count measure and build a semi-additive measure using the tabular designer.

Building Explicit Measures with DAX

As noted in Chapter 16, you can build a measure by accessing the measure grid within the BI model within Visual Studio 2010. Below are the steps to create a measure within the Adventure Works 2012 Tabular Model using the Product Inventory table.

1. Open the Adventure Works 2012 Tabular model within Visual Studio 2010. Ensure the model is within the Data View (Model ⇨ Model View ⇨ Data View).

2. Open up the Product Inventory Table by clicking on the tab of the same tab.

3. Click on any cell within the measure grid; this is any cell below the horizontal bar.

4. From here, you can type in your new calculated measure. For example, if I want to create a new measure [Total Units In] as shown in Figure 17-16 — which is the sum of the Product Inventory table [Units In] column — I can type:

```
Total Units In := SUM([Units In])
```

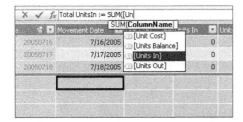

FIGURE 17-16

Do not worry if you do not create your DAX expression correctly for your measure. The IDE will warn you and prevent you from making any additional changes unless you first fix the incorrect expression (as shown in Figure 17-17).

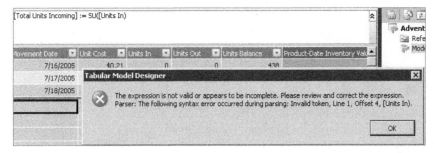

FIGURE 17-17

By creating this explicit measure, you are actually creating a calculated measure within an MDX script. In fact, all measures that are created are MDX script calculated measures. To visualize this, open up the Model.bim file as a file, not as a project. For those familiar with MDX calculation scripts, you will notice that the measure [Total Units In]:=SUM([Units In]) is simply the MDX calculated measure (as shown in Figure 17-18):

```
CREATE MEASURE 'Product Inventory'[Total Units In]=SUM([Units In]);
```

```
Model.bim* ×
                        <Command>
                            <Text>CALCULATE;
        CREATE MEMBER CURRENTCUBE.Measures.[__No measures defined] AS 1;
        ALTER CUBE CURRENTCUBE UPDATE DIMENSION Measures, Default_Member = [__No measures defined]; </Text>
                        </Command>
                        <Command>
                            <Text>-----------------------------------------------------------
        -- PowerPivot measures command (do not modify manually) --
        -----------------------------------------------------
        CREATE MEASURE 'Product Inventory'[Total Units In]=SUM([Units In]);
        CREATE MEASURE 'Product Inventory'[Total Units Out]=SUM([Units Out]);
        CREATE MEASURE 'Product Inventory'[Total Units Movement]=[Total Units In]-[Total Units Out];
        CREATE MEASURE 'Product Inventory'[Total Units]=CALCULATE(SUM([Units Balance]),LASTDATE('Product Inve
        CREATE MEASURE 'Product Inventory'[Total Inventory Value]=CALCULATE(SUM([Product-Date Inventory Value
```

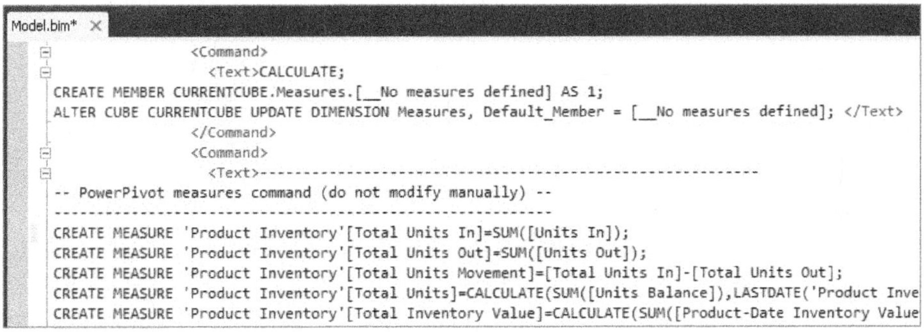

FIGURE 17-18

WHY CAN I PUT A MEASURE ANYWHERE IN THE MEASURE GRID?

If you are looking at the measure grid from the context of an SQL DBA or IT professional, you may be a tad confused about why a measure can go anywhere in the measure grid (I know I was). This may get more confusing within the context of tables. That is, above the measure grid (the horizontal bar), you see a list of tables. So, placing measures in any cell in a table does not make any sense.

Yet the measure grid was not designed with tables in mind. It was designed with Excel users in mind. That is, if you are an information worker, where you put your Excel calculations (calculated formulas, measures, etc.) is purely a function of where you want to put them within an Excel worksheet.

The context of a measure within the measure grid follows the same perspective of an Excel user: You have the ability to organize your measures in any way you see fit.

Implicit Measures

When you create a measure within PowerPivot by dragging a column from the PivotPivot Field List to the Values pane, an implicit measure has been created, as shown in Figure 17-19. That is, internally, PowerPivot creates a measure definition for the PowerPivot workbook. But it is important to note that within BISM Tabular models, you have to *explicitly* create measures (explicit measures) as described in the previous section.

FIGURE 17-19

Note that when you import a PowerPivot workbook into an Analysis Services Tabular project, as shown in Figure 17-20, the import process will convert the PowerPivot implicit measures into explicit measures (see Figure 17-21).

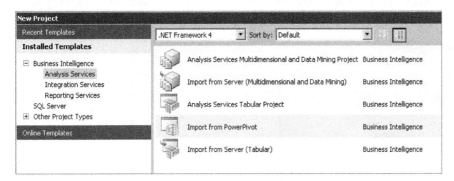

FIGURE 17-20

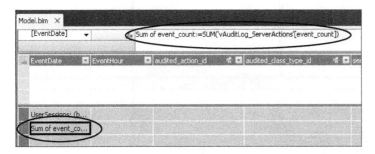

FIGURE 17-21

TURN OFF AUTOMATIC RECALCULATION WHEN ADDING MEASURES

If you find yourself in a situation where you have either a very large model or many measure expressions to define, switch the calculation mode to manual until after all your DAX expressions have been defined.

To change the calculation mode, select the Model ⇨ Calculation Options ⇨ Manual Calculation before you start creating your measures.

If you find that you need to calculate the measure as you work in manual calculation mode, you can start the calculation from the Model menu by clicking the Calculation Now option (Model ⇨ Calculate Now).

Change Measure Properties

Now that you have created an explicit measure, you may want to change the measure format or the measure description. To do this, look at the measure properties pane in the lower-right corner of the IDE (as noted in Figure 17-22).

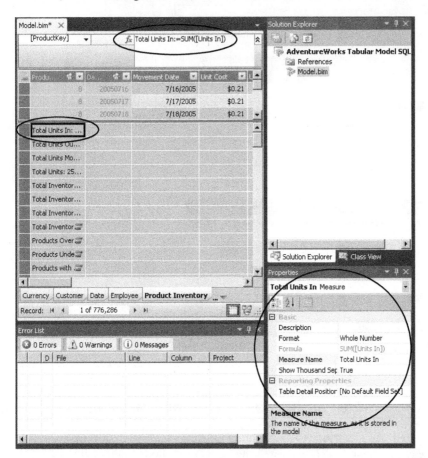

FIGURE 17-22

Within the properties pane, you can provide a Description by typing it in, then select the measure format by choosing the appropriate drop-down value, as shown in Figure 17-23.

Mimicking the Multidimensional Model

Measures in the tabular model are always in scope of the tables within the model. It is possible, however, to define measures together into a single table which has only hidden columns to look and feel to the client tool like measures in a multidimensional model.

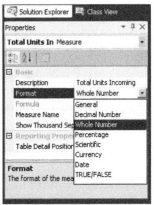

FIGURE 17-23

The steps in this section walk you through using a utility table to group measures together in a manner similar to that found in a multidimensional model.

1. Create the Model Measures table described in the Adding a New Table section earlier in this chapter. This table contains a single column and row, as shown in Figure 17-24.

FIGURE 17-24

2. From the Data Model View, find the Model Measures table. Select the NullColumn column and then right-click and choose Hide from Client Tools to hide the column.

3. In the first row of the Measures Grid, enter the following DAX expression:

```
Overall Sales:=[Reseller Total Sales] + [Internet Total Sales]
```

4. In the second row of the Measures Grid, enter the following DAX expression:

```
Internet Sales:=SUM('Internet Sales'[Sales Amount])
```

5. Save your model.

6. Click the Analyze in Excel button and use the Current Windows Users and Default perspective to test your model in Excel.

7. Select the Overall Sales and Internet Sales measures from the Model Measures table.

8. Drag the Category column from the Product table to the Row Labels box.

9. Verify that the measures perform as expected and mimic the behavior of measures within a multidimensional model. (See Figure 17-25.)

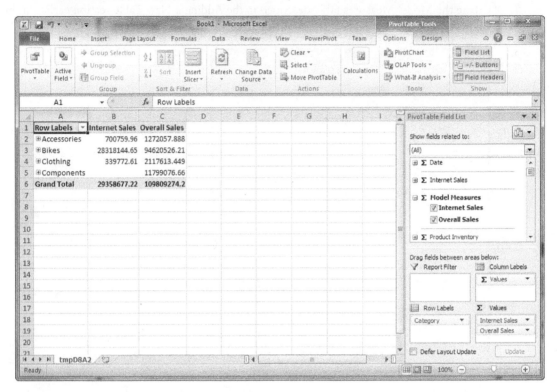

FIGURE 17-25

Building Semi-Additive Measures

Enter the following DAX expression and press Enter:

```
=RIGHT(" " & Format([MonthNumberOfYear],"#0"),2) & " - " & [EnglishMonthName]
```

For more information, please refer to "Semi additive measures in DAX/BISM Tabular" at http://msolap.wordpress.com/2011/08/13/semi-additive-measures-in-dax-bism-tabular/.

CREATING KPIS

Key Performance Indicators (KPIs) are mathematical constructs that enable a simple indicator graph to denote its business value. A common KPI is the traffic light KPI where green denotes something positive (for example, sales are up), yellow denotes something neutral (for example, sales are barely meeting targets), and red denotes something negative (for example, sales are down).

1. In the Model Data View (Model ➪ Model View ➪ Data View), select the Date table to make it active.

2. Click an empty cell in the measure grid so that you can create a new formula.

3. In the formula bar above the table, type the following formula to create the [Days in Current Quarter] measure:

   ```
   Days in Current Quarter:=COUNTROWS( DATESBETWEEN( 'Date'[FullDateAlternateKey],
   STARTOFQUARTER( LASTDATE('Date'[FullDateAlternateKey])),
   ENDOFQUARTER('Date'[FullDateAlternateKey])))
   ```

4. Repeat steps 1 through 3 to create the [Days in Current Quarter] measure as shown in Figure 17-26.

   ```
   Days Current Quarter to Date:=COUNTROWS(DATESQTD('Date'[FullDateAlternateKey]))
   ```

5. Select the Internet Sales table to make it the active table.

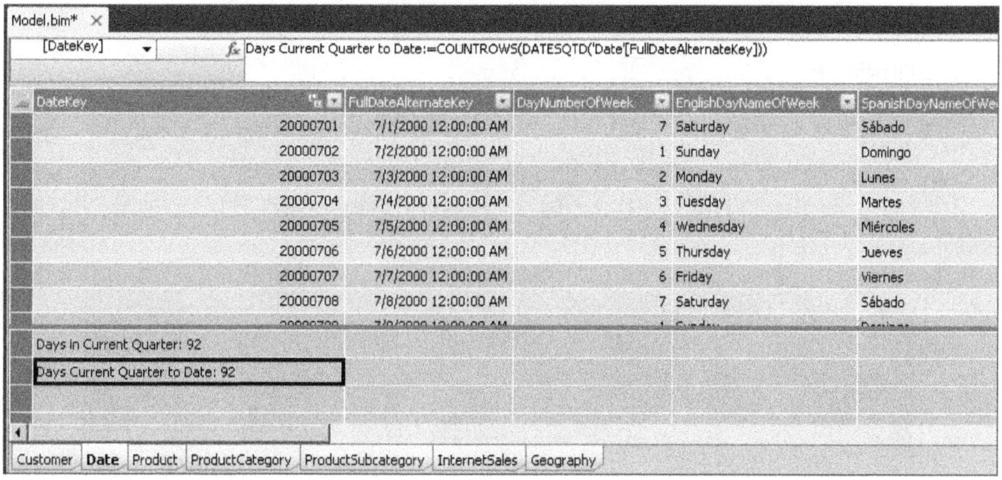

DateKey		FullDateAlternateKey	DayNumberOfWeek	EnglishDayNameOfWeek	SpanishDayNameOfWe
	20000701	7/1/2000 12:00:00 AM	7 Saturday	Sábado
	20000702	7/2/2000 12:00:00 AM	1 Sunday	Domingo
	20000703	7/3/2000 12:00:00 AM	2 Monday	Lunes
	20000704	7/4/2000 12:00:00 AM	3 Tuesday	Martes
	20000705	7/5/2000 12:00:00 AM	4 Wednesday	Miércoles
	20000706	7/6/2000 12:00:00 AM	5 Thursday	Jueves
	20000707	7/7/2000 12:00:00 AM	6 Friday	Viernes
	20000708	7/8/2000 12:00:00 AM	7 Saturday	Sábado

Days in Current Quarter: 92
Days Current Quarter to Date: 92

Customer **Date** Product ProductCategory ProductSubcategory InternetSales Geography

FIGURE 17-26

6. Click another empty cell in the measure grid, and in the formula bar above the table, type the following formula to create the [Internet Previous Quarter Sales] measure:

   ```
   Internet Previous Quarter Sales :=CALCULATE([InternetSalesAmount],
   PREVIOUSQUARTER('Date'[FullDateAlternateKey]))
   ```

7. Repeat the previous step to create the [Internet Current Quarter Sales] and [Internet Previous Quarter Sales Proportion to QTD] measures, as shown in Figure 17-27.

   ```
   Internet Current Quarter Sales=TOTALQTD([InternetSalesAmount],
   'Date'[FullDateAlternateKey])
   Internet Previous Quarter Sales Proportion to QTD:=[Internet Previous
   Quarter Sales]*([Days Current Quarter to Date]/[Days In Current Quarter])
   ```

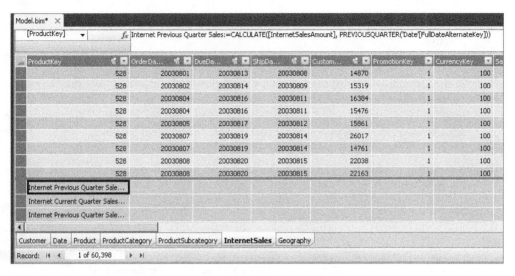

FIGURE 17-27

8. Click another empty cell in the measure grid, and on the formula bar above the table, type the following formula as shown in Figure 17-28:

```
Internet Current Quarter Sales Performance:=IFERROR([Internet Current Quarter
Sales]/[Internet Previous Quarter Sales Proportion to QTD], BLANK())
```

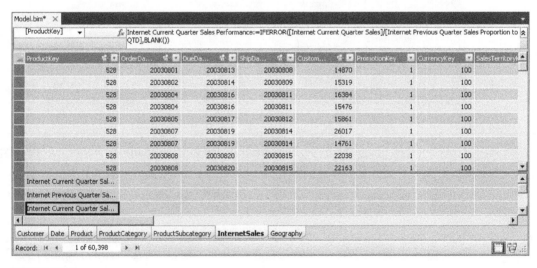

FIGURE 17-28

9. To create the KPI, in the measure grid, right-click the measure, and then click Create KPI, which opens the Key Performance Indicator dialog, as shown in Figure 17-29.

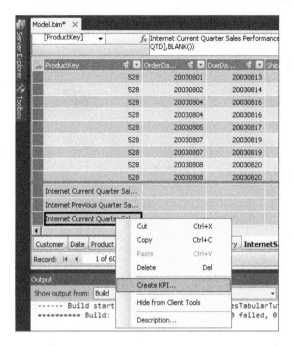

FIGURE 17-29

10. In the Key Performance Indicator dialog box, in the Define target value area, select the Absolute value option and type **1.1** in the Absolute value field; then press Enter.

11. In the Define status thresholds area, in the left (low) slider field, type **1**, and then in the right (high) slider field, type **1.07**.

12. In the Select icon style area, select the diamond (red), triangle (yellow), and circle (green) icon type.

13. Click OK to complete the KPI, as can be seen in Figure 17-30.

In the measure grid, notice the icon next to the Internet Current Quarter Sales Performance measure. This icon indicates that this measure serves as a Base value for a KPI.

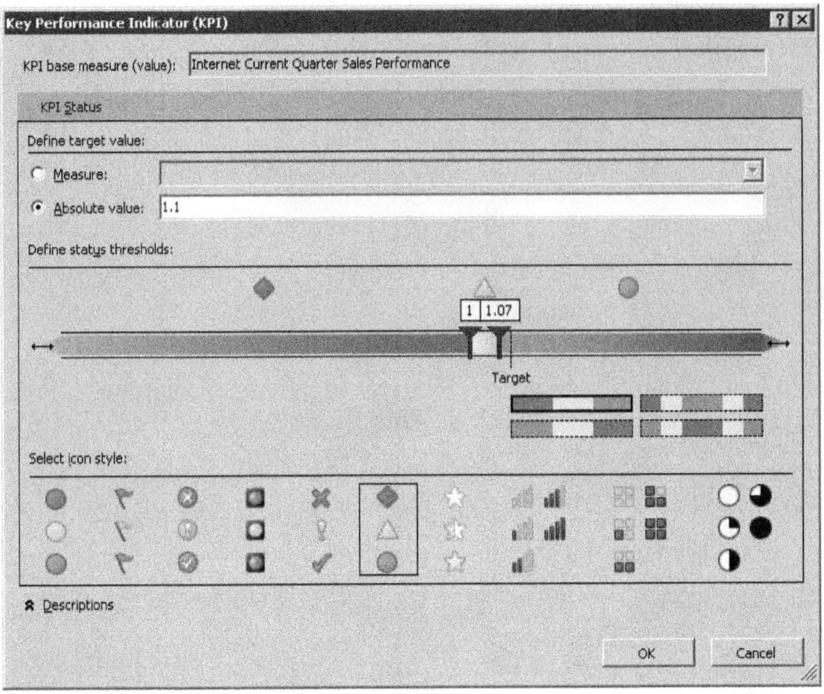

FIGURE 17-30

CREATING PERSPECTIVES

The purpose of a perspective is to provide a Model View specific to the business scenario to be achieved. With a perspective, the user sees only those tables, columns, measures, hierarchies, and KPIs applicable to that perspective instead of seeing all objects within the model (available in the Model Diagram or Model Data View). In this section, you create the Internet Sales perspective.

1. To start, click Model ⇨ Perspectives (see Figure 17-31).

2. In the Perspectives dialog, click the New Perspective button.

3. Rename the perspective to Internet Sales.

4. In the fields, select the Date, InternetSales, Product, ProductCategory, ProductSubcategory tables, and then click OK. The final Perspectives dialog view should be similar to Figure 17-32.

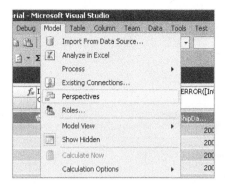

FIGURE 17-31

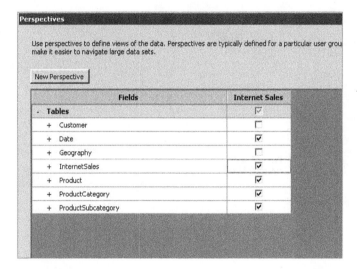

FIGURE 17-32

Now that you have created the Internet Sales perspective, you can view what objects are available in the perspective by clicking Model ⇨ Diagram View and then choosing the [Internet Sales] perspective in the Select perspective drop-down as noted in Figure 17-33.

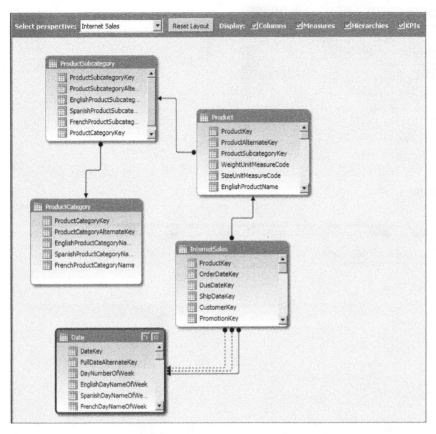

FIGURE 17-33

CREATING PARTITIONS

Partitions are an important component of any model because they allow you to break down large quantities of data into smaller, more manageable chunks. By partitioning data, you are able to distribute your data processing or data querying tasks into many processes instead of having a single process perform the task.

For example, in a table that contains one billion rows, if you were to place all of the data into a single partition — the default design when you create a single table — a single process or task will process or query all one billion rows. But if you were to partition this into, say, ten partitions of 100 million rows each, the result would be that ten tasks would perform ten 100 million row processes. The query or processing time would be the length of time to process 100 million rows instead of one billion rows — potentially ten times faster. This is especially advantageous today when there are multicore processers with the ability to execute many threads and processes in parallel. In Analysis Services 2012, creating partitions aids tabular BISM primarily with management operations involved in efficiently loading data into tables. Analysis Services 2012 does not support processing of partitions within a table that are to be done in parallel. However, you can process multiple tables in parallel.

There is a danger that, if you partition too much, too many data streams will need to be synchronized together. That is, if the partitions are too small, it will take more time to synchronize the parallel processes than it will take to actually query/process the data itself.

From a manageability perspective, a key facet of partitions is that they enable one set of data to be modified or processed while leaving the rest of the data untouched. By default, there is only one partition for your model, but you can quickly add partitions by following these steps:

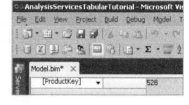

FIGURE 17-34

1. Start by clicking the Partitions icon, as highlighted in Figure 17-34.

2. From here, the Partition Manager dialog, shown in Figure 17-35, displays. The top of the dialog specifies what table you are modifying partitions for; choose InternetSales.

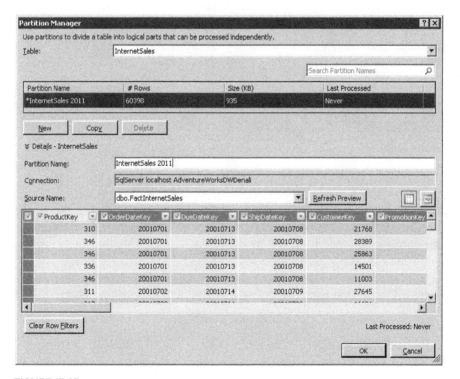

FIGURE 17-35

3. Change the partition name to InternetSales 2011, and click the Database icon button to modify the underlying SQL statement that populates the partition (refer to Figure 17-35).

4. Modify the partition so that the SQL statement includes the following WHERE clause. Figure 17-36 shows the associated Partition Manager dialog.

```
WHERE (([OrderDate] >= N'2001-01-01 00:00:00') AND ([OrderDate]
< N'2002-01-01 00:00:00'))
```

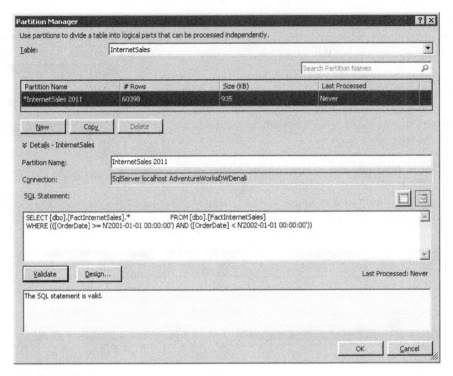

FIGURE 17-36

5. Click Validate to ensure the SQL statement is properly formed; the statement should be similar to the following. As you can see from the SQL statements, we are partitioning the data by a time period — in this case, by year. Within data warehouses and BI solutions, it is common to partition by a time period because data accumulates over time and it is common to query the data by a time period (current day, current week, current month, etc.).

```
SELECT [dbo].[FactInternetSales].*              FROM [dbo].[FactInternetSales]
WHERE ((([OrderDate] >= N'2001-01-01 00:00:00') AND ([OrderDate]
< N'2002-01-01 00:00:00'))
```

6. To create the partitions for 2002–2005, repeat the following steps:

    a. Click Copy to create a new partition based on the original InternetSales 2011.

    b. Rename the partition to InternetSales 200x where x is a number between 2 and 5.

    c. Modify the WHERE statement to the associated year, for example, for 2002:

    ```
    WHERE ((([OrderDate] >= N'2002-01-01 00:00:00') AND ([OrderDate]
    < N'2003-01-01 00:00:00'))
    ```

7. Click OK and the metadata will be saved. You will now need to reprocess the table so the model will be using the newly designed partitions.

8. To do this, ensure that the InternetSales table is chosen in the Model Designer, and click Model ⇨ Process ⇨ Process Partitions.

9. Ensure that process mode is set to Process Default, and check all the partitions you want to process, as noted in Figure 17-37.

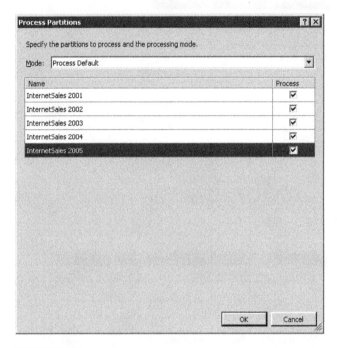

FIGURE 17-37

10. Click OK, and Visual Studio proceeds to process this tabular model. When completed, you see the Success icon within the Data Processing dialog, as noted in Figure 17-38.

11. Click Close.

12. To verify how the partitions have been built, click the Partitions icon (as noted previously in Figure 17-34) and take a view of the partition statistics within the Partition Manager icon as noted in Figure 17-39.

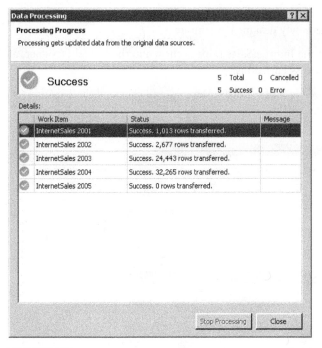

FIGURE 17-38

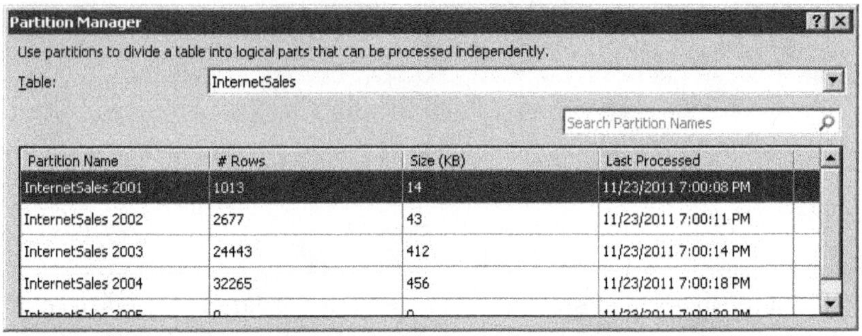

FIGURE 17-39

DirectQuery Partitions

In multidimensional BISM, you had the option to choose from the default MOLAP partition to ROLAP if you need real-time data from your relational system. You can set up tabular BISM partitions to retrieve data from the relational data source (specifically, SQL Server) every time you query the tabular BISM with the use of DirectQuery partition. SSAS provides additional configurations for DirectQuery partitions so that you can answer queries via cached data from DirectQuery partitions on Analysis Services. Before learning how to set up a DirectQuery partition, you need to learn the key constraints in SQL Server 2012 for DirectQuery partitions. They key limitations are:

➤   DirectQuery partitions are only supported when the data source is Microsoft SQL Server.

➤ Calculated columns are not supported when the tabular model is enabled.

➤ Certain DAX functions are not supported. For detailed information on what functions are supported please refer to http://technet.microsoft.com/en-us/library/hh213006.aspx.

➤ Analysis Services supports roles and permissions along with models with DirectQuery partitions. However, securing certain rows in the table (See the "Row Filters" section later in this chapter) is not supported in certain situations.

➤ The most important constraint is that you cannot use MDX to query tabular BISM with DirectQuery partitions. Hence, you will not be able to query the database from Excel. However, clients such as Power View (which you learn about in Chapter 23) can query the tabular model via DAX queries.

Even though there are certain key constraints with creating tabular models with DirectQuery partitions, you do have the benefit of creating a tabular model against a large data source from SQL Server and being able to create reports using Power View. Follow these steps to set up a DirectQuery partition.

1. Launch SSDT.

2. Create a new tabular model project named DirectQueryExample.

3. Create a new connection to the AdventureWorksDW relational database.

4. Import the FactInternetSales table and related tables into your tabular model.

5. Click on FactInternetSales table and open Partition Manager dialog.

6. Create two partitions by changing the query to retrieve data from the relational data source.

7. Right-click on Model.bim and select Properties.

8. In the Properties window change the property DirectQuery Mode from Off to On, as shown in Figure 17-40.

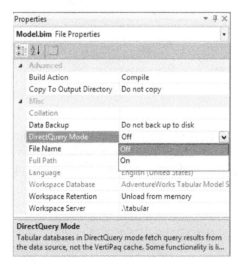

FIGURE 17-40

9. Launch the Partitions Manager for FactInternetSales table and you can now see one of the partitions marked as DirectQuery, as shown in Figure 17-41. You can only have a single partition in DirectQuery mode.

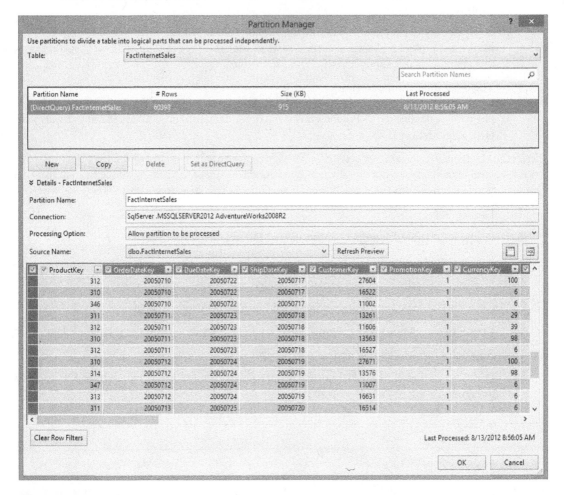

FIGURE 17-41

10. You can now change the overall caching settings for the entire database using the database property. Right-click on the database name DirectQueryExample in the Solution Explorer and select Properties. You will see the Query Mode option available, as shown in Figure 17-42.

The four options in the dialog are:

➤ **DirectQuery:** Data will be obtained from the relational data source.

➤ **DirectQuery with In-Memory:** DirectQuery mode should be turned on. Data can be loaded and cached in the model. Queries are served using DirectQuery data. Clients can override using the connection string property DirectQueryMode set to In-Memory.

➤ **In-Memory:** This is the default mode for tabular model partitions where data is loaded into the model.

➤ **In-Memory with DirectQuery:** DirectQuery model should be turned on. Queries use In-Memory data by default. Clients can use the DirectQueryMode connection string property to override and get data from the relational data source for partitions that have DirectQuery mode set.

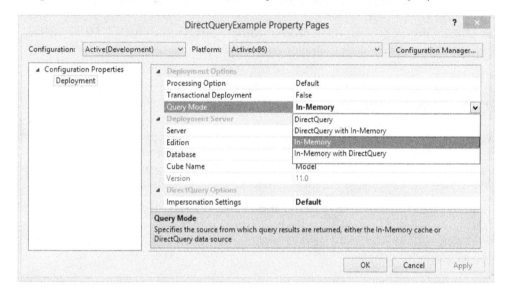

FIGURE 17-42

REAL-WORLD PARTITIONING TIPS

As a general rule, you will want to design your partitions so that they are approximately equal in size (by rows or by data size). The reason is that if partitions differ in size dramatically, you degrade the parallel performance of your query (or processing).

For example, as you can see in Figure 17-22, the number of rows ranges from 1,013 to 32,265 with the data sizes ranging from 14KB and 456KB. If four threads were to query the partitions from 2001 to 2004 in parallel, the 2001 and 2002 processes would complete much faster than the 2003 and 2004 partitions. Your query process would wait until all four threads were completed before going to the next step. If all four yearly partitions were equal in size, then all four threads would complete approximately the same time. That is, minimal latency between going from one set of tasks to another.

continues

(continued)

It is important to note that in the real world, it is common to have partitions that are broken out by equal time periods such as year, month, week, or day. More importantly, the Adventure Works DW design is not a good reflection of real-world design; it is a solid showcase of how to use the different features of Analysis Services.

One import factor to be aware of with partitions and tabular models in SQL Server Analysis Services 2012 is that partitions are to be used for manageability. Since SQL Server Analysis Services 2012 does not support parallel processing of partitions in a table, you cannot process multiple partitions in parallel. However, you can process partitions from multiple tables in parallel.

PROCESSING A TABULAR DATABASE

When you import data into your tabular model, SSDT sends a process command so that data from the relational data source can be processed and loaded into the model. There are several processing options for refreshing the data in a tabular model. After you have your tabular model deployed onto your server, you can process the entire database, a specific table, or a specific partition.

You can use SSMS to connect to a tabular database. If you right click on a database, table, or partition and click Process, you will see the Process dialog for that specific object with the corresponding processing options. The following table provides an overview of each object in a tabular database and its processing options.

OBJECT	PROCESSING OPTIONS
Database	ProcessDefault
	ProcessFull
	ProcessClear
	ProcessRecalc
Table	ProcessDefault
	ProcessFull
	ProcessData
	ProcessClear
	ProcessDefrag
Partition	ProcessDefault
	ProcessFull
	ProcessData
	ProcessClear
	ProcessAdd

The next table shows the descriptions of each tabular database object's processing option.

PROCESSING OPTION	DESCRIPTION
ProcessDefault	This is the default option that allows you to load data from the data source for all the objects that have not been processed, and then process all the dependent calculated columns, relationships, and hierarchies.
ProcessFull	This processes the entire object and any dependent objects even if the object has been processed. Performing ProcessFull on a database sends ProcessData followed by ProcessRecalc.
ProcessData	Loads data into corresponding tables or partitions.
ProcessClear	Clears all the data that has been loaded into the specified objects (a database, a set of tables, or partitions).
ProcessRecalc	This option is specific across the entire database and helps with processing all the calculated columns, relationships, and hierarchies.
ProcessDefrag	This option is used with a table and helps optimize the internal structures. This is typically used when you perform a series of ProcessAdd operations on a table.
ProcessAdd	This option helps to add only new rows to an existing table.

In this section we have shared the various processing options for each of the objects. Depending on your organizational needs and when you need to process your tabular BISM database, we recommend you use the right option along with the appropriate partition management strategy for each table.

CREATING AND APPLYING SECURITY ROLES

Last but certainly not least, you need to secure your model. Although both flavors of Analysis Services employ security roles, the security roles of the tabular model are analogous to those of a relational database. This is because you deal with rows within a table as opposed to multidimensional security. Nevertheless, the application of security roles between multidimensional and tabular is relatively similar.

Understanding Security Roles

There are two different security roles in Analysis Services — a server-based security role that allows you to administer the Analysis Services instance, and database roles that are specific to the models that are on that instance. These roles are assigned to Windows User or Group accounts that allow you to tie your Active Directory Federation Services (ADFS) account to the security role. This allows you to create only a single user (or groups of users) and assign roles to that user or group.

Within Analysis Services, you have three different basic permissions:

➤ **Read:** Members are provided read-only access to the data.

➤ **Process:** Members can process the model via script or package. Note that they cannot make changes to the model nor can they view the model in SSMS.

➤ **Administrator:** Members can perform Read and Process tasks as well as make modifications to schemas and view the model in SSMS.

There is also a None permission that allows you to query the model schema, but you are not allowed to query the data itself.

Row Filters

While the roles and the associated permissions are similar between the multidimensional and tabular modes, the application of security filters is different. Tabular mode is about holding tables and rows of data — therefore, the security context is row filtering (rather than dimensional filtering or cell security).

To apply a row filter to a table, you create a DAX expression that is assigned to that specific role. The steps below provide an example of how to apply the DAX expression

```
=Geography[CountryRegionCode] = "US"
```

to the [Internet Sales Access] role you will also create. With this filter, you will be able to limit Windows users assigned to the [Internet Sales Access] role to the rows associated with the geography of the US only.

To deny access to all rows for an entire table, use the =FALSE() function.

To read about roles in the SQL Server Analysis Services tabular model, visit
http://msdn.microsoft.com/en-us/library/hh213165(v=sql.110).aspx.

To create and apply security roles, follow these steps:

1. Go to the Model menu and click Roles, as shown in Figure 17-43.

2. In the Role Manager dialog, click New. You will see that a new role is created with the permission setting of None.

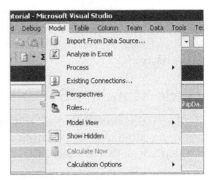

FIGURE 17-43

3. Rename the "Role" to your value — for example, Internet Sales Access. Apply the permissions desired (i.e., Read) and apply your own description (for example, Accessing Internet Sales Data), as noted in Figure 17-44.

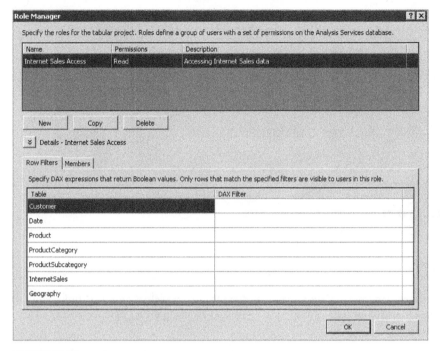

FIGURE 17-44

4. To ensure viewers under the Internet Sales Access have access to only US data, you can also apply a DAX formula in the Row Filters tab of this role. The DAX formula is noted below and can be seen in Figure 17-45.

```
=Geography[CountryRegionCode] = "US"
```

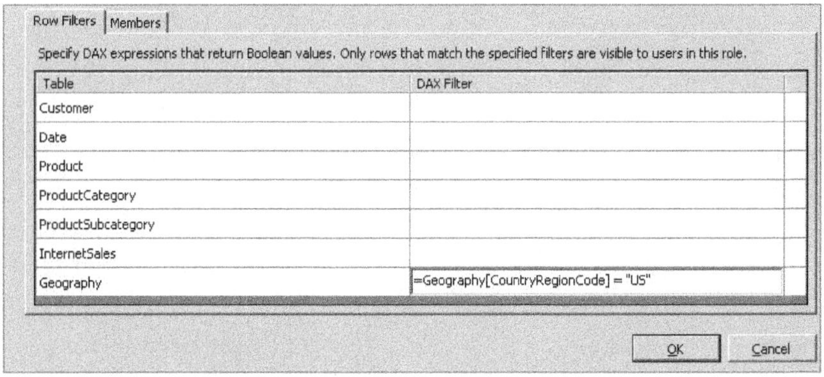

FIGURE 17-45

5. Add the members from Active Directory that you want to apply to this role. An example can be seen in Figure 17-46.

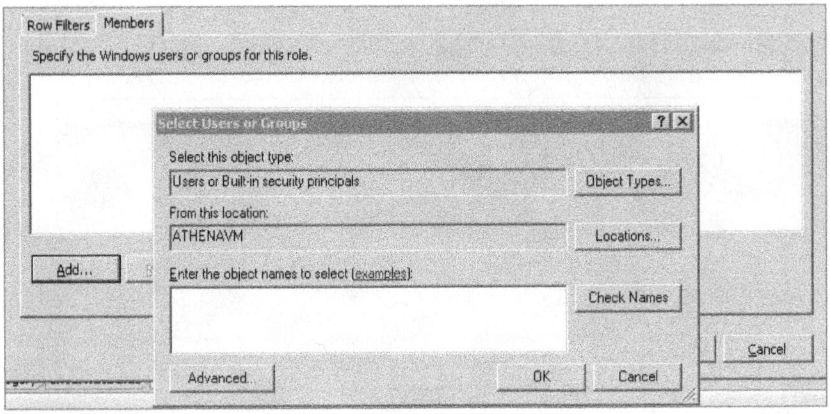

FIGURE 17-46

SUMMARY

In this chapter, you learned about enhancing the tabular model you created in Chapter 16 by using more complex hierarchies, enhancing measures, and creating KPIs, perspectives, and partitions, and applying security roles.

In the next chapters, you review DAX to better understand how to further enhance your tabular model.

18

Introduction to DAX

WHAT'S IN THIS CHAPTER?

➤ Introducing DAX language

➤ Introducing row context and filter context

➤ Categorizing DAX functions

➤ Discussing DAX usage

➤ Comparing DAX with MDX

DAX, an acronym for Data Analysis Expressions, is a language used to define and manipulate calculations as well as query data from tabular Business Intelligence Semantic Models (BISM). DAX was first introduced as part of PowerPivot for Excel, an Excel add-in for information workers to import, integrate, and analyze multiple tables with the help of calculations they were defining using DAX. In SQL Server Analysis Services 2012, DAX is supported against tabular BISM with additional enhancements including using DAX as a query language for clients to query data against tabular BISM. DAX provides a set of functions for business intelligence (BI) calculations, which are similar to Excel formulas, and there is overlap between the list of DAX functions and Excel functions. There are differences, and DAX contains new functions that don't exist within Excel. These DAX functions are designed to offer capabilities that focus on data analysis, particularly for related tables of data, and for dynamic analysis. The ability to define calculations that can be evaluated dynamically in many different contexts is a powerful tool, and prior to PowerPivot and DAX, these sorts of calculations often involved more complex multidimensional concepts and languages.

Excel users can learn how to perform data analysis using DAX formulas that look a lot like Excel formulas and provide additional capabilities and that are much easier to learn and use than the multidimensional constructs. BI professionals requested the ease of building BISM tabular models along with the performance offered with Vertipaq storage by PowerPivot. Hence, BISM tabular was extended to BI professionals via Tabular projects in SQL Server Data Tools (SSDT) along with a standalone Analysis Services server running in Vertipaq mode where Tabular models can be managed efficiently. In addition, the ability to query via DAX was added in SQL Server Analysis Services 2012.

This chapter introduces you to DAX formulas, calculations, functions, and how to use DAX as a query language.

SAMPLE DATA

This chapter uses a sample tabular model to demonstrate different DAX functions and concepts. The tabular model is based on relational data from the "Contoso" SQL Server relational database available from the Microsoft Download Center as part of Microsoft Contoso BI Demo Dataset for Retail Industry:

www.microsoft.com/downloads/details.aspx?displaylang=en&FamilyID=86866 2dc-187a-4a85-b611-b7df7dc909fc

Create an Analysis Services Tabular project in SQL Server Data Tools (SSDT) by importing two fact tables (FactSales and FactInventory) and nine related dimension tables along with the relationships between them if the relationships were defined in the data source. See Figure 18-1.

 Certain examples in this chapter use Excel to analyze the data in sample model.

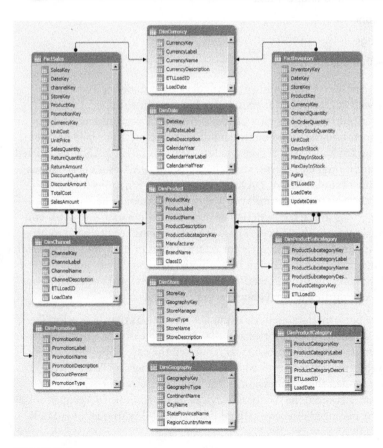

FIGURE 18-1

DAX FUNDAMENTAL CONCEPTS

In this section you learn the fundamental concepts for defining DAX calculations, also referred to as DAX formulas. You learn about the syntax, the various data types supported by DAX, and the fundamental concept of row and filter context, which is critical to understanding how SQL Server Analysis Services evaluates DAX calculations.

DAX Syntax

DAX formulas are used in tabular models to define calculated columns, measures, and row-level security. You learned about row-level security and how to use DAX in Chapter 17. You use DAX to enrich the sample model with calculated columns and measures after you learn the basics of DAX syntax.

DAX syntax is similar to Excel formulas: DAX uses the same sort of function composition and columns references in tables. DAX also extends the column referencing syntax to measures. Measures in tabular models belong to tables just like the columns. The names of columns must be unique within a table, and the names of measures should not match the column names within a table and must be unique across the database. To reference columns or measures in DAX formulas, the name of the column or measure should appear within square brackets. The column or measure name should also be preceded by the table name it belongs to in single quotes as shown here.

> Column reference – '*<Table Name>*'[*Column Name*]

> Measure reference – '*<Table Name>*'[*Measure Name*]

Example:

```
'FactSales'[Margin] = 'FactSales'[SalesAmount]-'FactSales'[TotalCost]
'FactSales'[Sum of SalesAmount] = SUM('FactSales'[SalesAmount])
```

The column and measure references described here are called *fully qualified references*. In some DAX formulas the table name may be dropped if the context hints at which table the column or measure belongs to. This type of reference is called a *partially qualified reference*. Because the measure names are unique across the database, they can always be referenced without the table name, unless the reference is used within another table that has a column with the same name.

Assume a sample schema with Table1 and Table2. Table1 has columns A, B, C and measures H and I. Table2 has columns A, B, E and measures C, F. The next example shows examples of DAX calculations with partially qualified references that are valid and invalid.

```
'Table1'[CalcColumn1] = [A] + [B]
'Table1'[CalcColumn2] = [H] * [F]
'Table1'[Measure3] = SUMX('Table2', [A] + [E])

'Table1'[CalcColumn4] = [A] + [E]            (unknown reference to 'E')
'Table1'[CalcColumn5] = [I] * [C]            (unknown reference to 'C')
'Table1'[Measure6] = SUMX('Table2', [A] + [C])   (unknown reference to 'C')
```

The DAX expression for `CalcColumn4` is invalid since E is not a valid column in Table1. The DAX expression for `CalcColumn5` and `Measure6` are invalid since column C appears both in Table1 and Table2 and needs to be explicitly referenced with the table name. The table name may drop the single quotes if it does not contain special characters (for example, space, ampersand, colon, and so on) and is not a keyword (for example `Table`, `Measure`, and so on). The table, column, and measure names are not case-sensitive.

DAX Data Types

DAX formulas use two types of objects: tables and scalar values. Each DAX function evaluates to either a scalar value or a table value. Table values are implicitly cast to scalar values if a table expression is used where a scalar value is expected. The implicit cast succeeds if the table contains a single column and no more than one row, otherwise it produces an error. DAX supports the following six data types for scalar values: *Integer, Real, Currency* (decimal number), *Boolean, Datetime* (values beginning with March 1, 1900), and *String.*

Calculated Columns and Measures

DAX formulas are used to create calculated columns and measures. *Calculated columns* are columns in a BISM tabular model that are defined using DAX formulas. After they are defined and calculated, they behave just like the rest of the columns (the columns that were imported from a data source) in the table. You can use them in reports and refresh them with the rest of the data. Depending on the nature of the DAX formula that defines them, they may be recalculated based on other changes in the model affecting the DAX formula. For example, if a calculated column formula depends on a certain column, then changing the data type of that column can trigger recalculation of the calculated column because it may affect the values in the calculated column. Measures are named formulas that do not have a specific value. Measures, just like columns, belong to a table. They are defined with a DAX formula and used in reporting to perform the calculation in various contexts. (You learn about row and filter context in the next section.) For example, if the measure formula is the sum of the sales amount, `SUM(FactSales[SalesAmount])`, then it can be evaluated for a given year or region. The sum of the sales amount does not have any specific value unless the context is not defined for evaluation. Calculated columns and measures can be referenced from other calculations defining calculated columns or measures. In summary, calculated columns get evaluated or calculated and stored at the time you process (load data) the BISM-tabular, whereas measures are evaluated at query time.

Row Context and Filter Context

One of the key concepts in DAX is the notion of the context in which a particular DAX formula is evaluated. This paragraph briefly introduces the notion of *row context* and *filter context*, which are discussed more with individual DAX functions and specific examples later in this chapter. Every DAX formula is evaluated in a certain context; it may be in the context of a specific row of a table (row context) or in the context of specific filters (filter context). For example, a DAX formula defining a calculated column is evaluated in the context of every row of the parent table. Column references evaluated in the row context of a parent table result in scalar values corresponding to the value of the column in the current row. The following steps create a *CityState* calculated column in a *DimGeography* table with the `[CityName]&","&[StateProvinceName]` DAX formula.

1. In the ContosoRetail tabular project, select the DimGeography table.

2. Right-click the header of the RegionCountryName column, and from the pop-up menu, select Insert Column.

3. A new column appears with the name CalculatedColumn1. Right-click its header, and rename it **CityState**.

4. Click the formula bar, type **=[CityName]&","&[StateProvinceName]** and press Enter.

   The calculated column formula is applied and the values are calculated, as shown in Figure 18-2. SQL Server Analysis Services evaluated the formula in the context of every single row of the DimGeography table. For example, in the context of the first row, the column reference [CityName] results in the value "Albany" and [StateProvinceName] results in "New York". The concatenation of these values result in "Albany,New York". Similarly the formula is evaluated for each row in the DimGeography table.

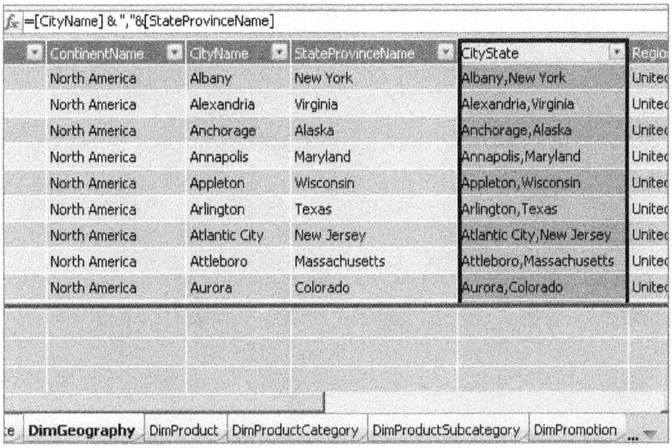

FIGURE 18-2

To understand DAX formula evaluation in a filter context, use a measure in an Excel PivotTable. Follow these steps to create a measure, and analyze the ContosoRetail model with Excel.

1. Select the FactSales table in the ContosoRetail tabular project. You may skip step 2 if a measure grid is shown for the FactSales table.

2. Right-click the FactSales table pane, and select Show Measure Grid, as shown in Figure 18-3.

3. The measure grid is now visible below the table area. Select the cell below the SalesAmount column.

4. Click the formula bar, type the following formula, and press Enter:

   Sum of SalesAmount:=SUM(FactSales[SalesAmount])

   (A colon-equals sign is used as an assignment notion in the measure definition.)

You should now see a Sum of SalesAmount measure in the measure grid, as shown in Figure 18-4. The measure grid reflects the value of the measure calculated for the entire table, which is the sum of all values in the SalesAmount column.

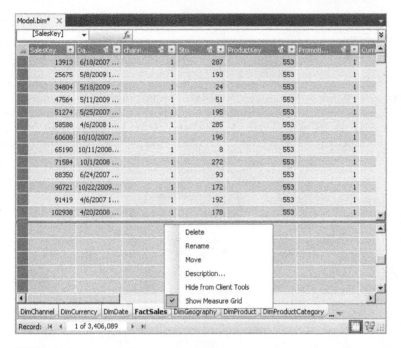

FIGURE 18-3

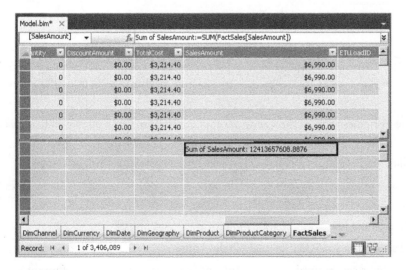

FIGURE 18-4

You next use this measure in Excel to understand DAX formula evaluation in a filter context.

1. On the Analysis Services toolbar, click the Analyze in Excel button to launch Excel with a PivotTable connected to the ContosoRetail tabular model (see Figure 18-5).

2. You can now see the Analyze in Excel dialog asking for the username or role to connect to the model perspective. Current Windows User and the (default) perspective are selected by default. Click OK.

3. Excel launches with a PivotTable connected to the model (see Figure 18-6). Check the Sum of SalesAmount Measure check box to add it to PivotTable Values.

FIGURE 18-5

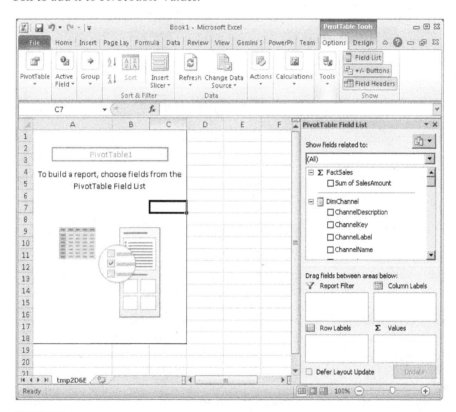

FIGURE 18-6

4. The Sum of SalesAmount Measure is now on the PivotTable showing the total sales amount. The result is the same as the measure grid, as shown in Figure 18-4. This is the result of evaluating the SUM(FactSales[SalesAmount]) formula for the entire data set.

5.   Right-click the ContinentName column of the DimGeography table, and select Add to Row
Labels (See Figure 18-7).

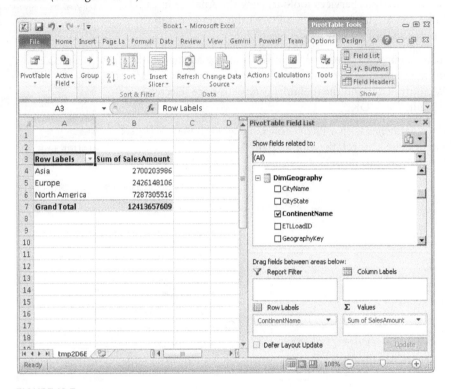

FIGURE 18-7

The PivotTable now reflects the Sum of SalesAmount for each continent and the Grand
Total corresponding to all the continents. What happens in the background is that the
SUM(FactSales[SalesAmount]) formula is evaluated in the context of a filter set on the continent
name. To calculate the sum of sales amount for Asia, the SUM(FactSales[SalesAmount]) is evaluated in the context of a filter: DimGeography[ContinentName]="Asia." The same filter is used for
Europe and North America by substituting "Europe" or "North America" for "Asia." The filter set
on a column automatically cross filters all related tables leaving out the rows that are not related to the
filtered values the column. In this example, rows from the FactSales table that are not related to Asia
are filtered out and not aggregated in the result of Sum of SalesAmount. You can add more filters to
the context by adding more fields to PivotTable Row and Column filters, a Report filter, or Slicers.

DAX OPERATORS AND BLANK VALUES

DAX supports the operators defined in the following table. DAX also supports the TRUE() and
FALSE() functions that evaluate to logical constants, and the BLANK() function that evaluates to a
blank value. A blank value in tabular models is similar to a NULL value in databases systems because
it represents the missing value in a field. In tabular models, a missing or empty value is referred as
blank because of the differences it has with traditional databases and the similarities it has with
Excel blank cells. In traditional databases arithmetic operations with NULL values evaluate to NULL

results, while DAX simply ignores the blank values in the calculation: BLANK()+1 evaluates to 1. This behavior is required to perform valid aggregations that ignore the blank values and aggregate the nonblanks. Aggregation of only blank values evaluate to a blank result: BLANK()+BLANK() evaluates to a blank value.

ARITHMETIC OPERATORS	
+	Addition
–	Subtraction
*	Multiplication
/	Division
^	Exponentiation
COMPARISON OPERATORS	
>	Greater than
<	Less than
>=	Greater than or equal to
<=	Less than or equal to
=	Equals
<>	Not equals
TEXT OPERATOR	
&	Concatenation
LOGICAL OPERATORS	
||	Logical OR
&&	Logical AND

DAX FUNCTION CATEGORIES WITH EXAMPLES

In addition to operators, DAX provides a list of functions that help with efficient data analysis. Approximately 50% of the DAX functions supported in SQL Server Analysis Services also have similar function names and equivalent results in Excel because DAX was initially targeted for information workers using PowerPivot for Excel. DAX provides functions that operate on tables as well as the ability to navigate between tables via relationships. Even though this capability appears to be similar to that provided by the VLOOKUP Excel function, the DAX functions provide more powerful functionality needed for advanced analytics. DAX also provides a set of functions that help to identify the current context of a calculation in which certain filters might have been applied, and time manipulation functions that help with the efficiency of calculations such as a year-over-year revenue growth calculation.

DAX functions can be broadly divided into eight categories: *Date and Time, Filter, Information, Logical, Math and Trigonometric, Text, Statistical,* and *Other.*

In this section you get a brief overview of the DAX functions with examples categorized based on their output or use. We have categorized examples in this way to show the input and output parameters taken by DAX functions and under what scenarios they will be used. Functions in the Logical, Math and Trigonometric (except SUM/SUMX), and Text categories are simple scalar functions that take scalar values as arguments and return a scalar value. Some functions in the Date and Time category are also simple scalar functions, and the rest are subcategorized as Time Intelligence functions. Functions in the Statistical category are aggregation functions that scan a table and perform a specific type of aggregation. Functions in the Information category can be subcategorized as simple scalar functions that provide information about specific scalar values; context information functions that provide information about the context the DAX formula is evaluated in; and connection information functions. The last subcategory of Information functions is part of row-level security, which will be covered in Chapter 19. Functions in the Other category are more BI-specific functions that perform table transformations, context manipulations, relationship navigations, and so on.

Scalar DAX Functions

The tables in this section show the Logical, Math and Trigonometric (except SUM/SUMX), Text, Simple Date and Time, and Simple Information functions. These are scalar functions that accept scalar values and return scalar values. Most of them are similar to the functions in Excel and have the same semantics. The following examples show you how to create calculated columns using scalar DAX functions. The calculated column NumberOfDaysOpen, as shown in Figure 18-8, is created with the following DAX formula:

```
INT(TODAY()-[OpenDate])
```

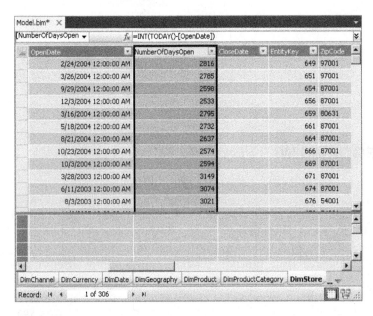

FIGURE 18-8

The formula calculates the difference between today's date and the store's open date and rounds it down to the nearest integer value for each row of the table. The difference of two Datetime values is a Datetime. Datetime values have numeric representation corresponding to the number of days past Dec 30, 1899, where the decimal part of the number represents the fraction of a day. The values in the NumberOfDaysOpen column corresponds to the number of full days the store is open. You can use the ROUND function to get not just full days, but also the nearest number of days (ROUND(TODAY()-[OpenDate], 0)). Some of the stores may be closed, and your calculation does not take that into account. To improve the calculation you should use the following DAX formula for the NumberOfDaysOpen column:

```
ROUND (
IF (
ISBLANK([CloseDate]),
TODAY(),
[CloseDate]
)-[OpenDate],
0
)
```

This formula first checks if the value of CloseDate column is blank for the current row and uses today's date as the last open date and CloseDate if it is not blank. The rest of the formula does not change; it calculates the difference between the last open date and the opening date and rounds up the difference to the number of days while implicitly casting the Datetime value to a numeric value. Figure 18-9 shows the final definition of the NumberOfDaysOpen column.

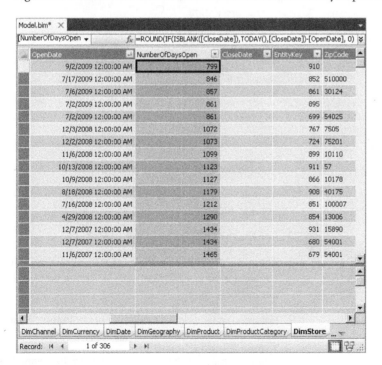

FIGURE 18-9

The following table shows the Logical functions.

FUNCTION NAME AND ARGUMENT	FUNCTION DESCRIPTION
AND (*Logical1*, *Logical2*)	Checks whether both arguments are TRUE, and returns TRUE if both arguments are TRUE. Otherwise returns FALSE.
FALSE ()	Returns the logical value FALSE.
IF (*LogicalTest*, *ResultIfTrue*, [*ResultIfFalse*])	Checks if a condition provided as the first argument is met. Returns one value if the condition is TRUE, and returns another value if the condition is FALSE. If the value is omitted then IF treats the return as an empty string.
IFERROR (*Value*, *ValueIfError*)	Evaluates an expression and returns a specified value if the expression returns an error; otherwise returns the value of the expression itself.
NOT (*Logical*)	Changes FALSE to TRUE, or TRUE to FALSE.
OR (*Logical1*, *Logical2*)	Checks whether one of the arguments is TRUE to return TRUE. The function returns FALSE if both arguments are FALSE.
SWITCH (*Expression*, *Value*, *Result* [,*Value*,*Result*],...[,*Else*])	Returns different results depending on the value of an expression.
TRUE ()	Returns the logical value TRUE.

The next table shows the Math and Trigonometric functions.

FUNCTION NAME AND ARGUMENT	FUNCTION DESCRIPTION
ABS (*Number*)	Returns the absolute value of a number.
CEILING (*Number*, *Significance*)	Rounds a number up to the nearest integer or to the nearest multiple of significance.
CURRENCY (*Value*)	Returns the value as a currency value.
EXP (*Number*)	Returns e raised to the power of a given number. The constant e equals 2.71828182845904, the base of the natural logarithm.
FACT (*Number*)	Returns the factorial of a number, equal to the series 1*2*3*...*, ending in the given number.
FLOOR (*Number*, *Significance*)	Rounds a number down, toward zero, to the nearest multiple of significance.

INT (*Number*)	Rounds a number down to the nearest integer.
ISO.CEILING (*Number*, [*Significance*])	Rounds a number up, to the nearest integer or to the nearest multiple of significance.
LN (*Number*)	Returns the natural logarithm of a number. Natural logarithms are based on the constant e (2.71828182845904).
LOG (*Number*, [*Base*])	Returns the logarithm of a number to the base you specify. If omitted, the base is 10.
LOG10 (*Number*)	Returns the base-10 logarithm of a number.
MOD (*Number*, *Divisor*)	Returns the remainder after a number is divided by a divisor. The result always has the same sign as the divisor.
MROUND (*Number*, *Multiple*)	Returns a number rounded to the desired multiple.
PI ()	Returns the value of Pi, 3.14159265358979, accurate to 15 digits.
POWER (*Number*, *Power*)	Returns the result of a number raised to a power.
QUOTIENT (*Numerator*, *Denominator*)	Performs division and returns only the integer portion of the division result.
RAND ()	Returns a random number greater than or equal to 0 and less than 1, evenly distributed.
RANDBETWEEN (*Bottom*, *Top*)	Returns a random number in the range between two numbers you specify.
ROUND (*Number*, *NumberOfDigits*)	Rounds a number to the specified number of digits.
ROUNDDOWN (*Number*, *NumberOfDigits*)	Rounds a number down, toward zero.
ROUNDUP (*Number*, *NumberOfDigits*)	Rounds a number up, away from zero.
SIGN (*Number*)	Determines the sign of a number. The function returns 1 if the number is positive, 0 (zero) if the number is zero, or −1 if the number is negative.
SQRT (*Number*)	Returns the square root of a number.
TRUNC (*Number*, [*NumberOfDigits*])	Truncates a number to an integer by removing the decimal, or fractional, part of the number.

The table below shows the Text functions.

FUNCTION NAME AND ARGUMENT	FUNCTION DESCRIPTION
BLANK()	Returns a blank value.
CONCATENATE(Text1,Text2)	Joins two text strings into one text string.
EXACT(Text1,Text2)	Compares two text strings and returns TRUE if they are exactly the same, FALSE otherwise. EXACT is case-sensitive but ignores formatting differences.
FIND(FindText,WithinText, [StartPosition],[NotFoundValue])	Returns the starting position of one text string within another text string.FIND is case-sensitive.
FIXED(Number,[Decimals], [NoCommas])	Rounds a number to the specified number of decimals and returns the result as text. It is possible to specify that the result be returned with or without commas.
FORMAT(Value,Format)	Converts a value to text according to the specified format.
LEFT(Text,[NumberOfCharacters])	Returns the specified number of characters from the start of a text string.
LEN(Text)	Returns the number of characters in a text string.
LOWER(Text)	Converts all letters in a text string to lowercase.
MID(Text,StartPosition, NumberOfCharacters)	Returns a string of characters from the middle of a text string, given a starting position and length.
REPLACE(OldText,StartPosition, NumberOfCharacters,NewText)	REPLACE replaces part of a text string, based on the number of characters you specify, with a different text string.
REPT(Text,NumberOfTimes)	Repeats text a given number of times. Use REPT to fill a cell with a number of instances of a text string.
RIGHT(Text,[NumberOfCharacters])	RIGHT returns the last character or characters in a text string, based on the number of characters you specify.
SEARCH(FindText,WithinText, [StartPosition],[NotFoundValue])	Returns the number of the character at which a specific character or text string is first found, reading left to right. Search is case-sensitive.
SUBSTITUTE(Text,OldText,NewText, [InstanceNumber])	Replaces existing text with new text in a text string.

TRIM(Text)	Removes all spaces from text except for single spaces between words.
UPPER(Text)	Converts a text string to all uppercase letters.
VALUE(Text)	Converts a text string that represents a number to a number.

The next table shows the Simple Date and Time functions.

FUNCTION NAME AND ARGUMENT	FUNCTION DESCRIPTION
DATE(Year, Month, Day)	Returns specified date as Datetime value.
DATEVALUE(DateText)	Converts a date in the form of text to a Datetime value.
DAY(Day)	Returns the day of the month, an integer value from 1 to 31.
EDATE(StartDate, Months)	Returns the date that is the indicated number of months before or after the start date.
EOMONTH(StartDate, Months)	Returns the date of the last day of the month, before or after a specified number of months.
HOUR(Datetime)	Returns the hour of the specified Datetime value as an integer value from 0 (12:00 A.M.) to 23 (11:00 P.M.).
MINUTE(Datetime)	Returns the minute of the specified Datetime value as an integer value from 0 to 59.
MONTH(Date)	Returns the month of the specified Datetime value as an integer value from 1 (January) to 12 (December).
NOW()	Returns the current date and time as a Datetime value.
SECOND()	Returns the second of the specified Datetime value as an integer value from 0 to 59.
TIME(Hour, Minute, Second)	Converts hours, minutes, and seconds given as integer numbers to a Datetime value.
TIMEVALUE(TimeText)	Converts a time in text format to a Datetime value.
TODAY()	Returns the current date as a Datetime value.

continues

(continued)

FUNCTION NAME AND ARGUMENT	FUNCTION DESCRIPTION
WEEKDAY(*Date*, [*ReturnType*])	Returns a number from 1 to 7 identifying the day of the week of a date. By default, the day ranges from 1 (Sunday) to 7 (Saturday). *ReturnType* parameter defines the beginning/end of the week. Supported values are 1 (week begins on Sunday/1 and ends on Saturday/7), 2 (week begins on Monday/1 and ends on Sunday/7), 3 (week begins on Monday/0 and ends on Sunday/6).
WEEKNUM(*Date*, [*ReturnType*])	Returns the week number for the given date and year according to the *ReturnType* value. The week number indicates where the week falls numerically within a year. *ReturnType* parameter defines the beginning of the week. Supported values are 1 (week begins on Sunday), 2 (week begins on Monday).
YEAR(*Date*)	Returns the year of a date as a four digit integer in the range 1900–9999.
YEARFRAC(*StartDate*, *EndDate*, [*Basis*])	Calculates the fraction of the year represented by the number of whole days between two dates. Basis parameter defines the type of day count basis to use. Supported values are 0 (US 30/360), 1 (actual/actual), 2 (actual/360), 3 (actual/365), and 4 (European 30/360).

The last table in this section shows the Simple Information functions.

FUNCTION NAME AND ARGUMENT	FUNCTION DESCRIPTION
ISBLANK(*Value*)	Checks whether a value is blank, and returns TRUE or FALSE.
ISERROR(*Value*)	Checks whether a value is an error, and returns TRUE or FALSE.
ISLOGICAL(*Value*)	Checks whether a value is a logical value (TRUE or FALSE), and returns TRUE or FALSE.
ISNONTEXT(*Value*)	Checks whether a value is not text (blank values are not text), and returns TRUE or FALSE.
ISNUMBER(*Value*)	Checks whether a value is a number, and returns TRUE or FALSE.
ISTEXT(*Value*)	Checks whether a value is text, and returns TRUE or FALSE.

Statistical DAX Functions

Functions in the Statistical category perform aggregations such as sums, counts, and averages. Some of the functions are similar to Excel aggregation functions, with the difference that they aggregate over a column of data as opposed to Excel functions that aggregate over a range of data.

DAX Aggregation functions perform eight types of aggregations: sum, average, count, max, min, rank, standard deviation, and variance. If you are familiar with Excel, you may notice that most of aggregation functions have the same names as Excel functions, whereas others have an X suffix. Two exceptions are the COUNTROWS and DISTINCTCOUNT functions, which do not exist in Excel. The functions without the X suffix take a column reference as an argument and perform corresponding aggregation over the values in that column. This functionality is similar to Excel, but it is limited for BI calculations. This is the reason DAX introduced extended versions of these functions that aggregate the results of given expressions for the rows of a table or table expression.

With the extended aggregation functions such as AVERAGEX, COUNTAX, COUNTX, MAXX, MINX, RANKX, STDEVX.P, STDEVX.S, SUMX, VARX.P, and VARX.S, you can construct formulas with the same behavior as their simplified counterparts. For example, AVERAGE(Table1[Column1]) is identical to AVERAGEX(Table1, Table1[Column1]). The simplified versions of aggregation functions are for simple syntax and compatibility with Excel aggregation functions. Aggregation functions scan the table specified in the first argument, evaluate the expression specified in the second argument for every row's context, and perform aggregation, such as sum, variance, or other, over the set of these values. The COUNTROWS function does not accept any scalar expression because it simply counts the rows in the table or in the result of table expression. The DISTINCTCOUNT function supports only the simple syntax accepting a column reference as the only parameter. It does not support arbitrary expressions for calculating number of unique values.

The following table lists the Statistical functions (including SUM/SUMX).

FUNCTION NAME AND ARGUMENT	FUNCTION DESCRIPTION
AVERAGE(*ColumnName*)	Returns the average (arithmetic mean) of all the numbers in a column.
AVERAGEA(*ColumnName*)	Returns the average (arithmetic mean) of all the values in a column.
AVERAGEX(*Table, Expression*)	Calculates the average (arithmetic mean) of a set of expressions evaluated for each row of the table.
COUNT(*ColumnName*)	Counts the number of cells in a column that contain numbers.
COUNTA(*ColumnName*)	Counts the number of cells in a column that are not empty. It counts not just rows that contain numeric values, but also rows that contain nonblank values, including text, dates, and logical values.

continues

(continued)

FUNCTION NAME AND ARGUMENT	FUNCTION DESCRIPTION
COUNTAX(*Table, Expression*)	Counts nonblank results when evaluating the result of an expression over a table. That is, it works just like the COUNTA function but is used to iterate through the rows in a table and count rows where the specified expressions results in a nonblank result.
COUNTBLANK(*ColumnName*)	Counts the number of blank cells in a column.
COUNTROWS(*Table*)	Counts the number of rows in the specified table or in a table defined by an expression.
COUNTX(*Table, Expression*)	Counts the number of rows that contain a number or an expression that evaluates to a number when evaluating an expression over a table.
DISTINCTCOUNT(*ColumnName*)	Counts the number of distinct values in a column.
MAX(*ColumnName*)	Returns the largest numeric value in a column.
MAXA(*ColumnName*)	Returns the largest value in a column, including any logical values and blanks.
MAXX(*Table, Expression*)	Evaluates an expression for each row of a table and returns the largest numeric value.
MIN(*ColumnName*)	Returns the smallest numeric value in a column. Ignores logical values and text.
MINA(*ColumnName*)	Returns the smallest value in a column, including any logical values and blanks.
MINX(*Table, Expression*)	Returns the smallest numeric value that results from evaluating an expression for each row of a table.
RANK.EQ(*Value, ColumnName, [Order]*)	Returns the rank of a number in a column of numbers. If more than one value has the same rank, the top rank of that set of values is returned. Supported values for *Order* are 0 (descending) and 1 (ascending).
RANKX(*Table, Expression, [Value], [Order], [Ties]*)	Returns the rank of specified value against the results of expression evaluated for each row in the specified table. Supported values for *Order* are 0 (descending) and 1 (ascending). Supported values for *Ties* are Dense (do not skip ranks after repeated values) and Skip (skip numbers after repeated values).
STDEV.P(*ColumnName*)	Calculates standard deviation based on the entire population given as arguments. Ignores logical and text values.

`STDEV.S(ColumnName)`	Estimates standard deviation based on a sample. Ignores logical and text values in the sample.
`STDEVX.P(Table, Expression)`	Estimates standard deviation based on the entire population that results from evaluating an expression for each row of a table.
`STDEVX.S(Table, Expression)`	Estimates standard deviation based on a sample that results from evaluating an expression for each row of a table.
`SUM(ColumnName)`	Returns the sum of all the numbers in a column.
`SUMX(Table, Expression)`	Calculates the sum of a set of expressions evaluated for each row of the table.
`VAR.P(ColumnName)`	Calculates variance based on the entire population. Ignores logical and text values in the population.
`VAR.S(ColumnName)`	Estimates variance based on a sample. Ignores logical and text values in the sample.
`VARX.P(Table, Expression)`	Estimates variance based on the entire population that results from evaluating an expression for each row of a table.
`VARX.S(Table, Expression)`	Estimates variance based on a sample that results from evaluating an expression for each row of a table.

Create the following calculated columns and measures in the ContosoRetail tabular model using aggregation functions.

1. Create the DAX measure Number of Sales in the FactSales table: `Number of Sales:=COUNTROWS(FactSales)` as shown in Figure 18-10. This measure calculates the number of rows in the FactSales table within the context it is evaluated in. If there are no sales for a given context, `COUNTROWS` returns a blank result.

2. Create the Number of Unique Products measure in the FactSales table: `Number of Unique Products:=DISTINCTCOUNT(FactSales[ProductKey])`. This measure calculates the unique number of products sold in the current context, as shown in Figure 18-11.

3. Create the Average Sales Count in Store measure in the DimStore table: `Average Sales Count in Store:=AVERAGEX(DimStore, [Number of Sales])` as shown in Figure 18-12. This measure evaluates the Number of Sales measure for every row in the DimStore table, which is the number of sales for a given store, and calculates the average of these numbers. The key point here is the context in which the Number of Sales measure is evaluated. It adds the DimStore table's row context into the filter context and then evaluates the expression. For example, evaluation of the Number of Sales measure for the first row of the DimStore table, where `[StoreKey]=273`, the FactSales table is filtered to contain only rows related to the store with ID of 273; then the number of rows is counted. This behavior is applied to every

measure evaluation that sets a difference between the evaluation of AVERAGEX(DimStore, [Number of Sales]) and AVERAGEX(DimStore, COUNTROWS(FactSales)). The latter does not add the row context of the DimStore table to the filter context before evaluating the COUNTROWS(FactSales) subexpression. Rows in the FactSales table are not restricted by the store in the current row context, and the subexpression evaluates to the same value for every row of the DimStore table.

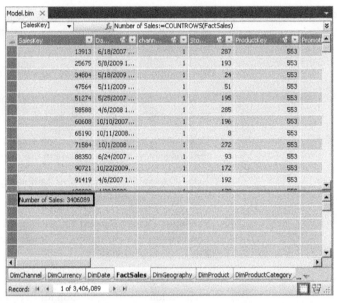

FIGURE 18-10

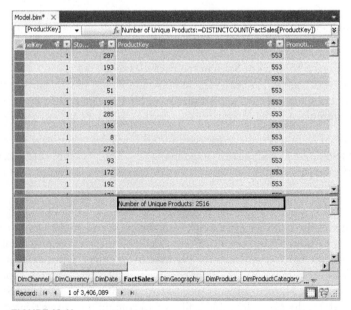

FIGURE 18-11

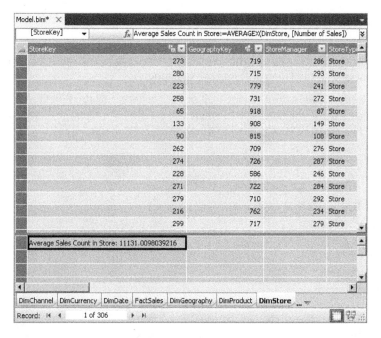

FIGURE 18-12

4. Create a StoreRank calculated column in the DimStore table with an =RANKX(DimStore, [Sum of SalesAmount], [Sum of SalesAmount], 0, SKIP) DAX formula, as shown in Figure 18-13. The RANKX function is evaluated for every row of the DimStore table. For a given row it first calculates the value of the third argument, which is the sum of sales in the selected store, and ranks it for the set of values calculated with the expression in the second argument for every row of the table specified in the first argument.

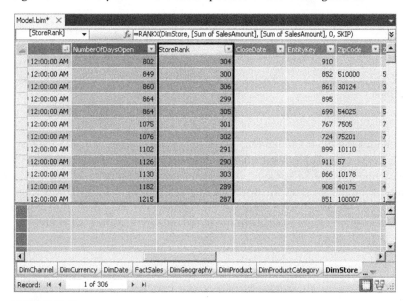

FIGURE 18-13

You can now use the previously defined measures to analyze the sales data in Excel along with the filter context.

1. Click the Analyze in Excel button on the Analysis Services toolbar to launch Excel with a PivotTable connected to the ContosoRetail tabular model.

2. Add a `DimStore[Average Sales Count in Store]` measure to the PivotTable values. Figure 18-14 shows the PivotTable with a single cell holding the Average Sales Count in Store measure. The measure is evaluated in a nonrestricted context.

FIGURE 18-14

3. Add `DimGeography[ContinentName]` and `DimGeography[StateProvinceName]` to the row labels of the PivotTable. Figure 18-15 shows the PivotTable with added fields in the row labels. Now the Average Sales Count in Store measure is evaluated for each cell individually averaging the number of sales for stores related to a specific Continent and State/Province. For each of the cells, you have a separate filter context in which the measure formula is evaluated. You may add more fields to the filter context by adding other columns to the row

and column labels. For example, adding `DimDate[CalendarYear]` to column filters can add another filter to the filter context of the measure evaluation.

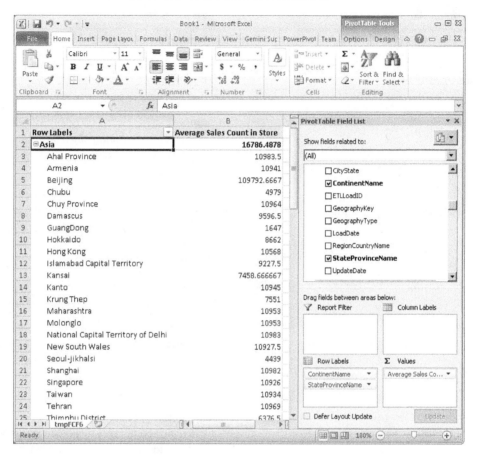

FIGURE 18-15

Other DAX Functions

Functions in the Other category are business intelligence (BI)-specific functions, which manipulate tables, filters, contexts, and relationships. The following table lists the functions in the Other category. In this chapter you learn the details only about some of these functions, including ALL, ALLEXCEPT, ALLNOBLANKROW, ALLSELECTED, CALCULATE, CALCULATETABLE, DISTINCT, EARLIER, EARLIEST, FILTER, LOOKUPVALUE, RELATED, RELATEDTABLE, USERELATIONSHIP, and VALUES. You learn the remaining functions in this category later in this chapter and in Chapter 19 while working with key BI problems and their solutions.

The following table shows the Other DAX functions.

Function Name and Argument	Function Description
ADDCOLUMNS(*Table,Name, Expression,*[*Name,Expression*]*,...*)	Returns a table with new columns specified by the DAX expressions.
ALL(*TableName*)	Returns all the rows in a table, ignoring any filters that might have been applied.
ALL(*ColumnName, [ColumnName,]...*)	Returns all distinct value combinations in specified columns, ignoring any filters that might have been applied. All columns must be from the same table.
ALLEXCEPT(*TableName, ColumnName, [ColumnName],...*)	Removes all context filters in the table except filters that have been applied to the specified columns. Returns all the rows in a table except for those rows affected by the specified column filters.
ALLNOBLANKROW(*TableNameOrColumnName*)	Returns all the rows except blank row in a table, or all the values in a column, ignoring any filters that might have been applied.
ALLSELECTED([*TableNameOrColumnName*])	Returns all the rows in a table, or all the values in a column, ignoring any filters that might have been applied inside the query, but keeping filters that come from outside.
CALCULATE(*Expression, [Filter], [Filter], ...*)	Evaluates an expression in a context modified by the specified filters. If evaluated in a row context, it also adds the row context to filter context.
CALCULATETABLE(*Table, [Filter], [Filter], ...*)	Evaluates a table expression in a context modified by filters. If evaluated in a row context, it also adds the row context to filter context.
CROSSJOIN(*Table, [Table], ...*)	Returns a table that is the crossjoin of specified tables or table expressions.
DISTINCT(*ColumnName*)	Returns a one-column table that contains the distinct (unique) values in specified column.
EARLIER(*ColumnName,[Number]*)	Returns the value in the specified column prior to the specified number of table scans. (The default is 1.)
EARLIEST(*ColumnName*)	Returns the value in the specified column for the first point at which there was a row context.

`FILTER(Table,FilterExpression)`	Returns a table that has been filtered with specified expression. A filter expression is a Boolean expression.
`FILTERS(ColumnName)`	Returns a table of the filter values applied directly to the specified column.
`GENERATE(Table1,Table2)`	The second table expression is evaluated for each row in the first table. Returns the crossjoin of the first table with these results.
`GENERATEALL(Table1,Table2)`	The second table expression is evaluated for each row in the first table. Returns the crossjoin of the first table with these results, including rows for which the second table expression is empty.
`KEEPFILTERS(Expression)`	Changes the CALCULATE and CALCULATETABLE function filtering semantics.
`LOOKUPVALUE(Result_ColumnName,Search_ColumnName, Search_Value, [,Search_ColumnName, Search_Value],...)`	Retrieves a value from a table corresponding to the values specified for search columns.
`RELATED(ColumnName)`	Returns a related value from another table.
`RELATEDTABLE(Table)`	Returns the specified table filtered by all related tables.
`ROLLUP(GroupBy_ColumnName, [GroupBy_ColumnName],...)`	Identifies a subset of columns specified in the call to SUMMARIZE function that should be used to calculate subtotals.
`ROLLUPGROUP( GroupBy_ColumnName, [GroupBy_ColumnName],...)`	Identifies a subset of columns specified in the call to SUMMARIZE function that should be used to calculate groups of subtotals.
`ROW(Name,Expression[,Name, Expression],...)`	Returns a single row table with new columns specified by the name and value calculated with DAX expressions.
`SAMPLE(Size,Table[,OrderBy,Order]...)`	Returns a sample subset from a given table expression. The rows are ordered by specified orders.
`SUMMARIZE(Table, [GroupBy_ColumnName], [GroupBy_ColumnName],... [,Name, Expression] [,Name,Expression]...)`	Creates a summary, the input table grouped by the specified columns. Additional columns are added with specified names and expressions.

continues

(continued)

Function Name and Argument	Function Description
TOPN(*N_Value,Table* [,*OrderBy_ Expression, Order*], [*OrderBy_Expression, Order*]..., [*Order*], [*Order*],...)	Returns a given number of top rows according to a specified expression. The table is ordered with specified orders before obtaining the top rows.
USERELATIONSHIP(*ColumnName1, ColumnName2*)	Specifies an existing relationship to be used in the evaluation of a DAX expression. The relationship is defined by naming, as arguments, the two columns that serve as endpoints.
VALUES(*TableNameOrColumnName*)	Returns a one-column table or a table that contains the distinct (unique) values in a column.
PATH(*ID_ColumnName, Parent_ColumnName*)	Returns a string that contains a delimited list of IDs, starting with the top/root of a hierarchy and ending with the specified ID.
PATHCONTAINS(*Path,Item*)	Returns TRUE if the specified *Item* exists within the specified *Path*.
PATHITEM(*Path,Position,*[*Type*])	Returns the nth item in the delimited list produced by the *Path* function.
PATHITEMREVERSE(*Path,Position,* [*Type*])	Returns the nth item in the delimited list produced by the *Path* function, counting backward from the last item in the *Path*.
PATHLENGTH(*Path*)	Returns the number of items in a particular *Path* string. This function returns 1 for the *Path* generated for an ID at the top/root of a hierarchy.

RELATED and RELATEDTABLE

You can use the RELATED and RELATEDTABLE functions to obtain values from a different table related to the current row (RELATED) or current context (RELATEDTABLE). Use these functions to create the following two calculated columns. Figure 18-16 shows the columns with calculated values.

```
DimProduct[ProductCategoryName]:=RELATED(DimProductCategory[ProductCategoryName])
DimProduct[ProductSales]:=SUMX(RELATEDTABLE(FactSales), FactSales[SalesAmount])
```

The ProductCategoryName column contains product category names for each product obtained from the related DimProductCategory table. The RELATED function uses the relationships between DimProduct, DimProductSubcategory, and DimProductCategory to obtain the value of ProductCategoryName corresponding to the current row context. The ProductSales column contains total sales amount for each of the products. For each row of the DimProducts table, the

RELATEDTABLE function adds the row context to the filter context and evaluates the FactSales table, resulting in the rows related to current product. Then, a summation of SalesAmount values is performed over the filtered table by the SUMX function.

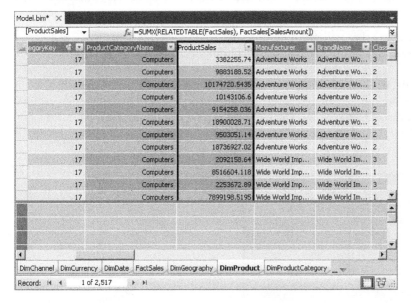

FIGURE 18-16

LOOKUPVALUE

The LOOKUPVALUE function is similar to the RELATED function in its semantics because it also obtains a value from a column in possibly a different table; however, it does not use any relationships for that. LOOKUPVALUE uses specified values for search columns to identify the value for the result column. It is similar to Excel's VLOOKUP function, but it has several differences. The search columns may belong to the same table as the result column or to related tables. The search value is a scalar expression that can be fully evaluated upfront. The expression used as a search value may not refer to any columns in the table being searched. Search values filter corresponding columns/tables and their related table. When all search column/value pairs have been applied, four outcomes are possible:

➤ If there are no rows, then a blank value is returned.

➤ If there is exactly one row, then the value in the result column is returned.

➤ If there are multiple rows and every value in the result column is identical to every other value, then that value is returned.

➤ If there are multiple rows and those rows contain more than one value in the result column, an error is returned.

The LOOKUP function operates on the base table that is not restricted by current filter context.

EARLIER and EARLIEST

If you have nested table scans, like in the case of nested aggregation functions or performing a table scan in a calculated column formula, use the `EARLIER` and `EARLIEST` functions to access a column value from the outer table scan.

To create a calculated column that will rank the stores based on their age using DAX `EARLIER` function, create a StoreRankBasedOnAge calculated column in the DimStore table with an `=COUNTROWS(FILTER(DimStore, [NumberOfDaysOpen] > EARLIER(DimStore[NumberOfDaysOpen])))+1` DAX formula, as shown in Figure 18-17. For every row in the `DimStore` table, the DAX formula filters the DimStore table so that it leaves only the rows that have a `NumberOfDaysOpen` value greater than the value in current row. Then, the calculated column formula counts the number of rows in the filtered table, which is essentially the number of stores that were opened earlier than the store in the current row.

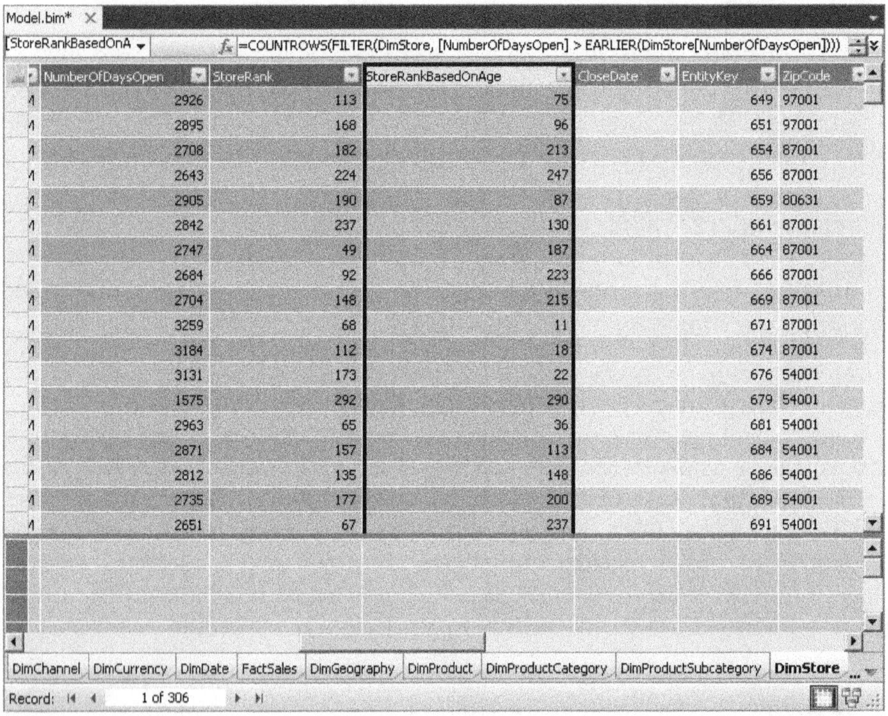

NumberOfDaysOpen	StoreRank	StoreRankBasedOnAge	CloseDate	EntityKey	ZipCode
2926	113	75		649	97001
2895	168	96		651	97001
2708	182	213		654	87001
2643	224	247		656	87001
2905	190	87		659	80631
2842	237	130		661	87001
2747	49	187		664	87001
2684	92	223		666	87001
2704	148	215		669	87001
3259	68	11		671	87001
3184	112	18		674	87001
3131	173	22		676	54001
1575	292	290		679	54001
2963	65	36		681	54001
2871	157	113		684	54001
2812	135	148		686	54001
2735	177	200		689	54001
2651	67	237		691	54001

FIGURE 18-17

VALUES and DISTINCT

The `VALUES` and `DISTINCT` functions return a table with a single column consisting of unique values in a specified column. The values in the column are restricted by the current filter context. There is a minor difference between these functions. The `VALUES` function returns all the values in a specified column including the blank row that might be generated due to referential integrity violations on one side of the relationships, whereas the `DISTINCT` function does not return the blank value.

FILTER

The FILTER function has simple semantics: for each row in a specified table or table expression, it evaluates the Boolean expression and returns only the rows that evaluated to TRUE. Follow these steps to create a measure that will calculate the number of active stores and analyze the number of active stores in different regions.

1. Create a Count of All Stores measure in the DimStore table with the DAX formula =COUNTROWS(DimStore).

2. Create a Count of Active Stores measure in the DimStore table with the DAX formula =COUNTROWS(FILTER(DimStore, [Status] = "On")), as shown in Figure 18-18.

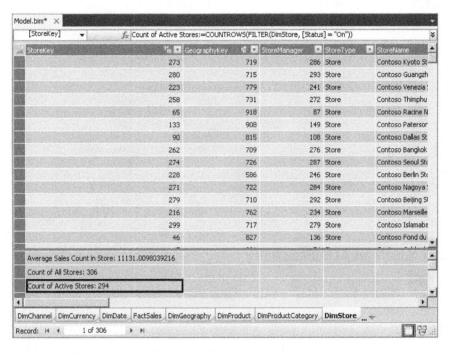

FIGURE 18-18

3. Click the Analyze in Excel button on the Analysis Services toolbar to launch Excel with a PivotTable connected to the ContosoRetail tabular model.

4. Add a DimStore[Count of Active Stores] measure to the PivotTable values.

5. Add a DimStore[Count of All Stores] measure to the PivotTable values.

6. Add a DimGeography[ContinentName] to the row labels.

Now your PivotTable should look like Figure 18-19. It shows that there are several inactive stores in North America.

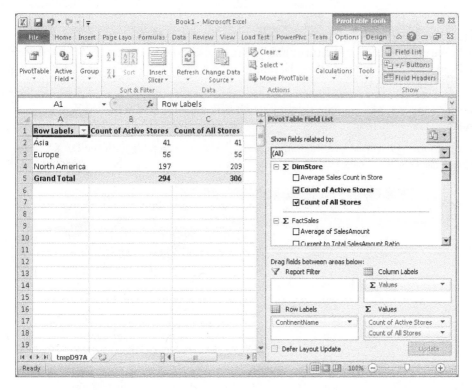

FIGURE 18-19

CALCULATE, ALL, and ALLSELECTED

The CALCULATE function is one of the most commonly used functions in DAX. It can change the filter context in which a given scalar expression is evaluated. If the CALCULATE function is used in a row context, it first adds the row context to the filter context; then it modifies the filter context with the filters specified in optional arguments. The CALCULATE function supports three types of filters:

➤ **Boolean filters** in the form of Boolean expressions: The CALCULATE function supports several restrictions on Boolean expressions:

    ➤ The expression cannot reference a measure.

    ➤ The expression cannot use the CALCULATE function.

    ➤ The expression cannot use any function that scans a table or returns a table, including aggregation functions.

➤ **Table filters** in the form of table expressions (DAX expressions that evaluate to a DAX table): These table filters restrict all related tables to the rows related to the specified table.

➤ **Active relationship modifiers** in the form of a USERELATIONSHIP function: If any inactive relationships are in the model, you can activate them by specifying them in a USERELATIONSHIP function inside a CALCULATE function. These type of filters modify the way related tables are filtered.

The ALL, ALLEXCEPT, ALLNOBLANKROW, and ALLSELECTED functions remove existing filters on certain tables and or columns. Follow these steps to learn more about the CALCULATE, ALL, and ALLEXCEPT functions.

1. Create a Current to Total SalesAmount Ratio measure in the FactSales table: Current to Total SalesAmount Ratio:=[Sum of SalesAmount] / CALCULATE([Sum of SalesAmount], ALL(FactSales)). This measure calculates the sum of the sales amount; then it calculates the sum of the sales amount a second time in a modified context in which the ALL function is applied on the FactSales table and returns the ratio of these two. The second time, the sum of sales amount is calculated for the entire FactSales table resulting in a total sales amount. See Figure 18-20.

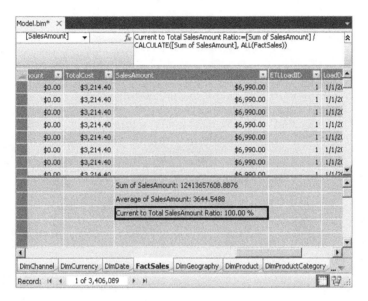

FIGURE 18-20

2. Use the Properties window to change the measure format to Percentage instead of General, as shown in Figure 18-21. Client applications such as Excel use the measure Format to apply given formatting to the values returned by measure evaluations.

3. Click the Analyze in Excel button on the Analysis Services toolbar to launch Excel with a PivotTable connected to the ContosoRetail tabular model.

4. Add a FactSales[Sum of SalesAmount] measure to the PivotTable values.

5. Add a FactSales[Current to Total SalesAmount Ratio] measure to the PivotTable values.

6. Add DimGeography[ContinentName] to the row labels. Now your PivotTable should look like Figure 18-22. The sum of the sales amount and corresponding ratio to the total is shown in the PivotTable.

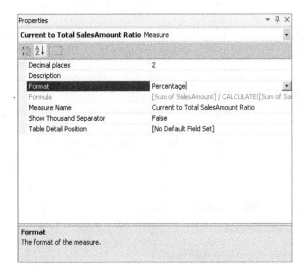

FIGURE 18-21

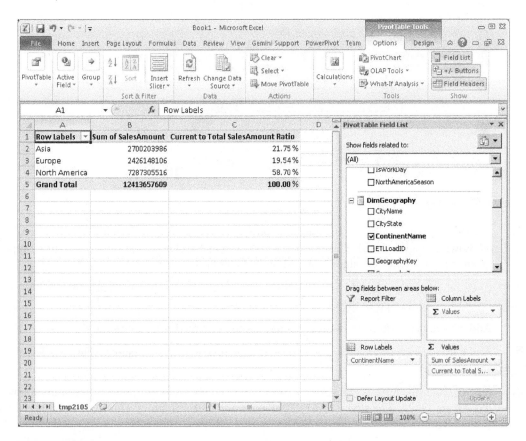

FIGURE 18-22

7. Remove the `FactSales[Sum of SalesAmount]` measure from the PivotTable values. Now you see only the ratio to the total sales amount for each region.

8. Add `DimDate[CalendarYear]` to column labels. In Figure 18-23 you see the ratio to the total sales amount for each continent and year, but this may not be what you want. What if you want to see the ratio of each continent's sale to the total for given year? To achieve the wanted result, you need to modify the DAX formula for the Current to Total SalesAmount Ratio measure. It should divide the sum of sales amount for the current context by the total sales amount for a given year. That is to ignore the filter on `DimGeography[ContinentName]` column but honor the context of `DimDate[CalendarYear]`.

9. Go to the ContosoRetail tabular project and change the measure formula to `Current to Total SalesAmount Ratio:=[Sum of SalesAmount] / CALCULATE([Sum of SalesAmount], ALLEXCEPT(FactSales, DimDate[CalendarYear]))`. Now it calculates the total sales amount for only a selected range of calendar years, as shown in Figure 18-23.

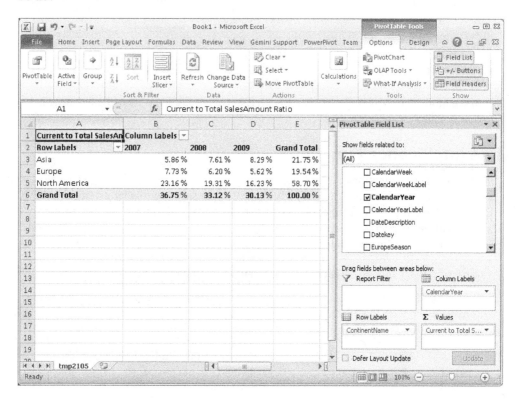

FIGURE 18-23

10. Go to Excel and refresh the PivotTable. The PivotTable now shows the ratio of each continent's sales amount to the total sales amount for each of the years. See Figure 18-24.

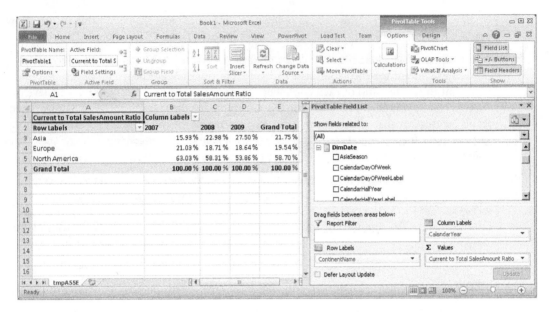

FIGURE 18-24

You see more examples with the CALCULATE function in Chapter 19 while learning key business problem solutions with DAX.

Time Intelligence Functions

Time Intelligence functions are composite functions that have knowledge about the calendar. They are a composite in the sense that you could achieve the same results by using other DAX functions; however, Time Intelligence functions provide ease of use and allow avoiding complex calculations around calendar specifics, such as the number of days in a month, leap year, and so on. The following table lists the Time Intelligence functions.

FUNCTION NAME AND ARGUMENT	FUNCTION DESCRIPTION
CLOSINGBALANCEMONTH (*Expression, Dates, [Filter]*)	Evaluates the expression at the last date of the month in the current context. *Filter* is set to the context of evaluation.
CLOSINGBALANCEQUARTER (*Expression, Dates, [Filter]*)	Evaluates the expression at the last date of the quarter in the current context. *Filter* is set to the context of evaluation.
CLOSINGBALANCEYEAR (*Expression, Dates, [Filter]*, *[YearEndDate]*)	Evaluates the expression at the last date of the year in the current context. *Filter* is set to the context of evaluation.

DATEADD(*Dates*,*NumberOfIntervals*, *Interval*)	Returns a table that contains a column of dates, shifted either forward or backward in time by the specified number of intervals from the dates in the current context. Supported values for *Interval* are year, quarter, month, and day.
DATESBETWEEN(*Dates*,*StartDate*, *EndDate*)	Returns a table that contains a column of dates that begins with the *StartDate* and continues until the *EndDate*.
DATESINPERIOD(*Dates*,*StartDate*, *NumberOfIntervals*,*Interval*)	Returns a table that contains a column of dates that begins with the *StartDate* and continues for the specified *NumberOfIntervals*. Supported values for *Interval* are year, quarter, month, and day.
DATESMTD(*Dates*)	Returns a table that contains a column of the dates for the month to date, in the current context.
DATESQTD(*Dates*)	Returns a table that contains a column of the dates for the quarter to date, in the current context.
DATESYTD(*Dates*, [*YearEndDate*])	Returns a table that contains a column of the dates for the year to date, in the current context. *YearEndDate* may specify the custom end of year.
ENDOFMONTH(*Dates*)	Returns the last date of the month in the current context for the specified column of dates.
ENDOFQUARTER(*Dates*)	Returns the last date of the quarter in the current context for the specified column of dates.
ENDOFYEAR(*Dates*, [*YearEndDate*])	Returns the last date of the year in the current context for the specified column of dates. *YearEndDate* may specify the custom end of year.
FIRSTDATE(*Dates*)	Returns the first date in the current context for the specified column of dates.
FIRSTNONBLANK(*ColumnName*, *Expression*)	Returns the first value in the column. The column returned is filtered by the current context, where the expression is not blank.
LASTDATE(*Dates*)	Returns the last date in the current context for the specified column of dates.
LASTNONBLANK(*ColumnName*, *Expression*)	Returns the last value in the column. The column returned is filtered by the current context, where the expression is not blank.

continues

(continued)

FUNCTION NAME AND ARGUMENT	FUNCTION DESCRIPTION
NEXTDAY(*Dates*)	Returns a table that contains a column of all dates from the next day, based on the first date specified in the dates column in the current context.
NEXTMONTH(*Dates*)	Returns a table that contains a column of all dates from the next month, based on the first date in the dates column in the current context.
NEXTQUARTER(*Dates*)	Returns a table that contains a column of all dates in the next quarter, based on the first date specified in the dates column in the current context.
NEXTYEAR(Dates, [*YearEndDate*])	Returns a table that contains a column of all dates in the next year, based on the first date in the dates column in the current context. *YearEndDate* may specify the custom end of year.
OPENINGBALANCEMONTH(*Expression*, *Dates*, [*Filter*])	Evaluates the expression at the first date of the month in the current context.
OPENINGBALANCEQUARTER (*Expression*, *Dates*, [*Filter*])	Evaluates the expression at the first date of the quarter in the current context.
OPENINGBALANCEYEAR(*Expression*, *Dates*, [*Filter*], [*YearEndDate*])	Evaluates the expression at the first date of the year in the current context.
PARALLELPERIOD(*Dates*, *NumberOfIntervals*, *Interval*)	Returns a table that contains a column of dates that represents a period parallel to the dates in the specified dates column in the current context with the dates shifted a number of intervals either forward in time or back in time. Supported values for *Interval* are year, quarter, month, and day.
PREVIOUSDAY(*Dates*)	Returns a table that contains a column of all dates representing the day that is previous to the first date in the dates column in the current context.
PREVIOUSMONTH(*Dates*)	Returns a table that contains a column of all dates from the previous month based on the first date in the dates column in the current context.
PREVIOUSQUARTER(*Dates*)	Returns a table that contains a column of all dates from the previous quarter based on the first date in the dates column in the current context.

PREVIOUSYEAR(*Dates*, [*YearEndDate*])	Returns a table that contains a column of all dates from the previous year given the last date in the dates column in the current context. *YearEndDate* may specify the custom end of year.
SAMEPERIODLASTYEAR(*Dates*)	Returns a table that contains a column of dates shifted one year back in time from the dates in the specified dates column in the current context.
STARTOFMONTH(*Dates*)	Returns the first date of the month in the current context for the specified column of dates.
STARTOFQUARTER(*Dates*)	Returns the first date of the quarter in the current context for the specified column of dates.
STARTOFYEAR(*Dates*, [*YearEndDate*])	Returns the first date of the year in the current context for the specified column of dates. *YearEndDate* may specify the custom end of year.
TOTALMTD(*Expression*,*Dates*, [*Filter*])	Evaluates the value of the expression for the month to date in the current context.
TOTALQTD(*Expression*,*Dates*, [*Filter*])	Evaluates the value of the expression for the dates in the quarter to date in the current context.
TOTALYTD(*Expression*,*Dates*, [*Filter*], [*YearEndDate*])	Evaluates the year-to-date value of the expression in the current context. *YearEndDate* may specify the custom end of year.

Most of Time Intelligence functions assume the existence of the Date table in the model. Some of the Time Intelligence functions also assume that the Date table is in granularity of days. As you can see in the tabular model you are working with in this chapter, the DimDate table in the ContosoRetail tabular model is in granularity of days. Follow these steps to mark it as a Date table.

1. From the main menu in SSDT, select Table ➤ Date ➤ Mark as Date Table, as shown in Figure 18-25.

FIGURE 18-25

2. In the Mark as Date Table dialog, the Datekey column is automatically detected as the unique identifier for the DimDate table, as shown in Figure 18-26. Click OK.

FIGURE 18-26

3. The DimDate table is now marked as a Date table and can be used in Time Intelligence functions.

Following are three subcategories of Time Intelligence functions:

➤ **Functions that return a single scalar value:** ENDOFMONTH, ENDOFQUARTER, ENDOFYEAR, FIRSTDATE, FIRSTNONBLANK, LASTDATE, LASTNONBLANK, STARTOFMONTH, STARTOFQUARTER, and STARTOFYEAR.

➤ **Functions that return a range of dates as a table that can later be used as a filter argument for the CALCULATE function:** DATEADD, DATESBETWEEN, DATESINPERIOD, DATESMTD, DATESQTD, DATESYTD, NEXTDAY, NEXTMONTH, NEXTQUARTER, NEXTYEAR, PARALLELPERIOD, PREVIOUSDAY, PREVIOUSMONTH, PREVIOUSQUARTER, PREVIOUSYEAR, and SAMEPERIODLASTYEAR.

➤ **Functions that evaluate a given expression for a time range:** CLOSINGBALANCEMONTH, CLOSINGBALANCEQUARTER, CLOSINGBALANCEYEAR, OPENINGBALANCEMONTH, OPENINGBALANCEQUARTER, OPENINGBALANCEYEAR, TOTALMTD, TOTALQTD, and TOTALYTD.

The following steps create measures in the ContosoRetail tabular model using Time Intelligence functions; use them to analyze the data in Excel.

1. Add a Sum of SalesAmount Prev Year measure to the FactSales table: Sum of SalesAmount Prev Year:=CALCULATE([Sum of SalesAmount], PREVIOUSYEAR(DimDate[Datekey])). The PREVIOUSYEAR function returns the range of dates prior to the range of dates in the current filter context. It modifies the range of dates in filter context and evaluates the Sum of SalesAmount measure for the previous year.

2. Add the Sum of SalesAmount To Date measure to the FactSales table: Sum of SalesAmount To Date:=CALCULATE([Sum of SalesAmount], DATESBETWEEN(DimDate[Datekey],

BLANK(), LASTDATE(DimDate[Datekey]))). The DATESBETWWEN function returns dates starting from the blank as the earliest date to the last date in the current context. It modifies the context set on dates to evaluate the Sum of SalesAmount measure for the date period starting from the beginning. Figure 18-27 shows both measure definitions.

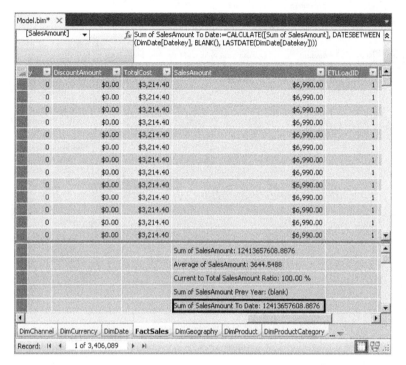

FIGURE 18-27

3. Click the Analyze in Excel button on the Analysis Services toolbar to launch Excel with a PivotTable connected to the ContosoRetail tabular model.

4. Add the following measures to the PivotTable values:

➤ FactSales[Sum of SalesAmount]

➤ FactSales[Sum of SalesAmount Prev Year]

➤ FactSales[Sum of SalesAmount To Date]

5. Add DimDate[CalendarYear] to the row labels. Figure 18-28 shows the PivotTable with all the fields.

➤ FactSales[Sum of SalesAmount] shows the sales amount for the selected year.

➤ FactSales[Sum of SalesAmount Prev Year] shows the sales amount for the previous year.

➤ FactSales[Sum of SalesAmount To Date] shows the sales amount from the beginning until the selected year.

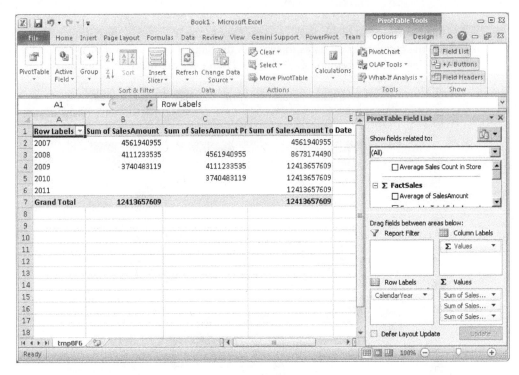

FIGURE 18-28

Chapter 19 provides additional examples of Time Intelligence functions.

Context Information Functions

You can use *Context Information* functions DAX formulas to check information about the filter context in which the formula is evaluated. The main purpose of these functions is to allow forking in a DAX formula evaluation depending on the filter context. For example, the following DAX construct allows avoiding any errors related to the table to scalar cast when there are multiple values in the current filter context:

```
IF(HASONEVALUE(DimDate[CalendarYear]), DimDate[CalendarYear], BLANK())
```

The formula checks if there is only one calendar year in the current context and uses that as a scalar or returns blank if multiple values are selected. Similarly you could check if a table or column contains a certain value and perform a calculation based on the condition.

The following table lists all Context Information functions.

FUNCTION NAME AND ARGUMENT	FUNCTION DESCRIPTION
CONTAINS(*Table*, *Column1*, *Value1* [*Column2*, *Value2*],...)	Returns TRUE if there exists at least one row where all columns have specified values.
HASONEFILTER(*Name*)	Returns TRUE if the specified table or column has one and only one filter.

`HASONEVALUE(ColumnName)`	Returns TRUE when there is only one value in the specified column.
`ISCROSSFILTERED(Name)`	Returns TRUE when the specified table or column is cross-filtered.
`ISFILTERED(ColumnName)`	Returns TRUE when there are direct filters on the specified column.
`ISSUBTOTAL(ColumnName)`	Returns TRUE if the current row contains a subtotal for a specified column and FALSE otherwise.

DAX AS A QUERY LANGUAGE

You learned how to use DAX as a formula language to define calculated column and measures. Analysis Services 2012 also supports DAX as a query language. The syntax for DAX queries is defined here:

```
DEFINE
MEASURE <TableName>[<MeasureName>] = <ScalarExpression>
MEASURE <TableName>[<MeasureName>] = <ScalarExpression>
...
EVALUATE
<TableExpression>

ORDER BY
          <ScalarExpression> [ASC | DESC]
          <ScalarExpression> [ASC | DESC]

START AT
          <ValueOrParameter>, <ValueOrParameter>, ...
```

The DEFINE, ORDER BY, and START AT clauses are optional, and you can leave them out of the query text.

The DEFINE clause enables you to define measures in the scope of the DAX query and use them in both EVALUATE and ORDER BY clauses. Measures defined in the DEFINE clause behave the same way as if they are defined in the model; they can reference other measures and columns defined in the model. The only difference is that these measures live only in the scope of the specific query. They cannot be referenced from other queries or other DAX formulas. A measure should be defined with its fully qualified name, meaning the parent table must be specified.

The EVALUATE clause defines the main DAX query to evaluate. The EVALUATE clause supports table expressions only; the result of a DAX formula must be a table, not a scalar expression. DAX does not support an implicit cast from a scalar value to a table; therefore, the outer DAX function used in a table expression after EVALUATE must return a table.

The ORDER BY and START AT sections are closely related. ORDER BY specifies the sorting to be applied to the result set. START AT provides a mechanism to have the results begin at a particular spot in the ordered set. Each item following the START AT clause maps to one of the ORDER BY expressions. The query may specify either a value at which to start or the name of a parameter that contains the value at which to start. The syntax for a parameter in the START AT clause can be @FOO where FOO is the parameter name. Using parameters instead of constant values in the START AT clause enables the starting values to be passed in as query parameters. The items following START AT are comma delimited, and there cannot be more items than are specified within the ORDER BY clause. The START AT items are used to filter the result set, removing any items that would have appeared in the report prior to the specified values. Following is an example that illustrates a DAX query:

```
DEFINE
        MEASURE FactSales[Max Discount] = MAXX(FactSales,
        RELATED(DimPromotion[DiscountPercent]))
EVALUATE
        FILTER(DimStore, [Max Discount] < 0.2)

ORDER BY
                DimStore[EmployeeCount] ASC,
                FactSales[Max Discount] DESC

START AT 50
```

In this example the Max Discount measure is defined in the FactSales table that calculates the maximum percent of discount in the current context. The query filters the DimStore table to include only the rows that had all promotions with less than a 20% discount. The result is sorted by the EmployeeCount column and the discount percentage. The rows that correspond to stores with less than 50 employees are removed from the result. DAX queries return the table in the form of a rowset.

You can use SQL Server Management Studio to send the DAX queries to Analysis Services 2012 server. Follow these steps to execute the preceding sample query.

1. Launch SQL Server Management Studio and connect to a local Analysis Services instance. Connect to the instance that hosts the ContosoRetail temporary tabular model.

2. The Databases folder in the SSMS Object Explorer window shows a database with a name that starts with ContosoRetail_ as shown in Figure 18-29. Right-click the database, and select NewQuery/MDX. The MDX Query editor window opens. The MDX Query editor allows editing and executing DAX queries just like MDX queries.

3. Copy and paste the preceding query text into the query editor window, as shown in Figure 18-30.

Execute the query by pressing F5 or clicking the Execute button on the SQL Server Analysis Services Editors toolbar. The result of the query appears in the Results window, as shown in Figure 18-31. Only two rows are returned by the query.

DAX queries typically use more table manipulation functions than scalar DAX formulas. For this reason, this section discusses some of DAX table functions.

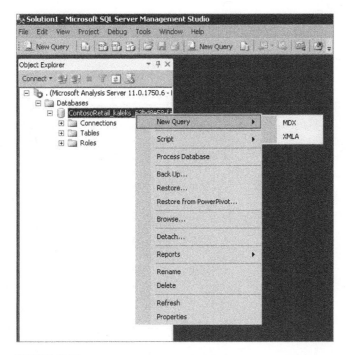

FIGURE 18-29

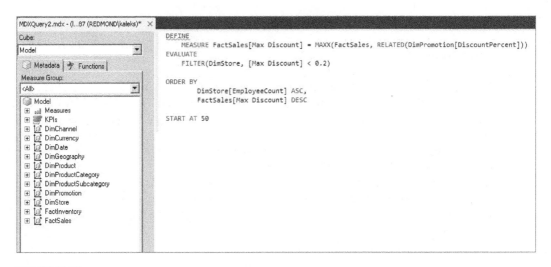

FIGURE 18-30

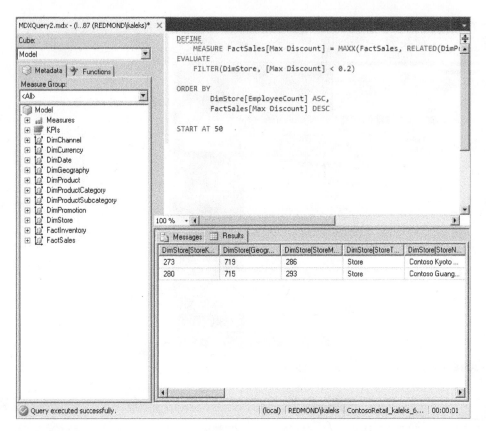

FIGURE 18-31

Use the TOPN and SAMPLE functions to limit the number of rows in a specified table. TOPN returns
the topmost *N* rows from the table based on the specified order. The TOPN function may actually
return more rows than requested if ties are in the data for the given ordering. Suppose there are five
distinct values followed by three equal values and the formula asks for the top six. The TOPN function returns eight rows in this scenario because there is no deterministic way to select the top six
rows. The SAMPLE function similarly returns a specified number of rows from the table by sampling
the rows. It returns the topmost and bottommost rows as well as other rows that are evenly distributed based on the specified order. Both functions do not guarantee the order of rows in the result.
Following are several DAX queries demonstrating the use of the TOPN and SAMPLE functions.

```
EVALUATE
        TOPN(5, DimStore, [Sum of SalesAmount])
```

The preceding query returns the five top stores that had the highest sales. Execute the query in SQL
Server Management Studio against the ContosoRetail database. Figure 18-32 shows the result of
the query. The stores in the result have one to five values in the StoreRank column. StoreRank is a
calculated column ranking the stores based on their sales amount. The result is not sorted because
there is no ORDER BY clause in the query.

```
EVALUATE
        SAMPLE(5, DimStore, [Sum of SalesAmount], 1)
```

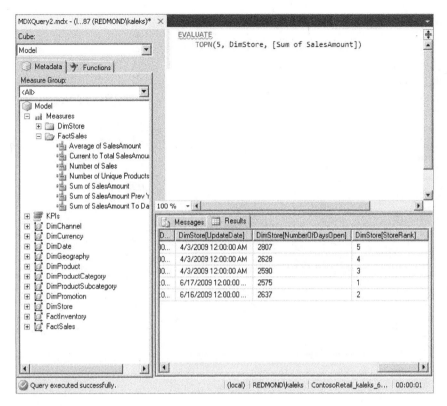

FIGURE 18-32

The preceding query returns the five stores sampled from the entire table based on their sales amount. Execute the query in SQL Server Management Studio against the ContosoRetail database. Figure 18-33 shows the result of the query. The stores in the result have evenly distributed rank values from 306 total stores, and the sampled set includes the topmost and bottommost rows from the ordered table.

The CROSSJOIN function takes any number of table expressions as inputs, evaluates each of the expressions independently, and returns the cross join of all these tables (all combinations of rows within these tables). Columns within the result of CROSSJOIN are referred by using the fully qualified column names from the arguments to this function. This means that such names must be unique and unambiguous. For example, the CROSSJOIN of a table with itself cannot be allowed. CROSSJOIN returns an error whenever the result contains duplicate column names. The relationships outgoing from the argument tables or table expressions are inherited by the result of CROSSJOIN. For example, the result of CROSSJOIN(FactSales, FactInventory) inherits all the relationships that the FactSales and FactInventory tables have. The result table does not have any incoming relationships because any primary key column from the argument table contains duplicate values in the result table. The following DAX query returns the cross join of all geographies and products.

```
EVALUATE
     CROSSJOIN(DimGeography, DimProduct)
```

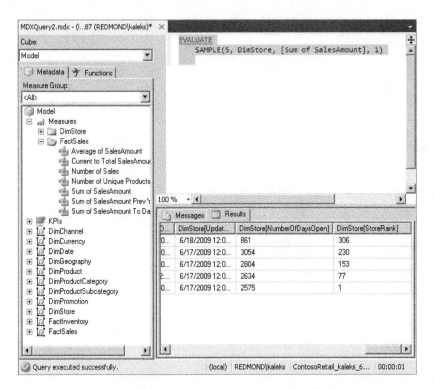

FIGURE 18-33

The GENERATE and GENERATEALL functions are similar to CROSSJOIN with a slight difference. They scan the first table and for each row evaluate the second table expression, then they cross join the current row from the first table with the result of the second table expression. The current row of the first table is in the row context but not in the filter context while evaluating the second table expression. The difference between GENERATE and GENERATEALL is that if the result of the second table expression is an empty table, then GENERATE removes the current row from the result while GENERATEALL adds the current row to the result with blank values corresponding to the columns from the second expression. The following DAX query cross joins each calendar year value with corresponding sampled products ordered based on their sales in the selected year. The CALCULATETABLE function is used to add the current row context (the calendar year value) to the filter context for evaluating the SAMPLE function. The filter on calendar year filters rows in the FactSales table affecting the value of the Sum of SalesAmount measure. The result has a cross join of the calendar year with the sampled five products. See Figure 18-34.

```
EVALUATE
      GENERATEALL (
VALUES (DimDate [CalendarYear]) ,
CALCULATETABLE (SAMPLE (5, DimProduct, [Sum of SalesAmount]))
)
ORDER BY  DimDate [CalendarYear], DimProduct [ProductKey]
```

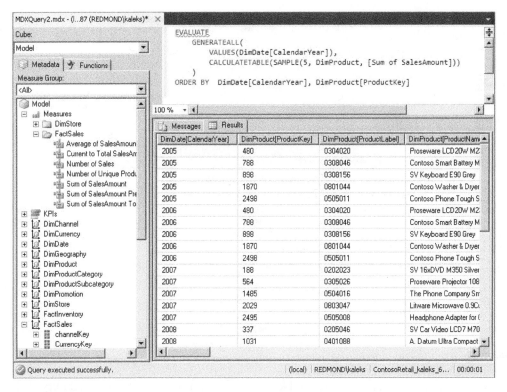

FIGURE 18-34

The ADDCOLUMNS function adds calculated columns to the table expression. The calculated columns are assigned the specified names and their values are populated by evaluating the specified DAX formula for every row in the table. The columns added by the ADDCOLUMNS function may be referenced by the name specified in the argument. For example, if the column name is specified as "bar", then the user may reference it with the following syntax: [bar]. The column name specified in the argument of ADDCOLUMNS may also include a table name such as "foo[bar]"; then the column may be referenced either with a nonfully qualified name [bar] or by a fully qualified name foo[bar]. This does not mean that there is a table foo in either the query or schema context; this is only a naming flexibility for the user. The following DAX query uses the ADDCOLUMN function to generate a report for sales amount per each calendar year. VALUES(DimDate[CalendarYear]) generates a single column table with all calendar year values, and ADDCOLUMNS evaluates the [Sum of SalesAmount] measure for every row of that table. The measure evaluation adds the row context to the filter context; therefore, the sum of sales amount is calculated for the current calendar year value. See Figure 18-35 for the result of the query.

```
EVALUATE
        ADDCOLUMNS (
                VALUES(DimDate[CalendarYear]),
                "Sales Amount", [Sum of SalesAmount]
        )
ORDER BY DimDate[CalendarYear]
```

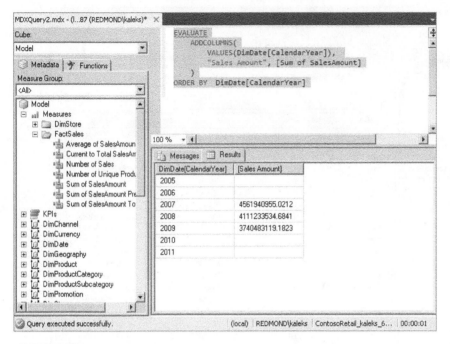

FIGURE 18-35

The SUMMARIZE function creates summary tables of data. It also combines the functionality of the ADDCOLUMNS function, meaning it allows adding new calculated columns to the result with specified names and DAX formulas. You can create the summary table by performing a GROUP BY operation. The first argument of SUMMARIZE is a table expression. The second set of arguments (GROUP BY columns) is a list of one or more column references that belong either to the table in the first argument or its related tables. For example, the following expression groups by the FactSales table with the calendar year and store keys:

```
SUMMARIZE(FactSales, DimDate[CalendarYear], FactSales[StoreKey])
```

The third set of arguments is a list of column name/expression pairs that you can use to define new columns in the result table similar to the ADDCOLUMNS function. The SUMMARIZE function first evaluates the table expression specified in the first argument; then it creates a new table containing the unique combinations of the column values specified in the second set of arguments (similar to selecting only the specified columns and applying a distinct operation over the rows in selected columns) and finally it adds the new columns specified in the third set of arguments by evaluating the specified DAX formulas for every row of the table. A difference from the ADDCOLUMNS function is that SUMMARIZE adds the row context to filter context before evaluating DAX expressions for new columns. Also, these DAX formulas may refer to the columns from the second set of arguments as if their values are already known. The following DAX query can generate a table with the calendar year, quarter, and month values along with their corresponding sales amount. Figure 18-36 shows the result of the query.

```
EVALUATE
     SUMMARIZE(
```

```
            DimDate,
            DimDate[CalendarYear],
            DimDate[CalendarQuarterLabel],
            DimDate[CalendarMonthLabel],
            "Total Sales", SUM(FactSales[SalesAmount])
        )
    ORDER BY
        DimDate[CalendarYear],
        DimDate[CalendarQuarterLabel],
        DimDate[CalendarMonthLabel]
```

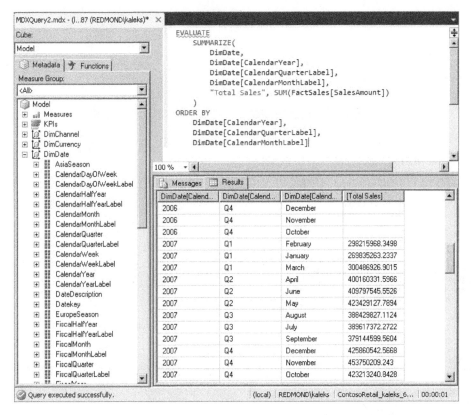

FIGURE 18-36

As you see, the query result shows the sales amount for each of the months of a given year or
quarter. It is often used to get the subtotals for a given level along with details of a lower level. For
example, you might want to see the subtotals of the sales amount for every quarter. For this, the
SUMMARIZE function supports the ROLLUP and ROLLUPGROUP constructs that specify the columns
for which subtotals are requested. For example, the following query produces the sales amount
for every month and the subtotals for every quarter and year. Figure 18-37 shows the result of the
query. Rows with blank calendar quarter labels correspond to subtotals for a given year, whereas
rows with blank calendar month labels correspond to subtotals for a given quarter. Blanks may also
be valid values for the columns in the result of SUMMARIZE; therefore, the differentiation of subtotal

rows may be nontrivial. For this reason, DAX supports the information function ISSUBTOTAL that returns TRUE if the current row is the subtotal for a specified column.

```
EVALUATE
SUMMARIZE(
            DimDate,
            DimDate[CalendarYear],
            ROLLUP(
                    DimDate[CalendarQuarterLabel],
                    DimDate[CalendarMonthLabel]
            ),
            «Total Sales», SUM(FactSales[SalesAmount])
        )
ORDER BY
        DimDate[CalendarYear],
        DimDate[CalendarQuarterLabel],
        DimDate[CalendarMonthLabel]
```

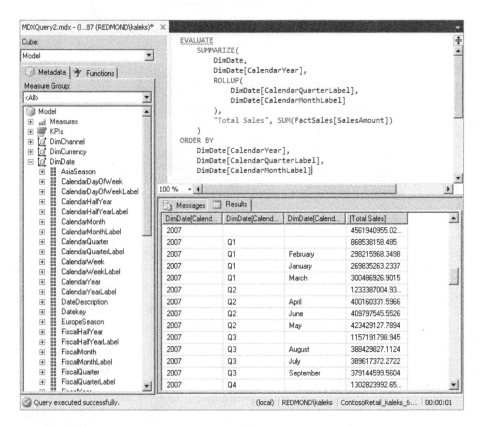

FIGURE 18-37

You can use the ROLLUPGROUP construct inside ROLLUP to generate a single subtotal for the entire group. If DimDate[CalendarQuarterLabel] and DimDate[CalendarMonthLabel] were specified inside ROLLUPGROUP in the preceding example, then there would be a single subtotal row for every year and not for quarters. The following example demonstrates the usage of ROLLUPGROUP and ISSUBTOTAL. It adds a new calculated column with a ISSUBTOTAL(DimDate[CalendarQuarter Label]) formula that has a value of TRUE if the current row is a subtotal for the calendar quarter and FALSE otherwise. The usage of ROLLUPGROUP eliminates the rows corresponding to subtotals for the calendar months.

```
EVALUATE
        SUMMARIZE(
                DimDate,
                DimDate[CalendarYear],
                ROLLUP(
                        ROLLUPGROUP(
                                DimDate[CalendarQuarterLabel],
                                DimDate[CalendarMonthLabel]
                        )
                ),
                "Total Sales", SUM(FactSales[SalesAmount]),
                "Subtotal", ISSUBTOTAL(DimDate[CalendarQuarterLabel])
        )
ORDER BY
        DimDate[CalendarYear],
        DimDate[CalendarQuarterLabel],
        DimDate[CalendarMonthLabel]
```

Use the ROW function to create a table with a single row. It enables DAX query users to query scalar DAX expressions by wrapping them inside the ROW function and forming a table with them. The ROW function takes a list of column names and DAX scalar expressions. For each pair it adds a column in a single row table and evaluates the DAX formula to calculate the value for a given column. The following query returns a table with a single row and two columns corresponding to the sum and average of the sales amount.

```
EVALUATE
        ROW(
                "Sum of SalesAmount", [Sum of SalesAmount],
                "Average of SalesAmount", [Average of SalesAmount]
        )
```

Use the FILTERS function to return the values of a given column in the current filter context that are restricted by filters applied directly on the specified column. For example, if there is a filter on the CalendarYear column, then FILTERS(DimDate[CalendarQuarterLabel]) returns all the values in the CalendarQuarterLabel column because there is no direct filter on it. The KEEPFILTERS function marks a table expression specified in the argument, so if it is added to the filter context, it does not change the existing filters. For example, if you have a FactSales[SalesAmount]>1000 filter on the SalesAmount column, then the KEEPFILTERS(FILTER(FactSales, FactSales[SalesAmount]<5000)) filter does not override the existing filter but intersects them, resulting in a filter on the SalesAmount column that is 1000<FactSales[SalesAmount]<5000.

The DAX query language is a powerful tool for generating reports based on Analysis Services Tabular models. Power View, which you learn about in Chapter 24, uses DAX queries to generate reports and charts based on Tabular models.

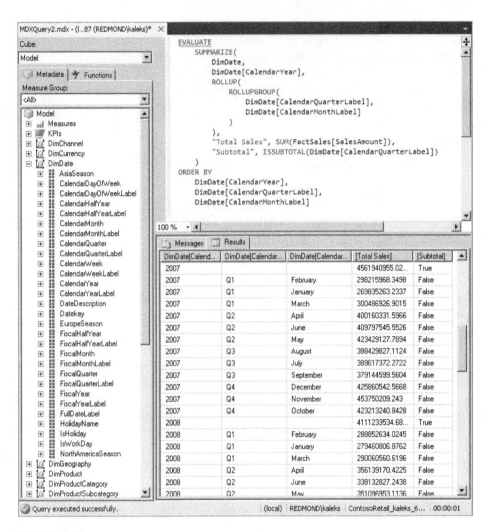

FIGURE 18-38

DAX AND MDX

As you learned in this chapter, DAX is both an expression language and query language similar to MDX. The main difference is that DAX operates with tables and columns, whereas MDX operates with dimensions and measure groups. DAX provides many functions similar to Excel functions with their syntax and semantics, which makes it easy to learn and start using. Many BI users familiar with Excel have a much shorter learning curve with DAX than with MDX. Along with the simple functions, DAX also provides more advanced functions that allow working with complex BI problems by manipulating tables, expression evaluation context, time periods, and so on.

On the other hand, MDX provides a richer arsenal of BI-specific functions. As a query language MDX is powerful for analytics, allowing querying a cell set with axes and values. The DAX query language is more report-oriented in which you expect a table with many rows and details.

When you connect a client such as Excel to tabular BISMs, Excel sends MDX queries to the model. At the same time you can connect a client such as Power View that sends DAX queries to the tabular BISM. Therefore, you can query the tabular BISM using MDX or DAX based on your client application and needs. When you connect to a tabular BISM, you can also see the multidimensional views where each table is mapped as a dimension and a measure group. The columns of the table are shown as attributes and measures within a table are part of the measure group of the table. Using an MDX query you can query the DAX measures as measures. There is an overlap in what you can achieve with both languages; choose the right language based on your applications' needs. There may be some performance implications choosing DAX or MDX, so you must evaluate the performance of your queries against your models.

SUMMARY

In this chapter you were first introduced to DAX as a formula or expression language. This chapter gave an overview of DAX with some examples of DAX expressions that involved various DAX functions and how DAX helps in data analysis by navigating between tables and iterating over rows in tables. The syntax of several DAX functions is similar to Excel functions when performing simple calculations, and it also provides rich functionality when performing complex BI analytics.

You also learned how to create calculated columns and measures using DAX formulas and use Excel to analyze the data using DAX measures so that you can better understand about Row context and Filter context semantics. Finally, you learned DAX as a query language and how to retrieve the data from your tabular BISM with the help of table manipulation functions and the EVALUATE syntax. You can query your tabular BISM via MDX or DAX, and you need to choose the right query language based on your applications' needs. In the next chapter you learn how to solve certain common business problems using SQL Server Analysis Services 2012, tabular BISM, and specific DAX calculations.

19

Advanced Topics in DAX

WHAT'S IN THIS CHAPTER?

➤ Parent-child hierarchies

➤ Cross-filtering with many-to-many relationships

➤ Role-playing dimensions

➤ Time-based averages

➤ Non-aggregatable attributes

In Chapter 18 you learned the basic concepts of DAX expressions and queries with several examples, and you became familiar with DAX functions, their categorization, and their purpose. In this chapter you take a list of typical Business Intelligence (BI) problems and solve them with tabular BISM with DAX. You learn how to define parent-child hierarchies using specific DAX functions, and how to analyze the data. Tabular models do not natively support many-to-many relationships, so this chapter shows you how to define many-to-many relationships between tables with DAX. You also learn various options for modeling role-playing dimensions. Finally, you also look at additional Time Intelligence function examples.

In this chapter you consider business scenarios and their implementation in BISM tabular using DAX. These scenarios include problems that do not have native DAX solutions and require special handling. The scenarios also include building parent-child hierarchies and performing aggregations for them, creating DAX calculations using cross filtering and performing time-based analysis using Time Intelligence functions. You walk through the scenarios step by step so that you understand how to define these, and you can design your tabular BISM efficiently for your specific organizational needs.

PARENT-CHILD HIERARCHIES

Parent-child hierarchies are one of the common hierarchy types in a business intelligence space by which people analyze the data. The most common parent-child hierarchy is the manager-employee relationship in which the manager is also an employee. SQL Server Analysis Services supports parent-child hierarchies natively for multidimensional BISM (refer to Chapter 8). Tabular BISM does not support defining parent-child hierarchies natively but SQL Server Analysis Services provides a set of DAX functions that help you define parent-child hierarchies.

To work with parent-child hierarchies, this section uses a specific tabular model. Create a new Analysis Services tabular model by importing the DimAccount and FactStrategyPlan tables from the ContosoRetail SQL Server database. SQL Server Data Tools (SSDT) automatically import the relationship between the two tables. Figure 19-1 shows the diagram of a tabular model.

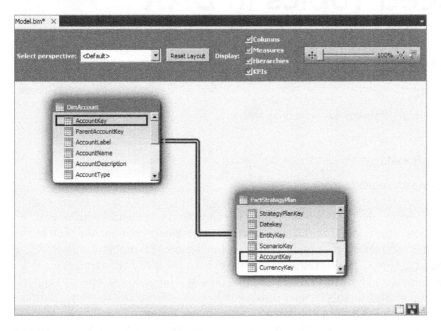

FIGURE 19-1

The DimAccount table has an AccountKey for every account and a ParentAccountKey pointing to parent account forming a parent-child relationship. In multidimensional models Analysis Services supports parent-child dimensions; however, tabular models do not support that notion in the schema level. To define the parent-child hierarchy based on the accounts and their levels, you need to define DAX calculations with the help of special DAX functions introduced in SQL Server Analysis Services 2012 and then create a hierarchy.

DAX provides the PATH function that builds the delimited path to the topmost level for a given row. For the ContosoRetail example it builds the path from a given account key to the topmost account. The PATH function takes two column references as arguments. The first argument is the column reference of the key column, whereas the second argument is the parent key column. Both columns must be from the same table. The PATH function starts by determining the current context for the key column by calculating the equivalent of CALCULATE(VALUES(<KeyColumn>)). The result must be a single value from the key column. When there are more than one or there are zero values for the key column in the current context, the PATH function returns an error. When there is a single value for the key column, then PATH returns a string that contains a delimited list of keys, (using a vertical pipe as the delimiter) starting with the top of the hierarchy and ending with the key value in current context. The string is constructed as follows:

1. Put the single key in the current context into the string (as the rightmost key in that string).

2. Look up the parent key, and if one exists, prefix the string with that parent key and a delimiter.

3. Repeat step 2 until there is no parent to be prefixed. The parent is considered to be empty if it is either a blank value or is equal to the key.

The PATH function is mainly used to define a calculated column in a table containing parent-child relationships between two columns within that table. The PATH function output is then used to generate different levels of hierarchy. Define a DimAccount[Path]:=PATH([AccountKey],[ParentAccountKey]) calculated column in the DimAccount table, as shown in Figure 19-2. The values in the Path column show that the account with AccountKey=1 is the topmost account, accounts with AccountKey=19 and 24 are on the second level, and so on.

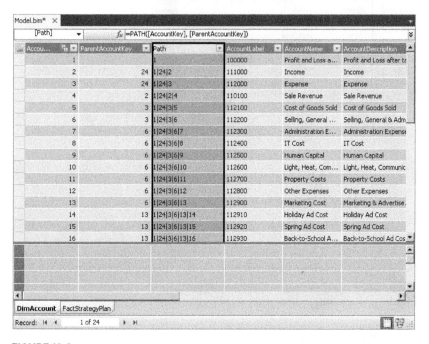

FIGURE 19-2

In addition to the `PATH` function, DAX provides several functions that operate on the values of the Path column.

The `PATHLENGTH` function takes a string containing a path value as an argument and returns the length of the path, which is useful for determining the level of a parent-child hierarchy for the current row context. Define a `DimAccount[PathLength]:=PATHLENGTH([Path])` calculated column in the DimAccount table. Figure 19-3 shows the new calculated column with populated values. The values in the PathLength column show seven levels in the hierarchy. To create the parent-child hierarchy, you must create a calculated column for each level of the hierarchy. DAX provides `PATHITEM` and `PATHITEMREVERSE` functions that return the value on a given level from the Path string. The `PATHITEM` function returns the item/value for a given level from the beginning of the string, whereas the `PATHITEMREVERSE` function returns the item/value for a given level from the end of the string.

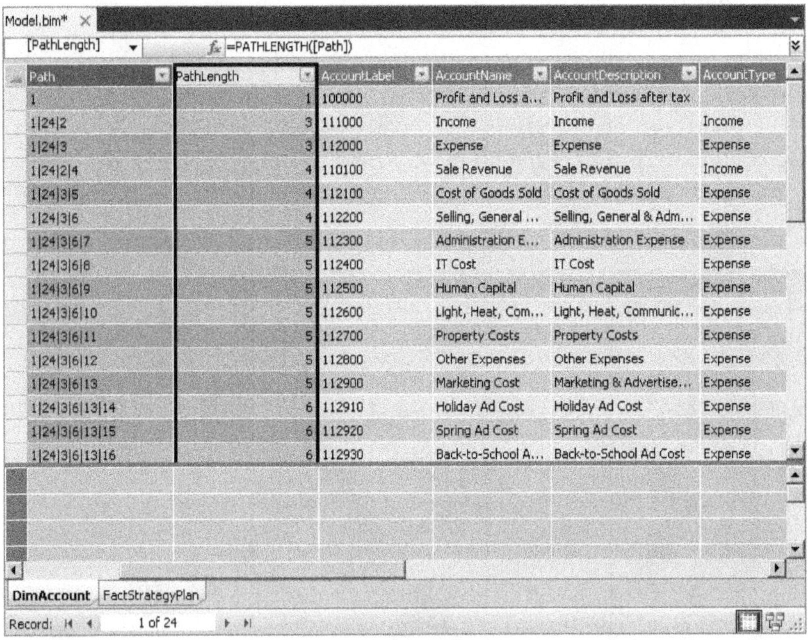

Path	PathLength	AccountLabel	AccountName	AccountDescription	AccountType
1	1	100000	Profit and Loss a...	Profit and Loss after tax	
1|24|2	3	111000	Income	Income	Income
1|24|3	3	112000	Expense	Expense	Expense
1|24|2|4	4	110100	Sale Revenue	Sale Revenue	Income
1|24|3|5	4	112100	Cost of Goods Sold	Cost of Goods Sold	Expense
1|24|3|6	4	112200	Selling, General ...	Selling, General & Adm...	Expense
1|24|3|6|7	5	112300	Administration E...	Administration Expense	Expense
1|24|3|6|8	5	112400	IT Cost	IT Cost	Expense
1|24|3|6|9	5	112500	Human Capital	Human Capital	Expense
1|24|3|6|10	5	112600	Light, Heat, Com...	Light, Heat, Communic...	Expense
1|24|3|6|11	5	112700	Property Costs	Property Costs	Expense
1|24|3|6|12	5	112800	Other Expenses	Other Expenses	Expense
1|24|3|6|13	5	112900	Marketing Cost	Marketing & Advertise...	Expense
1|24|3|6|13|14	6	112910	Holiday Ad Cost	Holiday Ad Cost	Expense
1|24|3|6|13|15	6	112920	Spring Ad Cost	Spring Ad Cost	Expense
1|24|3|6|13|16	6	112930	Back-to-School A...	Back-to-School Ad Cost	Expense

FIGURE 19-3

Create calculated columns in the DimAccount table, which correspond to the levels of the hierarchy, using the following DAX formulas. With this approach you simply flatten the parent-child hierarchy and create a regular user hierarchy on top of the flattened levels. Figure 19-4 shows the level calculated columns defined with the formulas below and their populated values.

```
DimAccount[Level1]:=PATHITEM([Path], 1)
DimAccount[Level2]:=PATHITEM([Path], 2)
DimAccount[Level3]:=PATHITEM([Path], 3)
DimAccount[Level4]:=PATHITEM([Path], 4)
DimAccount[Level5]:=PATHITEM([Path], 5)
```

```
DimAccount[Level6]:=PATHITEM([Path], 6)
DimAccount[Level7]:=PATHITEM([Path], 7)
```

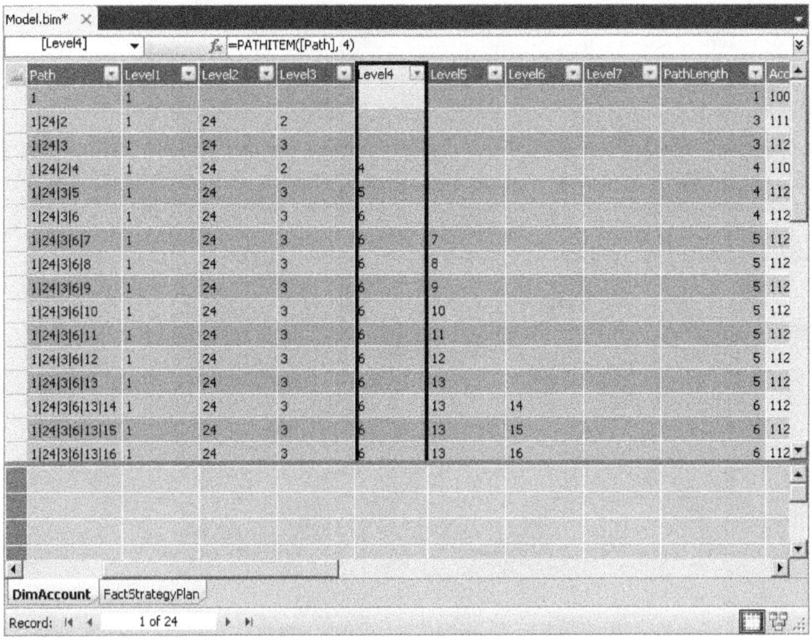

Path	Level1	Level2	Level3	Level4	Level5	Level6	Level7	PathLength	Acc
1	1							1	100
1|24|2	1	24	2					3	111
1|24|3	1	24	3					3	112
1|24|2|4	1	24	2	4				4	110
1|24|3|5	1	24	3	5				4	112
1|24|3|6	1	24	3	6				4	112
1|24|3|6|7	1	24	3	6	7			5	112
1|24|3|6|8	1	24	3	6	8			5	112
1|24|3|6|9	1	24	3	6	9			5	112
1|24|3|6|10	1	24	3	6	10			5	112
1|24|3|6|11	1	24	3	6	11			5	112
1|24|3|6|12	1	24	3	6	12			5	112
1|24|3|6|13	1	24	3	6	13			5	112
1|24|3|6|13|14	1	24	3	6	13	14		6	112
1|24|3|6|13|15	1	24	3	6	13	15		6	112
1|24|3|6|13|16	1	24	3	6	13	16		6	112

FIGURE 19-4

Now you can create a hierarchy based on the flattened levels of the parent-child hierarchy. However, it may not be the greatest idea to build a hierarchy on the key values in level columns; they are not useful for browsing the data. It is more helpful to have Account names instead of the key values in level columns. Use the following DAX formulas to modify level calculated columns to have account names for each level. The formulas look for the account name by setting a filter on the account key. Figure 19-5 shows the final values for level columns.

```
DimAccount[Level1]:=LOOKUPVALUE([AccountName],[AccountKey],PATHITEM([Path],1))
DimAccount[Level2]:=LOOKUPVALUE([AccountName],[AccountKey],PATHITEM([Path],2))
DimAccount[Level3]:=LOOKUPVALUE([AccountName],[AccountKey],PATHITEM([Path],3))
DimAccount[Level4]:=LOOKUPVALUE([AccountName],[AccountKey],PATHITEM([Path],4))
DimAccount[Level5]:=LOOKUPVALUE([AccountName],[AccountKey],PATHITEM([Path],5))
DimAccount[Level6]:=LOOKUPVALUE([AccountName],[AccountKey],PATHITEM([Path],6))
DimAccount[Level7]:=LOOKUPVALUE([AccountName],[AccountKey],PATHITEM([Path],7))
```

Follow these steps to create an Accounts hierarchy using the level calculated columns:

1. Switch to the diagram view.
2. Zoom in the DimAccount table, and select Level1-Level7 columns.
3. Right click the selection, and select Create Hierarchy, as shown in Figure 19-6. Name the hierarchy **Accounts**.

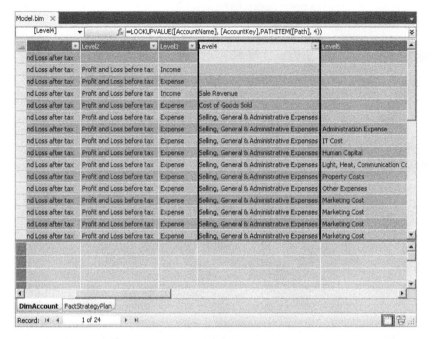

FIGURE 19-5

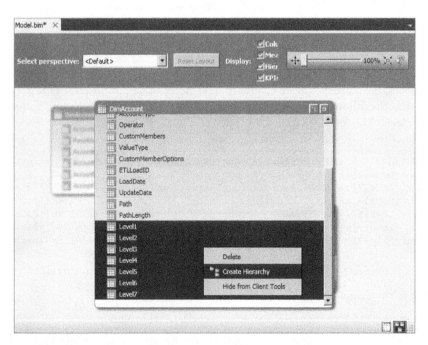

FIGURE 19-6

4. SSDT tries to create the hierarchy in the correct order based on the cardinalities of values in different columns. Figure 19-7 shows that the hierarchy is created in the wrong order: Level1 ➤ Level2 ➤ Level3 ➤ Level4 ➤ Level7 ➤ Level6 ➤ Level5. Drag and drop levels in the hierarchy to correct the order to match the following: Level1 ➤ Level2 ➤ Level3 ➤ Level4 ➤ Level5 ➤ Level6 ➤ Level7.

5. Switch to grid view. Now you have a hierarchy corresponding to the accounts in the DimAccount table.

Now that you have the hierarchy defined, consider adding a DAX measure that shows the amount on each of the accounts based on a planned strategy (the FactStrategyPlan table) and the operators defined for each of the accounts. As you can see, the Operator column in the DimAccount table associated a "+" or "−" operator with each account. These operators must be applied to the amount on every account when aggregating to parent account. For example, the account named Expense has a − operator, which means that its amount should be subtracted from its parent account (Profit and Loss Before Tax) when aggregating. The operator for a given account is not sufficient to determine how it should be aggregated to a given level. For example, if an account has a − operator and its parent has

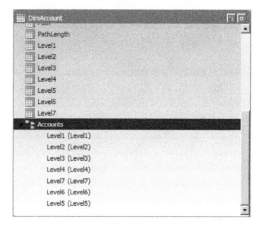

FIGURE 19-7

a − operator, too, it should be added to its grandparent amount when aggregating two levels up. To simplify the calculations you need to define operators (or a multiplier factor −1 or 1) for each level of aggregation. Use the following DAX formulas as calculated columns in the DimAccount table to define the multiplier factors for each level:

```
DimAccount[Level7Factor]:=
IF(LOOKUPVALUE([Operator],[AccountKey],PATHITEM([Path],7))="-",-1,1)
DimAccount[Level6Factor]:=
IF(LOOKUPVALUE([Operator],[AccountKey],PATHITEM([Path],6))="-",-1,1)* [Level7Factor]
DimAccount[Level5Factor]:=
IF(LOOKUPVALUE([Operator],[AccountKey],PATHITEM([Path],5))="-",-1,1)* [Level6Factor]
DimAccount[Level4Factor]:=
IF(LOOKUPVALUE([Operator],[AccountKey],PATHITEM([Path],4))="-",-1,1)* [Level5Factor]
DimAccount[Level3Factor]:=
IF(LOOKUPVALUE([Operator],[AccountKey],PATHITEM([Path],3))="-",-1,1)* [Level4Factor]
DimAccount[Level2Factor]:=
IF(LOOKUPVALUE([Operator],[AccountKey],PATHITEM([Path],2))="-",-1,1)* [Level3Factor]
DimAccount[Level1Factor]:=
IF(LOOKUPVALUE([Operator],[AccountKey],PATHITEM([Path],1))="-",-1,1)* [Level2Factor]
```

For every account, the preceding formulas calculate the factor by multiplying the accounts factor with all its parents up to the specified level. The multiplier factor for each account is calculated with this formula: IF(LOOKUPVALUE([Operator],[AccountKey],PATHITEM([Path],*<level>*))="-",-1,1), where *<level>* is the level of the current account in the path. However, this formula is multiplied with the parent's multiplier factor for a level up and so on until reaching Level1. Figure 19-8 shows the new calculated columns and their values.

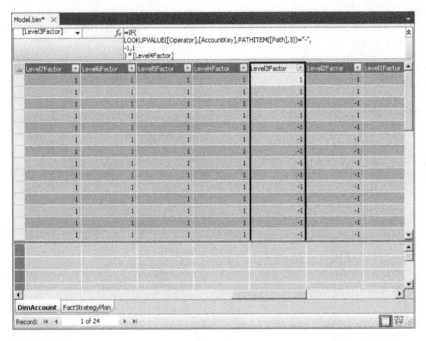

FIGURE 19-8

Now that you have the multiplier factors defined for each level, you can define a measure that performs the aggregation of amounts for each account. The measure should use the appropriate multiplier factor depending on which level it is evaluated for. For example, if the measure is evaluated for an account that is on Level2, the measure should use a multiplier factor from the Level2Factor column. Now, define the Aggregated Amount measure in the FactStrategyPlan table with the following formula:

```
Aggregated Amount:=SWITCH(
    MIN(DimAccount[PathLength]),
    7, SUMX(FactStrategyPlan,RELATED(DimAccount[Level7Factor])*[Amount]),
    6, SUMX(FactStrategyPlan,RELATED(DimAccount[Level6Factor])*[Amount]),
    5, SUMX(FactStrategyPlan,RELATED(DimAccount[Level5Factor])*[Amount]),
    4, SUMX(FactStrategyPlan,RELATED(DimAccount[Level4Factor])*[Amount]),
    3, SUMX(FactStrategyPlan,RELATED(DimAccount[Level3Factor])*[Amount]),
    2, SUMXFactStrategyPlan,RELATED(DimAccount[Level2Factor])*[Amount]),
    1, SUMX(FactStrategyPlan,RELATED(DimAccount[Level1Factor])*[Amount])
)
```

The DAX formula first tries to determine the level it is evaluating for by calculating MIN(DimAccount[PathLength]). Next, it performs aggregation over the FactStrategyPlan table and for every row by getting the multiplier factor for the related account to multiply with the amount in the current planned transaction. Now you can invoke Excel and analyze the data using the

`Aggregated Amount` measure. Follow these steps to build a PivotTable with an Accounts hierarchy and the `Aggregated Amount` measure:

1. On the Analysis Services toolbar, click the Analyze in Excel button to launch Excel with a PivotTable connected to the Accounts tabular model.

2. Add a `DimAccount[Accounts]` hierarchy to row labels.

3. Add a `FactStrategyPlan[Aggregated Amount]` measure to values.

4. Expand the Accounts hierarchy to see the accounts under Profit and Loss After Tax ➢ Profit and Loss Before Tax ➢ Expense ➢ Selling, General & Administrative Expenses to look at the Aggregated amount for the different accounts on different levels. Figure 19-9 shows the PivotTable.

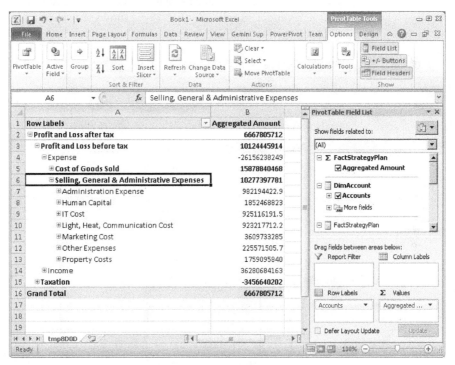

FIGURE 19-9

This solution works for more generic cases as well, when the accounts are marked not by "+" or "-" operators but positive, negative, or fractional weights. Multiplier calculated columns defined in the schema can serve the same purpose but have not just positive or negative values, but also accumulated factors for different accounts on different levels. You can also define an appropriate DAX expression if you do not want to roll up the value of a child to its parent.

CROSS-FILTERING WITH MANY-TO-MANY RELATIONSHIPS

To discuss cross filtering with many-to-many relationships, this section uses the CrossFilteringWithManyToMany Analysis Services tabular project based on the Adventure Works relational database. The content for this example is available on this book's page on Wrox.com in the Chapter 19 folder. This project uses the product sample Adventure Works relational database, which you have probably installed on your machine for earlier chapters. If not, download the relational database and restore or attach it to your SQL Server relational database instance. Open the tabular project CrossFilteringWithManyToMany; make sure you change the connection to the right Adventure Works relational database on your machine; and click Refresh/Process.

The tabular project has five tables: SalesOrderDetail, ProductVendor, Customer, Product, and Vendor. The SalesOrderDetail table is related to the Product and Customer table showing the details of every sales transaction. The ProductVendor table is related to the Product and Vendor tables showing what products each vendor supplies. Figure 19-10 shows the schema of the tabular model.

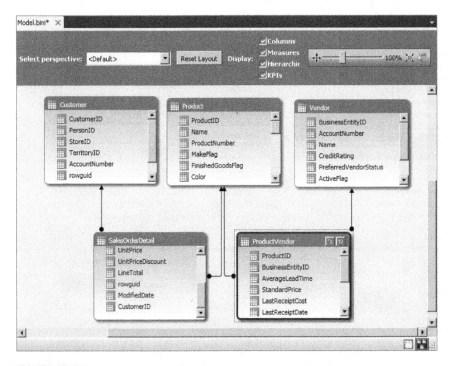

FIGURE 19-10

You need to understand more about filtering and cross-filtering in tabular BISM with examples before implementing the business solution to achieve cross-filtering with many-to-many relationships.

Filtering

Filtering is used when some rows of a given table are filtered out based on a condition. The filtering condition may be a simple or complex DAX expression within a tabular BISM, but it should be set on the rows of a given table. An example of table filtering is described by the following DAX expression:

1. The following expression filters the SalesOrderDetail table by removing rows for which the order quantity is more than 10:

```
FILTER(SalesOrderDetail, [OrderQuantity]>10)
```

2. The following expression filters the Customer table by removing rows that have an account number different from AW00011024:

```
CALCULATETABLE(Customer, [AccountNumber]="AW00011024")
```

When referring to these DAX expressions you can mention that they filter SalesOrderDetail and Customer tables respectively.

Cross-Filtering

Cross-filtering is used when some rows of a given table are eliminated in the current context based on a filter applied to a different (related) table. In DAX any filter applied to a table that is the one side of a relationship automatically cross-filters the table on the many side of the relationship. Following are several examples of cross-filtering:

➤ The following expression filters the Customer table by removing customers whose name is not Lisa. This automatically cross-filters the SalesOrderDetail table by removing sales transactions not made by customers with the name Lisa when a relationship has been defined between the SalesOrderDetail table and Customer table.

```
FILTER(Customer, [FirstName]="Lisa")
```

➤ The following expression filters the Product table by removing products with black color. This automatically cross-filters the SalesOrderDetail and ProductVendor tables by removing rows related to black products because there is a relationship between the SalesOrderDetail and ProductVendor tables.

```
CALCULATETABLE(Product, Product[Color]!="Black")
```

The examples in this section illustrate the cross-filtering automatically performed by DAX in tabular BISM. However, scenarios exist in which you want to cross-filter a table not directly related to the filtered table. For example, if a filter is on the Product table, you may want to cross-filter the Customer table by removing customers that did not purchase the selected products. This behavior is performed automatically; you need to design DAX expressions that promote the filter from the Product table to the Customer table. This next section can help you to design appropriate DAX expressions.

Cross-Filtering with DAX

DAX automatically cross-filters related table (tables that have relationship defined between them) by propagating a filter *from* the one side of the relationship *to* the many side. However, the filter is not propagated *to* the one side of the relationship *from* the many side. Follow these steps to add DAX calculations to the CrossFilteringWithManyToMany tabular model and build a PivotTable that shows the sales amount spent by each customer and the number of customers who purchased a given product.

1. Create a ProductName calculated column in the SalesOrderDetail table with this DAX expression: `SalesOrderDetail[ProductName]:=RELATED(Product[Name])`. The calculated column contains the name of the product sold in the current transaction, as shown in Figure 19-11.

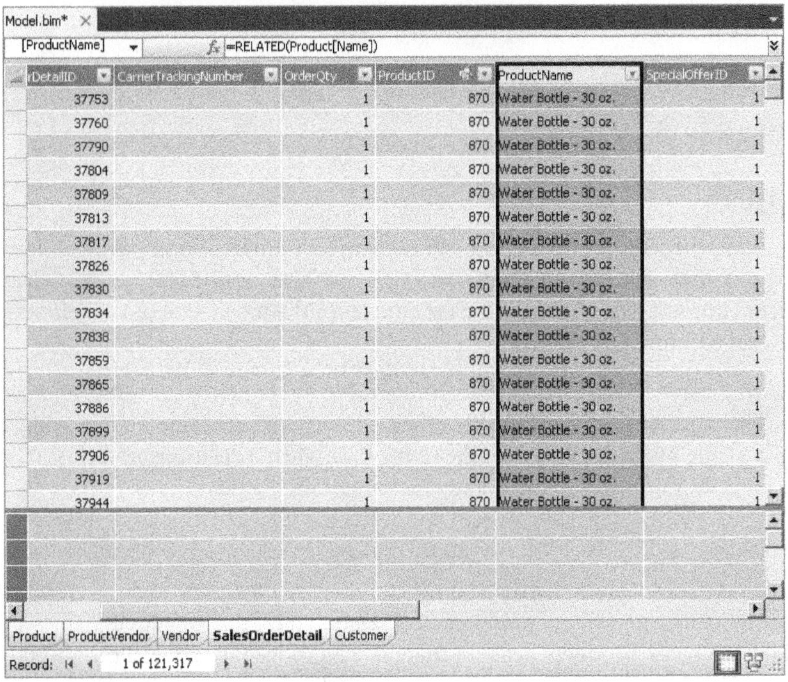

FIGURE 19-11

2. Define a measure `SalesOrderDetail[SalesAmount]:=SUM(SalesOrderDetail[LineTotal])` in the SalesOrderDetail table. The measure calculates the sum of the sales amount in the transactions for the given context, as shown in Figure 19-12.

3. Define a measure `Customer[Number of Customers]:=COUNTROWS(Customer)` in the Customer table. The measure calculates the number of customers in the given context, as shown in Figure 19-13.

4. On the Analysis Services toolbar, Click the Analyze in Excel button to launch Excel with a PivotTable connected to the CrossFilteringWithManyToMany tabular model.

5. Add a `Customer[FirstName]` column to the PivotTable row labels.

6. Add a SalesOrderDetail[SalesAmount] measure to the PivotTable values.

Figure 19-14 shows the PivotTable with both fields. You can see for each FirstName of the customers that the SalesOrderDetail table is cross-filtered automatically and the SalesOrderDetail[SalesAmount] measure is calculated for the cross-filtered rows.

8. Try the similar approach to get the number of customers that purchased a given product. Remove all the fields from the PivotTable and add SalesOrderDetail[ProductName] to row labels.

9. Add a Customer[Number of Customers] measure to the values. The PivotTable should look like Figure 19-15. As you can see the number of customers is not calculated in the context of the product in the row label. The reason is that the ProductName column is in the SalesOrderDetail table, and the filter does not automatically cross-filter the Customer table that is on the one side of the relationship.

To propagate the filter on the SalesOrderDetail table to the Customer table, you should define a new measure that explicitly sets the filter context with the DAX formula. You can use three possible solutions with DAX expressions to define the new measure:

➤ Customer[Number of Customers CF1]:=CALCULATE([Number of Customers], SalesOrderDetail)

This measure evaluates the Customer[Number of Customers] measure in the context of the SalesOrderDetail table. It explicitly adds filtered rows of the SalesOrderDetail table into the current filter context.

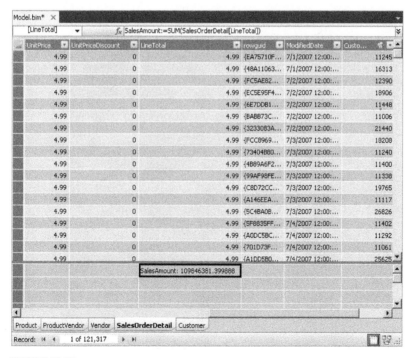

FIGURE 19-12

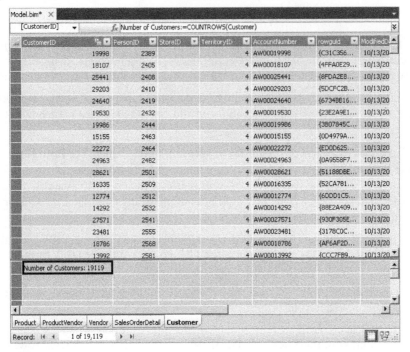

FIGURE 19-13

FIGURE 19-14

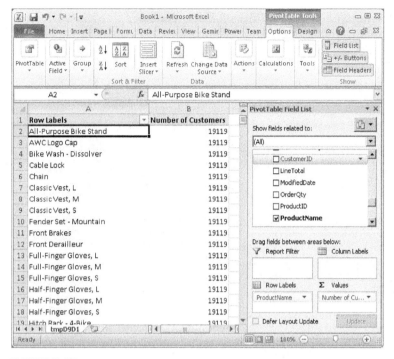

FIGURE 19-15

➤ `Customer[Number of Customers CF2]:=CALCULATE([Number of Customers], FILTER(Customer, [Number of Sales]>0))` where `[Number of Sales]` measure should be defined as `SalesOrderDetail[Number of Sales]:=COUNTROWS(SalesOrderDetail)`.

> This measure explicitly filters the Customer table by removing the rows that do not have related sales transactions in current context.

➤ `Customer[Number of Customers CF3]:=CALCULATE([Number of Customers], SUMMARIZE(SalesOrderDetail, Customer[CustomerID]))` `SUMMARIZE(SalesOrderDetail, Customer[CustomerID])`

> This returns the list of values from the `Customer[CustomerID]` column that has related sales transactions in the SalesOrderDetail table. The table of single `Customer[CustomerID]` filtered column acts as a table filter for CALULATE function and yields to the wanted result.

The third option appears a bit more complex than the first two; however, it is more optimal in terms of performance because it uses only a single (`Customer[CustomerID]`) column to propagate the filter to the Customer table. For the reason of efficient performance, the rest of this section uses the SUMMARIZE construct to propagate the filter from the many side of relationship to the table on one side of it.

Create a `Customer[Number of Customers CF3]:=CALCULATE([Number of Customers], SUMMARIZE(SalesOrderDetail, Customer[CustomerID]))` measure in the Customer table. As previously explained, the measure calculates the number of customers in the Customer table by cross-filtering it by any filters that exist on the SalesOrderDetail table. Figure 19-16 shows the measure.

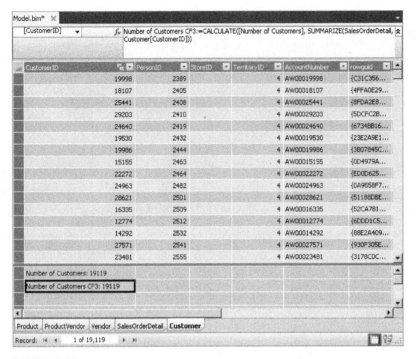

FIGURE 19-16

10. On the Analysis Services toolbar, click the Analyze in Excel button to launch Excel with a PivotTable connected to the CrossFilteringWithManyToMany tabular model.

11. Add a `SalesOrderDetail[ProductName]` column to the PivotTable row labels.

12. Add a `Customer[Number of Customers CF3]` measure to the values. The PivotTable should look like Figure 19-17. As you see, the number of customers is now calculated in the context of a given product name. With the DAX formula previously described, you could cross-filter the table on the one side of the relationship by the filter set on the table on the many side of it. Do not close Excel because you modify the PivotTable in the next step.

Now you are ready to extend this functionality to a more general case when there is a many-to-many relationship between two tables, or when there is a chain of many-to-many relationships between the tables you want to cross-filter. You can see that the solution for the generic case is not more complex than what you achieved with the previous DAX formulas.

The relationship between the Product and Customer tables is many-to-many because there are many customers that purchased any given product and there are many products that any given customer purchased. If you want to cross-filter the Customer table by any filter set on the Product table, you can simply use the method described earlier. The reason is that any filters set on the Product table automatically cross-filter the SalesOrderDetail table, which, in turn, cross-filters the Customer table just like you saw earlier. To confirm this, modify the PivotTable to set the filter not on the SalesOrderDetail table, but on the Product table.

Replace the `SalesOrderDetail[ProductName]` column on the PivotTable row labels with a `Product[Name]` column. This removes the filter from the SalesOrderDetail table and adds a filter on the Product table. As Figure 19-18 shows, the values for the `Customer[Number of Customers CF3]` measure did not change because the filter on the `Product[Name]` column filters the SalesOrderDetail table just like the `SalesOrderDetail[ProductName]` column did.

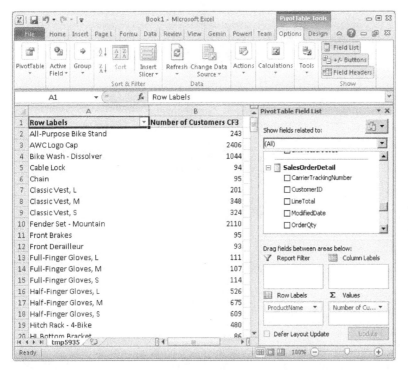

FIGURE 19-17

Consider the following problem: You need to find the amount each customer spent on products supplied by a selected set of vendors. A many-to-many relationship exists between the Product and Vendor tables because each product may be supplied by many vendors, and each vendor supplies many products. In the CrossFilteringWithManyToMany tabular model, a chain of many-to-many relationships exists between the Customer and Vendor tables. As the problem states, you need to cross-filter the Customer table by a filter set on the Vendor table. The filter set on the Vendor table automatically cross-filters the ProductVendor table, but it must be propagated to the Product table explicitly with DAX. Follow these steps to analyze the data in the PivotTable:

1. On the Analysis Services toolbar, click the Analyze in Excel button to launch Excel with a PivotTable connected to the CrossFilteringWithManyToMany tabular model.

2. Add a `Customer[FirstName]` column to the PivotTable row labels.

3. Add a `SalesOrderDetail[SalesAmount]` measure to the PivotTable values. The PivotTable now shows the amount spent by each of the customers for all products.

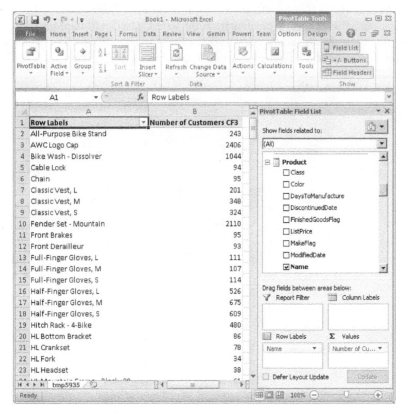

FIGURE 19-18

4. Insert a slicer based on the Vendor [Name] column. The PivotTable should now look like Figure 19-19.

5. Select the first vendor on the slicer. The expectation is that it is going to affect the amount shown on the PivotTable. However, it does not affect the SalesAmount measure value (see Figure 19-20) because the filter on the Vendor table is not propagated to the SalesOrderDetail or Product tables.

6. To propagate the filter from the Vendor or ProductVendor table to the context in which the SalesAmount measure is evaluated, you need to create a new DAX measure in the SalesOrderDetail table: SalesOrderDetail [SalesAmount CF3]:=CALCULATE([SalesAmount], SUMMARIZE(ProductVendor, Product[ProductID])). This measure evaluates the existing SalesAmount measure in the filtered Product table context, which automatically cross-filters the SalesOrderDetail table. Figure 19-21 shows the new measure defined.

7. Return to Excel PivotTable; refresh the field list to show the newly added measure; and replace the SalesAmount measure on PivotTable values with the SalesAmount CF3 measure. The new measure is affected by the changes of the slicer selection, as shown in Figure 19-22.

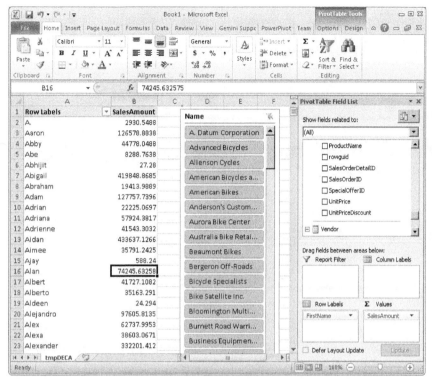

FIGURE 19-19

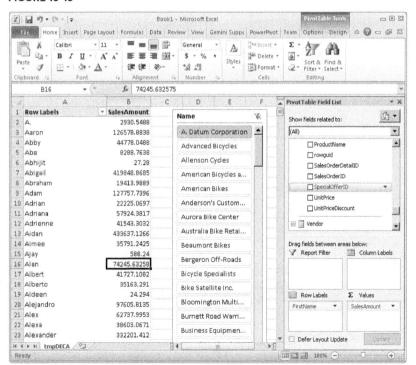

FIGURE 19-20

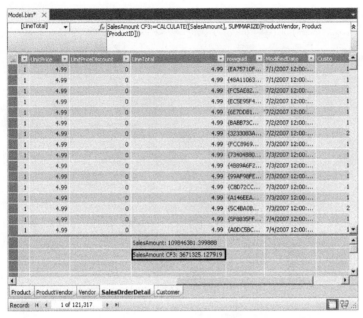

FIGURE 19-21

FIGURE 19-22

In a more generic scenario, if you have multiple tables that you want to propagate filters from, you must add a separate SUMMARIZE construct in the DAX expression for each of the tables that need to be filtered appropriately. You can try this as an exercise.

MULTIPLE RELATIONSHIPS BETWEEN TABLES

The term *role-playing dimension* (from Analysis Services Multidimensional models) refers to a dimension that can be instantiated into more than one cube dimension. For example, a date dimension may act as an "order date" or a "ship date" or a "delivery date." Discussing role-playing dimensions for Analysis Services tabular models is slightly different because tabular models do not support the notion of role-playing dimensions or role-playing tables. Instead, you can refer to it as to the generic problem of designing tabular models when multiple relationships exist between two tables. For example, consider the schema of a tabular model in Figure 19-23. The SalesOrderHeader table is a fact table of sales transactions and is related to the Customer, ShipMethod, and SalesPerson tables. In this section we discuss two ways to model multiple relationships between two tables and the benefits of each approach.

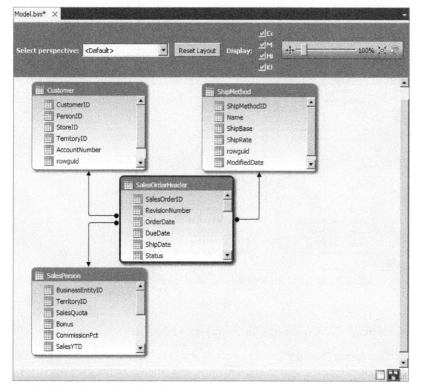

FIGURE 19-23

The SalesOrderHeader table has three date columns: OrderDate, DueDate, and ShipDate. To make the schema complete, you need to get the Date table and create relationships to these columns. You can model your tabular schema using two approaches depending on the usage of these relationships. The following two sections discuss possible approaches to this problem.

Multiple Instances of the Table

If you need to apply independent filters on each of the columns (OrderDate, DueDate, and ShipDate) in the table then you may need to import the same Date table multiple times with different names such as OrderDate, DueDate, and ShipDate. Get the RolePlayingDimensionsMT Analysis Service tabular project for this chapter on Wrox.com, download the content, open it in SSDT, and switch to diagram view. You see the schema, as shown in Figure 19-24.

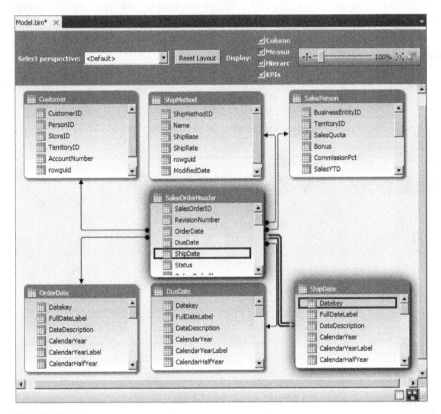

FIGURE 19-24

Follow these instructions to create DAX measures and analyze the data using multiple Date tables:

1. Create a `SalesOrderHeader[Number of Transactions]:=COUNTROWS(SalesOrderHea der)` measure in the SalesOrderHeader table. This measure calculates the number of transactions in the current context. You can use this measure to analyze the number of transactions for each salesperson for a given time frame. Figure 19-25 shows the measure definition.

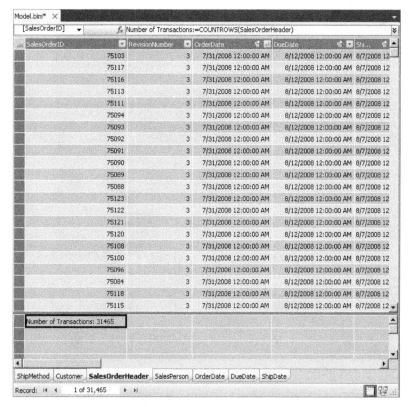

FIGURE 19-25

2. On the Analysis Services toolbar, click the Analyze in Excel button to launch Excel with a PivotTable connected to the RolePlayingDimensionsMT tabular model.

3. Add a `SalesPerson[FullName]` column to the row labels of the PivotTable.

4. Add a `SalesOrderHeader[Number of Transactions]` measure to the values of the PivotTable. Figure 19-26 shows the number of transactions for each salesperson.

5. Insert a slicer with the values of `OrderDate[CalendarYear]` and change the title to Order Year, as shown in Figure 19-27.

6. Similarly, insert slicers with the values of `DueDate[CalendarYear]` and `ShipDate[CalendarYear]`. Change their titles to Due Year and Ship Year, as shown in Figure 19-28. You can use the slicers to set filters on individual date columns (OrderDate, DueDate, and ShipDate). You can similarly add Order Month, Due Month, and Ship Month slicers and set even finer grain filters. For example, you can analyze how many sales transactions each salesperson made in November and shipped in December.

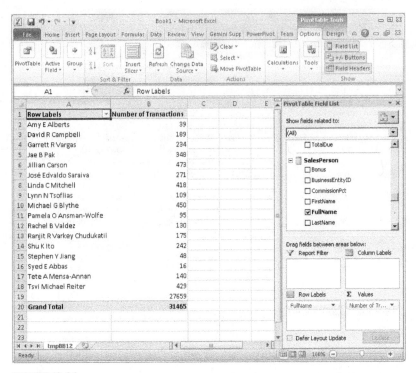

FIGURE 19-26

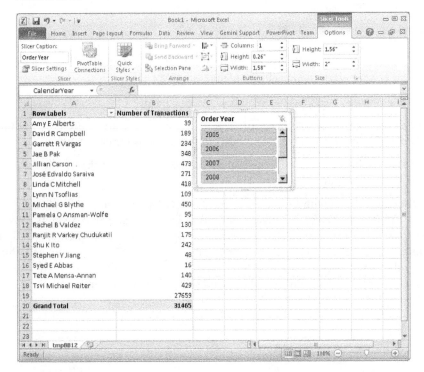

FIGURE 19-27

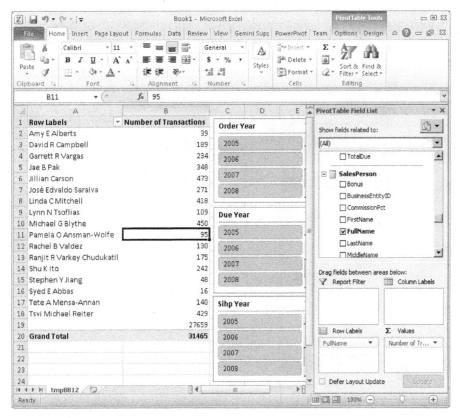

FIGURE 19-28

This approach of importing the same table multiple times to split the roles is useful when each role acts independently during filtering. This does not scale well when you have many roles and if there are other related tables. For example, if there were another table that the Date table was related to, you must import that related table several times as well. In addition to managing importing related tables, importing the same table multiple times along with related tables impacts both the space needed by the tabular model and performance during the import or refresh of the tables. In some scenarios, end users would like to see a single table to make it easier to understand the model and analyze the data. For example, it's easier for end users if there is one date table rather than three (because all three of them are date tables). Modeling your tabular database using multiple relationships between two tables is supported in SQL Server Analysis Services 2012 and can be done with the help of appropriate DAX expressions. You learn how to model this in the next section. Be aware that tabular BISM supports only one active relationship between two tables at any time, which is used for default calculations.

Multiple Relationships Between Two Tables

If you have correlated roles that you are going to filter identically, you need to consider creating multiple relationships between the SalesOrderHeader and Date tables. Open the

RolePlayingDimensionsMR Analysis Service tabular project in SSDT. You can see the schema, as shown in Figure 19-29, with three relationships between the SalesOrderHeader and Date tables. Only the `SalesOrderHeader[OrderDate]` ➤ `Date[Datekey]` relationship is active, whereas the other two relationships shown with dotted lines in Figure 19-29 are the inactive relationships.

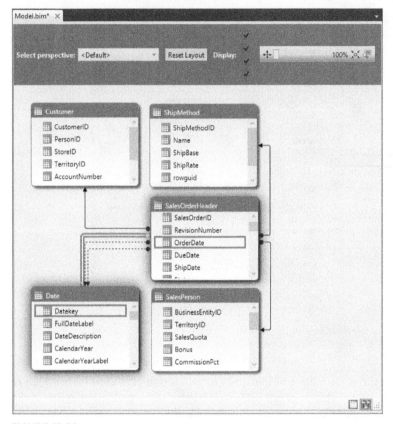

FIGURE 19-29

By default, any filter set on the Date table automatically cross-filters the related SalesOrderHeader tables using the active relationship. To cross-filter with a different relationship, you need to create a special DAX formula that explicitly propagates the filter using the given relationship. Follow these steps to create DAX calculations that allow cross-filtering of the SalesOrderHeader table with a given relationship:

1. Create a `SalesOrderHeader[Ordered Count]:=COUNTROWS(SalesOrderHeader)` measure in the SalesOrderHeader table. This measure calculates the number of transactions in the current context. The current context uses the active relationship to cross-filter the SalesOrderHeader table by any filter set on the Date table.

2. Create a `SalesOrderHeader[Due Count]:=CALCULATE([Ordered Count], USER ELATIONSHIP(SalesOrderHeader[DueDate], 'Date'[Datekey]))` measure in the SalesOrderHeader table. This measure calculates the number of transactions in the current context. However, it explicitly modifies the current context to use a SalesOrderHeader [DueDate] ➤ 'Date'[Datekey] relationship to cross-filter the SalesOrderHeader table by any filter set on the Date table.

3. Similarly create a SalesOrderHeader[Shipped Count]:=CALCULATE([Ordered Count], USERELATIONSHIP(SalesOrderHeader[ShipDate], 'Date'[Datekey])) measure in the SalesOrderHeader table. Figure 19-30 shows all the three measure definitions.

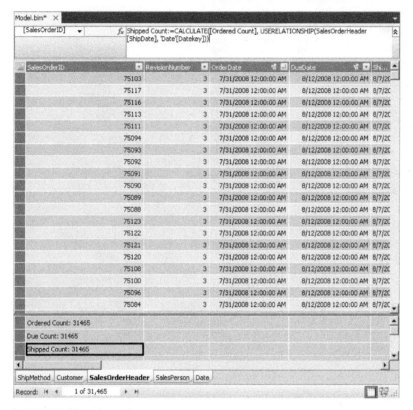

FIGURE 19-30

4. On the Analysis Services toolbar, click the Analyze in Excel button to launch Excel with a PivotTable connected to the RolePlayingDimensionsMR tabular model.

5. Add a SalesPerson[FullName] column to the row labels of the PivotTable.

6. Add SalesOrderHeader[Ordered Count], SalesOrderHeader[Due Count] and SalesOrderHeader[Shipped Count] measures to the values of the PivotTable. Figure 19-31 shows the number of ordered, due, and shipped transactions for each salesperson.

7. Insert slicers with the values of Date[CalendarYearLabel] and Date[CalendarMonthLabel] columns. The slicers enable you to filter the measures to see the number of ordered, due, and shipped transactions for a range of time, as shown in Figure 19-32.

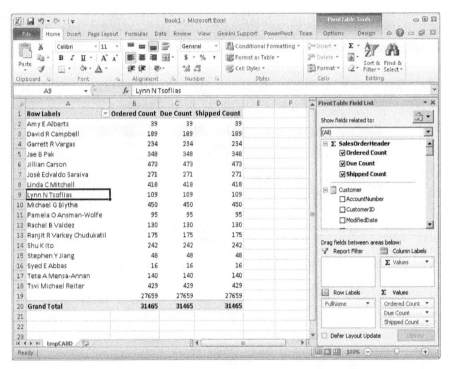

FIGURE 19-31

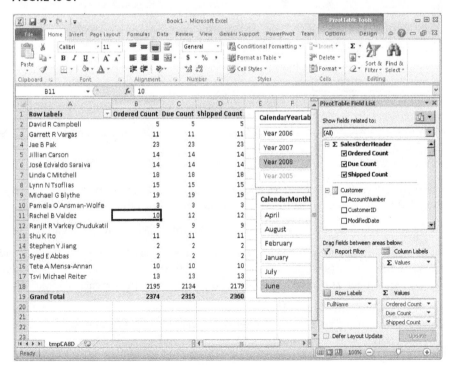

FIGURE 19-32

Having inactive relationships and allowing them on the measure calculation level is helpful when you try to use a single filter for multiple measures. However, it limits the flexibility of setting different filters on different roles during reporting. To summarize, the problem you try to solve determines the design you choose for the tabular model for role-playing dimensions. If you need the flexibility of individual filters for roles during reporting, you need to create multiple instances of tables for each row, and you need to create multiple relationships with DAX measures if you want a single filter applied for all roles.

TIME-BASED ANALYSIS

In this section you use the ContosoRetail tabular model that you built in Chapter 18. (It is also available with this chapter's download content on Wrox.com.) The business problem examples addressed in this section use Time Intelligence functions to achieve the calculations needed for analysis and reports. The ContosoRetail model has FactSales[Sum of SalesAmount Prev Year] and FactSales[Sum of SalesAmount To Date] measures that use Time Intelligence functions to calculate the sales amount for the same period in the previous year as well as for the period ending at the selected date. Consider the following problems for the ContosoRetail tabular model.

Moving Average

Consider calculating the average of daily sales amounts for the last 30 days. This problem is known as a moving average or rolling average. To get the average of daily sales amounts, you need to take the following logical steps:

1. Get a table of days that includes the last 30 days.

2. For every row (day) of the table from step 1, calculate the sum of the sales amount.

3. Calculate the average over the values from step 2.

For step 1 you can use the following expression: DATESINPERIOD(DimDate[Datekey], LASTDATE(DimDate[Datekey]), -30, Day). To ensure the expression returns the last 30 days for a given context, run the following DAX queries in SSMS. Figure 19-33 shows the result of the query.

The following query evaluates the DAX formula above in non-filtered context, and because the DimDate[Datekey] is in the granularity of days, it will return the last DimDate[Datekey] values corresponding to last 30 days.

```
EVALUATE
    CALCULATETABLE(
        DATESINPERIOD(
            DimDate[Datekey],
            LASTDATE(DimDate[Datekey]),
            -30,
            Day
        ),
        DimDate[CalendarYear]=2006
    )
```

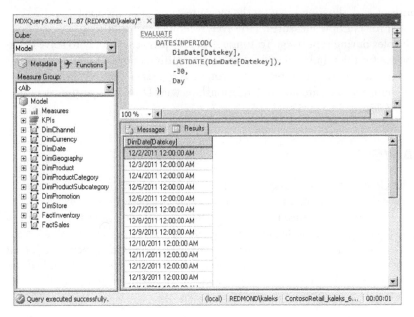

FIGURE 19-33

The following DAX query evaluates the DAX expression in the filtered DimDate table that has only one date: 12/31/2005. Because the LASTDATE (DimDate[Datekey]) subexpression is evaluated in the current filter context, it returns the last date of 12/31/2005, and the query returns the last 30 dates, corresponding to the last 30 days of 2005. DATESINPERIOD considers dates not only in the current filter context, but also for all dates in the DimDate[Datekey] column. This helps to avoid explicit removal of the filter context from the DimDate[Datekey] column with the ALL(DimDate[Datekey]) expression. Figure 19-34 shows the result of the query.

```
EVALUATE
    CALCULATETABLE (
        DATESINPERIOD (
            DimDate[Datekey],
            LASTDATE(DimDate[Datekey]),
            -30,
            Day
        ),
        DimDate[FullDateLabel]="2005-12-31"
    )
```

For step 2 you can use the ADDCOLUMNS function to add the sum of the sales amount for every row of the result of the previous formula, as shown by the DAX expression here:

```
ADDCOLUMNS (
    DATESINPERIOD (
        DimDate[Datekey],
        LASTDATE(DimDate[Datekey]),
        -30,
        Day
```

```
    ),
    "Sum of SalesAmount",
    [Sum of SalesAmount]
)
```

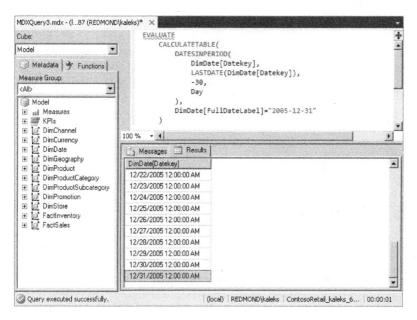

FIGURE 19-34

The DAX expression evaluates the FactSales[Sum of SalesAmount] measure in the context of every row of the date values in the table. As mentioned earlier, the measure evaluation first adds the row context to the filter context and calculates the sum of the sales amount for the current day. To verify that the formula works as expected, execute the following query in SSMS. The query should return a table with two columns: DimDate[Datekey] and [Sum of SalesAmount]. The result should have 30 rows corresponding to the last 30 days of the year 2007 and corresponding sums of sales amounts for each day. Figure 19-35 shows the result of the DAX query here.

```
EVALUATE
    CALCULATETABLE (
        ADDCOLUMNS (
            DATESINPERIOD (
                DimDate[Datekey],
                LASTDATE(DimDate[Datekey]),
                -30,
                Day
            ),
            "Sum of SalesAmount",
             [Sum of SalesAmount]
        ),
        DimDate[FullDateLabel]="2007-12-31"
    )
```

Figure 19-35 shows the result of the query.

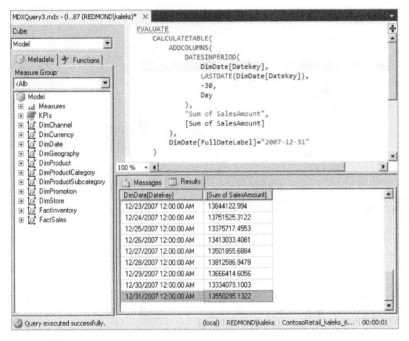

FIGURE 19-35

For step 3 you need to average the values in the [Sum of SalesAmount] column using the AVERAGEX function (See Figure 19-36). The following formula should calculate the moving average:

```
AVERAGEX(
    ADDCOLUMNS(
        DATESINPERIOD(
            DimDate[Datekey],
            LASTDATE(DimDate[Datekey]),
            -30,
            Day
        ),
        "Sum of SalesAmount",
        [Sum of SalesAmount]
    ),
    [Sum of SalesAmount]
)
```

Create the following measure in the FactSales table:

```
FactSales[MA of SalesAmount 30days]:=AVERAGEX(
    ADDCOLUMNS(
        DATESINPERIOD(
            DimDate[Datekey],
            LASTDATE(DimDate[Datekey]),
            -30,
```

```
        Day
    ),
    "Sum of SalesAmount",
    [Sum of SalesAmount]
),
[Sum of SalesAmount]
)
```

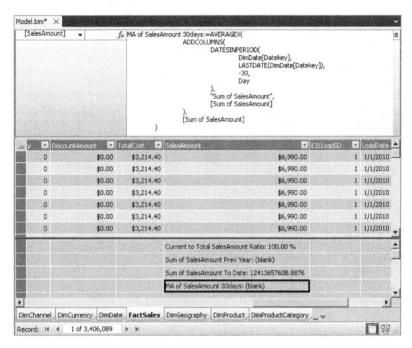

FIGURE 19-36

Follow these steps to analyze the ContosoRetail data using a moving average measure.

1. On the Analysis Services toolbar, click the Analyze in Excel button to launch Excel with a PivotTable connected to the ContosoRetail tabular model.

2. Add the following columns to the PivotTable row labels:

   ➤ DimDate[CalendarYearLabel]

   ➤ DimDate[CalendarMonthLabel]

   ➤ DimDate[CalendarWeekLabel]

   ➤ DimDate[CalendarDayOfWeekLabel]

3. Add the following measures to the PivotTable values:

   ➤ FactSales[MA of SalesAmount 30days]

   ➤ FactSales[Sum of SalesAmount]

The PivotTable now should look like Figure 19-37, which shows the daily sum of sales amount and the average for the last 30 days.

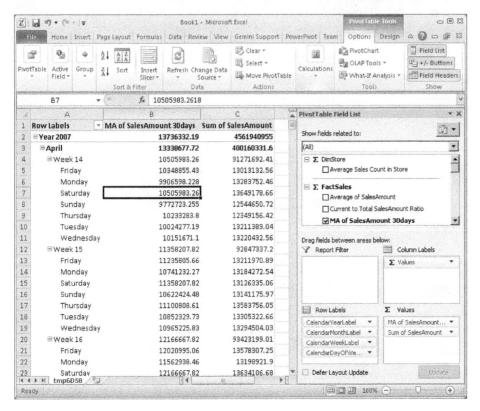

FIGURE 19-37

The measure formula does not overwrite the filter context for tables other than DimDate. It means you may slice and dice using other tables, such as DimChannel, DimProduct, and so on.

Opening and Closing Balance

This section discusses the business problem in which you need to find opening or closing inventory balances using the FactInventory table of the ContosoRetail tabular model. The FactInventory table consists of transactions in which the inventory was counted for various products in various stores. Each transaction identifies the date, store, product, and quantity in store. Inventory quantities do not add. If you count five bicycles one day and three bicycles a week later, the net result is that you have three bicycles. At any moment, the quantity in store is the last count that was taken of that product in that store. Although the number of given products do not add over time, they do add across products and stores.

The problem of finding opening and closing balances translates to finding the number of products in stores at the beginning and end of a given time period. To solve the problem, you need to define a measure that counts the number of products in inventory at any given point of time. The first step is to create a measure in the FactInventory table to calculate the sum of the number of products.

1. Create a `FactInventory[Products on Hand] := SUM(FactInventory[OnHandQuantity])` measure in the FactInventory table. This measure is not intended for reporting but will be used by other DAX expressions, so you may want to hide it from client tools. To do that, right-click the measure and select Hide from Client Tools. Figure 19-38 shows the measure.

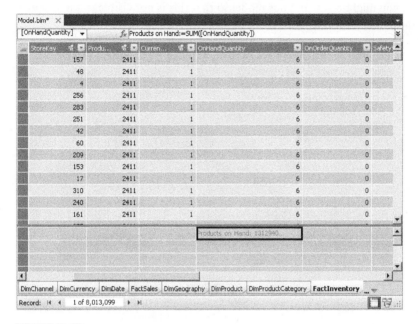

FIGURE 19-38

2. Create a DAX measure to group by products and stores and calculate the sum of the number of products on last transaction. The following DAX expression should group the FactInventory table by the `FactInventory[ProductKey]` and `FactInventory[StoreKey]` columns, and for each combination calculate the sum of quantities based on last transaction. The DAX expression `LASTNONBLANK(DimDate[Datekey], [Products on Hand])` passed as an argument to the `CALCULATE` function can set a filter on the `DimDate[Datekey]` column by filtering out all rows except the last transaction date, which is used for calculating the sum of quantity, as shown in the following DAX expression:

```
SUMMARIZE(
    FactInventory,
    FactInventory[ProductKey],
    FactInventory[StoreKey],
    "NumProducts",
    CALCULATE(
        [Products on Hand],
        LASTNONBLANK(DimDate[Datekey], [Products on Hand])
    )
)
```

3. To return the total number of products in inventory, you need to sum all the rows in the [NumProducts] column of the result table. Create the following measure in the FactInventory table that can help with this calculation. This is not the final measure yet because it looks at the transaction in a selected time period only. For example, if 2007 is selected, the products that were not counted during that year do not show up in the final result. Hence, we recommend hiding this measure from client tools and any intermediate measures you might create in your model so that this is not visible to the end user. Figure 19-39 shows the measure.

```
FactInventory[TotalProducts on Hand] = SUMX(
    SUMMARIZE(
        FactInventory,
        FactInventory[ProductKey],
        FactInventory[StoreKey],
        "NumProducts",
        CALCULATE(
            [Products on Hand],
            LASTNONBLANK(DimDate[Datekey], [Products on Hand])
        )
    ),
    [NumProducts]
)
```

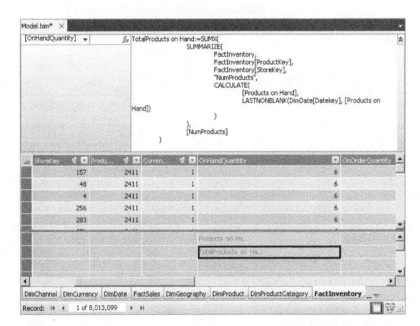

FIGURE 19-39

4. Define a new measure to scan all the dates up to the end of the selected range and calculate FactInventory[TotalProducts on Hand] by using a construct similar to that used in Chapter 18 for the FactSales[Sum of SalesAmount To Date] measure. The following measure calculates the total products in inventory as of the last day in a selected time period. Figure 19-40 shows the measure.

```
FactInventory[TotalProducts on Hand]:= CALCULATE(
    [TotalProducts Today],
    DATESBETWEEN(
        DimDate[Datekey],
        BLANK(),
        LASTDATE(DimDate[Datekey])
    )
)
```

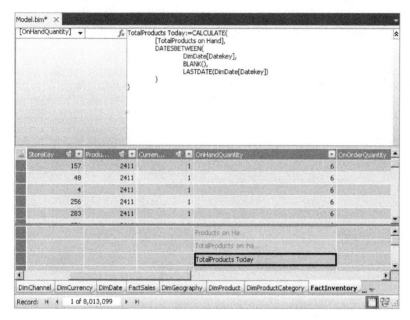

FIGURE 19-40

To find the number of products in inventory at the beginning and end of a selected period you need to define additional measures using the OPENINGBALANCE* and CLOSINGBALANCE* DAX functions. Follow these steps to create measures to calculate the opening and closing balance of the selected year:

1. Create the following measures in the FactInventory table:

```
FactInventory[ClosingBalanceYearQty]:=CLOSINGBALANCEYEAR(
    [TotalProducts Today],
    DimDate[Datekey]
)
FactInventory[OpeningBalanceYearQty]:=OPENINGBALANCEYEAR(
    [TotalProducts Today],
    DimDate[Datekey]
)
```

2. On the Analysis Services toolbar, click the Analyze in Excel button to launch Excel with a PivotTable connected to the ContosoRetail tabular model.

3. Add a DimProductCategory[ProductCategoryName] column to the PivotTable row labels.

4. Add a FactInventory[ClosingBalanceYearQty] measure to the PivotTable values.

5. Add a `FactInventory[OpeningBalanceYearQty]` measure to the PivotTable values.

6. Insert a slicer based on the `DimDate[CalendarYear]` column and select Year 2008. The PivotTable now shows the number of products in each product category in inventory for the beginning of 2008 and the end of 2008, as shown in Figure 19-41.

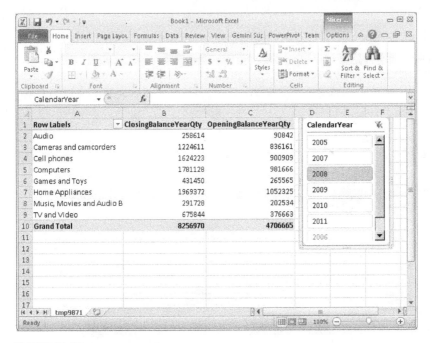

FIGURE 19-41

The preceding solution may have slow performance due to complex calculations. You can improve the performance by moving some of the DAX calculations into calculated columns that persist the results and simplify the measure calculations by using precalculated results.

NON-AGGREGATABLE COLUMNS

Once you have measures defined in your tabular BISM, querying a column along with a measure will also provide aggregated values. For example, assume you have a single table TransactionSales that contains transactions of sales for all products in each city/state. Assume you have SumOfSales as a measure that aggregates the sales. If you query this model in a client tool such as Excel, with "State" on rows and "SumofSales" as the value, you will get aggregated sales for each state along with the total. If you need to specify in the model to avoid clients querying total sales for all states, you can use one of the HASONEFILTER or COUNTROWS DAX functions. These functions help to evaluate if the DAX measure value is being calculated for each state or for all states. If you want to avoid aggregated results for a single column, such as State, you can use the HASONEFILTER DAX function as part of the measure, as follows:

```
SumOfSales = IF(HASONEFILTER(TransactionSales[State]), sum(Sales), NULL)
```

If you need to avoid clients querying subtotal aggregated data for an entire table, you can use the COUNTROWS DAX function.

SUMMARY

In this chapter you learned how to work with advanced DAX calculations to solve certain common business problems. In particular you learned how to build parent-child hierarchies using DAX functions and how to create calculations that aggregate the fact data for each level of the hierarchy. You learned how you can use DAX expressions to cross-filter related tables, and how to propagate filters set on tables related with many-to-many relationships.

This chapter also showed you how to work with role-playing dimensions in Analysis Services tabular BISM, discussing two approaches that you can consider for different purposes. Finally, you learned how to use Time Intelligence functions to solve problems such as calculating moving average and opening and closing balances. Understanding these common business problems and the examples shown in this chapter can help you solve additional business problems in your organization using the tabular BISM and DAX. The whitepapers from Microsoft, "DAX in the BI Tabular Model" (www.microsoft.com/en-us/download/details.aspx?id=28572) and "Securing the Tabular BI Semantic Model" (http://msdn.microsoft.com/en-us/library/jj127437.aspx) provide scenarios along with samples to help you understand additional business scenarios about how DAX helps solve those scenarios.

In Chapter 20 you learn how to use Excel 2010 to connect and analyze data in tabular and multidimensional BI semantic models. In Chapter 21 you learn how to set up SharePoint 2010 and PowerPivot for SharePoint so that you can publish PowerPivot for Excel solutions that contain tabular BI Semantic Models.

20

Analyzing Multidimensional and Tabular BISMs In Excel

WHAT'S IN THIS CHAPTER?

- ➤ Analyzing data using pivot tables
- ➤ Filtering data in pivot tables
- ➤ Grouping data in pivot tables
- ➤ Formatting data in Excel
- ➤ Sorting data with Excel
- ➤ KPIs, perspectives and translations
- ➤ Cube functions in Excel
- ➤ Pivot charts
- ➤ Local cubes
- ➤ Excel Services

You spend a good deal of time in this book exploring design and implementation options, but you haven't spent much time on the end-user experience — until now. In this chapter you learn about the many ways to present your aggregated data to the end user for analysis. You can slice the cube data, meaning that you present the data so that it can be looked at across some axis, or you can dice the data, which means that you drill down into the data by breaking it into smaller and smaller cubes.

In Chapter 1 you learned about the overall business intelligence stack from Microsoft. You learned that SQL Server Analysis Services (SSAS) is the business intelligence server that is the core of the business intelligence platform offering from Microsoft. As a developer, SQL Server

Data Tools (SSDT) and SQL Server Management Studio (SSMS) help you to analyze the SSAS data, but these are not suitable tools for end users making decisions based on SSAS data.

Various Microsoft Office products are available that leverage SSAS and present the SSAS data to end users in an effective way. One of the most widely used products to analyze data from SSAS is Microsoft Excel. Most of the customers use the pivot table functionality in Excel to analyze the data. You learn more about this in detail in this chapter. You also learn how to create offline cubes using Excel that you can share with your peers.

ANALYZING DATA IN EXCEL 2010

Microsoft Office Excel 2010, also called Excel 14, enables users to analyze, format, and visualize data using features such as Data Bars, Color Scales, and Icon Sets. With the release of SQL Server 2008 r2, you could install the PowerPivot for Excel add-in to leverage the power of Analysis Services running inside of Excel. In SQL Server 2012 you get an updated PowerPivot add-in, PowerPivot for Excel which you learned in Chapter 15. In this section you learn how to analyze SSAS 2012 data using a pivot table in Excel 2010.

Analyzing Data Using Pivot Tables

Having probably used Excel before, you might be familiar with the pivot table feature, especially considering that pivot tables date back to Excel Version 5. The pivot table feature can create reports for Excel users, which help them analyze data with ease. The pivot table feature can work on data stored in Excel or some other data source that Excel can access. The only requirement for using the pivot table with Analysis Services is that Excel can connect to the Analysis Services instance. In such a case, Analysis Services becomes a data source for Excel. Because there is a tight integration between Excel and Analysis Services, Excel is well aware of the Analysis Services models and objects and can present them effectively to the end users. As you might expect, Excel provides a wizard you can use to create pivot tables. It has advanced features that can even help you create what it calculates to be the best resulting layout.

As for the capabilities of a pivot table, they are similar in nature to the Cube Browser seen in SSDT — you can drag and drop dimensions and measures to analyze the data. Not only can you arrange data to best surface the information contained in it, but also the pivot table technology can sum the appropriate columns for you automatically. It is quite common for people to construct pivot tables to some planned configuration that is suited to act as a foundation for building charts and graphs. Charting and graphing capabilites come with Excel off the shelf, so you don't need to buy any additional software to use a pivot table in this way.

 Why is it called a pivot table? Why not call it what it actually is, a digital fulcrum for tabulated compilations? The name suggests the user can swivel or pivot on data that is tabular in nature. In the simplest possible terms, it is a way to display data so that it is easy to arrange and view how different columns interact with each other.

Within Excel a user has multiple ways to consume Analysis Services data. Users can create the following types of PivotTables:

➤ Native PivotTable to a multidimensional SSAS model

➤ Native PivotTable to a tabular SSAS model

➤ PowerPivot PivotTable to a tabular model

It is important to understand the features and limitations of each of the above approaches. Once a connection is made to a BISM, the Native PivotTable Field List shows the measures and attributes. Excel 2010 allows users to create pivot tables against both tabular BISM models and multidimensional BISM since Analysis Services exposes the multidimensional view of BISMs that Excel understands. In Chapter 15 you learned about the PowerPivot PivotTable connection to a tabular BISM that is created by PowerPivot. You will notice some limitations depending on where your tabular model resides. You take a closer look at some of the differences later in this chapter.

Creating a Pivot Table from a Tabular Model Using Analysis Services Data

To create a pivot table using tabular Analysis Services data as the source to populate the table, perform the following steps:

1. Download the AdventureWorksDW data file from this book's page on www.wrox.com and attach the SQL database.

2. Download the AdventureWorksTabular model project from this book's page on www.wrox .com.

3. Deploy the AdventureWorksTabular database to a tabular instance of Analysis Services running in tabular mode.

4. Launch Excel 2010.

5. Create a new blank workbook

6. Select the Data tab on the Excel Ribbon. You will see the various groups where the commands related to Data are organized.

7. In the Get External Data group, select From Other Sources as shown in Figure 20-1.

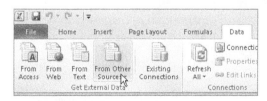

FIGURE 20-1

8. Select From Analysis Services. You should see the Data Connection Wizard dialog box shown in Figure 20-2.

9. On the Connect to Database Server page, enter the Analysis Services instance name where your Tabular mode Analysis Services instance is running.

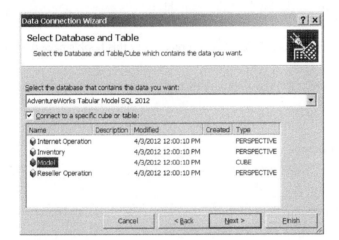

FIGURE 20-2

10. On the Select Database and Table page, select the AdventureWorksTabular database you deployed earlier and the Model cube (as shown in Figure 20-3) and click Next.

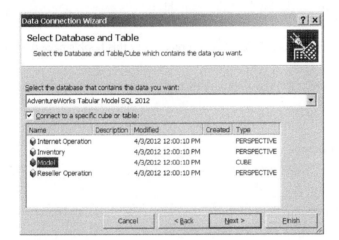

FIGURE 20-3

11. On the Save Data Connection File and Finish page, accept the defaults and click Finish.

12. In the Import Data dialog, select a location for your pivot table in the active worksheet, as shown in Figure 20-4, and click OK.

You should now see the pivot table along with the PivotTable Field List showing columns and measures in your Excel worksheet, as shown in Figure 20-5. The PivotTable Field List contains areas for adding items to the row, column, values, and report areas. To add a measure or a column to the pivot table, you just need to check the box next to the field item.

FIGURE 20-4

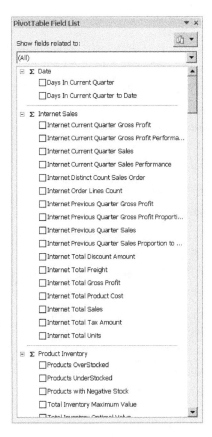

FIGURE 20-5

The objective of the previous exercise was to give you a perspective on pivot table functionality when connected to a Tabular BI Semantic Model. Users familiar with PowerPivot and the embedded tabular model expect the PowerPivot Field List and the ability to use PowerPivot functionality in the PivotTable. Since the BI Semantic Model includes both tabular and multidimensional models, PivotTable functionality was designed to provide a consistent experience when consuming tabular and multidimensional models. For this reason you see a tabular model the same way you would see a multidimensional model. A connection is made via Office Data Connection (ODC) much the same way a multidimensional model connection is made behind the scenes. To help you understand how to use Excel pivot tables connected to a BISM, we use the multidimensional model and highlight important functionality differences with tabular model connectivity as appropriate in each section in this chapter.

When you create a tabular model, you see tables, and columns and measures are parts of tables. However, when you connect this via Excel, you get the multidimensional view of the model. Hence, measures are under a measure group, and attributes and hierarchies are presented under a dimension; KPIs are shown separately in Excel. Therefore, in Excel you see each measure under a measure group, while columns (presented as attributes) and hierarchies are shown under dimension (table) names.

Creating a Pivot Table from a Multidimensional Model

To create a pivot table using multidimensional Analysis Services data as the source to populate the table, perform the following steps:

1. Download the AdventureWorksDW multidimensional project from this book's web page on www.wrox.com.

2. Deploy the AdventureWorksDW multidimensional database to a multidimensional instance of Analysis Services.

3. Launch Excel 2010 and create a new workbook.

4. Select the Data tab on the Excel Ribbon as shown in Figure 20-1.

5. In the Get External Data group, select From Other Sources as shown in Figure 20-1.

6. Select From Analysis Services. You should see the Data Connection Wizard dialog box shown in Figure 20-2.

7. On the Connect to Database Server page, enter the Analysis Services instance name for your multidimensional mode Analysis Services server and click Next.

8. On the Select Database and Table page, you will see the list of databases from SSAS. Select the AdventureWorksDW sample database you deployed earlier and the Adventure Works cube as shown in Figure 20-6 and click Next.

9. On the Save Data Connection File and Finish page, add a description for your data source connection and click Finish.

10. In the Import Data dialog, select a location for your pivot table in the active worksheet and click OK.

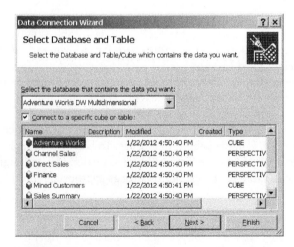

FIGURE 20-6

You should now see the pivot table along with the PivotTable Field List showing hierarchies and measures in your Excel worksheet. There's a lot of information in the PivotTable Field List and it can feel like information overload. The PivotTable Field List contains areas for adding items to the row labels, column labels, values, and report filter areas. To add a measure or a hierarchy to the pivot table you just need to check the box next to the field item.

Updating SSAS Connection Information

Excel 2010 provides a way to add additional connection string properties while connecting to SSAS. If you need to obtain or update connection information, perform the following steps:

1. On the Ribbon, select the Data tab.

2. In the Connections Group select Connections, as shown in Figure 20-7, to open the Workbook Connections dialog.

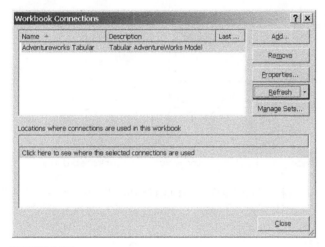

FIGURE 20-7

3. In the Workbook Connections dialog, click the connection you just created. For this example it is AdventureWorksTabular.

4. Click the Properties button. You should see the dialog shown in Figure 20-8.

5. In the Connection Properties dialog, click the Definition tab to see the connection string used to connect to SSAS.

When you create a connection to an SSAS instance, an ODC file is created to store all the information relevant to the connection. The file is by default saved at `%USERPROFILE%\My Data Sources \localhost Adventure Works DW Adventure Works.odc`. You can see the location of the file in the Connection File text box. For this sample connection, Excel 2010 has generated the following connection string to connect to your SSAS 2012 instance:

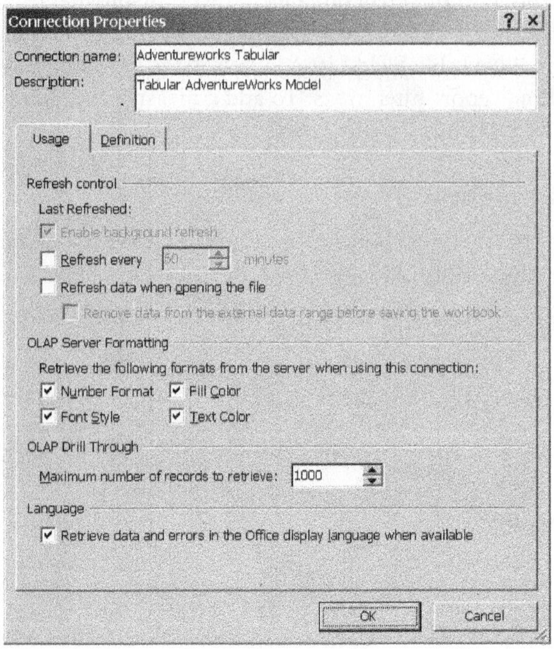

FIGURE 20-8

```
Provider=MSOLAP.5;Integrated Security=SSPI;Persist Security Info=True;
Data Source=localhost\tabular;Initial Catalog=AdventureWorksTabular;
```

You can edit the connection string and authentication settings in this dialog; then click OK to save the settings.

Analyzing Data in Pivot Tables

Now that you have learned how to view or edit connection strings used with SSAS, next you learn about data analysis using a pivot table. In the PivotTable Field List you can see the various measures in the AdventureWorks cube listed under each measure group followed by the list of dimensions. The attributes and hierarchies in a dimension are organized under folders as defined in the cube, as shown in Figure 20-9. You can also see the KPIs in the cube listed under a separate folder.

You learned earlier that the list of all the measures and dimensions might be overwhelming. Excel 2010 allows you a way to restrict the measures and related dimensions based on the measure group. You can utilize the Show Fields Related To drop-down menu to select a specific measure group:

FIGURE 20-9

1. Select the drop-down list box below Show Fields Related To, and select Internet Sales, as shown in Figure 20-10. Excel 2010 sends a list of discover statements to retrieve the corresponding list of measure groups and dimensions to populate the PivotTable Field List.

2. Navigate to the list of measures, and click the check box next to the Internet Sales Amount measure in the Internet Sales measure group. You now see the measure being added to the Values area in the PivotTable Field List and the value in the pivot table, as shown in Figure 20-10.

Excel 2010 sends the following MDX query to retrieve the `Internet Sales Amount` for the entire cube and shows the results in the pivot table:

```
SELECT
FROM [Adventure Works]
WHERE ( [Measures].[Internet Sales Amount] ) CELL Properties Value,
FORMAT_STRING,
LANGUAGE,
BACK_COLOR,
FORE_COLOR,
FONT_FLAGS
```

If you send the query using the MDX query editor in SQL Server Management Studio (SSMS) you see the same result of $29,358,677.22. Now analyze the Internet Sales Amount for various customers and years.

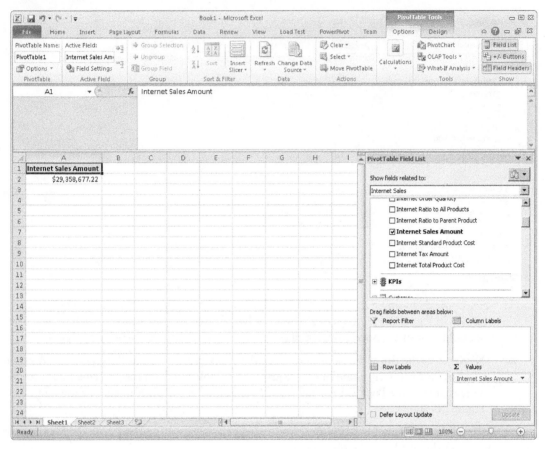

FIGURE 20-10

3. Scroll down in the PivotTable Field List, and click the check box for the Customer dimension's Customer Geography hierarchy. The Customer Geography hierarchy is added to Row Labels, and the customer countries along with the relevant sales amounts are shown in the pivot table.

4. Scroll down and click the Date dimension's Date.Fiscal hierarchy, as shown in Figure 20-11. Excel 2010 sends the following MDX query to retrieve the data:

```
SELECT NON EMPTY Hierarchize (
    {
        DrilldownLevel (
            { [Date].[Fiscal].[All Periods] },
            ,
            INCLUDE_CALC_MEMBERS
        )
    }
) Dimension Properties PARENT_UNIQUE_NAME,
HIERARCHY_UNIQUE_NAME ON COLUMNS,
NON EMPTY Hierarchize (
```

```
{
  DrilldownLevel (
    { [Customer].[Customer Geography].[All Customers] },
    ,
    ,
    INCLUDE_CALC_MEMBERS
  )
}
) Dimension Properties PARENT_UNIQUE_NAME,
HIERARCHY_UNIQUE_NAME ON ROWS
FROM [Adventure Works]
WHERE ( [Measures].[Internet Sales Amount] ) CELL Properties Value,
FORMAT_STRING,
LANGUAGE,
BACK_COLOR,
FORE_COLOR,
FONT_FLAGS
```

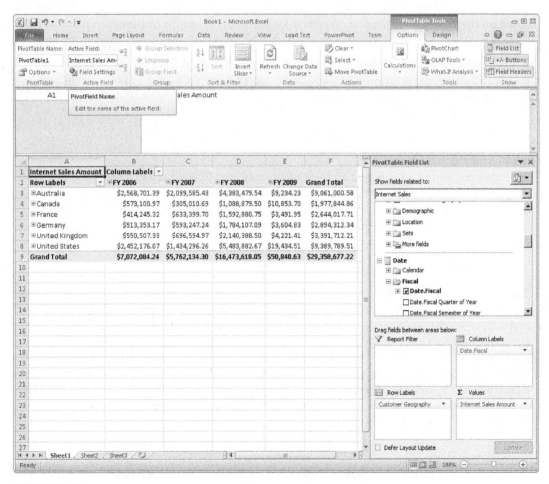

FIGURE 20-11

Excel 2010 understands the Time dimension that is specified in the cube and adds the hierarchy to the columns area. You see the top-level Date.Fiscal hierarchy members in the pivot table along with the [Internet Sales Amount], as shown in Figure 20-11. You can now see [Internet Sales Amount] data for various countries and various fiscal years. In one view you can see the sales trend for each country across various years and also a comparison of sales for a year across various countries. You can see a + symbol next to each member. The + symbol helps you to drill down further to analyze data under a specific member. Before drilling down, take a look at the MDX query sent by Excel so that you understand it. You can execute the MDX query in SSMS to retrieve the results. Figure 20-12 shows the MDX query results in SSMS.

If you hover over a specific member or a cell, you notice the corresponding properties in tool tips. You can also view the dimension or cell properties returned for each cell by double-clicking a member or a cell in SSMS. The results shown in SMSS are identical to the results you see in Figure 20-12, but the order in which the results are presented differs. The first row and first column of the results shown in SSMS are the final rows and columns you see in the pivot table, which correspond to the aggregated data corresponding to that specific member in the dimension based on the aggregation function specified for the measure. The members All Customers and All Periods shown in the table are actually the names of the All Members specified in the respective dimensions.

Excel generates a two-dimensional MDX query that requests data on the axes columns and rows in this example. For the dimension added on the columns of the pivot table (Date.Fiscal), the following MDX expression is specified:

```
NON EMPTY Hierarchize({DrilldownLevel({[Date].[Fiscal].[All Periods]})})
     DIMENSION PROPERTIES PARENT_UNIQUE_NAME ON COLUMNS
```

Start with the innermost function and work your way out. When you add a specific hierarchy to the pivot table, the member in the topmost level of that hierarchy is identified and used in the query. In the previous example, the All Member in the Date.Fiscal hierarchy, All Periods, is used. The DrilldownLevel MDX function is a function that can take multiple parameters. The syntax of the DrilldownLevel function is as follows:

```
DrilldownLevel( <Set>, [ ,<Level> | ,,<Index> ] )
```

The first argument to the DrilldownLevel function is a *Set*. The second and third arguments are optional. The DrilldownLevel function returns the members of the specified *Set* (provided as the first argument) that are one level lower than the level of the members specified in the set. If the optional *Level* parameter is specified, the function returns members one level below the specified level. If the set contains tuples, the index is used to reference the dimension for which the drill down has to be applied. In the query you are currently examining, the members at the Year level of the hierarchy Date.Fiscal is returned. You could have retrieved the members by specifying the MDX expression, but the DrilldownLevel function provides you with more options and is useful while drilling down to multiple levels, which is why Excel uses this function. Drilling down to multiple levels is discussed later in this section. Now, review the next MDX function using the Customer Geography hierarchy as shown in the following:

```
NON EMPTY Hierarchize({DrilldownLevel({[Customer].[Customer Geography].[All
     Customers]})}) DIMENSION PROPERTIES PARENT_UNIQUE_NAME
```

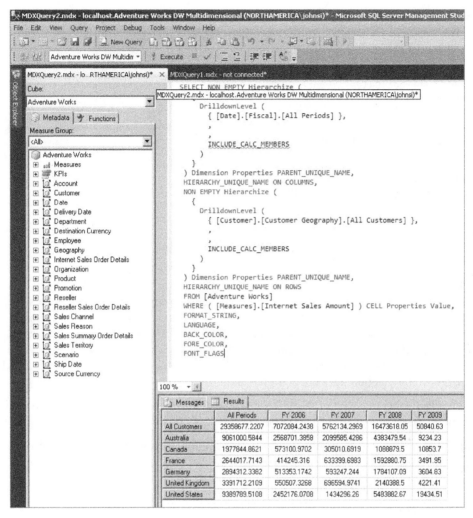

FIGURE 20-12

The result of the `DrilldownLevel` function is a set of members and is passed as an argument to the `Hierarchize` function. `Hierarchize` is an MDX function used for sorting the members in a set. The syntax is as follows:

```
Hierarchize( <Set> [, POST] )
```

The `Hierarchize` function takes a *Set* and returns the members in the set after a sort. If the second parameter POST is not specified, the default sort ordering of the hierarchy is used to sort the members in the set. If the parameter POST is specified, the members are sorted based on the default ordering, but the parent member will be at the end. This is illustrated by the following two MDX queries:

```
//MDX Query 1 -- Default sort ordering
SELECT Hierarchize (
    {
```

```
        DrilldownLevel (
          { [Customer].[Customer Geography].[Country] }
        )
      }
    ) ON 0,
    Measures.[Internet Sales Amount] ON 1
    FROM [Adventure Works]


    //MDX Query 2 -- Sort based on POST
    SELECT Hierarchize (
      {
        DrilldownLevel (
          { [Customer].[Customer Geography].[Country] }
        )
      },
      POST
    ) ON 0,
    Measures.[Internet Sales Amount] ON 1
    FROM [Adventure Works]
```

The first MDX query uses the default sort ordering of the hierarchy and returns the members in Country and State levels in the format {*<Country Member 1>, <State members for Country Member 1>, <Country Member 2>, <State members for Country Member 2> …*}. However, the second query that specified POST sorts the results as {*<State members for Country Member 1>, <Country Member 1>, <State members for Country Member 2>,<Country Member 2>, …*}. The Hierarchize MDX function does not eliminate duplicate members.

You have just learned about one part of the MDX query and why these functions are used to retrieve the results. Now it is time to examine the next part of the MDX query.

The keyword NON EMPTY is used to ensure empty values are eliminated in the results. To refresh your memory, following is the MDX query generated by Excel:

```
    SELECT NON EMPTY Hierarchize (
      {
        DrilldownLevel (
          { [Date].[Fiscal].[All Periods] }
        )
      }
    ) Dimension Properties PARENT_UNIQUE_NAME ON COLUMNS,
    NON EMPTY Hierarchize (
      {
        DrilldownLevel (
          { [Customer].[Customer Geography].[All Customers] }
        )
      }
    ) Dimension Properties PARENT_UNIQUE_NAME ON ROWS
    FROM [Adventure Works]
    WHERE ( [Measures].[Internet Sales Amount] ) CELL Properties Value,
    FORMAT_STRING,
    LANGUAGE,
    BACK_COLOR,
    FORE_COLOR,
    FONT_FLAGS
```

The outer SELECT query then retrieves the Internet Sales data for all the years only for United States.

The Report Filter

The Report Filter area in the PivotTable Field List also allows you to filter the data in the pivot table by hierarchies you add to the Report Filter area. Adding a hierarchy to the Report Filter allows you to create Excel reports that let the end user apply filters directly in the pivot table. Assume a scenario in which you want to analyze the [Internet Sales Amount] of customers in the United States to see if the customer's level of education has an impact. You might want to filter using one or more Education types. The following steps show you how to do the analysis using Report Filters:

1. Drag and drop the Customer Demographic Education attribute to the Report Filter area. You can notice Education added to the pivot table along with the default member shown next to it. By default, the filter allows only a single member filter. You can enable multimember selection in the filter in Excel. Continue with these steps to analyze the Internet Sales of customers who have a degree.

FIGURE 20-14

2. Drop down the list box next to the default member All Customers, and select the box next to Select Multiple Items, as shown in Figure 20-14.

3. Expand the + sign next to All Customers.

4. Deselect the check mark next to All Customers, and then select the members Bachelors and Graduate Degree.

5. Click OK.

You can now see the [Internet Sales Amount] for the United States has dropped from its previous value because the filter you applied includes only customers who have a degree. Excel 2010 sends the following MDX query to retrieve the results shown in the pivot table:

```
SELECT   NON EMPTY Hierarchize({DrilldownLevel(
                         {[Date].[Fiscal].[All Periods]})})
         DIMENSION PROPERTIES PARENT_UNIQUE_NAME ON COLUMNS ,
         NON EMPTY Hierarchize({DrilldownLevel(
                 {[Customer].[Customer Geography].[All Customers]})})
         DIMENSION PROPERTIES PARENT_UNIQUE_NAME ON ROWS
    FROM (
         SELECT ({[Customer].[Customer Geography].[Country].&[United States]})
               ON COLUMNS
         FROM (
             SELECT   ({[Customer].[Education].&[Bachelors],
                       [Customer].[Education].&[Graduate Degree]})
                     ON COLUMNS
             FROM [Adventure Works]
             )
         )
    WHERE ([Measures].[Internet Sales Amount])
    CELL PROPERTIES VALUE, FORMAT_STRING, LANGUAGE, BACK_COLOR, FORE_COLOR,
    FONT_FLAGS
```

In the MDX query you can see the nested subselect MDX statement used to filter the data being retrieved. First, the filter is applied to the United States using the subselect followed by another subselect for members having bachelor's and graduate degrees. The innermost subselect, which retrieves all members with degrees, gets evaluated first, followed by the subselect restricting the data to members of United States. The result of this subselect is a slice of the cube based on the restriction called a subcube. Finally, the [Internet Sales Amount] is retrieved based on the members requested in the columns and rows axes on the outermost MDX query.

The Row Filter

The pivot table also provides another way to perform the analysis based on Education. Instead of using the Report Filter, you can add the hierarchy to the Row and apply a filter there. To accomplish this go to the PivotTable Field List and drag the Education hierarchy from the Report Filter section to Row Labels underneath Customer Geography. You see the Education hierarchy as a second level in the Row area, as shown in Figure 20-15. The filter condition you applied to customers having a degree is still maintained.

	A	B	C	D	E	F
1						
2						
3	Internet Sales Amount	Column Labels				
4	Row Labels	FY 2006	FY 2007	FY 2008	FY 2009	Grand Total
5	Australia	$1,301,921.93	$1,167,074.94	$2,595,606.94	$4,688.00	$5,069,291.81
6	Bachelors	$987,499.54	$937,528.86	$1,993,629.64	$3,571.44	$3,922,229.49
7	Graduate Degree	$314,422.39	$229,546.08	$601,977.30	$1,116.56	$1,147,062.33
8	Canada	$271,478.17	$170,663.24	$556,319.17	$4,129.67	$1,002,590.25
9	Bachelors	$120,987.32	$77,482.91	$302,532.25	$2,160.02	$503,162.50
10	Graduate Degree	$150,490.86	$93,180.32	$253,786.92	$1,969.65	$499,427.75
11	France	$136,234.26	$242,053.50	$580,468.81	$1,193.78	$959,950.35
12	Bachelors	$89,627.49	$163,136.44	$375,652.47	$745.93	$629,162.33
13	Graduate Degree	$46,606.77	$78,917.06	$204,816.34	$447.85	$330,788.02
14	Germany	$233,539.10	$219,138.27	$749,052.18	$1,048.76	$1,202,778.31
15	Bachelors	$149,929.72	$159,738.59	$529,840.46	$822.06	$840,330.83
16	Graduate Degree	$83,609.38	$59,399.68	$219,211.72	$226.70	$362,447.48
17	United Kingdom	$311,491.44	$370,602.49	$1,086,944.29	$1,549.29	$1,770,587.51
18	Bachelors	$188,203.55	$252,071.41	$725,926.55	$930.75	$1,167,132.26
19	Graduate Degree	$123,287.89	$118,531.08	$361,017.74	$618.54	$603,455.26
20	United States	$1,312,715.50	$823,582.86	$3,210,430.22	$8,776.20	$5,355,504.77

Sheet1 / Sheet2 / Sheet3

FIGURE 20-15

Excel sends the following MDX query to retrieve the results shown in the pivot table. The following query is different from the one used to retrieve the pivot table data when you had Education as a Report Filter. First, the nested subselect statements used to restrict the cube data based on Customer Geography and Education have been combined into a single subselect statement. Second, the axes data on ROWS for the outermost SELECT statement includes a crossjoin of members of the Customer Geography as well as members of the Education hierarchies.

```
SELECT    NON EMPTY Hierarchize({DrilldownLevel(
                    {[Date].[Fiscal].[All Periods]})})
          DIMENSION PROPERTIES PARENT_UNIQUE_NAME ON COLUMNS ,
          NON EMPTY CrossJoin(  Hierarchize({DrilldownLevel(
                {[Customer].[Customer Geography].[All Customers]})}),
                Hierarchize({DrilldownLevel(
                {[Customer].[Education].[All Customers]})}))
```

```
            DIMENSION PROPERTIES PARENT_UNIQUE_NAME ON ROWS
FROM    (
        SELECT (
            {[Customer].[Customer Geography].[Country].&[United States]},
            {[Customer].[Education].&[Graduate Degree],
            [Customer].[Education].&[Bachelors]}) ON COLUMNS
        FROM [Adventure Works]
        )
WHERE ([Measures].[Internet Sales Amount])
CELL PROPERTIES VALUE, FORMAT_STRING, LANGUAGE, BACK_COLOR, FORE_COLOR,
FONT_FLAGS
```

Whenever there are multiple hierarchies in rows or columns, the pivot table creates an automatic grouping for each member in the hierarchy and creates a subtotal. In Figure 20-15 you can see a row showing the subtotal for each year. Because you wanted to analyze the data for bachelors and graduate degree customers, you need to restrict the visible members. You can change the filter selection from customers with degrees to customers with some sort of high school education by performing the following steps:

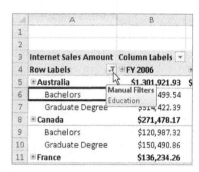

FIGURE 20-16

1. Select one of the members in the Education hierarchy such as Bachelors. Click the Filter icon next to Row Labels, as shown in Figure 20-16.

2. In the Select Field drop-down, make sure Education is selected, and then deselect Bachelors and Graduate Degree and select the High School and Partial High School members, as shown in Figure 20-17.

3. Click OK.

You now see the [Internet Sales Amount] of Customers with only some form of high school education. Applying the filter to the Row area has the benefit of allowing you to see data for each member in a separate row. Similar to applying a filter in the Row Labels area, you can also apply filters in the Column Labels area.

Drilling Down to Detailed Data

So far you have used the pivot table to analyze data using the axes rows, columns, and pages (Report Filter area); you have seen how to pivot on select members and view corresponding measure values. One of the key aspects to analyze OLAP data is not only viewing the aggregated data, but also drilling down or up to view member details as needed. The following steps show how to drill down to detailed data in pivot tables:

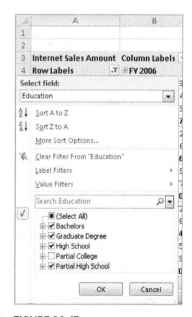

FIGURE 20-17

1. Update your pivot table so that Product Categories is added to the Report Filter section.

2. Remove the filter applied to the Education hierarchy by clicking the Row Labels filter and selecting all the members.

3. Remove the Education hierarchy by dragging and dropping the Education hierarchy from the Row Labels area in the PivotTable Field List to the area where all the measures and hierarchies are shown. Your pivot table should now contain Date.Fiscal in the Column Labels, Customer.Geography in the Row Labels that is filtered for the United States, Product.Product Categories hierarchy in the Report Filter, and Internet Sales Amount in the Values field.

4. To drill down to details of the Internet Sales within the United States, double-click the United States member. You now see that the level State-Province is shown in the row axis, and you see all the states within United States that have sales data, as shown in Figure 20-18. You can also drill down by clicking the + sign next to United States or by selecting the United States member and then clicking the Expand Entire Field icon in the Options tab on the Ribbon, as shown in Figure 20-19.

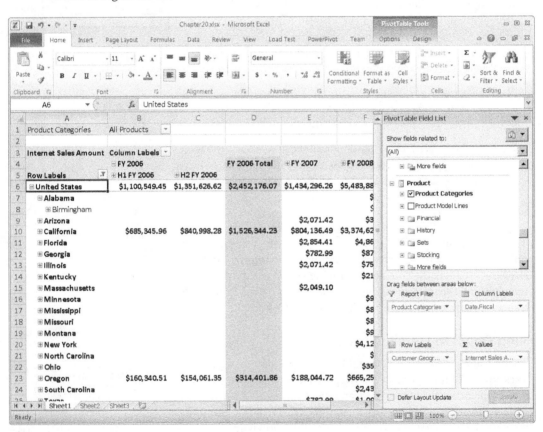

FIGURE 20-18

If you want to drill up from the current level, you can once again double-click the member United States or click the member and then click the Collapse Entire Field icon on the Options tab on the Ribbon. You can choose certain members after the drill down in the pivot table.

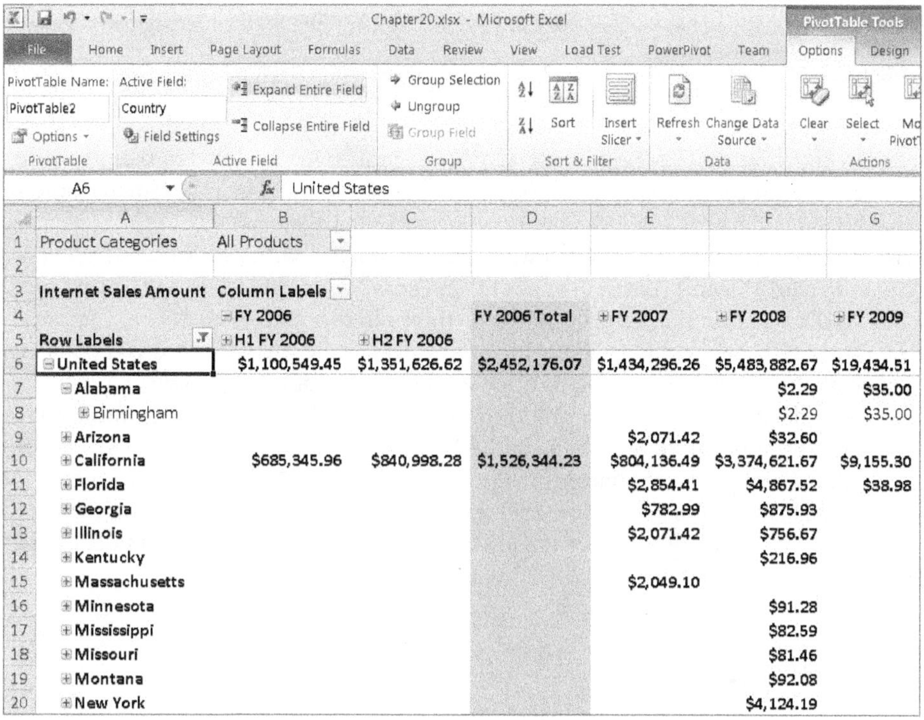

FIGURE 20-19

5. In the PivotTable Field List select the drop-down list next to the Country or State-Province level, and select the members Alabama, Arizona, and California, which are under United States.

6. On the column axis, drill down to the Month Level on Fiscal Year by double-clicking the first member for each level or clicking the + sign. Your pivot table shows the sales amount for three states within the United States for various fiscal years, with detailed data for the months in the first quarter of fiscal year 2006, as shown in Figure 20-20.

To understand the type of MDX query sent by Excel while drilling down to member details, you can use a simpler example in which your pivot table contains the Customer Geographies on Row Label without any filter on Country or State-Province, Product Categories on Report Filter, and Date.Fiscal on Column Label. Apply a drill down on the Column Label for the first member in Date.Fiscal, 2006. The following MDX query is sent by Excel 2010 to Analysis Services:

```
SELECT NON EMPTY Hierarchize( DrilldownMember({{DrilldownLevel(
                {[Date].[Fiscal].[All Periods]})}},
                {[Date].[Fiscal].[Fiscal Year].&[2006]}))
```

```
              DIMENSION PROPERTIES PARENT_UNIQUE_NAME,
              [Date].[Fiscal].[Fiscal Semester].[Fiscal Year] ON COLUMNS ,
        NON EMPTY Hierarchize( DrilldownLevel({
              [Customer].[Customer Geography].[All Customers]})})
              DIMENSION PROPERTIES PARENT_UNIQUE_NAME ON ROWS
FROM   [Adventure Works]
WHERE  ([Product].[Product Categories].[All Products],
        [Measures].[Internet Sales Amount])
CELL PROPERTIES VALUE, FORMAT_STRING, LANGUAGE, BACK_COLOR, FORE_COLOR,
FONT_FLAGS
```

The MDX functions `DrilldownMember` and `DrilldownLevel` are used in the preceding MDX query. The function `DrilldownMember` takes two sets — *Set1* and *Set2* — as parameters and returns a set that contains the drill down of members in *Set1* that are included in *Set2*. You can see that the innermost `DrilldownMember` is called with the sets `DrillDownLevel({[Date].[Fiscal]` `.[All Periods]})` and `{[Date].[Fiscal].[Fiscal Year].&[2006]}`. The first parameter is another MDX function that returns all the members in the Year level. `[Date].[Fiscal].[Fiscal Year].&[2006]` is one of the members in the first set and hence a drill down on this member results in the members `H1 FY 2006` and `H2 FY 2006`. Subsequent `DrilldownMember` functions drill down on the first half of fiscal year 2006 and the first quarter of fiscal year 2006, and Excel would generate a series of `DrilldownLevel` calls in the MDX query based on each level being drilled down. There is an optional third parameter for the `DrilldownLevel` MDX function, which takes the flag `RECURSIVE`. This prompts a recursive drill down on members in *Set1* based on the members in *Set2*. You can understand the behavior of the `RECURSIVE` flag by looking at the results of the following MDX queries:

```
SELECT    DrilldownMember(
          {DrilldownLevel({[Date].[Fiscal].[All Periods]})},
          {[Date].[Fiscal].[Fiscal Year].&[2006],
          [Date].[Fiscal].[Fiscal Semester].&[2006]&[1],
          [Date].[Fiscal].[Fiscal Quarter].&[2006]&[1]}, RECURSIVE) ON 0
FROM      [Sales Summary]
WHERE     ([Measures].[Sales Amount], [Product].[Product Categories].[All])
SELECT    DrilldownMember(
          {DrilldownLevel({[Date].[Fiscal].[All Periods]})},
          {[Date].[Fiscal].[Fiscal Year].&[2006],
          [Date].[Fiscal].[Fiscal Semester].&[2006]&[1],
          [Date].[Fiscal].[Fiscal Quarter].&[2006]&[1]}) ON 0
FROM      [Sales Summary]
WHERE     ([Measures].[Sales Amount], [Product].[Product Categories].[All])
```

Execute these queries in SSMS to see the results of the queries. The first query returns all the months of the first quarter of fiscal year 2006, but the second query returns only the members in the semester level for the fiscal year 2006. You have now successfully learned to drill down to details in your pivot table report and you learned more about the `DrilldownMember` and `DrilldownLevel` MDX functions.

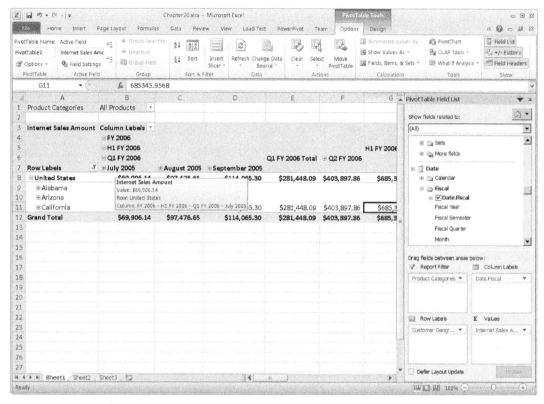

FIGURE 20-20

Analyzing Multiple Measures

So far you have been analyzing a single measure within your pivot table. Sometimes you might need to see more than one measure in your pivot table. For example, as an executive making financial decisions, you might need to analyze the Internet Sales along with the initial targets or to analyze the budgeted cost versus actual cost. In the Cube Browser within SSDT you could select multiple measures. In this section, you learn how to analyze multiple measures within a pivot table.

As an extension to the pivot table you analyzed in the previous section, assume you want to see the quantity ordered along with the sales amount in your pivot table. The following steps show you how to analyze the Internet Sales Amount along with Order Quantity:

1. Drill up to the fiscal year level on the Column Labels.

2. In the PivotTable Field List check the measure Internet Order Quantity. The measure is added to the Values section in the PivotTable Field List and the Values label for the measure is automatically added to the Column Labels section, as shown in Figure 20-21.

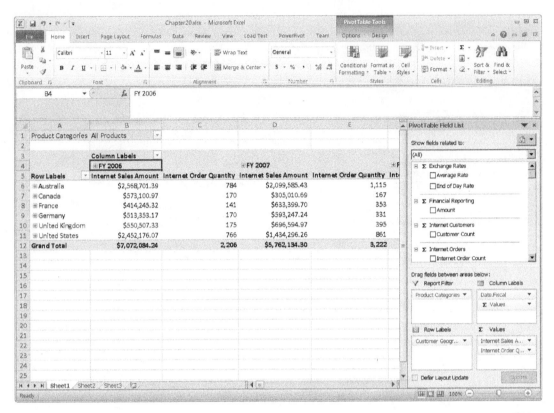

FIGURE 20-21

The pivot table now creates a new hierarchy called Values on the Columns axis and adds the two measures [Internet Sales Amount] and [Internet Order Quantity] to the Values area. If you move the Values hierarchy to the Row area, you get the layout shown in Figure 20-23. You can see the subtotals for each measure in separate rows. The MDX query sent to SSAS to populate the data in the pivot table includes a crossjoin of the Customer Geography hierarchy and a Set with the two measures Internet Sales Amount and Internet Order Quantity on the Rows axis.

Custom Grouping

When you analyze the results within a pivot table, you might want to group certain members and analyze the data for those specific members. For example, if you have sales data for all the countries, you might want to analyze the sales based on continents. If continent is not a level in the hierarchy, you might need to modify the cube design and add this information. Instead the pivot table helps you to group members and provide a name. Perform the following steps to group the countries' level of the Customer Geography hierarchy into two groups, North America and Europe, within the pivot table:

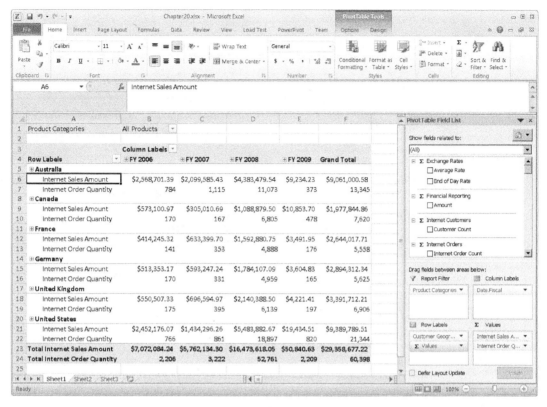

FIGURE 20-22

1. Remove Internet Order Quantity from the Values list so that Internet Sales Amount is the only value in the pivot table.

2. Hold down the Ctrl key, and select the members United States and Canada.

3. Right-click and select Group, as shown in Figure 20-23. You can also accomplish this by clicking the Group Selection button in the Group section of the Options tab on the Ribbon.

   A new group appears called Group 1. Under that group are the members United States and Canada. Excel uses the session cube feature of SSAS to create an intermediate level to group. Following is the query sent by Excel to SSAS:

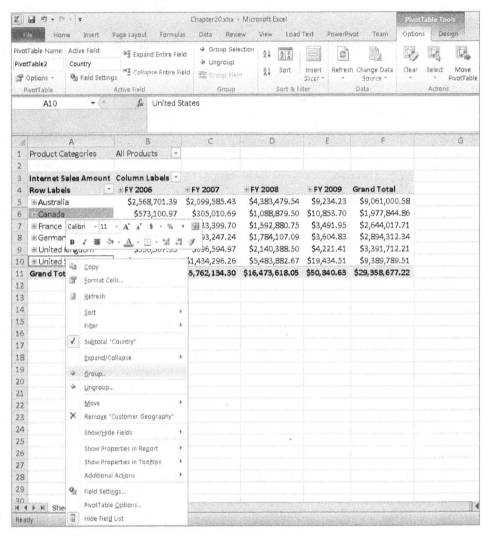

FIGURE 20-23

```
CREATE SESSION CUBE [Adventure Works_XL_GROUPING2] FROM [Adventure Works]
( MEASURE [Adventure Works].[Internet Sales Amount],
  MEASURE [Adventure Works].[Internet Order Quantity],
  MEASURE [Adventure Works].[Internet Extended Amount],
  ...
  DIMENSION [Adventure Works].[Ship Date].[Month Name] HIDDEN,
  DIMENSION [Customer].[Customer Geography] NOT_RELATED_TO_FACTS
  FROM _XL_GROUPING7
  (
    LEVEL [(All)],
    LEVEL [Customer Geography1] GROUPING,
    LEVEL [Country],
    LEVEL [State-Province],
```

```
LEVEL [City],
LEVEL [Postal Code],
LEVEL [Customer],
GROUP [Customer Geography1].[CountryXl_Grp_1]
(
    MEMBER [Customer].[Customer Geography].[Country].&[Canada],
    MEMBER [Customer].[Customer Geography].[Country].&[United States]
)
)
)
```

You can see that the create session cube statement is sent to SSAS where all the measures and dimensions are included and an intermediate level, [Customer Geography1], is created on the Customer Geography hierarchy. That level includes Canada and United States, as shown in the MEMBER lines in the code.

4. Select the cell containing the member Group1, and rename it to North America.

5. Create another group for France, Germany, and United Kingdom, and name it Europe. When you finish, the pivot table should look like Figure 20-24.

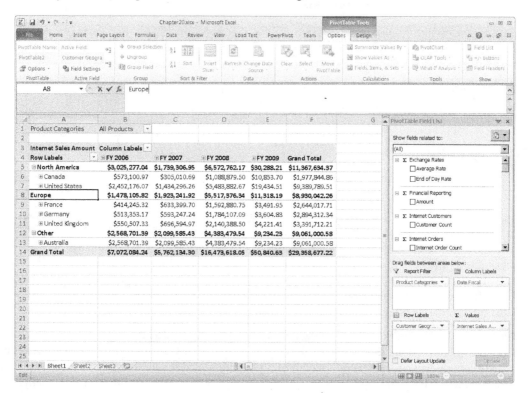

FIGURE 20-24

You have now successfully grouped members in the Customer Geography hierarchy without making design changes in the cube. As mentioned earlier, Excel uses the session cube feature of SSAS to create the intermediate levels. The intermediate levels persist only in the context of the current session and are not seen by other users. Totals are created for the new members North America and Europe, which allows the end user to drill down or drill up. If you click the drop-down list for Row Labels, you can see the new members created due to custom grouping along with the members in the Country level, as shown in Figure 20-25. If you double-click a cell containing a group member, you see that the double-click acts as a toggle switch to hide or show details in the next level. For example, if you double-click Europe, you can see the members France, Germany, and United Kingdom change from visible to hidden and vice versa. The groupings help you analyze the [Internet Sales Amount] for various continents across various fiscal years.

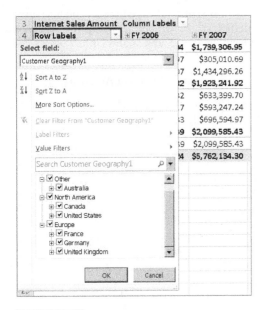

FIGURE 20-25

You can also create nested groups by grouping groups that have been created, such as grouping Europe and North America into a Northern Hemisphere group. The Grouping feature in Excel provides you with the flexibility to do multiple levels of grouping, which is useful when several members are in a hierarchy and you want to perform data analysis by grouping the members into several groups. You can ungroup a group of members by right-clicking the group name and selecting Ungroup from the context menu or clicking the Ungroup icon on the Ribbon under the Options tab in a similar manner as the grouping that was shown in Figure 20-23.

You must know the limitations of grouping hierarchy members in Excel pivot tables. Custom grouping is only available for multidimensional BISM, not tabular BISM. In addition, in multidimensional BISM you cannot group members of a parent-child hierarchy and hierarchies of ROLAP dimensions using Excel pivot tables. Having learned to use various options in the pivot table for data analysis, you now learn to present the data effectively to end users in the following sections.

Organizing Attributes in the PivotTable Field List

You can edit the folder names that the attributes belong to in SSDT. You change the folders for some customer attributes to help you organize information in a mailing list:

1. Launch SQL Server Data Tools.

2. Open the AdventureWorksDW multidimensional sample project.

3. In the Solution Explorer under Dimensions, double-click the Customer.dim dimension.

4. In the Attributes pane select Education.

5. Change the AttributeHierarchyDisplay property of the Education attribute in the Properties pane to Personal, as shown in Figure 20-26.

6. Make the same change to the Gender and Marital Status attribute properties.

7. Deploy the AdventureWorksDW multidimensional project onto your Analysis Services instance.

When your project finishes deploying, the server updated information that organizes and displays the hierarchies in the folder that you specified. This way you can organize the attributes the way you want in the PivotTable Field List for your end users. Now use the following steps to see the updated information within Excel:

1. Switch to your Excel application.

2. In the Ribbon select the Data tab.

3. In the Connections group select Refresh All.

4. View the Customer dimension in the PivotTable Field List.

The Customer dimension in the PivotTable Field List has been updated with a new folder called Personal, which now contains the attributes Education, Gender, and Marital Status, as shown in Figure 20-27.

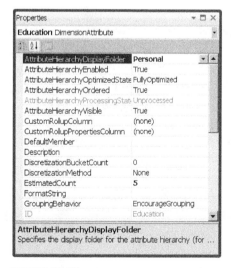

FIGURE 20-26

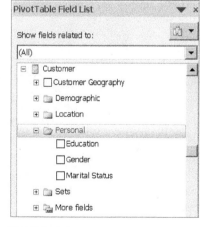

FIGURE 20-27

Number Formatting

If you are familiar with Excel, you might be aware that you can apply various kinds of formatting to a cell in Excel such as String, Number, and Currency. Excel requests the formatted value for the measures retrieved from Analysis Services cubes. It uses the formatted value to display the cell values. The measure InternetSaleAmount is of type Currency in the AdventureWorksDW sample database. That's why you see the InternetSalesAmount displayed as currency in the pivot table. If you change the formatting on the Analysis Services instance, Excel can display the new formatting. The following steps show how to change the formatting for the InternetSalesAmount from currency to three decimal places on your cube and see how this displays in Excel:

1. Open the Adventure Works cube in SSDT.

2. Select the InternetSalesAmount measure.

3. In the Properties window change the FormatString property from Currency to #,#.000 as shown in Figure 20-28.

4. Deploy the project to your Analysis Services instance.

5. Switch to your Excel application with the pivot table connected to the Adventure Works cube.

6. Select the Data tab on the Excel Ribbon.

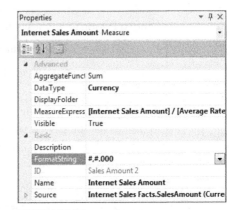

FIGURE 20-28

7. In the Connections group select Refresh All. The [Internet Sales Amount] now refreshes in the pivot table, and you see each cell value has three decimal places displayed, as shown in Figure 20-29. Perform the following three steps to get back to the original cube state for the subsequent exercises.

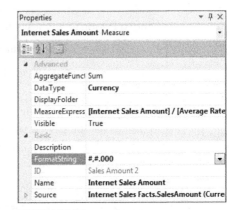

FIGURE 20-29

8. Switch back to SSDT.

9. Change the FormatString property of the [Internet Sales Amount] measure back to Currency.

10. Deploy the changes to your Analysis Services instance.

Highlighting Exceptions

Highlighting exceptions, which are also called bubbling up exceptions, provides a way to quickly read through the report and examine exceptions in the data. This is one technique that can help with faster data analysis, especially when you look at a pivot table with a large amount of data. SQL Server Analysis Services 2012 allows you to specify the background color for each cell value, which can be utilized by any Analysis Services client tool to highlight exceptions. You learned how to format the background color of cell values in Chapter 6. The following steps show you how to update the MDX script to specify background color for [Internet Sales Amount] based on its value and then view the results in Excel:

1. Switch to the SSDT that has the AdventureWorksDW 2012 sample project open.

2. Double-click the AdventureWorks.cube file to open the AdventureWorks cube in the cube editor, and select the Calculations tab.

3. In the Calculations tab click the icon to switch to Script View, as shown in Figure 20-30.

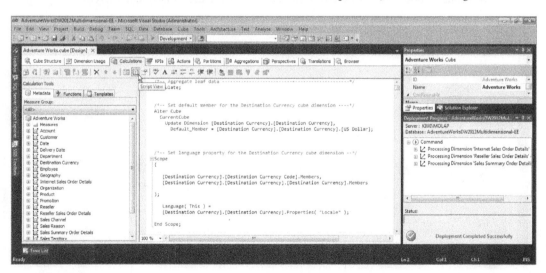

FIGURE 20-30

4. Scroll to the end of the MDX script, and add the following MDX expression in the MDX script editor, as shown in Figure 20-31:

```
//Adding background color
Scope ([Measures].[Internet Sales Amount]);
    Back_Color ( [Measures].[Internet Sales Amount] ) =
    IIF([Measures].[Internet Sales Amount]>100000,"65280","255");
End Scope;
```

This MDX expression specifies the background color based on the cell value. If the cell value is greater than 100000, the background color assigned is green (65280); otherwise a red background color (255) is assigned to the cell.

5. Deploy the updated AdventureWorksDW project to your Analysis Services instance.

6. Switch to the Excel application connected to the AdventureWorks cube, and on the Excel Ribbon select the Data tab.

7. In the Connections group select Refresh All.

The pivot table now refreshes with the updated data from your Analysis Services instance that contains the background cell values, as shown in Figure 20-32. Drill down on the cells corresponding to the United States members. You can see the background color applied to each state. This example shows a simple illustration of the background color. Typically the MDX expressions in the cubes for the background have appropriately highlighted the business objectives of your company. Having the background color highlight exceptions in the data helps you identify key areas to focus on to improve your business results. Perform steps 8 through 10 to return to the original cube state for the subsequent exercises.

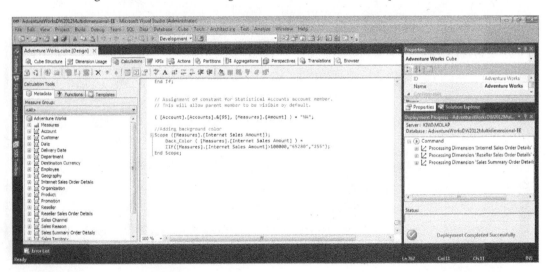

FIGURE 20-31

8. Switch back to SSDT.

9. Delete the MDX expression you added in this section for background color.

10. Deploy the AdventureWorksDW project to your Analysis Services instance.

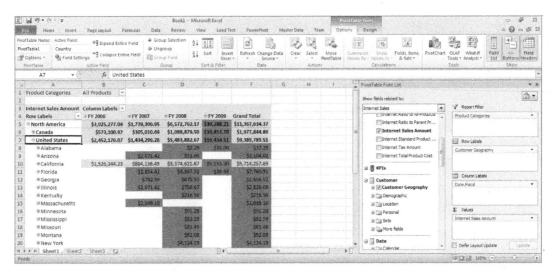

FIGURE 20-32

Viewing Member Properties

In Analysis Services 2008 you can define the relationship between attributes within a dimension using the Attribute Relationship page of the Dimension Designer. By default, all the attributes relate to the key attribute of a dimension because there is a one-to-many relationship. Member properties are properties that define certain aspects of a member. For example, a customer's name, age, and salary are properties of the customer. The Attribute Relationship page of the Dimension Designer also defines member properties, as you learned in Chapter 5. While analyzing the data in a pivot table, you may want to see the properties of a member. Excel provides two ways to see member properties within pivot tables: using tool tips or adding the data to the pivot table. The following sections show you how to view member properties within Excel.

Tool Tips

Tool tips provide you with an easy way to view the properties of members you analyze in the pivot table as you hover the mouse arrow over a specific member. To use tool tips, follow these steps:

1. Remove all the fields from your pivot table. You can do this by clicking the arrow on the right side of each attribute in the field areas of the PivotTable Field List and selecting Remove Field from the context menu, dragging each item from the field areas to the fields section, or unchecking the appropriate boxes in the fields section of the PivotTable Field List.

2. In the PivotTable Field List filter drop-down (Show Fields Related To), select [Internet Customers] and then add the Customer Geography and Customer hierarchies to the Row Labels.

3. Select the first Customer in North America, Aaron A. Allen, and hover the mouse over the member.

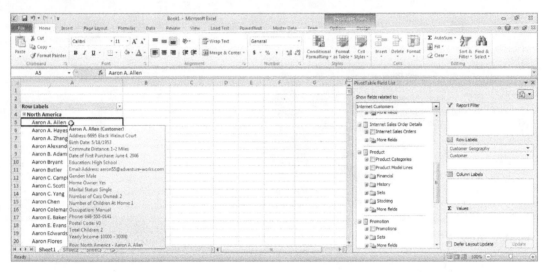

FIGURE 20-33

You see the member properties of the Customer Aaron A. Allen as a tool tip, as shown in Figure 20-33. Because the Customer hierarchy is the key attribute in the Customer dimension, you can see all the properties of the member from the Customer hierarchy. As you perform your data analysis in the pivot table and want to get more information about a specific member, this tool tip feature can help you understand the data better.

The Pivot Table Report

As an alternative to viewing the tool tips, Excel provides you with a way to have the member properties added into your pivot table. To use the pivot table from the previous section to view a member property as part of the pivot table report, follow these steps:

1. Right-click one of the Customer members, and on the context menu select Show Properties in Report Education.

2. Add the Date.Fiscal hierarchy to the Column Labels.

3. Add the Customer Count to the Values.

4. Expand the North America member to show the Countries in North America.

You now see the Education member property of each customer shown as a column in the pivot table, as shown in Figure 20-34. The member property added into the pivot table report is a column that appears before the attributes part of the Column Labels. Including all the member properties would make the pivot table difficult to analyze, so you should choose the appropriate member properties to include in the pivot table reports so that the end user can easily use those properties for effective data analysis.

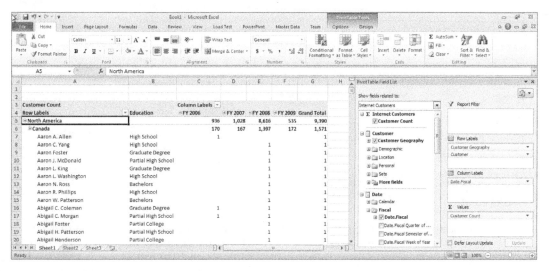

FIGURE 20-34

Sorting Data

You may have observed from the previous example that the list of members in a pivot table can be fairly long. To help you with further analysis, Excel 2010 provides you with new and simpler filtering and sorting options. In this section you learn how to sort in Excel 2010. Now return to analyzing Internet Sales by location:

1. Clear all the fields in the pivot table by removing the measures from values and hierarchies from Row Labels and Column Labels.

2. Select Internet Sales measure group as a filter in the PivotTable Field List.

3. Add the [Internet Sales Amount] to Values.

4. Add Customer Geography to the Row Labels.

5. Add Date.Fiscal to the Column Labels.

6. Drill down on the country France in the Customer Geography hierarchy, as shown in Figure 20-35.

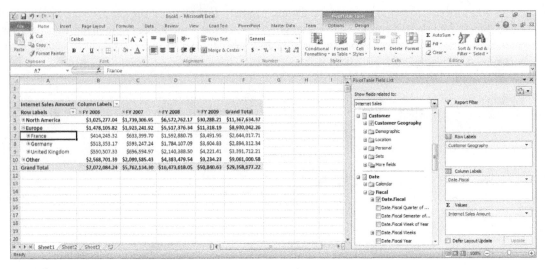

FIGURE 20-35

You now see the [Internet Sales Amount] for the various provinces in France for various fiscal years. However it is not easy to identify the provinces with minimum and maximum Internet sales for fiscal year FY 2006. Excel 2010 provides you with an easy way to sort the data in the pivot table that helps you easily identify the minimum and maximum InternetSalesAmounts.

7. Switch to the Home tab in the Excel Ribbon.

8. Select the [Internet Sales Amount] value for state Charente-Maritime and FY 2006.

9. In the Editing group, click the Sort & Filter icon (refer to Figure 20-35), and select Sort Smallest to Largest.

Excel sends the appropriate MDX query to retrieve the data from SSAS and sorts the members on the axes based on the column selected and cell values returned. You can now notice the pivot table has been sorted based on the [Internet Sales Amount] values for FY 2006, as shown in Figure 20-36. From the pivot table you can see that the province Pas de Calais doesn't have any Internet sales and the province Seine (Paris) has the maximum Internet sales. You can also see the year-to-year trend in Internet sales easily from this pivot table view.

Filtering Data

In the previous section you learned about sorting the data in pivot tables. When your pivot table is large with several hundred or thousands of members on rows or columns, data analysis becomes challenging. Excel 2010 provides you with three common ways to filter data in a pivot table. The three ways of filtering are based on Labels, Values, or Top 10. Label filters apply values such as the sales amount of the cities beginning with "Seine." Value filters help in filtering the data in the pivot table based on any of the measure values. For example, you might analyze the [Internet Sales Amount] data and apply a value to filter the data showing the [Internet Tax Amount] that is greater than a specific amount or even within a specific range. One of the most common data analysis requests is for the Top 10 values. The Top 10 filter helps you to quickly narrow down the pivot table to the Top 10 items so that you can analyze the Top 10 values efficiently. The following steps show you how to apply each of these filters and how they affect the data in the pivot table:

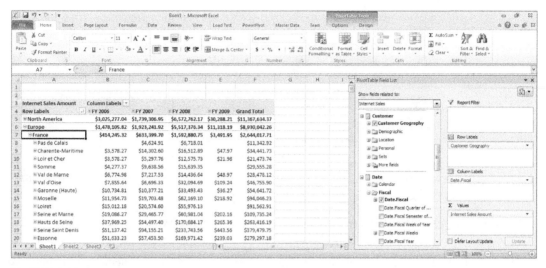

FIGURE 20-36

1. Right-click any State-Province in the country France, and on the context menu, select Filter Label Filters.

2. On the Label Filter dialog set the criteria to State-Province contains Seine, as shown in Figure 20-37, and click OK.

FIGURE 20-37

Excel sends the following MDX query to retrieve the data based on the filter condition. The MDX expression (InStr(1,[Customer].[Customer Geography].CurrentMember .member_caption,"Seine")>0) helps filter the members in the Customer Geography hierarchy that contain "Seine" in their member caption. InStr, a Visual Basic for Applications (VBA) function used in this expression, returns a value greater than 0 only when it finds the substring "Seine" in the member caption. Excel then uses the subselect MDX statement to filter the cube space to members in the Customer Geography hierarchy that contain the value "Seine" in their names. Because there are two groups created in the pivot table called Europe and North America, Excel has created a session cube with the name Adventure Works_XL_ GROUPING0, which is the name you see in the following MDX expression. The hierarchy for Customer Geography has been changed to Customer Geography1 within this session because the new levels have been created in the Customer Geography hierarchy.

```
SELECT  NON EMPTY Hierarchize( {DrilldownLevel({
            [Date].[Fiscal].[All Periods]})})
        DIMENSION PROPERTIES PARENT_UNIQUE_NAME ON COLUMNS ,
        NON EMPTY Hierarchize(DrilldownMember({{
            DrilldownMember( {{DrilldownLevel({
            [Customer].[Customer Geography].[All Customers]})}},
            {[Customer].[Customer Geography].[Customer Geography1].
```

```
                    [GROUPMEMBER.[CountryXl_Grp_2]].[Customer]].[Customer Geography]].
                    [All Customers]]]})}},
                 {[Customer].[Customer Geography].[Country].&[France]}))
              DIMENSION PROPERTIES PARENT_UNIQUE_NAME,
                 [Customer].[Customer Geography].[State-Province].[Country] ON ROWS
       FROM   (SELECT
                 Filter([Customer].[Customer Geography].[State-Province].Members,
                 (InStr(1,
                    [Customer].[Customer Geography].CurrentMember.member_caption,
                    "Seine")0)) ON COLUMNS  FROM [Adventure Works_XL_GROUPING0]
                 )
       WHERE ([Measures].[Internet Sales Amount])
       CELL PROPERTIES VALUE, FORMAT_STRING, LANGUAGE, BACK_COLOR, FORE_COLOR, FONT_
       FLAGS
```

The pivot table now filters to State-Provinces containing the word Seine in them, as shown in Figure 20-38.

3. Clear the Label filtering by right-clicking one of the State-Province members in France and selecting Filter Clear Filter State-Province on the context menu.

4. Filter the Column Labels to show only FY 2006 using the drop-down list next to it and selecting only FY 2006.

5. Right-click a member on Row Labels, and select Filter Value Filters.

6. In the Value Filter dialog, select the filter condition "is greater than" and have the value 600000, as shown in Figure 20-39.

You can now see the pivot table showing all the members in Customer Geography that have an [Internet Sales Amount] greater than $600,000 as shown in Figure 20-40.

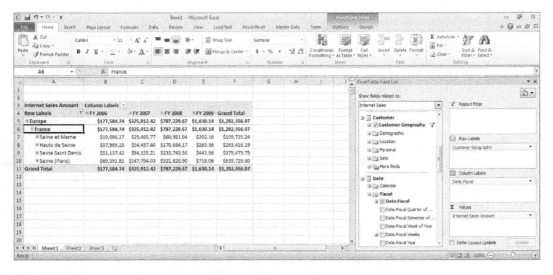

FIGURE 20-38

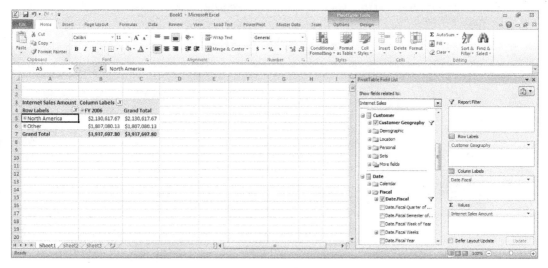

FIGURE 20-39

FIGURE 20-40

Excel sends the following query to retrieve the data from Analysis Services. In this query you can see the cube is initially filtered on Customer Geography members who have Internet Sales Amount greater than 600,000 using the subselect MDX clause, and then the outer SELECT clause retrieves the data for the pivot table including the two groups created in this specific session.

```
SELECT   NON EMPTY Hierarchize( {DrilldownLevel({
         [Date].[Fiscal].[All Periods]})})
         DIMENSION PROPERTIES PARENT_UNIQUE_NAME ON COLUMNS ,
         NON EMPTY Hierarchize(DrilldownMember({{DrilldownLevel(
         {[Customer].[Customer Geography].[All Customers]})}},
         {[Customer].[Customer Geography].[Customer Geography1].
         [GROUPMEMBER.[CountryXl_Grp_1]].[Customer]].[Customer Geography]].
             [All Customers]]],
         [Customer].[Customer Geography].[Customer Geography1].
         [GROUPMEMBER.[CountryXl_Grp_2]].[Customer]].[Customer Geography]].
             [All Customers]]],
         [Customer].[Customer Geography].[Customer Geography1].
         [OTHERMEMBER.[Customer]].[Customer Geography]].[All Customers]]]}))
         DIMENSION PROPERTIES PARENT_UNIQUE_NAME ON ROWS
FROM (
```

```
SELECT Filter( Hierarchize(
        [Customer].[Customer Geography].[Country].Members),
        ([Measures].[Internet Sales Amount]>600000)) ON COLUMNS
FROM (
    SELECT ( {[Date].[Fiscal].[Fiscal Year].&[2006]}) ON COLUMNS
    FROM [Adventure Works_XL_GROUPING0]
        )
    )
WHERE ([Measures].[Internet Sales Amount])
CELL PROPERTIES VALUE, FORMAT_STRING, LANGUAGE, BACK_COLOR, FORE_COLOR,
FONT_FLAGS
```

7. Remove the Value filter criteria specified earlier by clicking the Sort & Filter icon on the Home Ribbon and selecting Clear, as shown in Figure 20-41.

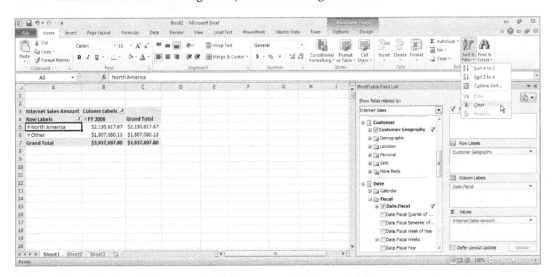

FIGURE 20-41

8. Click the member Europe, right-click, and select Ungroup.

9. Click the member North America, right-click, and select Ungroup. Now see how the Top 10 filter helps in easier data analysis. Assume you need to analyze the Internet sales of all the states within the United States and you want to identify the top 10 states' Internet sales based on gross profit. Perform the following steps in the pivot table to achieve the wanted results.

10. Drill down on the members of United States by clicking the + sign next to it.

11. Select one of the States within United States.

12. Right-click and select Filter Top 10.

13. In the Top 10 Filter for the State-Province hierarchy, select the Internet Gross Profit measure, as shown in Figure 20-42, and click OK.

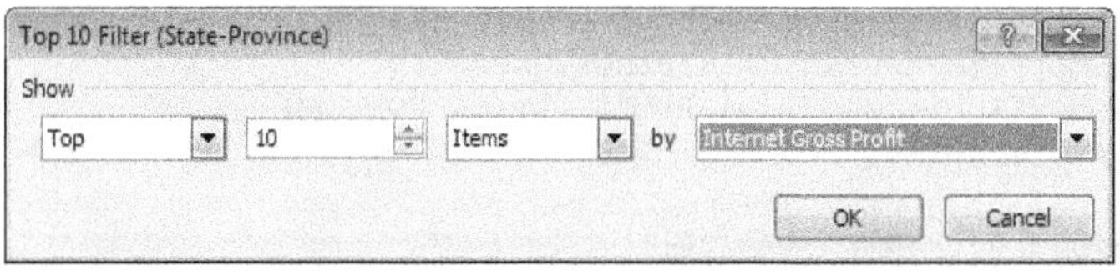

FIGURE 20-42

The number of states shown in the pivot table for United States now filters from 22 to the top 10 states, as shown in Figure 20-43.

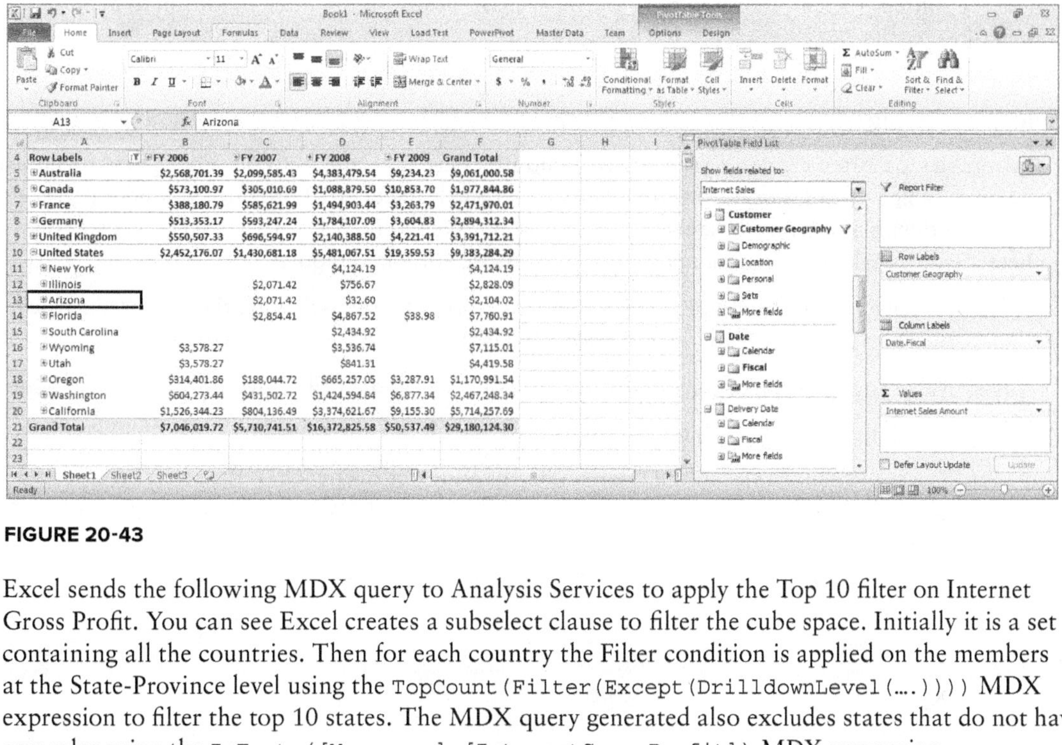

FIGURE 20-43

Excel sends the following MDX query to Analysis Services to apply the Top 10 filter on Internet Gross Profit. You can see Excel creates a subselect clause to filter the cube space. Initially it is a set containing all the countries. Then for each country the Filter condition is applied on the members at the State-Province level using the TopCount(Filter(Except(DrilldownLevel(….)))) MDX expression to filter the top 10 states. The MDX query generated also excludes states that do not have any sales using the IsEmpty([Measures].[InternetGrossProfit]) MDX expression.

```
SELECT    NON EMPTY Hierarchize({DrilldownLevel({
              [Date].[Fiscal].[All Periods]})})
          DIMENSION PROPERTIES PARENT_UNIQUE_NAME ON COLUMNS ,
          NON EMPTY Hierarchize(DrilldownMember({{DrilldownLevel(
              {[Customer].[Customer Geography].[All Customers]})}},
              {[Customer].[Customer Geography].[Country].&[United States]}))
          DIMENSION PROPERTIES PARENT_UNIQUE_NAME,
          [Customer].[Customer Geography].[State-Province].[Country] ON ROWS
FROM      (
          SELECT Generate(Hierarchize(
              [Customer].[Customer Geography].[Country].Members) AS
                  [XL_Filter_Set_0],
              TopCount(Filter(Except(DrilldownLevel([XL_Filter_Set_0].Current
```

```
                    AS [XL_Filter_HelperSet_0], , 0), [XL_Filter_HelperSet_0]),
            Not IsEmpty([Measures].[Internet Gross Profit])), 10,
            [Measures].[Internet Gross Profit])) ON COLUMNS
        FROM [Adventure Works]
        )
WHERE (([Measures].[Internet Sales Amount])
CELL PROPERTIES VALUE, FORMAT_STRING, LANGUAGE, BACK_COLOR,FORE_COLOR,
FONT_FLAGS
```

In this section you have learned the various ways you can filter the data in a pivot table. You also learned about the MDX queries sent by Excel during these filter conditions and identified that Excel uses the subselect MDX clause to filter the cube space based on the filter condition to achieve the final filter results.

Style and Design

Pivot tables are often created as reports that end users use for data analysis. That's why formatting the pivot table in an end-user-consumable way is critical. Excel 2010 provides you with preset styles to use on the pivot tables. These styles are shared between tables and other Excel objects. Follow these steps to make the existing pivot table an end-user-oriented report:

1. Remove the filter condition in the previous section by right-clicking the Sort & Filter icon on the Data tab of the Ribbon and selecting Clear.

2. Make sure your pivot table shows all the countries and a drill down only on United States.

3. Switch to the Design tab on the Ribbon, as shown in Figure 20-44.

You see various styles in the Design tab. If you hover over each of the styles, you see the style applied to your pivot table. This helps you to preview how a specific style will look on your pivot table report.

4. Choose the style for your pivot table (refer to Figure 20-44).

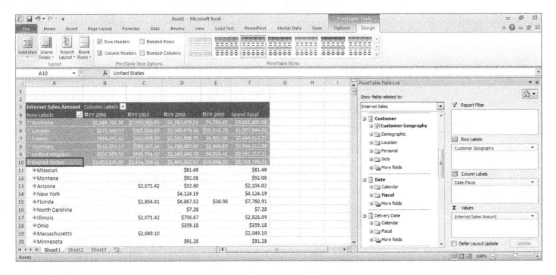

FIGURE 20-44

You can see that all the formatting in your pivot table is still available. Excel 2010 also allows you to create your own customized style. Refer to Excel 2010 documentation to learn about creating custom styles.

Excel 2010 Conditional Formatting

Excel 2010 has a conditional formatting feature that allows you to analyze the data efficiently in your pivot table. In this section you learn how you can set up conditional formatting with a few clicks. For this example you analyze the mountain bike product sales on various models delivered for various fiscal years so that you can determine which product models perform well without reviewing in detail the actual numbers.

1. Clear the fields in your pivot table by removing the measure in the Values area and the hierarchies in the Row Labels and Column Labels areas.

2. Select the Internet Ratio to All Products measure on Values.

3. Drag and drop Product Categories onto Row Labels.

4. Drag and drop Delivery Date.Fiscal Year onto Column Labels.

5. Drill down to Bikes Mountain Bikes. Notice the number of bikes.

6. Select the cell range that contains the ratios of mountain bikes delivered.

7. On the Home tab of the Ribbon, select the Conditional Formatting icon, and under Color Scales select the first option, Green-Yellow-Red Color Scale, as shown in Figure 20-45.

You now see the various colors applied to the data area you have selected. Red indicates the cells that have the least contribution to the sales, and green indicates the models that have contributed to the maximum sales. This method clearly helps you to analyze the pivot table data better because it visually differentiates the data.

 If you hover over the various color scales, you can preview them before selecting one.

The percentage does not need to be 100 percent for it to be green. Excel calculates the range of values based on the selection the user made. You also have the option to apply the other conditional formatting options in Excel 2010 such as Data bars or Top/Bottom Rules or Icon Sets. You can use any combination of these conditional formats to make your pivot table reports most efficient for data analysis for your end users. You should explore the various conditional formatting options in Excel 2010.

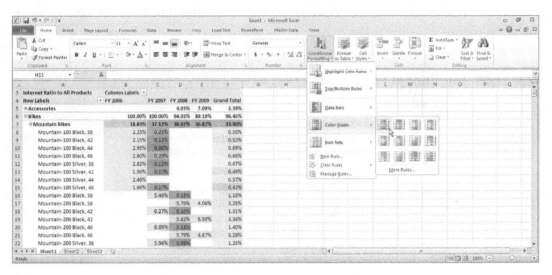

FIGURE 20-45

Perspectives and Translations

In Chapters 5 and 6 you learned about the Perspectives and Translations features supported by Analysis Services. Excel 2010 offers these features. In this section you learn how to use these features in pivot table reports.

Perspectives

Similar to views on relational databases, perspectives provide another layer for filtering data on the server. You can use perspectives as one of the ways to filter the data being viewed from your Analysis Services instance. The filter occurs on the Analysis Services server. Several perspectives are in the sample AdventureWorksDW database. The following steps show you how to create a new pivot table based on a perspective:

1. On a new worksheet in the Excel workbook, on the Ribbon select the Data tab, and select From Other Sources from Analysis Services.

2. In the Data Connection Wizard enter **localhost** for the server name, and click Next.

3. Select the AdventureWorksDW database in the Select Database and Table page of the wizard. You see the cubes and perspectives in the Adventure Works DW 2012 database.

4. Select the Finance perspective and click Next.

5. Accept the default name for the data connection file and click Finish.

6. Click OK in the Import Data dialog.

7. From the PivotTable Field List, add the Amount measure to the Values area, the Departments hierarchy to the Row Labels area, and the Date.Fiscal hierarchy to the Column Labels area.

You now see the pivot table created on the Finance perspective, as shown in Figure 20-46. You can see that the measure groups and the dimensions shown in the Field List are only the ones related to the Finance perspective. This is another way to filter the amount of meta data and data to be shown to the end user in the pivot table. When using perspectives for filtering in a pivot table, all the filtering of data and meta data occurs on the Analysis Services instance.

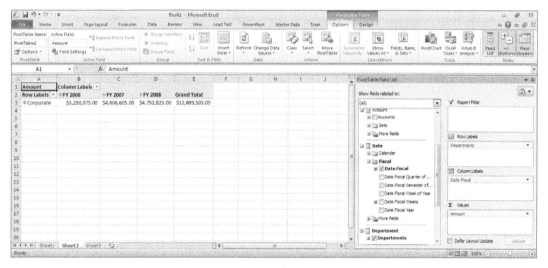

FIGURE 20-46

Translations

You learned about the Translations feature in SSAS in Chapters 5 and 6. When a client connects using a specific client locale such as Japanese, German, or French and if corresponding translations are defined in your multidimensional BISM for data and meta data, SSAS sends the appropriate captions specified for the locale. This SSAS feature is extremely useful when you design a multidimensional BISM for your organization where end users in various countries want to see the same data but with appropriate translated meta data. Normally, an end user has a localized version of Excel connecting to an SSAS instance and sees the localized information if the multidimensional BISM has been designed with translations. The locale-specific information is transferred by Excel. In this section you learn how to verify that an end user using a non-English locale will see translated meta data from Excel.

Assume you have created a multidimensional BISM for all users in your company with translations in French. You need to ensure that those using French Excel can see the translations. You can either install a French version of Excel to test this, or using your English version of Excel, test this by changing the connection string used to connect to SSAS. You need to update the connection string properties to inform Analysis Server to use specific locales. The AdventureWorksDW Sample has localized names in the database for Spanish and French. The following steps show you how to see the French data in your pivot table:

1. Switch to a new sheet in Excel, and select the Data tab.

2. Click Existing Connections, and select the connection to the AdventureWorks cube in the AdventureWorksDW database that you created earlier in this chapter, as shown in Figure 20-47, and click Open.

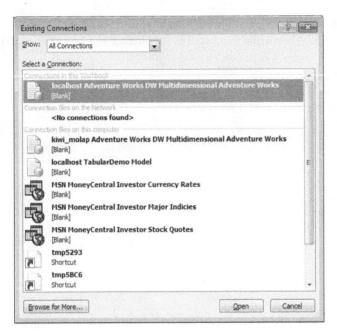

FIGURE 20-47

3. In the Import Data dialog, click the OK button.

4. Add the [Internet Sales Amount] to the Values area.

5. Add the Date.Fiscal hierarchy to the Column Labels.

6. Add Product.Product Categories to the Row Labels. You should now have a pivot table, as shown in Figure 20-48.

7. Click the Data tab on the Excel Ribbon. Then under the Connections group, click the Properties button.

8. In the Connection Properties dialog, switch to the Definition tab and add the text **LocaleIdentifier=1036** to the connection string, as shown in Figure 20-49.

9. Click OK.

Excel modifies your entry of LocaleIdentifier=1036 in the connection string to ExtendedProperti es="LocaleIdentifier=1036". You can see the updated connection string as shown if you click the Properties icon in the Connection group.

```
Provider=MSOLAP.5;Integrated Security=SSPI;Persist Security Info=True;Initial
Catalog=AdventureWorksDW;Data Source=localhost;Extended
Properties="LocaleIdentifier=1036";MDX Compatibility=1;Safety Options=2;
MDX Missing Member Mode=Error
```

FIGURE 20-48

FIGURE 20-49

Excel sends a series of discovers to retrieve the meta data and data to be shown in the pivot table with the updated connection string. The MDX query to retrieve the data for the pivot table is the same but Excel sends the additional property of LocaleIdentifier=1036. Analysis Services understands the French client (LocaleIdentifier=1036) and sends the translated data and metadata. Now your pivot table is updated to show the members of the Product and Date hierarchies in French captions, as shown in Figure 20-50. The actual Internet Sales Amount data values do not change. You have now successfully verified that your French users can connect to your multidimensional BISM and view your translations successfully. If you create an Excel report that the clients are going to use, you would actually need to update the saved connection string with the LocaleIdentifier=1036 property. You can do this by changing the connection's properties in the Workbook Connections dialog. You open the dialog by clicking the Connections button on the Data tab of the Ribbon.

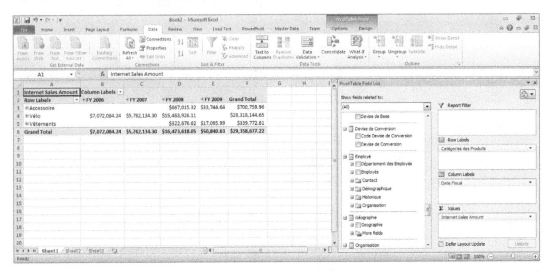

FIGURE 20-50

Key Performance Indicators

Key Performance Indicators (KPIs) are business measurements that track trends and progress toward some predefined goal. You learned how to define and use KPIs in Chapter 9. Excel 2010 understands SSAS KPIs and can retrieve and show the appropriate KPI icons within Excel. In this section you learn how to analyze data from Adventure Works using KPIs. The following steps show you how to review KPIs in pivot tables:

1. Change the language used by the connection string from the pivot table in the previous section to English by removing the LocaleIdentifier=1036 string in the Connection Property dialog.

2. Clear all the fields from your pivot table by removing them from Values, Row Labels, and Column Labels.

3. Navigate the PivotTable Field List, and add Date.Fiscal to the Row Labels.

4. Expand the KPIs folder, and then expand the [Growth In Customer Base] KPI. Add Value, Status, Goal, Trend to Values, as shown in Figure 20-51.

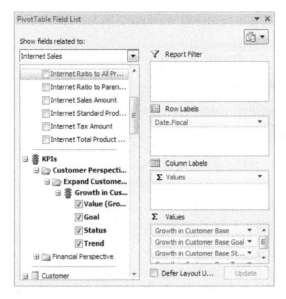

FIGURE 20-51

As shown in Figure 20-52, you see the Growth in Customer Base KPI's value, goal, status, and trend for various fiscal years. From the pivot table you can analyze that for FY 2006 there was no growth in customers because there was no previous year to compare against. Hence, the status doesn't matter in this case, and the trend is flat. For FY 2007 growth was 46 percent compared with the previous fiscal year, and the goal was 30 percent. Therefore, the KPI status indicator is green and the trend indicator is up.

FIGURE 20-52

The definitions of the KPIs are in the cube. Excel retrieves the KPIs using the following MDX query:

```
SELECT      {[Measures].[Growth in Customer Base],
             [Measures].[Growth in Customer Base Goal],
             [Measures].[Growth in Customer Base Status],
             [Measures].[Growth in Customer Base Trend]}
            DIMENSION PROPERTIES PARENT_UNIQUE_NAME ON COLUMNS ,
            NON EMPTY Hierarchize({DrilldownLevel({
                [Date].[Fiscal].[All Periods]})})
            DIMENSION PROPERTIES PARENT_UNIQUE_NAME ON ROWS
FROM [Adventure Works]
CELL PROPERTIES VALUE, FORMAT_STRING, LANGUAGE, BACK_COLOR, FORE_COLOR,
FONT_FLAGS
```

If you execute the MDX query in SSMS, you see the KPI values as numbers, as shown in Figure 20-53, which are the basis for the graphical information that is shown in Excel. Excel retrieves the numerical information defined on the multidimensional BISM for the KPIs and translates the values to appropriate KPI graphics in the pivot table. The graphical KPI helps you understand the data more easily than actual numbers. For example, green indicates the goal of 30 percent increase in customer base is being accomplished for a specific year, and red indicates the goal is not being accomplished for that specific year. Therefore, having a KPI graphic within the pivot table report enhances the end-users' ability to understand them easily and take appropriate business actions.

	Growth in Customer Base	Growth in Customer Base Goal	Growth in Customer Base Status	Growth in Customer Base Trend
All Periods	NA	NA	1	0
FY 2005	(null)	0.3	-1	0
FY 2006	(null)	0.3	-1	0
FY 2007	0.460562103354488	0.3	1	1
FY 2008	4.40409683426443	0.3	1	1
FY 2009	-0.94653112795773	0.3	-1	-1
FY 2010	-1	0.3	-1	1
FY 2011	(null)	0.3	-1	-1

FIGURE 20-53

Named Sets

Excel 2010 also shows the named sets defined in the SSAS multidimensional BISM in a folder called Sets under appropriate dimensions, as shown in Figure 20-54. This helps the end user or the person creating pivot table reports include the named sets directly in the pivot table rather than doing additional filtering in Excel. Experiment with including named sets within your pivot table.

Sheet Data Reports

As you saw in the previous section, pivot tables are useful for analyzing data and to a certain extent also help in creating Excel reports against SSAS. However, pivot tables do not provide the flexibility to create Excel reports such as asymmetric reports, inserting blank columns or rows to make the report suit specific formatting requirements. Excel 2010 introduced new functions that can retrieve data from SSAS. Excel 2010 also supports converting your pivot table into a sheet data report so that you can make additional enhancements to your Excel report to be viewed by your end users.

In this section you learn how to convert pivot tables to sheet data reports, learn about the new Excel functions to retrieve data from SSAS called cube functions, and learn about the benefits you gain from using sheet data reports.

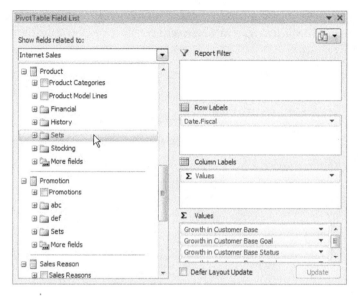

FIGURE 20-54

To convert an existing pivot table into a sheet data report, follow these steps:

1. Create a new sheet in your Excel workbook.

2. Create a pivot table connecting to the AdventureWorks cube on your SSAS instance with Customer Geography in the Row Labels, [Internet Sales Amount] in the Values section, and Date.Fiscal in the Column Labels. This is the same as the first pivot table you created at the beginning of this chapter (refer to Figure 20-12).

3. On the Ribbon, click the Options tab.

4. In the Tools group, click the OLAP Tools, and select Convert to Formulas, as shown in Figure 20-55.

Excel now converts the pivot table into regular Excel spread sheet data with formulas rather than member names and numbers in the cells. If you click each cell you can see the formula used to retrieve the data in the Excel formula bar, as shown in Figure 20-56. Each cell uses one of the cube functions available in Excel 2010. You see members retrieved using the CUBEMEMBER function and the numeric cell values retrieved using the CUBEVALUE function. You cannot drill down on the members as you do in the pivot table. However, if you had drilled down in your pivot table and then converted to the formulas, you would see members at the various levels seen in the pivot table at the time you converted to formulas.

You can now insert columns into the report and change the background color of the inserted columns to make the report more presentable to the end users, as shown in Figure 20-56. You can rename the Row and Column Labels if needed. Explore the enhancements to your Excel report. If you have page report filter conditions in your pivot table, those are also included when you convert to formulas. You still have the option to select members from this filter. Each cell has a separate cube function, so each cell in the spreadsheet can be queried separately from your SSAS instance. However, sending so many queries to SSAS would not be optimal. That's why Excel optimizes the number of queries being sent to an SSAS instance, and whenever feasible it batches data being retrieved for multiple cells into a single query.

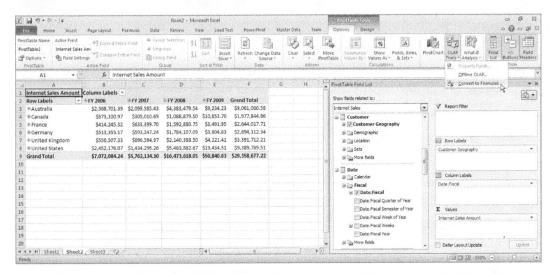

FIGURE 20-55

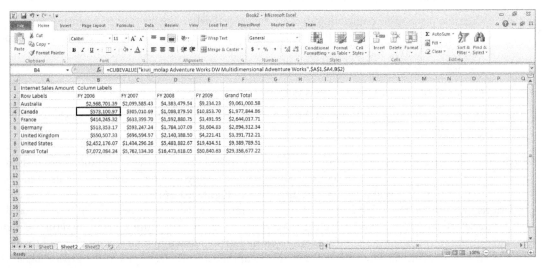

FIGURE 20-56

Perform the following steps to create a summary report for each country based on Internet Sales Amount with appropriate calculations. Here you create a table that shows the growth in sales from FY 2006 to FY 2007:

1. Select the six cells from members Australia down to United States, and press Ctrl+C to copy the data to your clipboard.

2. Paste the cells below the entire table, as shown in Figure 20-57.

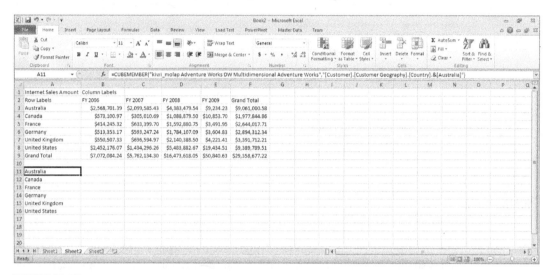

FIGURE 20-57

If you click each member you notice the new cells have the same formula. You can now calculate the percentage growth/increase in [Internet Sales Amount] between the years 2006 and 2007 and 2007 and 2008 in your aggregated report.

3. Enter **Countries** as a heading above the country members you pasted in step 2. Enter **2006-2007** and **2007-2008** in columns C and D in the same row that you entered the Countries heading. Enter **%Growth** in the cell above **2006-2007**.

4. For the cell corresponding to Australia and 2006-2007, cell number C13, enter the following formula: = (C3-B3) / C3.

5. Copy the formula from cell C13 to cells C14-C18. You can do this by clicking cell C13 and dragging the right-bottom corner of the selection box down to the member United States. The mouse cursor changes to a plus sign when you are at the right place to do the drag. You now see all the cells in the 2006-2007 column populated with data.

6. Copy and paste the formula from cell C13 to cell D13.

7. Similar to step 6, copy the formula from cell D13 to cells D14-D18.

8. Select all the cells between C13 and D18.

9. Click the % button in the Number section of the Home tab on the Ribbon, as shown in Figure 20-58, to format the cells as percentages.

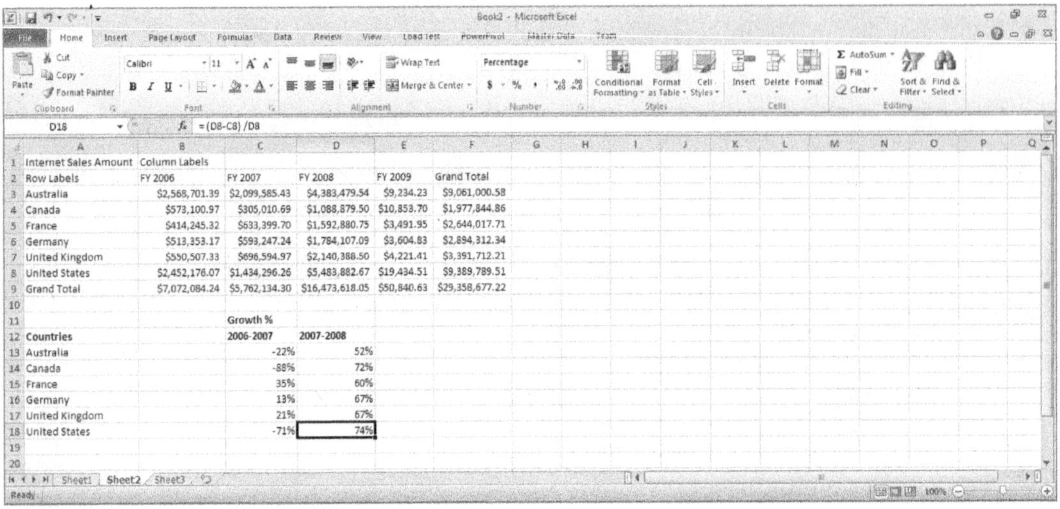

FIGURE 20-58

You can now see the summary report you have created shown in Figure 20-58. You have learned that you can refer to cells using cube functions that retrieve data from the SSAS instance and use the cells with formulas similar to regular cells in Excel spreadsheet reports such as copying, referencing other cells, and applying formatting. The cube functions therefore provide you with a higher flexibility and freedom to create custom reports than can be accomplished using pivot tables.

Cube Functions in Excel 2010

Most of the cube functions include the name of the connection to the cube as the first argument, and reference all the members used to obtain the values. You can retrieve the first member, Australia, using the cube function CUBEMEMBER with the following expression:

```
=CUBEMEMBER("localhost AdventureWorksDW Adventure
Works","[Customer].[Customer Geography].[Country].&[Australia]")
```

The first parameter is the connection information, and the second parameter is the name of the member to be retrieved. There is an optional caption parameter for the CUBEMEMBER function that is not utilized in this example.

The corresponding [Internet Sales Amount] for FY 2006 is referred to using the CUBEVALUE function and the following expression:

```
=CUBEVALUE("localhost AdventureWorksDW Adventure Works",$B$3,$B6,D$5)
```

The first parameter is the connection information, the second parameter references the measure name, Internet Sales Amount, and the third and fourth parameters correspond to the members to be utilized while retrieving the data. The CUBEVALUE function accepts a series of member expressions after the connection parameter.

Excel 2010 supports auto-completion for the cube functions to help you guide the parameters being passed. If you click a new cell and enter `=cubevalue("` you see the list of connections available, as shown in Figure 20-59. If you select one of the connections using Tab and then type double quotes to start the second parameter, you can see the list of dimensions available in the cube to be selected, as shown in Figure 20-60. This feature helps you to enter the correct member expression in the formula and saves you from having to remember the full MDX expressions needed to retrieve the data.

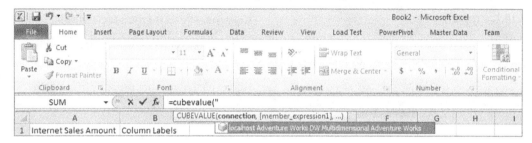

FIGURE 20-59

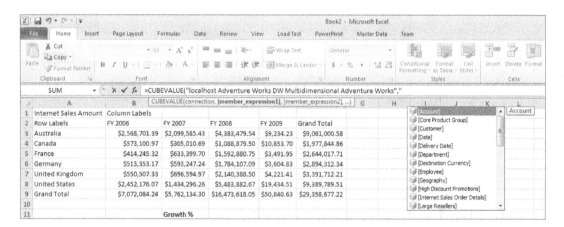

FIGURE 20-60

The following table lists the cube functions supported in Excel 2010 along with a brief description of each cube function:

CUBE FUNCTION NAME	DESCRIPTION
CUBEMEMBER (*connection, member expression, caption*)	Retrieves the member from a hierarchy.
CUBEVALUE (*connection, member expression1, member expression2*, and so on)	Retrieves the value based on the member expressions passed as parameters.
CUBEKPIMEMBER(*connection, kpi_name, kpi_property, caption*)	Retrieves values from KPIs. You need to specify the KPI name and the property value you need to retrieve as parameters.

continues

(continued)

CUBE FUNCTION NAME	DESCRIPTION
CUBESET(*connection, set_expression, caption,* [*sort_order*], [*sort_by*])	Returns MDX sets of values based on the set expression. This function allows you to specify the sort order for the members in the set.
CUBESETCOUNT (*set*)	Counts set items for the specified set.
CUBERANKEDMEMBER(*connection, set_expression, rank, caption*)	Retrieves the nth member of a hierarchy in a cube.
CUBEMEMBERPROPERTY(*connection, member_expression, member_property*)	Retrieves the member property of a member of a hierarchy.

Pivot Charts

Pivot charts allow you to view pivot table data graphically. Creating pivot charts is fairly quick in Excel 2010 and allows the end user to understand and interpret the data more easily than viewing it in a pivot table. Excel has various chart types and styles that you can easily switch to from the Ribbon. You can create the most efficient chart to analyze the data based on your business needs. The following steps show you how to create a pivot chart:

1. Create a new worksheet in your Excel workbook.

2. Create a pivot table with Customer Geography on the Row Labels, Internet Sales Amount in the Values section, and Date.Fiscal in the Column Labels.

3. On the Ribbon select the Insert tab.

4. In the Charts group select the Column option, and select the first 2-D column chart, as shown in Figure 20-61.

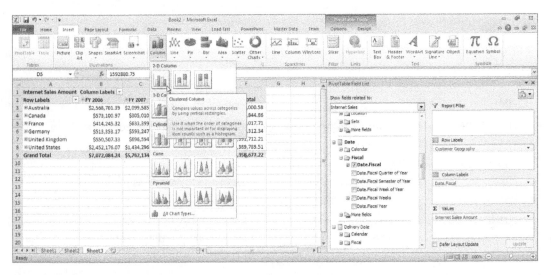

FIGURE 20-61

5. After you select the chart, experiment with different chart types by going to the Ribbon in the Chart group section and choosing the different chart types, as shown in Figure 20-62.

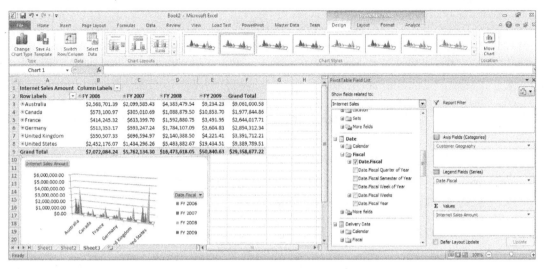

FIGURE 20-62

You can see that creating a pivot chart using the data in the pivot table was quite fast and provides you with better insight and the ability to interpret the data easily. The pivot chart has its own filtering pane where you can select a single member or multiple members in the pivot chart. The pivot chart and pivot tables are synchronized, so if you select a specific member on an axis, you also see the corresponding data being updated in the pivot table. Explore the various options of the pivot chart.

Local Cubes

Being busy executives, many consumers of business intelligence information want to access their cubes from the most remote of locations, such as from business class aboard a Boeing 747. Yes, some people actually find themselves with a laptop and no Internet connection. After you stop shivering from the thought of not being connected to the Internet, consider this alternative: You can create local cubes for your customers. With these offline cubes you can distribute an analytic environment to someone without a network connection. In other words, these customers do not need to have access to an Analysis Services instance to see the data. You can create local cubes directly by sending the DDL of the database or using Excel. Typically, local cubes are small sections of a server cube distributed to the end users to analyze the data offline. Customers using local cubes can do almost all the operations associated with online analysis. However, some restrictions exist that you need to be aware of while using local cubes.

The user creating a local cube from a server cube should have the ability to drill-through to the source data so that appropriate data can be retrieved from the server cube to form the local cube. Appropriate permission to see the source-level data is specified using a role that has specific access permissions to the cubes and dimensions in a database. Although local cubes behave similarly to a server cube in functionality, there are certain restrictions. Local cubes created from Analysis Services 2012 do not have the ability to execute stored procedures (.NET assemblies as well as COM DLLs). Hence, if the server cube has a stored procedure called while querying the cube, you could not send such queries against the local cube. Because the local cube is often a section of the server cube, some of the calculations in the MDX scripts might not access tuples because they are not available in the local cube. These are some things for you to consider during creation of local cubes that might be distributed to end users. To create a local (or offline) cube, follow these steps:

1. Create a pivot table connected to the sample Analysis Services database AdventureWorksDW that includes the hierarchies: Customer Geography in Row Labels, Date.Fiscal in Column Labels, Product Categories as a report filter, and the measure Internet Sales Amount in the Values area.

2. Select a cell in the pivot table to activate the Ribbon.

3. Select the Options tab, and then select the OLAP Tools within the Tools group.

4. Select Offline OLAP, as shown in Figure 20-63.

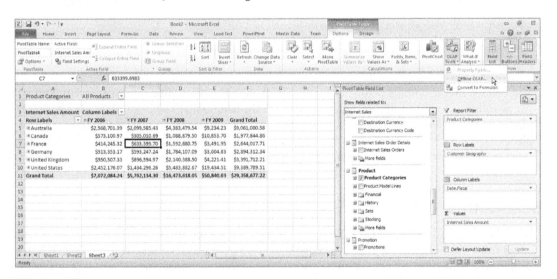

FIGURE 20-63

5. In the Offline OLAP Settings dialog, select Create Offline Data File, as shown in Figure 20-64.

6. Click the Next button in the welcome screen of the Create Cube File Wizard. You are now on the level selection page where you can choose the list of dimension hierarchies and the levels you want included in the offline cube file, as shown in Figure 20-65. In this dialog Excel shows the hierarchies of all the dimensions. By default, Excel selects the hierarchies included in the pivot table. You can alternatively add additional dimensions to your local cubes if you or the end users using the local cube would need them to analyze the data.

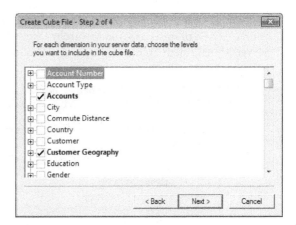

FIGURE 20-64

FIGURE 20-65

7. Traverse through the hierarchy selection, and only select the hierarchies: Customer Geography, Date Fiscal, and Product Categories. Click Next.

8. On the third page of the Create Cube File Wizard, you have the option to only include certain members, as shown in Figure 20-66. Review the hierarchy selections you made, and click Next.

9. On page 4 of the Create Cube File Wizard, provide a storage location where you have access to write a local cube file, and click Finish.

10. In the Offline OLAP Settings dialog (shown in Figure 20-67) select Offline OLAP, and click OK.

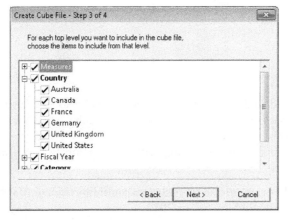

FIGURE 20-66

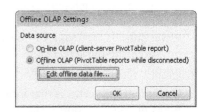

FIGURE 20-67

Following is the statement sent to the Analysis Services instance to create an offline cube with your selection of measures and hierarchy levels. You can also execute this statement from SQL Server Management Studio. SSAS sends a sequence of queries to retrieve data and then creates the local cube.

```
CREATE GLOBAL CUBE [Adventure Works] STORAGE 'C:\Users\Administrator\Documents\
Adventure Works.cub' FROM [Adventure Works]
(
      MEASURE [Adventure Works].[Internet Sales Amount],

      DIMENSION [Adventure Works].[Customer].[Customer Geography]
       (
             LEVEL [(All)],
             LEVEL [Country],
             LEVEL [State-Province],
             LEVEL [City],
             LEVEL [Postal Code],
             LEVEL [Customer]
      ),
      DIMENSION [Adventure Works].[Date].[Fiscal]
       (
             LEVEL [(All)],
             LEVEL [Fiscal Year],
             LEVEL [Fiscal Semester],
             LEVEL [Fiscal Quarter],
             LEVEL [Month],
             LEVEL [Date],
             MEMBER [Date].[Fiscal].[Fiscal Year].&[2006],
             MEMBER [Date].[Fiscal].[Fiscal Year].&[2007],
             MEMBER [Date].[Fiscal].[Fiscal Year].&[2008],
             MEMBER [Date].[Fiscal].[Fiscal Year].&[2009]
      ),
      DIMENSION [Adventure Works].[Product].[Product Categories]
       (
             LEVEL [(All)],
             LEVEL [Category]
      )
)
```

The operations, including drill up and drill down, appropriate member selections, and so forth, all of which you did online, can also be performed offline. After the offline cube (usually a subset of the server cube) is created, it can then be distributed to business decision-makers who do not need real-time access to the server cube. Experiment with performing drill-down and drill-up operations on the offline cube that you have created.

One important factor is that local cubes can only be created from multidimensional BISM. Tabular BISM does not support local cube creation in SQL Server 2012.

Excel Services

Excel Services is a hosted service within SharePoint 2010, which is part of the Office 2010 release. Excel Services enables you to upload and share Excel workbooks via web access for multiple users. Excel Services serves as an alternative to Office Web Components (OWC). With

Excel Services, users can share reports containing pivot tables, tables, and charts by simply publishing the reports on to their SharePoint site. After your report has been published in SharePoint, you can use Excel Services to access them via the Web.

SUMMARY

As a business intelligence application developer, you likely do your proof-of-concept browsing in SSDT, but using the cubes you've built for them, your customers can actually do the slicing and dicing in Excel pivot tables or by using Excel Services or Office Web Components technology. In this chapter you learned how Excel 2010 efficiently allows end users to generate effective reports from SSAS either using pivot tables or using the new cube functions in sheet data reports. SQL Server Analysis Services, Excel, and Performance Point Server together make a formidable business intelligence platform, and you should take advantage of that. Furthermore, most business professionals know Excel; it is a nearly ubiquitous application. Nonetheless, tools from other companies provide connectivity to and leverage from SQL Server Analysis Services 2012 each with their own value-add proposition. You can obtain more information about other client tools from www.ssas-info.com

21

PowerPivot for SharePoint

WHAT'S IN THIS CHAPTER?

➤ Using SharePoint and Excel Services

➤ Understanding PowerPivot servers for SharePoint

➤ Understanding PowerPivot Services for SharePoint

➤ Taking a look at workflow scenarios in PowerPivot for SharePoint

➤ Taking a look at new features in SQL Server 2012 for PowerPivot for SharePoint

➤ Installing and configuring PowerPivot for SharePoint

➤ Understanding optional setup steps for a multiserver environment

This chapter provides information on SharePoint services and servers in addition to information on setting up and configuring your PowerPivot for the SharePoint farm. This chapter also discusses the various different types of PowerPivot farms and how to effectively scale out your PowerPivot for the SharePoint farm. PowerPivot for SharePoint v1 had numerous complexities that often made deployment/configuration quite time-consuming. SQL Server 2012 has a number of new features and improvements that help address some of these issues.

One of the key concerns for IT administrators regarding Excel is the dissemination of undefined, unverifiable, and uncoupled spreadsheets, also known as *spreadmarts*, throughout the organization. Spreadmarts provide invaluable insights allowing analysts to solve complex business problems. Unfortunately, this insight can be overshadowed by the administrative overhead of attempting to manage the vast amount of data. Security, performance, and reliability can quickly become a challenge for an IT administrator.

SHAREPOINT 2010

SharePoint 2010 is a platform designed to make it easier for people to work together. SharePoint administrators can easily set up web sites and manage documents from start to finish while providing extensive reporting capabilities to allow businesses to make better decisions. SharePoint 2010 provides a way for organizations to easily secure and store important information.

Content management is just the beginning because SharePoint includes many built-in services. It enables users to quickly create wikis, blogs, and lists that contain their own custom content from their browsers. Word Services, Visio Services, and Excel Services enable users to view and edit Office documents in the browser directly — without the need to install the application software; all they need is a browser.

SharePoint workflows enable users to implement business processes on documents and items contained within the SharePoint farm. They help streamline complex business processes by packaging common application functionalities into mini-applications that enable a user to easily automate common tasks. For example, you can create a workflow that collects feedback on a document once that document is uploaded. After the document has been approved, the workflow can require a signature and then send an email to a particular email address.

Excel Services

Excel Services is one of the services available within SharePoint. It is the service that allows users to view Excel workbooks within SharePoint using their web browsers. As noted earlier (and throughout this book), one of the key concerns for Excel workbook users is the prevalent habit to create spreadmarts that are shared throughout an organization with lack of control or security. By having the creators of these workbooks upload the workbook to SharePoint, you can use SharePoint's security model to restrict or allow access to the workbook. You can also use SharePoint to share the Excel workbook systems that have only thin clients (that is, web browsers) readily available.

Comparing Excel and Excel Services

Excel Services provides end users with a similar experience to Excel desktop application.

As you can see, the screenshots showing the Excel client (Figure 21-1) and Excel Services (Figure 21-2) are similar. Keeping in mind the information workers (IW) who are consuming data within Excel Services, you can perform many of the functions that you can within the Excel client to read and understand the data, such as filtering the data. Figure 21-3 shows the same simple table within Excel Services filtered to the DatabaseGroup of Vendor.

Because many functions have been designed with the IW producer (that is, the analyst who regularly creates reports, compared to even more users who read the reports — the IW consumers) in mind, this means that the user must go back to Excel. To do this (refer to

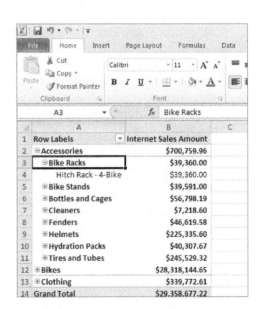

FIGURE 21-1

Figure 21-3), you need to click only on the Open in Excel button, and the Excel client opens with the same report.

FIGURE 21-3

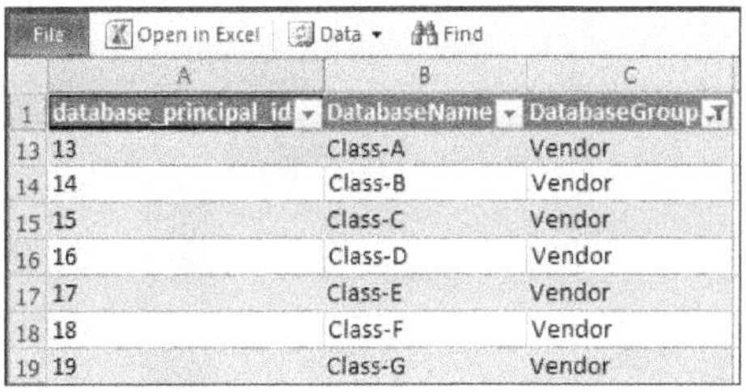

FIGURE 21-2

Excel Services and PowerPivot

The reason this chapter spotlights Excel Services (rather than the many other services within SharePoint) is because of PowerPivot's strong dependency on Excel in general. As noted earlier, PowerPivot is an add-in to the Excel 2010 client. PowerPivot augments and provides additional functionality to what already exists within Excel.

Going back to personas, the IW producer can make use of a familiar tool that is more powerful. For example, Figure 21-4 shows an Excel workbook that presents Healthcare Audit information. The IW producer has imported data from many disparate data sources (including server audit logs totaling more than 44 million rows), and joined them together to create this report.

But as an IW consumer, the analyst typically reads reports and does little data manipulation. Figure 21-5 shows the same report rendered by Excel Services.

Some notable similarities and differences exist between the two PowerPivot views. Within Excel Services, the IW consumer can make use of slicers and filtering to customize the view of data. Formatting between client and server is kept the same, including the conditional formatting of the numeric values. But an important function that is lacking in Excel Services (refer to Figure 21-5) is the Gemini Task Pane (refer to the right side of Figure 21-4).

This is an important difference, because the IW producer is the one who created the reports. Hence, the IW producer needs the Gemini Task Pane. This provides the ability to add different attributes such as slicers, labels, or values, and, ultimately, the ability to alter the entire look, feel, and, most important, the meaning of the report. The IW consumer, on the other hand, is provided with the ability to slice and filter as per the functionality available in Excel Services (refer to Figure 21-5). But while the IW consumer can customize the view of the report, the meaning of the report cannot be altered, which ensures report consistency throughout the organization.

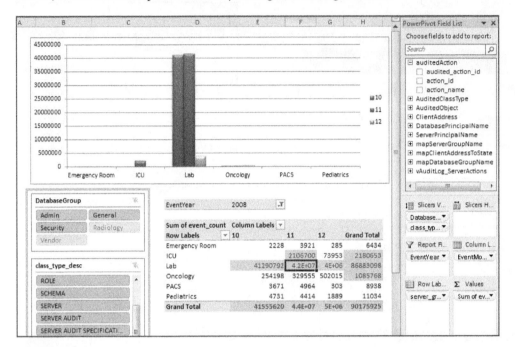

FIGURE 21-4

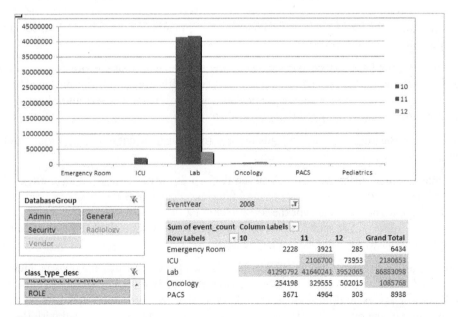

FIGURE 21-5

KEY SERVERS IN POWERPIVOT FOR SHAREPOINT

Now that you are familiar with the functionality and a few of the features of SharePoint Services, dive into the more technical details, starting with the SharePoint Services servers, and, in particular, the ones PowerPivot relies on.

Figure 21-6 shows the SharePoint Services server architecture. The following discussions examine the details depicted in this figure.

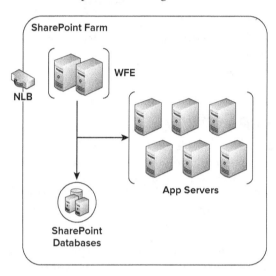

FIGURE 21-6

SharePoint Web Front End (WFE)

The SharePoint Web Front End (WFE) represents the web servers that the users access from their browsers. In addition to rendering web pages, it also uses Excel Web Access (EWA) to render the Excel workbooks calculated by Excel Services. For large deployments, there typically are multiple SharePoint WFEs.

To load balance between these servers, you should make use of a load balancer, whether it is hardware (for example, F5, Big IP, and so on) or software (for example, Windows Load Balancing Service or Linux LB service).

Because this is a common scenario, you should also be familiar with SharePoint Alternate Access Mapping (AAM). The basic principal of AAM is that you must tell SharePoint how to map Web requests (for example, viewing a workbook uploaded to a PowerPivot Gallery for the HR department) to the correct web application and site (for example, the correct URL for the application). Within load-balancing scenarios, the URL that a user types in the browser window (for example, `http://contoso.com/HR/Power%20Pivot%Gallery/default.aspx`) is not the URL that IIS will receive (for example, `http://192.168.0.1/HR/PP`). Hence, the purpose of AAM is to ensure that SharePoint can map the IIS-received URL to the correct site (that is, HR) and application (that is, PowerPivot Gallery).

For more information on AAM, take a look at Troy Starr's excellent blog series on the topic. Although the blogs were written for SharePoint 2007, the information is applicable to SharePoint 2010.

"What every SharePoint administrator needs to know about Alternate Access Mappings (Part 1 of 3)": http://bit.ly/LxnDF

"What every SharePoint administrator needs to know about Alternate Access Mappings (Part 2 of 3)": http://bit.ly/4vnHW5

"What every SharePoint administrator needs to know about Alternate Access Mappings (Part 3 of 3)": http://bit.ly/xbg2c

SharePoint Application Servers (App Servers)

When performing a complete SharePoint installation, all available services from Web access to Excel Services are installed. In large-scale environments, it is beneficial to have one set of servers act as WFEs (that is, turn off most services except for Web access) and another set of servers act as App Servers (that is, have certain services but not Web access). Therefore, the only real difference between a SharePoint WFE and a SharePoint App Server is that the latter does not have the Web services (Microsoft SharePoint Foundation Web Application) enabled.

Although this seems like a minor distinction, this is important to load balance the entire SharePoint farm. Web servers typically perform the task of simply rendering Web pages, so standard-commodity IIS servers (which you scale out) will be sufficient to perform these tasks. But, SharePoint App Servers typically perform more powerful tasks, whether it is the calculations performed by Excel Services, the search indexing by SharePoint Search Service, or the processing by the Analysis Services Engine Service. In these situations, you need to scale up each App Server — that is, have more memory, processors, and a powerful disk — as well as scaling out the servers.

Another important aspect within SharePoint is its capability to load balance services within the farm. For Excel Services and PowerPivot Services, they have their own health-monitoring services that enable the web services to determine the server instance that is "healthiest" when it assigns which user request goes to which server instance.

SharePoint Content Databases (Content dBs)

All the information stored within SharePoint (from the lists to Excel workbooks) is stored within a set of SQL Server databases known as the SharePoint content databases (or Content dBs, as shown in Figure 21-6). By default, documents such as Word documents and Excel workbooks are stored as a blob within the SQL database. As is typical with any SharePoint service, you can scale out the content databases to multiple databases placed on multiple servers to handle the load.

The profile of a SharePoint content database is similar to that of an online transaction processing (OLTP) environment, where there are a lot of transactions. With PowerPivot, these are large transactions because of the size of Excel workbooks and the VertiPaq database stored within it. So, some standard database optimization techniques do come into play, including file group configuration and having fast I/O for the underlying disk.

KEY SERVICES IN POWERPIVOT FOR SHAREPOINT

As noted in the previous sections, Excel Services is key to service dependency for PowerPivot for SharePoint. In addition, by default, the WFE (or Microsoft SharePoint Foundation Web Application) is another key service to render the Excel Services workbooks (via EWA). Other key services for PowerPivot for SharePoint include the following:

➤ Analysis Services Engine Service

➤ PowerPivot System Service

Now take a look at each of these.

Analysis Services Engine Service

Within the SharePoint farm, to access a VertiPaq instance, you connect to the Analysis Services Engine Service. This is a version of the Analysis Services Engine that runs the In-memory Business Intelligence (IMBI) engine, rather than the traditional Multidimensional Online Analytical Processing (MOLAP), Hybrid Online Analytical Processing (HOLAP), or Relational Online Analytical Processing (ROLAP) engines. For the self-service BI scenario that is delivered as part of PowerPivot Services (as part of SQL Server 2008 R2), the only supported way to access the Analysis Services IMBI engine is through SharePoint.

However, you can use tools such as SQL Server Profiler to debug the interactions against the service. More important, this version of the Analysis Services engine within SharePoint can be queried via MDX like any other client that can generate MDX. For example, Figure 21-7 shows a Report Builder Dashboard including charts and a bubble map that notes a Healthcare Server audit based on source location against a state map.

To show that this report from Report Builder is using the Excel workbook as its data source, Figure 21-8 shows the data source connection of this report. The data source provider isn't your traditional source server and database, but rather a URL to your Excel workbook within SharePoint.

To come full circle, Figure 21-9 shows the Report Builder 3.0 Query Designer, which is accessing the Excel workbook within SharePoint.

Figure 21-10 shows an excerpt of the SQL Server Profiler trace recording of when the Report Builder 3.0 Map report is accessing the Analysis Services Engine Service.

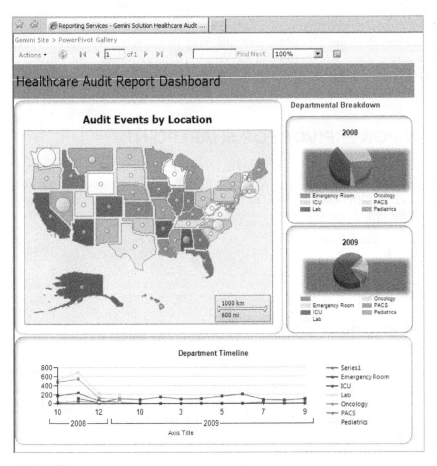

FIGURE 21-7

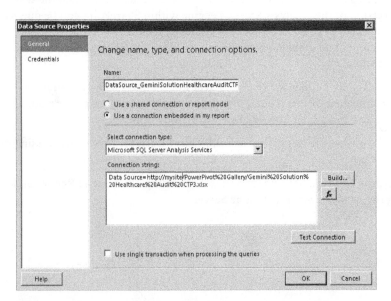

FIGURE 21-8

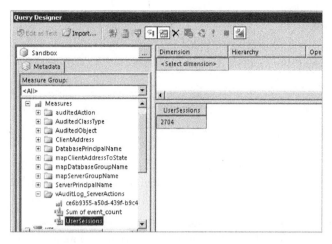

FIGURE 21-9

FIGURE 21-10

For those who are familiar with SQL Profiler (for Analysis Services), you can see the familiar EventClass = Query Begin with the TextData noting the familiar look of MDX.

```
SELECT NON EMPTY {
        [Measures].[UserSessions]
    } ON COLUMNS
    FROM [SandBox]
    CELL PROPERTIES...
```

Traditional SQL Server Analysis Service Client tools can query Analysis Services SharePoint Service.

Any client that can query a traditional Analysis Services Engine by way of MDX has the same capability against the Analysis Services Engine Service within the SharePoint farm without any modifications.

PowerPivot Mid-Tier Service

This service is also known as SQL Server Analysis Services PowerPivot System Service. To better understand this service, take a look at the following key features:

➤ Connectivity

➤ Data refresh

Connectivity

All communication from the SharePoint WFE to the Analysis Services Engine Service within the SharePoint farm is facilitated by this service. It is automatically installed on every server on which the Analysis Services Engine Service is installed.

Whenever Excel Services must connect to a PowerPivot sandbox, the PowerPivot System Service can determine if the sandbox already exists on all SharePoint App Servers that have an enabled and running Analysis Services Engine Service. If the sandbox already exists, then the PowerPivot System Service simply connects the WFE to it (that is, EWA on a WFE to Excel Services on an App Server to Analysis Services Engine Service on an App Server). If the sandbox does not already exist, it performs the following tasks:

1. User the PowerPivot health-monitoring service to determine which server is the healthiest.

2. Copy the Excel workbook to the Backup folder on this server.

3. Extract the database from the Excel workbook.

4. Copy the database to that server.

5. Attach the database to that Analysis Service Engine Service.

Finally, the PowerPivot System Service provides the pointer to the SharePoint WFE so that it can connect to that sandbox.

Data Refresh

The PowerPivot System Service is also responsible for performing a data refresh. As you can recall, data refresh is the PowerPivot feature that allows users to automatically connect to their external data source and refresh their PowerPivot for Excel workbooks with the latest data. Figure 21-11 shows an example of data refresh being enabled. (The numbers in the figure correlate to the steps that will be explained shortly.)

The information recorded on the data refresh page includes the user credentials to execute the data refresh. This is important because the service accounts within the SharePoint farm most likely will not have access rights to the data sources used to populate the workbook. Therefore, the PowerPivot System Service will impersonate the user credentials provided.

 These credentials are stored within the SharePoint Secure Store Service, which, as its name describes, securely stores the credentials such that impersonation is possible.

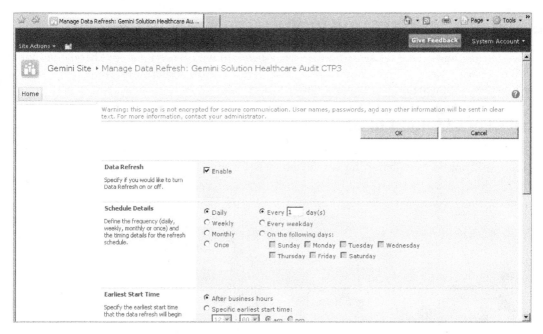

FIGURE 21-11

The PowerPivot System Service performs the automatic data refresh task to update the database within the PowerPivot for Excel workbook using the credentials within the Secure Store. For the PowerPivot System Service to perform the task of data refresh, it must do the following:

1. The Windows SharePoint Services Timer Service runs a PowerPivot timer job called the PowerPivot Data Refresh Timer Job every minute (by default).

2. The PowerPivot Data Refresh Timer Job calls the PowerPivot Service Application (PSA), which is a configurable, independent instance of the PowerPivot System Service (PSS) to read predefined schedules that are stored in the PowerPivot Application Database.

3. If the timer job finds a schedule in the PowerPivot Application database, the timer job hands the request to the PowerPivot Service Application (PSA).

4. The PowerPivot Service Application then impersonates the PowerPivot Unattended account or specified user to open the workbook from the content database

The SharePoint Timer Service kicks off the Mid-Tier Service for processing:

1. The Mid-Tier Service determines when the sandbox needs to be processed, maintains work queues, and controls throttling.

2. The Mid-Tier Service performs the tasks to connect to the necessary sandboxes.

3. With processing completed, the sandboxes are updated with the latest data. The Mid-Tier Service also updates the PowerPivot for Excel workbooks by placing the latest database into the workbook and resaving it to the SharePoint content database.

SERVICES ARCHITECTURE WORKFLOW SCENARIOS

Now that you understand the servers and services involved with PowerPivot for SharePoint, put this all into a better context. Take a look at three common workflow scenarios between all the servers and services within SharePoint to make PowerPivot work.

Excel Client Upload to SharePoint

First take a look at one of the more common scenarios concerning the upload of a PowerPivot for Excel workbook to your SharePoint site, as shown in Figure 21-12.

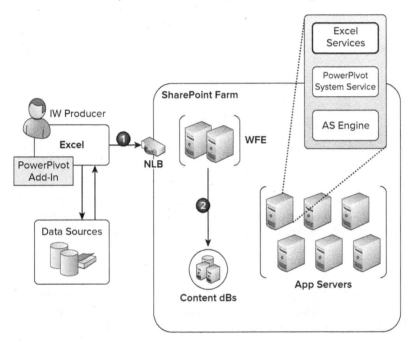

FIGURE 21-12

There is no difference between a SharePoint and PowerPivot for SharePoint workflow in this particular case. Following are the steps in the workflow:

1. The IW producer uploads a workbook to SharePoint by using Excel Save As or SharePoint Upload functionality. The workbook uploads to the SharePoint WFE.

2. In turn, the SharePoint WFE then stores the workbook within a SharePoint content database. By default, this is stored as a blob within the SharePoint database.

Your Excel workbook has a 2GB maximum size limitation.

Excel Services Rendering

Now that the workbook is uploaded to SharePoint (content database), your IW consumers will want to open up the workbook with SharePoint. This is reflected in Figure 21-13, with the numbered steps indicated in the diagram.

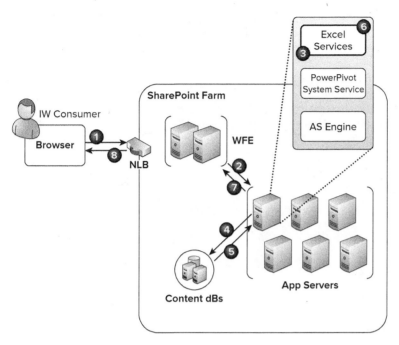

FIGURE 21-13

Following are a number of steps to make this happen:

1. The IW consumers request an Excel workbook against the SharePoint WFE from their browser.

2. Because it is an Excel Services request, the EWA component on the SharePoint WFE now makes the request to Excel Services on the App Server.

3. Excel Services has its own load balancer within the SharePoint farm, so the EWA request load balances (by default) to the healthiest App Server.

4. Excel Services requests from the SharePoint content database the originally requested workbook (from step 1).

5. Excel Services obtains the workbook and brings it back to the App Server.

6. Excel Services performs any calculations required from the workbook.

7. Excel Services pushes the data to the originating EWA component on the SharePoint WFE. EWA then renders the workbook to the browser.

8. The IW consumer can now work with this workbook.

Excel Services Server Action

Almost immediately after step 8, the IW consumer clicks on a slicer and performs some action that results in interacting with the data stored within the workbook. Figure 21-14 shows this process, again with the numbered steps indicated in the diagram.

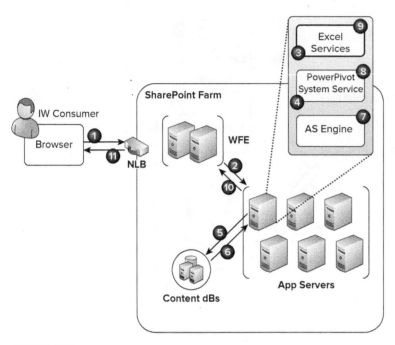

FIGURE 21-14

Following are the steps to make this happen:

1. The IW consumer makes a server action request (such as clicking on a slicer). The fact that this is a server action is transparent to the user.

2. Because it is an Excel Services request, the EWA component on the SharePoint WFE now makes the request to Excel Services on the App Server.

3. Excel Services has its own load balancer within the SharePoint farm, so the EWA request load balances (by default) to the healthiest App Server. Because it is a server action, Excel Services connects to the Analysis Services OLEDB provider.

4. This is your standard Analysis Services OLEDB provider, except that the call from Excel Services enables the IsHosted flag. In this case, the OLEDB provider knows to engage with the PowerPivot Mid-Tier Service. Similar to Excel Services, PowerPivot Mid-Tier Service has its own load-balancing service to help it determine the healthiest App Server. The purpose of this is to determine which App Server should host the Analysis Services Engine Service (which is discussed shortly).

5. The PowerPivot Mid-Tier Service makes a request for the Excel workbook from the SharePoint content database if Excel Services doesn't already have a workbook.

6. The PowerPivot Mid-Tier Service obtains the workbook and obtains any necessary meta data from the DefaultGeminiServiceAppDB database.

7. The PowerPivot Mid-Tier Service extracts the VertiPaq database from the workbook and attaches the database to the Analysis Services Engine Service. This attach command is the same traditional Analysis Services Engine attach statement.

8. Upon attaching the database, the PowerPivot Mid-Tier Service provides the location to Excel Services.

9. Excel Services connects to the Analysis Services Engine Service to perform its query and its calculations.

10. Excel Services then pushes the data to the originating EWA component on the SharePoint WFE. EWA then renders the workbook to the browser.

11. The IW consumer can now work with this workbook.

WHAT'S NEW

SQL Server 2012 PowerPivot for SharePoint has a number of new features and improvements that improve the overall experience. You also have many new administrative abilities and an improved PowerPivot for SharePoint setup experience.

New Administrative Capabilities

SharePoint 2010 Service Pack 1 is a prerequisite. The new administrative abilities in PowerPivot for SharePoint include many bug fixes, failover abilities, and some scalability enhancements. The default server allocation algorithm has also been changed to health-based instead of the 2008r2 default of round robin; this change enables PowerPivot for SharePoint to be more responsive to low memory situations.

You now have many more configuration options for your PowerPivot for SharePoint installation. Admins can modify the amount of database caching for each app server, frequency of cleanup, and even disable data refresh jobs based on failure rate. You have new capacity planning health rules for CPU, memory, and disk space; you can throw warnings if the server runs out of resources. You also have a mid-tier minidump ability in the unfortunate circumstance in which your PowerPivot for SharePoint server crashes.

Setup Improvements

SQL 2012 PowerPivot for SharePoint has a PowerPivot configuration tool similar to the Reporting Services configuration tool. This tool provides users with a consolidated and user-friendly interface for managing SQL Server 2012 PowerPivot for SharePoint and it simplifies common tasks such as creating the PowerPivot Service Application, managing features, and configuring the data refresh settings once installation is complete.

The PowerPivot configuration tool works by evaluating the SharePoint instance to determine which configuration options are available to the user. Users can then add, remove, upgrade, and configure features within the PowerPivot for SharePoint instance.

In order to use the PowerPivot configuration tool, you must be a SharePoint farm administrator, a server administrator for the Analysis Services instance, and db_owner of the SharePoint farm configuration database. SharePoint 2010 Service Pack 1 is also required prior to using the configuration tool. A shortcut to the PowerPivot configuration tool is found in the Configuration folder under the SQL Server 2012 program group.

POWERPIVOT FOR SHAREPOINT

If you have ever spent a late night digging through SharePoint ULS logs trying to get to the root of a weird PowerPivot for SharePoint issue, then this section is for you. When PowerPivot for SharePoint is installed and configured correctly, it is a thing of beauty. From the eye-catching thumbnail views of the PowerPivot Gallery to the unprecedented insight the management dashboard provides to IT departments, it is the ultimate BI Package. With that said, if you have experienced the joy of troubleshooting a failing PowerPivot data refresh job or an existing farm installation in v1, you may think otherwise.

PowerPivot for SharePoint has a lot of moving parts that can be scattered across numerous different servers in a SharePoint farm. As a result there are numerous different points at which a PowerPivot workbook request in SharePoint can fail.

Unfortunately, the benefits of PowerPivot for SharePoint v1 were often overshadowed by the complexities involved around integration with SharePoint. I've spent many a late night staring at SharePoint central admin, digging through ULS logs trying to get to the bottom of a PowerPivot for SharePoint issue. Sometimes I would get frustrated and send nasty emails to the product team at Microsoft…luckily they didn't take my comments personally. They listened to my feedback in addition to our customers' feedback and they implemented numerous improvements in SQL Server 2012 to address many of SQL Server 2008 R2's shortcomings.

Installation and Configuration

PowerPivot for SharePoint installation and configuration has numerous scenarios depending on the SharePoint farm configuration. This chapter discusses all the different configurations and when to use which installation. Some tips and tricks based on numerous complex farm installations are also discussed.

The first and easiest installation is the Single Server installation. Anyone starting out with PowerPivot for SharePoint should to go this route first. This option is good for new multimachine PowerPivot for SharePoint installations, which is explained later.

The second installation option discussed is the infamous existing farm install. This is an advanced configuration that can be tedious. This installation is not for the faint of heart. If you go this route you must back up your farm and read through the documentation for existing farm installs located in SQL Books Online.

New Server Installation

The new server installation installs all the required components for PowerPivot for SharePoint on a single machine. This install takes care of installing and configuring SharePoint for you. There are more than 15 steps that need to be completed manually with an existing farm installation that the new server installation handles for you.

If you plan a multiserver installation of PowerPivot and you are not limited to using an existing SharePoint farm, then a new server install is also the way to go. Specifically, you start with a single server and select a "new server" install. Then you can move the SQL databases (SharePoint config, content, and PowerPivot application databases) off this machine to one or more dedicated SQL machines. You may then add additional web front-end servers and application servers with PowerPivot for SharePoint installed as needed.

Existing Farm Installation

Installing PowerPivot to an existing SharePoint farm is an in-depth multiple-step process. There are ten steps to consider when planning an existing farm installation:

1. Install PowerPivot for SharePoint on one or more application servers.
2. Deploy the PowerPivot Web Application to web front-end servers.
3. Start Services on the Server.
4. Create a PowerPivot Service Application.
5. Configure Excel Services.
6. Configure Secure Store Service and Unattended Data Refresh Account.
7. Set Upper Limits on Disk Space Usage.
8. Increase Maximum Upload Size for SharePoint Web Applications and Excel Services.
9. Activate PowerPivot Feature Integration for Site Collections.
10. Verify Installation and Configuration.

For more detail about this topic, see the following whitepapers:

Existing farm installation: http://msdn.microsoft.com/en-us/library/gg144594(v=sql.105).aspx

Upgrade PowerPivot for SharePoint: http://technet.microsoft.com/en-us/library/ee210646(v=sql.110).aspx

Install PowerPivot for SharePoint: http://msdn.microsoft.com/en-us/library/ee210708.aspx

Scale Out Implementations

As PowerPivot for SharePoint grows with more users and larger workbooks, you may need to scale out your PowerPivot installation to handle the added load. You can take two common approaches to scaling out PowerPivot for SharePoint. (I stole the terminology from Dave Wickert.) Before I go into the two different approaches to scaling out PowerPivot for SharePoint, the first step in each approach is to scale out your SQL Servers.

Scale Out SQL

After you have a PowerPivot for SharePoint farm installation completed (single server installation) the first evolution for scaling out should be to move your SQL Server databases to a separate SQL machine. Specifically, you want to move the PowerPivot and SharePoint databases: PowerPivot application database, SharePoint configuration database, and SharePoint content database, respectively, to another physical machine. This is a best practice for any SharePoint farm and a best practice for

PowerPivot for SharePoint. You can easily use SQL Aliasing to accomplish this task. The required steps to accomplish this are discussed later.

Homogeneous Scale Out

The homogeneous scale-out approach is a simple and effective way to scale out your PowerPivot solution. You simply add additional PowerPivot for SharePoint servers, each server containing all required components for a PowerPivot for SharePoint install. Each server in the farm is configured the same where each one is a Web front end and an Application server. When the configuration completes, you can place a load balancer in front of all your servers and you are done.

Heterogeneous Scale Out

This is a dedicated architecture in which you specialize each machine in the cluster for a specific task. You may have a number of web front-end servers that are dedicated to the PowerPivot Web Service. You would have dedicated application servers running PowerPivot System Service, Excel Services, and other services. You can mix and match what services run on each server. You want to find the optimal mix of services for each server. For example you would not want to run the PowerPivot and SharePoint indexing service together on the same SharePoint machine because they are both memory-intensive. Excel Services, on the other hand, runs nicely with PowerPivot because Excel Services doesn't use a lot of memory whereas PowerPivot does. One consideration when growing your farm this way is you want to put in multiple of each of the dedicated machines; if one goes down, you will have some way to back up. In the Homogeneous scale out approach, each additional server is a backup because they all run the same services.

Verifying Your PowerPivot for SharePoint Setup

Now that you have completed the installation of PowerPivot for SharePoint, you should verify that this setup works properly. You also need to perform some additional configuration steps involving increasing the file size limits and Reporting Services integration. However, these steps should occur after verification, in case there are issues with your environment.

To verify your setup, perform three common tasks:

➤ Publish your Excel workbooks.

➤ View workbooks in PowerPivot Gallery.

➤ View workbooks in Excel Services.

Publishing Your Excel Workbooks

After you set up PowerPivot for SharePoint, you may already have the PowerPivot Gallery option, as shown in Figure 21-15.

If you do not, don't fret! You can create a new PowerPivot Gallery by going to your SharePoint Web application Ribbon and clicking Site Actions ⇨ More Options.

FIGURE 21-15

The Create Web dialog box appears. Under the Filter By section, choose Library, and then choose PowerPivot Gallery. Within this dialog, on the right side, type in the name of your new PowerPivot Gallery (for example, **My PowerPivot Gallery**) and click Create.

From here, it's just a matter of uploading your PowerPivot for Excel workbook to SharePoint. As a quick reminder, to do this, follow these steps:

1. Click your PowerPivot Gallery.

2. On the Ribbon, click Upload Document ➪ Upload Document.

3. The PowerPivot Gallery — Upload Document dialog appears, and from here, choose the file you want to upload.

4. Click OK and upload your file.

Upon initially uploading your workbook to the gallery, you may get the Hourglass view. The reason you see the hourglass is because PowerPivot is currently generating the thumbnails for the report preview that is part of the PowerPivot Gallery.

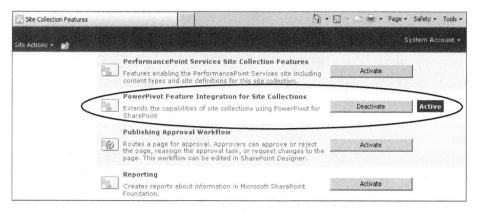

FIGURE 21-16

Viewing Workbooks in PowerPivot Gallery

Once uploaded to SharePoint, your PowerPivot workbooks will be available in the PowerPivot Gallery. The gallery is a Microsoft Silverlight application with multiple view options intended to create a more attractive and immersive user experience during browsing of all workbooks that have been uploaded to the library.

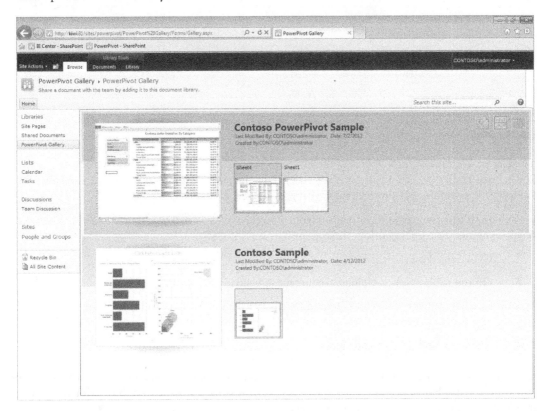

FIGURE 21-17

The default view (Figure 21-17) for the PowerPivot Gallery is a tabular view called Gallery. This view displays each workbook on a row with thumbnails of each worksheet listed sequentially. Three additional views are available as an alternate to the default view:

➤ **Theatre View:** The Theatre view (See Figure 21-18). features a thumbnail preview of each worksheet used to navigate below.

➤ **All Documents:** This is the standard layout for SharePoint libraries (See Figure 21-19) and does not use Microsoft Silverlight. This is the preferred view if you have a large number of PowerPivot workbooks in your library or if you are using versioning to check in and check out workbooks.

➤ **Carousel View:** Similar to the Theatre view with a centered preview area, the difference with this view (See Figure 21-20) is that the thumbnails that precede or follow the current thumbnail are immediately adjacent to the preview.

FIGURE 21-18

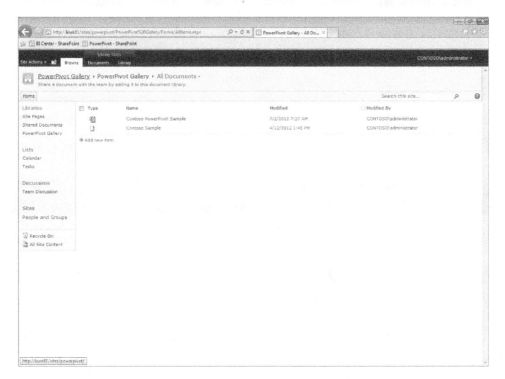

FIGURE 21-19

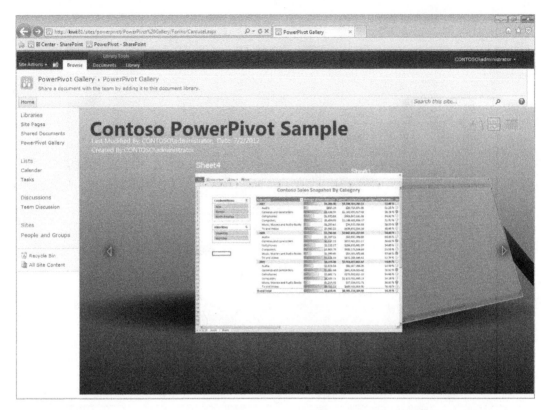

FIGURE 21-20

To switch between views in the PowerPivot Gallery, you will need to access the Library Tools by clicking the Library link (Figure 21-21) and then setting the Current View to your preferred view in the drop-down list.

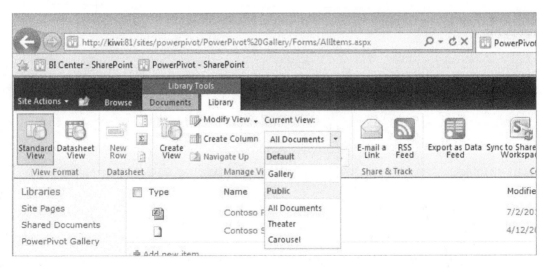

FIGURE 21-21

Once you have selected your preferred view, you can further refine the PowerPivot Gallery by selecting the Modify View option. This option allows you to control the template name, set an item limit, configure which attributes are displayed with the workbook thumbnails, control sort order as well as define filters.

Viewing Workbooks in Excel Services

When you click on one of the workbook thumbnails in the PowerPivot Gallery, the Excel Calculation Service is responsible for retrieving the workbook from the SharePoint content database and rendering it in the browser using the Excel Web Access Web Part. The look and feel of Excel Web Access is similar to Microsoft Office Excel and it allows you to view, interact and share PowerPivot workbooks from completely within the SharePoint portal site.

It is important to understand how the Excel Calculation Service, PowerPivot Service, and Analysis Services interact when viewing workbooks through Excel Services. Recall from the discussion in Chapter 7 that a subtle nuance exists when Excel Services initially loads a workbook. The PowerPivot Mid-Tier Service and the Analysis Services Engine Service are not engaged until a request for data is made by the Excel Calculation Service.

To force an interaction with PowerPivot and Analysis services, you will need to perform a server action such as a click on a slicer in the workbook that requires a data request from the PowerPivot Service. The PowerPivot Service would then forward the query on to the Analysis Service instance for processing.

OPTIONAL SETUP STEPS

Although the steps outlined here are optional, many of them are quite important for a multiserver PowerPivot for SharePoint environment. The section describes the following optional setup steps:

- ➤ Configuring the file size limits
- ➤ Turning off the external data warning on data refresh
- ➤ Integrating Reporting Services
- ➤ Adding more servers to your PowerPivot for SharePoint farm

Configuring File Size Limits

You may want to configure the file size limits of your SharePoint farm because, by default, SharePoint limits the upload size of your file to 50MB, and Excel Services limits the size of a workbook it can render to 10MB. Remember, for PowerPivot for Excel, the VertiPaq database resides within the workbook itself. Although compressed in comparison to the original source data, this is still larger than your typical Excel workbook.

So, although optional, it is recommended that you reconfigure SharePoint to handle much larger file sizes.

To increase Web application limits, follow these steps:

1. Go to SharePoint 2010 Central Administration ⇨ Application Management ⇨ Manage Web Applications (See Figure 21-22).

FIGURE 21-22

2. Select SharePoint-80 (which is the default Web application) and then, on the Ribbon, select General Settings ⇨ General Settings.

3. Change the Maximum Upload Size setting to the MB limits you want. The maximum allowed by SharePoint is 2,047MB.

To increase Excel Services limits, follow these steps:

1. Go to SharePoint Central Administration ⇨ Application Management ⇨ Manage Service Applications (See Figure 21-23).

2. Click your Excel Services application (hover over it and it will be clickable).

3. Click Trusted File Location, and then click http:// (the default file).

4. Under Workbook Properties, change the Maximum Workbook Size (the maximum is 2,000MB) and the Maximum Chart or Image Size to 100 (because of the larger chart images typically embedded within PowerPivot for Excel workbooks).

FIGURE 21-23

Turning Off the External Data Warning on Data Refresh

One of the common warnings that you will encounter is the following: "This workbook contains one or more queries that refresh external data." To optionally, suppress this warning on your SharePoint instance, follow these steps:

1. Go to SharePoint Central Administration ➪ Application Management ➪ Manage Service Applications.

2. Click your Excel Services Application.

3. Click Trusted File Location and then click `http://` (the default file) or the location you want to configure.

4. In the External Data section, uncheck the Refresh warning enabled option.

5. Click OK to save the configuration.

An alternative to making this configuration change for your default file, you can create a new trusted location for sites that contains your PowerPivot workbooks. You could then disable the "Warn on data refresh" setting for the new site. For more information, see `http://msdn.micro-soft.com/en-us/library/ff487971.aspx`.

Integrating Reporting Services

Two integration scenarios exist for integrating Reporting Services reports and PowerPivot workbooks. These scenarios involve PowerPivot as either the source or destination for report data.

Before discussing each scenario, there are a couple of pre-requisites that need to be considered. The minimum version for integrating Reporting Services with PowerPivot is SQL Server 2008 R2. Native mode and SharePoint integration modes are both supported, with SharePoint integration mode being preferred because it unifies the security model and simplifies the implementation process. Finally, be aware that authentication between Reporting Services and PowerPivot requires Windows Authentication.

The first integration scenario is using a PowerPivot workbook as a source of data for a Reporting Services report. Reports authored in both the Report Builder as well as the Report Designer can use a PowerPivot workbook as a source of data.

The MDX query designer is used to query the PowerPivot data as the underlying interface to PowerPivot is MDX. Connecting the Report Builder and Report Designer relies on the Microsoft SQL Server Analysis Services data, except the server name should be replaced with the path to the PowerPivot workbook.

Client dependencies must also be addressed if you are integrating PowerPivot data into a report. The report builder requires either PowerPivot to be installed on the workstation or SQL Server 2008 R2 ADOMD.NET libraries to be available within the SQL Server feature pack. The report designer requires the SQL Server 2008 R2 OLE DB Provider for Analysis Services to support PowerPivot data connections. Finally, to successfully deploy these reports, you must ensure that the ADOMD .NET provider is installed to the report server.

The second integration scenario is to use a Reporting Services report as a source and a PowerPivot workbook as the destination for the data. This scenario is made possible in Reporting Services by streaming report data directly to PowerPivot using an Atom feed.

The Atom feed is first exported from either the report manager or the report server page. Once exported, if the workstation has PowerPivot installed it can be consumed directly. Otherwise, an .atomsvc file containing the connect information will need to be saved and then imported into the PowerPivot workbook.

BI APPLIANCES

In the database world, appliances are server-class machines prepackaged with software configured for a specific type of workload; workload, architecture, software, and hardware are all considered when engineering the machine. Many different types of appliances are optimized for specific workloads such as database consolidation, data warehousing, virtualization, and messaging. The appliance may have custom installation scripts to streamline the deployment of various different products. The appliances are specifically tuned for the specific workload for which they are designed.

Microsoft and HP partnered to create an appliance tailored to the Microsoft BI stack called the HP Business Decision Appliance. The HP Business Decision Appliance is an HP ProLiant DL360 (two 6-core Intel Xeon 5650 processors) with 96GB of memory and eight 300GB enterprise drives. For detailed specs, see http://tinyurl.com/3f2ecls.

When deploying the HP Business Decision Appliance, the user is presented with an installation and configuration wizard that walks through the proper configuration of the following:

➤ Microsoft Windows Server 2008 R2 Enterprise Edition

➤ Microsoft SQL Server 2008 R2 Enterprise Edition with PowerPivot integration for SharePoint

➤ Microsoft SharePoint 2010 Enterprise Edition Prerequisites for SharePoint and PowerPivot

➤ Appliance Administration Console

➤ Appliance-specific SharePoint Home Page

One large benefit to an appliance is the customized installation and configuration it provides. The wizard takes the guesswork out of what can be a complicated installation. When the installation and configuration are complete, the server is operational and fully tuned for a BI workload. The system drives are mirrored, and the data drive is configured in a RAID 5 array for a total capacity of 1.5TB.

SUMMARY

In this chapter you learned about SharePoint services and key SharePoint Services. You also learned about setting up and configuring PowerPivot for a SharePoint farm. This chapter also discussed several types of PowerPivot farms and how to effectively scale your PowerPivot deployment.

In the next chapter, you will take a look at the enterprise considerations that need to be made when working with the BI Semantic Model (BISM).

PART V
Advanced Topics with Tabular BISM and Integration with PowerView

22

Introduction and Configuration of Power View

WHAT'S IN THIS CHAPTER?

➤ Learning about Power View architecture

➤ Reporting Services SharePoint Integrated Mode — installation and configuration

➤ Preparing model connections for the Power View tutorial

➤ Understanding data source connection options

In previous chapters, you learned how to create BI semantic models. In this chapter, you see how to install and configure Power View, which is part of SQL Server 2012 Reporting Services in SharePoint Integrated Mode. Power View enables you to interactively explore, visualize, and present data from PowerPivot workbooks and from tabular models hosted on an Analysis Server.

This chapter focuses on setting up Power View and its architecture, and configuring data connectivity for a variety of scenarios. It provides the basis for Chapter 23, which demonstrates how Power View enables business users to interactively explore and visualize data.

REPORTING SERVICES POWER VIEW

Power View is a feature of SQL Server Reporting Services 2012 in SharePoint Integrated Mode. The deployment consists of the following components that in the most basic scenario, you can install on one machine:

1. SharePoint Server 2010 with Service Pack 1

2. SQL Server 2012 Database Engine (alternatively SQL Server 2008 or 2008 R2 works, too)

3. SQL Server 2012 Reporting Services and Reporting Services Add-In

4. SQL Server 2012 PowerPivot for SharePoint

5. Optional: SQL Server 2012 Analysis Services standalone server instance in tabular mode

After you install these features, you can do the following:

➤ Access PowerPivot workbooks that you create in PowerPivot for Excel from SharePoint sites.

➤ Deploy the large sample FAA flight data model provided on the download site for this book.

➤ Build interactive Power View reports based on PowerPivot workbooks in SharePoint.

➤ Create Report Builder reports when you launch Report Builder in SharePoint.

Power View

Power View is a thin web client that launches in the browser from a published report or a tabular model available in SharePoint. The Power View application is hosted by the Reporting Services add-in for SharePoint on the web front end (WFE). Power View doesn't directly connect to the tabular model but uses the Reporting Services service application to authenticate users and connect to a tabular model, as shown by the dotted arrows in Figure 22-1.

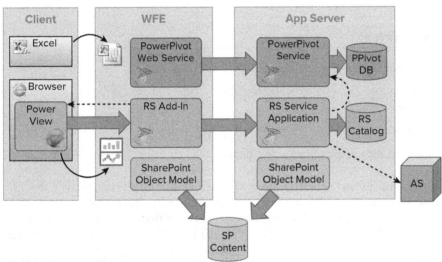

FIGURE 22-1

Legend for Figure 22-1:

   Excel PowerPivot workbook file

   Power View report (RDLX)

The tabular model can be an Excel PowerPivot workbook or a tabular model running on a SQL Server 2012 Analysis Services server. When you work in Power View, you don't need to know the names of servers or know about logins and permissions. Power View is automatically connected to the tabular model from which you launch Power View.

Power View saves reports to SharePoint with an RDLX file extension. The default click action for an RDLX file in a standard SharePoint document library launches Power View in presentation mode for the selected report. When Power View launches, it connects to the RS add-in and the RS service application to load the RDLX report in an in-memory user session.

Reporting Services

When Reporting Services is installed in SharePoint Integrated Mode, its integration with SharePoint is achieved through tightly coupled data sharing among the Reporting Services databases and the SharePoint databases. In this configuration, SharePoint becomes the primary mechanism for displaying, managing, and securing not only reports and models but data sources as well.

The SharePoint Service Application architecture (introduced in SharePoint 2010) enables you to distribute the load of different services to different physical machines. The consumers of the service in your SharePoint farm do not care where the service is physically located. An example of this distribution might be putting the PowerPivot service on a different server from the Reporting Services service and then putting the Excel service on yet another server. This enables you to mix and match services and physical hardware, depending on what you have available and what your load requirements are for each service.

The distribution can continue as the organization's needs multiply. A large organization usually has several servers that host various pieces of the SharePoint and Reporting Services scenario. A common approach is to distribute SharePoint among application servers and web front-end servers. Generally, a large, failsafe SQL Server cluster is used to host the multiple configuration and content databases of the SharePoint farm. There is also a computer that hosts the Reporting Services service and another server for the PowerPivot service.

Each of these scenarios breaks apart the pieces to gain stability and performance. In every scenario, however, the underlying architecture remains the same. The SharePoint database takes control of the Reporting Services objects. The objects are stored in the SharePoint databases but are synced with the Reporting Services database to improve report rendering performance.

One of the key benefits of SharePoint is that it provides users with a single access point to store all their business documents. A SharePoint site could be set up for the executive leadership team that includes all documents it requires on a daily basis. With Reporting Services in SharePoint Integrated Mode, reports are also stored in these same document libraries and are easily accessed and managed. One of the main benefits of storing the reports in the SharePoint libraries is that end users need to go to only their specific SharePoint site to obtain all their business documents, including their reports. The world of modern information workers and business users has become increasingly chaotic in a digital sense. Microsoft has made great strides in consolidating this into a single point of reference with the SharePoint site.

Reporting Services Add-in

The Reporting Services add-in for SharePoint installs on so-called web front-end (WFE) machines of your SharePoint deployment, as shown in Figure 22-1. The add-in provides services for both RDL and RDLX reports. For Power View specifically, the role of the RS add-in is as follows:

- ➤ Host the Power View application (XAP package).
- ➤ Host the Power View page (AdhocReportDesigner.aspx) to launch Power View from a model or a published RDLX report.
- ➤ Provide affinity and automatic fail-over to report server services in the farm for Power View user sessions.

Reporting Services Service Application

The Reporting Services service application is the central component of a SharePoint-integrated report server installation. For Power View specifically, the Reporting Services service application provides several services to enable a highly interactive experience in Power View:

➤ Data connections to the semantic model, including impersonation and delegation as configured and needed

➤ Query execution and data processing

➤ Fetching of web images hosted in a SharePoint site/document library or on external web server locations

➤ Configurable tracing and error logging for diagnostics and support

All Reporting Services service applications share a so-called catalog database to provide storage for internal meta data used by report server instances in a SharePoint farm.

PowerPivot for SharePoint

Chapter 21 offers detailed coverage of PowerPivot for SharePoint. To summarize, PowerPivot for SharePoint adds services and infrastructure to SharePoint to enable users to work with Excel PowerPivot workbooks. PowerPivot for SharePoint installs on top of SharePoint 2010 with SP1 and adds services and functionality to SharePoint to enable collaboration, sharing, and reporting for PowerPivot workbooks. PowerPivot for SharePoint consists of two main components that provide SharePoint the capability to host PowerPivot applications:

➤ **PowerPivot Service:** This service provides the capability to deploy and query PowerPivot workbooks. The service also includes the PowerPivot web service component that enables applications to connect to PowerPivot workbook data from outside the SharePoint farm. This includes reusing PowerPivot data from one workbook in other workbooks. The PowerPivot service provides refresh of external connections to data sources to keep the data current in a PowerPivot workbook. You can define a refresh schedule to automatically update data, such as at 7 a.m. every morning.

➤ **Analysis Services Service in Vertipaq Mode:** This is sometimes also called a PowerPivot database. It is an Analysis Services database instance running inside the SharePoint farm in tabular mode.

INSTALLING REPORTING SERVICES FOR SHAREPOINT

Assuming you already followed the steps in Chapter 21 to install and configure PowerPivot for SharePoint in your farm, you are ready to install the Reporting Services for SharePoint components, as well as an Analysis Services server in tabular mode.

To install and configure Reporting Services for SharePoint and Analysis Services, follow these steps:

1. You ran the SQL Server installation media to install PowerPivot for SharePoint, but you need to run it again to install the Reporting Services components and also Analysis Services in tabular mode. Start the SQL Server installation media, and then click the Installation tab.

2. Choose New SQL Server Stand-Alone Installation or Add Features to an Existing Installation.

3. On the Installation Type screen, confirm that the radio button Perform a New Installation of SQL Server is selected. The POWERPIVOT instance you installed is shown as well. You do not want to add features to this instance; you want to install a new instance for Reporting Services.

4. Enter the product key, and click Next.

5. Accept the terms of the licensing agreement, and click Next.

6. On the Setup Role page, confirm that the radio button SQL Server Feature Installation is selected, as shown in Figure 22-2, and click Next.

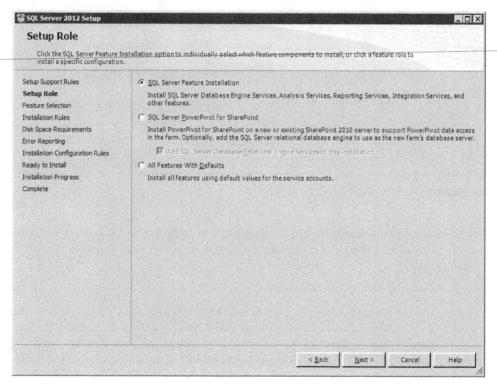

FIGURE 22-2

7. On the Feature Selection page, select Analysis Services, Reporting Services - SharePoint, and Reporting Services Add-In for SharePoint Products, as shown in Figure 22-3. Click Next to continue.

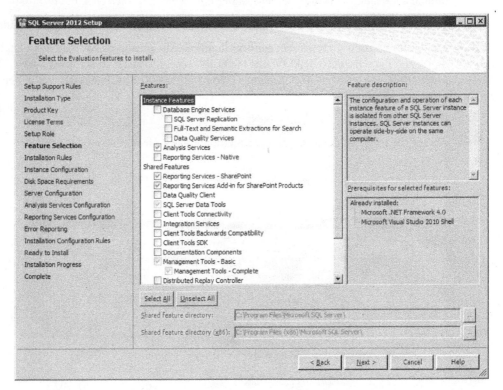

FIGURE 22-3

8. On the Instance Configuration screen, as shown in Figure 22-4, select the radio button to create a Default Instance. You can also provide a named instance, but in this example you use the default instance. Click Next to continue.

9. After reviewing the disk space requirements screen, click Next.

10. Enter the administrative account for SQL Server Analysis Services. This should be a domain account. In this example, you continue to use the same account for all services for the sake of simplicity and understanding the technology. Assuming your administrative account is part of the CONTOSO domain and is called Administrator, specify the service account configuration, as shown in Figure 22-5. After you enter the credentials, click Next to continue.

11. On the Analysis Services Configuration screen, be sure you have selected the radio button for Tabular mode, as shown in Figure 22-6. Then click Add Current User to add the logged-in user as administrator, and if it is different from the administrative user specified in the previous step 10, explicitly add that user as well. Click Next to continue.

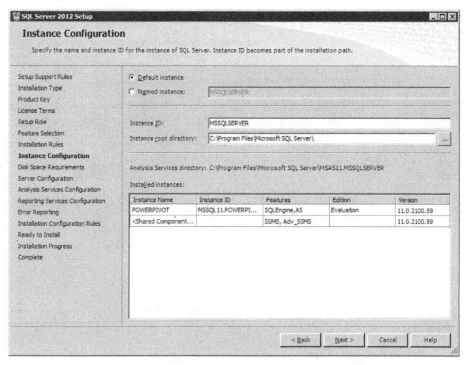

FIGURE 22-4

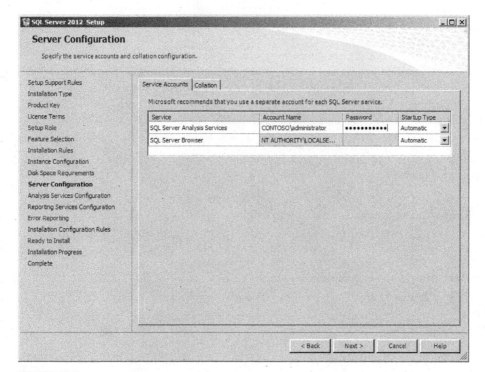

FIGURE 22-5

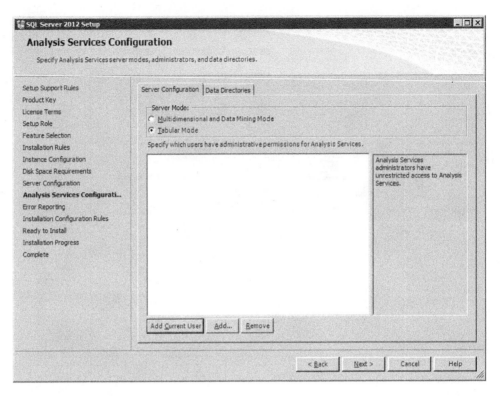

FIGURE 22-6

12. On the Reporting Services Configuration screen, the only option is to Install Only for SharePoint Integrated Mode. The Native mode installation options for Reporting Services are unavailable because you did not choose Native mode on the feature selection screen. After Reporting Services for SharePoint is installed in Integrated Mode, you use Central Administration, which is the management application for SharePoint, to configure Reporting Services. Click Next to continue.

13. Decide if you want to submit feedback to Microsoft, and then click Next on the Error Reporting screen.

14. The installation runs some tests and provides you with a simple report. Click Next on the Installation Configuration Rules screen to continue.

15. You see a summary of the installation, as shown in Figure 22-7. Click Install to begin the installation process.

16. When the installation is complete, you receive a report letting you know that everything installed correctly, as shown in Figure 22-8. Click Close to complete the installation process.

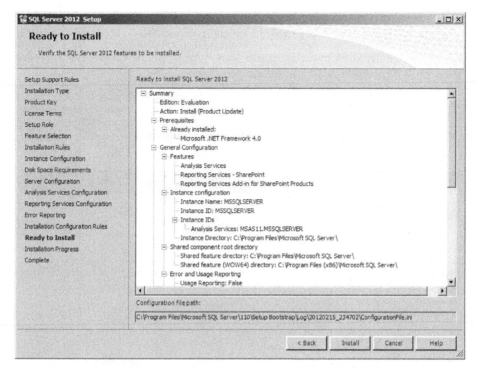

FIGURE 22-7

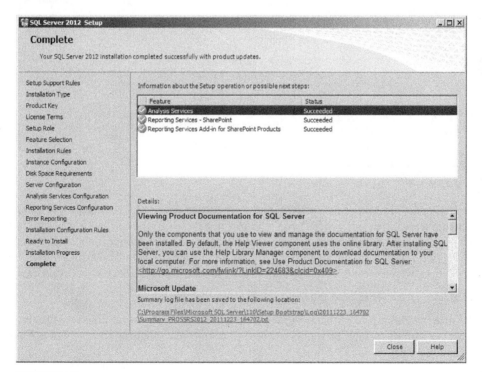

FIGURE 22-8

Now that Reporting Services is installed in SharePoint Integrated Mode, you need to create a Reporting Services service application in your SharePoint environment. To do so, follow these steps:

1. Open Central Administration by navigating to Start ➤ All Programs ➤ Microsoft SharePoint 2010 Products ➤ SharePoint 2010 Central Administration.

2. Click the Application Management tab on the left, and then click Manage Service Applications, located in the Service Applications section.

3. In the Ribbon at the top of the screen, click New. From the drop-down menu, select SQL Server Reporting Services Service Application, as shown in Figure 22-9.

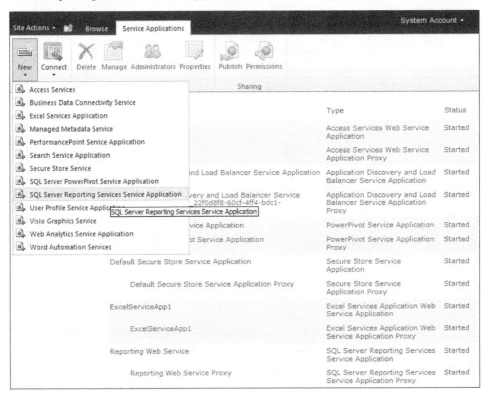

FIGURE 22-9

4. Enter a name for the service application, and then choose to create a new App Pool that the service application will run under. You could use an existing App Pool, but it is best practice to separate the Reporting Services service application from other service applications such as Excel Services. Separating the Reporting Services service into its own App Pool achieves process isolation, which creates an additional security layer to the SQL Server reporting data.

5. Enter a database server to hold the Reporting Services database.

6. Make sure that Windows Authentication is selected, and also choose to associate the service application with the default SharePoint site. The completed configuration is shown in Figures 22-10 and 22-11.

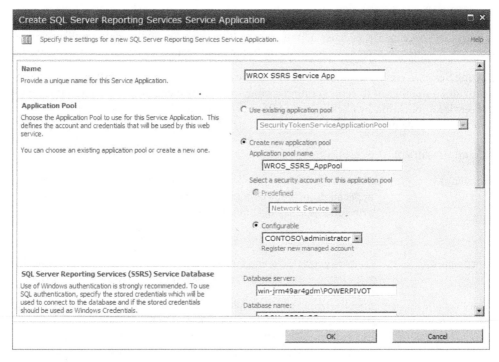

FIGURE 22-10

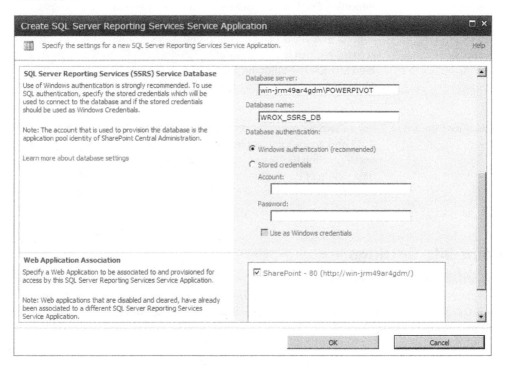

FIGURE 22-11

7. After the service application has been created, you see the status screen, as shown in Figure 22-12. Click OK to close it. You see the Reporting Services service application you created. You are now ready to begin using Reporting Services in SharePoint Integrated Mode.

The Reporting Services service application provides the integration with Reporting Services and, as a result, provides a number of different configuration screens. You can access the configuration section of the service application by clicking the SSRS service application you just created. The service application settings page provides the configuration settings, as follows.

CONFIGURATION SECTION	DESCRIPTION
System Settings	Defines the overall system settings for the Reporting Services service application. Includes configuration items such as the report settings, session settings, logging settings, security settings, and client settings.
Manage Jobs	Enables you to view and delete running reporting jobs.
Key Management	Enables you to view and manage encryption keys, including the ability to back up, restore, change, and delete keys.
Execution Account	Enables you to set credentials for data sources where a logged-in user does not execute the report. It is best practice to maintain a unique account for this execution account and provide only the minimum credentials required to access the needed data sources.
Email Settings	Reporting Services can deliver reports using e-mail. The settings on this page enable you to configure e-mail so that reports, processing notifications, and alerts can be sent to end users through e-mail. Using this screen, you can instruct Reporting Services to use an SMTP server and then provide the outgoing server information and FROM information. The FROM information is who the e-mail appears to be coming from to end users.
Provision Subscriptions and Alerts	For subscriptions, alerts, and scheduled reports to work with SQL Server 2012 and SharePoint, you must have the SQL Server Agent running, and Reporting Services must have access to it. You can find a detailed description of this feature in Microsoft's TechNet library at http://msdn.microsoft.com/en-us/library/hh231725(v=sql.110).aspx.

SharePoint Site Settings

When Reporting Services is installed in SharePoint Integrated Mode, a new section called Reporting Services is created in the SharePoint Site Settings, as shown in Figure 22-13. The new section allows the administrator to manage the server's shared schedules, manage the site's reporting services settings, and manage data alerts.

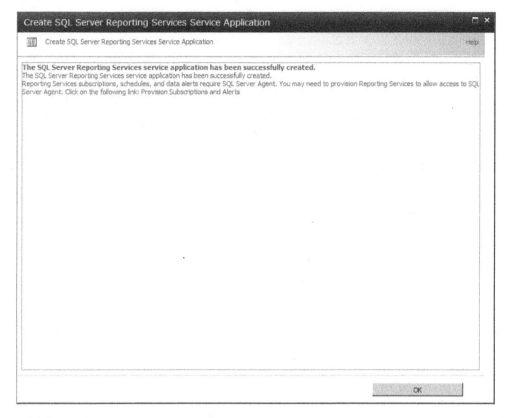

The following table describes the configuration of each of these features.

CONFIGURATION SECTION	DESCRIPTION
Manage Shared Schedules	Provides an interface for adding and managing scheduled reports. In addition, you can pause currently running schedules and start selected schedules on an ad hoc basis.
Reporting Services Site Settings	Enables you to configure settings for the SharePoint site, including enabling client-side printing, showing detailed error messages on remote computers, and enabling accessibility meta data in the HTML of the generated reports.
Manage Data Alerts	Provides an interface for administrators to view and manage the alerts set on reports by users. Using this screen, an administrator can both view and delete alerts. In addition, all the alerts for a specific report or all the alerts for a specific user can be viewed.

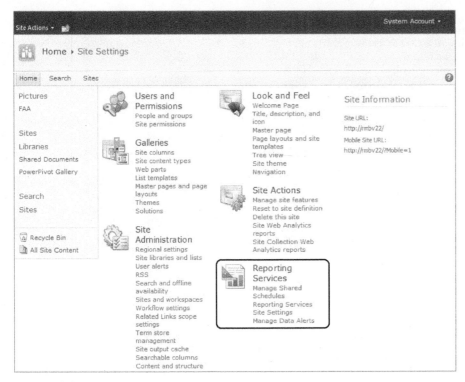

FIGURE 22-13

PREPARING MODEL CONNECTION FOR POWER VIEW TUTORIAL

Chapter 23 uses a large sample tabular database to provide a tutorial on Power View. You learn to explore its data, visualize insights, and share presentations of your analysis results.

The model database in the tutorial is an Excel PowerPivot workbook, created from publicly available datasets from the Federal Aviation Administration (FAA). The FAA is the national aviation authority of the United States, which has authority to regulate and oversee all aspects of civil aviation in the United States.

The FAA publishes a variety of datasets on airline traffic data, such as flight on-time performance, flight cancellations, flight-incidents with wildlife, and so on. The data is published through the Bureau of Transportation Statistics (BTS) at www.bts.gov.

The FAA.XLSX workbook was created by importing the raw datasets into PowerPivot for Excel, detecting and creating relationships between tables, and enriching the data with other datasets and images. The images, referenced from the PowerPivot workbook as image URL paths, are available as downloads on the Wrox download site next to the PowerPivot FAA sample workbook. However, you can create your own airline logo images instead of using the provided clipart images.

Deploying the FAA Flight Data Model

Follow these steps to upload the sample PowerPivot workbook as a new database in an Analysis Services server in tabular mode.

1. Locate the download for the FAA PowerPivot workbook on the Wrox download site for this book.

2. Download and save FAA.XLSX to the default backup folder of your Analysis Server deployment, typically located at: C:\Program Files\Microsoft SQL Server\MSAS11 .MSSQLSERVER\OLAP\Backup.

3. Go to All Programs ➤ Microsoft SQL Server 2012. Launch SQL Server Management Studio as the administrator by right-clicking the entry and selecting Run as Administrator.

4. In SQL Server Management Studio, connect to your Analysis Server instance.

5. When connected, right-click Databases, and select Restore from PowerPivot, as shown in Figure 22-14.

6. In the Restore from PowerPivot dialog, specify the location of FAA.XLSX as the backup file, and specify a database name as FAA, as shown in Figure 22-15. Click OK.

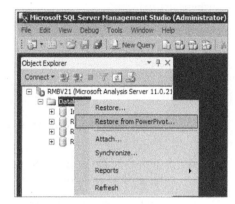

FIGURE 22-14

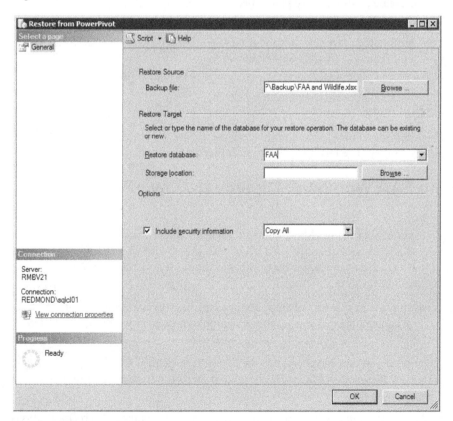

FIGURE 22-15

Creating SharePoint Image Library for FAA Airline Images

To create a new image library in SharePoint, follow these steps:

1. Log on as a user who has administrator or full control permissions on the SharePoint server.

2. In a browser window, navigate to `http://<YourSharePointServer>`.

3. In the SharePoint Ribbon, select Site Actions ➤ Manage Content and Structure.

4. In the Site Content and Structure page, select New ➤ List from the Ribbon.

5. On the next page, click Picture Library, as shown in Figure 22-16.

6. On the create picture library page, specify the name as **FAA**, and click Create.

7. You should now see a new picture library shown on the home of your SharePoint site, as shown in Figure 22-17.

8. Click the FAA link to navigate to the picture library.

9. Using the SharePoint Ribbon, upload all the airline images into the FAA picture library. The result should look similar to Figure 22-18.

FIGURE 22-16

Publishing FAA Workbook Directly to PowerPivot Gallery

In addition to uploading the workbook into an Analysis Services server, you can open the FAA workbook directly with Excel with the PowerPivot add-in installed. However, due to the large size of the workbook, it may take a minute to open and load all the data.

If you receive an error in subsequent steps about exceeding the maximum limit for file size, you can change this setting to publish/upload large PowerPivot workbooks, such as the FAA workbook, using these steps:

FIGURE 22-17

1. On your SharePoint server, launch the SharePoint Central Administration page from Start ➤ All Programs ➤ Microsoft SharePoint 2010 Products ➤ SharePoint 2010 Central Administration.

2. Under the heading Application Management, click the Manage Web Applications link.

FIGURE 22-18

3. Select SharePoint - 80, and then in the SharePoint Ribbon, click General Settings ➤ General Settings, as shown in Figure 22-19.

4. In the Web Applications General Settings dialog, navigate to the bottom of the page to the value Maximum upload size, and change the value from 200MB to 2047MB. Click OK.

5. For the setting to take effect immediately, open a command prompt in administrator mode, type the command **iisreset**, and press Enter to reset the Internet Information Services (IIS) applications.

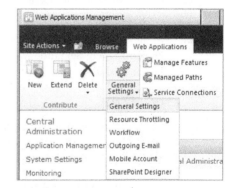

FIGURE 22-19

To publish the FAA workbook from Excel to SharePoint, follow these steps:

1. Switch to your machine with Excel and PowerPivot for Excel.

2. Open the FAA workbook.

3. In Excel, click File ➤ Save and Send ➤ Save to SharePoint ➤ Save As.

4. Enter **http://<YourSharePointServer>/PowerPivot Gallery** in the folder path of the Save As dialog, and click Save.

Alternatively, you can upload the FAA workbook directly in SharePoint following these steps:

1. Open a browser and navigate to `http://<yourSharePointServer>/PowerPivot Gallery`.

2. On the SharePoint Ribbon, select Documents ➤ Upload Document.

3. On the Upload dialog, browse to the location of the FAA workbook, and click OK to upload.

Creating Data Source Connections for Power View

Power View can connect to data using several different connection options, which are explained in more detail in the subsequent section "Configuring Data Source Connections." For the tutorial, you create two files, which you use in Chapter 23 to create a new Power View report from the published FAA workbook/database.

BI Semantic Model (BISM) Connection File

A BI semantic model connection file (.bism) connects Power View reports to BI semantic model data on a server or a workbook published in a SharePoint farm. There are similarities in how an Office data connection (.odc) file and a .bism connection file are defined and used. To create a .bism file, follow these steps:

1. Open a browser and navigate to `http://<yourSharePointServer>/Shared Documents`.

2. In the SharePoint Ribbon, select Documents ➤ New Document ➤ BI Semantic Model Connection, as shown in Figure 22-20.

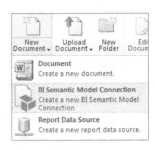

FIGURE 22-20

 If the menu option is missing, either you are logged in as a user who doesn't have permissions to create new content, or you did not correctly install and configure PowerPivot for SharePoint. Furthermore, in the RTM version of SQL Server 2012, the menu option for BI Semantic Model Connection shows the default new document icon. A future update (most likely SP1) will update that entry to use the updated BISM icon, as shown in Figure 22-20.

3. Specify the BISM connection file settings, as shown in Figure 22-21. Replace localhost with the server and optionally instance name (if you didn't install as default instance) of your Analysis Server in tabular mode where you uploaded the FAA database in the previous section, for example **MyServer\InstanceName**.

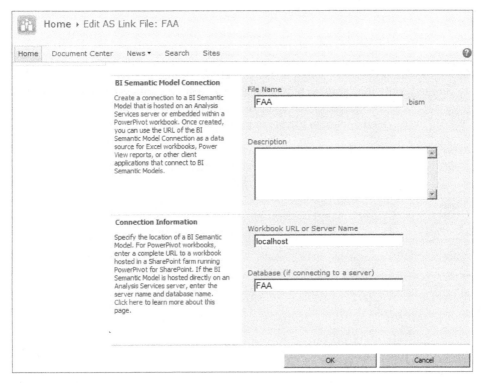

FIGURE 22-21

4. Click OK to create the BISM connection file. You should then see a new file in your document library, as shown in Figure 22-22.

Report Data Source (RSDS) Connection

Connection strings for semantic models in Report Data Sources can have the following formats:

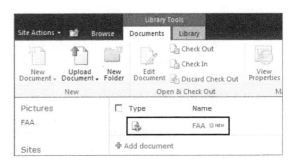

FIGURE 22-22

➤ Connecting to a PowerPivot workbook published in SharePoint by specifying the path of the workbook:

```
Data Source = http://<YourSharePointServer>/PowerPivot Gallery/FAA.xlsx
```

➤ Connecting to a tabular model on an Analysis Server by specifying server name and database name:

```
Data Source = <YourASServer>; Initial Catalog = FAA
```

To create an RSDS connection file, follow these steps:

1. In the document library where you just created a BISM connection file, select the SharePoint Ribbon, select Documents ➤ New Document ➤ Report Data Source.

2. In the data source properties page, specify connection settings, as shown in Figure 22-23. Make sure to specify the data source type as Microsoft BI Semantic Model for Power View. For the connection string, specify the name of your Analysis Server in tabular mode where you uploaded the FAA database in the previous section.

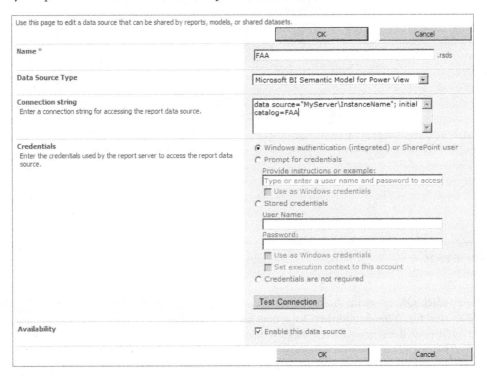

FIGURE 22-23

3. Click Test Connection to verify the connection can be successfully established.

4. Click OK to create the RSDS file. It should show as a new file in your document library.

CONFIGURING DATA SOURCE CONNECTIONS

This section explains several scenarios for data connection and authentication configurations for Power View. You can skip this section now if you want to walk-through the Power View tutorial in Chapter 23, and come back later to learn in depth about configuring data connections and authentication settings.

Power View is a thin web client that launches in the browser, which always connects to an artifact in SharePoint to open an existing report, or create a new report from a BI semantic model, as shown in Figure 22-24 and explained in the following table. Power View uses the Reporting Services service application for resolving and making actual data connections.

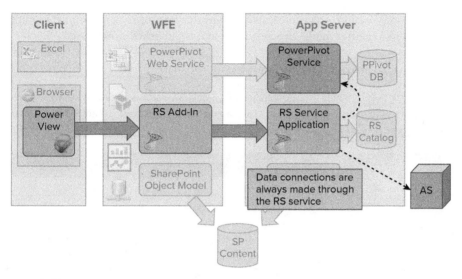

FIGURE 22-24

ICON	FILE TYPE	DESCRIPTION
	PowerPivot workbook (XLSX)	The PowerPivot workbook model is loaded and hosted by the PowerPivot service in SharePoint.
		If a PowerPivot workbook is published in PowerPivot Gallery, as shown in Figure 22-25, a new Power View report can be created directly from the workbook.
	BI Semantic Model (BISM) connection file	A BISM connection file points to a specific model that can be either a workbook or a database on an Analysis Services server. The BISM connection file effectively provides a redirect for the Analysis Services data provider when the connection is initially opened.
		A BISM connection can be used by Power View as well as other BI applications such as Excel.
	Report Data Source (RSDS)	A Report Data Source stores a full connection string and can be configured to store credentials with optional impersonation, as well as pass-through security.
		RSDS is a data source connection type used by Reporting Services clients only, such as Power View and Report Builder.
	Power View report (RDLX)	A published Power View report. Clicking an RDLX file in SharePoint opens the report in Power View presentation mode.

As explained in the previous section, you can create a connection to a BI semantic model in multiple ways. How you connect to a tabular model depends on how it is published or deployed.

Connecting to PowerPivot Workbooks

If a PowerPivot workbook is published in a PowerPivot Gallery, a business user can easily create a new Power View report using the workbook as its data source by selecting Create Power View Report, as shown in Figure 22-25.

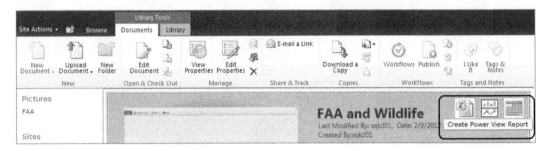

FIGURE 22-25

The connection string for using a PowerPivot workbook as a data source has the following format:
`Data Source=http://<SharePointSite>/PowerPivot%20Gallery/<WorkbookName>.xlsx.`

From a technical perspective, when a connection to a PowerPivot workbook is opened, Reporting Services uses the Analysis Services data provider to connect to the model through the PowerPivot service in SharePoint, as shown in Figure 22-26. The PowerPivot service checks whether the requested workbook is already loaded in its server instance. If needed, it loads the PowerPivot workbook on-the-fly from SharePoint as a new Analysis Services PowerPivot database.

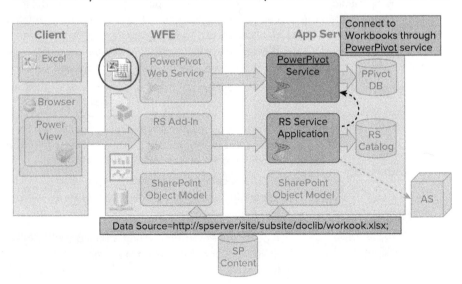

FIGURE 22-26

The PowerPivot service verifies that the Power View user has permissions to read the workbook and denies the connection otherwise.

Connecting to a BISM Connection File

A BI semantic model connection file (.bism) connects Excel or Power View reports to BI semantic model data on a server or a workbook published in a SharePoint farm. There are similarities in how an Office data connection (.odc) file and a .bism connection file are defined and used.

A BI semantic model connection is created and accessed via SharePoint. From a technical perspective, a BI semantic model connection provides an HTTP endpoint to a database. It simplifies tabular model access for business users who routinely use documents on a SharePoint site. They need to know only the location of the BI semantic model connection file or its URL to access tabular model databases.

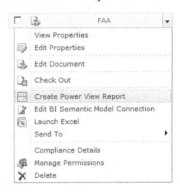

Creating BI semantic model connections enables quick launch commands on a BI semantic model connection in a document library. Quick launch commands open a new Excel workbook or options for editing the connection file. If Reporting Services is installed, you also see a command to create a Power View report, as shown in Figure 22-27. The default-click action for a .bism connection file is to create a new Power View report from the model connection.

FIGURE 22-27

From a technical perspective, when a Power View report is created from a .bism file in SharePoint, the Reporting Services service application provides a connection string pointing to the location of the .bism file, as shown in Figure 22-28. The Analysis Services data provider looks up the contents of the .bism file to connect and redirect to the actual model that the .bism points to.

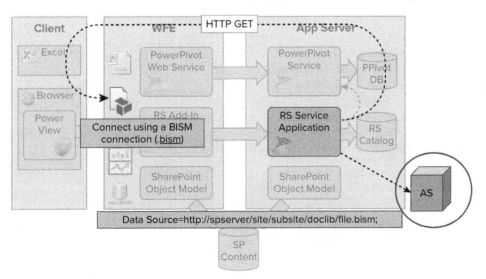

FIGURE 22-28

If the .bism file points to a workbook, the data provider communicates with the PowerPivot service, and the equivalent sequence of loading the workbook as a database and verifying user permissions is performed as explained in the preceding section for connecting to PowerPivot workbooks.

If the .bism file points to an external Analysis Services server, the data provider attempts to establish a connection with that server, which performs user authentication based on the actual end user who connects using the .bism file. Users who connect to tabular databases must have membership in a database role that specifies Read access. Roles are defined when the model is authored with SQL Server Data Tools, or for deployed models, by using SQL Server Management Studio.

Connecting to an RSDS

Report Data Sources (RSDS) were introduced in the initial version of SQL Server Reporting Services. A report server uses credentials to connect to external data sources that provide content to reports. Similar to .bism connection files, an RSDS simplifies tabular model access for business users who routinely use documents on a SharePoint site. They need to know only the location of the RSDS to access the model.

An RSDS provides many authentication configuration options. You can specify credentials that use Windows Authentication, database authentication, no authentication, or custom authentication. When sending a connection request over the network, the report server either impersonates a user account (and optionally sets the original user as execution context after the connection is successfully opened) or the unattended execution account.

Similar to .bism connection files, an RSDS connects Power View reports to BI semantic model data on a server or a workbook published in a SharePoint farm. An RSDS provides additional authentication configurations not available through .bism, which is explained in detail in the subsequent "Authentication Scenarios" section.

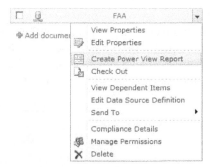

An RSDS connection is created and accessed via SharePoint and provides a quick launch command on its context menu to create a new Power View report, as shown in Figure 22-29. Note that the default-click action on a RSDS connection is to edit connection settings. Although .bism connection files are primarily used for Power View (and hence the default-click action creates a new Power View report from the model connection), RSDS serve significantly broader usage scenarios.

FIGURE 22-29

From a technical perspective, when a Power View report is created from a RSDS in SharePoint, the Reporting Services service application looks up the RSDS configuration settings in its catalog database, performs authentication and impersonation as specified, and then invokes the Analysis Services data provider to open the data connection to the PowerPivot workbook or a model database deployed on an Analysis Server, as shown in Figure 22-30.

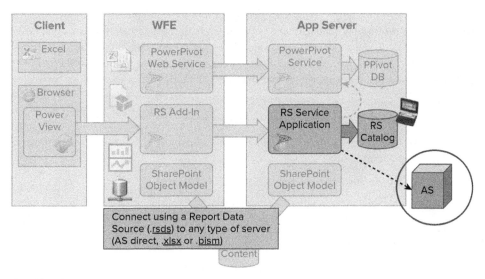

FIGURE 22-30

Authentication Scenarios

When connecting to a PowerPivot workbook published within the SharePoint farm, the tabular model inside the workbook is published on-the-fly to PowerPivot for SharePoint. As covered earlier, PowerPivot for SharePoint is a dedicated Analysis Services server in tabular mode running inside the SharePoint farm. Because workbooks are published on-demand (and automatically unloaded later when they are no longer used), there can be a significant latency when connecting to a model in a PowerPivot workbook initially. Deploying a PowerPivot workbook to a standalone Analysis Server makes it available as a permanent database on that server.

The authentication model for PowerPivot workbooks in SharePoint is based on the claims configuration for the SharePoint site with the PowerPivot workbook. Authorization for model data access in PowerPivot for SharePoint is based on whether the user has permissions to view and read the PowerPivot workbook. If you have read permissions, you can read all the data residing in the workbook.

In summary, authentication scenarios for PowerPivot workbooks published in a SharePoint farm are fairly straightforward. However, a standalone Analysis Server offers many additional capabilities for BI semantic models; you may want to leverage in an enterprise deployment. For example:

➤ Role-based security in the model

➤ Scalability and controlling load balancing when using dedicated servers

➤ Partitioning of model data

➤ DirectQuery, which enables running queries against the model directly against a SQL Server database, providing up-to-date data and security enforced in the underlying relational database.

However, connecting to standalone Analysis Services is not as simple. Typically, you have multimachine deployments, with multiple hops necessary between a client application (for example, Power View running in the browser of a business user), SharePoint web-front end, SharePoint services (for example, Reporting Services performing data connections and processing on behalf of Power View), and the Analysis Services server hosting the model database. You may need to consider the following questions:

> **Analysis Services supports only Windows authentication:**

> > Is Analysis Services running on the same machine as your SharePoint deployment? Frequently, that is not the case.

> > Is Analysis Services even running on the same domain?

> > Is Kerberos delegation enabled?

> > Do business users have read-permissions on the databases deployed on the Analysis Server?

> > Is row-level security enabled?

> **SharePoint Claims-Based Identity:** SharePoint 2010 supports two modes in which a client can authenticate with the platform: Classic mode and Claims mode. Reporting Services 2012 is fully integrated with both modes, including all types of SharePoint Claims authentication.

Windows identities are generally valid only for making a connection to one additional machine on behalf of the user (NTLM protocol) but not multiple machine-hops. The Kerberos protocol is a more secure protocol for Windows integrated authentication that supports ticketing authentication. A Kerberos authentication server grants a ticket in response to a client computer authentication request if the request contains valid user credentials and a valid Service Principal Name (SPN). The client computer then uses the ticket to access network resources.

Support for Claims authentication is a new feature in SharePoint 2010 and is built on Windows Identity Foundation. In a claims model, SharePoint Server accepts one or more claims about an authenticating client to identify and authorize the client. The claims come in the form of SAML (Security Assertion Markup Language) tokens and are facts about the client stated by a trusted authority. For example, a claim could state, "Robert is a member of the Enterprise Admins group for the domain Contoso.com." If this claim came from a provider trusted by SharePoint Server, the platform could use this information to authenticate Robert and to authorize him to access SharePoint Server resources. The types of claims supported for incoming authentication are Windows-Claims, forms-based authentication (FBA)-Claims, and SAML-Claims.

The Reporting Services 2012 web front-end component is claims-enabled to perform appropriate Claims authentication. It communicates the Claims token(s) to the Reporting Services service application. Using that approach the end users' identity can flow from a client application such as Power View running in the browser to the SSRS service application, even in a multimachine SharePoint farm scenario. The challenge to make successful model data connections is about connecting to a standalone SSAS server outside the SharePoint farm because Analysis Services supports only Windows authentication.

Comparison and Trade-offs

The following table provides an overview and comparison of the authentication configuration options available. Subsequent sections cover each of the four options in detail, specifically how to use BISM connection files and RSDS in each situation.

CRITERION	KERBEROS (BISM, RSDS)	BISM AND RS SERVICE ACCOUNT	RSDS AND STORED CREDENTIALS	RSDS AND EFFECTIVE USER
Easy to set up and configure	No	Yes	Yes	Yes
Enables row-level security based on end user	Yes	Yes	No	Yes
Manage user permissions on ...	SSAS	SSAS	RSDS	SSAS
Supports non-Windows users	No	No	Yes	No
Additional network hops (DirectQuery mode)	Yes	No	No	No
Clients Supported	Power View and Excel	Power View and Excel	Power View only	Power View only

Kerberos Delegation with BISM or RSDS

If the client authenticates with the WFE service by using Kerberos authentication (on a SharePoint site configured for Windows Classic authentication), Kerberos delegation can be used to pass the client's identity to the back-end system. Kerberos does not work in combination with SharePoint sites configured for Claims authentication.

As shown in Figure 22-31, using a BISM connection file or an RSDS configured as "integrated security," the end user's Windows identity can flow from Power View to the Reporting Services service application and connect as the end user's Windows identity to Analysis Services.

Permissions are directly managed in the model on the Analysis Services server. The drawback of Kerberos Delegation is that it is often complex to set up and configure correctly. You can find more information about Kerberos authentication in SharePoint 2010 in the documentation at http://technet.microsoft.com/en-us/library/gg502594.aspx.

BISM Connection and RS Service Account

If Kerberos is not configured, the Analysis Services data provider still attempts to make a Windows integrated security connection to the Analysis Server outside the SharePoint farm.

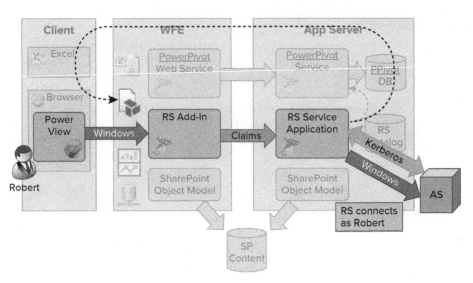

FIGURE 22-31

If that first connection attempt fails due to too many network hops, in case of a BISM connection file, the Analysis Services data provider automatically makes a second attempt using the process account that hosts the data provider with applying `EffectiveUserName=[client Windows identity]` on the connection.

The data provider runs inside the Reporting Services service application process, so if the RS service account is an administrator on the Analysis Server, this second connection attempt will succeed. The connection is opened as an AS administrator, with an explicit security context applied of the `EffectiveUserName` specified. `EffectiveUserName` is an AS data provider capability similar to `SetUser` in Transact-SQL.

Consequently, although the database connection was initially opened as an AS administrator, it effectively connects as the original end user. Commands executed on the opened connection are constrained to the permissions of that (lower-privileged) user, as shown in Figure 22-32.

Permissions are still directly managed in the model on the Analysis Services server. Configuring the Reporting Services service account as a Windows user that is also an administrator on a standalone Analysis Server may be a good alternative if configuring Kerberos Delegation is not an option.

RSDS and Stored Windows Credentials

If you need to support non-Windows Classic authentication, that is, Claims authentication, then this approach is the only option that enables Power View to run with models published to a standalone Analysis Server.

Figure 22-33 shows the RSDS configuration settings page, which, configured as shown, instructs the Reporting Services service application to impersonate the specified stored credentials as Windows identity, and then opens the connection to Analysis Services with that Windows user. You can limit the use of the RSDS impersonated connection through setting read-permissions in SharePoint on the RSDS file.

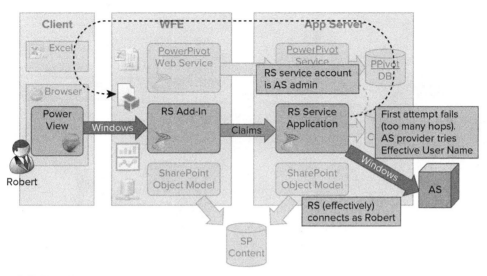

FIGURE 22-32

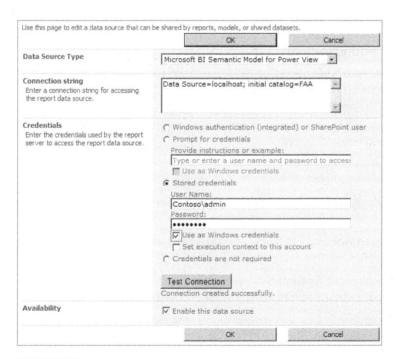

FIGURE 22-33

This approach enables you to control permissions in SharePoint on the RSDS file. You can enable model access to Power View users without the need to provide users read permissions on the back-end Analysis Server. Setting up a RSDS with stored Windows credentials for impersonation is easy, but it provides the same data view to all users because it is always the stored user identity that connects to the Analysis Services database, as shown in Figure 22-34.

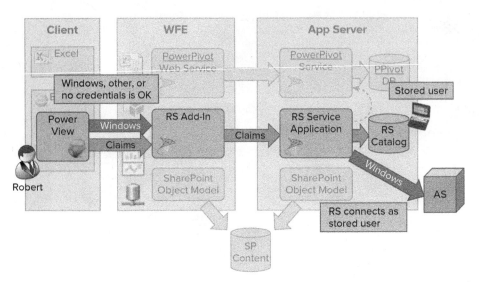

FIGURE 22-34

RSDS with Impersonation and EffectiveUser

This approach is similar to using a BISM connection file with the RS service account configured as an administrator on the Analysis Server, enabling the flow of the actual end user to the back-end database via the EffectiveUserName feature of the data provider.

The difference in this approach with using an RSDS is that you can chose administrator account settings per the RSDS you create in SharePoint. This also enables you to separate the identity of the RS service application from a set of AS back-end servers that you may want to host BI semantic models on, which provides further isolation from a security point of view.

Figure 22-35 shows an example of the RSDS configuration settings page. The implications of the settings are as follows:

1. The Reporting Services service application impersonates the specified stored credentials as Windows identity.

2. Then it opens the connection to Analysis Services impersonated as that Windows user. The impersonated user needs to be an administrator on the Analysis Server.

3. After the connection is opened, the data provider applies the security context of the EffectiveUserName explicitly specified by Reporting Services, based on the SharePoint-authenticated Power View user.

This approach enables you to control permissions in SharePoint on the RSDS file, and in addition in Analysis Services as the end user identity flows through to the model database, as shown in Figure 22-36.

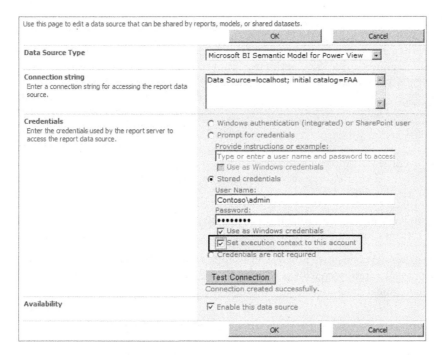

FIGURE 22-35

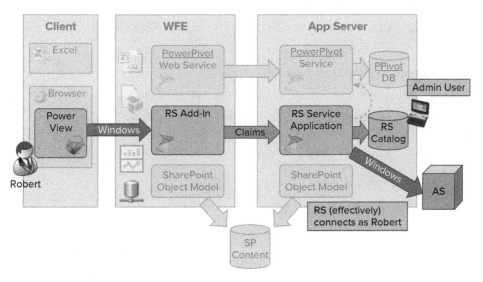

FIGURE 22-36

SUMMARY

In this chapter, you learned about the architecture and components of Power View and Reporting Services in SharePoint integrated mode. You performed an installation and configuration of all necessary components to be ready to use Power View.

You deployed the large FAA PowerPivot sample workbook, and learned about connection files that make it easy for end users to connect to models without the need to know connection strings or credentials.

You walked through several data source connection configuration scenarios depending on your authentication requirements in your environment. You learned about the capabilities and trade-offs of the available connection configuration options.

In the next chapter, you learn about analyzing and visualizing your tabular models with Power View and creating exciting presentations in the process!

Special thanks to our esteemed colleagues Bob Meyers and Sean Boon. Bob helped with the diagrams for describing authentication scenarios, and Sean helped with mashing up public FAA and other data for the sample model database.

Resources

➤ Installing Reporting Services SharePoint Mode Report Server for Power View and Data Alerting:

`http://msdn.microsoft.com/en-us/library/cc281311(v=SQL.110).aspx`

➤ Deployment Checklist: Reporting Services, Power View, and PowerPivot for SharePoint:

`http://msdn.microsoft.com/en-us/library/hh231687(SQL.110).aspx`

➤ Kerberos authentication in SharePoint 2010:

`http://technet.microsoft.com/en-us/library/gg502594.aspx`

➤ For more information about claims authentication, see "A Guide to Claims-based Identity and Access Control" (`http://go.microsoft.com/fwlink/p/?LinkID=187911`).

23

Visual Analytics with Power View

WHAT'S IN THIS CHAPTER?

➤ Gaining a quick overview of Power View

➤ Interactively exploring data in Power View

➤ Creating presentations with Power View

In this chapter you learn how to interactively explore, visualize, and present data from workbooks and model databases in Power View.

Power View, a new feature of Reporting Services 2012, provides intuitive ad-hoc reporting for business users such as data analysts, business decision makers, and information workers. Power View is a browser-based Silverlight application launched from SharePoint Server 2010 that enables users to present and share insights with others in their organization through interactive presentations. Data becomes a lot more impactful when it comes from a well-understood, quality-assured source, is shared and available to the people who need it, and presented in a format that helps share and explore insights easily. This is what the self-service Microsoft BI platform is about, tightly integrated with Microsoft Office and SharePoint.

SharePoint facilitates building BI portals and dashboards that contain Reporting Services reports (both business and Power View reports), Excel Services reports, data-alerting capabilities over reports, and PerformancePoint Services for scorecards and management dashboards.

INTRODUCTION TO POWER VIEW

Power View makes fast, interactive, visual analytics pervasive and accessible to business users and BI professionals. It enables them to easily create and interact with views of data from a tabular Business Intelligence Semantic Model (BISM), based on Excel PowerPivot workbooks published in a PowerPivot Gallery in SharePoint, or tabular models deployed to SQL Server 2012 Analysis Services server instances configured for tabular mode.

PowerPivot for Excel was originally introduced in SQL Server 2008 R2 for Excel 2010. Any workbooks you created with PowerPivot data can be uploaded in SharePoint, and you (and anyone else who has read permissions on the workbook file in SharePoint) can easily and quickly build highly interactive visualizations with Power View, connected to your existing Excel PowerPivot workbooks. You can quickly create a variety of visualizations, from tables and matrices to column, bar, line, and bubble charts, and sets of small multiple charts. An example of multiples in design mode is shown in Figure 23-1. For every visualization you want to create, you start with a table. You can then easily convert to other visualizations to determine which one best illustrates your data.

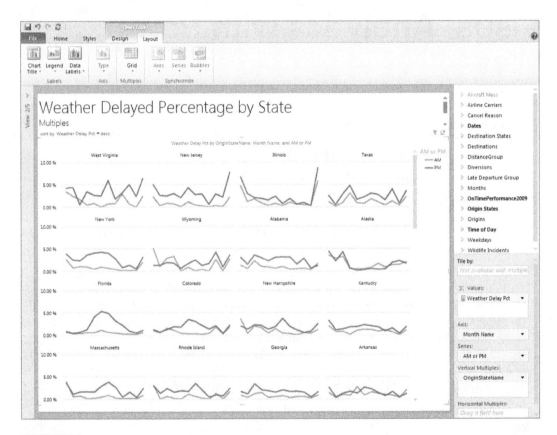

FIGURE 23-1

A Power View report is always *presentation-ready*. There is no switching between report design and preview modes (like Report Builder); instead, in each step you work with the real data. You don't need to create queries, Power View does it on your behalf automatically based on the tables and fields you explore and underlying meta data in the semantic model (for example, data types and relationships between tables).

You explore your data and visualize at the same time. A single report can contain *multiple views*. All the views are based on the same tabular model. Each view has its own visualizations, and filters on each view are for that view only.

Power View has reading and full-screen presentation modes, in which the field list, Ribbon, and other design tools are hidden to focus the attention on data visualizations and presenting, as shown in Figure 23-2.

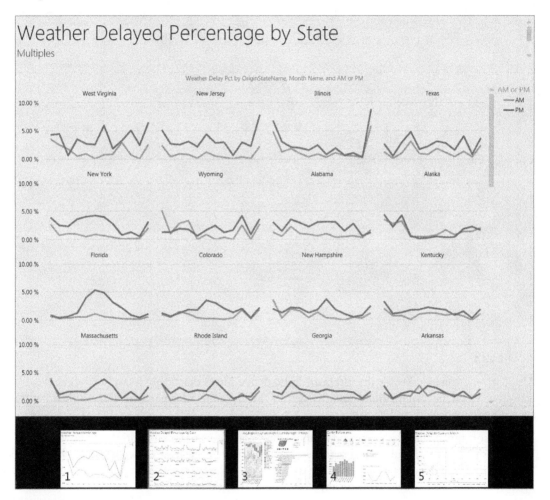

FIGURE 23-2

The report is fully interactive in presentation modes, with the same sorting, filtering, and highlighting capabilities available in other modes.

Power View provides several ways to filter data. Utilizing the meta data in the underlying tabular model, Power View knows the relationships between the different tables and fields in a report. Because of these relationships, you can use visualizations to filter and highlight all other visualizations in the same view, as shown in Figure 23-3, with one of the airlines selected in the right-hand chart, its contribution highlighted in the left hand-chart, and the data filtered in the top table.

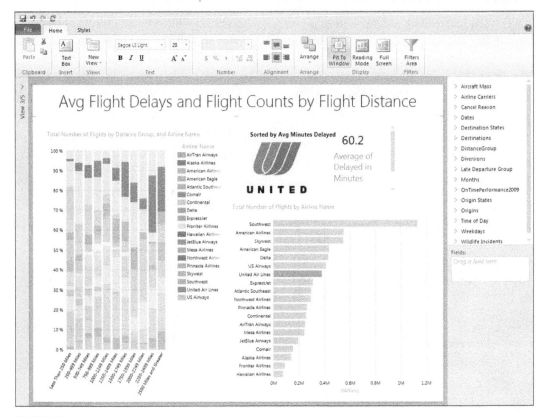

FIGURE 23-3

Alternatively, you can display the *filters area* and define filters that apply to an individual visualization or to all the visualizations on a view. You can leave the filter pane visible or hide it before switching to reading or full-screen mode.

You can sort tables, matrices, bar and column charts, and sets of small multiples in Power View. You sort the columns in tables and matrices, the categories or measures in charts, and the multiple field or the measures in small multiples. In each case, you can sort ascending or descending either on attributes, such as Product Name, or measures, such as Total Sales.

At any point, you can save your reports created with Power View back into SharePoint and share with other users, as shown in Figure 23-4.

You can print directly from Power View, as well as export an interactive version of your Power View report to PowerPoint presentations, as shown in Figure 23-5. Each view in Power View becomes a separate PowerPoint slide.

Interacting with Power View reports exported to PowerPoint is similar to interacting with Power View views in reading and full-screen modes: You can interact with the visualizations and filters added to each view, but you cannot create new visualizations or significantly modify the original visual analysis.

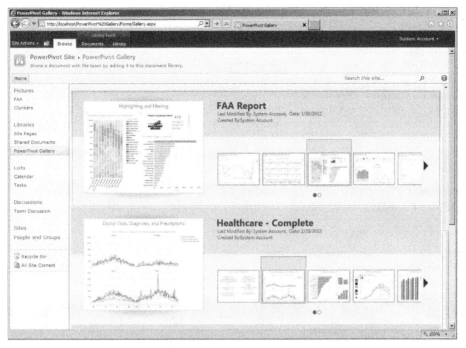

FIGURE 23-4

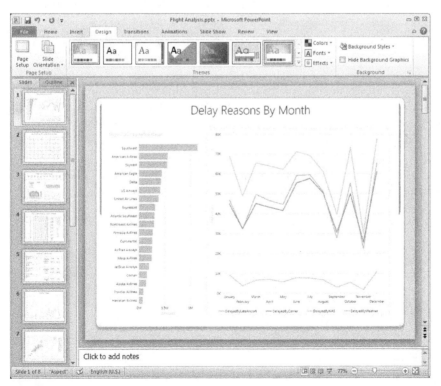

FIGURE 23-5

VISUAL ANALYTICS WITH POWER VIEW

In this section, you learn to interactively explore data in Power View and create compelling presentations.

Getting Started with Power View

Power View runs directly in the browser, using the Silverlight 5 browser plug-in. The first time you start Power View, it asks you to install the latest Silverlight browser plug-in if you don't have it yet.

Creating a New Power View Report

You start a new Power View report from a tabular model in a SharePoint Server 2010 document library or in a PowerPivot Gallery. The model can be

➤ An Excel PowerPivot workbook published in a PowerPivot Gallery.

   You create a new Power View report from a PowerPivot Gallery by clicking the Power View icon shown on the entry of a workbook, as shown in Figure 23-6.

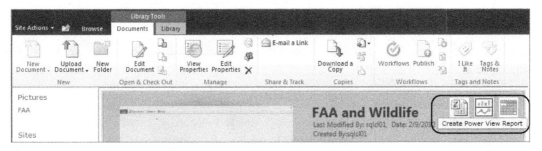

FIGURE 23-6

➤ A shared data source (RSDS) using a Microsoft Business Intelligence Semantic Model (BISM) data source type. The RSDS can point to either on an Excel PowerPivot file or to a tabular BISM deployed on an Analysis Services server.

   You create a new Power View report from an RSDS in a SharePoint document library by clicking the down arrow next to the RSDS file and selecting Create Power View Report, as shown in Figure 23-7.

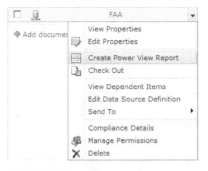

FIGURE 23-7

➤ A BISM connection file (.bism) that points to either an Excel PowerPivot file or to a tabular model deployed on an Analysis Services server.

You create a new Power View report from a BISM connection file in a SharePoint document library by either just clicking the file entry, or clicking the down arrow next to the BISM file, and selecting Create Power View Report, as shown in Figure 23-8.

FIGURE 23-8

For more information about RSDS and BISM connection files, see the section about Configuring Data Source Connections in Chapter 22.

The Power View design environment opens, and you see the view where you build your new report from a semantic model, as shown later in Figure 23-11. The Power View design environment has several main elements, which you learn in detail in the subsequent section about the Power View Design Experience.

Opening an Existing Power View Report

When you open reports in a PowerPivot Gallery, you can choose to open the report at a specific view, by clicking any of the preview images, as shown in Figure 23-9.

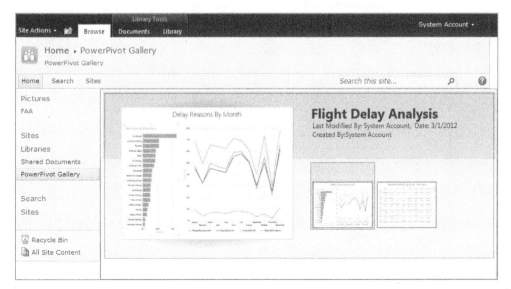

FIGURE 23-9

Clicking a preview image of a report in PowerPivot Gallery opens the report in reading mode. To open the report in edit mode, click the Edit Report icon in the upper-left corner of the report entry in PowerPivot Gallery.

To open a Power View report published in a regular SharePoint document library, simply click the file entry. To open a report directly in edit mode, click the down arrow next to the report, and then click Edit in Power View, as shown in Figure 23-10.

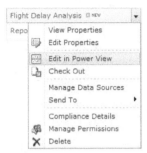

FIGURE 23-10

Introduction to the Power View Design Experience

The Power View design environment consists of several main elements, as shown in Figure 23-11.

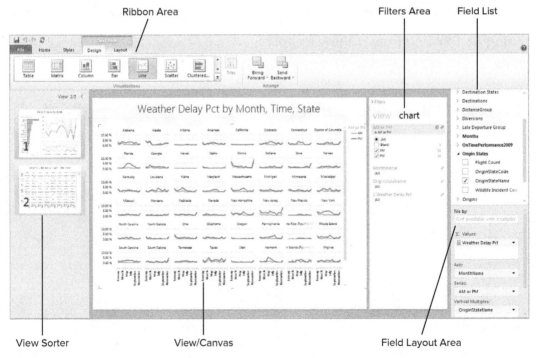

FIGURE 23-11

Power View has a Ribbon similar to that in Microsoft Office. The Home, Styles, Design, and Layout tabs are context-sensitive and contain buttons and menus for the most common tasks. The Design and Layout tabs appear only if you create or select a visualization on the *canvas*, and the tab contents change depending on the type of visualization. For example, a chart visualization provides options to modify the chart title and legend, and to synchronize chart axes.

The *canvas*, also called *view*, is of fixed size, similar to a PowerPoint slide, but unlike a Report Builder view. A Power View report can have many views, similar to a PowerPoint presentation consisting of many slides.

A view fits to the window using auto-fit mode by default. As you resize the browser window, or open panes such as the filters area, the view adjusts proportionally to fit the remaining window.

You can disable this behavior, and use scrollbars to view the different parts of the view. To stop the view from resizing to auto-fit to the window, deselect the Fit to Window button in the Ribbon of Power View.

Ribbon options are disabled (grayed out) if a particular action is not available based on what you selected in the view. For example, if a table has no measures, you cannot convert it to a chart, and all chart options are disabled on the Design tab.

The pane to the right of the canvas is the field list. The top half section displays the tables and fields available in the semantic model that your Power View report is based on. The lower half is the field well or layout section. It displays field grouping and layout options for the selected visualization in the canvas.

Creating a Table Visualization

As you click a field in the field list, Power View draws a table in the view, displaying your actual data and automatically adding column headings. You do not insert an empty table in the view or author a query. As you select more fields, they are added to the table in the view.

When you add a field to the view, you immediately see the actual values in that field — the same values you would see in reading and full-screen modes. Power View is always operating with the live data. The columns are formatted according to the field's data type, as defined in the model that the report is based on.

If an existing visualization is selected in the view, then clicking a field adds it to that visualization. If not, then the new field starts a new table visualization in the view.

For example, assuming you started a new Power View report from the FAA semantic model, go to the field list, expand Airlines (representing the Airlines model table), and select the Airline Name field. This creates a new table visualization, as shown in Figure 23-12. Airline Name also appears in the field well, shown as one of the fields used in the visualization.

Measures in a model table are fields marked with a Sigma (Σ) symbol in the field list. A measure is a numeric value that can be an aggregatable or non-aggregated value that typically indicates the size, quantity, or scale of something that is evaluated based on context. For example, Average Sales Amount can be a measure that gets evaluated based on the products and months selected by the user. Measures are defined in the tabular model that your report is based on. You need at least one measure to create a chart data visualization.

FIGURE 23-12

You can also use a *nonmeasure field* as a measure. To make use of this functionality in the tutorial, hover over the Airlines ➤ Flight Count field in the field list, click the drop-down arrow, and select Add to Table as Sum, as shown in Figure 23-13. The resulting table is shown in Figure 23-14 and also includes an automatic (sub)total aggregation at the bottom of the table. You can also change the aggregate function using the field well after a field is added as a measure. For example, if you have a field that is not aggregatable, such as a Rating field with values from 1 to 5, you could add it to a table and then set the aggregate to Average. Such a measure created in Power View is called an *implicit measure*.

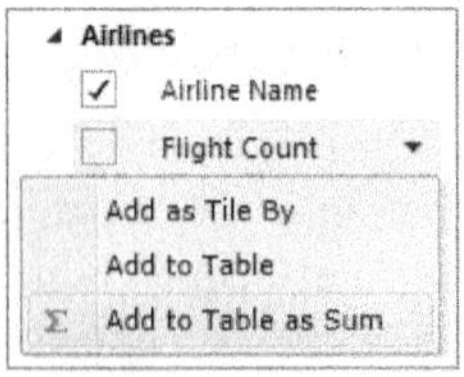

FIGURE 23-13

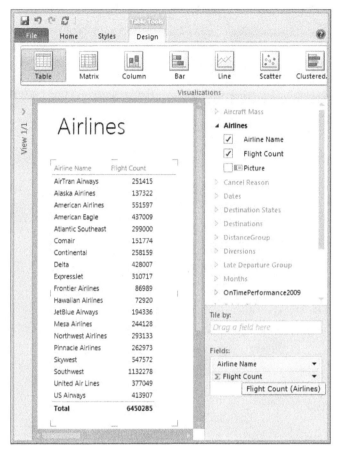

FIGURE 23-14

Converting Visualizations

You can quickly create a variety of visualizations in Power View, from tables and matrices to charts and sets of small multiple charts. For every visualization you want to create, start with a table, which you can then easily convert to other visualizations, to determine which one best illustrates your data.

To convert a table to other visualizations, ensure the table is selected in the view, and then click a visualization type in the visualizations gallery on the Table Tools Design tab. Figure 23-15 shows the table with airlines and flight counts created in the previous section converted into a bar chart.

FIGURE 23-15

Depending on the current fields and data in your table, Power View enables and disables different visualization types to give you the best visualization for that data. To start another visualization on the view, create another table by clicking into blank space of the view before selecting fields from the fields section of the field list.

Sorting Inside Charts

In Power View, you can sort data in tables, matrices, and bar and column charts. You can sort individual charts within small multiples. You can sort measures, such as Sales Amount, and nonmeasures, such as Airline Name. Sorting on various types of visualizations is explained in more detail later in this section.

Using the bar chart you created earlier in this chapter, you may notice that by default a chart is sorted ascending alphabetically by the category unless an explicit sort order is specified in the model.

To sort the chart of airlines ascending by flight counts, hover with your mouse over the top edge of the chart until you see a floating toolbar appear. The toolbar shows Sort By in the upper-left corner, then the name of the currently sorted field (that is, Airline Name) and then either asc for ascending or desc for descending.

You can click the field name to sort on a different value; alternatively, click the drop-down arrow to select a specific field to sort on, as shown in Figure 23-16.

FIGURE 23-16

Next, click asc to sort in the opposite direction, such that the airline with the highest flight count is shown at the top of the bar chart, as shown in Figure 23-17.

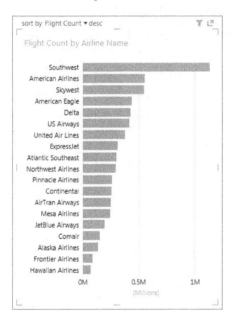

FIGURE 23-17

From launching Power View from the FAA model to gaining the insight that Southwest Airlines has the highest flight count recorded in the dataset of the FAA sample workbook database, you made only six mouse clicks (or less) and didn't use the keyboard at all.

Expanding Visualizations

All visualizations have a pop-out button in the upper-right corner, except for Tile visualization. When you click the button shown in Figure 23-18, the visualization expands to fill the entire Power View view, or if you are in reading or full-screen mode, to fill the entire window. When you click the pop-out button again, the visualization returns to its original spot in the report.

FIGURE 23-18

Filtering in Views

Power View provides several ways to filter and highlight data in reports. Based on the meta data in the underlying model, Power View knows the relationships between the different tables and fields in a report. This enables you to use visualizations on a view to automatically filter each other utilizing the underlying relationship information.

You start with building a visualization that analyzes the delay reasons for flights of airline carriers:

1. Click in an empty area of the current view (to ensure no visualization is selected).

2. In the field list, expand Months and select the MonthName field. This creates a new table on the view showing all month names.

3. In the field list, expand OnTimePerformance2009 and select the DelayedByLateAircraft field.

4. Using the Ribbon, convert the table into a column chart. As you resize the column chart, notice how the category axis and numeric y-axis automatically adjust to make optimal use of the visual view port. For example, Figure 23-19 shows a chart too narrow to fit all categories. Only a subset of the categories is visible, with a scroll bar to view the others. Figure 23-20 shows a chart that can fit all categories in its view. The category labels automatically adjust to improve readability. Figure 23-21 shows an even wider chart, in which category axis labels stack in two lines to utilize the available space optimally.

5. In the field list, select the following additional measures from the OnTimePerformance2009 table:

    ➤ DelayedByCarrier

    ➤ DelayedByNAS (National Air Space)

    ➤ DelayedByWeather

6. Select the chart, go to Chart Tools Layout in the Ribbon, click Chart Title, and select None. Select Legend ➤ Show Legend at Bottom.

    Figure 23-22 shows the resulting chart as stacked columns. This type of chart quickly shows the aggregated number of flights; not surprisingly the peaks for delays are during the December holiday and summer travel seasons.

7. In the Ribbon, switch to Chart Tools Design, and select Line to convert the column chart to a line chart, as shown in Figure 23-23. The line chart visualization shows clearly that overall for all carriers, delays due to National Air Space are the single most common type of delay consistently affecting flights' on-time performance.

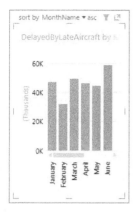

FIGURE 23-19

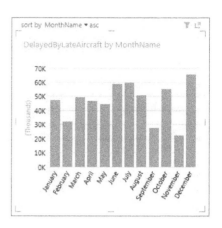

FIGURE 23-20

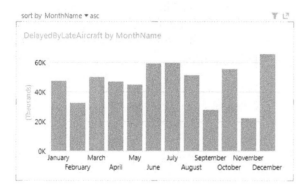

FIGURE 23-21

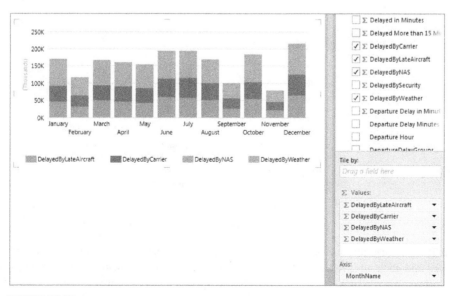

FIGURE 23-22

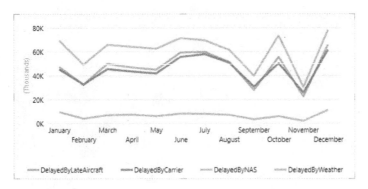

FIGURE 23-23

8. In your current view, locate the bar chart showing flight counts by airline. Click the bar for Southwest, and notice how the line chart with delay reasons automatically updates and filters to just flights by Southwest, as shown in Figure 23-24. The filter is applied with an animation to help you see the differences compared to the general trends compared to all airlines. In the case of the FAA data for on-time performance during 2009, the most common type of delay for Southwest was a late aircraft, unlike the general trend.

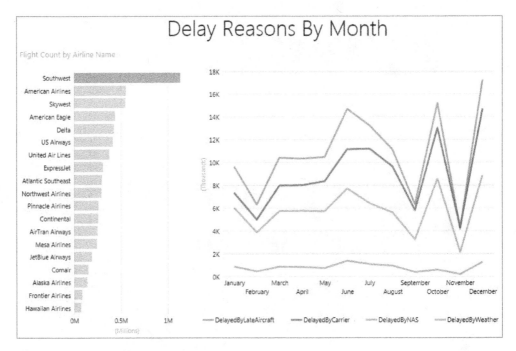

FIGURE 23-24

9. You can also perform multiselect for filtering. In the bar chart for flight counts, hold the Shift or Ctrl key and click additional airline names. This way you accomplish selection of multiple values; with each filter-click the line chart updates automatically, as shown in Figure 23-25.

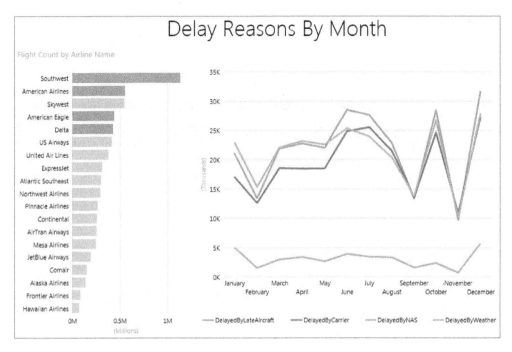

FIGURE 23-25

10. You can clear your chart filter value selection by clicking anywhere into the empty space of the bar chart for flight counts.

Multiple Views

You can create a report with multiple views in Power View, using the New View menu on the Home tab, as shown in Figure 23-26.

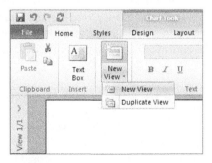

FIGURE 23-26

You can click through multiple views in a presentation, similar to PowerPoint. All the views in one report are based on the same model. You can copy and paste from one view to another, and duplicate whole views. If you save preview images of the views, an image of each view displays in the PowerPivot Gallery.

To explore the multiple view capability, create a second view in your report using the following steps:

1. Using the New View menu shown in Figure 23-26, create a new empty view.

2. In the field list, expand Months and select the MonthName field.

3. In the field list, expand OnTimePerformance2009 and select the Weather Delay Pct field.

4. Using the Ribbon, convert the table into a line chart, as shown in Figure 23-27. Not surprisingly, the chart reveals that weather delays are most common during the months of December and January due to winter conditions.

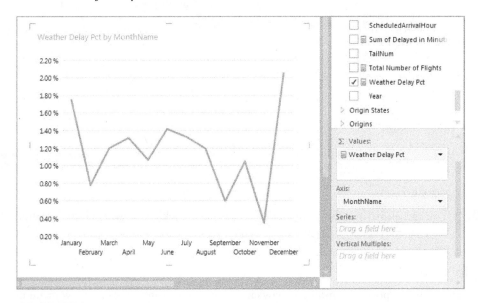

FIGURE 23-27

5. In the field list, expand Time of Day and select the AM or PM field. This automatically puts the field into the chart series. As you can see in the resulting chart in Figure 23-28, the underlying model contains an undesired (Blank) value that shows up in the chart as an extra series. You can filter out unwanted values using filters for the entire view or filters on a particular visualization.

6. Open the Filters Area for the selected visualization by clicking on the small filter icon in the floating toolbar of the chart, as shown in Figure 23-28.

7. The Filters Area appears and pre-populates with all fields currently used in the selected visualization. Click the AM or PM field within the filter pane. This expands the filter and automatically runs a query in the background to fetch the list of distinct values for the filter, as well as its counts. Select the individual filter values for AM and PM, as shown in Figure 23-29. As you select individual filter values, the chart visualization immediately updates.

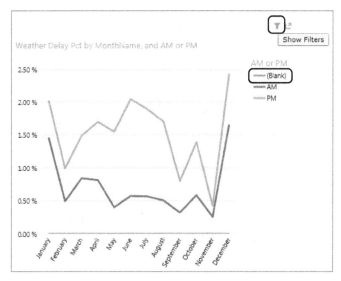

FIGURE 23-28

FIGURE 23-29

 Each view can have its own filters, but the UI visibility state of the Filters Area is constant: If the Filters Area is expanded on one view, it will be expanded on all views. As you move from view to view, in any mode, the state of the filter on each page persists: For example, if you have a filter for the Airline Name field filtering for one view for Southwest, when you leave the view and return to it, the filter will still be filtering for Southwest. When you duplicate a view, the filters are duplicated, too, along with the state of each filter. Saving the report also saves the state of each filter.

8. Minimize the Filters Area by clicking the arrow, as shown in Figure 23-30.

FIGURE 23-30

9. In the field list, expand Origin States and select the OriginStateName field. This changes the visualization into a small multiple (also known as Trellis chart), as shown in Figure 23-31. The chart multiples are automatically synchronized, both on the category axis and the value axis. This helps you visually compare and grasp information quickly, such as a higher percentage of flights in the afternoon is affected by weather delays than flights in the morning.

10. Set the number of multiples to display across and down using the Chart Tools Layout Ribbon, clicking the Grid button and selecting the wanted layout, as shown in Figure 23-32.

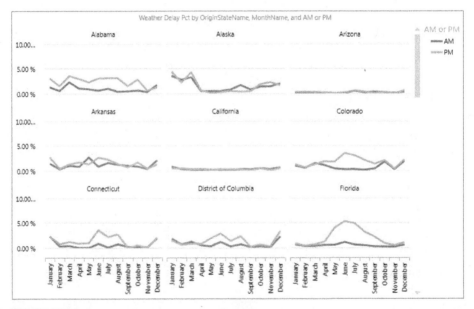

FIGURE 23-31

11. Expand the View Sorter by clicking the arrow icon next to the *View* pane shown in Figure 23-33.

You can navigate between views by simply clicking the thumbnail picture of a view. You can create a new view, duplicate a view, or delete a view, using the down-arrow menu on a given view, as shown in Figure 23-33.

You can re-order views using drag-and-drop within the View Sorter area.

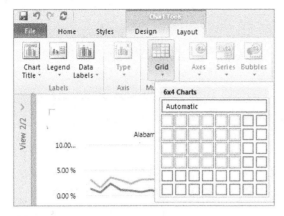

FIGURE 23-32

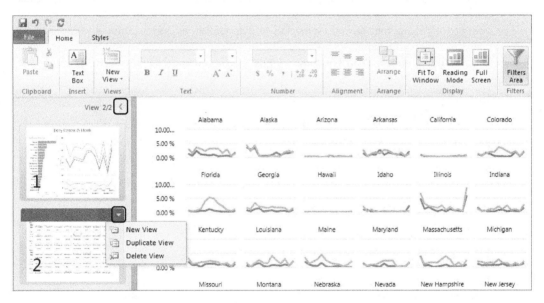

FIGURE 23-33

Saving Reports

You save a Power View report to the same SharePoint site and location as the model from which you launched Power View.

1. To save the report you created so far, click the Power View File menu, as shown in Figure 23-34, and click Save or Save As.

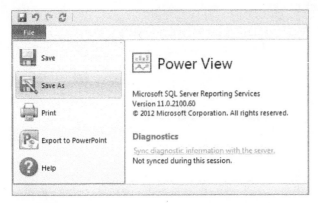

FIGURE 23-34

2. The first time you save the report, the default location is the folder where the model is located. To save it to a different location, browse to that location. For example, in the dialog navigate to the root of your SharePoint site, and select PowerPivot Gallery as save location, and specify a report name, as shown in Figure 23-35. By default, the Save preview images with the report check box is selected. For privacy reasons you may want to clear it and not save preview images.

FIGURE 23-35

View preview images are the images that Power View displays in the View pane in design mode. They are snapshots of a view. They are not real-time images, but they do refresh frequently. When you save a Power View report, by default these images are saved with the report. They are then displayed in the PowerPivot Gallery in SharePoint, just as Microsoft Excel worksheets are displayed. See Figure 23-36.

The first time you save a file, or when you save as, you have the option not to save the preview images. Consider not saving preview images if they display information that you consider potentially sensitive. The PowerPivot Gallery Carousel view displays images large enough to be readable. Views without preview images are shown with a watermark icon and a label, Preview Not Available.

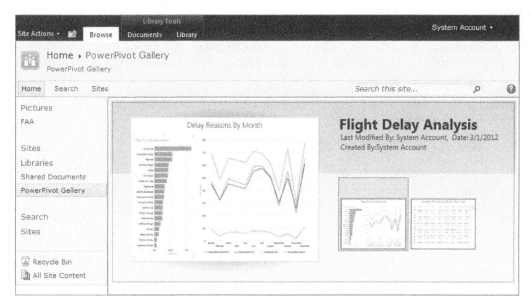

FIGURE 23-36

Also, if you open and view the views in a report that has preview images saved with it, when you save the report, you are saving the updated preview images. To avoid this, disable the preview images option on save.

Power View creates files with the RDLX file format. Currently, you can open reports in RDLX file format only with Power View but not with Report Builder. Similarly, you can open and edit reports in RDL file format with Report Builder but not in Power View.

Permissions for Power View

Power View uses SharePoint permissions to control access to Power View reports. If you have adequate permissions for a SharePoint folder, then you can open a Power View report in edit or reading mode. You can modify the report in edit mode as much as you want, but to save your changes you need Add Items permissions for the destination library or folder, or Edit Items permissions to overwrite an existing document.

Visualizations and Interactivity

Power View can create a variety of visualizations, from tables, cross-tabs (matrices), cards, tiles, to charts and sets of small multiple charts. For every visualization you want to create, you start with a table, which you can then easily convert to other visualizations, to determine which one best illustrates your data. To create a table, click a table or field in the field list, or drag a field from the field list to the view. For optimal performance, Power View does not fetch all data in a table at one time. It fetches more data as you scroll.

In this section, you convert tables to several types of visualizations, and you learn about synchronizing chart axes and several other capabilities.

Tile Visualizations

Tiles are containers with a dynamic navigation strip to help visualize master-detail relationships. You can convert a table or matrix to tiles to present tabular data interactively. As you navigate through values in the navigation strip, related information appears in data visualizations that you add to the container. All content in the container is automatically filtered by the selected value.

To create tile visualizations, you can continue with the report created in the previous subsection, using the following steps:

1.   Create a new empty view in your report.

2.   In the field list, expand DistanceGroup and select the Distance Group field.

3.   In the field list, expand OnTimePerformance2009 and select the OnTime Pct and Delayed by Carrier Pct fields.

4.   Using the Ribbon, convert the table into a column chart, as shown in Figure 23-37. The chart reveals that with increasing flight distance, the percentage of on-time flights overall decreases slightly. Flights delayed by the airline carrier tend to increase with flight distance, whereas other factors for delays are mostly independent of flight distance.

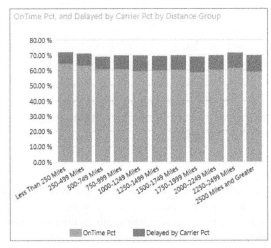

FIGURE 23-37

5.   In the field list, expand Airlines and drag the Picture field to the Tile by area in the field well, as shown in Figure 23-38.

6.   After you create a set of tiles, you can switch between two navigation styles using the Tile Tools Design tab on the Ribbon:

➤   A tab strip that displays values at the top of the tile container, as shown in Figure 23-39.

➤ A cover flow that display values at the bottom of the tile container, as shown in Figure 23-40.

FIGURE 23-38

As you navigate the tiles shown in Figures 23-39 and 23-40, you gain the insight that some carriers don't offer long-distance flights (for example, SkyWest and ExpressJet). There are also differences in on-time performance per carrier.

By default, Power View does not automatically synchronize the horizontal and vertical chart axes, series, and bubble size in charts in a tiles container. For each chart, it sets these scales based on the values in the chart on each individual tile. This makes each chart easy to read.

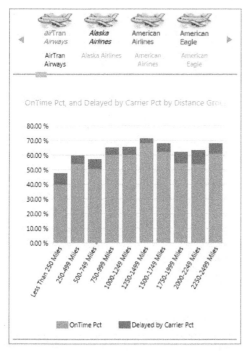

FIGURE 23-39

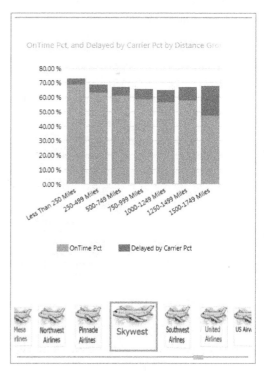

FIGURE 23-40

However, to simplify comparing chart values across multiple tiles, you can synchronize chart scales by following these steps:

1. Select the chart inside the tiles container.

2. On the Ribbon, select Chart Tools Layout.

3. Click the Axes drop-down, and select Same Across All Tiles for horizontal and vertical axis, as shown in Figure 23-41.

Synchronizing a chart category axis, such as flight distance, means that every category value is present for every chart, even if a value does not exist in a specific chart. As shown in Figure 23-42, Hawaiian Airlines has either short-distance or long-distance flights because Hawaii consists of several small islands close together (short-distance flights) but is far away from the North American continent (long-distance flights).

You can also add multiple visualizations side-by-side inside a tiles container. Those nested visualizations are automatically filtered by the selected value in the tile navigation strip. To add a new visualization for on-time flight performance by weekday automatically filtered by airline carrier, follow these steps:

1. Resize the tiles container to make room for a new visualization. Click into the empty space of the tiles container.

2. In the field list, expand Weekdays and select the Weekday field. Then expand OnTimePerformance2009 and select the OnTime Pct field.

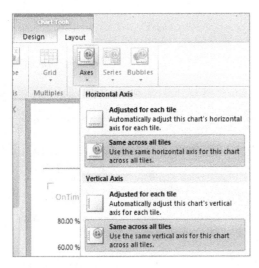

FIGURE 23-41

3. Using the Ribbon design tools, convert the table into a line chart.

4. Using the Chart Tools Layout, click the Axes drop-down and synchronize the vertical axis.

As you navigate the tiles, you can easily compare flight distance categories and on-time flights by weekday by airline carrier.

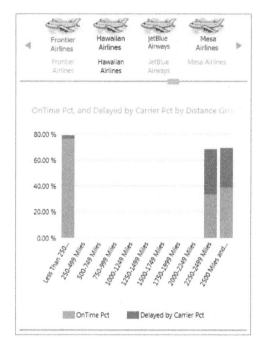

FIGURE 23-42

Highlighting in Visualizations

Charts can act as filters, using the relationships in the underlying model. This is interactive filtering, meaning that you can select values directly on the chart and have that filter other data regions on a view, as well as within a tile container. If you select one column in a column chart, this automatically

➤ Filters the values in all the tables and tiles, and bubble charts in the report.

➤ Adds highlighting to bar and column charts. It visually highlights the parts of other bar and column charts that pertain to that value. If values are cumulative, it shows the contribution of the filtered values to the original values. Otherwise, highlighting shows a relative comparison.

Figure 23-43 shows the tile container view created in the previous subsection. Navigate to Hawaiian flights, and then click the column for short-distance (less than 250 miles) flights. The chart for on-time flights by weekday highlights automatically and shows a relative comparison of the overall averages and the short-distance flight averages.

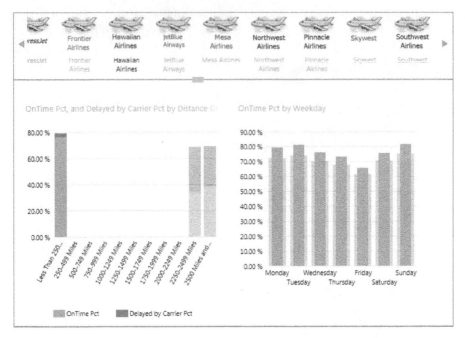

FIGURE 23-43

Matrix

You can convert a table to a matrix by adding row and column groups. Add column groups by dragging a field to the Column Groups area of the field well. For example, follow these steps to add a flight delay by originating airport by weekday analysis to your report:

1. Create a new empty view in your report.

2. In the field list, expand Origin States, and select OriginStateName. Then expand Origins and select Origin Code.

3. In the field list, expand OnTimePerformance2009 and select the Delay by Carrier Pct field.

4. Using the Ribbon, convert the table into a matrix. In the field list, expand Weekdays, click the down arrow next to the Weekday field, and select Add to Column Groups, as shown in Figure 23-44.

FIGURE 23-44

The resulting matrix visualization shown in Figure 23-45 shows grand totals and subtotals for each group by default. You can change this behavior using the Totals drop-down menu from the Ribbon, to only show totals on row groups, or column groups, or not at all.

OriginStateName	Origin Code	Monday	Tuesday	Wednesday	Thursday	Friday	Saturday	Sunday	Total
Alabama	BHM	9.21 %	5.92 %	7.16 %	9.42 %	9.38 %	7.98 %	9.93 %	**8.44 %**
	DHN	22.22 %	12.68 %	14.90 %	13.73 %	18.63 %	10.69 %	8.87 %	**14.68 %**
	HSV	6.40 %	4.98 %	5.60 %	5.99 %	6.97 %	8.12 %	8.21 %	**6.52 %**
	MGM	13.89 %	8.79 %	10.44 %	11.83 %	13.96 %	10.20 %	13.78 %	**11.88 %**
	MOB	9.19 %	6.12 %	6.20 %	7.74 %	7.48 %	6.15 %	7.90 %	**7.31 %**
	Total	**9.35 %**	**6.20 %**	**7.18 %**	**8.67 %**	**9.20 %**	**8.05 %**	**9.53 %**	**8.32 %**
Alaska	ADK				5.77 %			1.92 %	**3.85 %**
	ADQ	4.81 %	7.69 %	4.35 %	6.82 %	10.34 %	16.98 %	8.65 %	**7.91 %**
	AKN	18.18 %	27.27 %	9.09 %	36.36 %	45.45 %	45.45 %	54.55 %	**33.77 %**

FIGURE 23-45

Slicers

Slicers are another kind of filter, and they filter everything in the current view. Power View slicers look similar to slicers in PowerPivot for Excel. You create a single-column table from any field and convert it into a slicer. If the table has more than one column, the slicer icon in the Ribbon is disabled.

Each distinct value in the slicer acts as a button to select the value. As you hover over a slicer area, an icon appears in the top-right corner to clear (reset) the filter. You can create multiple slicers per view, as well as dependent slicers (based on relationships in the underlying model). For example, if you create two slicers, one for Product Categories and one for Products, when you click a category in the former, it filters the latter to show only products in that category. The filtering effects of all slicers are combined.

Figure 23-46 shows three slicers bound to independent fields, with the icon and tooltip for clearing the airline slicer shown when you hover with your mouse over the slicer area. Slicers can also be bound to image fields, such as the airline logo in the FAA sample model.

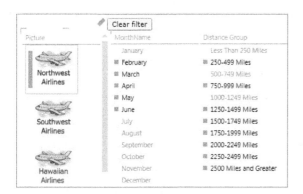

FIGURE 23-46

To select a particular slicer value, just click the value. The data is filtered in the report immediately. You can also select all except a certain set of values by resetting the filter with the button in the top corner, and then using Ctrl+click to unselect specific values. This shows overall values excluding the unselected values.

Selected slicer values are saved with the report. When you reopen a report, the selected slicer values are re-applied.

Filters

You learned about filters that affect an entire view in the previous section. You can also set visualization-level filters on tables, matrices, cards, and charts but not on tile containers or slicers. You can still set filters on the tables, matrices, and charts that are inside a tile container.

Like slicers, filters in the filters area are saved with the report and affect only one view or a specific visualization, not the entire report. Unlike slicers, filters are not shown directly in the view, so they do not take up any space in the view.

You can show or hide the filters area in design mode. If you make the filters area visible, it is also shown in reading and full-screen presentation modes. You can view filters for an individual visualization by hovering over its upper-right corner and then clicking the filter icon; refer to Figure 23-28 in the preceding section. This opens the filters area prepopulated with the fields used in the selected visualization.

You can drag additional fields from the field list to the filters area to create further filter conditions. You can use fields that are not in that visualization or anywhere on the view.

Power View provides basic and advanced filters:

➤ **Basic filters:** Numeric fields are automatically visualized as a range between the minimum and maximum value in the underlying data. You drag markers on a slider, or the overall slider, to set value ranges. For non-numeric fields, the filter visualization shows a list of values: The numbers after each value show how many records have that value: refer to Figure 23-29. If there are more than 500 distinct values in a field, you see a message that not all items are shown. Figure 23-47 shows examples of numeric and non-numeric filter visualizations.

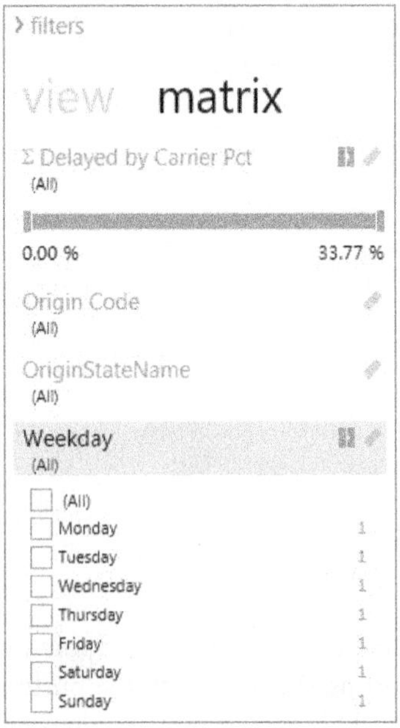

FIGURE 23-47

➤ **Advanced filters:** You can switch to the advanced filter mode by clicking the icon, as shown in Figure 23-48. In advanced mode, you can create more sophisticated filters using conditions such as Greater Than, Contains, Starts With. You can type all or part of a value to include or exclude.

FIGURE 23-48

Card, Callout Views

You can convert a table to a series of cards that display the data from each row in the table laid out in a card format, like an index card. There is an alternative visualization style available for cards, which is *Callout* and uses larger font sizes to draw the attention to key indicators of the card.

For example, follow these steps to add card and callout visualizations to your report:

1. Create a new empty view in your report.

2. In the field list click Airlines. This adds a table into the view with two fields shown by default. In addition, select the Flight Count field.

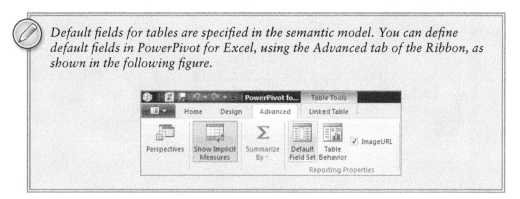

> *Default fields for tables are specified in the semantic model. You can define default fields in PowerPivot for Excel, using the Advanced tab of the Ribbon, as shown in the following figure.*

3. Convert the table into cards, using the visualization Ribbon, as shown in Figure 23-49.

4. In the field list, expand OnTimePerformance2009 and visualize several metrics on each card by selecting the following fields:

➤ EarlyArrival Count

➤ Late Arrival Count

➤ Cancelled

➤ OnTime Pct

➤ Delayed by Carrier Pct

➤ Weather Delay Pct

Figure 23-50 shows the resulting card visualization.

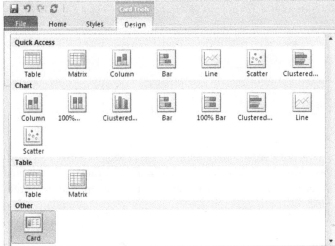

FIGURE 23-49

FIGURE 23-50

5. Select the card visualization on the view, create a copy (using the keyboard or the Ribbon menu) and paste. The copied card is automatically positioned into an area with free space. Because a callout style uses larger font sizes, remove the fields for EarlyArrival Count, Late Arrival Count, Delayed by Carrier Pct from the Fields list in the field well.

6. Click the Style drop-down on the Ribbon to convert the card layout into a callout layout, as shown in Figure 23-51. Figure 23-52 shows the resulting callout visualization.

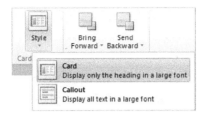

FIGURE 23-51

FIGURE 23-52

Zooming in Charts

Column and bar charts can show numerical, date, or non-numerical values on the x-axis. If the list of distinct non-numerical values is too long, the horizontal chart axis enables scrolling.

 If there are too many distinct values (more than 1,000) on the horizontal axis of a column or bar chart, Power View automatically retrieves a representative sample of the data instead of the full set. This helps you get an idea of the characteristics of the full value range, while still providing fast performance. You can then narrow down the range of values using filters and slicers.

For numerical and date values, the chart axis enables zooming, as shown in Figures 23-53 and 23-54. The first chart shows the percentage of flights delayed by weather throughout the entire year. The second chart shows the same data zoomed to the time period of November and December. You can zoom by dragging the markers on the horizontal axis to narrow the time window. You can scroll through the entire date range by dragging the slider.

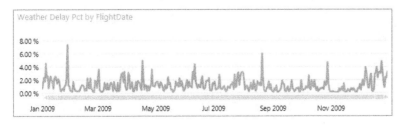

FIGURE 23-53

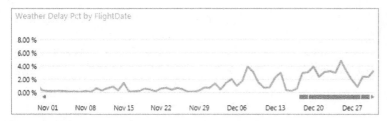

FIGURE 23-54

To create the chart shown, follow these steps:

1. Create a new empty view in your report.

2. In the field list, expand OnTimePerformance2009 and select FlightDate and Weather Delay Pct fields.

3. Convert the table into a line chart using the Ribbon.

4. Zoom in by dragging the markers on the horizontal axis to narrow the time window. Scroll through the entire date range by dragging the slider.

Scatter and Bubble

Scatter and bubble charts are an effective way to visualize a lot of related data in one chart. They help you understand and present patterns and clustering of data values. In scatter charts, the x-axis displays one measure and the y-axis displays another, making it easy to see the relationship between the two values for all the items in the chart. In a bubble chart, a third measure controls the size of the data points.

For this tutorial on scatter, bubble, and animated charts, you use the `Population Statistics.xlsx` PowerPivot workbook, provided on the Wrox download site for this book. You can follow these steps:

1. Upload `Population Statistics.xlsx` into the PowerPivot Gallery.

2. After you refresh the gallery site in the browser, click the Create Power View Report icon next to the Population Statistics workbook. This launches a new Power View report.

3. In the field list, expand Population Stats and select the Males per 100 Females field. The Power View field well shows the Average aggregate function applied by default, as shown in Figure 23-55. The default aggregation for each field is defined in the semantic model, but if you want you can change the aggregation function in Power View.

FIGURE 23-55

When designing a model, you can define the default aggregation function for client tools using PowerPivot for Excel. Select the column in the PowerPivot window, go to the Advanced tab, and choose the function from the Summarize By drop-down, as shown in the following figure.

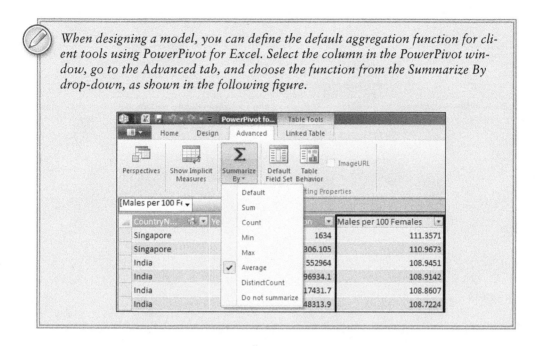

4. Convert the table into a scatter chart using the Ribbon.

5. Add the following additional fields from Population Stats by clicking

➤ CountryName (Since it is a non-numeric field, Power View automatically groups by country name.)

➤ MedianAge (The chart maps it to y-axis.)

➤ TotalPopulation (The chart maps it to bubble size.)

The resulting chart is shown in Figure 23-56. It visualizes effectively that the median age of the population of Germany and Japan is fairly old, whereas India and China have a young average population. It also shows that the Russian Federation has a high ratio of female population.

Animated Timeline Charts

Timeline charts are effective to visualize change over time. You can add a time dimension to scatter and bubble charts, with a Play Axis. The field used for the Play Axis in Power View can be of any data type; it is not restricted to be a time dimension.

The Population Statistics model contains historical population data as well as future projections for various countries. Continuing from the bubble chart created in the previous section, follow these steps to add a Play Axis:

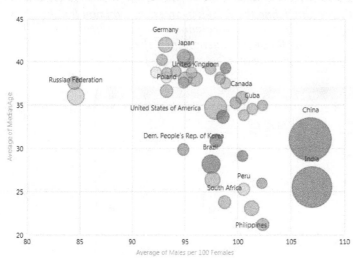

Average of Males per 100 Females, Average of MedianAge, and Average of TotalPopulation by Co

FIGURE 23-56

1. In the field list, click the down arrow next to the Year field, and select Add as Play Axis, as shown in Figure 23-57.

FIGURE 23-57

2. Hover with the mouse over the bubble chart until the Filter icon appears in the top-right corner. Click the Filter icon to narrow the list of countries you are interested in. For example, select the following country for the CountryName filter on the chart: Austria, Brazil, Canada, China, France, Germany, India, Japan, Russian Federation, United Kingdom, and United States of America.

The bubble chart shows a timeline axis, with the range of available values in the data. By default, the timeline is positioned at the last value (last frame of animation), as shown in Figure 23-58.

FIGURE 23-58

You can drag the Play Axis marker with the mouse to a particular location, such as 2010, as shown in Figure 23-59. As you change the Play Axis position, the watermark text of the chart updates and shows the current value.

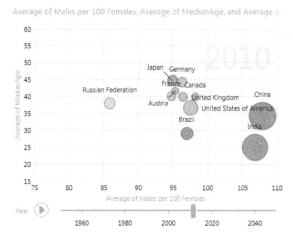

FIGURE 23-59

When you click the Play button, the bubbles travel and adjust in size to show how the values change based on the timeline. You can pause at any point to investigate the data in more detail.

When you can click a bubble on the chart, you can see its history in the trail the bubble follows over time. For example, Figure 23-60 shows the trend for Germany, which had an imbalance in the male/female population ratio and a young population following World War II. The average age of the population increases as time progresses due to recovery and high living standards.

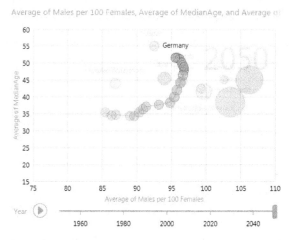

FIGURE 23-60

Figure 23-61 shows the trend for the Russian Federation. After World War II, Russia's male population began to recover. In the 1990s, a demographic crisis began to impact Russian males that coincided with the dissolution of the Soviet Union and the fall of the Berlin Wall. There is debate over the cause of this, but one of the theories points at a rise in alcoholism following that time period.

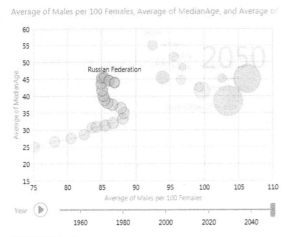

FIGURE 23-61

Refreshing Data in a Power View Report

If Power View is connected to a tabular BISM in Direct Query mode, you get to see real-time data from the underlying relational database. However, if the database is not optimized or large, those queries may not finish with subsecond response time. While a long running request is in progress, the Refresh button in the top-left corner (Quick Access Toolbar) of Power View changes temporarily into a Cancel button. You can click the Cancel icon, and Power View is immediately responsive afterward.

You can refresh the data in a Power View report at any point without refreshing the page, by clicking the Refresh button on the Power View Quick Access Toolbar.

The Quick Access Toolbar for Power View contains buttons for undo, redo, save, and refresh/cancel, as shown in Figure 23-62.

FIGURE 23-62

 If you click the Refresh button in your browser, and then click Leave This Page, you lose whatever changes you have made to the report since you last saved it.

Presenting and Exporting in Power View

A Power View report is always in a presentation ready state; you can browse your data and present at the same time, as you work with real data. Power View offers reading and full-screen presentation modes. Furthermore, you can export an interactive version of the report to PowerPoint.

You built a fairly comprehensive set of analyses in the previous sections about FAA flight and Population Statistics data as Power View reports. Now it is time to present your findings.

For this section, you can either use the reports you built in the previous section or upload the pre-built `Flight Delay Analysis.rdlx` sample report to your SharePoint site.

Reading and Presentation Mode

Reading and full-screen presentation modes hide the Ribbon and other design tools to provide more room for the visualizations. The report is still fully interactive, with filtering, sorting, and highlighting capability.

If you open an existing report by clicking a RDLX document in SharePoint, the report is opened in reading mode. If you are in design mode, you can switch to reading mode using the Ribbon.

Figure 23-63 shows the Flight Delay Analysis report in reading mode. You can navigate between views using the keyboard (cursor left/right, page up/down), or using the navigation button in the bottom-right corner of the reading mode screen.

FIGURE 23-63

If you click the preview icon in the bottom-left corner of the reading mode screen, a navigation panel appears at the bottom of the browser window, as shown in Figure 23-64. You can navigate between views by scrolling and clicking on preview images.

FIGURE 23-64

Full-screen presentation utilizes the entire screen, with no browser frame, as shown in Figure 23-65. Full-screen presentation mode has identical interactivity (filtering, sorting, and highlighting).

If the filter pane is visible in design mode, it is also available in reading mode and presentation mode to interact.

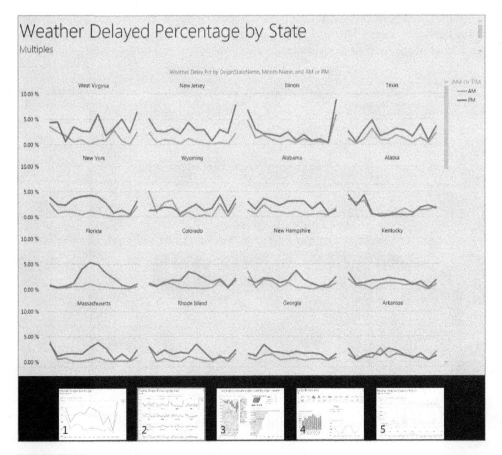

FIGURE 23-65

Printing Views

You can print a Power View report from design or reading modes using the File menu and clicking Print. Power View prints one view at a time: the current view. The view always prints in landscape orientation, regardless of settings in the Print dialog box. It prints exactly what you see in the view. For example, Power View prints the selected tile in a tile container, the filters area if it is expanded, or the current frame of a scatter or bubble chart with a Play Axis.

PowerPoint Export and Interactivity

Power View supports PowerPoint export. There are no add-ons required; it works out-of-the-box with PowerPoint 2007 and newer.

You can export an interactive version of your Power View report to PowerPoint, using the Export option from the Power View File menu, as shown in Figure 23-66. Each view in Power View becomes a separate PowerPoint slide.

FIGURE 23-66

Interacting with Power View reports exported to PowerPoint is similar to interacting with views in Power View reading and full-screen modes. In PowerPoint's slide show and reading view modes, you can click to activate the view and then utilize full Power View presentation interactivity while in PowerPoint.

You can export a Power View report to PowerPoint following these steps:

1. In the Power View file menu, click Export to PowerPoint, as shown in Figure 23-66.

2. Save the new PowerPoint presentation. You can save the PowerPoint file anywhere locally or into the SharePoint site.

Access to the original Power View report on a SharePoint server is required for enabling interactivity of the views inside a PowerPoint presentation. If you open a saved PowerPoint file with Power View contents and you do not have access to the original Power View report on a SharePoint server, then you can see only the placeholder images in all PowerPoint modes (normal, slide show, and reading view) and the Power View views are not interactive.

3. If you have not yet saved the Power View report, you are prompted to save it now. You cannot export a Power View report to PowerPoint without saving it first.

4. To generate the PowerPoint export, Power View navigates through each view and captures a higher resolution thumbnail image. After the export phase is complete, save the PowerPoint presentation, and open the saved presentation in PowerPoint. PowerPoint opens in normal view. A static image of each view is centered on a separate slide, as shown in Figure 23-67.

5. In PowerPoint, click Enable Editing. You can modify the PowerPoint presentation as you would any other, with styles and other enhancements. These will not affect the Power View views because they remain opaque areas on the slide. The font and size of text in the Power View views also remains unaffected.

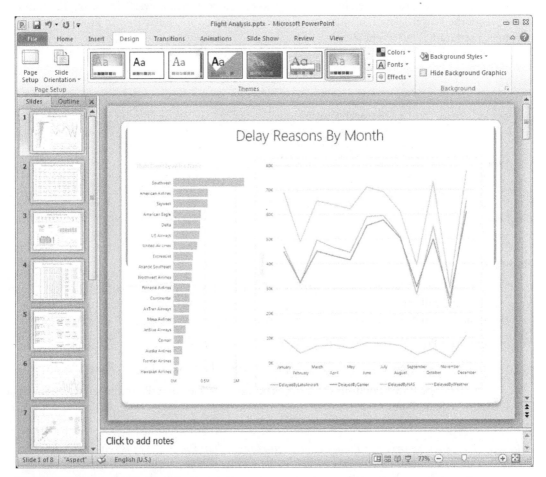

FIGURE 23-67

6. In the lower-right corner, click the Reading View or Slide Show button.

7. To interact with the visualizations in PowerPoint slide show or reading view mode, in the lower-right corner of the slide, click Click to Interact (shown in Figure 23-68) to load the live Power View report from the SharePoint server.

8. When the report is live, you can utilize all interactivity options of Power View presentation mode inside PowerPoint, such as filtering shown in Figure 23-69.

If you have chosen not to save preview images with the Power View report, when the PowerPoint presentation opens you see placeholder images.

When you update and save the original Power View report in Power View, the next time you view the PowerPoint presentation in slide show or reading view mode, you see the updates to the Power View views.

FIGURE 23-68

Tips and Tricks for Power View

This section provides a list of tips and tricks, and answers frequently asked questions.

➤ **Grayed-out fields in the field list:** Sometimes a field is grayed out in the fields section of the field list when you have a visualization selected. If so, it means a relationship is not defined between the fields already in the visualization and the field in the fields section of the field list. Relationships need to be defined in the tabular model, either using PowerPivot for Excel, or in SQL Server Data Tools.

➤ **Grayed-out icons in the Ribbon:** Power View's Ribbon is context-sensitive based on the visualization selected in the current view. When an icon on the Ribbon is grayed out, it means that action is not available for the currently selected on the view. For example, if a table has no measures, then all the chart icons are disabled on the Design tab. You need at least one measure for a chart.

➤ What settings are controlled and configured in the model?

FIGURE 23-69

➤ Visibility of which fields display in the field list.

➤ Data types and data formats.

➤ Whether a numeric field is a measure or nonmeasure by default.

➤ Whether the sort order for a field that is used as a nonmeasure is controlled by the sort order of a different field. For example, sorting for a MonthName field might be controlled by a MonthNumber field, so the months are in chronological rather than alphabetical order.

➤ In a card visualization, which text field displays prominently as the title (Default Label defined in Table Behavior in PowerPivot for Excel).

➤ In a card visualization, which image field appears prominently on the left (Default Image defined in Table Behavior in PowerPivot for Excel).

➤ Whether fields with potentially duplicate values, such as customer names, are grouped by the field or by the related key field. For example, you cannot group on binary image fields — Power View implicitly groups on the unique identifier defined for that table.

➤ Whether the aggregate function for a measure can be changed in the report.

➤ For external images, whether the image URL or the image itself displays in the report (determined by the field's ImageURL setting on the Advanced tab in PowerPivot).

➤ Show all rows or columns, even if they have no data (outer join). Sometimes you want to see all the rows in a table, even if some of them have no values. (This is called an outer join.) For example, say you have a table of regions, cities, stores, and sales totals. Maybe you want to see all the stores in a region, even if some have no sales, or all the cities, even if some cities have no stores.

You might also want to see all the columns in a matrix, even if some have no data. For example, you could have a column for each year, and you want to see all the years, even those with no values.

You can control the setting for each field independently, by clicking the drop-down arrow next to the field name in the Values box in the layout section of the field list, and then click Show items with no data, as shown in Figure 23-70.

FIGURE 23-70

SUMMARY

In this chapter you learned about analyzing and visualizing the tabular BI Semantic Models with Power View, and creating exciting presentations in the process, including exporting to PowerPoint and showing interactive Power View visualizations inside PowerPoint!

Resources

Power View: see *Professional SQL Server 2012 Reporting Services* by Paul Turley, et al. (Wrox, 2012, ISBN: 978-1-118-10111-7).

INDEX